Marketing Management
A Relationship Approach

Pearson Education

We work with leading authors to develop the strongest educational materials in marketing, bringing cutting-edge thinking and best learning practice to a global market.

Under a range of well-known imprints, including Financial Times Prentice Hall, we craft high quality print and electronic publications which help readers to understand and apply their content, whether studying or at work.

To find out more about the complete range of our publishing, please visit us on the World Wide Web at: www.pearsoneduc.com

Marketing Management
A Relationship Approach

Svend Hollensen

An imprint of **Pearson Education**

Harlow, England · London · New York · Reading, Massachusetts · San Francisco · Toronto · Don Mills, Ontario · Sydney
Tokyo · Singapore · Hong Kong · Seoul · Taipei · Cape Town · Madrid · Mexico City · Amsterdam · Munich · Paris · Milan

Pearson Education Limited

Edinburgh Gate
Harlow
Essex CM20 2JE

and Associated Companies throughout the world

Visit us on the World Wide Web at:
www.pearsoneduc.com

First published 2003

© Pearson Education Limited 2003

ISBN 0 273 64378 9

British Library Cataloguing-in-Publication Data
A catalogue record for this book is available from the British Library

Library of Congress Cataloging-in-Publication Data

Hollensen, Svend.
  Marketing management : a relationship approach / Svend Hollensen.
    p. cm.
  Includes bibliographical references and index.
  ISBN 0-273-64378-9 (pbk.)
  1. Relationship marketing. 2. Marketing--Management. 3. Relationship
marketing--Case studies. I. Title.

  HF5415.55 .H65 2002
  658.8--dc21

                                        2002070854

10 9 8 7 6 5 4 3 2 1
07 06 05 04 03

Typeset in 9.5/12pt Stone Serif
Printed by Ashford Colour Press Ltd., Gosport

Contents

Part IV Developing marketing programmes   447

11 Product and service decisions   449

12 Pricing decisions   486

Preface

The development of marketing theory and practice is undergoing a paradigm shift from a transactional to a relationship orientation. As many companies are still relying on the traditional marketing approach, this book will bridge the gap between **relationship marketing** (RM) and traditional (transactional) Marketing (TM).

In the traditional transactional approach, **marketing management** is about planning, coordinating, and controlling marketing activities that are aimed at satisfying customer needs and desires – and receiving money from sales.

In recent years, marketing has been undergoing considerable self-examination and internal debate. The overriding emphasis in the 'traditional' marketing approach is on acquiring as many customers as possible. Evidence is mounting, however, that traditional marketing is becoming too expensive and is less effective.

Many leading marketing academics and practitioners have concluded that many of the long-standing practices and operating modes in marketing need to be evaluated, and we need to move towards a relationship approach that is based on repeated market transactions and mutual gain for buyers and sellers.

The 'new paradigm' is commonly referred to as relationship marketing (RM). Relationship marketing is not a new idea. Before the advent of mass production and mass media, relationship marketing was the norm; sellers usually had first-hand knowledge of buyers, and the successful ones used this knowledge to help keep customers for life.

Relationship marketing reflects a strategy and process that integrate customers, suppliers, and other partners into the company's design, development, manufacturing, and sales processes.

Fundamentally, relationship marketing draws from traditional marketing principles. Marketing can be defined as the process of identifying and satisfying customers' needs in a competitively superior manner in order to achieve the organization's objectives. Relationship marketing builds on this.

The customer is still fundamental to a marketing relationship. Marketing exists to efficiently meet the satisfaction of customer needs, as well as those of the marketing organization. There is a considerable body of knowledge in social sciences that sheds light on the many facets of human relationships. We draw from these sources to further our understanding of consumer relationships.

Marketing exchange seeks to achieve satisfaction for the consumer and the marketing organization (or company). In this latter group we include employees, shareholders, and managers. Other stakeholders (like competitors, financial and governmental institutions) are also important. As we shall see later in case study 1.1, relationships can cover a wide range of organizations in the environment e.g.

- governmental institutions
- industry associations
- European Union (EU) institutions
- religious groups.

However, the main focus of this book is still on the relationships between the firm and its closest external bodies, primarily the customers.

In the transactional approach, participants focus exclusively on the economic benefits of the exchange. Even though in relational exchange the focus widens, economic benefits remain important to all of the partners in marketing relationships.

With the relationship approach in mind, an integrated view of marketing management will be presented. To do this, the latest research findings in marketing management and related disciplines are summarized. Yet, marketing management is still a very practical discipline. People still have practical needs, firms still face practical problems, and solutions still have to work in real life. Most marketers cannot and should not hide in labs. Marketing is a social science based on theories and concepts, but it also requires that most marketers meet with people, observe them, talk to them, and understand their activities. In essence, marketing is a dialogue between sellers (marketers) and buyers (customers). This book reflects this applied approach. Together with important concepts and theories, my experience that has been obtained through work with numerous companies – large and small, domestic and international – for many years will be drawn on.

Target audience

This book is written for people who want to know how the relationship and the traditional marketing approach (in combination) affect the development of effective and efficient marketing plans. This book is aimed primarily at students, MBA/graduate students and advanced undergraduates who wish to go into business. It will provide the information, perspectives, and tools necessary to get the job done. My aim is to enable you to make better marketing decisions.

A second audience for this book is the large group of practitioners who want to build on the existing skills and knowledge already possessed. The book is of special interest to the manager who wishes to keep abreast of the most recent developments in the 'marketing management' field.

Unique features of this book

This marketing text tries to integrate the 'new' relationships approach in the traditional process of developing effective marketing plans. Compared to other marketing management books this text will attach more importance to the following themes.

Buyer-seller relationships

The guiding principle of this textbook is that of building relationships between buyers and sellers. Relationships is a growing trend and for good reason. Dramatic changes in the marketing environment are presenting immense new opportunities for companies that really build and retain relationships with customers. Relationship marketing emphasizes the tremendous importance of satisfied, loyal customers. Good customer relationships happen when all employees within the organization develop the sensitivity and desire to satisfy customers' needs and wants. It may be argued that the traditional concept of marketing (as exemplified later in Chapter 1) does not adequately reflect the recognition of the long-term value of a customer. The argument is that many of the traditional definitions of marketing, although stressing the importance of customer needs and satisfaction, are essentially concerned with maximizing the profitability of each transaction. Instead they should seek to develop long-term relationships with customers, which cannot easily be duplicated by competitors.

Buyer-seller interaction on a global scale

Today's companies are facing fierce and aggressive competition. Today most firms compete not only locally and nationally, but globally as well. Companies that have never given a thought to internationalization now also face competition in their home market from international companies. Thinking globally also requires an understanding of the international diversity in buying behaviour and the importance of cross-cultural differences, both in the B-t-C and B-t-B market. This cross-cultural approach is centred on the study of the interaction between buyers and sellers (and their companies) who have different national and/or cultural backgrounds.

Creating competitive advantage through relationships together with other companies

Greater emphasis is given to the development of competitive advantage, and consequently to the development of resources and capabilities and competences within the organization and with other companies. Relationship marketing seeks to build a *chain of relationships* (networks or value net) between the organization and its main stakeholders, including customers, suppliers, distribution channel intermediaries, and firms producing complementary products and services. Relationships to competitors are also considered.

Cross-functionalism

Marketing is not an isolated function. A marketer's ability to effectively implement a strategic marketing programme depends largely on the cooperation and competence of other functional areas within the organization. Consequently, substantial attention is given to the interfunctional approach of marketing management. This includes: the concept of competitive advantages, **cross-functional teams** in the development of new products, **supply chain management**, internationalization, quality management, and ethics.

Outline

The book is structured around the two main steps involved in marketing management, i.e. the decision-making process regarding formulating, implementing, and controlling a marketing plan:

- Step 1: Analysis of the internal and external situation (Parts I and II)
- Step 2: Planning and implementation of marketing activities (Parts III, IV and V)

The schematic outline of the book in Figure 1 shows how the two main steps are divided into five parts. The book has a clear structure according to the *marketing planning process* of the firm (Figure 1). Based on an analysis of the competitive advantages of the firm (Part I) and the analysis of the external situation (Part II), the firm is able to develop marketing strategies (Part III) and marketing programmes (Part IV). Finally, the firm has to implement and control its activity in the market and if necessary make changes in the marketing strategy (Part V).

Figure 1 The structure of the book

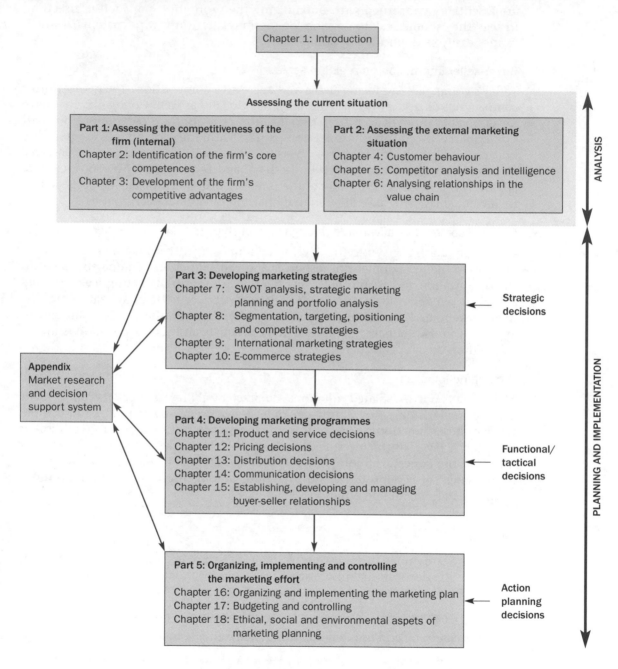

Throughout the book this marketing planning process is seen in a relationship approach, as a supplement to the transactional approach.

The market research function gives a very important input to all the five phases (parts) of this decision-making process, with a possible feedback to the marketing information system (MIS). Therefore this section of the book is an Appendix, but a very important one, as the past marketing experiences are stored in the marketing information system, which may add important contributions to new marketing decision-making processes – i.e. for making better marketing decisions.

Pedagogical/learning aids

Many aids to student learning come with the book. These include:

- *chapter learning objectives*: tell the reader what he/she should be able to do after completing each chapter.
- *case studies*: there are two case studies in each chapter, one at the start and one at the end. Each case study also contains questions.
- *exhibits*: examples from the real world to illustrate the text and the marketing models.
- *summaries*: each chapter ends with a summary of the main concepts.
- *discussion questions*: at the end of each chapter the discussion issues are presented as questions.
- *glossary*: a glossary on page 761 provides quick reference to the key terms in the book.

Supplementary material to accompany the book can be downloaded by lecturers from **www.booksites.net/hollensen**.

Table 1 shows the case studies in this book.

Table 1 Case studies in the book

Chapters	Case titles/subtitles	Location of headquarters	Target market area and type
1. Introduction	**1.1 Coca-Cola** Reconsidering the marketing strategy for Muslim dominated markets after September 11, 2001	USA	USA/World B-t-B
	1.2 Kamis Company A Polish spice supplier is penetrating grocery stores in eastern Europe	Poland	Eastern Europe B-t-B and B-t-C
2. Identification of the firm's core competences	**2.1 Microsoft and Lego** Different competences help create global competitiveness for both companies	USA /Denmark	World B-t-C
	2.2 Amazon and Toys 'R' Us Pooling competences to form a single online toy store	USA	World B-t-C

Table 1 continued

Chapters	Case titles/subtitles	Location of headquarters	Target market area and type
3. Development of the firm's competitive advantage	**3.1 Teepack Spezialmaschinen** Establishing customer relationships to manufacturers of tea brands	Germany	World B-t-B
	3.2 BBC Worldwide Ltd Creating global competitiveness through relationships	UK	World B-t-B and B-t-C
4. Customer behaviour	**4.1 BASF** An ingredients supplier for the worldwide cosmetics industry seeks new relationships	Germany	World B-t-B
	4.2 Manchester United Trying to establish a global brand through an alliance with New York Yankees	UK	USA/World B-t-C
5. Competitor analysis and intelligence	**5.1 Viagra** A pharmaceutical superstar is facing future competition	USA	World B-t-C
	5.2 Virgin Cola Trying a comeback in the USA	UK	USA B-t-C
6. Analysing relationships in the value chain	**6.1 Jordan** Philips and Jordan: development and marketing of an electrical toothbrush for the world market	Norway/Holland	World B-t-B and B-t-C
	6.2 Dandy Chewing Gum A specialist in the development of competitor alliances	Denmark/France	France/Russia World B-t-B and B-t-C
7. SWOT analysis, strategic marketing planning and portfolio analysis	**7.1 Microsoft's X-Box** Online gaming through an alliance with Japan's NTT Communications	USA	World B-t-C
	7.2 Ford Motor Company Driving into the world golf car market	USA	World B-t-B and B-t-C
8. Segmentation, targeting, positioning and competitive strategies	**8.1 Ballygowan** International segmentation of the mineral water market	Ireland	World B-t-B and B-t-C
	8.2 BMW's Mini A cult classic makes a comeback	Germany	World B-t-C
9. International marketing strategies	**9.1 Skagen Designs** Marketing of Scandinavian designed watches to the USA and the rest of the world	USA	USA/World B-t-C
	9.2 ITE (Hugo) and IO Interactive (Hitman) Two 'born globals' in the computer games industry	Denmark	World B-t-B and B-t-C
10. E-commerce strategies	**10.1 Nokia** Club Nokia's website creates customer loyalty	Finland	World B-t-C
	10.2 Gameplay.com The online games marketer is undergoing a turbulent time	UK	World B-t-B and B-t-C

Table 1 continued

Chapters	Case titles/subtitles	Location of headquarters	Target market area and type
11. Product and service decisions	11.1 Swatch Watch A blockbuster product is needed	Switzerland	World B-t-C
	11.2 Joyco India A bubblegum manufacturer outmanoeuvres Perfetti with Boomer in head-on competition	Spain	India B-t-C
12. Pricing decisions	12.1 Electrolux An alliance with Toshiba to break into the Japanese market for household appliances	Sweden	Japan B-t-B and B-t-C
	12.2 Harley-Davidson Is the image justifying the price level?	USA	USA/World B-t-C
13. Distribution decisions	13.1 Denka Holding A Danish furniture group in an international franchise expansion	Denmark	World B-t-B and B-t-C
	13.2 Red Bull The energy drink that gives you 'wings' attempts to penetrate US distribution channels	Austria	World B-t-C
14. Communication decisions	14.1 Autoliv The Autoliv-Volvo communication strategy for the launch of a post-crash safety system	Sweden	World B-t-B and B-t-C
	14.2 Heineken Can the Heineken-Paulaner relationship provide new value for customers in the world beer market?	Holland/Germany	World B-t-B and B-t-C
15. Establishing, developing and managing buyer-seller relationships	15.1 Celador Productions How to maintain relationships with the international entertainment market beyond the Who Wants To Be A Millionaire? show	UK	World B-t-B and B-t-C
	15.2 Alcatel Space Creating a network of relationships in the global satellite market	France	France/World B-t-B and B-t-C
16. Organizing and implementing the marketing plan	16.1 Adidas-Salomon Splits into three divisions to sharpen consumer focus	Germany	World B-t-C
	16.2 Teekanne Marketing planning for international expansion of branded tea sales	Germany	World/USA B-t-C
17. Budgeting and controlling	17.1 Condomi Marketing budget consequences of an aggressive pricing and promotion strategy in the British condom market	Germany	UK B-t-C
	17.2 SCA (Svenska Cellulosa Aktiebolaget) Planning and budgeting for increased market shares in the world tissue market	Sweden	World/USA B-t-B and B-t-C
18. Ethical, social and environmental aspects of marketing	18.1 Pokémon Ethical issues in marketing to children	Japan	World
	18.2 Body Shop A company with ethical values	UK	World

In the development of this text a number of reviewers have been involved, whom I would like to thank for their important and valuable contribution. Especially, I would like to thank Professor Martin G.M. Wetzels, Technical University Eindhoven, Holland and Ass. Professor Christer Kedström, Lund University, Sweden.

I am grateful to my publisher Pearson Education. During the writing process I had the pleasure of working with a team of editors, whom I thank for their encouragement and professionalism in transforming the manuscript into the final book. Especially, I would like to thank development editor, Louise Lakey for her encouraging comments during the last part of the process.

Throughout the writing period there has only been one constant in my life – my family. Without them, none would have been possible. Thus it is to my three girls – my wife, Jonna, and my two daughters, Nanna and Julie – that I dedicate this book.

Svend Hollensen
Sønderborg, Denmark

About the author

Svend Hollensen is an Associate Professor of International Marketing at the University of Southern Denmark. He holds an M.Sc. (Business Administration) from Aarhus Business School. He has practical experience from a job as International Marketing Co-ordinator in a large Danish multinational enterprise as well as from being International Marketing Manager in a company producing agricultural machinery.

After working in industry he received his Ph.D. in 1992 from Copenhagen Business School.

He has published articles in journals and is the author of two case books which focus on general marketing and international marketing (published by Copenhagen Business School Press). Furthermore he is the author of *Global Marketing: A Market-responsive Approach*, published by Financial Times Prentice Hall and now in its second edition. It has also recently been translated into Russian and Chinese.

The author may be contacted via:

University of Southern Denmark
Grundtvigs Allé 150
DK-6400 Sønderborg
Denmark

Fax: +45 65 50 12 92
e-mail: **svend@sam.sdu.dk**

Guided tour

Part openings
Each part opener has a structure map that allows you to get a clear picture of how the part is set out and how the various chapters relate to each other.

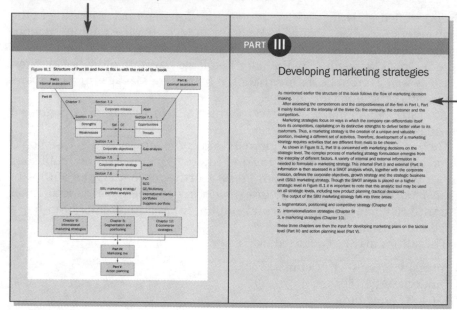

Part introductions
These give an overview of the topics to be covered in the part chapters.

Learning objectives
Each chapter begins with a set of learning objectives, which show the skills and knowledge you should have achieved by the end of the chapter.

Questions
The questions at the end of the introductory case study test your understanding of what you have just read and highlight areas to think about before beginning to read the chapter.

Opening case study
There is an introductory case study in each chapter, which gives a flavour of the material in that chapter.

End of chapter case study

Each chapter ends with a case study that will help you reflect on and analyse theories raised in the chapter.

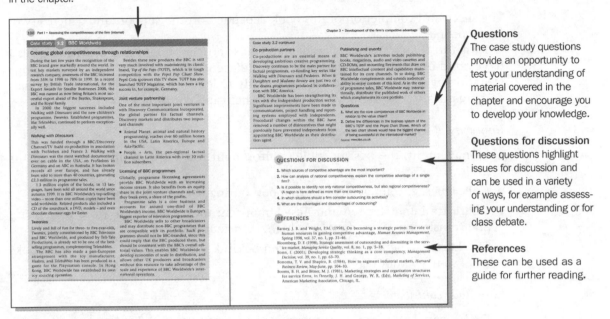

Questions
The case study questions provide an opportunity to test your understanding of material covered in the chapter and encourage you to develop your knowledge.

Questions for discussion
These questions highlight issues for discussion and can be used in a variety of ways, for example assessing your understanding or for class debate.

References
These can be used as a guide for further reading.

Web resources

A downloadable Instructor's Manual is available to lecturers at http://www.booksites.net/hollensen, which contains teaching notes on the 36 case studies included in the book and model answers to the discussion questions. All of the figures and tables in the book can also be downloaded as PowerPoint files from the site.

Acknowledgements

The successful completion of this book depended on the support and generosity of many people.

I wish to thank the many academics whose articles, books and other materials I have cited or quoted. However, in this preface it is not possible to acknowledge everyone by name. In particular I am deeply indebted to the following individuals and organizations. I thank you for all your help and contributions.

University of Southern Denmark:

- Management: the best possible environment for writing and completing this project.
- Colleagues: encouragement and support during the writing process.
- Charlotte Lund Hansen and Aase Simonsen: took care of the word processing and translation of my drafts in a highly efficient manner.
- The Library, Ole Krogh and the team behind him: provided articles and books from sources worldwide.

Case study contributors:

- Dr Mohan Lal Agrawal, Services Management Center, Lucknow, India: case study: Green Card Israel (available on the book website).
- Dr Pallab Paul, Department of Marketing, University of Denver: case study: Open House of Israel (available on the book website).

Publisher's acknowledgements

We are grateful to the following for permission to reproduce copyright material:

Figure 1.2 reprinted from Payne, A. (ed.) (1995) *Advances in Relationship Marketing*, with permission from Kogan Page; Figure 2.6 reprinted from *European Management Journal*, vol. 18, no. 2, N. Kumar, L. Scheer and P. Kotler, From market driven to market driving, © 2000 with permission from Elsevier Science, Figure 11.4 reprinted from *Industrial Marketing Management*, vol. 30, S. Stremersch, S. Wuyts and R.T. Frambach, The purchasing of full-service contracts, © 2001 with permission from Elsevier Science and Figure 18.4 reprinted from *International Marketing*, S. Paliwoda, with permission from Elsevier Science; Figures 2.9, 2.12, 3.3, 3.8, 6.13, 6.14, 7.13, 9.3, 9.6, 9.9, 9.10, 9.13, 9.14, 10.2, 10.6, 10.8, 10.12, 11.2, 11.7, 11.8, 11.11, 11.12, 12.5, 13.8, 13.9, 14.2, 14.5, 14.7, 17.4, 17.5, 17.6, A.1, A.2 and A.5 and Tables 11.1, 12.1, 14.3, 14.7 reprinted from Hollensen, S. (2001) *Global Marketing: A market responsive approach*, 2nd edition, Figure 9.2 reprinted from Jeannet, J.P. (2000) *Managing with a Global Mindset*, Figure 15.2, Figure 9.4 reprinted from Tayeb, M. (2000) *International Business: Theories, policies and practices*, p.383, Figure 11.5

reprinted from Baker, M. and Hart, S. (1999) *Product Strategy and Management*, p.175, Figure A.3 reprinted from Wright, L.T. and Crimp, M. (2000) *The Marketing Research Process*, 5th edition, p.380, with permission from Pearson Education; Table 3.1 reprinted from Burton, J. (1995) Composite strategy: the combination of collaboration and competition, *Journal of General Management*, vol. 21, no. 1, pp.1–23 and Figure 9.8 reprinted from Welch, L.S. and Loustarinen, R. (1988) Internalization: evolution of a concept, *Journal of General Management*, vol. 14, no. 2, pp.36–64, with permission from Braybrooke Press; Figure 4.1 reproduced with permission from Luvigel EM, BASF Aktiengesellschaft; Exhibit 4.6 reproduced with permission from Grundfos; Table 5.1 reprinted with permission from *Marketing Management*, published by the American Marketing Association, B.H. Clark (1998), vol. 7, no. 4, pp. 8–20, Figure 8.4 reprinted with permission from *Marketing Management*, published by the American Marketing Association, J. Barron & J. Hollingshead, January/February (2002), pp. 24–28, courtesy J. Barron & J. Hollingshead and the Monitor Group, Figure 9.5 reprinted with permission from *Journal of International Marketing*, published by the American Marketing Association, C.A. Solberg (1997), vol. 5, no. 1, pp. 9–30, and Figure 9.12 reprinted with permission from *Journal of Marketing*, published by the American Marketing Association, I. Ayal & J. Zif (1979), vol. 43, Spring, pp. 84–94; Figure 5.6 reproduced with permission from The Virgin Drinks Company Limited; Figure 6.1 reprinted from Håkansson, H. and Johanson, J. (1987) *Industrial Technological Development: A network approach*, p.17, with permission from Thomson Learning; Figure 6.16 reprinted from Rafiq, M. and Ahmed, P.K. (2000) Advances in the internal marketing concept: definition synthesis and extension, *Journal of Services Marketing*, vol 14, no. 6, pp.449–462, Table 11.2 reprinted from Onkvisit, S. and Shaw, J.J. (1993) *International Marketing: Analysis and strategy*, 2nd edn, Figure 13.4 reprinted from Pirog III, S.F. and Lancioni, R. (1997) US–Japan distribution channel cost structures: is there a significant difference? *International Journal of Physical Distribution and Logistics Management*, vol. 27, no. 1, pp.53–66, Figure 18.3 reprinted from Wu, H.J. and Dunn, S.C. (1995) Environmentally responsible logistics systems, *International Journal of Physical Distribution and Logistics Management*, vol. 25, no. 2, pp.20–38, with permission from MCB University Press; Figure 8.11 reprinted from *Marketing Management: The millennium edition* 10/e by Kotler, Philip, © 2000, adapted by permission of Pearson Education, Inc., Upper Saddle River, NJ, and Figure 9.11 reprinted from *Global Marketing Management* by Keegan, Warren J., ©1995, adapted by permission of Pearson Education, Inc., Upper Saddle River, NJ; Figure 8.12 reproduced with permission from BMW Group; Figure 9.1 reproduced with permission from Skagen Designs; Figure 10.1 reproduced from *Nokia Annual Report 2000* with permission from Nokia Group; Figures 10.10 and 10.11 reprinted from Segil, L. (2001) *Fast Alliances: Power your E-business*, copyright © 2001 John Wiley & Sons, Inc., Figure A.6 reprinted from McDaniel Jr, S. and Gates, R. (1993) *Contemporary Market Research: An applied orientation*, copyright © 1993 John Wiley & Sons, Inc., this material is used by permission of John Wiley & Sons, Inc.; Figure 11.9 first published in *The Journal of Brand Management*, vol. 7, no. 4, in a paper by Dave Allen entitled 'The ACID Test™: a communications tool for leadership teams who want to interact with the whole organisation' and Table 15.2 first published in *The Journal of Brand Management*, vol. 8, no. 3, in a paper by Brian Wansink and Scott Seed entitled 'Making brand loyalty programs succeed', Henry Stewart Publications (www.henrystewart.co.uk); Figure 12.8 reprinted from Simon, H. and Kucher, E. (1993) The

European pricing bomb – and how to cope with it, *Marketing and Research Today*, February, pp. 25–36, copyright © ESOMAR 2001; Figure 13.10 reproduced with permission from Red Bull; Figure 16.7 reprinted from C. Homburg, J.P. Workman Jr & O. Jensen (2000), *Academy of Marketing Science Journal*, vol. 28, no. 4, pp.459–479, copyright © 2000 by Sage Publications, Inc., reprinted by permission of Sage Publications, Inc.; Figure 17.8, Table 17.8 and Figure 17.10 reproduced with permission from SCA.

In some instances we have been unable to trace the owners of copyright material, and we would appreciate any information that would enable us to do so.

Introduction

After studying this chapter you should be able to:

- describe how marketing management is placed in the overall company strategy.
- compare and discuss the differences and similarities between the traditional (transactional) marketing approach and the relationship marketing approach.
- explain what implications the relationship marketing approach has on the traditional (transactional) marketing mix (the four Ps).
- describe and discuss the three different organizational forms of relationship marketing.

Case study 1.1 Coca-Cola

Reconsidering the marketing strategy for Muslim dominated markets after September 11, 2001

While Coca-Cola has succeeded in penetrating nearly every country of the world, it has never been able to separate itself from the image of an overpowering US brand. This was underlined by a peculiar moment in October 2001 in Indonesia, when hundreds of Muslim teenagers, thirsty from calling for a boycott of US goods, gulped down Coca-Cola's Sprite and Fanta drinks. Other US companies have also been targeted. Days before the demonstration by Indonesian youths, protesters in another Indonesian city bombed a Kentucky Fried Chicken outlet. Nike has protected its overseas plants with security guards. The US attacks on Afghanistan after September 11, 2001 have stirred anger in Muslim dominated countries in the Middle East and south-east Asia. Coca-Cola stands for so much of what the USA stands for. This has forced Coca-Cola, along with other multinationals, to reconsider its marketing strategy in these areas.

From a business point of view, it would matter little if Coca-Cola's sales dropped significantly in the Middle East. Coca-Cola's revenues there represent less than 2 per cent of its global business and in Iraq, Syria and Afghanistan it has no operations. But the region has always been a sore point for Coca-Cola and one where, during the past few decades, the company is trying to win customers back from PepsiCo, its arch-rival (Table 1.1).

The company's relations with Arab nations have been sensitive since it opened the first **franchised** soft drinks plant in Israel in the 1960s. Coca-Cola's biggest boast is that it is in almost 180 countries – a feat matched by few other companies. The current crisis comes at a time when Coca-Cola is trying to minimize its American prowess and is marketing local brands in more and more countries. Such a task is more difficult when its familiar red-and-white swirl logo is being heralded as a symbol of US terrorism.

The Middle East is not one of Coca-Cola's biggest markets, but what it does worry about is whether anti-US sentiment there will translate to other countries such as the Philippines or

Case study 1.1 continued

Table 1.1 Market share for soft drinks in Muslim dominated countries

	Egypt	Lebanon	Jordan	Saudi-Arabia	Pakistan
	Market share, %				
Coca-Cola	55	31	40	23	25
Pepsi	37	65	55	74	71
Others	8	4	5	3	4
Total	100	100	100	100	100
Total market, million cases	170	47	31	250	109

Malaysia. These countries are important for the company. Any unrest in the Philippines would affect the economy and therefore affect consumption patterns.

The Coca-Cola management in Atlanta, USA, is concerned about the market position of Coca-Cola in the Middle East. They are considering which marketing measures to implement in order to improve the relationships with main players in the Muslim soft drinks market. Or perhaps they should keep a low profile and withdraw from the Muslim market?

If Coca-Cola should choose to strengthen relationships in the Muslim soft drinks market it is considering doing it by approaching:

- end consumers (by advertising)
- main distributors (retail chains) in the markets

- religious (Muslim) leaders
- governments in Muslim countries
- US Government/Secretary of Commerce
- US commercial attaché
- other groups.

Questions

1. If you were asked, would you (at the time) recommend that Coca-Cola should withdraw from the Muslim markets or should it strengthen relationships with one or more groups in or around the Muslim soft drinks markets?

2. If Coca-Cola chooses to remain pro-active in the Muslim countries, which group should Coca-Cola approach in order to strengthen relationships?

Source: adapted from Lui (2001).

1.1   Introduction

This chapter introduces marketing management in a relationship approach. The chapter contrasts the traditional (**transactional**) **marketing** (TM) concept with the **relationship marketing** (RM) approach. The marketing management process is introduced in the form of a hierarchical planning model.

This book will bridge the gap between the traditional **marketing planning** approach and the 'new' relational marketing (RM) approach.

This chapter will start by discussing where the marketing management strategy is placed in the overall company strategy. The book is structured (Figure 1.1) according to the hierarchical marketing management process.

Figure 1.1 **Structure of the book in relation to hierarchical marketing management process**

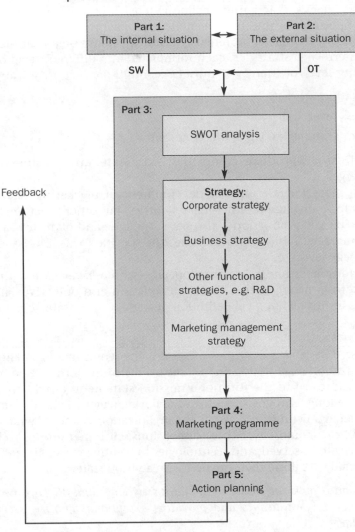

The marketing management process

1.2

Though it is not always the case, the starting point for the marketing management process and the **marketing plan** should be the corporate strategy.

Marketing strategy

Although strategy first became a popular business buzzword during the 1960s, it continues to be the subject of widely differing definitions and interpretations. The following definition, however, captures the essence of the term:

> **A strategy is a fundamental pattern of present and planned objectives, resource deployments, and interactions of an organization with markets, competitors, and other environmental factors.**

This definition suggests that a strategy should specify what (objectives to be accomplished), where (on which industries and product markets to focus), and how (which resources and activities to allocate to each product/market to meet environmental opportunities and threats) and to gain a competitive advantage.

Rather than a single comprehensive strategy, many organizations have a hierarchy of interrelated strategies, each formulated at a different level of the firm. The three major levels of strategy in most large, multi-product organizations are:

1. corporate strategy

2. business-level strategy

3. functional strategies, e.g. marketing strategy.

In small, single-product companies, corporate and business-level strategic issues merge.

Our primary focus is on the development of marketing strategies and programmes for individual product-market entries, but other functional departments – such as R&D and production – also have strategies and plans for each of the firm's product markets. Table 1.2 summarizes the specific focus and issues dealt with at each strategy level.

The traditional strategy literature operates with a *hierarchical* definition of strategic marketing management. The terms mission and objectives all have specific meanings in this hierarchical definition of strategy and strategic management.

Mission

As suggested in Table 1.2 a firm's mission is the senior management's view of what the organization seeks to do and become over the long term. Often, this view of the future is expressed in the form of a mission statement: a publicly available summary of the long-term goals of a firm's senior managers. This corporate mission can be considered a definition of what the organization is and of what it does. Ideally the definition should cover three dimensions: customer groups to be served, customer needs to be served, and technologies to be utilized (Abell, 1980).

McDonald's combine their mission with a vision statement:

Our vision is to be the world's best 'quick service restaurant'. This means opening and running great restaurants and providing exceptional quality, service, cleanliness and value.

Source: www.mcdonalds.com.

Objectives

Objectives in the hierarchical definition of strategy are the specific performance targets that firms aspire to in each of the areas included in a firm's mission statement. It is usually not enough for a firm just to assert that it wants to be a leader in its industry or that it wants to become a major diversified company. In addition, a firm needs to specify what it means to be a leader in its industry, what being a major diversified company means. Often, objectives are stated in financial or economic terms. Thus for one firm being a 'leader' in an industry may mean having the largest market share, but for other firms leadership might mean being the most profitable firm in the industry, having the highest-quality products, or being the most innovative. In the same way, being a major diversified company may mean unrelated diversification across a wide variety of industries for one firm and it may

Table 1.2 Different planning levels in the company

Strategy components	Corporate strategy	Business strategy	Marketing strategy
Scope/mission	Corporate domain – which businesses should we be in?	Business domain – which product markets should we be in within this business or industry?	• Target market definition • Product-line depth and breadth • Branding policies
Strategy	Corporate development strategy • **Conglomerate diversification** (expansion into unrelated businesses) • Vertical integration • Acquisition and divestiture policies	Business development strategy Concentric diversification (new products for existing customers or new customers for existing products)	• Product-market development plan • **Line extension** and product elimination plans
Goals and objectives	Overall corporate objectives aggregated across businesses • Revenue growth • Profitability • ROI (**return on investment**) • Earnings per share • Contributions to other stakeholders	Constrained by corporate goals Objectives aggregated across product-market entries in the business unit • Sales growth • New product or market growth • Profitability • ROI • Cash flow • Strengthening bases of competitive advantage	Constrained by corporate and business goals Objectives for a specific product-market entry • Sales • Market share • Contribution margin • Customer satisfaction
Allocation of resources	• Allocation among businesses in the corporate portfolio • Allocation across functions shared by multiple businesses (corporate R&D, MIS)	• Allocation among product-market entries in the business unit • Allocation across functional departments within the business unit	Allocation across components of the marketing plan (elements of the marketing mix) for a specific product-market entry
Sources of competitive advantage	Primarily through superior corporate financial or human resources; more corporate R&D; better organizational processes or synergies relative to competitors across all industries in which the firm operates	Primarily through competitive strategy; business unit's competences relative to competitors in its industry	Primarily through effective product positioning; superiority on one or more components of the marketing mix relative to competitors within a specific product market
Sources of synergy	Shared resources, technologies, or functional competences across businesses within the firm	Shared resources (including favourable customer image) or functional competences across product markets within an industry	Shared marketing resources, competences, or activities across product-market entries

| Exhibit 1.1 | **Retro marketing** |

Retro marketing is combining the old with the new, usually in the form of old styling with current technology and design.

One example is the 'new' Volkswagen Beetle, which combines the distinctive bubble shape of the old Beetle with the latest automotive technology to produce a 21st-century car with 20th-century styling. Another example includes the Chrysler PT Cruiser, a pastiche of the upright sedans of the late 1930s.

We also see new big-budget movies of old low-budget television series (Charlie's Angels, Mission Impossible, Lost in Space).

The TAG Heuer watch may look like the 1930s original, but where there was once a mechanical escapement there is now a solar powered microchip.

The Marlboro cowboy was retro from day one and the brand has continued to advertise itself with idealized images of the past.

Source: adapted from Brown (1999).

mean a relatively narrow product and industry focus for another. In this hierarchical definition of strategy, comparing actual behaviour with objectives is the way that managers can know whether they have fulfilled a firm's mission.

With a mission and objectives in place, a firm, according to the hierarchical definition of strategy, can then turn its attention to strategies. Strategies, here illustrated by the marketing strategy, thus become the means through which firms accomplish their objectives and mission.

Marketing plan

In most organizations strategic planning is an annual process, typically covering just the year ahead. Occasionally, a few organizations may look at a practical plan that stretches three or more years ahead. To be most effective, the plan must be formalized, usually in written form, as an identifiable marketing plan. The process of marketing management and the development of a marketing plan is no different from any other functional area of management in that it essentially comprises four key tasks.

Analysis

The starting point of marketing management decisions is analysis. Customers, competitors, trends and changes in the environment, and internal strengths and weaknesses must each be fully understood by the marketer before effective marketing plans can be established. Analysis in turn, requires information using systematic market research and **marketing information systems**.

Planning

The second task of the manager is the planning process. The marketing manager must plan both long-term marketing direction for the organization (strategic planning), including, for example, the selection of target markets, and the marketing programmes and tactics that will be used to support these strategic plans.

Implementation

Both strategic and tactical plans must, of course, be acted upon if they are to have any effect. The implementation tasks of marketing management involve such activities as staffing, allocating tasks and responsibilities, budgeting, and securing any financial and other resources needed to carry out the plans. Actions include activities, like placing an advert in the right media, delivering products, doing customer surveys, etc.

Control

The fourth, and sometimes neglected, task of the manager is measuring and evaluating progress against objectives and targets established in plans. **Control** of marketing plans can be problematical, with difficulties associated with both measuring marketing performance and pinpointing cause and effect. For example, market share – a frequently used measure of marketing performance and hence a basis for marketing control – needs very careful analysis and interpretation if it is to provide a useful basis for controlling the **effectiveness** of marketing strategies and plans. Both qualitative and quantitative techniques of control should be used by the marketing manager and include budgetary control, control of marketing mix effectiveness and, from time to time, a full **marketing audit**.

In the following the strengths and weaknesses of the hierarchical approach to marketing planning will be highlighted.

Strengths of the hierarchical approach to marketing planning

The hierarchical approach has three important strengths. First, it emphasizes the link between strategy and performance. Virtually all strategic management researchers, and most practising managers, are interested in the relationship between the actions taken by a firm and a firm's performance. The hierarchical definition provides explicit criteria for judging the performance quality of a firm's strategies – good strategies enable an organization to reach its objectives and fulfil its mission; bad strategies make it more difficult for a firm to reach its objectives and fulfil its mission.

Second, this hierarchical definition focuses on the multiple levels of analysis that are important in formulating and implementing strategies. These levels of analysis vary in their degree of abstraction. Company missions are very abstract concepts. They specify what a firm wants to become but say little about how a firm will get to where it wants to go. Objectives translate missions into specific goals and targets and thus are less abstract. Strategies specify which actions firms will take to meet their objectives. Plans, the least abstract concept, focus on specific actions that need to be taken to implement strategies.

By emphasizing the multiple levels of analysis in the strategic management process, hierarchical definitions appropriately emphasize the need in organizations to gather information, ideas, and suggestions from all parts of the firm in order to formulate effective strategies. In this conception of strategy, each part of a firm plays an important role. Senior managers specialize in establishing missions and objectives, divisional managers specialize in strategy formulation, and functional managers focus their efforts on tactics. No one of these tasks is more important than any other. Missions and objectives will never be achieved without strategies and tactics. Strategies without missions and objectives will be unfocused. Strategies without tactics are usually not implemented. And plans without strategies or missions are not likely to improve a firm's performance.

A third strength of the hierarchical definition is that it emphasizes that strategy, in order to have an impact on performance, cannot remain simply an idea in an organization. Rather, it must be translated, through resource allocation, into action. An organization's mission is often a statement of an idea, or a manifestation of the values, of top management. However, by itself, a mission statement is likely to have little impact on a firm's performance. Rather, this mission statement must be linked with objectives, strategies, and tactics. In choosing objectives, strategies, and tactics, managers must make tough decisions, set priorities, and allocate resources. Firms that translate their mission into actions increase the probability that they will improve their performance.

Weaknesses of the hierarchical approach to marketing planning

The most important weaknesses of the hierarchical approach are as follows. First, it has a very underdeveloped notion of the external competitive environment's impact on strategy formulation and implementation. Mission statements summarize where the senior management want an organization to be in the long run, but the development of these statements is encouraged to focus inward. In choosing a mission, senior managers are encouraged to look inward, evaluating their own personal priorities and values. Certainly, this kind of analysis is an important step in developing a firm's mission.

Indeed, part of this book is devoted to this kind of internal analysis. Such an analysis, however, must be linked with the external analysis (Part II) in order for firms to choose missions, objectives, strategies, and thus marketing plans, that will add value to the firm.

A second weakness of the hierarchical definition is that it tends to focus, almost exclusively, on formal, routine, bureaucratic strategy-making processes. In this definition, strategic choices are made through systematic study and analysis. These analyses result in coherent, self-reinforcing sets of strategies that, taken together, lead a firm to reach its objectives and mission. There is little doubt that many organizations choose at least some of their strategies in this logical and systematic way. An enormous amount of research on formal strategic planning suggests that more and more firms are adopting explicit and formal planning systems to choose their strategies. The hierarchical definitions presented in Figure 1.1 tend to emphasize this formal, systematic aspect of choosing and implementing strategies.

Yet not all strategies are chosen in this way. Small and medium sized enterprises (**SMEs**) choose strategies by discovering an unanticipated opportunity and exploiting that opportunity to improve performance resulting in 'emerging strategies' (Mintzberg, 1987; Mintzberg and Waters, 1985). Firms also choose strategies 'retroactively' – that is, they engage in certain kinds of behaviour over time, and then, only after that pattern of behaviour has existed, senior managers label these actions as a coherent or consistent strategy. Some firms stumble into their strategy by chance. All these are ways that firms can choose strategies, yet none of them is consistent with the formal, systematic strategic management process presented in Figure 1.1.

A third weakness of hierarchical approaches to defining strategy and strategic management is that, despite their apparent rigour and clarity, they often fail to give significant guidance to managers when they are applied in real organizations. There are literally thousands of objectives that an organization could choose to support any given mission statement. Which objectives a firm should choose, which should be given priority, and which should be ignored are questions that must be answered logically and with ideas that are not provided in the hierarchical definition. Moreover, there may be thousands of different strategies that firms could choose to support any given set of objectives. Which particular strategies a firm should choose goes beyond the hierarchical model.

1.3 The traditional (transactional) marketing (TM) concept versus the relationship marketing (RM) concept

The American Marketing Association (AMA), an international organization of practitioners and academicians, defines marketing as follows:

Marketing is the process of planning and executing the conception, pricing, promotion, and distribution of ideas, goods, and services to create exchanges that satisfy individual and organizational objectives.

This definition describes what the traditional (transactional) marketing concept is: the conception, pricing, promotion and distribution of ideas, goods and services. Moreover, the definition implies a list of activities for the marketer to undertake: the planning and execution of these four elements of competition so that individual and organizational objectives are satisfied.

Another characteristic of transactional marketing is the belief that independence of choice among marketing players creates a more efficient system for creating and distributing marketing value. Maintaining an arm's length relationship is considered vital for marketing efficiency. Industrial organizations and government policy makers believe that independence of marketing players provides each player freedom to choose his/her transactional partners on the basis of preserving their own self-interests at each decision point. This results in the **efficiency** of lowest cost purchases through bargaining and bidding.

The so-called **4Ps** are the epitome of what should be done and are also known as the marketing mix. This transactional micro-economic and teacher-friendly marketing framework is straightforward to understand and use. Indeed, in the 1950s and 1960s the 4Ps approach proved very successful. In the USA this was the era of mass manufacturing and **mass marketing** of packaged consumer goods and, because of that, marketing was often more about attracting than retaining customers.

The model of transaction marketing (as in the 4Ps) rests on three assumptions:

1. there is a large number of potential customers
2. the customers and their needs are fairly homogeneous
3. it is rather easy to replace lost customers with new customers.

Looking at today's markets and certainly when moving from consumer markets to industrial and service markets this approach may not be appropriate.

The relationship marketing (RM) concept

According to the traditional (transactional) marketing concept the major focus of marketing programmes has been to make customers buy, regardless of whether they are existing or new customers. Often only a small part of the marketing budget has explicitly been allocated directly towards existing customers.

Since the 1980s academics have been questioning this approach to marketing (e.g. Grönroos 1996; Gummesson, 1999). They argue that this approach to marketing is no longer broad enough because of the importance of customer retention, the changes in the competitive environment and the limitations of transaction marketing.

In Europe, this new direction of marketing thought was mainly initiated by IMP (Industrial Marketing and Purchasing Group).

According to Gordon (1998), p. 9

> *Relationship marketing is the ongoing process of identifying and creating new value with individual customers and then sharing the benefits from this over a lifetime of association. It involves the understanding, focusing and management of ongoing collaboration between **suppliers** and **selected customers** for mutual value creation and sharing through interdependence and organizational alignment.*

RM not only attempts to involve and integrate suppliers and customers. Besides a need for focusing on customer retention, Payne (1995) emphasizes that RM indicates a shift towards the organization of marketing activities around cross-functional functions. Payne (1995) presents a model (Figure 1.2) where six markets need to be considered if the customer is to be served satisfactorily.

Customers remain the prime focus in the centre of the model but as shown in Figure 1.2 there are five other markets where a detailed marketing strategy may be needed.

Figure 1.2 The relationship marketing's six markets models

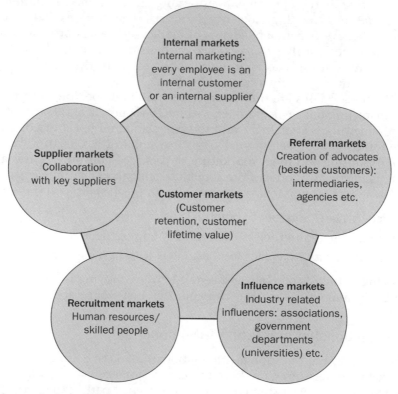

Source: after Payne (1995), p. 31.

RM attempts to involve and integrate customers, suppliers, and other infrastructural partners into a firm's developmental and marketing activities. Such involvement results in close interactive relationships with suppliers, customers or other value chain partners of the firm.

Relationships are the fundamental asset of the company. More than anything else – even the physical plant, patents, products, or markets – relationships determine the future of the firm. Relationships predict whether new value will continue to be created and shared with the company. If customers are amenable to a deepening bond, they will do more business with the company. If employees like to work there, they will continue along their **learning curve** and produce more and better. If investors and bankers are happy with their returns, they will continue to keep their funds in the company.

Thus, the development of relationship marketing points to a significant **paradigm** shift in marketing: competition and conflict to mutual cooperation, and independence and choice to mutual interdependence, as illustrated in Figure 1.3.

Today many companies realize the importance of the RM approach but most companies still operate with a mixture of the TM and RM approaches. Some firms are attaching more weight to RM than others, and vice versa.

RM emphasizes cooperation rather than competition and consequent conflict among the parties. It also emphasizes cooperation rather than competition and consequent conflict among the marketing players. The exchange-based transactional marketing approach is based on a notion of mass markets where individual customers are anonymous. The goal is to make customers choose one particular **brand** over competing brands. This easily creates a situation of competition between the marketer and the customer.

Figure 1.3 Transactional and relationship marketing

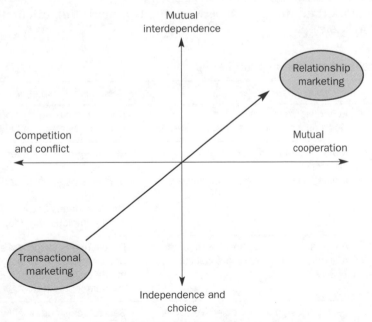

Source: adapted from Sheth and Parvatiyar (1995) p. 400.

In transaction marketing situations, customers, as unidentified members of a segment, are exposed to a number of competing products, and they are supposed to make independent choices from among the available options. The two parties have conflicting interests. The starting point is that the customer does not want to buy; he or she has to be persuaded to do so.

In RM, where interactions and cooperation exist at some level, the customer and the supplier or service provider are not totally isolated from each other. The relationship is based on value creation in interactions between the supplier or service provider and the customer. Cooperation is required to create the value that the customer is looking for. Of course, this does not mean that conflicts could not exist; however, cooperation is the driving force, not conflict.

In situations where there are a limited number of customers and/or where continuous interaction with customers occurs, a relationship approach is relatively easy to adopt, if this is considered profitable and appreciated by the customers. This is the case in many **business-to-business** markets and in service markets. When a firm has mass markets with limited direct contact with its customers, a relationship approach is less obvious.

Importance of customer retention

Recently, evidence has been provided about the value of long-term customer relationships and on how to improve performance by focusing on customer retention instead of single sales. It suggests that it can be up to ten times more expensive to win a customer than to retain a customer – and the cost of bringing a new customer to the same level of profitability as the lost one is up to 16 times more (Peppers and Rogers, 1993). Further evidence is provided by Lindgreen and Crawford (1999) who show that increasing customer retention from 80 per cent to 94 per cent in a food catering business quadrupled the value of its average customer. Moreover, existing satisfied customers can make up about two-thirds of the volume for an average business (Vavra, 1995).

Some important differences between the two marketing orientations are highlighted in Table 1.3.

Table 1.3 Transactional and relationship marketing

Category	Transactional marketing	Relationship marketing
Focus	Economic transaction. Decision focus on product/brand and 4Ps.	Decision focus on relationships between firms in a network and individuals.
The marketing environment	Marketing rules are very clear, defined and constant. Market is bound by countries and regions.	Marketing rules are relatively clear, defined and constant. Market is relatively bound by network and alliances. The boundaries between firms are blurred, if not completely eroded.
Parties involved	A firm and buyers are involved in a general market. Distant and impersonal contact.	Dyadic relationships: sellers, buyers, and other firms. Face-to-face, close interpersonal contacts based on commitment and trust.
Goals	Each party's goals and objectives, while similar, are geared to what is best for them.	Shared goals and objectives ensure common direction.

Table 1.3 continued

Category	Transactional marketing	Relationship marketing
Managerial intent	Transaction/sales volume and creating new customers are considered a success. Customer attraction (to satisfy the customer at a profit).	Keeping the existing customers, retention, is considered to be a success. Satisfy the customer, increase profit, and attain other objectives such as increased loyalty, decreased customer risk, etc.
Production focus	Mass production.	**Mass customization**.
Communication	Communications structured and guarded.	Open communication avoids misdirection and bolsters effective working relationships.
Customers	Low customer interactivity. Customers are less knowledgeable and informed.	High customer interactivity. Customers are aware and informed. Their feedback can be immediate.
Competitive advantage/ differentiation	The quality of the product is important for differentiation. The marketing mix can be used for the differentiation.	Creativity is important for differentiation. Long-term and close relationships, adaptation, putting the customer at the centre of the organization is a source of differentiation.
Balance of power/sharing	Active seller – less passive buyers. Suspicion and distrust. Each party wary of the motives and action by the other. Sharing limited by lack of trust and different objectives. Often opportunistic behaviour.	Seller and buyer mutually active and adaptive (interdependent and reciprocal). Mutual trust forms the basis for strong working relationships. Sharing of business plans and strategies.
Organization/managerial level	Functional marketers (e.g. sales manager, product development manager). Marketing is a concern of the marketing department.	Managers from across functions and levels in the firm. Everyone in the organization is a part-time marketer. Specialist marketers (e.g. key **account managers**).
Formality	Formal (yet personalized via technology).	Formal and informal (i.e. at both a business and social level).
Duration	Discrete (yet perhaps over time). Short-term.	Continuous (ongoing and mutually adaptive, may be short or long-term).
General advantages/ disadvantages	Advantage: independence of buyer and seller.	Advantage: intimate knowledge of needs and markets (developed over time), which has been likened to reading the minds of customers.
	Disadvantage: the firm is in a vulnerable situation if a competitor makes a better offer to the customer.	Disadvantage: the firm is in a vulnerable situation if its business supplier (customer) disappears.

Source: adapted from Payne (1995), Lindgreen *et al*. (2000), Zineldin (2000).

It has been said that transaction marketing is too simplified a framework for today's businesses as they are confronted with many competitive challenges. In the 1990s, markets have generally become mature and there is only little possibility for product differentiation. Therefore, customer retention is becoming more important.

RM suggests that the company should focus on the ultimate market segment and serve customers as individuals. Companies can give individual customers, or logical groups of customers (where serving the individual uniquely makes no sense to either customer or supplier) the value each wants by using technology appropriately throughout the **value chain**. Often this means taking apart existing business processes and inserting technology into them. For example, when the **Internet** is used for online ordering, the process for purchasing has been redesigned.

However, all this does not exclude transaction marketing. In a way transaction marketing and RM become part of the same fundamental paradigm: *focus on customer satisfaction*.

Although RM is a strong strategic concept, its implementation requires the use of powerful instruments. This instrumental dimension was largely neglected in the early academic discussion of the RM concept. Nevertheless, most companies and scholars do use the transactional paradigmatic framework when identifying adequate marketing instruments for building and maintaining relationships with customers.

1.4 Balancing the transactional and relationship concepts throughout the book

This book links between the traditional marketing approach and the relationship marketing (RM) approach. Some chapters (Chapters 2–5) concentrate more on the traditional marketing approach, whereas Chapter 6 attempts to draw all the factors together into a true relationship approach (between-the-boxes approach)

in Figure 1.4 indicates that the actors (firm, customer and competitor) are treated more independently of the relationship approach. In other words, these three chapters have a more traditional marketing approach, without focusing on the relationships to other important players in the value chain.

These relationships (double arrows between firm and the other actors) are then covered in Chapter 6, which also includes the firm's relations to suppliers and complementors. Hence, though there seems to be a paradigm shift going on from the transactional to the relationship marketing approach, most companies still are practising a mixture of both.

1.5 How the RM concept influences the traditional marketing concept

In the following, some of the consequences of a relationship orientation for the traditional four marketing parameters (4Ps) are given.

Figure 1.4 Balancing the concepts of transactional and relationship marketing

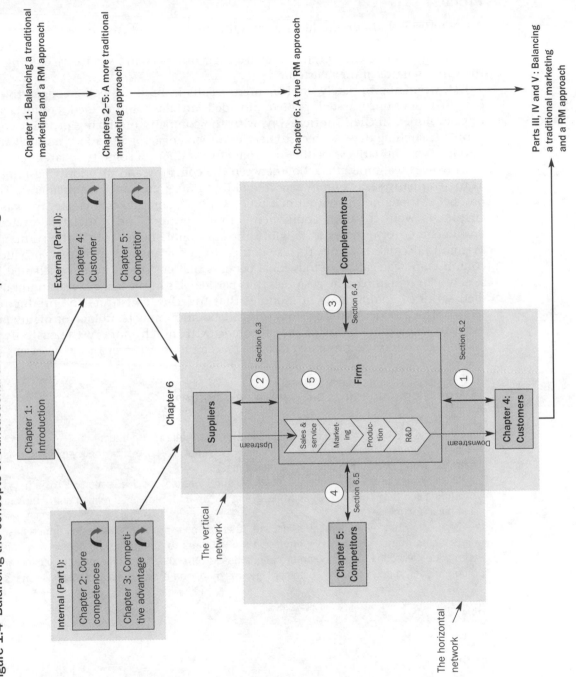

Chapter 1: Balancing a traditional marketing and a RM approach

Chapters 2–5: A more traditional marketing approach

Chapter 6: A true RM approach

Parts III, IV and V : Balancing a traditional marketing and a RM approach

External (Part II):
Chapter 4: Customer
Chapter 5: Competitor

Internal (Part I):
Chapter 2: Core competences
Chapter 3: Competitive advantage

Chapter 1: Introduction

Chapter 6

Complementors

Section 6.4
3

Section 6.3
2

Section 6.2
1

Suppliers

The vertical network

Upstream

Firm
5
Sales & service
Market-ing
Produc-tion
R&D

Downstream

Chapter 4: Customers

Section 6.5
4

Chapter 5: Competitors

The horizontal network

Product

A key impact of RM on product policy is the integration of customized elements in what were previously standardized products for mass markets. Modern information technology allows firms to individualize their products and services according to the varying needs of their customers.

RM, when appropriately implemented, results in products being cooperatively designed, developed, tested, piloted, provided, installed, and refined. Products are not developed in the historical way, with the company producing **product concepts**, researching these with customers, and then engaging in various research and development initiatives, leading to product introduction some time later. Rather, RM involves real-time interaction between the company and its priority customers as the company seeks to move more rapidly to meet customer requirements. The product is therefore the output of a process of collaboration that creates the value customers want for each component of the product and associated services. Products are not bundles of tangible and intangible benefits that the company assembles because it thinks this is what customers want to buy. Rather, products comprise an aggregation of individual benefits that customers have participated in selecting or designing. The customer thus participates in the assembly of an unbundled series of components or modules that together constitute the product or service. The product resulting from this collaboration may be unique or highly tailored to the requirements of the customer, with much more of the customer's knowledge content incorporated into the product than was previously the case.

Exhibit 1.2	Permission marketing: old wine in new bottles

A new buzzword is permission marketing.

Customers do not want to be bombarded with information on products they do not want or need. What customers want is a genuinely personal dialogue with their suppliers. It is merely a step towards true one-to-one marketing.

The concept seeks to reduce the costs of, and increase positive responses to, a mass marketing campaign by more selective targeting. However, it remains a refinement of the old and failed techniques.

Permission marketing is product-focused. It seeks more prospects interested in purchasing specific items. The goal of permission marketing is to substitute all mass marketing techniques with one-to-one communications based on a thorough knowledge of customer requirements; a sophisticated customer life cycle map; and a high degree of responsiveness to customer events.

Source: adapted from Godin, S. (1999), Kelly (2001).

Price

Traditional marketing sets a price for a product, perhaps discounting the price in accordance with competitive and other marketplace considerations. The price seeks to secure a fair return on the investment the company has made in its more or less static product.

Relationship oriented pricing is centred on the application of price differentiation strategies. The pricing should correspond to **customer lifetime values**. This proposal represents an attempt to estimate the net present value of the current and future potential of various customers or customer segments.

In relationship marketing, the product varies according to the preference and dictates of the customer, with the value varying commensurately. So when customers specify that a product should have a specific feature and that certain services should be delivered before, during, and after the sale, they naturally want to pay for each component of the package separately. Just as the product and services are secured in a process of collaboration, so too will the price need to reflect the choices made and the value created from these choices.

Business-to-business marketers, especially for larger capital goods and installations, have typically engineered the products and services to customer requirements and negotiated the prices of their services. But customers have not often been involved in all aspects of the value chain and the price/performance **trade-offs** that sellers have thought were necessary. RM invites customers into the pricing process, and all other value-related processes, giving customers an opportunity to make any trade-offs and to further develop trust in the relationship.

Distribution

The general message of RM for distribution is that it should get closer to the customer. Conventional marketing thinking sees distribution as the channel that takes the product from producer to consumer. In the case of the computer industry, Dell sees distribution as a direct sales approach, primarily using the Internet, telephone sales and order placement, whereas IBM uses many approaches to distribution, including its own stores, a direct sales force, and retailers that resell the firm's personal computers. RM instead considers distribution from the perspective of the customer, who decides where, how, and when to buy the combination of products and services that constitute the vendor's total offering. Seen this way, distribution is not a channel but a process. The process allows customers to choose where and from whom they will obtain the value they want. Continuing the computer example just mentioned, the customer can choose whether to buy an off-the-shelf model from a reseller and take it home immediately, order one to be built to individual preferences at the factory and shipped within a week or so, or have one configured in-store that will be available within a few days. It thus may be more accurate to think of distribution as placement, giving customers choices with regard to the locations at which they will specify, purchase, receive, install, repair, and return individual components of the products and services. That is, whereas traditional marketing considers a product as a bundled package of benefits, RM unbundles the product and service and allows the customer to initiate a placement decision for each element.

Communication (promotion)

Traditional marketing sends smoke signals for all within a specific market segment to see. 'Buy me', the signals say to all who can see them. RM instead gives individual customers an opportunity to decide how they wish to communicate with the enterprise, how often, and with whom. Mass promotion becomes support to build equity in the firm or brand, rather than a means to influence purchase directly.

The RM approach indicates the need for integrated communication and the demand for interactive communication.

Technology can make promotion become communication because technology can help individuals to interact more frequently and more effectively. For the producer in the B-t-B market this communication may involve opportunities for supplier and customer to interact at the strategic level – considering each other's plans, customers, strategies, and initiatives – so that both can consider how best to be interdependent over the planning horizon. It may also tie into the customer and supplier's information and communications system, letting staff in each firm feel as though they work with the other in an integrated way. In this way, the lines between supplier and customer can be further blurred.

Producers in the B-t-C market could relate and communicate in much the same way with their channel intermediaries, such as the retailers. And now, with technology, customers can be interactively and uniquely engaged. Using technologies such as the Internet, computer-telephony integration at call centres, intelligence at point of sale, kiosks, smart cards, and interactive voice response, companies can give consumers a host of options for communicating with the company and have information on hand to engage, inform, and direct each customer with complete knowledge as to the customer's preferences and behaviours.

Part 4 of this book further develops the implications of the RM approach on the traditional 4P marketing mix (product, price, place, promotion).

1.6 Different organizational forms of RM

It is important to understand the nature of relationship. The boundaries of RM have been discussed since RM was first investigated in the 1970s (Healy *et al.*, 2001).

It is possible to study relationships in different contexts. Figure 1.5 presents a context where it is possible to study relationships in three ways.

Figure 1.5 Forms of relationships

Dyadic relationship	Chain of relationships	Networks
Example	*Example*	*Example*
Explanation A dyadic buyer-seller relationship that tends to ignore the role of other elements in the distribution channel and the role of other stakeholders.	*Explanation* The relationship is still dyadic but goes beyond the buyer-seller relationship to include all marketing activities directed towards establishing, developing, and maintaining successful relational exchanges in the total vertical value chain. This results in several dyadic relationships along the vertical chain.	*Explanation* A more complex structure of relationships or networks involving three or more parties.

Exhibit 1.3	Relationship between university and industry

Companies generally expect that their cooperation with public or private research centres and universities will provide:

- an interpretation and understanding of the research (whatever it may be)
- access to a pool of expertise and to scientific networks
- an analysis of the practical aspects of technological innovation
- a proposal of feasible scientific and technological options which takes into account advice and external opinions
- information on scientific and technological trends
- a renewal of scientific and engineering skills within that industry.

The Pirelli Tyre Company cooperates in a consortium with Milan Politecnico, the University of Southampton, the University of Milan and the University of Akron. These associations involve optical technologies as well as amplification techniques that are useful in the transmission of signals via cable. Historically, as Pirelli's research teams had always placed a particular emphasis on these specific fields of research, its collaboration with the universities complements well its strategic orientations.

The success of a cooperative working relationship of this sort appears to be strongly influenced by several factors:

- an awareness of the diversity in motivation and culture
- a mutual or convergent interest: commercial success on one hand, greater recognition on the other
- the strategic character of the project
- a long-term association
- highest quality management methods
- clear and realistic objectives
- transparent contracts, particularly when the financial considerations and the publications that are associated with a cooperation programme are under the aegis of the contract
- direct and regular interactions
- on-site availability of appropriate resources
- precise and clear modalities of control.

Supported by this example, we can conclude that the success of university-industry cooperation is especially dependent upon four aspects:

- *confidentiality* which must be strict and unconditional with respect to third parties
- the *mutuality of the interests* at stake, i.e. the programme must be tantamount to a 'win-win' strategy
- a *continuity* in the relationship between the participants
- the *rapid exploitation* of results.

Source: adapted from **www.Pirelli.com**.

The dyadic relationship is the basic irreducible building block of inter-firm relationships. It can be used as the basis for studying a number of marketing phenomena ranging from buyer-seller relationships, salesperson-purchasing **agent** interactions to inter-firm relationships and **strategic alliances**.

Thus a chain of relationships' key distinction from RM is that although the unit of analysis is still dyadic, the dyad can be other than one buyer-seller relationship. Furthermore, more than one dyad can be involved in any given exchange.

From the relationship background, network theory evolved when researchers started looking beyond simple dyadic relationships and began to concentrate their research effort on the more complex structures of networks.

Network theory has been based on the players-activities-resources model which suggests that networks are dynamic entities exhibiting interdependence and connectedness between actor bonds, activity links and resource ties (Hakansson and Johanson, 1992; Hakansson and Snehota, 1995). Nets which involve three or more players place great emphasis on the role of marketing in building and managing relationships with a company's many **stakeholders**, which could include suppliers, competitors, governments, and employees as well as customers.

1.7 Summary

Over the last decade, considerable emphasis has been placed on the importance of relationship marketing (RM). The re-orientation of marketing has been at the expense of the traditional approach to marketing, that is transaction marketing (the 4Ps). However, the premises of this book are that transactional marketing is still relevant and should be practised concurrently with various types of RM.

In RM customers take a much more active role than they normally are given. The success of RM also, to a large extent, depends on the attitudes, commitment and performance of the employees. If they are not committed to their role as part-time marketers and are not motivated to perform in a customer oriented fashion, the strategy fails. Besides customers and internal employees the stakeholder view also includes other players in the RM process: suppliers, competitors and other external players.

The chapter ends with a categorization of RM into three forms of organization: dyadic relationships, chain of relationships and networks. The classic dyadic buyer-seller relationship tends to ignore the role of other stakeholders whereas networks are a more complex structure of relationships involving several stakeholders.

Case study 1.2 Kamis Company

A Polish spice supplier is penetrating grocery stores in eastern Europe

It all started in 1991, when Kamiński, after a brief stay in a trading company dealing in food-stuffs from the former Soviet Union, decided to establish his own company. His only starting capital was a diploma from Warsaw University's Organization and Management Department, and his hands-on knowledge of both the domestic and foreign food markets. He submitted an application for a loan along with a business plan to PKO BP bank. His application was refused, but he did not give up. Kamiński met the bankers and convinced them to support his idea.

Ten years ago, Kamiński (37 years old) employed only a handful of people, producing 20 spices from imported raw materials. Today, his company employs 1000 people and produces nearly 200 types of seasoning spices. Kamis' 1996 sales totalled zl.88 million, with an operating profit of 20 per cent every year. Kamis imports raw materials and produces its seasonings at a factory near Warsaw. The company supplies them to 20,000 Polish stores. Kamis' researchers have even invented a seasoning mix for the most important Polish dish – bigos (Polish hunters' stew, made from sauerkraut and meat).

Kamiński remains the chairman and only shareholder in the company. The company's real name is Kamis-Przyprawy Company.

Competition

Kamiński credits his success to the fact he has filled a niche that has only recently attracted foreign competition. The Kamis brand is known to 64 per cent of Poles. The company makes 25 per cent of all seasonings sold in bags, 74 per cent of those sold in jars, and 10 per cent of all mustard sales. Its closest rival, Kotanyi of Austria, controls only 3 per cent of the Polish market, and France's Ducros accounts for only 1 per cent.

Generally, many of the large spice manufacturers are promoting themselves actively in eastern Europe, among them are Maggi (Germany), Knorr (Austria), Van den Bergh Foods (UK) and McCormick & Company (USA).

International expansion

His life's goal is to see his company grow. Despite many foreign offers, he does not plan to sell his shares to anyone. Another goal is expansion outside Poland. He hopes to see the sale of Polish-made seasonings in Belarus, Russia, Ukraine and the Baltic states. Kamis seasonings have already reached these markets thanks to independent distributors and his own (local) sales representatives. They deliver the products only in the main cities (Moscow, Saint Petersburg, Kiev and Bucharest). Kamis foresees establishing new companies in these areas, and would eventually like to repeat the pattern in southern Europe. Kamiński has chosen this strategy because of the difficulty of expanding the range of products, some of which could be difficult to sell in the Polish market.

The structure of grocery retailing is quite different in eastern Europe compared to western Europe. Many grocery stores in eastern Europe are still very small, but there is a tendency towards fewer and larger retail **chain stores**.

Some facts about markets in eastern Europe

Table 1.4 compares the market in eastern Europe with the main markets in western Europe.

Kamis' use of the marketing mix

The competitive advantages of Kamis in the eastern European spice market are:

- own distribution. The competitors mainly use local distributors
- quality of the spices
- packaging
- point-of-sale displays. With its distribution Kamis can arrange special displays in the bigger stores more easily.

The price Kamis can charge for its products in the big cities of Russia and Ukraine is 40–50 per cent higher than in Poland. However, Kamis' prices are not higher than the foreign competitors. In the cities where Kamis products are available, the cost of living is high, so it is the normal market price.

▶

Case study 1.2 continued

Table 1.4 European sales of herbs and spices, 1999

	Per capita volume (kg)	Per capita value (US$)
Bulgaria	0.26	0.82
Czech Republic	0.27	2.66
Hungary	0.36	2.82
Poland	0.18	3.13
Romania	0.01	0.04
Russia	0.10	1.89
Slovakia	0.24	2.68
Ukraine	0.08	0.31
France	0.13	3.41
Germany	0.11	3.72
Italy	0.04	1.40
UK	0.14	2.83

Source: adapted from Euromonitor, Consumer Europe 1999.

The company spends a lot of money on television commercials and print adverts in women's periodicals. Kamiński worries that they are too expensive for the company, but sees them as a necessary marketing tool.

In one of the latest Kamis TV commercials in Poland there is an Indiana Jones-type person travelling around the world, looking for the best and most exotic spices. He returns to Poland to offer these spices to the housewives.

Questions

1. Is it relevant to consider the RM approach for a company like Kamis?

2. Which country in eastern Europe (outside Poland) should be the first priority for Kamis?

3. What is the most critical marketing parameter for Kamis, when it tries to penetrate grocery stores in other eastern European countries?

Source: Voice Business (1997) www.kamis.pl

QUESTIONS FOR DISCUSSION

1. What are the similarities between relationship marketing (RM) and transactional marketing (TM)?

2. How does a RM strategy differ from a TM strategy?

3. Which kind of industries could benefit from the use of RM versus TM and vice versa?

4. In which situations would customers not be expected to be interested in RM?

REFERENCES

Abell, D. (1980), *Defining the Business: The starting point of strategic planning*, Prentice-Hall, Englewood Cliffs, NJ.

Brown, S. (1999), Retro marketing: yesterday's tomorrows, today! *Market Intelligence and Planning*, vol. 17, no. 7, pp. 363–76.

Godin, S. (1999), *Permission Marketing*, Simon & Schuster, New York.

Gordon, I. H. (1998), *Relationship Marketing*, John Wiley & Sons, Canada Ltd.

Grönroos, C. (1996), Relationship marketing: strategic and tactical implications, *Management Decision*, vol. 34, no. 3, pp. 5–14.

Gummesson, E. (1999), *Total Relationship Marketing – Rethinking marketing management: From 4Ps to 30 Rs*, Butterworth-Heinemann, Oxford.

Hakansson, H. and Johanson, J. (1992), 'A model of industrial networks', *in* Axelsson, B. and Easton, G. (Eds), *Industrial Networks: A new view of reality*, pp. 28–34, Routledge, London.

Hakansson, H. and Snehota, I. (Eds) (1995), *Developing Relationships in Business Networks*, Routledge, London.

Healy, M., Hastings, K., Brown, L. and Gardiner, M. (2001), The old, the new, and the complicated – A trilogy of marketing relationships, *European Journal of Marketing*, vol. 35 no. 1/2, pp. 182–93.

Kelly, S. (2001), Seeking permission for ultimate goal in true one-to-one marketing, *MAD*, March 16.

Lindgreen, A. and Crawford, I. (1991), 'Implementing, monitoring and measuring a programme of relationship marketing', *Marketing Intelligence & Planning*, vol. 17, no. 5, pp. 231–9.

Lindgreen, A., Davis, R., Brodie, R. J. and Buchanan-Oliver, M. (2000), Pluralism in contemporary marketing practices, *International Journal of Bank Marketing*, vol. 18, no. 6, pp.294–308.

Liu, B. (2001), Coca-Cola helps quench thirst during boycott of US goods, *Financial Times*, October 26.

Mintzberg, H. (1987), The strategy concept 1: five Ps for strategy, *California Management Review*, Fall, pp. 11–24.

Mintzberg, H. and Waters, A. (1985), On strategies, deliberate and emergent, *Strategic Management Journal*, vol. 6, pp. 257–72.

Payne, A. (Ed.) (1995), *Advances in Relationship Marketing*, Kogan Page, London.

Peppers, D. and Rogers, M. (1993), *One-to-One Future: Building relationships one customer at a time*, Currency/Doubleday, New York.

Sheth, J. N. and Parvatiyar (1995), The evolution of relationship marketing, *International Business Review*, vol. 4, no. 4, pp. 397–418.

Vavra, T. G. (1995), *Aftermarketing: How to keep customers for life through relationship marketing*, Business One Irwin, Homewood, II.

Voice Business, (1997), no. 51–2, December 21–8, pp. 478–9.

Zineldin, M. (2000), Beyond relationship marketing: technologicalship marketing, *Marketing Intelligence Planning*, vol. 18, no. 1, pp. 9–23.

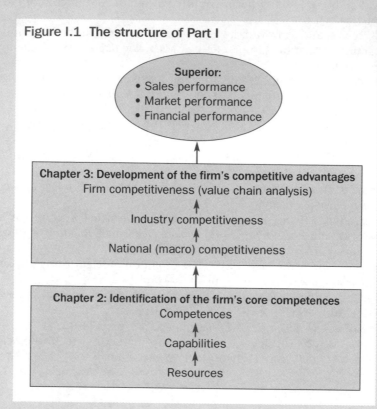

Figure I.1 The structure of Part I

Superior:
- Sales performance
- Market performance
- Financial performance

Chapter 3: Development of the firm's competitive advantages
Firm competitiveness (value chain analysis)

Industry competitiveness

National (macro) competitiveness

Chapter 2: Identification of the firm's core competences
Competences

Capabilities

Resources

Assessing the competitiveness of the firm (internal)

When the international economy was relatively static, competition was a 'war of position' in which firms occupied competitive space like squares on a chessboard. The key to competitive advantage was where a firm chose to compete. How it chose to compete was also important but secondary – a matter of execution. However, as markets fragment and product life cycles accelerate, dominating existing product segments becomes less important. In today's dynamic business environment a firm's success depends on anticipation of market trends and quick response to changing customer needs. The essence of strategy is not the structure of a firm's products but the dynamics of its behaviour. In future the goal is to identify and develop the hard-to-imitate organizational capabilities that distinguish a firm from its competitors in the eyes of customers.

Part I covers the necessary internal analysis to assess the competitive advantages of the firm with regard to its customers and other stakeholders in the external environment, which is the focus of Part II.

The structure of Part I is shown in Figure I.1.

Chapter 2 identifies the firm's core competences, based on the assessment of its resources and capabilities. Capabilities can be described as what an organization does as opposed to what is has (resources or assets). Chapter 3 then continues with how the core competences might be used in the development of competitive advantages, from the macro-level (country-specific advantages) to the micro-level (value chain analysis).

Chapter 2

Identification of the firm's core competences

LEARNING OBJECTIVES

After studying this chapter you should be able to:

- explain the difference between the resource-based view (RBV) and the market-orientation view.
- describe and explain different strategy options in the RBV.
- explain the connection between the RBV and RM.
- describe and discuss the concept of the value chain.

Case study 2.1 Microsoft[1] and Lego[2]

Different competences help create global competitiveness for both companies

On January 10, 2001 Microsoft Corp. and Lego Company announced the formation of a sweeping global alliance that would result in new services and enhanced products and technologies for consumers around the world. The synergy between Lego Company's family content, Microsoft's worldwide consumer network (www.msn.com), and Microsoft's software and service expertise, provides a business platform to deliver an environment where consumers can create and explore.

What kind of value will Lego deliver to Microsoft in this alliance?

Microsoft's products have been driven by office efficiency and adult markets. Not much thought has been given to children. With the help of the Lego brand's powerful relationship with children and families all over the world — based on values of imagination, creativity, fun and learning – Microsoft will be in a better position to create a unique sales platform for this customer group, when the marketing of the X-box starts.

Lego will develop products for Microsoft's proposed X-box games console. In addition, Lego will use Microsoft's Windows Media technology for future products for its Lego Studio, the website that enables children to produce their own films.

Lego will advertise Microsoft's website MSN on its site. It will use Microsoft technology such

[1] Founded in 1975, Microsoft Corp. is the world leader in software, services and Internet technologies for personal and business computing. The company offers a wide range of products and services designed to empower people through great software – any time, any place and on any device.

[2] The family-owned Lego Company was founded in Denmark in 1932. The company is the world leader in providing quality products and experiences that stimulate children's creativity, imagination and learning. It does so through activities that encourage hands-on, minds-on creation, fun, togetherness and sharing of ideas. These activities include the development and marketing of computer-based play and educational materials, such as the award-winning Lego Mindstorms product line. By the year 2005, the company wants the Lego brand to be the strongest in the world among families with children.

Case study 2.1 continued

as its Passport and Kids Passport on its website to aid online shopping.

Lego will facilitate the integration of Microsoft.net services and technologies throughout its global enterprise network to increase the productivity of its users and availability of content, while reducing total cost of ownership.

What kind of value will Microsoft deliver to Lego in this alliance?

Lego products will be advertised on Microsoft's MSN – the world's second most popular Internet portal with 200 million page views per month (Lego products are already sold via both its own website and via the eShop on MSN). Consumers are able to experience the world of Lego in a virtual environment by exploring MSN Kids channel for the latest Lego games and activities as well as purchase the physical products through MSN eShop. In addition, Lego will have an advertising presence in targeted areas of MSN.

Lego will have the opportunity to work as content provider for Microsoft's MSN Kids channel. Lego has also been named a game developer for the new X-box for gamers of all ages.

The firms say that other joint marketing exercises are anticipated in the near future.

That personal relationships are also important in international business relationships can be seen from the fact that Microsoft chief Bill Gates and the owner of Lego, Kjeld Kirk Kristiansen, have been meeting for a long time and they have a shared philosophy about how to make a difference for children.

Questions

1. Which of the two partners will benefit most from the alliance?

2. What kind of further joint marketing exercises could both companies benefit from in the future?

Source: adapted from BBC News (2001a), Lego (2001).

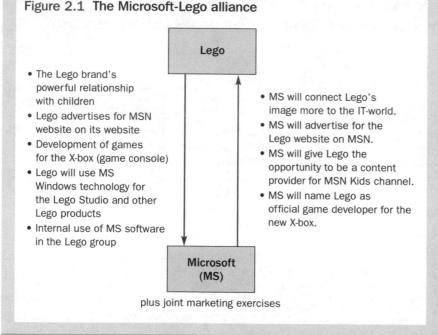

Figure 2.1 The Microsoft-Lego alliance

Lego

- The Lego brand's powerful relationship with children
- Lego advertises for MSN website on its website
- Development of games for the X-box (game console)
- Lego will use MS Windows technology for the Lego Studio and other Lego products
- Internal use of MS software in the Lego group

- MS will connect Lego's image more to the IT-world.
- MS will advertise for the Lego website on MSN.
- MS will give Lego the opportunity to be a content provider for MSN Kids channel.
- MS will name Lego as official game developer for the new X-box.

Microsoft (MS)

plus joint marketing exercises

2.1 Introduction

Understanding competitive advantage is an ongoing challenge for decision makers. Historically, competitive advantage was thought of as a matter of position, where firms occupied a competitive space and built and defended market share. Competitive advantage depended on where the business was located, and where it chose to provide services. Stable environments allowed this strategy to be successful, particularly for large and dominant organizations in mature industries.

This ability to develop a sustained competitive advantage today is increasingly rare. A competitive advantage laboriously achieved can be quickly lost. Organizations sustain a competitive advantage only so long as the services they deliver and the manner in which they deliver them have attributes that correspond to the key buying criteria of a substantial number of customers. Sustained competitive advantage is the result of an enduring value differential between the products or services of one organization and those of its competitors in the minds of customers. Therefore, organizations must consider more than the fit between the external environment and their present internal characteristics. They must anticipate what the rapidly changing environment will be like, and change their structures, cultures, and other relevant factors so as to reap the benefits of changing times. Sustained competitive advantage has become more of a matter of movement and ability to change than of location or position.

The question of an enduring value differential raises the issue of why a firm is able to achieve a competitive advantage. To answer this, it is necessary to examine why and how organizations differ in a strategic sense. Identifying strengths and weaknesses requires introspection and self-examination. It also requires much more systematic analysis than has been done in the past.

From capability to advantage

How well a company assembles the capabilities that a new business requires determines how successful it is at gaining and keeping positional advantage. Some capabilities are more important than others, and combinations are generally harder to imitate than individual capabilities. The business builder's challenge begins with the need to assemble the capabilities that are most critical to making money in the business. Lasting competitive advantage comes only when companies assemble combinations of capabilities that are difficult to imitate.

Competitive advantage may not call for superior capabilities in every area of a business. But control of the most important capabilities can determine how much of the value of a growing business will flow to its owner. For every opportunity, it is important to distinguish the capabilities that influence competitive success from those that are merely necessary to stay in business. Capabilities that are less critical can be outsourced or controlled by others.

2.2 Roots of competitive advantage

Two theoretical perspectives are particularly relevant for understanding how firms deploy scarce resources to create competitive excellence. These are: **market orientation view** (MOV) and the **resource-based view** (RBV).

There is, however, a potential conflict between these two perspectives in the sense that one (MOV) advocates the advantages of outward-looking responsiveness in adapting to market conditions, while the other (RBV) is inward looking and emphasizes the rent-earning characteristics of corporate resources and the development of corporate resources and capabilities. Quite simply, from a marketing viewpoint, if strategy becomes too deeply embedded in corporate capabilities, it runs the risk of ignoring the demands of changing, turbulent marketing environments. Yet from a resource-based perspective, marketing strategies that do not exploit a company's distinctive competences are likely to be ineffective and unprofitable.

However, we argue that *competitive positioning* provides a way of reconciling this potential conflict – see Figure 2.2. Later we will argue that the **value-chain based view** (VBV) represents a balanced view of the RBV and MOV.

We will now look at the two theoretical perspectives.

2.3   The resource-based view (RBV)

Most firms that apply a relationship marketing approach are probably somewhere in this stage of the transition process. A true transition towards a relationship marketing strategy requires a focus on competences and resources in the relationship (because partners in the relationship use each other's resources (Grönroos, 1996)). This section focuses on identification of a single firm's competences from a RBV.

According to the resource-based theory, which has its roots in economic theory (e.g. Penrose, 1959) and early strategy theory (Selznick, 1957; Ansoff, 1965), the long-term competitiveness of a company depends on its resources that differentiate it from its competitors, that are durable, and that are difficult to imitate and substitute (e.g., Grant, 1991; Fahy, 2002).

Various definitions and classifications or resources have been proposed in the literature. The most important in the current context are briefly described here.

Figure 2.2 The resource-based view versus market orientation

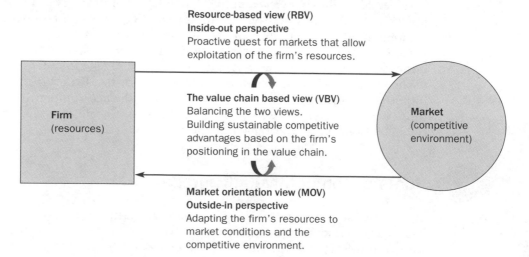

Resources

The resources of the firm in the competence-based approach are typically classified into two types: tangible and intangible resources. Tangible resources are inputs into a firm that can be seen, touched and/or quantified. They include assets like plant and equipment, access to raw materials and finance, a trained and skilled workforce and a firm's organisational structure. Intangible resources range from intellectual property rights like patents, trademarks and copyrights to the know-how of personnel, informal networks, organizational culture and a firm's reputation for its products. The dividing line between the tangible and intangible is often unclear, and how they are classified varies a little from one writer to another. Despite the problems with classification, proponents of the competence-based approach agree on the relative importance of the two types of resource. Although it is clear that both types of resource are required for any business to operate, competence-based theorists argue that intangible resources are the most likely source of competitive advantage. The reason for this, it is argued, is that, being less visible, they are more difficult to understand and imitate than tangible resources. As such they are therefore more likely to be a source of competitive advantage.

I use the word 'resource' as the most generic term to qualify the basic unit of asset, skill, ability, expertise, knowledge, etc. owned and controlled by one firm. Grant (1991) describes six types of resources: technological, financial, physical, human, organizational, and reputation. Resources are extremely diverse as shown in Figure 2.3 (examples are given in brackets).

Figure 2.3 Resource profile

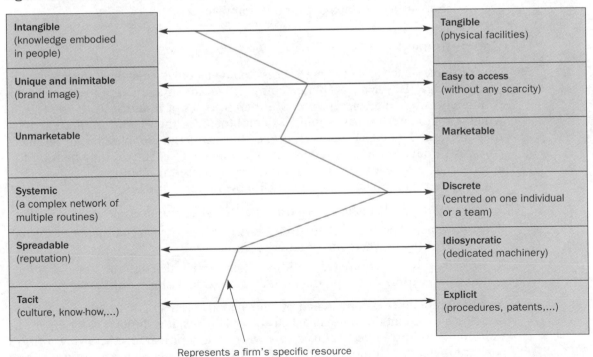

Represents a firm's specific resource profile measured on six criteria

The dotted line in Figure 2.3 represents a specific resource (e.g. technical) measured on six criteria. However, the resource-based theory does not consider all resources possessed by a company, but focuses only on critical (or strategic) resources, i.e. those that are the basis of the company's sustainable competitive advantage. To determine such resources, various authors have proposed a number of 'tests' (see also Grant, 1991; Prahalad and Hamel, 1994), the most important of which are:

- competitive superiority test, which evaluates if and to what extent the research contributes to differentiating the company from its competitors

- imitation test, which analyses actual and potential competitors' difficulty in imitating the resource, due, for example, to its physical uniqueness, path dependency, casual ambiguity or economic deterrence

- duration test, which measures if the resource's benefits will also be generated in the long term

- appropriateness test that verifies if the company owning the resource is able to exploit the advantages generated in the market

- substitutability test, which assesses how difficult it is for competitors to replace the resource with an alternative that gives the same advantages.

The very basis of RBV is to increase the ability of the firm to act upon, shape and transform its environment. The objective is no longer to adapt to the environmental forces but to choose a strategy that allows the best exploitation (the best return) of resources and competences given the external opportunities. It means taking into account the external opportunities but with the objective of creating value beyond existing market standards. As a consequence, the strategic options for a firm are derived from its resource profile: the business portfolio is an output of the search of applications carried out for one competence.

Competence

One resource – such as a privileged access to raw material – may be a source of competitive edge. However, a greater competitive advantage should emerge from competences, i.e. the combination of different types of resources. It is the way in which the resources are assembled, or combined, for the execution of an activity that creates the difference between firms. This distinctive combination of resources emerges through organizational learning. Competence examples may be found in engineering knowledge, production expertise or marketing abilities.

Competence may be described by the following three attributes:

1. *proprietariness*: a competence is a firm-specific set of resources.
2. *learning*: a competence results from years of experience accumulated in a small number of fields (where the firm may dominate).
3. *pervasiveness*: a competence is diffused pervasively throughout the entire firm and exists within several product lines (or strategic business units (SBUs)).

A **core competence**, as articulated by Prahalad and Hamel (1990), has three traits: it makes a contribution to perceived customer benefits; it is difficult for competitors to imitate; and it can be leveraged to a wide variety of markets. Knowing a firm's core competence is important for developing strategy. By concentrating on their

| Exhibit 2.1 | Honda's competences in small engines |

A famous example of a business strategy that was clearly based on a focus on a core competency is Honda's application of small engine technology to a variety of products requiring small engines (motorcycles, jet skis, lawn mowers, etc.).

When Honda introduced motorcycles in the US market, it had focused most of its attention on selling its higher value (but problem-plagued) motorcycles through a dealer network. At the same time, it introduced a series of much smaller motorcycles with little fanfare through sporting goods stores. While their larger motorcycles floundered competing against the likes of firmly established Harley-Davidson, Honda's smaller engine motorcycles found a ready audience with a more utilitarian 'nicest people' demographic group. This turned out to be Honda's beachhead into the US marketplace.

The ability to concentrate on customers and understand their changing needs is the first step in the value chain based view.

Although it is true that the small engines in both the motorcycles and the scooters were Honda's core competence, that core competence alone did not ensure success. Honda succeeded because it also looked to the other end of the value chain – it listened to what the customer wanted.

It turned out to be both a customer and a product very different from what Honda had envisioned. Honda quickly refocused its distribution channels and adjusted its product mix to meet the unexpected market demand. In the long term, Honda was able to refocus its efforts and eventually capture market share in the higher value motorcycle market.

Source: adapted from Prahalad and Hamel (1990), Webb and Gile (2001).

core competence and outsourcing other activities, managers can use their company's resources in four ways: they maximize returns by focusing on what they do best; they provide formidable barriers against the entry of competitors; they fully utilize external suppliers' strengths and investment that they would not be able to duplicate; and they reduce investment and risk, shorten cycle times, and increase customer responsiveness.

Figure 2.4 shows the connection between resources, core competences, sustainable competitive advantages and competitive excellence.

Resources alone are not a basis for competitive advantage. It is the way in which resources are integrated with each other to perform a task or an activity that provides the capability for an organization to compete successfully in the marketplace. This being the case, the most important resource for any organization is the skill and knowledge possessed by the organization's employees. It is this skill and knowledge acquired over time and embedded in the firm's culture that influences how it operates and determines its success.

Whether or not resources and capabilities have the potential to become core competences depends on how difficult they are for competitors to acquire and how valuable they are to the firm as a basis for competitive advantage. When they are rare, difficult to imitate, non-substitutable and they allow a firm to exploit opportunities or neutralize threats, then they can be considered core competences and serve as the basis of an organization's sustained competitive advantage.

A resource becomes a source of sustainable competitive advantage only if it passes several tests. First, it must be competitively superior and valuable in the

Figure 2.4 The roots of competition

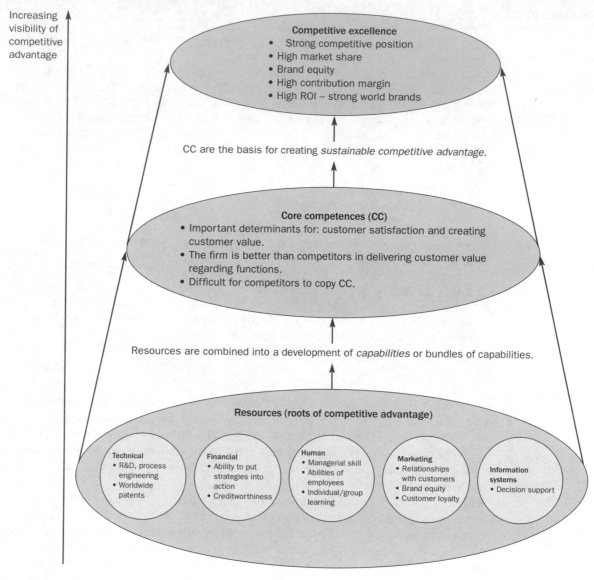

Source: inspiration from Grant (1991).

product market. Second, it must be difficult to imitate. Third, it must not be easy to replace by an alternative capability. Fourth, it must be durable. Fifth, it must be difficult to move. If the capability can move with an employee, it is the employee, not the corporation that will acquire the value.

Some individual capabilities may pass the tests. A world-class brand, for example, will continue to confer advantage on its owner. But few individual capabilities are unassailable, and even a first-to-market advantage can fade away without proper support. The key to sustaining competitive advantage as a business grows is to assemble a bundle of distinctive capabilities that together satisfy the criteria.

The capabilities in the bundle can be built in-house, borrowed by means of alliances, or acquired out of house. As each new capability is added to the bundle, greater competitive advantage accrues because the combination becomes more difficult for competitors to imitate or substitute, and more difficult for employees to acquire from the company.

2.4 Resource-based strategy options

The typical resource-based strategy is to identify, develop, protect, exploit, deploy and renew resources – that are difficult to copy – in order to generate sustainable competitive advantage in business units. Figure 2.5 tries to capture the fundamentals of such a strategy along two axes: resources and customer types.

Examples of the four strategy options will now be given.

Exploit resources in existing business

Developing close relationships is important in the global environment. Firms can leverage the **reach** of their international distribution. In some industries, developing a relationship with a local partner can help to defuse protectionism. In cultures with long time frames, firms seek to develop relationships before conducting business. Relationships are particularly useful in reducing opportunistic behaviour in areas of the world that are less legalistic than the western world. A strong relationship with a local partner can be used to leverage a firm's other assets internationally. Relationships are useful to buffer the inevitable disruptions and uncertainties that characterize international business.

Figure 2.5 Four different resource-based strategy options

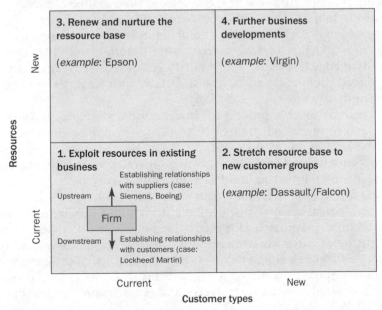

Source: Adapted from Wernerfelt (1984), Jolly (2000).

Relationships with customers: Lockheed Martin (USA)

In the defence aerospace business, Lockheed Martin has close relationships with its defence agency customers. Its managers call this competence 'customer intimacy', and it involves satisfying not only its own objectives, but those of its customers. Its deeply shared motto is: 'The customer's mission is our mission!' The close relationship with the customer enables Lockheed Martin to understand and satisfy the varied needs that exist in the client organization. It gauges and tries to satisfy the different needs of politicians in the capital, of generals in the defence department, of technicians in the field and, as part of the ongoing servicing and support. Consequently, Lockheed Martin strives to reduce the customer's total project cost, which is quite different from the initial purchase price (Mascarenhas *et al.*, 1998).

Relationships with suppliers: Siemens (Germany)

Siemens produces large capital equipment such as power generation, telecommunications and transportation equipment. Siemens markets these items in over 120 countries. Historically, German companies have had close relationships with German banks (supplier of financing). Siemens, in particular, has had a close relationship with Deutsche Bank, with executives sitting on each other's boards. This close relationship with a major German bank provided Siemens with ample, low-cost financing for its customers, enabling the firm to make international sales to many countries. Siemens' international competitors based in other countries may not have this close relationship with their banks and cannot exercise such a financial advantage (Mascarenhas *et al.*, 1998).

Boeing (USA)

Despite its historic competence in the design and production of aeroplanes, Boeing was facing both increasing competition from Europe's Airbus and rising labour costs in the USA. Airbus was state-owned until the mid-1980s and the bulk of its planes are produced in the four member countries: France, Germany, Spain and the United Kingdom. International cost-conscious customers, such as Japan Air Lines, were increasingly demanding local sourcing in return for plane orders. Senior management at Boeing reasoned that international sourcing could provide a competitive edge if it could better satisfy customer needs, and if overseas production reduced production costs, and if Airbus, with stronger unions, did not have the flexibility to source internationally.

To develop a reliable process for international sourcing, however, Boeing first had to determine which items of the plane should be outsourced, and which should be kept in-house. Boeing decided to retain wing design and production in-house because it was a critical component (affecting safety, lift, efficiency, strength) and one in which it had accumulated substantial expertise.

Boeing also had to determine which suppliers could be relied on. Boeing's existing technological competence in plane design and production proved useful in setting technical standards for potential suppliers. It developed a detailed, hierarchical protocol for evaluating suppliers with regards to the design team (the prospective supplier's ability to meet the technical specifications), project management (the supplier's ability to execute projects on time), procurement (the supplier's ability to meet cost budgets), and senior management (the supplier's history with other projects).

After choosing suppliers, Boeing developed an audit procedure to check not only the end products, but the process through which they were produced at the suppliers. This audit involved weekly visits to some of its suppliers. Suppliers had to develop a planning system for their projects and had to adhere to a protocol for safety and configuration management (how proposed design changes were to be managed and communicated). Suppliers were required to provide extensive documentation to Boeing. Electronic mail was not used for communication because of potential piracy. To facilitate communication and coordination, all suppliers were placed on a common software platform developed by Dassault and a computer-aided design package that allowed concurrent three-dimensional interactive design (Mascarenhas *et al.*, 1998).

Stretch resource base to new customer groups

The 'market stretcher' company directs its strategy towards the exploitation of its initial resources into multiple markets. This is market-related diversification. For high-technology firms, the basic principle is to capitalize on the technological platform of the firm. Using a specific resource or a given competence (combination of resources) developed over years of learning, this company expands the range of its activities by constantly increasing the number of new customers' markets and applications.

Dassault

The French firm Dassault is one of Europe's largest aerospace companies. It is well known for its outstanding expertise in military jet aeroplanes such as the Mirage and the Rafale (it designed and built the first jet fighter in France in 1949). Using its expertise in the design and manufacturing of jet aeroplanes (as well as after-sales service), Dassault launched the Falcon family of business jets, designed for non-military customers, at the beginning of the 1970s. The company currently has a family of four Falcon business jets (for transcontinental and even worldwide transportation). The reservoir of expertise embodied in military activities enabled the company to launch in 1985, for example, the first certified business jet with carbon fibre wing (Jolly, 2000).

Renew and nurture the resource base

Here the rationale is to enlarge the firm's resource base so that it can serve the same customers or markets but often with new technologies. Such behaviour often characterizes technology-related diversification.

This is not always a comfortable strategy as the firm must always be at the cutting edge of technological competition and at the same time, R&D investment must always be recovered very quickly.

Epson

Epson is a Japanese manufacturer and marketer of electronic products known for its wide array of imaging products. Computer printers represent the core product of the company. Epson relies on several technologies to serve this printing need: dot matrix (using the company's advanced micro piezo technology), black and white/colour inkjet and black and white/colour laser printers. These technologies serve the same generic printing needs for business as well as home markets. Some products are designed for professional markets, such as specialized printers for photographers or large format printers for architects. Epson's core strategy on printers is nevertheless changing as the company recently started diversification into products for image capture (including scanners and digital cameras) and also video projectors.

Further business developments

With this option the company is expanding its range of customer groups and simultaneously renewing its resource portfolio. Obviously, such a strategy option is very difficult to implement, because it requires simultaneously a combination of the second and third options.

Virgin

Virgin began in the 1970s with a UK student magazine and a mail-order record retailer. The power of the Virgin brand name is equal to Richard Branson's personal reputation. Today, the Virgin brand is used in connection with such diversified businesses as planes, trains, soft drinks, music, mobile phones, holidays, cars, wines, publishing and bridal wear. Virgin has created over 200 companies worldwide and employs over 25,000 people.

2.5 Market orientation view (MOV) compared to the resource-based view

The MOV or fit model suggests that the firm adapts its assets to its environmental constraints in order to obtain a fit with the environment. Basically, MOV is about adapting to the market environment (Kohli and Jaworski, 1990). However, adaptation to different customers in different countries can be an expensive **business model** as illustrated with Tetra Pak in Table 2.1. In this regard you get very satisfied customers but the costs involved in producing this **customer value**/satisfaction might also be very high.

Table 2.1 summarizes the main differences between the RBV and the MOV.

Figure 2.6 The business system of Ikea

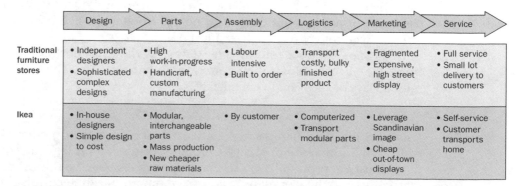

	Design	Parts	Assembly	Logistics	Marketing	Service
Traditional furniture stores	• Independent designers • Sophisticated complex designs	• High work-in-progress • Handicraft, custom manufacturing	• Labour intensive • Built to order	• Transport costly, bulky finished product	• Fragmented • Expensive, high street display	• Full service • Small lot delivery to customers
Ikea	• In-house designers • Simple design to cost	• Modular, interchangeable parts • Mass production • New cheaper raw materials	• By customer	• Computerized • Transport modular parts	• Leverage Scandinavian image • Cheap out-of-town displays	• Self-service • Customer transports home

Source: reprinted from *European Management Journal*, vol. 18, no. 2, N. Kumar, L. Scheer and P. Kotler (2000) from market driven to market driving, © 2000 with permission from Elsevier Science.

Table 2.1 Main differences between the resource-based view and the market orientation view

	Market orientation view (MOV)	Resource-based view (RBV)
Basic principle	Adapt firm's resources to the requirements of its competitive environment, i.e. to key success factors.	Pro-active quest for environments that allow the best exploitation of the firm's resources.
Strategic analysis	Centred on industry structure and market attributes.	Emphasis on internal diagnosis.
Formulation process	Outside-in.	Inside-out.
Source for competitive edge	Market positioning in relation to local competitive environment.	Firm's idiosyncratic set of resources and competences.
Examples: Lipparini and Fratocchi (1999)	**Tetra Pak** The Swedish company Tetra Pak develops, manufactures and markets complete packaging systems for liquid and semi-liquid foods as well as equipment required for their distribution. The Tetra Pak architecture is derived from, and based on, relationships. The relational aspects that the company considered when it set up a production activity in a given country mainly concerned customer companies or governments. Even today, Tetra Pak seeks to become part of local culture, rapidly acquiring a network identity, which is the direct result of its relational capability. Market-orientation leads to location of production activities where the need for a given product arises, for example, the creation of a paper-processing facility in Brazil after verifying the demand for its packaging systems at potential customers, e.g. producers of liquid foods. Its customers in Brazil would like to be close to the Tetra Pak processing plant because the logistics function is a critical factor in continuity of supplies, given that the customers must necessarily use Tetra Pak material for their machines. IT links with its packaging material stocks enable Tetra Pak to predict the re-**order point** and adjust production of the nearest paper-processing facility.	**Ikea** Ikea, the world's biggest home furniture manufacturer, is an example of how value can be created by renouncing a number of activities in the value chain and focusing on its own resources/competences and on relations with customers and suppliers. The Ikea formula comprises high quality design, a global sourcing system, products that the customers take home and assemble, and sales outlets that are also entertainment and service points. The cost savings generated by outsourcing activities like assembly and delivery allow the company to charge lower prices than its competitors. The company has approximately 2000 suppliers in over 50 countries, and 30 purchasing centres worldwide have the task of seeking out suppliers able to fit into its value system with good-quality, low-cost products. The final decision is taken by designers in Sweden, where Ikea's operational HQ is located. Suitable computerized international coordination and support structures help suppliers source raw materials on the best terms. See also Figure 2.6 for an illustration of IKEA's business system.

As both views (models) have advantages and disadvantages, a way of bridging the gap between the RBV and the MOV will now be covered.

2.6 The value chain based view (VBV)

The RBV focuses on what the firm has, whereas the VBV focuses on what the firm does. In addition, the VBV also integrates some elements of the MOV, but it does not ignore the costs of performing the activities.

Resources per se do not create value. Rather, value creation results from the activities in which the resources are applied.

The foundation of competitive advantage is a product and/or service that provides value to the business' customers. Value is the *differences* between the benefits customers realize from using the product and the costs they incur in finding, acquiring, and using it (see Figure 2.7).

The components driving customer benefits include product values, service values, technical values, and commitment value. The components driving cost fall into two categories: those that relate to the price paid, and those representing the internal costs incurred by the customer. These components can be unbundled into salient attributes. Commitment to value, for example, includes investment in personnel and customer relations. Internal cost might reflect set-up time and expense, maintenance, training, and energy.

If the benefits exceed the costs, then a customer will at least consider purchasing your product. For example, the value to an industrial customer may be represented by the rate of return earned on the purchase of a new piece of equipment. If the cost reductions or revenue enhancements generated by the equipment justify the purchase price and operating costs of the equipment through an acceptable return on investment, then value has been created.

Thus, the value of products is a function of buyer purchasing criteria (Porter, 1985, pp.141–3). Variation in buyer purchasing criteria gives rise to selective adaptation of products or differentiation. Differentiated products can command a higher price if they provide a better match with buyer purchasing criteria.

Figure 2.7 Customer value as benefits minus costs

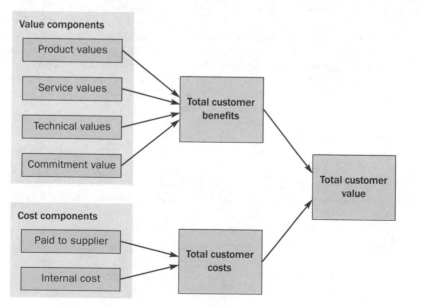

Exhibit 2.2   The value chain of Acme Axles, Inc.

Acme Axles, Inc. (a disguised name) makes custom-designed axles, wheels, and related parts for trailers, tractors, generators, welders, and other equipment requiring axle systems. Acme differentiates itself from competitors by providing fast on-time delivery of high-quality, custom-designed axles.

The value chain outline for Acme and the axle industry is shown in Figure 2.8.

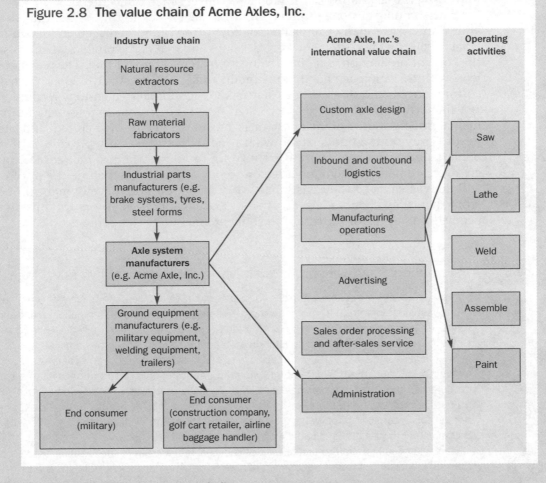

Figure 2.8 The value chain of Acme Axles, Inc.

There are three levels of value chain analysis:

● The industry value chain consists of the different firms in the vertical supply chain.

● The company's (Acme Axle, Inc.) internal value chain consists of the different functions in the company.

● Operational activities of a certain function (only the detailed description of operational activities is shown).

Natural resource extraction (i.e. ore mining and rubber plantations), raw material fabrication (i.e. steel foundries, and tyre manufacturers), and industrial parts manufacturing are the supplier links in the value chain. Customer links include military and non-military ground equipment manufacturing. These downstream manufacturers use the axle systems as components of the equipment such as welding trailers, airport baggage handling trailers, golf carts, and tractors.

Source: adapted from Donelan and Kaplan (1998).

Customer value is defined either by the cost reductions that the product can provide in the customer's activities or by the performance improvements that the customer can gain by using the product. Porter's generic strategies of cost or differentiation (1980) are aimed at improving either the cost or value of a product relative to the average of the industry.

Technology development is performed to either reduce the cost of a product, particularly through process improvements, or to raise the commendable price by improving the adaptation of the product to buyer purchasing criteria.

Understanding customers' **perceptions** of value is key to this part of the process and is one where many companies fall down. Too often, management determines what it believes the customer wants, develops and makes the product, then adds up the costs of production and puts a standard margin on top of that. The major problems with this approach are that the product may not effectively address changing customer needs and that the price may be too high for created customer value.

Value-driven companies spend enough time with customers to obtain a fundamental understanding of their customers' businesses and of their current and latent needs. They want to understand what product features really provide customer benefits, and which ones are merely going to add to the product cost without giving customers any additional reason to buy. They also determine the price that will deliver value to their customers early in the product development process. From that, they deduct their target profit and give their engineers and operations people firm targets for the cost of the final product or its components.

Exhibit 2.3	Information management at Caterpillar creates competitive advantage

The manufacturer of machines for building contractors, Caterpillar, shows several examples of the relevance of information management. Caterpillar uses information management and relationship management to construct an effective value chain through the dealer network. Given the commitment to the distributor organisation, many decisions are simplified.

A critical design criterion for the machines is that they can be repaired economically and conveniently, and their highly integrated manufacturing and distribution systems are designed so that they can replace a part in any machine anywhere in the world within 48 hours. Caterpillar competitors' customers typically wait four or five days for a part. The reason for Caterpillar's competitive advantage in this regard is that they have integrated both customers (dealers) and sub-suppliers into their business systems.

The role of information to create market knowledge comes from the learning aspects of the manufacturer/distributor partnership relationships. Another aspect of information management concerns the productivity of Caterpillar and distributor inventories, and customer equipment. The remoteness of many construction sites means that there are serious problems when parts of equipment break dowm. Caterpillar have begun to resolve such problems by installing sensors on each machine that automatically spot problems which may occur and sends an electronic alert to the local dealer's field technician through his portable computer. The symptoms and diagnosis are validated by a technician who determines the necessary actions. The computer program identifies the parts and tools required to effect a repair. The technician can then use another feature of the program to order parts from storage and issues replenishment orders as and when required. The computer program contains best-practice repair procedures and, on completion of the repair, will update the equipment's service record and issue an invoice. It can also handle electronic payments.

Source: adapted from Walters and Lancaster (2000).

Superior value

Delivering value may not be enough to achieve competitive advantage though. Excellent quality is no advantage if your competitors all have similar offerings. Competitive advantage requires that the value of your product or service is superior to that of your competitors. The major challenge here is that your competitors are providing a moving target by continuously improving the value they provide.

Competitive advantage can be accomplished by providing the greatest level of benefits through a differentiation strategy. It can also be accomplished by enabling a customer to achieve the 'lowest life-cycle cost' compared to comparable products. It is important to recognize that lowest life-cycle cost does not require the lowest purchase price. Lowest life-cycle cost can be achieved by helping the customer reduce start-up, training, or maintenance costs.

The value chain

Porter's work (1985) is the key reference on value chains and value configuration analysis for competitive advantage.

Value chains are created by transforming a set of inputs into more refined outputs. The strategic challenges associated with managing a value chain are related to manufacturing products with the right quality at the lowest possible cost. The ways to reduce costs – or increase value – are primarily found through economies of scale, efficient capacity utilization, learning effects, product and information flows, and quality measures. Critical drivers of value creation in chains also include the interrelationships between primary activities, on the one hand, and product development, marketing and service, i.e. support activities, on the other hand.

The firm's value chain as, for example, shown in Figure 2.10 provides a systematic means of displaying and categorizing activities. The activities performed by a firm in any industry can be grouped into the nine generic categories.

At each stage of the value chain there exists an opportunity to contribute positively to the firm's competitive strategy by performing some activity or process in a way that is better than the competitors, and so providing some uniqueness or advantage. If a firm attains such a competitive advantage, which is sustainable, defensible, profitable and valued by the market, then it may earn high rates of return, even though the industry may be unfavourable and the average profitability of the industry modest.

In competitive terms, value is the amount that buyers are *willing to pay for what a firm provides them (perceived value)* less the sacrifices that the customers offer to obtain access to the value (e.g. money, time). A firm is profitable if the value it commands exceeds the costs involved in creating the product. Creating value for buyers that exceeds the cost of doing so is the goal of any generic strategy. Value, instead of cost, must be used in analysing competitive position, since firms often deliberately raise their costs in order to command a premium price via differentiation. The concept of buyers' perceived value will be discussed further in this chapter.

The value chain displays total value and consists of value activities and margin. Value activities are the physically and technologically distinct activities that a firm performs. These are the building blocks by which a firm creates a product that is valuable to its buyers. Margin is the difference between total value (price) and the collective cost of performing the value activities.

Competitive advantage is a function of either providing comparable buyer value more efficiently than competitors (lower cost), or performing activities at comparable cost but in unique ways that create more customer value than the competitors are able to offer, and, hence, command a premium price (differentiation). The firm might be able to identify elements of the value chain that are not worth the costs. These can then be unbundled and produced outside the firm (outsourced) at a lower price.

Value activities can be divided into two broad types, *primary activities* and *support activities*. Primary activities are the activities involved in the physical creation of the product, its sale and transfer to the buyer, as well as after-sales assistance. In any firm, primary activities can be divided into the five generic categories. Support activities support the primary activities and each other by providing purchased inputs, technology, human resources and various firm-wide functions.

Primary activities

The primary activities of the organization are grouped into five main areas: inbound **logistics**, operations, outbound logistics, marketing and sales, and service.

1. Inbound logistics are the activities concerned with receiving, storing and distributing the inputs to the product/service. These include materials, handling, stock control, transport, etc.
2. Operations transform these various inputs into the final product or service: machining, packaging, assembly, testing, etc.
3. Outbound logistics collect, store and distribute the product to customers. For tangible products this would involve warehousing, material handling, transport, etc.; in the case of services it may be more concerned with arrangements for bringing customers to the service if it is in a fixed location (e.g. sports events).
4. Marketing and sales provide the means whereby consumers/**users** are made aware of the product or service and are able to purchase it. This would include sales administration, **advertising**, selling, etc. In public services, communication networks, which help users access a particular service, are often important.
5. Services cover all the activities, which enhance or maintain the value of a product or service, such as installation, repair, training and spare parts.

Each of these groups of primary activities is linked to support activities.

Support activities

These can be divided into four areas.

1. *Procurement.* This refers to the process of acquiring the various resource inputs to the primary activities (not to the resources themselves). As such, it occurs in many parts of the organization.
2. *Technology development.* All value activities have a 'technology', even if it is simply know-how. The key technologies may be concerned directly with the product (e.g. R&D, product design) or with processes (e.g. process development) or with a particular resource (e.g. raw material improvements).
3. *Human resource management.* This is a particularly important area, which transcends all primary activities. It is concerned with the activities involved in recruiting, training, developing and rewarding people within the organization.
4. *Infrastructure.* The systems of planning, finance, quality control, etc. are crucially important to an organization's strategic capability in all primary activities.

Exhibit 2.4	McDonald's goes into a win-win relationship with Pret à Manger, a UK sandwich chain – concentrating on each partner's competences

McDonald's Corp. has acquired a minority interest in the UK-based Pret à Manger, a quick service food company that serves mainly sandwiches, snacks and hot beverages at lunchtime.

Pret à Manger was launched in 1986 by Julian Metcalfe, Sinclair Beauchamp, Andrew Roalfe and Harvey Smyth, all whom will retain majority ownership and management control.

In the alliance, McDonald's provides Pret à Manger with the resources to grow its business outside the UK, where it has more than 100 outlets. The long-term strategy of Pret à Manger is to seek a greater share of the international informal eating-out market by capturing meal occasions that do not make sense for McDonald's to offer.

McDonald's faces a number of challenges in trying to deliver growth. The prospect of a maturing burger sector and saturated outlet distribution could mean that further expansion will only lead to volume cannibalization. McDonald's other alternative is to experiment with other types of prepared food – such as sandwiches. Furthermore, Pret's cultural skills and entrepreneurial verve would be valuable to the McDonald's business model.

In an attempt to allay fears among its loyal customers that the McDonald's buy may taint Pret à Manger's reputation for offering 'high quality, natural food', the chain is distributing leaflets to its customers explaining the new partnership.

Sources: adapted from American Marketing Association (2001), Farnham (2001).

Infrastructure also consists of the structures and routines of the organization, which sustain its culture.

Having looked at Porter's complex value chain model, a simplified version will be used in most parts of this book (Figure 2.9). This simplified version of the value chain is characterized by the fact that it contains only the primary activities of the firm.

Figure 2.9 A simplified version of the value chain

Research and development	Production	Marketing	Sales and service
Technology	Purchasing	Marketing info. system	Sales force management
Research	Scale economies	Distribution	Merchandising
Development	Productive capacity	Prices	Logistics/transportation
Patents	Productivity	Communication	Terms of sale/delivery
Product features	Component parts	Technical literature	Terms of payment
Technical specification	Assembly	Packaging	Inventory
Product performance	Material flow	Product argumentation/	Customer service (BDA
Design	Production technology	(versus competing	service – before, during
Engineering	Quality management	products)	and after purchasing)
Product quality	Manufacturing cycles	Brand positioning	

←——— Upstream ———————————————————— Downstream ———→

Source: Hollensen (2001), p. 16.

As indicated in Figure 2.9, a distinction is also made between the production-oriented, 'upstream' activities and the more marketing-oriented, 'downstream' activities.

From value chain to value constellation

As markets are getting more complex the value chain of the single firm cannot be seen independently from the value chains of other actors in the market network (Prahalad and Ramaswamy, 2000).

Normann and Ramirez (1993) argue that strategic analysis should focus on the value-creating system itself within the different players – suppliers, business partners, customers and internal employees work together to co-produce value.

Although value activities are the building blocks of competitive advantage, the value chain is not a collection of independent activities, but a system of interdependent activities. The value chains of different players are related to each other by linkages within the total industry. Linkages are relationships between the way in which one value activity is performed and the cost or performance of another.

In understanding the competitive advantage of an organization, the strategic importance of the following types of linkage should be analysed in order to assess how they contribute to cost reduction or value added. There are two kinds of linkage (Figure 2.10):

- *Internal linkages* between activities within the same value chain, but perhaps on different planning levels within the firm.
- *External linkages* between different value chains 'owned' by the different players in the total value system.

Figure 2.10 Model of some inter- and intra-firm relationships

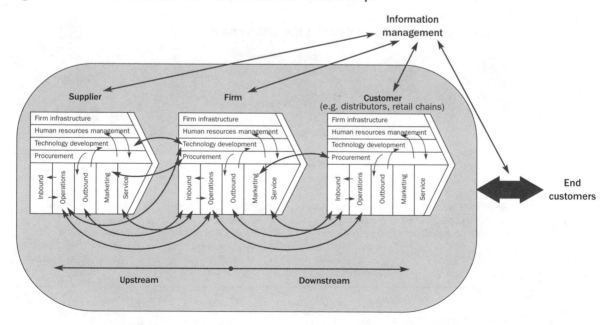

Source: adapted from Lings (2000), p. 34.

Normann and Ramirez (1993) use the term value constellation to describe the 'chain' of different players' value chain and their relationships (see Figure 2.10). The global furniture chain Ikea is used as an example of the new logic of value. Ikea's goal is not to create value for customers but to mobilize customers to create their own value from the company's various offerings.

Figure 2.10 also stresses the importance of information management as a tool for coordinating information between the different players in the value chain.

| Exhibit 2.5 | **Intel uses its competence to sell consumer products** |

Until now the California-based company Intel has derived 80% of its sales and profits from microprocessors. However, it has been affected by the global downturn in computer sales, and as a result cut the price of its Pentium 4 chips by up to 19% in 2001, in a bid to stimulate demand.

Over recent years, Intel has recognized the danger of only making chips for PCs, and has made a foray into other areas of technology to encourage PC purchase. By extending the value of PCs with consumer products, it in turn hopes to drive demand for PCs based on the Pentium 4.

Source: adapted from BBC (2001), Brabbs (2001).

Internal linkages (see also Figure 2.10)

There may be important links between the primary activities. In particular, choices will have been made about these relationships and how they influence value creation and strategic capability. For example, a decision to hold high levels of finished stock might ease production scheduling problems and provide a faster response time to the customer. However, it will probably add to the overall cost of operations. An assessment needs to be made of whether the added value of extra stock is greater than the added cost. Sub-optimization of the single value chain activities should be avoided. It is easy to miss this point in an analysis if, for example, the marketing activities and operations are assessed separately. The operations may look good because they are geared to high-volume, low-variety, low-unit-cost production. However, at the same time the marketing team may be selling quickness, flexibility and variety to the customers. When put together these two potential strengths are weaknesses, because they are not in harmony, which is what a value chain requires. The link between a primary activity and a support activity may be the basis of competitive advantage. For example, an organization may have a unique system for procuring materials. Many international hotels and travel companies use their computer systems to provide immediate quotations and bookings worldwide from local access points.

External linkages

One of the key features of most industries is that a single organization rarely undertakes all value activities from product design to distribution to the final consumer. There is usually a specialization of roles, and any single organization usually participates in the wider value system, which creates a product or service. In understanding how value is created, it is not enough to look at the firm's internal value chain alone. Much of the value creation will occur in the supply and distribution chains, and this whole process needs to be analysed and understood.

Suppliers have value chains (upstream value) that create and deliver the purchased inputs used in a firm's chain. Suppliers not only deliver a product, but also can influence a firm's performance in many other ways. For example, Benetton, the Italian fashion company, managed to sustain an elaborate network of suppliers, agents and independent retail outlets as the basis of its rapid and successful international development during the 1970s and 1980s.

In addition, products pass through the value chain channels (channel value) on their way to the buyer. Channels perform additional activities that affect the buyer and influence the firm's own activities. A firm's product eventually becomes part of its buyer's value chain. The ultimate basis for differentiation is a firm and its product's role in the buyer's value chain, which determine the buyer's needs. Gaining and sustaining competitive advantage depends on understanding not only a firm's value chain, but how the firm fits into the overall value system. See also strategy 1 in Figure 2.4 for some examples of upstream and downstream relationships.

There are often circumstances where the overall cost can be reduced (or value increased) by collaborative arrangements between different organizations in the value system. It will be seen in Chapter 9 that this is often the rationale behind **joint ventures** (e.g. sharing technology in the international motor manufacture and electronics industries).

Exhibit 2.6	**Lego is refocusing its basic competences**

In March 2001, Lego announced that it had turned a £45 million profit in 1999 into a £90 million loss in 2000. Lego owns probably the most popular and successful children's toy ever invented.

Lego has spent the past 20 years battling against a changing world. After launching the building bricks in 1958, it enjoyed growth for 20 years, and managed to penetrate the US market after some hiccups. The patent on the bricks expired in 1981, opening the way for an array of competitors. In the 1990s, the growth of video and computer games outstripped that of construction toys, and in 1998 Lego recorded its first loss. This prompted the company to drop its long aversion to commercial tie-ins and it linked up with Star Wars, Disney and Microsoft.

Lego has pulled out of manufacturing wristwatches and publishing books, and instead licenses these activities to third parties. Lego has also looked hard at its existing licensing deals, such as that with Danish firm Kabooki (which produces the Lego Wear clothing line). In addition, investment in new Legoland parks has been reduced.

In *Marketing Week* (2001) there was a statement about Lego:

Still, many parents would prefer their children to play with Lego rather than sit in front of the television or a computer game – it is a constructive toy rather than a destructive one like many PlayStation games. Some are surprised that Lego is launching a television station. 'Leave it to the professionals', says one observer. The brand risks losing its position as the creative, constructive alternative to watching the television and the more decadent end of the video games market.

In March 2002, the Lego management announced that the £90 million loss in 2000 had turned into a £42 million profit in 2001, due to success with a new Harry Potter product and the so-called Bionicle line.

Question: Do you agree with this statement in *Marketing Week* about Lego?

Sources: adapted from *Marketing Week* (2001), www.lego.com

Figure 2.11 The virtual value chain as a supplement to the physical value chain

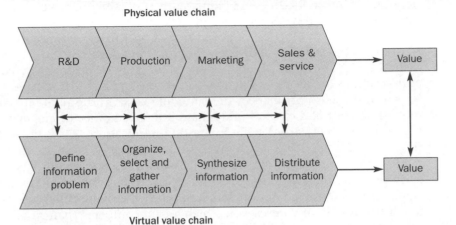

By introducing the virtual value chain, Rayport and Sviokla (1996) have extended the conventional value chain model, which treats information as a supporting element in the value-adding process (see Figure 2.11).

Each of the physical value-chain activities might make use of one or all four information processing stages of the virtual value chain, in order to create extra value for the customer. That is the reason for the horizontal double arrows (in Figure 2.11) between the different physical and virtual value-chain activities.

In this way (in relation to Figure 2.11), information can be captured at all stages of the physical value chain. Obviously such information can be used to improve performance at each stage of the physical value chain and to coordinate across it. However, it can also be analysed and repackaged to build content-based products or to create a new line of business.

A company can use its information to reach out to other companies' customers or operations, thereby rearranging the value system of an industry. The result might be that traditional industry sector boundaries disappear. The CEO of Amazon.com, Jeffrey P. Bezos, clearly sees his business as not bookselling, but the information-broker business.

2.7 Internationalizing the value chain

International configuration and coordination of activities

All internationally oriented firms must consider an eventual internationalization of the value chain's functions. The firm must decide whether the responsibility for the single value chain function is to be moved to the export markets, or is best handled centrally from head office. In principle, the value chain function should be carried out where there is the highest competence (and the most cost effectiveness), and this is not necessarily at head office.

A distinction immediately arises between downstream and upstream activities on Figure 2.9. The location of downstream activities, those more related to the buyer, is usually tied to where the buyer is located. If a firm is going to sell in Australia, for example, it must usually provide service in Australia, and it must have salespeople stationed in Australia. In some industries it is possible to have a single sales force that travels to the buyer's country and back again; other specific downstream activities, such as the production of advertising copy, can sometimes also be performed centrally. More typically, however, the firm must locate downstream activities in each of the countries in which it operates. In contrast, upstream activities and support activities are more independent of where the buyer is located (Figure 2.12). However, if the export markets are culturally close to the home market, it may be relevant to control the entire value chain from head office (home market).

This distinction carries some interesting implications. First, downstream activities create competitive advantages that are largely country specific: a firm's reputation, brand name and service network in a country grow largely out of its activities and create entry/mobility barriers largely in that country alone. Competitive advantage in upstream and support activities often grows more out of the entire system of countries in which a firm competes than from its position in any single country.

Second, in industries where downstream activities or other buyer-tied activities are vital to competitive advantage, there tends to be a more multi-domestic pattern of international competition. In many service industries, for example, not only downstream activities but frequently upstream activities are tied to buyer location, and global strategies are comparatively less common. In industries where upstream and support activities such as technology development and operations are crucial to competitive advantage, global competition is more common.

For example, there may be a large need in firms to centralize and coordinate the production function worldwide to be able to create rational production units that are able to exploit economies of scale. Furthermore, as customers increasingly join regional cooperative buying organizations, it is becoming more and more difficult to sustain a price differentiation across markets. This will put pressure on the firm to coordinate a European price policy.

The distinctive issues of international strategies, in contrast to domestic, can be summarized in two key factors of how a firm competes internationally. The first is

Figure 2.12 Centralizing and decentralizing value chain functions

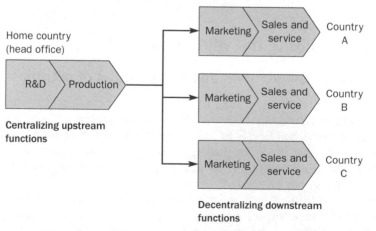

Source: Hollensen (2001), p. 20.

called the configuration of a firm's worldwide activities, or the location where each activity in the value chain is performed, including the number of places. The second factor is called coordination, which refers to how identical or linked activities performed in different countries are coordinated with each other (Porter, 1985).

| Exhibit 2.7 | Identifying key competences at Daimler-Benz |

The case of Daimler-Benz provides a good example of the management of technological competences. This internal process takes two to three months, and involves the group's senior management. External consultants corroborate the internal analysis and further develop the opinions gathered from the business units. The process is summarized in the nine main phases shown in Table 2.2.

Table 2.2 Stages in identification of key competences at Daimler-Benz

Stages	Level of identification
Phase 1	Products, clients and markets.
Phase 2	Key factors of success (KFS): • the characteristic that the customer will perceive • internal processes.
Phase 3	Future market trends and the evolution of KFS.
Phase 4	Identification of areas of key competences.
Phase 5	Initial formulation of key competences.
Phase 6	Multi-criteria checking: • excellence • the basis of a competitive advantage • contributions made to the value created for the customer • sustainable yet difficult to imitate • can create value in new markets.
Phase 7	Fine-tuning and honing of these critical competences: • contacts with customers and competitors • interview with experts • return to phases 5 and 6 of the loop.
Phase 8	Needs analysis in terms of the key competences: • elaboration of a plan for improving the present situation • definition of a strategy that makes it possible to transplant new competences onto the existing ones and combine the existing and the new competences.
Phase 9	Study of competences other than key competences • can they be outsourced? • analysis of the competences that should be retained.

Daimler-Benz launches this internal process by drawing up comparisons with competitors in each of its business units' main markets. It then tries to identify, through a multi-criteria analysis, competences that could one day become key competences. The results are checked against the perceptions of clients, competitors and experts. This step facilitates the fine-tuning of key competences.

Source: adapted from Quelin (2000).

2.8 Summary

Competences are the skills, knowledge and technologies that an organization possesses on which its success depends. Although an organization will need to reach a threshold level of competence in all its activities, it is likely that only some of these activities are core competences. These core competences underpin the ability of the organization to outperform the competition and therefore must be defended and nurtured. Core competences concern those resources that are fundamental to a company's strategic position.

In the chapter, three basic perspectives on identification of core competences have been presented:

- resource based view (RBV): an Inside-out perspective
- market orientation view (MOV): an Outside-in perspective
- value chain based view (VBV): between the RBV and the MOV.

The RBV emphasizes the importance of firm-specific assets and knowledge.

The underlying approach of the RBV is to see the firm as a bundle of tangible and intangible resources, and to see some of these resources as costly to copy and trade. A firm's resource position can lead to sustained competitive advantage.

Especially in knowledge-intensive firms, distinctive capabilities consist of intangible resources.

In contrast to the MOV, which takes the environment as the critical factor determining an organisation's strategy, the RBV assumes that the key factors for success lie within the firm itself in terms of its resources, capabilities and competences. The choice of the firm's strategy is not dictated by the constraints of the environment but is influenced more by calculations of how the organization can best exploit its core competence relative to the opportunities in the external environment.

The MOV is basically about adapting to the market environment by concentrating mainly on customers and their needs.

The VBV integrates elements of both the RBV and the MOV, but it does so without ignoring the costs of performing the activities. The value chain provides a systematic means of displaying and categorizing activities. Value activities can be divided in different ways:

- primary and support activities
- upstream and downstream activities.

At each stage of the value chain the firm seeks to add value and thus compete with its rivals. The simplified version of the value chain used throughout the book contains only the primary activities of the firm. The value chain is not a collection of independent activities but a system of interdependent activities. The firm's value chain activities are also related to other actors' value chains. Competitive advantages are created if the firm can:

- offer better perceived value for customers
- perform the value chain activities at a lower cost than competitors.

Case study 2.2 Amazon[3] and Toys 'R' Us[4]

Pooling competences to form a single online toy store

On August 10, 2001, Toys 'R' Us Inc. CEO John H. Eyler Jr and Amazon.com CEO Jeffrey P. Bezos announced they were pooling their expertise to form a single online toy store. New Jersey-based Toysrus.com would choose and buy toys, using its parent's buying power to get the best toys. Amazon, in Seattle, would run the store on its site, ship the products, and handle customer service. Now both expect to become profitable much sooner than they could individually.

Background

There were many problems in closing this deal and many remain. During Christmas 1999, Amazon got its buying wrong and was left with a pile of unsold toys. Amazon had to book losses of US$39m, on total sales of US$95m.

Toys 'R' Us and its toysrus.com website had problems with delivery, especially in the run-up to Christmas 1999. Thousands of US customers did not receive their orders in time, and the Federal Trade Commission fined the company US$350,000.

The process towards the alliance

The first contracts between Amazon and Toys 'R' Us were established in February 2000. However, selling to consumers through an alliance is much tougher than it looks. Both firms must set aside their pride and do what works for customers and investors. How Amazon.com and Toys 'R' Us did it provides a guide to how others might solve problems in e-tailing.

To see if an alliance would fit with customers, who often complain about the unpleasant ambience of Toys 'R' Us stores, Amazon ran focus groups with both Amazon and Toys 'R' Us customers in April. The results were promising: customers said they associated Toys 'R' Us with deep selection, something Amazon also strives for.

Meanwhile, Toysrus.com announced a deal with Japan's Softbank Venture Capital, on February 24. For 20% of the company, Softbank paid US$57 million, which allowed Toysrus.com to add and improve distribution centres, hire management, and improve customer service.

At the same time, Amazon's financial power was starting to fade as dot.com shares dropped sharply. Investors became fed up with the money-losing dot.coms. Amazon's shares dropped 36%, to US$48 a share, from early February to early April 2001.

During spring and summer 2000 negotiations went into a more intensive stage with senior managers constantly phoning between meetings in Seattle, New York, and Chicago.

On July 28, Eyler flew to Seattle to meet with Bezos and his team. They devised code names to prevent leaks: the deal was named Project Stream, after Amazon's headquarters near the water in Seattle.

Although the deal was largely complete, the timing and the finances were not, according to Bezos – how much Amazon's annual fee should be, how it should share revenue, and what it

---

[3] Amazon.com is the Internet's leading retailer in books, music, DVDs, and Videos. Amazon.com began trading on the web in July 1995 and today offers Earth's biggest selection, along with online auctions and free electronic greeting cards. Amazon.com seeks to be the world's most customer-centred company, where customers can find and discover anything they might want to buy online. Amazon.com lists more than 18 million unique items including books, CDs, toys, electronics, videos, DVDs, tools and hardware, lawn and patio items, kitchen products, software, and video games. Through Amazon.com zShops, any business or individual can sell virtually anything to Amazon.com's more than 23 million customers, and with Amazon.com Payments, sellers can accept credit card transactions, avoiding the hassles of offline payments. The company also participates in sothebys.amazon.com, the leading auction site for guaranteed art, jewellery and collectibles, at **www.sothebys.amazon.com**. Amazon.com operates two international websites: **www.amazon.co.uk** and **www.amazon.de**.

[4] Toys 'R' Us is the world's leading retailer for toys and currently operates 1552 stores; 707 toy stores in the USA, 469 international toy stores, including franchise stores, 201 Kids 'R' Us children's clothing stores, 137 Babies 'R' Us stores and 38 Imaginarium stores. The company also sells merchandise through its Internet sites at **http://www.toysrus.com**, **http://www.babiesrus.com** and **http://www.imaginarium.com** and through mail order catalogues. Toys 'R' Us is a leading global Internet retailer for toys and children's products. Toysrus.com, an affiliate of Toys 'R' Us, Inc., combines one of the world's most recognizable brands with unparalleled expertise in the toy and children's industry. In July, Toysrus.com launched Babiesrus.com, an online e-resource partnership with Babies 'R' Us. According to Media Metrix, in 1999 Toysrus.com became one of the fastest-growing e-commerce sites on the Internet.

Case study 2.2 continued

would get per toy sold. Amazon wanted assurances that Toysrus.com would allocate enough toys to the site and that the parent company would support it with marketing. To avoid paying too much, Toysrus.com wanted the longest fixed-price deal it could get, and the teams argued over how much Toys 'R' Us branding, such as its giraffe logo, the site would carry.

The result

The final agreements were signed on August 9, 2000. At the press conference on August 10, Bezos called the deal with Toys 'R' Us 'a match made in heaven. They know toys better than anybody, and we know e-commerce better than anybody'.

The relationship would go far beyond Amazon's existing partnerships, which essentially charged other **e-tailers** cash to promote their stores on Amazon's site. Amazon had a tried and tested distribution network with plenty of excess capacity, while Toysrus.com had merchandizing and purchasing expertise. If the two joined forces, they could dominate online toy sales, estimated by Forrester research Inc. to to be US$3.6 billion, or 10% of the overall toy market by 2004.

Under the 10-year agreement, each company will take care of different aspects of the two online stores: Toysrus.com, in collaboration with its parent, will select, purchase and manage inventory; Amazon will house the stores' inventory in its US warehouses and handle development of the site and front-end operations like taking orders and customer service.

In a joint statement, the companies said the terms of the agreement allow for it to be expanded globally. Amazon will receive regular fixed cash payments, an extra payment for every toy sold, and a small percentage of total revenue. Amazon will also receive warrants entitling it to buy 5% of the joint web venture.

Toys 'R' Us, meanwhile, carries the inventory risk, but stands to receive the online profits – if it can make any.

Toys 'R' Us chief executive John Eyler said sales had to increase 300% to 400% for the venture to become profitable.

Questions

1. Identify the core competences of Amazon.com and Toys 'R' Us. How are these competences in harmony with each other?

2. Does the Amazon–Toys 'R' Us relationship make sense from a resource based view (RBV) and a market orientation view (MOV)?

3. What are the chances that the partnership will turn out to be a financial success?

Sources: Burnett (2000), Financial Times (2000) Green (2000), Kong (2000), Martinez (2000), Schwartz (2000), Wingfield and Bulkeley (2000).

QUESTIONS FOR DISCUSSION

1. Explain the differences between the RBV, MOV and VBV.

2. What is the connection between RBV and the RM approach?

3. What is the purpose of the value chain?

4. Why is it relevant to make a split between upstream and downstream activities in the value chain?

5. Is the value chain also a relevant model for services?

6. How can the firm create competitive advantage by the use of resources and competences in the firm?

REFERENCES

American Marketing Association (2001), McDonald's takes a small bite into UK sandwich chain, *Daily News*, **www.ama.org**, January 31.

Ansoff, H. I. (1965), *Corporate Strategy*, McGraw-Hill, New York.

BBC (2001), Intel to sell consumer products. *BBC News*, **http://news.bbc.co.uk**, January 2.

BBC News (2001a), *Microsoft and Lego link* **http://news.bbc.co.uk/hi/english/business**, January 10.

Brabbs, C. (2001), Intel must get beyond its chipmaker image, *Marketing*, London, April 26, pp.21–2.

Burnett, V. (2000), Amazon and Toys 'R' Us forge alliance for online retail stores, *Financial Times*, August 10.

Donelan, J. G. and Kaplan, E.A. (1998), Value chain analysis: a strategic approach to cost management, *Journal of Cost Management*, March–April pp. 7–15.

Fahy, J. (2002). A resource-based analysis of sustainable competitive advantage in a global environment, *International Business Review*, vol. 11, no. 1, pp. 57–77.

Farnham, J. (2001), Pret and McDonald's, *MAD*, February 8.

Financial Times (2000), Amazon and Toys 'R' Us rewrite rules of the game. A shift from clicks and mortar to large-scale combinations of online and offline retailers may be about to become a trend in Jackson, *Financial Times*, August 14.

Grant, R. M. (1991), The resource based theory of competitive advantage: implications for strategy formulation, *California Management Review* (Spring), pp.114–35.

Green, H. (2000), Double play, *Business Week*, New York, October 23.

Grönroos, C. (1996), Relationship marketing: strategic and tactical implications, *Management Decision*, vol. 34, no. 3 pp. 5–14.

Hollensen, S. (2001), *Global Marketing: A market responsive approach*, Financial Times/Prentice Hall, Harlow, 2nd edn.

Jolly, D. (2000), Three generic resource-based strategies, *International Journal of Technology Management*, vol. 19, no. 718, pp. 773–87.

Kohli, A.K. and Jaworski, B.J. (1990), 'Market orientation: the construct, research propositions, and managerial implications', *Journal of Marketing*, vol. 54, no. 2, pp. 1–18.

Kong, D. (2000), Amazon, Toys 'R' Us team for online toy store. Complementary skills unite rivals, *USA Today*, August 11.

Kumar, N., Scheer, L. and Kotter, P. (2000), From market driven to market driving, *European Management Journal*, vol. 18, no. 2, April, pp. 129–42.

Lego (2001), *Lego Company and Microsoft Corp. announce a shared dream*, **http://www.lego.com/info/** press release, Redmond, WA., and Billund, Denmark, January 10.

Lings, I. N. (2000), Internal marketing and supply chain management, *Journal of Services Marketing*, vol. 14, no. 1, pp. 27–43.

Lipparini, A. and Fratocchi, L. (1999), The capabilities of the transnational firm, *European Management Journal*, vol. 17, no. 6, pp. 655–67.

Marchand, D. A. (1999), 'Hard IM choices for senior managers. Part 10 of Your guide to Mastering Information Management', *Financial Times*, April 5.

Marketing Week (2001), A brick too far, *Marketing Week*, London, March 15.

Martinez, M. J. (2000), Amazon.com Teams with Toys 'R' Us, *Washington Post*, August 10.

Mascarenhas, B., Beveja, A. and Jamil, M. (1998), Dynamics of core competencies in leading multinational companies, *California Management Review*, vol. 40, no. 4, Summer, pp. 117–32.

Normann, R. and Ramirez, R. (1993), From value chain to value constellation: designing interactive strategy, *Harvard Business Review*, July–August, pp. 65–77.

Penrose, E. (1959), *The Theory of the Growth of the Firm*, John Wiley & Sons, New York.

Porter, M. (1980), *Competitive Strategy: Techniques for analyzing industries and competitors*, Free Press, New York.

Porter, M. (1985), *Competitive Advantage: Creating and sustaining superior performance*, Free Press, New York.

Porter, M. E. (1986), Competition in global industries: a conceptual framework, *in* Porter, M. E. (Ed), *Competition in Global Industries*, Harvard Business School Press, Boston, MA.

Porter, M. (1990), *The Competitive Advantage of Nations*, Free Press, New York.

Prahalad, C.K. and Hamel, G. (1990), The core competence of the corporation. *Harvard Business Review*, May–June, pp. 79–91.

Prahalad, C. K. and Hamel, G. (1994), Strategy as a field of study: why search for a new paradigm? *Strategic Management Journal*, 15, pp. 5–16.

Prahalad, C. K. and Ramaswamy, V. (2000), Co-opting customer competence, *Harvard Business Review*, January–February, pp. 79–87.

Quelin, B. (2000), Core competencies, R&D management and partnerships, *European Management Journal*, vol. 18, no. 5, October, pp. 476–87.

Rangone, A. (1999), A resource-based approach to strategy analysis in small–medium sized enterprises, *Small Business Economics*, vol. 12, pp. 233–48.

Rayport, J. F. and Sviokla, J. J. (1996), Exploiting the virtual value chain, *McKinsey Quarterly*, no. 1, pp. 21–36.

Schwartz, E. (2000), Amazon, Toys 'R' Us in e-commerce tie-up, *Infoworld*, Framingham, August 14.

Selznick, P. (1957), *Leadership in Administration*, Row, Peterson & Co., Evanston, ILL.

Walters, D. and Lancaster, G. (2000), Implementing value strategy through the value chain, *Management Decision*, vol. 38, no. 3 pp. 160–78.

Webb, J. and Gile, C. (2001), Reversing the value chain, *Journal of Business Strategy*, March–April, pp. 13–17.

Wernerfelt, B. (1984), A resource-based view of the firm, *Strategic Management Journal*, vol. 5, no. 2, pp. 171–80.

Wingfield, N. and Bulkeley, W. M. (2000), Amazon.com, Toys 'R' Us agree to combine online toy stores, *Wall Street Journal*, New York, August 11.

Chapter 3

Development of the firm's competitive advantage

LEARNING OBJECTIVES

After studying this chapter you should be able to:

- define the concept 'international competitiveness' in a broader perspective from a macro level to a micro level.
- discuss the basic sources of competitive advantages.
- explain how 'economies of speed' can be used as a competitive advantage.
- explain how Porter's traditional competitive-based five forces can be extended to a relationship (five sources model).
- define the steps in competitive benchmarking and explain how these steps are related to the outsourcing decision process.
- explain the purposes and motives for outsourcing activities.
- discuss the advantages and disadvantages of outsourcing.

Case study 3.1 Teepack Spezialmaschinen GmbH

Establishing customer relationships to manufacturers of tea brands

Teepack (www.teepack.de) is a specialized manufacturer of tea bag machines for the world's best-known brands of tea and herb and fruit teas, such as Lipton, Pickwick, Twinings, and Lyons/Tetley.

Teepack is a sister company of Teekanne[1], the leading tea, herb, and fruit tea packing company in Germany with the Teefix and Teekanne brand.

The invention of the automatic tea bag-packaging machine by Teepack in 1949 revolutionized the tea market with the double-chamber tea bag. It meant that production

volumes could be increased dramatically. The latest generation of these machines is capable of production speeds of almost 400 tea bags per minute, i.e. about 2 billion per year.

The tea bag – produced on Teepack machines – is the most sold double-chamber tea bag in the world. Important benefits are

- considerably larger space between the two bag chambers
- Maximum tea bag stability and durability without adding glue or heat sealing.

Up to now the popularity of the practical tea bag has continued to grow. For example, in Germany, 82% of tea sales are in double-chamber tea bags. In the USA, the figure is about 90%, and in Europe, excluding the UK, the figure is about

[1]. The Teekanne Group has production and sales subsidiaries in seven countries: Germany, USA, Italy, Spain, Czech Republic, Poland, and Austria. Total turnover of the group is about €300 million and there are over 1700 employees in the group.

Case study 3.1 continued

100%. Even in Australia, the double-chamber tea bag has convinced the consumers. Down under, sales of the British tea bag and the double-chamber tea bag are about the same.

For over 50 years, Teepack has been the number one producer of tea bag packaging machines in the world. Teepack has sold more than 2000 Constanta packaging machines. Owing to Teepack's packaging machines, Lipton leads in the international tea market. Up to 1957, Teepack had sold more than 100 tea bag packaging machines in the USA.

Technical innovation resulted in Teepack engineers developing a new, even more efficient machine, 'Perfecta'. Since 1990, more than 200 'Perfecta' machines have been sold worldwide.

Today, Teepack has a market share of about 70% of the global tea bag machine market.

Questions

Please visit www.teepack.de before you answer the questions. You can also get a good impression of the tea bag production process at:

http://www.teekanne.de/50jahre/machinen/machinen. htm. Click on the Teepack-video. 12:10 minutes.

1. Explain how Teepack has developed its competitiveness in the global tea bag packaging machine market.

2. Describe the different ways by which Teepack can develop and maintain customer relationships.

Source: www.teepack.de, www.teekanne.de.

3.1 Introduction

Competitiveness is how effective and efficient a firm is, relative to its rivals, at serving customers and resellers. Effectiveness has to do with the quality of products, market share, and profitability; efficiency has to do with response speed and low costs. Both effectiveness and efficiency ultimately depend on competitive rationality – the strength of the firm's competitive drives and its decision-making skills.

The topic of this chapter is how a firm creates and develops competitive advantage in the international market. The development of a firm's international competitiveness takes place interactively with the business environment. The firm must be able to adjust to customers, competitors and public authorities. To be able to participate in the international arena, the firm must have established a competitive basis consisting of resources, competences and relations to others in the international arena.

3.2 General sources of competitive advantage

Depending on the degree of internationalization of its business, a company has access to different general sources of competitive advantage. A globally operating company may derive competitive advantage from qualities that are perhaps not available to firms with a regional or domestic focus, such as:

- economies of scale
- economies of scope
- strategic thinking as a core competence
- exploitation of local advantages
- ability to provide global services

- company-specific competitive advantages
- the ability to use human resources in developing competitive advantage.

Each factor will now be discussed in detail.

Economies of scale (efficiencies of global scale and volume)

Economies of scale are often the main feature of a market. The theory is that the greater the economies of scale, the greater the benefits accruing to those with a high sales volume. As a result, the competition to achieve larger market share is intense. Economies of scale can come about because larger plants are more efficient to run, and their cost per unit of output may be relatively less. There may be overhead costs that cannot be avoided – even by the smaller organizations – but can be spread over larger volumes by the bigger firms. Economies of scale may also be the result of learning. With increasing cumulative production the manufacturer learns more and finds more efficient methods of production. All of these effects tend to increase competition by offering incentives to buy market share in order to become the lowest-cost producer. By the same token economies of scale also produce significant barriers against new entrants to the market. The higher the initial investment, the more difficult it is to justify the investment for a new entry. But such economies of scale do not always last forever.

Hence, where economies through large-scale operations are substantial, a firm will do all it can to achieve scale economies. Attempts to capture scale economies may lead a firm to compete for market share aggressively, escalating pressures on other firms. A similar situation occurs when a business' fixed costs are high and the firm must spread them over a large volume. If capacity can only be added in large increments, the resulting excess capacity will also intensify competition.

Experience effects are based on size over time, rather than size at a particular point in time. The experience effect reflects the improvements (usually resulting in lower costs) that result from economies of scale, learning and improved productivity over time.

For example, capital costs do not increase in direct proportion to capacity. Higher capacity results in lower depreciation charges per unit of output, lower operating cost in the form of the number of operatives, lower marketing, sales, administration, and research and development costs, and lower raw materials and shipping costs. It is generally recognized, however, that cost reductions apply more to the value-added elements than to bought-in supplies. In fact, the Boston Consulting Group discovered that costs decrease by up to 30 per cent for every cumulative doubling of output. This phenomenon (a so-called 70 per cent **experience curve**: every time production output doubles, the unit cost falls to 70 per cent of the former cost) is shown in Figure 3.1(a). This experience curve would be typical for the production function, whereas the experience curve is less sensitive for value functions like marketing and product development (Figure 3.1(b)). The reason is that these functions are more innovative in nature. While there are many implications for marketing strategy, particularly in relation to pricing policy, discussion will be confined to the product/market implications.

Large economies of scale exist when there are high fixed versus **variable costs** in the predominant business model. Large organisations can amortize the fixed costs over greater volumes, which gives them a big advantage over small competitors.

Figure 3.1 Experience curves in different functions

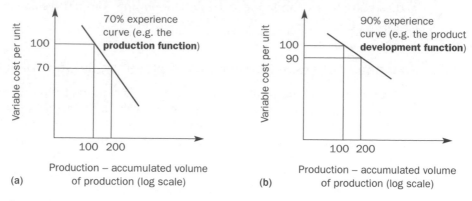

Source: adapted from Czepiel (1992), p. 154.

Exhibit 3.1	Economies of scale at generic drug manufacturers

The focus of generic drug manufacturers is on efficiency (in order to compete on price). The competences required to compete operationally are mainly linked to efficiency in production. This includes the ability to identify economies of scale and capacity utilization, as well as better linkages between the different activities. They are also connected to an efficient flow of goods. This implies the ability to continually improve the logistics connected to a very complex flow of people, technologies and materials. Another critical competence is negotiating skills, allowing the firm to continuously reduce the costs of suppliers by making sure they reduce costs, and reducing both transaction and linkage costs. Furthermore, the relationships needed for generic drug makers to compete operationally include a set-up with suppliers and customers that facilitates an efficient flow of information and products. Also, close contacts with customers and a limited number of suppliers may limit transaction costs. The relationships developed by successful generic drug makers are largely aimed at cutting cost and improving flows. This may imply reducing the number of suppliers and increasing the business with the remaining partners.

Source: adapted from Haanes and Fjeldstad (2000).

However, Toyota taught the western world that many fixed cost can be reduced. By reducing in-process inventories, set-up times for machinery, and the overhead costs inherent in an inventory-intensive batch-manufacturing process, Toyota flattened the scale economics of assembling a car. CAD (computer-aided-design) systems had a similar effect on reducing the fixed cost of designing a new model. As a result, there is no relationship between a car producer's market share and its profitability. Analogous innovations have flattened scale economics in steel, electric-power generation and computers – and rendered transitory what were once thought to be sustainable advantages.

Strategists in industries that today see leading companies enjoying scale-based competitive advantage ought to ask themselves if the fundamental trade-offs that create today's high fixed costs might change. Consider Intel. A barrier to potential competitors is the US$700 million cost to design a new family of microprocessors and the US$3 billion needed to build a new fabrication facility. However, disruptive technologies such as Tensilica's modular microprocessor architecture are flattening the scale economics of design. And small fabrication facilities, or mini-fabs, could reduce the fixed costs of production. Such technologies take root at the bottom end of the market first, but their capabilities are improving all the time (Christensen, 2001).

For example, global efficiencies of scale allowed Asian manufacturers of VCRs to move along the experience curve. The Asian VCR manufacturers could sell their products at lower prices than was possible for US manufacturers serving only the regional market. Consequently, US manufacturers no longer produce VCRs.

Economies of scope (transfer of resources, experience, ideas and successful concepts across products and markets)

A second source of competitive advantage, intertwined with scale economics, has been breadth of product range. For example, through the 1970s, Caterpillar's scope gave the company an unassailable advantage in construction equipment against smaller competitors such as Komatsu. Only Caterpillar was large enough to absorb the complexity-driven overhead costs of developing, manufacturing and distributing a full product range. Caterpillar's dealers did not need to carry equipment from other manufacturers in order to offer customers what they needed. Caterpillar's huge installed base of equipment in the field meant its dealers, who were the largest dealers in each market, could afford to stock the part necessary to offer 24-hour delivery of any spare part to any Caterpillar owner. No competitor could match this at that time.

Scope economies are also derived from activities in interrelated geographical markets. If they are strong, a sustainable advantage in one market can be used to build sustainability in another. The term scope economy is not just a new name for synergy; it actually defines the conditions under which synergy works. To achieve economies of scope, a company must be able to share resources across markets, while making sure that the cost of those resources remains largely fixed. Only then can economies be effected by spreading assets over a greater number of markets.

Global companies can transfer resources between business units in different parts of the world. These resources may include personnel (such as experienced production managers), funds (global organizations usually have a lower capital cost than domestic firms), and superior market information. Firms such as Kraft-Jacobs-Suchard, the Swiss chocolate and coffee manufacturer owned by Philip Morris, transfer their managers to operations where they need their specific know-how, for example in the growing markets of eastern Europe, and profit from the capital transfer capacity of their company to respond quickly to market opportunities wherever they occur.

A global company is also able to transfer experience, ideas and successful concepts from one country to another. McDonald's country managers in Europe, for example, meet regularly to compare notes on products and promotional ideas, but also how to avoid waste, and to discuss whether such ideas might be appropriate in other markets. Faster knowledge transfer and learning result in superior customer benefits through lower prices and improved product and service features.

Finally, global companies often have a stronger brand reputation than can be achieved by domestic companies. As travel and communication across national boundaries increase, this potential for transfer of brand reputation is likely to grow.

Competitive advantage is a constantly moving target. The most successful firms know how to keep moving, always staying alert and pro-active. Today, time represents a powerful source of competitive advantage and includes managing time in production and service delivery, in new product development and introduction, and in sales distribution.

Time can be expressed in a variety of ways: cycle time, **time to market**, new product development time, time elapsed between order placement and payment, and real-time customer responsiveness. Time-based competitors focus on both activity and system delivery times as measures in all phases of their operations.

All *time-based competition (TBC)* uses process strategies to reduce one or more of the various types of **lead times** faced by the company. They are implemented using such tactics as team building, organizational flattening, flexible manufacturing systems and simultaneous engineering. The key challenge facing any company attempting to implement TBC is to ensure that there is a proper fit between how the company competes in the marketplace, the specific TBC process strategies selected, and the specific implementation tactics used.

By competing on time, a company enjoys first-entrant advantages that include higher pricing, higher market share, improved customer service, and productivity improvement. The goal of TBC, like just-in-time, is to eliminate all wasted time from activities in the value chain. Such time-reduction methods can be seen in overlapping product development activities through simultaneous engineering, improving communication channels between various functions (including customers and suppliers), through set-up times, and smoothing production flow. The underlying premise of TBC is that the company fastest at responding to market needs will lead the rest.

The time-based competitor is able to use customer feedback to offer new products in less time, quickly discontinuing products that do not sell well. In an early example of TBC, Yamaha was overwhelmed when Honda responded to its challenge in motorcycles. Honda launched many of new motorcycle models in just a few months. Yamaha was forced to admit defeat and retreat from its position as market leader. Honda's gain of market share and its market dominance were a direct result of time-based strategies.

A strategy built on leadership alone or flexible manufacturing alone would not have been sufficient for Honda because Yamaha could have matched it on each score. Honda's competitive advantage came from optimizing synergies between time-based characteristics of lower prices, flexible processes, top quality and heightened awareness of consumers via consumer service programmes.

However, that TBC is not everything is shown by the VCR industry, where success in controlling the industry standard perhaps can indicate all competitive advantages in other areas.

Sony, as the first-to-market initially had many competitive advantages over JVC, e.g. innovation and differentiation. Yet losing in the industry standard war to JVC's VHS format, due to a lack of network building, diminished Sony's many competitive advantages in the VCR business. Sony had to abide by the standard set by JVC and reduce its own Betamax system to a niche product, hurting its performance in the business (Ma, 2000a).

The first-generation approach to speed has been radical in many ways. Managers in North America and Europe changed forever how they thought about manufacturing, for example. Borrowing from the Japanese, they introduced methodologies, which helped to boost production speed and to match supply and demand more accurately. As the speed of manufacturing and service delivery increased, attention shifted upstream toward the much longer, less tangible product-development process. By breaking down functional barriers and introducing concurrent design processes, companies cut product development time by 30 per cent or more.

Today the focus is also on strategy. The companies that can make decisions fast, change direction nimbly, and figure out when to enter and exit markets will enjoy competitive advantage.

Speed plays an increasingly important role in more traditional strategic moves, such as mergers and acquisitions. Traditionally, acquisitions were used to buy earnings and remove competitors in mature markets. Now, innovation and access to capabilities drive many mergers and aquisitions. In those cases, senior managers must identify, execute, and assimilate acquisitions very quickly or they will lose the deal. Partnerships can substantially enhance a company's ability to move swiftly by enabling it to focus on what it does best and fastest. Sun Microsystems and Cisco Systems are highly regarded when it comes to design and marketing, but they turn to contract manufacturers Jabil, Flextronics, and Solectron for product supply in all but the newest technologies. Not only are the contract manufacturers faster today, but their focus will keep them faster tomorrow (Meyer, 2001).

Strategic thinking as a core competence

The ability to think strategically is crucial to remaining competitive in an increasingly turbulent and global environment. Strategic thinking should be driven by a strong sense of organizational purpose and a vision of the desired future for the organization.

A crucial element of strategic thinking is the ability to take a holistic perspective of the organization and its environment. This requires an understanding of how different problems and issues are connected with each other, how they influence each other and what effect one solution in a particular area would have on other areas.

Taking a holistic approach requires the ability to distance oneself from day-to-day operational problems and to see how problems and issues are connected to the overall pattern that underlies particular details and events (Bonn, 2001).

Heracleous (1998) made the distinction between strategic planning and strategic thinking by an analogy to *single-loop learning* and *double-loop learning*. In his view, the former is analogous to strategic planning, the latter to strategic thinking. He claimed that single-loop learning involves thinking within existing assumptions and taking actions based on a fixed set of alternatives. Double-loop learning, in contrast, challenges existing assumptions and develops new and innovative solutions, leading to potentially more appropriate actions. Like single-loop learning and double-loop learning, strategic planning and strategic thinking are interrelated in a dialectical process and are equally important for effective strategic management.

Exploitation of local advantages

One might expect that global companies are less well situated than local firms to exploit local advantages, such as closeness to the market and working with distributors on a personal basis. However, domestic marketers, especially those located in

Exhibit 3.2

Intel's development of competitive advantage

Intel is an innovator. Its initial dominance in the computer memory device business derived from its technical innovation and mould-breaking products. Intel's dominance in microprocessors for PCs started with the 8080 microprocessor, and later the 8086. Its 8088 microprocessor, an 8-bit version of the 8086, was chosen by IBM when it launched its PC in 1981. Intel's constant innovation in microprocessors helped it produce a score of new products in its X86 and Pentium series. Innovation propels Intel's successive dominance in its core business.

Despite its dominance in the microprocessor business, Intel does not rely solely on its strong market position to fend off rivals. Instead, Intel is a fierce competitor, a paranoid warrior embodying the aggressive spirit of its CEO, Andy Grove. Its constant introduction of new-generation chips, – 286, 386, 486, Pentium, Pentium MMX and Pentium Pro – ensures that Intel always has a competitive edge over rivals which imitate Intel's designs. In Intel's hyper-competitive business environment, Intel's real advantage is being faster than its rivals (time-based competitiveness). Intel challenges and competes against itself to expand the technological boundary.

Intel's unique strengths lie in its technical capability to develop mould-breaking products. Critical to its success are also its capabilities in manufacturing and marketing. With its superior design capabilities, Intel was able to develop innovative products that set the industry standard.

Sticking to the logic that high switching costs prevent customers from shifting easily between different technological standards, Intel lately has focused its effort to support the momentum of Pentium computers, the latest being Pentium 4 (2001).

To establish a dominant position in any business, a firm needs commitment. Intel´s commitment was to microprocessors. Intel also made its commitment because of its belief in relationships and in the technical problems that would need to be solved. It was the willingness of major computer manufacturers like Compaq to build the 486-based computers that largely influenced Intel's decision. Intel knew very well the value of complementors whose products enhance the value of Intel products. For instance, its cooperative relationship with Microsoft helped define the PC standard. The complementarity of Intel's microprocessors and Microsoft's operating systems allowed the two firms to dominate the PC hardware and software businesses for the last two decades.

Although Intel, Microsoft and major computer makers fight to claim the value created in the PC business, these firms also cooperate to explore new ways to enhance the total value. For instance, Intel's *Intel Inside* campaign not only effectively promoted its brand to end customers, but also enhanced the credibility of computer manufacturers' products, because it makes sense to communicate to the end customers that your computers are based on a dominant standard in microprocessors. Intel provided rebates on its chips and lured manufacturers to collaborate on its *Intel Inside* campaign.

Designing and manufacturing complement each other. To speed the design process, Intel designers involved manufacturing early in the chip design process, ensuring that the chips could be manufactured economically. Intel possesses manufacturing facilities all over the world. In order to enhance its manufacturing quality and productivity, it has closed inefficient plants, enhanced clean-room discipline, and used more automation. Both its designing and manufacturing capabilities jointly define Intel's unique technical competence that makes it possible to introduce new generations of chips to the market quickly.

Intel's marketing capability allows it to go beyond its immediate customers – major computer makers who adopt Intel's microprocessors – and connect directly with its end customers. Its *Intel Inside* campaign has become one of the best-staged advertising and

Exhibit 3.2 continued

promotion schemes in history, alongside such classical examples as NutraSweet and Dolby. Since its introduction in 1990, Intel has become a well-known customer brand. As a result, customers, whether they are computer literate or not, would insist on having Intel inside their computers, thinking that it must be something good and essential if so many major names in the computer business like IBM, Compaq and Dell relentlessly promote it.

Source: adapted from Ma (2000a).

small countries, are often under-financed, lacking in well-qualified management, and not highly competitive in nature. The additional resources available to global marketers, coupled with a more professional marketing orientation, may make them better prepared to seek out and exploit local advantages.

Ability to provide global services

Global companies have the ability to provide global services. Increasingly, customers in industrial and consumer markets are looking for more complete products, including pre- and post-sale services. In particular, services that can be delivered through technology (such as international investment) may be performed more efficiently or more fully by global marketers. This is one of the reasons why former national telecommunications companies such as Deutsche Telekom seek strategic partnerships to improve their competitive position. For example, in March 2002 Deutsche Telekom announced a partnership with Microsoft.

Company-specific competitive advantages

In general, a company can identify its specific sources of competitive advantage by running through its list of distinctive competences for the markets under consideration.

Distinctive competences may become competitive advantages if the firm can successfully transform them into benefits for potential customers or relevant stakeholders. The distinctive competence of highly flexible low-cost production, for example, can only become a competitive advantage when it can be transformed into low-priced customized products. Customers and stakeholders will have a high propensity to develop preferences and long-term relationships with the provider of such benefits if they are highly attractive to them. Competitive advantages are strongest when they are unique to the firm, that is, when they cannot be duplicated easily. The family ties of owners and managers of Taiwanese and Hong Kong-based companies with business people from the People's Republic of China, for example, give them a competitive advantage over US companies in obtaining joint-venture contracts with Chinese firms. A marketer should not overlook, however, the possibility that competitors might develop capabilities quite fast through acquisitions, mergers or cooperation. Finally, a competitive advantage only exists if the customers and stakeholders are ready to value the benefits offered, such as paying a good price or providing goodwill.

The ability to use human resources in developing competitive advantage

The success of marketing and especially RM is, to a large extent, dependent on the attitudes, commitment and performance of the employees. If they are not committed to their role as part-time marketers and are not motivated to perform in a customer-oriented fashion, the strategy fails. Hence success in the marketplace requires initial success internally in motivating employees and getting their commitment to the pursuit of a relationship marketing strategy. RM is, therefore, highly dependent on a well-organized and continuous **internal marketing** process.

Human capital theory (Lepak and Snell, 1999) distinguished general skills and firm-specific skills of human resources. General skills are skills possessed by individuals that provide value to a firm and are transferable across a variety of firms. For example, all competitor firms have the potential to accrue equal value from acquiring employees with knowledge of general management, the ability to apply financial ratios, or general cognitive ability. Specific skills, on the other hand, provide value only to a particular firm and are of no value to competing firms. For example, the knowledge of how to use a particular technology used only by one firm or knowledge of a firm's policies and procedures provide value to that firm but usually would not be valuable to other firms.

Because general skills provide equal value to all firms, one would expect that, given even moderately efficient labour markets, these would not be a source of competitive advantage for any one organization. To seek to gain sustained competitive advantage through general skills would be futile. On the other hand, there are two reasons that this does not imply that these skills are not important. First, general skills are necessary for maintaining competitive parity. For example, basic reading and writing skills are general skills that will not provide competitive advantage to any one firm; however, a firm that hired many employees who could not read and write would be at a considerable disadvantage in the marketplace. Second, most organizations have defined the 'new deal' between the firm and its employees. One avenue to sustained competitive advantage is to provide employees with the necessary training and development that ensures them marketability to other firms (i.e. general skills). Firms that fail to invest in general skills will be unable to attract and retain competent employees.

In addition, while general skills are applicable across organizations and thus most likely to result in only competitive parity, this does not mean that the importance of general skills should be ignored – they add value.

Greater potential for sustainable competitive advantage stems from investment in firm-specific skills. One avenue is to focus on developing a firm-specific skill base within an organization because these skills cannot be easily duplicated by competitors. These skills provide competitive advantage because they provide value to the firm, but they are not easily marketable by the employees who possess them. One can accomplish this through investing in constant training and development of employees to perform work processes and procedures that are specific to the firm. In fact, central to the concept of organizational learning is the process of developing and disseminating tacit knowledge (i.e. firm specific knowledge) throughout the firm (Senge, 1990). The firm benefits from these firm-specific skills while providing employees with the opportunity for growth and development.

The importance of firm-specific skills highlights the potential shortsightedness of outsourcing most or all of a firm's training and development activities. Outsourced activities such as these provide general rather than firm-specific skills most effectively. While some training firms may be able to develop tailor-made programmes for specific firms, these are not feasible when proprietary technologies and processes exist. In addition, the training firm, which develops the tailor-made programmes, consequently acquires the skills and can theoretically (although not ethically and possibly not legally) exploit them with competing firms. For these reasons, while some training activities can and should be outsourced, outsourcing all training activities is not likely to gain sustainable competitive advantage through people (Barney and Wright, 1998).

3.3 Introduction of a holistic model of competitiveness: from macro to micro level

The theory of firm competitiveness implicitly assumes that the 'competitiveness of nations' is not simply based on country-specific factors but heavily influenced by firm-specific factors, as the latter is deeply ingrained in and shapes the former.

On the other hand, the competitive advantage developed by a firm in its home market is determined to a significant extent by the national business environment, with benefits being derived from access to resources and skills and competitive pressures derived from other national firms creating the need to invest and innovate.

The need to understand the advantages gained by firms in industries in these countries is valuable for the individual firm in seeing what it is about its own location that can determine its ability to gain competitive advantage.

It is relevant to look at why a nation becomes the base for successful international competition in an industry, or how it is that firms in an industry from a particular country can create competitive advantage, and then sustain it over time.

This section focuses on the three levels of analysis – nation, industry, and firm (see Figure 3.2)

Figure 3.2 Three levels of international competitiveness

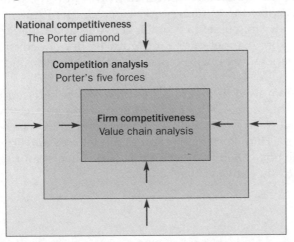

Recently, however, the concept of 'bloc competitiveness' is receiving more and more attention as economic unions of nations (blocs) such as the European Union (EU), the North American Free Trade Area (NAFTA), the Association of South-East Asian Nations (ASEAN), and Asia Pacific Economic Cooperation (APEC) emerge (Cho, 1998; Proff, 2002). Bloc competitiveness is especially important for the 15 countries that form the EU. The prime purpose of establishing the union was undoubtedly to combine the competitiveness of each nation and strengthen the resulting overall competitiveness as a whole. For instance, there are 16 manufacturers of railway rolling stock in the EU, and only two competing companies have formed an alliance. Strategic alliance would be a good way to strengthen the competitiveness of European companies, and therein lies the competitiveness of the EU.

Japanese companies also point to the importance of bloc competitiveness. From the late 1980s, Japanese companies expanded their strategic partners from traditional subcontractors in Japan to foreign companies that have advantages in competitiveness. Ricoh, an optical instrument maker, established Taiwan Li-Kwang in Taiwan to carry out production in Taiwan and exports. Its sister company in Senchen, Tai-Lian Opticals, is a joint venture that provides components. To build this company, Ricoh joined Mitsubishi Corporation and set up Gastra Trading in Hong Kong, which in turn formed an alliance with Wan-Hai Investment Co. The purpose of this joint venture with the Hong Kong company was to gain easy access to information on investing in mainland China and to have more access to Chinese government. This case clearly shows that Ricoh considers east Asian countries as a loosely organized bloc. This Japanese company is creating bloc competitiveness, which comes from combining the competitive advantages of various nations in that part of the world.

To enable an understanding of the development of a firm's international competitiveness in this broader perspective, a holistic model in three stages (see Figure 3.3) will be presented:

1. Analysis of national competitiveness (the Porter diamond)
2. Competition analysis in an industry (Porter's five forces)
3. Firm competitiveness and value chain analysis: (a) competitive triangle; (b) **benchmarking**.

The analysis starts at the macro level and then moves into the firm's competitive arena through Porter's five forces framework. Based on the firm's value chain, the analysis concludes with a discussion of which activities and functions in the value chain are the firm's core competences (and must be developed internally in the firm) and which competences must be placed with others through alliances and market relations.

The graphical system used in Figure 3.3 (which will be referred to throughout this section) places the models after each other in a hierarchical windows logic, where you move from stage 1 to stage 2 by clicking on the icon box 'Firm strategy, structure, and rivalry'. Here Porter's five forces model appears. From stage 2 to 3 you click the middle box called 'Market competitors/buyers' and the model for a value chain analysis/competitive triangle appears.

Figure 3.3 Development of a firm's international competitiveness

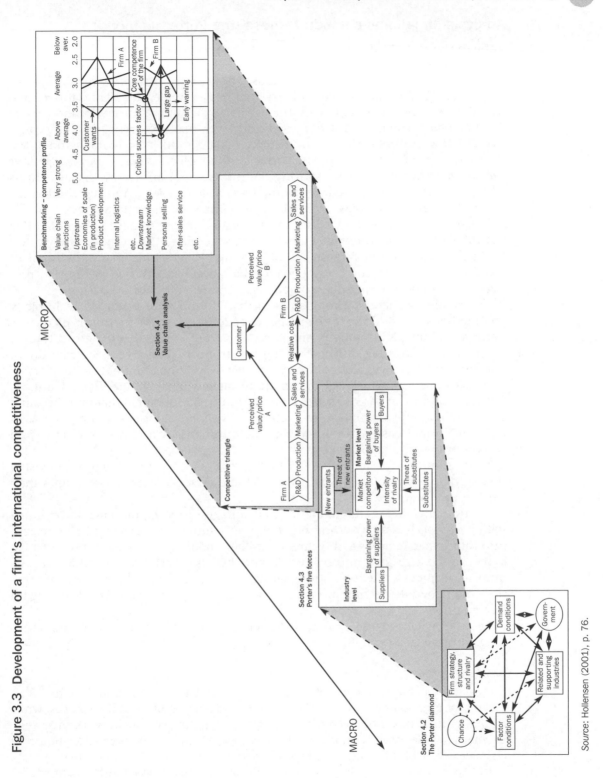

Source: Hollensen (2001), p. 76.

Analysis of national competitiveness (the Porter diamond)

Though the analysis of national competitiveness represents the highest level in this book (Figure 3.3), several writers (e.g. Cho, 1998) have argued that also some kind of regional competitiveness exists, because the national diamonds within regions (e.g. North America and EU) are interrelated. For example, Canada's national diamond is highly integrated with the US. This double diamond framework is described by Rugman and D'Cruz (1993). However, the heterogeneity among countries in, for example, the EU or NAFTA makes it difficult to talk about the competitiveness of trading blocs. Porter (1990) called his work *The Competitive Advantage of Nations*, but as a starting point it is important to say that it is firms which are competing in the international arena, not nations. Yet, the characteristics of the home nation play a central role in a firm's international success.

Taking the examples Porter uses to support the theory of national competitive advantage will make the issue global. Why is Germany the home of the world's leading companies in luxury cars and chemicals? Why is Switzerland the home of leading companies in confectionery and pharmaceuticals? Why has the USA produced world leaders in personal computers, software and credit cards?

The home base shapes a company's capacity to innovate rapidly in technology and methods, and to do so in the proper directions. It is the place from which competitive advantage ultimately emanates, and from which it must be sustained. Competitive advantage ultimately results from an effective combination of national circumstances and company strategy. Conditions in a nation may create an environment in which a firm can attain international competitive advantage, but it is up to a company to seize the opportunity. The national diamond becomes central to choosing the industries to compete with, as well as the appropriate strategy. The home base is an important determinant of a firm's strengths and weaknesses relative to foreign rivals.

Understanding the home base of foreign competitors is essential in analysing them. Their home nation yields advantages and disadvantages. It also shapes their likely future strategies.

A firm gains important competitive advantages from the presence in its home nation of world-class buyers, suppliers and related industries. They provide insight into future market needs and technological developments. They contribute to a climate for change and improvement, and become partners and allies in the innovation process. Having a strong cluster at home unblocks the flow of information and allows deeper and more open contact than is possible when dealing with foreign firms.

Let us now take a closer look at the different elements in Porter's diamond beginning with the factor conditions.

Factor conditions

Each nation possesses factors of production (land, labour, and capital), which can mean that a nation such as Russia has a large endowment of natural resources, while Holland does not. Some countries possess a highly educated workforce (e.g. Germany) while others do not (e.g. Ethiopia). Depending on the type and amount of resources available, the nation will tend to favour some industries rather than others.

In this connection it is important to mention that the most enduring competitive advantages for nations are created by those factors that have the least degree of mobility.

At one extreme, we have climate with no mobility. Finland will never be a major producer of citrus fruit, no matter what government and industry do to try to change the rest of the national diamond.

At the other end of the mobility scale we have capital, probably the most mobile of the factors of production. Over the years we have seen enormous increases in the flow of foreign capital in the industrialized and developing countries of the world. This can be seen as part of the process of global economic integration. Technology and the loosening of currency restrictions throughout the world have improved the flow of capital across nations and suggest that differences in capital availability are no longer likely to constitute a very stable competitive advantage for an area.

Gaining competitive advantage is not just a matter of looking at the quality and amount of the production factors, however; all the parts of the 'diamond' will have an influence. For example, a company that wishes to innovate must have access to skilled labour suppliers who can provide the necessary materials and know-how and the commitment to take the line of action that leads to competitive pressure and advantage.

Labour shortages and a lack of storage and production space led Japanese car manufacturers to automate their production processes earlier than their counterparts in other nations, and to develop space-saving, lean production techniques such as **just-in-time** inventory management systems.

Demand conditions

The nature and size of home demand is represented in the right-hand box of Porter's diamond (Figure 3.3). There is an interaction between scale economies, transportation costs and the size of the home market. Given sufficiently strong economies of scale, each producer wants to serve an extensive market from a single location. To minimize transportation costs, the producer chooses a location with large local demand. When scale economies limit the number of production locations, the size of a market will be an important determinant of its attractiveness. Large home markets will also ensure that firms located there develop a cost advantage based on scale and often on experience as well.

An interesting pattern is that an early large home market that has become saturated forces efficient firms to look abroad for new business. For example, the Japanese motorcycle industry with its large home market used its scale advantages in the global marketplace after an early start in Japan. The composition of demand also plays an important role.

A product's fundamental or core design nearly always reflects home market needs. In electrical transmission equipment, for example, Sweden dominates the world in the high-voltage distribution market. In Sweden there is a relatively large demand for transporting high voltage over long distances, as a consequence of the location of population and industry clusters. Here the needs of the home market shaped the industry that was later able to respond to global markets (with ABB as one of the leading producers in the world market).

The sophistication of the buyer is also important. The US government was the first buyer of computerchips and remained the only customer for many years. The price inelasticity of government encouraged firms to develop technically advanced products without worrying too much about costs. Under these conditions, the technological frontier was clearly pushed much further and much faster than it would have been had the buyer been either less sophisticated or more price sensitive.

Other examples of these effects can be observed in the Japanese consumer electronics industry. Because of its highly concentrated urban centres and the relative lack of land available for expansion, the Japanese have been forced earlier than other nations to focus on miniaturization and the efficient use of space. The Japanese are also highly sophisticated and knowledgeable purchasers of consumer electronics, as audio equipment is considered a status item in Japan. Japanese consumers conduct considerable research before making their purchases, and are among the first consumers to identify and demand the next generation of product features. All of these demand characteristics provide Japanese consumer electronics manufacturers with the impetus and information necessary to provide the most efficient products with cutting-edge features and designs.

Related and supporting industries

In part, the advantages of clustering come from a reduction in the transportation costs for intermediate goods. In many other cases, advantages come from being able to use labour which is attracted to an area to serve the core industry, but which is available and skilled for supporting industries. Coordination of technology is also eased by geographic proximity. Porter argues that Italian world leadership in gold and silver jewellery has been sustained in part by the local presence of manufacturers of jewellery-making machinery. Here the advantage of clustering is not so much transportation cost reductions, but technical and marketing cooperation. In the semiconductor industry, the strength of the electronics industry in Japan (which buys the semiconductors) is a strong incentive to the location of semiconductor manufacturers in the same area. It should be noted that clustering is not independent of scale economies. If there were no scale economies in the production of intermediate inputs, then the small-scale centres of production could rival the large-scale centres. It is the fact that there are scale economies in both semiconductors and electronics, coupled with the technological and marketing connections between the two that give rise to clustering advantages.

Firm strategy, structure and rivalry

One of the most compelling results of Porter's study of successful industries in ten different nations is the powerful and positive effect that domestic competition has on the ability to compete in the global marketplace. In Germany, the fierce domestic rivalry among BASF, Hoechst and Bayer in the pharmaceutical industry is well known. Furthermore, the process of competition weeds out inferior technologies, products and management practices, and leaves as survivors only the most effiicient firms. When domestic competition is vigorous, firms are forced to become more efficient, adopt new cost-saving technologies, reduce product development time, and learn to motivate and control workers more effectively. Domestic rivalry is especially important in stimulating technological developments among **global firms**.

The small country of Denmark has three producers of hearing-aids (Oticon, Widex and Danavox), which are all among the top ten of the world's largest producers of hearing-aids. In 1996, Oticon and Widex fought a violent technological battle to be the first in the world to launch a 100 per cent digital hearing-aid. Widex (the smaller of the two producers) won, but forced Oticon at the same time to keep a leading edge in technological development.

Chance

When we look at the history of most industries, we also see the role played by chance. Perhaps the most important instance of chance involves the question of who comes up with a major new idea first. For reasons having little to do with economics, **entrepreneurs** will typically start their new operations in their home countries. Once the industry begins in a given country, scale and clustering effects can cement the industry's position in that country.

Government

Governments play a powerful role in encouraging the development of industries that will assume global positions within their own borders. One way governments do this is through their effect on other elements of the national diamond. Governments finance and construct infrastructure, providing roads, airports, education and healthcare, and can support the use of alternative energy (e.g. wind farms) or other environmental systems that affect factors of production.

From the firm's point of view, the last two variables, chance and government, can be regarded as exogenous variables which the firms must adjust to. Alternatively, the government may be considered susceptible through lobbying, interest organizations and mass media.

In summary, we have identified six factors that influence the location of global industries: factors of production, home demand, the location of supporting industries, the internal structure of the domestic industry, chance and government. We have also suggested that these factors are interconnected. As industries evolve, their dependence on particular locations may also change. For example, the shift in users of semiconductors from the military to the electronics industry has had a profound effect on the shape of the national diamond in that industry. To the extent that governments and firms recognize the source of any locational advantages that they have, they will be better able to both exploit those differences and anticipate their shifts.

Competition analysis in an industry

The next step in understanding a firm's competitiveness is to look at the competitive arena in an industry, which is the top box in the diamond model (see Figure 3.3).

One of the most useful frameworks for analysing the competitive structure has been developed by Michael E. Porter. Porter (1980) suggests that competition in an industry is rooted in its underlying economic structure and goes beyond the behaviour of current competitors. The state of competition depends upon five basic competitive forces, as shown in Figure 3.3. Together, these factors determine the ultimate profit potential in an industry, where profit is measured in terms of long-term return on invested capital. The profit potential will differ from industry to industry.

To make things clearer, we need to define a number of key terms. An industry is a group of firms that offer a product or class of products that are close substitutes for each other. Examples are the car industry and the pharmaceutical industry (Kotler 1997, p. 230). A market is a set of actual and potential buyers of a product and sellers. A distinction will be made between industry and market level, as we assume that the industry may contain several different markets. This is why the outer box in Figure 3.3 is designated 'industry level' and the inner box 'market level'.

The industry level consists of all types of players (new entrants, suppliers, substitutes, buyers and market competitors), which have a potential or current interest in the industry.

The market level consists of players with a current interest in the market: that is, buyers and sellers (market competitors). At the end of this chapter, this market will be further elaborated as the buyers' perceived value of different competitor offerings will be discussed.

Although division into these two levels is appropriate for this approach, Levitt (1960) pointed out the danger of '**marketing myopia**' where the seller defines the competition field (i.e. the market) too narrowly. For example, the European luxury car manufacturers showed this myopia with their focus on each other rather than on the Japanese mass manufacturers, who were new entrants into the luxury car market.

The goal of competition analysis is to find a position in industry where the company can best defend itself against the five forces, or can influence them in its favour. Knowledge of these underlying pressures highlights the critical strengths and weaknesses of the company, shows its position in the industry, and clarifies areas where strategy changes yield the greatest pay-off. Structure analysis is fundamental for formulating competitive strategy.

Each of the five forces in the Porter model comprises a number of elements that combine to determine the strength of each force, and its effect on the degree of competition. Each force will now be discussed.

Exhibit 3.3 **The Porter 5-forces model in use**

Porter's 5-forces model is useful in answering the following question: how large is the profit potential in a certain industry? This is an example from the metal container industry.

Figure 3.4 Porter's 5-forces model in the metal container industry

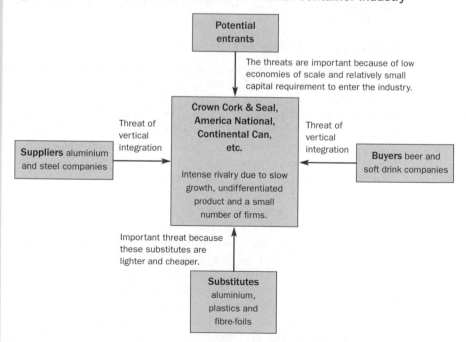

Exhibit 3.3 continued

Bargaining power of suppliers

Aluminium companies: there are only four suppliers of aluminium and these companies are much more concentrated than the metal container industry. These firms have vast resources and pose a credible threat in terms of forward integration.

Steel companies: there are few suppliers of tin-plated steel and they also pose a credible threat in terms of forward integration. Aluminium and steel companies can also exert a good deal of bargaining power over metal can manufacturers.

Bargaining power of buyers

Buyers of cans are very large and powerful. The cost of can is a significant part of their costs. Cans are a commodity bought in large quantities. There is low customer loyalty. Buyers pose a credible threat in terms of backward integration and can exert a great deal of power over metal can producers.

Threat from substitute products

Aluminium's lighter weight could help in transport costs. It is easier to lithograph, producing a better reproduction at lower cost. It is also favoured over steel as a recycling material. Plastics are generally lighter and resistant to breakage. Fibre-foil is 20 per cent lighter and 15 per cent cheaper than a steel can. These substitutes pose a significant threat to tin-plated steel.

Threat of entry

Economies of scale in this industry are quite low and as such cannot be used as an entry barrier. Capital investment is certainly not an entry barrier. Brand loyalty is absent and, therefore, is not an entry barrier. The metal container industry then has very low barriers to entry but is not an attractive (high-margin) industry.

Intensity of rivalry among existing competitors

This is a slow growth, mature industry. A metal container is largely an undifferentiated product, forcing the customers to choose on the basis of price. The presence of close substitutes and low entry barriers keeps prices down. The existence of very powerful buyers and very powerful suppliers also keeps container prices down. Therefore, price competition is quite intense.

In summary, the major trends characterizing the metal container industry are:

● the continuing threat of in-house manufacture

● the emergence of plastic as a viable packaging material

● steady competition from glass as a substitute for aluminium in the beer market

● the emergence of the soft drinks industry as the largest end user of packaging, with aluminium one of the main materials used

● the diversification of, and consolidation among, packaging producers.

Given these factors, the profit potential in the metal container industry is expected to be low.

Source: adapted from Harvard Business School (1990), Furner and Thomas (2000).

Market competitors (degree of rivalry)

The intensity of rivalry between existing competitors in a market depends on a number of factors.

- *The concentration of the industry*: numerous competitors of equal size will lead to more intense rivalry. There will be less rivalry when a clear leader (at lest 50 per cent larger than the second) exists with a large cost advantage.
- *Rate of market growth*: slow growth will tend towards greater rivalry.
- *Structure of costs*: high fixed costs encourage price cutting to fill capacity.
- *Degree of differentiation*: commodity products encourage rivalry, while highly differentiated products, which are hard to copy, are associated with less intense rivalry.
- *Switching costs*: when **switching costs** are high because the product is specialized, the customer has invested a lot of resources in learning how to use the product or has made tailor-made investments that are worthless with other products and suppliers (high asset specificity), rivalry is reduced.
- *Exit barriers*: when barriers to leaving a market are high due to such factors as lack of opportunities elsewhere, high vertical integration, emotional barriers or the high cost of closing down plant, rivalry will be more intense than when **exit barriers** are low.

Firms need to be careful not to spoil a situation of competitive stability. They need to balance their own position against the well-being of the industry as a whole. For example, an intense price or promotional war may gain a few percentage points in market share, but lead to an overall fall in long-term industry profitability as competitors respond to these moves. It is sometimes better to protect industry structure than to follow short-term self-interest.

In some industries, previously 'unassailable' product differentiation advantages have been eroded, to be replaced by intense rivalry. In the US cigarette market, for example, discount brands have been capturing an increased share of sales, rising from less than 5 per cent in 1981 to 30 per cent in 1992. In response to this trend, Philip Morris recently began discounting the price of its brand leader, Marlboro. Philip Morris concluded that such discounts were necessary to maintain Marlboro's market share, although they resulted in a 40 per cent reduction in pre-tax profits from its US tobacco operations.

On the other hand, some brand names continue to protect firms from intense rivalry. Despite the cola wars of the 1970s and 1980s, Coca-Cola remains among the world's best-known brands. By carefully exploiting that product differentiation advantage, especially overseas (thereby avoiding confrontations with PepsiCo), Coca-Cola was able to obtain huge profits during the last ten years.

The fast-food business is an example of an industry that for years was able to avoid high rivalry and price competition through the implementation of product differentiation strategies. Different fast-food firms focused their marketing efforts on different segments of the fast-food industry – for example, McDonald's for children, Taco Bell for Mexican food, Kentucky Fried Chicken for chicken. However, the use of product differentiation as a rivalry-reducing strategy has broken down in the fast-food industry and has been replaced by fierce price competition.

Relationships between US and Japanese car companies are also now characterized by less rivalry than they were a few years ago. Through much of the 1980s, US and Japanese car firms competed on price, performance, quality, and service. However, since the mid-1980s, these former direct competitors have learned to cooperate with each other – through joint ventures and strategic alliances – in ways that have reduced rivalry and increased profits. Now, whenever Mazda sells a car in the US market, Ford benefits; whenever Mitsubishi sells a car in the United States, Chrysler benefits; and so forth. Indeed, a recent effort to establish import quotas reducing the number of Japanese cars that could be imported into the United States did not receive required political support from US car companies. The use of cooperative strategies has enabled US car companies to reduce the threat of rivalry.

Suppliers

The cost of raw materials and components can have a major bearing on a firm's profitability. The higher the bargaining power of suppliers, the higher the costs. The bargaining power of suppliers will be higher in the following circumstances:

- supply is dominated by few companies and they are more concentrated than the industry they sell to
- their products are unique or differentiated, or they have built up switching costs
- they are not obliged to contend with other products for sale to the industry
- they pose a credible threat of integrating forwards into the industry's business, i.e. they seek control of the next level of the vertical chain
- buyers do not threaten to integrate backwards into supply, i.e. the buyers of the supplier's goods (firms in the middle box of Porter's five forces) do not want to control the supply
- the market is not an important customer for the supplier group.

Much of Microsoft's power as a supplier of software to the PC industry reflects its dominance in the operating systems market, where MS-DOS and Windows remain the de facto standard for most personal computers. For now, at least, if a company wants to sell personal computers, it is going to need to interact with Microsoft.

A firm can reduce the bargaining power of suppliers by seeking new sources of supply, threatening to integrate backward into supply, and designing standardized components so that many suppliers are capable of producing them.

This has been particularly common in the electronics industry, where a potential supplier will develop a unique technology and a firm wishing to use the technology will need to redesign its entire product to do so. Before redesigning its product, a firm will often require the original supplier to license several other firms that can also be its suppliers. With these multiple, less threatening suppliers in place, a firm is more willing to redesign its product to take advantage of the new technology.

Many Japanese firms have taken an alternative approach to managing the threat of suppliers. Suppliers can be a threat when a buyer depends on a supplier more than the supplier depends on the buyer. A way to create a balance in this dependence is for a supplier to purchase a substantial equity position in its critical customer and for a customer to purchase a substantial equity position in its critical supplier. This cross-equity holding gives both parties incentives to cooperate. Indeed, this ownership structure can be thought of as a form of strategic alliance. Such cross-equity ownership is very common in Japan. Indeed, it is not unusual for four or five of the largest equity holders in a Japanese firm to be major suppliers to that firm. These large equity holders will include not only suppliers of raw material and parts but also suppliers of capital (that is, banks) and suppliers of labour (company labour unions). These cross-equity relations tend to be very stable and form the basis of very cooperative relations among Japanese firms and their suppliers. Recently, several US and European firms have begun to implement similar cooperative approaches to managing supplier relations.

Buyers

The bargaining power of buyers is higher in the following circumstances:

- Buyers are concentrated and/or purchase in large volumes.
- Buyers pose a credible threat of intergrating backwards to manufacture the industry's product. Buyers are likely to integrate backwards when the supplies they purchase are a significant portion of the costs of their final products. In this context, buyers are likely to be very concerned about the costs of their supplies and constantly on the lookout for cheaper alternatives, including the possibility of backward vertical integration. For example, the metal can is approximately 40 per cent of the final cost of a can of Campbell's soup (Christensen, 2001). To reduce this cost and gain control over a significant portion of its **total costs**, Campbell Soup Company has vertically integrated backward and has become one of the largest can-manufacturing companies in the world.
- Products they purchase are standard or undifferentiated.
- There are many suppliers (sellers) of the product.
- Buyers earn low profits, which create a great incentive to lower purchasing costs.
- The industry's product is unimportant to the quality of the buyer's products, but price is very important.

Firms like McDonnell-Douglas and Westinghouse that sell a significant amount of their output to the US Department of Defense recognize the influence of this buyer on their operations. Recent reductions in defence spending have forced defence companies to try even harder to reduce costs and increase quality to satisfy government demands. All these actions reduce the economic profits of these defence-oriented companies.

Firms in the industry can attempt to lower buyer power by increasing the number of buyers they sell to, threatening to integrate forward into the buyer's industry, and producing highly valued, differentiated products. In supermarket retailing, the brand leader normally achieves the highest profitability partially because being number one means that supermarkets need to stock the brand, thereby reducing buyer power in price negotiations.

Substitutes

The presence of substitute products can reduce industry attractiveness and profitability because they put a constraint on price levels.

If the industry is successful and earning high profits, it is more likely that competitors will enter the market via substitute products in order to obtain a share of the potential profits available. If there are high prices for coffee, for example, tea will become more attractive.

The threat of substitute products depends on the following factors:

- the buyer's willingness to substitute
- the relative price and performance of substitutes
- the costs of switching to substitutes.

In the textile industry, several chemical companies have developed substitutes for traditional textiles. These chemical substitutes include rayon and nylon. However, over the years, several traditional textile companies have developed the skills needed to make these new textiles as well as more traditional textiles. Overall, the threat of substitutes has been lessened, and it is now moderate to low.

The threat of substitute products can be lowered by building up switching costs. These costs may be psychological. Examples are the creation of strong distinctive brand personalities, and maintaining a price differential commensurate with perceived customer values.

The rising price of crude oil in the 1970s and 1980s made several energy substitutes – wind energy and solar energy – look economically attractive. Rather than simply focusing on crude oil, most international oil companies began diversifying their operations to include one or more of these substitute energy sources. As long as the price of crude oil was high, these energy substitutes were important components of the business of these firms. However, the fall of oil prices in the late 1980s prompted most of these firms to **divest** these diversified operations. Such divestitures were consistent with the observation that these activities were no longer close substitutes for crude oil. On the other hand, oil companies like BP have been advertising in the UK that they are involved in alternative energy sources such as wind farms.

New entrants

New entrants can serve to increase the degree of competition in an industry. In turn, the threat of new entrants is largely a function of the extent to which barriers to entry exist in the market. Some key factors affecting these entry barriers include the following:

- economies of scale
- product differentiation and brand identity, which give existing firms customer loyalty
- capital requirements in production
- switching costs – the cost of switching from one supplier to another
- access to distribution channels.

Because high barriers to entry can make even a potentially lucrative market unattractive (or even impossible) to enter for new competitors, the marketing planner should not take a passive approach but should actively pursue ways of raising barriers to new competitors.

High promotional and R&D expenditures and clearly communicated retaliatory actions to entry are some methods of raising barriers. Some managerial actions can unwittingly lower barriers. For example, new product designs that dramatically lower manufacturing costs can make entry by newcomers easier.

Although numerous challenges are associated with erecting barriers to entry, there are nevertheless examples of industries where such barriers have been created. In breakfast cereals, for example, product differentiation – in the special form of brand proliferation – has continued for many decades. It is now the case that virtually every combination of grain, sugar, and artificial colour that could be invented has already been invented. Moreover, breakfast cereals take up a large percentage of the available shelf space in most grocery stores. Entry into this market is very difficult, because incumbent firms have already filled just about all possible entry points. It appears that the soft-drinks industry, with the introduction of caffeine-free colas, sugar-free colas, fruit-based soft drinks, and clear colas, is moving in a similar direction, making entry into this market very difficult.

The collaborative 'five sources' model

Porter's original model is based on the hypothesis that the competitive advantage of the firm is best developed in a very competitive market with intense rivalry. The five forces framework thus provides an analysis for considering how to squeeze the maximum competitive gain out of the context in which the business is located – or how to minimize the prospect of being squeezed by it – on the five competitive dimensions that it confronts.

Over the last decade, however, an alternative school (e.g. Reve, 1990; Kanter, 1994; Burton, 1995) has emerged which emphasizes the positive role of cooperative (rather than competitive) arrangements between industry participants, and the consequent importance of what Kanter (1994) has termed 'collaborative advantage' as a foundation of superior business performance.

An all-or-nothing choice between a single-minded striving for either competitive or collaborative advantage would, however, be a false one. The real strategic choice problem that all businesses face is where (and how much) to collaborate, and where (and how intensely) to act competitively.

Put in another way, the basic questions that firms must deal with in respect of these matters are as follows.

- Choosing the combination of competitive and collaborative strategies that are appropriate in the various dimensions of the industrial environment of the firm.

- Blending the two elements together so that they interact in a mutually consistent and reinforcing manner which is not counterproductive.

- In this way, optimizing the firm's overall position, drawing upon the foundation and utilization of both collaborative and competitive advantage.

This points to the imperative in the contemporary context of complementing the competitive strategy model with a sister framework that focuses on the assessment of collaborative advantage and strategy. Such a complementary analysis, which is called the *five sources framework* (Burton, 1995) is outlined below.

Corresponding to the array of five competitive forces that surround a company – as elaborated in Porter's treatment – there are also five potential sources for the building of collaborative advantage in the industrial environment of the firm. These sources are listed in Table 3.1.

| Exhibit 3.4 | Roche Diagnostic Systems – developing competitiveness through focusing on customer satisfaction |

In 1969 Roche Diagnostic Systems began as a small, yet global division of F. Hoffmann-La Roche, which has its headquarters in Switzerland and its largest affiliates in the USA, Italy, France, and Japan. The division's business centred on diagnostic instrumentation and test reagents for clinical and drug testing professionals. By 1990, the products included blood cultures, chemistry (and later, haematology) instruments, drug testing kits, pregnancy tests, and tumour monitoring assays.

Roche Diagnostics was primarily a product and innovation driven company that would address very different customer segments. The result was that Roche Diagnostics was never a primary supplier or partner to customers in any one segment. Not surprisingly, the company seldom achieved its profit objectives.

When Jean-Luc Belingard assumed responsibility for the division in 1990, he focused on customer-driven strategies to achieve service quality through systematically measured customer satisfaction.

The first step in this measurement of customer satisfaction was a focus groups with customers. The goal of the focus groups was to gain understanding of the critical interactions between Roche Diagnostics and its customers.

The customer metrics used in the satisfaction survey included numerous factors such as the speed of response for engineers and technical representatives, the speed of hotline response, and the percentage of problems that were sorted out first time.

When Roche Diagnostics began its customer service focus, most customers would have rated themselves as 'satisfied' with the service from Roche. The division's new management quickly learned, however, that having 'satisfied' customers was not generating the expected profits. The management realized that satisfaction was not enough – customers had to be 'delighted' with Roche for the division to succeed. But efforts to move customers beyond mere satisfaction would have been wasted if they were not demonstrably linked to divisional profitability.

However, the proportion of 'very satisfied' customers grew, as did its sales and profits. Roche Diagnostics went from a low-growth division to the fastest growing competitor within its industry and in the F. Hoffmann-La Roche worldwide healthcare group.

After the division rarely met profit objectives for nearly 20 years, its new focus helped the company exceed all profit expectations within a 5-year period.

Source: adapted from Keiningham *et al.* (1999).

In order to forge an effective and coherent business strategy, a firm must evaluate and formulate its collaborative and competitive policies side by side. It should do this for two purposes.

● To achieve the appropriate balance between collaboration and competition in each factor of its industry environment (e.g. relations with suppliers, policies towards customers/channels).

● To integrate them in a way that avoids potential clashes and possibly destructive inconsistencies between them.

This is the terrain of composite strategy, which concerns the bringing together of competitive and collaborative endeavours.

Table 3.1 The five sources model and the corresponding five forces in the Porter model

Porter's five forces model	The five sources model
Market competitors	Horizontal collaborations with other enterprises operating at the same stage of the production process or producing the same group of closely related products (e.g. contemporary global partnering arrangements among car manufacturers).
Suppliers	Vertical collaborations with suppliers of components or services to the firm – sometimes termed vertical quasi-integration arrangements (e.g. the *keiretsu* formations between suppliers and assemblers that typify the car, electronics and other industries in Japan).
Buyers	Selective partnering arrangements with specific channels or customers (e.g. lead users) that involve collaboration extending beyond standard, purely transactional relationships.
Substitutes	Related diversification alliances with producers of both complements and substitutes. Producers of substitutes are not natural allies, but such alliances are not inconceivable (e.g. collaborations between fixed-wire and mobile telephone firms in order to grow their joint network size).
New entrants	Diversification alliances with firms based in previously unrelated sectors, but between which a blurring of industry borders is potentially occurring, or a process (commonly due to new technological possibilities) that opens up the prospect of cross-industry fertilization of technologies/business that did not exist before (e.g. the collaborations in the emerging multimedia field).

Source: Burton (1995).

Value chain analysis/benchmarking

Until now we have discussed the firm's international competitiveness from a strategic point of view. To get closer to the firm's core competences, we will now look at the market-level box in Porter's five forces model, which treats buyers and sellers (market competitors). Here we will look closer at what creates a competitive advantage among market competitors towards customers at the same competitive level.

The competitive triangle

Success in the marketplace is dependent not only upon identifying and responding to customer needs, but also upon our ability to ensure that our response is judged by customers to be superior to that of competitors (i.e. high perceived value). Several writers (e.g. Porter, 1980; Day and Wensley, 1988) have argued that causes of difference in performance within a market can be analysed at various levels. The immediate causes of differences in the performance of different firms, these writers argue, can be reduced to two basic factors.

● The *perceived value* of the product/services offered, compared to the perceived sacrifice. The *perceived sacrifice* includes all the 'costs' the buyer faces when making a purchase, not only the *purchase price*, but also acquisition costs, transportation, installation, handling, repairs and maintenance (Ravald and Grönroos, 1996). In the models presented, the (purchase) price will be used as a representative of the perceived sacrifice.

● The firm-related *costs* incurred in creating this perceived value.

These two basic factors will be further discussed later in this section.

The more value customers perceive in a market offering relative to competing offerings, and the lower the costs in producing the value relative to competing producers, the higher the performance of the business. Hence, firms producing offerings with a higher perceived value and/or lower relative costs than competing firms are said to have a competitive advantage in that market.

This can be illustrated by the 'competitive triangle' (see Figure 3.3). There is no one-dimensional measure of competitive advantage, and perceived value (compared to the price) and relative costs have to be assessed simultaneously. Given this two-dimensional nature of competitive advantage, it will not always be clear which of the two businesses will have a competitive advantage over the other.

In Figure 3.5, firm A will clearly have an advantage over firm B in case I, and clearly have a disadvantage in case IV, while cases II and III do not immediately allow such a conclusion. Firm B may have an advantage in case II, if customers in the market are highly quality conscious and have differentiated needs and low price elasticity, while firm A may have a similar advantage in case II when customers have homogenous needs and high price elasticity. The opposite will happen in case III.

Even if firm A has a clear competitive advantage over firm B, this may not necessarily result in a higher return on investment for A, if A has a growth and B a hold policy. Thus performance would have to be measured by a combination of return on investment and capacity expansion, which can be regarded as postponed return on investment.

While the relationship between perceived value, relative costs and performance is rather intricate, we can retain the basic statement that these two variables are the cornerstone of competitive advantage. Let us take a closer look at these two fundamental sources of competitive advantage.

Perceived value advantage

We have already observed that customers do not buy products, they buy benefits. Put in another way, the product is purchased not for itself but for the promise of what it will 'deliver'. These benefits may be intangible: that is, they may relate not to specific product features but rather to such things as image or reputation. Alternatively, the delivered offering may be seen to outperform its rivals in some functional aspect.

Figure 3.5 Perceived value, relative costs and competitive advantage

		Perceived value (compared to the purchase price)	
		Higher for A	Higher for B
Relative costs	Lower for A	I	II
	Lower for B	III	IV

Perceived value is the customer's overall evaluation of the product or service offered. So, establishing what value the customer is actually seeking from the firm's offering (value chain) is the starting point for being able to deliver the correct mix of value providing activities. It may be some combination of physical attributes, service attributes and technical support available in relation to the particular use of the product. This also requires an understanding of the activities, which constitute the customer's value chain.

Unless the product or service on offer can be distinguished in some way from its competitors, there is a strong likelihood that the marketplace will view it as a 'commodity', and so the sale will tend to go to the cheapest supplier. Hence the importance of seeking to attach additional values to the offering to mark it out from the competition.

What are the means by which such value differentiation may be gained? If we start in the value chain perspective, we can say that each activity in the business system adds perceived value to the product or service. Value, for the customer, is the perceived stream of benefits that accrue from obtaining the product or service. Price is what the customer is willing to pay for that stream of benefits. If the price of a product or service is high, it must provide high value, otherwise it is driven out of the market. If the value of a product or service is low, its price must be low; otherwise it is also driven out of the market. Hence, in a competitive situation, and over a period of time, the price that customers are willing to pay for a product or service is a good measure of its value.

Exhibit 3.5	Creating customer value at a winter sports destination

The purpose of building a conceptual model for the strategic management of a winter sports destination is to identify how the strategic tasks (concerned with creating strategic success) and strategic management (implementation of strategy) of the destination relate to the goals and activities of the destination. In constructing this relationship the elements identified through breaking down the value creating process have been applied based on an analogy of the destination being a multi-divisional firm. This model suggests that activities be split into two main levels, a strategic level and an operational level. The conceptual model presented in Figure 3.6 allows for the application of different organizational structures of the destination.

The value creation process in a destination is not well explained by the chain configuration because of the non-sequential production process in a destination. In the chain, the output of one activity is the input of the next activity. In a destination, value to the customer is achieved through the collection of discrete service providers: a network. The configuration logic suggested in their value network may be adapted to develop a value configuration related to a destination value creation system.

The operational level consists of the bundle of business units represented by the individual service providers (private companies and public services) which deliver the tourism product – the transfer value to destination customers (or the primary activities in the value 'fan'). The operational level also includes the service units' value contribution as related to the environment (natural, cultural, and social) of the tourism product. In the value configuration terminology these activities are support activities for the performance of the primary activities.

The strategic level embodies the destination strategic organizational level and the two main strategic tasks. The first of these (task 1) is the management of the configuration of

Exhibit 3.5 continued

Figure 3.6 A conceptual model of a winter sports destination

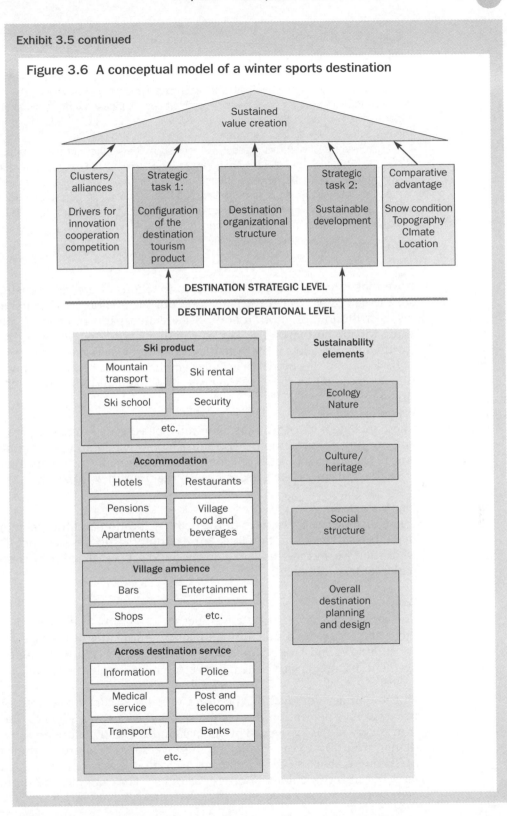

Exhibit 3.5 continued

the destination tourism product (the mix of business units), and the second (task 2) is the management of sustainable development (the sustainability elements – natural, cultural, and social elements and overall planning and design).

The tourism product (supply-side) configuration of a destination (task 1) is the combination of discrete services in terms of both quality and quantity supplied by the destination's operational level of service providers.

Typically, services in this respect will consist of: the ski product (lift systems, sports activities, ski schools, ski guides, ski rentals, repair services, etc.); the accommodation (accommodation facilities, restaurants, kindergarten, etc.); the village ambience (entertainment, events, shops, etc.); and the services (banks, telecommunications, transport, medical service, police, information, etc.). The important aspect of strategic positioning is embodied in the configuration of the tourism product.

Source: adapted from Flagestad and Hope (2001).

If we look especially at the downstream functions of the value chain, a differential advantage can be created with any aspect of the traditional 4P marketing mix: product, distribution, promotion and price are all capable of creating added perceived value for the customer. The key to whether improving an aspect of marketing is worthwhile is to know if the potential benefit provides value to the customer.

If we extend this model, particular emphasis must be placed upon the following (see Booms and Bitner, 1981; Magrath, 1986; Rafiq and Ahmed, 1995).

People

These include both consumers, who must be educated to participate in the service, and employees (personnel), who must be motivated and well trained in order to ensure that high standards of service are maintained. Customers identify and associate the traits of service personnel with the firms they work for.

Physical aspects

These include the appearance of the delivery location and the elements provided to make the service more tangible. For example, visitors experience Disneyland by what they see, but the hidden, below-ground support machinery is essential for the park's fantasy fulfilment.

Process

The service is dependent on a well-designed method of delivery. Process management assures service availability and consistent quality in the face of simultaneous consumption and production of the service offered. Without sound process management, balancing service demand with service supply is extremely difficult.

Of these three additional Ps, the firm's *personnel* occupy a key position in influencing customer perception of product quality. As a consequence, the image of the firm is very much influenced by the personnel. It is therefore important to pay particular attention to the quality of employees and to monitor their performance. Marketing managers need to manage not only the service provider–customer interface, but also the actions of other customers. For example, the number, type and behaviour of other people will influence a meal at a restaurant.

Relative cost advantage

Each activity in the value chain is performed at a cost. Getting the benefits from the product or service to the customer is thus done at a certain 'delivered cost' which sets a lower limit to the price of the product or service if the business system is to remain profitable. Reducing the price will thus imply that the delivered cost be reduced first by adjusting the business system. As mentioned earlier, the rules of successful business may be described as *providing the highest possible perceived value to the final customer, at the lowest possible delivered cost.*

A firm's cost position depends on the configuration of the activities in its value chain versus that of competitors and its relative location on the cost drivers of the activity. A cost advantage is gained when the cumulative cost of performing all the activities is lower than the competitors' cost. This evaluation of the relative cost position requires an identification of each important competitor's value chain. In practice, this step is extremely difficult because the firm does not have direct information on the costs of the competitors' value activities. However, some costs can be estimated from public data or interviews with suppliers and distributors.

Creating a relative cost advantage requires an understanding of the factors that affect costs. It is often said that 'big is beautiful'. This is partly due to economies of scale, which enable fixed costs to be spread over a greater output, but more particularly it is due to the impact of the *experience curve.*

The experience curve is a phenomenon that has its roots in the earlier notion of the learning curve. The effects of learning on costs were seen in the manufacture of fighter planes for World War II. The time taken to produce each plane gradually fell as learning took place. The combined effect of economies of scale and learning on cumulative output has been termed the experience curve. The Boston Consulting Group estimated that costs decreased on average by 15–20 per cent each time cumulative output doubled.

Subsequent work by Bruce Henderson, founder of the Boston Consulting Group, extended this concept by demonstrating that all costs, not just production costs, would decline at a given rate as volume increased. In fact, the relationship that the experience curve describes is between real unit costs and cumulative volume.

This suggests that firms with greater market share will have a cost advantage through the experience curve effect, assuming that all companies are operating on the same curve. However, a move towards a new manufacturing technology can lower the experience curve for adopting companies, allowing them to leap-frog more traditional firms and thereby gain a cost advantage even though cumulative output may be lower. The general form of the experience curve and the above-mentioned leap-frogging to another curve are shown in Figure 3.7.

Leap-frogging the experience curve by investing in new technology is a special opportunity for SMEs and newcomers to a market, since they will have (as a starting point) only a small market share and thereby a small cumulative output.

The implications of the experience curve for the pricing strategy will be discussed further in Chapter 12. According to Porter (1980), there are other cost drivers that determine the costs in value chains.

- *Capacity utilization*: underutilization incurs costs.
- *Linkages*: costs of activities are affected by how other activities are performed. For example, improving quality assurance can reduce after-sales service costs.

Figure 3.7 Leap-frogging the experience curve

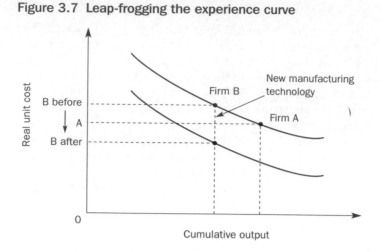

- *Interrelationships*: for example, different SBUs' sharing of R&D, purchasing and marketing will lower costs.
- *Integration*: for example, outsourcing of activities to sub-suppliers can lower costs and raise flexibility.
- *Timing*: for example, firms that are first-to-market in a market can gain cost advantage. It is cheaper to establish a brand name in the minds of the customers if there are no competitors.
- *Policy decisions*: product ranges, level of service and channel decisions are examples of policy decisions that affect costs.
- *Location*: locating near suppliers reduces in-bound distribution costs. Locating near customers can lower out-bound distribution costs. Some producers locate their production activities in eastern Europe or the Far East to take advantage of low wage costs.
- *Institutional factors*: government regulations, **tariffs**, local content rules, etc. will affect costs.

Competitive benchmarking

The ultimate test of the efficiency of any marketing strategy has to be in terms of profit. Those companies that strive for market share, but measure market share in terms of volume sales, may be deluding themselves to the extent that volume is bought at the expense of profit.

Because market share is measured retrospectively, we need to utilize continuing indicators of competitive performance. This will highlight areas where improvements in the marketing mix can be made.

In recent years a number of companies have developed a technique for assessing relative marketplace performance, which has come to be known as *competitive benchmarking*. Originally the idea of competitive benchmarking was literally to take apart a competitor's product, component by component, and to compare its performance in a value engineering sense with your own product. This approach has often been attributed to the Japanese, but many western companies have also found the value of such detailed comparisons.

The concept of competitive benchmarking is similar to what Porter (1996) calls operational effectiveness (OE), meaning performing similar activities better than competitors perform them. However, Porter (1996) also thinks that OE is a necessary but not a sufficient condition for outperforming rivals. Firms also have to consider strategic (or market) positioning, meaning the performance of different activities from rivals or performing similar activities in different ways. Only a few firms have competed successfully on the basis of OE over a long period. The main reason is the rapid diffusion of best practices. Competitors can rapidly imitate management techniques and new technologies with support from consultants.

However, the idea of benchmarking is capable of extension beyond this simple comparison of technology and cost effectiveness. Because the battle in the marketplace is for 'share of mind', it is customers' perceptions that we must measure.

The measures that can be used in this type of benchmarking programme include delivery reliability, ease of ordering, after-sales service, the quality of sales representation and the accuracy of invoices and other documentation. These measures are not chosen at random, but are selected because of their importance to the customer. Market research, often based on in-depth interviews, would typically be employed to identify what these **key success factors** are. The elements that customers identify as being the most important (see Table 3.2) then form the basis for the benchmark questionnaire. This questionnaire is administered to a sample of customers on a regular basis: for example Deutsche Telekom carries out a daily telephone survey of a random sample of its domestic and business customers to measure customers' perceptions of service. For most companies an annual survey might suffice; in other cases, perhaps a quarterly survey, particularly if market conditions are dynamic. The output of these surveys might typically be presented in the form of a competitive profile, as in the example in Table 3.2.

Most of the criteria mentioned in Table 3.2 relate to downstream functions in the value chain. Concurrently with closer relations between buyers and suppliers, especially in the industrial market, there will be more focus on the supplier's competences in the upstream functions.

Development of a dynamic benchmarking model

On the basis of the value chain's functions, we will suggest a model for the development of a firm's competitiveness in a defined market. The model will be based on a specific market as the market demands are assumed to differ from market to market, and from country to country.

Before presenting the basic model for the development of international competitiveness I will first define two key terms.

- *Critical success factors* are those value chain functions where the customer demands or expects the supplier (firm X) to have a strong competence.

- *Core competences* are those value chain functions where firm X has a strong competitive position.

The strategy process

The model for the strategy process is shown in Figure 3.8.

Table 3.2 Competitive benchmarking (examples with only few criteria)

Examples of value chain functions (mainly downstream functions)	Customer					Own firm (Firm A)					Key competitor (Firm B)				
	Importance to customer (key success factors)					How do customers rate performance of our firm?					How do customers rate performance of key competitor?				
	High importance		Low importance			Good				Bad	Good				Bad
	5	4	3	2	1	5	4	3	2	1	5	4	3	2	1

Uses new technology
High technical quality and competence
Uses proved technology
Easy to buy from
Understands what customers want
Low price
Delivery on schedule
Accessible for enquiries
Takes full responsibility
Flexible and quick
Known contact person
Provides customer training
Takes account of future requirements
Courteous and helpful
Specified invoices
Gives guarantees
ISO 9000 certified
Right first time
Can give references
Environment conscious

Figure 3.8 Model for development of core competences

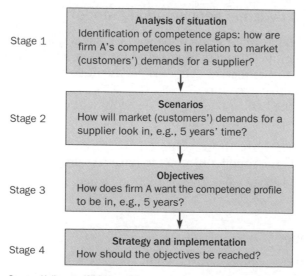

Source: Hollensen (2001), p. 95.

Stage 1: Analysis of situation (identification of competence gaps)

We will not go into details here about the problems there have been in measuring the value chain functions. The measurements cannot be objective in the traditional way of thinking, but must rely on internal assessments from a firm's representatives (interviews with relevant managers) supplemented by external experts ('key informants') who are able to judge the market's (customers') demand now and in the future.

The competence profile for firm A in Figure 3.3 (top-right) is an example of how a firm is not in accordance with the market (customer) demand. The company has its core competences in parts of the value chain's functions where customers place little importance (market knowledge in Figure 3.3).

If there is a good match between the critical success factors and firm X's initial position, it is important to concentrate resources and improve this core competence to create sustainable competitive advantage.

If, on the other hand, there is a large gap between customers' demands and the firm's initial position in critical success factors in Figure 3.3 (as with the personal selling functions), it may give rise to the following alternatives:

- improve the position of the critical success factor(s)
- find business areas where firm A's competence profile better suits the market demand and expectations.

As a new business area involves risk, it is often important to identify an eventual gap in a critical success factor as early as possible. In other words, an 'early warning' system must be established that continuously monitors the critical competitive factors so that it is possible to start initiatives that limit an eventual gap as early as possible.

In Figure 3.3, the competence profile of firm B is also shown.

Stages 2 and 3: Scenarios and objectives

To be able to estimate future market demand, different scenarios are made of the possible future development. These scenarios are first described generally, and then the effect of the market's future demand or expectations on a supplier's value chain function is examined.

By this procedure the described gap between market expectations and firm A's initial position becomes more clear. At the same time, the biggest gap for firm A may have moved from personal sales to, for example, product development. From knowledge of the market leader's strategy it is possible to complete scenarios of the market leader's future competence profile.

These scenarios may be the foundation for a discussion of objectives and of which competence profile the company wants, in, say five years' time. Objectives must be set realistically and with due consideration of the organization's resources (the scenarios are not shown in Figure 3.3).

Stage 4: Strategy and implementation

Depending on which of firm A's value chain functions are to be developed, a strategy is prepared. This results in implementation plans, which include the adjustment of the organization's current competence level.

3.4 Outsourcing – a strategic decision framework based on customers' evaluation

After the dynamic benchmarking process the firm might have an idea about whether it should perform a certain value chain activity itself or if it should consider letting somebody else do it, e.g. outsource the activity.

It is important for a firm to decide which competences to keep in-house and which to outsource. The underlying assumption is that a firm should outsource non-core activities to be able to focus more on the core competence.

Over the last number of years, **outsourcing** has become an important issue for many organizations. The potential for outsourcing has moved from peripheral activities such as cleaning and catering to critical activities such as design, product development, IT, manufacturing, logistics and marketing/advertising.

What is outsourcing? The word outsourcing defines the process of transferring the responsibility for a specific business function from an internal employee group to an external partner. An example of outsourcing (and how the boundary of the firm is 'reduced') is shown in Figure 3.9.

Though there might be differences, in- or outsourcing and make or buy analysis will be regarded as synonyms in this book.

Outsourcing is a contractual agreement between the firm and one or more suppliers to provide services or processes that the firm is currently providing internally. The fundamental difference between outsourcing and any other purchasing agreement is that the firm contracts-out part of its existing internal activity. There are many reasons why a company may choose to outsource and it will rarely be for one single reason.

The three most obvious reasons are listed in Table 3.3.

The hybrid situations enable the two organizations supporting the same market to share resources and increase revenue through synergistic relationships.

As indicated, one of the reasons why firms have outsourced a number of their primary supply chain activities is that the costs of remaining up to date in a multitude of value chain activities has become financially onerous. Where technology moves the fastest, the problem is the most serious. It would not be a surprise to learn, therefore, that a number of the pioneering outsourcers have been in the IT sector (see Exhibit 3.6).

Figure 3.9 Example of primary supply chain outsourcing in an IT firm

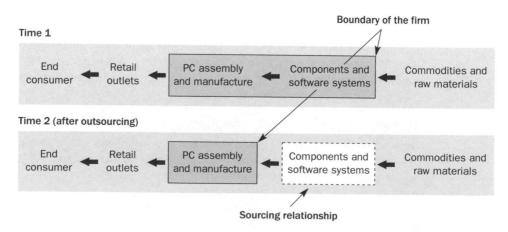

Table 3.3 Reasons why companies outsource

Rationale	Description	Benefits
Cost reduction	Outsourcing to another party to reduce cost of operations.	• Improve efficiency • Increase return on assets • Improve profitability
Revenue generation	Contracting with another party to provide products or services which the outsourcing firm cannot offer on its own.	• Increase revenue (new products to existing and/ or new customers) • Reduce risk • Improve efficiency
Hybrid situations	Collaborations, alliances, partnerships, etc., with two or more like parties in the same business line to offer complementary products or services.	• Improve return on investment • Increase capability utilization • Create economies of scope by offering a broader product concept to customers

Source: adapted from Bloomberg (1998, p. 7).

Exhibit 3.6

Outsourcing at IBM – a success and a failure

One of the pioneers of outsourcing was IBM, although its experience has become one of the great stories of postwar capitalism. At the beginning of the 1980s, IBM outsourced many of the major components for its early PC – a radical departure. The early evidence was that this decision had worked well for Big Blue. By utilizing the expertise of Intel, Microsoft and a host of other companies, IBM was able to get its product to market in little over a year. This was a performance that left its main rival, Apple, behind and allowed it to build a share of the PC market of 41 per cent by 1985. It was the fact that IBM had created a 'virtual organization' through outsourcing that received much of the credit for this exceptional performance. At the time, in the early 1980s, many pointed to the IBM experience as the model for doing business in the future. However, later in the decade IBM encountered problems that were directly attributable to its decision to outsource. These problems developed in three stages.

First, the open architecture of the IBM PC meant that competitors could imitate the IBM format and make their products compatible with IBM's products. The second stage was that once this had happened, IBM's suppliers, especially Intel and Microsoft, began to sell their products to IBM's competitors. As a result, IBM's PCs became largely indistinguishable from those of the competition. Suddenly, Big Blue found itself operating in a highly competitive market, with little that gave it a sustainable competitive advantage.

In the third and final stage, IBM decided to advance its PC as a means of fighting back. However, this meant it had to put back together the network of suppliers that combined to produce the early models. IBM could not act alone because it no longer possessed all the necessary capabilities to bring a PC to market. Unfortunately for IBM many key suppliers were not willing to cooperate and, indeed, were making their money from assisting IBM's competitors to erode its market share even further. The result of all this was that by 1995 IBM accounted for only about 7 per cent of the world PC market.

Today (2002) the PC business is not a core business for IBM. The profit margins are very low, but still IBM is number 3 in the world market after Compaq and Dell. Today IBM earns much more from IT – consulting and servicing IT for large companies, functioning as an ASP (application service provider).

Source: adapted from Chesbrough and Teece (1996), Lonsdale and Cox (2000).

An outsourcing/insourcing framework

The stages involved in the outsourcing framework are illustrated in Figure 3.10. The stages will now be described.

Figure 3.10 Outsourcing – a decision framework

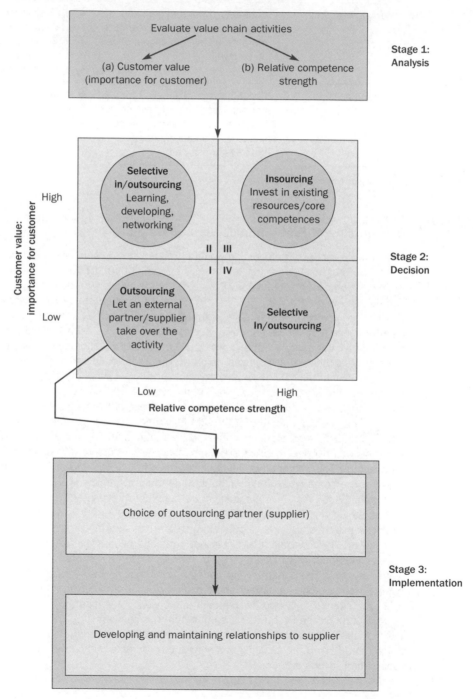

Stage 1: Analysis

Stage 1a: Evaluating customer value (KSF)

Activities with high customer value are often key success factors (KSF), which are central to the firm successfully serving the need of potential customers in each market. To point out KSFs, customers are asked if the firm's value chain activities are adding value for them. This is done by asking about the importance of activities (see also the questionnaire in Table 3.2).

Stage 1b: Evaluating the firm's relative competence strengths

Focusing attention on customer needs and competitive advantage will involve applying the firm's distinctive capabilities to meet these needs. Here, each selected activity must be benchmarked against the capabilities of all potential external providers of that activity. This will enable the company to identify its *relative* performance for each activity (also illustrated in Table 3.2 questionnaire).

The depth of evaluation of the organization's value chain can take place at the activity (such as logistics) or sub-activity (materials handling) level depending on the particular circumstances of the organization.

Stage 2: Decision about in/outsourcing

Stages 1a and 1b identify the disparity between the sourcing company and potential external providers of the core activities. It allows companies to focus on whether it will be detrimental to their competitive position to outsource activities such as research and development, design, engineering, manufacturing, marketing and service, both in the short and long term.

Before the final decision the firm must identify and measure the costs associated with either retaining the activity in-house or outsourcing the activity.

In Box I in Figure 3.10 the firm faces one of its value chain activities, which only delivers low customer value, and the firm is also relatively poor in performing the activity (low relative competence strength). In this situation it is more appropriate for the company to outsource the activity to external suppliers that are more competent and have a lower cost base.

Unlike Box I, Box III is a situation where the company can focus resources on the activities where it can achieve pre-eminence and provide high customer perceived value. For example, if a company has leadership in a core activity then this activity should be held and further developed within the company in order to maintain and build this core competence.

In Boxes II and IV the outcome can be either keeping the activity in-house or outsourcing depending on the specific situation. The situation in Box II is very similar to the evaluation of the activity of **'personal selling'** in Figure 3.3. In this situation the firm could outsource the activity (because it is not good at performing the activity) or it could try to develop its competence level and move it from Box II to Box III, because the activity is very important for the customer.

The outcome of Box IV could also be a selective in/outsourcing depending on the situation. Perhaps this firm is able to transfer its high relative strength in these activities to another industry or a new customer group who would value it more. This would be a reverse situation where the firm itself would function as a sub-supplier to another outsourcing company.

Stage 3: Implementation

If the outcome of stage 2 is outsourcing (Box I), the firm believes it can be more flexible by outsourcing activities than performing activities internally by being in a better position to react rapidly to market changes and be more responsive to customer change. This strategy will result in the company gradually becoming a 'systems integrator' in which it manages and coordinates a network of best production and service providers. Such a strategy is based on the premise that the company should outsource those activities (both production and service) where it can develop no strategic advantage itself.

From this analysis of potential suppliers, the company will filter out any potential suppliers that are unsuitable (see also screening of potential suppliers in Figure 4.12). If it is found that there are no suppliers suitable with which to initiate a relationship, then the company may pursue an 'Invest to perform internally' strategy. However, if the company has found a suitable supplier, then it should form a relationship while leveraging its own capabilities by focusing resources on high value-added activities.

A number of issues have to be addressed before the actual outsourcing to the chosen supplier can take place. The company may wish to maintain the knowledge (design skills, management skills, manufacturing, etc.) that enable the technology of the activity to be exploited, even when it is being provided by another partner. Therefore, it is important that the company controls the new product development and design process, as these are the activities that will drive future growth. The company may establish a partnership relationship or strategic alliance with a supplier in order to exploit their capabilities. This involves an intensive collaborative working relationship with the prospective partner.

If the company has succeeded in developing a best-in-world core competence, it would never outsource it. The company may even prefer to build defensive rings of essential competences that customers insist it have or that protect its core competence – as Sony has done (Exhibit 3.7).

Exhibit 3.7	Sony, an outsourcing company

Sony, as one of the largest electronics manufacturers in the world, certainly enjoys market power because of its strong market position globally, e.g., its dominant position in the personal stereo segment of the personal electronics market. Its efficient manufacturing capability and outsourcing expertise provide operating advantages. Sony is a firm that is known to be a pioneer, not a follower. Innovation lies at the heart of the whole corporation. It constantly launches new products and models to overwhelm the me-too competitors. And Sony is a company that is willing to make commitments, for good or bad, even when a technology's commercial viability is uncertain. Its commitment to the Betamax format in the VCR industry caused it to lose out in that lucrative market because it failed to become the industry standard. Sony failed to establish its leadership position in its business system of fellow VCR producers. The same can be said about its stubbornness in going alone on Mini-Disc and Digital Audio Tape (DAT), and not sharing its format through network alliances.

Nonetheless, one has to appreciate Sony's remarkable consistency and discipline in implementing its strategy: it is both a pioneer and the proprietary beneficiary of its new technology. Sony's miniaturization skills have often been cited as a classical example of corporate

Exhibit 3.7 continued

Figure 3.11 The structure of Sony, an outsourcing company

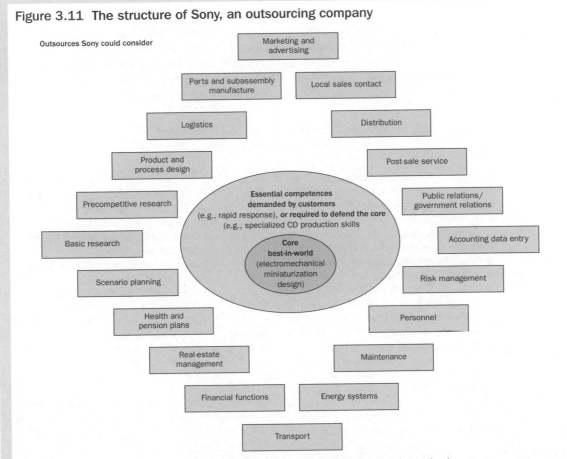

Source: adapted from Quinn (2000), p. 20, with permission from Los Angeles Times Syndicate International.

core competence (Figure 3.11) which enables it to enjoy a commanding lead in portable and pocket-size electronics (Prahalad and Hamel, 1990).

Its unique capability lies in quickly adopting new knowledge and technology. In this sense, Sony is definitely a leading company in time-based competition.

Although it favours proprietary technology, Sony is also no stranger to cooperation and learning-inspired collaborative arrangement. To tackle technical challenges and share risks in R&D, in the late 1970s and early 1980s, Sony jointly developed the CD format with Philips. Once it learned enough from its partner and ironed out major technical obstacles, it decided to make a greater commitment to manufacturing facilities faster than Philips did and pre-empt the worldwide market for CD players. Philips saw the CD format as essentially a high-end consumer product, whereas Sony treated it as the future industry standard and a potential blockbuster for the firm, which would succeed its colour TV and Walkman as the next star product and help sustain its growth.

Source: after Ma (2000b), Quinn (2000).

Advantages and disadvantages of outsourcing

Outsourcing can create a number of economic advantages. However, there are also a number of risks in outsourcing, which may create perceived disadvantages (see Table 3.4).

These disadvantages are mostly of a psychological nature and if managed effectively do not lead to financial losses. For example, partnering with a third-party introduces a host of new outlooks, personalities, and demands that can produce new problems. These challenges include a more complicated level of communication, insecurity in the workforce, and the risk of high **transaction costs**.

Table 3.4 Advantages and disadvantages of outsourcing

Advantages	Disadvantages
• Offers significant cost savings across a wide range of low-margin, non-differentiated services as well as additional income opportunities. • Outsourcing non-critical functions permits a company to increase its financial resources. • Eliminates investments in fixed infrastructure. • Allows for greater quality and efficiency. • Permits increased access to functional expertise. • Outsourcing provides a competitive advantage and creates new revenue streams by allowing suppliers to offer services that would otherwise require considerable expense and commitment of personnel. • Using an outside provider allows suppliers to test market demand for a product or service in a less risky, more cost-effective way than creating the service internally with service resources.	• Requires a change in management mind set. • Requires a new and more complicated level of communication. • Introduces a host of new outlooks, personalities, and demands that can produce new problems. • Introduces insecurity to the workforce and unions. • Monitoring and evaluating the performance of suppliers is a difficult task. • Outsourcing functions that have customer contact risks alienating customers. • Outsourcing benefits may not be realized in the short term. • Long-term contracts which feature short-term savings may prove expensive later (resulting in high transaction costs).

Source: adapted from Bloomberg (1998), p. 7.

The biggest barrier to outsourcing is that it requires a change in management mind set. Many managers fear the loss of control or conflict of interest and fail to compare the cost and benefit of using internal support organizations. Managers faced with an outsourcing decision often construe the financial cost and loss of control over individuals as their justification for not outsourcing, but fail to consider the long and short term savings to the organization.

Motivating employees for the change towards outsourcing is not an easy task. However, the risk associated with outsourcing can be offset and controlled if managed properly.

3.5 Summary

The main issue of this section is how the firm develops competitive advantage in the international marketplace. The sources of competitive advantage are:

- economies of scale (scale efficiencies)
- economies of scope (transfer of resources across products and markets)

- economies of speed (time-based competition advantages)
- exploitation of local advantages
- ability to provide global services
- ability to use 'human resources' (HR) (HR are especially important for RM and internal marketing).

A three-stage model allows us to understand the development of a firm's international competitiveness in a broader perspective.

Analysis of national/regional competitiveness

The Porter diamond indicates that the home base plays a central role in the firm's international success.

Competition analysis

Here the firm itself is the unit of analysis. Porter's five forces model suggests that competition in an industry is rooted in its underlying industry structure. The state of competition depends on five basic competitive forces, which determine profit potential in an industry.

Value chain analysis

According to the competitive triangle it can be concluded that firms have competitive advantage in a market if they offer products or services with the following characteristics:

- a higher perceived value to the customers
- lower relative costs than the competing firms.

Influenced by core competency thinking, many companies have been attempting to reorganize their value chains and focus on a number of core activities, in which they can achieve and maintain a long-term competitive advantage and outsource all other activities where they do not have high relative competence strength.

While the motives for outsourcing are normally specific to the particular situation, some commonly cited reasons are to:

- reduce cost
- improve quality, service and delivery
- improve organizational focus
- increase flexibility
- facilitate change.

The biggest obstacle to outsourcing is that the management may fear that they would lose control. However, the risks associated with outsourcing can be offset and controlled if managed properly.

Case study 3.2 BBC Worldwide

Creating global competitiveness through relationships

During the last few years the recognition of the BBC brand grew markedly around the world. In ten key markets surveyed by an independent research company, awareness of the BBC increased from 55% in 1998 to 78% in 1999. In a recent survey by British Trade International, for the Export Awards for Smaller Businesses 2000, the BBC was named as now being Britain's most successful export ahead of the Beatles, Shakespeare, and the Royal Family.

In 2000 the biggest successes included *Walking with Dinosaurs* and the new children's programme, *Tweenies*. Established programmes, like *Teletubbies*, continued to perform exceptionally well.

Walking with Dinosaurs

This was funded through a BBC/Discovery Channel/TV Asahi co-production in association with ProSieben and France 3. *Walking with Dinosaurs* was the most watched documentary ever on cable in the USA, on ProSieben in Germany and on ABC in Australia. It has broken records all over Europe, and has already been sold to more than 40 countries, generating £2.3 million in programme sales.

1.3 million copies of the books, in 13 languages, have been sold all around the world since autumn 1999. It is BBC Worldwide's top-selling video – more than one million copies have been sold worldwide. Related products also included a CD of the soundtrack, a DVD, models – and even chocolate dinosaur eggs for Easter.

Tweenies

Lively and full of fun for three- to five-year-olds, *Tweenies*, jointly commissioned by BBC Television and BBC Worldwide, and produced by Tell-Tale Productions, is already set to be one of the best-selling programmes, complementing Teletubbies.

The BBC has also made a pan-European arrangement with the toy manufacturer, Hasbro, and *Teletubbies* has been produced as a game for the Playstation console. In Hong Kong, BBC Worldwide has established its own toy sourcing operation.

Besides these new products the BBC is still very much involved with maintaining its classic brand, *Top of the Pops* (TOTP), which is in tough competition with the *Pepsi Pop Chart Show*. Pepsi Cola sponsors this TV show. TOTP has also launched TOTP Magazine, which has been a big success in, for example, Germany.

Joint venture partnership

One of the most important joint ventures is with Discovery Communications Incorporated, the global partner for factual channels. Discovery markets and distributes two important channels:

● Animal Planet: animal and natural history programming, reaches over 80 million homes in the USA, Latin America, Europe and Asia-Pacific.

● People + Arts, the pan-regional factual channel in Latin America with over 10 million subscribers.

Licensing of BBC programmes

Globally, programme **licensing agreements** provide BBC Worldwide with an increasing income stream. It also benefits from an equity share in the joint venture channels and, once they break even, a share of the profits.

Programme sales is a core business and accounts for around one-third of BBC Worldwide's income. BBC Worldwide is Europe's biggest exporter of television programmes.

BBC Worldwide sells to other broadcasters and may distribute non-BBC programmes that are compatible with its portfolio. Such programmes should not be BBC-branded, since this could imply that the BBC produced them, but should be consistent with the BBC's overall editorial values. This enables BBC Worldwide to develop economies of scale in distribution, and allows other UK producers and broadcasters without this resource to take advantage of the scale and experience of BBC Worldwide's international operations.

Case study 3.2 continued

Co-production partners

Co-productions are an essential means of developing ambitious creative programming. Discovery continues to be the main partner for factual programmes, co-funding key series like *Walking with Dinosaurs* and *Predators*. *Wives & Daughters* and *Madame Bovary* are just two of the drama programmes produced in collaboration with BBC America.

BBC Worldwide has been strengthening its ties with the independent production sector. Significant improvements have been made in communications, project handling and reporting systems employed with independents. Procedural changes within the BBC have removed a number of disincentives that might previously have prevented independents from appointing BBC Worldwide as their distribution agent.

Publishing and events

BBC Worldwide's activities include publishing books, magazines, audio and video cassettes and CD-ROMs, and mounting live events that draw on BBC intellectual content and capabilities maintained for its core channels. In so doing, BBC Worldwide complements and extends audiences' ability to enjoy content of this kind. As in the case of programme sales, BBC Worldwide may, internationally, distribute the published work of others which complements its core portfolio.

Questions

1. What are the core competences of BBC Worldwide in relation to the value chain?
2. Define the differences in the business system of the BBC's TOTP and the Pepsi Chart Shows. Which of the two chart shows would have the biggest chance of being successful in the international market?

Source: www.bbc.co.uk

QUESTIONS FOR DISCUSSION

1. Which sources of competitive advantage are the most important?
2. How can analysis of national competitiveness explain the competitive advantage of a single firm?
3. Is it possible to identify not only national competitiveness, but also regional competitiveness? (A region is here defined as more than one country.)
4. In which situations should a firm consider outsourcing its activities?
5. What are the advantages and disadvantages of outsourcing?

REFERENCES

Barney, J. B. and Wright, P.M. (1998), On becoming a strategic partner. The role of human resources in gaining competitive advantage, *Human Resource Management*, Spring 1998, vol. 37, no. 1, pp. 31–46.

Bloomberg, D. F. (1998), Strategic assessment of outsourcing and downsizing in the service market, *Managing Service Quality*, vol. 8, no. 1, pp. 5–18.

Bonn, I. (2001), Developing strategic thinking as a core competency, *Management Decision*, vol. 39, no. 1, pp. 63–70.

Bonoma, T. V. and Shapiro, B. (1984), How to segment industrial markets, *Harvard Business Review*, May–June, pp. 104–10.

Booms, B. H. and Bitner, M. J. (1981), Marketing strategies and organization structures for service firms, *in* Donelly, J. H. and George, W. R. (Eds), *Marketing of Services*, American Marketing Association, Chicago, IL.

Brownlie, D. (2000), Benchmarking your marketing process, *Long Range Planning*, vol. 32, no. 1, pp. 88–95.

Burton, J. (1995), Composite strategy: the combination of collaboration and competition, *Journal of General Management*, vol. 21, no. 1, pp. 1–23.

Chesbrough, H. and Teece, D. (1996), When is virtual virtuous? Organizing for innovation, *Harvard Business Review*, January–February, pp. 68–70.

Cho, D. S. (1998), From national competitiveness to bloc and global competitiveness, *Competitive Review*, vol. 8, no. 1, pp. 11–23.

Christensen, C. M. (2001), The past and future of competitive advantage, *MIT Sloan Management Review*, Winter, pp. 105–9.

Czepiel, J. A. (1992), *Competitive Marketing Strategy*, Prentice-Hall, Englewood Cliffs, NJ.

Day, G. S. (1984), *Analysis for Strategic Marketing*, West Publishing, New York.

Day, G. S. and Wensley, R. (1988), Assessing advantage: a framework for diagnosing competitive superiority, *Journal of Marketing*, vol. 52, no. 2, pp. 1–20.

Flagestad, A. and Hope, C. A. (2001), *Tourism Management,* 22, pp. 445–61.

Furner, O. and Thomas, H. (2000), The rivalry matrix: understanding rivalry and competitive dynamics, *European Management Journal*, vol. 18, no. 6, pp. 619–37.

Grunert, K. G. and Ellegaard, C. (1992), The concept of key success factors, *in Marketing for Europe: Marketing for the future* (Proceedings of the 21st Annual Conference of the European Marketing Academy), EMAC, pp. 505–24.

Haanes, K. and Fjeldstad (2000), Linking intangible resources and competition, *European Management Journal*, vol. 18, no. 1, February, pp. 52–62.

Hamholtz, E. and Lacey, J. (1981), *Personnel Management: Human capital theory and human resource accounting*, Institute of Industrial Relations, UCLA, Los Angeles, CA.

Harvard Business School (1998), *Crown Cork & Seal in 1989. Sheila M. Cavanaugh, 1993, Rev. May 29*, Harvard Business School, Case 9–793–035.

Heracleous, L. (1998), Strategic thinking or strategic planning?, *Long Range Planning*, vol. 31, no. 3, pp. 481–7.

Hollensen, S. (2001), *Global Marketing: A market responsive approach*, Financial Times/Prentice Hall, Harlow, 2nd edn.

Kanter, R. M. (1994), Collaborative advantage: the art of alliances, *Harvard Business Review*, July–August, pp. 96–108.

Keiningham, T. L., Goddard, M. K. M., Vavra, T. G. and Iaci, A. J. (1999), Customer delight and the bottom line, *Marketing Management*, vol. 8, no. 3, Fall, pp. 57–63.

Ketelhöhn, W. (1998), What is a key success factor, *European Management Journal*, vol. 16, no. 3, June, pp. 335–40.

Kotler, P. (1997), *Marketing Management*, Prentice-Hall, Englewood Cliffs, NJ.

Krutten, J. (1999), Benchmarking in the pharmaceutical industry, *Marketing Health Services*, vol. 19, no. 3, pp. 14–22.

Lepak, D. P. and Snell, S. A (1999), The human resource architecture: toward a theory of human capital allocation and development, *The Academy of Management Review*, vol. 24, no. 1, pp. 31–48.

Levitt, T. (1960), Marketing myopia, *Harvard Business Review*, July–August, pp. 45–56.

Lonsdale, C. and Cox, A. (2000), The historical development of outsourcing: the latest fad? *Industrial Management & Data Systems*, vol. 100, no. 9, pp. 444–50.

Ma, H. (2000a), Competitive advantage and firm advantage, *Competitiveness Review*, vol. 10, no. 2, pp. 15–32.

Ma, H. (2000b), Towards an advantage-based view of the firm, *Advances in Competitive Research (ACR)*, vol. 8, no.1, pp. 34–59.

Magrath, A. J. (1986), When marketing service's 4 Ps are not enough, *Business Horizons*, May–June, pp. 44–50.

Meyer, C. (2001), The second generation of speed, *Harvard Business Review*, pp. 24–5.

Olian, J. D., Durham, C.C. and Kristof, A.L. (1998), Designing management training and development for competitive advantage: lessons for the best, *HR – Human Resource Planning*, vol. 21, no. 1, pp. 20–31.

Porter, M. E. (1980). *Competitive Strategy*, The Free Press, New York.

Porter, M. (1985), *Competitive Advantage*, The Free Press, New York.

Porter, M. E. (1990), *The Competitive Advantage of Nations*, The Free Press, New York.

Porter, M. E (1996), What is strategy?, *Harvard Business Review*, November–December, pp. 61–78.

Prahalad, C. K. and Hamel, G. (1990), The core competence of the corporation, *Harvard Business Review*, May–June, pp. 79–91.

Proff, H (2002), Business unit strategies between regionalisation and globalisation, *International Business Review*, vol. 11, no. 2, pp. 231–50.

Quinn, J. B. (2000), Outsourcing innovation: the new engine of growth, *Sloan Management Review*, summer, pp. 13–27.

Rafiq, M. and Ahmed, P. K. (1995), Using the 7 Ps as a generic marketing mix, *Marketing Intelligence and Planning*, vol. 13, no. 9, pp. 4–15.

Ravald, A. and Grönroos, C. (1996), The value concept and relationship marketing, *European Journal of Marketing*, vol. 30, no. 2, pp. 19–30.

Rayport, J. F. and Sviokla, J. J. (1996), Exploiting the virtual value chain, *McKinsy Quarterly*, no. 1, pp. 21–36.

Reve, T. (1990), The firm as a nexus of internal and external contracts, *in* Aoki, M., Gustafsson, M. and Williamson, O. E. (Eds), *The Firm as a Nexus of Treaties*, Sage, London.

Rugman, A. and D'Cruz, J. (1993), The double diamond model of international competitiveness: the Canadian experience, *Management International Review*, vol. 33, special issue, pp. 17–39.

Senge, P. (1990), *The Fifth Discipline*, Doubleday, New York.

Sheth, J. N. and Sharma, A. (1997), Supplier relationships: emerging issues and challenges, *Industrial Marketing Management*, vol. 26, pp. 91–100.

Tampoe, M. (1994), Exploiting the core competences or your organization, *Long Range Planning*, vol. 27, no. 4, pp. 66–77.

Webster, F. and Wind, Y. (1972), *Organizational Buying Behavior*, Prentice-Hall, New York.

Zairi, M. and Ahmed, P. Z. (1999), Benchmarking maturity as we approach the millennium?, *Total Quality Management*, no. 4/5, July, pp. 810–16.

Figure II.1 The structure of Part II

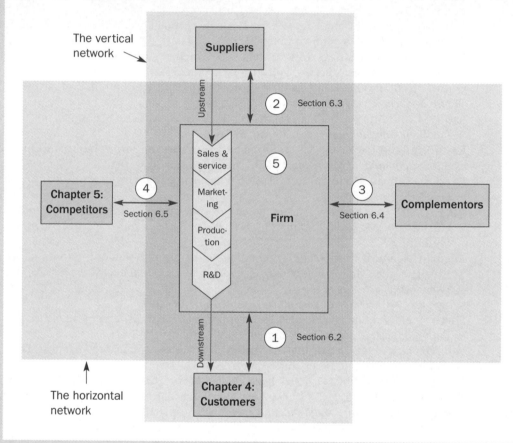

Assessing the external marketing situation

Part II looks at the environment in which marketing operates. The marketing environment consists of a *micro-environment* and a *macro-environment*.

The macro-environment consists of the larger societal forces which effect the whole micro-environment:

- *demographic environment*: population size and growth trends, age structure of population, changes in family structure.
- *economic environment*: income distribution, purchasing power etc.
- *political environment*: laws, government agencies, growth of public interest groups.

The ethical, social and environmental aspects and how they affect and shape the marketing plan will be analysed in Chapter 18.

The micro-environment consists of forces and players close to the firm such as customers, suppliers, complementors and competitors. The structure of Part II (Figure II.1) shows how these players via Chapter 6 are connected in a value net approach.

The focus of this part is the micro-environmental factors and the relationships between the central players.

Chapters 4 and 5 start by analysing the most important issues of two of the most important players shown in Figure II.1:

- the customer 'box'
- the competitor 'box'.

Customers and competitors have been chosen for further analysis because they receive the most attention among managers in firms. These two types of player are also both represented in the model, labelled 'the competitive triangle'.

Chapter 6 tries to analyse the relationships between the most important players in the value net.

The analysis in Chapters 4 and 5 contains the more traditional approach to customer and competitor behaviour and analysis. This analysis forms the basis for the analysis of the relationships between the important players in the micro-environment.

Part I (Assessment of the internal conditions) and Part II constitute the input for the later development of marketing strategies (Part III) and the marketing plan (Part IV) and its implementation (Part V).

Chapter 4

Customer behaviour

LEARNING OBJECTIVES

After studying this chapter you should be able to:

- understand why consumers make purchase decisions.
- identify and discuss the main motives behind buying behaviour on the B-t-C market.
- understand how customers make purchase decisions.
- identify the various types of buyer in organizational markets and determine their distinct needs, wants and motivations.
- identify different organizational buying situations.
- describe and discuss the organizational buying process.
- identify and understand the factors influencing the organizational buying process.
- evaluate the roles of members of the buying centre.
- understand the link between consumer demand and B-t-B marketing.
- understand what is meant by customization.

Case study 4.1 BASF

An ingredients supplier for the worldwide cosmetics industry seeks new relationships

In recent years there has been an increasing globalization in the cosmetics industry. The multi-national marketers (like Unilever) have grown via acquisitions of national companies or even other smaller multi-nationals.

Manufacturers of cosmetic and personal care brands are increasingly outsourcing their chemical manufacturing as well as many of their R&D needs to specialized chemical companies. The brand manufacturers are looking to consolidate their vendor base, and deal with vendors that can supply a multitude of ingredients. The German multi-national BASF is one of these ingredients suppliers.

BASF

BASF is a transnational chemical company that aims to increase and sustain its corporate value through growth and innovation. The company's product range includes high-value chemicals, plastics, colorants and pigments, dispersions, automotive and industrial coatings, agricultural products and fine chemicals as well as crude oil and natural gas.

With sales in 2000 of €35.9 billion and a workforce of 100,000 employees, BASF is one of the world's leading chemical companies and also one of the leading ingredients suppliers for the personal care industry.

Case study 4.1 continued

BASF is now introducing a liquid thickener, Luvigel®EM for cosmetics formulations (a skincare product), which reduces manufacturing time and provides better thickening (see Figure 4.1).

The personal care market

The personal care market is growing by 1–2% per year. Personal care multi-nationals are increasingly asking specialty companies for help in new product development to offset the price declines.

The total personal care market in the USA and Europe is illustrated in Table 4.1.

Table 4.1 Personal care market, 1999

	USA	Europe
	Share	
Skin care[1]	30%	32%
Hair care	21%	25%
Make-up products[2]	17%	12%
Fragrances	14%	14%
Oral care	12%	11%
Antiperspirants and deodorants	6%	6%
Total	100%	100%
Total market (personal care) (US$ billion)	$26	$28

[1] Includes shaving products, body washes, and sun protection lotions.
[2] Includes nail care products.
Source: adapted from Brown and Walsch (2000).

The target market for BASF's Luvigel®EM is the skincare market. Among the potential customers for Luvigel®EM are L'Oréal, Unilever, Estée Lauder, Procter & Gamble, Benckiser Group, Revlon, Boby Shop, Wella, and Boots the Chemist.

L'Oréal (France)

L'Oréal SA is one of the world's largest hair care, cosmetics and fragrances groups with consolidated sales of FFf75.4bn (£7.7bn) in 1998, of which FFr61.5bn (£6.3bn) derived from cosmetics, with FFr16.4bn (£1.7bn) of the cosmetics figure coming from the perfumes and beauty division. Brands include Lancôme skincare products, cosmetics and perfumes, and fragrances grouped under the Prestige & Collection division, including Giorgio Armani, Cacherel, Ralph Lauren, Guy Laroche, Paloma Picasso and Lanvin. The perfumes and beauty division also markets Biotherm and Helena Rubinstein cosmetics.

L'Oréal's other operating arms include Salon (with the L'Oréal Professional, Inné, Kérastase and Redken brands), Consumer (with the L'Oréal, Laboratoires Garnier and Gemey brands) and Active Cosmetics (with Vichy, Phas, and La Roche-Posay products). L'Oréal also operates in luxury goods (with the Lanvin fashion house) and in dermatological products. It also owns Synthélabo, France's third-largest pharmaceutical group.

In the UK, L'Oréal has a leading presence in hair care and cosmetics and is undoubtedly the market leader in fine fragrances, with a portfolio of famous brands which includes the top-selling Anaïs Anaïs, plus Eden, Loulou and Noa (all in the Cacharel 'house'); Giorgio Armani's Dazzling, Emporio Armani and Gio; Lancôme's Trésor, Pôeme, Ô, and Ô Oui; Paloma Picasso's Mon Parfum, Paloma Picasso and Temptations; Ralph Lauren's Polo Sport Woman and Romance, and the mass-market Vanderbilt. The majority of L'Oréal's fragrances are marketed as eau de toilettes, eau de parfums and parfums, and most also include a complementary range of toiletries.

Unilever

One of the largest global consumer goods businesses, Unilever is an Anglo-Dutch conglomerate, operated jointly by Unilever NV, Rotterdam, and the London-based Unilever plc. Unilever's activities are grouped into two operating divisions: foods, and home and personal care. The worldwide sales in 1999 reached £27.3 bn. Unilever employs 246,000 people (1999). The personal care division includes the Elida Fabergé business and brands such as Dove, Lynx, Brut, Impulse, Lifebuoy, Lux, Mentadent, Pepsodent, Pond's, Salon Selectives, Signal, Sunsilk and Vaseline. The division also includes fragrances marketed under the Calvin Klein, Elizabeth Arden, Fabergé, Karl Lagerfeld and Parfums International 'houses', including cK one, cK be, Contradiction, Escape, Eternity and Obsession (Calvin Klein); Cerruti,

Case study 4.1 continued

Figure 4.1 BASF's Luvigel® EM

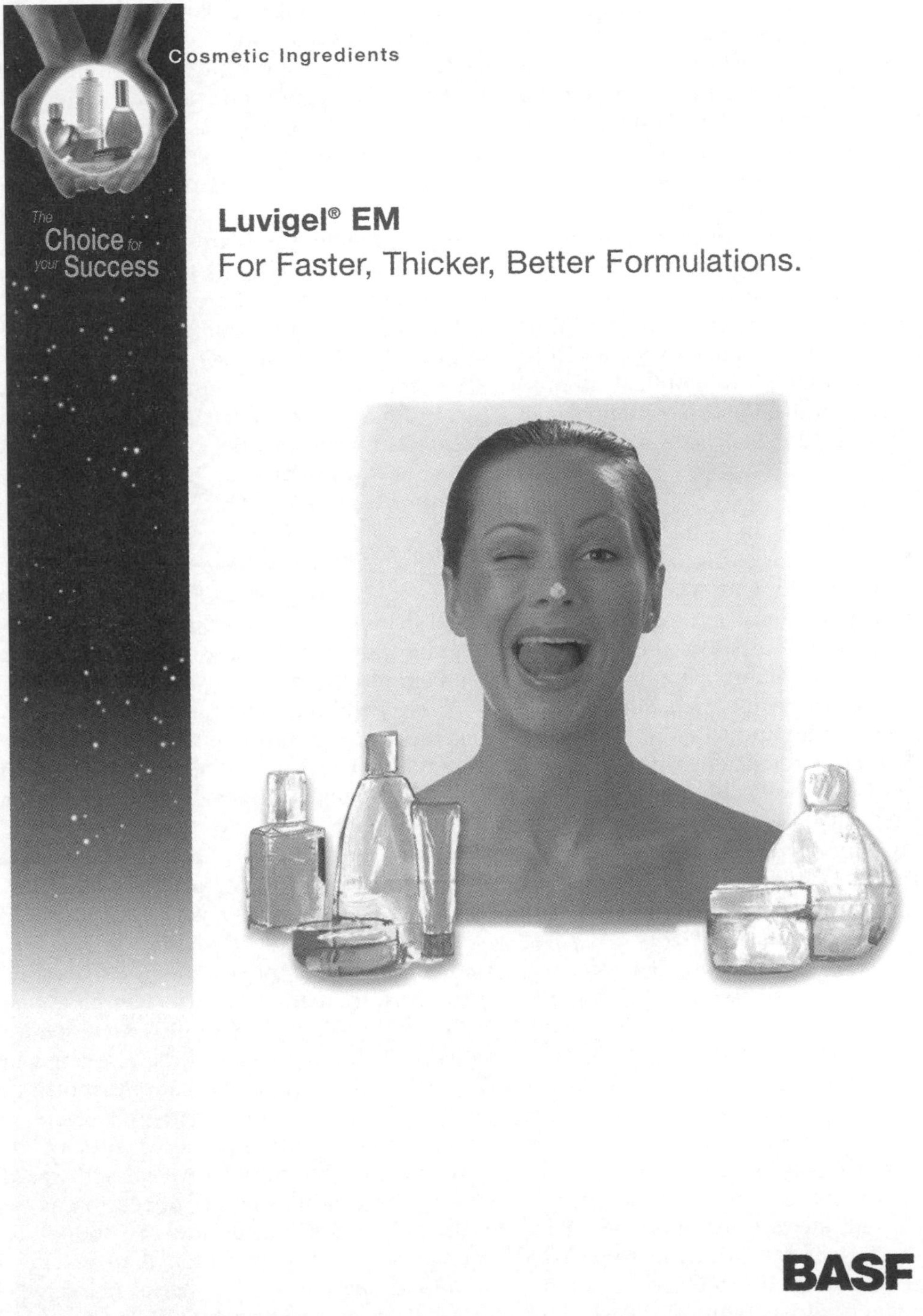

Case study 4.1 continued

Chloe, 5th Avenue, Narcisse, Splendor, Sunflowers and True Love (Elizabeth Arden); Addiction and Fusion (Fabergé); Sun Moon & Stars (Lagerfeld) and Very Valentino (Parfums International). cK one, launched in 1994, was the pioneer in light, unisex fine fragrances and the launch campaign was generally acknowledged by the industry to have been a model of its kind, bringing affordable designer fragrances to a younger audience. cK one was followed in 1996 by cK be. Claims by some commentators that the new fragrance would cannibalize sales of cK one have been strenuously refuted by Calvin Klein.

In September 1999, Unilever announced its intention to reduce the number of brands in its business from around 1600 to 400. While full details are not yet available, weaker brands in all areas of the business are likely to be affected.

Estée Lauder (USA)

The Estée Lauder Companies Inc., founded in 1946, is one of the major cosmetic and toiletries companies in the world, with a key presence in the prestige skin care market, most notably in North America. The company's skin care and sun care products are sold in approximately 100 countries under the well-established brand names of Estée Lauder and Clinique. In recent years Estée Lauder strengthened this focus on cosmetics and toiletries through the acquisition of companies that take it into new sectors or new price positions. The company segments its business into four categories: skin care, colour cosmetics, fragrances and hair care. Hair care represents a new business category for Estée Lauder and sales in this area now relate predominantly to the Aveda business, which it acquired in December 1997. Within the skin care market, the company's focus is on the global Estée Lauder and Clinique brands together with the Prescriptive and Origins brands. The brands are designed to be complementary and allow women to 'move on' to the next brand at various stages of their life. Notably, the Clinique and Origin brands are targeted at younger consumers, Prescriptives to women in the 30–45 year-old age bracket and Estée Lauder is marketed to women older than 45. The main differences between the brands lie in their areas of emphasis in skin care: whether they are promoted as preserving the skin's youthfulness and elasticity, or as reducing the signs of ageing. The Estée Lauder brand comprises a comprehensive range of skin care products under the parent branding. The Clinique brand is designed to address individual skin types and needs, with products based on a strong dermatological expertise. Both the Estée Lauder and Clinique brands include sun care variants, and the Prescriptives and Origins brands also cover a comprehensive range of products.

In fiscal 1999, the company achieved global sales of US$4 billion, with strong growth of 9.5%, compared with 7% in 1998. Both operating and net profits have shown strong growth over recent years. In 1999, operating profit grew 11.7% to US$457 million. In 1999, the number of employees was 17,700.

Procter & Gamble (USA)

Procter & Gamble is one of the very few international manufacturers to achieve the objective of creating truly global brands, such as Oil of Olay, Pampers and Pantene Pro-V.

As a general principle, the company seeks to develop and retain brand loyalty among consumers by offering consistently high quality and value-for-money on innovative products, which are supported by high advertising investment.

Within the perfumes and fragrances market, the Hugo Boss brand is strong and has developed broad regional coverage.

The personal care division of Procter & Gamble consists of other well-known brands. In fragrances, the company owns Giorgio Beverly Hills, with Giorgio, Giorgio Aire, Giorgio Holiday, Hugo Woman and Ocean Dream; Laura Biagotti, with Venezia and Laura Biagotti, and Le Jardin and Rapport, marketed under the world-famous cosmetics brand, Max Factor.

In the UK, the most recent launch was the Oil of Olay products range, priced to compete with mid-market brands such as Boots No. 7 and Revlon, and with which it hopes it will double its share of the cosmetics market. This shows that its cosmetics brands are essentially

Case study 4.1 continued

mass market brands reflecting the importance of that category in the market as a whole.

Benckiser Group (Germany)

The Coty brand is owned by the German household products and detergents group, Benckiser, and is probably the leading single supplier of mass fragrances to the European market.

Based in Ludwigshafen and established in 1925, the Benckiser group is family-owned through the parent company Joh A Benckiser GmbH and operates in the detergents and household cleaning markets in addition to the toiletries and cosmetics market. Having bought about 25 companies in the last decade, Benckiser is now concentrating on a process of organic growth with the emphasis on expanding existing market positions, developing an international strategy and restructuring several major subsidiaries.

The firm divided its international business into the two divisions of cosmetics and household cleaning products in 1996.

The cosmetics product range includes brands like Adidas, Chanson d'Air, Chanson d'Eau, Exclamation, L'Airmant, Mellow Musk, Monsoon Eau, Quiddity by Chipie, Vanilla Fields, Vanilla Musk and Wild Musk. Coty also markets the Davidoff line of fine fragrances, including Cool Water for Woman. The company has been one of the most highly active in developing the youth fragrance sector in Europe, particularly with the launch of Quiddity in its distinctive, lifestyle-linked, CD-style packaging.

Revlon (USA)

The US cosmetics and fragrance supplier Revlon Inc. reported net sales of $2.252 billion (£1.4 billion) in 1998, 0.6% up on the previous year. Operating income fell by more than 40% to $124.6 million, which the company ascribed to the effect of global economic problems in its international business and to retailer consolidation in the USA, which brought wide-ranging changes to consumer buying patterns and trade inventory levels.

Revlon's Charlie has long been the best-selling mass-market fragrance in the UK. The company has retained the brand's high profile through continuous marketing and by the addition of variants, including Charlie Blue, Charlie White, Charlie Red, and Charlie Sunshine.

Body Shop (UK)

See Case Study 18.2 for more details.

Wella (Germany)

In 1998, the Wella Group recorded a turnover of DM4321 million, an increase of 2% on 1997. In the same year, group profits grew 29% to reach DM130 million due to cost cutting measures during 1998.

Europe accounted for 63% of group sales in 1998, followed by America with 23% and the Asia, Africa and Pacific region with 13%.

Wella markets a comprehensive range of hair care products for both consumer and professional salon use, which are increasingly being promoted under the Wella umbrella brand.

Since 1995, Wella has concentrated on its core businesses of hair care and fragrances, divesting its activities in the skin care, bath and shower products, health food and decorative cosmetics sectors.

As well as the brand manufacturers there is also a big **private brand** supplier in the UK:

Boots the Chemist

Boots operates as the UK's leading chemist chain with more than 1300 Boots the Chemist in the UK and Ireland. Boots is one of Europe's largest suppliers of private-label toiletries and cosmetics. Boots the Chemist accounts for 17.5% of the colour cosmetics market with its No.7 and 17 brands and has a share of just over 13% of the facial skin care sector. Skin care products are also sold under the Botanics, Skin Kindly and Natural Collection sub-brands.

Questions

1. Which of the potential customers presented in the case study should BASF approach for its liquid thickener Luvigel®EM?

2. Describe the possible decision-making process of the buyer of Luvigel®EM.

Source: adapted from Brown and Walsch (2000).

4.1 Introduction

This chapter deals mainly with the behaviour of customers in the B-t-C and the B-t-B markets. This analysis is then used as an input for Chapter 6 (especially Section 6.2) where the firm's relationships with the customers are analysed.

To a producer or service provider a market is where the product or service is sold or delivered and the profits generated. The seller or marketer defines the market in types of customer. Thus, a market consists of all the potential customers sharing particular wants and needs who might be willing to engage in change to satisfy wants or needs. Once the potential customers' wants and needs are backed by their purchasing power, an actual market is formed.

The market concept applies equally to service. The term market can even represent a powerful concept in the not-for-profit sectors. Although **not-for-profit organizations** do not refer to the target population they serve as a market, every not-for-profit organization has clients or customers. Hence, in the long run, it is the customers – with their purchasing power – who will decide what the market really is. They set the boundaries and their purchases decide what products or services will remain in the market. Thus, to understand the market, the firm must understand the customer.

There are different types of customer depending on whether the firm is approaching the business-to-consumer market (B-t-C) or business-to-business market (B-t-B).

The firm (producer) may not sell directly to the consumers (end users). Instead, many firms sell to the B-t-B market (see Figure 4.2). Here, the firm may serve as a sub-supplier to other businesses (larger original equipment manufacturers (OEMs))

Figure 4.2 Customers in B-t-C and B-t-B markets

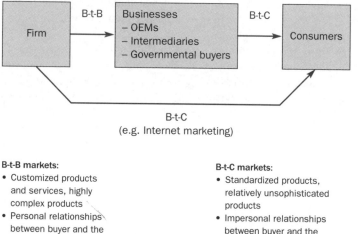

B-t-B markets:
- Customized products and services, highly complex products
- Personal relationships between buyer and the selling firm/salesperson – reliance on personal selling
- Sophisticated buyers
- More rational buying; more customer emphasis on risk-reduction; less customer emphasis on self-expressive benefits of brands

B-t-C markets:
- Standardized products, relatively unsophisticated products
- Impersonal relationships between buyer and the selling firm – more reliance on mass market advertising
- Buyers growing in sophistication
- Often more emotional buying – customer perception of functional, emotional and self-expressive benefits of brands

which may use a firm's component in its final product. The differences and similarities between B-t-B and B-t-C markets have long been debated, especially given the dynamic nature of the business environment in both markets (Mudambi, forthcoming). Figure 4.2 summarizes some relevant comparisons and the main characteristics of B-t-B and B-t-C.

The firm may also have governmental organizations or intermediaries as buyers. Lately, many Internet firms (like Amazon and Dell) have begun to cut the distribution chain by selling directly to consumers.

The outline and structure of this chapter can be illustrated as shown in Figure 4.3.

In both B-t-C and B-t-B markets, the customer decision-making process forms the basis for the segmentation of the two markets.

Customer decision making is essentially a problem-solving process. Most customers – whether individual consumers or organizational buyers – go through similar mental processes in deciding which products and brands to buy. Obviously,

Figure 4.3 Structure of Chapter 4

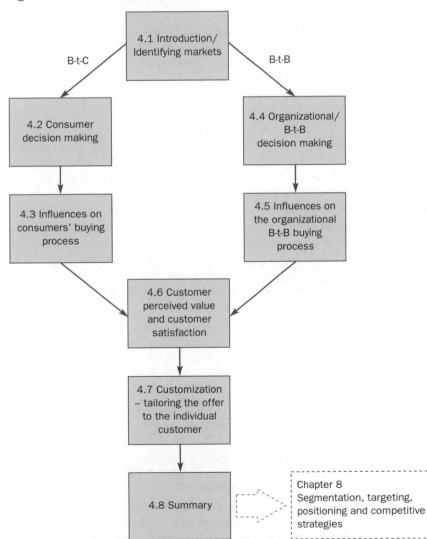

though, various customers often end up buying very different things because of differences in their *personal characteristics* (needs, benefits sought, attitudes, values, past experiences, and lifestyles) and *social influences* (different social classes, **reference groups**, or family situations).

Market segmentation is as important in business markets as it is in the marketing of consumer goods and services. Segmenting the market may, for example, enable the sales force to emphasize different sales arguments in different segments and the firm can tailor its operations and marketing mix to each segment.

Thus, the more marketers know about the factors affecting their customers' buying behaviour, the greater their ability to design strategic marketing programmes to fit the specific concerns and desires of these segments. This chapter examines the mental processes that individual consumers go through when making purchase decisions – and the individual and environmental factors affecting these decisions. Our discussion provides a useful framework for choosing, organizing and analysing information about current and potential customers for a particular product or service.

Irrespective of whether the firm is in the B-t-C or B-t-C market, the starting point is to define who the current customers are. The answer is not always obvious as there may be many people involved in the purchase and use of a particular product or service. Customers are not necessarily the same as consumers. A useful way to approach customer definition is to recognize five main roles that exist in many purchasing situations. Often several, or even all, of these roles may be held by the same individuals, but recognizing each role separately can be a useful step in targeting marketing activity more accurately.

The roles in this **buying centre** are as follows.

- *The initiator*. This is the individual (or individuals) who initiates the search for a solution to the customer's problem. In the case of the purchase of a chocolate bar it could be a hungry child who recognizes her own need for sustenance. In the case of a supermarket the re-ordering of a particular product line which is nearly sold out may be initiated by a stock controller, or even an automatic order processing system.

- *The influencer*. Influencers are all those individuals who may have some influence on the purchase decision. A child may have initiated the search for a chocolate bar, but the parents may have a strong influence on which product is actually bought. In the supermarket the ultimate customers will have a strong influence on the brands ordered – the brands they buy or request the store to stock will be most likely to be ordered.

- *The decider*. Another individual may actually make the decision as to which product or service to purchase, taking into account the views of initiators and influencers. This may be the initiator or the influencer in the case of the chocolate bar. In the supermarket the decider may be a merchandiser whose task it is to specify which brands to stock, what quantity to order, and so on.

- *The purchaser*. The purchaser is the individual who actually buys the product or service. He or she is, in effect, the individual who hands over the cash in exchange for the benefits. This may be the child or parent for the chocolate bar. In industrial purchasing it is often a professional buyer who, after taking account of the various influences on the decision, ultimately places the order, attempting to get the best value for money possible.

- *The user*. Finally comes the end user of the product or service, the individual who consumes the offer. For the chocolate bar it will be the child. For the goods in the supermarket it will be the supermarket's customers.

What is important in any buying situation is to have a clear idea of the various people who are likely to have an impact on the purchase and consumption decision. Where the various roles are undertaken by different individuals it may be necessary to adopt a different marketing approach to each. Each may be looking for different benefits in the purchase and consumption process. Where different roles are undertaken by the same individuals, different approaches may be suitable depending on what stage in the buy/consume process the individual is at the time.

A central theme of this book is that most markets are segmented; in other words, different identifiable groups of customers require different benefits when buying or using essentially similar products or services. Identifying who the various customers are and what role they play then leads to the question of what gives them value. For each of the above members of a **decision-making unit** (DMU), different aspects of purchase and use may give value.

4.2 Consumer decision making

Approaches to understanding consumer buying behaviour draw heavily on the other social sciences.

The company also has a strong role to play in designing and providing appropriate stimulation to the purchase decisions. The process is dynamic as there is an interaction between the buyer and the environment. The consumer actively participates in the process by searching for information on the alternatives available, by providing evaluations of products and services, and by expressions of risk. In this process the company also plays an active role by manipulating the variables that are under its control. The company modifies the marketing mix to accommodate the demands expressed by consumers. The more successful it is in matching its marketing mix with expressed and latent demands in the market, the greater the possibility is that consumers will buy the company's products now and in the future. Consumer behaviour is determined by a host of variables studied in different disciplines. Consumer behaviour may be described as a relationship between a stimulus of some kind, such as a new product, the way information about the innovation is processed by the consumer, and the response the consumer makes having evaluated the alternatives (Figure 4.4).

The stimulus is captured by the range of elements in the marketing mix which the company can manipulate to achieve its corporate objectives. These stimuli derive from the product or service itself, or from the marketing programme developed by the company to support its products and services. A number of symbolic stimuli derive from the use of media such as television. Stimuli also include many of the conditioning variables discussed above. Chief among these are the cultural and social influences on consumer behaviour and the role of reference groups.

Process refers to the sequence of stages used in the internal process of these influences by the consumer. This sequence highlights the cause-and-effect relationships involved in making decisions. The processes include the perceptual, physiological and inner feelings and dispositions of consumers towards the product or service being evaluated.

The third component refers to the consumer's response in terms of changes in behaviour, awareness and attention, brand comprehension, attitudes, intentions and actual purchase. This response may indicate a change in the consumer's psychological reaction to the product or service. As a result of some change in a stimulus, the consumer may be better disposed to the product, have formed a

Figure 4.4 The SPR (SOR) model

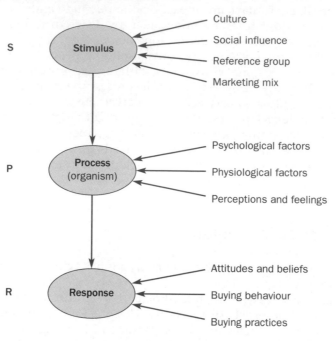

better attitude towards it, or believe it can solve a particular consumption-related problem. Alternatively, the response may be in the form of an actual change in purchasing activity. The consumer may switch from one brand to another or from one product category to another. Consumer responses may also take the form of a change in consumption practices, whereby the pattern of consumer behaviour is changed. Supermarkets frequently offer incentives to get people to shop during slack periods of the week, which involves a change in shopping practice.

Generally speaking, a great deal of interest is focused on responses that involve buying or the disposition to buy. Manufacturers spend considerable sums of money in developing and promoting their products, creating brands and otherwise designing marketing effort to influence consumer behaviour in a particular way. At the same time, consumers may be more or less disposed to these efforts. Through the influence of external stimuli and internal processing mechanisms, a convergence may occur between consumer wants and needs, and the products and services provided. On other occasions, no such convergence occurs.

It is known, however, that the same degree of interest may not be displayed for all products and services. For some products and services, consumers like to be heavily involved. Some purchases are planned, while others are unplanned and may even arise as a result of impulse. These are among the various outcomes or responses, which arise in the stimulus process response model of consumer behaviour.

The decision-making processes consumers use when making purchases vary. Different buyers may engage in different types of decision-making processes depending on how highly involved they are with the product. A high-involvement product for one buyer may be a low-involvement product for another.

The decision processes involved in purchasing high- and low-involvement products are quite different (Figure 4.5). The following sections examine the mental steps involved in each decision process in more detail.

Figure 4.5 Customer involvement in the buying decision

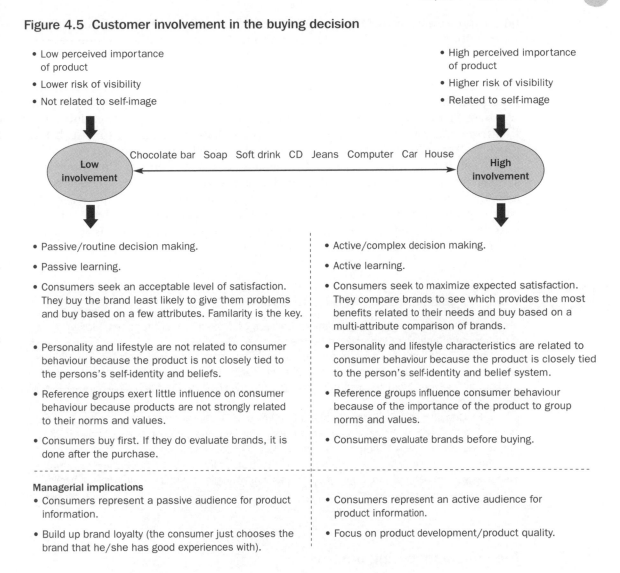

- Low perceived importance of product
- Lower risk of visibility
- Not related to self-image

- High perceived importance of product
- Higher risk of visibility
- Related to self-image

Low involvement ⟷ High involvement

Chocolate bar Soap Soft drink CD Jeans Computer Car House

- Passive/routine decision making.

- Passive learning.

- Consumers seek an acceptable level of satisfaction. They buy the brand least likely to give them problems and buy based on a few attributes. Familarity is the key.

- Personality and lifestyle are not related to consumer behaviour because the product is not closely tied to the persons's self-identity and beliefs.

- Reference groups exert little influence on consumer behaviour because products are not strongly related to their norms and values.

- Consumers buy first. If they do evaluate brands, it is done after the purchase.

- Active/complex decision making.

- Active learning.

- Consumers seek to maximize expected satisfaction. They compare brands to see which provides the most benefits related to their needs and buy based on a multi-attribute comparison of brands.

- Personality and lifestyle characteristics are related to consumer behaviour because the product is closely tied to the person's self-identity and belief system.

- Reference groups influence consumer behaviour because of the importance of the product to group norms and values.

- Consumers evaluate brands before buying.

Managerial implications
- Consumers represent a passive audience for product information.

- Build up brand loyalty (the consumer just chooses the brand that he/she has good experiences with).

- Consumers represent an active audience for product information.

- Focus on product development/product quality.

Determinants of consumer involvement

Consumer involvement is frequently measured by the degree of importance the product has to the buyer. Laurent and Kapferer (1985), for example, indicate a number of factors that influence the degree to which consumers become involved in a particular purchase. The most important factors are:

- perceived importance of the product
- **perceived risk** associated with its use.

The level of involvement with any product depends on its perceived importance to the consumer's self-image. High-involvement products tend to be tied to self-image, whereas low-involvement products are not. A middle-aged consumer who feels (and wants to look) youthful may invest a great deal of time in her decision to buy a sport-utility vehicle instead of an estate car. When purchasing an ordinary light bulb, however, she buys almost without thinking, because the purchase has nothing to do with self-image. The more visible, risky, or costly the product, the higher the level of involvement.

Involvement also influences the relationship between product evaluation and purchasing behaviours. With low-involvement products, consumers generally will try them first and then form an evaluation. With high-involvement products, they first form an evaluation (expectation), then purchase. One reason for this behaviour is that consumers do not actively search for information about low-involvement products. Instead, they acquire it while engaged in some other activity, such as watching television or chatting with a friend. This is called *passive learning*, which characterizes the passive decision-making process. Only when they try the product, do they learn more about it. In contrast, high-involvement products are investigated through *active learning* – part of an active decision-making process – in order to form an opinion about which product to purchase.

Exhibit 4.1	McDonald's is seeking alternatives for beef

As a consequence of the BSE crisis in Europe, McDonald's has launched McFarmer, a burger made entirely out of pork, in Germany.

McDonald's decision to create a pork-related burger comes as German consumers become increasingly reluctant to buy beef products. Earlier, the crisis forced the multinational fast-food giant to drop print adverts informing the public about the beef used for its products.

A McDonald's spokeswoman admitted that sales of beefburgers have recently declined but would not reveal any figures. A growing number of McDonald's customers, however, have switched to the vegetable burger – launched 14 years ago – and to chicken and fish burgers.

Other meat products are suffering from the BSE problem. Even a German favourite – sausages – are being regarded with suspicion as many varieties contain certain levels of beef.

Source: adapted from *Adage Global* (2001).

The consumer buying process

For a better understanding of consumer buying behaviour, marketers have broken the decision-making process into the five steps described below. These are shown in Figure 4.6, along with a description of how one consumer made a high-involvement purchase. For low-involvement purchases, the first three steps may be skipped. As involvement increases, each step takes on greater importance, and more active learning occurs.

Step 1: Problem identification

Consumers' purchase decision processes are triggered by unsatisfied wants or needs. Individuals perceive differences between ideal and actual states on some physical or sociopsychological dimension. This motivates them to seek products or services to help bring their current state more into balance with the ideal.

We human beings are insatiable – at least with respect to our sociopsychological needs – but we are limited by time and financial resources. It is impossible for us to

Figure 4.6 The consumer decision-making process

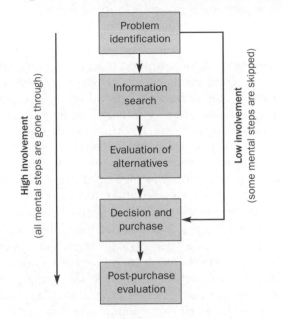

satisfy all our needs at once. We tend instead to try to satisfy the needs that are strongest at a given time. The size of the gap between our current and our desired state largely determines the strength of a particular need.

If you are thirsty, you may simply run out and buy a soft drink. In a high-involvement purchase the recognition of a need may arise long before it is acted upon. In the case of a house, the cost may prevent you from acting on your need for several years.

Step 2: Information search

Having recognized that a problem exists and might be satisfied by the purchase and consumption of a product or service, the consumer's next step is to refer to information gained from past experience and stored in memory for possible later use.

The information search consists of thinking through the situation, calling up experiences stored in memory (internal search), and probably seeking information from the following.

- Personal sources include family members, friends, and members of the consumer's reference group.

- Commercial sources refer to information disseminated by service providers, marketers, and manufacturers and their dealers. They include media advertising, promotional brochures, package and label information, salespersons, and various in-store information, such as price markings and displays.

- Public sources include non-commercial and professional organizations and individuals who provide advice for consumers, such as doctors, lawyers, government agencies, travel agencies, and consumer-interest groups. Consumers are usually exposed to more information from commercial sources than from personal or public sources. Consumers do, however, use information from different sources for different purposes and at different stages within the decision-making process. In general, commercial sources perform an informing function for consumers. Personal and public sources serve an evaluation and legitimizing function.

Each source has its benefits and drawbacks. Because services are tangible, difficult to standardize, and their production and consumption inseparable, they are more difficult to evaluate than products. Thus, most services are hard to assess until they are being consumed after purchase (e.g. cruises and restaurant meals). Indeed, some services are difficult to assess even after they have been consumed. Even when products are very expensive and ego-involving, some consumers are unlikely to conduct an exhaustive search for information before making a decision. Why? Because of the costs involved. Perhaps the biggest cost for most people is the opportunity cost of the time involved in seeking information. They give up the opportunity to use that time for other, more important or interesting activities, like work.

Another information-search cost is the possible negative consequence of delaying the decision too long. For example, a consumer has only a limited time to decide whether to take advantage of a special deal offered on a specific cruise. Finally, there are psychological costs involved in searching for information. Collecting information can be a frustrating task, often involving crowded stores and rude salespeople. Also, some consumers become frustrated and confused when they have a lot of complex information to evaluate before making a choice. Consequently they cut their information search short.

Step 3: Evaluation of alternatives

Consumers differ in their approach to evaluation, but a number of aspects are common. Products or services are viewed by individuals as bundles of attributes. Consumers find it difficult to make overall comparisons of many alternative brands because each brand might be better in some ways but worse in others. Instead, consumers simplify their evaluation task in several ways. First, they seldom consider all possible brands; rather, they focus on their invoked set – a limited number they are familiar with that are likely to satisfy their needs.

Second, consumers evaluate each of the brands in the invoked set on a limited number of product factors or attributes (Figure 4.7). They also judge the relative importance of these attributes, or the minimum acceptable performance of each. The set of attributes used by a particular consumer and the relative importance of each represent the consumer's choice criteria.

Cars are seen as transport, safety, prestige, speed and carrying capacity. Some attributes are more important than others, so consumers allocate different levels of importance weights to each attribute identified. Some buyers will view safety as more important than speed. The company can divide the market into segments according to the attributes which are important to different groups.

Consumers tend to develop a set of beliefs about where each product or brand is in regard to each attribute. This set of beliefs about a particular brand is referred to as the brand image. For a particular consumer, the brand image of a BMW may be that it is expensive, reliable and fast, while the brand image of a Lada may be that it is cheap, plain and slow.

Figure 4.7 Selected attributes consumers use to evaluate alternative products or services

Category	Specific attributes
Cost attributes	Purchase price, operating costs, repair costs, cost of extras or options, cost of installation, trade-in allowance, likely resale value
Performance attributes	Durability, quality of materials, construction, dependability, functional performance (e.g. acceleration, nutrition, taste), efficiency, safety, styling
Social attributes	Reputation of brand, status image, popularity with friends, popularity with family members, style, fashion
Availability attributes	Carried by local stores, credit terms, quality of service available from local dealer, delivery time

Step 4: The purchase decision

The purchase decision emerges from the evaluation of alternatives. The consumer may decide not to buy and save the money or spend it on a different item altogether. Or he may want to play safe by deciding to purchase a small amount for trial purposes, or by leasing rather than buying. The decision to buy often occurs some time before the actual purchase. The purchase is a financial commitment to make the acquisition. It may take time to secure a mortgage or car loan.

Consumers shopping in a retail store intent on purchasing one brand sometimes end up buying something different. This happens because the consumer's ultimate purchase can be influenced by such factors as being out-of-stock (no outside cabins on a particular cruise), a special display, or a message from a salesperson ('I can get you a better deal on a similar cruise if you can go two weeks later').

Step 5: The post-purchase evaluation

The purchase evaluation stage results in satisfaction or dissatisfaction. Buyers often seek assurance from others that their choice was correct. Positive assurance reinforces the consumer's decision, making it more likely that such a purchase will be made again. Positive feedback confirms the buyer's expectation.

Consumers are more likely to develop brand loyalty to services than to products because of the difficulty of obtaining and evaluating information about alternative services as well as, in some cases, the extra costs involved. Also, in some cases repeated patronage brings additional benefits such as preferential treatment (getting an appointment with your doctor) and the service provider getting better insights into the consumer's tastes/preferences.

Even when a product performs as expected, consumers may doubt whether they made the best possible choice. Such doubts are called **cognitive dissonance**.

Doubts about whether the best possible purchase has been made can be reduced in two ways. First, they can simply withdraw from their decision – take the product back and ask for a refund (difficult to do with a service). A second way to reduce dissonance is for consumers to be convinced they really did make the best choice. Many people, thus, continue to seek information about their chosen brand *after* a purchase. Marketers play an active role in dissonance reduction by reinforcing consumers' purchase decisions via, for example, follow-up letters assuring customers they made a wise decision and that the firm stands behind the product should anything go wrong.

Exhibit 4.2

Skoda is considering new customer groups

The Czech word Skoda means pity or shame. Thus, on spying a passing Skoda car, Czechs used to say, 'there goes a shame', and nobody would argue. Skoda's press officer is Milan Smutny, whose surname means sad. However, Skoda's image has changed.

When Volkswagen beat Renault in 1991 to buy a 70% stake in Skoda for US$650 million, its plan was simple. First, transform the company with German management and lots of cash (over US$2 billion so far, but – importantly – from Skoda's own cash flow, not from VW's); then exploit Czech engineering talent, low labour costs and Skoda's access to central European markets.

This formula has worked well. Analysts reckon that Skoda is the most successful former Communist company anywhere. Production has tripled since 1991. In 1997, Skoda overtook Fiat's Polish affiliate as central Europe's largest car manufacturer. Despite a three-year recession in the Czech Republic, Skoda has doubled its sales since 1995 to US$3.2 billion, and in 1999 it made a respectable profit of US$75 million.

The growth has been driven by exports. In 1991, around 30% of Skodas were sold abroad; now around 80% are exported. Skoda has plants in Poland and Bosnia, and one on the way in India. Its controlled expansion into western Europe has continued apace, especially into Germany, the firm's biggest western market.

Skoda is hoping to expand its customer base beyond its traditional target audience of mature, cost-conscious customers whilst ensuring that this core sector of its business is not disappearing.

The brand is enjoying something of a revival under its new owners but, despite having one of the most loyal customer bases in the sector, its marketing activity has remained small – the existing database currently holds just 35,000 names.

As part of this move to appeal to a different generation of car buyers, online adverts are among the media elements to be used in the campaigns.

Source: adapted from *Customer Loyalty Today* (2000), Boleslav (2001).

4.3 Influences on consumers' decision making

Even if some consumers have a similar involvement they buy different brands for different reasons. Some of the important psychological variables that affect a consumer's decision-making process include needs, perception, memory, and attitudes. The consumer's personal characteristics, such as **demographic** and **lifestyle** variables etc. influence these psychological factors – see Figure 4.8.

Figure 4.8 Hierarchy of variables affecting individual consumer behaviour

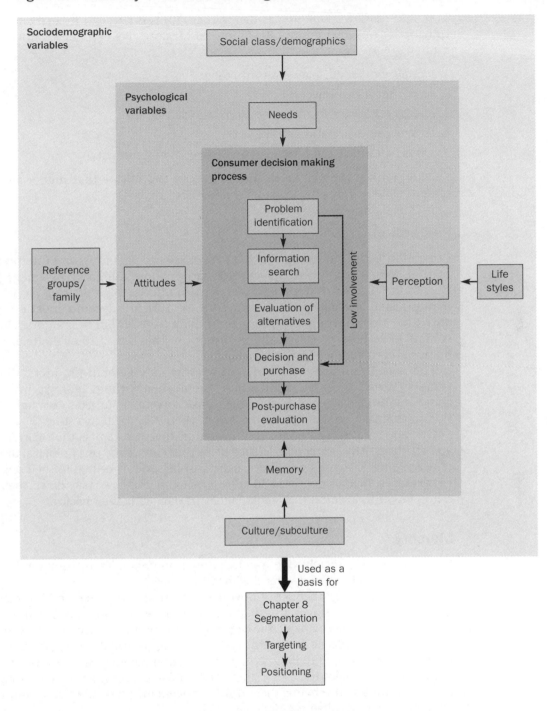

Needs

Abraham Maslow's famous classification (1970) is often used by marketers to help categorize consumer desires. According to Maslow, five basic needs underlie most human goals:

1. *physiological*: food, water, warmth, sleep
2. *safety*: security, protection
3. *love and belonging*: family, friendship, and acceptance
4. *esteem*: prestige, status, self respect
5. *self actualization*: self fulfilment and personal enrichment.

Maslow ranked the five needs in a hierarchy to indicate that higher level needs tend to emerge only after lower level needs are satisfied.

Perception

Perception is the process by which a person selects, organizes, and interprets information. When consumers collect information about a high-involvement product they follow a series of steps, or a hierarchy of effects. Exposure to a piece of information, such as a new product, an advert, or a friend's recommendation, leads to attention, then to comprehension, and finally to retention in memory. Once consumers have fully perceived the information, they use it to evaluate alternative brands and to decide which to purchase.

The perception process is different for low-involvement products. Here, consumers store information in their memories without going through the above-mentioned steps. Exposure may cause consumers to retain enough information so that they are familiar with a brand when they see it in a store.

Consumers also tend to avoid information that contradicts their current beliefs and attitudes. This perceptual defence helps them avoid the psychological discomfort of reassessing or changing attitudes, beliefs, or behaviours central to their self-images. For example, many smokers avoid anti-smoking messages, or play down their importance, rather than admit that smoking may be damaging their health.

Memory

Consumers are also selective in what they remember. Thus, they tend to retain information that supports what they believe.

There are different theories of how the human memory operates, but most agree that it works in two stages. Information from the environment is first processed by the short-term memory, which forgets most of it within 30 seconds or less because of inattention or displacement by new incoming information. Some information, however, is transferred to long-term memory, from where it can be retrieved later.

In long-term memory, a vast amount of information may be held for years or even indefinitely. It remains there until replacement by contradictory information through a process called interference.

Consumers are bombarded with promotional messages. Marketers hope that the more often their brand name is seen, the more likely consumers will be to process information about it.

Attitudes

An attitude is a positive or negative feeling about an object (say, a brand) that predisposes a person to behave in a particular way toward that object.

Attitudes are often described as consumer preferences – a like or dislike for products or their characteristics. Marketers usually think of attitudes as having three components: cognitive, affective, and behavioural. The cognitive aspect refers to knowledge about product attributes that are not influenced by emotion. The affective component relates to the emotional feelings of like or dislike. The behavioural element reflects the tendency to act positively or negatively. In other words, attitudes toward purchasing a product are a composite of what consumers know about its attributes.

Generally, marketers use their knowledge of consumer attitudes to make sure that strategies are consistent with consumer tastes and preferences. From time to time, marketers attempt to change consumer attitudes, usually by influencing one of the three components.

Socio-demographic variables

Age/social class/demographics

The consumer's age category has a major impact on spending behaviour. For example, older consumers choose more products related to medical care and travel, and choose fewer products in home furnishings and clothing than do younger age groups; the presence of young children obviously affects the purchasing of a variety of goods and services. Teenagers spend a great deal of money on films, soft drinks, and fast foods, for example.

The world population will continue to grow. The trend has occurred for two reasons. One is the lowering of the death rate, and the other is ageing 'baby boomers'. The **baby boom** is the name for the tremendous increase in births that occurred in most western countries between 1946 and 1965, in the 20 years following World War II. The generation born between 1965 and 1976 is often called Generation X. Generation X is smaller than the baby boom generation, but they are expected to overtake baby boomers as a primary market for many product categories at the beginning of this millennium. Another group of consumers came into being between 1977 and 1995, when adult baby boomers began having children, creating an 'echo' of the baby boom. The oldest members of this group are in their mid-20s. We will use the term Generation Y for this group. They are growing up very accustomed to computers and the Internet.

Marketers increasingly look at social class from a global perspective. In some societies – such as India and Brazil – class distinctions are clear, and status differences are great. In others – such as Denmark and Canada – differences are less extreme. In countries with strong class differences, where people live, the cars they drive, the types of clothing they wear, how much they travel, and where they go to college is largely determined by social class.

In a country with a more homogeneous class structure, such as Sweden or Denmark, it is not uncommon for executives from all levels to work as a team, so for example, Americans of various ranks are accepted as well.

Lifestyles

Two people of similar age, income, education, and even occupations do not necessarily live their lives in the same way. They may have different opinions, interests, and activities. As a result, they are likely to exhibit different patterns of behaviour – including buying different products and brands and using them in different ways for different purposes. These broad patterns of activities, interests, and opinions – and the behaviours that result – are referred to as lifestyles. To obtain lifestyle data, consumers are asked to indicate the extent to which they agree or disagree with a series of statements having to do with such things as price consciousness, family activities, spectator sports, traditional values, adventurousness, and fashion. Lifestyle topologies have been developed by researchers in other countries.

Culture/subculture

Culture has perhaps the most important influence on how individual consumers make buying decisions. Culture is the set of beliefs, attitudes, and behaviour patterns shared by members of a society and passed on from one generation to the next. Cultural values and beliefs tend to be relatively stable over time, but they can change from one generation to the next in response to changing conditions in society.

Cultural differences create both problems and opportunities for international marketers, particularly for such products as food and clothes. By taking cultural values into account, companies adjust to the particular customs of people in different countries. Values are the shared norms about what it is right to think and do. They reflect what society considers to be worthy and desirable. Marketers need to understand values so their actions are not counter to what consumers in a given market consider to be acceptable.

A **subculture** is a group of people with shared values within a culture. There are many groups of people in the USA (e.g. Hispanics and Jews) who share common geographic, ethnic, racial, or religious backgrounds. They continue to hold some values, attitudes, and behaviour patterns that are uniquely their own.

Reference groups/family

All consumers live with, depend on, and are nurtured by other people. We influence and are influenced by those with whom we have frequent contact – friends, colleagues, and family members. We are also influenced by people we know only indirectly through the mass media.

Reference groups are people whose norms and values influence a consumer's behaviour (Kotler, 2000).

The family

The family is especially important to marketers because it forms a household, which is the standard purchase and consumption unit.

How does the family make buying decisions? Here the marketers generally look at three important aspects.

1. How do families make decisions as a group?
2. What roles can various members play in a purchase decision?
3. How does family purchase behaviour change over time?

In research on families of European descent Lee and Collins (2000) found that several coalitions emerged in family decisions.

Exhibit 4.3	SoapWorks challenges the large detergent manufacturers by approaching consumers who are concerned with health

In 1994, 33-year-old Amilya Antonetti's infant son had health problems after she had used one of the standard detergent brands. Amilya lives in northern California, and she thought it had something to do with the chemicals used in the detergents from Procter & Gamble and other detergent manufacturers. Therefore, she began developing anti-allergenic cleansing detergents.

Books and experts on natural remedies helped, and so did talking to other mums with other problems. Words from her grandma were: keep it simple, baking soda, vinegar, soda ash, borax, lemons, and grapefruits.

When Amilya Antonetti began to talk seriously about breaking into the $4.7 billion US-laundry detergent market, in 1994, industry veterans told her she had to be joking. It's been difficult, but five years later, Antonetti now has shelf space in 5000 stores from California to Florida. She generated revenues of $10 million in 2000.

Since 1994 Antonetti has expanded the product range to include also shower body wash, shampoo, and soap bars.

In order to pay her 52 employees and make a profit that she admits is on the low end for the industry, Antonetti says she budgets no more than $60,000 a year for advertising. That's less than the cost of a single 30-second commercial on prime-time network television, which can cost from $80,000 to $400,000. And it's minuscule compared with the $119 million that brand giant Clorox reports as its advertising expenses just for the first quarter of 2000.

SoapWorks has doubled its revenues each year since its launch, but as is typical at growing companies, Antonetti and husband Karp, who serves as chief financial officer, are grappling with chronic cash flow problems. Moreover, with every advance Antonetti makes in the market, she runs into new demands for costly promotions.

To step up production, and thereby increase profit margins without boosting prices, Antonetti has decided she needs to bring in outside investors. It's just that she hasn't yet found the right ones. If SoapWorks does get capital, the challenge for Antonetti will be staying true to her vision.

Amilya's concept originated from within herself, from her problems with her son. That has resonated with other mothers and other women who have been attracted to joining her cause.

Sources: adapted from Osborne (2000), information on **www.soapworks.com**.

In particular, fathers and daughters appeared to work together, especially older daughters (aged between 12 and 19). However, this coalition was weakened when there were two daughters in the family, as the daughters seemed to side with their mother against the only male in the family. Also mothers and sons seemed to work best together, particularly when there were two sons in the family. There is also evidence that this coalition was strong where it was a son who was the oldest child. It seemed to be the older daughters who were the key players in this family interaction.

The marketing implications of Lee and Collins (2000) are as follows. In order to increase the effectiveness of promotional campaigns towards families, marketers must examine the relative influence of family members at each stage of the decision-making process for each product category under consideration. It is suggested that segmentation of some family markets on the basis of the type of household structure and demographics may also be useful. Further, during the development of promotional campaigns, marketers may wish to direct messages regarding decision making to family members who dominate particular stages of the decision process.

The influence of various family members varies substantially across countries. Generally speaking, the more traditional the society, the more men hold the power. In the more egalitarian countries – such as the Scandinavian countries – decisions are more likely to be made jointly. As women become better educated and have more buying power in Europe and Japan, more **joint decisions** will happen.

Not all families consist of a mother, a father, and children. Still more households consist of only one person, or several non-relatives, or a single parent with children (see Exhibit 4.4).

Exhibit 4.4

Example of loyalty: store loyalty versus brand loyalty

The following data is based on a household panel survey by GfK Nürnberg.

Many consumers describe themselves as more store loyal than brand loyal. Figure 4.9 shows both. Brand loyalty is drawn on the x-axis and is measured as the share of all purchases within a product group taken by the most preferred brand. Store loyalty is measured similarly, as the number of visits to the most preferred outlet expressed as a proportion of all shopping trips undertaken for any one product category.

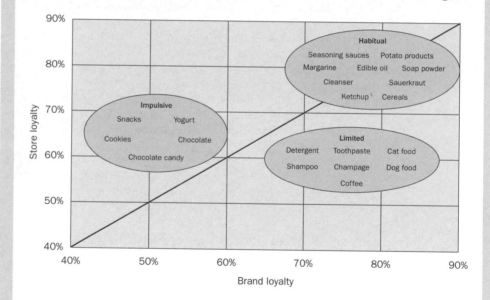

Figure 4.9 Intensity of brand and store loyalty for fast moving consumer goods

Source: Thurau and Hansen (2000), p. 37, with permission from Springer Verlag.

Above the bisecting line, store loyalty is higher than brand loyalty, and this case applies above all to product categories where impulse buying is very common; sweets, snack products, yoghurts, chocolates etc. Nevertheless, brand loyalty in these product categories is still relatively high, at around 50%. Very high rates for brand loyalty can be seen for products like cereals, soups, potato products, sauces, dog food, coffee and other products typically purchased repeatedly; loyalty rates reach 80% and higher. Brand loyalty for these products is generally a little bit higher than store loyalty, but all in all we have to conclude that loyalty is a widespread phenomenon.

Source: adapted from Thurau and Hansen (2000), p. 37.

Figure 4.10 Key consumer expenditure/investment

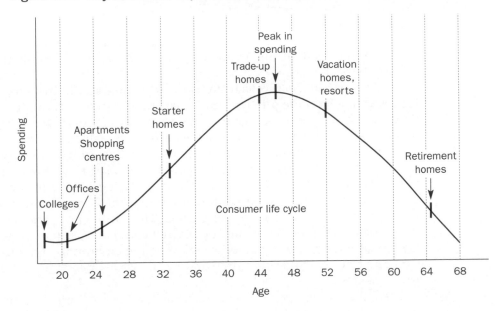

Family life cycle (FLC)

The **family life cycle** describes the progress a household makes as it proceeds from its beginning to its end. Each stage reflects changes in a unit's purchasing needs and, hence, the difference in expenditure patterns – for instance, young married couples without children (DINKs = double income no kids) are often very affluent because both spouses work. They are a major market for luxury goods, furniture, cars, and vacations.

Dent (1999) noticed a link between US birth rates and economic growth: a 47-year lag between birth and the time Americans reach their peak earning and spending years (see Figure 4.10). Using that correlation, Dent now predicts that the Dow Jones Industrial Average will nearly quadruple to 41,000 by 2008 – the year the number of 47-year-old boomers peaks. As the less numerous Generation X enter their heavy spending years, he sees the stock market then drifting into a deflationary decline – that is, until the 83 million members of Generation Y reach their economic prime in another dozen years (Dent, 1999; Weiss, 2000).

Dent (1999) describes how every generation of consumers makes predictable purchases over the course of their lifetime. At age 47, consumers finally reach their spending peak, after which children leave home and family spending declines. Fortunately, investors can capitalize on this spending curve by matching large generational cohorts to their anticipated behaviour in the marketplace.

4.4 Organizational B-t-B decision making

The marketing of goods and services to other businesses, governments, and institutions is known as business-to-business marketing. It includes everything but direct sales to consumers. The products are marketed from one organization to another, until the one at the end of the chain sells to the final consumer.

Organizational markets consist of all individuals and organizations that acquire products and services which are used in the production of products and services demanded by others. The demand for most products and services arises because of a **derived demand** for the finished products and services that the company produces. About half of all manufactured goods in most countries are sold to organizational buyers.

The market behaviour, which affects the demand for industrial products and services, is generally quite different from that experienced in consumer markets. The differences arise mainly in regard to the behaviour of industrial buyers, the types of products and services purchased, and the purposes for which they are purchased.

Buying is performed by all organizations: manufacturing firms, service firms and not-for-profit organizations in the public and private sectors. Organizational buying is a complex process, which may be divided into a number of stages taking place over time. People with different functional responsibilities are usually involved in the industrial buying process. Their influence varies at the different stages, depending on the product or service being purchased. In broad terms, organizational buying is influenced by factors in the environment, by the nature and structure of the organization itself and by the way the buying centre in the company operates.

There is a strong correlation between the level of a country's economic development and its demand for industrial goods and services. Thus, countries with a basically agrarian economy demand mainly farm equipment and supplies plus public sector purchases including military equipment and supplies. This is in contrast with highly developed countries, which are strong markets for high-technology products.

Identifying buyers in organizational markets

Buyers in organizational markets are typically manufacturers, intermediaries or customers in the public sector. To identify them it may be necessary to segment the market.

Manufacturers as customers

Manufacturers buy raw materials, components, and semi-finished and finished items to be used in the manufacture of final goods. Manufacturers tend to be concentrated in particular areas of a country, and hence may more easily be served than consumer markets where the population is dispersed. Furthermore, buying power for certain products tends to be concentrated in a few hands, since a few manufacturers frequently account for most of the production of specific industrial products.

Intermediate customers (resellers)

Intermediate customers are organizations which buy and sell to make a profit. They are sometimes referred to as resellers. Normally they make very few changes to the products handled. **Wholesalers** and retailers are the largest intermediaries in this market, but other specialized distributors also exist, which may also provide additional services.

Intermediate customers are also concerned with the derived demand further down the distribution channel for the products they carry. They are particularly concerned about product obsolescence, **packaging** and inventory requirements, since all three variables are important considerations in their financial well-being.

Public sector markets

The public sector market is in reality a myriad of markets. It consists of institutional markets like schools, hospitals, prisons and other similar public bodies. It also consists of direct sales to government departments such as the health service and education departments. In most countries with an active public sector, the annual budgets of many of these institutions can be larger than the expenditure of organizations in the private sector.

Public sector tendering procedures

Many different purchasing terms are used in public sector purchasing, but it is possible to establish two broad categories of these. The first category contains terms, which refer to the extent of the publicity given to a particular public sector tender or contract, while the second category contains terms based on the discretion available to the awarding authority within the public service itself.

Where it is judged that many suitable qualified suppliers exist, the publicity given to a particular tender notice is widespread. The opposite is the case where the number of potentially suitable suppliers is limited. Three tendering procedures, each implying a different level of publicity, may be identified:

- open tendering
- selective tendering
- private contracting.

Open tendering procedures arise when an invitation to tender is given the widest publicity. In this situation, an unlimited number of suppliers have the opportunity of submitting bids. *Selective tendering procedures* occur when the invitation to tender is restricted to a predetermined list of suppliers. In this case, the invitation to tender normally takes the form of invitations sent to these suppliers. *Private contracting procedures* refer to the situation where the awarding authority contacts suppliers individually, usually a single supplier.

Buying situations

B-t-B buying behaviour is influenced by two overall organizational considerations. Organizations that have significant experience in purchasing a particular product will approach the decision quite differently from first-time buyers. Therefore attention must centre on buying situations rather than on products. One firm may see the purchase of a new computer as a new task because of the firm's lack of experience in this area, whereas another firm may see the same situation as a **modified re-buy**. Therefore, a marketing strategy must begin with identifying the type of buying situation the buying firm is facing.

Three types of buying situations have been delineated: new task, modified re-buy, and **straight re-buy**.

New-task buying

This occurs when an organization faces a new and unique need or problem – one in which buying centre members have little or no experience in buying and, thus, must expend a great deal of effort to define purchasing specifications and to collect information about alternative products and vendors. Each stage of the decision-making process is likely to be extensive, involving many technical experts and administrators. The supplier's reputation for meeting delivery deadlines, providing adequate service, and meeting specifications is often a critical factor in selling a product or service to an organization for the first time. Because the buying-centre members have limited knowledge of the product or service involved, they may choose a well-known and respected supplier to reduce the risk of making a poor decision.

When confronting new-task buying, organizational buyers operate in a stage of decision making referred to as extensive problem solving. The buyers and decision makers lack well-defined criteria for comparing alternative products and suppliers, but they also lack strong predispositions toward a particular solution.

A modified re-buy

This occurs when the organization's needs remain unchanged, but buying centre members are not satisfied with the product or the supplier they have been using. They may desire a higher-quality product, a better price, or better service. Here buyers need information about alternative products and suppliers to compare with their current product and vendor. Modified re-buys present good opportunities for new suppliers to win an organization's business if they can offer something better than the firm's current vendor.

Limited problem solving best describes the decision-making process for the modified re-buy. Decision makers have well-defined criteria, but are uncertain about which suppliers can best fit their needs. In the consumer market, college students buying their second computer might follow a limited problem-solving approach.

A straight re-buy

This involves purchasing a common product or service the organization has bought many times before. Such purchases are often handled routinely by the purchasing department with little participation by other departments. Such purchases are almost automatic, with the firm continuing to purchase proven products from reliable, established vendors. In straight re-buy situations, all phases of the buying process tend to be short and routine. Even so, when large quantities are involved, the need for quality assurance, parity pricing, and on-time delivery to minimize inventory requires a competent salesforce to help the supplier maintain a continually satisfying relationship with the buyer over time. Indeed, the rapid spread of computerized reordering systems, logistical alliances and the like have made the development and maintenance of long-term relationships between suppliers and their customers increasingly important in the purchase of familiar goods and services.

For routine purchases or straight re-buys, the Internet is being used to streamline the purchasing process. To this end, firms are adopting electronic (e) procurement systems, joining trading communities or turning to electronic marketplaces that have been designed specifically for their industry (for example buying steel in the car industry).

Routine problem solving is the decision process organizational buyers employ in a straight re-buy. Organizational buyers have well-developed choice criteria to apply to the purchase decision. The criteria have been refined over time as the buyers have developed predispositions toward the offerings of one or a few carefully screened suppliers.

The buy grid model

The buying process always begins when someone in the organization recognizes a problem that can be solved by a purchased product or service (Figure 4.11). Sometimes the problem is nothing more than the company running out of regularly purchased items, in which case the purchasing professional determines the quantity needed and reorders the product or service. This would be a straight re-buy situation. Recognizing the problem (stage 1), determining the product and quantity (stage 3), and evaluating the performance of the product or service (stage 8), are found in all three types of buying situations. Therefore, a minimum of three stages is found in all organizational purchases.

The new-task situation is the most complex buying situation and therefore involves all eight buying stages. As we go to the right of Figure 4.11 some of the buying stages are left out because of the reduced complexity of the buying situation. We find the least number of buying stages in straight re-buy.

Figure 4.11 also suggests that some activities at each stage and their execution differ. More people are involved in organizational purchase decisions; the capability

Figure 4.11 The extended buy grid model

Characteristics	Buying situation		
	New task	Modified re-buy	Straight re-buy
Buying stages			
1. Recognition of a problem/need	Always	Always	Always
2. Determination of characteristics and quantity of products/services needed	Always	Sometimes	Never
3. Determination of the product/service desired and quantities needed	Always	Always	Always
4. Search for potential suppliers and preliminary evaluation of their suitability	Always	Sometimes	Never
5. Acquisition and initial analysis of proposals (samples) from suppliers	Always	Sometimes	Never
6. Evaluation of proposals and selection of supplier(s)	Always	Sometimes	Never
7. Selection of an order routine	Always	Always	Always
8. Performance, review, feedback and evaluation	Always	Always	Always
Impotance of buying decision	High ←	→	Low
Degree of interaction between buyer and seller	High ←	→	Low
Number of criteria used in supplier selection	Many ←	→	Few

Source: adapted from Robinson *et al.* (1967), De Boer *et al.* (2001).

of potential suppliers is more critical; and the post-purchase evaluation process is more formalized. We will examine other unique features of each stage of the organizational purchase decision process next.

1. Recognition of a problem or need

The organizational purchasing process starts when someone in the firm recognizes a need that can be satisfied by buying some product or service. Thus, while consumers may buy things impulsively to satisfy psychological or social needs, most organizational purchases are motivated by the needs of the firm's production processes and its day-to-day operations.

An organization's demand for goods and services is a derived demand, which, as we noted earlier, comes from its customers' demands for the goods and services it produces. Fluctuations in economic conditions can produce change in the sales of an organization's goods or services, which, in turn, can result in rapid changes in production schedules and in accumulations or depletions in the firm's materials and parts inventories. As a result, the organization's purchase requirements for materials and parts can change dramatically in a short time.

In some cases, need recognition may be almost automatic, as when a computerized inventory control system reports that an item has fallen below the reorder level or when a piece of equipment wears out. In other cases, a need arises when someone identifies a better way of carrying out day-to-day operations. For example, a production engineer might recommend the purchase of a new machine that would increase production and thus reduce costs.

Changes in the company's strategy, resulting in a need for producing a new product line, may also result in a 'new-task' buying situation. Needs then may be recognized by many people within the organization, including users, technical personnel, top management, and purchasing agents.

Instead of simply monitoring inventories and reordering when they run low, some firms attempt to forecast future requirements so as to plan their purchases in advance.

Requirements planning governs the purchase of raw materials and fabricating components as well as supplies and major installations. One result of such planning is the signing of long-term purchase contracts, particularly for products projected to be in short supply or to a projected increase in price. Requirements planning can also lead to lower costs and better relations between a buyer and its suppliers.

2. Determination of characteristics and quantity of needed product or service

The need for particular goods and services is usually derived from a firm's production or operation requirements and, therefore, must meet specific technical requirements. Technical experts from the firm's R&D, engineering, and production departments are thus often involved early in the purchase decision. When the firm needs a unique component or piece of equipment, it might even seek help from potential suppliers in setting the appropriate specifications. For example, car manufacturers consult their parts suppliers before finalizing other specifications for a new model. Indeed, as we have seen B-t-B marketers increasingly involve major customers in the process of developing new products and product improvements to help ensure that those items will meet the needs and specifications of potential buyers.

3. Determination of the product or service desired and quantities needed

When specifications for the desired product or service are to be determined, purchasing (and possibly other departments) may perform a value analysis. This systematic appraisal of an item's design, quality, and performance requirements helps to minimize procurement costs. It includes an analysis of the extent to which the product might be redesigned, standardized, or processed using cheaper production methods. A cost analysis that attempts to determine what the product costs a supplier to produce is also a part of a value analysis. Such information helps the purchasing agent better evaluate alternative bids or negotiate favourable prices with suppliers.

Sometimes a firm has the option of making some components or performing some services internally ('make'), or buying them from outside suppliers (outsourcing). See also section 3.4 for a further discussion of outsourcing.

Economic considerations typically dominate such decisions, although in the long term other factors may be important (for instance, overdependence on a single supplier).

4. Search for potential suppliers and preliminary evaluation of their suitability and qualifications

Once the specifications and workable solutions have been determined and precisely described, the buying organization searches for alternative sources of supply. Here the purchasing department can exercise much influence as it provides most of the data for possible vendor sources. Figure 4.12 illustrates a process for screening potential suppliers.

Figure 4.12 Screening of potential suppliers

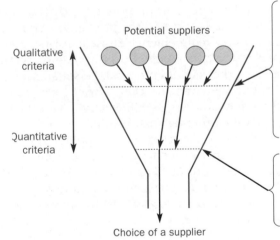

Screening criteria regarding 'supplier choice'

'Softcore' screening

Firm policy:
– Screening out potential suppliers who do not fit into the supplier portfolio and the supplier policy of the firm

Co-operation between the firm and the supplier:
– There should be a fit between the 'company values' of the two firms
– Both firms should be able to benefit from the co-operation

'Hardcore' screening (weights, scores)

Evaluation of supplier capabilities: production, technical support, R&D (number of new product introductions per year) etc. (see also Table 4.13)

Qualitative criteria

Potential suppliers

Quantitative criteria

Choice of a supplier

If new potential suppliers are involved, the purchasing department typically engages in an in-depth investigation before qualifying that firm as a potential supplier. Such an investigation would include information such as the firm's finances, reputation for reliability, and the ability to meet quality standards, information that can be obtained from personal sources (such as salespeople, **trade shows**, other firms, and consultants) and non-personal sources including catalogues, advertising, and trade literature.

For existing suppliers the firm may evaluate the performance quite frequently, and there is often considerable information about that supplier's quality of performance on file.

5. Acquisition and initial analysis of proposals (samples) from suppliers

Requests for specific proposals are made to qualified vendors in this phase. In a straight re-buy situation, the buyer may simply contact the chosen vendor to obtain up-to-date information about prices, delivery times, and mode of shipment, so phases 4 and 5 may be skipped. For modified re-buys, more time might be spent on the analysis of the proposals submitted. New-task buys probably would take the most time and months may go by before a final decision is made.

6. Evaluation of proposals and selection of supplier(s)

Like individual consumers, organizational buyers evaluate alternative suppliers and their offerings by using a set of choice criteria reflecting the desired benefits. The criteria used and the relative importance of each attribute vary according to the goods and services being purchased and the buyer's needs. Always important is the supplier's ability to meet quality standards and delivery schedules. Price is critical for standard items such as steel desks and chairs, but for more technically complex items, such as computers, a broader range of criteria enters the evaluation process and price is relatively less important.

The various potential suppliers and their proposals are then analysed to determine which vendor or vendors can best match the product or service specifications and the desired price and delivery requirements. Subsequent negotiations may be needed to produce the desired results relative to prices, delivery and long-term commitment or other aspect of the vendor's proposal. Personal tastes and personalities cannot be ruled out, but the company that is well liked and can give the customer the best overall product and service will generally win the order, plus the strong possibility of a long-term partnering relationship.

Another factor that can influence the selection of suppliers is reciprocity, which occurs when an organization favours a supplier that is a customer or potential customer for the organization's own products or services. Although this situation sometimes causes inappropriate bonds between buyer and supplier, it can also develop into a rewarding long-term partner relationship. An example of Chrysler's supplier evaluation is given in Figure 4.13.

7. Selection of an order routine

After the selection of supplier, orders are forwarded to the vendor, and status reports are sent to the user department. The inventory levels will be established, and the just-in-time routines will be determined, if such a possibility exists. The user department views this phase as just the beginning. Delivery, set-up, and training, if necessary, will then happen.

Figure 4.13 An example of supplier evaluation (Chrysler Corporation)

Supplier name_____ Shipping location_____	Type of product_____ Annual sales dollars_____					
	5 Excellent	4 Good	3 Satisfactory	2 Fair	1 Poor	0 N/A
Quality (45%)						
Defect rates	___	___	___	___	___	___
Quality of sample	___	___	___	___	___	___
Conformance with quality programme	___	___	___	___	___	___
Responsiveness to quality problems	___	___	___	___	___	___
Overall quality	___	___	___	___	___	___
Delivery (25%)						
Avoidance of late shipments	___	___	___	___	___	___
Ability to expand production capacity	___	___	___	___	___	___
Performance in sample delivery	___	___	___	___	___	___
Response to changes in order size	___	___	___	___	___	___
Overall delivery	___	___	___	___	___	___
Price (20%)						
Price competitiveness	___	___	___	___	___	___
Payment terms	___	___	___	___	___	___
Absorption of costs	___	___	___	___	___	___
Submission of cost savings plans	___	___	___	___	___	___
Overall price	___	___	___	___	___	___
Technology (10%)						
State-of-the-art-components	___	___	___	___	___	___
Sharing R&D capability	___	___	___	___	___	___
Ability and willingness to help with design	___	___	___	___	___	___
Responsiveness to engineering problems	___	___	___	___	___	___
Overall technology	___	___	___	___	___	___
Buyer_____Date_____ Comments_____						

Source: Boyd *et al.* (1998), p. 133, with permission from McGraw-Hill.

A good proportion of all industrial buying involves a purchasing contract. This streamlines the buying decision, making it a straight re-buy situation.

Contracts such as these enable a firm to standardize its purchasing activities across many locations. They can also introduce cost savings through scale economies (quantity discounts) and a reduction in paperwork. One problem with long-term legal contracts, though, is that they must specify precisely all the details of a purchase agreement, including product specifications, prices, credit terms, etc. But, in today's rapidly changing economic and technical environments, it can be difficult for the parties to foresee accurately what their needs and market conditions will be like months or years into the future. And it can be difficult to adjust the terms of a contract in response to unforeseen product improvements, market conditions, or cost improvements. Such inflexibility is one reason for the recent popularity of more informal relationships and alliances between suppliers and their major customers – relationships based more on flexibility and trust between the parties than on detailed legal contracts.

8. Performance review, feedback and evaluation

When a purchase is made and the goods delivered, the buyer's evaluation of both product and supplier begins. The buyer inspects the goods on receipt to determine whether they meet the required specifications. Later, the department using the product judges whether it performs to expectations. Similarly, the buyer evaluates the supplier's performance on promptness of delivery, and post-sales service.

In this phase the user department determines whether the purchased item has solved the original problem. Because this time can be a difficult phase for the vendor (since some of the variables are not completely controlled by him), it behoves the buying organization to analyse the performance and provide feedback to all the interested parties for further evaluation. Feedback that is critical of the chosen vendor can cause the various members of the decision-making unit to re-examine their views. When this re-examination occurs, views regarding previously rejected alternatives become more favourable.

In some organizations this process is done formally, with written reports being submitted by the user department and other persons involved in the purchase. This information is used to evaluate proposals and select suppliers the next time a similar purchase is made. This formal evaluation and feedback process enables organizations to benefit from their purchasing mistakes and successes.

In other organizations (especially in SMEs with limited personnel resources) step 8 is done more informally.

The steps in the buying process described above apply primarily to 'new-task' purchases, where an organizational customer is buying a relatively complex and expensive product or service for the first time. At the other extreme is the 'straight re-buy', where a customer is reordering an item it has purchased many times before (office supplies, bulk chemicals). Such repeat purchases tend to be much more routine. Straight re-buys are often carried out by members of the purchasing department with little participation by other employees, and many of the activities involved with searching for and evaluating alternative suppliers are dropped. Instead, the buyer typically chooses from among suppliers on an 'approved' list, giving weight to the company's past satisfaction with those suppliers and their products and services.

From the seller's viewpoint, being an approved supplier can provide a significant competitive advantage, and policies and procedures should be developed to help maintain and develop such favoured positions with current customers. Many firms have developed **key account** management programmes and cross-functional customer service teams to help preserve the long-term satisfaction of their largest customers. Also, suppliers are offering new technologies – such as Internet-based reordering systems – and forming alliances with their customers to help them make their reordering process more efficient while simultaneously increasing the likelihood they will continue to reorder from the same supplier.

For potential suppliers not on a buyer's approved list, the strategic marketing problem is more difficult. A non-approved supplier's objective must be to move the customer away from the automatic reordering procedures of a straight re-buy towards a situation where the buyer is willing to consider new suppliers.

Kraljic's purchasing model

The purchasing function has a substantial impact on the total cost to a firm and thereby on the potential profit. Choosing the right suppliers has become increasingly important as they account for a large part of the value creation related to the buying firm's products and services. Thus, managing the firm's supplier base is becoming an essential strategic issue. Kraljic's (1983) model aims at matching external resources provided by suppliers with the internal needs of the buying firm.

In this portfolio, the perceived importance and complexity of a purchasing situation is identified in terms of two factors: profit impact and supply risk (Figure 4.14). Profit impact includes such elements as the (expected) monetary volume involved with the goods and/or services to be purchased and the impact on (future) product quality. Indicators of supply risk may include the availability of the goods or services under consideration and the number of potential suppliers. Depending on the values of these factors, purchases (and therefore the related supplier selection decisions) can be grouped according to Kraljic's classification into strategic, bottleneck, leverage and routine purchases.

Let us try to relate the buying situation in the buy grid model (Figure 4.11) to the four categories in Kraljic's model (Figure 4.14).

Leverage items typically involve modified re-buy situations. There are many suppliers to choose from while the high value (and saving potential) of the items justifies a pro-active search and frequent selection of suppliers. However, the execution of the first steps in the process (problem definition, formulation of criteria and prequalification) is often decoupled from the final choice. The first three steps result in the so-called approved vendor lists. Final (frequent) choices are made from these approved vendor lists.

Figure 4.14 Supplier selection model

	Low-supply risk/low complexity	High-supply risk/high complexity
Low-profit impact/low value added	**Routine items** Many suppliers Rationalize purchasing procedures Systems contracting Automate/delegate	**Bottleneck items** Monopolistic supply market Long-term contracts Develop alternatives (internally) Contingency planning
High-profit impact/high value added	**Leverage items** Many suppliers available Competitive bidding Short-term contracts Active sourcing	**Strategic items** Few (difficult to switch) suppliers Medium/long-term contracts Supplier development/partnership (develop alternatives externally) Continous review

Source: adapted from De Boer *et al.* (2001), Kraljic (1983).

In case of a routine item, there are many suppliers that could supply the item. However, because of the low value of the item, it will not pay off for the firm to search frequently for and select suppliers. Moreover, usually a whole set of related routine items (e.g. stationery) is assigned to one (or two) suppliers in order to achieve a highly efficient ordering and administration procedure. The choice of the supplier is fixed for a reasonable period of time. Intermediate changes in the desired or required items are dealt with by the current supplier. Irrespective of such specific changes in the items requested and/or actually purchased, the appropriateness of the supplier is typically reconsidered periodically and if necessary a new (adaptive) selection will take place.

In case of bottleneck and strategic items, the choice of the supplier is also more or less fixed. Small changes in the specification of the items are automatically dealt with by the existing supplier. However, the reason for this is very different from that in the routine case. In these cases with a high supply risk, there are virtually no suppliers to choose from immediately, either because of a unique specification (i.e. a very strong resource tie between the buying company and the supplier) or because of the scarcity of the material. As a result, the choice set is often much smaller. Decision models are primarily used as means for periodic evaluation (monitoring) of the existing supplier.

The framework implicitly also addresses the impact of (inter-firm) relationships between the buyer and the seller on the selection process and the use of decision models. Depending on the substance and the strength of the relationship, the nature of the decision alternatives may differ. For example, in new task situations, where it is unlikely that the buying company has ever been in contact with the suppliers, the decision alternatives are primarily shaped by the offerings of these suppliers, i.e. the products or services they produce. In modified re-buys and especially in straight re-buys for strategic and bottleneck items however, the interaction between buyer and supplier is likely to be more intense and relationships may have been going on for a long time.

4.5 Influences on buying process

In this chapter we have already seen how the buying situation influences the B-t-B buying process.

The eight-stage model of the organizational buying process provides the foundation for explaining other forces that influence a particular buying decision of an organization. Figure 4.15 shows how **organizational buying behaviour** is influenced by four major categories of forces. The four major forces are:

1. environmental forces (e.g. growth rate of the economy)
2. organizational forces (e.g. the size of the buying)
3. group forces (e.g. the influence of the buying centre)
4. individual forces (e.g. personal preferences).

Figure 4.15 Forces influencing the organizational buying process

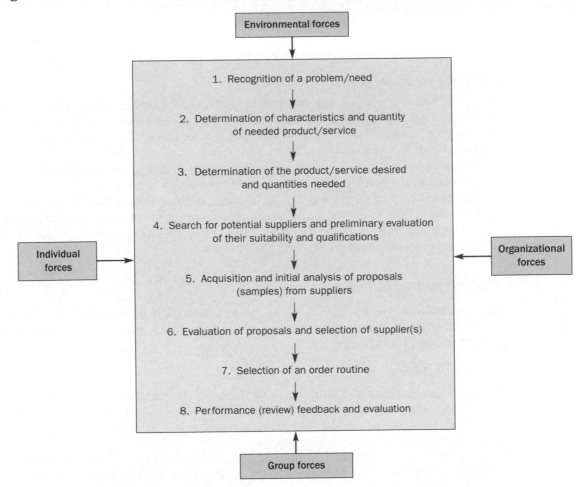

Environmental forces

A projected change in business conditions, a technological development, or a new piece of legislation can drastically alter organizational buying plans. Such environmental influences define the boundaries within which buyer-seller relationships develop in the business market.

Economic Influences

Because of the derived nature of industrial demand, the marketer must also be sensitive to the strength of demand in the ultimate consumer market. The demand for many industrial products fluctuates more widely than the general economy. Firms that operate on a global scale must be sensitive to the economic conditions that prevail across regions. A wealth of political and economic forces dictate the vitality and growth of an economy.

The economic environment influences an organization's ability and, to a degree, its willingness to buy. However, shifts in general economic conditions do not affect all sectors of the market evenly. For example, a rise in interest rates may damage the housing industry but may have minimal effects on industries such as paper, hospital supplies, and soft drinks. Marketers that serve broad sectors of the organizational market must be particularly sensitive to the differential impact of selective economic shifts on buying behaviour.

Technological Influences

Rapidly changing technology can restructure an industry and dramatically alter organizational buying plans. Notably, the Internet and **e-commerce** have changed the way firms and customers (whether they be consumers or organizations) buy and sell to each other, learn about each other, and communicate.

The marketer must also actively monitor signs of technological change and be prepared to adapt the marketing strategy to deal with new technological environments.

Because the most recent wave of technological change is as dramatic as any in history, the implications for marketing strategists are profound and involve changing definitions of industries, new sources of competition, changing **product life cycles**, and the increased globalization of markets.

Organizational forces

An understanding of the buying organization is based on the strategic priorities of the firm, the role that purchasing occupies in the organization, and the competitive challenges that the firm confronts.

Strategic solutions

Organizational buying decisions are made to facilitate organizational activities and to support the firm's mission and strategies. A business marketer who understands the strategic priorities and concerns that occupy key decision makers is better equipped to deliver the desired solution.

To provide such customer solutions, the business marketer requires an intimate understanding of the opportunities and threats that the customer is confronted with.

Strategic role of purchasing

In many firms, purchasing strategy is becoming more closely tied to corporate strategy (Nellore and Söderquist, 2000). Compared to traditional buyers, recent research suggests that more strategically oriented purchasing managers are:

● more receptive to information and draw it from a wide variety of sources;
● more sensitive to the importance of longer-term supplier relationships, questions of price in relation to performance, and broader environmental issues;
● more focused on the competences of suppliers in evaluating alternative firms.

Moreover, these purchasing managers are evaluated on performance criteria that are more tightly linked to strategic performance.

Given rising competitive pressures, purchasing managers are increasingly using rigorous cost modelling approaches to identify the factors that drive the cost of purchased goods and services.

To secure competitive advantage, purchasing managers are also tieing purchasing strategies more directly to corporate goals to increase product quality, accelerate product development, capitalize on new technologies, or respond more quickly to changing customer expectations. Indeed, leading purchasing organizations have learned that these results can only be achieved by building close relationships with suppliers and by using B-t-B Internet-based marketplaces.

As purchasing assumes a more strategic role in the firm, the business marketer must understand the competitive realities of the customer's business and develop/produce better value for customers – in the form of products, services and ideas that improve the performance goals of the customer organization.

An organization that centralizes buying decisions will approach purchasing differently from a company where purchasing decisions are made at individual user locations. When purchasing is centralized, a separate organizational unit is given authority for purchases at a regional, divisional, or headquarters level. There seems to be a trend towards centralized purchasing. Why? First, through centralization, purchasing strategy can be better integrated with corporate strategy. Second, an organization with multiple plant locations can often achieve cost savings by pooling common requirements. Third, the nature of the supply environment can also determine whether purchasing is centralized. If the supply environment is dominated by a few large sellers, centralized buying may be particularly useful in securing favourable terms and proper service. If the supply industry consists of many small firms, each covering limited geographical areas, decentralized purchasing may achieve better support.

Finally, the location of purchasing in the organization often hinges on the location of key buying influencers. If engineering plays an active role in the purchasing process, the purchasing function must be close organizationally and physically.

The organization of the marketer's selling strategy should parallel the organization of the purchasing function of key accounts. To avoid disjointed selling activities and internal conflict in the sales organizations, and to serve the special needs of important customers, many business marketers have appointed key account managers to take care of coordinating a key account's centralized and dispersed requirements, often on a global level (Pardo, 1999; Holt, 2000).

Group forces

Multiple buying influencers and group forces are critical in organizational buying decisions. The organizational buying process typically involves a complex set of smaller decisions made or influenced by several individuals. The degree of involvement of group members in the procurement process varies from routine re-buys, in which the purchasing agent simply takes into account the preferences of others, to complex **new task buying** situations, in which a group plays an active role throughout the decision process.

The business marketer address three questions.

- Which organizational members take part in the buying process?
- What is each member's relative influence in the decision?
- What criteria are important to each member in evaluating a prospective supplier?

The salesperson who can correctly answer these questions is ideally prepared to meet the needs of a buying organization and has a high probability of becoming the chosen supplier.

The buying centre

A group of people in the organization who make a purchase decision are said to form the buying centre, sometimes referred to as the decision-making unit (DMU).

The concept of the buying centre provides rich insights into the role of group forces in organizational buying behaviour. The buying centre consists of those individuals who participate in the purchasing decision and who share the goals and risks arising from the decision.

Roles for members of the buying centre have been classified as: users, influencers, buyers, deciders and **gatekeepers** (Webster and Wind, 1972). The importance of different organizational roles varies according to the phase of the buying process. The make-up of a buying centre in terms of members and the roles fulfilled changes depending on organizational factors, the organization size and the buying situation.

Roles can be conceived fairly easily for purchasing products such as production materials. It is more difficult to specify roles for services.

Determining who within the company is the user of transportation for inbound materials or outbound products, who is the gatekeeper or who has the decider role is a difficult task. It is quite likely that several individuals occupy the same role within the buying centre.

Users

Users are those within the buying centre who will actually use the product being purchased. In manufacturing firms, for example, they are the employees who operate or service production equipment. When components are purchased, the users assemble the parts. In hospitals and other healthcare facilities, users may be nurses, physicians, or the technicians who operate medical equipment. Users with a high degree of expertise may help develop product specifications. They are especially important in the last phase of the buying process, follow-through. They can provide valuable feedback to sales representatives about how well the product performs. Users can influence the buying decision in a positive way by suggesting the need for purchased materials and by defining standards of product quality, or in a negative way by refusing to work with the materials of certain suppliers for any of several reasons.

Influencers

Influencers are members of the firm who directly or indirectly influence buying or usage decisions. They exert their influence by defining criteria which constrain the choices that can be considered in the purchase decision, or by providing information with which to evaluate alternative buying actions. Technical personnel are significant influencers, especially in the purchase of equipment or the development of new products or processes.

Buyers

Buyers have formal authority for selecting the supplier and managing the terms of the purchase. Depending upon the nature of the organization and its size, buyers may have such titles as purchasing manager, purchasing agent or buyer, or this responsibility and authority may reside with people other than those designated specifically as buyers – the production manager, for instance.

Deciders

Deciders are those members of the buying organization who have either formal or informal power to determine the final selection of suppliers. The buyer may be the decider, but it is also possible that the buying decision is made by somebody else and that the buyer is expected to ensure proper implementation of the decision.

In practice, it is not always easy to determine when the decision is actually made and who makes it. An engineer may develop a specification that can only be met by one supplier. Thus, although purchasing agents may be the only people with formal authority to sign a buying contract, they may not be the actual deciders.

Often the selling organization solidifies its relationship with the buying centre over time, which is called creeping commitment. The seller gradually wins enough support to obtain the order. In competitive bidding situations, the decision to purchase occurs when the envelopes are opened. In these cases, however, much depends on how the specifications are drawn up in the first place. Some salespeople work closely with the buying organization at that stage to change the specifications and influence the decision in their favour.

Gatekeepers

Gatekeepers control the flow of commercial (outside) information into the buying organization. Purchasing agents have been referred to as gatekeepers because they are often the first people that sales representatives contact. They are responsible for screening all potential sellers and allowing only the most qualified to gain access to key decision makers.

The control of information may be accomplished by disseminating printed information, such as advertisements, or by controlling which salesperson will speak to which individuals in the buying centre. For example, the purchasing agent might perform this screening role by opening the gate to the buying centre for some sales personnel and closing it to others.

As mentioned earlier, the buying process is seldom the same from one firm to the next, or even from one purchase to the next within a given firm. In each case, the decision-making process of the buying organization is affected by a number of factors.

The background of the buying centre members affects the buying process. Purchasing agents, engineers, users, and others in the organization have expectations that are formed largely by their experience.

Organizational buying is influenced by sources of information such as sales people, **exhibitions** and trade shows, direct mail, press releases, journal advertising, professional and technical conferences, trade news, and word-of-mouth.

So far, much of our discussion has focused on the buying centre. A more formalized buying centre, the buying committee, is used extensively in the resellers' market and by many business organizations, particularly when purchasing is centralized. In the resellers' market, organizations such as food chain retailers form buying committees that meet on a regular basis to decide on new product purchases.

Individual forces

Individuals, not organizations, make buying decisions. Each member of the buying centre has a unique personality, a particular set of experiences, a specified organizational function, and a perception of how best to achieve both personal and organizational goals. Importantly, research confirms that organizational members who perceive that they have an important personal stake and commitment in the buying decision will participate more forcefully in the decision process than their colleagues. To understand the organizational buyer, the marketer should be aware of individual perceptions of the buying situation.

4.6 Customer perceived value and customer satisfaction

In this book, customer satisfaction and customer value are closely linked together though assessing customer perceived value sometimes goes beyond tracking customer satisfaction.

Delivering superior value to customers is an ongoing concern of management in many business markets. Knowing where value resides from the standpoint of the customer has become critical for suppliers because greater levels of customer satisfaction lead to greater levels of customer loyalty and repeat buying. This again leads to a higher degree of commitment and, ultimately, higher market share and higher profit (see Figure 4.16). In fact, delivering superior value to customers is key to creating and sustaining long-term industrial relationships.

As seen in Figure 4.16, we will concentrate on the measurement of customer satisfaction in this section. Later on we will discuss the implications of customer satisfaction on other key measures.

Figure 4.16 Firm X's customer satisfaction model – an example

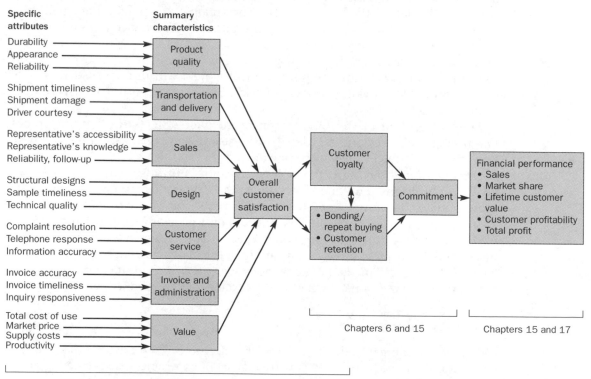

Measuring customer satisfaction/customer value

Value is perceived subjectively by customers. Customers are not homogeneous; therefore, different customer segments perceive different values for the same product. Different people in the customer organization are involved in the purchasing process. Whereas in some cases, firms may have established a formal buying centre, in other cases the people may be part of an informal group. Also, the number of people involved in the purchasing process and their positions may vary across customer organizations.

These members of a buyer's organization have different perceptions of a supplier's value delivery. Therefore, in a customer value audit, it is necessary to identify and assess the value perceptions of all key people involved in the purchasing process. Such a multiple-person approach is considered to be more reliable by far than single-person studies.

In addition, within the supplier's organization, opinions of how customers view the company's products differ among functional areas, i.e., general management, marketing and sales management, salespeople or customer service personnel. With value perceptions differing between customers and suppliers and even within these organizations, identifying and bridging perceptual gaps become critical steps in value delivery.

Two examples of customer satisfaction surveys are given in Exhibits 4.5 and 4.6.

Exhibit 4.5	**Measurement of Firm X's customer satisfaction**

Firm X produces a component subassembly sold to about 150 customers. All customer firms were included in the research. In each firm, three or four functional areas were involved in the purchase decision and use of the product, so each of those areas was included, for a sample of 500 current customers. Two hundred past customers and an equal number of competitors' customers were also surveyed.

The questionnaire had three parts:

● demographic data
● determining the relative importance of each attribute
● measuring Firm X's performance on each attribute.

Current and past customers were asked to rate Firm X's actual performance. For the competitors' customers, a disguised approach was used. Those respondents were asked to assess the top four firms in the industry, one of which was Firm X.

If the respondents had no actual experience with a particular firm, they were asked to present their perceptions of what they thought the firm was like. Initially, respondents were asked to rate the importance of each of seven broad categories. Then, for each category, they were asked to rate the importance of each attribute on a seven-point scale, with 1 representing not important and 7 representing very important. Firm X's performance was measured using a seven-point scale, with 1 representing very poor performance and 7 representing very good.

Once the performance evaluations and importance ratings from current and previous customers were collected, the overall mean value was plotted for the sample of each characteristic by combining the results into a performance/importance grid (Figure 4.17).

Exhibit 4.5 continued

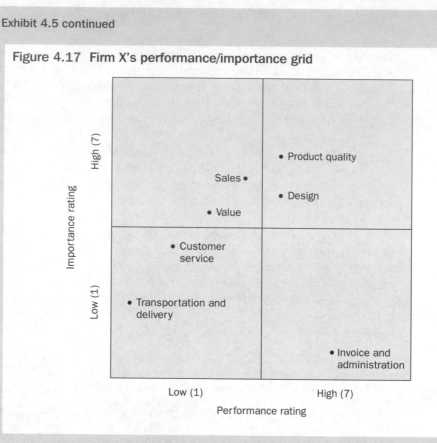

Figure 4.17 Firm X's performance/importance grid

Firm X's executives were delighted to notice that their quality improvement efforts had not been misdirected. Both product quality and design were essential to customers, and Firm X was viewed as reasonably good in both characteristics, though there was certainly room for improvement. More troubling were the sales and value characteristics. Both areas were reasonably important to customers, but performance was much weaker than expected. Customer service was apparently a little less important than sales and value, but its performance was also worse. These three characteristics held some very clear potential for improving customer satisfaction. Because transportation was contracted out to a trucking firm, the problems in shipment timeliness and transit damage would require a joint effort to resolve. The new automated billing system was apparently working well; customers rated performance on invoice and administration fairly highly. However, this function was not important to the customers.

Source: adapted from Naumann *et al*. (2001).

Exhibit 4.6	Measurement of customer satisfaction at Grundfos

Facts about the Grundfos Group (www.grundfos.com)

Products

With an annual production of 10 million pump units, Grundfos is one of the world's leading pump manufacturers. Circulator pumps, submersible pumps, and centrifugal pumps are the three major product groups. Today, Grundfos is the world's largest manufacturer of circulator pumps, with approximately 40 per cent of the world market for these pumps. In 2000 the net turnover for the Grunfos Group was approximately €1.3 billion.

In addition to pumps, Grundfos manufactures electric motors for the pumps and has considerable production of electric motors for separate merchandising. Furthermore, Grundfos develops and sells state-of-the-art electronics for pump controls and other systems.

Applications

Circulator pumps are used for heating, ventilation and air-conditioning in houses, office buildings, hotels, etc. In industry the pumps are used in processes as well as in the area of plant maintenance; they are also important built-in parts in OEM products. In the water-supply and waste-water segment Grundfos offers a wide range of reliable pumps for irrigation, greenhouses and for municipal, private and industrial water supply as well as sewage applications.

Global extension

The Grundfos Group is represented by 58 companies in 43 countries. In addition, Grundfos products are merchandised by distributors in a large number of countries.

Customers

Typical customers of Grundfos pumps are: installers, wholesalers, contractors, OEMs, consultants, end users. The following questionnaire is different for each customer group. Specific questions are drawn for each customer group from the following full list of questions.

Source: adapted from www.grundfos.com.

Exhibit 4.6 continued

Please help us to improve ...

Respondent name	Your name:
Customer/company name	Company name:
Address 1	Address 1:
Address 2	Address 2:
Zip/postal code	Zip/postal code:
City	City:
State	State:
Phone number	Phone number
Your e-mail address	Your e-mail address:

Current contact details

To enable Grundfos to maintain an accurate listing of customer contacts, please check that the contact details above are correct. If details are incorrect or missing please write the correct details in the right side above.

Your general opinion

	No, not at all	No	Neither/ nor	Yes	Yes, very much
In general are you satisfied dealing with Grundfos?	☐	☐	☐	☐	☐
Is Grundfos a supplier worth recommending to others?	☐	☐	☐	☐	☐
Is Grundfos your preferred supplier of pumps?	☐	☐	☐	☐	☐

Your overall satisfaction

In the left side below please mark the one box which most accurately reflects the importance of each feature in relation to your organisation. In the right side please mark the box which most accurately represents your level of satisfaction with Grundfos.

Not Important	Less Important	Quite Important	Very Important	Extremely Important			Very dis-satisfied	Dissatisfied	Neither/ nor	Satisfied	Very satisfied
☐	☐	☐	☐	☐	A	Telephone contact	☐	☐	☐	☐	☐
☐	☐	☐	☐	☐	B	Grundfos product quality	☐	☐	☐	☐	☐
☐	☐	☐	☐	☐	C	Grundfos sales personnel	☐	☐	☐	☐	☐
☐	☐	☐	☐	☐	D	Order handling and delivery performance	☐	☐	☐	☐	☐
☐	☐	☐	☐	☐	E	Product technical support	☐	☐	☐	☐	☐
☐	☐	☐	☐	☐	F	Maintenance and repair services	☐	☐	☐	☐	☐
☐	☐	☐	☐	☐	G	Product information and documentation	☐	☐	☐	☐	☐
☐	☐	☐	☐	☐	H	Supporting your sales	☐	☐	☐	☐	☐
☐	☐	☐	☐	☐	I	Complaints handling	☐	☐	☐	☐	☐

Specific quality aspects

Based on your recent experiences please rate Grundfos' quality level on the following specific items. You may not feel able to assess all items, in which case please simply skip it and proceed to the next.

Telephone contact

	Very poor	Poor	Fair	Good	Excellent
A1 Telephone/switchboard access and waiting time	☐	☐	☐	☐	☐
A2 Ease of getting in contact with the person you need to talk with	☐	☐	☐	☐	☐

Additional comments/problems experienced regarding Grundfos' telephone contact:

_____

_____

Exhibit 4.6 continued

Please help us to improve ...

Product quality

	Very poor	Poor	Fair	Good	Excellent
B1　Suitability of our product range as compared with your needs	☐	☐	☐	☐	☐
B2　Reliability and durability of our products	☐	☐	☐	☐	☐
B3　Ease to install and user-friendliness of products	☐	☐	☐	☐	☐

Additional comments/problems experienced regarding Grundfos' product quality:

_____
_____

Grundfos sales personnel

	Very poor	Poor	Fair	Good	Excellent
C1　Accessibility of Grundfos sales staff	☐	☐	☐	☐	☐
C2　Giving prompt and accurate responses to your inquiries	☐	☐	☐	☐	☐
C3　General technical understanding of applications	☐	☐	☐	☐	☐
C4　Courtesy and responsiveness of sales staff	☐	☐	☐	☐	☐

Additional comments/problems experienced regarding Grundfos' sales personnel:

_____
_____

Order handling and delivery

	Very poor	Poor	Fair	Good	Excellent
D1　Quotations are provided promptly and accurately	☐	☐	☐	☐	☐
D2　Prompt confirmations of orders and delivery time	☐	☐	☐	☐	☐
D3　Prompt, adequate notice if a delivery is delayed	☐	☐	☐	☐	☐
D4　Ability to offer products for delivery when you need them	☐	☐	☐	☐	☐
D5　Consistently meeting delivery dates on time as promised	☐	☐	☐	☐	☐

Additional comments/problems experienced regarding Grundfos' order handling and delivery:

_____
_____

Product technical support

	Very poor	Poor	Fair	Good	Excellent
E1　Provision of competent product selection assistance	☐	☐	☐	☐	☐
E2　Provision of quick solutions to your technical problems	☐	☐	☐	☐	☐
E3　Product training offered by Grundfos	☐	☐	☐	☐	☐

Additional comments/problems experienced regarding Grundfos' technical support:

_____
_____

BE › THINK › INNOVATE ›　　　　GRUNDFOS ⋈ ▶

Exhibit 4.6 continued

Please help us to improve ...

Maintenance and repair service

	Very poor	Poor	Fair	Good	Excellent
F1 Speed of pump repair service offered	☐	☐	☐	☐	☐
F2 Ability to supply spare parts when you need them	☐	☐	☐	☐	☐
F3 Fairness of warranty decisions	☐	☐	☐	☐	☐
F4 User-friendly service manuals and spare parts lists	☐	☐	☐	☐	☐

Additional comments/problems experienced regarding Grundfos' maintenance and repair service:

_____

_____

Product information and documentation

	Very poor	Poor	Fair	Good	Excellent
G1 Information regarding new products	☐	☐	☐	☐	☐
G2 Understandable and informative catalogues and data leaflets	☐	☐	☐	☐	☐
G3 User-friendly installation and operating instructions	☐	☐	☐	☐	☐

Additional comments/problems experienced regarding Grundfos' product information and documentation:

_____

_____

Supporting your sales

	Very poor	Poor	Fair	Good	Excellent
H1 Provision of advertising and promotional support	☐	☐	☐	☐	☐

Additional comments/problems experienced regarding Grundfos' sales support:

_____

_____

Complaints handling

	Very poor	Poor	Fair	Good	Excellent
I1 General attitude towards complaints	☐	☐	☐	☐	☐
I2 Speed of complaints handling	☐	☐	☐	☐	☐
I3 Ability to provide an acceptable solution	☐	☐	☐	☐	☐

Additional comments/problems experienced regarding Grundfos' complaints handling:

_____

_____

Partnership development

	Very poor	Poor	Fair	Good	Excellent
J1 Responsiveness to your business needs and special requests	☐	☐	☐	☐	☐
J2 Attention to what could go wrong and then take measures to prevent or minimise problems	☐	☐	☐	☐	☐
J3 Grundfos' commitment to achieve continous improvements in serving your business needs	☐	☐	☐	☐	☐

Additional comments/ problems experienced regarding the Grundfos partnership:

_____

_____

UserId / Password

3

BE > THINK > INNOVATE >

GRUNDFOS

Exhibit 4.6 continued

Please help us to improve ...

Grundfos' reputation

Please mark to what extent you find that the statements below are good descriptions of your colleagues' or customers' impressions of Grundfos.

	No, not at all	No	Neither/ nor	Yes	Yes, very much
Grundfos has a reputation for high quality	☐	☐	☐	☐	☐
Grundfos develops environmentally friendly products	☐	☐	☐	☐	☐
Grundfos is the leader in pump technology	☐	☐	☐	☐	☐

Your business with Grundfos

What percentage of your annual pump purchases this year do you expect to buy from Grundfos?

_____

If you had to prioritise, which one thing may GRUNDFOS improve first of all, in the way we are serving your business?

_____

_____

	Yes	No
Will you help us to further improve our service to you by answering this survey again next year?	☐	☐

	Printed questionnaire	On the Internet
If 'Yes', how do you prefer to reply to any future survey?	☐	☐

Thank you for completing this questionnaire, and helping us to offer a better service to you in the future.

BE ＞ THINK ＞ INNOVATE ＞

GRUNDFOS

Customer satisfaction, loyalty and bonding

The first qualitative criterion is customer satisfaction. Satisfaction arises if the customer's experience fulfils or exceeds expectations. When satisfaction and customer penetration are cross-referenced as in Table 4.2, the upper left corner is the most interesting, where **penetration** is high, but satisfaction low. This situation may arise when satisfaction and loyalty are changing at different rates.

With weak loyalty, customer recommendations or friendly customer feedback cannot be expected. Well-founded loyalty (upper right corner of Table 4.2), where there is high quantitative loyalty and satisfaction, should be the aim, if all the benefits of loyalty are to be enjoyed.

Table 4.2 Customer satisfaction loyalty and bonding

	Low satisfaction	High satisfaction
High customer penetration	Weak loyalty	Well-founded loyalty
Low customer penetration	No loyalty	Potential loyalty

Source: adapted from Thurau and Hansen (2000), p. 33.

On the other hand, loyalty may be missing even though there is customer satisfaction, for example where there is some kind of barrier to a more intensive relationship. If this is the case, then these barriers have to be broken down if RM is to be successful.

Customer bonding may be seen as a process which influences customers, and customer loyalty as the result of this process. We can take three different perspectives in defining customer bonding and loyalty. These perspectives are described in more detail below (see also the summary in Table 4.3).

Suppliers will define customer bonding as a bundle of activities which builds up intensive relationships with customers, including contact opportunities, barriers to a change of supplier or creation of customer preferences for the supplier (which may be based on technology, materials, staff, etc.).

Table 4.3 Customer bonding: three different perspectives

Supplier	Supplier-customer relationship	Customer
Customer bonding activities	Purchase behaviour	Attitudes and intentions
Building up contact centres, barriers to change, customer preferences etc.	Interaction between supplier and customer, atmosphere in supplier-customer relationship	Satisfaction, preferences, willingness to repurchase from, or contact, supplier
Customer bonding = bundle of activities which achieve a closer customer relationship	Customer loyalty = consecutive transactions (exchange of information, goods or money) between supplier and customer within a certain time period, good atmosphere in the relationship	Customer loyalty = positive attitude towards supplier combined with a willingness to perform further transaction

Source: adapted from Thurau and Hansen (2000), p. 31.

Looking at the relationships between supplier and customer, customer loyalty can be defined and measured in terms of the amount and the quality of transactions between both parties. Transactions cover, for example, the number of contacts or shopping visits, or the degree of customer penetration (the proportion of a customer's total buying volume accounted for by one supplier). The qualitative side of transactions refers to the atmosphere in which they take place, i.e. the climate of the relationship during the contact between both sides.

Customers will declare themselves loyal to a supplier through feelings and perceptions of (high) satisfaction, through positive attitudes and through certain preferences for the supplier, meaning that customers will be willing to repurchase from this supplier.

Increasing customer skills through investments in customers

One effective way in which manufacturers might increase customer retention could be to increase customers' post-purchase skills through targeted investments in the customers themselves. Such a strategy is based on an interpretation of the *customer as a co-producer* in the value-creation process. If such a strategy is to succeed, a significant amount of product value must be initially inaccessible to the customer (e.g. the customer should be unable to use certain product features). At the same time, it must be possible to give the consumer access to this additional value by increasing his or her skills. Such an increase in customer skills should produce a higher level of customer satisfaction and also have positive effects on other dimensions of the quality of the customer-company relationship. Hence, an investment in customers aims to improve their post-purchase skills, for example by increasing their ability to use the full range of product features or to maintain the product adequately (Thurau and Hansen, 2000).

4.7 Customization – tailoring the offer to the individual customer

Traditional marketing often views the customer as a passive participant in the exchange process until the time of the sale. Customization sees the customer as an active participant at every stage of the product development, purchase and consumption process, and as the co-producer of the product and service offering.

Instead of accepting off-the-shelf products, customers are creating their own products, from configuring computers to building their own CDs. New products no longer come fully formed out of the laboratories, but arise through an interactive process of working directly with the market. Each customized product is a result of a co-design and production process of the customers and the firm. When this process is repeated across a number of customers, new insights emerge about customer preferences. Attributes and offerings that are not attractive can be dropped and those that are frequently requested can be enhanced.

By combining customer configuration with a mass production strategy, companies can also use the insights from the customized products to shape their mass-produced line. Customer design choices may catch emerging trends.

Early customization efforts were in the form of 'made to order' products and services (e.g., furniture or tailored suits), which, however, had long lead times and were not tied to flexible manufacturing systems. The recent advances in flexible manufacturing coupled with the collection of detailed information about customers, and advances in **database marketing** and its associated analyses enables firms to offer products tailored to customers' needs (customization), but at costs that are almost the same as that of standardized production and mass marketing. This shift is illustrated in Figure 4.18.

As shown in Figure 4.18, mass customization changed the centuries-old trade-off between tailoring a product to the needs of specific customers and the costs or time associated with delivering the desired product. Continuing innovations in flexible manufacturing, inventory management, and integration of global supply chains have provided further impetus in favour of delivering customized products quickly and at reasonable costs.

Individually and collectively, customers now have the means to directly influence a company's policies and strategies. For example, the growth of online product communities is profoundly altering the power structure in the exchange process.

Database marketing offers alternative approaches by which firms can tailor individual offerings and products to increase customer loyalty, volume of purchases, and repeat purchases. First, companies that have made a commitment to one-to-one marketing are good at managing this information and communications process. In this way, companies can actually offer customers fewer options than mass marketers, because only the relevant options are visible. Second, firms can use innovative software to offer creative recommendations to a purchaser of music, movies, books, etc., based on related products purchased by other customers who

Figure 4.18 The process towards customization

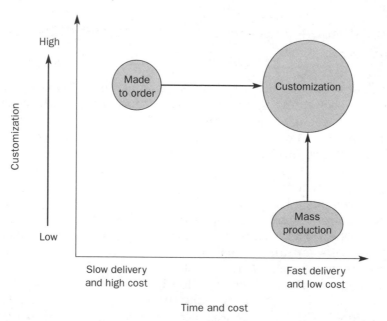

Source: adapted from Wind and Rangaswamy (2001), p. 18.

purchase the same product(s). Third, companies can ask customers to provide them information about their preferences, and then design products and services to conform to the stated preferences.

While traditional marketing environments (mass-produced products sold through mass markets to target segments) will continue to play an important role in the economy, and while an increasing number of companies experiment with mass customization and personalization, the new type of marketing characterized by customization represents a growing and increasingly important segment of the business. In the online environment, marketers are able to better identify customer preferences and either focus their messages and products and services on meeting the needs of each individual, or allow the customer to customize the message and products and services they desire.

The challenges of customization

Customization also raises a number of challenges including issues related to obtaining information from customers, the identification of the intangible factors that can make or break an offering, enhanced customer expectations, the need for limiting the complexity of options, and the required changes to the entire marketing and business strategy of the firm.

In the following, some of these challenging factors are discussed (Wind and Rangaswamy, 2001).

Knowledge exchange with customers

A key challenge is that for customization to work effectively there needs to be exchange of information and knowledge between companies and customers. This requires the company to 'open up' some of its internal processes and structures to its customers. It also requires customers to be willing to share their attitudes, preferences, and purchase patterns with the company on an ongoing basis. Currently, the knowledge transfer occurs because of the novelty of the new medium, and because both the customers and the company become better off to some extent with such a knowledge transfer. However, with increasing online competition and concerns about privacy, companies need to design privacy guidelines and incentive structures carefully to facilitate the knowledge exchange between themselves and their customers.

First, consider the privacy aspects. It is important to recognize that companies can obtain and provide information useful for customization without having to know the identity of the customer.

Second, consider the incentive aspects. Customers must feel that they benefit in some measurable way by providing information to the company. This is more likely to happen if the company puts in place a structure in which it brings in its own knowledge in the service of its customers.

Real-time conjoint analysis studies that allow the company to assess consumers' preferences while offering the consumers the results, as an aid in their decision process, have great potential to offer value to both the company and the consumers.

In general, as consumers become more empowered, one can also see the further development of search engines and **decision support systems** to help consumers make better decisions including the customization of the product and services they design and the associated information they seek.

Higher customer expectations

The customization process creates higher expectations on the part of customers. They expect the product they receive to match their wants and needs perfectly. If it fails to meet these higher expectations, they are likely to be far more disappointed and dissatisfied than if they had bought a standard product.

Companies need to have the marketing and manufacturing capabilities to maintain a one-to-one relationship and to deliver what the customer wants efficiently. At the core of Dell's customized computer sales is an assembly process that can rapidly deliver exactly what the customers request. Yet these technological solutions have to be augmented with a marketing communication programme aimed at managing customer expectations.

Limiting the options offered to customers

The temptation in the customization process is to give customers too many options, but this may lead to psychological shutdown. The key is to offer just the right amount of variety so customers are presented with the right choices without being overwhelmed.

The decision of how much customization to offer depends not only on consumers' preferences and ability to handle the choices, but also on the nature of the product and its requirements to assure quality performance, capabilities of the available technology, the competitive offerings, and the implications of the target positioning, and value proposition.

One way to limit the options to the feasible set is to present standardized option packages, as is common in the car industry. This gives customers a starting point in developing more customized products. The car industry uses these options very effectively, but does not do as good a job at inviting customers to use these options packages. The manufacturers generally offer many options, but customers typically buy the cars that are on display.

4.8 Summary

Consumers' decision-making processes are classified largely on the basis of high and low involvement with the product and the extensiveness of the search for information. High-involvement products or services are psychologically important to the consumer. To reduce the psychological and financial risks associated with buying a high-involvement item, consumers engage in a complex decision-making process. The five major steps in the process are problem identification, information search, evaluation of alternatives, purchase, and post-purchase evaluation. The way in which these steps are carried out differs between products and services.

Most purchase decisions have low consumer involvement. Therefore, consumers do not engage in an extensive search for information or make a detailed evaluation of alternative brands. Such search-and-evaluation behaviour is more likely to occur with products than with services. Buying behaviour is strongly influenced by psychological and personal characteristics that vary across individual consumers and countries. Information and social pressures received from other people influence consumers' wants, needs, evaluations, and preferences for various products and brand names.

By definition organizational customers can be grouped into three main categories:

- good and services producers (raw materials, components, software, office supplies)
- intermediates (resellers)
- public organizations/government.

Organizational buyers purchase goods and services for further production for use in operations, or for resale to other customers. In contrast, individuals and households buy for their own use and consumption. These two types of markets also differ in numerous other ways, including their demand characteristics, their market demographics, and their buyer-supplier relationships.

The buying task is determined by three interrelated factors:

- the newness of the problem to the decision makers
- the information needs of the people in the buying centre
- the number of new alternative products and/or suppliers to be considered.

Based on these factors, there are three buying situations: straight re-buy, modified re-buy, and new-task buying. Organizational purchasing often involves people from various departments.

The individuals involved in the buying process form what is called a buying centre and share information relevant to the purchase of a particular product or service. One of the marketer's most important tasks is to identify which individuals in the buying centre are responsible for a particular product, determine the relative influence of each, identify the decision criteria of each, and understand how each group member perceives the firm and its products.

These participants in the buying process can be grouped as users, influencers, gatekeepers, buyers, and buy in larger quantities – and purchase more complex and expensive goods and services – than consumers do. Differences between the business and consumer markets are summarized in Table 4.4.

Table 4.4 Differences between the business and consumer markets

	B-t-B market	B-t-C market
Market structure	Geographically concentrated Relatively few buyers Oligopolistic competition	Geographically dispersed Mass markets (often millions) Pure competition
Size of purchase	Often extremely large	Usually small
Buyer behaviour	Functional involvement Rational/task motives prevail Stable relationships Professionalism, expertise	Family involvement Social/emotional motives prevail Less buyer-seller loyalty Less trained, often inexperienced
Buying influences	Committees, technical experts, and management are all involved in decision making (buying centre)	The individual, household members, friends and relatives
Decision making	Distinct, observable stages Often group decisions	Vague, mental stages Usually individual decisions
Supplier relationship	Long-term contracts and supplier involvement	Many single purchases

The Internet is playing an increasing role in both B-t-B and B-t-C markets. Websites enable organizations to promote brand values, reduce printing costs, attract and qualify prospects and leads, and foster customer loyalty. Sites can also expand the customer database, provide customer service, and showcase and sell products.

The interactive age is providing businesses with the potential to strengthen RM and generate new customers. Consumers benefit from the Internet through better possibilities of providing relevant information (quality, prices etc.) when comparing and evaluating product or brand alternatives in the buying process.

Case study 4.2 Manchester United

Trying to establish a global brand through an alliance with New York Yankees

Manchester United has developed into one of the most famous and financially successful football clubs in the world, being recognized in virtually every country, even countries with little interest in the sport. In December 2000 Manchester United was rated the world's richest football club for the third year in a row by Deloitte & Touche.

Manchester United's 1999 summer tour of Australia and China has helped to raise the international profile of the brand further. The four-match tour attracted huge crowds, with about 70,000 spectators per game. The tour was designed to take the club to places where there was support and where they could build upon it. The overseas supporters of Manchester United do not get many opportunities to see the team play live.

Prior to the Asian-Pacific tour an agreement was signed between the club, sportswear suppliers Umbro and the Australian Woolmark company to market a new fabric for the club's shirts for the 2000-2001 season.

Furthermore, the club has launched a free Internet service (www.manutd.com). Although it was not the first UK club to offer free Internet access – Arsenal launched its venture as early as the summer of 1997 – it has been the first to offer its service with a worldwide audience in mind.

1999 was a fantastic year for Manchester United when they won the treble: The Premier League (National) Championship, the FA Cup and the European Champions League.

In 2000 and 2001, they won their 6th and 7th Premiership titles. Manchester United was also the winner of the International Cup for the first time.

In the following we will present some key figures from the Manchester United financial report 2000. Turnover, all of which arises from the Group's principal activity, can be broken down into its main components as shown in Table 4.5. In 2001, the profit before tax was £21.8 million.

Table 4.5 Manchester United key figures

	2000 £million	1999 £million
Gate receipts and programme sales	36.6	41.9
Television	30.5	22.5
Sponsorship	18.5	17.5
Conference and catering	6.7	7.2
Merchandising and other	23.6	21.6
Total turnover	116.0	110.7
Operating profit before amortization of players and exceptional costs	30.1	32.3
Net interest receivable	0.5	1.7
Profit before player trading and exceptional costs	30.6	34.0
Other costs	13.8	11.6
Profit before tax	16.8	22.4

Turnover

Turnover for the year 2000 amounted to £116 million compared to £110.7 million in 1999.

Case study 4.2 continued

The increase was mainly derived from increased television income as a result of the revamped European Champions League, although this was partially offset by a reduction in gate receipts due to fewer games being played at Old Trafford during the year 2000.

Television income rose significantly from £22.5 million to £30.5 million in 2000. Additional revenue was received from the revamped and extended European Champions League and from the three competitions in which the team participated as reigning European champions, the UEFA Super Cup, the World Club Championship and the Inter Continental Cup.

In 2000, merchandizing turnover was boosted by the launch of a number of official Manchester United retail outlets overseas in conjunction with international retail partners.

During 2000, Manchester United's flagship stores opened in Singapore, Dublin, Kuala Lumpur (Malaysia) and Cape Town (South Africa). In addition, the two financial services products launched in 1998, the 'Save and Support' savings account and the Manchester United MasterCard, have been very successful and assisted in the increase in turnover in this area.

Other promotional activities in 2000 were as follows.

Sponsorship and new media

- £30 million four-year sponsorship deal with Vodafone.
- New £1.6 billion FA Premier League television contracts from season 2001/02.
- Expanded online access to the Club through the official website: www.manutd.com.
- MUTV – the TV channel that lives and breathes Manchester United, seven days a week.

However, MUTV, the joint venture television channel with BSkyB (owning 10 per cent of Manchester United shares) and Granada, continued to incur losses in the year although at a lower level.

The Manchester United team reached the quarter finals of the European Champions League before being eliminated by the eventual winners, Real Madrid. The operating profit from this competition was £16.9 million (1999 – £8.8 million), representing 56 per cent (1999 – 27 per cent) of the operating profit before player amortization. This competition is therefore an increasingly important element in Manchester United's overall earnings.

In April 2001, Manchester United was eliminated again in the quarter finals of the Champions League, this time by Bayern Munich. After this happened the shares of Manchester United began to fall and it has been a problem since.

Hotels

Manchester United has interests in two hotel projects. The Quality Hotel adjacent to the Old Trafford stadium in which Manchester United has a 25 per cent stake continues to trade profitably. The company has recently taken a 31.4 per cent stake in a 120 bedroom hotel (Sleep In) to be built adjacent to the Trafford Centre shopping complex, just a couple of miles from Old Trafford.

Sponsorship

Manchester United's objective is to seek new alliances, which will encourage and reward investment in the club to the mutual advantage of both parties. This new model is based upon aligning with a company. It could contribute to the fan base with added value products and services, which were previously unavailable to them.

The new arrangement with Vodafone combines a traditional sponsorship element with a transactional aspect, with Manchester United benefiting from both. It will also link the mobile, multi-media operator in the development of a wireless Internet access portal.

ManUMobile has been launched as the first WAP-service of its kind to provide all the latest club news as it happens. Text messages provide live match day updates, kick-off times and other stories as they happen. The WAP site provides full news, match information, player biographies and a lot more, enabling supporters to keep up to date with their favourite team wherever they are.

Case study 4.2 continued

Finally, a partnership with McVitie's Jaffa Cakes has also been established which creates an official sponsor for their Academy.

Though the senior management of Manchester United is satisfied with the financial results in 2000 they are a little worried about the sharp increase in the staff costs, especially of the players. Lately, David Beckham has pushed his salary further ahead of the other players in the club.

Manchester United enters an alliance with the famous US baseball team New York Yankees

On February 7, 2001 the two sporting goliaths Manchester United and YankeeNets (The New York Yankees' parent company) joined marketing forces. In many respects, the United-Yankees' marriage is a match made in heaven. They are the leaders of their sports – so ridiculously rich, attractive and successful that people either love them or hate them.

This tie-up is just the latest instalment of Manchester United's quest for world domination and there can be no doubt that it is the dominant global brand within football.

The Manchester United name is known far beyond the boundaries of Europe, from Africa to China, from India to Latin America. It was widely noted that the words 'football club' had been removed from its logo recently and Manchester United is referred to as a marketing brand.

This was obviously not what many club supporters wanted to hear and there were serious concerns voiced about the 'Americanization of Manchester United'. The evidence for this is certainly not lacking, as the YankeeNets deal followed an agreed US$440m, 15-year licensing deal with Nike, starting in August 2002.

YankeeNets also finalized a deal in December 2000, along similar lines to the Manchester United tie-in, in order to link up with American football team, the New York Giants. This is certainly not an exclusive deal and both are free to look elsewhere for other relationships to bolster their positions of commercial power.

The British may well be getting all worked up about the potential fallout from the deal and its impact on football, but the fact remains that the average American simply does not care about soccer or 'English football'. The average US man is incredibly 'americentric' in his sports preferences, which means ice hockey, baseball, basketball and American football.

It is interesting to note that women's football has a strong presence in the USA, with many of the US squad now being high-earning celebrities. However, the men's game in the USA does not attract the glitz and glamour that it is associated with in most of the rest of the world, possibly because it is often thought of as a girls' game there.

Still, the staff at YankeeNets apparently know the North American sports markets better than anyone and they believe that football has developed positively in the USA over the past ten years. They are confident that there is definitely a market for what they call Manchester United content in the USA. Their expertise will certainly help the club in preparations for its mooted pre-season tour of North America in the summer of 2003, which is also when the American Soccer Federation is trying to bring the FIFA World Club Championship to the USA.

It may well be the case that in cities such as New York there is enough of an immigrant population to make a Manchester United marketing programme viable. The other strong link may be with the Latin American countries, which care passionately about football, but which are also quite keen on baseball.

Of course, the concern is how many people in the UK really do or possibly care about baseball? Certainly not enough to fill Old Trafford in Manchester.

The overall consensus is that in the short term this deal means little more than joint merchandising, but it is the medium and longer term that could be interesting.

Although the cultural and social factors do not point towards Americans becoming passionate football lovers in the near future, it might also be dangerous to ignore the alliance between the two marketing juggernauts.

Case study 4.2 continued

Questions

1. How would you describe Manchester United customers on the:

    (a) B-t-C market
    (b) B-t-C market?

    Which of the two markets is most important for Manchester United?

2. What are the short-term and long-term benefits and pitfalls of the Manchester United-New York Yankees alliance for both partners?

3. What are the prerequisites for establishing Manchester United as a global brand?

4. Is the Manchester United-New York Yankees alliance the right way for realizing a global brand strategy?

Source: adapted from: BBC (2001), MAP (2001)

QUESTIONS FOR DISCUSSION

1. What specific factors at the time of purchase may affect the buying decision on the B-t-C market?

2. What is the difference between Generations X and Y?

3. How does the demand for industrial products differ from the demand for consumer products?

4. What are the major differences between consumer and industrial buying behaviour?

5. How does the buying situation by class of purchase affect the organizational buying process?

6. What are the differences between the traditional 'buy grid' model and the 'extended buy grid' model?

7. Describe government buying procedures. Why is market orientation less important when selling to governments?

8. What is the buying centre in a company? Describe its functions and the implications for the selling organization.

REFERENCES

Adage Global (2001), *McDonald's taps DDB German shop for pork burger launch*, **www.adageglobal.com**, April 24.

BBC (2001), Defeat hits Man Utd shares, *BBC News*, **http://news.bbc.co.uk**, April 19.

Boleslav, M. (2001), Slav Motown, *The Economist*, January 4.

Boyd, H.W., Walther O.C., Larréché, J.C. (1998), *Marketing Management*, Irwin /McGraw-Hill, 3rd edition.

Brown and Walsch (2000), Formulators outsource to make up lost margins, *Chemical Week*, New York, Dec. 6, pp. 51–62

Customer Loyalty Today (2000), 'Unattractive' Skoda builds database for 2001 push, *Customer Loyalty Today*, August 25.

De Boer, L., Labro, E. and Morlacchi, P (2001), A review of methods supporting supplier selection, *European Journal of Purchasing & Supply Management*, vol. 7, pp. 75–89.

Dent, H.S. (1999), *The Roaring 2000s Investor*, Simon and Schuster, New York.

Friedrich, S.A (2000), Was ist 'Core' und was ist 'Non-core'? *IO Management*, no. 4, pp. 18–23.

Holt, S. (2000), Managing global networks: the role of the global account manager, *IMP Conference 2000*, Bath (CD-ROM article).

Kotler, P. (2000), *Marketing Management*, Prentice Hall, Englewood Cliffs, NJ.

Kraljic, P. (1983), Purchasing must become supply management, *Harvard Business Review*, vol. 61, no. 5, pp. 109–17.

Laurent, G. and Kapferer, J. (1985), Measuring consumer involvement profiles, *Journal of Marketing Research*, vol. 22, no. 2, pp. 41–53.

Lee, C. K.-C. and Collins, B. A. (2000), Family decision making and coalition patterns, *European Journal of Marketing*, vol. 34, no. 9, pp. 1181–98.

MAP (2001), United look to conquer America, *MAP*, March 13.

Maslow, A.H. (1970), *Motivation and Personality*, Harper & Row Publishers Inc., 2nd ed.

Mudambi, S. (forthcoming), Branding importance in business-to-business markets: three buyer clusters, *Industrial Marketing Management*.

Naumann, E., Jackson, D.W. and Rosenbaum, M.S (2001), How to implement a customer satisfaction program, *Business Horizons*, January–February, pp. 37–46.

Nellore, R. and Söderquist, K. (2000), Portfolio approaches to procurement – analysing the missing link to specifications, *Long Range Planning*, vol. 33, pp. 245–67.

Osborne, J. (2000), Bootstrap marketing: taking on Procter & Gamble, *Inc. Magazine*, October 1, pp. 20–2.

Pardo, C. (1999), Key account management in the business-to-business field: a French overview. *Journal of Business & Industrial Marketing*, vol. 14, no 4, pp. 276–90.

Robinson, P. J., Faris, C. W and Wind, Y. (1967), *Industrial Buying and Creative Marketing*, Allyn and Bacon, Boston.

Thurau, T. H. and Hansen, U. (2000), *Relationship Marketing – Gaining competitive advantage through customer satisfaction and customer retention*, Springer Verlag, Berlin/Heidelberg.

Webster Jr, F. E. and Wind, Y. (1972), A general model for understanding organizational buying behaviour, *Journal of Marketing*, vol. 36, April, pp. 12–19.

Weiss, M. J. (2000), The demographic investor, *American Demographics*, December (outline on **www.demographics.com**).

Wind, J. and Rangaswamy, A. (2001), Customerization: the next revolution in customization, *Journal of Interactive Marketing*, vol. 15, no. 1, winter, pp. 13–32.

Chapter 5

Competitor analysis and intelligence

LEARNING OBJECTIVES

After studying this chapter you should be able to:

- integrate competition into an environmental analysis.
- discuss competition and competitors at different levels:
  - budget competition
  - core benefit competition
  - product class competition
  - brand competition.
- specify the levels in competitor awareness.
- describe how to design a competitor intelligence (CI) system.
- evaluate the information sources for CI.
- specify the contents of a competitor audit.
- evaluate the strengths and weaknesses of competitors.
- assess current strategies of main competitors.
- give examples of how to evaluate the strengths and weaknesses of competitors.
- assess current strategies of main competitors.
- outline possible response patterns of main competitors.

Case study 5.1 Viagra

A pharmaceutical superstar is facing future competition

The US pharmaceutical industry has been restructured. There have been several mergers and acquisitions.

Astra and Zeneca are now one company, Hoechst Marion Roussel and RhonePoulenc Rorer merged to become Aventis, and Roche acquired Genentech. Pfizer and Warner-Lambert are now Pfizer, Inc., Glaxo Wellcome and SmithKline Beecham have formed GlaxoSmithKline. Furthermore, Monsanto has merged with Pharmacia & Upjohn, and is now known as Pharmacia Corporation.

Today Pfizer is one of the top five pharmaceutical companies in the world. In 1998, one of the most publicized product introductions took place when Pfizer introduced Viagra, a drug for erectile dysfunction (ED). The company helped replace the harsh-sounding term 'impotence' with the softer erectile dysfunction or ED, perhaps easing conversation with physicians and between spouses on the subject.

Viagra is an oral treatment for erectile dysfunction, a condition that to varying degrees affects 50 per cent of men over the age of 40

▶

Case study 5.1 continued

(a conservative estimate), and is significantly associated with depression, coronary artery disease, diabetes, high blood pressure and possibly high cholesterol.

Viagra increases blood flow to the penis, so that when a man is sexually aroused he can achieve and maintain an erection. Viagra alone, without sexual stimulation and arousal, will not cause an erection. One significant drug interaction became apparent within the first few months of Viagra's release, when a small number of patients taking organic nitrates – such as nitroglycerine – for heart conditions experienced lowered blood pressure, dizziness, angina and even heart attacks. As a result, Pfizer was compelled to issue a letter warning physicians of that contra-indication in May 1998, and to concede that heart patients – a large group of men with ED – could not be helped by Viagra.

New pills for ED are now in the late stages of clinical trials. There were at least five Viagra-like drugs in development at the end of 2001. We are going to see drugs that stimulate the brain rather than working by increasing blood flow to penile arteries. This is a completely different mechanism, and there will be different patients responding to it.

Before Viagra, the costs associated with assessing and treating ED were prohibitive. Treatments included injection therapy, which costs about US$25 per shot. Penile prostheses cost US$15,000 to US$20,000 per implant and a sexually active 50-year-old man could expect to have multiple implants over the course of his life.

The oral therapy, which improves blood flow to the penis, represents a more cost-effective option. The major cost associated with Viagra is the US$8–10 cost of the pill itself. The pill takes up to an hour to work and is effective for approximately five hours. During the first year of treatment with an average utilization of about once a week, costs are about US$675, an amount that drops to about US$450 per patient in each subsequent year due to the minimal evaluation and follow-up required.

Lower cost is not the drug's sole attraction. Viagra has a broad spectrum of efficacy, regardless of the patient's age, the cause of the ED or its severity. Overall, 70 per cent of men with ED will respond to treatment regardless of the cause of their dysfunction. The drug is well tolerated. The side effects, which are typically mild to moderate, most commonly include headaches, flushing and indigestion. Less often, the user may experience blue-tinged or blurry vision, or visual sensitivity to light. Viagra is contra-indicated for patients taking nitrates.

Within six months (in November 1998), Viagra had problems. The US Food & Drug Administration had received reports of 130 deaths in patients taking Viagra, more than half of them cardiovascular (heart)-related. Prescriptions had plummeted, and analysts had slashed their sales estimates.

However, Pfizer turned the bad news around. When the bad news about heart attacks hit in November 1998, the company was already racing to complete a follow-up safety study in Sweden. In tests on patients with both cardiovascular disease and ED, Viagra once again proved effective. And the heart-attack rate turned out to be no greater than for patients receiving a placebo.

Advertising for Viagra

A direct-to-consumer campaign is expected to be comparable in scope and spending to the ones Pfizer has used for Viagra. Pfizer spent US$53 million on Viagra's US adverts in 1999.

Pfizer sponsored a Viagra car in the Nascar circuit. And early in 2000, Pfizer hired bands to play on a half-mile of beachfront in Rio de Janeiro while doctors in booths interviewed prospective patients about ED and other conditions.

Financial results

Sales of Viagra, hailed at its launch as the most successful drug of all time, were expected to reach US$1.2 billion in 2000 (total Pfizer sales were about US$18 billion in 2000).

Other uses of Viagra

Now Pfizer's goal is to broaden the medical uses of Viagra. Two new possibilities for using Viagra have appeared.

Case study 5.1 continued

Viagra for women

The company has spent millions of dollars testing the drug on women. Viagra would work in women in a similar way to how it works in men, by increasing blood flow to the genitals. In women, it may also increase lubrication. Some women simply feel sexually excited after taking Viagra (*Independent*, 2000). Early results have been disappointing, but Pfizer still hopes to identify a segment of women who do respond.

Viagra for diabetes sufferers

Viagra may have another use – reducing indigestion caused by long-term diabetes. Research work with mice has shown that Viagra, in conjunction with the standard diabetes treatment insulin, can help a condition known as gastroparesis, caused when the pyloric muscle leading out of the stomach will not relax and let food empty into the intestine. Viagra affects a specific muscle in the penis that needs to relax before an erection can occur. Apparently it also has that muscle-relaxing effect in the diabetic. The condition, marked by bloating, pain, vomiting and occasional dehydration, affects nearly 75 per cent of people who have had diabetes for more than five years. Trials using Viagra in diabetic people are being planned.

In the USA alone, there are about 16 million diabetes sufferers.

New competitors are coming up

The drugs that may pose the most serious threat to Viagra are Cialis (made by Eli Lilly and Icos Corporation) and Vardenafil (made by Bayer).

Researchers presenting the results of human trials of Cialis said the drug was as effective as its rival, but without some of that product's side effects. Scientists told the World Meeting on Impotence Research in Australia that Cialis worked in up to 85 per cent of patients and did not cause the visual problems and facial flushes seen in some Viagra users.

Bayer is also conducting trials of an impotence drug called Vardenafil. However, Cialis is furthest along in clinical trials.

The Phase II trial did not resolve whether Cialis would be safe for cardiac patients. Because Viagra may not be taken with common heart medications called nitrates, any competitor that could overcome that risk would have a clear market advantage. Many impotence patients are elderly men with heart trouble.

Participants in the Phase II trial of Cialis were told to take the medication whenever they wished to have sexual intercourse. The maximum dose was one pill per day. Cialis will now enter Phase III clinical trials, the final phase before approval. It is unclear if heart patients will participate in those experiments.

In November 2000, Pfizer lost a UK court battle after charging that drugs such as Cialis would infringe the company's patents.

Edward Nodder, a specialist in intellectual property at the law firm Bristows, said: 'This is a very serious blow for them. The basic concept of Viagra is now unprotected and there's no barrier to others.'

Questions

You are invited as a marketing consultant at one of Pfizer's management meetings to give an input regarding some actions to the new competitive threats.

1. What kind of competitive intelligence would you gather to decide what counteractions Pfizer should take in response to the future competitor products?

2. How do you consider the future market development for drugs against ED?

3. What can Pfizer do to expand the actual market for Viagra?

Source: *Business Week* (2000), Dyer and Clark (2000), Griffith (2000), *Irish Times* (2000), *The Independent* (2000).

5.1 Introduction

Except for a minor section dealing with interaction between competitors (Section 5.3) this chapter is mainly about how to analyse competitors, their behaviour and their strategies. A more comprehensive analysis of competitor relationships is given in Chapter 6 (Section 6.5).

Competitor intelligence (CI) is the publicly available information and other types of information on competitors, current and potential, that is an important input in formulating a marketing strategy. No general would order an army to march without first fully knowing the enemy's position and intentions. Similarly, before deciding which competitive moves to make, a firm must be aware of the perspectives of its competitors. CI includes information beyond industry statistics and trade gossip. It involves the close observation of competitors to learn what they do best and why and where they are weak.

In most western countries the development has resulted in a major intensification of **competitor analysis**. The reasons for increasing CI are:

● increasing competition between companies
● deregulation
● liberalization
● globalization
● periods of economic recession
● reduced product and service differentiation.

Factors inhibiting the growth of CI include:

● data protection
● different legislation from country to country
● fear that competitive intelligence is unethical
● fear of counter-intelligence
● failure of competitive strategies to yield the expected gain.

The use of CI is increasing gradually. There is growing awareness of the need to have a competitor strategy, which is every bit as important as the customer strategies that are already commonplace (West, 1999).

In terms of their use of CI, companies seem to go through a series of stages (see Figure 5.1). At the first stage is competitor awareness. This stage is entered soon after a company is formed, or even before, when the start-up is being planned. Being competitor aware means that the key competitors are known and that there is some knowledge – usually incomplete and certainly unverified – about their products, their prices, the clients they have succeeded in winning business from, the market sectors they service and the staff they employ.

The organization that is competitor aware rarely uses the data that it holds other than for occasional ad hoc tactical exercises, such as competitive pricing decisions, or as an input to a business plan that has to be submitted to an external organization, such as a bank.

As companies grow they tend to become competitor sensitive, both in terms of their awareness of the damage competitors can inflict on their business and the need to win orders by competing more effectively. Unfortunately, being competitor sensitive does not always increase the demand for information on competitors. An alarming proportion of competitor sensitive companies continue to rely exclusively on informal information flows from their sales forces, business contacts and the trade press, rather than from a structured intelligence programme. When they do use sources other than the informal information channels the prime motive is usually emulation. They seek to copy what they perceive to be the best of their competitors' practices. There is nothing wrong with emulation as a business process, providing it is factually driven using such techniques as reverse engineering and competitor benchmarking, but it represents a very limited source of data that can be derived about competitors' activities.

The organization that is competitor intelligent is one that devotes serious resources to studying its competitors and anticipating their actions. This includes identifying competitors' physical and intangible resources; studying their organizations and their methods in as much detail as possible; and developing knowledge of their strategies and potential plans. The competitor intelligent organization is continuously aware of the threats posed by competitors, the nature and seriousness of those threats and what needs to be done to counteract them. They recognize the need to look forward to anticipate competitive actions and to predict the likely responses to actions they are proposing to take themselves. They are also aware that the most serious threats may arise from companies that are not yet active in their business sector.

There is a close parallel between the growth in competitor analysis, and the development of customer analysis. There was a time when organizations were only customer aware. Interest in competitive strategy was nurtured by the publication of books such as Michael Porter's *Competitive Advantage* and *Competitive Strategy* in the 1980s. This was accompanied by a short flirtation with marketing warfare that focused on beating the competition by adopting military tactics.

Figure 5.1 Development of competitive intelligence

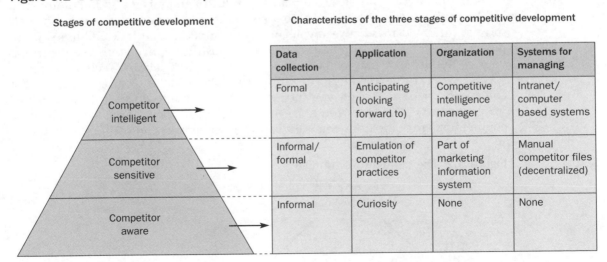

| Stages of competitive development | Characteristics of the three stages of competitive development |

	Data collection	Application	Organization	Systems for managing
Competitor intelligent	Formal	Anticipating (looking forward to)	Competitive intelligence manager	Intranet/ computer based systems
Competitor sensitive	Informal/ formal	Emulation of competitor practices	Part of marketing information system	Manual competitor files (decentralized)
Competitor aware	Informal	Curiosity	None	None

Source: adapted from West (1999).

Competition is good for customers as it means that companies have to try harder or lose their customer base. In many markets competition is the driving force of change. Without competition, companies only satisfy: they provide satisfactory levels of customer value (satisfaction) but fail to excel. The conflict between improving customer value and costs is illustrated by the competitive triangle (Figure 5.2).

This framework recognizes that for firm A to be a winner in the competition, it is no longer sufficient to be good at satisfying customers' needs (producing customer value). Companies also have to produce at a lower cost than other competitors (here competitor B).

When developing a marketing strategy (Chapter 7), companies need to be aware of their own strengths (S) and weaknesses (W), customer needs (O, opportunities) and the competitors (T, threats). Altogether these four elements represent the SWOT analysis, which in Chapter 7 will be used as a basis for developing the firm's marketing strategy. The focus of this chapter will be on analysing competitors at the strategic and tactical level.

Strategic intelligence looks to the future and allows an organization to make informed decisions concerning future conditions in the marketplace and/or industry. *Tactical intelligence* looks at the present. This level of intelligence provides decision makers with the information necessary to monitor changes in the company's current environment and helps them search for new opportunities. To maximize the potential benefit of CI, the strategic and tactical levels must be coordinated. Because all the partner companies identified coordination as a high priority, these businesses create, continuously improve, and use CI systems, processes, and products that enable this to happen. Moreover, all of these companies believe that coordinating strategic and tactical intelligence with sales and marketing has led to a strengthening in competitive positions as well as increases in customer satisfaction and retention.

Competitive analysis flows out of customer analysis. To truly know how you compare with your competitors, you first need to understand your customers' wants and needs. Then you must identify both current and potential competitors in both your served and unserved markets. Industry analysis is also important. You need to know about the suppliers to your industry as well as the channels which serve as intermediaries between you and your competitors and the end users. These players have an impact on your competitive position. Once you have identified your competitors, it may be possible to group them by factors, such as degree of specialization or degree of globalization, to make it easier to discern patterns of competitive behaviour. Now you should be in a position to do an in-depth analysis of competitors' strategies. You must be careful not to focus simply on what your competitors are doing now. You must consider where your competitors are going.

Figure 5.2 The competitive triangle

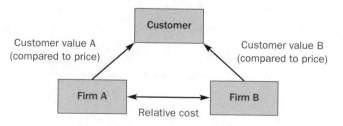

This chapter focuses on eight issues.

1. Who are our competitors? (Section 5.2)
2. How are the competitors interacting? (Section 5.3)
3. How do we learn about our competitors? (Section 5.4)
4. What are the strengths and weaknesses of our competitors (competitor audit)? (Section 5.5)
5. Market commonality and resource commonality. (Section 5.6)
6. What are the objectives and strategies of our competitors? (Section 5.7)
7. What are the response patterns of our competitors? (Section 5.8)
8. How can we set up an organization for CI? (Section 5.9)

Exhibit 5.1   **Apple Computer versus Microsoft in the 1980s**

Apple Computer capitalized on changes in society and technology to initiate the home desktop PC market. While other companies would have a greater role later on, Apple was the first. Apple's response to the competitive market changed when IBM entered. Apple immediately saw IBM as the competitor to fear the most and developed a strategy of differentiation from IBM: IBM's other competitors saw the market differently and sought to emulate IBM as much as possible. Apple, seeking to out-compete IBM, completely missed the role of software – and Microsoft – in the marketplace. When Microsoft became the market standard, Apple, operating on a different standard, lost its market position.

Apple failed to see the influence of economies of scale on software development; as a result, the number of software titles developed for Apple products was rapidly outpaced by those developed for IBM compatible products.

Source: adapted from Glitman (2000).

5.2   Who are our competitors?

The danger when identifying competitors is that competitive myopia prevails (Levitt, 1960). According to Levitt's thesis, the mission of a business should be defined broadly: an airline might consider itself in the holiday business; a railway company should not consider other railway companies as competitors but rather consider themselves as in the transport business, competing with other transport methods like roads and air.

Later on Levitt's proposition was contradicted by some practical examples: among them was Coca-Cola, which in the early 1980s extended its business from being a soft drinks marketer to being a beverage company. Subsequently, the company bought three wine companies.

Competition for a certain product can be defined clearly at every level of the hierarchy shown in the examples of Figure 5.3.

The number of competitors grows as you go outwards from the centre. However, the terms industry and product class do not get to the heart of competition or market definition.

A good definition of an industry is the following:

Figure 5.3 Examples of competition against colas

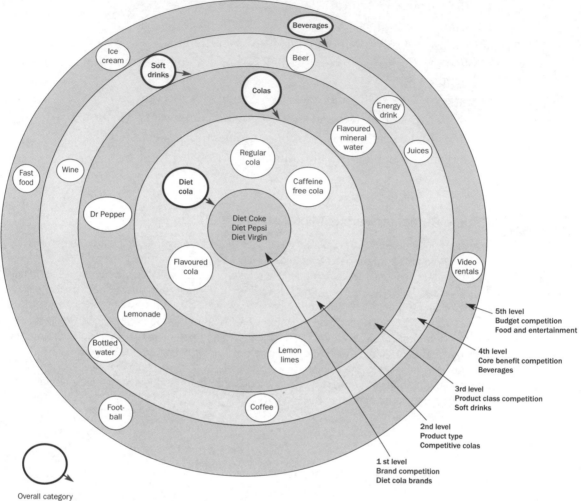

An industry should be recognizable as a group of products that are close substitutes to buyers, are available to a common group of buyers, and are distant substitutes for all products not included in the industry.

The key part of this definition is the fact that competition is defined by the customer, not by the marketing manager; after all, it is the customer who determines whether two products or services compete against each other.

An alternative way to define the competition that better incorporates the customer's perspective is also shown in Figure 5.3. The narrowest definition of competition that results in the fewest competitors would include only products or services of the same product types or brands. For a diet cola brand the narrowest way to define competition would be to include only the other diet cola brands.

Although there may be some product variations such as capacity, the most direct competitors are the brands that look like yours (first level of competition).

This narrow definition might be useful in the short term because these brands are your most serious competitors on a day-to-day basis. It is also a convenient definition of competition because it mimics the way commercial data services (e.g. A. C. Nielsen) often measure market shares. However, this narrow definition may set an industry standard for looking at competition and market shares in a way that does not represent the true underlying competitive dynamics. Thus, the product type level, though perhaps providing the set of the closest competitors, is too narrow for a longer-term view of competition.

The second level of competition is based on products that have similar features and provide the same basic function. In this type of competition, called product type competition, more brands are considered to be competitors like Coca-Cola classic, Pepsi One, Caffeine Free Diet Pepsi.

At the third level (product class competition), other competitors are considered to be other soft drink brands like Sprite, Dr Pepper and 7-Up. At the fourth level the products are competing generically because they satisfy the same need. In Figure 5.3 it is the need of thirst or the need of enjoying a beverage together with others.

The point is that there is a critical difference between generically defined competitors and product form or product category competition. The latter two are inward oriented, whereas generic competition is outward oriented. Product type and product class competitors are defined by products that look like yours. Generic competitors are defined by looking outside the firm to the customers. After all, the customer determines what products and services solve the problem at hand. Although in some cases there may be a limited number of ways to solve the same problem or provide the same benefit, in most instances focusing on the physical product alone ignores viable competitors.

The final level of competition (level 5) is the most general level, as many products and services are discretionary items purchased from the same general budget.

A person shopping in a department store in the housewares area faces many other discretionary items for the home that are unrelated to making coffee or quenching thirst. Products such as pots and pans and knives may find their way into the shopping basket and could be viewed as substitutable in the budget. This kind of competition is called budget competition.

5.3 How are the competitors interacting?

A competitive interaction occurs when a set of firms engages in a series of behaviours that affect each other's outcomes and/or behaviours over time. In this situation, the competitors are 'at war', in other situations the interaction might be peaceful.

At a more general level, one can think of an interaction as consisting of a sequence of events, occurring as follows. Our firm and the competitor firm engage in a set of actions (e.g. marketing mix) that provoke a particular customer response.

While no interaction can be completely controlled, research and experience suggest that companies can influence competitive interactions to their advantage. To do so, though, they must know how to identify competitors, recognize their behaviours and the consequences, and then design effective actions and reactions.

Between two firms A and B, three types of interaction are possible (see Table 5.1): each competitor is aware of the other's effect on it. When neither competitor is aware of the other, the interaction is an implicit one. When one firm is aware of

Table 5.1 Types of competitive interactions

		Firm A	
		Aware	*Unaware*
Firm B	*Aware*	*Explicit* Relationship behaviours (benign or hostile)	*Asymmetric* Firm A – Ignorance Firm B – Stealth
	Unaware	*Asymmetric* Firm A – Stealth Firm B – Ignorance	*Implicit* Market behaviours (customer-mediated)

Source: reprinted with permission from *Marketing Management*, published by the American Marketing Association, B. H. Clark (1998), vol. 7, no. 4, pp. 8–20.

the interaction but the other is not, the interaction is asymmetric. Each type of interaction is characterized by a typical pattern of behaviours.

In an *explicit interaction*, each firm is aware of its relationship with the other and attempts to manage that relationship to its advantage. The relationship behaviours may be benign or hostile. In a benign situation, the two firms work to maximize the profits of both partners in the interaction by engaging in positive behaviours such as joint marketing or product development, or at least by avoiding negative behaviours such as price cuts. In a hostile situation, each firm tries to gain a sustainable advantage over the other, maximizing its own gains. Explicit interactions are what we usually think of when we consider competitor interactions, such as Coca-Cola and Pepsi.

In an *implicit interaction*, the relationship is characterized by market behaviours alone. Customer response to the two competitors' actions creates certain outcomes for both organizations, but each firm is ignorant of the other's effect on its business. This is most common in markets with a large number of small competitors. For example, all restaurants in a given city compete with each other to some degree. This also occurs when different companies meet the same needs in very different ways.

In an *asymmetric interaction*, the aware firm has the opportunity to exercise stealth, taking actions that the ignorant competitor will not see. Stealth may allow a firm to steal business from competitors without their knowledge. Asymmetry often arises from differences in firm size: the small firm knows well that it is in an interaction with the large firm, but for the large firm the small firm is inconsequential.

5.4 How do we learn about our competitors?

CI activities can theoretically be performed by any person or department in an organization, not just by marketing or corporate strategy personnel. Traditional CI activities, unlike acts of corporate espionage, include obtaining publicly disseminated or publicly accessible information (such as analysing annual reports) and engaging in routine transactions in open product markets (such as buying and testing a competitor's newest product). These activities are generally viewed as being both legal and ethical.

| Exhibit 5.2 | Cooperating with competitors |

What are the advantages of competitors – or presumed competitors – cooperating with one another in certain spheres, even as compete in others? For example, *USA Today* competes with *Chicago Tribune* for readers and advertisers. On a basic level, they could work together on joint literacy programmes in the schools to get children reading newspapers. But take it further. The *Chicago Tribune* has a big Sunday paper, while *USA Today* has no weekend edition. The *Chicago Tribune* now uses its Sunday printing press to print *USA Today* during the week, because *USA Today* is going to be printed by someone, and the *Chicago Tribune* can make more money by utilizing its capacity more effectively. *USA Today* can save money by having the *Chicago Tribune* do it for less.

The two papers are competitors but also 'complementors'. Similarly, Mastercard and Visa compete for merchants and card members, but cooperate with terminals and fraud prevention measures. Pharmaceutical companies cooperate in disease-recognition campaigns, such as promoting testing for osteoporosis. They create a bigger market for osteoporosis medicines, and then compete for the expanded market.

Read more about competitor alliances in Section 6.5.

Source: adapted from Competitive Intelligence Magazine (1999).

Once a firm has decided to engage in CI, it can choose from the following classifications of CI (Hannon, 1997).

Pro-active or reactive CI

By definition, a pro-active approach involves conscious, premeditated acts to avoid being surprised. Pro-active tactics include periodic surveillance, continuous monitoring, and targeted studies. These acts are more offensive, since they target and investigate identifiable and realistic threats. On the other hand, reactive, more defensive, approaches are more likely to be undertaken in response to competitive threats, whether they are actually realized or merely expected. Of course, there are numerous cost/benefits trade-offs that affect how pro-active or reactive a company can be at any given time.

Formal or informal CI

Formal acquisition is usually much quicker, better organized, and more responsive. As might be imagined, it is usually also more expensive. Practically speaking, most formal corporate intelligence systems have at their core a staff that is charged with responsibility for CI operating procedures such as developing a modus operandi for the routine submission of competitor reports. Alternatively, informal intelligence activities, which are the norm for many western organizations, are often uncoordinated, unfocused, and shallow. Not surprisingly, they are usually less expensive. When companies adopt a reactive approach, whether by design or default, individual employees, departments, and **strategic business units** may all be engaged in intelligence activities. Unfortunately, these efforts, more often than not, are disjointed, ineffective, and inefficient.

No matter how formally or informally the competition is to be monitored, it is imperative for firms to a least identify those competitors who merit surveillance and determine if there are appropriate information sources for finding out more about these companies.

Essentially, three sources of CI can be distinguished: what competitors say about themselves, what others say about them, and what employees of the firm engaged in competitive analysis have observed and learned about competitors. Much information can be obtained at low cost.

As far as information from its own sources is concerned, the company should develop a structured programme to gather competitive information. First, a detailed information gathering programme must be developed. Second, salespeople may be trained to carefully gather and provide information on the competition, using such sources as customers, distributors, dealers, and former salespeople. Third, senior marketing people should be encouraged to call on customers and speak to them in-depth. These contacts should provide valuable information on competitors' products and services. Fourth, other people in the company who happen to have some knowledge of competitors should be encouraged to channel this information to an appropriate office.

Information gathering on the competition has grown dramatically in recent years. Almost all large companies designate someone specially to seek CI. SMEs will normally not have the resources for that.

The information gathering techniques, summarized below, are all legal, although some may involve questionable ethics. A responsible company should carefully review each technique before using it to avoid practices that might be considered illegal or unethical.

Gathering information from internal employees and employees of competing companies

Firms can collect data about their competitors through interviews with new recruits or by speaking with employees of competing companies.

When firms interview, e.g. students for jobs, they may pay special attention to those who have worked for competitors, even temporarily. Job seekers are eager to impress and often have not been warned about what they can and cannot divulge.

Companies send engineers to conferences and trade shows to question competitors' technical people.

Probably the oldest tactic in corporate intelligence gathering, companies hire key executives from competitors to find out what they know.

Gathering information from competitors' customers

Some customers may give out information on competitors' products. The close cooperative relationship that engineers cultivate with the customer's staff often enables them to learn what new products competitors are offering.

Gathering information from competitors' suppliers

A firm and its main competitor are sometimes supplied by the same subcontractor. As many firms today have close relations with their suppliers, some information exchange may be possible.

Gathering information by observing competitors or by analysing physical evidence

Companies can get to know competitors better by buying their products or by examining other physical evidence. Companies increasingly buy competitors' products and take them apart to determine costs of production and even manufacturing methods.

| Exhibit 5.3 | At Xerox the sales people are important sources of CI |

Judith M. Vezmar, Vice President, US Customer Operations, Xerox Corporation, talked about an occasion when CI was very useful.

'At Xerox, we have a competitive hot line for our sales people to phone in competitive information. We use our sales force to identify where the competition is located, who our potential customers are, what industries they're in, what applications they have, and even why they bought from the competition.

'Here's an example of how important these "eyes and ears" are. Early last year we received competitive information indicating that a competitor was planning, for the first time, to offer service on Xerox products. One of our competitor's service reps told one of our service technicians that he was being trained to service our products. Our service rep went to his manager and that information was passed up through the channel into the competitive intelligence group.

'We verified the information with about three additional clues, one of which was rather obvious – an ad the competitor had placed in the classifieds for people with Xerox product experience. This allowed us to announce a counter-strategy as the competitor was about to announce its new service strategy.'

Source: adapted from Vezmar (1996).

Gathering information from published materials and public documents

This type of material could be:

● financial reports of the firm
● government reports
● company presentation brochures
● company portraits in industry journals.

Most of this information can be found on the Internet.

Why the Internet is a good source of CI

Internet resources will provide an array of basic information. To paraphrase the old saying, 'All that glitters is not gold', one should be reminded that just because it is on the Internet does not mean it is accurate. WWW is not the source of data, it is the contact connect symbol. The analyst must document the author, method of data collection, date, publisher location, and purpose of printing the data.

All too frequently, novices think they have an authoritative report if a portion of a report is dotted with Internet footnotes. Experienced researchers question the authenticity of data until there has been an opportunity to assess the **reliability** of the Internet (or any) data source. Although sales exaggerations affect few people, the same practice on the Internet could lead to vastly different conclusions unless the information and source credibility are questioned by those who use information in making important strategic decisions.

Falsifying data on the Internet is rare. However, the inability to police the Internet could lead to inaccurate if not intentionally false data inputs. Always keep in mind the fact that it is up to the data collector to verify the quality of the information taken from the Internet.

Types of CI available

In the broadest sense, data sources are either free or available for a fee. Paid-for services are of three types:

1. a database that charges a monthly fee for access to the data provided
2. services that provide data to subscribers on a per-inquiry basis
3. research reports which one can acquire from research firms.

Subscription services

There are many online data links that will give subscribers access to special databases. A subscription to Lexis-Nexis is one possibility. Subscribers can get up-to-date information direct from Lexis-Nexis (**www.lexisnexis.com**). Lexis contains legal materials, whereas Nexis is not focused on legal issues, but is concerned about future interaction.

Lexis-Nexis is one of the leading business intelligence providers. Over 30,000 sources are covered; 3 billion searchable documents make up their service. Over a million new documents are added every week.

Nexis will provide reports on a regular basis (such as Lexis monthly). Each of these Lexis-Nexis monthly updates provides a list of any new articles on a selected subject that have been published in the past month.

There are many other subscription services on the Internet. Some additional examples are:

- Dun & Bradstreet (**www.dnb.com**). There is also a Dun & Bradstreet On-Line giving selected operating ratios by SIC code, credit reports, etc.
- Hoovers, (**www.hoovers.com**) provides profiles on corporate firms listed in one directory. A great deal of financial data is available.
- Moody. (**www.moodys.com**) is useful to check out the credit rating of competition.
- **www.databaseamerica.com** provides current information on competitors' products and strategies.
- Phoenix Consulting Group (**www.intellpros.com**) provides competitive intelligence and counter-intelligence services.
- Fuld & Company (US) (**www.fuld.com**) is a pioneering company in the CI field. Offers detailed description of CI, seminars and consulting services.
- Aware (UK) (**www.marketing-intelligence.co.uk**) provides CI for businesses in Europe and the UK.
- Compentia (US) (**www.compentia.com**) provides customized research related to CI and strategic planning.
- Current Analysis (**www.currentanalysis.com**) brings action-oriented CI to clients within 24–28 hours of a significant development.
- Free Internet sources: high on any list of first websites for those who want to start building CI systems using Internet sources should be industry or trade associations. Similarly, professional associations can provide valuable data.

Sources of general information

Perhaps one of the more interesting CI developments on the Internet can be found when one looks at any of the various free news retrieval services. These services are of special interest because they are delivered to your computer as often as every 15 minutes. In some cases, you are reading material prior to publication dates.

Suppose you are doing business throughout Europe or the USA. How can you track news of special interest to your business? Here are some of the possibilities:

- Corporate Information.com (US) (**www.corporateinformation.com**) – you can search by company name (250,000 company profiles).
- Wright Research Center (US) (**http://profiles.wisi.com**) has detailed descriptions and financial analysis of about 20,000 companies.
- Comfind (US) (**www.comfind.com**) has information on products, industries and companies.
- Society of Competitive Intelligence Professionals (**www.scip.org**) offers assistance, articles, and advice.
- Lycos online (**www.companiesonline.com**) lists links for company information.

Free online annual reports (PDF-format):

The following are useful sources of annual reports.

- Report Gallery (**www.reportgallery.com**) has about 2200 annual reports available from US companies.
- Investor Relations Information Networks (IRIN) (**www.irin.com**) covers US companies.
- Company Annual Reports On-Line (CAROL) (**www.carol.co.uk**) covers European companies.
- **www.c-direct.ne.jp** has annual reports from Japanese companies. It has both a Japanese and an English version.

5.5 What are the strengths and weaknesses of our competitors?

Having identified our competitors and described how to collect CI the next stage is to complete a competitor audit in order to assess their relative strengths and weaknesses.

Whether competitors can carry out their strategies and reach their goals depends on their resources, capabilities and their resulting strengths and weaknesses. A precise understanding of competitor strengths and weaknesses is an important prerequisite for developing competitor strategy.

This information will enable predictions to be made about the competitor's future behaviour and reactions. It is not sufficient to describe how the competitor is performing in terms of market share and profits. A competitive analysis must diagnose how the competitor has managed to generate such performance outcomes, be they good or bad. In particular, it locates areas of competitive vulnerability. Military strategy suggests that success is most often achieved when strength is concentrated against the enemy's greatest weakness.

The process of assessing a competitor's strengths and weaknesses may take place as part of a marketing audit. As much internal, market and customer information as possible should be gathered. For example, financial data concerning profitability, profit margins, sales and investment levels, market data relating to price levels, market share and distribution channels used, and customer data concerning awareness of brand names, and perceptions of brand and company image, product and service quality, and selling ability may be relevant.

Not all of this information will be accessible, and some may not be relevant. The management needs to decide the extent to which each piece of information is relevant or not. For example, the management must decide how much to spend on measuring customer awareness and perceptions through market research. This process of data gathering needs to be managed so that information is available to compare our company with its chief competitors on the key factors for success in the industry.

A four-stage model, as represented by a competitive benchmarking, can then be used as follows (the result of the competitive benchmarking can be seen in the upper right corner of Figure 3.3).

1. Identify the major attributes that customers value. Ask customers what features and performance levels they look for in choosing a supplier or a product. Different customers will mention different features and benefits (value chain functions). Assess the importance of different attributes. Rate or rank the importance of different functions to customers. The highest ranked functions are called key success factors (KSFs).
2. Assess the company's and the competitors' performance on different value functions.
3. Examine how customers rate the company's performance against a specific major competitor on an attribute-by-attribute basis. The key to gaining competitive advantage is to take each customer segment and examine how the company's offer compares to that of its major competitor. If the company's offer exceeds the competitor's offer on all important attributes, the company can charge a higher price and earn higher profits, or it can charge the same price and gain more market share. However, if the company is seen as performing at a lower level than its major competitors on some important attributes, it must invest in strengthening those attributes or finding other important attributes where it can gain an edge on the competitor.
4. Monitor customer values regularly. The company must review customer values and competitors' standings periodically if it wants to remain strategically effective.

The competence profile for firm A in Figure 3.3 is an example of how a firm is not in accordance with the market (customer) demand in the form of key success factors. The company has its core competences in parts of the value chain's functions where customers place little importance (e.g. market knowledge).

If there is a generally good match between key success factors and firm A's initial position, it is important to concentrate resources and improve this core competence to create sustainable competitive advantages.

If, on the other hand, there is a large gap between customers' demands and the firm's initial position in key success factors as shown in Figure 3.3 (as with the personal selling functions), it may give rise to the following alternatives:

● improve the firm's initial position
● find business areas where firm A's competence profile better suits the market demand and expectations.

As a new business area involves risk, it is often important to identify an eventual gap in a critical success factor as early as possible. In other words, an early warning system must be established that continuously monitors the critical competitive factors so that it is possible to start initiatives that limit the size of an eventual gap as early as possible.

In Figure 3.3, the competence profile of firm B is also shown.

Assessing a competitor's strengths and weaknesses begins with identifying relevant techniques and assets in the industry. Weaknesses might include resource limitations or lack of capital investment. Ways of attacking competitors' strengths and weaknesses include the following.

● Attack geographic regions where a rival has a weak market share or is exerting less competitive effort.

● Attack buyer segments that a rival is neglecting or is poorly equipped to serve.

● Attack rivals that lag on quality, features or product performance; in such cases, a challenger with a better product can often convince the most performance-conscious customers of lagging rivals to switch to its brand.

● Attack rivals that have done a poor job of servicing customers. In such cases, a service-oriented challenger can win a rival's disenchanted customers.

● Attack rivals with weak advertising and brand recognition; a challenger with strong marketing skills and a good image can often take sales from lesser-known rivals.

5.6 Market commonality and resource commonality

Chen (1996) proposed a model where both market commonality (market overlap) and resource similarity (resource overlap) affect the awareness and motivation to take actions and await competitive responses (see Figure 5.4). In this model, a competitor's likelihood of response is influenced by both market commonality and resource similarity.

The *high market commonality* between Amazon.com and Barnes & Noble explains the fierce competition between these two companies. Amazon.com became, in a few years, the leading online bookseller in the USA. Barnes & Noble was the largest bookstore chain in the world. It sold books only in the USA and owned at least one store in every major US city. At the end of 1996, it operated 11.5 million square feet of selling space and had more than 20,000 employees. This market commonality explains the 1997 entry of Barnes & Noble into the online market and the subsequent moves and counter-moves of the two companies. On January 28, 1997, Barnes & Noble publicly announced that it planned to become the exclusive bookseller on America Online's (AOL's) Marketplace and to launch its own website later in the spring. On March 10, Barnes & Noble announced that its website would feature a personalized book recommendation service that the company had been working on since 1996. On March 18, Barnes & Noble went online at AOL with a deep discount policy. Barnes & Noble launched its own website (bn.com) on May 13, 1997. Amazon reacted by reducing its prices, once on June 10, 1997 and again on November 21, 1997. Later, on September 17, 1999, Amazon launched zShop to sell rare and out-of-print books matching a service that had been offered by bn.com since November 1998.

Figure 5.4 Possibilities of cooperation between two competitors A and B, showing market and resource product commonality

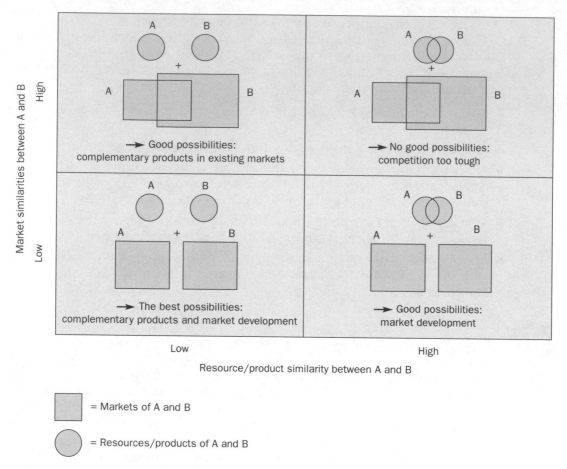

Source: adapted from Chen (1996).

The *high resource commonality* between Amazon and eBay also explains the fierce rivalry between these two companies. The two firms are both pure online businesses with few tangible resources. Their main resources are their customer bases. eBay runs the largest person-to-person auction website, connecting some 3.8 million buyers and sellers worldwide. It helps people buy and sell collectibles and antiques as well as many other goods normally sold through flea markets, antique stores and classified advertisements. The success of eBay's dynamic pricing system has been considered as a threat to Amazon's dominance of the online retail industry. So, on March 30, 1999, Amazon's president Jeff Bezos launched Amazon's auctions in direct competition with eBay. As a reaction, eBay recently polled members on whether they'd like to see fixed-price auctions (many said yes) and dealer storefronts. This was a direct counter-attack against Amazon's fixed-price business model.

5.7 What are the objectives and strategies of our competitors?

Knowing a competitor's objectives is crucial to predicting how it will respond to changes in the environment, and if strategic changes are likely. Also, a company's strategies are driven by its goals and objectives. For example, in the USA K-mart was always alarmed by Wal-Mart's entry and expansion efforts into areas promising high growth potential.

Understanding the objectives of competitors can give guidance to strategy development on three levels. Goals can indicate where the company is intending to develop and in which markets, either by industry or internationally, major initiatives can be expected. The areas of expansion could indicate markets that are to be particularly competitive but may also signify that companies are not so committed. Where the intention is profitable coexistence, it is often better to compete in areas that are deemed of secondary interest to major companies rather than to compete directly.

Reward structures for staff can also indicate objectives. Where sales staff, for example, are rewarded on a **percentage of sales** commission that practice suggests that sales volume (rather than profitability) is a key objective.

When competing against a diversified company, ambitious goals in one sector may indicate that commitment to another is diminishing. Equally, very large and diversified companies may often not be able to take advantage of their enormous financial strengths because of their unwillingness to make strategic shifts in their resources. There is also a chance that financially driven companies may be unwilling to take the risks of new ventures, preferring instead to pick the bones of those who were damaged in taking the risk.

Also indicative of future goals can be the *ownership structure* of the competitor. Competitors owned by employees and/or managers may set a higher priority on providing continuity of employment than those owned by conventional shareholders. Likewise, competitors in the public sector may set higher priorities on social goals than profitability. Competitors owned as part of diversified conglomerates may be managed for short-term cash rather than long-term market position objectives.

Assessing competitors' current strategies

Assessing the current strategy involves asking the basic question: 'What exactly is the competitor doing at the moment?' This requires making as full a statement as possible of what competitors are trying to do, and how they are trying to achieve it.

Three main sets of issues need to be addressed with regard to understanding current competitor strategies, as follows.

1. *Identification of the market* or markets they have chosen to operate in: their selection of target markets.

2. Identification of the way in which they have chosen to operate in those markets: the *strategic focus* they are adopting with regard to the type of competitive advantage they are trying to convey.

3. The supporting *marketing mix* that is being adopted to enable the positioning aimed for to be achieved.

Beyond these three core elements of strategy it can also be helpful to assess the organization of the marketing effort – the structures adopted – to facilitate implementation of the strategy.

Identification of competitors' chosen markets

Prices

Competitors' prices will often be an indicator of the target market. In grocery retailing, for example, Aldi and Netto have consistently pursued a minimum-range, low-price strategy in attempts to attract price-sensitive, bulk grocery purchasers rather than compete directly with industry leaders such as Tesco and J. Sainsbury on quality and service.

Product features

The features built into products and the type and extent of service offered will be good indicators of the types of customer the competitor is seeking to serve. In the car industry, for example, the products made by Jaguar, a **subsidiary** of Ford, indicate clearly the types of customers being pursued. Skoda, now owned by Volkswagen, on the other hand, offers very different cars to the market, suggesting a completely different target market.

Advertisements and other promotional materials can also give clues as to what the target markets are. The wording of advertisements indicates the values the advertiser is attempting to convey and imbue in the product or service offered. Traditional Volvo advertising has clearly focused on safety, which appeals to safety-conscious, middle-class families. BMW advertising concentrates on technical quality and the pleasures of driving, suggesting a younger target market. The media in which the advertisements appear, or the scheduling adopted, will also give indications of the target market aimed for. Similarly, the distribution channels the competitor chooses to use to link the customer with offerings may give clues as to the targets it is aiming for.

Competitors' strategic focus

As discussed in the competitive triangle model, there are two main routes to creating a competitive advantage. The first is through low costs relative to competitors. The second is through providing valued uniqueness, differentiated products and services that customers will be willing to pay for.

Competitors may be focusing on cost reducing measures rather than expensive product development and promotional strategies. If competitors are following this strategy it is more likely that they will be focusing research and development expenditure on process rather than product development in a bid to reduce manufacturing costs.

Information about a competitor's cost structure is valuable, particularly when considering a low-cost strategy. Such cost structure information should include the competitor's overhead, all costs, investments in assets, and size of labour force.

The most effective competitors compete on the basis of value, offering superior quality, price and reliability. A company with exclusive access to specific raw materials establishes a differential advantage over its competitors. Strategically manoeuvring the variables of the marketing mix can give the company a special edge over competitors. The **cost leadership** route is a tough one for any firm to follow successfully and requires close, relentless attention to all cost drivers. As noted above in the UK grocery market, Aldi and Netto have adopted this rigorous approach, restricting product lines and providing a 'no-frills' service.

Providing something different, but of value to customers, is a route to creating competitive advantage that all players in a market can adopt. The creative aspect of this strategy is to identify those differentiating features on which the firm has, or can build, a defensible edge. Signals of differentiation will be as varied as the means of differentiation. All are highly visible to competitors and show the ground on which a given supplier has chosen to compete.

Strategies can also be defined in terms of competitive scope. For example, are competitors attempting to service the whole market, a few segments or a particular niche? If the competitor is a niche player, is it likely that it will be content to stay in that segment or use it as a beachhead to move into other segments in the future? Japanese companies are renowned for their use of small niche markets as springboards for market segment expansion (e.g. the small car segments in the USA and Europe).

Knowing the strategic thrust of competitors can help our strategic decision making. For example, knowing that our competitors are considering expansion in North America but not Europe will make expansion into Europe a more attractive strategic option for our company.

Competitors' supporting marketing mix

Analysis of the marketing mix adopted by competitors can give useful clues as to the target markets at which they are aiming and the competitive advantage they are seeking to build with those targets. Analysis of the mix can also show areas where the competitor is vulnerable to attack.

The four Ps

Product

At the product level, competitor analysis will attempt to deduce positioning strategy. This involves assessing a competitor product's target market and differential advantage. The marketing mix strategies (e.g. price levels, media used for promotion, and distribution channels) may indicate the target market, and market research into customer perceptions can be used to assess relative differential advantages.

Companies and products need to be continuously monitored for changes in positioning strategy. For example, Volvo's traditional positioning strategy based on safety has been modified to give more emphasis to performance.

Price

Analysis of competitor pricing strategies may identify gaps in the market. For example, a firm marketing vodka in the USA noted that the leader offered products at a number of relatively high price points but had left others vacant. This enabled the firm to position its own offerings in a different market sector.

Place

Understanding the distribution strengths and weaknesses of competitors can also identify opportunities. Dell, for example, decided to market their PCs direct to businesses rather than distribute them through office retail stores where their established competitors were already strong.

Promotion

Both the message and the media being used by competitors warrant close analysis. Some competitors may be better than others at exploiting new media such as satellite or cable. Others may be good in using public relations. Again, analysis will show where competitors are strong, and where they are vulnerable.

Exhibit 5.4 | **Fidelity used 'Jeopardy' in its CI process**

John Prescott, Professor of Business Administration, University of Pittsburgh talked about how to get CI into employees' thinking.

'One of my favorite incentives was at Fidelity. To help their sales force with CI, they created a 'Jeopardy' game. They gave the sales force a lot of information prior to the sales meeting. Then, at the sales meeting, they played 'Jeopardy' to allow the sales force to see how much of this they actually absorbed. They have a lot of fun with this game at the sales meeting. The sales people like the process, and it helps institutionalize CI issues.'

Source: adapted from Prescott (1998).

5.8   What are the response patterns of our competitors?

The ultimate aim of competitor analysis is to determine competitors' response profiles – that is, how a competitor might behave when faced with various environmental and competitive changes.

To succeed in predicting a competitor's next move, the marketing manager has to have a good feel for the rival's situation, how its managers think, and what its options are. Doing the necessary research can be time consuming since the information comes in bits and pieces from many sources. But scouting competitors well enough to anticipate their next moves allows managers to prepare effective countermoves and to take rivals' probable actions into account in designing the best course of action.

In evaluating the response patterns of our competitors the following questions are important.

● Is the competitor satisfied with the current position? If yes, this competitor may allow indirect competitors to exploit new markets without being perturbed. Alternatively, if this competitor is trying to improve its current position, it may be quick in chasing market changes or be obsessed by improving its own short-term profits performance. Knowledge of a company's future goals will clearly play an important part in answering this question.

● What likely moves or strategy shifts will the competitor make? History can provide some guide as to the way that companies behave. Goals, assumptions and capabilities will also give some guidance to how the company can effectively respond to market changes. After looking at these a company may be able to judge which of its own alternative strategies is likely to result in the most favourable reaction on the part of the competitors.

● Where is the competitor vulnerable? In a competitive market success is best achieved by concentrating strength against weakness. It is foolish for a firm to attack a market leader in areas where it is strongest.

Exhibit 5.5	Role play in CI as a predictor of competitive behaviour

At last, it's time to pull all of this together and come to something you can really use. Here are the vital sub-steps:

● Write a 'competitive novel'. If the competitor were a novel, what would be going on inside the heads of its key characters (including how they think about you)? Try this as an actual written exercise.

● Role play possible sequels to the story so far. Given what you've learned of the goals and assumptions that drive the competitor (and those that drive your own company), how would they respond to actions you have planned? How would you then respond? Play two or more rounds against your plans, not in an effort to absolutely predict what the competitor's actions will be, but to understand what kinds of moves they would consider, and to make sure that you are prepared to deal with the consequences.

● Assess results and identify new questions. Nothing is static in the competitive world. As you assess the results of your effort, new questions will arise. Given the possible response scenarios you've developed, it may now be important to know, for instance, whether they could launch their new product in 7 months, or whether it has to be 18. These critical questions become worthy of further research, analysis, and monitoring.

Source: adapted from House (2000).

The complacency of leaders in markets can provide major opportunities. The competitor's own feeling of invulnerability may be their own weakness that could lead them to a downfall. What will provoke the greatest and most effective retaliation by the competitor?

Whereas market leaders may accept some peripheral activity, because of the low margins they perceive, or the low market volume involved, other actions are likely to provoke intense retaliation. This is often the case in price sensitive markets, where one competitor reduces the price (e.g. reducing petrol prices) in the hope of gaining market share. Sometimes the market leader may even go to the business press and claim that every price cut would be matched. Sometimes this step prevents a fierce price war.

A result of the above is that most competitors fall into one of four categories.

1. *The laid-back competitor.* A competitor that does not react quickly or strongly to a rival's move. Reasons for a slow response vary. Laid-back competitors may feel their customers are loyal; they may be milking the business; they may be slow in noticing the move; they may lack the funds to react. Rivals must try to assess the reasons for the behaviour.

2. *The selective competitor.* A competitor that reacts only to certain types of attacks. It might respond to price cuts, but not to advertising expenditure increases. Shell and Q8 are selective competitors, responding only to price cuts but not to promotions. Knowing what a key competitor reacts to gives its rivals a clue as to the most feasible lines of attack.

3. *The tiger competitor.* A competitor that reacts swiftly and strongly to any assault. Procter & Gamble does not let a new detergent come easily into the market.

4. *The stochastic competitor.* A competitor that does not exhibit a predictable reaction pattern. There is no way of predicting the competitor's action on the basis of its economic situation, history, or anything else. Many SMEs are stochastic competitors, competing on miscellaneous fronts when they can afford to.

| Exhibit 5.6 | **First-mover advantages for Pepsi's distributor in Vietnam** |

Until the surrender of Saigon, the Chuong Duong Beverage Factory bottled Coca-Cola, and the Vietnamese consumed 500 million bottles of Coke annually. With the advent of communism, the name of Saigon was changed to Ho Chi Minh City, and Coca-Cola was officially banned from Vietnam as the USA imposed an embargo on its enemy.

International Beverage Company (IBC) was a relatively small business in Tann Thoi Hiep, a village near Ho Chi Minh City. IBC was a relatively insignificant soft drinks firm, with 200 employees. In 1993, PepsiCo signed a memorandum of understanding to hand over a license to IBC once the US-imposed trade embargo was removed. In early February 1994, the USA dropped the 19-year-old ban on Vietnam. A few hours later, IBC began making Pepsi-Cola, while Ogilvy and Mather released a television advert, which they had produced for Pepsi.

Coca-Cola in Vietnam

In 1993, Coca-Cola Indochina agreed on a US$24 million joint venture with the state-controlled soft drinks producer, Chuong Duong Beverages, in Ho Chi Minh City. Target production was to be 90 million litres annually. However, the central authorities rejected the application to produce Coca-Cola in Ho Chi Minh City.

In response, Coca-Cola applied to establish Coca-Cola Ngoc Hoi Soft Drink Co. Ltd, a joint venture with Vinalimex. This project, near Hanoi in the North of the country, would have an annual capacity of 8.5 million cases. A problem for Coca-Cola – and an advantage for IBC – was that this venture needed facilities, which had yet to be built.

The rejection of Coca-Cola's Chuong Duong plans gave Pepsi a head start in Ho Chi Minh City. Although Coca-Cola's joint venture near Hanoi was approved, it would take months to build a factory. As long as Coca-Cola could not be produced in Vietnam, IBC grew and prospered, making, bottling and distributing Pepsi and 7-Up. Within weeks, IBC's market share jumped from an insignificant proportion to 55 per cent. IBC increased its staff from 220 employees in 1993 to 700 in 1994. Sales soared from 27 billion dong in 1993 to 171 billion dong in 1994.

Source: adapted from Dana (1999).

The aim of this step is to force a company to look beyond its own moves and towards those of its competitors and, like a great player of chess, think several moves ahead. It involves a firm thinking of its moves in a broad, strategic framework rather than the incremental manner in which strategies often emerge. Or, by following a series of seemingly small incremental shifts in pricing and promotion, a firm may be perceived to be making a major play in the marketplace and incur the wrath of major players.

5.9 How can we set up an organization for CI?

Competitive, or business, intelligence is a powerful new management tool that enhances a firm's ability to succeed in today's highly competitive global markets. It provides early warning intelligence and a framework for better understanding and countering competitors' initiatives. Competitive activities can be monitored in-house or assigned to an outside firm.

Within the organization, competitive information should be acquired both at the corporate level and at the SBU level. At the corporate level, competitive intelligence is concerned with competitors' investment strengths and priorities. At the SBU level, the major interest is in marketing strategy, that is, product, pricing, distribution, and promotion strategies that a competitor is likely to pursue. The true pay-off of CI comes from the SBU review.

The CI task can be assigned to a SBU strategic planner, to a marketing person within the SBU who may be a market researcher or a product/market manager, or to a member of staff. Whoever is given the task of gathering CI should be allowed adequate time and money to do a thorough job.

International CI structures

When establishing an international CI structure, there are several ways of constructing the responsibilities based on geographic information needs, resources

---

Exhibit 5.7   **Shadow teams in CI**

Shadow teams provide a way of integrating the firm's internal knowledge with external competitive intelligence. Shadow team members should represent a cross-functional composite, drawn from the organization's best and brightest people. Each team's mission is to 'shadow' a chosen, key competitor and to learn everything possible about the rival from published data, firm personnel, network connections etc. As information is collected and analysed, the shadow team becomes a knowledge base that may soon operate as a think tank.

Shadow Team Case Study: pharmaceutical firm

A medium-size US pharmaceutical firm structured shadow teams around ailment classifications. During scanning activities, a shadow member heard a rumour from a US Food and Drug Administration contact, which was corroborated by a field sales person, that a new drug positioned to rival the firm's market leader was close to receiving approval. An upcoming conference gave the shadow team an opportunity to gather intelligence and validate – or refute – the rumour. Network connections identified the academic institution that was conducting the competitor product trials. During an evening cocktail party, shadow team members independently engaged scientists in discussions about chemistry and related topics. In time, they learned about the trials (although the product or sponsor was never noted by name), confirmed the rumour and, just as important, identified new procedures employed in clinical testing.

At the same time, the shadow team was charged with finding out why competitors were constantly beating the firm to market with new categories of drugs. Their experience with competitor scientists at the conference influenced the team's decision to launch a counter-intelligence investigation of their own firm. They learned that their own scientists, both in-house and those contracted to run clinical trials, behaved in the same way as the scientists at the conference, by discussing chemical issues close to the trials.

This firm obtained two results from this.

● It launched a campaign to bolster its product's market share.

● A programme was created to enhance awareness of protecting intellectual property and competitive information throughout the organization. The shadow team drove home the importance of not only learning, but of guarding knowledge.

Source: adapted from Rotherberg, Marist College and Associates (1999).

available and anticipated demand. When anticipated demand is low, the assignment of international responsibilities should probably fall to the initial project analyst. When anticipated demand is high or moderate, more formal structures are beneficial.

Limited human resources/additional responsibilities

When staffing is limited, a single individual may need to be assigned to cover the entire world. A better format though is to divide the world's regions among the CI team. If only a single region is of interest, such as Latin America, and the CI team has two full-time analysts, then assign each one half of the region; one would have South America, while the other would focus on, say, Central America, Mexico and the Caribbean. This division allows familiarity with and understanding of the culture, people, governments and commercial structures to grow. If only specific countries are being examined, then split them equally among the analysts.

Expanded human resources/single responsibility

In the event that budget or staffing can allow for specialists in specific international regions, based on demand, assign those responsibilities accordingly. A critical component of a single responsibility focus is the ability to maintain perspective within the scope of the organization as a whole. The danger of confusing significant and insignificant information can be a problem when analysts are not able to maintain size and scope perspectives.

Should the CI team be able to hire someone specifically for an internationally focused intelligence assignment, background and experience in that culture may be preferable, but education and international orientation are the primary objectives. Specific requirements include active reading and listening skills to break down artificial or secondary barriers caused by translation; interest and enjoyment in working with people from other socio-economic backgrounds and cultural upbringing, and awareness of the home culture's biases, expectations and beliefs. In other words, hire someone who understands and is sensitive to these facts.

For example, US citizens typically prefer space between themselves and those around them and tend to depend on schedules and set times. Latin Americans tend to interact when physically closer, and are patient when the meeting scheduled at 1 pm takes place at 4 pm.

5.10 Summary

This chapter has explored the key issues in analysing competitors and creating competitive advantage. Firms need to understand their competitors because corporate success results from providing more value to customers than the competition (competitive triangle). To prepare an effective marketing strategy, a company must study its competitors as well as its actual and potential customers.

Competitor analysis and CI focus on competitor identification, an audit of competitor capabilities (strengths and weaknesses), their objectives and strategies and prediction of response patterns. The aim is to provide a basis for creating a competitive advantage, anticipating future actions, and estimating how they will react to future actions our company may take.

There is no doubt that competitive pressure will continue to intensify in all markets. The forces that are active now are unlikely to diminish in the near future. Increasing numbers of companies will start to collect CI from internal and external sources and the number of specialists from whom they can outsource will grow.

As important as a competitive orientation is in today's global market, companies should not overdo the emphasis on competitors. Companies should manage a good balance of consumer and competitor monitoring.

In the next chapter we shall see that it might be beneficial to enter into relationships with former competitors.

Case study 5.2 Virgin Cola

Trying a comeback in the USA

'Virgin Cola is about challenging duopolies and geting a piece of the cake' Richard Branson, founder of Virgin, at the introduction of Virgin Cola in 1994.

Virgin – the third most recognized brand in the UK – is now trying to become a global brand name of the 21st century. It is involved in airlines, trains, finance, soft drinks, music, mobile phones, holidays, cars, wines, publishing, and bridal wear. What ties all these businesses together are the values of the brand and the attitude of people. Virgin consists of over 200 companies worldwide, employing over 25,000 people. The total revenues around the world in 1999 exceeded £3 billion (US$5 billion).

The name Virgin was suggested to Branson as a means of portraying the idea of commercial innocence combined with a certain shock value. For Richard Branson, 'The brand is the most single important asset that we have; our ultimate objective is to establish it as a major global name. That means we need to have a number of core businesses with global potential' (Vignali, 2001).

Virgin Cola has always had a large task on its hands, with Coke and Pepsi retaining such a stranglehold. Richard Branson set his sights on the number two spot when he launched the brand as a joint venture with Canadian drinks company Cott in 1994 (he bought Cott's stake in 1998). Yet Virgin Cola is still lagging. According to A.C. Nielsen, Virgin had sales of £28.6 million in audited retail outlets in the UK in 1999, while Coke had sales of £620.4 million.

Virgin Cola is produced by Virgin Drinks (formerly Virgin Cola).

The Virgin Cola story

In 1994, following the success of previous business ventures, Branson launched himself and The Virgin Group into a completely different product area, the global cola market. His rationale stemmed from the urge to challenge the two major global giants within the cola market. His motive was to shake up the cola market. Thus, using the fun image of the Virgin brand to exploit this new market, the cola war began (Vignali, 2001) (Figure 5.6).

The history of Virgin cola is as follows.

1994
- Virgin Retail Group and the Canadian Cott Corporation announce the formation of the Virgin Cola Company Ltd through a joint venture.
- Virgin Cola launched in the UK.

1995
- Virgin Cola launched in Japan.

1996
- Virgin Cola launched in France.

1998
- Virgin Cola launched in Belgium and South Africa.
- Virgin Cola facilities established in the USA on the east and west coasts, using an extensive network of new age beverage distributors.
- Virgin bought out Cott Corporation's share in the company.

▶

Case study 5.2 continued

Figure 5.6 Virgin soft drinks

1999

● New markets targeted in China and South America.

The Virgin Cola advertising and image

Virgin Cola spends relatively little on advertising, compared with Coke and Pepsi. In 2001 it spent £5 million in the UK. Glenn Harrison, creative director at international branding consultancy Tango, said following the image building of Virgin Cola (Witt 2000):

The Virgin brand is a manifestation of one man's personality, confident enough to challenge the establishment (Coca-Cola and Pepsi), yet still in touch with giving consumers a better deal. This is central to Virgin's appeal.

I'd love Virgin Cola to really have a crack at the established cola brands in the way Virgin Atlantic has challenged BA. It needs to go out on a limb and reflect the confidence of the Virgin brand. Virgin Cola has not created a reason to exist. Virgin products seem to work best in markets where there is a deficiency in quality, cost

and/or emotional return to the consumer. It seems to have forgotten this in creating a brand whose point of difference is that it is a girlie cola drink which doesn't taste as good as Coke and Pepsi.

This low product quality perception may not have been so bad if the branded competition weren't very good marketers, did not have much money or if own-label didn't have its act together.

However, none of these situations exist. Coke and Pepsi are more than good enough at marketing – spending their massive budgets to ram home a constant message and offer great deals in supermarkets. At the other end of the spectrum, own-label and its best mate Perfectly Clear are putting massive pressure on quality and value. And this leaves Virgin Cola between a rock and a hard place.

The US and UK cola market

In the UK, the majority of carbonated drinks are consumed by people aged between 12 and 20. In the USA, the market is dominated by consumers between the ages of 24 and 30. Owing to increased competition and more variety, today's consumers are more likely to experiment with different flavours of carbonated drinks than just cola. This is becoming very popular in the USA, while in the UK this trend is just beginning.

The leading brands such as Coca-Cola and Pepsi have so far been able to hold on to their market through fierce promotion strategies and diversification into new types of carbonated drinks. Innovation and brand image are the key to their success.

The US soft drinks market is larger and more mature than the UK soft drinks market. In the USA the soft drinks market in 1998 was US$50 billion and it is expected to increase by 5 per cent per year. In fact, the USA has the largest soft drinks market, by value and volume, in the world. Soft drinks sales in the UK were US$8 billion (Vignali, 2001).

Virgin Cola in the UK

Six years after Richard Branson wagered he would shave off his beard if Virgin Cola had not overtaken Pepsi in the UK by the year 2000, figures show Virgin with 5–7% market share of cola sales, compared with approximately 20% for Pepsi. One industry insider said that Virgin

Case study 5.2 continued

has done everything in its power to make a success of the brand. It always plays the underdog, but if you look at the size of the Virgin Group, it is not short of money to spend when it wants to. Ultimately, people just did not want to buy its product (Buxton, 2000).

The rest of the case study is about Virgin's efforts to increase market share in the USA where Virgin Cola launched the brand for the first time in 1998.

Virgin Cola in the USA

The name might imply shyness, innocence or inexperience, but UK-based Virgin Cola marched onto the US beverage scene in 1998 with a brash attitude and the intention of taking on the cola giants. The style was a trademark of company owner, British entrepreneur Richard Branson, and it had previously put Virgin soft drinks in the ranks of Coke and Pepsi in England.

Branson kicked off Virgin's US debut by travelling through New York City's Times Square in a tank to symbolize the war he wished to wage on the Coca-Cola and Pepsi-Cola brands. The brand's first marketing campaign in the USA challenged consumers to 'say something' by sounding off while standing on a Virgin Cola soapbox. Both ploys were in true Branson style, which served him well in the creation of Virgin Atlantic Airways and Virgin Megastores, and made the beverage brand popular in the United Kingdom. So why didn't it turn out to be a success in the United States?

Bob O'Brien, managing director at Virgin Drinks USA, admits that when the brand was launched in 1998 on the west and east coasts, it did not meet the high standards set for the launch (Theodore, 2000)

According to O'Brien the Virgin Cola marketing campaign had three problems:

1. Supply didn't keep up with demand. Consumers who saw Branson's public relations blitz couldn't find the product in stores and quickly lost interest. There were people who were saying 'we've been looking for years, and we can't find it'. There was some frustration at the consumer level in terms of interest being created and not being fulfilled.

2. Too narrow a product line. In a world where consumers are used to many beverage options, Virgin had only two products, a cola and a diet cola.

3. The company overestimated consumer knowledge of the Virgin brand name in the USA. The Virgin brand name has much greater equity in the UK. People recognize the brand name and Richard Branson is a far better known figure in the UK than he is in the USA.

Another factor is that the USA already has very successful colas. Consumers are not necessarily looking for alternative cola brands, but increasingly looking for a wider range of soft drinks and other non-alcoholic beverages. That is why, rather than continue what would surely be a losing battle against the major cola companies, Virgin has made new product development one of its key strategic decisions. It will put a major effort behind broadening its line-up to include functional and new age beverages. The company changed its name early in 2000 to Virgin Drinks USA to better represent its new mission: still focusing on the soft drinks, but to make a broader type of beverage to fulfil the emerging drinks needs.

Two examples of broadening the product concept are as follows.

New flavours in the existing line of carbonated soft drinks

The first thing the company did was broaden its line of carbonated soft drinks with two new flavours, Virgin Lem'n Lime and Virgin Orange, a tangerine and orange flavoured soft drink. It also brought Virgin's proprietary 'Cur-V' bottle to the United States. Nicknamed 'Pammy' in the UK, after actress and Branson friend Pamela Anderson Lee, the bottle will maintain its curves, but have a more politically correct image in the USA.

New energy drink

The company has also introduced Virgin Hi-Energy, a passion fruit flavoured energy drink with taurine, caffeine, vitamins B6, B12 and pantothenic acid, and ginseng. The product uses

Case study 5.2 continued

the Virgin logo, but is packaged in a slim can. Hi-Energy is just the first in a series of other new functional and new age beverages that are on the way.

Furthermore, the company has also moved its Virgin Drinks Headquarters from Los Angeles to Wilton, CN., which allows it to take better advantage of synergies with other Virgin properties, such as Virgin Atlantic Airways, which is based nearby, and the Virgin Megastores music and entertainment retail outlets. The close proximity to the other Virgin companies has provided both better corporate benefits, and several potential marketing partners.

Richard Branson will continue to play an important part in the brand's marketing. He is an incredible asset of the company. He is a PR machine.

New relationships in distribution

Virgin Drinks USA has realized that the beverage distributors might be a little hesitant to take on Virgin products after its difficult start in 1998. The sales team has to spend much of their time on the road, explaining the company's mission.

The company tries to obtain a good distribution coverage in the areas they have chosen as their target markets. A good distribution coverage can really help support awareness building. If Virgin Cola is not on the shelf, it is really in big trouble. The best marketing in the world is not going to help you if your product is not available for sale where people are making buying decisions.

Although the brand made its initial debut in 12-ounce cans and 2-litre bottles, the focus is now on the single-serve bottle and the convenience store market that is so influential to alternative beverages. The company has created a dedicated, branded cold box (cold drink equipment) and vending equipment to serve those retail customers (key accounts) who are interested in creating long-term relationships. Virgin thinks it can bring great value not only to the consumer, but to the beverage distributors with whom it is partnering now and in the future.

Virgin Drinks are currently available on the east and west coasts. Virgin believes that it will have full nationwide distribution in a couple years. Virgin is going to be very focused on both coasts and the south, and if the time is regarded as being right, it will pick up more markets.

Questions

1. What have been the main reasons for the disappointing performance of Virgin Cola (Virgin Drinks division)?

2. Which segmenting, targeting and positioning strategy would you recommend to Virgin Drinks for its comeback in the US market? (Use Tables 5.2 and 5.3.)

Source: Buxton (2000), Theodore (2000), Virgnali (2000), Witt (2000).

Table 5.2 US soft drinks market shares by company

1999 Rank	Companies	Market share (%)	Cases (millions)
1	Coca-Cola Co.	44.1	4377.5
2	PepsiCo	31.4	3119.5
3	Dr Pepper/7-Up (Cadbury)	14.7	1455.1
4	Cott Corp.	3.1	310.0
5	National Beverage	2.1	205.0
6	Royal Crown	1.2	115.4
7	Big Red	0.4	35.7
8	Seagram's	0.3	29.0
9	Monarch Co.	0.1	12.3
10	Private label/other	2.6	270.5
	Total Industry		9930.0

Table 5.3 US soft drinks market shares by brand

1999 Rank	Brands	Market share (%)	Cases (millions)
1	Coke Classic	20.3	2018.0
2	Pepsi-Cola	13.8	1371.8
3	Diet Coke	8.5	843.0
4	Mountain Dew	7.1	705.0
5	Sprite	6.8	671.5
6	Dr Pepper	6.3	630.0
7	Diet Pepsi	5.1	503.0
8	7-Up	2.1	204.9
9	CF Diet Coke	1.8	175.2
10	Barq's Root Beer	1.1	109.2

QUESTIONS FOR DISCUSSION

1. Why is competitor analysis essential in today's turbulent business environment?

2. What are the major steps in conducting a competitor analysis?

3. How does an industry's structure affect the intensity of competition?

4. What are the major sources of competitor intelligence?

5. How would you design a CI system?

6. How far is it possible to predict a competitor's response to marketing actions?

REFERENCES

Business Week (2000), How Viagra revived after a cold shower, *Business Week*, New York, August 28.

Buxton, P. (2000), Bitter truth Virgin is loath to swallow, *Marketing Week*, London, vol. 23, no. 8, March 23, pp.21–2.

Chen, M.-J. (1996), Competitor analysis and interfirm rivalry: toward a theoretical integration, *Academy of Management Review*, vol. 21, no, 1, pp. 100–34.

Clark, B. H. (1998), Managing competitive interactions, *Marketing Management*, vol. 7, no. 4, pp. 8-20.

Competitive Intelligence Magazine (1999), Managing your CI career, *Competitive Intelligence Magazine*, vol. 2, no. 3 July–Sept (**www.scip.org**).

Dana, L. P. (1999), International Beverage Company, *British Food Journal*, vol. 101, no. 5/6, pp. 479–82.

Drott, M. C. (2000), Personal knowledge, corporate information: the challenges for competitive intelligence, *Business Horizons*, April–May, pp. 31–7.

Dyer, C. and Clark, A. (2000), Pfizer loses Viagra battle: competitors ready to move in after patent on impotence drug is ruled invalid, The *Guardian*, London, November 9.

Furrer, O. and Thomas, H. (2000), The rivalry matrix: understanding rivalry and competitive dynamics, *European Management Journal*, vol. 18, no. 6, December.

Geroski, P. A. (1999), Early warning of new rivals, *Sloan Management Review*, Spring, pp. 107–16.

Glitman, E. (2000) Comprehending 'Irrational' competitor actions through futures-based analysis, *Competitive Intelligence Magazine*, vol. 3, no. 4, October–December.

Griffith, V. (2000), New drug threatens Viagra's reign, *Financial Times, Companies & Finance International*, November 29.

Hannon, J.M. (1997), Leveraging HRM to enrich competitive intelligence, *Human Resource Management*, vol. 36, no.4, winter, pp. 409–22.

House, D. (2000), Getting inside your competitor's head: a roadmap for understanding goals and assumptions, *Competitive Intelligence Magazine*, vol. 3, no. 4, October–December. (**www.scip.org**)

Irish Times (2000), Home news: Pfizer loses its exclusive patent in Viagra case, *Irish Times*, November 9, 2000.

Kotler, P. (2000), *Marketing Management*, Prentice Hall, Englewood Cliffs, NJ.

Levitt, T. (1960), Marketing myopia, *Harvard Business Review*, July–August, p. 46.

Porter, M. E. (1980), *Competitive Strategy*, The Free Press, New York.

Porter, M. (1985), *Competitive Advantage*, The Free Press, New York.

Prescott, J. (1998), Leveraging information for action: a look into the competitive and business intelligence consortium benchmarking study', *Competitive Intelligence Review*, vol. 9, no. 1, Spring.

Rotherberg, H. N. (1999), Marist College and Associates, Fortifying strategic decisions with shadow teams: a glance at product development. For keeping tabs on competitors, the shadow (team) knows, *Competitive Intelligence Magazine*, April–June, vol. 2. no. 2. (**www.scip.com**)

The Independent (2000), It gives me energy and puts me in the mood: Viagra is finding favour on the black market as an aphrodisiac for women. But does it work? And is it safe? *The Independent – Health*, London, October 26.

Theodore, S. (2000), Mainstream alternatives, *Beverage Industry*, New York, vol. 91, no. 10, pp. 42–3.

Vezmar, J. M. (1996), Competitive intelligence at Xerox, *Competitive Intelligence Review*, vol. 7, no. 3, Fall.

Vignali, C. (2001), Virgin Cola, *British Food Journal*, vol. 103, no. 2, pp. 131–45.

West, C. (1999), Competitive intelligence in Europe, *Business Information Review*, vol. 16, no. 3, September, pp. 143–50.

Witt, J. (2000), Preparing Virgin cola for the fight of its life, *Marketing*, London, November 2, p. 23.

Chapter 6

Analysing relationships in the value chain

LEARNING OBJECTIVES

After studying this chapter you should be able to:

- discuss the reasons and motives why firms go into relationships.
- describe and understand the concept of the 'value net' model.
- explain and discuss how relationships with suppliers and customers can add value in the total vertical chain.
- describe the phases in the development of a relationship.
- show and explain which factors determine a possible termination of inter-firm relationships.
- explain and discuss how horizontal relationships with competitors and complementors can add value to the customers.
- explain the difference between B-t-C and B-t-B relationships.
- explore how internal marketing relationships can add value to the relationships with customers.

Case study 6.1 Philips and Jordan

Development and marketing of an electrical toothbrush for the world market

Jordan is a family owned international manufacturer of mechanical oral hygiene products, household and painting tools, based in Oslo, Norway. Jordan branded toothbrushes can be found in more than 100 countries on all five continents. Jordan is the leading toothbrush in more European countries than any other brand.

Jordan's total sales in 1999 were US$115 million of which about 60 per cent came from oral care products (this includes dental sticks and dental floss as well as toothbrushes).

The group recorded a loss before tax of US$3.5 million in 1999 as against a profit of US$4.3 million the year before.

The group's financial position is sound, with very good liquidity. Jordan AS, the parent company, has a book equity of US$30 million, which corresponds to an equity ratio of 62 per cent.

The oral care/toothbrush market

The world oral care market has an estimated retail value of US$8.5 billion. Electric toothbrushes represent 5–10 per cent of the oral care market and the segment is growing rapidly. Already 10–15 per cent of the western population have electric toothbrushes and this figure is expected to rise to as much as 30–50 per cent in the next few years. It is expected that 4.2 million electrical dental care appliances will be sold this year in the USA and 3.7 million in Europe.

Case study 6.1 continued

Jordan's toothbrush markets

Norway, Sweden, Denmark, Finland and the Netherlands are Jordan's primary markets for oral care products. In Norway, Jordan's toothbrushes have a market share of 73 per cent, in Finland the market share is about 39 per cent, in Sweden and Denmark the share is 25 per cent, and, in Holland, 20 per cent.

Alliance with Philips[1]

As a consequence of the strong market growth in electrical toothbrushes Philips and Jordan announced in April 1997 that they were combining their expertise to form what would be one of the strongest alliances ever established in oral care. The first fruit of the alliance was a new electrical toothbrush: the Philips/Jordan 2-action Plaque Remover that was launched in 1998.

Jordan's experience was the perfect match for Philips, one of the world's leading producers of personal care appliances and renowned for technological research and innovation. Jordan, a global player in mechanical oral care, and a European market leader, is currently ranked fourth in the world. With 160 years experience in brush design and manufacture, Jordan brought to the alliance its broad knowledge of the oral care field.

Extensive clinical trials showed conclusive proof that the 2-Action Plaque Remover provides the best interdental reach and gum protection available. For researching and testing personal care products (including dental care products), Philips has its own dedicated research institute, the Philips Personal Care Institute.

Hence, with the new 2-Action Plaque Remover, the Philips-Jordan alliance was ready to attack the market leader owned by Gillette, Braun Oral-B, which has about 40 per cent of the world market for electrical toothbrushes.

Recently, Procter & Gamble's Colgate Actibrush has also entered the electrical toothbrush market. The lower-priced product was introduced in April/May 2000 and by the end of 2000 Actibrush had generated US$115 million in sales and had reached 50 countries. Also GlaxoSmithKline introduced its Aquafresh powerclean battery powered toothbrush in April 2001.

Philips makes a new move in the electrical toothbrush market

In August 2000, Philips announced that it had signed an agreement to acquire Optiva Corporation, the US-based manufacturer of the Sonicare® sonic toothbrush. With approximately 600 employees and annual sales of US$175 million, Optiva is the market leader (35–40 per cent market share) together with Braun Oral-B.

The Sonicare line is sold through a broad set of US distribution channels, including over 32,000 retail outlets (e.g. Target, Walgreens, Costco, Bed Bath & Beyond and Macy's) as well as through dental professionals. Sonicare differs from conventional power brushes by employing sonic technology. It cleans with a combination of 31,000 brush strokes per minute and gentle sonic waves. Sonicare has been clinically shown to remove nearly twice as much plaque between teeth as a manual brush. Sonicare's safety and efficacy has been confirmed in studies published in 40 research reports and abstracts from over 80 different investigators, including 18 universities in North America and Europe. To date, more than 7 million Sonicare® sonic toothbrushes have been sold, mainly in the USA.

In January 2001, Optiva Corporation changed its name to Philips Oral Healthcare.

Questions

1. What were the strategic benefits for Philips and Jordan in creating an alliance?
2. What would be the benefits for Philips of the Optiva acquisition? How would Optiva benefit from the acquisition?
3. If you were a part of the Jordan senior management group, how would you react to Philips' acquisition of Optiva?

Source: Chemist & Druggist (2001), Cordona (2000), Nelson (2001), Philips (1997), Philips (2000), Philips (2001).

[1] Royal Philips Electronics is one of the world's biggest electronic companies and Europe's largest, with sales of €37.9 billion in 2000. It is a global leader in colour television sets, lighting, electric shavers, colour picture tubes for televisions and monitors, and one-chip TV products. Its 219,400 employees in more than 60 countries are active in the areas of lighting, consumer electronics, domestic appliances, components, semiconductors, and medical systems.

6.1   Introduction

It is impossible to make sense of what happens in a firm or how to manage it without taking a relationship view of a company. This means that it is not enough to discuss the activities that a single firm performs. We need to understand how these activities are linked to the activities of the company's suppliers, its customers and indeed to their customers. Because a firm's activities evolve within its relationships with others, each may have to do things that they do not really like, or they may be unable to do the things that they want. Hence, companies are dependent for their success on their relationships with customers and suppliers and with others. Many of the strategic choices that a company makes will be in response to the actions of these other companies.

In turn, the outcome of a firm's strategy will always depend on the actions of others, and how they react to what the company does. In this way a firm's strategy may be thought of as a kind of game, because there is nothing predetermined about the consequences of the various choices a firm might take. In a market where relationships matter, these games of action and reaction are complex and their results are vital to the firms involved.

Relationships enable firms to develop competitive advantage by leveraging the skills and capabilities of their partners to improve the performance of the total value chain. Firms no longer compete as individual companies; they compete as groups of companies that cooperate to bring value to the ultimate consumer. Across virtually all sectors of the economy, relationships have reshaped the interactions of companies.

In his classic 'From 4Ps to 30Rs' work, Gummesson (1994, 1999) identified 30 types of relationships. The relationships are divided into four levels:

1. *Classic market relationships (R1–R3)* are the *supplier-customer dyad*, the *triad of supplier-customer-competitor*, and the *physical distribution network*, which are treated extensively in general marketing theory.

2. *Special market relationships (R4–R17)* represent certain aspects of the classic relationships, such as the *interaction in the service encounter* or the *customer as member of a loyalty programme*.

3. *Mega relationships (R18–R23)* exist above the market relationships. They provide a platform for market relationships and concern the economy and society in general. Among these are *mega marketing* (lobbying, public opinion and political power), *mega alliances* (such as the NAFTA, setting a new stage for marketing in North America), and *social relationships* (such as friendship and ethnic bonds).

4 *Nano relationships (R24–R30)* are found below the market relationships, that is relationships inside an organization (*intra*-organizational relationships). All internal activities influence the externally bound relationships.

Compared to this comprehensive approach to RM, the following analysis of relationships (the value net) is mainly focused on the four closest players in the **micro-environment**, plus relationships to internal employees. (These are the classic market relationships and the nano relationships in the Gummesson terminology.

The value net

The value net (Figure II.1, p. 104) shows the relationships with other players in the value chain.

The value net reveals two fundamental symmetries. Vertically, customers and suppliers are equal partners in creating value. The other symmetry is on the horizontal for competitors and complementors. The mirror image of competitors is complementors. A complement to one product or service is any other product or service that makes the first one more attractive, i.e., computer hardware and software, hot dogs and mustard, catalogues and overnight delivery service, red wine and dry cleaners. The value net helps you understand your competitors and complementors 'outside in'. Who are the players and what are their roles and the interdependences between them? Re-examine the conventional wisdom of 'Who are your friends and who are your enemies?' The suggestion is to know your business inside out and create a value net with the other players. Increase demand for whatever your customer sells.

The starting point of Figure II.1 is the player bonds, but according to Håkansson and Johanson (1997) and Håkansson and Snehota (1995), relationships between these players can be characterized along three dimensions that comprise the substance of those relationships. Closely connected to the value net (Figure II.1) is the so-called ARA network, where the players (actors) are supplemented with resources and activities (Figure 6.1).

Figure 6.1 The ARA network

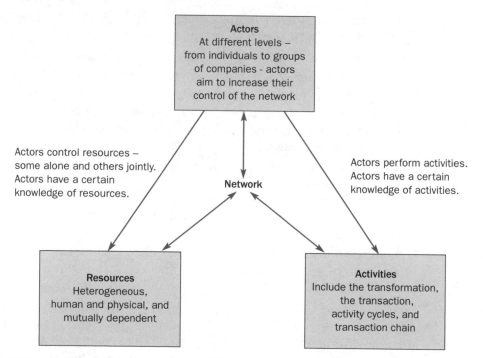

Source: adapted from Håkansson and Johanson (1987), p. 17.

Player bonds

The characteristics of a company in a business market are largely defined by the relationships that bind it to others and through which it acts.

The individual players in Figure 6.1 will learn about each other, they will invest in their relationship, and social exchange between them will increase their knowledge of each other and build up a certain trust.

Resource ties

Resources are required to perform the commercial activities of the firm. Resources are not independent, but rely on each other to be productive. A relationship is also a way of tying the resources of two companies together. A company's resources are of little real value until they are activated through interaction with other companies. It is through a relationship that a company can make use of its own resources and activate those that are controlled by a counterpart for its own benefit. This activation means that the resources of one company are likely to become oriented toward a specific use and will be tied to the resources of other companies. These resource ties between companies are essential both to innovate in using resources and to develop new ones.

Activity links

Activities are processes involved in the production of goods and services. Relationships also link the different activities of suppliers and customers to each other. Activity links are the basis of ideas such as **total quality management** that cut across a company's boundaries.

This is why questions about the most appropriate business relationships have been so important when introducing them. Activity links between companies are valuable because they give the companies involved the chance to rationalize some of the operations that are important for their success.

Because relationships are substantial, they are not easy to change quickly and changes are likely to incur significant costs, both in disruption and in developing new relationships. This tends to make business markets rather stable.

In the following sections the different activity links of the actor relationships are further described.

To fully understand the actor relationships it is also very important to grasp the five dependence dimensions that can exist between two firms in a relationship (Håkansson and Snehota, 1995; Svensson, 2002):

1. *Technical dependence*: when two firms use compatible equipment and adapt their mutual business activities to each other in a technical sense.

2. *Time dependence*: when two firms have time-based needs or synchronization of their mutual business activities.

3. *Knowledge dependence*: when the interaction processes between two firms result in learning each other's strengths and weaknesses. This interaction creates awareness and knowledge about each other's ability to solve problems.

4. *Social dependence*: the interaction between two firms is often based on personal relationships. This means that the social atmosphere and the personal chemistry between the involved executives affects the activities in a business relationship.

5. *Economic/juridical dependence*: the formal dependence that may exist between two firms, such as written agreements. It strengthens the dependence between two firms' business activities in an economic and juridical sense.

In relation to Figure II.1, the relationship to customers (1) is normally the main issue in marketing books. But in this chapter the success with customer/relationship is regarded as very dependent on what is happening in relationships 2–5 (Figure II.1).

Therefore, the following sections deal with the different relationships in more detail.

6.2 Customer relationships

The simplest reason why firms seek to develop ongoing relationships with their customers is that it is generally much more profitable to retain existing customers than continually seek to recruit new customers to replace lost ones. There have been many exercises to calculate the effects on a company's profits of even a modest improvement in the rate at which customers defect to competitors.

RM signifies that the firm should seek to have close relationships with its customers. Please note that in this section, customers may cover both end buyers and distributors/resellers.

What is meant by a relationship, and how is it developed? As illustrated by the following quotes, in essence this new approach means a focus on long-term interactions between a marketer and its customers, instead of a short-term transactional approach:

> *Relationship marketing is the process of identifying and establishing, maintaining, enhancing, and when necessary terminating relationships with customers and other stakeholders* (Grönroos, 1996, p. 7).

> *Relationship marketing has the aim of building long-term satisfying relations with key parties – customers, suppliers, distributors – in order to earn and retain their long-term preference and business* (Kotler, 2000, p. 13).

In the development of relationships, managers have to realize that the customer is no longer interested in buying a product. The product, in fact, is no more than an artefact around which customers have experiences. What's more, customers are not prepared to accept experiences fabricated by companies. Increasingly, they want to shape those experiences themselves, both individually and with experts or other customers.

Prahalad and Ramaswamy (2000) distinguish between personalization and customization.

Customization assumes that the manufacturer will design a product to suit a customer's needs. It is particularly pronounced on the Internet, where consumers can customize a host of products and services such as business cards, computers (like Dell), and greeting cards.

Personalization, on the other hand, is about the customer becoming a co-creator of the content of experiences. To provide personalized experiences, companies must create opportunities for customers to experiment with and then decide the level of involvement they want in creating a given experience with the company. Since the level of customer engagement cannot be predetermined, companies will have to give consumers as much choice and flexibility as possible, both in the channels of distribution and communication and in the design of products. But

| Exhibit 6.1 | **Lean dealership: car dealers build a relationship with the consumer** |

The European motor retail industry is currently facing an unprecedented number of major forces for change. For car dealer businesses to survive, they must clearly demonstrate to consumers that they represent the best possible channel for the acquisition and maintenance of consumers' motoring needs. They must also demonstrate to manufacturers that they represent the best route to market for them.

The consumption of motoring is currently delivered by the interaction between three primary players:

● *Consumers* have a demand for mobility, at a cost which maximizes value in their perception.

● *Manufacturers* (and their upstream supply chains) wish to generate shareholder value by designing, producing and marketing new cars. Greater customer loyalty is also a goal that manufacturers seek because it reduces their own substantial customer acquisition costs. Traditionally, such loyalty has been achieved by careful new product development that meets the future wants and needs of its current customers.

● *Dealers* wish to generate value by being the distribution channel for new cars between manufacturers (in one location). These and many other retailers also deal with the location and resale of used cars and with the maintenance of all cars.

Let us elaborate further on the dealers' perspective and their interest in building relationships with consumers. In the lean dealership, salespeople use their time not only to sell cars, but also to sell after-care. They become customer account managers. Sales training on the brand already gives them good product knowledge, and with extra training and checklists they could do basic diagnosis and book customers in for service and repair. They use an integrated IT system to schedule a customer's car into the workshop – perhaps at a specific time of day convenient for them.

Each salesperson should have a personal technician linked to him or her and each of them has a nominated substitute in case of holidays or illness. These two are supported by a team of specialists. Dealers that have tried the idea of personal technicians in the past found it difficult to implement, primarily because they do not manage the consumer demand.

In the lean dealership, customer account managers aim to have regular contact with most customers for their after-sales needs. During this activity, managers will steadily gather increasing amounts of information about the customer's motoring needs. In particular, they would understand more about their customers':

● wants and needs (job/income change, family size change, new drivers, hobbies or interests, etc.)

● financial commitments (broad income levels and outstanding loan status)

● propensity to replace their car(s).

The better the customer account manager understands the customers' likely wants and needs, the more likely he or she is to be able to satisfy them with an appropriate car at an appropriate price at an appropriate time.

Source: adapted from Jackson (1985).

companies can also help direct their customers' requirements and expectations by guiding public debate about the future technology and its impact on new products on the market.

However, managing the variety of customer experiences is not the same as managing variety in products. It is about managing the interface between a company and its customers – the range of experience transcends the company's products. Managers must develop a product that shapes itself to users' needs, not the other way around. But as noted, customers evolve over time through their experience with a product. The product has to evolve in a way that enables future modifications and extensions based both on a customer's changing needs and on the company's changing capabilities.

Developing buyer-seller relationships – the marriage metaphor

Over the past 15 years the analogy between building business relationships and personal relationships (marriage) has been utilized extensively. Certainly there are some interesting parallels between them, and by considering the personal aspects of relationship development it is possible to arrive at a better understanding of the business issues.

A theoretical life-cycle model of relationships proposed by Dwyer *et al.* (1987) identified five stages of relationship development – awareness, exploration, expansion, commitment and dissolution (see Figure 6.2).

The linking stages seem to be:

● meeting (awareness)
● dating (exploration)
● courting (expansion)

Figure 6.2 Stages in buyer-seller relationship development

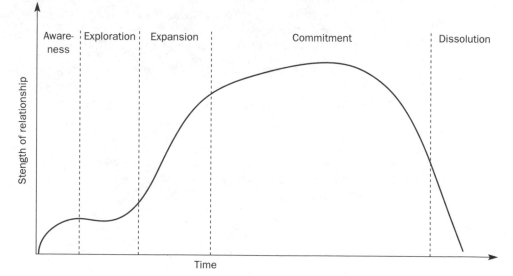

Source: adapted from Dwyer *et al.* (1987).

| Exhibit 6.2 | Soft drinks and clothing – it is all about creating linkages with end consumers |

In 1999, soft drink manufacturer PepsiCo launched a range of branded clothes aimed at the UK youth market. This followed Coca-Cola, which launched a range of branded clothes earlier that year.

When Coca-Cola re-entered the clothing market it already had licensees manufacturing 100,000 products in over 40 countries, though these were more promotional items than proper fashion ranges. Coca-Cola stated that the return of the company to fashion was necessary because 'consumers feel a special connection with Coca-Cola – more than just a drinking experience'.

PepsiCo already had a range of clothing, which had been available in the USA for some time, but this is the first time its UK licensing programme had been extended to include clothes. It is unknown whether PepsiCo planned to open any high street sales outlets, although this was thought to be unlikely.

Source: adapted from Centaur Communications (1999).

- marriage (commitment), and possibly
- divorce (dissolution of relationship).

Their model proposed that a relationship begins to develop significance in the exploration stage when it is characterized by the attempts of the seller to attract the attention of the other party. The exploration stage includes attempts by each party to bargain and to understand the nature of the power, norms and expectations held by the other. If this stage is satisfactorily concluded, an expansion phase follows. Exchange outcomes in the exploratory stage provide evidence as to the suitability of long-term exchange relationships. The commitment phase of a relationship implies some degree of exclusivity between the parties and results in the information search for alternatives – if it occurs at all – being much reduced. The dissolution stage marks the point where buyer and seller recognize that they would be better able to achieve their respective aims outside the relationship.

Dissolution stage

A relationship can be considered to have ended when no activity links or resource ties exist between the parties involved in the relationship. Although personal bonds may remain, both parties perceive the relationship as ended.

In supplier-customer relations some customers may stop buying the firm's products. This is an effective exit strategy. However, most business relationships are very complicated, involving activity links and resource ties.

For inter-firm relationships, it is likely that the closer the parties are, the more concerned the firms will be about the other 'losing face' due to ending the relationship.

Before developing a model of relationship termination, the factors that characterize a business relationship (commitment, trust, satisfaction, quality of alternatives, satisfaction, dependence, trust, social and other bonds) prior to termination must be considered. These factors can not only provide a cause for the termination, but impact greatly on the types of strategies firms utilize when ending relationships. For example, the fact that superior alternative partners exist may be sufficient to motivate a firm to terminate a relationship.

Morgan and Hunt (1994), Hocutt (1998), and Giller and Matear (2001) proposed that the propensity to leave a relationship flows directly from commitment and that there is a strong negative relationship between commitment and propensity to leave the relationship (Figure 6.3).

The relationship termination process begins with an event triggering the termination and extends through to the consequences of the termination on both parties and the connected network.

A trigger is any factor that alters the current state of the relationship in such a way that the termination process is initiated. Although the trigger starts the process, it is not necessarily the reason why the relationship is terminated. A trigger can occur long before the actual termination takes place and it can be a factor internal to the company such as relocation of the organization, or an external factor such as a downturn in the economy causing a cutback in spending. A trigger is essentially dissatisfaction with an event, which will then provoke a reaction. Since the actual termination of a relationship is achieved through a series of acts,

Figure 6.3 A model for relationship termination

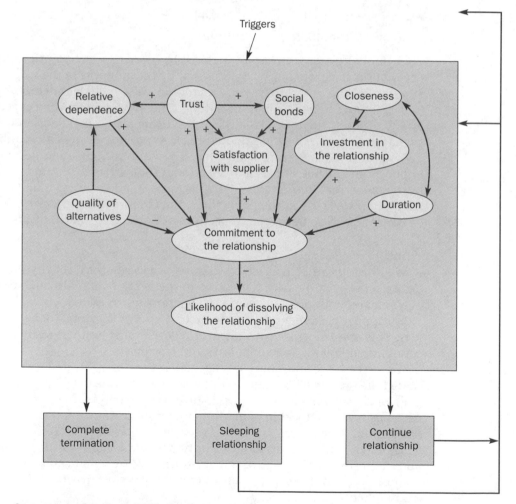

Source: adapted from Hocutt (1998), Giller & Matear (2001).

knowledge about the alternative ways of acting will provide a sound basis to understand inter-firm relationship termination better.

Satisfaction with supplier

It is important to stress the importance of continuously assessing customer satisfaction in a relationship. It is proposed that satisfaction with the supplier acts as a mediating variable between two related variables, trust and social bonds, and the outcome variable of commitment to the relationship (Hocutt, 1998).

Trust

It is a precondition for increased commitment. Therefore, the relationship dissolution model proposes that trust directly influences commitment, but the relationship between trust and commitment is also mediated by satisfaction with the supplier and relative dependence.

Social bonds

Individuals may develop strong personal friendships that tend to hold a relationship together. Buyers and sellers who have a strong personal relationship are more committed to maintaining the relationship than less socially bonded partners.

Qualities of alternatives

The firm's inability to replace a partner may be considered as an indication of the dependence on its partner. If there is a wide array of high-quality partners, dependence and commitment to the relationship will be low, and vice versa.

Relative dependence

Relative dependence can be defined as a partner's perceived difference between its own and its partner's dependence on the relationship. The firm with the greater relative dependence has, by definition, relatively greater interest in sustaining the relationship. The higher the level of relative dependence on the service provider, the higher the level of commitment to the relationship.

Investment in the relationship

Anderson and Weitz (1989) found that the greater the level of investment made by a manufacturer in a relationship, the greater the increase in that manufacturer's commitment to its relationship with the distributor. Investment in the relationship acts as a mediating variable between closeness of the relationship and level of commitment. Closeness influences the size of the investment in the relationship, which in turn influences commitment.

Closeness

A relationship is classified as close when it is characterized by high interdependence.

Duration

A firm's attachment to another reflects the prior history of learning and socialization of partners during their involvement. Hence, a longer relationship will result in higher barriers to dissolving the partnership.

From Figure 6.3 it appears that relationships can be terminated to varying degrees. Of course we can have a situation with a complete termination where there is no intention or possibility for the relationship to be reactivated in the future. But we may also see a situation where a relationship has been terminated, but bonds still exist between the firms that allow for the relationship to be reactivated some time in the future. This type of termination is referred to as a *sleeping relationship*.

Finally, we may see a situation where the relationship just confirms where it was temporarily interrupted after the partners have discussed the structure of the future relationship.

Managerial implications

Managers may consider relationship termination as a strategic decision. Firms should evaluate which relationships to initiate, which to develop, which to continue to invest in and also which to discontinue. Once a firm has made the decision to discontinue or terminate a relationship, it should be aware that there is a range of termination strategies which may be employed. The firm could be looking for strategies that could be labelled 'beautiful exits' (Alajoutsijärvi *et al.*, 2000). A beautiful exit is achieved by a strategy that minimizes damage occurring to the disengager, the other party and the connected network.

In fact there is a lot to learn from all types of personal relationships, not just marriage. After all, business relationships are not impersonal; they depend entirely on the people who represent the supplier and the customers. There are interesting parallels with the Chinese concept of Guanxi, which involves different levels of personal commitment and connections.

The implications for business of the marriage metaphor are:

- choose your partner carefully
- structure the partnership carefully
- devote time to developing the relationship
- maintain open, two-way communication
- be entirely trustworthy.

It is important to point out that not all personal relationships progress to a marriage, monogamous or polygamous, and it is equally appropriate that not all marketing partnerships have to, or are even able to, develop beyond the friendship stage.

Exhibit 6.3 | **Nescafé establishes relations with its end customers by supporting charity**

Nescafé is using its relational database for a string of direct marketing initiatives designed to strengthen the emotional ties between consumers and its range of coffee brands.

It is sending mailshots which highlight its support for leading charities, using the names on its database. In the first tranche of the two-year campaign, Nescafé emphasized its cash injections to Kids' Clubs Network, Shelter, Macmillan Cancer Relief and the British Red Cross. Nescafé also launched a Nescafé website and run on-pack promotions to reinforce its commitment to worthy causes.

Nescafé admits it had not used its database effectively in the past, but views the new venture as a 'window' for building a closer rapport with consumers.

Nescafé marketing manager, Simon Hardy, said: 'This is a new departure for us, but one which we know our consumers want. Each charity will also run its own marketing featuring Nescafé as title sponsor'.

Source: adapted from Walker (1999).

The nature of the customer and the behaviour spectrum

The behaviours of buyers and sellers interact with fundamental characteristics of the exchange environment to define the nature of their relationship. This section will use some basic elements of each sphere to describe a continuum of trading relations.

Jackson (1985) suggests that business marketers should assess 'the time horizon within which a customer makes a commitment to a supplier and also the actual pattern the relationship follows over time'. Figure 6.4 highlights the typical characteristics of customers at the end points of the account behaviour spectrum: **always-a-share customers** (transactional exchange) and **lost-for-good customers** (collaborative exchange).

Always-a-share and lost-for-good represent different ends of a continuum of exchange situations. Sellers will retain customers by giving good service and responding to customer needs. Differentiating the offering on dimensions that forge structural ties and create exit barriers will tend to move the relationship toward the lost-for-good variety. For example, an always-a-share supplier might move from a fill-in role to become a major supplier by meeting customer criteria for becoming a preferred supplier. The standards for preferred supplier vary from firm to firm, but often include quality programmes, employee safety and training efforts, and delivery specifications.

The always-a-share customers

These customers can allocate their purchases to several vendors. A period of no purchases can be followed by a period of high purchases.

Figure 6.4 The marketing relationship continuum

Always-a-share customer Transaction focus	Lost-for-good customer Relationship focus
• Lower switching costs (suppliers are largely interchangeable) • Smaller investment actions • Single sale • Discontinuous customer contact • Focus on product features • Short-term scale • Little emphasis on customer service • Limited commitment to meeting customer expectations • Quality is the concern of production staff • Low transaction costs • Lower importance	• High switching costs • Substantial investment actions, especially in procedures and lasting assets • Customer retention • Continuous contact • Focus on product benefits and the technology behind • Long-term scale • High emphasis on customer service • High commitment to meeting customer expectations • Quality is the concern of all staff • High transaction costs • Higher importance: strategic, operational and personal
Examples of products: Print services, office supplies, bulk chemicals, PCs' supplies	*Examples of products:* Telecommunication systems, franchises, computer systems (e.g. CRM systems)

Source: adapted from Jackson (1985).

The always-a-share customer purchases repeatedly from some product category, displays less loyalty or commitment to a particular supplier, and can easily switch part or all of the purchases from one vendor to another. Because of low switching costs, these customers may share their patronage over time with multiple vendors and adopt short-term commitments with suppliers.

The lost-for-good customers

Relationships cemented by switching costs are called *lost-for-good relationships* because the prospects of a customer making a costly switch to a competitor followed by a costly return to the first are remote – probably weaker than a cold-call prospect. It is not likely that the customer would pay the switching costs again to return to the first firm.

Customers are tied to a system. They face significant switching costs which may include:

- specific investments
- cancellation penalties
- set-up costs for a new supplier
- retraining
- finding and evaluating a new supplier.

The lost-for-good customer makes a series of purchases over time, and views the commitment to a particular supplier as relatively permanent. Once won, this type of account is likely to remain loyal to a particular supplier for a long time. If lost, however, it is often lost for good.

The behaviour of many customers in the business market is somewhere between a pure transaction focus and a pure relationship focus. The particular position that a customer occupies depends on a host of factors: the characteristics of the product category, the customer's pattern of product usage, and the actions taken by both the supplier and the customer.

Implications for relationship marketing strategies

Business marketers often have a portfolio of customers who span the whole customer behaviour spectrum. Some emphasize low price and a transaction perspective while others place a premium on substantial service and desire a more collaborative relationship. Indeed, some customers fall somewhat in the middle of the account spectrum and represent accounts that might be effectively upgraded to a level that adds value to the relationship for both parties. To develop responsive and profitable relationship marketing strategies, special attention must be given to four areas: selecting accounts, developing account-specific product offerings, implementing relationship strategies, and evaluating relationship strategy outcomes.

A relationship with customers targeted on strong and lasting commitments is especially appropriate for lost-for-good accounts. Business marketers can sensibly invest resources in order to secure commitment and to aid customers with long-term planning. Given the long-term nature and the considerable stakes involved, customers are concerned both with marketers' long-term capabilities and with their immediate performance. Because the customers perceive significant risk, they demand competence and commitment from the selling organization.

If we transfer this to Figure 6.5, the upper figure ('bow-tie') illustrates the always-a-share and the lower figure ('diamond') illustrates the lost-for-good. In the traditional 'bow-tie' relationship, the purchasing agent and the salesperson assume the primary roles in the exchange process.

Relational exchanges, in contrast, have a structure similar to the 'diamond' where the boundaries between the firms become more opaque. Interactive, cross-functional teams now openly exchange ideas for improving efficiency and effectiveness (see Figure 6.5). The goal is to create new value together.

Perhaps the most important prerequisite for the 'diamond' model is the need for a high level of 'connectivity' between the firm and its strategic suppliers. This implies not just the exchange of information on demand and inventory levels, but multiple, collaborative working relationships across the organizations at all levels. It is increasingly common today for companies to create supplier development teams that are cross-functional and, as such, are intended to communicate with the equivalent customer management team in the supplying organization (Kothandaraman and Wilson, 2000).

Behavioural conditions in buyer-seller relationships

The key dimensions in the basic behavioural conditions for establishing and developing buyer-seller relationships are as follows.

Bonding/goal compatibility

Bonding is defined as the part of a business relationship that results in two parties (customer and supplier) acting in a unified manner toward a desired goal.

Figure 6.5 Organization of buyer-seller relationship

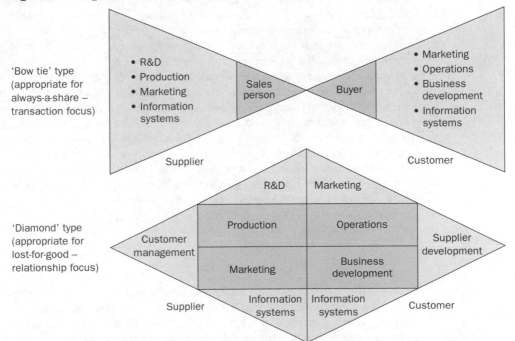

Partners in the relationship must share mutually achievable goals although the goals do not have to be the same. It would be unrealistic to expect that partners would share the same goals as each probably has different parts of the value chain, such as to source product exclusively from a certain key supplier. However, it is likely that both share the goal of better meeting the needs of the end customer. Given the economics of the different levels of the supply chain, one partner might focus on reducing the total cost of ownership, whereas the other partner might look at accessing a new market segment as its major goal.

Exhibit 6.4	Speedo's relations with its retailers

Speedo is a leading international brand company of professional swimwear, based in the UK. Like many companies today, Speedo has set up different, parallel structures for managing its diverse customer base.

Its current organization comprises three distinct interface structures: first, a traditional sales organization with a large and dispersed field salesforce who deal with the small independent sports stores. They have traditionally been the mainstay of the business and represented in the past the main channel of distribution. For Speedo, however, the sports stores are low volume customers that are spread all over the country and therefore best dealt with by individual salespeople. The company's concern for these relationships is manifested in the strong emphasis they place on an experienced, well-qualified salesforce with a high level of employee retention.

The portion of the business accounted for by the second customer segment, major high street retailers and sports multiples, has gradually increased over the last few years to approximately 50%, with the prospect of a further rise to 80% in the near future. The shifting balance and the concentration within this channel of distribution leverages the relationship value, which in turn justifies the resource-intensive account structure Speedo maintains to deal with these customers. The work between the dedicated account managers and their counterparts on the retailer side is facilitated by the provision of back-up support from other functions within the company.

Finally, Speedo started an even closer cooperation with two potentially high growth customers in 1999. The relationship project and the corresponding interface structure are still in a trial phase but both parties' commitment is high. One of the clients is Sports Division, Europe's biggest independent sports retailer with approximately 120 high street stores, additional in-store concessions as well as a number of superstores. For Speedo, the relationship is crucial because aside from the high economic relationship value, Sports Division shares its interest, stocking only leading brands and not own label products. The initiative for the project came from the operations director who is still in charge of the implementation and who assigned an account development team to work exclusively on this one account. The team members have been selected to match the retailer's supply management team and both teams' target is to improve the effectiveness and efficiency of the supply chain.

Source: adapted from Christopher and Jüttner (2000).

Trust

Trust is the belief that one's alliance partner will act in a predictable manner, will keep his or her word, and will not behave in a way that negatively affects the other. This last point is particularly salient under conditions where one partner might feel vulnerable due to a heightened dependence on the other.

In many alliances, partners are compelled to share information or knowledge that lies near, if not at, the core of their business. Trust diminishes the concern that this knowledge might be expropriated and used later to compete against the partner. This fear is very real among managers of small companies that seek alliances with larger companies. These managers fear that the larger firm is using the relationship to gain knowledge for its own benefit.

Empathy

Empathy is the dimension of a business relationship that enables the two parties to see the situation from the other's perspective. It is defined as seeking to understand somebody else's desires and goals. It involves the ability of individual parties to view the situation from the other party's perspective in a truly cognitive sense. The empathy dimension plays a major role in Chinese business relationships (Gaunxi framework) and is also apparent in western business relationships (Buttery and Wong, 1999).

Reciprocity

Reciprocity is the part of a business relationship that causes either party to provide favours or make **allowances** for the other in return for similar favours or allowances to be received at a later date. It covers the interdependence for mutual benefit and equality of exchanged values between two individuals.

These behavioural factors emphasize the importance of personal social ties in business relationships. Business relationships are built on friendships, and friendships are built upon a variety of social interactions. The individual's networks are also the enablers and driving forces of many firms' internationalization. This is a phenomenon well known to marketing practitioners, but has received little attention among academics (Axelsson and Agndal, 2000).

Relationships in B-t-B markets versus B-t-C markets

For many years RM was conceived as an approach for the inter-organizational B-t-B markets. Recently, however, the domain of RM has been extended to incorporate innovative applications in mass consumer markets. Much has changed in a few years. Recent applications of RM in consumer markets have been facilitated by developments in direct and database marketing within an increasingly competitive and fragmented marketplace.

In Table 6.1 the major differences between B-t-B and B-t-C relationships are highlighted.

One-to-one marketing relationships

According to Peppers *et al.* (1999), one-to-one marketing means being willing and able to change your behaviour toward an individual customer based on what the customer tells you and what else you know about that customer.

One-to-one relationship marketing is often expressed as being synonymous with relationship marketing, but is treated here as an extension of the initial effort that results from the ever-increasing personalization of promotional efforts in a variety of industries.

The two obvious approaches are either segmentation or personalization. Segmentation is information distributed to narrow, well-defined bands of target customers – an approach used for years. Conversely, personalization is information

Table 6.1 Comparison of B-t-C and B-t-B relationships

Characteristic	Business-to-consumer (B-t-C)	Business-to-business (B-t-B)
1. Relationship form.	Membership. The individual acknowledges some relationship (though informal affiliation with the organization).	Working partnership, just-in-time exchange, co-marketing alliance, strategic alliance, distribution channels relationship.
2. Average sale size; potential lifetime value of the customer to the selling firm.	Normally small sale size; relatively small and predictable lifetime value of the customer; limit on the amount of investment in relationship on any single customer.	Normally large and consequential; allows for large and **idiosyncratic investments** in a single relationship.
3. Number of customers.	Large number; requires large overall investment in relationship management, but low investment per customer.	Relatively fewer customers to spread investment in relationships over.
4. Seller's ability and cost to replace lost customer.	Normally can be replaced quickly at relatively low cost.	Large customers can be difficult and time consuming to replace.
5. Seller dependence on buyer.	Low for any single customer.	Varies based on customer size; can be devastating.
6. Buyer dependence on seller.	Normally has more alternatives, low switching costs, and switching can be made quickly.	Viable alternatives can take time to find, switching costs can be high, and changes impact multiple people in the organization.
7. Purchasing time frame, process, and buying centre complexity.	Normally a short time frame, simple process, and simple buying centre where one or two individuals fill most buying roles.	Often a long time frame, complex process; may have multiple individuals for a single buying role; may be subject to organizational budget cycles.
8. Personal knowledge of other party.	Relatively few contact points with seller even when loyal user; seller's knowledge of buyer often limited to database information.	Multiple personal relationships; multiple inter-organizational linkages.
9. Communication used to build and sustain relationships.	Dependence on non-personal means of contact; seller's knowledge generally limited to database information of customers.	Emphasis on personal selling and personal contact; customer knowledge held in multiple forms and places.
10. Relative size.	Seller normally larger than buyer.	Relative size may vary.
11. Legal.	Consumer protection laws often favour consumers.	Relationships governed by prevailing contract law as well as industry standard regulations and ethics.

Source: adapted from Gruen (1995).

distributed and designed to be one-to-one. The historical methods for collecting data for either segmented or personalized databases have been direct mail and **tele-marketing**. One-to-one relationships can be enhanced today by most firms using the Internet, which gives the opportunity of personal addressed marketing communications. One-to-one marketing goes hand in hand with customization. It is all about generating feedback so that marketers can learn more about customers' preferences with future offers being tailored to those preferences.

The intention of one-to-one marketing is to increase the value of a customer base by establishing a learning relationship with each customer. The customer tells you of some need, and you customize your product or service to meet it. The theory behind one-to-one marketing is simple, with implementation being another matter. Effectiveness will require differentiating customers and interacting with them.

The emphasis on the customization of products and services to meet the very specific needs of individual customers is altering the manufacturing requirements of most firms. New technology has emerged that permits such emphasis on individualism in the final product. Mass customization is the term used to describe the ability of manufacturers to make almost instant changes in the production process to individualize output in quantities as small as one. This technology coupled with the emphasis on relationships has permitted the pursuit of relationship marketing on a one-to-one basis. Mass customization will further drive relationship marketing with its associated demands for greater understanding of each customer within the seller's marketing umbrella. This additional emphasis will spur marketers to find new and better ways of gaining customer information and keeping it current.

Bonding in buyer-seller relationships

The following is mainly developed for the service sector, but the bonds described are applicable to the majority of B-t-B relationships. Liljander and Strandvik (1995) define bonds as 'exit barriers that tie the customer to the service provider and maintain the relationship'.

The authors propose ten different types of bonds between the customer and the seller: legal, economic, technological, geographical, time, knowledge, social, cultural, ideological, and psychological bonds. The authors point out that the first five bonds can be managed by a service firm while the remaining five are difficult for a firm to measure and manage.

1. A *legal bond* is a contract between a customer and a service provider. As mentioned earlier, the present study views legal bonds as belonging to the legal factor group.

2. An *economic bond* refers to a situation in which price reductions are used as incentives towards the customers. The economic bond belongs to the economic factor group.

3. A *technological bond* refers to a situation in which the customer is required to use repair/maintenance facilities and/or original spare parts from a manufacturer. As described earlier, the technological bond belongs in the technological factor group.

4. A *geographical bond* describes the limited possibility to buy a service because of distance. The present study views the geographical bond as belonging to the contextual factor group.

5. A *time bond* illustrates the situation where a service provider may be used because of suitable business hours. The present study categorizes the time bond as belonging to the procedural factor group.

6. A *knowledge bond* means that a customer gains knowledge about a service provider. As mentioned earlier, the knowledge bond belongs in the information factor group.

7. A *social bond* exists when a customer and a service provider know each other well. As mentioned earlier, social bonds belong in the social factor group.

8. A *cultural bond* exists when a customer identifies with certain companies or products made in certain countries. The cultural bond belongs in the contextual factor group.

9. An *ideological bond* indicates personal values, for example a preference for 'green' or environmentally sound products. The ideological bond is part of the social factor group.

10. A *psychological bond* refers to a customer being convinced of the superiority of a certain service provider. The present study sees the psychological bond as belonging to the social factor group.

Figure 6.6 presents one suggestion for the relationship of the concepts of bonds and commitment over time. It illustrates the holistic view of bonds, i.e. that their combination dictates the state of commitment and no bond operates in isolation from others. Bond is proposed as a term to be used for ties, and the resulting state would be called 'commitment', i.e. a combination of interrelated bonds that evolve in the bonding process in the course of the relationship. Further, the state of commitment and the combination of bonds are perceived in their own way by both parties in the relationship.

Figure 6.6 Development of bonds and commitment over time

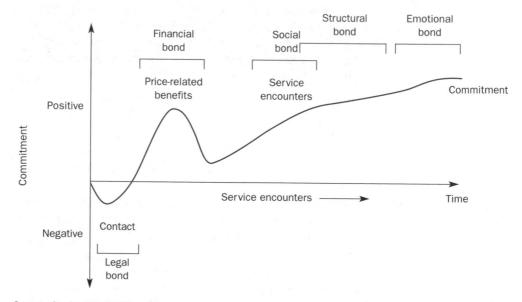

Source: after Arantola (2000), p. 51.

Commitment may be positive or negative. In semantic terms the idea of a negative bond may seem odd – how could a tie be measured on the minus scale? However, the concept helps in assessing the negative situations when bonds act as exit barriers for a customer who wants to exit. The customer perceives ties and the situation is perceived as negative. This situation is illustrated in Figure 6.6 with the legal bond, where the customer is bound by a legal agreement that prevents an exit. In Figure 6.6, the financial bond results in positive commitment in the following ways. The customer perceives being tied to the supplier due to relationship investment or special pricing, and perceives the relationship as beneficial and positive. Financial bonds are usually rather short term (as seen in Figure 6.6), but a service encounter may immediately build a positive emotional bond, or it may take a couple of months for the first bonus voucher to arrive and build a positive economic bond. When positive bonds develop, elements of loyalty such as repeat experiences and positive attitude are also present.

The role of encounters in RM

Encounters can be considered to be the period of time during which a customer directly communicates with a specific product or service. We can see these encounters as '**moments of truth**'. In this approach, an encounter is not limited to personal interaction, but includes customer contact with physical facilities and other tangibles.

Communication is defined as the process of *assigning meaning*. Each perception we have of our environment involves a transactional process between ourselves and the object(s) we perceive. Each participant's perception of the other in an encounter is a transaction between the qualities of this other and the participant's interpretation of these qualities. You form a *relationship* with the other participant in a dyadic encounter when you become aware that this other person is aware of you. Your participation in a specific encounter means that it will have an effect on you, irrespective of whether you are primarily creating or deciphering the message. In any transaction, each participant is simultaneously sending and receiving.

A person is aware that he or she is in a relationship when he or she is aware of being perceived by the other party. A relationship is therefore formed during a specific encounter when the following elements are present:

● you and another are interacting;

● you are aware of the other's behaviour;

● the other is aware of your behaviour;

● as a result, you are aware that the other is aware, and the other is aware that you are aware.

A relationship is formed when two people are aware of both each other and the other's awareness. But this is only the beginning of a potential relationship. The key to building a relationship and sustaining communicative behaviour is in the way in which each participant adjusts to the other.

The awareness of being perceived by the other party at the start of a relationship is not limited to interpersonal encounters where customers have face-to-face contact with employees, although the potential for creating relationships in such encounters is rather high. The relationship might well be created and maintained during encounters with a mediated human contact, e.g. via phone, fax, email or the Internet, or through encounters involving no human contact, e.g. interaction with a company through an ATM. The complexity of interaction decreases where there is no face-to-face human contact; responses are reduced to verbal or written expressions in the mediated human encounter, while interaction during an encounter with no human contact is limited to automatic predesigned response patterns performed by or through mechanical and electronic equipment.

In Figure 6.7, encounters have been categorized using two factors: *degree of human interaction* and *intensity of the relationship bond*. The latter describes the extent to which a single encounter contributes to relationship bonding. Figure 6.7 distinguishes seven types of encounter and positions them according to these two factors.

Internationalization of encounter-based strategies

Companies that have been able to establish and maintain lasting relationships with customers in their home markets might be interested in exploring the potential for transferring encounter-based relationship strategies to other markets. Although the ground rules for establishing relationships might be the same all over the world, the prevailing (cultural) conditions underpinning the formation and consolidation of relationships with customers may be different in parts of the world.

The management have to be aware of the considerably higher complexity of the environment under consideration (compared to a purely domestic market) when a

Figure 6.7 Typology of encounters based on the degree of human interaction and the intensity of the relationship bond

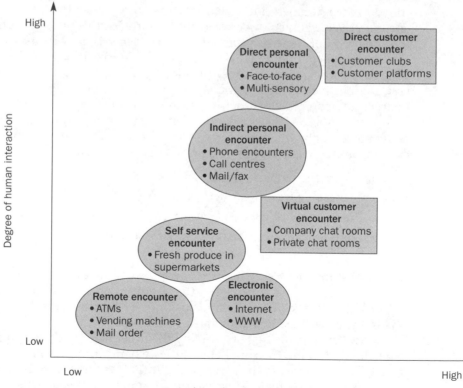

Source: Thurau and Hansen (2000), p. 283, with permission from Springer Verlag.

company takes and implements decisions concerning the standardization of encounters with the aim of establishing customer relationships in foreign cultures. A careful assessment of the opportunities for encounter standardization should provide an efficient and effective basis for establishing and maintaining relationships with customers, provided the product and/or service on offer is able to satisfy customer expectations.

Buyer-seller relationships in a cross-cultural perspective

International strategic alliances are being used with increasing frequency in order to keep up with the rapidly changing technologies, gain access to specific foreign markets and distribution channels and create new products. Strategic alliances are becoming an essential feature of companies' overall organizational structure, and competitive advantage depends not only on the firm's internal capabilities, but also on its types of alliances with other companies.

Formation of international strategic alliances brings together managers from different organizations, different national origins, with differences in the partners' cultural bases. Nationality is the key personal attribute that shapes the interaction among managers. Managers with similar attributes, values and perceptions would be more likely to have strong ties with each other than managers with dissimilar attributes, values and perceptions. Thus a shared nationality is a basis for managers to establish and maintain strong network ties.

Capitalizing on an effective understanding of this culture can be used by the seller to achieve a competitive advantage in developing and maintaining long-term buyer-seller relationships. The age of the person in the buyer's organization with whom the seller interacts can play a major role in establishing relationships. The age factor has cultural consequences of its own. The older the buyer, the more his or her experience is integrated into the decision process.

Thus, it is interesting that companies which do business in an international context can handle the cultural complexity and heterogeneity. Good handling of cultural heterogeneity implies that the company can cope well in different cultural environments.

The success and the possibility of building both national and international co-operative relations depend on the interaction of the persons who want to establish the relation (Axelsson and Agndal, 2000, p. 4).

Distance reduction in international strategic alliances

The formation of collaborative alliances among organizations is touted as a significant strategy that organizations can use to cope with the turbulence and complexity of their environments. An international strategic alliance is commonly defined as:

> Relatively enduring inter-firm cooperative agreements, involving cross-border flows and linkages that utilise resources and/or governance structures from autonomous organisations in two or more countries, for the joint accomplishment of individual goals linked to the corporate mission of each sponsoring firm (Parkhe, 1991, p. 581).

The inter-firm distance is the degree to which the cultural norms etc. in one country are different from those in another country. Inter-firm distance creates difficulties for managers when they adapt to the different cultures. Thus greater cultural distance may lead to misunderstandings, friction, and conflict between managers. The distance is also often referred to as the psychic distance. For international companies trying to use strategic alliances as a competitive weapon, it is crucial to identify the factors that reduce the distance between the partners. Figure 6.8 shows the possible factors that are believed to influence the distance reduction.

The dyadic relationship does not appear as an isolated entity, but as part of a larger context. Any company has to maintain relationships with several other players and some other relationships occur in the development of a certain relationship. Each relationship then appears to be embedded in or connected to some other relationships, and its development and functions cannot be properly understood if these connections are disregarded.

The interaction approach model takes four basic elements into consideration when assessing the importance and influence of interaction.

1. The *interaction process*, which expresses the exchanges between the two organizations along with their progress and evolution throughout time.

2. The *participants* in the interaction process, meaning the characteristics of the supplier and the customer involved in the interaction process.

3. The *environment* within which the interaction takes place.

4. The *atmosphere* affecting and being affected by the interaction.

The manipulation and control of these variables is of particular importance in international business and is a resource-intensive and time-consuming process. The interaction approach places the emphasis on processes and relationships; buyers and sellers are seen as active participants in long-term relationships that involve complex patterns of interaction.

Since this section tries to explain the distance reduction by focusing on the atmosphere that has developed it seems relevant to define the concept of atmosphere. The concept of atmosphere is here defined as

> *the emotional setting, in which business is conducted. It constitutes the working environment for the individuals in their interaction with each other (Hallén and Sandström, 1991, p. 113).*

Figure 6.8 Factors influencing the inter-firm distance

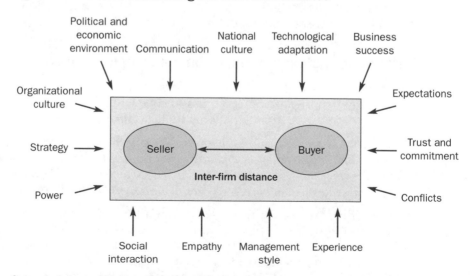

Source: preliminary work by Anna Marie Dyhr Ulrich, Ph.D. Researcher at the University of Southern Denmark.

As a result of research on interaction processes five atmosphere criteria are suggested. These are cooperation/conflict, power/dependence, trustworthiness/commitment, expectations and closeness/distance (Håkansson 1982).

While focus in this section is on distance reduction, we only want in the following to discuss distance in detail.

Psychic distance/closeness

The psychic closeness/distance is used here to denote the degree of familiarity with regard to mainly cultural but also social aspects.

Researchers of psychic distance are not very precise about the exact concept. These are factors that should hinder and hamper the information flow between a company and its market, e.g. differences in language, culture, political systems, level of education, level of development.

A problem with the psychic distance concept is that it relates to individuals' cognitive understanding instead of the whole company's behaviour. There is no objective goal, but a distance that exists in human thought, and the distance perceived depends on how the individual regards the world. The term 'psychic' refers to the individual perception.

In empirical studies, Hofstede (1983,1992) introduced the concept of cultural distance as a measure of the distance between nations. Cultural distance is a potentially powerful determinant of the way relationships can develop.

The cultural distance is often used as a synonym for the psychic inter-firm distance. International business literature shows little consensus regarding an exact definition of the concept of distance. Here the perceived distance is considered as:

the distance between the home market and a foreign market resulting from the perception and understanding of cultural, business, organizational and personal differences.

The inference is that distance is a consequence of a number of interrelated factors, of which perception is a major determinant. Perception is an interpretation of data, and is, therefore, highly subjective in terms of an individual's personal experience and value systems; as value systems are largely a product of cultural background, it could be argued that culture has an influence on perception.

Cultural influence on the perceived distance and the interaction of the alliance partners

If perception is influenced by culture, and perception is used to interpret those factors, which constitute the distance, it is clear that culture has an influence on distance.

The concept of distance is multidimensional in connection with international buyer-seller relationship building. We suggest that the following cultural dimensions affect the distance:

- different understanding of the national and industry culture
- different understanding of the organizational culture
- different personal behaviour because of different mental programming.

The national culture is only one level in the cultural hierarchy that influences the parties' behaviour and perception. The national culture must be seen as the basic, arranging structure for how to handle business activities. Throughout time, many researchers have defined the concept of culture. In this section the perception of culture will be based on Hofstede's definition. He defines culture as: 'The collective programming of the mind which distinguishes the members of one category of people from another' (Hofstede, 1994, p. 1). He has laid down five criteria, based on what the national, cultural differences are thought to be. The five criteria are: power distance, individualism versus collectivism, masculinity versus femininity, uncertainty avoidance and long-term versus short term-orientation (Hofstede, 1994).

As Figure 6.9 shows, the initial distance 1 between a buyer and a seller (from different countries) is influenced by the psychological characteristics of the buyer and the seller; the firm's organizational culture, and the national and industrial culture to which the firm belongs. Figure 6.9 also shows how the initial distance 1 at the beginning of the relationship is reduced to distance 2 through the interaction process of the two partners.

In this context distance 2 (in Figure 6.9) is relevant for further discussion. Distance 2 represents a psychic distance which can only be reduced by an intercultural learning process. Every culture has recognized patterns of behaviour and communication which make communication easier. However, in different cultures there are also recognized patterns which are specific to that culture. In the learning process, the company learns about these patterns which are specific to the culture. The company learns which methods are the most effective.

Figure 6.9 Reducing the distance in a cross-cultural relationship

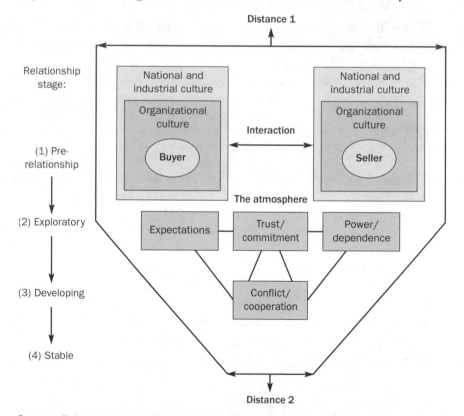

Source: preliminary work by Anna Marie Dyhr Ulrich, Ph.D. Researcher at the University of Southern Denmark.

The different cultural levels influence an individual's perception and behaviour. People with different cultural backgrounds and different mental programming[1] are involved in the interaction. This results in different interpretations of behaviour, performance, rules, routines, etc., which often make it difficult – on the personal level – to build and extend social connections (Hallén & Sandström, 1991, p. 108). The culture levels (national and industry culture, organizational culture and personal level) are supposed to have a mutual influence and effect on each other, which is difficult to separate.

6.3 Supplier relationships

Suppliers can do much more than deliver reasonably priced items on request. The supplier relationships represent some of the most important assets of a company and should thus be considered and treated with a similar logic to other types of investment. Exploiting some of the potential of a supplier requires that the operations of the two companies become more closely integrated in the various facets of the relationship. This involves extensive and intense interpersonal interaction, coordination of various activities, and mutual adaptation of resources, which entail costs for both companies.

It has been estimated that purchased materials and services account for between 50 per cent and 80 per cent of the total cost of a manufactured product, and it was further estimated that suppliers account for 30 per cent of the quality problems and 80 per cent of the product lead time (Burton, 1988). Additionally, with the application of just-in-time sourcing, buyer-supplier relationships have become increasingly important. A new partnership-like relationship between buyer and supplier is required; it is characterized by strategic emphasis, **single sourcing**, and continuous improvement in cost, service, and flexibility.

Han *et al.* (1993) describe a strong industry shift toward reducing the number of suppliers with whom the buyer does business. That marks a change from the traditional arm's-length relationship between buyers and suppliers. At present, companies are paying more attention to their relationships with suppliers. A good, reliable supplier base can give a firm an edge in its competitive environment. A close, long-term buyer-supplier relationship allows the partners to exploit certain economies that would not otherwise be realized under the traditional adversarial approach.

It has been particularly emphasized that buying companies tend more and more to:

- outsource non-critical activities
- establish close partnership relationships with suppliers
- reduce and trim their supplier bases.

The impression is that these changes in supply strategy reflect a growing awareness of the role supplier relationships can play in a company's strategy and are an attempt to better exploit this potential. This evolving perspective on purchasing efficiency has been beneficial to many companies and has generally been acclaimed by researchers and consultants.

---

[1] For further details see Hofstede, 1983.

Outsourcing to suppliers is linked to business strategies aiming at enhanced specialization and at a focus on core competence. Increasing technical complexity and diversity make it more and more difficult for a company to stay at the cutting edge in several different areas of technology at the same time. Earlier recommendations of arm's-length relationships to suppliers to avoid dependency and keep prices down have been replaced by an emphasis on the benefits that can be reaped from close relationships.

Buyer-supplier relationships have received increased attention in the light of new management philosophies and techniques and the knowledge that effective buyer-supplier relationships will significantly contribute to a firm's strategic success. According to the main articles published in both practitioner and academic journals, it appears that the buyer-supplier relationship has played a more important role in organizations in the past few years.

The rest of this section approaches buyer-supplier relationships by comparing a traditional adversarial relationship with cooperative relationships. The advantages and disadvantages of each with respect to the bargaining power of the buyer and supplier are discussed. Various scenarios of buyer-supplier relationships are explored (e.g. where there are one, few, or multiple buyers/suppliers representations), and the bargaining power of each scenario is discussed. Further, the two approaches are evaluated and a hybrid approach proposed. Finally, a conclusion and assessment of the results are provided.

Traditional adversarial relationships

The adversarial approach is derived from a transaction-based theory as it explains how firms interact with one another to minimize total production and transaction costs. The cooperative approach, on the other hand, is more closely associated with behavioural and negotiation theory. These conflicting theories, therefore, involve the differences in assumptions regarding market-induced economic theory and behavioural theory at an interpersonal level.

Several academics criticized the adversarial relationship and praised the cooperative relationship as the approach certain to dominate the future of buyer-supplier relationships. Although there is a clear trend toward cooperative buyer-supplier relationships, the adversarial system and other scenarios are still viable and commonly found in practice.

The role of power in adversarial buyer-supplier relationships

Because of increased emphasis on quality, just-in-time production, and outsourcing of subassemblies, there have been more cooperative buyer-supplier relations. The superiority of the buyer and supplier partnership has not, however, been unequivocally established in practice.

Under the adversarial approach of buyer-supplier relationships, buyers will attempt to reduce the power of their suppliers by maintaining multiple sources with low volume of supply, thereby avoiding any uniqueness in the relationship that might make the cost of switching suppliers high. In that environment, the buyer searches for readily available substitute materials that will help keep supplier prices under control. Moreover, by avoiding long-term commitments and keeping options continually open, a buyer can always transfer its patronage quickly and easily to those suppliers that, at any given time, are the most efficient and technically advanced in their operations.

Exhibit 6.5	Springer Verlag's relations with its supplier of paper, Hallsta

Axel Springer Verlag is one of Germany's biggest publishing firms, founded in 1946. Springer publishes a large number of daily newspapers as well as weekly and monthly magazines. *Die Welt*, *Welt am Sonntag*, *Hamburger Abendblatt*, *Bild* and *Bild am Sonntag* are among the most important. Springer has production units in Berlin, Ahrensburg, Essen-Kettwig and Darmstadt. The Springer Group has about 12,000 employees and had a turnover of DM 4.8 billion in 1998. Springer purchases 450,000 tonnes of paper every year.

The Swedish paper producer Hallsta was founded in 1915 and is one of three paper mills within Holmen Paper, which in turn is owned by the Modo Group. Hallsta has a capacity of 650,000 tonnes of paper and employs about 1000 people. This makes Hallsta one of Europe's biggest producers of paper.

Springer is one of Hallsta's biggest and also therefore most important customers. Holmen/Hallsta and Springer have been doing business since the 1940s. Springer buys a large share of Hallsta's paper production for the *Bild am Sonntag*'s edition of 2.5 million copies. *Bild am Sonntag* was launched in 1956 and has since then been printed on paper from Holmen and Hallsta.

Springer also uses other resources such as printing presses and printing ink. In total, Springer buys different types of paper from about 15 different suppliers and negotiates with another 5–7 manufacturers of paper. Of the total volume 75 per cent is imported and the rest is purchased from German paper producers. For *Bild am Sonntag*, Springer has two main suppliers, Hallsta and a production unit within Stora Enso, situated in Finland. Hallsta and the Stora Enso unit have both informal and more formal meetings that to some extent are initiated by Springer.

A very typical example that shows Springer's role in relation to its suppliers and how Springer coordinates the resource use at its suppliers is the episode when Hallsta wanted to change the paper quality that the mill supplied Springer for *Bild am Sonntag*. However, in order to change the quality Holmen/Hallsta also had to convince the Stora Enso unit to produce the same paper quality. The reason is that Springer's purchasing philosophy is to always keep at least two suppliers for each paper quality if possible. Therefore Springer contacted Stora Enso and asked if the Finnish unit would accept producing the same quality that Hallsta wanted to supply Springer with. The Stora Enso unit agreed to do this and Hallsta then provided the Stora Enso unit with the paper grade's technical specification. In order for changes to take place an involvement from at least one other firm was necessary.

This exhibit also shows that two competitors (Hallsta and Stora Enso) can both benefit from cooperating on certain issues.

Source: adapted from Wedin, (2000).

Buyers can coordinate closely with a large number of suppliers mainly through information technology and the aggressive use of overt economic pressure of the kind prescribed in the supplier-as-competitor approach. A buyer can keep suppliers under pressure by making certain that no more than a small percentage of its total purchases come from any one supplier.

Shifts in the bargaining power of buyers, relative to their suppliers, depend on the size and concentration of buyers, the quality of information buyers possess regarding suppliers and their products and costs. A buyer can exercise tremendous power if it is large enough and if the supplier is vulnerable. The large buyer groups can purchase in huge quantities at preferential prices that give them additional bargaining power toward their suppliers.

Cooperative relationships

Compared with the traditional adversarial system, the cooperative buyer-supplier relationship encourages more advanced management and production systems (such as total quality management and just-in-time) and foresees a more extended cooperative interaction in product design and technological development between buyer and supplier. The incentive to develop such an interaction arises in the context of operations and can form the basis for medium- to long-term contracts. Thus, buyer-supplier relationships change from prevalently commercial transactions based on price to a cooperative relationship based on the the overlap between strategic planning in buyers and sellers.

The evolution of the buyer-supplier relationship from an adversarial approach to a cooperative one is usually accompanied by a reduction in the number of suppliers. The emphasis for the buyer is placed on developing close cooperative relationships with a relatively small number of carefully selected suppliers with a long-term partnership in mind. That relationship requires a high degree of interdependence between the buyer and supplier and offers significant economies of cooperation, which can help improve both firms' profitability. In fact, buyers and suppliers acknowledge that their reciprocal dependency is increasing because the areas of interaction are growing. It is exactly that greater reciprocal involvement that tends to raise the switching costs of the relationship, making the relationship more balanced and stable, yet more binding for each firm. However, this cooperative relationship between the buyer and supplier, which involves the shifting of responsibilities and power, seems to be rather removed from reality and practice.

In a cooperative buyer-supplier relationship, when a buyer maintains a small base of suppliers and uses just-in-time sourcing, some responsibilities and costs are shifted from the buyer to the supplier. Specifically, the supplier may become responsible for quality, delivery, packaging, design, and inventory.

Further, because it would be difficult for buyers to substitute suppliers, a small base of suppliers can reduce the power of buyers resulting in the increased power of any given supplier. The buyer would then become increasingly dependent on the supplier, risking potential harm in the buyer-supplier relationship. To overcome the potential risk, buyers and suppliers should try to create mutual dependency, resource abundance, and homogeneity of goals and intents. They should reduce the motivation, rather than the ability of suppliers to exercise their power. The buyer should encourage the supplier to invest in a new plant, new warehousing facilities, or new delivery vehicles, thereby increasing the switching costs for the supplier and ensuring dependence on the buyer. A trustworthy buyer or supplier is one who does not act in a purely self-serving manner, accurately discloses relevant information when requested, does not change supply specifications, and generally acts ethically. This type of trust should govern cooperative buyer-supplier relationships. The key to a stable, mutually beneficial buyer-supplier partnership over time is understanding how performance problems may enter a relationship and how they can best be eliminated.

Bargaining power in buyer-supplier relationships

The bargaining power is affected by the proportion of a firm's business allocated to one particular buyer or supplier. Figure 6.10 depicts various possible scenarios with

Figure 6.10 The matrix of power structure for buyer-supplier relationships

Buyer \ Supplier	One	Few	Multiple
One	**Cooperative system** ①	Unequal distribution of power	Unequal distribution of power
Few	Unequal distribution of power	**Balanced power or protection** ②	Unequal distribution of power
Multiple	Unequal distribution of power	Unequal distribution of power	**Adversarial system** ③

respect to the power structure between buyer and supplier, concentrating primarily on the amount of business (volume of sales or production) given to a buyer or supplier. The focus of the power structure and the bargaining power is on individual firms rather than on entire markets or industries.

Figure 6.10 shows a set of distinct scenarios for various buyer-supplier relationships. The cells are intended to be specific and represent nine unique scenarios. Only the three possible buyer-supplier scenarios with an equal number of firms will be considered.

One buyer, one supplier (cooperative system)

In this situation a buyer chooses only one supplier or vice versa. It is also called single sourcing; a supplier receives the entire business or volume of the operation of a buyer with respect to some materials.

Single-sourcing is commonly found in cooperative relationships. After a careful selection process, one supplier is chosen to fulfil all the needs for one particular part or subassembly or service. In this situation, the buyer is usually very vulnerable – especially if the supplier can switch to other customers for business. This dependency exists because the supplier has invested considerable money in equipment to achieve price reductions and quality improvement. That usually makes it difficult for a buyer to find another supplier, as another supplier may not be willing to make a similar investment.

A significant amount of the R&D expenditure has been shifted to the supplier. Other suppliers and the OEM may lack the required knowledge to replace the existing supplier.

Technical and product know-how has been transferred to the supplier, who might pose a threat of forward vertical integration or employ knowledge to the benefit of the buyer's competitors.

Personal relationships between the buyer's purchasing department and the supplier may have developed because of close cooperation. The buyer's purchasing department may be reluctant to search for alternative suppliers and serve as a gatekeeper, not even permitting competitors to bid.

From the supplier's standpoint, the majority of its output goes to only one buyer. Although long-term contracts, information-sharing, and inter-firm cooperation are intended to alleviate uncertainty, the supplier has to rely, to a large extent, on the goodwill of the buyer. Often buyers use their leverage to gain access to a supplier's confidential information, financial records, cost structure, labour contracts, and so on.

A supplier's investment in special equipment and R&D projects could go to waste if the buyer discontinues its business with the supplier, especially if there are no guarantees or legal protection provided for the supplier.

Few buyers, few suppliers (balanced power or protection)

In this situation a buyer or supplier has a fairly balanced choice in selecting its trading partner and protecting its business.

A few buyers/suppliers can mean two or more buyers or suppliers. Buyers use dual suppliers or a few suppliers to protect themselves against possible shortages, strikes, and other emergencies that may be caused by having a single supplier. Similarly, suppliers protect themselves against possible loss of business that may result from a buyer's bankruptcy or a decline in sales volume. Buyers can maintain competition among their existing suppliers by decreasing the volume for underperforming suppliers and increasing the volume of good suppliers who have a lower share of the overall volume. Buyers may choose to have two or more suppliers if their product design and technological requirements cannot be adequately met by a single supplier.

Suppliers may choose dual buyers or a few buyers if they believe they possess the capabilities to satisfy the demand and technological needs of more than one buyer simultaneously. That can lead to a supplier's ability to charge high rates for its parts and materials. This type of relationship, common in Japan, presents multiple opportunities and challenges for both buyers and suppliers. If the balance of power between a buyer and supplier changes, other types of scenarios can emerge.

Multiple buyer, multiple suppliers (adversarial system)

In these situations buyers can temporarily choose any number of suppliers as their trading partners or vice versa. Both buyers and suppliers are primarily motivated by economic benefits derived from their business.

The overriding goal in such a relationship is profit. Buyers and suppliers in this scenario attempt to maximize their profit at the expense of other firms. A buyer maintains multiple suppliers with little volume for each. The buyers choose or drop suppliers on the basis of cost. If a new supplier is able to supply the same parts and materials at a lower cost, the buyer will not hesitate to replace the higher-cost supplier with a lower-cost supplier. The reverse of this situation could be equally true for a supplier who wishes to replace a buyer. Most of the discussion presented in the adversarial buyer-supplier relationship section of this section is applicable to that scenario as well.

In the other scenarios shown in Figure 6.10 there is more or less unequal distribution of power between buyer(s) and seller(s). If there are fewer buyers than suppliers, buyers attempt to force prices down, bargain for higher quality products or services, or play one supplier off against another. The buyers' power increases if switching costs are low, buyers have full information, and buyers use their potential to integrate backwards.

The conditions that make the suppliers powerful tend to be similar to conditions that make buyers powerful in the case of few buyers and multiple suppliers. Suppliers' power increases if few substitutes exist for suppliers' products and services, suppliers' products are differentiated or switching costs are high, and suppliers threaten forward integration.

Depending on market situation, it is possible to sum up the power relationship between buyer and seller as shown in Figure 6.11

Figure 6.11 provides a description of some of the key attributes that one might expect to find if one were trying to position buyer and supplier relationships using the power matrix. The power matrix is explained in more detail elsewhere, but it is constructed around the idea that all buyer and supplier relationships are predicted on the relative value and the relative scarcity of the resources that are exchanged between the two parties.

In the buyer dominance box, the buyer has power attributes relative to the supplier that provide the basis for the buyer to leverage the supplier's performance on

Figure 6.11 The attributes of buyer and supplier power

Buyer dominance	Interdependence
• Few buyers/many suppliers • Buyer has high share of total market for supplier • Supplier is highly dependent on buyer for revenue with limited alternatives • Supplier switching costs are high • Buyer's switching costs are low • Buyer's account is attractive to supplier • Supplier offerings are customized • Buyer search costs are low • Supplier has no information asymmetry advantages over buyer	• Few buyers/few suppliers • Buyer has relatively high share of total market for supplier • Supplier is highly dependent on buyer for revenue with few alternatives • Supplier switching costs are high • Buyer's switching costs are high • Buyer's account is attractive to supplier • High degree of dependence between buyer and supplier (balanced power) • Buyer search costs are high • Supplier has significant information asymmetry advantages over buyer
Independences	**Supplier dominance**
• Buyer has relatively low share of total market for supplier • Supplier is not dependent on buyer for revenue and has many alternatives • Supplier switching costs are low • Buyer's switching costs are low • Buyer's account is not particularly attractive to supplier • Supplier offerings are standardized • Buyer search costs are relatively low • Supplier has only limited information asymmetry advantages over buyer	• Few buyers/few suppliers • Buyer has low share of total market for supplier • Supplier is not at all dependent on the buyer for revenue and has many alternatives • Supplier switching costs are low • Buyer's switching costs are high • Buyer's account is not attractive to the supplier • Supplier offerings are not customized • Buyer search costs are very high • Supplier has high information asymmetry advantages over buyer

Vertical axis: Attributes of buyer power relative to supplier (High / Low)

Horizontal axis: Attributes of supplier power relative to buyer (Low / High)

quality and/or cost improvement, and ensure that the supplier receives only normal returns.

In the interdependence box, both the buyer and the supplier possess resources that require the two parties to the exchange to work closely together, since neither party to the exchange can force the other to do what it does not wish to do. In this circumstance, the supplier may achieve above-normal returns but must also pass some value to the buyer in the form of less-than-ideal returns, as well as some degree of innovation.

In the independence box, neither the buyer nor the supplier has significant leverage opportunities over the other party, and the buyer and the supplier must accept the current prevailing price and quality levels. Fortunately for the buyer, this price and quality level is often not that advantageous for the supplier because the supplier has few leverage opportunities (other than buyer ignorance and incompetence) and may be forced to operate at only normal returns.

In the supplier dominance box, the supplier has all of the levers of power. It is in this box that one would expect the supplier to possess many of the isolating mechanisms that close markets to competitors and many of the barriers to market entry that allow above-normal returns to be sustained. In such an environment, the buyer is likely to be both a price and quality receiver.

As well as the possible buyer-supplier power structures to consider, there is huge potential in exploiting better the opportunities offered by coping with suppliers. However, potential benefits are not reaped automatically. The focus has shifted from buying well towards managing within relationships (Gadde and Snehota, 2000).

Reverse marketing

Firms increasingly realize that rapidly changing market conditions require significant changes in their purchasing function. In more and more firms, purchasing is becoming pro-active and of strategic importance. This phenomenon has been referred to as **reverse marketing**. As the term implies, there are clear similarities with the marketing concept (Biemans and Brand, 1995). The phenomenon was described in Chapter 4, in the section about supplier selection in the B-t-B market.

Reverse marketing describes how purchasing actively identifies potential subcontractors and offers suitable partners a proposal for long-term cooperation. Similar terms are pro-active procurement and buyer initiative (Ottesen, 1995). In recent years, the buyer-seller relationship has changed considerably. The traditional relationship, in which a seller takes the initiative by offering a product, is increasingly being replaced by one in which the buyer actively searches for a supplier that is able to fulfil its needs.

Many changes are taking place in the utilization of the purchasing function, as shown in Figure 6.12.

Implementing a reverse marketing strategy starts with fundamental market research and with an evaluation of reverse marketing options (i.e. possible suppliers). Before choosing suppliers the firm may include both present and potential suppliers in the analysis as well as current and desired activities.

Based on this analysis the firm may select a number of suitable partners as suppliers and rank them in order of preference.

Figure 6.12 Supplier development

	Current activities	New activities
Existing suppliers	Intensify current activities	Develop and add new activities
New potential suppliers	Replace existing suppliers Add suppliers: secure deliveries	Develop new activities not covered by existing suppliers

6.4 Complementor relationships

Closely connected to the tendency towards competitor relationships are relationships with complementors. These are based on collaborations between manufacturers of complementary functions and/or products.

In Figure 6.13, two different types of coalition are shown in the value chain perspective. These are based on the possible collaboration pattern along the value chain. In Figure 6.13 two partners are shown, A and B, each having its own value chain. Three different types of value chain partnership appear:

- *upstream-based collaboration (1)*: A and B collaborate on R&D and/or production
- *downstream-based collaboration (2)*: A and B collaborate on marketing, distribution, sales and/or service
- *upstream/downstream-based collaboration (3)*: A and B have different, but complementary competences at each end of the value chain.

In such collaboration, each partner has a strategic resource that the other needs and so they are prepared to develop some form of extended exchange mechanism in order to expedite the process. For example, it could involve the transfer of technology in exchange for knowledge and understanding of a market. The resources involved are, by definition, strategic in nature. They are the long-term, relatively stable bases upon which the organizations create value in the product offerings that they exchange.

Figure 6.13 Collaboration possibilities for partners A and B in the value chain

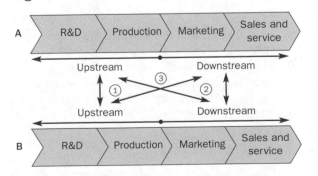

Source: Hollensen (2001), p. 274.

Types 1 and 2 represent the so-called Y coalition and type 3 represents the so-called X coalition.

Y coalitions

Partners share the actual performance of one or more value chain activities. For example, joint production of models or components enables the attainment of scale economies that can provide lower production costs per unit. Another example is a joint marketing agreement where complementary product lines of two firms are sold together through existing or new distribution channels, and thus broaden the market coverage of both firms.

X coalitions

Partners divide the value chain activities between themselves. For example, one partner develops and manufactures a product while letting the other partner market it. Forming X coalitions involves identifying the value chain activities where the firm is well positioned and has its core competence. Take the case where A has its core competences in upstream functions, but is weak in downstream functions. A wants to enter a foreign market, but lacks local market knowledge and does not know how to get access to foreign distribution channels for its products. Therefore A seeks and finds a partner, B, which has its core competences in the downstream functions, but is weak in the upstream functions. In this way A and B can form a coalition where B can help A with distribution and selling in a foreign market, and A can help B with R&D or production.

In summary, X coalitions imply that the partners have asymmetric competences in the value chain activities: where one is strong, the other is weak and vice versa. In Y coalitions, on the other hand, partners tend to be more similar in the strengths and weaknesses of their value chain activities.

The so-called **co-branding** is closely connected to the downstream-based collaboration.

Co-branding

The term co-branding is relatively new to the business vocabulary and is used to encompass a wide range of marketing activity involving the use of two or more brands. Thus co-branding could be considered to include:

- *Sponsorship*, where Marlboro sponsors the Ferrari team in Formula 1.
- *Licensing*, where Mattel has been granted the worldwide rights to manufacture a Ferrari-branded range of boys' and girls' toys including vehicles, dolls, soft toys, and games and puzzles. Licensed products, especially with entertainment properties, can sometimes have a limited shelf life. Using a licence like Pokemon could be very short term. Others, such as Sesame Street or Disney's Mickey Mouse, could go on practically for ever.
- *Retailing*, where BP hosts Safeway mini-stores.
- *Retail co-promotion*, where McDonald's and Disney get together.
- *Manufacturing collaborations*, for examle, the Mercedes-Swatch car.

| Exhibit 6.6 | The Esso-Tesco alliance in the UK |

An example of a co-branding arrangement is the tie-up between Esso and Tesco to establish 24-hour mini-supermarkets (Tesco Express) at petrol stations.

Esso brings its brand strength, its array of well-sited locations and its operational expertise in running petrol stations competitively. Tesco brings its own brand strength, its knowledge of consumer buying patterns and lifestyles, its purchasing expertise and market power, its distribution infrastructure and its operational expertise in running supermarkets.

The tie-up with Esso offers Tesco Express the benefit of rapid, high profile expansion of its operating locations in prime sites, increasing customer awareness of the Tesco Express proposition and values. It enables Tesco Express to achieve critical mass more quickly than it could have using standalone locations.

The two brands are important elements of the proposition. Both Esso and Tesco convey such strong signals to the UK buying public with respect to their core offerings that the partners would destroy value by creating a new brand to describe a venture that is so close to their core businesses.

Companies which do not enjoy such brand power in their markets would have more difficulty in accelerating the growth of new services on the back of their brands and might prefer to set up a formal alliance with a new brand identity.

Motives for co-branding

The basis for any cooperative arrangement is the expectation of synergies, which create value for both participants, over and above the value they would expect to generate on their own.

Co-branding is a form of cooperation between two or more brands with significant customer recognition, in which all the participants' brand names are retained. It is of medium to long-term duration and its net value creation potential is normally too small to justify setting up a new brand and/or legal joint venture. (The Mercedes-Swatch car is an exception here.)

Logic and experience confirm that the stronger the brands are that form the co-brand, the more likely it is that their identities will be preserved, whatever the extent of co-operation. If the participants were to destroy significant value by aban-

| Exhibit 6.7 | Co-branding: Pepsi-Cola + Starbucks = Starbucks Frappuccino |

One of the big US successes in co-branding of the past few years has been Pepsi-Cola's alliance with Seattle's Starbucks Corp. In 1994, the two companies formed a joint venture to produce and market ready-to-drink (RTD) coffee drinks in Starbucks outlets as well as retail channels. Starbucks Frappuccino has become the leading RTD coffee product with more than 50 per cent market share.

'By combining our efforts, we were able to enter a beverage category that was virtually untapped,' said Pepsi-Cola spokesman Bart Casabone. 'The partnership enables both Pepsi and Starbucks to leverage the strengths of each partner. Starbucks brings a premium trademark and coffee expertise, whereas Pepsi brings beverage expertise and distribution excellence.' Indeed, with Pepsi's distribution network, Starbucks Frappucino is now available in more than 200,000 retail outlets, according to the coffee company.

Source: adapted from Steinriede (2000).

doning very powerful brands and investing resources in another name instead, the net value creation potential would be severely reduced.

Duration

How long cooperative relationships last depends very much on the life cycle of the products and/or the characteristics of the markets involved.

The relationship between McDonald's and Disney where McDonald's uses the latest Disney movie on its product range will typically last for three to four months and can best be defined as a co-promotion.

At the other extreme, Mercedes-Benz and Swatch are co-operating on the development, manufacture and launch of a new urban vehicle, a process likely to take five years. This cooperation is taking place in a joint venture.

Similarly, a number of airlines are cooperating on routes, flights and customer marketing in major global initiatives, like the Star Alliance. These initiatives have no evident end-point at all, have new brand identities created for them, and are generally described as alliances.

In between these extremes lie a number of arrangements usually referred to as co-branding and/or ingredient branding, such as Intel with a variety of PC manufacturers to co-brand its machines with the 'Intel inside' logo. But these arrangements are also without fixed end-points.

It appears that the envisioned duration strongly influences the categorization of many instances of co-branding, but it is not the only discriminating factor. Longer-term cooperations generally imply more extensive sharing of assets and expertise, with the potential to generate more shared value.

Values endorsement co-branding

This level of cooperation is specifically designed to include endorsement of one or other's brand values and positioning or both. In fact, it is often the principal reason for the tie-up.

In recent years many charities have launched co-branded 'affinity' credit cards with a bank or credit card company, in fact so many that the concept has been somewhat devalued, but the principle remains intact. This is a win-win situation for the bank, the charity and the customer. The charity benefits from extra revenue, the bank gets extra transaction volume along with the kudos of charitable associations and the customer feels that they are contributing to a worthwhile cause.

So the essence of value endorsement co-branding is that the two participants cooperate because they have, or want to achieve, alignment of their brand values in the customer's mind. This substantially decreases the pool of potential partners for any projected co-branding deal and increases the value creation potential.

Le Cordon Bleu's co-branding deal with Tefal offers a more conventional example of value endorsement co-branding. Le Cordon Bleu is a French culinary academy whose brand has become synonymous with the highest standards of cooking. Tefal, a leading French cookware manufacturer, was launching its new Integral range of high quality cookware and negotiated for the endorsement of Le Cordon Bleu in its marketing campaign.

This helped to build brand awareness for Tefal Integral, it endowed the Integral brand with strong associations of culinary quality, particularly as Le Cordon Bleu academy's chefs were shown to be using Integral cookware and endorsing its quality values. The chief executive officer of Le Cordon Bleu knowingly staked his brand's values and reputation on the co-branded products.

Both companies were able to reinforce their complementary brand reputations through the tie-up and stimulate increased sales revenues for the co-branded products. This highlights the importance of appropriate partner selection.

Ingredient branding

The rationale here is that a brand noted for the market-leading qualities of its product supplies that product as a component of another branded product. Despite the similarities between co-branding and ingredient branding there is also an important difference, as indicated in Figure 6.14.

Co-branding

In the case of co-branding, two powerful and complementary brands combine to produce a product that is more than the sum of their parts and relies on each partner committing a selection of its core skills and competences to that product on an ongoing basis.

This was the case some years ago when Bacardi Rum and Coca-Cola marketed a bottle with the finished mixed drink 'Rum-and-Coca-Cola'.

Ingredient branding

Normally the marketer of the final product (**OEM**) creates all of the value in the consumer's eyes. But in the case of Intel and NutraSweet, the ingredient supplier is seeking to build value in its products by branding and promoting the key component of an end product. When promotion (pull strategy: see Figure 6.14) of the key component brand is initiated by the ingredient supplier, the goal is to build awareness and preference among consumers for that ingredient brand. Simultaneously, it may be the manufacturer (OEM) that seeks to benefit from a recognized ingredient brand. Some computer manufacturers are benefiting from the quality image of using an Intel chip.

Figure 6.14 Illustration of co-branding and ingredient branding

Co-branding

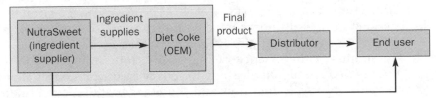

Ingredient branding

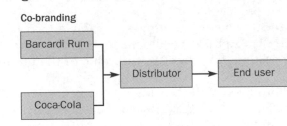

Source: Hollensen, (2001), p. 421.

| Exhibit 6.8 | Procter & Gamble is linking up with Tupperware in a global alliance |

Procter & Gamble (P&G), the world's biggest advertiser, has linked up with Tupperware, more famous for selling its products through 'parties', in a global marketing alliance. Despite their different sizes (P&G has an annual turnover of US$38 billion, Tupperware has US$1.1 billion), both companies hope to gain from the alliance.

P&G will use Tupperware's home-selling expertise to market directly to consumers and to trial new products. The Tupperware parties have offered P&G the chance to test consumer reaction prior to conventional marketing drives before it commits large-scale marketing investment.

P&G markets about 300 brands, including Oil of Olay, Pampers and Ariel, to almost 5 billion consumers across 140 countries.

The alliance follows an experimental venture in the USA and Europe during spring 1999. P&G introduced its new Swiffer duster product exclusively to Tupperware parties, before rolling it out using traditional marketing methods. Tupperware offered containers for Swiffer refills.

Source: adapted from Michalczyk (1999).

However, ingredient branding is not suitable for every supplier of components. An ingredient supplier should fulfil the following requirements.

- The ingredient supplier should be offering a product that has a substantial advantage over existing products. DuPont's Teflon, NutraSweet, Intel chips and the Dolby noise reduction system are all examples of major technological innovations, the result of large investment in R&D.

- The ingredient should be critical to the success of the final product. NutraSweet is not only a low-calorie sweetener, but has a taste that is nearly identical to that of sugar.

An important part of the value for IBM, Compaq or any other PC manufacturer of co-branding with Intel is the reputation that Intel enjoys in the PC marketplace for the manufactured quality and functional performance of its Pentium microprocessors. Quality and performance are core values for the Intel Pentium brand and they migrate through to the PC product.

The categorization of ingredient branding as a value added tool is justified because there is an identifiable physical component – the chip – contained in the product as sold to the customer. Without it, the value of the product would be greatly diminished.

Cars provide a good illustration of the benefits of ingredient co-branding. They are the most expensive branded purchases that most consumers ever make, so the manufacturers want to attach strong emotional and intuitive values to them in addition to their rational benefits and values. Many of the car companies, particularly the global volume producers, have found that co-branding deals enable them cost-effectively to reinforce particular brand images and customize their products. Various premium car manufacturers use Bose audio products. The use of such a strongly branded item, associated in the consumer's mind with high quality, is heavily promoted with the car's advertising to reaffirm the premium positioning of the vehicle.

In summary, the essence of ingredient co-branding is that a manufacturer (OEM)/ingredient supplier wishing to convey focused messages about the attributes and values of its product uses and promotes branded components whose own brand image reinforces the desired attributes and values.

The ingredient supplier benefits by guaranteeing sales volumes at the same time as reinforcing the attributes of its product brand. The manufacturer (OEM) benefits by confirming the attributes and image of its product while sharing the marketing costs.

6.5 Competitor relationships

The relationships between competitors have not been analysed to the same extent as vertical relationships. Cooperative relationships between vertical players, i.e. buyer and sellers, are more easy to grasp as they are built on a distribution of activities and resources among players in a supply chain. Horizontal relationships, on the other hand, are more informal, invisible, and more based on social exchanges.

When competitors are involved in resource exchange alliances, competition introduces some problems. The dilemma is that in creating an alliance with a competitor, an organization is, in effect, in the business of making them more competitive. Thus, in addition to competition within the alliance for value being created (local competition) there is also competition in the marketplace (extended competition). At its simplest, it is not obvious why any organization would enter into such an alliance.

For collaboration to succeed, each partner must contribute something distinctive: basic research, product development skills, manufacturing capacity, access to distribution. The challenge is to share enough skills to create advantage over companies outside the alliance while preventing a wholesale transfer of core skills to the partner. This is a very thin line to walk. Companies must carefully select what skills and technologies they pass to their partners. They must develop safeguards against unintended, informal transfers of information. The goal is to limit the transparency of their operations.

Hence, firms can proactively seek to cooperate with their competitors, suppliers or clients to gain access to complementary technological competences. Many firms in the microcomputer and mobile telephone terminals sectors have created alliances with firms in the energy sector to jointly develop increasingly miniaturized, but more durable batteries, which are decisive characteristics in the marketing of microcomputers and mobile phones.

Hamel *et al.* (1989) found that there are differences in the competitor alliance motives between Asian and western companies. Many Asian companies enter competitor alliances to enhance their technology, product and distribution competences. On the other hand, western companies enter competitor alliances to avoid investment and save costs in the upstream part of the value chain.

Based on Easton (1992) and Bengtsson and Kock (1999) the competitor alliances are categorized into five groups (Figure 6.15). The five categories of competitor alliances will now be discussed and some managerial implications are also given for each category.

Conflict

Conflict between competitors occurs when the strategies they employ are largely directed at each other with the aim of destruction. The strongest version of conflict requires that an organization has as its single overriding objective the effective destruction of a specific competitor.

Figure 6.15 Five types of relationships between a firm and its competitor

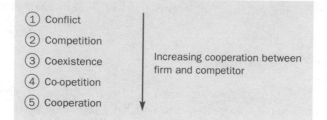

In the early 1980s, a number of authors took upon themselves the task of transferring the principles of war and battle, as codified by generations of military strategists such as Von Clausewitz, into the business arena. Organizations cannot only seek to destroy existing competitors, but also to prevent the emergence of new ones. Pre-emptive strategies may be used to render it unlikely that a new competitor survives.

Competition

In competition, organizations seek their goals through third parties (i.e., customers) and act within the rules of the game but with an eye on competitors. This mode of competition is the one upon which most marketing strategy models are based.

The dominance of economies has led to rational, structural, analytical, and aggregate models of intercompetitor behaviour (e.g. Porter, 1980). According to the competition type, an action-reaction pattern arises as competitors follow each other; if one of the competitors launches a new product line, the other will immediately follow. Interaction is therefore simple and direct. Power and dependence are equally distributed among the competitors, based on functional and psychological factors. Norms are based on informal rules as the acceptance of rules of play are widespread, and competitors set their goals independently. A common feature is that these goals are similar in structure and they can only be reached by acquiring resources from the same buyer.

A firm having a strong position and no need for external resources held by the competitor will probably focus on a relationship based on competition. The advantage of competition is that it forces companies to undertake measures not always required by customers in order to constantly improve their business.

Coexistence

Central to the concept of coexistence is independence. Coexistence competitors are either independent, perceive themselves to be independent, or choose to behave as if they were independent. Independence may be defined in terms of goals, or actions, or both.

The coexistence relationship does not include any economic exchange, merely information and social exchanges. Moreover, bonds are not present, as the competitors usually know about each other, but do not interact with each other. Power is commonly derived from a firm's dominating position or strength, and this means that dependence is present, as the smaller firms are in the hands of the larger firm. There is distance between the competitors, based on psychological factors. Trust must be regarded as high, but informal, as one firm is dependent on the other firm not interfering with it. Norms are informal and quite strong, though the rules of play are not discussed. The competitors' goals are stipulated independently.

The competing firms may choose independently not to compete on price. More commonly, they may decide not to poach key competitor employees. Previously, it was suggested that one of the characteristics of competition is that there are rules of conduct.

A firm with a weak position in the business network compared to a competitor who is not interested in cooperation can try to establish a relationship containing coexistence. The advantage of coexistence is that smaller companies have the opportunity to further develop their businesses in interactions with customers, and hence the disadvantage is that the competitors do not force each other to further develop new solutions which are not demanded by customers.

Co-opetition

It may be argued that one single relationship can comprise both cooperation and competition, that two firms can compete and cooperate simultaneously. In any specific relationship elements of both cooperation and competition can be found, but one or the other of these elements can in some cases be tacit. If both the elements of cooperation and competition are visible, the relationship between the competitors is named co-opetition.

This relationship can include both economic and non-economic exchanges. Power in the cooperative side of the relationship is based on functional aspects in accordance with the value chain. In the competitive side of the relationship, power is based on the firm's position and strength. In a similar manner, dependence arises in two ways. When cooperating, dependence is stipulated in formal agreement, or is based on trust. When competing, the dependence is related to the firm's strength and position in the business network, and is more equally distributed. Conflicts are rare in cooperation, but in competition they arise frequently. There are also clear norms when cooperating, partly based on the formal agreement. When competing, invisible norms are a part of the competition climate. The distance or proximity is functional or psychological. Goals are jointly stipulated when competitors cooperate. This is not the case when they compete. The goals in competition are often object-oriented.

A firm with a strong position, but lacking resources held by the competitor, must focus on a co-opetitive relationship. This relationship comprises both cooperation and competition and must be regarded as the most useful one, as the companies in some respect help and to some extent force each other to develop. Through long-term co-opetition, firms will learn about each other and what the other is capable of both by analysing the other firm's patents and products, and by participating in common developmental projects. Consequently, new and creative solutions can be shared, and money saved. Through co-opetition, new products can be developed more cost-effectively, as each firm contributes with its own core competence. This means that firms can stay within their core businesses and still offer a wider range of problem solutions to their customers than if the company worked on its own.

Within the process, firms develop mechanisms that attempt to deal with competitiveness within the relationship. They may, for example, place limits around the competition, e.g., geographical or project boundaries, to contain the competitive arena from the start. As the relationship progresses they may seek methods and techniques to differentiate themselves in the marketplace, such as different brand propositions, alternative distribution channels or target different market segments (Perks and Easton, 2000).

For example, two competitors can complement each other by creating new markets, but will compete when it comes to separating the markets. Hence, organizations may make the same products, but not compete in the same markets or segments or may not compete in the same way (Bengtsson and Kock, 2000). However, the two competitors have to be careful not to be seen to be engaging in anti-competitive behaviour.

Exhibit 6.9	Competitor relationship: Corel (WordPerfect) forms alliance with Microsoft (Word)

In October 2000 the Canadian software maker Corel announced that it had formed a strategic alliance with Microsoft and that Microsoft had bought US$135 million worth of Corel's preferred shares. Corel said it would work with Microsoft in testing, developing and marketing Microsoft's Internet business strategy. It will work with Microsoft on product offerings, trade show events and websites.

Source: adapted from *New York Times* (2000).

Cooperation

Compared with the other forms of relationships here described, cooperation calls forth a great variety of forms, types, and mechanisms. The exchanges are frequent, comprising business, information and social exchange. All types of bonds can arise, though social, knowledge and legal/economic bonds are the most frequent. Though the competitors cooperate it does not mean that they do not compete, and perhaps they even distrust each other.

Cooperation among competitors may be divided broadly into formal and informal relationships.

Formal relationships

Formal relationships are, in general, planned, managed, and overt. Formal dyadic relationships are those concerned largely with direct interaction between competitors. Within formal relationships, a distinction is made between dyadic activity and joint activity through investment in a third party (joint venture).

Joint ventures are created by two or more companies as a separate organizational entity. In doing so they transfer assets to the joint venture. The higher the proportion of assets transferred the more the joint venture begins to resemble a merger.

Joint ventures may or may not involve competitors. To the extent that they do, anti-trust problems become more important.

Joint research and development and new product development represent the most salient and, currently, highly fashionable form of joint activity. Competitors can fail to cooperate in the early stages precisely because they see a competitive advantage disappearing. Similarly, cooperators may fail to compete once the fundamental research work has been completed.

Joint distribution of competing products is not uncommon, but it usually involves a separate distribution operation or channel operated as a joint venture, or the use of one organization's facilities by another, rather than a set of joint activities as such. Consortia represent a form of joint activity (not a dyadic relationship, but more like a network) that encompasses many of the functions of the organizations concerned. Although the consortium may be organized through a joint venture structure, this is not strictly necessary. In the markets for large-scale projects of various kinds, the companies involved have long experience of the formation and management of consortia and have organizational forms that allow them to operate the temporary coalitions which such consortia represent. Members of many consortia are not necessarily competitors, but complementary suppliers. Large projects demand high-capacity manufacturing or construction facilities, and human and financial resources. However, a single company may not be capable of executing the project by itself.

Almost any aspect of a single firm's activity may be performed jointly. Competitors may act together in the supply market in order to stabilize prices (e.g., in commodity markets). In the oil industry OPEC represents an organization of 'competing' countries that aims to stabilize oil prices at a relatively high level.

One form of dyadic competitor alliance in formal relationships is subcontracting. Normally, subcontracting involves putting out part of the manufacturing process to a specialist supplier, which may incidentally be part of a competitor. This will occur every time an assembler buys from the upstream unit of an integrated manufacturer (vertical alliance). There is, however, a more direct horizontal relationship that can occur, and which might be called a capacity agreement. These agreements, which are usually informal for obvious reasons, are used to allow manufacturers to overcome temporary capacity constraints. Typically, a manufacturer finds that it is unable to fulfil a contract or order in the time allowed and approaches a competitor to carry out part of the work. Clearly, the manufacturing processes must be rather general in nature.

Informal relationships

Informal relationships are built on social norms and trust. These norms, and sometimes formal agreements, adjust the distribution of power and dependence among the competitors, which means that conflicts are rare. Informal relationships are more likely to be unplanned, random, and based upon individual or social premises. Furthermore, competitors have common goals, and closeness of goals is based on functional and psychological factors.

The modes that operate more on the individual level are more informal in nature. These modes can, in turn, be categorized as involving transfers of people, information, and social norms.

Individuals moving from one competitor to another provide a potential link and a powerful means by which cooperation between them can be achieved. Such an individual brings with him or her the existing relationships from the organization left behind. These relationships may reduce with time, but are unlikely to disappear.

The individual provides a potential communication mode. In many industries movement of employees between competitors is common, and the resultant network of personal relationships is an important input for the implementation of the firm's marketing strategy.

Individuals may move singly, or they may move together, forming a new company. If the individuals form a company as part of a planned process of organizational development, it is called a spin-out. If, however, the new company has no connection with its parent the usual term is spin-off. Spin-outs are formal, planned moves and, in most situations, do not lead to competition between parent and new company. By contrast, spin-offs are informal, and may be either acrimonious or harmonious depending on the circumstances of the parting.

In summary, if the firm, on the other hand, needs resources held by the competitor and does not have a strong position, cooperation is the best option. The advantage of cooperation is related to development, but the function of cooperation is the access to resources rather than a driving force or pressure to develop. Through cooperation a company can gain competence, market knowledge, reputation, access to other products, and other resources of importance for its business.

The worst case scenario is if a firm transfers a key resource that allows a competitor a huge increment in competitive advantage while being unable to leverage the resource acquired in the same way. The best case scenario is where it turns out that the two partners discover that they are not really competing or move to such a position as a result of the strategic alliance. However, communication about prices among marketing competitors may be dangerous either because of the anti-trust implications or because of the danger of misjudging the costs and benefits of a particular exchange.

In the sections on conflict and competition the main source of information was to be found in economics. By contrast, work on cooperation appears to be the province of writers on organization, particularly those concerned with the relatively new field of inter-organizational relations.

6.6 Internal marketing (IM) relationships

Parallel to relationships that curb the free market mechanism outside the company, there is an internal market consisting of groups communicating to other groups within the organization. Internal marketing is considered to be the process of creating market conditions within the organization to ensure that internal employees' wants and needs are met. This will be the best basis for creating a relationship with external players.

Rafiq and Ahmed (2000) have defined internal marketing as

> *a planned effort using a marketing-like approach to overcome organizational resistance to change and to align, motivate and inter-functionally co-ordinate and integrate employees towards the effective implementation of corporate and functional strategies in order to deliver customer satisfaction through a process of creating motivated and customer-orientated employees.*

Figure 6.16 shows the relationships between the criteria for IM and the implementation of one particular organizational strategy that is at the heart of service organizations, namely, service quality. The relationships indicated in Figure 6.16 are derived directly from the IM literature. This will be the best basis for creating relationships with external players. Internal marketing emerged from services marketing. Its purpose was to get the front-line personnel – who have interactive relationships with external customers – to handle the service encounter better and with more independence. The distinction between internal and external marketing becomes blurred.

Figure 6.16 A model for internal marketing

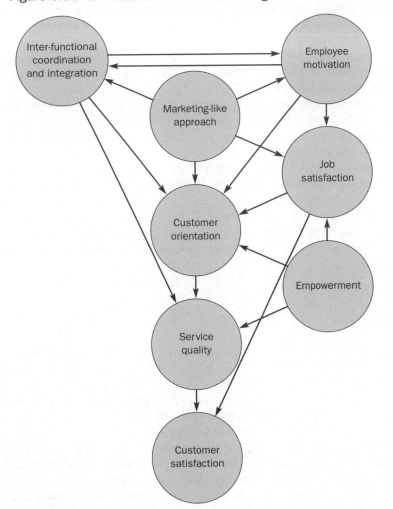

Source: Rafiq and Ahmed (2000), p. 455.

For instance, the motivation of employees via marketing-like activities was implicit in the early stages of the evolutionary development of IM. Grönroos (1981) and others also recommend the marketing-like approach to improve the inter-functional coordination and hence customer orientation. Inter-functional coordination and integration are in later stages. In later stages of the evolutionary development of IM, the central reason for interest in IM was its contribution to effective implementation of strategy via increased inter-functional coordination and employee motivation.

At the centre of this framework is customer orientation, which is achieved through a marketing-like approach to the motivation of employees, and inter-functional coordination. The centrality of customer orientation reflects its importance in the marketing literature and its central role in achieving customer satisfaction and hence organizational goals.

The objective of internal marketing within RM is to create relationships between management and employees and between functions. The personnel can be viewed as an internal market, and this market must be reached efficiently in order to prepare the personnel for external contacts. Efficient internal marketing becomes an antecedent to efficient external marketing. Techniques from external marketing can be applied internally, mainly from the areas of promotion and communications. However, traditional ways of internal mass marketing – such as the distribution of memos and internal magazines – is insufficient. To a large extent, internal marketing must be interactive. An **intranet** can help, but the social event is also important. At the start of a sales season, large groups gather to learn, to be entertained, and to mix socially for a day or two.

Training and education can be seen as tools for internal marketing. Disney has its own university, and McDonald's has its Hamburger University.

Internal marketing can be based on personal and interactive relationships as well as on a certain amount of mass marketing. Traditional activities to reach employees have often been routinely performed and have built more on bureaucratic principles and wishful thinking than on professional marketing and communications know-how.

6.7 Summary

Relationships, rather than simple transactions, provide the central focus in marketing. It is not enough to discuss the activities that a single firm performs. RM includes relationships or networks among companies and their suppliers, lateral partnerships among competitors, government, and not-for-profit organizations, internal partnerships with business units, employees, and functional departments, and buyer partnerships with intermediate and ultimate customers. Collectively, these represent complex arrays of relationships among organizations, which are carried out through information transfers. In this chapter, we have limited our understanding and analysis to how the activities are linked to the activities of a company's suppliers, competitors, complementors, customers, and employees (the value net).

A company's activities evolve within its relationships with these organizations.

Relationship with customers

The always-a-share customer and the lost-for-good customer represent opposite ends of a continuum of exchange situations. The always-a-share customer displays less loyalty to a particular supplier, whereas the lost-for-good customer remains loyal to a particular supplier for a long time.

Relationship with suppliers

The adversarial approach is derived from a transaction-based theory as it explains how firms try to minimize the total production costs by maintaining multiple sources in order to reduce the power of their suppliers with the co-operative relationships. On the other hand, the company develops a close relationship with a small number of selected suppliers.

Relationship with competitors

Four different types of relationship have been identified, taking the trade-off between cooperation and competition into account: competition, coexistence, co-opetiveness, and cooperation.

Relationship with complementors

These are based on collaboration between manufacturers of complementary functions and/or products.

Relationship with internal employees

The employees can be viewed as an internal market. Internal marketing is considered to be the process of creating market conditions within the organization to ensure that the internal employees' wants and needs are met. This will be the best basis for creating relationships with external organizations.

The development of a customer relationship can be explained by use of the marriage metaphor: awareness, exploration, expansion and termination (dissolution). The decision to terminate is considered to be due to the interaction of a trigger event and the existing state of the relationship. The factors that characterize an inter-firm relationship cannot only provide a cause for the termination, but impact greatly on the strategies firms utilize when ending a relationship. A model of inter-firm relationship termination was proposed and propositions regarding choice and use of relationship termination strategies were explored.

Case study 6.2 DANDY CHEWING GUM

A specialist in development of competitor alliances

The Danish chewing gum manufacturer Dandy (www.dandygroup.com), with around 2000 employees, produces about 25,000 tonnes of chewing gum per year. It is sold in more than 70 countries. In 2000, Dandy's total net turnover increased to DKK 1850 million, a 20 per cent increase on the year before. The profit in 2000 was DKK 91 million against DKK 25 million in 1999. Dandy has sales companies in 22 countries and production takes place in three factories in Vejle, Novogrod and in Africa.

Dandy's mission is: 'We create smiles'. And their vision is to be the world's best chewing gum company. The company will constantly offer consumers the best taste and the best products. It wants traders to regard it as the best chewing gum supplier. And it aims to be an attractive business partner through innovation,

flexibility, speed and cost awareness, and work together towards a common goal. It believes that cooperation, networks and partnerships are the way forward.

Background

Dansk Tyggegummi Fabrik A/S was founded in 1915 as an ordinary confectionery factory. The founder was Holger Sørensen. His first chewing gum, Vejle Tyggegummi, was put on the market in January 1927. After World War II the company chose the the name Dandy, as an expression of something new and exciting.

World War II put a stop to any further development. Restrictions and lack of raw materials slowed down production considerably. Holger Sørensen died in 1943 and Erik Bagger-Sørensen took charge of the company together with his

▶

mother. After the war Erik Bagger-Sørensen gained sole responsibility for managing the company and exports began again. A raw material licence of US$1000 was granted on condition that chewing gum was exported for 3 × US$1000.

The export office was established in 1946 and exports gradually increased in a sporadic way to countries which had not been hit by the war.

Dandy's main brand, Stimorol, was introduced in 1956. In 1978 it was followed by a sugar-free version. 1959 was the start of a more systematic internationalization of Dandy. That year Dandy was approached by a slightly eccentric Dutch man called Mr Kamphuis. He had tasted the product and believed it would be a good supplement to the tobacco products he already sold. Under the management of Mr Kamphuis, Stimorol became a success in Holland, and the product is still a market leader in Holland.

The first sales subsidiary was established in Belgium in 1965 in cooperation with Mr Kamphuis. In the 1970s other sales subsidiaries followed in Sweden, Switzerland, Germany and France. Today Dandy operates with distributors and agents in markets where they have no sales subsidiaries. In the 1990s, Dandy established several sales subsidiaries in eastern Europe. Dandy was also the first chewing gum manufacturer to establish its own production in Russia – this gave Dandy a first-to-market advantage in this market, and today Dandy shares the Russian market with Wrigley, with each having 50 per cent market share.

Products

There are two main types of chewing gum: sticks (the flat oblong chewing gum) and dragée (the tablets). The trend in the market is towards the dragée-type and that is also where Dandy has specialized its resources.

One of Dandy's core competences lies in the coating process of dragée-type chewing gum. The tablets are coated with a mixture of water, sweeteners and flavourings, which form an outer shell. Coating is an advanced process requiring constant electronic monitoring of temperature and air humidity.

There are three main parts to Dandy's business:

● own brands, Stimorol, V6 and Dirol
● medical chewing gum (Fertin)
● development and production of chewing gum as a sub-supplier of private brands for chewing gum manufacturers and private labels for retail chains. Dandy works with large chain stores in Europe and the USA, developing stores' own brands (retail brands).

Dandy's own brands

Dandy develops, produces and markets its own brands, Stimorol, V6 and Dirol. Stimorol was the first sugar-free product on the market and is one of the biggest chewing gum brands in Europe. In 2000, it was the market leader in Switzerland, Denmark, and Belgium.

Dirol and V6 are well-known brands on the market for dental chewing gum – protecting teeth against acids that cause tooth decay. They contain the active ingredient carbamide, which neutralizes the acids in plaque. The target for V6 is the 20 to 40-year-old age group and for Dirol the target group is 15 to 30-year-olds. V6 Junior is aimed at 5 to 10-year-olds and Dirol Kids at 9 to 12-year-olds.

Stimorol, V6 and Dirol are sold through Dandy's existing distribution system (via sales subsidiaries and agents to retail chains). The brands are marketed with the aid of strong international television and cinema commercials and outdoor advertisements on posters, buses and kiosks. V6 is sold in western Europe and Dirol in eastern Europe, central Asia, the Middle East and southern Africa.

The market is changing a great deal. From being sweet, brightly coloured and full of sugar, chewing gum today is quite a different product with a content intended to provide some functional benefits for customers. The trend is now changing from chewing gum as a lifestyle product to chewing gum as a product which includes some functional benefits. Consumers will increasingly be demanding products which in

Case study 6.2 continued

addition to tasting good and adding to their sense of well-being will also, for example, provide fresh breath, help keep teeth white, reduce the acid content in the mouth after meals, protect teeth against caries, etc.

Medicinal chewing gum

The pharmaceutical company Fertin, which makes medicated gum, was founded in 1978 and is one of the European market leaders in this sector.

Fertin is an expert in relation to the addition and controlled release of active ingredients in chewing gum. The company has knowledge of how a substance can be placed in the centre of coating, how to camouflage an unpleasant medicinal taste and the rate at which flavour and active substances are released from a chewing gum tablet. This know-how is based on years of working with leading scientists and educational institutions.

Fertin cooperates with international pharmaceutical companies for the development and production of private brands, such as Nicotinell nicotine chewing gum, which Fertin produces for Novartis, and the dental chewing gum Aquafresh, produced for GlaxoSmithKline.

The most important markets for Fertin are Europe, the USA, Australia, the Middle East and South-East Asia.

Distribution of chewing gum

Chewing gum is distributed to supermarkets, shops, and kiosks in nearly all countries. Chewing gum is an impulse buy. The display and position of products within shops determines which brand consumers choose. For this reason, Dandy is always developing display stands and other advertising material specially adapted for the most strategic locations in each type of retail outlet.

Competitors

Dandy's main competitor is Wrigley, which (like Dandy) also only has chewing gum in its product range. Wrigley is the global market leader in the chewing gum industry with a market share of about 30 per cent. Wrigley's turnover is 8–9

times higher than Dandy's. Wrigley is market leader in Europe's two biggest markets, the UK and Germany. The main competitors and their market share is shown in Table 6.2.

Table 6.2 World chewing gum market competitors 1999

Manufacturer	Country	Share of world market
Wrigley	USA	35%
Warner-Lambert (Adams)	USA	23%
Lotte	Japan	10%
Nabisco	USA	5%
Dandy	Denmark	5%
Kraft Jacobs Suchard (KJS)	France	4%
Perfetti	Italy	3%
Joyco	Spain	1%
CSM Leaf	Holland	1%
Cadbury (Hollywood)	UK/France	1%
Others		12%
Total		100%

Source: adapted from material provided by Dandy, November 2001.

The competitive structure is very different from region to region. However, Wrigley and Warner Lambert play an important role in every region (Table 6.3), and they are true global players. Other manufacturers, like Dandy, are regional players and are only strong in certain regions. Then there are also local players, like Tong Yang, which only have a presence in specific countries.

Many chewing gum manufacturers (like Cadbury/Hollywood in France or Warner Lambert/Adams in the USA) are part of large multi-national confectionery companies.

Partnerships – Dandy – a strong partner

Of all the chewing gum companies in the world, Dandy has had the greatest growth over the past decade. One of the main reasons for the high growth is the alliances which Dandy has entered. These alliances have often been with potential competitors like the ones described here. Cooperation with Dandy means a strong

Case study 6.2 continued

Table 6.3 Competitor positions in the regional markets

South America	North America	Western Europe	Eastern Europe	India, Africa, Middle East	Pacific rim
Wrigley	Wrigley	Wrigley	Wrigley	Warner-Lambert	Lotte
Warner-Lambert	Warner-Lambert	KJS	Dandy	Wrigley	Wrigley
KJS	LifeSavers	Perfetti	Warner-Lambert	Dandy	Hai Tai
Cadbury Sta.	(Nabisco)	Warner-Lambert	Leaf	Bim Bim	Joyco
Dos en uno	Canels	CSM Leaf	Perfetti	Perfetti	Warner-Lambert
Arcor		Dandy	KJS	Royal Beech	Leaf
Confiteca		Joyco		Nut	Tong Yang
Caramelos-Ryal		Lamy Lutti		Kent	Ezaki Gilico
				Baycan	
				Joyco	
				Ulker	
				Nahda	
				Cadbury	

Source: adapted from material provided by Dandy, November 2001.

partnership right from conception to sales to consumers. The company has many years' experience with the development of chewing gum, and its product development department has considerable expert knowledge about chewing gum and flavour creation. This helps ensure the constant optimization and development of products with the right texture, taste and flavour duration – guaranteeing high quality chewing gum with exactly the flavour the consumer desires.

Co-operation and networks are the way forward for Dandy. Only with this way it can ensure continued development and growth, as Dandy is only a minor player in the global chewing gum market. That is why the company has entered partnership agreements with a series of large international companies for the production and distribution of chewing gum (Table 6.4).

We will now focus on Dandy's alliances with the two competitors, KGFF (in the French chewing gum market) and Joyco (in the Russian chewing gum market).

The Dandy–KGFF alliance in France

By the end of the 1980s Dandy had a sales subsidiary with approximately 60 employees in France. At that time, the chewing gum market in France was divided so that the Hollywood brand, produced by the US owned Kraft General Foods France (KGFF), was in a very strong position – an almost monopolistic position. KGFF's Hollywood brand controlled 80 per cent of the market, whereas Dandy's Stimorol represented 7 per cent. KGFF was in a strong position for sticks, but it had rather old-fashioned production technology for dragées. The latter was (and it still is) Dandy's core competence. The production technology for dragées is much more complex than for sticks, which in principle is cutting the chewing gum into rectangles.

Inter-firm and inter-personal distances

In September 1986, Dandy was contacted by a company agent from KGFF's parent company, Kraft General Foods in the USA, to see if they could visit them in Vejle. In passing, it should be noted that Kraft General Foods at that time (before the acquisition by Philip Morris in December 1988) was the world's second largest producer of food.

Dandy's managing director, Holger Bagger-Sørensen (HBS), was actually rather tired of these discussions as they were always about acquisition of Dandy. However, Dandy's management decided to meet briefly with KGFF,

Case study 6.2 continued

Table 6.4 Dandy's alliance partners over time

Alliances	Year	Purpose
KGFF (Cadbury) France	1986	Production and distribution agreement in France and Belgium.
Lotte	1986	Distribution agreement in Russia.
Albert Heijn, Holland	1990	Production of private labels for own stores.
Kesko	1992	Production of private label chewing gum.
GlaxoSmithKline	1994	Production of Aquafresh (private brand) in Germany, UK, USA, Denmark and southern Europe.
Novatis Healthcare	1995	Production of nicotine chewing gum.
CSM Leaf, Holland	1998	Distribution agreement for Russia/CIS.
Unilever	1998	Production of Mentadent and Signal, private brand especially for southern Europe.
Aldi in Denmark, Germany, Holland and Belgium	1998	Production of private label for own stores.
Delhaize, Belgium	1999	Production of private label for own stores.
Morrison, UK	2000	Production of private label for own stores.
Elite, Israel	2000	Production of private label for own stores.
Bergi, Italy	2000	Production of private label for own stores.
Joyco, Spain	2000	Distribution agreement in Russia/CIS. Joyco produces Dandy's bubble gum.
Colgate Palmolive	2001	Production of functional chewing gum for Canada and the USA.
Kroger, USA	2001	Production of private label for own stores.
Sweet 'n' Low, USA	2001	Production of private label for own stores.

Bold indicates the two alliances explained here

Source: adapted from material provided by Dandy, November 2001.

so HBS sent marketing director Poul Ernst Rasmussen (PER) to Copenhagen to welcome the directors of Kraft General Foods (who arrived on a private aeroplane) in order to find out the real reason for their visit. HBS and PER participated in the following meeting in Vejle along with the French director general of KGFF, a US director from headquarters, and the company agent.

At the start of the meeting everybody engaged in small talk in order to sound each other out, as HBS puts it. However, it soon turned out that Kraft General Foods had not come to buy Dandy. They had noticed Dandy's special core competence in dragées and had come to discuss the possibilities of cooperation. When the representatives from Dandy heard that things started to develop.

The meeting in Vejle was positive and in the minutes HBS wrote as follows:

In the long run they may hope to acquire Dandy, but in the short run they are interested in a strategic alliance ...... We expressed that principally we are interested in alliances, seeing that the big companies are getting bigger, and that we, being one of the smaller, if not, will get under pressure. We are competitive because we invest in new technology etc., this being necessary because we produce chewing gum only. Our sales in France are high, but we don't make any profit, are very vulnerable because of the difficult business conditions (50 per cent discounts and payments for listing in Food, which is further complicated by the fact that we have one product only), and the sales force necessary.

▶

Case study 6.2 continued

The next six months went by, finding out more about each other. In this connection HBS said:

It takes time to convince each other that you really want to cooperate. What Dandy feared was that: 'Big brother is here to get you'. At the same time, KGFF might fear that Dandy would not be able to deliver 2000 tonnes of chewing gum in time and in the proper quality.

Immediately after the first meeting only HBS and PER knew of the project. Later, when calculations were to be made, the remaining two members of the senior management team, the production manager and the financial controller, were informed. All four people kept the project group secret for a while.

Six months and a number of meetings with KGFF later, the key points of the contract between the two companies had been defined and were to be discussed. At this point Dandy's management also felt that cooperation with KGFF would most likely become a reality, and therefore Dandy involved more people. Among other things Dandy and KGFF formed a mutual

project group. The group was to plan production in detail so that time scales could be worked out.

In 1988 the ultimate contract between Dandy and KGFF was ready to be signed. The contract contained the conditions under which both parties agreed to make the resources available (Figure 6.17).

KGFF was to do the following for Dandy:

● distribution of Dandy's Stimorol in France. In the first year, KGFF had to sell at least 90 per cent of Dandy's average sales during the past few years.

● production of Dandy's 'sticks'. Here, KGFF had a more advanced technique as they had invested in a new factory at that time.

Dandy was to undertake the following for KGFF:

● production of KGFF's dragée (their Hollywood brands), a total of about 2000 tonnes per year of total Dandy production of about 16,000 tonnes.

● try to market KGFF's Hollywood brands through Dandy's distribution facilities in

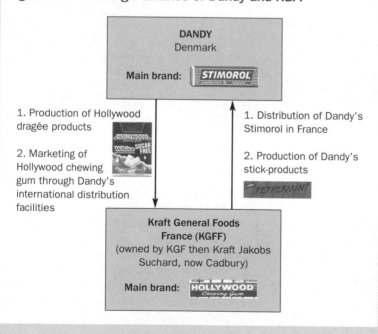

Figure 6.17 Strategic alliance of Dandy and KGFF

Case study 6.2 continued

places where Hollywood was in a weak position (at that time they were only powerful in France, Belgium and Switzerland). Dandy's distribution facilities were much more extensive than those of KGFF in other European markets.

Further, Dandy and KGFF wanted to cooperate on the following:

● cooperation on purchasing: exchange of knowledge about supplier prices, terms of delivery, etc.

● product development: a mutual development programme in gum base[2].

Not all of these elements were realized. For Dandy, the most important was the production of the 2000 tonnes of dragées for KGFF.

After concluding the agreement, Dandy closed down its French subsidiary with only limited losses. A year went by before Dandy started to produce KGFF's dragées because KGFF had to phase out a factory in Italy first.

Of course, the cooperation with KGFF was not unproblematic. If you consider the different sizes of the two companies, Dandy's essential interest was to maintain and develop the alliance, as the agreement meant a great deal to Dandy. Therefore, Dandy made much of pointing out how KGFF would benefit from the cooperation:

● cost savings because KGFF should pay interest and depreciate the DKK40 million – the price of a new factory in Denmark

● profit on buying and production development cooperation

● as Dandy had a special sales manager in France who often visited the stores, Dandy could often give KGFF some good advice about merchandising for both the Stimorol and the Hollywood brands.

Further, 2–3 times a year Dandy's management held meetings with KGFF's management in order to discuss the overall lines for quantities, prices, timetables, development projects, etc.

One problem was that part of the management from Kraft General Foods in France,

originally owned by Philip Morris (now by Cadbury), was no longer employed by KGFF. Some of the new managers may not have felt committed to the original contract, and therefore it was important for Dandy to develop social relationships with the new managers.

Dandy now sold about 900 tonnes of Stimorol per year to the French market through KGFF's distribution facilities as well as the 2000 tonnes per year to KGFF. The market share for Stimorol in France did increase even though the subsidiary company was closed down. Furthermore, the alliance with KGFF was the beginning of Dandy's entering into new alliances with other chewing gum producers around the world, like the next one with Joyco. Dandy was able to use the experience acquired by working with KGFF to reduce the cultural distance with other international chewing gum producers that they would find it worthwhile to build a strategic alliance with.

We will now look at how Dandy has developed its competences in building alliances since the KGFF alliance in 1986. We will analyse this from the perspective of the Dandy-Joyco alliance, an alliance established 15 years later than the Dandy-KGFF alliance.

The Dandy-Joyco alliance in Russia/CIS

In 2000, Dandy entered into an alliance with the Spanish company Joyco (**www.joycogroup.com**), the confectionery part of the Agroline Group.

Joyco background

Joyco is a dynamic group of bubblegum and sweet companies. It was founded in 1977 and became national leader in only ten years. During the 1980s and 1990s it expanded rapidly, extending to more than 70 countries worldwide. The Joyco Group has its headquarters in Spain where there is a state-of-the-art R&D centre, which develops products and technologies for all the group companies.

Today, the Joyco Group comprises numerous companies, partnerships and joint ventures. The Group employs 2700 people in nine factories and sales offices worldwide. Joyco has factories in Spain, India, China, Mexico, Poland, the

---

[2] A raw material which is contained in chewing gum.

Case study 6.2 continued

USA, Italy, France, the Philippines, and Russia and a presence in many more countries through commercial offices and exports.

Joyco states that the consumers are the heart of its vision and the company is passionate about providing the consumer with taste and fun.

History

In 1977, the Spanish sweet company was born. The company became known for its entrepreneurial spirit and passion for fun. The company started under the name General de Confiteria, a small company with big plans to establish a presence in the gum industry. In 1979, the company launched Bang-Bang, Spain's first soft bubblegum and the company's first hit. In 1983, the company launched a new brand, Trex, which soon became the most popular Spanish chewing gum brand. In 1985, it was followed by a new gum hit: Boomer.

At that time the company was the leading Spanish sweet maker and it was time to think more globally. In 1988, the company became the first international confectioner to enter the Chinese market. Joyco ventured into Poland in 1992 and the following year built a factory there. In 1993 the company entered a joint venture in India and developed an extensive national distribution network. In 1995, it built a factory there. At the same time the Boomer brand became market leader in India (see Case Study 11.2 for more detail). By 1996, the company exported to more than 70 national markets. In 2000, the company opened a new joint venture in China, with the aim of becoming market leader in confectionery in the medium term. And in 2001 Joyco moved into a new market with the signing of a joint venture in the Philippines.

Products

Chewing gum brands

Boomer is the flagship brand of the group. Boomer is available in three formats: single units, multi-pack and roll. The brand is synonymous with its super hero Boomerman. Other brands are Bang-Bang, Trex, Ta-Ta, Dunkin and Licor del Polo, a dental chewing gum.

Chocolate and other sweet brands

The most popular chocolate brands are: Duvalin, Lunctas and Dunketas. The best-known sweet brand is Pim Pom, the company's lollipop brand. Pim Pom is available in various different flavours, After Dinner, Chimos and Chunkys.

The gum sector constitutes 58 per cent of Joyco's overall sales, sweets account for 27 per cent of sales, and chocolate bars 15 per cent.

Some country details

The joint venture in China is the nation's leading producer of gum. The local brand Ta-Ta dominates the bubblegum segment with a market share of almost 60 per cent.

The company is Spain's largest gum manufacturer, with a 50 per cent share of the bubblegum market. In addition to the brands Boomer and Trex, the company is introducing a new dental chewing gum, Licor del Polo (based on a leading tooth hygiene brand, Henkel).

The joint venture in Mexico is among the leaders in the local confectionery industry. The company has recently introduced the brands Boomer and Trex.

The subsidiary in Poland has established a strong distribution network. The brand Boomer is market leader in the bubblegum segment. Joyco Italy is the firm's oldest branch. It was set up in 1985 to manage the European markets. The company in France has marketing and sales teams. Joyco France has recently introduced a customer tracking system well equipped to track local trends.

The joint venture in the Philippines is aiming to become market leader in chewing gum and lollipops in the domestic market as well in the Asian region. In India, the gum market is highly competitive with the presence of several global players. Today the Boomer brand has a 55 per cent share of the bubblegum market.

Dandy's alliance with Joyco

Joyco wanted to penetrate the Russian market with its bubble gum, Boomer, but it did not have a distribution network. Therefore Joyco became interested in using the well-established and comprehensive distribution network of Dandy, which has about 1800 Russian sales representatives visiting all types of shops. In

Case study 6.2 continued

Russia, shops in general are much smaller than in western Europe and North America. Joyco takes advantage of Dandy's distribution network in Russia (Figure 6.18) in a kind of piggy-back solution. Furthermore, the alliance with Joyco was based on a reciprical agreement (Figure 6.19).

Joyco uses Dandy's distibution system not only in Russia/CIS but also in Sweden and Denmark. In return Joyco produces Dandy's bubblegum on Dandy's production plant in Novgorod, Russia. Dandy still has bubblegum in its product range, but it is now concentrating much more on the dragée type.

The distance reduction in the Dandy-Joyco alliance started with two meetings between the CEO and senior management of the two

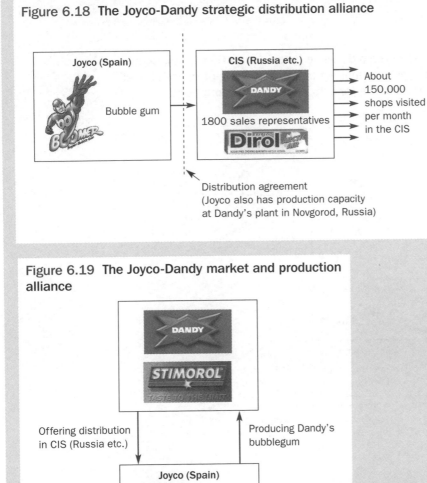

Figure 6.18 The Joyco-Dandy strategic distribution alliance

Figure 6.19 The Joyco-Dandy market and production alliance

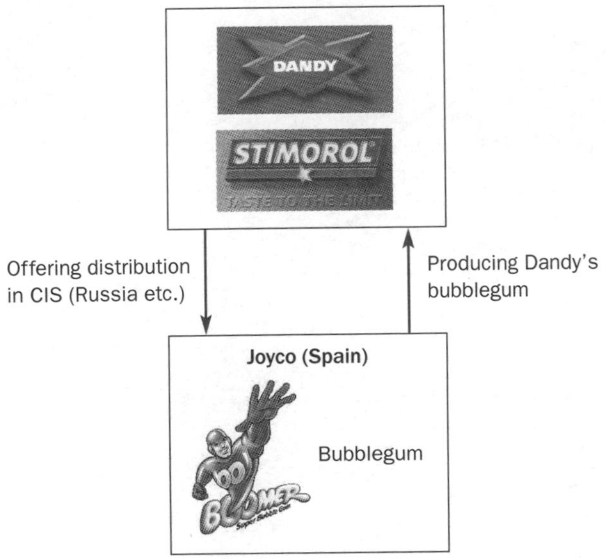

Case study 6.2 continued

companies. In contrast to the Dandy-KGFF alliance, this part of the process only lasted a few weeks. Relations between employees in different departments were then established (see Figure 6.20).

These relations on departmental and employee level were developed in order to learn the organizational culture and the routines of the partner.

This was a quick transition from the bow-tie type relationship to a diamond type relationship (Figure 6.20).

Questions

1. What kind of competitor relationships are the Dandy-KGFF alliance and the Dandy-Joyco alliance?

2. How are Dandy's competences in the value chain used in the alliances to create value for both partners?

3. What should Dandy's future product market strategy be? Should they develop their own brands (Stimorol, Dirol and V6) or should they function more as a sub-supplier to large multinational confectionery or healthcare/pharmaceutical companies?

Source: www.dandygroup.com, material from Dandy.

Figure 6.20 **Reducing the psychic distance in the Joyco-Dandy alliance: (a) bow-tie type relationship at the beginning of negotiations; (b) diamond type relationship later on in negotiations**

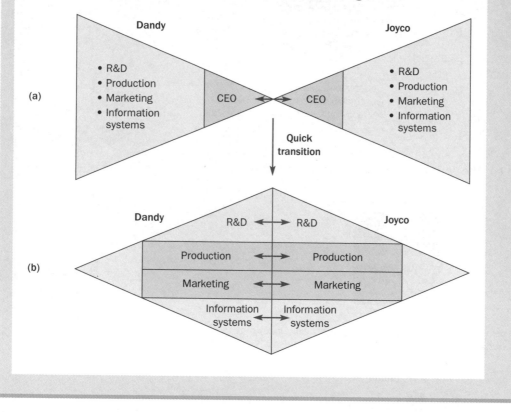

QUESTIONS FOR DISCUSSION

1. What are the main differences between B-t-C and B-t-B relationships?

2. What might be the advantages and disadvantages of creating relationships with consumers for a manufacturer?

3. Motorola and Hewlett-Packard compete in some markets, are supplier and customer, respectively, for each other in various markets, share suppliers in other markets, often have the same customers, and have relationships in yet other markets. What should be done by the firms to achieve joint goals, minimize conflicts, and protect core assets?

4. Some consulting companies argue that by properly incorporating suppliers in the product development process, firms can cut the cost of purchased parts and materials by as much as 30 per cent. Discuss how a buyer-supplier relationship might create these costs savings.

5. Discuss the possibilities for a manufacturer who wants to integrate consumers into the product development process.

6. Explain how distance in cross-cultural buyer-seller negotiation can be reduced.

7. Dell has entered into a relationship with IBM's Global Service Division. Under this agreement, IBM will now provide the service support for Dell's big customers. Evaluate the benefit of the relationship to Dell and IBM.

8. Relationships often involve more than the salesperson and a purchasing agent ('bow tie' model). Often, both a whole selling team and a whole buying team are involved. Describe the interactions between buyer and seller in the 'diamond' model.

REFERENCES

Alajoutsijärvi, K., Møller, K. and Tähtinen, J. (2000), Beautiful exit: how to leave your business partner, *European Journal of Marketing*, vol. 34, no. 11/12, pp. 1270–89.

Anderson, E. and Weitz, B. A. (1989), Determinants of continuity in conventional industrial channel dyads, *Marketing Science*, vol. 8, Fall, pp. 310–23.

Arantola, H. (2000), *Buying Loyalty or Building Commitment – An empirical study of customer loyalty programs*, Swedish School of Economics and Business Administration, Helsinki, research report.

Axelsson, B. and Agndal, H. (2000), Internationalization of the firm: a note on the crucial role of the individual's contact network. Paper presented at the IMP Conference, Bath, 7–9 September.

Bengtsson, M. and Kock, S. (1999), Cooperation and competition in relationships between competitors in business networks, *Journal of Business and Industrial Marketing*, vol. 14, no. 3, pp. 179–93.

Bengtsson, M. and Kock, S. (2000), 'Coopetition' in business networks – to cooperate and compete simultaneously, *Industrial Marketing Management*, vol. 29, pp. 411–26.

Biemans, W. G. and Brand, M. J. (1995), Reverse marketing: a synergy of purchasing and relationship marketing, *International Journal of Purchasing and Materials Management*, Summer, pp. 28–37.

Brown, P. J. (2000), Satellites: the next generation, *Broadcasting & Cable*, New York, July 31, pp. 48–50.

Bullock, C. (2000), Alcatel Space cashes in on global joint ventures, *Interavia*, Geneva, December, pp. 45–7.

Burton, T. T. (1988), JIT/repetitive sourcing strategies: tying the knot with your suppliers, *Production and Inventory Management Journal*, vol. 29, no. 4, pp. 38–41.

Buttery, A. A. and Wong, Y. H. (1999), The development of a Guanxi framework, *Market Intelligence & Planning*, vol. A, no. 3, pp. 147–54.

Centaur Communications (1999), *Kids Marketing Report*, Centaur Communications, London, October 28.

Chemist & Druggist (2001), More power to Aquafresh sales (GlaxoSmithKline launches battery-powered toothbrush), *Chemist and Druggist*, September 25, p. 8 .

Chen, M. J. (1996), Competitor analysis and interfirm rivalry: toward a theoretical integration, *Academy of Management Review*, vol. 21, no. 1, pp. 100–34.

Christopher, M. and Jüttner, V. (2000), Developing strategic partnerships in the supply chain: A practioner's perspective, *European Journal of Purchasing & Supply Management*, vol. 6, pp. 117–27.

Conway, T. and Swift, J.S. (2000), International relationship marketing: the importance of psychic distance, *European Journal of Marketing*, vol. 34, no. 11/12, pp. 1391–413.

Cordona, M. M. (2000), Colgate challenges Gillette dominance in electric brushes, *Advertising Age*, Chicago, vol. 71, no. 14, April 3, pp. 10-11.

Cox, A. (2001), Understanding buyer and supplier: a framework for procurement and supply competence, *Journal of Supply Chain Management*, Spring, pp. 8-15.

Dwyer F. R., Schurr, P. H. and Oh, S. (1987), Developing buyer and seller relationships, *Journal of Marketing*, vol. 51, April, pp. 11–27.

Easton, G. (1992), Industrial networks: a review, *in* Axelsson, B. and Easton, G. (Eds) *Industrial Networks – A new view of reality*, Routledge, London, pp. 3–27.

Ford, D. (1979), Developing buyer-seller relationships in export marketing, *Organisation, Marknad och Samhälle*, vol. 16, no.5.

Ford, D. (1984), Buyer/seller relationships in international industrial markets, *Industrial Marketing Management*, vol.13, no. 2.

Ford, D. (1998), *Managing Business Relationships*, John Wiley & Sons.

Gadde, L.-E. and Snehota (2000), Making the most of supplier relationships, *Industrial Marketing Management*, vol. 29, pp. 305–16.

Giller, C. and Matear, S. (2001), The termination of interfirm relationships, *Journal of Business & Industrial Marketing*, vol 16, no. 2, pp.94–112.

Grönroos, C. (1981), Internal marketing – an integral part of marketing theory, *in* Donnelly, J. H. and George, W. E. (Eds), *Marketing of Services*, American Marketing Association Proceedings Series, pp. 236–8.

Grönroos, C. (1996), Relationship marketing: strategic and tactical implications, *Management Decision*, vol. 34, no. 3, pp. 5–14.

Gruen, T. W. (1995), The outcome set of relationship marketing in consumer markets, *International Business Review*, vol. 4, no. 4, pp. 449–69.

Gummesson, E. (1994), Making relationship marketing operational, *International Journal of Service Industry Management*, vol. 5, no. 5, pp. 5–20.

Gummesson, E. (1999), *Total Relationship Marketing*, Butterworth Heinemann, London.

Håkansson, H. (Ed.) (1982), *International Marketing and Purchasing of Industrial Goods*, John Wiley & Sons, Chichester.

Håkansson, H. and Johanson, J. (1987), *Industrial Technological Development: A network approach*, Croom Helm, London.

Håkansson, H. and Johanson, J. (1992), A model of industrial networks, *in* Axelsson B. and Easton G. (Eds) *Industrial Networks: A view of reality*, Routledge, London.

Håkansson, H. and Snehota, I. (1995), *Developing Relationships in Business Networks*, Thomson, London.

Hallén, L. and Sandström, M. (1991), Relationship atmosphere in international business, *in* Paliwoda, S. J. (Ed.), *New Perspectives on International Marketing*, Routledge, London.

Hallén, L. and Wiedersheim, P. F. (1979), Psychic distance and buyer-seller interaction, *Organisasjon, Marked og samfunn*, vol. 16, no. 5, pp. 308–24.

Hallén, L. and Wiedersheim, P. F. (1984), The evolution of psychic distance in international business relationships, *in* Hagg, I. and Wiedersheim, P. F. (Eds), *Between Market and Hierarchy*, University of Uppsala.

Hallén, L., Johanson, J. and Mohamed, N. S. (1987), Relationship strength and stability in international and domestic industrial marketing, *Industrial Marketing & Purchasing*, vol, 2, no. 3.

Hamel, G., Doz, Y. and Prahalad, C. K. (1989), Collaborate with your competitors – and win, *Harvard Business Review*, vol. 67, no. 1, pp. 133–9.

Han, S. L., Wilson, D. T. and Dant, S. P. (1993), Buyer-supplier relationships today, *Industrial Marketing Management*, vol. 22, pp. 331–8.

Harbert, T. (2000), Beaming business abroad. Electronic Business; Highlands Ranch; June; pp. 76–84.

Harrigan, K. R. (1985), An application for clustering for strategic group analysis, *Strategic Management Journal*, vol. 6, pp. 55-73.

Hocutt, M.A. (1998), Relationship dissolution model: antecedents of relationship commitment and the likelihood of dissolving a relationship, *International Journal of Service Industry Management*, vol. 9, no. 2, pp. 189–200.

Hofstede, G. (1983), National cultures in four dimensions: a research-based theory of cultural differences among nations, *International Studies of Management and Organization*, vol. 13, no. 1–2.

Hofstede, G. (1992), *Kulturer og Organisationer – Overlevelse i en grænseoverskridende verden*, J.H. Schulz Grafisk A/S, Copenhagen.

Hofstede, G. (1994), The business of international business is culture, *International Business Review*, vol. 3, no. 1.

Hollensen, S. (2001), *Global Marketing: A market responsive approach*, Financial Times/Prentice Hall, Harlow 2nd edn.

Hörnell, E., Vahle, J.-E. and Wiedersheim, P. F. (1973), *Export och Utlandsetableringar*, Almqvist & Wiksell.

Jackson, B. B. (1985), Build customer relationships that last, *Harvard Business Review*, vol. 63, November/December, pp. 120–8.

Johanson, J. and Mattsson, L.-G. (1987), Interorganizational relations in industrial systems: a network approach compared with the transaction-cost approach, *International Studies of Management and Organization*, vol. 17, no. 1.

Johanson, J. and Vahle, J.-E. (1999), The internationalization process of the firm: a model of knowledge development and increasing foreign market commitments *in* Buckley, P. J. and Ghauri, P. N., *The Internationalization of the Firm, A reader*, Thomson Business Press, 2nd edn.

Johanson, J. and Wiedersheim, P. F. (1975), The internationalization of the firm – four Swedish cases, *Journal of Management Studies*, October.

Johanson, M., Polsa, P. E. and Törnroos, J. Å. (1999), Business network in different cultural contexts: Western – Russian – Chinese, *Paper presented at the 15th IMP Conference*, Dublin.

Kiff, J. S. (2000), The lean dealership – a vision for the future: from hunting to farming, *Marketing Intelligence & Planning*, vol. 18, no. 3, pp. 112–26.

Kothandaraman, P. and Wilson, D. T. (2000), Implementing relationship strategy, *Industrial Marketing Management*, vol. 29, pp. 339–49.

Kotler, P. (2000), *Marketing Management*, Prentice Hall, Englewood Cliffs, NJ.

Liljander, V. and Strandvik, T. (1995), The nature of customer relationship, *in* Swartz, T.A., Bowen, D.E. and Brown, S.W. (Eds), *Advances in Services Marketing and Management: Research and practice*, JAI Press, London, pp. 141–67.

Mazurkiewicz, G. and Hall, J. R. (1999), Honeywell-Blue Dot alliance partners contractors with profitable accessories, *Air Conditioning, Heating & Refrigeration News*, Troy, Dec. 27.

McCurry, J. W., Rozelle Jr., W. N., Isaacs, M., Owen, P. and Woodruff, C. (2000), Glen Raven: textiles' visionary global merchant, *Textile World*, June, pp. 1–35.

Michalczyk, I. (1999), P&G signs home Tupperware deal, *Marketing*, London, Nov. 4.

Morgan, R. M. and Hunt, S. D. (1994), The commitment-trust theory of relationship marketing, *Journal of Marketing*, vol. 58, July, pp. 20–38.

Nelson, E. (2001), Colgate's net rose 10% in period, new products helped boost sales, *Wall Street Journal*, New York, February 2.

New York Times (2000), Corel and Microsoft form alliance, *New York Times*, October 3, p. 12.

Nordström, K. A. and Vahle, J.-E. (1994), Is the globe shrinking? Psychic distance and the establisment of Swedish sales subsidiaries during the last 100 years, *in* Landeck, M. (Ed.), *International Trade: Regional and global issues*, St Martins Press.

O'Grady, S. and Lane, H. W. (1996), The psychic distance paradox, *Journal of International Business Studies*, Second Quarter.

Ottesen, O. (1995), *Buyer Initiative: Ignored, but imperative for marketing management – towards a new view of market communication*, Tidvise Skrifter, no. 15, adverlung for Okonomi, Kultur og Samfunnsfag, Stavanger College, Norway.

Parkhe, A. (1991), Interfirm diversity, organisational learning, and longevity in global strategic alliances, *Journal of International Business Studies*, vol. 22.

Peppers, D., Rogers, M. and Dorf, B. (1999), Is your company ready for one-to-one marketing?, *Harvard Business Review*, vol. 77, January–February, pp. 151–60.

Perks, H. and Easton, G. (2000), Strategic alliances: partner as customer, *Industrial Marketing Management*, vol. 29, no. 4, July, pp. 327–38.

Philips (1997), *Philips and Jordan sink their teeth into oral toothbrush with new alliance*, April 8 (press release).

Philips (2000), *Philips to acquire Optiva Corporation, maker of the Sonicare® sonic toothbrush*, August 22 (press release).

Philips (2001), *Name change for Optiva*, January 9 (press release).

Porter, M. E. (1980), *Competitive Strategy*, The Free Press, New York.

Prahalad, C. K. and Ramaswamy, V. (2000), Co-opting customer competence, *Harvard Business Review*, January–February, pp. 79–87.

Rafiq, M. and Ahmed, P. K. (2000), Advances in the internal marketing concept: definition synthesis and extension, *Journal of Servies Marketing*, vol. 14, no. 6, pp. 449–62.

Smith, B. A. (1999), New launchers seek commercial market share, *Aviation Week & Space Technology*, New York, December 13, pp. 50–2.

Steinriede, K. (2000), Alliances provide marketing edge, *Beverage Industry*, New York, Feb.

Svenson, G. (2002), The measurement and evaluation of mutual dependence in specific dyadic business relationships, *Journal of Business and Industrial Marketing*, vol. 17, no. 1, pp. 56–74.

Thurau, T. H. and Hansen, U. (2000), *Relationship Marketing: Gaining competitive advantage through customer satisfaction and customer retention*, Springer Verlag, Berlin–Heidelberg.

Wedin, T. (2000), Value creation in industrial networks, Contribution to the IMP Conference, Bath, September 7–9.

Walker, C. (1999), Nescafé blends relations with new charity support, *Precision Marketing*, November 8, News.

Figure III.1 The structure of Part III and how it fits in with the rest of the book

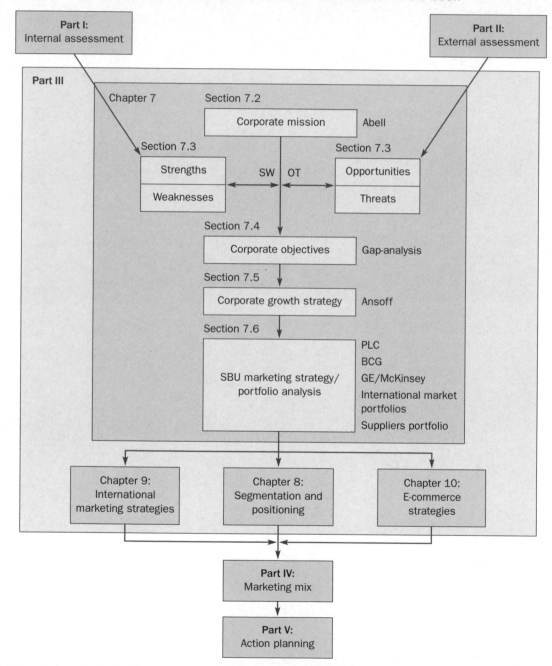

Developing marketing strategies

As mentioned earlier the structure of this book follows the flow of marketing decision making.

After assessing the competences and the competitiveness of the firm in Part I, Part II mainly looked at the interplay of the three Cs: the company, the customer and the competitors.

Marketing strategies focus on ways in which the company can differentiate itself from its competitors, capitalizing on its distinctive strengths to deliver better value to its customers. Thus, a marketing strategy is the creation of a unique and valuable position, involving a different set of activities. Therefore, development of a marketing strategy requires activities that are different from rivals to be chosen.

As shown in Figure III.1, Part III is concerned with marketing decisions on the strategic level. The complex process of marketing strategy formulation emerges from the interplay of different factors. A variety of internal and external information is needed to formulate a marketing strategy. This internal (Part I) and external (Part II) information is then assessed in a SWOT analysis which, together with the corporate mission, defines the corporate objectives, growth strategy and the strategic business unit (SBU) marketing strategy. Though the SWOT analysis is placed on a higher strategic level in Figure III.1 it is important to note that this analytic tool may be used on all strategic levels, including new product planning (tactical decisions).

The output of the SBU marketing strategy falls into three areas:

1. segmentation, positioning and competitive strategy (Chapter 8)

2. internationalization strategies (Chapter 9)

3. e-marketing strategies (Chapter 10).

These three chapters are then the input for developing marketing plans on the tactical level (Part IV) and action planning level (Part V).

Chapter 7

SWOT analysis, strategic marketing planning and portfolio analysis

LEARNING OBJECTIVES:

After studying this chapter you should be able to:

- describe the stages in strategic market planning.
- understand the nature of corporate strategy and how it is connected to the SBU marketing strategy.
- describe and understand the role of SWOT analysis in strategic marketing.
- understand when and how to use different strategic tools in strategic market planning.
- describe the two downstream portfolio models: the BCG and GE models.
- discuss advantages and disadvantages of these models.
- explain the different levels of international portfolio analysis.
- explain the purposes of integrating a supplier portfolio model in a marketing analysis.
- understand how a supplier can be involved in product development with the manufacturer.

Case study 7.1 Microsoft's X-Box

Online gaming through an alliance with Japan's NTT Communications

The stakes in Microsoft's head-to-head battle with Sony are great: the world games console market is estimated to be worth US$20 billionn a year. In its Internet gaming push, Microsoft has formed an alliance with the Japanese Internet and telecommunications company NTT Communications.

Together, the two companies will develop Internet access via the X-Box, facilitate games distribution and other high-speed services, and make it possible for Japanese customers to play games with each other over the Internet.

Microsoft believes the Japanese market offers great growth potential. In Japan, online gaming has been relatively undeveloped. Online gaming

trials started in 2001 and online services will be launched in 2002.

The deal with NTT is seen as part of the games makers' search for new and alternative distribution methods for their products. In its choice for a new games console Microsoft thinks that consumers are looking for what is going to make the next generation of online gaming, and being first-to-market is critical.

Microsoft, founded in 1975, is the worldwide leader in software, services and Internet technologies for personal and business computing. NTT Communications is a wholly owned Internet and long-distance calling service arm of the telecoms

Case study 7.1 continued

carrier Nippon Telegraph, and NTT DoCoMo is 64% owned by the group.

The competitor – Sony PlayStation 2

Sony's PlayStation 2 has also been built with future networking and Internet access in mind. But Sony has said it will wait until broadband Internet access is widely available before it equips its console with a modem. Sony has predicted that a broadband will be widely available by 2005. However, this is not the opinion of NTT Communications' president, Masanobu Suzuki. He said 'we believe this new service will contribute to the popularization of broadband (in Japan)'. Sony may not have specific plans to link its PlayStation 2 with its Internet service provider subsidiary. However, Sony Computer Entertainment (SCE) and Japanese mobile phone giant NTT DoCoMo plan to launch PlayStation games on mobile phones.

The idea is that owners of NTT DoCoMo's i-mode Internet phone will be able to turn to their phones in spare moments to play PlayStation 2 games. And players will be able to compete with each other whether they are connected to a phone, a personal computer or a television.

This is part of Sony's plan to upgrade its mobile phone handset operations and focus more on mobile computing products.

Questions

1. Put Microsoft's X-Box and the Windows product in a BCG matrix. Explain the positions and their implications.

2. Is it a good idea for Microsoft to carry out market testing for online gaming in Japan?

3. Comment on the statement of Microsoft's Japanese partner, NTT Communications' president, Masanobu Suzuki, on online gaming.

4. Who do you think will be the winner in the global games console market?

Source: adapted from: BBC (2001).

7.1　Introduction

A strategic approach to marketing has a number of advantages. First, a strategic emphasis helps organizations orient themselves toward key external factors such as consumers and competition. Instead of just projecting past trends, the goal is to build market-driven strategies that reflect customer concerns. Strategic plans also tend to anticipate changes in the environment rather than just react to competition. Another reason strategic marketing is important is that it forces you to take a long-term view.

The structure of this chapter will follow the phases in the corporate marketing planning process.

7.2　Corporate mission

A formal organization exists to serve a purpose. This purpose may take a variety of forms and may be classified in a number of ways according to the viewpoints of a particular organization.

A well-defined organization provides a sense of direction to employees and helps guide them towards the fulfilment of the firm's potential. Managers should ask, 'What is our business?' and 'What should it be?' The idea is to extract a purpose from a consideration of the firm's history, resources, distinctive abilities, and environmental constraints. A mission statement should specify the business domains in which the organization plans to operate, or more broadly, for example, 'we are an office productivity company'. The firm should try to find a purpose that fits its present needs and is neither too narrow nor too broad.

Determining a corporate mission that fulfils these requirements is by no means easy. Some companies spend two or three years redefining their corporate mission and still manage to produce a corporate mission statement that is not particularly useful or relevant. But what precisely is the nature of such a statement?

To be useful and relevant, a business definition should ideally fulfil a number of criteria. The following represents the more important of these criteria when thinking about how to define a business:

- The definition should be neither too broad nor too narrow. Definitions such as 'we are in the business of making profits' or 'we produce pens' are not really useful. Effective mission statements should cover product line definition, market scope and growth direction.

- Ideally, the definition should encompass the three dimensions of what Abell (1980) refers to as the 'business domain'. These three dimensions are customer groups to be served, customer needs to be served and technologies to be utilized.

7.3 SWOT analysis

SWOT (strengths, weaknesses, opportunities and threats) analysis is a technique specially designed to help identify suitable marketing strategies for company to follow.

A SWOT analysis encompasses both the internal and external environments of the firm. Internally, the framework addresses a firm's strengths and weaknesses on key dimensions such as financial performance and resource; human resources; production facilities and capacity; market share; customer perceptions of product quality, price, and product availability; and organizational communication. The assessment of the external environment includes information on the market (customers and competition), economic conditions, social trends, technology, and government regulation. When performed correctly, a SWOT analysis can drive the process of creating a sound marketing plan. SWOT analysis can be especially useful in discovering strategic advantages that can be exploited in the firm's marketing strategy. In this section, we will explore the benefits of a SWOT analysis and discuss guidelines for conducting a productive one.

The effective use of SWOT analysis provides the following four key benefits to the manager creating the marketing strategy.

- *Simplicity*. SWOT analysis requires no extensive training or technical skills to be used successfully. The analyst needs only a comprehensive understanding of the firm and the industry that it operates. Because specialized training and skills are not necessary, the use of SWOT analysis can actually reduce the costs associated with strategic planning.

- *Collaboration*. Because of its simplicity, SWOT analysis fosters collaboration and open information exchange between the managers of different functional areas. By learning what their colleagues do, what they know, what they think, and how they feel, the marketing manager can solve problems and fill voids in the analysis before the marketing strategy is finalized. The SWOT analysis framework provides a process that generates open information exchange in advance of the actual marketing strategy development process.

- *Flexibility*. Also closely related to its simplicity is the flexibility of SWOT. It can enhance the quality of an organization's strategic planning even without extensive marketing information systems. However, when comprehensive systems are present, they can be structured to feed information directly into a SWOT framework. In addition, the presence of a comprehensive marketing information system, even though it is not needed, can make repeated SWOT analyses run more smoothly and efficiently.

- *Integration*. SWOT analysis can also deal with a wide variety of information sources. SWOT analysis allows the planner to integrate and synthesize diverse information, both of a quantitative and qualitative nature. It organizes information that is widely known, as well as information that has only recently been acquired or discovered.

SWOT analysis can help push the planning team toward agreement as it uncovers potentially harmful disagreements. All of these different forms of information are inherent to, and sometimes problematic for, the strategic planning process. SWOT analysis helps transform this information from a weakness of the planning process into one of its major strengths.

Conditions for an effective and productive SWOT analysis

The degree to which a firm receives the full benefits of a SWOT analysis will depend on the way the framework is used. If done correctly, SWOT can be a strong catalyst for the planning process. If done incorrectly, it can be a great waste of time and other valuable resources. To ensure that you receive the full benefits, you should:

- stay focused
- collaborate with other functional areas
- research issues from the customer's perspective
- separate internal issues from external issues.

Stay focused

A major mistake planners often make in conducting a SWOT analysis is to complete only one generic SWOT analysis for the entire organization (corporate SWOT).

Instead you have to decide which organizational level is being analysed and then start the SWOT analysis there. However, as shown in Figure 7.1 SWOT analyses at the different levels are interlinked.

So when we say SWOT analyses, we really mean SWOT analyses. In most firms there should be a series of analyses, each focusing on a specific organizational level and/or a specific product/market combination. Such a focus enables the marketing manager to focus on the specific marketing mix being used in a given market. This focus also allows the manager to analyse the specific issues that are relevant to the particular product/market. If needed, separate product/market analyses can be combined to examine the issues that are relevant for the entire strategic business unit, and business unit analyses can be combined to create a complete SWOT for the entire organization. The only time a single SWOT would be appropriate is when an organization has only one product/market combination.

Figure 7.1 The link between SWOT analyses and different organizational levels

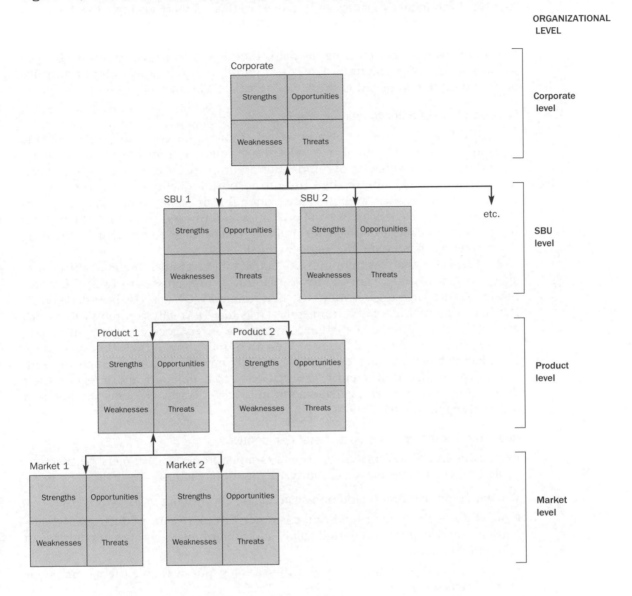

Besides increased relevance, another major benefit of a focused SWOT analysis is its ability to identify knowledge gaps. The identification of such gaps depends on the firm's ability to gather market intelligence.

The requirement of staying focused is also true when we talk about competitors. Information on competitors and their activities is an important aspect of a well-focused SWOT analysis. The key is not to overlook any competitor, whether a current rival or one that is not yet a competitor. As we discussed in Chapter 5, the firm will focus most of its efforts on brand competition. As the SWOT analysis is conducted, the firm must watch for any current or potential direct substitutes for its products. Product and total budget competitors are important as well. Looking at all types of competition is important because many planners never look past brand competitors. Thus, although the SWOT analysis should be focused, it must not be myopic. Even industry giants can lose sight of their potential competitors by focusing exclusively on brand competition. Kodak, for example, had always taken steps to maintain its market dominance over rivals such as Fuji, Konica, and Polaroid in the film industry. However, entering the market for digital cameras completely changed Kodak's set of competing firms. Kodak was forced to turn its attention to giants like Sony and Canon in the fast-growing market for digital cameras.

Collaborate with other functional areas

The SWOT analysis should be a powerful stimulus for communication outside normal channels. The final outcome of a properly conducted SWOT analysis should be an amalgamation of information from many areas. Managers in product development, production finance, inventory control, quality control, sales, advertising, customer service, and other areas should learn what other managers see as the firm's strengths, weaknesses, opportunities, and threats. This allows the marketing planner to come to terms with multiple perspectives before actually creating the marketing strategy and the marketing plan.

As the SWOT analyses from individual areas are combined, the marketing manager can identify opportunities for joint projects and **cross-selling** of the firm's products. In a large organization, the first time a SWOT analysis is undertaken is the first time that managers from some areas have formally communicated with each other. Such cross-collaborations can generate a very good environment for creativity and innovation. Moreover, research has shown that the success of introducing a new product, especially a radically new product is extremely dependent on the ability of different functional areas to collaborate and integrate their differing perspectives. This collaboration must occur across divisions and between different organizational levels.

Research issues from the customers' perspective

Every issue in a SWOT analysis must be examined from the customers' perspective. To do this, the analyst must constantly ask questions such as:

- what do our customers (and non-customers) believe about us as a company?
- what do our customers (and non-customers) think of our product quality, customer service, price and overall value, and promotional messages in comparison to our competitors?
- what is the relative importance of these issues, not as we see them, but as our customers see them?

Examining every issue from the customers' perspective also includes the firm's internal customers: its employees. Some employees, especially front-line employees, are closer to the customer and can offer a different perspective on what customers think and believe. Other types of stakeholders, such as **brokers** and investors who are involved in providing capital for the firm, should also be considered. The SWOT analysis forces managers to change their perceptions to the way customers and other important groups see things. The contrast between these two perspectives often leads to the identification of a gap between management's version of reality and customers' perception. It is like putting a mirror in front of the manager and saying: 'this is how customers look at you – is this also how you see yourself?'

Separate internal issues from external issues

As you conduct a SWOT analysis, it is important to keep the internal issues separate from the external ones. Internal issues are the firm's strengths and weaknesses, while external issues refer to opportunities and threats in the firm's external environments.

The failure to understand the difference between internal and external issues is one of the major reasons for a poorly conducted SWOT analysis. This happens because managers tend to get ahead of themselves by listing their existing marketing strategies and tactics as opportunities. Opportunities and threats exist independently of the firm. Strategies and tactics are what the firm intends to do about its opportunities and threats relative to its own strengths and weaknesses.

SWOT driven strategic marketing planning

In the previous section we looked at the conditions for conducting an effective SWOT analysis.

Now, we will consider how a firm can use its set of strengths, weaknesses, opportunities, and threats to drive the development of strategic plans that will allow the firm to change its current marketing strategy and achieve its goals and objectives. Remember that SWOT analysis should not be an academic exercise to classify information correctly. Rather, it should serve as a catalyst to facilitate and guide the creation of marketing strategies that will produce the desired results. The process of organizing information within the SWOT analysis can help the firm see the difference between where it thinks it is, where others see it as being, and where it hopes to be.

To address these issues properly, the marketing manager should appraise every strength, weakness, opportunity, and threat to determine its total impact on the firm's marketing efforts. This assessment will also give the manager an idea of the basic strategic options that might be available to emphasize the firm's capabilities or convert/minimize its weaknesses and threats. One method of conducting this SWOT assessment is to create and analyse the SWOT matrix. Let's look at how a marketing manager might conduct this assessment.

These are two main steps in a SWOT analysis (see Figure 7.2). In this process the assessment of the firm's strengths and weaknesses involves looking beyond the firm's current products. The manager should also assess the firm's business processes that are key to meeting customers' problems rather than specific products.

Step 1: The matching of strengths and opportunities

The key to the successful achievement of the firm's goals and objectives depends on the ability of the firm to transform key strengths into capabilities by matching them with opportunities in the marketing environment. Capabilities can become competitive advantages if they provide better value to customers than competitors' offerings.

When we refer to capabilities or competitive advantage, we usually speak in terms of real differences between competing firms. After all, capabilities and competitive advantage stem from real strengths possessed by the firm. However, the capabilities and competitive advantage that any firm possesses are often based more on perception than reality. Most customers make purchase decisions based on their own perceptions of the firm's capabilities and advantages. How customers see a company is how that firm is. Regardless of the facts about a company, if

Figure 7.2 Turning the SWOT analysis into a strategic tool for gaining competitive advantage

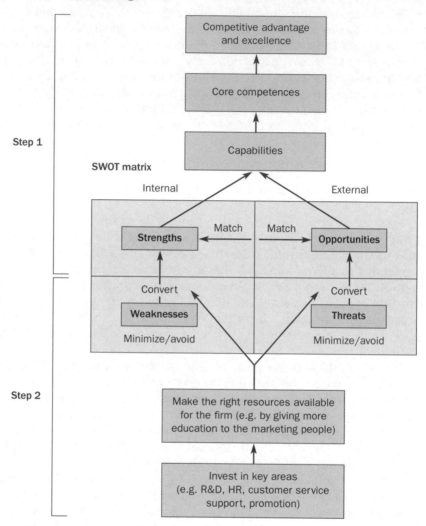

customers perceive the company as slow to react, impersonal, or having excessively high priced or out-of-date products, that is quite simple the way that firm is.

Effectively managing customer's perceptions has been a challenge for marketers for generations. The problem lies in developing and maintaining capabilities and competitive advantage that customers can easily understand, and that solve specific customers' needs. Capabilities or competitive advantage that do not translate into specific benefits for customers are of little use to a firm.

Successful firms attempt to get very close to their customers by seeking their input on how to make the firm's goods and services better or how to solve specific customer problems. These firms also attempt to create long-term relationships between themselves and their customers.

As outlined in Chapter 3 a firm must possess certain core competences to be able to implement a market strategy of competitive excellence. Before a competitive advantage can be translated into specific customer benefits, the firm's target market(s) must recognize that its competences give it an advantage over the competition (see Chapter 3).

Step 2: Converting weaknesses and threats

Firms can convert weaknesses into strengths, and even capabilities, by investing strategically in key areas (e.g. R&D, customer support, promotion, employee training) and by linking key areas more effectively (such as linking human resources to marketing). Likewise, threats can often be converted into opportunities if the right resources are available. Finding new markets for a firm's products could be a viable conversion strategy.

In some cases, weaknesses and threats cannot be successfully converted in the short or long term. When this occurs, the firm must adopt strategies that avoid these issues or minimize their repercussions. One such strategy is to become a niche marketer. Another strategy for minimizing or avoiding weaknesses and threats is to reposition the product. Changes in demographics, declining sales, or increasing competition are common reasons for product **repositioning**. Despite a company's best efforts, some weaknesses and threats simply cannot be minimized or avoided. When this situation occurs, the firm is said to have a limitation. Limitations occur most often when the firm possesses a weakness or faces a threat that coincides with one of its opportunities. Limitations can be particularly troublesome if they are obvious to consumers. How does a company deal with its limitations? One way is to diversify, thus reducing the risk of operating solely within a single business unit or market.

The manager has several potential marketing activities that can be used to take advantage of capabilities and convert weaknesses and threats. At this stage, however, there are likely to be many potential directions for the manager to pursue. Because most firms have limited resources, it is difficult to accomplish everything at once. The manager must prioritize all potential marketing activities and develop specific goals and objectives for the marketing plan.

| Exhibit 7.1 | **Kellogg shows consideration for its weaknesses in snack food** |

In October 2000, cereal giant Kellogg bought biscuit and cracker maker Keebler Foods. For Kellogg, a move beyond cereals is necessary. It gains access to Keebler's strong direct distribution system, which is hailed as one of the industry's best. Keebler has relationships with convenience stores that Kellogg will be able to capitalize on, and therefore expand the sales base for its products.

Cereal and breakfast-food maker Kellogg has watched the sales of its ready-to-eat cereals stagnate over the last few years. Kellogg has struggled to get its product mix right, and has made efforts to become less reliant on cereal sales.

Domestic cereal sales account for about 37% of Kellogg's US revenues. With the addition of Keebler and its tasty brands of snack foods, Kellogg's revenue-reliance on US cereal sales will drop to 27%.

It looks like both partners win with the deal. Kellogg enters the fast growing snack-food market with established and popular brands, and gets access to an efficient and successful distribution system. This will help the lagging cereal giant grow more than it could by just selling cereals. Keebler gets a small price premium on its current valuation, plus the opportunity to jump into a larger international market with Kellogg.

Source: adapted from Lofton (2000).

7.4 Corporate objectives

Broadly, setting objectives involves a company in considering the following two questions:

- Where do we wish to go?
- When do we intend to arrive?

Without an answer to these questions, a company can be likened to a ship without a compass; it can move, but it lacks a clear sense of direction. More specifically, objectives:

- provide for a *sense of purpose* in a company. Without objectives, companies lack the means to focus and organize their efforts.
- help a company to *achieve consistency* between the various levels of decision making, and between the different functions.
- help to *stimulate effort*; they provide a basis for motivating individuals to achieve them.
- provide the *basis for control* in a company. Unless we know precisely what is required, it is difficult, if not impossible, to know the extent to which we have achieved it.

In order to fulfil these important functions, objectives must have certain characteristics. Objectives should be:

- *quantified*. Quantitative objectives with respect to both levels of performance and time reduce the risk of their being vague or ambiguous.
- *acceptable* and *agreeable* to those charged with the responsibility of attaining them. It is pointless setting objectives if they are not acted upon – or if the effort to achieve them is given grudgingly. A frequent reason for objectives being unacceptable is that they are felt to be too difficult or impossible to achieve.
- *consistent*. As we shall see shortly, often companies have a variety of objectives as opposed to a single one. It is important that these multiple objectives do not conflict one with another in such a way that the achievement of an objective in one area is inconsistent with the achievement of objectives in others. For example, an objective of improved profitability may be inconsistent with an objective of maximum sales.

Having discussed the functions of objectives, and the characteristics that objectives ideally should possess if they are to serve these functions, we can now turn our attention to the variety of corporate objectives that a company might set.

In economic analysis it is often asserted that a firm has one, and only one, objective: namely to maximize its total profits. In addition to profit objectives, it is now recognized that companies may have a variety of objectives encompassing a spread of activities. Some of the most frequently encountered objectives and their corresponding performance criteria/measures are shown in Table 7.1.

Whatever the mix of objectives, it must be remembered that the objectives themselves relate to some point in the future, hence the importance of specifying a time-scale for their achievement. For an existing business there will also be a past.

Table 7.1 Common objectives, their performance criteria and measures

Objectives	Performance criteria	Possible measure or indexes
Profit and financial objectives	Profitability	• Profit • Profit as percentage of sales • Contribution margin • Return on investment (ROI)
	Contribution to owners	• Earnings per share • Price/earnings ratio
	Utilization of fixed assets	• Capacity utilization • Fixed assets as percentage of sales
Growth objectives/ marketing objectives	Per cent yearly growth	• Sales • Unit sales • Profits
	Competitive strengths	• Market share • Brand awareness • Brand preference
	Contribution to customers	• Price relative to competitors • Product quality • Customer satisfaction • Customer retention • Customer loyalty
Social responsibility objectives	Contribution to employees	• Wage rates, benefits • Personnel development, promotions • Employment stability, turnover
	Contribution to society	• Contributions to charities or community institutions • Growth in employment

It is possible, therefore, to measure the past and current performance of the company with respect to those areas in which it has objectives for the future. Management can then compare where it wishes to be (objectives) with where it is likely to be on the basis of a projection from past performance. Any difference constitutes what is referred to as a planning gap, which would cause some kind of gap analysis. This notion of a planning gap is illustrated in Figure 7.3.

The gap stems from the difference between future desired profit objectives and a forecast of projected profit based on past performance and following existing strategy.

If there is a planning gap, a number of options are available; the intention however is to close the gap. For example, the gap could be closed by revising objectives downwards. Such a step might be taken where the initial objectives are unrealistic. Alternatively, or in addition, the gap could be closed by actions designed to move the company off the projected curve and towards the desired curve.

This next step in the process of corporate planning is the formulation of strategies.

Figure 7.3 The planning gap

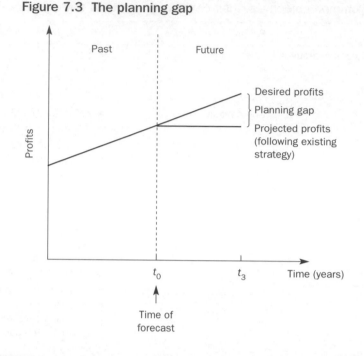

Duracell versus Energizer batteries – two multinationals are considering their portfolios in batteries

Younger consumers, especially in their teens and early 20s, need endless supplies of batteries to operate all their electronic products, and promise to fuel market growth for years to come.

As a result of the introduction of new products over the last five years and a growing need by consumers for portable power sources to operate their consumer electronics products, the US batteries market has blossomed into a US$5 billion business. Consumers say they buy batteries based on brand awareness and the trust factor. That may be a key reason why private labels have not done well in this category and several brands have dominated the market. Duracell and Energizer have been locked in a battle for market supremacy.

The US market for batteries

The Gillette Company, through subsidiary Duracell Global Business Management Group, captured the largest share of the market in 2000, accounting for about 50% of total market value.

Energizer Holding Inc. captured about 25% of the total market in 1999. Despite producing the Energizer line of alkaline batteries, the nation's second most popular brand, the company market share fell from 31% in 1998.

Rayovac captured 15% of the market in 2000, compared to a 9.5% market share in 1998, attributed to strong sales of both alkaline batteries and the company's Renewal brand, which is the US's leading line of rechargeable batteries.

Matsushita's Panasonic batteries accounted for 4% of the market in 1999.

In May 1999, Energizer Holding Inc. had to withdraw an advertising campaign. This Energizer campaign – which featured the Energizer bunny torturing, crushing and pummelling competitive batteries – based its superiority claim on battery performance tests conducted for a Popular Electronics magazine article published in January 1999. Gillette contended, and the court agreed, that the testing protocols used in the article were unscientific, unreliable and did not reflect the way batteries perform for consumers in real life.

Sources: Duracell (1999), Maremont (2001), Marketing Week (1998), Progressive Grocer (2000).

7.5 Corporate growth strategy

A strategy for reaching long-term objectives needs to be developed specifically for each SBU. **Market penetration**, product development, **market development**, and diversification are the four basic product strategies (Figure 7.4) for closing the planning gap. Each cell in the Ansoff matrix presents distinct opportunities, threats, resource requirements, returns and risks, and will now be discussed.

Market penetration

The most frequently used strategy is to take the existing product in the existing market and try to obtain an increased share of that market. The two ways in which this can be achieved are by increasing sales to existing customers and by finding new customers in the same market. The first strategy means persuading users to use more of the product on more occasions, perhaps by replacing an indirect competitor. Alternatively, the strategy may be to use the product more often without any need to take business from competitors.

The second strategy takes business directly from competitors by increasing both penetration and market share. This can be achieved either by changing the product offering or by changing the positioning of the product offering.

With this option, product improvement is also an option. An example of a company following such a tactic is Japan-based Komatsu, Caterpillar's most important competitor in the market for earthmoving and construction equipment. They have taken a significant market share by continually raising the quality of their products,

Figure 7.4 The Ansoff product-market matrix

	Current products	New products
Current markets	**Market penetration strategies** • Increase market share • Increase product share • Increase frequency of use • Increase quantity used • New applications	**Product development strategies** • Product improvements • Product-line extensions • New products for same market
New markets	**Market development strategies** • Expand markets for existing products • Geographic expansion • Target new segments/ customer groups	**Diversification strategies** • Vertical integration • Forward integration • Backward integration • Diversification into related businesses (concentric diversification) • Diversification into unrelated businesses (conglomerate diversification)

Source: adapted from Ansoff (1957).

which allowed an extension of warranties, and by extending the range of their products' application through improved technologies. A company may attempt to expand a market that they already serve by *converting non-users to users* of their product. This can be an attractive option in new markets when non-users form a sizable segment and may be willing to try the product given suitable inducements. Thus when Carnation entered the powdered coffee whitening market with Coffeemate, a key success factor was its ability to persuade hitherto non-users of powdered whiteners to switch from milk. Former users can also be targeted. Kellogg has targeted former breakfast cereal users (fathers) who rediscover the pleasure of eating cornflakes when feeding their children. Market expansion can also be achieved by *increasing usage*. Colman attempted to increase the use of mustard by showing new combinations of mustard and food. Kellogg has also tried to increase the usage (eating) rate of its cornflakes by promoting eating them in the evening as well as at breakfast.

Market development

This entails the marketing of current products to new customer groups and new regions.

New customer groups

The promotion of nylon for new customer groups accounted for the growth in sales of nylon, which was first marketed as a replacement for silk in parachutes, but expanded into shirts, carpets, tyres etc.

Geographic expansion

Geographic expansion is appropriate when important competitors are opening up new markets, or when opportunities in new markets will be available for only a short time. These characteristics are often found in high-tech industries like computer technology and advanced circuit technology. The speed with which new computer chips, for example, can be matched by competitors means that they are marketed globally as quickly as possible to take advantage of product superiority for as long as possible.

Geographic expansion also becomes necessary when intense price competition in slow-growing markets leads to diminishing profit margins. To achieve higher sales volumes, the company introduces its products in markets where few product modifications are required. Eastman Kodak, for example, faced with strong competition from Japan's Fuji and Germany's Agfa-Gevaert (both penetrating growing US, European and Japanese markets) turned to China, where 35 mm film sales have quintupled since the early 1980s, to roughly 120 million rolls in 1995. Only one of the country's seven domestic makers, Lucky Film Corp., had a truly national brand in 1996. While just 12 per cent of China's 1.3 billion people owned a camera, picture taking is fast becoming as popular as it is in Japan. By the end of the decade, China is expected to overtake Japan, becoming the world's second-largest film market, behind the USA. But competition is unavoidable. With less than 30 per cent of the Chinese film market and an even smaller share of photographic paper in 1996, Kodak remains behind. Fuji leads in film and is fighting a price war with Agfa-Geveart for that company's leading share of the photographic-paper market. (Jobber, 1998).

Product development

This strategy involves a major modification of the goods or service, such as quality, style, performance, or variety.

A company follows its basic strategy of product market development, allocates resources to a limited number of markets and focuses its operations on the development of new products in these areas. This approach is appropriate if the company is well established in its markets and lacks the motivation, ability or knowledge to adapt to a new environment. Product market development is most appropriate when the current product market has matured and new product markets are growing fast in existing markets.

An offer of 'high performance' versions of existing car models can be used to extend the ranges to additional customers. Similarly, adding vitamins to orange juice will possibly cause some existing users to increase their usage but may also attract new users.

Diversification

This option concerns the development of *new products for new markets*. This is the most risky option, especially when the entry strategy is not based upon the core competences of the business. Firms must be aware of diversification simply because the grass looks greener in the new market.

One obvious example is the tobacco companies that have diversified – often at considerable cost – into areas as varied as cosmetics and engineering. However, diversification can also be a positive move to extend the application of existing expertise.

Honda's move from motor cycles to cars (based on its core competence in engines) and Sony's move into 8 mm camcorders (based on its core competences in miniaturization and video technology) extended the application of existing expertise.

Disney Corporation diversified from cartoons to theme parks and television broadcasting. Heinz has steadily and successfully extended beyond its core ketchup business; its Weight Watchers brand is now worth hundreds of millions of dollars. But it should be noted that, like many other similarly successful diversifications, Heinz's strategy was built on a logical extension of the company's existing strengths.

Vertical integration is one way for corporations to diversify their operations. *Forward integration* occurs when a firm moves downstream in terms of the product flow – as when a manufacturer acquires a wholesaler or retail outlet. *Backward integration* occurs when a firm moves upstream by acquiring a supplier. For example, Compaq has strengthened its position in computer software markets by acquiring several software developers.

Concentric diversification occurs when a firm internally develops or acquires another business that does not have products or customers in common with its current business, but that might contribute to internal synergy through the sharing of production facilities, brand names, R&D know-how, or marketing and distribution skills. Thus, Sara Lee has made more than 60 acquisitions in recent years, most involving businesses that could benefit from the firm's well-respected brand and its distribution strengths in grocery stores.

Conglomerate diversification, the riskiest diversification of all, moves into completely new areas. For example, British Aerospace decided to apply the huge cash flow from its defence business to investments in car, construction and property. The company never found the expected synergy and either divested the acquisitions or reported large losses (Economist, 1995).

Ansoff's product-market matrix is probably one of the best-known frameworks for delineating overall corporate strategies. A second and increasingly popular group of techniques aimed at the identification and selection of corporate strategies is also based on analysing appropriate marketing strategies. These are the so-called portfolio models and they will be discussed in the next section.

7.6 SBU marketing strategy/portfolio analysis

The definition of the unit of analysis for **portfolio planning** is a critical stage and one that is often poorly done in practice. The components of a firm involved in portfolio analysis or businesses are called strategic business units, or SBUs. Managers within each of these business units decide which objectives and strategies to pursue. Senior corporate managers typically reserve the right to grant final approval of such decisions to ensure their overall consistency with corporate objectives and resource allocations across SBUs in the company portfolio. Lower-level general managers, however, conduct much of the analysis on which such decisions are based. These managers are more familiar with a given SBU's products and customers, and ultimately they are responsible for implementing its strategy.

Ideally, strategic business units have the following characteristics.

- *A homogeneous set of markets to serve with a limited number of related technologies.* Minimizing diversity across an SBU's product market entries enables the unit's manager to better formulate and implement a coherent and internally consistent business strategy.

- *A unique set of product markets,* in the sense that no other SBU within the firm competes for the same customers with similar products. Thus, the firm avoids duplication of effort and maximizes economies of scale within its SBUs.

- *Control over those factors necessary for successful performance,* such as production, R&D and engineering, marketing, and distribution. This does not mean an SBU should not share resources – such as manufacturing plant or a sales force – with one or more other business units. But the SBU should determine how its share of the joint resource is used effectively to carry out its strategy.

- *Responsibility for their own profitability.*

As you might expect, firms do not always meet all of these ideals when creating business units. There are usually trade-offs between having many small homogeneous SBUs versus large but fewer SBUs that managers can more easily supervise.

Portfolio analysis was originally intended for use at the SBU level, where these are generally defined as subsidiaries which can operate independently as businesses in their own right. In reality, however, boundaries are seldom clear-cut and the problems of definition can be substantial.

Practitioners have often used the portfolio models (e.g. the BCG model) to look at products rather than business units or to provide a pictorial presentation of international markets. These applications do not conform strictly to those for which it was originally intended, but its value as a means of presenting much information still remains, providing the limitations of the matrix are kept in mind.

Where products are selected as the unit of analysis it is important that market shares and growth rates reflect the more specific market sectors in which they are operating.

Product life cycle (PLC)

In relation to portfolio models, the most important message the PLC can bring to management is that of cash flow. The model offers a clear reminder that the launch of a new brand requires significant investment that can last from its launch to the end of the growth phase, which can be a longer period than most organizations allow for. In addition, the more successful the new brand, the greater the investment needed.

This proposition suggests that products are born, grow to maturity, and then decline, much like plants and animals. During the introductory period, sales grow rapidly but the high expenses mean that no profits are made. Near the end of the growth stage, the rate of expansion of sales begins to slow down and profits reach a peak. During the maturity phase, sales reach their peak and profits are slowly eroded by increasing competition. If nothing is done to revive declining products, they eventually have to be dropped. However, sometimes it is hard to know when a product is leaving one stage and entering the next. The life-cycle concept helps managers think about their product line as a portfolio of investments.

Most organizations offer more than one product or service, and many operate in several markets. The advantage here is that the various products – the **product**

Figure 7.5 Product life cycle

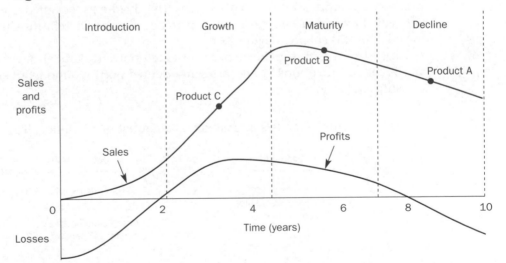

portfolio – can be managed so that they are not all in the same phase in their life cycles. Having products evenly spread out across life cycles allows for the most efficient use of both cash and human resources. Figure 7.5 shows an example of such life-cycle management and some of the benefits that can be obtained from a well-managed product portfolio. The current investment in C, which is in the growth phase, is covered by the profits being generated by the earlier product B, which is at maturity. This product had earlier been funded by A, the decline of which is now being balanced by the newer products. An organization looking for growth can introduce new goods or services that it hopes will be bigger sellers than those that they succeed. However, if this expansion is undertaken too rapidly, many of these brands will demand investment at the beginning of their life cycles, and even the earliest of them will be unlikely to generate profits fast enough to support the numbers of later launches. Therefore, the producer will have to find another source of funds until the investments pay off.

7.7 Introduction to portfolio models

Relationship marketing attempts to involve and integrate customers, suppliers and other partners into the firm's development of marketing actitivies.

Portfolio models have their foundation in Markowitz's (1952) pioneering portfolio theory for the management of equity investments. Since then, portfolio models have been widely used in strategic planning, essentially at the SBU level.

The portfolio models discussed in this chapter tend to focus on the downstream relationships to the customers (market). Portfolio models have been used in strategic planning and marketing, but their application to the field of purchasing has been limited. This seems, however, to be changing, as procurement management has become more strategic. This is why the dyadic aspect of interdependence between buyer and suppliers, the upstream aspects of relationships, are also included in this chapter (Figure 7.6).

We will start with the downstream-oriented portfolio models (Sections 7.8, 7.9 and 7.10) and then look at an upstream-oriented portfolio model of supplier relationships in Section 7.11.

Figure 7.6 Portfolio models in upsteam and downstream relationships

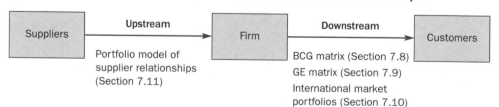

7.8 The Boston Consulting Group's growth-share matrix – the BCG model

One of the first – and best known – of the portfolio models is the growth-share matrix developed by the Boston Consulting Group in the late 1960s. The Boston Matrix offers a useful map of an organization's product strengths and weaknesses as well as the likely cash flows. It was reasoned that one of the main indicators of cash generation was relative market share, and market growth rate was indicative of cash usage. Figure 7.7 shows the Boston Matrix. It is well worth remembering that one of the key underlying assumptions of this matrix is the expectation that the position of products in their markets will change over time. This assumption is, of course, the incorporation of the product life-cycle thinking discussed earlier.

Figure 7.7 presents an example of the share/growth matrix in which six product lines (A–F) make up the portfolio. A light blue circle represents the current position, and a dark blue circle the forecast future position. The area of the circle is proportional to the product's contribution to company sales volume.

Figure 7.7 shows also the two factors which underlie the Boston Consulting Group's approach. Market share is used because it is an indicator of the product's ability to generate cash; market growth is used because it is an indicator of the product's cash requirements. The measure of market share used is the product's share *relative* to the firm's largest competitor. This is important because it reflects the degree of dominance enjoyed by the product in the market. For example, if

Figure 7.7 The BCG model

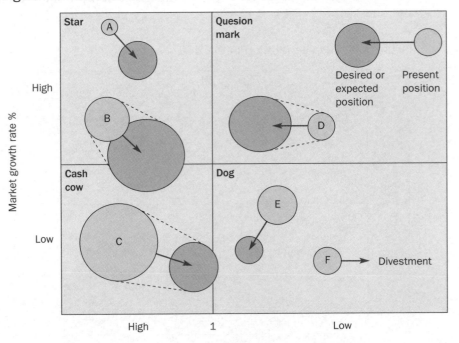

company A has 20 per cent market share and its biggest competitor also has 20 per cent market share, this position is usually less favourable than if company A had 20 per cent market share and its biggest competitor had only 10 per cent market share. The relative ratios would be 1:1 compared with 2:1. It is this ratio, or measure of market dominance, that the horizontal axis measures.

Market growth rate

The vertical axis recognizes the impact of market growth rate on cash flow. This dimension acts as a proxy, or more easily measured substitute, for the more difficult to assess product life cycle and reflects the strategies and associated costs typical over the cycle. At product launch costs are likely to far outstrip revenues. R&D costs will need to be recouped, production capacity created and market beachheads established. Typically during the launch and introductory phases of the life cycle, cash flow will be negative and hence there will be a need to invest cash generated elsewhere (or borrowed from external sources) in the venture.

As the product becomes established in the market, revenues will pick up, but the venture is likely to remain cash hungry because of the need to make further capital investment.

In Figure 7.8 the change is shown as a negative cash flow when the growth rate is high and a positive cash flow when the growth rate is low (mature markets). During the decline phase of the life cycle, margins are likely to come under increasing pressure, but investment can be kept to a minimum. Products at this phase of the cycle are typically managed for cash, which is then invested in the next generation of products to ensure life (from new products) after death (of the old ones).

Figure 7.8 Cash generation in the BCG matrix

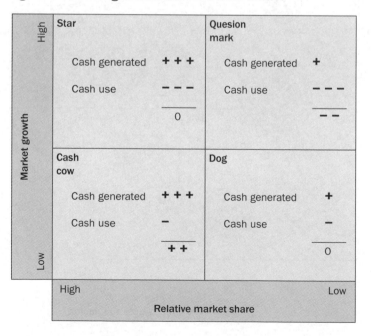

Relative market shares

The horizontal axis of the BCG model depicts relative market share. While market growth rate has been found to be a useful indicator of cash use (or the need for investment), market share has been found to be related to cash generation. Higher market shares, relative to competitors, are associated with better cash generation because of economies of scale and experience curve effects. The experience curve concept, also developed by the Boston Consulting Group in the 1960s, forms the foundation for this relationship, but further supporting evidence comes from the influential **Profit Impact of Marketing Strategy (PIMS)** study of the 1970s and 1980s. Relative market share is in effect used as a proxy for profitability, the underlying premise being that dominant share leads to superior profitability.

Each of the four cells in the growth-share matrix represents a different type of business with different strategy and resource requirements. The implications of each are discussed below.

Question marks

Businesses in high-growth industries with low relative market shares are called question marks or problem children. Such businesses require large amounts of cash, not only for expansion to keep up with the rapidly growing market, but also for marketing activities (or reduced margins) to build market share and catch the industry leader. If management can successfully increase the share of a question mark business, it becomes a star. But if they fail, it eventually turns into a dog as the industry matures and the market growth rate slows.

Stars

A **star** is the market leader in a high-growth industry. Stars are critical to the continued future success of the firm. As their industries mature, they move into the bottom-left quadrant and become cash cows. Paradoxically, while stars are critically important, they often are net users rather than suppliers of cash in the short term. This is because the firm must continue to invest in such businesses to keep up with rapid market growth and to support the R&D and marketing activities necessary to stave off competitors' attacks and maintain a leading market share. Indeed, share maintenance is crucial for star businesses to become cash cows rather than dogs as their industries mature.

Cash cows

Businesses with a high relative share of low-growth markets are called **cash cows** because they are the primary generators of profits and cash in a corporation. Such businesses do not require much additional capital investment. Their market shares are stable, and their share leadership position usually means they enjoy economies of scale and relatively high profit margins. Consequently, the corporation can use the cash from these businesses to support its question marks and stars (as shown in Figure 7.8). However, this does not mean the firm should necessarily maximize the business's short-term cash flow by cutting R&D and marketing expenditures to the bone – particularly not in industries where the business might continue to generate substantial future sales. When firms attempt to harvest too much cash from such businesses, they risk suffering a premature decline from cash cow to dog status, thus losing profits in the long term.

Dogs

Low-share businesses in low-growth markets are called dogs because, although they may generate some cash, they typically generate low profits, or losses. Divestiture is one option for such businesses, although it can be difficult to find an interested buyer. Another common strategy is to harvest dog businesses. This involves maximizing short-term cash flow by paring investments and expenditures while the business is gradually phased out.

The relationship between the BCG model and the concept of PLC

The product portfolio matrix approach propounded by the Boston Consulting Group may be related to the product life cycle by putting the introduction stage in the question mark quadrant; growth starts toward the end of this quadrant and continues well into the star quadrant. Going down from the star to the cash cow quadrant, the maturity stage begins. Decline is positioned between the cash cow and the dog quadrants (see Figure 7.9). Ideally, a company should enter the product-market segment in its introduction stage, gain market share in the growth stage, attain a position of dominance when the product-market segment enters its maturity stage, maintain this dominant position (with a generation of cash for new products) until the product-market segment enters its decline stage, and then determine the optimum point for removing the product.

This ideal PLC is often in contrast to the typical PLC flow which is represented by the dotted line in Figure 7.9.

Figure 7.9 The BCG model and the product life cycle

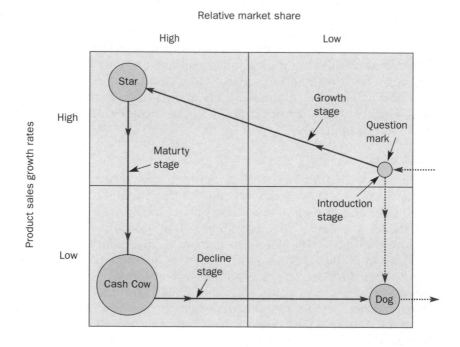

The advantages of the BCG model

The advantages of the BCG model are as follows.

1. It fulfils a human desire for taxonomy, classifying a complex mix of different businesses. It is easy to grasp, has an attractive presentation and uses catch phrases and terms which are easy to memorize and have a clear link to strategy. These may be poor reasons for using a strategic tool, but they make it an effective means of communication in an area where little else is clear.

2. Research has provided some evidence to support the Boston matrix. It embodies simple ideas with cash flow implications which are intuitively appealing to managers. The PIMS study has been a particularly fruitful source of support for the Boston matrix.

3. Simplicity is probably the Boston matrix's greatest virtue. It brings together a number of very important strategic issues and allows them to be presented and understood quickly. Fashion has led to the popularity of the Boston matrix. This means it is an idea that is well understood and liked by many managers and therefore one which allows communication between headquarters and SBUs. It has become part of the common business vocabulary.

4. One of the most informative uses of the Boston matrix is to plot competitors' positions along with the firm's own. This gives a valuable insight into their position (especially their cash position), indicates how they may behave in the future, and shows the relative strengths and weaknesses of the firm's own brands.

The disadvantages of the BCG model

The BCG model is not without problems and limitations. Some of the more frequent criticisms are as follows.

1. Defining the relevant industry and market served (i.e. the target market segments being pursued) can present problems. Market share varies depending on the definition of the corresponding product/market. Hence, a product may be classified in different cells, depending on the market boundaries used. For example, Coke Classic holds about a 24 per cent share of the US soft-drinks market, but less than 8 per cent of the market for all beverages. Given that consumers substitute other beverages – such as coffee, bottled water, and fruit juice – for soft drinks to varying degrees, which is the most appropriate market definition to use?

2. Many critics have argued that the BCG growth share matrix is an oversimplification of product markets and can lead to insufficient management attention to the range of factors that is important in marketing strategy. For example, the matrix is based on only two key factors – market growth and relative market share. While the matrix specifies appropriate investment strategies for each business, it provides little guidance on how best to implement those strategies. While the model suggests that a firm should invest cash in its question mark businesses, it does not consider whether there are any potential sources of competitive advantage that the business can exploit to successfully increase its share. Simply providing a business with more money does not guarantee that it will be able to improve its position within the matrix.

3. Market growth rate is an inadequate description of overall industry attractiveness. For one thing, market growth is not always directly related to profitability or cash flow. Some high-growth industries have never been very profitable because low entry barriers and low capital requirements have enabled supply to grow even faster, resulting in intense price competition. Also, rapid growth in one year is no guarantee that growth will continue in the following year.

4. Relative market share is inadequate as a description of overall competitive strength. The assumption is that an experience curve resulting from a combination of scale economies and other efficiencies gained through learning and technological improvements over time leads to continuing reductions in unit costs as a business's relative market share increases. But a large market share within an industry does not always give a business a significant cost advantage – especially when the product is a low-value-added item.

5. The model implicitly assumes that all business units are independent of one another except for the flow of cash. If this assumption is inaccurate, the model can suggest some inappropriate resource allocation decisions. For instance, if other SBUs depend on a dog business as a source of supply, or if they share functional activities, such as a common salesforce, harvesting that dog might increase the costs or reduce the effectiveness of the other SBUs.

6. The BCG portfolio framework was developed for balancing cash flows. It ignores the existence of capital markets. Cash balancing is not always an important consideration. Partly because of limitations and criticisms of the BCG growth share matrix, a number of product-market portfolio techniques now use several factors to analyse strategic business units instead of only the two found in BCG's growth share matrix approach. Working in conjunction with McKinsey & Co., General Electric USA (GE) has developed one of the more popular of these multiple-factor **screening** methods.

7.9 General Electric market attractiveness – business position matrix (GE matrix)

In the GE matrix, SBUs are evaluated using the two factors of *market attractiveness* and *competitive position*. In contrast to the BCG approach, each of these two dimensions is, in turn, further analysed into a number of sub-factors that underpin each factor.

The market attractiveness-business position portfolio assessment model was developed by General Electric USA and designed to overcome some of the problems of models such as the BCG matrix.

The classic analysis of attractiveness is contained in the nine-cell GE matrix, which also includes a study of the competitive strength of a supplier. Other similar matrices are the Shell directional policy matrix, and the Arthur D. Little product-market evolution portfolio. Each is a logical refinement of the heavily criticized Boston Consulting Group (BCG) matrix. The replacement of the single BCG factor of market growth with the more complex multi-dimensional market attractiveness on the vertical axis, and, on the horizontal, using measures of competitive strength instead of the single factor of relative market share makes the nine-cell alternative far stronger as an analytical tool.

Figure 7.10 Compiling the GE matrix and making conclusions based on it

Step 1:
Determining the factors
(only shown for hydraulic pumps)

The SBU only, e.g. hydraulic pumps		Weight ×	Rating (1–5)	=	Score/ value
Market attractiveness	Overall market size	0.20	4		0.80
	Annual market growth rate	0.20	5		1.00
	Historical profit margin	0.15	4		0.60
	Competitive intensity	0.15	2		0.30
	Technological requirements	0.15	4		0.60
	Inflationary vulnerability	0.05	3		0.15
	Energy requirements	0.05	2		0.10
	Environmental impact	0.05	3		0.15
	Total	1.00			3.70

		Weight ×	Rating (1–5)	=	Score/ value
Business strength	Market share	0.10	4		0.40
	Share growth	0.15	2		0.30
	Product quality	0.10	4		0.40
	Brand reputation	0.10	5		0.50
	Distribution network	0.05	4		0.20
	Promotional effectiveness	0.05	3		0.15
	Productive capacity	0.05	3		0.15
	Productive efficiency	0.05	2		0.10
	Unit costs	0.15	3		0.45
	Material supplies	0.05	5		0.25
	R&D performance	0.10	3		0.30
	Managerial personnel	0.05	4		0.20
	Total	1.00			3.40

Step 2:
Estimate position of SBUs in the GE matrix

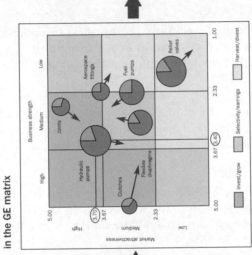

Step 3:
Strategic implications of SBU positions

		Business strength		
		High	Medium	Low
Market attractiveness	High	**Protect position** • Invest to grow at maximum sustainable rate • Concentrate effort on maintaining strength	**Invest to build** • Challenge for leadership • Build selectively on strengths • Reinforce vulnerable areas	**Build selectively** • Specialize on limited strengths • Seek ways of overcoming weaknesses • Withdraw if indications of sustainable growth are lacking
	Medium	**Build selectively** • Invest heavily in most attractive segments • Build up ability to counter competition • Emphasize profitability by raising productivity	**Selectivity/manage for earnings** • Protect existing programme • Concentrate investments in segments where profitability is good and risk is relatively low	**Limited expansion or harvest** • Look for ways to expand without high risk; otherwise, minimize investment and rationalize operations
	Low	**Protect and refocus** • Manage for current earnings • Concentrate attractive segments • Defend strengths	**Manage for earnings** • Protect position in most profitable segments • Upgrade product line • Minimize investment	**Divest** • Sell at time that will maximize cash value • Meanwhile cut fixed costs and avoid investment

Source: adapted from La Rue T. Hosmer (1982), p. 310, Kotler (2000), pp. 71–2, Day (1986) p. 204.

Compiling the GE matrix

As shown in Figure 7.10 the process of compiling the GE matrix consists of the following three major steps:

- Step 1: Determine the factors and the position of the SBU in the GE matrix
- Step 2: Prepare the GE matrix (estimate position of SBUs)
- Step 3: Make strategic recommendations based on the GE matrix.

The five sub-steps in step 1 are:

1. list the products and services that you intend to include in the analysis
2. determine factors contributing to market attractiveness
3. determine factors contributing to business position
4. establish ways of measuring market attractiveness and business position
5. rank each strategic business unit according to whether it is high, medium or low on business strength; and high, medium or low on market attractiveness.

Products and services

The list can consist of: countries, companies, subsidiaries, regions, products, markets, segments, customers, distributors or any other unit of analysis that is important. The GE can be used at any level in an organization and for any kind of SBU.

Factors

In order to use the GE matrix, the strategic planner must first determine the various factors contributing to market attractiveness and business position. The total list of possible factors to include could look like Table 7.2.

Ranking each SBU

After selecting some important factors from the list, the strategic planner should try to estimate the position of the single SBUs in the GE matrix. Within the matrix, the circle size represents the size of the market and the shaded part the share of the market held by the SBU.

The positions of these SBUs could then give implications for different strategies (step 3). The three cells in the upper-left corner indicate strong SBUs in which the company should invest or grow. The diagonal cells stretching from the lower left to the upper right indicate SBUs that are medium in overall attractiveness. The company should be selective and manage for earnings in these SBUs. The three cells in the lower-right corner indicate SBUs that have low overall attractiveness.

Advantages and disadvantages of the GE matrix

Advantages

- The GE matrix uses several factors to assess SBUs instead of only two, and is also based on return on investments rather than simply cash flow.
- The GE analysis is much richer than the BCG analysis because more are factors taken into account, and it is more flexible.
- Much of the value of such a tool lies in the discussion and debate necessary to identify and weight relevant factors.

Table 7.2 Factors contributing to market attractiveness and competitive position

Attractiveness of your market	Competitive position of your business (business strengths)
Market factors	
Size (value, units or both)	Your share (in equivalent terms)
Size of key segments	Your share of key segments
Growth rate per year:	Your annual growth rate:
– total	– total
– segments	– segments
Diversity of market	Diversity of your participation
Sensitivity to price, service features and external factors	Your influence on the market
Cyclicality	Lags or leads in your sales
Seasonality	
Bargaining power of upstream suppliers	Bargaining power of your suppliers
Bargaining power of downstream suppliers	Bargaining power of your customers
Competition	
Types of competitor	Where you fit, how you compare in terms of products, marketing capability
Degree of concentration	
Changes in type and mix	Service, production strength, financial strength, management
Entries to and exits from market segment	Segments you have entered or left
Changes in share	Your relative share change
Substitution by new technology	Your vulnerability to new technology
Degrees and types of integration	Your own level of integration
Financial and economic factors	
Contribution margins	Your margins
Leveraging factors, such as economies of scale and experience	Your scale and experience
Barriers to entry or exit (both financial and non-financial)	Barriers to your entry or exit (both financial and non-financial)
Capacity utilization	Your capacity utilization
Technological factors	
Maturity and volatility	Your ability to cope with change
Complexity	How strong your skills are
Differentiation	Types of your technological skills
Patent and copyrights	Your patent protection
Manufacturing process technology required	Your manufacturing technology
Socio-political factors in your environment	
Social attitudes and trends	Your company's responsiveness and flexibility
Law and government agency regulations	Your company's ability to cope
Influence with pressure groups and government representatives	Your company's aggressiveness
Human factors, such as unionization and community acceptance	Your company's relationships

Disadvantages

- The technique is much more complex than the BCG approach, and requires much more extensive data gathering and processing.

- Evaluation and scoring of SBUs is subjective. Subjectivity can be a problem, especially if planners are inexperienced in exercising the judgement required.

- Another limitation is the unproven relationship between influencing factors and the overall factors (market attractiveness and business position) themselves. For instance, management recognizes that its company's technological innovativeness gives it a strong status in the market, but the form and the direction of that relationship is not specified or easily quantifiable. Again, informed debate about the nature and form of such relationships can be highly beneficial.

Despite the limitations and practical difficulties in assessing future changes and strategic choices to deal with them, the technique has useful implications for marketing strategy. The limitations may be somewhat minimized if management uses informed judgement throughout the assessment. The model can be used to build up a qualitative picture of the product portfolios of its own or other companies hence also providing a useful insight into competitors' market positions and business strengths.

7.10 International portfolio analysis

To decide which markets should be served, management must simultaneously examine the attractiveness of potential product and country markets and the firm's competitive position in the markets. On the one hand, management will try to focus the activities of the firm on the most attractive markets. On the other, it has to consider the firm's ability to build on or develop competitive advantages in those markets.

A potential method of simultaneously analysing the attractiveness of markets and the competitive position of the firm (its business units, product range or products) in those markets is portfolio analysis. The matrix used for international portfolio analysis is very similar to the GE matrix, but factors such as political and financial risk, transferability of funds, taxes and subsidies, or the potential for standardization influence the portfolio structure. These factors have to be introduced to the comparison to increase the information level included in the analysis. A highly profitable market can be threatened by political unrest, religious upheavals, or restrictive laws concerning business.

Figure 7.12 shows an example of how a country is positioned in an international portfolio. The principle behind the positioning process is the same as with the GE matrix.

The corporate portfolio analysis provides an important tool to assess how to allocate resources not only across geographic areas, but also across the different product businesses (Douglas and Craig, 1995). The global corporate portfolio represents the highest level of analysis and it might consist of operations by product businesses or geographic areas.

As illustrated in Figure 7.13 Unilever's highest level of analysis is its different product businesses. With this global corporate portfolio as a starting point, the fur-

Exhibit 7.3

Gillette's international market portfolio in wet shaving

The Gillette Company, founded in 1901, currently has 61 manufacturing facilities in 25 countries. It is a major global consumer goods company with distributors and retailers in more than 200 countries and territories worldwide.

Gillette's strong, sustained growth in razors and blades reflects the outstanding market performance of its technologically superior products. Among these is the Sensor family of shaving systems, which continues to perform well globally. Research indicates that Gillette currently holds the number one position worldwide in men's wet shaving but also in selected female grooming products, such as wet shaving products and hair depilation devices.

Figure 7.11 outlines the strength of Gillette's businesses worldwide and the market attractiveness at the end of 1999 (by market growth). Note that the axes are reversed compared to Figure 7.12.

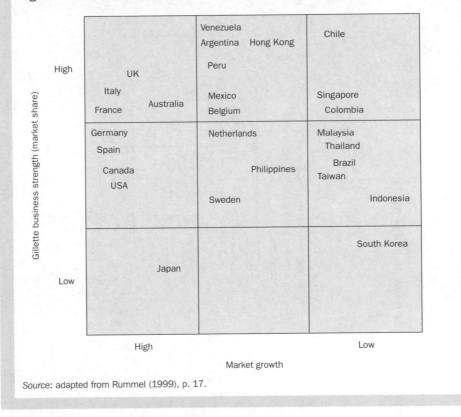

Figure 7.11 Gillette's international market country portfolio

Source: adapted from Rummel (1999), p. 17.

ther analysis of single corporate product businesses can go in a product factor, a geographic factor or a combination of the two factors.

It appears from the global corporate portfolio in Figure 7.13 that Unilever´s foods business is characterized by high market attractiveness and high competitive strengths. However, a more distinct picture of the situation is obtained by analysing underlying levels. This more detailed analysis is often required to give an operational input to specific market-planning decisions.

Figure 7.12 Country positioning in the international portfolio

Step 1:
Factors of country attractiveness and competitive strength

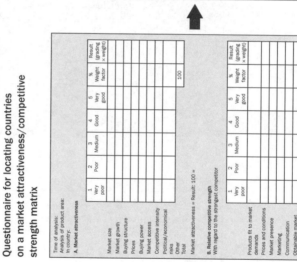

Step 2:
Questionnaire for locating countries on a market attractiveness/competitive strength matrix

Step 3:
Strategic implications of country positions

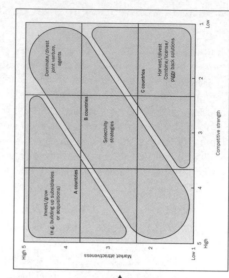

Figure 7.13 Unilever's global portfolio

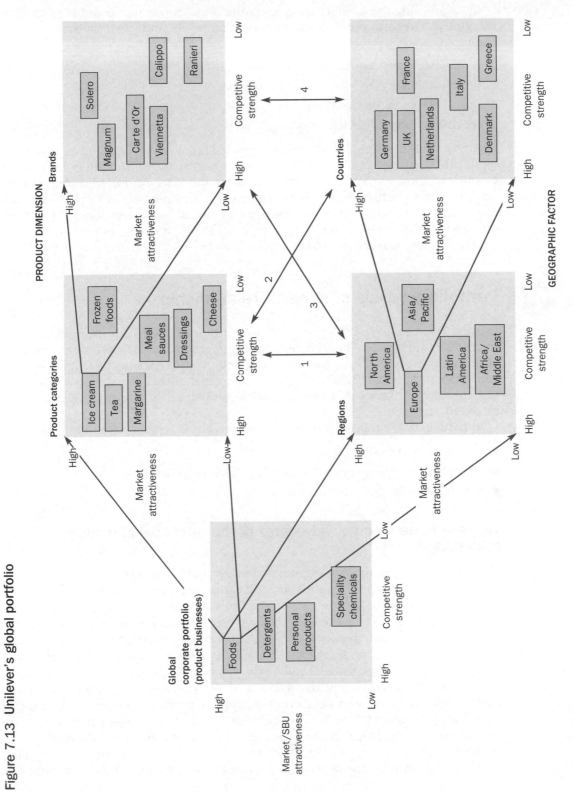

Source: Hollensen (2001), p. 209.

By combining the product and geographic dimensions it is possible to analyse the global corporate portfolio at the following levels (indicated by the arrows in Figure 7.13):

1. product category by region (or vice versa)
2. product category by country (or vice versa)
3. region by brand (or vice versa)
4. country by brand (or vice versa).

Of course, it is possible to make further detailed analysis of, for example, the country level by analysing different customer groups (e.g. food retailers) in certain countries. Thus, it may be important to assess the interconnectedness of various portfolio units across countries or regions. A customer (e.g. a large food retail chain) may have outlets in other countries, or the large retailers may have formed cross-border alliances in retailing with central purchasing from suppliers (e.g. Unilever) – see also section on retailing.

7.11   Portfolio analysis of supplier relationships

During the past two decades, the strategic importance of firms' supply side has increased considerably. These changes are commonly referred to as a shift from purchasing to supply management. According to this perspective, competitive advantage no longer resides with a firm's own capabilities, but rather with the relationship and linkages that the firm can establish with external organizations, including suppliers.

In particular, it has been emphasized that buying firms tend more and more to:

● outsource non-critical activities
● establish close 'partnership' relationships with suppliers
● reduce and trim their supplier base.

Why are there so many advocates of the relationship focus in marketing?

The transaction cost approach argues that every arm's-length transaction involves a transaction cost in search, negotiation and other associated activities. This leads to inefficiencies instead of efficiencies for the firms engaged in exchange transactions.

Relationship marketers, therefore, believe that interdependencies reduce transaction costs and generate higher quality while keeping management costs lower than exchange marketing. In short, better quality at a lower cost is achieved through interdependence and partnering among the value chain players.

The primary objective of this section is to describe some important considerations when analysing and developing a supplier portfolio. Based on the Kraljic (1983) supplier portfolio model, the approach in this study suggests that power and the risk of opportunistic behaviour are only two factors influencing the appropriate strategy when managing supplier relationships. Therefore, the portfolio of supplier relationships associated with purchases is categorized based on the relative supplier attractiveness and the strength of the relationship between the buyer and the supplier (Olsen & Ellram, 1997).

The portfolio model in Figure 7.14 illustrates an example of a firm by representing each relationship with a circle where the size of the circle illustrates the current allocation of resources to the relationship. This is often equivalent to the yearly value of purchase at that particular supplier. In Figure 7.14 the firm has 14 suppliers.

The relative supplier attractiveness describes the factors that make a company choose a specific supplier. It is necessary to use a contingency approach, because the factors and especially their importance will vary from company to company. Figure 7.14 contains some important factors that could be used to evaluate the relative supplier attractiveness. Therefore, it is important to emphasize that the company has to do this. The current supplier should be compared with alternative suppliers to determine the attractiveness. The list is not comprehensive, and firms may benefit from including other more specific factors. It is important that the company discusses which factors are important and allocates a weight to each relevant factor.

The financial and economic factors include an evaluation of the supplier's margins, financial stability, scale and experience, and the barriers to the supplier's entry and exit. An assessment of the economic factors also includes an evaluation of the slack that is a measure of the effect of the supplier's activities on the reduction of the buyer's internal economic process costs. The performance factors include a traditional evaluation of delivery, quality, price, etc. The technological factors include an assessment of the supplier's ability to cope with changes in the technology and an assessment of the current and future strength and types of the supplier's technological capabilities, the supplier's current and future capacity utilization, the supplier's design capabilities, the speed in development, and the supplier's patent protection.

The organizational, cultural, and strategic factors include an evaluation of the relationship's influence on the company's overall supply chain position. An evaluation of the possibility of opportunistic behaviour and other internal and external factors is also important. Finally, the group of other factors includes an assessment of the supplier's ability to cope with general changes in the environment. These changes could include changes in legislation, supply condition, or the level of competition. Another important factor could be the safety record of the supplier.

The strength of the relationship describes the factors that create bonds between two companies. Figure 7.14 illustrates some factors that could be evaluated; it is not comprehensive.

The economic factors describing the strength of the relationship include the value of the purchase, the importance of the buyer in terms of the percentage of the supplier's sales being purchased by the buyer, and the cost of exiting that market. In this situation, the transaction-specific investments will create exit costs, because the investments cannot be transferred to other customers or suppliers.

The character of the exchange relationship describes characteristics of the exchange situation that creates stronger bonds between the companies.

Strategic implications of the suppliers' portfolio

The two 'extreme' situations (cells 3 and 7) will be used as examples for the strategic implications.

Cell 3 includes the supplier relationships where the supplier has a high relative attractiveness and the relationship is relatively strong. The strategy for these relation-

Figure 7.14 The portfolio of suppliers

Step 1:
Factors influencing the relative supplier attractiveness

Financial and economic factors
- The supplier's margins
- The supplier's financial stability
- The supplier's scale and experience
- Barriers to the supplier's entry and exit
- Slack

Performance factors
- Delivery
- Quality
- Price

Technological factors
- The ability to cope with changes in technology
- The types and depth of supplier's current and future technological capabilities
- The supplier's current and future capacity utilization
- The supplier's design capabilities
- The supplier's speed in development
- The supplier's patent protection

Organizational, cultural, and strategic factors
- Influence on the company's network position
- The internal and external integration of the supplier
- The strategic fit between buyer and supplier
- Management attitude/outlook for the future
- Senior management capability
- Compatibility across levels and functions of buyer and supplier firm
- General risk and uncertainty of dealing with the supplier
- Feeling of trust in relations with the supplier

Other factors
- Ability to cope with changes in the environment
- Safety record of the supplier

Step 2:
Factors influencing the strength of the relationship

Economic factors
- Volume or dollar value of purchase
- Importance of the buyer to the supplier
- Exit costs

Character of exchange relationship
- Types of exchange
- Level and number of personal contacts
- Number of other partners
- Duration of the exchange relationship

Cooperation between buyer and supplier
- Cooperation in development
- Technical cooperation
- Integration of management

Distance between the buyer and the supplier
- Social distance
- Cultural distance
- Technological distance
- Time distance
- Geographic distance

Step 3:
Compilation of the supplier portfolio

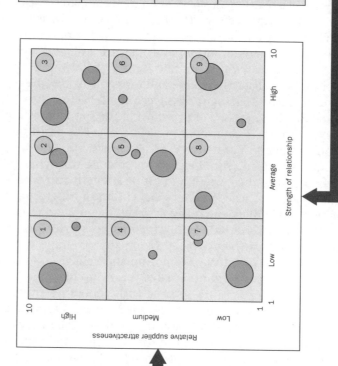

Source: adapted from Olsen and Ellram (1997), pp. 106–7.

ships could be to reallocate resources among different activities in order to maintain a strong relationship. Strong relationships are costly because coordination, adaptation and interaction entail costs. Increasing involvement usually means a substantial increase in relationship and supply handling costs, but may, under certain circumstances, lead to lower direct procurement and transaction costs. However, the main rationale for strong relationships is to achieve cost benefits, for instance, through taking advantage of supplier skills and developing capabilities to improve the quality of the customer's end product. Increased involvement makes sense only when the increased relationship costs are more than offset by relationship benefits. Reaping these benefits most often requires non-standardized solutions and customer specific adaptations. High-involvement relationships are associated with investment logic.

Cell 7 includes relationships with low supplier attractiveness combined with a weak relationship. These relationships need attention because a reasonable strategy would be to change the supplier.

Weak relationships may lead to higher direct procurement costs and transaction costs. On the buyer side, there may be costs for adapting internal resources to fit with what suppliers have to offer. In the absence of good coordination, the buyer might be obliged to build up inventories as a buffer against possible risks. Furthermore, in order to enssure availability of supplies, the customer might tend to use many suppliers, resulting in increased supply handling costs.

At first sight it does not seem right that the firm offers so many resources to the relationship with the 'big size circle' supplier in cell 7. However, before changing the supplier, it is important to reconsider the supplier's influence on the company's network position. The supplier could be important in relation to other members of the network (other suppliers or customers). This could be an important reason to maintain the supplier. Other strategies include outsourcing the purchase or using systems contracting to enhance the supplier attractiveness.

Supplier types

Based on the assessment of the supplier portfolio model it is possible to develop a typology which breaks the suppliers into four categories (Figure 7.15). The following analyses the involvement of partner suppliers into one of the key activities of the firm, product development.

Involvement of partner suppliers in product development

In many industries, manufacturing companies give suppliers increasing responsibilities with regard to the design, development and engineering of products. The overall aims are to make better use of suppliers' technological capabilities and expertise and to improve (short-term) product development efficiency and effectiveness.

In terms of efficiency, supplier involvement can lead to the reduction of development costs and the reduction of development lead-time. This is mainly achieved by preventing, reducing or introducing design changes earlier by means of early and intensive communication with the supplier ('right first time' development).

In terms of effectiveness, supplier involvement may lead to the reduction of product cost and the increase of product value. This can be achieved by mobilizing and leveraging supplier expertise.

Apart from improving (short-term) development project performance in terms of effectiveness and efficiency, manufacturers may have an interest in collaborating with suppliers in product development to achieve long-term benefits. One

Figure 7.15 Four categories of suppliers

Contractual suppliers.
Obtain a product by simply specifying out of the supplier's
catalogue. No need for any discussions concerning the
product being bought.

Child suppliers.
Involve the supplier after all the specifications have been
cleared and simulated so that the supplier can deliver to
OEM specifications.

Mature suppliers.
Involve the supplier after the initial work of identifying overall
design and critical dimensions has generated the critical
(or rough) specification. The critical (or rough) specifications
contain functional data and rough envelopes of functionality.
The supplier is entrusted to deliver the system within the
quality and budget constraints as decided jointly.

Partner suppliers.
Involve the supplier from the first instant and trust in his
or her abilities to understand the interfaces and deliver a
product that is compatible with all the necessary interfaces
within the budget and quality levels decided jointly.

Increasing commitment involvement into the activities of the firm

Source: adapted from Nellore and Söderquist (2000), pp. 253–4.

common long-term goal involves getting (long-term) access to the technological knowledge of suppliers. Ultimately, manufacturers may even have an interest in influencing supplier decisions with regard to the kind of technologies to invest in, in order to provide the best conditions for future technological collaboration (Wynstra *et al.*, 2001). However, it has been pointed out (Wynstra *et al.*, 2001) that not all efforts regarding supplier involvement in product development do result in the envisaged benefits; there are several problems to overcome.

There may be problems that cannot be attributed only to the manufacturer or the supplier, but which are primarily connected to the relationship between the two. Problems like a lack of communication and trust may lead to unclear agreements and diverging expectations, which hinder the collaboration's effectiveness and efficiency. Significant problems arise when the manufacturer fails to communicate clearly to suppliers what it expects from them, especially in terms of development responsibility for the products developed.

A lack of trust between the two parties may also hinder collaboration, as both parties will see large potential risks. Because of that, it may be especially difficult to collaborate with new suppliers, which may be necessary, for example, when the manufacturer needs a new type of component it has not used before.

Furthermore, manufacturers may end up selecting suppliers with little or limited experience in joint product development, for example due to supplier selection criteria only focusing on price. Weighting technological and innovative capabilities more heavily in supplier selection could improve the results of supplier involvement.

Despite the difficulties with supplier involvement, it can result in major benefits, both in the short and long term.

7.12 Summary

Developing a successful marketing strategy requires activities to be chosen that are different from competitors'. The structure of this chapter has followed the main phases in the complex marketing planning process, where the end result emerges from the interplay of different factors.

A corporate mission is the reason why a firm exists. It can be considered as a definition of what the organization is and what it does.

SWOT analysis structures the internal and external information into four categories:

- strengths and weaknesses (internal)
- opportunities and threats (external).

The SWOT analysis serves as a catalyst for structuring the creation of marketing strategies that will produce the desired result. It focuses on creating competitive advantage by matching company strengths to market opportunities. Furthermore, it provides guidance on how the firm might structure its marketing strategy to convert weaknesses and threats, and minimize or avoid those weaknesses and threats that cannot be converted.

Corporate objectives state where the firm intends to be at some specific time in the future. A corporate growth strategy describes how the long-term objectives will be achieved. According to the Ansoff product-market matrix there are four options: market penetration, market development, product development, and diversification.

A SBU marketing strategy concerns how to create competitive advantage in each of the SBUs (combination of products/markets). The portfolio models (PLC, BCG, GE/McKinsey etc.) guide the development of strategic alternatives for each of the company's SBUs and new business possibilities. In this way, this chapter has described the 'corporate' input to the later formulation of marketing plans.

In order to manage a firm's collection of SBUs, products or markets (countries), three downstream portfolio models were presented.

- the Boston matrix (BCG model), where businesses are positioned in terms of market growth rate and relative market share, is certainly one of the best known.
- General Electric pioneered another matrix (GE model) which is more marketing oriented. In this portfolio model, each business is rated in terms of market attractiveness and competitive position.
- the international market portfolio is very similar to the GE model in its structure.

Furthermore an upstream oriented supplier portfolio was presented. This portfolio approach is a three-step approach to managing supplier relationships. The first step is to classify the components into the different factors of the portfolio model. The second step is to classify the suppliers based on their attractiveness to the firm (manufacturer) and the strength of the buyer-supplier relationship. Finally, strategies are drawn up to improve the supplier's strength and/or relationship with the buyer, in order to deliver the desired component optimally.

Portfolio models have been criticized both for their general structure, in which the different factors are only approximate estimations of the parameters that are supposed to be measured, and for their limited applicability in specific fields such as marketing and purchasing. This might be due to the fact that companies focus too much on developing very complex factors in order to classify components, customers or suppliers, and become confused. The classification is not an end in itself, but a means to aid in the development of appropriate action plans.

Involving suppliers in product development can result in major benefits in terms of money and time. Supplier involvement in product development holds great potential, both in the short and long term, but few companies seem to be able to realize these benefits. A large part of the unfulfilled potential is due to common problems such as lack of communication and trust, insufficient supplier abilities and internal resistance at the manufacturer. Also, it requires a great deal of thinking and effort. Primarily, it presupposes active management on behalf of the manufacturer, both in the short and long term, supported by adequate organizational and human resources.

Case study 7.2 Ford Motor Company

Driving into the world golf car market

As part of a new and innovative product line, Ford announced on January 10, 2000 that it would begin offering a golf car by the end of the year, taking on such industry giants as E-Z-Go and Club Car. Ford unveiled its plans on the opening day of the 2000 Detroit Automotive Show at Cobo Arena.

The 'low speed, closed-community vehicle', as Ford describes its golf car, is part of the automative company's new environment-friendly TH!NK product line. Other battery-operated product offerings are an electric bike and a fully fledged electric road car called the TH!NK City.

The retail price for the golf car, known as the Neighbor, is about US$6000, and the car was introduced in November 2000.

The global golf car market

Nearly a million golf cars are hired out by courses around the world. Three major players, E-Z-Go (USA), Club Car (USA), and Yamaha Motor Company (Japan) dominate the market. The three manufacturers have about 80% of the world golf car market.

USA

The USA is a golfer's paradise with 16,000 courses nationwide (the UK has fewer than 3000 golf courses). Despite the tradition of amateur golfers using caddies and the fact that golf cars are prohibited on the PGA Tour almost all these courses have golf cars. The total number of golf cars in operation nationwide is about 800,000.

Europe

In Europe there has been a 54% increase in the number of courses in ten years. The number of golfers is increasing 7% each year (www.golf-research.com). England has more golf cars in operation in Europe than any other country. Spain, however, leads the way in regard to the average number of golf cars per course, with over 23 (Table 7.3). Norway has very few golf cars (just 38 in all), which could be explained by the type of terrain the golf courses are built on.

Tables 7.4 and 7.5 show how the number of cars and fleet size is affected by tourism. Tourist courses (defined as being those where over 50% of the rounds are played by tourists) average three times as many cars as non-tourist courses. Over one-fifth of tourist courses have a fleet of over 20 cars. The market for new golf cars is shown in Table 7.6.

As well as the USA and Europe, Japan is also an important market for golf cars. There are currently about 2300 golf courses in Japan and the total number of golf cars owned by them is about 154,000. The annual market demand for new units is estimated at 14,000.

Case study 7.2 continued

Table 7.3 Average number of golf cars per course

Country	Number of golf cars per course
Spain	23.2
Portugal	15.8
Italy	15.6
Belgium	8.4
France	6.6
Luxembourg	6.3
Austria	6.1
The Netherlands	4.4
Germany	3.3
Wales	2.9
Switzerland	2.9
Finland	2.7
England	2.3
Denmark	2.2
Sweden	2.1
Eire	1.8
Northern Ireland	1.1
Scotland	1.1
Norway	0.8

Source: adapted from Golf Research Group.

Table 7.4 Golf cars and tourism

	Number of courses	Courses with golf cars (%)	Total no. of cars	Cars per course
Non-tourist	2335	58	9939	4
Tourist	374	79	4527	12

Source: adapted from Golf Research Group.

Table 7.5 Distribution of fleet size

	1–3	4–10	11–20	Over 20	Total
Non-tourist	52%	31%	10%	7%	100%
Tourist	28%	32%	19%	21%	100%

Source: adapted from Golf Research Group.

Table 7.6 The market for new golf cars

	USA	Europe
Total market (000s)	140	80
Manufacturer	%	%
E-Z-Go	40	21
Club car	30	31
Yamaha Motor Company	20	32
Others	10	16
Total	100	100

Source: adapted from Golf research and other public sources.

The three major players will now be described.

E-Z-Go

E-Z-Go was founded in 1954 in Augusta, Georgia, USA. From these early days, E-Z-Go has grown into the world's largest manufacturer of golf cars and utility vehicles. In 1961, E-Z-Go became part of Textron, a global, multi-industry company, with access to the resources needed for worldwide expansion. E-Z-Go has the largest sales and service network in the golf car industry.

Club Car

Club Car is also based in Augusta, Georgia, USA, and is part of Ingersoll-Rand. Club Car has 35 years' experience in the production of golf cars and on March 9, 2001 it announced that it had produced its millionth golf vehicle.

Club Car is one of the three largest manufacturers of golf cars in the USA with a market share of about 30%. Club Car employs 1400 people worldwide with about 1200 working in the Augusta area.

Yamaha

On February 23, 2001, Yamaha Motor Co. celebrated the production of its 800,000th golf car. Yamaha began golf car production in 1975.

Production takes place in Japan and the USA. Yamaha's total production of golf cars is about 50,000 units per year of which about 60% go to the USA and the rest to other countries.

By constantly responding to the needs of the golf industry and supplying a wide range of models including 2-passenger types, standing

Case study 7.2 continued

caddie types, 4- and 5-passenger types, electro-magnetic guidance system models and electric powered models, Yamaha has succeeded in maintaining a market share in Japan of about 57%.

The Ford launch of the golf car

Ford executives emphasize that the initial market focus of their golf car is closed communities, resorts, work environments, and golf courses in the USA and Europe. When the vehicle is off road, it can reach 40 km/h and meets all of the new federal safety standards for such public-access vehicles, including a full complement of lights and turn signals, windscreen wipers and three-point safety belts.

The vehicle comes in 2- or 4-seat versions with the 2-seater offering a 'golf package', according to Rob Stevens, president of the TH!NK Mobility Group LLC, a separate wholly owned company established by Ford to market the new line of battery-powered vehicles. The 4-seater can be converted into a utility vehicle.

Rob Stevens considers the new golf car a luxury golf car, but also an 'and' car. Ford thinks that people want more than a golf car. John Wallace, director of the TH!NK Group, added, 'We're an automotive company and this is something that works great on the golf course and gives you more on the road'.

As indicated above, Ford is certainly interested in going after the golf car fleet industry.

Currently, Ford's US$6000 price tag might prove to be prohibitive for many golf courses. The average price of golf fleet cars is usually US$3200–3500.

According to Ron Skanes, manager of communications and media relations for E-Z-Go, the new Ford golf car ('TH!NK Neighbor') looks like more of a car than a golf car. He added, 'so far, the information we have is they [Ford] will target Sun cities [communities], that sort of thing. Targeting to the golf course market is a totally different animal'.

Outside of golf, though, Ford is on par with its competitors in the personal car/neighbourhood market. According to Skanes, Club Car's equivalent to Ford's TH!NK Neighbor is the Fairway Villager. Its suggested retail price with all options is about US$6000. E-Z-Go's equivalent, called the Freedom, costs about $5500 with all options.

Questions

1. What are the main differences in buying behaviour of golf cars for:
   (a) closed communities for older people
   (b) golf courses?
2. Prepare a SWOT analysis for Ford's entry into the golf car market.
3. Prepare a marketing strategy for penetration of Ford's golf car into golf courses around the world.

Source: adapted from Kaufman (2000).

QUESTIONS FOR DISCUSSION

1. How can corporate objectives be derived from the corporate mission?
2. What is the purpose of a SWOT analysis?
3. How can a SWOT analysis be carried out? What are the critical issues?
4. What are the differences between marketing objectives and marketing strategies?
5. What purpose may a product portfolio serve in the context of a marketing strategy?
6. What is the meaning of relative market share in the BCG model?
7. What are the advantages and disadvantages of using portfolio models in strategic marketing planning?
8. What is the purpose of integrating supplier portfolio models in marketing planning?
9. Why is it important to involve suppliers in product development?

REFERENCES

Abell, D. (1980), *Defining the Business: The starting point of strategic planning*, Prentice Hall, Englewood Cliffs, NJ.

Ansoff, H. I. (1957), Strategies for diversification, *Harvard Business Review*, September–October, pp. 113–24.

BBC (2001) *Microsoft's X-Box goes online*, **http://news.bbc.co.uk**. News, Thursday March 29

Day, G.S. (1986), *Analysis for Strategic Market Decisions*, West Publishing Co., St Paul, MN.

Douglas, S. P. and Craig, C. S. (1995), *Global Marketing Strategy*, McGraw-Hill, New York.

Duracell (1999) *The Gillette Company prevails in lawsuit against Ralson Purina*, **http://www.duracell.com**, press release, May 13.

Economist (1995), A tale of two conglomerates, *Economist*, November 18, p. 20.

Gadde, L. E. and Snehota, I. (2000), Making the most of supplier relationships, *Industrial Marketing Management*, vol. 29, pp. 305–16.

Hollensen, S. (2001), *Global Marketing: A market responsive approach*, Financial Times/Prentice Hall, Harlow, 2nd Edn.

Hosmer, La Rue T. (1982), *Strategic Management*, Prentice-Hall, Upper Saddle River, NJ.

Jobber, D. (1998), *Principles and Practice of Marketing*, 2nd edn, McGraw Hill, New York.

Kaufmann, S. (2000), Ford introduces new golf car, *Golf Week*, October 1, p. 10 (**http://www.golfweek.com**).

Kotler, P. (2000), *Marketing Management*, Prentice Hall, Englewood Cliffs, NJ.

Kraljic, P. (1983), Purchasing must become supply management, *Harvard Business Review*, vol. 61, pp. 109–17.

Lofton, L. (2000), *Kellogg and Keebler: A tasty combo*, **www.tool.com** (News) 27 October.

Maremont, M. (2001), Gillette plans to pour its energies into reviving Duracell – marketing strategy includes a coppertop label, but signals an avoidance of price cuts, *Wall Street Journal*, New York, March 28, p. 6.

Marketing Week (1998), Duracell combats new Energizer range with extra-strength launch, *Marketing Week*, London, February 26, p. 10.

Markowitz, H. (1952), Portfolio selection, *Journal of Finance*, March, p. 7.

Nellore, R. and Söderquist, K. (2000), Portfolio approaches to procurement, *Long Range Planning*, vol 23, pp. 245–67.

Olsen, R. F. and Ellram, R. L. (1997), A portfolio approach to supplier relationships, *Industrial Marketing Management*, vol. 26, pp. 101–13.

Progressive Grocer (2000), Batteries, *Progressive Grocer*, New York, August, p. 26.

Rummell, J. (1999), What's new at Gillette?, *Global Cosmetic Industry*, New York, no. 4, October, pp. 16–18.

Wynstra, F., Van Weele, A. and Weggemann, M. (2001), Managing supplier involvement in product development: three critical issues, *European Management Journal*, vol. 19, no. 2, pp. 157–67.

Chapter 8

Segmentation, targeting, positioning and competitive strategies

LEARNING OBJECTIVES

After studying this chapter you should be able to:

- understand the importance and meaning of market segmentation.
- identify and discuss the various bases for segmenting B-t-C markets and B-t-B markets.
- outline how firms select target segments.
- explain the differences between various strategic approaches to target marketing, undifferentiated, differentiated and concentrated marketing.
- comprehend what is involved in positioning a product or service against competitors.
- explain the difference between positioning in the B-t-C market and B-t-B markets.

Case study **8.1** Ballygowan

International segmentation of the mineral water market

The concept of bottling and selling bottled water from Eire was first developed by Geoff Read, founder of the Ballygowan brand, in the early 1980s. In 1984, after extensive market research, Ballygowan bottled water was introduced into test outlets. These included delicatessens, small grocers and supermarkets. The positive results of the test marketing indicated that broader, full-scale distribution was feasible.

In 1984, Ballygowan was restructured as part of a joint market venture agreement between Geoff Read and Richard Nash Co. Ltd, one of Eire's long established soft drink manufacturers.

In 1987, the US beverage giant, Anheuser Busch, purchased a 50.1% stake in Ballygowan. The Americans, who had recently launched their Budweiser beer brand in Eire, were looking for a premium European water to compete with Perrier. In 1989, Ballygowan bought the share-

holding of Anheuser Busch back, making it a wholly owned Irish company.

In 1993, Ballygowan was bought by Cantrell and Cochrane Group, one of Eire's largest drinks companies. Management of Ballygowan was placed in the hands of Clonmel-based Showerings (Ireland) Ltd, whose range of brands include Bulmers, Stag, Ritz, Cidona, Britvic, Babycham and Snowball.

In April 1995, Ballygowan acquired Aquaporte Ltd, the brand leader in the Irish water cooler market, renaming it Ballygowan Water Cooler Division. This division sells water coolers for offices.

The geographical location of the Ballygowan source in the south-west corner of Eire is an important factor. The strong prevailing winds from the Atlantic ensure that the area is free of pollution. High rainfall also plays an important

Case study 8.1 continued

role. This area is also totally free of industry and intensive farming.

Ballygowan's total sales reached IR£25 million in 1999.

The Irish market for mineral water

The market in Eire for bottled water is valued at almost IR£50 million per annum. It now stands at 54 million litres.

Since 1990 consumption of bottled water in Eire has grown by an average of 20% per annum. In 1998, it grew by 15%, mainly as a result of strong growth in the grocer and water cooler sectors. This growth was expected to continue.

The grocer sector accounts for 74% of total volume, water coolers for 19% and the licensed trade for 7%.

Annual per capita consumption in Eire is 15 litres. This represents an increase of 10 litres per head since 1991. 15 litres is still well below the European average, suggesting there is considerable room for growth in the Irish market. Irish consumers now drink more bottled water per person than in the UK.

The sector in the Irish bottled water market which is enjoying the most dynamic rate of growth is still (non-sparkling) water. This accounted for 70% of total volume in 1998.

Ballygowan remains the undisputed leader in the Irish bottled water market with a share of 50% followed by Tipperary mineral water.

The competitive situation in the European mineral water market

The global bottled water market underwent dramatic changes in brand ownership in 1992, when the Swiss food giant Nestlé bought all Perrier's mineral water brands except Volvic, which was sold to BSN (now known as Groupe Danone). Today Nestlé (with brands like Perrier and Vittel) and Danone (with brands like Evian and Volvic) are the world's leading mineral water producers.

Domestic producers continue to have a significant presence, despite increasing consolidation, in France (Groupe Neptune with Castel), Italy (San Benedetto), Spain (Vichy Catalan) and Benelux (Spadel from Belgium is the market leader with 29% of total value sales in 1997). We have seen that this dominance of local producers is also prevalent in Ireland.

Characteristics of four major mineral water markets are shown in Table 8.1.

Ballygowan's export markets

Exports account for about 45% of Ballygowan's total volume sales. Markets include Northern Ireland, France, Germany, and Italy. In Northern Ireland, Ballygowan has 50% market share.

Market research in 1999 confirmed that Ballygowan is the largest bottled water brand in the UK pub trade. It is also the fastest growing sparkling water brand in the UK grocery sector.

Britvic Soft Drink Company Ltd is Ballygowan's largest distributor in the UK. Other brands within the Britvic portfolio include Pepsi, 7-Up, Tango, Robinsons and Ribena.

Ballygowan is the main bottled water brand to be supplied to the US military in the UK. It is also shipped to US forces stationed in Germany.

Questions

1. Explain differences in buying behaviour for
   (a) bottles of mineral water
   (b) water coolers.

2. Based on the information in the case study (including Table 8.1), where should Ballygowan target its marketing resources?

3. How should Ballygowan penetrate your chosen market?

Sources: Business and Finance (1999), Beverage Industry (2000 a, b, c), Prince (2001), Townsend (2001).

Table 8.1 Characteristics of four major mineral water markets (sales in hotels, restaurants and catering are not included) in 1999

	UK	France	Germany	USA
Market sectors (millions litres)	Type Flavoured 33 Still 518 Carbonated 290 Total 841	Type Flavoured 125 Still 5750 Carbonated 1120 Total 6995	Type Flavoured 63 Still 2308 Carbonated 3758 Total 6129	Type Flavoured 139 Still 4709 Carbonated 315 Total 5163
Market shares (%)	Companies (brands) Premier Waters Ltd 17 Perrier Vittel (UK) Ltd 9 Eden Valley Mineral Water Co. Ltd 5 Highland Ltd 5 Strathmore Ltd 2 Spadel (UK) Ltd 1 Coca-Cola Schweppes Beverages Ltd 1 Ballygowan Ltd 1 Private label 45 Other 14 Total 100	Companies (brands) Group Danone (Evian) 40 Perrier Vittel SA 26 Groupe Neptune SA 12 St Amand 8 Private label 12 Other 2 Total 100	Companies (brands) Gerolsteiner Brunnen GmbH & Co 11 Die Blauen Quellen Mineral- und Heilbrunne AG 6 Mineralbrunnen berkingen- Teinach AG 4 Visla Brunnen 3 Apollinaris Schweppes GmbH & Co. 3 Coca-Cola Schweppes Beverages Ltd 2 Frankenbrunnen 2 Rheinfelsquell 2 Richard Haringer Getränke 2 Private label 4 Other 61 Total 100	Companies (brands) Nestlé SA (Perrier, Poland Spring) 19 Group Danone SA (Evian) 11 PepsiCo 6 McKesson BHOC 4 Suntory Ltd 3 Private label 3 Other 2 Other 2 Other 2 Other 3 61 Total 100
Distribution of mineral water and comments (%)	Channels Supermarkets/hypermarkets 69 Other stores 13 Small food outlets 9 General merchandisers 4 Outdoor 3 Vending machine 1 Other 1 Total 100 In the supermarkets/hypermarkets J. Sainsbury and Tesco are the two leading mineral water retailers. As demand grows, mineral water is starting to be delivered to British homes by milkmen.	Channels Supermarkets/hypermarkets 75 General merchandiser 15 Small food outlets 5 Other stores 2 Outdoor 2 Vending machine 1 Total 100 The three giants of the hypermarket operators are Carrefour, Leclerc and Intermarché, the latter being mainly large supermarkets. Wholesalers are under threat as large supermarkets and hypermarkets are increasingly dealing directly with manufacturers. Very hot summer weather will drive impulse sales through local outlets.	Channels Supermarkets/hypermarkets 39 Specialist bulk stores 32 Traditional food retailers 17 Discount stores 8 Other 4 Total 100 Unlike other food markets, traditional retailers hold a comparatively high share of the distribution breakdown (17%) because mineral water is seen as an everyday essential item. Discount stores are of particular importance for the distribution of carbonated mineral water, predominantly selling private label products.	Channels Supermarkets/hypermarkets 43 Small food outlets/superettes 21 Vending machine 15 General merchandisers 11 Other stores 8 Outdoor 2 Total 100 Private label sales accounted for over 26% of volume sales distribution in 1999, reflecting the strength of major supermarket/hypermarket retailers. Vending is a convenient, clean way for consumers to obtain water.
Comments on consumer profiles	Private label products have benefited from the fact that mineral water is a fairly homogenous product, making pricing the most important consideration for many consumers. Mineral water is consumed more by women than by men in the UK. This is particularly noticeable with sparkling water where consumption by females is almost twice the level of male consumption. Consumers in higher income socio-economic groups drink much more mineral water than lower earners.	According to a study carried out by Credoc (a consumer research body) in 1998, 35.6% of French households refused to drink tap water. The low share of the carbonated type is due to the fact that most French people continue to drink still water with meals. Flavoured waters, particularly the sparkling variety, can compete more directly with soft drinks and therefore appeal to a younger market. The emergence and popularity of five litre bottles demonstrates that more and more people are using mineral water not only for drinking, but also for preparation of tea, coffee and in cooking.	The Germans are the fourth largest group of mineral water consumers in Europe behind the Italians, French and Belgians with a per capita consumption of 97 litres in 1999. The trend towards a healthy lifestyle is responsible for the recent surge in the number of teenagers who drink mineral water. Climate also plays an important role in the consumption of mineral water, with 85% of Bavarians drinking it regularly, compared to 72% of their northern counterparts.	Mineral water consumption is higher among women than it is among men, as the former tend to be more conscious about their eating habits and the latest health trends. Consumers between the ages of 35 and 44 consume mineral water more frequently than consumers in other age groups. Consumption is related to household income, as usage is highest in wealthier households. Consumption is lowest among consumers aged 65 and over, a group which has not accepted the concept of paying for water, when tap water is free.

Source: adapted from different sources.

8.1 Introduction

Market segmentation has long been considered one of the most fundamental concepts in marketing. Ever since Smith (1956) published his article in *Journal of Marketing*, market segmentation has become a dominant concept both in marketing theory and in real-world applications. It not only provides one of the major ways of implementing the marketing concept but also directs a firm's marketing strategy and resource allocation among different markets and products.

Market segmentation is the process of dividing a market into distinct groups of buyers with similar requirements. It has become increasingly important in the development of marketing strategies for at least three reasons.

1. Population growth has slowed, and more product markets are maturing. This, in turn, sparks more intense competition as firms seek growth via gains in market share as well as in an increase of **brand extensions**.

2. There is an important trend toward **micro-segmentation** (one-to-one marketing). This trend has been accelerated in some industries by new technology such as computer-aided design, which has enabled firms to mass customize many products such as designer jeans and cars. For example, many car companies are using a flexible production system that can produce different models on the same production line. This enables the company to make cars to order. More specialized media have also sprung up to appeal to narrow interest groups, e.g. special interest magazines, radio programmes, cable TV, Internet.

3. Expanding disposable incomes, higher educational levels, and more awareness of the world have produced customers with more varied and sophisticated needs, tastes, and lifestyles than ever before. This has led to an increase in goods and services that compete with one another for the opportunity of satisfying some groups of consumers.

Generally, marketers cannot use averages. Instead, they use segmentation, targeting, and **positioning** to define unique consumer groups, select those they wish to serve, and then integrate the marketing mix to establish a unified image of the product relative to the competition.

Pitfalls with segmentation

Despite all the advantages with market segmentation there are also problems involved (Gibson, 2001).

Segmentation is descriptive not predictive

Segmentation and the research to implement it are designed to describe markets as they exist today. In contrast decisions are based on the expectation of a certain favourable future outcome, and the only information useful to the decision maker is information about the likelihood of that expected outcome. In short, a description of the market as it currently exists, before a decision is made, is irrelevant to making a decision about future events.

Segmentation assumes homogeneity

Segmentation asserts that customers are so different they cannot be averaged and therefore must be classified into segments. However, within defined segments, it assumes customers are not different and can be averaged.

In fact, the fundamental assumption of customer heterogeneity is true, radically true. Customers are different not only at the market level, but at the segment level. This heterogeneity is apparent to anyone looking at the individual respondents in any study. The fact that we seldom look prevents us from seeing and accepting this reality.

Segmentation assumes competition-free segments

Competitors are considered when choosing the target segment, and segments with strong competitors are disqualified. However, once the target segment is selected, competitors are ignored.

The consequences of ignoring competitors can be dangerous. For example, Coca-Cola found that cola drinkers preferred sweeter cola. Repeated paired product comparison tests showed the new sweeter Coca-Cola was preferred over regular Coke. Yet, the new sweeter Coca-Cola failed because the market already had a sweeter cola – Pepsi Cola.

Segmentation may define the wrong segment

The target segments finally selected in traditional segmentation research may exclude significant numbers of real prospects and include significant numbers of non-prospects.

It is a feature of segmentation that when any one segment is selected as a target, prospects in the other segments are excluded.

Because of the segmentation, targeting and positioning are critical. You simply can not be a leading-edge marketer without these three steps. The activities required to accomplish each stage are described in the following sections. The structure of Chapter 8 is shown in Figure 8.1.

A market segment is a homogeneous group of customers with similar needs, wants, values, and buying behaviour. Each segment is an arena for competition.

Market segmentation is the process by which a market is divided into distinct customer subsets of people with similar needs and characteristics that lead them to respond in similar ways to a particular product offering and strategic marketing programme.

Each segment will vary in size and opportunity. Since it may be difficult to appeal successfully to each segment, companies select certain ones for emphasis and will try to satisfy them more than competitors – this is called target marketing.

Positioning means creating an image, reputation, or perception in the minds of consumers about the organization or its products relative to the competition. The company appeals to customers in the target segments by adjusting products, prices, promotional campaigns, service, and distribution channels in a way consistent with its positioning strategy.

These three decision processes – market segmentation, market targeting, and positioning – are closely linked and have strong interdependence (see Figure 8.2). All must be well considered and implemented if the firm is to be successful in managing a given product-market relationship.

Figure 8.1 Chapter outline

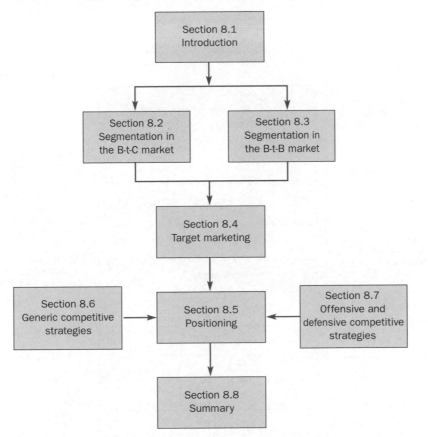

It is important to keep the distinction between product differences and market segments in mind. Market segments should not be defined by product names or characteristics. Markets are made up of customers (people and organizations).

Factors favouring market segmentation

A firm has the option of adopting a market aggregation strategy or a segmentation strategy. Most companies adopt the latter. A market aggregation strategy is appropriate where the total market has few differences in customer needs or desires, especially when the product can be standardized. It is also appropriate where it is operationally difficult to develop distinct products or marketing programmes to reach different customer segments; that is, not all segmentation schemes can be used.

The benefits of segmentation more than offset the difficulties involved in identifying individual market segments. These factors favouring segmentation fall into three main categories.

Better strategic allocation of marketing resources

The strategic benefits of segmentation are sometimes overlooked. Targeted plans and programmes, based on identified needs and habits of specific markets, result in better allocation of company resources and higher profits.

Figure 8.2 The three step market segmentation and positioning process

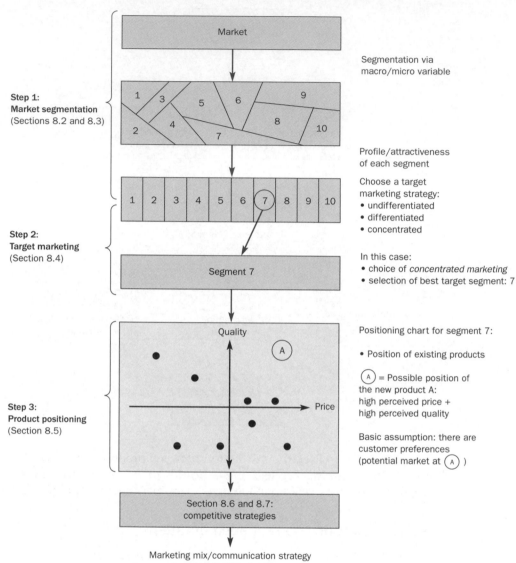

Most successful business strategies are based on market segmentation and a concentration of resources in the more attractive segments. Segmentation should focus on subdividing markets into areas in which investments can gain a long-term competitive advantage.

Creation of more effective marketing programmes

Segmentation helps in the design of marketing programmes that are most effective for reaching homogeneous groups of customers. The seller can create separate marketing programmes aimed at more completely satisfying the needs of different buyers. This creates a competitive advantage.

Better opportunities for new product or market development

The seller is in a better position to spot and compare new product or market opportunities as well as potential threats. Often, a careful analysis of various segments reveals one or more groups whose specific needs and concerns are not being satisfied by existing competitive offerings. Such open segments may represent attractive opportunities for development of new products or innovative marketing approaches; for example, the laptop computer.

When a firm seeks to expand its volume, effective market segmentation analysis will uncover the degree of customer satisfaction by comparing each segment's needs against the offering of other suppliers. Low current satisfaction indicates a marketing opportunity, assuming the firm can do better than its competitors and produce an acceptable profit.

When a firm merely wants to maintain market share, constant surveillance of individual market segments will usually spot competitive or environmental threats.

Factors discouraging market segmentation

Special organizational and environmental problems may discourage market segmentation. Not every perceived opportunity becomes a profitable venture. Some of the specific instances in which segmentation in business markets is not useful are as follows.

1. Heavy users or buyers make up such a large proportion of the sales volume that they appear to be the only relevant target. Public utilities consume such large quantities of coal for generating electricity that they dwarf other users of coal.

2. The market is so small that marketing to a portion of it is not profitable. Therefore, a brand or product would have to appeal to all segments and level of users.

Requirements for effective market segmentation

An effective and useful segmentation scheme should define market segments according to five criteria.

Adequate size

Marketers evaluate the degree to which the segments are large or profitable enough to be worth considering for separate marketing cultivation. It involves a trade-off between customer homogeneity and scale effects.

Measurability

Marketers evaluate the degree to which information on particular buyer characteristics exists or can be obtained. There is often a need for a combination of specific (e.g. age) and abstract segmentation variables.

Accessibility

Marketers evaluate the degree to which the firm can effectively focus its marketing efforts on chosen segments. Segmentation variables must identify members in ways that facilitate their contact.

Responsiveness

Marketers assess the degree to which segments respond differently to different marketing mix elements, such as pricing or product features. Segmentation variables must maximize behavioural differences between segments.

Compatibility

Marketers evaluate the degree to which the firm's marketing and business strengths match the present and expected competitive and technological state of the market.

Thus, the art of market segmentation involves identifying groups of consumers that are sufficiently large, and sufficiently unique, to justify a separate marketing strategy. The competitive environment of the market segment is also a factor that must be analysed.

Business firms segment their markets primarily to allocate their resources more effectively and to maximize return on investment. Unfortunately, a segmentation strategy involves added costs in obtaining and analysing data, and in developing and implementing separate marketing and manufacturing plans to serve each segment effectively. The strategy must therefore result in additional sales volume and profits to justify its costs. Before implementing a segmentation strategy, the marketer should develop an estimate of the costs versus the benefits.

Two common segmenting methods

Segmentation can be quite complicated because most markets are complex. There are many different types of customers, and, as we have seen, literally thousands of variables can be used to segment them. Marketers typically use one of two approaches in selecting variables and grouping customers. The *top-down segmentation method* starts with all consumers and seeks meaningful variables for subdividing the entire market. The *bottom-up* segmentation starts with a single potential customer and adds others with similar characteristics. Anyone without those characteristics is placed in a new segment, and the process continues. In other words, rather than the whole market, the focus is on one segment at a time. The following is based on the top-down method.

Identifying segmentation variables

The total market is heterogeneous, meaning it has many types of buyers. Market segmentation divides the total market into homogeneous subgroups, or clusters with similar characteristics. We then can inspect each subgroup in greater detail. Without a well-focused picture of the market, it is virtually impossible to create a powerful marketing strategy.

How is segmentation done? First, the marketer must select a way of categorizing potential customers into subgroups. A segmentation variable is any descriptive characteristic that helps separate all potential purchasers into groups. Examples include gender, age, and income. Variables are then subdivided into categories. For example, within the gender variable, the two categories are male and female. Categories may be very broadly or very narrowly defined.

There are many ways of dividing a market into segments. These ways of dividing a market (segmentation variables) can vary from the B-t-C market to the B-t-B market. The next two sections deal with segmentation in:

● the B-t-C market
● the B-t-B market.

Once the segmentation scheme is developed, you need to describe, or profile, each group in more detail. The market segment profile compiles information about a market segment and the amount of opportunity it represents. The profile may include: the number of current and potential buyers; the potential number of products these buyers may purchase; the amount of revenue the segment may provide; and the expected growth rate. In addition to size and growth, other criteria used to select targets include competitive factors, cost and efficiency factors, the segment's leadership qualities, and the segment's compatibility with the company's vision, objectives, and resources.

8.2 Segmentation in the B-t-C market

Figure 8.3 lists the categories and variables commonly used for segmentation in the B-t-C market. The left side of Figure 8.3 shows the trade-off problem of using segmentation variables from the different categories of segmentation variables. The use of the socio-demographic variables results in a high degree of measurability (easy and cheap to use, often based on **secondary data** or desk research), but they would perhaps only have low relevance for marketing planning. As we move down the list in Figure 8.3 to **psychographic** and 'benefit sought' variables, the implications for the formulation of marketing strategies and plans become more relevant and meaningful.

But all the various variables are important and would be likely to be used to some extent in the segmentation of a given market. Thus, marketers might try to define segments using a combination of benefit, behavioural, and physical factors, even though this requires the combination of **primary data** (field research) – see also the Appendix.

The socio-demographic variables

Variables like gender, age, family life cycle, household type, and income are used in demographic segmentation. This type of information is readily available. Demographics are very useful in categorizing different tastes and preferences. An added benefit is that it's relatively easy to measure and project the composition and size of demographic segments for the next 5, 10, or 15 years (high degree of measurability in Figure 8.3). Consequently, this kind of segmentation is an excellent tool for long-range strategic planning as well as short-term marketing.

Different locations vary in their sales potential, growth rates, customer needs, cultures, climates, service needs, and competitive structures, as well as purchase rates for a variety of goods. Consequently, one of the most common ways to segment a market is by geography.

Figure 8.3 Segmentation criteria for the B-t-C market

Segmentation variables		Examples
Sociodemograhic variables	Age	Under 2, 2–5, 6–11, 12–17, 18–24, 25–34, 35–49, 50–64, 65 and over
	Gender	Male, female
	Geography	Regions, countries, cities, metropolitan areas, counties and blocks
	Life cycle family	Young, single; newly married, no children; couples with youngest child under 6; youngest child 6 or over; older couples with dependent children; older couples without dependent children; older retired couples; single
	Income	Under £15,000, £15,000–24,999, £25,000–74,999 etc.
	Occupation	Professional, manager, clerical, sales, supervisor, blue collar, homemaker, student, unemployed
	Education	Some high school, graduated high school, some college, graduated college
	Events	Birthdays, graduations, anniversaries, national holidays, sporting events
	Race and ethnic origin	Anglo-Saxon, African-American, Italian, Jewish, Scandinavian, Hispanic, Asian
	Religion	Protestant, Catholic, Jewish, Muslim
	Social class	Lower-lower, upper-lower, lower-middle, middle, upper-middle, lower-upper, upper-upper
Behaviouristic	Readiness	Unaware, aware, interested, knowledgeable, desirous, intend to buy, trial
	Media and shopping habits	Magazine subscriber, cable user, mall, convenience stores, Internet-shopper
	Ability and experience	None, novice, expert, professional, nonuser, first-time user, regular user, former user
	Loyalty	Switcher, moderate, high loyalty
	Usage frequency	Heavy (daily), weekly (medium), light (monthly)
	Innovativeness	Innovators, early adopters, **early majority,** late majority, laggards
Psychographic	Lifestyle	Actualizer, fulfiller, achiever, experiencer, believer, striver, maker, struggler
	Personality	Compliant, aggressive, detached, sensory, intuitive, thinking, feeling
Benefits sought	Delivery	Convenience, speed, flexibility
	Product features	Safety, reliability, taste, packaging
	Price/service	Low, medium, high

Degree of measurability — High (top) to Low (bottom)

City

Segmentation by city is often used by global companies. Coca-Cola knows that soft drink consumption relates to population size. With the exception of New York City and Los Angeles, all metropolitan areas of more than 10 million are located outside the USA. So it's no mystery why Coca-Cola markets globally. A city's population size alone does not always provide enough segmentation information, so marketers think about other factors. Some metropolitan areas are known for their industry expertise: in Hollywood it's films; in Silicon Valley, computer software.

Events

These include a varied set of activities ranging from national holidays, sports, and back-to-school week, to personal events such as birthdays, anniversaries, and weddings. Each requires a specific marketing programme.

Race and ethnic origin

More and more companies are targeting three segments via specialized marketing programmes. Motorola has run separate advertising campaigns for its papers and mobile phones to African-Americans, Asian Americans, and Hispanics. Spiegel and *Ebony* magazine have combined to produce a direct-mail catalogue designed to provide clothing that meets the style, colour, and fit of African-Americans. Efforts, so far, have been successful.

However, it is important to remember that ethnic segments are not homogeneous. There are demographic differences within ethnic groups. For many people, race has nothing to do with their buying behaviour. Consequently, other forms of segmentation may work much better.

Social class

Every social class has its status groupings based largely on similarities in income, education, and occupation. Because researchers have long documented the values of the various classes, it is possible to infer certain behaviour concerning a given product. For example, the middle classes tend to place more value on education, family activities, cleanliness, and being up to date than do lower-class families. In the international field, one has to be careful in using social class as a segmentation variable since the differences among classes can become blurred, as they do in the Scandinavian countries. In the USA, many of the criteria used to define class status seem to some to be no longer applicable as the nation becomes increasingly fragmented into dozens of distinct subcultures, each with its own unique tastes and ambitions.

Behaviouristic variables

These variables reflect the behaviour of customers towards a specific product. Behaviouristic segmentation categorizes consumers based on people's awareness, product and media uses, and actions. Past behaviour is one of the best predictors of future behaviour, so these variables require an understanding of what consumers have previously done. The variables include purchase volume, purchase readiness, ability and experience, loyalty, media habits, and shopping behaviours.

Segmentation by readiness

For many products, potential users go through a series of stages that describe their readiness to purchase. These stretch all the way from being unaware of a product, through trial, leading up to loyalty. Readiness is a useful segmentation variable, particularly for new products. This scheme is often used in adjusting the communications mix.

Segmentation by media and shopping habits

A broad range of media and shopping habits can be used to categorize shoppers. For example, some people subscribe to cable, others do not; some prefer shopping at department stores or on the Internet and so forth. These variables focus on accessibility of target customers. Those who shop only in malls are accessed differently from those who prefer Internet-shopping or catalogue shopping at home.

Segmentation by ability and experience

The performance of products is determined by the ability and experience of its user. Consequently, ability is an excellent segmentation variable for almost any skill-based product. For example, the marketing of software games for PCs, skis, tennis rackets, and golf equipment is targeted to ability segments. This is due in large part to the performance requirements of these products. As performance requirements increase, new technologies produce products with higher performance capabilities but generally require more skill.

Segmentation by loyalty

As we have discussed, a key goal of firms is to create brand loyalty. Some consumers are naturally loyal to particular product categories. There are many ways to look at loyalty, but the most popular seems to be the most straightforward. It looks at switchers, moderately loyal, and highly local categories. Switchers may select a different brand with nearly every purchase. They may actually seek variety or they simply do not care which brand they buy. Moderately loyal customers have a preference for a brand but will switch if it is convenient to do so. Loyal buyers have strong preferences. Not all buyers are loyal to a single brand within a product class. Some people have two or three that are equally acceptable.

Usage frequency

This is important because in many markets a small proportion of potential customers makes a high percentage of all purchases (the '80–20' rule, 20 per cent of buyers purchase 80 per cent of the volume of any product). It is amazing how true this is for many products. Heavy users can be extremely important to companies. Consequently, most marketers divide the market into heavy, moderate, and light users, and then they look for characteristics that may explain why some people consume vastly greater amounts. Therefore, the marketing costs are lower per unit of sales.

Still, marketing strategists need to realize that competition for heavy users can be extreme. If medium or light users are being ignored, they may provide a marketing opportunity. For example, giants like Coca-Cola and Pepsi are always targeting students. They spend a great deal of money to be represented on campus in order to 'capture' students.

Innovativeness

This is concerned with how individuals and organizations vary in their capacity and desire to innovate. This is particularly true for the **adoption** of new products. There are substantial differences between early and late adopters. Thus, each of the various adopter groups can be considered as a segment. All too frequently, current customers are not considered an important segment despite their value over time and their being easy to identify.

Psychographic variables

Segmentation by lifestyle, or personality, groups consumers on the basis of their activities, interests, and opinions. From such information it is possible to infer what types of products and services appeal to a particular group, as well as how best to communicate with individuals in the group. Lifestyle has been used to describe, for example, the **benefit segments** for sportswear.

Psychographic and lifestyle segmentation links geographic and demographic descriptors with a consumer's behavioural and psychological decisions. Psychographic variables used alone are often not very useful to marketers; however, they can be quite useful when joined with demographic, geographic, and other data. Lifestyle is a person's distinctive mode of living. It describes how time and money are spent and what aspects of life are important. The choice of products, patterns of usage, and the amount of enjoyment a person gains from being a consumer are all part of a lifestyle. Consider the difference between people who are physically fit from exercise and proper nutrition and those who are out of shape from high-fat diets and sedentary living. Since there are so many lifestyles, the trick is to identify them in the context of your company's marketing strategy.

Benefits sought variables

Customer needs are expressed in benefits sought from a particular product or service. Individual customers do not have identical needs and thus attach different degrees of importance to the benefits offered by different products. In the end, the product that provides the best bundle of benefits – given the customer's particular needs – is most likely to be purchased.

Since purchasing is a problem-solving process, consumers evaluate product or brand alternatives on the basis of desired characteristics and how valuable each characteristic is to the consumer – choice criteria. Marketers therefore can define segments according to these different choice criteria in terms of the presence or absence of certain characteristics and the importance attached to each. Firms typically single out a limited number of benefit segments to target. Thus, for example, different car manufacturers (such as Volvo) have emphasized different benefits over the years, such as reliability, safety, and high mileage versus styling, quickness, and status.

Benefits sought must be linked to usage situations. There is ample evidence that usage often strongly affects product choice and substitutability. Thus, the appropriateness of product attributes varies across different usage environments. Any attempt to define viable segments must recognize this fact; for example, consumer needs vary in different usage situations for many products.

For example, toothpaste consumers can be segmented into sensory, sociable, worrier, and independent segments. Sociable consumers seek bright teeth; worriers seek healthy teeth. Aqua packaging could indicate fluoride for the worrier segment, and white (for a white smile) for the sociable segment (Kumar and Naspal, 2001).

Mittal and Katrichis (2000) found that the attributes important to newly acquired customers were not the same as the ones that were important to loyal customers.

A survey among credit card holders showed that the format of the statement and the performance of the customer service representative are more important for new rather than loyal customers. Conversely, the promotional benefits associated with the card and adequacy of credit limit were more important to loyal customers than to new ones.

Based on these insights, the credit card company redesigned its communication strategy for customer attraction. It started emphasizing its attractive interest rate, the quality of its customer service department, and its statements' easy-to-read and user-friendly format. With regard to loyal customers, the firm undertook an internal campaign to reassess the credit limit of all customers, then made appropriate revisions. The company also launched a series of research studies to identify special benefits that customers desired, and then offered these benefits to customers. Finally, the company revised its customer satisfaction philosophy to a segmented focus on the different needs of the newly acquired and loyal customer (Mittal and Katrichis, 2000).

| Exhibit 8.1 | Segmentation in work ('salty snacks in the workplace') |

Some time ago the consulting firm Monitor Group did a segmentation job for a client in the food and beverage sector. The scope of the segmentation was defined around the marketing objective – *selling more of the client's snacks in the setting of the workplace*. A team was established with members from both the client and Monitor Group.

Once the scope was established, the first step was to identify a number of proxy segmentation variables that were both actionable and meaningful. The team brainstormed a long list of segmentation variables, which were scored and then tested. One of the more interesting results here is how powerful relatively simple demographic variables turned out to be. After the brainstorming and quantitative testing it turned out that age, gender, and 'nature of occupation' were the most powerful segmentation variables. Figure 8.4 illustrates the frame for segmentation of 'salty snacks in the workplace'.

After setting up the segmentation frame the next step was to create profiles of each segment. The data for this came from multiple sources, ranging from existing quantitative and qualitative customer research to the experiences and latent knowledge of the team and the broader organization.

After evaluating each segment (cell) the following segment turned out to be the most relevant target group: 'labour intensive' male consumers (18–35 years old) in manufacturing jobs. The team then created an in-depth profile (customer portrait) of this target group.

Purchase and usage environment

- Predominantly men working in suburban or rural settings.

- Find work physically demanding and repetitive – they are usually standing or moving around and constantly on their feet.

- Work environment likely to be unpleasant – least likely to work in an environment with heating or air conditioning.

Exhibit 8.1 continued

Figure 8.4 Segmentation for selling 'salty snacks' in the workplace

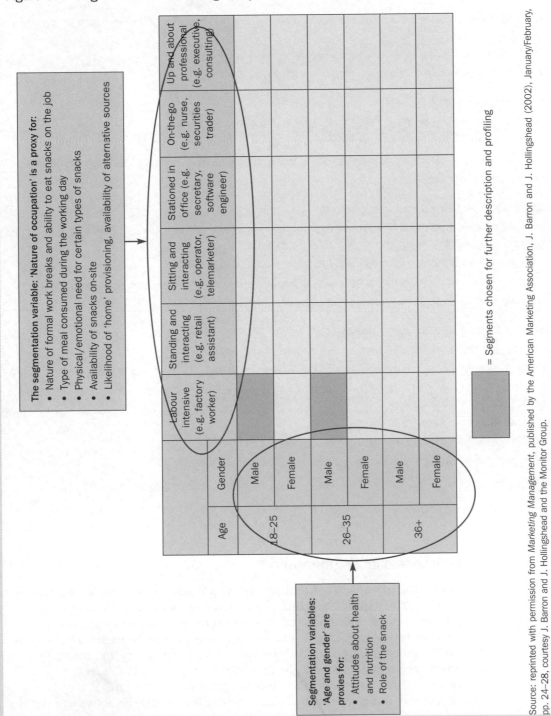

The segmentation variable: 'Nature of occupation' is a proxy for:
- Nature of formal work breaks and ability to eat snacks on the job
- Type of meal consumed during the working day
- Physical/emotional need for certain types of snacks
- Availability of snacks on-site
- Likelihood of 'home' provisioning, availability of alternative sources

= Segments chosen for further description and profiling

Segmentation variables: 'Age and gender' are proxies for:
- Attitudes about health and nutrition
- Role of the snack

Source: reprinted with permission from *Marketing Management*, published by the American Marketing Association, J. Barron and J. Hollingshead (2002), January/February, pp. 24–28, courtesy J. Barron and J. Hollingshead and the Monitor Group.

Exhibit 8.1 continued

- Break room without kitchen is primary facility where they can relax, socialize, and consume snacks.
- The most commonly available snacks are chips, pretzels, and sweets.
- Although they purchase most snacks at work, they are more likely than any other segment to bring snacks from home.
- Least likely to consume snacks outside scheduled breaks or mealtimes.
- Have to walk the farthest of all segments to get their snack source.

Desired experience

- Want a snack that tastes good during both meal and non-meal occasions.
- More likely during non-meal occasions to want a snack that provides energy.
- More likely during non-meal occasions to use a snack that helps them cope with their work environment.
- Want a snack that is fun.

Product/service beliefs and associations

- More likely than other segments to believe that snacks satisfy physical needs (taste and refreshment) rather than emotional needs (personal, reward, escape).
- More likely than other segments to enjoy the taste of chips and pretzels.
- More likely than other segments to believe that 'healthy' snacks will improve their work performance.
- Only segment to prefer competitor product over client product.

Resulting purchase and usage behavior

- Most likely to use vending machines as their source of snacks.
- Chips and pretzels are their top choice of snack for both meal and non-meal occasions.
- Client brands consumed more often during non-meal occasions, but at the same rate as competitor brands during meal occasions.
- Medium bag is the package of choice.
- Most likely segment to use a single serving bag during meal times.
- More likely to consume a snack in social settings than other segments.

This in-depth target group profiling then formed the basis for the creation of targeted marketing plans.

Source: adapted from Barron and Hollingshead (2002).

Multidimensional segmentation

In segmenting markets, most researchers use a single set of variables, such as demographics, psychographics, product category-related attitudes, product usage-related behaviours, derived importance from joint exercises, or latent structures.

The acid test for successful market segmentation is to demonstrate that the derived segments respond differently to variations in the marketing mix. Unfortunately, many segmentation schemes fail this key test.

However, there is no reason to limit the basis for segmentation to only one type of variable when many criteria actually determine buyers' response to offerings in the category. These criteria are multi-dimensional, encompassing attitudes, needs, values, benefits, means, occasions, and prior experience, depending on the product or service category and the buyer.

A segmentation scheme based on only one set of variables may have limited utility to the firm because various users of segmentation schemes have different needs. For example, product development managers may want the market segmented on perceived values and benefits sought; marketing communications managers may want it divided into groups of buyers with similar needs, desires, or psychographic profiles, and sales managers may prefer segmentation based on sales potential or profitability.

Market segmentation based on multiple dimensions, using separate segmentation schemes for each one, is often more useful and more flexible for planning marketing strategy and executing marketing tactics. Thus, researchers may consider different segmentation variables for buyers using different bases concerning product-user identity (i.e. performance needs, means, and desires).

8.3　Segmentation in the B-t-B market

The concept of B-t-B segmentation has gained increasing attention among academic researchers (Goller *et al.*, 2002) Since B-t-B customers, like B-t-C consumers, differ in their needs, resources, and buying attitudes, a practical approach to understanding these differences is to identify variables by which potential buyers can be segmented. Market segmentation attempts to identify groups of firms that are similar in their purchasing needs, product expectations, and responses to marketing programmes. These firms do not have to be similar in company structure, size, or end markets, although similarity in such factors can provide a basis for more finely tuned segmentation. We will discuss this point further later.

Business marketing managers attempt to find the best product-market match, that is, the most likely customers for each of their products.

Given the considerable difference between business customers, marketers find it difficult to determine which segmentation variables are the most or least likely to provide a desirable fit. Compounding the problem, Bonoma and Shapiro (1983) state that most business marketers use segmentation as a way to explain what has happened rather than as a means to plan and predict what will happen.

There is no magic formula for segmenting the business market. The marketer should try different variables, either alone (which may be sufficient in some cases) or in combination. For segmentation variables to be meaningful, however, they must involve characteristics that are easily identified, understood, and discernible. B-t-C markets are typically segmented on the basis of demographic and psychographic variables. The B-t-B marketer typically segments organizations on the basis of size and end use, and organizational buyers on the basis of decision style and other criteria. Thus, the business or organizational market can be segmented on several bases, broadly classified into two major categories: macro-segmentation and micro-segmentation.

Macro-segmentation centres on the characteristics of the buying organization and situation, thus dividing the market by such organizational characteristics as size and geographic location.

In contrast, micro-segmentation requires a higher degree of market knowledge, focusing on the characteristics of decision-making units within each macro-segment – including buying decision criteria, perceived importance of the purchase, and attitudes towards vendors. Wind and Cardozo (1974) recommend a two-stage approach to business market segmentation: identify meaningful macro-segments, and then divide the macro-segments into micro-segments.

Variables forming the macro-segments and micro-segments would include the following.

Macro-variables include:

- *industry*, e.g. agriculture, mining, construction, manufacturing, reselling, finance, services
- *organizational characteristics*, e.g. size, plant characteristics, location, economic factors, customers' industry, competitive forces, purchasing factors
- *end use markets*, e.g. manufacturers of end products, commercial contractors, wholesalers and retailers, banks and other financial institutions
- *product application*, e.g. components in specific end products, consumer home or recreational usage, resale, production line or office productivity.

Micro-variables include:

- *organizational variables*, e.g. purchasing stage, customer experience stage, customer interaction needs, product innovativeness, organizational capabilities
- *purchase situation variables*, e.g. inventory requirements, purchase importance, purchasing policies, purchasing criteria, structure of the buying centre
- *individual variables*, e.g. personal characteristics, power structure.

One of the most famous and cited segmentation models for the B-t-B market will now be presented and discussed.

Bonomo and Shapiro's (1983) macro/micro-segmentation process

Figure 8.5 shows the five nests advocated by Bonoma and Shapiro in their macro/micro approach to business market segmentation. Working from the outside to the inside, the analyst would start with the first nest, demographics.

Demographics

The variables in the demographic nest are the industry, company size, and company location, all relating to the customer's needs and usage patterns. Industry provides a broad understanding of product and service needs. Company size affects the size of a potential order, which forces the seller's attention on to its own ability to produce and manage the delivery of the product. Customer location impacts on the seller's salesforce organization, its territorial placement, and associated physical distribution factors.

Operating variables

The second nest, operating variables, contains three relatively stable components: company technology, user/non-user status, and customer capabilities. Company technology, both product and manufacturing process, can determine buying needs. The technology used indicates the company's needs for tooling, test instruments, components, and appropriate support systems. Product and brand-use status would help to isolate common experiences with a brand or product, thus enabling the seller to categorize similar buyers. Customer capabilities include organizational

Figure 8.5. The 'nested' approach to segmentation

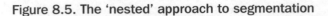

Demographics
- Industry
- Company size
- Location

Operating variables
- Technology
- User/non-user status
- Customer capabilites

Purchasing approaches
- Organization of DMU
- Purchasing policies
- Purchasing criteria

Situational factors
- Urgency
- Product application
- Size of order

MACRO ⟶   MICRO

Personal characteristics
- Motivation
- Risk perceptions
- Buyer-seller perception
- Matching

Source: adapted from Bonoma and Shapiro (1983).

strengths and weaknesses that could help to classify a company's attractiveness and its 'fit' with the seller's abilities to provide satisfaction.

Purchasing approaches

The third nest, purchasing approach, investigates five components: the organization of the purchasing function (decision-making unit (DMU)) power structures, buyer-seller relations, general purchasing policies, and purchasing criteria. The organization of the purchasing function helps to determine the size, location, and levels of authority that exist in a customer's purchasing unit, which affects the size, location and cost of the seller's salesforce. Power structures that exist within specific customers have an impact on the type of suppliers they would choose. As discussed earlier, the seller could pursue a firm with a powerful engineering unit that dominated purchasing, or the potential customer's power base could lie in the manufacturing department and/or the general manager. Either situation would help to determine required salesforce talents, product/service features to emphasize, and the broad outline for a successful selling strategy. These interrelations were discussed at length in Chapter 4. General purchasing policies, such as leasing, bidding, and doing business with only well-established vendors, would dictate policy to those suppliers willing to do business within these constraints. Purchasing criteria are those product and organizational benefits deemed necessary for vendors to satisfy before a buyer-seller relationship can be established.

Situational factors

The fourth nest, situational factors, has three components: urgency of order fulfilment, product application, and size of order. Urgency of order fulfilment would be a function of the customer's inventory on hand, and the availability of suppliers to meet their needs in the allocated delivery time. The use of just-in-time purchasing practices would carry further implications. Product application challenges the seller's ability to satisfy both technical product needs and product servicing. Size of the order would suggest that a seller concentrate on those customers whose normal orders would mesh with the seller's production economies of scale.

Personal characteristics

The fifth and last nest analyses the potential fit between the buying centre member's personal characteristics and those of the seller. These factors include motivation, individual perceptions, acceptance of risks by the seller, personal attention to buyer demands, and the matching of the buyer's personality traits with similar sales representatives' personality traits.

The nesting approach encourages the integration of all five nests starting at the macro level and moving down to the micro level for successful industrial market segmentation. However, as previously mentioned, market segmentation involves definite costs. The more a market is segmented, the more expensive it is. Thus, the degree of market segmentation depends on how detailed customer knowledge must be for effective use, As the marketer moves from macro-segmentation into micro-segmentation, more intimate knowledge of potential market segments is required, and this will increase the costs of segmentation. While macro-variables can be obtained easily from available secondary data sources, this is not the case with micro-variables.

Operational and personal attributes can also change significantly from one buying situation to another, even within the same company. Therefore, as Bonoma and Shapiro (1983) argue, market segmentation should begin with macro-variables, working inward to the more personal areas only as far as necessary. In other words, once the segmentation scheme seems 'good enough', further efforts should cease.

Criticism of Bonoma and Shapiro's nested approach

The following criticism has been made of the approach:

● There is little attention to customer needs, except the box labelled 'situational factors' (Mitchell and Wilson, 1998).

- There is little insight into which of these variables may be most useful and in what combination or sequence.
- When moving from outside into the nest, when should the marketer stop looking for relevant variables?
- Systematic methods (like Bonoma and Shapiro) have limited relevance when there are few customers and the market is concentrated. Then a single customer can change everything on the market due to its role or its weight. One single event can ruin instantaneously the most serious analysis. Furthermore, in industrial environments, data are rare, uncertain, changing, and unreliable, which does not fit with rigorous methods. Consequently, industrial companies often have difficulty in segmenting their markets.

In such a case Millier (2000) suggests a combination of intuition and rationalization in segmentation.

A relationship approach to B-t-B segmentation

This section thus presents an alternative framework for the segmentation of industrial markets – one based on the nature of the buyer-seller relationship and which seeks to tap into the interests of both parties.

The two factors in the proposed model are:

- buyer loyalty
- value to the seller.

These factors are closely indicative of the 'relationship' value to both the buyer and the customer. The simplified two-dimensional framework is shown in Figure 8.6. The interpretation of the matrix is simple and largely self-explanatory, although the underlying rationale is both sound and capable of implementation.

Figure 8.6. Proposed relationship segmentation framework

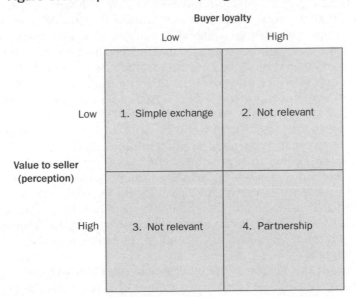

Segmenting in the partnership case (4) needs a deep understanding of the customers' characteristics, needs, and future directions, whereas the same information would be too costly, time consuming to collect and too comprehensive to use when segmenting in the simple exchange, case (1) (Freytag and Clarke, 2001).

Freytag and Clarke (2001) propose a two-step selection process. The first step is finding attractive future segments for further evaluation. The second step is the selection of the target segment and involves the company and the segments. The aim of this process is to find a perfect match between segment demands and an optimal use of the company's resources and capabilities.

In this way segments are developed in the interaction between the company and potential market segments. The demands that the relationship's development will require from the involved parties need to be identified and considered. The seller in particular will be required to make adaptations and commitments, but they may also be needed from the buyer. In many situations, the wants and needs of the customer will be developed in interaction between the parties.

A result of this two-step segmentation selection process may be that segments that seem attractive are not selected because they do not suit the resources and capabilities of the seller firm.

When evaluating to decide which segments the company should focus on, it is advantageous to find a synergy between the segments. The closer segments are to each other regarding customer needs and technology, the less they require of the company's resources.

The fundamental premise of the methodology is that market segmentation is most effective when it reflects genuinely the interests and practices of both buyer and seller. The same cannot be claimed for conventional industrial segmentation practices that commonly revolve around the use of available secondary data (e.g. demographic data) and/or existing production or sales organization (e.g. industrial application) (Elliott and Glynn, 2000).

Thus, the logic for the proposed approach is that, while it is acknowledged that value to the buyer is complex and multi-dimensional, the buyer's interests will be fundamentally reflected in its loyalty to the seller (either historically or in the future). This reflects that while, undoubtedly, many industrial buyer-seller relationships are mutual and long lasting, in a significant portion of cases, particularly in larger mass industrial markets, some buyers do not seek a deep and reciprocal relationship. Such buyers will be seeking to maximize value around a single transaction or short-term relationship. They have no loyalty, nor do they expect it. Partly as a result of history, in which the government was a monopoly supplier, most buyers neither have experience, nor seek a long-term relationship, with their supplier, and many will buy simply on the basis of a fractionally lower price, whilst others are dominated by 'inertia' (as distinct from 'loyalty'). Much of government purchasing which requires competitive tendering will reinforce this lack of loyalty.

Conversely, the seller's interest will be reflected in the *lifetime financial value of the customer*. Before target markets are actually chosen by the firm, identified segments must be evaluated with respect to their profitability, i.e. the cost of serving and maintaining them as it relates to the potential sales revenue. This involves an empirical investigation of such factors as average purchase size, purchase frequency, likelihood of switching, costs of servicing, purchase of consumables, and after-sales service, recommendations etc.

Calculation of this customer lifetime value to the seller will rely, typically, on the analysis of a representative sample of customer histories extending over five to ten years (see also Section 17.3 regarding customer lifetime value).

Segmented 'lifetime financial value' analysis may indicate that smaller, but regular buyers contribute a greater profit margin and lifetime value than single large purchasers.

Clearly, in the ideal situation there will be a symmetry in the interests of both parties as shown in cells 1 and 4, with sellers preferring the 'partnership' relationship. As shown in cell 1, the seller's best interests are served by focusing on the current transaction, lowering its cost and maximizing the value of the transaction without risking losing the deal.

Where there is a mismatch in both parties' expectations, then the likely consequence is that, while the deal will proceed, it will result in adverse consequences for both parties. In the case of cell 2, the seller will receive a gain on the transaction, but the buyer will feel exploited and will not re-purchase, even though that would be his preference. In the case of cell 3, the seller will over-invest in what he perceives to be a valuable customer, only to see the customer desert the seller after the transaction, notwithstanding the seller's investment in the relationship.

Moreover, the proposed typology embraces the central concepts of customer relationships, customer value and customer loyalty and incorporates them into the important process of market segmentation in industrial markets.

The symmetry in the interest of buyers, customers, and sellers (suppliers) is also reflected in a negotiable and bilateral 'fit-seeking' process where suppliers frame tentative segments (based on initial research) subject to exploration with well-placed key managers. This would encourage the development of evolutionary segmentation that focuses not only on consumer needs, but also on supplier needs, because these are mutually synergistic. The process would also help to develop the sort of long-term relationships between supplier and customer that help to ensure that supplier offerings are developed in line with customer expectations and needs.

Reverse segmentation

The notion of reverse segmentation is a convenient expression to highlight a process that parallels segmentation, a process whereby customers select suppliers that meet particular criteria (e.g. quality, financial stability, investors in relationships approaches, ethical stances, delivery reputation, collaborative product development strategies). By implication, a supplier able to exhibit appropriate 'reverse segmentation' criteria to a customer (and such criteria may well shift from customer to customer) can become significantly more attractive – not least through their evident customer understanding. Similarly, active seeking of particular reverse segmentation criteria could become a significant segmentation variable, especially for those organizations seeking to focus on long-term supplier-customer relationships (e.g. in the car components industry or in corporate sponsorship markets) (Mitchell and Wilson, 1998).

Thus, the reverse segmentation (supplier segmentation) is widespread in the car industry, where the success of Japanese firms has often been attributed to close supplier relationships, or a partner model of supplier management. Various studies suggest that, compared to arm's-length relationships, Japanese-style partnerships result in superior performance because partnering firms (Dyer *et al.*, 1998):

- share more information and are better at coordinating interdependent tasks
- invest in dedicated or relation-specific assets which lower costs, improve quality, and speed development
- rely on trust to govern the relationship, which is a highly efficient mechanism that minimizes transactions costs.

On the other hand, because suppliers only work primarily with one customer, they do not have opportunities to learn from multiple customers. Consequently, this impedes the supplier's abilities to learn and upgrade its technological capabilities.

Dyer *et al.* (1998) found that the Japanese car makers Nissan and Toyota were the most effective at strategically segmenting suppliers to realize the benefits of both the arm's-length and partner models. Independent Japanese suppliers such as Bridgestone (tyres) and Mitsubishi Belting Co. (belts, hoses) realized economies of scale by selling their relatively standardized products to all car makers. Moreover, these suppliers made fewer investments in assets dedicated to a particular car maker. Car makers provided less direct assistance to these suppliers mainly because the benefits of assistance to the supplier would more easily spill over to competitors. In contrast, more affiliated and smaller suppliers like Nippondenso and Calsonic made substantial investments in relation-specific assets and coordinated activities closely with car makers through frequent face-to-face interactions. Toyota and Nissan provided significantly more assistance to affiliated suppliers to help them lower production costs, improve quality, and minimize inventories. Toyota and Nissan had greater incentives to assist these suppliers since their own success (i.e. ability to differentiate their products) is closely tied to the success of these particular suppliers (a 'win-win' situation).

| Exhibit 8.2 | Values of world consumers |

The research firm Roper Starch Worldwide has carried out research about personal values of people around the world. To ensure comparability across cultures a list of about 60 personal values was given to 30,000 respondents aged 13–65 in about 60 countries. Each respondent was interviewed in his or her own home and rated each value as a guiding principle in his or her life.

Consumers worldwide share many of the same values (Table 8.2). 'Protecting the family' ranks as the world's top value, by a wide margin. 'Honesty' ranks second, and 'health and fitness' third.

Table 8.2 The world's top ten personal values

Rank	Value	Per cent who say value is 'extremely important'
1	Protecting the family	47
2	Honesty	38
3	Health and fitness	31
4	Self-esteem	28
5	Self-reliance	27
6	Justice	27
7	Freedom	27
8	Friendship	26
9	Knowledge	26
10	Learning	25

Source: adapted from Roper Starch Worldwide (2000), p. 4.

Exhibit 8.2 continued

At the same time, regional variations exist. In North America, for instance, individuality, romance, excitement, adventure, and social tolerance are rated higher. In Latin America, romance, sex, spirituality, traditional gender roles, and faith are more important. Western Europe puts more emphasis on sex, leisure, freedom, social tolerance, and having fun. For eastern Europe, material security, enduring love, sex, justice, and freedom are rated higher.

In developed Asia, living for today, having fun, stable personal relationships, and enjoying life are important. In a region once steeped in tradition, this signals a significant change and the need for marketers to acknowledge these shifting values. For developing Asia, where socio-economic stability is far less established, status, power, public image, wealth, and the traditional value of respecting ancestors are disproportionately more important values.

North America, Latin America, western and eastern Europe, and developed and developing Asia each share at least six of the world's top ten values. Though the world's top values are the same across countries and regions, some values exhibit hugely differing trends from culture to culture, giving a great amount of insight to those countries and cultures (see Table 8.3). For example, respecting one's elders is the most important value in Vietnam, but ranks a low 46th in Germany.

Table 8.3 The world's biggest value gaps

	Where it's highly ranked	Where it's not highly ranked
Respecting ancestors	Vietnam (1)	Germany (46)
Faith	Indonesia, Egypt, and Saudi Arabia (1)	France (45)
Friendship	Germany (1)	South Africa (26)
Freedom	Argentina, France, Italy, and Spain (2)	China (40)
Knowledge	India (2) and Singapore (3)	Egypt (34)
Stable relationships	UK and Japan (3)	Venezuela (43)
Self-reliance	Mexico (3) and Russia (4)	Saudi Arabia (33)
Ambition	Egypt (6) and Saudi Arabia (7)	Italy (55)
Romance	Thailand (9)	India (56)
Looking good	Egypt (13)	Japan and China (54)
Sex	UK, Czech Republic and Poland (19)	Egypt, South Africa, Japan, India, and Thailand (57)

Source: adapted from Roper Starch Worldwide (2000), p. 5.

Source: adapted from Roper Starch Worldwide (2000).

8.4 Target marketing

Market targeting is not the same as market segmentation. As discussed earlier, market segmentation is the process of dividing a market into groups of potential customers who are similar in needs, expectations, and response to marketing stimuli. The seller selects variables that identify this market and develops a marketing mix that best fits the market's expectations and anticipated response.

Target marketing is the process of selecting one or more of these market segments and developing products and programmes that are tailored for each segment.

Once the segments have been identified, management must evaluate the opportunities each segment offers.

Large multi-nationals can operate in many market segments, but most new entrants into a given market have to select one or a few segments. Limited financial and managerial capacities prevent broader activity as it might spread their resources too thinly and set them up as a takeover target. The number of segments in which a company competes is determined by its shared goals, the flexibility of its manufacturing base, and the heterogeneity of the market's requirements.

In order to select the right segment as a target market, a manager can compare the future potential of different segments using the same set of criteria and then prioritize them to decide which segments to target and how resources and marketing efforts should be allocated. One useful analytical framework managers can use for this purpose is the market attractiveness/business position matrix. At the corporate level, managers use such models to allocate resources across businesses, or at the business-unit level to assign resources across product-markets. In principle, it is the Mckinsey/GE model (Chapter 7).

A number of strategies can help guide a manager's choice of target markets. Three of the more common of these are undifferentiated, differentiated and concentrated marketing strategies. They are illustrated in Figure 8.7.

Undifferentiated (mass) marketing

Undifferentiated marketing treats all the customers the same. Companies look for desires that are common to most potential customers and then try to design products that appeal to everyone. By focusing internally on a single or a few products, companies can streamline manufacturing, distribution, and even promotion in order to improve quality and gain cost efficiencies (economies of scale). But the standardized product may fail to meet individual customer needs.

This strategy requires substantial resources, including production capacity, and good mass marketing capabilities. Consequently, it is favoured by larger business units or by those whose parent corporation provides substantial support.

An example is in the start-up phase of many website businesses, such as **portals** that engage in attracting as many visitors as possible. The value of customers to the firm primarily is measured by their sheer numbers; specifically, by how many people view the advertising at a site. The key value measure is stock-market capitalization, which is heavily skewed toward the site that attracts the most traffic. The type of customer matters little; in fact, at this stage it is premature to speak of customer relationships.

The key business problems at this stage relate to generating a market presence quickly before other competitors achieve a critical mass of customers.

Establishing brand recognition and identity is critical to creating traffic. Strong brands (e.g. Yahoo, AOL) simplify the decisions customers must make about how to access the market. The expectation is that these brands will eventually convert impression into purchase behaviour.

As long as companies keep the price relatively low and competitive alternatives are unavailable, an undifferentiated marketing strategy can be successful. However, competition is tough. Companies that once thrived are being threatened by rivals who use more targeted approaches, such as differentiated or concentrated marketing.

Figure 8.7 Three strategies in customer targeting

Charateristics	Undifferentiated marketing	Differentiated marketing	Concentrated/one-to-one marketing
	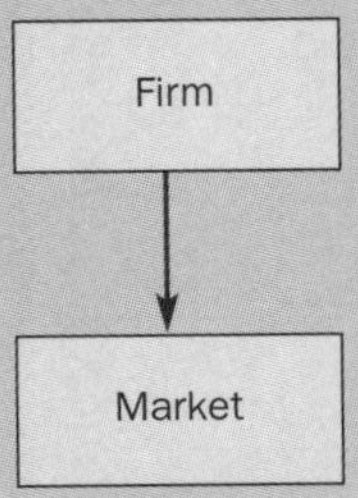 Firm → Market	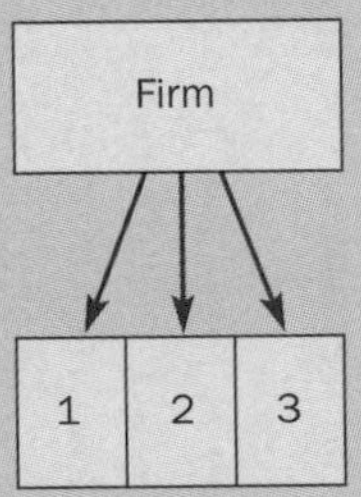 Firm → 1 2 3	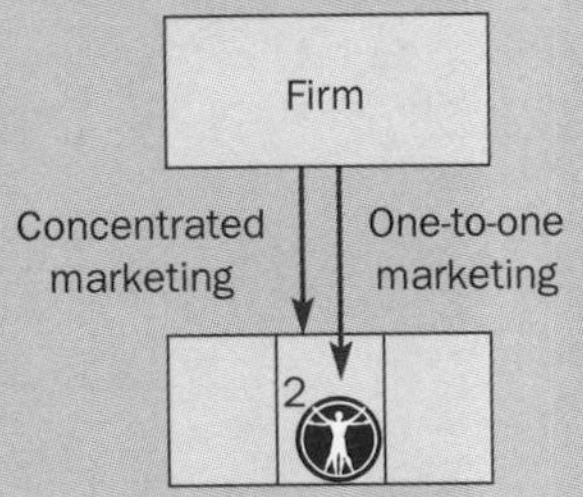 Firm (Concentrated marketing / One-to-one marketing) → 2
Definition	All customers are treated the same, regardless of actual differences	Customers grouped into high-level market segments	Customers are treated and act differently based on their unique profiles
Goal	Acquire mass of people viewing, drive traffic	Acquire and begin to develop customer relationships, drive revenue	Development and retention of customers, customer profitability
Needed capabilities	Mass marketing, branding	Value proposition design, customer relationship management	Experience management, profitability management
Research methods	Anticipate customer priorities through information acceleration, lead user analysis	Segmentation on needs, behaviour, targeting models	Customer profitability in market tests. Customer lifetime value

Differentiated marketing

Differentiated marketing serves each segment with the marketing mix matched specifically to its desires and expectations. The advantage of differentiated marketing is that wants and needs are satisfied better for each targeted segment. The disadvantage is that it may also cost more, because several marketing mix strategies are typically required.

Again, we will try to connect this strategy option to an example from e-business (Wyner, 2000).

A web business that anticipated making a profit from e-commerce (rather than solely from mass advertising) might want to structure its offerings to accommodate the needs of specific segments, e.g. affinity groups around specific topics such as travel, sports, and home improvement.

Many established businesses fit this description; they clearly can not survive with a mass-market, customer-selection process and a 'one size fits all' value proposition. Examples include conventional retailers, car makers, and providers of entertainment such as theme parks.

The key measure of customer value is revenue that comes directly from customers, rather than from other sources such as advertisers. To maximize revenue, it is critical to identify customer needs and requirements and to develop differentiated offerings that have a competitive advantage.

Getting large numbers of customers to visit a website is not sufficient; they must also be buyers. Customer relationship development becomes important, including cross-selling additional products to maximize revenues across the entire product and service portfolio. Increasing the depth of the relationship with customers has significant economic benefits, in some cases exceeding the value of new customer acquisition.

Concentrated (niche) marketing

This strategy involves serving one or more segments that, while not the largest, consist of substantial numbers of customers seeking somewhat specialized benefits from a supplier.

Such a strategy is designed to avoid direct competition with larger firms that are pursuing the bigger segments. For example, overall coffee consumption is down substantially, but the sales of gourmet coffees have boomed in recent years. Companies pursuing this strategy must make sure they have a great deal of knowledge about their major target segment.

Concentrated marketing has worked extremely well for new companies or companies entering new areas of the world. By gaining a foothold in a core market, a company can build the financial strength, experience, and credibility needed for expansion to other similar segments.

Niche marketing is another strategy worth mentioning. A niche is a very small market that most companies ignore because they do not perceive adequate opportunity. The smallest possible niche is the individual. Marketing to one customer is called *one-to-one marketing* (also illustrated in Figure 8.7).

Peppers *et al.* (1999) use a questionnaire to identify a firm's readiness for using one-to-one marketing on a daily basis.

A business can achieve superior profitability if it can give each customer the best offer for him or her, provided there is an efficient and effective fulfilment capability.

Issues of customer loyalty and retention have become increasingly important because it is often more profitable to keep an existing customer than to find new ones.

This customer selection process is possible in businesses with detailed individual customer level information, such as financial service companies that capture virtually all customer transactions in digital form. Customers can be grouped into categories based on their past use of products and services. There is no need to use higher-level groups (such as a high or low frequency transaction on credit cards) when customers can be identified with particular product features that suit them (such as specific interest rates, annual fees, and reward programmes).

An emerging type of business design goes beyond selecting customers based on refined targeting to individuals and enables individual customers to build their own 'offer' (individualized self selection). Customers select what they want to meet their own needs.

This web based technology is used to develop a digital customer interface enabling each individual to choose from potential products that are exactly what the customer wants. These 'choiceboards' are becoming more common, and as commerce becomes increasingly electronic, they promise to capture significant market shares.

In financial services, for example, a customer can select mutual funds from a vast selection of offerings through fund networks. Choiceboards in the PC business allow the customer to design completely a personal computer to incorporate the desired functionality.

Dell is an example of a company that has essentially become a customer-specific web store, where customers can design their own computer.

8.5 Positioning

Once the segmentation process gives a clear picture of the market and the target marketing strategy has been selected, the positioning approach can be developed.

Success requires a sustainable strategy that is differentiated from competitors. A higher probability of success can be achieved if the marketing mix is arranged so that it is unmatched by competitors.

Positioning is the process of creating in the mind of consumers an image, reputation, or perception of the company and/or its products relative to competitors. Positioning (or repositioning) then, is the perceived fit between a particular product and the needs of the target market. The positioning concept must be defined relative to competitive offerings and consumer needs.

Thus, the following critical question needs to be answered. 'How can a business position its offering so that customers in the target market perceive it as providing the desired benefits, thereby giving it an advantage over current and potential competitors?' The choice of market position is a strategic decision with implications not only for how the firm's product or service should be designed but also for detailing the other elements of the strategic marketing programme. Each of the marketing mix elements is capable of making a contribution to the positioning of a product.

A positioning analysis can take place at the company product category, and brand levels. At the product category level, the analysis examines customers' perceptions about types of products they might consider as substitutes to satisfy the same basic need. Suppose, for example, that a company is considering introducing a new instant breakfast drink. The new product would have to compete with other breakfast foods, such as bacon, eggs, and breakfast cereals. To understand the new product's position in the market, a marketer could obtain customer perceptions of the new product concept relative to likely substitute products on various critical attributes. Figure 8.8(a) shows a product positioning map constructed from such information. The two attributes defining the product space are price and convenience of preparation. The proposed new drink occupies a distinctive position because customers perceive it as a comparatively low-cost, convenient breakfast food.

Once competitors introduce similar brands into the same product category, a marketer needs to find out how the brand is perceived compared with competitors. Thus, Figure 8.8(b) shows the result of a positioning analysis conducted at the brand level. It summarizes customer perceptions concerning three existing brands of instant breakfast drinks. This brand level analysis is very useful for helping marketers understand a brand's competitive strengths and weaknesses and for determining whether the brand should be repositioned to differentiate it from competitive products.

Once the perceptions are plotted, most marketers want to know the consumer's ideal position. The ideal position is the one most preferred by each consumer.

Finally, what is the difference in positioning on the B-t-C market and B-t-B market? The principles in the two markets are the same. What matters is that the customer (and prospective customer) sees the merits in your positioning and that you link other strategies to this positioning in order to deliver the 'promise' implied by the positioning decision. If you claim to be a comprehensive supplier, you must be a comprehensive supplier to sustain customer support. And the same goes for other choices.

However, in the B-t-B market company image considerations, rather than brand image building factors are determinants of perceived positioning strategies. The

Figure 8.8 Positioning at product and brand level

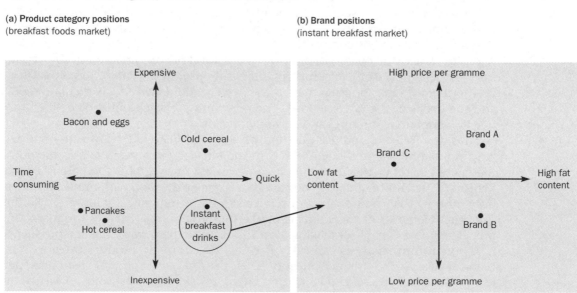

(a) Product category positions
(breakfast foods market)

(b) Brand positions
(instant breakfast market)

Source: adapted from Busch and Houston (1985), p. 450.

Exhibit 8.3   ## Positioning of US TV talk shows

Oprah Winfrey faced a dilemma when she realized that her own show had migrated toward the lower left quadrant of Figure 8.9, which she felt was out of alignment with her own values. The star near Larry King marks the position many executives preferred. Shows like Rikki Lake and Jerry Springer have a sensationalism that appeals to many viewers, but many believe their value to society is questionable. Oprah decided to move her show back to its original position in the upper right quadrant.

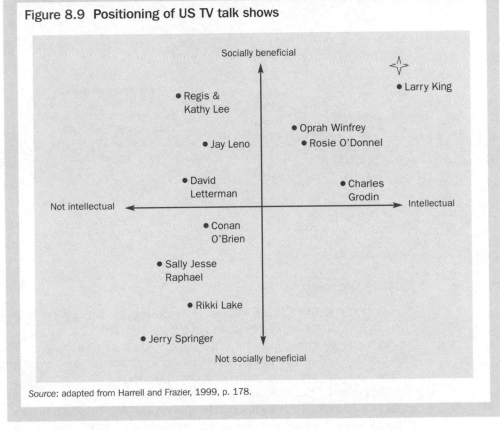

Figure 8.9 Positioning of US TV talk shows

Source: adapted from Harrell and Frazier, 1999, p. 178.

brand-image-led positioning strategies that are prevalent in consumer goods marketing do not transfer well to business marketing (Kalafatis *et al.*, 2000).

8.6   # Generic competitive strategies

Porter (1985) states that there are only three potentially successful generic strategies to outperforming other firms in an industry: overall cost leadership, differentiation and focus. Figure 8.10 shows Porter's thoughts in a modified way.

Figure 8.10 Generic strategies

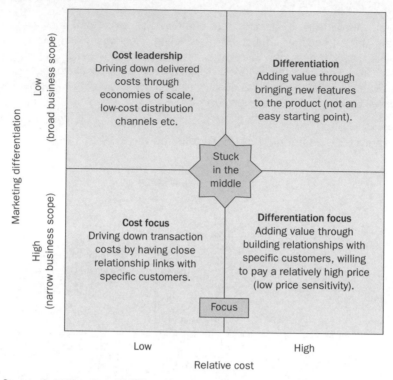

Source: adapted from Porter (1985), p. 12.

Cost leadership

A cost leadership strategy focuses on gaining advantages by reducing economic costs below the costs of competitors. This alternative has come to prominence in recent years, as companies have invested vast sums to achieve economies of scale. Many segments in the industry (broad industry focus) are served and great importance is placed on minimizing costs on all fronts.

Markets have been expanded to entire continents to support massive new plant as in the European car industry. Here, Hyundai has implemented a cost-leadership strategy with its emphasis on low priced cars for basic transportation.

There are many reasons why an individual firm may have a cost advantage over its competitors. The two most important sources of cost advantages are **economies of scale** and **economies of scope**.

Economies of scale

Economies of scale reflect the efficiencies that come with size. Fixed costs such as administration, facilities, equipment, staff and R&D can be spread over more units. Cost advantages arise where a producer derives economies of scale by having a large sales volume. Fixed costs can then be spread over a greater output. In addition there are the added benefits of what is called the 'experience curve'. The experience curve is similar to the learning curve with which we are familiar as people. As we perform a task or job again and again, we develop our skills. In time we become more efficient at doing the task or job. The experience curve extends this concept to show that efficiency increases and value added costs decline as the volume of production increases. Where a firm has the predominant market share, it should be able to reap the benefits of experience and hence enjoy cost advantages. These same benefits do not apply, however, where a firm has deliberately sought to increase its market share by buying it through price reductions, increased marketing effort and product development at the expense of long-term profitability.

Economies of scope (synergy)

Economies of scope (synergy) is where a business enjoys an advantage because it is linked to another business within the same enterprise. Both enterprises may benefit from shared resources, and in so doing reduce costs or investment. They may also be able jointly to offer a combination of complementary products. Synergy often results from some commonality in two operations, such as:

● R&D
● operating costs
● plant usage
● company or brand image and its impact on the market
● distribution
● sales or advertising.

In addition, it often produces increased revenues, decreased operating costs or reduced investment.

The implications of cost advantages for the marketing strategy is that they can be used to reduce prices or to earn higher margins at the same price. A preferable alternative, however, may be to reinvest in the product rather than run the risk of initiating price wars. Thus cost leaders are often market standard products that are believed to be acceptable to customers. Heinz and United Biscuits are believed to be cost leaders in their industries. They market acceptable products at reasonable prices which means that their low costs result in above-average profits.

One of the problems with this Porter generic strategy is that there can be only one lowest cost producer in any market, and to achieve this, the organization tends to focus too much on internal operational matters. This often involves significant capital investment, which relies on a period of relative stability in order to get a full return on the investment. The major risk is that the firm could lose touch in a dynamic marketplace, especially one where technology is changing.

Differentiation

It is not an easy task to create competitive advantage in a situation where the firm has relatively high costs. Differentiation removes the product from the most direct elements of competition by differentiating the marketing mix to the different buyer groups in the industry.

Differentiation strategies are usually associated with a premium price, and higher than average costs for the industry as the extra value to customers (e.g. higher performance) often raises costs. The aim is to differentiate in a way that leads to a price premium which is greater than the cost of differentiating. Differentiation gives customers a reason to prefer one product over another.

An important way in which a firm can attempt to differentiate its products is through linking different functions within the firm. For example, in selling computers and IT solutions, IBM has been very successful in linking the sales and service function. When a customer purchases an IBM mainframe computer it is not just buying a big box with electronic components. Instead, it is buying a relationship with IBM – a relationship that includes high levels of service and technical support. At IBM, the relationship with the company does not end with the purchase of a computer; it begins with this purchase.

Differentiation focus

With this strategy a firm aims to differentiate within one or a small number of target market segments. Focusing on the special needs of the segment means that there is an opportunity to differentiate the product offering from competitors and also charge a higher price. This could still result in a profitable business, in spite of the relatively high costs.

An example of differentiation focus can be seen in Harley-Davidson's decision to stay in the heavyweight motorcycle segment, where it had distinctive styling. Other companies following this strategy are Rolex (watches) and Porsche (sports cars).

Cost focus

With this strategy a firm seeks a cost advantage with one or a small number of market segments or single customers. By dedicating itself to a specific segment or a specific customer the cost focuser can seek economies that may be ignored or missed by broadly targeted competitors. By creating a close relationship with a few important customers, the firm can drive down the transaction costs associated within the buyer-seller relationship.

Porter argues that failure to make the choice between cost leadership, differentiation and focus strategy means that a company is stuck in the middle (see also Figure 8.9) with no competitive advantage, resulting in poor performance (Porter, 1985).

Some researchers have suggested that the most effective strategy for some situations is systematic oscillation between cost leadership and differentiation (Gilbert and Strebel, 1988).

Exhibit 8.4

Levi Strauss and other companies are approaching gay men and lesbians

Levi Strauss, the USA's largest clothing advertiser, sponsored *Inside Out*, a 12-page advertorial supplement in the November 1998 issue of *Out* magazine. The advertorial, selling Dockers khaki pants, features ten men and women who are openly homosexual as part of a campaign that includes contributions from Levi Strauss and its Red Tab Foundation to two organizations that help gay youth and fight homophobia in schools.

Levi Strauss is one of a growing number of companies targeting products at gay men and lesbians, from cars to computers. Even a new toothpaste, Mentadent Crystal Ice, is being advertised by Unilever, the consumer products giant, in *The Advocate*, the US national gay and lesbian news magazine.

Source: adapted from Elliott (1998).

Indeed, the strongest situation could be where a firm enjoys the benefits of both a cost advantage and a value advantage. Streamlined, automated production facilities coupled with active and effective product differentiation strategies have enabled many Japanese consumer goods manufacturers to achieve very strong competitive positions which are very difficult to dislodge.

Honda motorcycles have maintained their initial success in the USA by consistent action to sustain a competitive advantage based on distribution and brand image in addition to low cost realized through high volume production.

8.7 Offensive and defensive competitive strategies

If a market cannot be expanded through new users, new uses, and increased frequency of purchase, a 'build market share' strategy may be a relevant alternative. This implies gaining marketing success at the expense of the competition.

A successful strategy amounts to combining attacking and defensive moves to build a stronger position in the chosen marketplace. In recent years several authors, most notably Kotler and Singh (1981), and Ries and Trout (1986), have drawn an analogy between military warfare and competitive battles in the marketplace. Their basic contention is that lessons for the conduct of business strategy can be learned by a study of warfare and the principles developed by military strategies.

Offensive strategies

As indicated when a build objective is pursued in a market that cannot, for one reason or another, be expanded, success must, by definition, be at the expense of competitors.

In the battle with competitors, organizations must decide on what dimensions to attack or defend. This decision is based, in part, on the size of the firm relative to its competitors. It will also depend on the strategies that are viable in a particular industry.

Kotler and Singh have identified five competitor confrontation strategies (see Figure 8.11) designed to win sales and market share.

Frontal attack

A frontal attack means taking on a competitor head-on. This is one of the most difficult and dangerous of all marketing strategies. To be successful, the firm must have a substantial marketing advantage or considerable resources. For instance, the firm might have a similar product, but be able to sell it at a lower price.

The requirement of a similar 3 : 1 advantage to ensure success in a commercial frontal attack has been suggested (Kotler and Singh, 1981). Some question this 3 : 1 force, but all agree, however, that to defeat a well-entrenched competitor, who has built a solid market position, requires substantial superiority in at least one key area of the marketing programme.

IBM's attack on the PC market in the early 1980s is a classic example of the frontal attack. The market pioneer (Apple) was attacked partly as a defensive move by IBM as the company saw the likelihood that PCs would become executive workstations and hence threaten IBMs traditional dominance of the mainframe business market. There were several aspects to IBM's attack on the market. It was spear-

Figure 8.11 **Attack strategies**

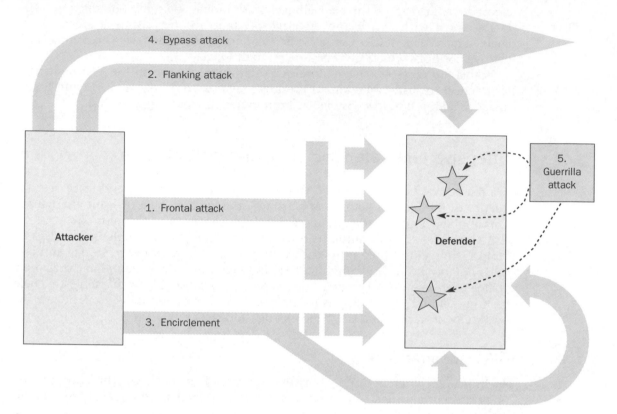

Source: reprinted from *Marketing Management: The millennium edition* 10/e by Kotler, Philip, © 2000, adapted by permission of Pearson Education, Inc., Upper Saddle River, NJ.

headed by a technological improvement (16-bit processors gave increased power and speed over the competing 8-bit machines.)

At the same time IBM made the technical specification of its machines widely available to software houses and other peripheral equipment manufacturers so that software became readily available and soon established an industry standard ('IBM-compatible'). The creation of the industry standard was made possible by the use of that prime marketing asset – the IBM name and reputation. Finally, a massive promotional campaign was launched in the small business market. The results were not only a dominant share of the markets for IBM, but they also managed to encourage the further growth of the market as a whole.

Flanking attack

In contrast to the frontal attack the flanking attack seeks to concentrate the aggressor's strengths against the competitor's weaknesses. In warfare, a flanking attack would seek to shift the battleground away from the enemy's strength to the unguarded or less well-defended flanks. A flanking attack is appropriate for segments of the market where customer needs are not being fully met. This may simply mean fighting in geographical regions, where the competition is weak. More likely, it means bringing out new products for emerging segments of the market. Flanking addresses gaps in existing market coverage of the competition. This strategy has been used very effectively by Japanese corporations.

The entry of Japan into the UK car market is a classic example of a flanking strategy. In cars especially, the Japanese took advantage of the OPEC-induced oil crisis of the early 1970s to cater to customer needs in the small car segment. The Japanese cars were cheap, reliable and offered good fuel consumption to the hard-hit motorist. Having established a toehold in the market, the Japanese car manufacturers have subsequently moved into other segments. Timing can be crucial to a successful flanking strategy. The Japanese entry into the US small car market was timed to take advantage of the recession and power. The strategy requires the identification of competitor weaknesses, inability or unwillingness to serve particular sectors of the market.

Encirclement

This involves attacking the defender from all sides to spread its resources thinly by probing on many fronts at once. Again, superior resources are required.

In business there are two approaches to the encirclement attack. The first is to attempt to isolate the competitor from the supply of raw materials on which it depends and/or the customers it seeks to sell to. The second approach is to seek to offer an all-round better product or service than the competitor. After their original flanking attack on the small car market, the Japanese used an encirclement attack aimed at many segments simultaneously with many different brands.

Bypass attack

A bypass attack is one of non-confrontation. The firm diversifies into unrelated products or diversifies into new markets for existing products as Marks & Spencer has done with its move into financial services.

Bypass attacks are most prevalent in high-technology markets, where a challenger puts its efforts into bypassing existing technology and winning the battle for the next generation of technology to be brought to the market. Such a move needs significant funding, but it can put the winner in an almost impregnable position.

Such a technological leap-frogging happened when Casio bypassed the Swiss analogue watches with digital technology.

Guerrilla attack

Guerrilla warfare entails small, intermittent attacks on a competitor. One goal might be to gain small amounts of market share while provoking minimal competitive reaction.

Guerrilla tactics may be the only feasible option for a small company facing a larger competitor. Such tactics allow the small company to make its presence felt without the dangers of a full frontal attack. By being unpredictable, guerrilla activity is difficult to defend.

One of the most long lasting guerrilla actions is Virgin Atlantic's campaign against British Airways (BA). Despite being in an alliance that carries more people across the Atlantic than BA, Virgin Atlantic still successfully positions itself as the little victim of BA's alliance with American Airlines.

Defensive strategies

Defensive strategies exist to counter each offensive strategy. In defending market share, the firm also has several alternatives: Kotler and Singh (1981) suggest six basic holding strategies.

Position defence

This involves erecting barriers around the company and its markets to shut out competition. The military analogy is the opposite side of the wall from the siege. The defender creates the largest walls and moats possible and sits tight until the aggressor gets weary, or finds other more pressing priorities, and withdraws. The main risk in this strategy is marketing myopia. Redesigning or reformulating your product can keep you one step ahead of the competition.

Flanking defence

This is the defending parallel to flanking attack. The aggressor seeks to concentrate strength against the weaknesses of the defender, often (especially in military warfare) using the element of surprise to gain the upper hand.

A flanking defence requires the company to strengthen the flanks, without providing a weaker and more vulnerable target elsewhere.

Pre-emptive defence

This follows the philosophy that the best form of defence is to attack first. The objective is to strike a physical or demoralizing blow which will prevent the aggressor from attacking in the first place.

Counter-offensive

Where deterrence of a potential attack before it occurs may be the ideal defence, a rapid counter-attack to 'stifle' the aggression can be equally effective. The essence of a counter-offensive is to identify the aggressor's vulnerable spots and to strike hard. The counter-offensive defence is most effective where the aggressor has become vulnerable through overstretching resources.

One example is where the defender attacks the competitor's home territory so that it has to divert its efforts into protecting its existing products. For example, some US firms have entered the Japanese market mainly to force Japanese firms that had entered the US market to reconcentrate their efforts back in their home market.

Mobile defence

This involves creating a flexible response capability to enable the defender to shift the ground which is being defended in response to environmental or competitive threats and opportunities. When a company's major market is under threat a mobile defence may make strategic sense. The two options are diversification and market broadening. A classic example of a company using diversification as a form of mobile defence was Philip Morris diversifying into the confectionery and food business when its cigarette market was threatened.

The mobile defence is an essential strategic weapon in markets where technology and/or customer wants and needs are changing rapidly. Failure to move with these changes can result in making the company vulnerable to a flanking or bypass attack.

Strategic withdrawal

A strategic withdrawal requires giving up untenable ground to reduce overstretching and allow concentration on the core business that can be defended against attack. The company has to define its strengths and weaknesses, and then to hold on to its strengths while divesting (or outsourcing) its weaknesses. This results in the company concentrating on its core business.

By the end of January 2001 the Swedish mobile telephone manufacturer, Ericsson, outsourced production of mobile telephones to a US partner, while keeping the value-adding R&D function within the Ericsson company.

Strategic withdrawal is usually necessary where the company has diversified too far away from its core skills and distinctive competences that gave it a competitive edge.

8.8 Summary

This chapter has focused on two interrelated decisions that are involved in the formulation of a strategic marketing programme for a product-market entry – market segmentation, market targeting and positioning.

Market segmentation separates potential customers into several groups or segments with distinctive characteristics. Customers within a segment should have similar wants, needs, and preferences; they should have similar media habits and buying patterns. The group should be large enough to justify attention, and data about individuals in each segment should be available.

Two common segmenting methods are the top-down method and the **bottom-up method**. The top-down method begins by selecting segmentation variables and assigning customers to the category they fit. The bottom-up method starts with the unique characteristics of one potential customer. Each time someone with unique characteristics is discovered, a new segment is added.

For the B-t-C market, typical segmentation variables are geographic and demographic factors, ethnic factors, psychographic and behaviouristic factors, and desired benefits.

In the B-t-B market two segmentation stages may be required. The first, macro-segmentation, divides the market according to the organizational characteristics of the customer, while micro-segmentation groups the customers by the characteristics of the individuals who influence the purchasing decision. Product usage and geographical locations are examples of macro-segmentation variables, while purchase influence, loyalty, and area of expertise are micro-segmentation variables.

Micro-segmentation centres on key characteristics of the decision-making unit and requires a higher level of market knowledge.

Target marketing focuses on selecting groups of customers so marketers can more clearly understand their specific wants and needs and adjust accordingly.

Market targeting may use a market-attractiveness matrix as an analytical framework to help managers decide which market segments to target and how to allocate resources and marketing efforts.

The three basic target marketing strategies are undifferentiated, differentiated, and concentrated marketing.

Undifferentiated marketing treats all customers alike and is similar to mass marketing. For this strategy to work, companies generally must have significant cost advantages. Differentiated marketing involves serving several segments but adjusting the marketing mix for each. It usually requires decentralized decision making. Concentrated marketing focuses on one segment or only a few. Because differentiated and concentrated strategies consider customer needs and wants within a certain group of customers, they are far superior to an undifferentiated strategy.

Positioning creates in the mind of consumers an image, reputation, or perception of the company and/or its products relative to competitors. It helps customers understand what is unique about a company and its products.

Positioning seeks to maximize a product's performance relative to competitive offerings and to the needs (benefits sought) of one or more targeted market segments.

Marketers can use a positioning map to depict how customers perceive products according to certain characteristics. For business products, a commodity, differentiated, or speciality positioning strategy can be used. Products are often positioned by benefit, by price and quality, by the time of use or application.

Positioning analysis can take place on different levels: company, product category, and brand levels. The main difference between positioning in the B-t-C and B-t-B markets is that in business markets company image considerations rather than brand image building are determinants of positioning strategies.

Successful marketing strategies are often based on differentiation, market focus, and lower costs. Firms must identify windows of opportunity and select appropriate attack and defence strategies to reach organizational goals.

Military analogies have been drawn upon to identify strategic options under the conditions of conflict and competition. The strategies of frontal, flank, encirclement, bypass and guerrilla attacks provide five options for companies wishing to build sales and/or market share. Position, flank, pre-emptive, counter-offensive and mobile defences and strategic withdrawal are options for companies defending sales and/or market share against aggressive competitors.

Case study 8.2 BMW's Mini

A 'cult' classic makes a comeback

To the British, it's a national icon – the car that's owned and loved by everyone from students to pop stars to royalty. It was typically identified with students and as a second car for British housewives. To the Japanese, it's a cult classic with a sales niche of its own. Its contribution to car history was its practical design – wheels pushed out to the corners, transverse engine and front-wheel drive.

The Mini is one of the world's best-selling cars, with 5.3 million produced to date. The original Mini was launched on August 26, 1959, by the British Motor Corp. (BMC), in response to fuel rationing introduced by the Suez crisis.

The totally redesigned Mini, the first since the Mini introduction in 1959, was launched worldwide in 2001–2002. The new Mini was launched first in the UK in July 2001 and in the rest of Europe in autumn 2001. The car re-entered the USA in early 2002, priced at around US$18,000, slightly more than the old version sold for in 1999. Asia will follow, including Japan, where the old Mini has achieved cult status.

BMW's new brand strategy is to position the Mini as a premium brand in the entry-level, small-car category, competing mainly against the VW Beetle and DaimlerChrysler's Smart car.

The Mini has not been redesigned since it first rolled off the assembly line at former owner Rover's Birmingham, UK, plant in 1959. BMW bought the Rover Group in the mid-1990s. In March 2000, BMW sold Rover Cars to a UK consortium and Land Rover to Ford Motor Co.; BMW kept only the Mini.

In 1999, Japan was the Mini's largest market, as BMW sold 14,000 of the cars globally. The car has not been sold in the USA, however, since 1967.

BMW executives said they hope the Mini will attract a customer younger than the average BMW driver. In the USA, BMW said it expects early demand for the Mini to come from nostalgic baby boomers but hopes eventually to

Case study 8.2 continued

attract 20–34-year-olds, who are more individu-alistic, and experimental, and take more risks than a typical BMW owner.

BMW plans to build 100,000 Minis at a reno-vated plant in Oxford, UK, during the first full year of production. BMW has spent £520 mil-lion on the plant where the car will be built. Analysts expect the car maker's profit this year will be reduced by about €100 million with the launch of the Mini.

The company should be selling about 200,000 to justify the development and approach profitability, analysts said.

BMW saw the Mini as the jewel in the Rover crown, and still seems convinced that the Mini will sell well – despite its relatively high price. The car is really not much more than a good looking two-seater with a big boot, or a very small rear seat.

The new Mini will not be sold as a small car for the masses, but as a nippy, hip car for the young and image-conscious with money to burn.

The Mini's life cycle will be short if it is not seen as practical. That is the whole point for BMW; it wants to establish something beyond a trendy, fashion car. They know it is going to be fast, sporty, good-looking, with good build qual-ity, but can it reach out to buyers who need it to do a job?

The German car maker, which gets about 86% of sales from its 3-series and 5-series cars, expects to introduce new models over the next decade.

BMW in the USA

The BMW Group has announced that the Mini will return to the USA after an absence of more than three decades. Only 10,000 were sold in America between 1960 and 1967, when imports were halted because of new safety and emissions regulations. The original Mini was priced at US$1295 in 1960. BMW executives will not reveal official prices for the new model, but say that a base model will start at about US$18,000.

In the USA, the Mini's goal is to draw new buyers to BMW who cannot afford a BMW. The British-built car will be targeted at trend-setting individuals.

Figure 8.12 **The new Mini**

Case study 8.2 continued

The global advertising campaign of BMW's Mini

The main tagline of the global Mini campaign is *'Feel Me'*, communicating the experience of climbing down into the little car. *'Drive Me'* stresses the unique experience of driving the small front-wheel car. Many say it is like driving a go cart. *'Protect me'* stresses safety features like six air bags. *'Dress me'* tells users they have countless options to customize their Mini with exterior paints, interior finishes and music systems. The main thrust of the Mini's marketing in the UK at the end of 2001 was 'It's a Mini adventure'.

Statistics on the US car industry

The sales volumes in different US sectors are shown in Table 8.4.

Table 8.4 Sales volume in different sectors

Sectors	Million vehicles 1995	1999
Bus/van/sport utility	3.4	4.7
Heavy trucks	0.3	0.4
Large/luxury cars	1.7	1.8
Medium-sized cars	3.9	4.0
Pick-ups	2.8	3.3
Small cars	2.9	2.8

Source: adapted from Euromonitor.

The Big Three car manufacturers, GM, Ford and DaimlerChrysler, accounted for 72.6% of the market in 1999 (Table 8.5).

GM failed to reach the company's goal of 30% market share, yet still maintained the largest percentage, with a 29.2% volume share of the car/off-road vehicle/recreational vehicle/pick-up market in 1999.

Toyota and Honda increased their share of the market to 8.7% and 6.4%, respectively, in 1999, counterbalancing a deepening economic crisis that hurt sales throughout Asia and eastern Europe.

Table 8.5 Companies' share of US market, 1999

Companies	% volume
General Motors Corporation	29.8
Ford Motor Company	26.1
DaimlerChrysler AG	16.7
Toyota Motor Company	8.7
Honda Motor Company Ltd	6.4
Others	12.3
Total	100.0

Source: adapted from Euromonitor.

In March 1999, Ford acquired Volvo's passenger car business for US$6.5 billion, raising its volume market share to 26.1%. GM increased its stake in Suzuki to 10% in late 1998, and raised its share of Isuzu to 49% in early 1999.

Despite the fact that Ford lays heavier emphasis on increasing profit than capturing market share, the company further closed the gap between itself and GM in 1999. DaimlerChrysler increased its market share to 16.7% of volume sales in 1999.

Table 8.6 shows the projected changes in US households from 1998 to 2008. The growth rate of married-couple households without children will far outpace that of couples with kids, and nonfamily households will grow at a slightly faster rate than family households. Household formations may be changing, but it is the presence of children that really determines the type of new vehicles adults drive home from the showroom (Table 8.7).

Households with children are the most likely to buy minivans. Traditional households, married couples with children, lead the way. Single parents rank second, but they are even more likely to go for sport utility vehicles and small and medium-sized cars.

Statistics on the German car industry

Statisitics about the passenger car market in Germany are given in Table 8.8. Statistics on brand awareness are given in Table 8.9.

Case study 8.2 continued

Table 8.6 Change in US households from 1998–2008 (000s)

	1998	2008	Change	Per cent Change
All households	102,022	112,433	10,411	10.2%
Family households, total	70,938	77,864	6,926	9.8%
Married couples without children under 18	28,977	34,335	5,458	18.8%
Married couples with children under 18	25,166	25,155	–11	0.0%
Female householder, no husband	12,917	14,061	1,144	8.9%
Male householder, no wife	3,878	4,213	335	8.6%
Non-family households, total	31,084	34,569	3,485	11.2%
Living alone, total	25,691	28,780	3,089	12.0%
Females living alone	15,154	17,255	2,101	13.9%
Males living alone	10,537	11,525	988	9.4%
Living with non-relatives	5,393	5,789	396	7.3%
Female householder	2,124	2,334	210	9.9%
Male householder	3,269	3,455	186	5.7%

Source: adapted from TGE Demographics.

Table 8.7 Share of new-vehicle purchases, July 1998–June 1999

	Married couples with children	Married couples without children	Multiple adults with children	Multiple adults without children	One adult with children	One adult living alone
Small car	11.8%	11.1%	14.8%	13.5%	17.4%	15.9%
Mid-size car	18.4%	21.3%	19.1%	21.6%	21.0%	22.7%
Large car	1.3%	4.0%	1.4%	2.9%	0.9%	2.4%
Sports car	4.2%	4.5%	4.8%	5.0%	4.5%	5.6%
Luxury car	6.7%	10.1%	6.7%	9.2%	6.7%	9.0%
Minivan	14.6%	7.5%	10.6%	5.5%	11.5%	4.6%
Sport utility vehicle	22.0%	19.4%	19.9%	18.8%	21.2%	19.5%
Pick-up truck	19.6%	21.3%	21.6%	22.7%	15.9%	19.8%
Full-size van	1.4%	0.8%	1.1%	0.8%	0.9%	0.5%
Total	100%	100%	100%	100%	100%	100%

Source: adapted from The Polk Company.

Case study 8.2 continued

Table 8.8 Passenger car market in Germany

| | Car possession by type of car* (Value as index) | | | | | | |
	Superminis	Small cars	Medium sized cars	Large cars	Sports car	Multi-purpose vehicle	Off-road vehicle
Potential in millions	3.41	6.21	5.41	2.30	0.82	1.21	0.44
Men	90	100	108	99	114	101	96
Women	113	100	90	101	82	99	105
Age							
Under 30 years	112	107	82	71	147	96	72
30–39 years	96	96	104	77	99	146	100
40–49 years	114	108	118	135	156	134	150
50–59 years	111	103	117	133	67	71	118
Over 59 years	66	86	78	93	24	38	60
Education							
Elementary school, no apprenticeship	60	65	65	55	93	45	107
Elementary school, apprenticeship	85	94	85	74	67	82	103
Higher education, no Advanced level	110	107	101	95	109	104	102
Advanced level/student	119	110	133	164	142	138	90
Size of household							
1 person	73	63	42	48	110	43	46
2 persons	94	98	97	118	98	54	72
3 persons	103	113	121	96	101	94	145
4 persons and more	118	111	114	106	97	191	125
Marital status							
Single	115	96	80	78	164	97	66
Married	98	105	116	111	81	107	119
Divorced	83	76	47	78	92	62	52
Occupation							
Self-employed, professional	110	108	141	265	207	199	323
Managers	142	128	147	245	194	139	128
Employees in higher wage bracket	115	97	120	106	87	115	69
Employees in medium wage bracket	100	95	95	59	71	58	43
Employees in lower wage bracket	97	102	56	20	83	58	113
Manual	80	96	79	43	66	79	67
Net income per household							
0–2,999 DM	73	75	40	20	64	37	58
3,000–3,999 DM	81	102	88	60	66	85	76
4,000–4,999 DM	97	98	119	98	71	108	101
5,000–5,999 DM	132	114	141	166	143	108	171
6,000–6,999 DM	149	108	133	164	157	236	110
7,000 DM or more	159	149	184	311	267	183	191

* Index value: licence owners = 100.

Source: adapted from Der Markt der Automobile (1999).

Case study 8.2 continued

Table 8.9 Awareness of car brands in Germany (% of licence owners)

Car manufacturer	Total brand awareness	Of positive attitude towards brand
German manufacturers		
Audi	97	68
BMW	97	67
Ford	95	37
Mercedes-Benz	98	62
Opel (GM)	97	50
Porsche	89	48
VW	99	69
European manufacturers		
Alfa Romeo	78	34
Citroën	83	14
Fiat	90	16
Lancia	64	17
Peugeot	85	23
Renault	88	25
Rover	67	27
Saab	64	19
Seat	75	12
Skoda	68	10
Volvo	85	37
Asian manufacturers		
Kia	44	5
Daewoo	54	6
Subaru	57	6
Daihatsu	58	4
Hyundai	58	6
Suzuki	68	10
Mitsubishi	75	16
Nissan	79	17
Honda	82	25
Mazda	83	23
Toyota	84	24

Source: adapted from FAME 98/99.

Questions

1. In general, how can the personal car market be segmented? Which segmentation criteria would be relevant?

2. Give a proposal for the segmentation, targeting and positioning strategy of the Mini in:
   (a) the USA
   (b) Germany.

Sources: Fortune (1998), Der Markt der Automobile (1999), Adage Global (2000), Advertising Age (2000), American Demographics (2000), Automotive Industries (2000), Marketing (2000), Motor (2000), Ward's Auto World (2000) BBC (2001), CNN (2001).

QUESTIONS FOR DISCUSSION

1. What benefits are to be gained from market segmentation, as opposed to treating the market as a single entity?

2. What stages are involved in identifying market segments?

3. Is market segmentation always a good idea? Under which conditions, if any, might segmentation be unnecessary or unwise?

4. Can market segmentation be taken too far? What are the potential disadvantages of over-segmenting a market? What strategy might a firm pursue when it believes that the market has been broken into too many small segments?

5. Which variables or descriptors might be most appropriate for segmenting the market for the following products and services? Explain your reasoning.
   (a) Breakfast cereals.
   (b) Personal computers (PCs).
   (c) Software, games for PCs.
   (d) Lawnmowers.
   (e) Photocopiers.
   (f) Wind turbines.

6. Explain the idea of positioning and why products are repositioned periodically.

REFERENCES

Adage Global (2000), BMW awards German shop global launch of new Mini, **www.adageglobal.com** Daily News, September 30.

Advertising Age (2000), BMW puts $40 mil effort behind its revamped Mini, *Advertising Age*, Chicago, vol. 71, no. 42, October 9, pp. 34–6

Automotive Industries (2000), Risking brand image with new brand, *Automotive Industries*, vol. 18, no.10, October, pp. 30–1

Barron, J. and Hollingshead, J. (2002), Market segmentation work: successful marketing really does begin with effective segmentation, *Marketing Management*, January/February, pp. 24–28.

BBC (2001), A new life for the Mini, May 22, **http://news.bbc.co.uk**.

Beverage Industry (2000a), Bottled water comes of age, *Beverage Industry*, New York, vol. 91, no. 9, September, pp. 26–9.

Beverage Industry (2000b), Bottled water soars, *Beverage Industry*, New York, vol. 91, no 9, September, pp. 22–6.

Beverage Industry (2000c), State of the industry, *Beverage Industry*, New York, vol. 91, no 7, July, pp. 38–40.

Bonoma, T. V. and Shapiro, B. P. (1983), *Segmenting the Industrial Market*, D.C. Heath and Co., Lexington.

Busch, P. S. and Houston, M. J. (1985), *Marketing Strategic Foundations*, Richard D. Irwin, Burr Ridge, IL.

Business and Finance (1999), Ballygowan: the 'Hoover' of the Irish water industry in just fifteen years, *Business and Finance*, September 23.

CNN (2001), BMW rolls out new Mini, May 22. **http://cnnfn.cnn.com**.

Der Market der Automoblie (1999), Fakten '99, Focus, **www.focus.de/medialine**.

Dyer, J. H., Cho, D. S. and Chu, W. (1998), Strategic supplier segmentation, *California Management Review*, vol. 40, no. 2, Winter, pp. 57–77.

Elliott, G. and Glynn, W. (2000), Segmenting industrial buyers by loyalty and value, IMP Conference, Bath, UK.

Elliott, S. (1998), Levi Strauss begins a far-reaching marketing campaign to reach gay men and lesbians, *New York Times*, New York, Oct. 19. p. 11.

Fortune (1998), BMW – Takes its own route, *Fortune*, October 26, pp. 103–8.

Freytag, P. V. and Clarke, A. H. (2001), Business to business market segmentation, *Industrial Marketing Management*, vol. 30, pp. 473–86.

Gibson, L. D. (2001), Is something rotten in segmentation?, *Marketing Research*, Spring, pp. 20–5.

Gilbert, X. and Strebel, P. (1988), Developing competitive advantage, *in* (Eds) Quinn, J. B. Mintzberg, H. and James, R. M., *The Strategic Process*, Prentice-Hall, Englewood Cliffs, NJ.

Goller, S., Hogg, A. and Kalafatis, P. (2002), A new research agenda for business segmentation, *European Journal of Marketing*, vol. 36, no. 1/2, pp. 252–71.

Harrell, G. D. and Frazier, G. L. (1999), *Marketing: Connecting with customers*, Prentice-Hall, Englewood Cliffs NJ.

Kalafatis, S. P., Tsogas, M. H. and Blankson, C. (2000), Positioning strategies in business markets, *Journal of Business & Industrial Marketing*, vol. 15, no. 6, pp. 416–37.

Kotler, P. (2000), *Marketing Management: The millennium edition*, Pearson Education, Inc., Upper Saddle River, NJ, 10th edn.

Kotler, P. and Singh, R. (1981), Marketing warfare in the 1980s, *Journal of Business Strategy*, Winter, pp. 30–41.

Kumar, V. and Naspal, A. (2001), Segmenting global markets: look before you leap, *Marketing Research*, Spring, pp. 8–13.

Marketing (2000), BMW picks Rover man to market new Mini, *Marketing*, London, September 7, pp. 5–6.

Millier, P. (2000), Intuition can help in segmenting industrial markets, *Industrial Marketing Management*, vol. 29, no. 2, March, pp. 147–55.

Mitchell, V.-W. and Wilson, D.F. (1998), Balancing theory and practice, *Industrial Marketing Management*, vol. 27, pp. 429–45.

Mittal, V. and Katrichis, J. M. (2000), Distinctions between new and loyal customers, *Marketing Research*, vol. 12, no. 1, Spring, pp. 26–32.

Motor (2000), 'The mini's back ... after 30 years', *Motor*, New York, vol. 193, no. 4, April, pp. 51–2.

Peppers, D., Rogers, M. and Dorf, B. (1999), Is your company ready for one-to-one marketing?, *Harvard Business Review*, January–February, pp. 151–60.

Porter, M. E. (1980), *Competitive Strategy*, Free Press, NY.

Porter, M. E. (1985), *Competitive Advantage: Creating and sustaining superior performance*, Free Press, New York.

Prince, G. W. (2001), Rock the boat, *Beverage World*, April 15, pp. 53–7.

Ries, A. and Trout, J. (1986), *Positioning: The battle for your mind*, McGraw-Hill, New York, 2nd edn, pp. 1–210.

Roper Starch Worldwide (2000), Re-mapping the world of consumers, *American Demographics*, October (**www.demographics.com**).

Smith, W. (1956), Product differentiation and market segmentation as alternative marketing strategies, *Journal of Marketing*, vol. 21, July, pp. 3–8.

Townsend, M. (2001), Record demand as healthier lifestyles take off but the tap stuff is just as good, Bottled water floods in, *The Express*, March 6, p. 10.

Ward's Auto World (2000), BMW previews new mini, *Ward's Auto World*, Detroit, vol. 36, no. 10, October, pp. 33–4.

Wind, Y. and Cardozo, R. N. (1974), Industrial market segmentation, *Industrial Marketing Management*, vol. 7, pp. 153–66.

Wyner, G. A. (2000), Customer selection, *Marketing Research*, vol. 12, no. 1, Spring, pp. 42–4.

Chapter **9**

International marketing strategies

LEARNING OBJECTIVES

After studying this chapter you should be able to:

- explain the difference between a market responsive strategy and a global integrated strategy.
- define the term 'globalization'.
- discuss the reasons (motives) why firms internationalize.
- explain the role of the individual manager in the firm's internationalization procedure.
- analyse models and theories explaining firms' internationalization processes.
- explain the term 'born global' and its connection to Internet marketing.
- explain the relevance of a relationship for an SME serving as a subcontractor.
- identify and classify different market entry modes.
- identify the factors to consider when choosing a market entry strategy.
- explain the difference between standardization and adaptation strategies.
- discuss why intercultural negotiation is a great challenge in international marketing.

Case study 9.1 Skagen Designs

Marketing of Scandinavian designed watches to the USA and the rest of the world

In January 2001, Charlotte and Henrik Jorst admire the scenery of the Sierra Nevada Mountains from their recently acquired house at Reno, Nevada. They can look back at ten hectic but successful years. Their company was founded in an apartment in New York, from where the first marketing took place. The two entrepreneurs started selling relatively expensive watches bearing a logo that US companies might use as company presents. During the Gulf Crisis it was, however, very difficult to sell watches in that price range. Therefore, in 1990 Charlotte and Henrik visited a watch fair in Basel, Switzerland, in order to find a manufacturer who was able to produce their own designs

at a lower price. They found a Danish owned company, Comtech Watches, with headquarters in Aarhus and a factory in Hong Kong. Since then this company has been an extremely important strategic partner for Skagen Designs in connection with product development and production of the watches. Through the years Charlotte, Henrik and the family behind Comtech have become very close friends.

In 1992 Charlotte and Henrik had an annual turnover of US$800,000, primarily through an advertisement on the back page of a big mail-order catalogue for 'Father's Day'. Events then followed in quick succession. In 1995, the department store Bloomingdale's stocked the

Case study 9.1 continued

Skagen Design watches, and afterwards other retail chains like Macy's, Nordstrom and Watch Station have followed. In addition, the watches are sold in big gift shops and design shops.

By 1998 Skagen Designs had an annual turnover of almost US$20 million, and in 1999 the turnover had increased to approximately US$25 million. In 1999 Inc. Magazine's 'Inc. 500' appointed the company one of the fastest growing companies in the USA.

The core competences of Skagen Designs are as follows:

- development of new watch concepts following fashion trends
- keeping a close eye on everything
- quick decisions
- well-developed partnership with the 'upstream' specialist (Comtech Watches), which is in charge of the specific product development and production at competitive prices.

Charlotte and Henrik have divided the work between them as follows. Charlotte is primarily in charge of sales and marketing, while Henrik is in charge of the company's finance and administration.

In the USA the watches are sold at very competitive prices compared with other designer watches, i.e. typically about US$110.

Skagen Designs – the story in brief

1986
Party at Carlsberg. Even if Henrik had brought his girlfriend, he managed to make Charlotte Kjølbye his neighbour at dinner, and they fell head over heels in love with each other. Shortly after the party Carlsberg sends Henrik Jorst to New York. From New York, Henrik Jorst manages Carlsberg's USA sales. Charlotte stays on for a year and a half in Denmark, but in spite of the short and uncommitted acquaintance they keep in close contact on the phone. Then she joins him in the USA.

1990
Henrik Jorst quits his job at Carlsberg. In Henrik's opinion Carlsberg does not understand the USA. He wants to be able to put more pressure on the key market and expose Carlsberg much more. Charlotte walks about the streets of New York trying to sell the Danish Jacob Jensen watches to watchmakers. She started working for an **advertising agency**, but she cannot stand working for managers whom she has to humour. In 1989 she got a job as a model and also a job as the seller of Danish advertisers' watches. Once they have the Jacob Jensen agency, the family business has started and they are working round the clock. But they have hardly any money. Charlotte gives birth to a daughter, Christine.

1991
Spring in New York, and the Jorst family take the advertisers' watches to a trade fair. At this fair several retailers notice the watches and wonder why the two Danes present them as advertisers' watches and not branded goods. 'Produce watches! We will sell them'. During the summer they produce 800 copies of four different watches of their own designs. Several months later all the watches are sold. Perhaps they will succeed.

1992
Sitting at the dinner table Henrik and Charlotte design 30 different models, all labelled 'Skagen Denmark'. In a New York street Charlotte meets one of the managers from the mail order giant 'The Sharper Image'. She takes a chance, and yes, he puts the Skagen watches on the back page of the 'Father's Day' catalogue. Everything is sold. From the apartment in New York Henrik and Charlotte have a turnover of DKK5.6 million (US$800,000).

1993
Taxes, what about taxes? Henrik Jorst makes some enquiries. There are not many states in the USA where business taxes are almost zero. In Florida and Nevada this is, however, the case. One day they fly to Incline Village at Lake Tahoe – one of the world's best ski resorts. They lose their hearts and buy a house that is much too expensive, but big. The company moves into every room, from kitchen cupboards to garage. They still do it all by themselves. Charlotte becomes pregnant and gives birth to their daughter Camilla.

Case study 9.1 continued

1995

Five years after starting the company. Now, it becomes really big. Bloomingdale's takes the watches on trial. Sold out – in one single day. Everyone wants the Skagen watches that now have cult status. They engage employees in a small, rented office not far from their home at the lake. After a year the office is too small, and after another year the same happens again.

1998

The magazine, Inc., puts Skagen Designs on the list of the 250 fastest growing, privately owned companies. During five years the turnover has increased by almost 1200 per cent. The 1997 turnover amounts to DKK106 million. Finally, the rest of the company moves out of the villa at Lake Tahoe. New headquarters are opened in Reno, and Charlotte's Danish Design sells for DKK200 million, almost US$30 million.

1999

A complete range of watches, pens and sunglasses is in stock. The number of employees is approaching 100. Henrik gives Charlotte a horse as a present for their ten year wedding anniversary. The family moves from Lake Tahoe to a large house of 650 square metres on the outskirts of Reno. It is situated on the top of a hill with a beautiful view of the Sierra Nevada Mountains.

2000–2002

Another increase in turnover can be expected. Henrik and Charlotte still control all products that they design and approve themselves.

Products

During recent years Skagen Designs has developed from being just a watch company to being a company that launches designer products e.g. sunglasses, office accessories and homewares. Figure 9.1 shows an example of a product line from Skagen Designs.

Markets

Until now Skagen Design's marketing has primarily focused on the US and Danish markets. The volume of the watch market in various countries given in Table 9.1, and the value in Table 9.2.

Figure 9.1 A product line from Skagen Design: Ultra Slim Line

Marketing the watches

In the USA the products from Skagen Designs are launched through fashion papers like *Vogue*, *InStyle*, *GQ* and *Accessories*. Further, TV shows like Jeopardy and Wheel of Fortune are sponsored as well as actors in the series Ally McBeal and The Practice.

Competitors

As a fashion company Skagen Designs is competing with all big international companies designing watches like Calvin Klein, Coach, Guess, Gucci, Swatch, Alfex, and Jacob Jensen. Most of these companies possess a financial strength many times bigger than that of Skagen Designs.

▶

Case study 9.1 continued

Table 9.1 Volume of watch market in various countries, 1999

Country	Total sales volume (000s)	Sales volume per 1000 people
Austria	3,080.0	381.0
Belgium	2,089.0	204.3
Bulgaria	345.0	42.0
Canada	355.0	11.6
China	12,452.0	9.8
Czech Republic	594.5	57.8
Denmark	1,079.0	202.7
Finland	642.0	124.3
France	12,812.0	216.8
Greece	1,885.0	179.1
Hungary	253.4	25.1
Ireland	652.0	173.6
Italy	14,110.0	245.2
Netherlands	2,992.0	189.2
Norway	896.0	200.9
Poland	1,726.0	44.6
Portugal	2,140.0	214.2
Romania	497.0	22.1
Russia	28,007.7	191.9
Slovakia	391.1	72.5
Spain	7,945.0	201.6
Sweden	1,615.0	182.3
Taiwan	2,775.0	125.1
Ukraine	375.0	7.6
United Kingdom	15,048.2	253.5
USA	226,565.2	838.4

Source: different public sources.

Table 9.2 Value of watch market in various countries, 1999

Country	Value (US$ million)	Value (US$ per capita)
Austria	235.8	29.2
Belgium	177.0	17.3
Bulgaria	5.8	0.7
Canada	26.9	0.9
China	308.4	0.2
Czech Republic	15.8	1.5
Denmark	102.9	19.3
Finland	40.9	7.9
France	679.4	11.5
Germany	862.9	10.5
Greece	85.9	8.2
Hungary	5.4	0.5
Ireland	8.8	2.3
Israel	32.9	5.5
Italy	1,158.1	20.1
Japan	1,646.4	13.0
Mexico	18.4	0.2
Netherlands	177.4	11.2
New Zealand	28.0	7.3
Norway	74.9	16.8
Poland	29.0	0.8
Russia	180.9	1.2
Singapore	428.0	135.3
Slovakia	10.0	1.9
South Africa	49.8	1.2
Spain	668.0	16.9
Sweden	103.7	11.7
Switzerland	561.3	78.6
Taiwan	21.3	1.0
Ukraine	9.1	0.2
United Kingdom	953.0	16.1
USA	12,797.3	47.4

Source: different public sources.

Questions

As an expert in international marketing Charlotte and Henrik have called you in to obtain valuable input in connection with the international expansion of Skagen Designs. In the following questions, please specify your assumptions if necessary. State the reasons for your answers.

1. Discuss how the three internationalization theories can be applied to Skagen Designs.

2. What screening criteria should Skagen Designs use in connection with the choice of new markets for its assortment of watches?

3. Make a specific choice of new markets for Skagen Designs.

4. Which market entry mode should Skagen Designs use in the chosen markets?

5. Skagen Designs is considering selling its watches online. What problems and possibilities do you see for Skagen Designs in this connection?

Source: different public sources.

Introduction

International marketing is important because the world has become more globalized. The growth of global business activities offers increased opportunities. International activities can be crucial to a firm's survival and growth. By transferring knowledge around the globe, an international firm can build and strengthen its competitive position.

However, the primary role of marketing management, in any organization, is to design and execute effective marketing programmes. Companies can do this in their home market or they can do it in one or more international markets. Expanding internationally is enormously expensive, in terms of both money and, especially, senior management time and commitment. Due to the high cost, expanding internationally must generate added value for the company beyond extra sales. In other words, the company needs to gain a competitive advantage by expanding internationally. So, unless the company gains by doing this, it should probably stay at home.

The task of global marketing management is complex enough when the company operates in one foreign national market. It is much more complex when the company starts operations in several countries. Marketing programmes must, in these situations, adapt to the needs and preferences of customers that have different levels of purchasing power as well as different climates, languages and cultures. Moreover, patterns of competition and methods of doing business differ between nations and sometimes also within regions of the same nation. In spite of the many differences, however, it is important to hold on to similarities across borders. Some coordination of international activities will be required, but at the same time the company will gain some synergy across borders, in the way that experience and learning acquired in one country can be transferred to another.

There are two main forces that determine the route of internationalization.

Forces for national market responsiveness

Often customer characteristics and desired benefits, key competitors and their strategies, or the nature of the market infrastructure, differ from one market to another, which requires the firm to modify substantially its competitive positioning to compete effectively. Consequently, a firm must modify its domestic positional advantage to each market (market responsiveness) to be successful (see Figure 9.3). For example, Ariel had to modify existing detergent products as well as its positioning and develop new products to match differences in washing habits, water conditions, and use of washing machines in different parts of the world. It was initially developed in Europe as a low-temperature detergent powder with an environmentally friendly version. In India, it has been marketed as a pre-soak, and in the USA as Cheer, an all-purpose detergent. Differences in the cost and availability of local resources may also suggest the desirability of tailoring the development of a competitive position and the value delivered to customers from one market to another.

In this case, the geographic dispersion of activities provides greater contact with customers and competitors. In particular, if the firm emphasizes customization of its offerings, proximity to customers may enable it to provide rapid response and tailoring of product and services to meet specific customer needs. For example, Hyundai's computer division established an assembly plant in California to be close to consumers and competitors, though there are substantial production efficiencies in centralization. Proximity to customers may provide a significant advantage, especially if there are differences in customer demand from one location to another (Craig and Douglas, 2000). Mostly downstream activities, such as marketing and distribution, are by their very nature geographically dispersed.

Forces for global coordination/integration

Interdependencies between markets are growing as a result of the flow of goods, people, and information across national boundaries. As a result, in assessing its overall competitive advantage in global markets, a firm needs to consider the strengths and weaknesses of its competitive positions in each country's market and how these interact to influence deployment of resources worldwide.

In this case, concentration of the firm's value-creating activities offers several advantages insofar as scale economies can provide the firm with a cost advantage relative to competitors in serving a given market. Equally, concentration enables the use of superior or highly specialized skills and expertise or an accumulation of specialized knowledge relating to product design, creation of advertising copy, or other functions. For example, Procter & Gamble concentrates R&D on detergents in three centres located in the USA, Japan, and Europe. Each centre works on different problems and shares the results to develop new products or product formulations for different markets. Similarly, Unilever has three new product development centres that work on new product ideas for the entire organization (Craig and Douglas, 2000).

If we observe traditional learning in many international companies, the assignment of managerial responsibility along territorial lines inevitably means that managers learn from events that take place in their assigned countries. In the extreme, managers only learn what happens in their own geographic territory, and would even disregard events occurring elsewhere (100 per cent national market responsiveness). This would mean that the company is competing globally on the basis of individual country-specific learning curves (Figure 9.2(a))

Figure 9.2(b) represents the opposite situation. This is the true global learning organization. Here, events occurring at different locations throughout the world would be plotted on to a single, global learning curve. Managers would incorporate the learning of other colleagues from the global organization into their own activities. The learning and experience in one market might be used in other markets. Since many learning events occur on a globally pooled basis, managers can come down their own learning curve more rapidly, thus enhancing their own and the firm's competitiveness. Each local organization, thus organized, would compete on the strength of all the lessons learned, and not simply the local ones. All units would be stronger, more intelligent, and more competitive than if they were operating on their own.

As a reaction to pressures from international markets, both **LSEs** (large-scale enterprises) and **SMEs** (small and medium-sized enterprises) evolve towards a globally integrated but market-responsive strategy. However, the starting point of LSEs and SMEs is different (see Figure 9.3). The huge global companies have traditionally based their strategy on taking advantage of 'economies of scale' by launching standardized products worldwide. These companies have realized that a higher degree of market responsiveness is necessary to maintain competitiveness on national markets. On the other side, SMEs have traditionally regarded national markets as independent of each other. But as international competences evolve, they have begun to realize

Figure 9.2 The global learning organization

(a) Existing model

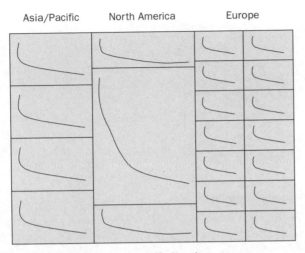

Individual country-specific learning curves

(b) New model

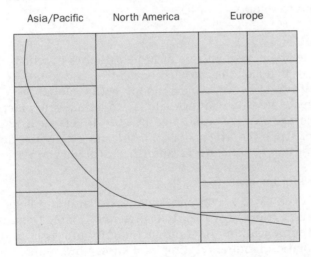

Source: after Jeannet (2000), p. 13, with permission from Pearson Education.

that there are similarities between their different international markets. They recognize the benefits of coordinating the different national marketing strategies in order to utilize economies of scale in R&D, production and marketing.

In summary there are different reasons for the firm to consider globalization as a strategic imperative.

Figure 9.3 Global integration/market responsiveness grid: the future orientation of LSEs and SMEs

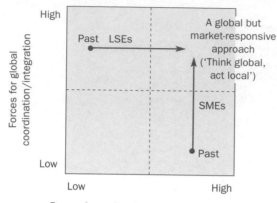

Source: Hollensen (2001), p. 5.

The growth imperative

Companies have no choice but to persist in a never-ending quest for growth if they wish to garner rewards from the capital markets and attract and retain the best talent. For many industries, developed country markets are quite mature. Thus, the growth imperative generally requires companies to look to emerging markets, e.g. China and India, for fresh opportunities.

The cost imperative

Whenever the value chain sustains one or more activities in which the minimum efficient scale (of research facilities, production centres, and so on) exceeds the sales volume feasible within one country, a company with a global presence will have the potential to create a cost advantage relative to a domestic player within that industry. Hence, companies are stimulated by cost drivers such as economies of scale, economies of scope (i.e. the gains from spreading activities across multiple product lines or businesses), sourcing advantages, and application across countries.

The knowledge transfer imperative

No two countries, even close neighbours such as Holland and Belgium, are completely alike. So when a company expands its presence to more than one country, it must adapt at least some features of its products and/or processes to the local environment. This adaptation requires creating local know-how, some of which may be too specific to be relevant outside the particular local market. However, in many cases, local product and/or process innovations are at the cutting edge and have the potential to generate global advantage by transferring know-how across borders.

Globalization of customers

The term 'globalization of customers' refers to customers that are worldwide corporations (such as the soft drinks companies served by advertising agencies). When the customers of a domestic company start to globalize, the company must follow the customers. Three reasons dictate such an alignment. First, the customer may strongly prefer worldwide consistency and coordination in the sourcing of products and services. Second, it may prefer to deal with a small number of supply partners on a long-term basis. Third, allowing a customer to deal with different supplier(s) in other countries poses a serious risk that the customer may replace your firm with one of these suppliers, even in the domestic market.

Globalization of competitors

If your competitors start to globalize and you do not, they can use their global stronghold to attack you in at least two ways. First, they can develop a first-to-market advantage in capturing market growth, pursuing global scale efficiencies, profiting from knowledge transfer, and providing a coordinated source of supply to global customers. Second, they can use a multi-market presence to cross-subsidize and wage a more intense attack in your own home markets. It is dangerous to underestimate the rate at which competition can accelerate the pace of globalization. A compromise between the forces of globalization and the forces of localization (national market responsiveness) is 'global strategy', which in part reflects the aspirations of a global strategy approach, while the necessity for local adaptations and tailoring of business activities (i.e. 'glocalization') is simultaneously acknowledged.

| Exhibit 9.1 | MTV comes back in Japan with a more localized concept |

In January 2001, MTV could be seen in 341 million households in 139 countries. After failing once in Japan, MTV went on air again in January 2001 as a 24-hour Japanese language service on cable and satellite TV. The channel replaced a local music channel called Vibe, which had 2.8 million viewers.

Japan is already flooded with music channels, but MTV felt that its new partner and heavy reliance on local content, combined with MTV's expertise in the international music marketplace, would help it succeed this time around, even though the competition is stiffer.

Part of the problem MTV had before in its 1992–8 run in Japan was that it was broadcast under a licensing arrangement with electronics company Pioneer Corp. No MTV executives held day-to-day decision-making positions.

The split came over differences in fees and content. Around 75% of the music videos on the old MTV channel were foreign, but in the Japanese music market local acts represent about 80% of the market in terms of sales.

MTV plans to work with its local partners to build its Internet based marketing as well as animated fare.

Source: adapted from Adage Global (2000a).

'Glocalization'

There is a continuum from the local adaptations of worldwide strategies on one side, and the universal or global strategies without adaptations on the other. In an empirical context, the global strategy approach is more like a managerial utopia, though any kind of genuine or true global strategy will not be successfully implemented worldwide. A worldwide strategy has at least to be adapted to local conditions, characteristics, and circumstances to a certain extent. Nevertheless, it is a matter of thinking globally, but acting locally, i.e. acting and thinking 'glocally'.

Apparently, in most areas it is not suitable to apply a genuine or true global strategy, since local adaptations of the business activities usually have to be taken into consideration in the marketplace.

Domino's Pizza is a good example of a company that has benefited from adapting its business model when it entered India. Unlike KFC, Domino's was successful in its initial entry into India, primarily because it tailored its approach to the Indian culture and lifestyle. Even though pepperoni pizza is one of the most popular items for Domino's in other markets, the company dropped it from the menu to show respect for the value Hindus place on the cow. Domino's also tailored other toppings, such as chicken, ginger, and lamb, to suit Indian taste buds.

Marketing practitioners face five main decisions in connection with the international marketing process. Figure 9.4 shows the five phases of the decision process linked to the information needed in each phase.

In a study of recently internationalized US firms, Yip *et al.* (2000) conclude that the firms using a systematic sequence of steps in the internationalization process (Figure 9.4) are better performers than the firms which do not. The more systematic the approach, the better the performance (Yip *et al.*, 2000, p. 10). Hence, in the remaining sections of this chapter the phases of Figure 9.4 will be discussed further.

Figure 9.4 Major steps in international marketing planning

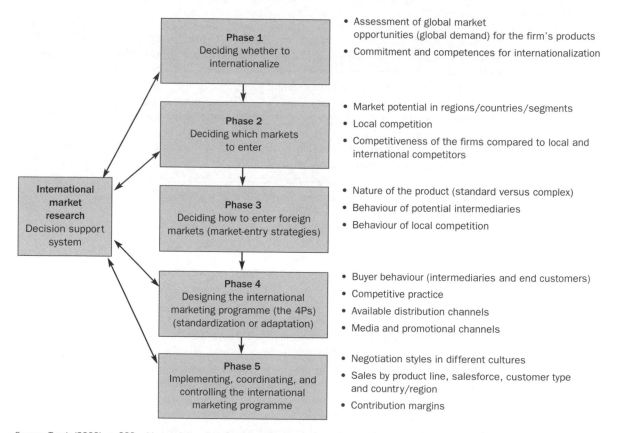

Source: Tayeb (2000), p. 383, with permission from Pearson Education.

As development and implementation of the marketing programme, phases 4 and 5 are major issues in Parts IV and V of this book, in this section coverage of phases 4 and 5 will be limited to:

- standardizing or adaptating the international marketing programme
- how to negotiate in foreign cultures (reduction of psychic distances).

Exhibit 9.2 **J. Sainsbury runs into trouble in Egypt**

When J. Sainsbury, the established British supermarket chain, moved into Egypt at the beginning of 2000, it was with hopes of obtaining big profits from being the first to bring wide scale western supermarket techniques to the 40-year-old socialist retail scene. The company may still do that. But after months facing boycotts, and losses, J. Sainsbury is rethinking Egypt.

The popular view was that shopping at the new store was as bad as committing adultery or stealing, which is the equivalent of an Islamic fatwa, though it lacked the official approval of the religion's leaders.

The 40-year-old socialist retail system had resulted in a very long distribution channel with high retail prices. Eventually J. Sainsbury agreed not to lower prices below Egyptian wholesaler levels. The popular view changed, but by October 2000, new troubles surfaced. Anti-Israeli protestors, fed by rumours, made J. Sainsbury a chief target of a wider consumer boycott against western products that included McDonald's, Coke and Pepsi. The Egyptian subsidiary lost US$15 million on US$58 million sales in the half-year ending October 2000.

Egypt's Prime Minister Atef Ebeid has met with Sainsbury managers to try to help them cut through some of the bureaucracy they faced.

Other foreign supermarket chains are undaunted by Sainsbury's experience. Carrefour of France is planning three hypermarkets in Cairo and Alexandria by 2002 and a total invest-ment of US$233 million over ten years.

If Sainsbury's competitors take note, the lessons learned from J. Sainsbury could help to introduce much more competition.

Source: adapted from Postlewaite (2001).

9.2 Phase 1: Deciding whether to internationalize – initiation of internationalization

In the international marketing literature, the 'staying at home' alternative is not discussed thoroughly. However, Solberg (1997) argues that with limited interna-tional experience and a weak position in the home market there is little reason for a firm to engage in international markets. Intead the firm should try to improve its performance in its home market. This alternative is cell 1 in Figure 9.5.

If a firm finds itself in a global industry as a dwarf among large multi-national firms, then Solberg (1997) argues that the firm may seek ways to increase its net worth so as to attract partners for a future buy-out bid. This alternative (cell 7 in Figure 9.5) may be relevant to SMEs selling advanced high-technology components (as sub-suppliers) to large industrial companies with a global network. In situations with fluctuations in global demand, the SME (with limited financial resources) will often be financially vulnerable. If the firm has already acquired some competences in

Figure 9.5 The nine strategic windows

		Industry globalism		
		Local	Potentially global	Global
Preparedness for internationalization	Mature	3. Enter new business	6. Prepare for globalization	9. Strengthen your global position
	Adolescent	2. Consolidate your export markets	5. Consider expansion in international markets	8. Seek global alliances
	Immature	1. Stay at home	4. Seek niches in international markets	7. Prepare for a buy-out

Source: reprinted with permission from *Journal of International Marketing*, published by the American Marketing Association, C. A. Solberg (1997), vol. 5, no. 1, pp. 9–30.

international business operations, it can overcome some of its competitive disadvantages by going into alliances with firms representing complementary competences (cell 8). The other cells in Figure 9.5 are further discussed by Solberg (1997).

The fundamental reason for internationalization, in most firms, is to make money. But as in most business activities, one factor alone rarely accounts for any given action. Usually a mixture of factors results in firms taking steps in a given direction.

Table 9.3 provides an overview of the major motivations to internationalize. They are differentiated into proactive and reactive motives. *Pro-active* motives represent stimuli to attempt strategy change, based on the firm's interest in exploiting unique competences (e.g. a special technological knowledge) or market possibilities. *Reactive* motives indicate that the firm reacts to pressures or threats in its home market or in foreign markets and adjusts passively to them by changing its activities over time.

Table 9.3 Major motives for starting export

Pro-active motives	Reactive motives
● Profit and growth goals	● Competitive pressures
● Managerial urge	● Domestic market: small and saturated
● Technology competence/unique product	● Overproduction/excess capacity
● Foreign market opportunities/market information	● Unsolicited foreign orders
● Economies of scale	● Extended sales of seasonal products
● Tax benefits	● Proximity to international customers/psychological distance

Source: Albaum *et al*. (1994), p 31, with permission from Pearson Education, Inc., Upper Saddle River, NJ.

For internationalization to take place, someone or something within or outside the firm (so-called change agents) must initiate it and carry it through to implementation. Perceptive managements gain early awareness of developing opportunities in overseas markets. They make it their business to become knowledgeable about these markets, and maintain a sense of open-mindedness about where and when their companies should expand overseas.

Often, managers enter a firm having already had some global marketing experience in previous jobs and try to use this experience to further the business activities of their new firm. In developing their goals in the new job, managers frequently consider an entirely new set of options, one of which may be global marketing activities.

The role of the individual manager's network

Axelsson and Agndal (2000) show how the individual manager's network or relations from the past can function as enablers and driving forces for internationalization. Thus it becomes meaningful to distinguish between two network levels, the firm and the individual. While firm networks have received considerable attention in recent years, the role of individual networks has largely not been explored in international business research.

Axelsson and Agndal (2000) identify the following six categories of the individual's network that could be the basis for the driving forces of the firm's internationalization:

1. contact from past or present workplace
2. other professional contacts, friends from school, etc.
3. contacts from clubs (Rotary, golf, etc.)
4. family, extended family
5. personal friends, friends' friends
6. life history.

Once the firm has 'decided' (pro-active or passive) to internationalize, there are several routes that will now be explored.

Inward internationalization (importing)

Welch and Loustarinen (1993) claim that inward internationalization (importing) may precede and influence outward internationalization (international market entry and marketing activities) – see Figure 9.6.

A direct relationship exists between inward and outward internationalization in the way that effective inward activities can determine the success of outward activities, especially in the early stages of internationalization. The inward internationalization may be initiated by:

● the buyer: active international search of different foreign sources (buyer initiative or reverse marketing).
● the seller: initiation by the foreign supplier (traditional seller perspective).

When moving from inward to outward internationalization, the buyer's role (in country A) shifts to seller, both to domestic customers (in country A) and to foreign customers. Through interaction with the foreign supplier, the buyer (importer) gets

Figure 9.6 Inward/outward internationalization: a network example

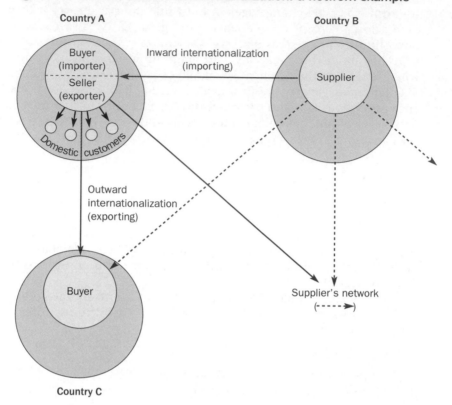

Source: Hollensen (2001), p. 37.

access to the network of the supplier, so that at some later time there may be an outward export to members of this network. In some cases, inward foreign licensing may be followed by outward technology sales.

The Uppsala model

The Scandinavian stages model of entry suggests a sequential pattern of entry into successive foreign markets, coupled with a progressive deepening of commitment to each market. The model in illustrated in Figure 9.7.

Figure 9.7 implies that commitment to additional markets as a rule will be made in small steps, both in the commitment to the market and in the countries or regions entered. There are, however, three exceptions. First, firms that have large resources can take larger internationalization steps as they are still relatively small in comparison with their resources. Second, when market conditions are stable and homogeneous, relevant market knowledge can be gained in ways other than experience. Third, when the firm has considerable experience from markets with similar conditions, it may be possible to generalize this experience to any specific market (Johanson and Vahlne, 1990).

The geographical factor in Figure 9.7 shows that firms enter new markets with successively greater psychic distance. Psychic distance is defined in terms of factors such as differences in language, culture and political systems, which disturb the

Figure 9.7 The Uppsala model: an incremental approach to internationalization

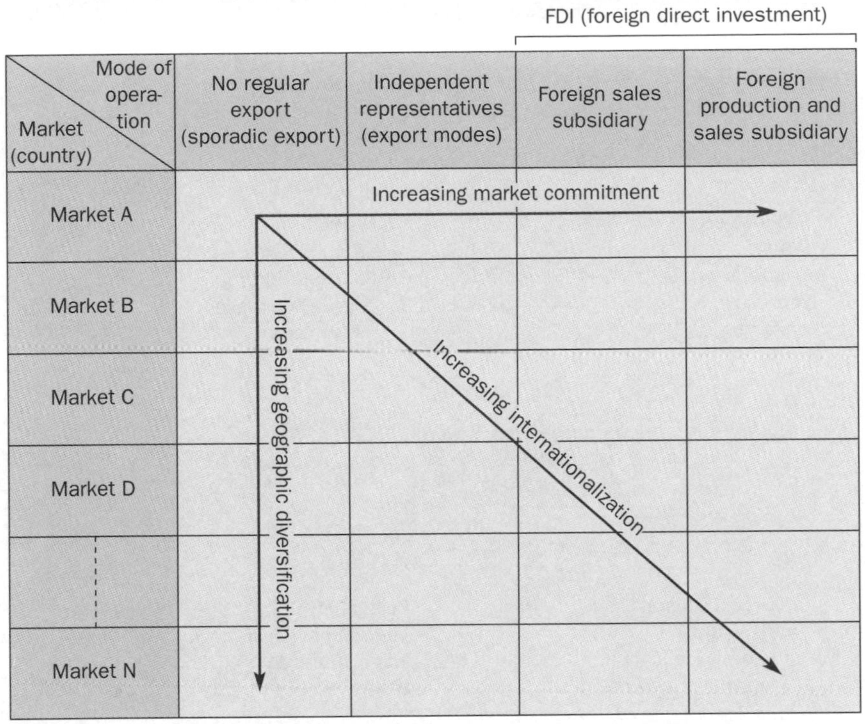

Source: adapted from Forsgren and Johanson, 1975, p. 16.

flow of information between the firm and the market. Thus firms start internationalization by going to those markets they can understand most easily. There they will see opportunities, and there the perceived market uncertainty is low.

The original stage model has been extended by Welch and Loustarinen (1988), who operate with six factors of internationalization (see Figure 9.8).

1. *sales objects (what?)*: goods, services, know-how and systems
2. *operational methods (how?)*: agents, subsidiaries, licensing, franchising, management contracts
3. *markets (where?)*: political/cultural/psychic/physical distance differences between markets
4. *organizational structure*: export department, international division
5. *finance*: availability of international finance sources to support the international activities
6. *personnel*: international skills, experience and training.

The transaction cost analysis (TCA) model

Transaction costs emerge when markets fail to operate under the requirements of perfect competition ('friction free'); the cost of operating in such markets (i.e. the transaction costs) would be zero, and there would be little or no incentive to impose any impediments to free market exchange. However, in the real world there

Figure 9.8 Factors of internationalization

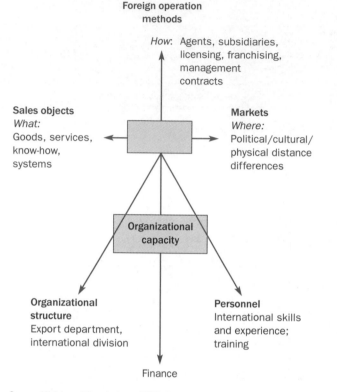

Source: Welsh and Loustarinen, 1988. Reproduced with permission from The Braybrooke Press Ltd.

is always some kind of 'friction' between buyer and seller, resulting in transaction costs (see Figure 9.9).

The transaction costs analysis (TCA) framework argues that cost minimization explains structural decisions. Firms internalize, that is, integrate vertically, to reduce transaction costs.

Transaction costs can be divided into different forms of costs related to the transaction relationship between buyer and seller. The underlying condition for the following description of the cost elements is this equation:

transaction costs = ex ante costs + ex post costs
$$= \text{(search costs + contracting costs)} + \text{(monitoring costs + enforcement costs)}$$

The network model

The basic assumption in the network approach is that the international firm cannot be analysed as an isolated actor, but has to be viewed in relation to other actors in the international environment. Thus, the individual firm is dependent on resources controlled by others. The relationships of a firm within a domestic network can be used as connections to other networks in other countries. In a situation with international customers and competitors, the less internationalized firm can be pulled out of the domestic market by its customers or complementary suppliers to the customers. Sometimes the initial step abroad can be rather large.

Figure 9.9 **The principles of the TCA model**

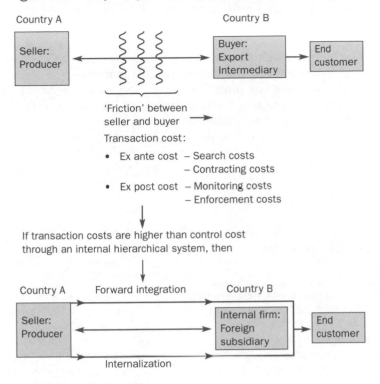

Source: Hollensen (2001), p. 53.

Born global

In recent years research has identified an increasing number of firms that certainly do not follow the traditional pattern in their internationalization process. In contrast, they aim at international markets or maybe even the global market right from the start (Oviatt and Mcdougall, 1994). Such firms have been named 'born globals'. Born globals are typically SMEs with fewer than 500 employees and annual sales under US$100 million. They rely on cutting-edge technology in the development of almost unique product or process innovations. But the most distinguishing feature of born global firms is that they tend to be managed by entrepreneurial visionaries, who view the world as a single, borderless marketplace from the time of the firm's founding. Born globals are small, technology-oriented companies that operate in international markets from the start. There is growing evidence of the emergence of born globals in numerous countries of the developed world. The born global phenomenon suggests a new challenge to traditional theories of internationalization (Rasmussen *et al.*, 2001).

The case of born globals may be similar to the situation of the 'late starter' or the 'international among others' (Johanson and Mattson, 1988). In the latter situation both the environment and the firm are highly internationalized. Johanson and Mattson (1988) point out that internationalization processes of firms will be much faster in internationalized market conditions, because the need for coordination and integration across borders is high. Since relevant partners or distributors will often be occupied in neighbouring markets, firms do not necessarily choose neighbouring markets to expand into. In the same vein their 'establishment chain' need not follow the traditional way because strategic alliances, joint ventures, etc. are much more prevalent; firms seek partners with supplementary skills and resources. In other words, the internationalization processes of firms will be much more individual and situation specific in internationalized markets.

It seems obvious that the phenomenon born global must be about how fast a company appears on the international markets. Therefore, it is relevant to deal with the speed of the internationalization process.

Various factors can accelerate the internationalization process and its speed, while others slow down the process in SMEs (Table 9.4). The more distinct the accelerating factors of the SMEs, the more they resemble a born global. Case study 9.2 is about two firms in the computer games industry which have two different degrees of born global.

Table 9.4 Factors for SMEs which accelerate and decelerate the internationalization process

Accelerating factors	Decelerating factors
1. SMEs are flexible and can adapt to changed market conditions. It is easier to develop new products and adjust the organization in a SME than in a large company.	1. It is difficult for SMEs to obtain economies of scale when making the product or service – and consequently the SME can only compete internationally on price with difficulty.
2. SMEs can make quick decisions. They can move rapidly from one product or market to another.	2. It is difficult for the SME to obtain the relevant competence (human resources) to operate internationally. It is more attractive/safe to work for a large company.
3. Technologically SMEs are allowed to work with a small part of the value chain (or a small part of the product range) often so small that large companies are not interested.	3. It is harder for the SME to get relevant information about international markets – and harder to assess the amount of information.
4. SMEs aim at operating in a very small niche (often worldwide) and in this way they can develop a very specific competence.	4. It may be more difficult for the SME to obtain credit and get access to the necessary capital.

The Internet revolution offers new opportunities for young SMEs to establish a global sales platform by developing e-commerce websites. Today many new and small firms are born globals in the way that they start up on the Internet and sell to a global audience via a centralized e-commerce website. However, after some time many of these firms realize they cannot expand global sales to the next level without having some localized e-commerce websites.

9.3 Phase 2: Deciding which markets to enter

After considering the initial phase of internationalization (Section 9.2), this section follows the process of selecting the right international market. In this stage environmental forces (economic, political/legal and socio-cultural forces) are used as inputs to the selection process of the target markets for developing the international marketing mix.

This chapter will not go into details about the international environmental factors. Instead, we will explore the screening process leading to the selection of a target market.

An illustration of the whole international market segmentation/screening process (IMS) is shown in Figure 9.10.

According to Figure 9.10, the number of markets is reduced by 'coarse', macro-oriented screening methods based on criteria such as:

- restrictions in the export of goods from one country to another. Papadopoulos *et al.*, (2002) include 'trade barriers' as a very important input variable in their model explaining 'international market selection' (IMS)
- **gross national product (GNP)** per capita
- cars owned per 1000 of the population
- government spending as a percentage of GNP
- population per hospital bed.

When screening countries it is particularly important to assess the political risk of entering a country. Over recent years, marketers have developed various indices to help assess the risk factors in the evaluation of the potential market opportunities. One of these indices is the business environment risk index (BERI). BERI measures the general quality of a country's business climate (see Hollensen, 2001), pp. 195–6 for a further discussion of the BERI model).

The model in Figure 9.10 begins by regarding the world market as the potential market for a firm's product. However, if the firm only regards western Europe as a possible market the firm may start the screening process at this lower level. The closer we move in the screening process (Figure 9.10), the greater the use of primary data (personal interviews, field research, etc.), as well as screening from internal criteria. Furthermore, the firm may discover a *high **market potential*** in some geographic segments. However, this is not the same as a *high sales potential* for the firm's product. There may be some restrictions (e.g. trade barriers) on the exporting of products to a particular country. Also the management of the company may have a certain policy only to select markets which are culturally similar to the home market. This may exclude distant countries from being selected as target markets, though they may have a high market potential. Furthermore, to be able to transform a high market potential into a high sales potential, there must be a harmony between the firm's competences (internal criteria) and the value-chain functions that customers rate as important to them. Only in this situation will a customer regard the firm as a possible supplier, equal to other possible suppliers. This segmentation selection process (matching segment attractiveness with a firm's resources and competences) is similar to the one proposed by Freytag and Clarke (2001), which is described in Section 8.3.

In general, Figure 9.10 is based on pro-active and systematic decision making by the firm. This is not always a realistic condition, especially not in SMEs, where a pragmatic approach is required. Often, firms are not able to segment from their own criteria but must expect to be evaluated and chosen (as sub-suppliers) by much larger firms. The pragmatic approach to IMS can also give rise to the firm choosing customers and markets with a background similar to the managers' own personal network and cultural background.

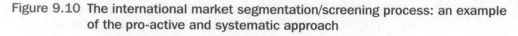

Figure 9.10 The international market segmentation/screening process: an example of the pro-active and systematic approach

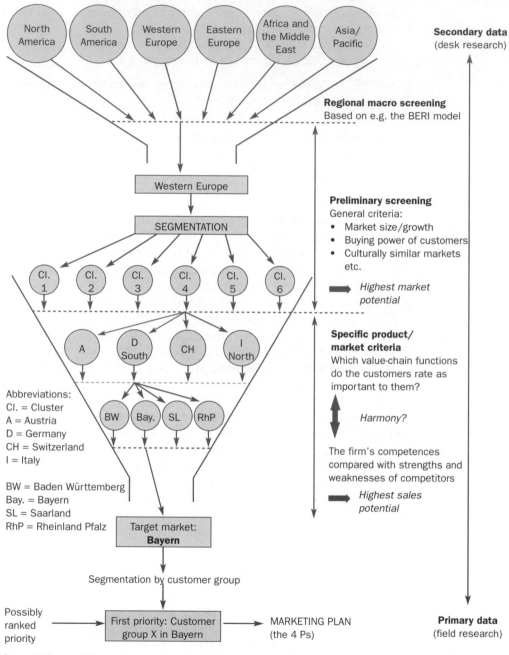

Source: Hollensen (2001), p. 202.

A further screening variable that could be built into the selction of the target market is the learning potential. There are two drivers of the learning potential of any market (Gupta and Govindarajan, 2000). The first is the presence of sophisticated and demanding customers for the particular product or service. Such customers force a company to meet very tough standards for product and service quality, cost, cycle time, and a host of other attributes; accelerate its learning regarding tomorrow's customer needs; and force it to innovate constantly and continuously. France and Italy are leading-edge customer markets for the high fashion clothing industry – a fact of considerable importance to a company such as Du Pont, the manufacturer of Lycra and other textile fibres.

The second driver of a market's learning potential is the pace at which relevant technologies are evolving there. This technology evolution can emerge from one or more of several sources: leading-edge customers, innovative competitors, universities and other local research centres, and firms in related industries. Therefore, the strategic importance of a market is a joint function of both market or sales potential and learning potential.

When the firm (from the screening model in Figure 9.10) has chosen the target market, the choice of *market expansion strategy* is the next key decision in the international marketing strategy.

The choice of a market expansion strategy is a key decision in international marketing. First, different patterns are likely to cause the development of different competitive conditions in different markets, over time. For example, a fast rate of growth into new markets that have short product life cycles can create entry barriers for competitors and give rise to higher profitability. On the other hand, a purposeful selection of relatively few markets for more intensive development can create higher market shares, implying stronger competitive positions.

In designing their strategy, firms have to answer two underlying questions:

- will they enter markets incrementally (the waterfall approach) or simultaneously (the shower approach)? (see Figure 9.11)

- will entry be concentrated or diversified across international markets?

Figure 9.11 The incremental strategy (waterfall approach) and simultaneous strategy (the shower approach in a LSE with a global presence): sales in different types of country

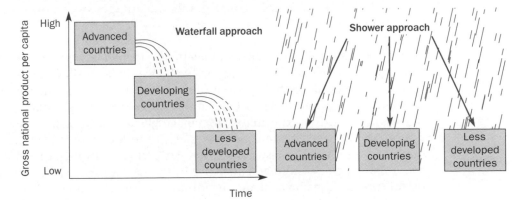

Source: reprinted from *Global Marketing Management* by Keegan, Warren J., © 1995, adapted by permission of Pearson Education, Inc., Upper Saddle River, NJ.

The use of waterfall or shower approach (spread of global expansion)

Entry on an incremental basis (waterfall approach), especially into small markets, may be preferred where a firm lacks experience in foreign markets and wishes to edge gradually into international operations. Information about, and familiarity with, operating in foreign markets are thus acquired step by step. This strategy may be preferable if a company is entering international markets late and faces entrenched local competition. Equally, if a firm is small and has limited resources, or is highly risk averse, it may prefer to enter a single or a limited number of markets and gradually expand in a series of incremental moves rather than making a major commitment to international expansion immediately.

Some companies prefer a rapid entry into world markets (shower approach) in order to seize an emerging opportunity or forestall competition. Rapid entry facilitates early market penetration across a number of markets and enables the firm to build up experience rapidly. It also enables a firm to achieve economies of scale in production and marketing by integrating and consolidating operations across these markets. This may be especially desirable if the product or service involved is innovative or represents a significant technological advance, in order to forestall pre-emption or limitation.

In summary, an accelerated speed of global expansion (shower approach) is more appropriate under the following conditions (Gupta and Govindarajan, 2000).

It is easy for competitors to replicate your recipe for success

This possibility is obvious for fast food and retailing companies where it is easy for competitors to take a proven concept from one market and replicate it in another unoccupied market with a relatively small investment. This phenomenon is also observable in other, very different types of industries as well, such as personal computers and software. The rapid globalization of companies like Compaq, Dell, and Microsoft reflects their determination to prevent replication and/or pirating of their product concepts in markets all around the world.

Scale economies are extremely important

Very high economies of scale give the early and rapid globalizer massive first-to-market advantages and handicap the slower ones for long period of time. This is precisely why rapid globalizers in the tyre industry, such as Goodyear, Michelin, and Bridgestone, now hold considerable advantages over slower ones, such as Pirelli and Continental.

Management's capacity to manage (or learn how to manage) global operations is high

Consider experienced global players like Coca-Cola, Unilever, and ABB. Should such companies successfully introduce a new product line in one country, it would be relatively easy and logical to globalize it rapidly to all potential markets around the world. Aside from the ability to manage global operations, the speed of globalization also depends on the company's ability to leverage its experience from one market to another. The faster the speed with which a firm can recycle its learning about market entry and market defence from one country to another, the lower the risk of spreading managerial and organizational capacity too thinly.

| Exhibit 9.3 | Benetton is penetrating the Iranian market |

In March 2000 fashion giant Benetton, one of Italy's most familiar brand names, was in talks that could spread the company's bold colours and attention grabbing advertising to Iran. The store in Tehran would not be the company's first in the Middle East: it already had operations in Egypt and Israel. But it would be a controversial move, given Iran's relationship with the West for the last 20 years.

Not that controversy has changed the company's plans in the past. The company's advertising campaigns have attracted headlines around the world for their controversial subject matter. And political correctness has never influenced Benetton's choice of store locations. The company, which does business in 120 countries, also operates stores in Cuba. Iran obviously represents a limited market at best, but the Iranian market entry could be a political statement that would fit in well with the company's image.

Some local media speculated that Benetton's market entry might not be aimed at opening stores but instead at producing clothes in Iran. But the company's spokesman said that theory was groundless, because Iran's textile industry was not up to date. He said technology transfer was also unlikely, since it was unclear how Benetton would benefit.

Source: adapted from Adage Global (2000b).

Concentrated or diversified approach

The question of concentrating or diversifying at the country level can be combined with concentration or diversification at the customer (segment) level. The resulting matrix (Figure 9.12) illustrates the four possible strategies, as follows:

- Cell 1: few customer groups/segments in few countries
- Cell 2: many customer groups/segments in few countries
- Cell 3: few customer groups/segments in many countries
- Cell 4: many customer groups/segments in many countries.

Figure 9.12 The market expansion matrix

		Market/customer target group	
		Concentration	Diversification
Country	Concentration	1	2
	Diversification	3	4

Source: reprinted with permission from *Journal of Marketing*, published by the American Marketing Association, I. Ayal and J. Zif (1979), vol. 43, Spring, pp. 84–94.

9.4 Phase 3: Deciding how to enter foreign markets (market entry strategies)

Once the firm has chosen target markets abroad the question arises as to the best way to enter those markets. An international market entry mode is an institutional arrangement necessary for the entry of a company's products, technology and human capital into a foreign country or market. Figure 9.13 shows the classical distribution systems in a national consumer market.

The chosen market entry mode can be regarded as the first decision level in the vertical chain that will provide marketing and distribution to the next actors in the vertical chain. In Chapter 13 we well take a closer look at the distribution systems at the national level.

Some firms have discovered that an ill-judged market entry in the initial stages of a firm's internationalization can threaten the firm's future market entry and expansion activities. It is common for the initial method of entry that is chosen to become the way that further markets are entered and new products are sold through the same established channels. If the initial entry mode was problematic this mode be carried on to further market entries. The inertia in changing entry modes delays the transition to a new entry mode. The reluctance of firms to change entry modes once they are in place, and the difficulty involved in so doing, makes the mode of entry decision a key strategic issue for firms operating in today's rapidly internationalizing marketplace.

For most SMEs, the market entry represents a critical first step, but for established companies the problem is not how to enter new emerging markets, but how to exploit opportunities more effectively within the context of their existing network of international operations.

Figure 9.13 Examples of different market entry modes

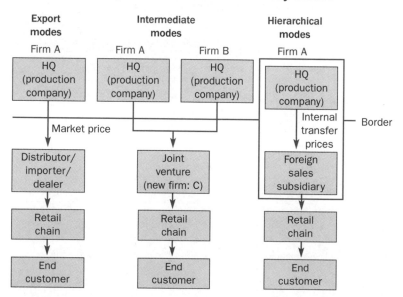

Source: Hollensen (2001), p. 230.

There is, however, no ideal market entry strategy, and different market entry methods might be adopted by different firms entering the same market and/or by the same firm in different markets.

As shown in Figure 9.13, three broad groupings emerge when one looks at the assortment of entry modes available to the firm when entering international markets. There are different degrees of control, risk and flexibility associated with each of these different market entry modes. For example, the use of hierarchical modes (investment modes) gives the firm ownership and thereby high control, but committing high resources to foreign markets also represents a higher potential risk. At the same time, high resource commitment creates exit barriers, which diminish the firm's ability to change the chosen entry mode in a quick and easy way. So the entry mode decision involves trade-offs, as the firm cannot have both high control and high flexibility.

Figure 9.13 also shows three examples representing the main types of market entry mode. By using hierarchical modes, transactions between independent parties are substituted by intra-firm transactions, and market prices are substituted by internal transfer prices.

Many factors should be considered when deciding on the appropriate market entry mode. Hollensen (2001) discusses these different factors and how they influence the entry mode decision. For example, the intermediate or alliance-based modes (e.g. joint ventures) are often appropriate under the following conditions (Hyder and Ghauri, 2000; Gupta and Govindarajan, 2000).

Sociocultural distance between home country and host country is high

The more dissimilar and unfamiliar the target market, the greater the need for the firm to rely on a local partner to provide know-how and networks. Conceivably, the firm could obtain the requisite local knowledge and competences through acquisition. However, in highly dissimilar and unfamiliar markets, its ability to manage an acquired subsidiary is often very limited. Ford's decision to enter the Indian market through the joint venture (JV) mode rested partly on the company's need to rely on an experienced and respected local partner, Mahindra & Mahindra.

The risk of asymmetric learning by the partner is (or can be kept) low

In a typical JV, two partners pool different but complementary know-how into an alliance. Ongoing interaction between their core operations and the alliance gives each an opportunity to learn from the other and appropriate the other's complementary know-how. In effect, this dynamic implies that the alliance often is not just a cooperative relationship, but also a learning race. If Firm A has the ability to learn at a faster rate than Firm B, the outcome is likely to be asymmetric learning in favour of Firm A. Thus, over time, Firm A may seek to dissolve the alliance in favour of doing it alone in competition with a still-disadvantaged Firm B.

Government regulations require local equity participation

Historically, many countries with formidable market potentials, such as China and Brazil, have successfully imposed the JV option on foreign entrants, even when all other considerations might have favoured the choice of complete ownership.

As many SMEs are involved with subcontracting and developing relationships we will now look at subcontractors' possibilities for internationalizing their business.

Developing relationships in international subcontracting

A subcontractor can be defined as a person or a firm that agrees to provide semi-finished products or services needed by another party (main contractor) to perform another contract to which the subcontractor is not a party. According to this definition, the characteristics of subcontractors that distinguish them from other SMEs are as follows.

- Subcontractors' products are usually part of the end product, not the complete end product itself.

- Subcontractors do not have direct contact with the end customers, because the main contractor is usually responsible to the customer.

Many changes are taking place in the utilization of the purchasing function:

- Reduction in the number of subcontractors.

- Shorter product life cycles, which increase the pressure to reduce the time to market (just-in-time).

- Upgraded demands on subcontractors (zero deficits). In addition, firms are demanding that their suppliers become certified under quality standards. Those that do not comply may be removed from the supplier list.

- Purchasing no longer just serves the purpose of getting lower prices. The traditional arm's-length relationships are increasingly being replaced by long-term partnerships with mutual trust, interdependence and mutual benefits.

Implementing a **reverse marketing** strategy starts with fundamental market research and with an evaluation of reverse marketing options (i.e. possible suppliers). Before choosing suppliers the firm may include both present and potential suppliers in the analysis as well as current and desired activities.

Based on this analysis the firm may select a number of suitable partners as suppliers and rank them in order of preference.

The position of subcontractors in the vertical production chain is shown in Figure 9.14.

In the original equipment manufacturer (**OEM**) contract, the contractor is called the OEM or 'sourcer', whereas the parts suppliers are regarded as 'manufacturers' of OEM products (subcontractors or sub-suppliers). Typically the OEM contracts are different from other buyer-supplier relationships in the way that the OEMs (contractors) often have much stronger bargaining power than the subcontractors. However, in a partner-based buyer-supplier relationship, the power balance will be more equal. There are cases where a subcontractor improved its bargaining and went on to become a major force in the market (Cho and Chu, 1994).

The internationalization process has been described as a learning process by the Uppsala school. Generally speaking, it is something that can be described as a gradual internationalization. According to this view, the international development of the firm is accompanied by an accumulation of knowledge in the hands of management and by growing capabilities and propensities to manage international affairs. The main consequence of this way of thinking is that firms tend to increase their commitment toward foreign markets as their experience grows. The number of adherents to this theory has grown, but there has also been much criticism of it.

Figure 9.14 Possible internationalization of system suppliers

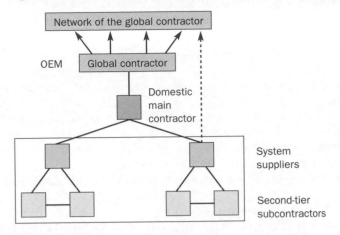

Source: Hollensen (2001), p. 323.

The main problem with the Uppsala model is that it seems to suggest the presence of a deterministic and mechanistic path that firms implementing their internationalization strategy must follow. Sometimes it happens that firms leap-frog one or more stages in the establishment chain; at other times firms stop their internationalization altogether (Welch and Loustarinen, 1988).

There is a central difference with regard to internationalization among contractors and subcontractors. The internationalization of subcontractors is closely related to their customers. The concept of a subcontractor indicates that the strategies of such a firm, including its internationalization strategy, cannot be seen in isolation from the strategies of its partner, the contractor. Therefore, the internationalization of a subcontractor may show irregular paths, such as leap-frogging.

In collaboration with other specialized subcontractors, system suppliers may be involved in international system supplies by taking over the management of whole supplies of subsystems (Figure 9.14).

Systems supplies result in the development of a new layer of subcontractors (second-tier subcontractor). Through the interaction between a system supplier and a domestic main contractor, the system supplier can get access to the network of a global contractor (the dotted line in Figure 9.14) because of the network/contract between the contractor and the global contractor. For example, a Japanese car seat supplier supplies the Japanese Toyota factory (domestic main contractor). This can eventually give the supplier access to other Toyota factories around the world (global contractors) and their global networks.

In many cases the collaboration between the subcontractors will be characterized by exchange of tacit, not easily transferable knowledge. The reason for this is that the complete subsystem is frequently based on several fields of competence, which have to be coordinated by use of **tacit knowledge** and communications.

| Exhibit 9.4 | **US coffee bars struggle to penetrate the Italian market** |

In Italy, neighbourhood coffee bars are ubiquitous, but so far US coffee giants like Starbucks and Barnies have yet to get a foothold in Italy.

It's not because of a lack of coffee drinkers. A coffee roasters' association survey showed that Italians drink more coffee per capita than any other country in the world – about 900 cups per year for every man, woman and child, almost three times the per capita consumption in the USA.

Indeed, espresso is the leading style of coffee in Italy; with the country's 110,000 coffee bars serving 75 million cups every day, accounting for three-quarters of the nation's total coffee consumption. Most Italians either drink espresso coffee with a small drop of milk in it or they prefer a ristretto, a very small and dense jolt of caffeine.

Meanwhile, coffee drinks that are popular in the USA and elsewhere – such as cappuccino or American-style coffee – are hardly consumed at all in Italy, where purists consider them watered-down versions of the real thing.

When Italians step into a (coffee) bar, they do not sit down and in a minute they are gone again. Many do it four or five times a day; they do not have time to sit down with a big mug of coffee.

Still, there may be hope for the US coffee giants: the coffee roasters' association said nearly two-thirds of the respondents in its survey said they would pay extra for high-quality coffee. The trick, an association spokesman said, is convincing Italians that a big glass of US-style coffee represents a high-quality drink.

Source: adapted from Adage Global (2001).

9.5 Phases 4 and 5: Design and implementation of the international marketing mix

Since the beginning of the 1980s, the term 'globalization' has increasingly become a matter of debate. Levitt's contribution (Levitt, 1983) provoked much controversy concerning the most appropriate way for companies to become international. Levitt's support of the globalization strategy received both support and criticism. Essentially, the two sides of this debate represented local marketing versus global marketing and focused on the central question of whether a standardized, global marketing approach or a country-specific differentiated marketing approach has the most merits.

There are different forces in the international environment that may favour either 'increasing globalization' or 'increasing adaptation' of a firm. Which force will win not only depends on the environmental forces but also on the specific international marketing strategy that the firm might favour.

Hence, a fundamental decision that managers have to make regarding their global marketing strategy is the degree to which they should standardize or adapt their global marketing mix. The following three factors provide vast opportunities for marketing standardization.

Globalization of markets

Customers are increasingly operating worldwide and are characterized by an intensively coordinated and centralized purchasing process. As a countermeasure,

| Exhibit 9.5 | The UK-based B&Q penetrates the Chinese home improvements market |

Home improvements retailer B&Q has opened its biggest store yet, in China (Shanghai), where it hopes to increase its outlets from 4 – including the new store – to 58 by 2005.

Shanghai has experienced a building boom as the city government has pulled down city centre slums and built extensive new suburbs. A flat in these new districts needs partition walls, doors and floors as well as kitchen equipment and bathrooms, as they are handed over as bare shells.

Chinese customers' lifestyles and DIY needs means that in many ways B&Q has to operate quite a different business model from stores in the UK. The new Shanghai store will offer some ranges and products seen in UK stores, but no wallpaper. The concept of gardening does not really exist as space is so limited. B&Q will offer customers soft furnishings, but the garden centre, a major part of the UK format, will play a small role.

Source: BBC (2001).

manufacturers establish a global key account management in order to avoid individual country subsidiaries being played off against each other in separate negotiations with, for example, global retailers.

Globalization of industries

Many firms can no longer depend on home markets for sufficient scale economies and experience curve effects. Many industries, such as computers, pharmaceuticals and automobiles, have high R&D costs which can be recouped only via worldwide high-volume sales.

Globalization of competition

As a consequence of the worldwide homogenization of demand, the different markets are interrelated. Therefore the firms can plan their activities worldwide and attempt to establish a superior profile with regard to other global competitors. Hence, country subsidiaries no longer operate as profit centres, but are viewed as parts of a global portfolio.

The standardized marketing concept can be characterized by two features. The standardization of marketing processes is mainly concerned with a standardized decision-making process for cross-country marketing planning. By standardizing the launch of new products, controlling activities, etc., rationalization of the general marketing process is sought.

The standardization of marketing programmes and the marketing mix is concerned with the extent to which individual elements of the 4Ps can be unified into a common approach for different national markets.

These two characteristics of standardization are often interrelated: for many strategic business units, process-oriented standardization is the precondition for the implementation of standardized marketing programmes.

Many authors discuss standardization and adaptation as two distinct options. The commercial reality, however, is that few marketing mixes are totally standardized or adapted. Instead it is more relevant to discuss degrees of standardization.

The results indicate that there are different ways of realizing a **standardized concept** within the marketing mix. In the case of products it is possible to standardize the package at least on an average level. Difficulties arise as far as the pricing policy is concerned. For example, it is possible to reach a standardized price position only for disposable nappies. So Procter & Gamble selects only those markets that possess the necessary purchasing power to pay a price within the target price range. In the case of alcoholic drinks, it is nearly impossible to gain a standardized price positioning due to legal constraints. In Denmark, for example, consumers have to pay twice as much for the same Johnny Walker whisky as in Germany because of tax regulations. However, in many cases it is possible to use one brand name worldwide. There are negative effects connected with particular names in a few cases; you have to change brand names to avoid these unintentional images.

Negotiation in foreign cultures (reduction of psychic distances)

From, for example, Hofstede's (1980) work we see that there are differences (gaps) between national cultures. If we go to the individual level we talk about the psychic distance which can also be influenced by the differences in organizational culture between the parties involved. Conway and Swift (2000) conclude that the higher the level of psychic distance (between a buyer and a seller from two different cultures), the greater the time and effort required to develop successful long-lasting business relationships.

In negotiations, the most fundamental gap influencing the interaction between buyer and seller is the difference between their respective cultural backgrounds. The end of Section 6.2 further discussed how these gaps between sellers and buyers can be reduced. This cultural distance can be expressed in terms of differences in communication and negotiation, the concepts of time, space or work patterns, and the nature of social rituals and norms.

9.6 Summary

The global integration/market responsiveness grid shows the advantage of integrating both factors in the global strategy. Marketing programmes must adapt to the needs and preferences of different customers that have different levels of purchasing power as well as different languages and cultures. But in order to move towards a global learning organization it is important to hold on to similarities across borders and gain some global synergy.

The motives for internationalization are differentiated into pro-active and reactive motives. Pro-active motives represent internal stimuli to attempt strategy change, based on the firm's interest in exploiting unique competences or market possibilities. Reactive motives indicate that the firm is reacting to pressures or threats in its home market or in foreign markets and adjusting passively to them.

For internationalization to take place, someone or something (triggers) inside or outside the firm must initiate it and implement it. The individual manager is very important in driving the internationalization process forward.

Three internationalization models have been presented.

Uppsala model

This is a gradual learning-by-doing process. Additional market commitments should be made in small incremental steps:

- choose new geographic markets with small psychic distances from existing markets
- choose an entry mode with few marginal risks.

Transaction costs analysis model

Where there are high transaction costs (caused by friction between buyer and seller, firms should internalize activities (i.e. implement the global marketing strategy in wholly owned subsidiaries).

Network model

The relationships of a firm in a domestic network can be used as bridges to other networks in other countries. Such direct or indirect bridges to different country networks can be important in the initial steps abroad and in the subsequent entry into new markets.

Seen from the perspective of the international marketer, market entry modes can be classified into three groups:

- export modes: low control, low risk, high flexibility
- intermediate modes (contractual modes): shared control and risk, split ownership
- hierarchical modes (investment modes): high control, high risk, low flexibility.

It cannot be stated categorically which mode is the best. There are many internal and external conditions which affect this choice and it should be emphasized that a manufacturer wanting to engage in global marketing may use more than one of these methods at the same time. There may be different product lines, each requiring a different entry mode.

Standardization and adaptation of the international marketing strategy are presented as two distinct options. However, in reality a few international marketing strategies are totally standardized or adapted. Instead it is more relevant to discuss degrees of standardization or adaptation. At the start of negotiations between two partners from different cultures, there is a psychic distance between them. To reduce this psychic (cultural) distance, cross-cultural training of negotiators is required.

Case study 9.2 ITE (Hugo) and IO Interactive (Hitman)

Two 'born globals' in the computer games industry

The global computer games industry

In 2000 computer games had an annual turnover of €13 billion in the USA and Europe. Annual increases in this market are about 20%, and competition with the film industry is still keener.

According to a study by Informa Media Group PLC – referred in Maio (2001) (see Table 9.5) – the world market for entertainment games is expected to rise more than 70% (to US$85 billion) over the period 2001 to 2006.

The total market for hardware will continue to grow but its share of the total world market is expected to fall from 24% to 21%.

According to the study (Maio, 2001) the biggest growth is expected to come from games played via mobile phones. The mobile phone games market was expected to reach US$800 million in 2001, and is expected to rise to US$11 billion by 2006. The interactive television games market is expected to hit US$62 billion in sales in 2006, with online games reaching US$5.7 billion.

Games revenue from the Internet, interactive TV and mobile phones accounted for 3% of the industry total in 2001. This proportion is set to increase to 27% by 2006. However, console games will continue to be the dominant platform, increasing by 73% from US$18.8 billion to US$32.6 billion during that period.

Revenues in the games industry have overtaken the film industry, and it is the most widespread form of entertainment. Via the Internet computer games have become enormously popular. The online game Everquest has 300,000 active players from all over the world.

About 60% of all Americans, 145 million people, are playing computer games. 35% of Americans regard computer games as the most entertaining pastime – twice as many as film, TV, and books. In five years the average American is expected to spend more time on computer games than on books and magazines. The active gamers spend on average ten hours

Table 9.5 World market for entertainment games (hardware and software) by category

	2001		2006 (projected)	
	US$ billion	%	US$ billion	%
Hardware				
Console hardware (primarily Nintendo's GameCube, Playstation 2 and Microsoft's X-Box)	9.2	18	14.3	17
Handheld (Gameboy etc.)	2.7	6	3.4	4
Software				
Console software	9.6	19	18.3	21
PCs (including Arcades)	21.0	42	19.0	22
Handheld (Gameboy)	2.9	6	3.8	4
Rental (e.g. from video rental stores)	3.1	6	4.6	5
Online (via Internet)	0.6	1	5.7	7
Interactive TV (via cable)	0.1	0	6.2	7
Mobile phone	0.8	2	11.0	13
Total	50.0	100	86.3	100

Source: adapted from Maio (2001).

Case study 9.2 continued

per week, on either PC games or console games (Tarr, 2001).

The big switch from film to games has many consequences. By 1992 Nintendo had a bigger profit than all US film companies and the three biggest TV networks combined. The latest James Bond film, Golden Eye, was a solid film success, but when Nintendo launched the Golden Eye game, turnover doubled. Recently, there has been an attempt to transfer computer games to movies. Tomb Raider: Lara Croft had its first performance in the USA in June 2001. Preliminary figures show that the movie has been a commercial success in spite of the fact that production costs were more than US$100 million (Seiler and Snider, 2001).

A company like Electronic Arts (EA), the world's largest producer of games software, has a market value of about €8 billion and employs 3800 people, including 1800 games developers in 13 locations in five countries. In three years its turnover has doubled to €1.65 billion. The company systematically works at buying rights to develop games based on books, films, and sport. Recently the company bought the games rights to the Harry Potter books.

Today, EA has the sole games rights to icons like James Bond, Tiger Woods, and FIFA. EA has recently put online games into an independent business. The goal is to establish a strong position in the rapidly growing online market. In March 2000, EA entered into an agreement with America Online (AOL) for the sole rights to AOL's games channel. The agreement gives EA access to AOL's 60 million online customers (Andersen and Stokholm, 2000).

In addition to computer games the console market is growing. It is expected to be dominated by the following three products: Nintendo's Gamecube, Sony's Playstation 2, and Microsoft's X-Box. A pessimistic estimate is 150–200 million private games consoles worldwide by 2005.

Interactive Television Entertainment (ITE)

Ivan Sølvason 'invented' the screen charmer Hugo in 1990 and made him famous in Denmark in one evening. A few years later

nobody in Denmark would have anything to do with him, and Sølvason was on the verge of bankruptcy. Today Hugo is more popular than ever. He has appeared in 37 countries on four continents. In 2001 turnover was expected to be about US$10 million of which 90% was expected to come from exports. There were about 90 employees (in mid-2001).

In 1987, Ivan Sølvason, a probationary clerk in his mid-twenties, was editor of the magazine *Computer*. In the evening he was busy programming games for the home computers of that time, the Amiga and Commodore 64. The first games were failures.

However, the following year, Ivan Sølvason was back – this time with a new company and a moderate order from Nordisk Film. The company wanted a computer game for Danish TV2's new entertainment programme. Sølvason's proposition was the ice bear Oswald who could be directed by the viewers from ice floe to ice floe with push-button phones. Before long the phrase 'Isn't that just too bad! We'll have another try' was a permanent part of Danish classrooms, offices, and homes. A positive scourge was born. At the same time TV2 could boast of being the first station in the world to let the viewers direct their own computer game. This was echoed in the media, but money was still scarce. Sølvason sold the first Oswald to Nordisk Film for US$12,000, while his successor, Super Oswald, was sold for only US$10,000.

However, Nordisk Film soon needed a new game concept. Oswald had clearly shown that by putting colloquial dialogue into the computer game the programme could cause much comment. The idea of letting viewers participate in the game from their living rooms was also to be continued, but otherwise Sølvason's team was given a free rein.

From the moment Hugo croaked his first 'Hello... anybody there?' on TV2 in the autumn of 1990 he was a big sales hit. ITE attacked every attempt to take advantage of Hugo's name and reputation. This resulted in more than 170 lawsuits against Danish producers and advertisers. The compensation only covered the lawyer's fees, but for the company it was important that

▶

Case study 9.2 continued

Hugo maintained his identity as a figure with whom a family with young children could feel confident. Having looked at the turnover that Hugo's name provided one can understand that his integrity had to be protected. The chocolate factory, Cloetta, thus increased its share of the Danish confectionery market from 4 to 35% during the 18 months the factory's Hugo campaign lasted. The Danes managed to eat more than 60 tonnes of Hugo sweets in this period.

When the Danish magazine offered the Hugo game to its readers in a Christmas campaign, sales reached 30,000. Thus Hugo became the best selling computer game in Denmark, and soon his face was to found everywhere. There was a flood of money at ITE. The basement in Copenhagen was replaced by a more presentable home. The Danish company thought it had a global product – Hugo was to be presented to the world market. While the Hugo fever was still raging in Denmark, the ITE staff went to the film festival in Cannes to tell foreign TV bosses about the Danish screen charmer – however, without success.

At the same time Nordisk Film expressed a wish for new figures in the Hugo game. They obtained new figures: Hugo's wife, Hugoline, his three little troll children, the witch Afskylia, and several new paths were added to the game. Development costs were enormous, and in spite of **royalties** from all the Hugo products, ITE was losing money. At the beginning of 1992, ITE was on the verge of bankruptcy. The third visit to Cannes in the spring of 1993 was make or break for the company. ITE did, however, succeed in persuading a large Spanish channel to test the concept. After some exciting months with impatient creditors, orders from France, Turkey and Finland kept the company afloat.

In 1993, ITE was really on the road to success on the international market. ITE had each TV station develop its own concept with Hugo in the centre. In this way ITE could ensure that the new programmes were adapted to the individual markets with high ratings from the beginning. This success was subsequently used to market Hugo to new stations.

Since then there has been no let-up. Interactive TV shows followed in rapid succes-sion, among others the football game Crazy Cartoon Soccer, which TV2 had used in its sports transmissions.

In Sweden, Hugo is the most popular children's programme ever. And in Brazil Hugo received 1.8 million viewer calls in one evening many times. But Hugo is a linguistic genius: he speaks about 20 languages fluently.

The computer games

In 1994 Hugo moved from TVs to PCs, which were starting to become common in Danish homes. The digital Hugo is a success. In a continuation of the TV success, the three-dimensional Hugo lives his own game life. He is on CD-ROM, DVD/video, Gameboy and Playstation.

ITE uses different distributors around the world. In Nordic countries the company used Electronic Arts (EA) from September 2000, after its distributor until then, Egmont Interactive, decided to concentrate solely on Sony Playstation and its games. (See also Figure 9.15.)

More than 5 million Hugo games have been sold, and already 50,000 orders have been placed in advance for the 3D animation for the new Playstation version. At the same time Hugo is available on the Internet with eight new games. Furthermore, he will get his own book club in cooperation with Carlsens Forlag. A CD-ROM comes with the book.

ITE also has a good income from other products, among others Thout & Neck, which sells well in southern America, and the football game Crazy Cartoon Soccer.

Even though ITE has delivered 65 shows to a local American network, the company has had difficulties in establishing itself in the USA.

Hugo is about to become an international film star. The costs for the 3D animated movie, *Hugo and the Diamond Moon*, will amount to €13.33 million. The movie will have its first performance at the end of 2002.

ITE is considering opening a giant Hugo amusement park in Denmark. Ivan Sølvason is still the senior manager and owner of ITE ApS and he has kept all rights relating to Hugo. The expansion plans for the Hugo concept are, however, restrained by the fact that ITE needs

Case study 9.2 continued

further capital for developing new product concepts. This is why ITE is looking for financial partners.

IO Interactive

IO Interactive was founded in 1998, and in 1999 the company was incorporated in the Egmont group (Nordisk Film/Egmont owns 47% of the shares in IO Interactive). The new manager of IO Interactive, Janos Flösser, was headhunted from Nordisk Film. At once he began providing financial capital for developing the first game (Hitman). Eidos was contacted – together with EA, it is one of the world's largest distributors and producers of games software and behind several games hits. Eidos immediately became interested in the Hitman concept. IO Interactive borrowed €2.27 million from Eidos in order to develop Hitman. In this way IO Interactive acted as sub-supplier to Eidos, which took care of financing and distribution. IO Interactive had, however, gained experience in the global market, because Eidos distributed the game and left the player contact to IO Interactive.

Hitman was originally to be launched in the spring of 2000, but the project was delayed, and Hitman was officially offered for sale at Christmas 2000. In general, 80% of games software are sold in December. Prior to that Hitman was made available in a demonstration version, which was downloaded more than 300,000 times.

Hitman is a 3D-shooter game, in which you play a ruthless, bald, hired assassin with the code name 47. The game is inspired by films like *The Godfather*. The company is developing Hitman 2, a game for PCs, Playstation 2, and perhaps future consoles like the X-Box and Nintendo Gamecube.

International launch of Hitman

About a month after launch, Hitman had sold 250,000 copies. 100,000 copies were sold in the USA, 24,000 in the UK, and 33,000 in Germany. The rest were sold in a number of markets, including Denmark, where the game topped the sales list. These are good sales figures, particularly when compared with other big star titles in computer games. However, the launch of Hitman was affected by several foolish commercial blunders. Releasing the game in the USA before Europe was the biggest blunder, as it resulted in a large flow of pirate copies from the USA to the rest of the world. That blunder may have cost Hitman 50% of sales during the first month. Another blunder is that the game can easily be copied.

Every time a copy of Hitman is sold IO Interactive receives royalties. At present Hitman has sold 250,000 copies all over the world, but the Danish company will not make a profit until sales reach 420,000. Until then all the money goes to Eidos. Once sales have passed 420,000 copies, every copy sold will generate about €7.5 (10% royalty) for IO Interactive. This amounts to a turnover of US$17 million (at an average price of US$40).

IO Interactive might have made a bigger profit by distributing the game itself, but this would have meant investment in distribution and marketing in the range US$10–20 million. In this way the relationship with Eidos is a risk-minimizing business model for IO Interactive, and at the same time it has made the company a well-known games developer in international circles.

Janos Flösser expects Hitman to sell 5–600,000 copies, but IO Interactive's expectations for the next version of Hitman are about 1.5 million copies. In computer circles a PC game is a top seller when it reaches sales of 300,000.

IO Interactive's expectations for game consoles like Sony's Playstation 2, Nintendo's Gamecube and Microsoft's X-Box are high because of the increasing interest and growth in the market.

Conclusion

The total industry value chain is illustrated in Figure 9.15. Until now most computer games have been sold to offline PCs without access to the Internet. In future a larger proportion of

▶

Case study 9.2 continued

Figure 9.15 Value chain in the computer games industry

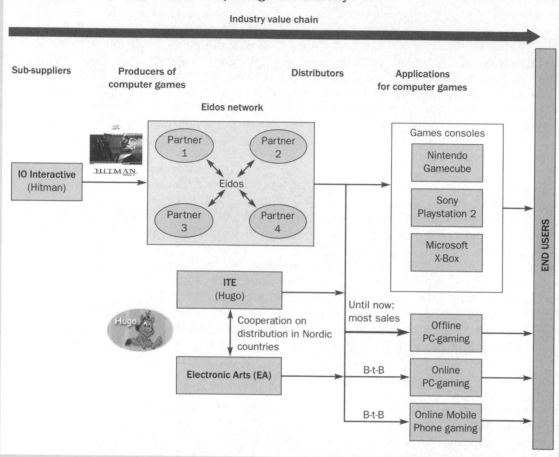

games is expected to be distributed to games consoles, or through Internet suppliers or mobile phone companies offering these services to their subscribers. The trend towards online games is being accelerated by the development of broadband services with the effect that in future advanced games can be distributed over the Internet or the mobile phone network. This part of the market will be characterized as business-to-business. Direct B-t-B customers become owners of Internet portals (e.g. AOL, Jubii) or mobile phone companies. When Internet and TV merge, TV companies (or suppliers of channels for cable TV) will also be possible B-t-B customers for online games.

IO Interactive is positioned further back in the value chain than ITE, as IO Interactive can primarily be considered games developer for Eidos. Eidos is one of the large firms in the market, and the relationship with Eidos offers IO Interactive an opportunity of getting into its international network, and perhaps getting in touch with other producers or distributors who can benefit from IO Interactive's competences in developing games. In any case, the access to Eidos' distribution network has meant that right from the start IO Interactive is a genuine born global.

In contrast to IO Interactive, ITE wanted to do everything itself, and its internationalization follows the traditional pattern, where a

Case study 9.2 continued

company is in the home market for some years before it begins to internationalize. The reason why this process also contains elements of the born global phenomenon is that once the internationalization began, ITE exported the Hugo troll to more than 30 countries within a year or two. As mentioned before, ITE tries to avoid attaching itself too closely to one worldwide distributor. As can be seen in Figure 9.15 ITE uses EA in Nordic countries.

Questions

1. Compare the born global phenomenon with regard to the internationalization of ITE and IO Interactive.

2. What further internationalization do you see for the two companies?

Source: The information for this case study is based on various Danish newspapers. You can also visit ITE's homepage www.ite.dk or www.ite4fun.com, and IO Interactive's homepage www.ici.dk, from where you can download an evaluation version of Hitman. There is also a link to the main distributor, Eidos.

QUESTIONS FOR DISCUSSION

1. What are the main differences between global marketing and marketing in a domestic context?

2. What is meant by the concept psychic distance?

3. Do you think that cultural differences between nations are more or less important than cultural variations within nations? Under what circumstances are each of them important?

4. Why is the screening of foreign markets important?

5. Explore the factors that influence the international market selection process.

6. Why is exporting frequently considered the simplest way of entering foreign markets and favoured by SMEs?

7. Explain the shift from seller to buyer initiative in subcontracting.

8. Explain why international negotiations may differ from country to country.

REFERENCES

Adage Global (2000a), Daily news, www.adageglobal.com, August 29.

Adage Global (2000b), Benetton courts controversy by eyeing up Iranian markets www.adageglobal.com, March 21.

Adage Global (2001), US-style coffee bars struggle to crack Italian market, www.adage-global.com, Daily News, February 14.

Albaum, G., Strandskov, J., Duerr, E. and Dowd, L. (1994), *International Marketing and Export Management*, Addison-Wesley, Reading, MA, (2nd edn).

Andersen, K. S. and Stokholm, F. (2000), Spilindustri: 'Hitman' udfordrer game-gigan-terre, *Børsens Nyhedsmagasin*, November 13, p. 16.

Axelsson, B. and Agndal, H. (2000), *Internationalization of the Firm: A note on the crucial role of the individual's contact network*, IMP Conference, Bath, September.

Ayal, I. And Zif, J. (1979), Market expansion strategies in multinational marketing, *Journal of Marketing*, vol. 43, Spring, pp. 84–94.

BBC (2001), B&Q opens Shanghai megastore, *Business News*, www.bbc.co.uk, August 8.

Cho, D.-S. and Chu, W. (1994), Determinants of bargaining power in OEM negotiations, *Industrial Marketing Management*, vol. 23, pp. 342–55.

Conway, T. and Swift, J. S. (2000), International relationship marketing: the importance of psychic distance, *European Journal of Marketing*, vol. 34, no. 11/12, pp.1391–413.

Craig, C. S. and Douglas, S. P. (2000), Configural advantages in global markets, *Journal of International Marketing*, vol. 8, no. 1, pp. 6–26.

Forsgren, M. and Johanson, J. (1975), *International Företagsekonomi*, Norstedts, Stockholm.

Gupta, A. K. and Govindarajan, V. (2000), Managing global expansion: a conceptual framework, *Business Horizons*, March–April, pp. 45–54.

Hofstede, G. (1980), *Culture's Consequences: International differences in work-related values*, Sage, Beverley Hills, CA.

Hollensen, S. (2001), *Global Marketing: A market responsive approach*, Financial Times/Prentice Hall, Harlow, 2nd edn.

Hyder, A. S. and Ghauri, P. N. (2000), Managing international joint venture relationships, *Industrial Marketing Management*, vol. 29, pp. 205–18.

Jeannet, J. P. (2000), *Managing with a Global Mindset*, Financial Times/Prentice Hall, Harlow.

Johanson, J. and Mattson, L. G. (1988), Internationalization in industrial systems, *in* Hood, N. and Vahlne, J. E. (Eds), *Strategies in Global Competition*, Croom Helm, UK.

Johanson, J. and Vahlne J. E. (1990), The mechanism of internationalization, *International Marketing Review*, vol. 7, no. 4, pp. 11–24.

Keegan, W. (1995), *Global Marketing Management*, Prentice-Hall, Englewood Cliffs, NJ.

Levitt, T. (1983), The globalization of markets, *Harvard Business Review*, vol. 61, no. 3, May/June, pp. 92–102.

Maio, P. (2001), Video-game industry is seen expanding at a rapid clip during next five years, *Wall Street Journal*, New York, May 25.

More, C. M., Fernice, J. and Burt, S. (2000), Brands without boundaries: the internationalization of the designer's brand, *European Journal of Marketing*, vol. 34, no. 8, pp. 919–37.

Oviatt, B. M. and McDougall, P. P. (1994), Towards a theory of international new ventures, *Journal of International Business Studies*, vol. 25, pp. 45–64.

Papadopoulos, N., Chen, E. and Thomas, D. R. (2002), Towards a tradeoff model for international market selection, *International Business Review*, vol. 11, pp. 165–92.

Postlewaite, S. (2001), How a fatwa altered Sainsbury's strategy. Supermarket struggles against local bias, **http://www.adageglobal.com**, March 12.

Rasmussen, E. S., Madsen, T. K. and Evangelista, F. (2001), The founding of the Born Global company in Denmark and Australia: sensemaking and networking, *Asia Pacific Journal of Marketing and Logistics*, vol. 13, no. 3, pp. 75–107.

Seiler, A. and Snider, M. (2001), Lara Croft's greatest leap: Hollywood raids the video game industry's treasures with Tomb Raider, *USA Today*, June 15.

Solberg, C. A. (1997), A framework for analysis of strategy development in globalizing markets, *Journal of International Marketing*, vol. 5, no. 1, pp. 9–30.

Svensson, G. (2001), 'Globalization' of business activities: a 'glocal strategy' approach, *Management Decision*, vol. 39, no. 1, pp. 6–18.

Tarr, G. (2001), Interactive gaming industry targets entertainment lead, *Twice*, New York, vol. 16, no. 13, May 28, pp. 44–5.

Tayeb, M. (2000), *International Business*, Financial Times/Prentice Hall, Harlow.

Welch, L. S. and Loustarinen, R. K. (1988), Internationalization: evolution of a concept, *Journal of General Management*, vol. 14, no. 2, pp. 36–64.

Welch, L. S. and Loustarinen, R. K. (1993), Inward-outward connections in internationalization, *Journal of International Marketing*, vol. 1, pp. 44–56.

Yip, G. S., Biscarri, J. G.and Monti, J. A. (2000), The role of the internationalization process in the performance of newly internationalizing firms, *Journal of International Marketing*, vol. 8, no. 3, pp. 10–35.

Chapter 10

E-commerce strategies

LEARNING OBJECTIVES

After studying this chapter you should be able to:

- explain the reasons for the rapid development of e-commerce.
- explore how e-commerce functions in the main market types: B-t-B, B-t-C, C-t-B, C-t-C.
- discuss 'disintermediation' (bypassing resellers).
- discuss possible alternative routes for profitable e-commerce strategies.
- explain how online trust is a precondition for creating long-lasting relationships between the web marketer and the customer.

Case study 10.1 Nokia

Club Nokia's website creates customer loyalty

Nokia is the world leader in mobile communications. In 2000:

- net sales totalled €30.4 billion (US$27 billion)
- the company employed over 60,000 people
- Nokia had a global network of distribution, sales and customer services
- there were production facilities in 10 countries
- research and development was undertaken in 15 countries
- products were sold in over 130 countries.

Nokia estimated that 405 million handsets were sold worldwide in 2000, a 45% increase from the previous year, but short of analysts' expectations for sales of 420 million.

Similarly, the 128 million handsets that Nokia said it sold in 2000 (market share 31.6%), while in line with the company's published estimates, and 64% higher than the previous year, disappointed analysts, some of whom had expected the Finnish company to sell as many as 135 million handsets.

Nokia's principal rivals, US-based Motorola and Sweden's Ericsson, both saw their market share eroded. For the first time, Nokia has a market share more than double that of its nearest competitor (Motorola). Aside from Nokia, the big winner was German group Siemens, which increased its market share to 8.6% – and fourth place worldwide – from 5.5% in the previous quarter. In the process, it overtook France's Alcatel and Japan's Panasonic.

The Nokia brand has become one of the most valuable in the world and is one of the company's key assets in securing long-term shareholder value. Apart from worldwide recognition as an excellent information technology company, more than 50% of the population aged between 16 and 75 on three continents now have spontaneous awareness of Nokia.

The mobile phone industry is changing

As customers become more sophisticated and demand more from their handsets, they are looking for new value when it comes to choosing what to buy (Figure 10.1).

▶

Case study 10.1 continued

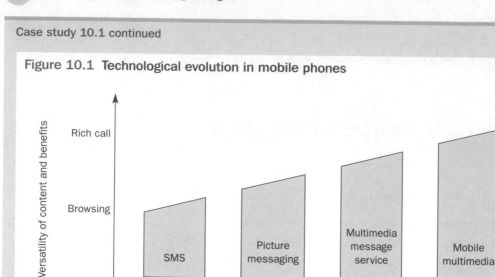

Figure 10.1 Technological evolution in mobile phones

Source: Nokia Annual Report 2000, p. 8.

In global terms, the market for mobile phone manufacturers continues to show impressive growth. In 1992 there were only about 10 million people in the world with a mobile phone. One estimate for the global mobile subscriber base at the end of 2000 is about 715 million, continuing to rise to over 1 billion in the first half of 2002 – a hundred-fold rise in a decade.

As indicated earlier, the total number of handsets sold in 2000 was about 405 million – up from 280 million in 1999. In 2001, the total was estimated at between 500 and 550 million.

Market growth is slowing down as more and more people have mobile phones. However, for an industry of this size, market growth continues to be attractive.

On the other hand, the product life cycle of a mobile phone is around two years and the upgrade or replacement market is expected to grow from 40–50% today, to 70–80% in the next few years.

With the Internet spreading to mobile phones the number of possible peer-to-peer or consumer-to-service connections is exploding and the way in which we are using our mobile phones is expanding. This offers tremendous new market opportunities.

Since customers are now familiar with the technology, and use it every day, the trend will be towards mobile phones that provide exactly what customers want. As it is estimated that, in future, 70–80% of new mobile phones will be bought by people who already own one, maintaining customer loyalty is of vital importance to Nokia.

Club Nokia

The consequence of the market development is that new categories of mobile phones are being developed. New features, functions and services are on the way to suit today's more sophisticated customers. Games, music and imaging are among new features in store for the ever growing band of Nokia mobile phone owners who are keeping in touch with the company through Club Nokia (www.nokia.com/clubnokia). The club, which became available in all Nokia regions during 2001, is open to every Nokia phone owner and, so far, several million people in over 20 countries have registered to join.

Club Nokia is all about information, support and fun. Through its customized website, the club caters for every type of customer interaction and features high quality call centre support and service back-up.

Case study 10.1 continued

Club Nokia is a multi-channel service including WAP, WWW, and SMS access with personalization as a key feature. Nokia will focus on services that enhance and complement the handset such as ring tones. A recent feature enables members to customize and send extra pictures to Nokia picture messaging-enabled mobile phones. They can also compose their own ring tone or download a choice of caller group icons.

In the first year, members receive free e-mail and phone support from the Club Nokia Careline. The careline answers specific enquiries about phones and Club Nokia itself. Should a phone need attention, it directs members to the nearest service point.

Questions

1. Explain the purpose of Club Nokia. Do you agree that it is better to have Club Nokia online (as a website) rather than offline?

2. Visit Club Nokia's website (click from **www.nokia.com**). Do you agree that Club Nokia is able to create customer loyalty?

3. In autumn 2001, Nokia launched a new mobile phone accessory, the digital Nokia Music Player HDR-1. With the Nokia Music Player, users will be able to listen to an integrated FM stereo radio and downloadable audio/music files, as well as use it as a hands-free kit for their phone. Using the Nokia Music Player, it is possible to download AAC and MP3 music files via the Nokia Audio Manager PC software installed on your PC. With the 32 MB memory card, the Nokia Music Player can hold up to nine hours of audio, depending on the encoding format and quality. As the Nokia Music Player requires only one AAA battery, it can easily be used as a stand-alone device.

(a) Should the Nokia Music Player be marketed online, offline or both?

(b) Would the choice of Club Nokia as the distribution channel for the Nokia Music Player be a good decision, or should Nokia choose another e-commerce strategy?

Source: Nokia financial report 2000 and press releases, BBC (2001), DBC (2001), Kapner (2001).

10.1 Introduction

Electronic commerce on the Internet, or e-commerce, has experienced rapid growth during its infant years. Some academics (e.g. Van Hooft and Stegwee, 2001) argue that the 'e' will soon be dropped and that e-commerce will be business as it comes to be generally understood. In this chapter, various existing models and theories will be used. We argue that these models and thories still apply when looking from a new e-commerce perspective. Examples will be given of possible applications to demonstrate the use of these models. However, we do not aim at giving an exhaustive and complete description; organizations are too different from each other and new developments arise every day. Every model and every example will have to be adapted to fit within a specific situation.

Fundamentally, e-commerce is concerned with electronic data information interchange. The term e-commerce is used in this book because it deals with all transactions that are Internet-based whereas e-business specifically refers to transactions and relationships between organizations.

The extra value created by this information trading may also be illustrated by the synergies between the physical and the virtual value chain (see Figure 2.11). Virtual activities do not eliminate the need for physical activities. The complementarity of virtual activities and physical activities often has the effect that a virtual activity places greater demands on physical activities elswhere in the value chain. For example, direct ordering makes warehousing and shipping more important. Such effects underline the fact that virtual applications are not stand-alone technologies; they must be integrated into the overall value chain (Porter, 2001).

The value that can be realized through e-commerce will be partly determined by the extent to which different value-chain activities of a firm are interconnected with suppliers, manufacturers, and customers, allowing simultaneous flow of information about multiple transactions to these parties. For example, by placing an order with payment option form on the Internet, customers can quickly customize their orders. The information can be routed directly to the manufacturers and suppliers in real time. The transactions created in real time not only will increase the competitive intensity with regard to speed and efficiency of the business, but will also place a heavy demand on organizations to manage customers' information for their future use. By tracking customer information, a firm becomes aware of customer preferences and tastes, and can also make targeted efforts in meeting those demands earlier than its competitors.

In e-commerce, information is not viewed as a by-product of the strategic activities performed around the physical value chain because it begins to play a strategic role in itself. Therefore, strategic activities in the virtual value chain are performed with and around information. Therefore, it becomes imperative that businesses integrate virtual chain activities with physical activities for offering customized products and services as shown in Figure 2.11. While virtual value-chain activities provide information access to customers, suppliers and manufacturers, and make a large part of the transactions transparent, physical value-chain activities make it possible for them to be realized by fulfilling customer orders and assembling final products and services.

The key is to think about the Internet as a trading centre or market, although in a virtual environment. In the future, it will pervade many areas of our lives where we will sell, trade, invest, talk, inform and meet new people. Perhaps the most appropriate image of the Internet is as a marketplace for information trading. In addition, many transactions will involve money, tendered in digital form rather than currency. Digital information, not just as money, will be the new medium of exchange in this market.

E-commerce is simply part of the new means of communication that has been opened up by the development of the Internet. A useful definition of e-commerce is the use of the Internet for the exchange of information of value, more specifically orders and payments between businesses and between businesses and consumers. In essence, e-commerce is the secure trading of goods, information or services and, in the main, is conducted using Internet technologies.

As a new channel for commercial transactions, the use of e-commerce will open up fresh sources of revenue and opportunities for organizations that have carefully structured strategies (Fraser *et al.*, 2000).

The use of e-commerce and, more specifically, the Internet, is just like any other element that the business marketer employs to accomplish the firm's mission: it must be focused, based on objectives, and directed at specific target segments. For the marketer, the Internet can be viewed as:

- a communication device to build customer relationships
- an alternative distribution channel
- a valuable medium for delivering services to customers

- a tool for gathering marketing research data
- a method for integrating members of the supply chain.

In short, the Internet does not usually replace existing channels of distribution; rather it supports or supplements them. In a similar way, it does not eliminate the selling function; rather it facilitates the salesperson's efforts and enhances the effectiveness and efficiency of the sales function. To be successful, business marketers must integrate the Internet and e-commerce into the overall marketing strategy.

Depending on how it is applied, e-commerce has the potential to increase revenue by creating new markets for old products, creating new information-based products, and establishing new service delivery channels to serve and interact with the customer better. E-commerce also results in *lower transaction costs* by enabling better coordination in the sales, production, and distribution processes (or better supply chain management), and by consolidating operations and reducing overheads.

The supplier is able to provide low-cost access to both order entry and order tracking, 24 hours a day, seven days a week. Transactions that do not require in-person services can be handled in a cost-effective manner on a website, while the firm can devote more staff to working with higher margin customers requiring personal attention. The result is reduced costs for both types of transactions.

The development of the Internet as a new distribution channel will result in a shift of power from the manufacturers and the traditional retail channels to the consumers. This increasing consumer power can be explained in the following way.

- *The search for convenience*: the Internet gives people a new tool to gather information and purchase more easily than through traditional channels.

- *The incorporation of the Internet into the purchase process*: pre-purchase and post-sale use of the Internet is exploding, regardless of where the product is bought.

- *A shift in loyalties*: consumers reward online merchants with higher repeat-purchase behaviour.

- *Future buying plans*: survey results indicate an increasing consumer disposition to buy online (IDC, 2000a; Boston Consulting Group, 2000).

Today's technology only scratches the surface of efficient comparison shopping and product search. The development of automated buying profiles, networked buying clubs, and online auctions will bring greater price competition to the Internet. Merchants must be prepared to live up to 'we will match any price' marketing guarantees.

Competing on the Internet is different from the traditional industrial world. Competition no longer takes place in the physical marketplace, but in a **market space** (Rayport and Sviokla, 1996). This computer-mediated environment has profound implications for how business is transacted between buyer and seller. The nature of a transaction is different in that it is based on information about the product or services rather than on their physical appearance or attributes. The context of the transaction is different; instead of taking place in a physical world, it occurs in a computer-mediated environment with the buyer conducting the transaction from a personal computer screen. Consequently, to be a player in many industries does not require physical infrastructure like buildings and machinery; a computer and communications platform are sufficient.

Like so many buzz words in use today, e-commerce tends to mean different things to different people. For the purpose of introducing the subject, e-commerce is defined here as:

the enablement of a business vision supported by advanced information technology to increase the effectiveness of the business relationships between trading partners.

Examples of e-commerce transactions are:

- an individual purchases a book on the Internet
- a government employee reserves a hotel room over the Internet
- a business calls a toll-free number and orders a computer using the seller's interactive telephone system
- a retailer orders merchandise using an EDI network or a supplier's **extranet**
- a manufacturing plant orders electronic components from another plant within the company using the company's intranet
- an individual withdraws funds from an automatic teller machine (ATM).

10.2 Comparison between the industrial economy and the digital economy

E-commerce is more than home shopping. It encompasses a range of electronic interactions between organizations and their up- and downstream trading partners. Many of their transactions have been occurring for quite some time, long before the Internet opened to commercial traffic. Platforms for e-commerce that precede the Internet include the use of Minitel in France for inter-organizational commercial transactions, as well as the use of EDI over private networks.

The Internet has become a powerful business tool. This new approach to the communication and distribution of information and services has transformed the fundamental dynamics behind many social and business interactions. The barriers and obstacles which often accompanied traditional commerce are giving way to new business approaches.

Consumers, producers and distributors now all have flexible, fast and inexpensive ways of participating in the market for products and services round the world. Individual and corporate customers can approach the marketplace differently as the variety and depth of information on products and services speed up decision-making processes. Moreover, this new virtual marketplace is providing a significant boost to economic activity.

The Internet's unprecedented impact on the way the world does business stems from the way it has altered basic business dynamics. The dynamics that have shaped markets and market leaders since the 19th century – dynamics rooted in an industrial economy – have been replaced with a new set of fundamental principles based on a digital economy.

In the industrial economy, manufacturing dominates. The production of goods is the principal driver of economic activity. In the digital economy, knowledge and relationships dominate. It is a world where information and ideas are becoming more important than physical objects.

In the industrial economy, the most serious market barriers were lack of a distribution infrastructure and lack of capital. These significant entry barriers in the physical world meant first-to-market advantage could typically be measured in years. The Internet, however, has turned traditional distribution models upside down. With distribution models changing and capital easier to obtain, markets are wide open and first-to-market advantage is now measured in months. The new distribution barrier is 'e-distribution', or the first-to-market advantage earned by companies that are able to lock up exclusive business relationships with the new e-business drivers, such as the leading web portals. Becoming an exclusive retail partner of a portal such as America Online, for example, would enable a retailer to leap-frog ahead of its competition.

Although e-commerce transactions are performed with and through information, the need for performing physical activities cannot be completely eliminated, because a number of back-end activities are still performed physically. This is because a number of back-end activities require tangible materials, tools, and technologies. For example, a book or a manual can easily be captured, codified, and downloaded electronically. However, for writing a book or a manual, groups of writers or engineers need to visit the site of their inspiration in person and experiment with a number of alternatives before perfecting their craft. In e-commerce, though a number of activities can be replaced electronically, there still remains a need to perform some basic functions physically. Therefore, in e-commerce, success will depend on the ways the physical and virtual value-chain activities are matched and integrated.

10.3 Types of products that can be sold over the Internet

The products sold in e-commerce markets can roughly be grouped into two categories: physical products and purely digital goods and services.

Physical products

Marketing physical products over the web has led to some of the biggest success stories in e-commerce. The key to success is marketing that takes advantage of the interface and the networked environment. Transferring a conventional mail-order business to the web adds little value.

The potential advantages of the Internet include the scope for real-time interaction within a vast networked community, the possibility of using sophisticated market mechanisms, and the illusion of almost infinite inventory (when an intermediary acts for many suppliers).

Digital goods and services

This category includes information goods and services, such as financial information, news services, reference and learning materials, entertainment and multimedia products, software distribution services, distributed database services and remote computation services. In addition, the Internet has spawned innovative digital products such as online gaming, chat rooms, search engines, online advertising, telephone yellow pages and certification services. These products are characterized by being difficult to value and easy to copy.

Companies use different strategies to price and market these goods. They include customization and bundling, bundling valuable content with advertising to provide 'free' goods, introducing different versions of the same product to suit different users, charging subscriptions and, most important, using market mechanisms to help set price.

The individualization of goods

The digital world, in which information can be acquired and processed with ease, lets sellers tailor their products to individual customers. Further, the electronic environment allows companies to respond quickly to consumer feedback.

The ease of customization, and the ability to adapt to variations in consumer preferences, lead to the possibility of individualizing goods in the electronic markets. As each consumer will prefer (and be offered) a different version of the basic product, the total perceived value of the same (basic) product may be higher than with only one version of the product.

One weakness of the Internet is that it can realistically reproduce only two of our five senses, namely, sight and sound. One cannot feel, smell or taste products that are advertised on the web. This limitation will restrict the kind of products that can be sold over the Internet.

The suitability of the Internet for marketing to consumers depends to a large extent on the characteristics of the products and services being marketed. It is therefore necessary to explicitly consider product and service characteristics and the ease of carrying out the transaction when evaluating the impact of the Internet.

Exhibit 10.1 | **The online divorce-booking market**

It is sad but true that in the USA, the divorce rate now stands at 50 per cent (in the UK, the divorce rate is 40 per cent). Divorce is no longer the stigma it once was and for many it is just another factor in their increasingly complex lives. American marketers are recognizing this fact of life more than ever and are building it into their advertising, products and services.

In the USA, each state has a different divorce law, so getting divorced can be both a legal and financial minefield. As a consequence, a host of websites has emerged that are devoted to the subject of divorce. Many of them take different views – from Stopyourdivorce.com and Divorceasfriends.com to Split-up.com and the Do-It-Yourself Divorce kit offered on Divorceonline.com. In this way you can organize your divorce online.

In many cases there are children to consider. Supportkids.com is an Internet-based service that claims to have collected more than US$50m (£34m) of overdue child support payments for thousands of families. It takes a percentage of the money it recovers from the offending parent.

Source: adapted from Devaney (2001).

10.4 The global rise and structure of e-commerce

Forrester Research predicts that within three years, online commerce will reach US$6.8 trillion in 2001 from US$657 billion in 2000 (Global Reach, 2001). This huge amount includes Forrester's projection for both business-to-business and business-to-consumer transactions online. The firm projects that although North America accounted for nearly 80 per cent of worldwide e-commerce in 2000, that will shift as Asian and European nations become more active.

The figures show that North America will have 51 per cent of the world e-commerce, Japan 13 per cent, Germany 5.7 per cent in 2004. The figures are shown in Table 10.1 by region.

Table 10.1 Projected split of e-commerce in 2004

Region	Share (%)
North America	51
Asia/Pacific	24
Europe	23
Latin America	2
Total	100

Source: adapted from Global Reach (2001), www.glreach.com.

The e-commerce growth in all regions will be healthy, but Asia/Pacific and western Europe will accelerate the fastest between 2000 and 2004.

According to Global Reach (2001) (Table 10.2), one in six European adults used the Internet to seek pricing or product information for products and services. The total number of people in 2001 with access to the Internet was 420 million.

Global Reach (2001) found that the USA and Canada still account for the largest proportion of the world's Internet access, with 41 per cent of the global audience. Europe, the Middle East and Africa are responsible for 27 per cent of the world's Internet population, followed by Asia Pacific (20 per cent) and Latin America (4 per cent) – these figures are not shown in Table 10.2.

One in 11 adults made an online purchase in the same period. Denmark, Sweden and Switzerland led the region in terms of web browsing and purchasing, while Belgium/Luxembourg, Italy and Spain had relatively few people browsing or purchasing via the Internet.

According to Global Reach (2001) only Sweden comes close to the USA, where 64 per cent of all web surfers shop online each month and 30 per cent buy online.

In the Asia-Pacific region, adults in Australia and New Zealand are most likely to use the Internet to seek information about products and services, with one in four adults turning to the Internet. Purchasing online is also common in Australia and New Zealand, as well as South Korea. Only a very small proportion of people in Hong Kong, Taiwan and Singapore have bought goods and services online.

If a South Korean browses the Internet for information on goods or services, he or she is much more likely to buy than is the case in other countries. Three in five South Koreans who browse convert that investigation into a purchase. By contrast, only one-third of adults from Hong Kong or Taiwan who browse for information then go on to buy.

Table 10.2 World Internet access and use

Country	Percentage of people with Internet access, age 16+		Worldwide online browsing and purchasing behaviour, past six months, adults 16+ (percentage)	
	Access at home	Access at work	Browsing for products	Purchasing products
Australia	50	30	24	10
Austria	42	27	25	12
Belgium/Luxembourg	39	23	12	5
Denmark	58	38	39	16
Finland	49	37	28	11
France	22	17	12	6
Germany	35	22	22	11
Hong Kong	58	23	13	4
Ireland	46	25	17	8
Italy	34	14	10	3
Netherlands	56	28	28	11
New Zealand	51	31	29	12
Norway	53	38	24	14
Singapore	56	21	19	7
Spain	20	11	8	3
South Korea	57	17	18	11
Sweden	61	41	46	26
Switzerland	43	31	32	17
Taiwan	50	19	13	4
UK	46	26	19	11
USA	65	40	64	30

Source: adapted from www.thestandard.com, June 13, 2001, Nielsen/NetRating.

Demographic shift on the Internet

After years of slowly converging, the profile of the average adult US and European Internet user looks like the profile of the average population, according to research done by TheStandard (Partore, 2001).

The demographic shift – from **early adopters** of new technology who were young, relatively wealthy and predominantly male, to average people – is important because it validates the Internet as a mainstream marketing, advertising and research platform. Though Internet users still have an above average household income, the Internet has been adopted by nearly every demographic segment of the US and European population.

The most noticeable demographic shift is seen in Internet use by gender. Female web surfers have overtaken men in numbers in the USA, and are surging on to the Internet in the Asia-Pacific region. Other trends show that women are more efficient in their web behaviour than men, and women are showing an increasing willingness to purchase online.

Women were later adopters of the Internet, but are making up for that lag now, and the speed with which they are coming online means that women must become a priority for most e-tailers. Women spend less time online as they generally know what they are looking for and leave once they achieve their goal. E-marketers should take this tendency into account by ensuring that their sites focus on ease and convenience.

Languages used on the web

In 1999, 54 per cent of all Internet users were English speaking, but by 2001, Internet users were predominately non-English speaking – 55 per cent of Internet users did not speak English as their first language (Global Reach, 2001). The language groups that most significantly attack the dominance of English on the Internet are those in the Asia-Pacific region (primarily Japanese and Chinese) and Latin America. Of course this has also to do with the increasing penetration of the Internet in these areas of the world.

The growth of the non-English-speaking market will mean that it will become imperative for companies to offer multiple-language websites.

The introduction of the euro as a single currency

The next two years are set to bring dramatic changes in Europe: not only are most European countries going online at an unprecedented rate, but 12 countries of the European Union have phased out their own currency and accepted a common currency (the euro) at the beginning of 2002. It is widely thought that the combination of these two factors will stimulate e-commerce.

10.5 Types of e-commerce – defining new business models

The impact of e-commerce on the economy extends far beyond the monetary value of e-commerce activity. Businesses use e-commerce to develop competitive advantage by providing more useful information, expanding choice, developing new services, streamlining purchasing processes, and lowering costs. The Internet also imposes price discipline as customers have access to price and product information from many sources.

The different e-commerce markets may be divided into four categories, as shown in Table 10.3. The four markets will be discussed further.

Table 10.3 Four different e-commerce markets

	Business	Consumer
Business	**B-t-B** • EDI relations • GM, Ford and DaimlerChrysler join forces in sourcing car parts in e-markets	**B-t-C** • Dell • eToys • CDnow
Consumer	**C-t-B** (reserve auctions) • PriceLine • HobShop (earlier name: Accompany) • LetsBuyIt	**C-t-C** (traditional auctions) • eBay • QXL

| Exhibit 10.2 | **Perfume giants stop online retailer in France** |

Legal challenges from top international luxury goods and cosmetics marketers including L'Oréal, Yves Saint Laurent and the LVMH Group forced Parfumsnet to temporarily shut down its online perfume counter (www.parfumsnet.fr) in France.

Parfumsnet, which was launched in 1999 by former L'Oréal employees, suggests that the perfume marketers' principal objective is not to protect brand image, but rather to establish full control over online sales. Company executives say that their catalogue has low prices and e-commerce services that threaten the manufacturers' own Internet plans.

The perfume marketers asserted that unlicensed sales at the Internet site violated their right to operate selective distribution networks across the 15-member European Union.

European courts have long allowed luxury goods producers wide leeway to control marketing and distribution. Leading members of this group are unwilling to allow Internet-based discount merchants like Parfumsnet to enter their selective distribution networks, created to protect brand quality.

The perfume manufacturers have filed 16 related legal complaints against the site in French courts. Cosmetic giant L'Oréal is the most aggressive, filing individual suits seeking court injunctions banning online sales of perfume brands including Armani, Biotherm, Cacharel, Guy Laroche, Lancôme, Lanvin, Ralph Lauren, Paloma Picasso and Helena Rubinstein.

The LVMH luxury group has filed suits to protect brands including Christian Dior, Givenchy, Guerlain and Kenzo, while Yves Saint Laurent Beauté has already won injunctions banning sales of perfumes under the YSL and Van Cleef and Arpels brands.

Parfumsnet has appealed against the court decision. Rather than targeting the **selective distribution** networks, it demands that courts recognize the Internet as a new market meriting inclusion in existing distribution policies.

Parfumsnet continues to operate parallel sites in Italy and Spain.

Source: adapted from Adage Global (2000).

Today the B-t-B market volume is four times bigger than the B-t-C market; according to Durlacher (2000).

Business-to-business (B-to-B) e-commerce

Electronic-based commerce is not a new phenomenon in the B-to-B market. Instead of Internet-based solutions, many industries have been using **electronic data interchange (EDI)** for years to streamline business processes and reduce the cost of doing business. Suppliers, manufacturers, wholesalers, distributors and retailers share inventory information and send orders, invoices and shipping data electronically. EDI enhances the flow of information and goods through the supply chain and eliminates manual re-entry of data, thereby eliminating errors and costly delays.

EDI is used for the exchange of structured data between the computer systems of trading partners. It is frequently used as an electronic replacement for traditional paper documents such as the order form or invoice but EDI is well developed also in the world of finance and administration. In essence, EDI is used for the exchange of structured data between the originators and recipients of such information. EDI can be defined as

the transfer of structured data, by agreed message standards, from one computer system to another by electronic means.

A brief explanation of the terms used in this definition will help readers understand the concept, which is also known as paperless trading.

- The use of *structured data* refers to a precise, recognized method of assembling data. Such data items as item code, customer reference, delivery point and limit price all come together to form a purchase order invoice, packing list, acknowledgement of order, etc.

- The phrase *by agreed message standards* implies that discrepancies between documents (an invoice is one such document) will be minimized by providing a fixed and agreed method of specifying and presenting the data. Much effort has been expended by respected national and international standards organizations in producing standards for presenting the data, via syntax rules and message guidelines.

- The definition also uses the phrase *from one computer system to another*, and implies that the two systems belong to distinct organizations. However, EDI can be used for both intra-company and inter-company communications.

- The phrase *by electronic means* implies no human intervention.

Traditional EDI, however, is expensive and time consuming to implement. Many smaller companies simply cannot justify the price of entry. According to *Business Week*, adding a single trading partner to an EDI network can cost up to US$50,000. In contrast, some Internet-based EDI links cost less than US$1000, making them affordable for a much broader audience.

EDI on the web supports much a richer exchange of information. Traditional EDI supports only highly structured documents such as purchase orders and invoices. The Internet supports the exchange of multimedia information, including engineering drawings, full-colour photographs, audio and even video clips. As a result, Internet-based EDI fosters much tighter relationships among participants, providing a sense of teamwork and shared goals, and enabling all components and systems of a value chain to communicate with each other. Today, EDI has further developed and hybrid solutions are now available, most of them based on web technology.

Many of the same advantages that arise from retail e-commerce hold for business-to-business e-commerce. For example, e-commerce can permit businesses to increase the services they can offer their business customers. By opening an immediate and convenient channel for communicating, exchanging and selecting information, e-commerce is allowing firms to reconsider what functions they should perform in-house and which are best provided by others. The new technology has helped to create new relationships and to streamline and augment supply chain processes. As these changes are occurring, the roles of logistic and financial intermediaries (e.g. FedEx, UPS, American Express) are expanding.

These changes will result in aggressive growth rates in the B-t-B market during the next few years (Barrat and Rosdahl, 2002).

Figure 10.2 illustrates the shift from EDI to Internet-based B-t-B e-commerce. In the Internet-based e-commerce marketplace (or E-hubs as Kaplan and Sawhney (2000) call them) there are two methods of price determination.

Aggregation mechanism (fixed pricing)

This brings a large number of buyers and sellers together in one industry-specific portal (or vertical portal). These e-hubs reduce transaction costs by providing one-stop shopping.

PlasticsNet.com, for example, allows plastics processors to issue a single purchase order for hundreds of plastics products sourced from a diverse set of suppliers. The aggregation mechanism is static in nature because prices are pre-negotiated (fixed pricing).

Matching mechanism (dynamic pricing)

Unlike the static aggregation mechanism, the matching mechanism brings buyers and seller together to negotiate prices on a dynamic and real-time basis. The matching mechanism works best in the following settings (Kaplan and Sawhney, 2000):

- products are commodities or near-commodities and can be traded sight unseen
- trading volumes are massive in relation to transaction costs
- buyers and seller are sophisticated enough to deal with dynamic pricing
- companies use spot purchasing to smooth the peaks and troughs of supply and demand
- logistics and fulfilment can be conducted by third parties, often without revealing the identity of the buyer or seller
- demand and prices are volatile.

Of special interest are the so-called 'reverse aggregators'. Reverse here means that the e-hubs attract a large number of buyers and then bargain with suppliers on their behalf.

By gathering together the purchasing power of many buyers, particularly small and medium-sized buyers, the reverse aggregators can negotiate price reductions. In some industries volume discount can approach 20 per cent. The purchasing e-hub can reduce procurement transaction costs by outsourcing the procurement function.

While business-to-business e-commerce is a global phenomenon, the North American market currently dominates. The $700 billion North American market is twice the size of business-to-business e-commerce in the rest of the world combined (US$330 billion). It is likely that North America will retain its significant lead over the next few years, but the global dynamics of business-to-business e-commerce will shift. In western Europe, which lags 18 months behind North America in e-commerce adoption, several countries have accelerated their e-commerce investment and will significantly close this gap. Asia and Latin America remain further behind, but this may change rapidly as global supply chains go online. For local suppliers in local markets, business-to-business e-commerce presents significant growth opportunities, as they expand their networks and customer bases by accessing new export markets.

By 2003, North American business-to-business e-commerce will reach $3 trillion. In the rest of the world, it will reach US$1.8 trillion.

Also by 2003, more than 65 per cent of all business-to-business e-commerce purchases will be in the retail, motor vehicle, shipping, industrial equipment and high technology sectors, and cost savings rather than strategic opportunities will drive most of the initial growth. Companies which have moved aggressively into business-to-business e-commerce will have cost savings on materials of up to 15 per cent as purchasing and record keeping processes are simplified (Boston Consulting Group, 2000).

Figure 10.2 The development of B-t-B e-commerce

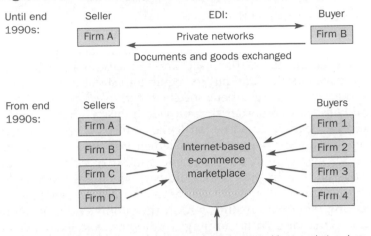

Internet-based e-marketplace, which is created by e-market makers,
(e.g. Chemdex, Vertical Net etc., which develop e-marketplaces of buyers
and sellers within a particular industry or geographic region).

Source: Hollensen (2001) p. 343.

| Exhibit 10.3 | **Will online build-to-order (BTO) cars be the future business model?** |

The online build-to-order (BTO) PC did wonders for Dell Computer Corp. when it opted to overhaul its business model to give consumers the opportunity to purchase a customized computer. Now car manufacturers are planning to the same, but nobody expects it to be easy.

The car industry will introduce a BTO manufacturing and sales approach over four years to improve market responsiveness and bolster sagging profits.

Spurred by the possibilities of e-business, several of the major manufacturers, such as Ford, General Motors, DaimlerChrysler, Volkswagen and Toyota. have launched initiatives that could see the beginning of the end of Henry Ford's one-size-fits-all manufacturing process that formed the basis of the motor industry for the best part of a century.

Manufacturing cars is a much more complicated process than building computers in all the various aspects of the value chain: retail/distribution, product design, manufacturing and procurement. Most car models come in thousands of possible configurations, the parts are bought from many suppliers and fulfilment is achieved through a vast network of independent dealers.

The industry will have to simplify the vehicle-configuration process by combining separate options into packages. Car makers will also need to establish distribution centres with adequate suppliers of base vehicles that can be customized in a timely fashion to meet the customers' specific orders.

While supply chain issues are crucial for any BTO initiative to be successful, change will also have to come in the retail segment. Replacing the current sales-driven remuneration system with one based on customer satisfaction would be a good starting point.

Dealerships and manufacturers could invest cost savings from reduced vehicle inventories into new retailing processes that will steer the consumer's interest away from pricing considerations and point it toward other value propositions, such as emotional aspects, to create a unique buying experience for the customer.

Sources: adapted from Information from Ford Motor Co., www.ford.com, General Motors Corp. www.gm.com, McGrath (2001)

Vertical and horizontal hubs in B-t-B e-commerce

When a mass of sellers and buyers exists in the content aggregator hub, distribution channel efficiencies can be realized through minimized searching as well as through automated transaction facilitation. Success in this model requires the content aggregator to be a 'contextual marketplace' and to focus on a specific factor in order to attract the mass of sellers and buyers required to sustain its benefit to the channel. Specialization occurs along either a specific function or process (Figure 10.3).

Vertical hubs are web portals that provide industry-specific goods, services, and information for participants in a particular industry. Generally, vertical hubs possess extensive industry-specific knowledge, but tend to lack business-process expertise. SciQuest.com in the life sciences industry, e-Steel in the steel industry, and PlasticsNet.com in the plastics industry are among today's leading vertical hubs. To maintain a buyer and seller mass, the vertical aggregator must focus on building long-term relationships within the supply chain. Providing a one-stop market space that offers a broad range of products and extensive domain-specific content is imperative to sustaining relationships. Moreover, the potential success of vertical hubs is directly related to the extent of existing barriers in the channel, such as fragmentation among the industry's buyers and sellers, inefficiency in the existing supply chain, and a relatively high number of key suppliers and buyers. Equally important to potential success is the hub's industry knowledge, existing industry relationships, and technological ability to create integrated catalogues and sophisticated search engines.

Figure 10.3 Vertical and horizontal hubs

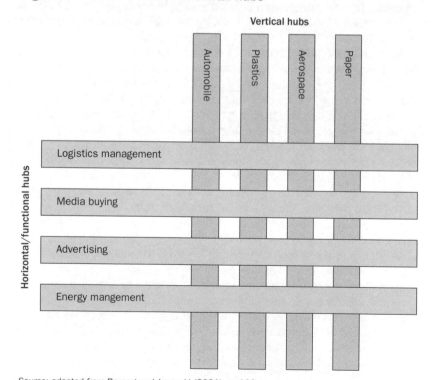

Source: adapted from Rayport and Jawarski (2001), p. 100.

Horizontal or functional hubs focus on providing the same function across different industries. Functional hubs possess business-process expertise, but tend to lack extensive industry-specific knowledge. Examples of functions currently represented include global logistics monitoring and tracking (Celarix), employee benefits administration (Employease), and project management (BidCom). Success is associated with the degree of process standardization, the aggregator's process knowledge and workflow automation expertise, the ability to provide meaningful content across industries, and the ability to customize for industry-specific differences.

Horizontal aggregators can generate profits from the sale of the software necessary for back-office processes, as well as from transaction fees or advertising fees realized from the online market space. Ariba, a facilitator of procurement across industries, is one of the most recognized functional hubs. It connects buyers and sellers and boasts total automation for the procurement process – from the employee placing the order, through the internal approval process, to eventual fulfilment.

Nevertheless, Ariba and other functional hubs have a hurdle to overcome. They are only effective if the processes are universal across all buyers and sellers. If clients cannot use their intermediary for the majority of transactions, they must maintain some traditional processes, thereby minimizing the intermediary's utility.

Unless vertical hubs find closely related domains where they can leverage their assets, they find it difficult to diversify into other vertical markets. Horizontal hubs, because of their low ability to deliver industry-specific content, run the risk of becoming back-end service providers to vertical hubs. Eventually, vertical hubs will

---

Exhibit 10.4	**3M avoids channel conflict on the web**

Rather than compete with resellers for online sales, 3M has discovered a way to help build channel partners' web sales while building its own.

3M in St Paul, Minnesota, is working with its resellers to create e-showrooms-virtual, co-branded online stores that help resellers sell more of 3M's products. In the e-showrooms, 3M uses the so-called microsite, which has lots of information in it and tries to create a highly engaging brand experience.

The e-showrooms provide content about the 3M products that the distributors' sites have no space for. The e-showrooms enable 3M to provide the end user with the appropriate content on the products and provide control over how the end user views the product and facilitates the sale.

3M has an e-showroom in place for its ergonomic products including wrist rests, document holders, and computer screen filters. When customers enter the showroom, through a banner or a hyperlink on the distributor site, they can customize the type of information they will receive by choosing what type of user they are from three choices provided: a moderate computer user, an intensive computer user, or an ergonomic professional. Each showroom is customized for each of the three types of customer. 3M has different levels of products and highlight the appropriate products for different segments. Each showroom incorporates the distributor's branding with 3M's, as well as the distributor's product numbers and pricing. The distributor handles all fulfilment and pockets the money on sales.

3M brings the information and the distributor brings the customers. The customer gets 3M's expertise in ergonomics and the distributor's online offerings put all of this together and the result is a win-win situation for all parties involved.

Source: adapted from Galen (2000).

probably form patchwork alliances with horizontal hubs or, alternatively, 'meta-hubs' may emerge where multiple vertical hubs will share a common back-end and functional service.

Potential vertical aggregator competitors must have domain experience and established relationships in the industry they wish to penetrate. Likewise, potential horizontal aggregators must have a substantial differentiation to attract buyers and sellers who would incur high switching costs in building a relationship with a new horizontal aggregator.

Buyers and sellers conducting business through e-hubs can benefit from lower transaction costs, productivity gains by employees within transaction processes, and better prices.

Business-to-consumer (B-t-C) e-commerce

Many of the advantages of e-commerce were first exploited (in the mid-1990s) by retail e-businesses such as Amazon.com, eTrade, and Auto-by-tel that were created as Internet versions of traditional bookstores, brokerage firms, and car dealerships. Freed from the geographic confines and costs of running actual stores, such firms could deliver almost unlimited content on request and could react and make changes in close to real time. Compared to traditional retail or catalogue operations, this new way of conducting business is changing cost structures. The emergence of these e-businesses has made their competitors consider their own e-commerce strategies, and many now operate their own online stores (e.g. Barnes & Noble, Merill Lynch).

E-businesses do more than simply provide alternative shopping sites; they can also expand existing markets and even create new ones. Not included in the cost savings listed above are the additional value that Internet-based businesses can provide in terms of increased information and choice and time savings. These advantages make it possible for buyers and sellers to come together in significantly more efficient ways than would otherwise be possible. For example, musicfile.com serves as a clearing house where music collectors and retailers can advertise their deleted vinyl records and CDs, and buyers can post their wants.

The move towards providing goods and services through a digital medium does not need to be all or nothing. In the retail business, the web store and the physical store can support each other in many different ways, capitalizing on natural complements. These include cross-promotions, joint-service provisions, and value-added services. Cross-promotions are perhaps the most straightforward example of a natural complement. Web stores may provide the bargains that people may expect when shopping on the Internet, but also offer coupons for in-store purchases. Marketers are accustomed to the use of loss-leaders to increase store traffic, and realize that once in the store, other purchases for non-discounted merchandise are more likely. A physical store can use its website to highlight local events, such as a reading or performance at the store, helping to bring in traffic. The web store may also provide information about additional services which are available at the store that also add value to products purchased online. A company might use e-mail for direct marketing not only to advertise the website, but also to provide information about in-store products and services. Some services might be provided jointly, leveraging the investment in physical and web presence. A good example would be when a computer store offers a product online, but provides installation and repair services at its premises for customers purchasing from its website. The web store may also function as a source of value-added service for customers who have purchased or plan to purchase goods at the physical store.

With the emergence of grocery websites customers gain convenience by shopping online. A local grocery store then delivers the chosen items. Finally, a number of stores have initiated in-store web kiosks as a means of lowering costs and improving service. In-store shoppers can search for products that are not on display, gather in-depth information without taking up the salesperson's time, and even purchase or pay for products for immediate or subsequent delivery. These various complementary approaches represent a sampling of strategies a retailer might use to leverage its investment in physical and web distribution channels.

Consumer-to-business (C-t-B) e-commerce

This type of e-commerce is a kind of **'reverse auction'** where the buyer (consumer) rather than the seller initiates the transaction.

LetsBuyIt and MobShop (formerly Accompany) are direct competitors in this C-t-B market. The business principle of both companies is that consumers join together to drive down the price of products through the benefits of bulk buying. The time of the sale is announced in advance. As more customers join the buying circle, the price of the product continues to fall for the entire group. Online reverse auctions appear to be a quick and easy way to reduce the buying price. However, Emiliani and Stec (2002) have pointed out that gross savings are often eroded by direct and indirect losses, which may result in a net saving that may be unattractive given the amount of time needed to secure it.

Both LetsBuyIt and MobShop launched their first co-buying sites in April 1999, but the geographical markets of the two companies are different: MobShop is mainly based in North America, whereas LetsBuyIt mainly targets the European market. At the start of 2001 LetsBuyIt ran into serious financial problems, like many other Internet firms at that time.

A more radical form of pricing is the rise of customer-set pricing. The old mass-market model was that manufacturers and retailers set prices and customers paid them. Priceline.com and DealTime.com offer a reverse model of pricing, in which customers propose the prices (e.g. for products such as airlines, hotels, and mortgages) and producers determine whether they will accept them. This approach is more likely to work for non-customized products, such as airline seats, where the customer can easily shop around for the lowest price on the same product from a variety of sources.

Consumer-to-consumer (C-t-C) e-commerce

This e-commerce type covers the new fashion for consumer-to-consumer auctions. They are not so much a new marketplace as a new form of entertainment. Auctions did not develop by chance; for many products they suit both buyers and sellers. Fixed prices did not develop by chance; for many (standardized) products they suit both buyers and sellers. However, despite these reservations, the new auction-pricing portals will not disappear, because it is great fun for many people. The bidding and close interaction between buyers and sellers promotes a sense of community – a near addiction that keeps them coming back.

The US-based eBay Inc. is the world's largest and most popular person-to-person trading community on the Internet. eBay pioneered online person-to-person trading by developing a web-based community in which buyers and sellers are brought together in an efficient and entertaining auction format to buy and sell personal items such as antiques, coins, collectibles, computers, memorabilia and toys. The eBay service permits sellers to list items for sale, buyers to bid on items of interest and all eBay users to browse through listed items in a fully automated, topically arranged, intuitive and easy-to-use online service that is available 24 hours a day, seven days a week

The eBay-user spends 130 minutes a month at the site – ten times more than the typical Amazon-user. Of all consumer e-commerce spending in 1998, some 15 per cent came through auctions (Business Week, 1999b).

Amazon's response to this development came on April 12 1999 when Amazon announced its plans to acquire the Internet-based auction company, LiveBid.com Inc., after eBay also approached the company about a possible buyout. In *Business Week* 1999b) Jeffrey Bezos, Amazon CEO, was asked if he thought that the dynamic pricing of auctions would come to other products of Amazon.com. He answered (Business Week, 1999b):

> *No, no, no. Auction pricing is most useful when it's hard to assess a fair value. So that means either that the thing you are selling is unique, or maybe it's not unique, but its value fluctuates rapidly. Stock prices are sort of like that. For most things, fixed prices are more efficient. The reason is that you don't have to negotiate. You don't want to negotiate the price of simple things you buy every day.*

This answer is in line with the principles of the transaction cost analysis model which implies that transaction costs increase when the transactions are characterized by a high degree of complexity.

The proportion of eBay's customers outside North America is still under 5 per cent, but the company is trying to boost these numbers with its purchase of some local Internet firms.

QXL.com is eBay's direct European competitor. It is a pan-European auction community, conducting consumer-to-consumer and business-to-consumer auctions across seven countries in western Europe.

10.6 Exploring buying behaviour in the e-commerce market

This section deals with buying behaviour in the two main markets: the business-to-consumer (B-t-C) market and the business-to-business (B-t-B) market.

Segmenting and exploring consumer behaviour in the B-t-C market

Hofacker (1999) divides Internet users into two main segments, hedonistic surfers and utilitarian searchers.

Hedonistic surfers use a website by experiencing it in the same way they do films and sports events. Often there is a strong non-verbal aspect to the hedonistic experience – the images are quite important. Surfers are relatively unfocused and their browsing is spontaneous. The goal is escapist, to achieve immersion in the site, or at least a high degree of personal enjoyment either through stimulation or pleasure or both. The idea is to gather interesting and exciting experiences from the web.

A unique site works best for these surfers, one which is novel and interesting. They can be drawn into a website via links everywhere and advertising banners on other sites.

In contrast to hedonistic surfers, *utilitarian searchers* are on a mission and they have a work mentality. The utilitarian searcher uses the web in a way that is instrumental and rational. Such a visitor is looking for some kind of specific information. A well-organized and searchable site works best for these seekers.

Utilitarian searchers often use search engines and they can often find a web address that is easy to guess.

We will now discuss consumer buying behaviour in the B-t-C market. Despite the fundamental difference between the marketplace and the virtual market space, one principle still holds true in both worlds: the marketer must understand how the consumer makes decisions as to purchase choice before he/she can effectively respond to these demands.

Figure 10.4 provides an overview of the main differences between marketplace and market space in the consumer decision process. Of course, iteration exists between the different stages. Each of these stages will now be examined in turn and compared in the context of the marketplace and the market space.

Figure 10.4 Consumer purchasing decision process: the market place verus the market space

	MARKETPLACE		MARKET SPACE
Consumer issues:	Marketing issues:		Marketing issues:
• Need awareness • Problem definition • Problem articulation	• Consumer identification • Problem recognition • Stimulate search interest	Problem recognition	• Database to know customer better • Anticipate needs/wants • Response to problems
• Sources of information • Accessibility of information • Reliability of information	• Attract searchers • Provide information	Information search	• Advertising in the marketplace media • Links from other sites • Quality of information • Push technologies
• Comprehensiveness of information • Trust and confidence in information • Trial and sampling	• Influencing purchase criteria • Provide testing/sampling opportunities • Build brand preference	Evaluation of alternatives	• Virtual communities and user groups endorsements • Simulation and testing opportunities
• Negotiation process • Transaction process	• Management of the exchange process • Management of supply	Choice/ Purchase	• Ease of ordering and delivery, payment, security, conditions
• After-sales support • Relationship support	• Service support • Problem recovery • Relationship management	Post-purchase behaviour	• Online support • Relationship building with consumer, user groups and virtual communities

Source: reprinted from *European Management Journal*, vol. 16, no. 5, P. Butler and J. Peppard (1998) Consumer purchasing on the Internet: process and prospects, © 1998 with permission from Elsevier Science.

Problem recognition

The first stage, consumer decision, triggers all subsequent activity. The consumer is compelled to fill the gap between the actual and the desired state. When problem awareness is reached, problem recognition may be triggered by a number of external and internal factors.

In traditional markets, conventional marketing communications stimulate demand via conventional media, e.g. an advertisement on television. However, on the Internet the medium is new, and so new kinds of communication are required. In the traditional mass marketing approaches much of the audience will not be interested, and there is considerable wastage. But new information technologies fundamentally change that. Computer-mediated environments enable identification of individual consumer wants and needs, and the subsequent design and delivery of individual and customized communications.

Information search

The information gathered, either from internal sources (e.g. memory) or external sources (e.g. discussions, brochures, sales promotions) provides the basis for this stage. The marketplace imposes limitations on information. Economic and access barriers constrain what can be known efficiently, and consequently what can realistically be evaluated. On the Internet, however, intelligent shopping agents can scan the entire web to find the data necessary for comparison. The relevant criteria can be presented and explained and can be ordered to suit individual needs.

The management of information is the primary role of the agent or broker in the marketplace. The intermediary function is here largely based on information provision and exchange. This is the effective function of travel agents, for instance. But, in the market space, when an airline sets up its own website with interactive flight information and booking facilities, for example, then the traditional intermediary is bypassed in a classic case of **disintermediation**. As channel disintermediation and re-intermediation become important, a match between information content and consumer requirements also becomes important. As individuals come to utilize the Internet for consumer purchases, a situation of perfect information is almost attainable. However, it must be noted that consumers' sense of uncertainty can actually increase as they gain more information. Information overload occurs when we learn more about the alternatives available to us, and the search becomes psychologically costly.

Evaluation of alternatives

In the marketplace, word-of-mouth communication, and family, colleagues and friends, are a central influence at this stage. In the market space, new reference groups appear. The virtual community, consisting of discussion groups of interested parties, can have the power of the traditional reference groups, but with even greater quality and quantity of information. A simple version of a virtual community is Amazon.com's open book reviews, whereby a potential buyer can read book reviews by other visitors.

Purchase decision

This stage involves decisions on where and how to buy. *Where* to buy is a decision regarding the choice of seller. Competition on the web is driven by sellers attempting to build more exciting and interesting sites than their competitors, attracting the right customers to those sites, and providing superior shopping experiences to induce purchase. *How* to buy concerns the nature of the transaction and contract. Many of the products and services currently available to individual consumers on the Internet are digital, e.g. software and upgrades, or easily physically transported, e.g. music CDs and books. The future broadening of the base will require particular analysis of physical delivery issues. The actual delivery routines for such a service are probably more complex than the ordering, packing and payment routines. Whereas the order can be met within the one organization and under one roof, the logistics of physical delivery of relatively bulky but relatively low-value grocery orders is an entirely different proposition.

Post-purchase behaviour

In this stage the actual sale should be perceived as a starting point rather than an end. How the customer takes delivery of the product, how the product is used, the degree and satisfaction, quality of the service, customer complaints and suggestions are all critical to understanding consumer behaviour. This, of course, applies both in the marketplace and in the market space.

The main difference between relationship development in the two types of markets is that the market space emphasizes high technology, and is more characterized by the power of information and communication technologies to satisfy customer needs and thereby continue business relationships. For the seller in the market space the big issue is keeping the website up to date. Post-purchase activity involves consumers returning to the seller's site with queries, for new information, and to repurchase.

The Internet model of retailing (e-tailing)

The online model of retailing contains some or all of the following features. Depending on the product type, it allows the customer to access online information about the product, place an order, pay for the product and, in the case of digital products (such as software, music, video, etc.), have them delivered instantaneously over the Internet. Because of the nature of online retailing, a number of advantages over traditional physical retailers can be identified.

Advantages of e-tailing

The advantages are as follows.

- *Wide reach*. Using the Internet, online retailers create a platform for advertising and selling their merchandise potentially to the whole Internet community, which provides them with a much wider reach than physical retailers.
- *Exhaustive product selection*. Because of the digital nature of the business, which provides virtually unlimited storage capacity, it is possible to offer a large selection of products that was previously impractical.
- *Few infrastructure requirements*. Offering a wide range of products does not require nearly as much physical infrastructure as is the case with traditional retailers, since information is stored electronically.
- *Unlimited opening hours*. Online stores are also not restricted by limited opening hours; instead, customers can access retailing websites in their own time.
- *High degree of scalability*. In order to respond to increasing client numbers and expand into new markets, an e-tailer only needs to add computer servers to the computer infrastructure.

Disadvantages of e-tailing

However, there are inevitably problems associated with this e-tailing model.

- Since online retailers have no direct face-to-face contact with customers, severe drawbacks arise.
- It is difficult and/or time consuming for pure e-tailers to build a brand name. This is in part due to the number of web offerings that makes it difficult for a brand name to stand out from the mass of links and banner advertisements that clutter the screen.
- It is also more difficult to establish trust with potential customers, who are accustomed to receiving face-to-face help and advice from a salesperson at the local store. Pure online retailers have to rely on other means to establish trust.
- Associated with the lack of physical contact is also the difficulty of handling physical flow. This includes issues such as fitting and trying out products, merchandise delivery and product returns.

The convergence of the two retailing models into 'clicks and mortar'

Concluding from the above discussion of traditional and online retailing, both business models have a number of advantages as well as drawbacks. In the attempt to eliminate or minimize such drawbacks, the emerging trend in the industry is the convergence of the two models of retailing. The result is '**clicks and mortar**'. In other words, traditional retailers are now increasingly moving into the online world while e-tailers are increasingly moving into physical infrastructure. The reasons underlying this convergence and examples of companies which have shifted their operations away from either the pure physical or pure online model towards a mixed one, the so-called 'clicks-and-mortar', will now be described (Enders and Jelassi, 2000).

Traditional stores move online and become clicks and mortar

One of the reasons why traditional retailers have not embraced the Internet was the fear of cannibalizing their own sales. It was not long before they realized that if they were not willing to cannibalize their own sales, others would do it to them. Furthermore, since the Internet is expected to have a large penetration in the short to medium term, physical retailers are now positioning themselves in this emerging market space.

An example of this is the world's largest book retailer Barnes & Noble, which operates over 1000 bookstores throughout North America, attracting over 300 million visitors annually. In 1999, it launched its web-based subsidiary barnesandnoble.com in partnership with Bertelsmann, the German media firm. The size and market power of the parent company provides barnesandnoble.com with a strong leverage as it can tap into the large customer database and use the physical stores to acquire new online customers.

Based on the specific preferences of book club members, promotions are tailored to different reading interests (e.g. a science fiction book club).

Selling both through existing physical stores and through the Internet allows **bricks and mortar** retailers to leverage the strength of each channel. Customers who want to touch and feel products or who are in need of personal assistance will be catered for. At the same time, they have the opportunity to browse and search for products through the Internet conveniently, at any time and in any place, and either have the goods delivered to them or pick up the products themselves at the bookstore. If a purchased product does not fulfil customer expectations, it is easy to return it to the store for a refund. For retailers who already have a large store network with a well-known brand, it is also easier to become established online. If a customer knows that there is a bookstore where he/she can go if problems arise, he/she will be more inclined to make a purchase there than in a store that only exists online.

Online retailers move into conventional infrastructure and become clicks and mortar

Most online retailers (e-tailers) thought initially that they could outsource the handling of physical goods to external providers, allowing them to focus on the web-based retailing of the business, which is easily scaleable. The idea was essentially that they could serve millions of customers and create substantial revenues while at the same time outsourcing the cost-intensive goods handling to external providers. However, as it turned out, the integration between e-tailers and goods handlers was not as smooth as expected. Problems that have arisen include running short on products, delivering the wrong products or delivering them late. In order to address these problems, pure e-tailers are moving into the physical front-end of the value chain by slowly adding warehouses or even physical retail stores.

An example is Amazon.com, which significantly expanded its warehousing capacity during 1999, building over 3 million square feet of warehouse, which included seven new warehouses in the USA, one in the UK and one in Germany. Overall, it had 3.5 million square feet at the end of 1999, which is ten times more than in 1998. The goal is to develop a distribution infrastructure to meet long-term growth and provide Amazon.com customers with fast reliable shipping that comes directly from the company. The distribution facilities allow Amazon.com to increase the number of books, CDs, videos and other products, e.g. toys, through an alliance with Toys 'R' Us, which has decided to let Amazon.com take care of its online business. These products are kept on hand for immediate shipment to customers and thus are delivered faster as a result of greater availability, quicker processing and shorter delivery times. In addition to speed, Amazon.com is also trying to maintain a high level of customer service satisfaction. Until now, Amazon.com has not been able to generate any profits for its owners, but this may be about to change. In the fourth quarter of 2001, Amazon had its first quarterly profit.

Generally, any products that can be delivered in a digital format (such as software, music or printed documents) are likely to experience a radical shift towards the online retailing model. The reason for this shift is that for these products, there is no substantial reason for the customer to visit a physical store. In the music industry, for example, consumers will increasingly be able to select the songs they want to buy through an online website and then receive them directly over the Internet. This can all be done at much lower marginal unit costs than in the traditional format and with a much higher degree of customization for the individual customer. However, it is likely that consumers will still also look for the shipping experience in a physical store. If physical stores continue to be an important part of the shipping experience, those retailers who manage to integrate their online retailing with physical in-store retailing are likely to come out ahead.

| Exhibit 10.5 | eBay's role as a network orchestrator in the value chain |

The orchestrator's role is characterized by creating a network of contract manufacturers and suppliers connected to one another and to itself by a powerful set of network applications running on its proprietary extranet. Cisco itself was withdrawing from those parts of the industry value chain where it lacked pre-eminent advantage.

Orchestrators then set about establishing a platform across which the network participants will interact. For Cisco, this platform is the Cisco Connection Online, a web-based channel for organizing and circulating information generated by the company's customers and partners. For eBay, the platform is the auction software that brings into being a community of sellers and buyers (Figure 10.5).

In effect, eBay provides the product-management and distribution links of the value chain, while the company's specialist partners, such as Billpoint, Visa, iShip, Paybyweb, Tradeable and UPS, handle direct payment, shipping and other essential services.

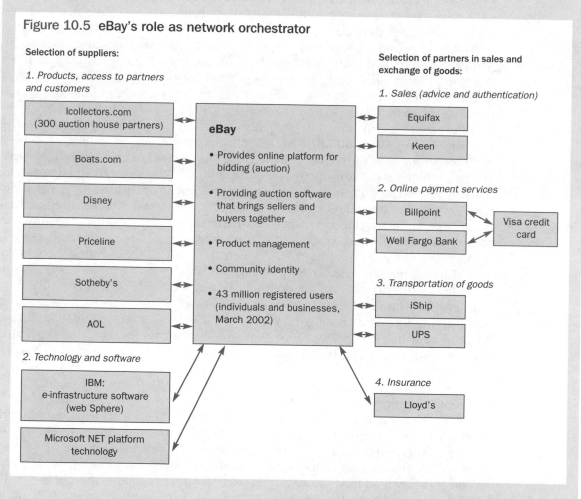

Figure 10.5 eBay's role as network orchestrator

Source: adapted from Häski and Lighton (2001).

Exploring business behaviour in the B-t-B market

Web information systems hold great potential to streamline and improve business-to-business transactions. Instead of regarding the Internet as a mere sales channel, companies also utilize emerging technologies to cut costs out of the supply chain by streamlining procurement processes and improving collaboration. In times of intense competition and increasingly open markets, the ability to achieve efficiency improvements can become key to commercial success.

We will look now at how businesses make buying decisions and how they can be supported by an e-commerce information system. A conceptual framework is introduced in Figure 10.6. The inter-organizational transactions are analysed from a process-oriented perspective. We distinguish between four phases: information, negotiation, settlement, and after-sales and transaction analysis.

Participants

Transactions usually involve three categories of participants: buyers, sellers, and inter-mediaries. Buyers and sellers are the active groups in terms of exchanging goods and services (sellers) for some form of recompense (buyer). Regarding the third group, intermediaries, we will expand the role from a traditional distributor of goods as described earlier. The intermediaries are supposed to offer a variety of services to support and facilitate transactions. This includes financial institutions such as banks, credit card companies and insurance brokers; providers of shipping, logistics and warehousing services; and consultants, industry associations and market researchers offering advice, product data or market information. Providers of information technology to automate transactions or to help set up electronic marketplaces can be characterized as intermediaries as well.

In the case of business-to-business transactions, both buyers and sellers are business organizations, whereas business-to-consumer and consumer-to-consumer transactions involve end consumers or private households as buyers or sellers, respectively.

Figure 10.6 The buyer/seller transaction process model

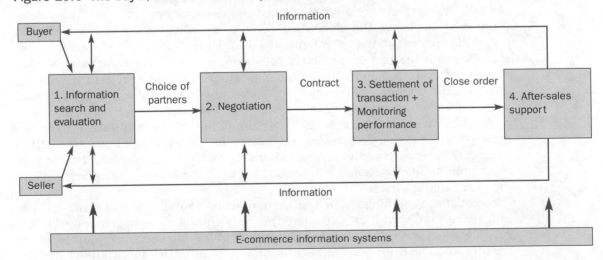

Source: Hollensen (2001), p. 352.

In the following we refer to the four phases of the buyer/seller transaction process model (Figure 10.6). In particular the role of the e-commerce information system will be described.

Phase 1: Information search and evaluation

In the information phase of a transaction, both buyers and sellers look for information. In the marketplace, buyers locate information sources such as product catalogues, use them to scan product listings, obtain offerings from prospective suppliers, and gather additional information about products, vendor or transaction-specific requirements. Before a purchasing transaction can be performed, internal approval frequently has to be obtained from senior management.

The information phase comprises both searching for a particular electronic catalogue or source of information and locating required information and commodities within the information repository. In this phase, buyers and sellers are not yet focused on specific transaction partners. Information gathering and knowledge creation are at the centre of attention, and information is the primary object of exchange between prospective transaction partners.

A variety of web-based information systems and other applications are available to provide support for the information phase of a transaction. Electronic catalogues, for example, feature comprehensive product descriptions and search tools, configuration support for complex purchases, workflow routing for approval processes, and access to additional information such as market research data and product reviews. Catalogues can be provided by suppliers, set up by the buyer, or developed by a third party. They can be hosted on the supplier's web server, or be integrated into internal systems. Links to back-end systems provide access to human resources data, as they are required to manage purchasing authorization.

Phase 2: Negotiation

Of all transaction phases, the negotiation phase shows the broadest range of variations ranging from simple processes where price is the most important factor (always-a-share), to very complex arrangements where the buyer–seller relationship is regarded as a long-term strategic partnership (lost-for-good), according to Jackson (1985). Negotiations are often perceived as processes where a small number of prospective customers and sellers (often only one participant on each side) bargain on product prices and the other terms of a deal. The parties jointly identify possible solutions with the goal of reaching a consensus, usually in the form of a contract. Bargaining processes alter with decisions whether to accept or reject the offering, and with the outlining of counter-suggestions until a mutually satisfactory agreement is reached. As prospective buyers and seller start communicating directly with each other, interaction is the centre of attention. In this phase, influence is the primary object of exchange between the transaction partners. Not every transaction process features such complex negotiations. In fact, the negotiation phase is very often quite simple or even non-existent, such as in the case of retail purchases and pre-negotiated contracts.

Negotiations can range from a single transaction to multiple-year contracts. The longer the time span that is covered, the more complex the structure of the bargaining process tends to be. In the following, we focus on complex forms of negotiations (be it for one transaction or a large number), but acknowledge the simpler forms as well.

Information systems support negotiations in a number of ways. They can provide transaction information and decision support by assessing the value of specific offerings, by identifying new bargaining options, and by increasing the negotiator's productivity. Participants may improve their bargaining positions through additional online information, such as the volume of previous business, supplier performance, or spending patterns.

Phase 3: Settlement of transaction and monitoring performance

Upon execution of the contract the objects of the transaction are exchanged according to the conditions previously stipulated. In addition, the settlement phase regularly includes some form of mutual performance monitoring. After the rather unstructured negotiation phase, the process of executing a transaction can be relatively straightforward. It is formally initiated as soon as a purchase order is confirmed by the supplier. The supplier ships the goods (often in collaboration with a third party, for example a local provider of logistic services), announces the shipment, and sends out a corresponding invoice. At the buyer side, orders are tracked, items are received, and payment is initiated after matching the invoice with the delivery. Naturally, there are many variations on this standard scenario. Consider, for example, the differences between the shipment of physical goods and the online delivery of information goods.

In the settlement phase of a transaction, activities and procedures are comparatively well defined, as they are part of the contract. Thus, attention centres on execution and efficiency. At this point, the main objects of exchange are goods and services. Information technologies to support transaction settlement may include EDI systems on the web and various tools to process orders internally and between transaction partners, facilitate order tracking, and support payment processes.

Phase 4: After-sales analysis

After a transaction has taken place, both sellers and buyers store the transaction data to provide after-sales support (seller), or to assess supplier performance and analyse internal buying patterns (buyer). At the buyer side, the information flow is often split. While the purchase data is stored with central procurement, the end user keeps the product-related documentation. In case of unexpected irregularities, it is often the end user who contacts the supplier (e.g. to request a repair). Without proper access to the transaction file, communication problems and delays can occur. Capturing, storing, and managing data are vital at this point. As in the first phase (information), it is mainly information that is being exchanged between buyer and seller.

The electronic support of after-sales activities ranges from simple e-mail services to automated help desks and sophisticated electronic maintenance manuals. Ideally, systems to support after-sales and transaction analysis provide central access to the transaction information. **Data warehousing** applications support the storing, accessing and processing of large amounts of data. They allow the firm to assess supplier performance, analyse internal buying patterns, provide the basis for consolidating corporate purchasing, and improve future bargaining positions with suppliers. At the supplier side, data about past transactions – including information of system configurations, preferred payment options, and so forth – support the maintenance process and subsequently improve the quality of the information phase of future transactions.

B-t-B e-commerce models

In Figure 10.7 a business classification scheme is described, the categorization depending on the number of sellers and buyers (Barnes-Vieyra and Claycomb, 2001).

Cell 1: One seller to one buyer

This is similar to the EDI situation – see Figure 10.2.

Cell 2: One seller to many buyers

In practice this situation results in two different cases.

One seller to many buyers

To be successful in B-t-B e-commerce in the one seller to many buyers model, a company must strive to create channel strategies that incorporate e-commerce with traditional channels. As the buyer realizes greater utility from the e-commerce channel, so should the firm's traditional distribution channels. Leading companies advise involving the customer, as well as people from every business function who deal with the customer, in the development of new channels. For example, personal selling will see greater efficiency in finding new prospects, customer data collection, and productivity.

The vast amount and quality of customer information facilitated by e-commerce is a powerful knowledge management tool for sales professionals. It improves customer needs analysis and product configurations, ultimately allowing the salesperson to provide effective and efficient one-to-one solutions. The idea is to provide a buying situation in which customers' efforts are minimized by offering

Figure 10.7 B-t-B e-commerce models

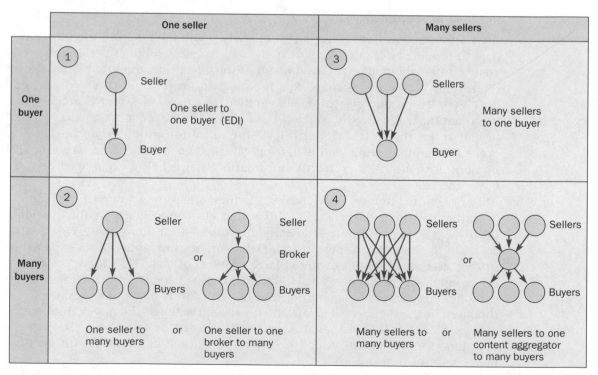

them options and allowing them to take advantage of the channel that best fits their needs.

A competitive advantage can be realized in this model. Cisco provides perhaps the best example of how a company can flourish as a result of B-to-B e-commerce. Regardless of strong competitors, Cisco continually gains market share as a result of the added utility provided to its customers. Its online offerings include user-friendly configurations of complex products, product catalogues, order placement, and after-sales service. As more and more customers use Cisco's website, greater profitability is realized through reduced technical and customer support costs as well as lower costs in traditional communication processes such as printing and shipping.

One seller to one broker to many buyers

In its simplest form, the one seller to one broker to many buyers model is an online auction where the online auction house is the broker. It offers the best opportunity for greater profitability in industries where highly differentiated or perishable products and services can be marketed to disparate buyers with varying perceptions of product value. Commodity markets can also benefit from this model. Although the market pressures remain and are likely to increase through a greater level of buyer information, opportunities exist for reduced costs in timely and efficient transactions. Unlike the previous model, this one is less concerned with content and more with providing a market space free of traditional distribution constraints.

The one seller to one broker to many buyers model offers potential benefits for buyers and sellers of specific markets. Buyers benefit from lower costs associated with searching and information gathering, and gain power in the market as information becomes more prevalent. Sellers with highly differentiated or unique products stand to benefit most from the auction model.

Cell 3: Many sellers to one buyer

Many large companies insist that procurement be handled electronically, refusing to do business with suppliers unable to make such transactions. Buyers realize transaction cost savings and greatly benefit from the lower costs inherent in electronic bidding processes: less need for personal contact, reduced resources required in manual form processing, and the ability to infer price competitiveness by observing activity among suppliers. The buyer has the information advantage and the seller typically is in a price-taker position. The rapid communication associated with instantaneous electronic purchase orders, invoices, and shipping documentation versus the waiting time involved in unlinked administrative processes offers the benefit of reduced cycle time. The time necessary to communicate new demands is minimal. Small firms are expected to benefit as well through greater opportunities to bid. Internet protocol processes allow participation in bidding previously barred by cost and technical complexity.

Cell 4: Many sellers to many buyers

The many sellers to many buyers model seeks to provide a market space where the distribution channel ceases to be serial in nature and any market player has the opportunity to transact with any other player. Any participant in any given transaction may be either a buyer or a seller. Although this model promises the best chance for economic impact, it is probably also the most challenging to implement because success depends on all buyers and sellers having compatible software.

The many sellers to content aggregator to many buyers model includes an intermediary (the content aggregator) that hosts an electronic marketplace for buyers and sellers to meet, acting as a hub for commerce. This electronic intermediary is commonly referred to as a hub or portal within the e-commerce industry.

Both supplier firms (sellers) and buying firms should decide for themselves which of the B-t-B models would best provide a sustainable competitive advantage. In particular, supplier firms (including content aggregators and brokers) must decide what features would maximize buyer satisfaction and increase purchasing.

A trend is the increase in products becoming commodities, or commoditization. As buyers gain access to more and more information, there is a diminished effect on suppliers' abilities to differentiate their goods and services. This is particularly true with the many sellers to many buyers model. To combat this effect, suppliers must identify niche markets too small to appeal to competitors, innovate to stay ahead, or create a monopoly. Paradoxically, the same forces that are driving commoditization are also permitting its antithesis – mass commoditization. Buyers should look for purchasing models that will allow them to obtain low prices as well as products customized to their particular needs.

10.7 Disintermediation in e-commerce – myth or reality?

According to transaction cost analysis (TCA), firms will choose the entry and distribution mode that economizes on transaction costs, in particular the coordination cost between producer and intermediaries.

Today, as information technology continues its rapid increase in performance at lower cost, information infrastructures are now within the reach of individual consumers. The potential for transformation in the value chain of many firms is thus far greater now than it has been in the past, as technology begins to enable producers to interact directly with consumers. It has been noted that intermediaries add significant costs to the value chain, which are reflected in higher prices of products or services to the end customers. One fundamental question, therefore, is to what extent producers would take advantage of direct electronic links with consumers, and whether, in the process, intermediaries will be eliminated from the value system.

The essential argument is that the use of IT allows manufacturers to internalize activities that have been traditionally performed by intermediaries. Producers will capture value and, in the resultant redistribution of profits along the value system, traditional intermediaries will disappear. Benjamin and Wigand (1995) argue that if transactions take place directly between manufacturers and consumers, both manufacturers and consumers will benefit: the manufacturers will try to retain a higher portion of surplus value or profits that are generated along the value system, while the consumers will benefit from both a larger choice and lower prices. In other words, the network's ability to support direct exchanges efficiently will increase both producer and consumer welfare. Thus, it is predicted that manufacturers will sell directly to consumers, and consumers will prefer to buy directly from manufacturers.

Thus the myth has been that the Internet will eliminate the need for intermediaries. Early predictions called for *disintermediation* (e.g. Wunderman, 1998), that is, the disappearance of physical distribution chains as people move from buying through distributors and resellers to buying directly from manufacturers. The reality is that the Internet may eliminate the traditional physical distributors, but in the transformation process of the value chain new types of intermediaries may appear. So the disintermediation process has come to be balanced by a re-intermediation force – the evolution of new intermediaries tailor-made for the online world (Figure 10.8).

The traditional distribution model is linear. The manufacturer builds products. Wholesalers and distributors aggregate products from multiple manufacturers and bring them through several levels of distribution in small lots to resellers who deal directly with consumers. The value added in the distribution chain lies in shipping, warehousing and delivering products.

With the Internet, value chains are being deconstructed and reconstructed in different ways – into value webs. This process has given rise to a new class of intermediaries. Companies such as Yahoo! aggregate information and make it easier to access information and see new possibilities of doing business. The value added is no longer in logistic aggregation but rather in information aggregation. Consumers come to these sites looking for information and opportunities to purchase.

Companies such as Amazon.com and E*Trade are dramatically changing traditional models of selling goods and services by acting as a new type of intermediary. These new types of intermediaries offer new opportunities for existing companies as well as start-ups. Companies need to examine their current value chain and determine how the Internet might change it. Then they can adapt their business processes to take advantage of the new model, thereby protecting their major sources of revenue and also developing new ones.

For example, consider the airline industry. In the physical economy, who are the distributors of travel tickets? Thousands of travel agents, spread around the world. In the online economy, who are the distributors? Travel-related websites such as Microsoft's Expedia, among others. Consider another point: in some big US cities various reports indicate that almost 20 per cent of car sales take place on Internet sites. The distribution channels have not gone away; they have simply shifted to new intermediaries.

Figure 10.8 Disintermediation and re-intermediation

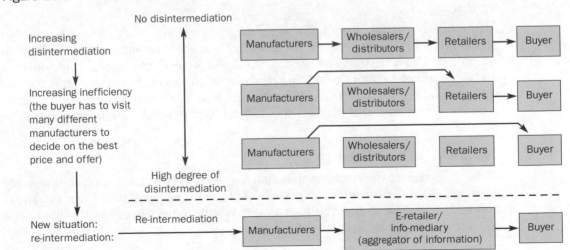

Source: Hollensen (2001), p. 355.

Building trust on the web

In the rush to build Internet businesses, many executives concentrate all their attention on attracting customers rather than retaining them. However, the cost of attracting new customers far exceeds the cost of retaining current customers. When Reichhold and Schefter (2000) asked web shoppers to name the attributes of e-tailers that were most important in earning their business, the number one answer was 'a website I know and trust'. All other attributes, including lowest cost and broadest selection, lagged far behind.

Hence, before the firm can gain the loyalty of customers they first have to gain their trust. Trust is an important issue in web marketing. Consumers may have to provide personal information about themselves, such as address and credit card information, and every interaction may be recorded. Since the risk is higher when purchasing from an unfamiliar web business than in the conventional market, long-term relationships are more desirable, which further increases switching costs.

For example, millions of customers felt comfortable letting Amazon store their names, addresses, and credit card numbers in its ordering system. The resulting convenience – customers can make repeat purchases with just one click – has become a critical competitive edge. It is one of the biggest reasons customers keep coming back – to buy not just books but also CDs, videos, hardware, and other products. If customers did not trust Amazon, if they feared that their credit card numbers might be accessed by someone else, they would never share their personal information and Amazon would lose its competitive position.

Trust is built methodically through a step-by-step process in which the consumer and marketer exchange value. Each time the customer shares some personal information, the marketer should be ready to reward the consumer with personalized services and richer experiences. The mutual give-and-take balance eventually leads to an advanced trust-based collaboration.

A four stage 'trust building' model (Dayal et al., 1999) is shown in Figure 10.9. In principle, the model may be used both for the B-t-C and B-t-B markets.

Attraction

At the first stage, the customer browses the site and even makes a transaction. No real relationship exists between the marketer and the customer, and none may be warranted. The best strategy is to provide the browsers with relevant information and experiences without demanding personal information. The customer is providing the marketer with the customer's time and attention together with some browser information and maybe also a general view of what the customer thinks of the site.

User-driven personalization

At the second stage, consumers start shaping web pages to their specific tastes. For example, CDNow customers can personalize their home pages with favourite artists and wish lists. The company shows that it is willing to deliver some value to the consumer before gaining financially.

Figure 10.9 The e-trust building process

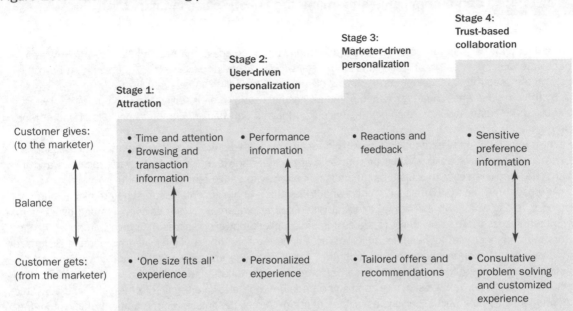

Source: adapted from Dayal et al. (1999), p. 68.

Marketer-driven personalization

In the third stage, marketers begin using insights provided by the customer to send information back to them. Thus, CDNow uses its knowledge of a consumer (developed at the earlier stages of trust) to suggest products he or she might like.

Wise and Morrison (2000) show how www.Mysimon.com uses decision-support software to offer tailored purchase advice in a variety of product categories. This allows the buyer to compare the offerings of many suppliers. It helps customers to sort through an array of purchase decisions, decide which product features are important to them, and then see how well the available offerings match up with their requirements. As the process continues, CDNow learns the consumer's preferences and tries to offer what he or she really likes. It is worth emphasizing that marketers should rein in their urge to make immediate use of data mining and personalization technologies to create user-specific communication. Too often the customers are bombarded with promotional offers as soon as the marketer obtains an e-mail address.

Trust-based collaboration

At the final stage, the marketer and the consumer work together on a very intimate basis. The customer allows the marketer access to the most sensitive personal or company information and the customer in turn gains customized experiences and consultative problem solving. Only a few online marketers have reached this level of trust with their customers in the B-t-C market. However, in the B-t-B market this stage is more prevalent.

Exhibit 10.6   Can e-commerce streamline the US car-parts industry?

The current situation

The industry for car-parts is fragmented, and has many intermediaries. The parts makers sell their wares to giant warehouse distributors. These giants in turn sell goods to smaller players called 'jobbers' that have their own warehouses to hold local inventory. The big distributors also sell to various retailers.

By the time the wheel bearing or a motor mount has been sold to an installer who has put it into a vehicle and billed the customer, more than half the price paid for that part has gone into the pockets of one or more intermediaries.

This profusion of players adds days to vehicle-repair times. It leads to chronic problems with excess inventory, mix-ups and availability. Moreover, with so many buffers between the far-flung parts factories and the commuter who is stuck with a faulty car, there is no easy way to gauge product demand.

At present (Figure 10.10), all information about the supply chain is contained in separate places and protected by those who have it. The major focus of the OEM at present is toward its suppliers and distributors, who then access the dealers to get to the customer. Suppliers, however, access their own warehouse distributors, who connect with jobbers, and installers as well as retailers. It is a complicated distribution system to say the least. Of course, warehouse distributors can bypass the jobber altogether and go directly to the installer and the retailer. The suppliers can also go to the retailers directly. Methods of communication include post, phone, fax, face to face, and some e-mail. All the arrows are going to the right, and very little information is coming back. Everyone uses rates of return to make estimates on the amount of inventory that is needed, since no one has clear information. There is huge waste in the system.

Can iStarXchange remove the inefficiencies?

iStarXchange was formed in February 2000 as a joint venture of Toyota Motor Sales, USA, in Torrance, CA, and i2 Technologies of Irving, TX. The latter company is a leading producer of supply chain management software.

Figure 10.10 The existing distribution system in the US car-parts industry

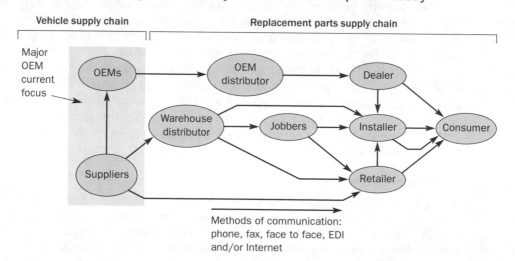

Source: Segil, L. (2001) *Fast Alliances: Power your E-business*, copyright © 2001 John Wiley & Sons, Inc., this material is used by permission of John Wiley & Sons, Inc.

Exhibit 10.6 continued

Toyota recognized that it would benefit if more and more of its customers and customers' customers placed their orders online. In addition, using the Internet permits all participants to share data, thereby leading to greater efficiencies in planning and inventory management.

After studying the subject extensively, Toyota concluded that rather than invest in an Internet system just for itself, it would be far better to sponsor the development of a market space that could be used by all participants in the original equipment market and car-parts market.

Figure 10.11 outlines the changes that iStarXchange would bring to the industry. Now the jobbers, OEMs, suppliers, and wholesale distributors connect with the dealers, installers, and retailers to serve the customer. All communications are Internet based, with information going in all directions. Every time something is sold, the inventory levels are updated and true demands will be passed back through the system to enable the calculation of real inventory figures. Whereas now every manufacturer has the overhead of huge distribution centres the new system eliminates the need for the inventory levels that currently exist in the value chain.

Labour costs also decrease since there will be no need for employees to tell customers what is in the catalogue and at what prices. At present, the jobbers serve the purpose of information flow, but with the new system their jobs are most at risk. There are 25,000 in the USA alone.

In the future, suppliers (manufacturers) of car parts can look at the end of the value chain and see what the product is doing.

However, some auto parts manufacturers are still reluctant to sell online. One parts manufacturer that is wary of selling directly over the Internet is Tenneco Automotive Inc., a US$3.3 billion-a-year supplier of suspension and exhaust-system parts. Even though Tenneco could sell directly to repair shops online, the company is not even considering it. Tenneco needs the middlemen, it says, particularly for its distribution networks, which move and deliver a lot of the company's products. Tenneco is using the web to take orders from a handful of its bigger customers – mostly big warehouse distributors and retail repair chains, which are using the system to buy exhaust system parts. But the company is not allowing repair shops to use that system.

Figure 10.11 Streamlining the value chain in the US car-parts industry

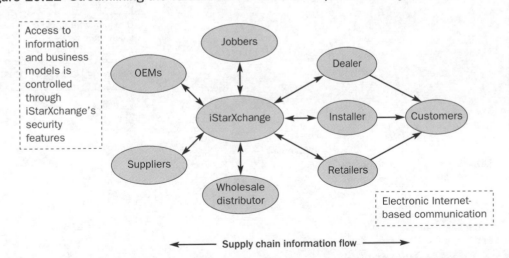

Source: Segil, L. (2001) *Fast Alliances: Power your E-business*, copyright © 2001 John Wiley & Sons, Inc., this material is used by permission of John Wiley & Sons, Inc.

Sources: Freeman (2000), Segil (2001).

10.8 Developing a dynamic e-commerce strategy

Many commercial websites have moved from providing basic company and product information to becoming an integral part of product and service launch strategies. Yet many firms are realizing that even this more coordinated approach is not taking full advantage of the Internet.

Figure 10.12 explores the development of a firm's web strategy from a low-level strategy with the same one-way communication to a fully integrated e-commerce strategy, where the customer feels that he or she is treated on a one-to-one interactive basis. We will now look at the three commitment levels in detail.

Level 1: One-to-many broadcast

Companies use the Internet for something that could be considered little else than a formal presence. These companies feel that they have to be present on the web, but do not follow any concrete **marketing objectives** with the establishment of their website.

The motivation of management in establishing such a page is most probably mainly reactive: as competitors move on to the web, it is felt that a presence has become necessary. Often, however, management will doubt that few if any customers or prospects will ever care to go near the site. The only tangible benefit from the web is seen in the ability to use it in traditional marketing channels in order to project a high-technology image, an image of a company that keeps abreast with the latest developments. Although such an Internet 'strategy' will certainly not

Figure 10.12 Increasing commitment to e-commerce

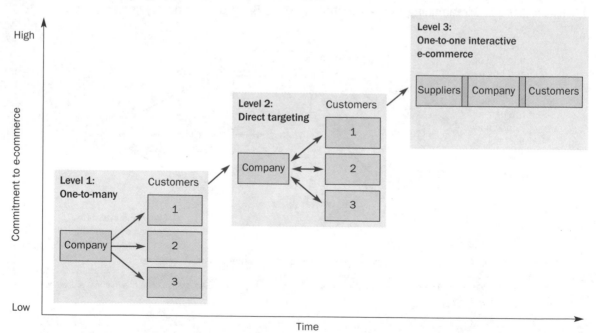

Source: Hollensen (2001), p. 358.

double the company's turnover, it can nonetheless be an economically plausible move because investment is low.

The web representation is regarded as an additional tool to channel information on a firm's products or services to potential and existing customers. Companies following this strategy do consider that the web is a useful tool, but perceive it to be no different from the traditional one-to-many marketing channels. The focus of such a web presence will therefore lie in the firm providing as much information as possible through the web rather than establishing a dialogue with the customer. Consequently, these companies will spend considerable time designing their website and ensuring the information is complete, accurate and kept up to date. The site will be easy to access, quick to load, and easily found using search engines. Products or services may be displayed in great detail in this virtual showroom to enhance their visibility and exposure in the marketplace and thus increase the probability of purchase.

However, these sites will not be designed as a communication device. The site will not explicitly encourage customer feedback such as service requests or complaints beyond product enquiries. Moreover, if customers want to purchase a product they will often have to use the traditional channels to do so. In summary, these informational sites represent company and product brochures. Economically speaking this is a valid strategy for companies that rely heavily on mass communication. The web presence will allow these firms to keep their customers and prospects constantly up to date. It will also decrease the amount of printed information and the likelihood of having boxes full of outdated brochures awaiting disposal.

Level 2: Direct targeting

For the firms on this level, the key difference between traditional marketing media and the new web marketing is the degree of interactivity. Communication is no longer based on businesses feeding information to customers. Rather, the customers play an active role not only in looking for information relevant to the specific product and service needs in their buying process, but also in communicating these needs to the company. Hence, some degree of segmentation is possible. In some cases, the customers can also buy standard products on the website. The interaction (feedback) is still not at the highest level, as the basic exchange of information takes place through e-mail.

The most fundamental capability of a website is the presentation of information about products, services, people, events or ideas. websites with a strategic orientation emphasize both the gathering (feedback) and **diffusion** of information. It is possible to evaluate the extent to which an organization fulfils the informing function by examining the efforts to exchange information with key stakeholders. These stakeholders are customers, investors, suppliers, affiliates, employees, managers, and community members. In addition to providing information on the company's vision, history, products and services, many websites include information on organizational structure, finance, recruiting, executive teams and customer surveys.

After establishing a presence on the Internet, one of the primary objectives of a new website is to attract a variety of interested parties to visit the company's site.

This is done in a variety of ways. It may simply be a matter of mentioning the address of the firm's home page in all possible connections. On the other hand, the company may have found differences among the customers and have differentiated the home page for its different customer groups around the world.

Many companies try to duplicate their US e-commerce strategy in European countries, but it is not as easy as it might seem. Companies cannot create a single website and expect to reach customers and distributors around the world.

Global e-commerce with one worldwide standardized website will probably not be successful in the long run, but for the small company (born global) it may be the only way to get started in global e-commerce, without using too many resources. The moment a company has to deliver physical goods, it has to deal with legislation (e.g. tariff barriers, VAT). It also has to deal with cultural, legal and ethical and language barriers.

Let us explore the language barrier further. Today, there are only seven countries where English is the primary language spoken, about half a billion people, and where the combined economies represent 30 per cent of the world's economy. The combined population of these countries represents 8 per cent of the world's population. Companies that continue to target this small fraction of the world market will miss out on capturing a large potential market.

According to the latest statistics (**http://www.euromktg.com/glostats**), 91 million people access the Internet from English-speaking countries, whereas 80 million people access the Internet in other languages. Recent figures from Forrester Research state that 80 per cent of European-based corporate sites are multilingual. (See **http//www.glreach.com/eng/ed/art/reasonsforglobal.html**.)

An example of the use of multilingual websites is Eastman Kodak Co., which has region-specific versions of its Kodak.com websites in 16 countries. Also, search engines like Yahoo! and Alta Vista have country-specific websites, at least in their major markets.

Level 3: One-to-one interactive

This is the final level, where we see a high degree of interaction between buyer and seller. Here, the company is moving from providing company and product information to becoming an integral part of the whole vertical value chain from supplier to end consumer. This virtual integration works faster than level 2 (direct targeting) by blurring traditional boundaries between suppliers, manufacturers and customers in the value chain. Dell Computers gained the position as a market leader in the personal computer industry by using this model (Magretta, 1998).

A website that supports e-commerce can provide an important strategic asset for a business. A successful site has many benefits:

- it tightens relationships with existing customers and business partners
- it offers new revenue-generating opportunities, through new channels as well as new business models
- it offers opportunities to reduce costs by streamlining processes
- it provides a competitive advantage.

Building a site can represent a significant investment in time and resources. A haphazard approach often results in wasted money and lost opportunity. To be successful, companies must integrate e-commerce into their overall business strategies and processes. They must understand the role of e-commerce in the context of other revenue-generating channels as well as re-engineering and cost-reduction initiatives.

Companies must also recognize that e-commerce may have a dramatic impact on existing business models and distribution channels. It may be necessary to redefine the current business model and perhaps modify relationships with the current channel or supply chain – or develop entirely new relationships or supply chains. Some industries will be more affected than others by the supply chain transformation that the Internet is causing. In some industries, a complete redefinition of the business model may be the only way to maintain a competitive edge. As a result, a careful examination of the existing business model and how e-commerce may affect it is essential for success in the online arena.

The following phases are involved in developing and implementing a successful e-commerce strategy.

- Identification of the process, product or business area that is most applicable for an e-commerce initiative.

- The company's e-commerce goods. Questions that need to be answered include:
  - what portion of the business will e-commerce represent in 12 months, two years and five years?
  - what volume of business does the company expect over the next five years?
  - what level of return on investment does the company expect?
  - how will return on investment be measured?
  - what cost savings can the company realize through e-commerce?
  - will online sales reduce the sales volumes in existing channels? If so, what will be the impact on each channel?

- Definition of internal and external groups. Defining the audience or customer is one of the primary tasks because it determines how and when internal and external groups should be involved. This includes identifying internal audiences, such as marketing, sales, sales channel, finance, IT and other internal groups, as well as external customers, suppliers, vendors, resellers and other business partners. This element of the overall plan affects many other aspects of the e-commerce system, from site design to online marketing techniques.

- Evaluation of competitor strategies. The company's traditional competitors may already have an e-commerce initiative. It is essential to identify what these competitors are doing. Are they aggressively pursuing an e-commerce strategy or are they taking a wait-and-see approach? Are they extending their existing offerings to the new channel or are they creating an entirely new business? Although current competitors are a threat, non-traditional competitors often represent the biggest competitive risk. These are the companies that find new ways to reconstruct traditional value chains into value webs – gaining a significant head-start over companies that simply move existing business processes to the Internet.

- Integration of e-commerce with existing distribution channels and partners. E-commerce is one component of an overall business value chain. It integrates with existing business processes and systems, and should complement existing channels rather than compete with them.

● Putting the right internal competences/skills in place. Moving into electronic commerce requires new skills, knowledge and expertise in the three areas of strategy, technology and creativity.

  – Strategic planning must be approached in a totally different way because of the dynamic nature of the Internet. Therefore the time perspective of strategic plans in the physical firms (e.g. five years) should normally be shortened to perhaps one year in Internet firms.

  – Internet technologies are rapidly evolving, and keeping pace with the new developments is difficult. Technological expertise involves in-depth understanding of current hardware and software solutions, new technologies, site development, systems integration and security issues.

  – Creative skills involve more than just basic website design. This discipline encompasses the entire user experience – what users see, how they navigate, how they obtain information and how they conduct transactions. It also encompasses the audience development activities that drive traffic to the site. Marketing and promotional techniques that are effective in traditional media do not always translate well into the online marketplace.

After considering these phases, the company can then design and implement the desired e-commerce system. This also involves creating a web presence, which is creative and adds value in order to get customers to come back for more. The company can keep their site focused on the strategic benefits for customers by managing what the Strategic Interactive Group (**www.sig.bsh.com**) has called the '4 Cs' of the web.

Content

When people come to your site, they want to find something there. The challenge is to work out what people want and how they want to interact with it. It is all about having the right content, in the right format, with the right functionality. As with any communication medium, the right mix of information and creative content is needed. And because the web is a different medium from print or TV, managing content for the web takes different approaches and requires the integration of marketing and technology skills.

Camera

Can the firm bring products or services to the market that customers value? Can they bring them to market in a way that adds value over other types of distribution? If yes, they are differentiating themselves from other companies.

Customization

Unlike other media and channels, the web is ideal for directing customers to the information and products they want, and for providing them with another, often easier, mode of transaction.

Community

If the firm can create a sense of community on the web, they have an advantage because people will come back to the site over and over again, just like people come back to their favourite magazines, TV shows, and retail stores. Community is a powerful return mechanism for the web.

10.9 Creating and maintaining relationships in e-commerce through 'stickiness'

One of the major strategies for value creation through e-commerce is 'stickiness' – the ability of websites to draw and retain customers. The following presents different ways by which companies can draw and retain customers in e-commerce (Zott *et al.* 2000).

Loyalty programmes – reward customers for their loyalty

Loyalty programmes are not a new idea as a means of encouraging repeat purchasing. Rewarding buyers with something that can be accumulated and redeemed for goods and services has long been popular in the real world. Doing this leads to more frequent purchasing by a given customer and greater sales volume in the long term.

Award programmes also help establish a better relationship between the seller and the buyer. In return for the reward, the seller can accumulate information about the buyer's purchasing patterns and preferences and is then able to serve him or her better in the future.

Globally, loyalty programmes are best known through a few players in specific industries, e.g. airlines that reward frequent fliers with free tickets.

Personalization of product or customization of service

Another means of keeping customers is by tailoring products or services to fit their particular personality or tastes. Tailoring can take various forms – products can be made to order, or personalized by the seller, or the interface (i.e. the web page that the customer sees when visiting the website) can be adapted, or customized by the consumer. These tailoring tactics are possible when the firm has adequate knowledge about the consumer. Companies have the opportunity to build a closer relationship with the customer by using the information that the customer gives upon registering or opening an account.

It can be used to speed up the purchasing process by calling up previous orders or payment information, to cross-sell other products, and to increase the level of service that a user receives. Knowing a consumer's tastes is also a good marketing tool. Targeted product offerings can be made by selective banner advertising, or by sending e-mails notifying clients about special offers, enticing the consumer to return to the site and make a purchase.

Personal information about the user can also be gathered by the placement of '**cookies**', a common means of recognizing a repeat user when he or she returns to a site.

Build online (virtual) communities

A community can be seen as a group in which individuals come together based on an obligation to one another, or as a group in which individuals come together for one purpose.

Communities of users, known as user groups, have a long history in the B-t-B market. Such groups provide a useful forum for users to share experiences, solve problems, meet peers at conferences and events, and explore other companies. Online communities with real-time 'chat' have been a feature of the Internet since it started. Newsgroups were the primary driver for the growth of the Internet during the 1994–5 period. The rapid rise of America Online (AOL) was driven by its ability to generate vibrant communities through chat and online messaging.

Creating online communities has benefits for both consumers and vendors. Consumers are able to share their experiences, access competing vendors and ideas, and shape the content they receive.

One of the most popular ways of building online communities seems to be the chat room. In this model, people connect through the website and communicate in real time with other users with similar interests. Other forms of community include game-playing communities and communities of knowledge. In the former, users play against each other through the website, enter tournaments, and join discussion groups, sharing their opinions and experiences.

However, the community concept is not limited to speciality sites. Any firm that is able to identify common interests amongst users, and then provide a medium where they can interact, share information, and build interest around the product, can build a community.

Compared with sites which allow interaction between site and participant only, multi-directional interaction among participants benefits greatly from an increased number of members – in fact, the value of such an exchange, or marketplace, increases in proportion to the square of the number of participants.

Communities that rely on user-generated content will become more attractive as destination sites. As momentum picks up, growth breeds growth. Once a user or a member has come into a community, it is naturally in their interest to encourage other people to join. This phenomenon results in 'viral marketing' – not only do users actively do promotional work for a company, but the number of marketers increases exponentially as new members are added to the pool.

All the site owners need to do is to channel and support this content effectively. Increasing the number of community members to the site means further value and profits, in the form of advertising revenues and greater e-commerce opportunities (Figure 10.13).

According to Figure 10.13, the four elements needed to create value in online communities are as follows.

Transaction attractiveness

An online community site must offer members not only entertainment but also a sense of involvement and even ownership. Communities require a truly bottom-up view of brand building, whereby the customers create the content and are, in a sense, responsible for it. This view contrasts with many brand strategists' traditional top-down view of business, where products and services are created by organizations and sold to customers. Members of the community generate content for the site, influence its growth and determine its evolution. Visitors to community sites should be able to sense the presence of others like themselves who have visited or are currently visiting the same site, and see the results of their participation in the growth of the site. For example, when you buy a book on Amazon.com, the site will tell you that 'other people who bought this book also bought ...'. While no direct communication with other users has taken place here, the visitor feels that their presence on the site has added value to his/her experience.

Figure 10.13 Creating value in online communities

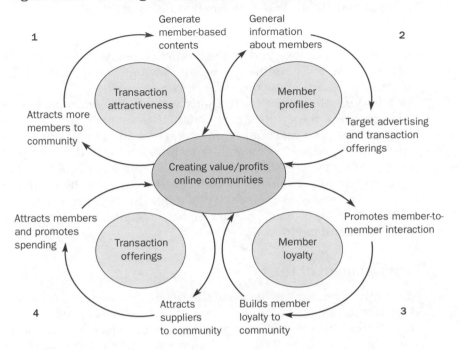

Member profiles

Typically visitors become members by free online registration on the site. In this way the site owner can gather a lot of useful information about the community members. Companies can learn a great deal about what makes their own sites successful by building a community and listening to the feedback this generates. Feedback provided on community forums tends to be more honest and accurate than market surveys, although care should be taken in assessing how representative the more vocal members of a community are.

Member loyalty

Community members are given the chance to participate in discussions and interact with other members. This is achieved through the use of community tools such as discussion boards, live chat, and member mailboxes. A good community experiences repeat visits from users and is able to attract their attention for long periods of time. By creating member loyalty, communities build significant barriers for entry for new competitors in a field, and allow a company to capitalize on being first-to-market. Nobody likes to chat in an empty room, and if users seek buyers or sellers they will find more of them in the busiest forum. While a business model, content and features may be easy to replicate, an established community is extremely difficult to move.

Transaction offerings

Perhaps the most compelling reason for building a community is that a community is conducive to transactions and e-commerce. Through the presence of relevant content, other interested people will become part of the transaction process, just as fellow shoppers and shop assistants are a part of the real-life buying experience. People do not like to shop in an empty store. As in the real world, community members make decisions about where to shop and what to buy based on the apparent popularity and image of a store or product line, on the availability of store personnel for advice and guidance, and on the counsel of friends and fellow shoppers.

An example of an online community with all the elements mentioned above except the transaction offerings is Sony Playstation.

An important element for the Sony Playstation community is the continuing addition of new content (e.g. new games) that members perceive as valuable. Such content helps to retain current members and to attract new ones. New members, in turn, help stimulate the community by bringing fresh ideas and perspectives. The new content also allows the community management to guide the future direction of the community. Examples of such content generated by community organizers are product reviews or company evaluations. In the Sony Playstation community the organizers also encourage the members to contribute with new ideas for future applications and products.

Establishment of trust

Lack of trust and security is one of the largest impediments to e-commerce growth, especially in Europe, because it is one of the main reasons consumers do not purchase online. This mistrust stems partly from the lack of physical representation, since buyers cannot touch and feel products on the Internet, and partly from concerns regarding credit card abuse (IDC, 2001).

Customers may be more likely to trust a seller who shows a well-known partner or brand, or by making a connection to their history as a conventional operation.

Companies may also post each others' banners on their sites, often in exchange for a share of revenue for sales from transactions originating at the partner site. This allows firms that do not have strong brand recognition to ally with an established brand and gain credibility by association.

10.10 The legal environment of e-commerce

Companies that conduct e-commerce are subject to the same laws, regulations and taxes that govern the operations of all businesses. Companies operating on the web face at least one complicating factor as they try to follow the laws. A company that uses the web immediately becomes an international business, and as such the company can become subject to many more laws, more quickly, than it would if it had been a traditional company tied to one specific physical location. Furthermore any country's legal issues are difficult to interpret and follow because of the newness of e-commerce and the unsettled nature of the laws. Some of the legal issues (in different countries) on which companies might need to seek specific legal advice are: ownership of the company's domain names (URLs), advertising and marketing standards, and taxation on e-commerce.

If the Internet is used to promote and sell products overseas, the company has to be aware of the various marketing legislation in the different countries. For example, Germany has specific laws that prohibit explicit comparisons between products.

One interesting issue is the data protection and privacy laws. The European Union's comprehensive privacy legislation, the Directive on Data Protection, became effective on October 25 1998. It requires that transfers of personal data take place only to non-EU countries that provide an 'adequate' level of privacy protection.

The USA and the EU have been trying to set common rules on data privacy. The USA is concerned that strict EU laws would stop companies from sending some data to the USA from the EU. The USA also says the EU rules are likely to give US consumers a false sense of security because such rules are impossible to enforce. In November 1999, the US Commerce Department released a plan to issue 'safe harbor' regulations that would protect US companies operating in Europe from sanctions under a new EU law as long as they meet certain guidelines. The EU, meanwhile, is concerned that the USA will not enforce privacy guidelines strictly enough. It also wants the USA to set clear rules that allow consumers access to their own personal information that has been collected by businesses. The outcome of these negotiations between the USA and the EU is not yet clear.

10.11 Summary

During the last few years there has been an explosion of online commercial activity enabled by the Internet. This is generally referred to as electronic commerce (e-commerce), with a major component of e-commerce being electronic transactions taking place on Internet-based markets (electronic markets, or e-markets).

The development of the Internet as a new direct distribution channel has resulted in a shift of power from the manufacturers and the traditional retail channels to the consumers.

Generally, the development of e-commerce in Europe has lagged behind the development in the USA. A major factor inhibiting the growth of consumer e-commerce in Europe is lack of confidence in online security. However, for those selling via the Internet, the new European currency, the euro, will make it easier to do business, and give encouragement to companies selling to European customers. Since Europeans will now be able to shop and compare prices at the click of a mouse, they will be more favourably inclined towards e-commerce.

The B-t-B market volume of e-commerce is much bigger than for the B-t-C market – four times bigger, according to some research results. The reason for this difference is that e-commerce is not a new phenomenon in the B-to-B market. Instead of Internet-based solutions, many industries have been using electronic data interchange (EDI) for years to streamline business processes and reduce the cost of doing business.

The main difference between buying behaviour in the marketplace and the virtual market space is that the market space emphasizes high technology, and is more characterized by the power of information and communication technologies to satisfy customer needs and thereby continue business relationships.

The myth has been that the Internet will eliminate the need for intermediaries. Early predictions called for disintermediation, that is, the disappearance of physical intermediaries as people moved from buying through distributors and resellers to buying directly from manufacturers. The reality is that the Internet may eliminate the traditional distributors, but the transformation process of the value chain has given rise to a new class of intermediaries. Companies such as Yahoo! aggregate information and make it easier to access new information and see new business possibilities. The value added is no longer in logistics aggregation but rather in information aggregation.

Three alternative strategy levels of e-commerce commitment have been presented:

- Level 1: one-to-many strategy where the Internet presence is a company and product brochure.
- Level 2: direct targeting where the company starts selling on the Internet.
- Level 3: one-to-one interactive e-commerce.

At level 3, the company is moving from providing company and product information to becoming an integral part of the whole vertical value chain from supplier to end consumer. This virtual integration works faster than level 2 (direct targeting) by blurring traditional boundaries between suppliers, manufacturers and customers in the value chain.

Companies that conduct e-commerce must be subject to the same laws, regulations and taxes that govern operations of all businesses. But a company that uses the web immediately becomes an international business, and as such the company can become subject to many more laws, more quickly, than if it were a traditional company tied to one specific physical location. Furthermore many countries' legal issues are difficult to interpret and follow because of the newness of e-commerce.

The Internet is a powerful tool for strengthening relationships, but the basic laws and rewards of building loyalty have not changed. Keeping a central focus on trust helps marketers understand how to build loyalty. Only by sustaining trust can marketers expect to establish enduring relationships with customers.

What are the drivers and barriers of e-commerce?

Drivers
For the supplier:

- reduced working capital (less inventory, reduced administration)
- global reach
- more efficient distribution (disintermediation means fewer distribution channels)
- ability to develop relationships with customers.

For the customer:

- more choices (greater product depth and global reach)
- ease of purchase and monitoring delivery
- more individual products (via mass customization of products)
- cost savings
- faster product cycle time (ordering, shipping, billing)
- in the B-t-B market the customer has better possibilities of swapping between suppliers than with EDI.

Barriers (for both supplier and customer)

- When entering the global market there may be different barriers to different countries: language barriers, cultural barriers, limited Internet access, different legislation, logistical barriers, etc.

Exhibit 10.7	**Boo.com – the fashion e-tailer rises from the grave**

Clothes are not easy to sell on the Internet – you cannot feel them and you cannot try them on. Boo.com was planned to be the first truly global fashion e-tailer in that it would offer customers service in the language of their choice. Boo.com planned to offer fashions in the USA and Europe from dozens of international companies, including Adidas, Puma, and North Face, and niche labels like Cosmic Girl and Vans that had a cult following, but were difficult to find in chain stores. Boo.com planned to launch worldwide, creating a global brand from scratch. Boo.com described its vision as 'bringing beautiful clothes to the world'.

The name Boo.com was selected by the company's three founders, Ernst Malmsten, Kajsa Leander and Patrik Hedelin, because it was regarded as short, catchy, and otherwise meaningless in major languages – much along the same line as names such as Amazon, Yahoo, Google, and eBay.

Boo.com's fashion-conscious virtual personal shopper, Ms Boo, would guide users through the shopping process and provide real-time individual advice, complete with a sophisticated attitude. Boo.com's online interactive magazine, Boom, would have international features on everything from sporting and clubbing to hard news and trend reports.

With some delay, Boo.com finally launched its site on November 2, 1999. At this time, there were about 300 employees at Boo.com. However, from the beginning the extensive use of advanced technology had many drawbacks to Boo.com's customers. The website had been built for high speed user access and required a Flash plug-in and the latest web browsers to allow users to view the site's advanced features. This resulted in less than 25% of those who tried to access the website succeeding. The site was immediately inundated with user complaints. The main outcry came from Macintosh users who could not access the site at all.

Boo.com's clothing remained no cheaper than in the shops, leading consumers to question the point of an Internet e-tailer that could not offer cheaper prices than conventional stores. The negative press on Boo.com kept building. 'There was high expectation before we launched,' Malmsten said. 'People treat us like a big nasty corporation that's been running for years, and we're just a start-up.'

As May 2000 approached, Malmsten felt a sense of desperation. Technology shares were doing badly, and many were predicting the end of the Internet bubble. Boo.com had only US$500,000 left in the bank and there was no further word from its investors. Malmsten and Leander realized that they needed to raise US$30 million to keep going. They did not succeed in raising the money and in May 2000 Boo.com was put into liquidation.

On 30 May 2000, Ben Narasin, CEO of Fashionmall.com, the US fashion portal, flew to London to buy the Boo.com's brand, web address, advertising materials, and online content. Fashionmall.com paid around US$450,000 for the remains of Boo.com. Boo.com reopened as an Internet fashion portal on October 30, 2000, with approximately ten employees from Fashionmall.com taking care of Boo.com's online sales.

Ben Narasin has wondered what he should do with the resurrected brand and what products he should sell on the new Boo.com site. He was also concerned about the possibility that people familiar with the old Boo.com brand name would feel 'cheated' upon arriving at the new site.

Do you have any recommendations for Ben Narasin, concerning his worries?

Sources: adapted from: Stockport *et al.* (2001), www.boo.com.

- Web technology is not user friendly.
- Security fears.
- E-commerce is not suitable for certain types of product, for example 'tactile' products (fashion clothes) or very complex products or projects, where face-to-face communication is necessary.
- Conflicting interests (e.g. distributors, who may be bypassed, have another interest to the manufacturer).
- WWW = World Wide Wait (poor performance leading to slow downloads).

Case study 10.2 Gameplay.com

The online games marketer is undergoing a turbulent time

Gameplay was founded in early 1999 to establish an online computer games portal through the acquisition of various assests and companies and to raise funds to develop such business.

The online games market is very turbulent. With many of the first wave of start-ups now gone, established developers and big players are poised to make a move on the market. If 2000 was the year of the start-up, then with the onset of dot.com gloom, the online games market looks very different now.

As with nearly all consumer sectors, Gameplay has suffered with 2001 market downturn and the slowdown in advertising spend. Gameplay was forced to announce major restructuring in February 2001, cutting its staff from 700 to 400 employees. However, the industry analysts are very optimistic about the growth in this sector.

The market for online games

Online games take a variety of forms, ranging from simple head-to-head games, such as chess and backgammon, to complex, turn-based strategy games and action games. Many PC games manufacturers now build multi-player functionality into their products as a matter of course.

Analysts agree that the online games sector is set to grow over the next five years. For example, Datamonitor has suggested that in the USA and western Europe, online revenues from subscription and pay-per-play games will rise from US$61 million in 1998 to US$680 million in 2003. Datamonitor also suggests that by 2003, revenue from online games will represent 13 per cent of all online content revenues, with compound annual growth rates in excess of 62 per cent – much faster than other predicted growth rates in the online sector.

The next five years are likely to see the expansion of faster Internet access through cable modems and ADSL technologies. Increased Internet access speeds and capacity will particularly assist those applications which need a high bandwidth, and applies particularly to computer games. It is also believed that the increasing rates of penetration of these broadband technologies are likely to assist businesses such as that of Gameplay.com given that speed is an essential element in playing many online games.

The strategy of Gameplay.com

From the start, Gameplay has had the strategy of becoming the leading online games destination and community. Gameplay allows customers to buy games, talk about games or play games on a number of platforms, including online (web/broadband), IDTV and WAP.

Gameplay now offers a pan-European, multi-platform games destination across four channels or business areas.

Direct channel

The direct channel comprises both mail-order and e-commerce. The two outlets are synergistic, and Gameplay offers one of the largest ranges of games and accessories with next-day delivery as standard. The company's continually increasing buying power enables it to offer customers games up to 15 per cent below high-street retail prices. It now has mail-order and e-commerce platforms in both the UK and Germany.

Case study 10.2 continued

Online Gameplay.com

This is an online community incorporating Wireplay, Europe's largest dial-up gaming network. Currently it supports 120 titles. Wireplay is an important tool for retention of customers – it is this thriving and loyal multi-player community that differentiates Gameplay.com from its competitors.

IDTV (Interactive Digital TV)

This comprises premium games channels with standalone games, quiz games, multiplayer games and T-commerce.

Gameplay is currently building partnerships with a number of key UK and European television and cable partners. It has signed deals with BskyB, Telewest, Cable & Wireless and NTL, and is in discussion with various potential partners. This part of the business currently represents 23 per cent of total turover.

In February 2001 Gameplay announced another agreement with one of the leading European pay TV platforms, Viasat. The deal involves Gameplay integrating its state-of-the-art interactive TV Games channels into Viasat's digital platform offering Viasat subscribers a suite of premium games, a prize quiz and in the future a television commerce channel selling video games. The service is accessible via Viasat's highly successful Everyday.TV portal. The agreement is for four years.

Steen Ulf Jensen, CEO of Pay TV for Viasat Broadcasting commented:

We are very pleased to announce this partnership with Gameplay. Viasat were looking for a launch partner who could deliver a high quality sustainable service in the games areas of our 'everyday.TV' portal. The strengths and depth of Gameplay's iTV product is best of breed in our opinion and their commercial model is very much in keeping with our own. Gameplay's current products and future development strategy also underline their comprehensive understanding of the digital TV viewer who requires a digital TV service, which stays fresh and remains interesting. Gameplay's service will be key in helping convert our new digital subscribers into interactive digital customers and then keeping them.

WAP gameplay mobile

This comprises wireless Internet services that are accessible via WAP phones. This channel features a top ten chart of games, a news channel featuring reviews and release dates of these titles, and online quiz games.

Competitors

Many traditional retailers already have e-commerce websites with computer games being either a small or major part of the products available. It is assumed that such companies have an internal conflict between full price traditional sales and discounted price online sales, which will prevent many of them from matching Gameplay's prices in the short and medium term. However, other online games marketers are appearing.

Electronic Arts is the world's largest games developer and has had a series of games hits including The Sims and the FIFA series. It has already launched its online venture EA.com in the USA and is anticipating a European launch before the end of 2002. In the USA it has partnered with AOL and has been using the Internet service provider's marketing muscle to go on a major customer acquisition spree.

UK firm Eidos, responsible for the hit Tomb Raider franchise, already claims to have a number of multi-player online games. However, unlike EA, it is holding back most of its online strategy until the advent of broadband which many in the games industry see as the holy grail.

Anco, which has been responsible for a number of sports games including the Alex Ferguson Player manager series, also has significant web ambitions. It recently created a dedicated online division for its newly launched online football game Playasmanager, which it is looking to take worldwide.

The latest development

On February 6 2001 Gameplay announced how it will organize its activities in the future, and where it will focus its resources. The group was divided into two distinct operation divisions: the Technology Division and the Boxed Games

Case study 10.2 continued

Division. Non-core business and activities were closed or sold.

As a result of these changes, the group's strategy will focus more directly on developing the Technology Division and the expansion of boxed games from a lower cost base. This restructuring programme resulted in the loss of 275 jobs throughout the group, which included some 54 head-office positions.

The cost reductions have mainly taken place in the Boxed Games Division.

- The UK call centre and distribution operations in Leeds were amalgamated on to one site.

- The UK operation closed its eight retail outlets. Whilst proving the concept and producing significant revenues, the high operating costs of the existing locations made it difficult for the board to see a path to profitability without significant expansion of the chain.

- E-commerce websites were no longer operated locally in each territory. They are now run centrally and served in the local language to each European subsidiary.

- There was also be some rationalization to reduce the cost base in Germany.

- It was also the directors' intention to reduce activities in France where it had proved difficult to see a route to profitability within the time frame required by the board.

In late 2001 the management group of Gameplay.com made a mangement buy-out where they took over the company and invested in it too.

Questions

1. How is Gameplay able to sell boxed games cheaper than through established bricks-and-mortar retailers?

2. Who are the target customer groups of Gameplay?

3. How do you see the future competitive situation in this industry?

4. How should Gameplay increase its brand awareness?

5. Is it still realistic to seek to establish Gameplay.com as Europe's leading online games portal and community?

Sources: Datamonitor (1999), Gameplay (1999, 2000, 2001), Gorritz and Medina (2000), New Media Age (2001).

QUESTIONS FOR DISCUSSION

1. Explain the term virtual value chain.
2. Explain what is meant by electronic commerce.
3. What are transaction costs and why should they be considered in e-commerce?
4. 'The web represents a pull medium for marketing rather than a push medium'. Discuss.
5. What types of distribution channel conflict are caused by the Internet?
6. How does the demographic profile of Internet users differ from the general population of a country?
7. Explain the main benefits that a company selling fast-moving consumer products could derive by creating a website
8. Describe sticky features that websites use to attract and keep visitors. Why is stickiness important to companies operating websites?
9. Why do companies that create global web strategies need to accommodate cultural differences and can they turn them to their advantage?
10. For the following stages in the buying process, explain how the Internet can be used to help achieve the communication objectives: supplier search, evaluation and selection, purchase, post-purchase.

11. Why is the Internet a suitable medium for one-to-one marketing?

12. 'Companies should spend a higher proportion of their website budgets on promotion than on designing and developing the site'. Discuss.

13. 'It is inevitable that the transparency of information on products and price on the web will drive down product prices'. Discuss.

REFERENCES

Adage Global (2000), Perfume giants force halt to online retailer in France, *Daily News*, November 8, **http://www.adageglobal.dom**.

Barnes-Vieyra, B. and Claycomb, C. (2001), Business-to-business e-commerce: models and managerial decisions, *Business Horizons*, May–June, pp. 13–20.

Barratt, M. and Rosdahl, K. (2002). Exploring business-to-business market sites, *European Journal of Purchasing and Supply Management*, vol. 8, pp. 111–22.

BBC (2001), Nokia sales prompt telecoms slump, *BBC News*, January 9.

Benjamin, R. and Wigand, R. (1995), Electronic markets and virtual chains on the information highway, *Sloan Management Review*, Winter, pp. 62–72.

Boston Consulting Group (2000), *The Race for Online Riches – E-Retailing in Europe* (**http://www.bcg.com/new_ideas/new_ideas_subpage3.asp**).

Business Week (1999a), A hard sell online? Guess again – clothes, furniture, even food are starting to move, *Business Week*, July 12, pp. 78–80.

Business Week (1999b), In the ring: eBAY vs. Amazon.com, *Business Week*, May 31, pp. 49–55.

Butler, P. and Peppard, J. (1998), Consumer purchasing on the Internet: process and prospects, *European Management Journal*, vol. 16, no. 5, October, pp. 600–10.

Computer Economics (1999), Internet usage according to language, *Computer Economics*, July 6, (**http://www.glreach.com/globstats/**).

Cyber Dialogue (2000), *American Internet Survey* (**http://cyberatlas.internet.com/big_picture/demographics/article/0,1323,5911_246241,00.html**).

Dayal S., Landesberg, H. and Zeisser, M. (1999), How to build trust online, *Marketing Management*, vol. 8, no. 3, Fall, pp. 64–71.

Datamonitor (1999), *Revenues from consumer online content publishing*, Datamonitor, April.

DBC (2001), Nokia increases market share, *DBC Business*, January 5.

Department of Commerce (1999), Chapter 1: Electronic commerce in the digital economy *in The Emerging Digital Economy II*, (**http://www.ecommerce.gov/ede/chapter1.html**).

Devaney, P. (2001), Advertisers target the divorce-booking market, *MAD*, January 25 (**www.mad.co.uk**).

Durlacher (2000), *Business to business e-commerce: investment perspective*, Durlacher Research Ltd, London.

Emiliani, M.L. and Stec, D.J. (2002), Realizing savings from online reverse auctions, *Supply Chain Management: An International Journal*, vol. 7, no. 1, pp. 12–23.

Enders, A. and Jelassi, T. (2000), The converging business models of Internet and bricks-and-mortar retailers, *European Management Journal*, vol. 18, no. 5, pp. 542–50.

Financial Times (1999), 'Gucci doubles its net profit for third quarter', *Financial Times*, Companies & Finance Section, December 11.

Fraser, J., Fraser, N. and McDonald, F. (2000), The strategic challenge of electronic commerce, *Supply Chain Management: An International Journal*, vol. 5, no. 1, pp. 7–14.

Freeman, S. (2000), Stalled in the fast lane: the auto-repair-parts system is definitely broken. Can e-commerce fix it? E-commerce special report, *Wall Street Journal*, July 17.

Galen, C. (2000), How 3M avoids channel conflict on the Web, *Sales and Marketing Management*, New York, June, p. 34.

Gameplay (1999), *Introduction of Gameplay.com to Alternative Investment Market (AIM) of the London Stock Exchange*, Gameplay, London.

Gameplay (2000), Gameplay announces restructuring to shorten timetable to profitability, Gameplay, London, Press release, February 6.

Gameplay (2001), Gameplay announces interactive TV agreement with pan Scandinavian digital platform Viasat, Press release, February 12.

Gartner Group (2000), *GartnerGroup forecasts worldwide business-to-business e-commerce to reach $7.29 trillion in 2004*, Gartner Group, Connecticut, January.

Global Reach (2001), *Global Reach Express: Global Internet trends report from Nielson*, June 23 (**www.glreach.com**).

Global Report (1999), *The world's online populations* (**http://cyberatlas.internet.com/ big_picture/demographics/article/0,1323,5911_246241,00.html**).

Gorritz, C. M. and Medina, C. (2000), Encouraging girls with computers through software games, *Communication of the ACM*, vol. 43, no. 1, pp. 42–9.

Häski, R. and Lighton, J. (2001), The future of the networked company, *The McKinsey Quarterly*, no. 3, pp. 26–39.

Hofacker, C. F. (1999), *Internet Marketing*, Digital Springs, Inc., 2nd edn.

Hollensen, S. (1999), *Globalization of Internet-based services: the case of Amazon.com*, AIMS Conference 1999 (**http://www.indiainfoline.com/bisc/amaz.html**).

Hollensen, S. (2001), *Global Marketing: A market responsive approach*, Financial Times/Prentice Hall, Harlow, 2nd edn.

IDC (2000a), *Europe sees big gains in Internet usage, 2000* (**http://cyberatlas. internet.com/big_picture/demographics/article/0,1323,5911_281021,00.html**)

IDC (2000b), *A preview of IDC's consumer survey: European Internet and eCommerce*, IDC European Internet Center (PowerPoint presentation, **http://www.idc.com**).

IDC (2001), *User Perception of Internet Security – A European consumer survey*, **www.idc.com**, document IS01H.

Jackson, B. (1985), Build customer relationships that last, *Harvard Business Review*, November–December, pp. 120–8.

Jardine, A. (1999), Laura Ashley site to offer net sales, *Marketing*, London, December 9.

Kaplan, S. and Sawhney, M. (2000), E-hubs: the new B2B marketplaces, *Harvard Business Review*, May–June, pp. 97–103

Kapner, S. (2001), A Nokia report rattles telecommunications shares, *New York Times*, Jan. 10.

Kotha, S. (1998), Competing on the Internet: the case of Amazon.com, *European Management Journal*, vol. 16, pp. 212–22.

Lake, D. (1999), Spotlight: how big is the US net population, *The Standard: Intelligence for the Internet Economy*, November 29.

Lohse, G.L. and Spiller, P. (1999), Internet retail store design: how the user interface influences traffic and sales, *Journal of Computer Mediated Communication*, vol. J, no. 2, December, pp. 1–20.

Magretta, J. (1998), The power of virtual integration: an interview with Dell Computer's Michael Dell, *Harvard Business Review*, March–April, pp. 73–84.

McGrath, D. (2001), The road to build-to-order cars will likely be a bumpy one, *Microtimes*, no. 219, March 28, pp. 15–19.

Mediamark Research (1999), *Spotlight: How Big is the US Net Population?*, (**http://www.the standard.com/metrics/display/0,2149,1071,00.html**).

New Media Age, (2001), New players, same game, *New Media Age*, March 15.

Nusbaum, A. (2000) Web cuts out entire order of middlemen: Information Technology Internet in Japan: B-t-B e-commerce is threatening the livelihoods of thousands of intermediaries, *Financial Times*, January 11.

Partore, M. (2001), *Online Consumers Now the Average Consumer*, **www.thestandard.com**, July 12.

Porter, M. E. (2001), Strategy and the Internet, *Harvard Business Review*, March, pp. 63–78.

Ranchhod, A. and Gurau, C. (2000), Marketing on the Internet: observations within the biotechnology sector, *International Journal of Physical Distribution & Logistics Management*, vol. 30, no. 7/8, pp. 697–709.

Rayport, J. F. and Sviokla, J.J. (1996), Exploiting the virtual value chain, *McKinsey Quarterly*, no. 1, pp. 21–36.

Rayport, J. F. and Jaworski, B.J. (2001), *e-Commerce*, McGraw-Hill/Irwin.

Reichhold, F. and Schefter, P. (2000), E-loyalty – your secret weapon on the web, *Harvard Business Review*, July–August, pp. 105–13.

Segil, L. (2001), *Fast Alliances: Power your E-business*, John Wiley & Sons, Inc.

Stockport, G. J., Kunnath, G. K. and Sedick, R. (2001), Boo.com – the path to failure, *Journal of Interactive Marketing*, vol. 15. no. 4, Autumn, pp. 56–70.

Thompson, M. J. (1999), *Customer Feeding Frenzy: E-retailers vie for $185 billion*, **http://www.thestandard.com**, November 15.

Van Hooft, F. P. C. and Stegwee, R. sA. (2001), E-business strategy: now to benefit from a hype, *Logistics Information Management*, vol. 14, no. 1/2, pp. 44–53.

Wise, T. and Morrison, D. (2000), Beyond the exchange: the future of B2B, *Harvard Business Review*, November–December, pp. 86–96.

Wunderman, W. (1998), The future of selling via the Internet. The online progress of disintermediation, *Web Commerce Today*, no. 10, May 15.

Zott, C., Amit, R. and Donlevy, J. (2000), Strategies for value creation in e-commerce: best practice in Europe, *European Management Journal*, vol. 18, no. 5, pp. 463–75.

Figure IV.1 The structure of Part IV

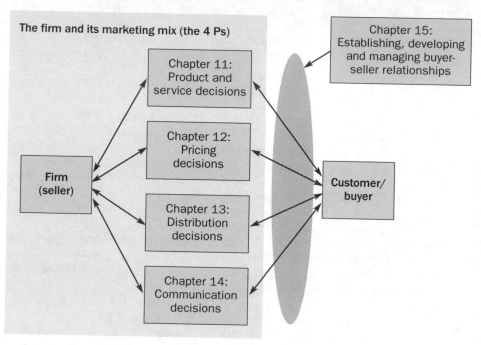

PART IV

Developing marketing programmes

Functional plans (e.g. production, R&D, financial, HR) are designed to transform the strategic plans of the corporate and divisional levels into tactical actions that govern the day-to-day operations of the various functional departments within each business unit. It is at this functional level of planning that each organization finds out the degree to which the desired outcomes expressed in the mission statement and marketing goals can be realized and applied in practical terms.

In the typical organization, each business function has a potential impact on customer satisfaction. Under the marketing concept, all departments should try to think of the customer and work together to satisfy customer needs and expectations.

This part will of course discuss the traditional 4 Ps of the marketing mix (Chapters 11–14) but it will also integrate the new stream of managing buyer-seller relationships (Chapter 15). Figure IV.1 shows the structure of Part IV.

Increasingly, goods and services will be treated as a way of creating value together with individual customers, and the customer's role in the production will be more important. That is the reason why Chapter 15 is included as an attempt to expand the traditional '4 P' thinking. Chapter 15 tries to combine the more short-term marketing mix with the more holistic approach of establishing and retaining long-term relationships with customers.

Plans must be specific to the organization and to its current situation. There is not one system of planning but many systems, not one style but many styles, and a planning process must be tailor-made for a particular firm in a specific set of circumstances.

Chapter 11

Product and service decisions

LEARNING OBJECTIVES

After studying this chapter you should be able to:

- explain the mix of product and service elements.
- explore levels of a product offer.
- define the categories of service.
- determine the 'service quality gap'.
- explore the stages in 'new product development'.
- discuss different forms of the product life cycle.
- discuss what it means to develop new products for foreign markets.
- discuss the term brand equity.
- define and explain the different branding alternatives.
- discuss how the Internet might be integrated in future product innovations.

Case study **11.1** Swatch Watch

A blockbuster product is needed

Nicolas G. Hayek (chief executive of Swatch Group Ltd) who revolutionized the watch business in the 1980s is looking for his next breakthrough. He is putting a Swatch wristwatch phone on the market, as well as a watch equipped for Internet access. He is also working with Hewlett-Packard to develop even more advanced watches.

The Swiss watch industry

In the 1970s, after repeated crises in the Swiss watch industry, the two largest firms in this sector (ASUAG and SSIH), which were among the largest watch manufacturers in the world, were in trouble. Foreign competition, in particular the Japanese watch industry, with its mass production of cheap new electronic products and new technology, was rapidly establishing a strong foothold in the market.

Finally, both ASUAG and SSIH faced bankruptcy. Already some foreign competitors were offering to buy prestigious watch brand names such as Omega, Longines and Tissot. Nicolas G. Hayek, today Chairman of the Board and Chief Executive Officer of the Swatch Group and at that time CEO of Hayek Engineering, received an assignment to assess the chances of survival and to develop a strategy for the future of both companies. In 1983, as a result of his study, several measures were recommended to be implemented to turn the companies around. The most famous were the merger of ASUAG and SSIH into SMH and the launching of a low cost, high technology watch – the Swatch. These measures, together with some others, made the SMH Group the largest watch-making company (in value) five years later.

Case study 11.1 continued

The Swatch Group adopted its present name in 1998 (since 1986 it had been called SMH Swiss Corporation for Microelectronics and Watch-making Industries Ltd). The change has been made because of the difficulty in adapting the name and its abbreviation SMH into other languages.

The Swatch Group Ltd in Biel, Switzerland is today the largest manufacturer of finished watches in the world. In terms of sales the Swatch Group represents 22–25% of watch sales in the world. In 1998, the Group produced more than 118 million watches. The Swatch Group has some 50 production centres situated mainly in Switzerland, but also in France, Germany, Italy, the USA, US Virgin Islands, Thailand, Malaysia and China.

The Swatch Group offers watches in all price and market categories:

- Blancpain and Omega, in the luxury and prestige segment
- Rado and Longines in the top range
- Tissot, Certina, Mido, Balmain, Hamilton and Calvin Klein in the middle segment
- Swatch, FlikFlak and Lanco in the basic segment
- Endura produces 'private label' watches whose prices vary according to the customer's wishes.

But the Swatch Group is not only a watchmaking group. Microelectronics and micromechanics represent another important part of its operations. The Swatch Group is also active in the service sector (including sports timing which measures the time at most of the Olympic Games and multiple international sports events) and in the field of telecommunications and the car sector.

The principal focus of today's largest manufacturer of finished watches in the world will remain the watch industry.

Where is the new blockbuster product?

Hayek, who owns nearly 40% of Swatch, is riding high. Fuelled by Asia's recovery and record US consumer spending, in 1999 Swatch turned in its best performance since 1992, and its share price doubled. Sales were up 10.9% to US$2.2 billion and profits jumped an estimated 20% to US$258 million. Sales increased further to US$2.5 billion and profits to US$404 million in 2000. Yet sustaining that pace will be tough, because the watch market is growing less than 5% a year.

Hayek's quest for a blockbuster new product is also proving difficult. A couple of attempts have misfired, including the first prototype wrist phone that was too bulky to market and a stake in DaimlerChrysler's troubled Smart Car project, which Swatch sold back to the car maker. Some doubt that his newest offerings will fare much better. While the mobile phone industry is racing toward the Internet, the Swatch wrist phone has been launched without Internet access. The Internet Swatch is an awkward contraption that has to be used with a computer terminal and a special mousepad.

Time is running short for Hayek, aged 72. He plans to step aside from day-to-day management, probably turning that job over to his son. Meantime, the quest for a hot product goes on. One possibility: a watch with a smart chip that acts as a credit card. Who knows?

Questions

1. Evaluate the global Swatch Watch product portfolio.
2. Do you think that Nicolas G. Hayek will succeed with his idea about a wrist watch credit card?

Source: www.swatchgroup.com.

11.1 Introduction

The product decision is among the first decisions that a marketing manager makes in order to develop a marketing mix. This chapter examines product-related issues and suggests conceptual approaches for handling them. Also discussed are product development, brand (labelling) strategies and service policies.

What is a product?

Products, or services, are the vital ingredients of the market offering and are the vehicles for providing customer satisfaction. The product is the object of the exchange process, the thing which the producer or supplier offers to a potential customer in exchange for something else which the supplier perceives as equivalent or greater value. Conventionally, this something else is money. In the absence of money, we must resort to barter or counter trade where goods are traded against other goods. It follows that for an exchange to occur someone must have a demand for the object in question and be willing to exchange money or other assets, which are seen as possessing value.

Two particularly important ideas have been introduced in the discussion of demand preference and substitutability. Preference defines the extent to which a consumer will favour one product over another, while substitutability reflects how well one product may take the place of another. The latter qualification is particularly important to marketers because it is similar to brand switching.

Importance of service

According to Samiee (1999), 25 per cent of the global merchandise trade belongs to the service category. The value of global trade in services has been growing by over 10% per year and this trend is expected to continue. It is seen from the definition of a product that services often accompany products. Increasingly it is accepted that because buyers are concerned with benefits or satisfaction this is a combination of both tangible products, and intangible services (Baker and Hart, 1999). As Figure 11.1 shows, the mix of a product and service element may vary substantially.

Figure 11.1 Combination of service and product for different products

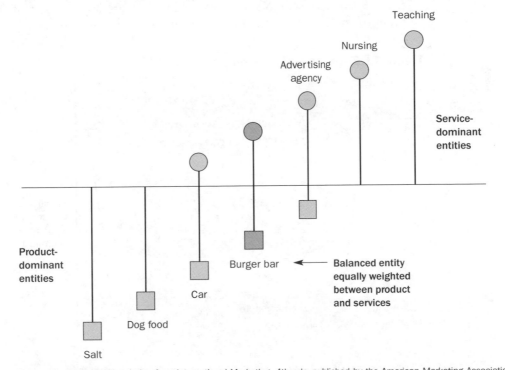

Source: reprinted with permission from *International Marketing*, 4th edn, published by the American Marketing Association, M. R. Czinkota and I. A. Ronkainen (1995).

11.2   The components of the product offer

In creating an acceptable product offer for international markets, it is necessary to examine first what contributes to the total product offer. Kotler (2000) suggests that there are five levels of the product offer which should be considered by marketers in order to make the product attractive to international markets. In the product components of Figure 11.2 we include not just the core physical properties, but also additional elements such as packaging, branding and after-sales service that make up the total package for the purchaser.

We can also see from Figure 11.2 that it is much easier to standardize the core product benefits (functional features, performance, etc.) across borders than it is to standardize the support services, which often have to be tailored to the business culture and sometimes to individual customers.

11.3   Service strategies

Characteristics of services

Before considering possible international service strategies, it is important to consider the special nature of global service marketing. Services are characterized by the following features.

● *Intangibility*. As services like air transportation or education cannot be touched or tested, the buyers or services cannot claim ownership or anything tangible in the traditional sense. Payment is for use or performance. Tangible elements of the service, such as food or drink on airlines, are used as part of the service in order to confirm the benefit provided and to enhance its perceived value.

Figure 11.2 The three levels of a product

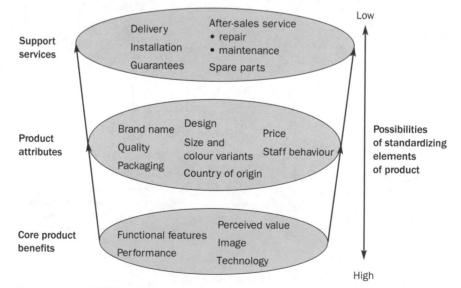

Source: Hollensen (2001), p. 396.

- *Perishability*. Services cannot be stored for future usage – for example, unfilled airline seats are lost once the aircraft takes off. This characteristic causes considerable problems in planning and promotion in order to match supply and demand. To maintain service capacity constantly at levels necessary to satisfy peak demand will be very expensive. The marketer must therefore attempt to estimate demand levels in order to optimize the use of capacity.

- *Heterogeneity*. Services are rarely the same because they involve interactions between people. Furthermore, there is high customer involvement in the production of services. This can cause problems of maintaining quality, particularly in international markets where there are quite different attitudes towards customer service.

- **Inseparability**. The time of production is very close to or even simultaneous with the time of consumption. The service is provided at the point of sale. This means that economies of scale and experience curve benefits are difficult to achieve, and supplying the service to scattered markets can be expensive, particularly in the initial setting-up phase.

Categories of service

All products, both goods and services, consist of a core element that is surrounded by a variety of optional elements. If we look first at the core service products, we can assign them to one of three broad categories depending on their tangibility and the extent to which customers need to be present during service production. These categories are presented in Table 11.1.

Table 11.1 Three categories of service

Categories of service	Characteristics	Examples (service provider)	Possibilities of worldwide standardization (hence utilizing economies of scale, experience effects, lower costs)
People processing	Customers become part of the production process. The service firm needs to maintain local geographic presence.	Education (schools, universities). Passenger transportation (airlines, car rental). Healthcare (hospitals). Food service (fast food resturants). Lodging service (hotel).	No good possibilities: because of 'customer involvement in production', many local sites will be needed, making this type of service very difficult to operate globally.
Possession processing	Involve tangible actions to physical objects to improve their value to customers. The object needs to be involved in the production process, but the owner of the object (the customer) does not. A local geographic presence is required.	Car repair (garages). Freight transport (forwarding agent). Equipment installation (electrician). Laundry service (laundrette).	Better possibilities: compared to people-processing services, this involves a lower degree of contact between the customer and the service personnel. This type of service is not so culture-sensitive.
Information-based services	Collecting, manipulating, interpreting and transmitting data to create value. Minimal tangibility. Minimal customer involvement in the production process.	Telecommunication services (telephone companies). Banking. News. Market analysis. Internet services (producers of homepages on web, database providers).	Very good possibilities: worldwide standardization from one central location (single sourcing) because of the 'virtual' nature of these services.

Source: Hollensen (2001), p. 399.

Determining the service quality gap

Quality is often considered to be one of the keys to success. The competitive advantage of the firm is said to depend on the quality and value of its goods and services.

Figure 11.3 illustrates how quality factors are connected to traditional marketing activities resulting in a perceived service quality. Good total quality is obtained when the gap between the customer's expected service quality and perceived service quality is zero or very small, meaning that perceived service quality meets the customer's expectations of the expected service quality. If expected service quality is much higher than the perceived service quality, the gap will be large and the total service quality will be low, even if the perceived service quality, measured in an objective way, is good.

As shown in Figure 11.3 the customer's expected service quality and perceived service quality is a function of a number of factors, most of which can be controlled by the company. The expected service quality is highly influenced by the firm's marketing and communication tools. The image and word of mouth factors, as well as public relations, are only indirectly controlled by the firm. Also the needs of the customers and their past experience with the company may also have an impact on their expectations.

On the other hand, what really counts is the quality as it is perceived by the customers (perceived service quality). Basically, the perceived service quality has two factors; a *technical* or outcome factor, and a *functional* or process-related factor. The hotel guest will be provided with a room and a bed to sleep in, the airline passenger will be transported from one place to another, a company may get its goods transported from its warehouse to a customer. These are examples of the technical quality factor. What the customers basically receive in their interaction with a firm

Figure 11.3 The total service quality gap

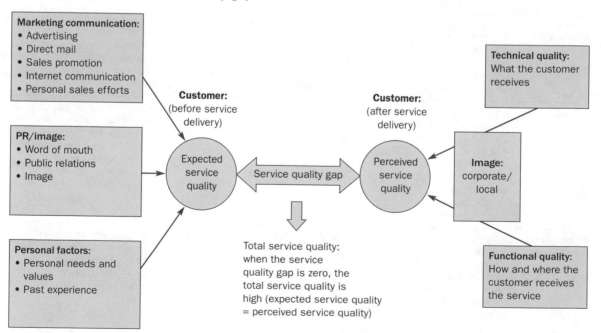

is clearly important to them and their quality perception. It is what the customer is left with, when the service production process and its buyer-seller interactions are over. Sometimes this dimension can be measured relatively objectively by customers because of its characteristic as a technical solution to a problem. However, as there are a number of interactions between the service provider and the customer, the customer will also be influenced by the way in which the technical quality is transferred to him or her. This is called the functional quality of the process. It is easy to see that the functional quality cannot be evaluated as objectively as the technical factor; it is frequently perceived very subjectively. The two quality factors, what and how, are not only valid for services. The technical solution for a customer provided by, for example, a machine – in the production function – is part of the overall technical quality perceived by this customer. But attempts to tailor this machine to the specific demands of a customer is an additional value and therefore part of the overall functional quality which the customer experiences.

The technical quality of a service process is normally a prerequisite for good quality. It has to be at an acceptable level. The definition of an acceptable level depends on the firm's strategy and the needs and expectations of the customers. However, once the outcome is good enough, this becomes transparent, and should not be used as a way of differentiating the product or service.

The functional quality (how) perception is also influenced by elements of the physical environment. The where aspect is considered to be part of the how factor, which is logical because the perception of the process clearly is dependent on the service process in, for example, a restaurant.

Usually the service provider cannot hide behind brand names or distributors. In most cases the firm, its resources and its operating methods are visible to the customers. The firm's corporate and/or local image is therefore of the utmost importance to most services. It can affect the perception of quality in various ways. If the provider has a favourable image in the minds of the customers, minor mistakes will probably be forgiven. However, if mistakes often occur, the image will be damaged.

As far as the perceived service quality is concerned, the image can be viewed as a filter, as illustrated in Figure 11.3 (Grönroos, 2000).

After-sales services (AS)

Customer service provides one important means by which a company can tailor its offerings to the needs and desires of its customers. By offering good service, a company assures consumers that it stands behind its products and projects a reliable and high quality image. Customer services offered after the sales transaction is completed are of crucial importance in this respect. Here, AS is defined as those activities in which a firm engages after purchase of its product that minimize potential problems related to product use, and maximize the value of the consumption experience. Researchers have suggested that AS consists of a number of elements. Here, AS is conceptualized as consisting of: the installation and start-up of the purchased product, the provision of spare parts for products, the provision of repair services, technical advice regarding the product, and the provision and support of warranties.

AS adds to the product's value and is often treated as an integral part of the product. Levitt (1983) suggests that because the provision of AS enhances product value

Exhibit 11.1	Product definition in the airline business

The airline product is more than the simple availability of a seat for travel on a particular route, though this is surely the core benefit. In fact, the product should not be seen as a physical item but a group of services matching, to a greater or lesser extent, the consumers' requirements. The extended and augmented aspects of the product include factors of safety, comfort and convenience, with the latter covering the frequency of departures, services – including ticketing and baggage handling – luggage allowance, etc. Moreover, the product concept can be extended still further if there are associated services such as car rental, hotel reservation, excursions, etc.

Airlines have recognized the differentiation possible in bundling certain features of the in-flight and ground services and typically two or three classes have been offered. The parallel use of branding is prevalent to convey that the aircraft's space and seating is allocated to provide additional levels of comfort and service. Whilst higher classes offer superior services, it is seating related factors that have been frequently cited as the most preferred aspects. For example, a survey of frequent business travellers reported four out of five were concerned with seat size.

As many aspects of the airline product may only be assessed through experience, marketing activity is aimed initially at the encouragement of trial and then customer retention. Promotional communication for the former purpose is frequently image laden to build on the specific facets of the product mix incorporated in the airline brand or class, such as reference to the quality of cuisine. Attention to service delivery in all its aspects is necessary for inducing the satisfaction that leads to repeat purchasing. Of course, there should not be gaps between customer expectation, based on the image communicated, and the reality of the experience. The experience will consist of many tangible and intangible factors.

Source: adapted from Driver (2001).

in a manner similar to other intangible product components, these service elements should be regarded as part of the augmented product (Asugman *et al.*, 1997).

The potential financial importance of these services has been called to the attention of corporations. Herbig and Palumbo (1993) suggested, 'Profit margins for aftermarket services are typically about 15% to 25% before taxes, whereas those for products are only 7% to 11% … Often, up to 25% to 40% of corporate revenues and from 20% to 50% of corporate profits can be generated from the aftermarket service components of a business'.

Customer support in after-sales service

Goffin and New (2001) suggest that there are seven key elements of customer support in B-t-B after-sales service:

- *Installation.* For many products, the first element of product support following the sale is installation. For complex products, or where safety issues are involved, personnel from the manufacturing company or their representatives usually perform this.

- *User training.* The complexity of some types of equipment means that manufacturers must provide good training for users. For example, the successful implementation of new manufacturing equipment often depends on extensive training. Many products include functions, which help users learn to use them more efficiently; these can range from simple help functions to full computer training packages.

- *Documentation*. Most products require some form of documentation. Typical forms of documentation cover equipment operation, installation, maintenance and repair. Good documentation can reduce support costs (Miskie, 1989).

- *Maintenance and repair*. Historically, this has always been an important element of customer support. Maintenance is necessary to clean, refurbish or replace parts or equipment which otherwise would be liable to fail. If equipment fails, fast and efficient repair is essential in many markets because down-time costs are very high – often many times the price of spare parts or service. Manufacturers need to have effective logistics for the management of customer support engineers and the movement of spares, the parts used in repairs.

- *Online support*. Telephone advice on products is important in many industries. Product experts give online consultations to customers to help them use products more efficiently, or sometimes to trace the cause of faults.

- *Warranty*. Manufacturers' warranties reduce the financial risk of owning products. Over the working lifetime of a product, support costs can be high and so many manufacturers offer customers the possibility to purchase an extended warranty.

- *Upgrades*. Customers may be offered the opportunity to enhance the performance of existing products. For example, computer upgrades increase the working lifetimes of products.

Over the years there has been a change in the relative importance of different elements of customer support. In the past, when many products had high failure rates, the most important aspect of support was fast and reliable repair. New technologies have now typically led to more reliable products. However, increased product complexity (which is often software based) means that the importance of user training and online support has increased.

Full service contracts

Based on Stremersch *et al.* (2001), 'full service' can be defined as

> **a comprehensive bundle of products and/or services, that fully satisfies the needs and wants of a customer related to a specific event or problem.**

The concept of a full service strategy is clearly related to the concepts of 'bundling' and 'systems selling'. Bundling can be defined as 'the offering of groups of products and/or services as a package'.

Thus, the concept of full service is composed of two conceptually distinct components, that is, a bundling strategy (a bundle of products and/or services); and an extension in customer need fulfilment (that fully satisfies the needs and wants of a customer related to a specific event or problem).

In Figure 11.4 these components are examined in the following way.

- *Bundling strategy*. Does the supplier firm bundle its products and/or services? Within this component three types are distinguished: pure components (unbundled offer), mixed bundling (components are available in a bundled as well as an unbundled offer), and pure bundling (components are only available in a bundled offer).

- *Extension in need fulfilment.* This component comprises the extent to which customer needs are satisfied by the supplier firm; the three levels of customer need fulfilment are indicated in Figure 11.4, that is, single, extended, and total.

Figure 11.4 positions full-service strategies relative to other (B-t-B) marketing strategies. It illustrates that firms pursuing a full-service strategy can be challenged on two factors. Competitive offerings may compete with full-service suppliers by focusing on satisfying specific customer needs, either by means of bundled or unbundled offers. Alternatively, competitors may choose to satisfy multiple needs by offering different unbundled solutions. This approach may appeal to customers seeking high levels of flexibility in their purchasing behaviour.

Therefore, it is clear that industrial customer firms will evaluate full-service offerings differently from mere product or service offerings. These differences are likely to be related to both the purchasing criteria used as well as the purchasing process itself. The high degree of comprehensiveness and potential implications for full-service contracts is likely to positively influence both more of the DMU (decision making unit) members and the DMU's heterogeneity.

In the research of service maintenance contracts, Stremersch *et al.* (2001) found that maintenance companies (and OEMs) will have to broaden their marketing and sales approach in a horizontal as well as a vertical way. Higher management levels are involved in the buying process as well as other departments. Furthermore, other buying motives will come into play through the involvement of different people. Maintenance firms will also have to be prepared for a longer decision-making process and develop specific tools, for instance to calculate the total cost of ownership, for specific phases throughout the extended buying process.

Figure 11.4 The full-service concept

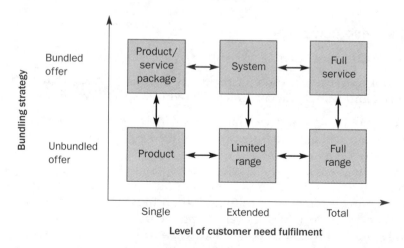

Source: reprinted from *Industrial Marketing Management*, vol. 30, S. Stremersch, S. Wuyts and R. T. Frambach (2001) The purchasing of full-service contracts, © 2001 with permission from Elsevier Science.

11.4 New product development (NPD)

Long-term success is dependent on the ability to compete with others. One of the most important conditions for achieving this is to ensure that your firm's products are superior to the competition, by adding new competitive products to the product portfolio.

The traditional NPD model involves the following stages in product development: **idea generation**, screening, concept development and testing, business analysis, product development and testing, **test marketing**, commercialization or launch (Baker and Hart, 1999, pp. 154–7).

The multiple convergent process model

Baker and Hart (1999) have suggested the following multiple convergent process model (Figure 11.5) which has been derived from the idea of parallel processing.

In the multiple convergent approach, there are tasks that must be carried out in different internal departments (research and development, marketing, engineering/design, manufacturing) and carried out in cooperation with external partners (suppliers and customers). Hence, the total number of different actors/departments involved in the NPD process is six, as illustrated in Figure 11.5. The tasks have to be carried out simultaneously and the results must converge at some point, which is likely to happen several times due to the iterations in the process.

Consequently, there are multiple convergent points that link the activity-stage model to the decision-stage models. The extent of involvement of internal and external groups will be determined by the firm's specific needs in the product development process.

One of the advantages of this model is that it recognizes the involvment of external partners in the product development process. There is growing interest in the need for supplier and customer involvement in the NPD. From the customers, the firm can benefit from new product ideas and product adaptations to specific customer needs. The supplier can contribute with supplier innovation and just-in-time techniques.

Product platform/modularity in NPD

The modular approach to product development is an important success factor in many markets. By sharing components and production processes across a product platform, companies can develop differentiated products efficiently, increase the flexibility and responsiveness of their manufacturing processes, and take market share away from competitors that develop only one product at a time.

The modular approach is also a way to achieve successful mass customization – the manufacture of products in high volumes that are tailored to meet the needs of individual customers. It allows highly differentiated products to be delivered to the market without consuming excessive resources.

Product modularity consists of designing a platform that is a collection of assets that are shared by a set of products. These assets can be divided into four categories (Robertson and Ulrich, 1998), as follows:

- *Components*: the part designs of a product, the fixtures and tools needed to make them, the circuit designs, and the programs burned into programmable chips or stored on disks.

Figure 11.5 The multiple convergent process model for NPD

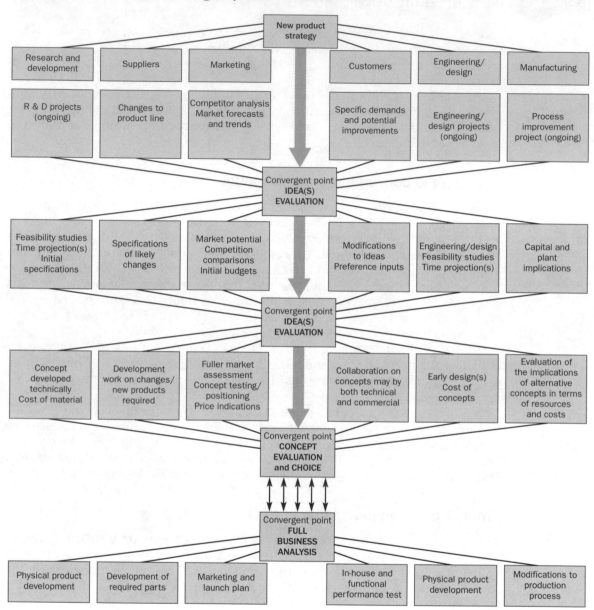

Source: after Baker and Hart (1999), p. 175.

- *Processes*: the equipment used to make components or to assemble components into products and the design of the associated production process and supply chain.
- *Knowledge*: design know-how, technology applications and limitations, production techniques, mathematical models, and testing methods.
- *People and relationships*: teams, relationships among team members, relationships between the team and the larger organization, and relationships with a network of suppliers.

This general product platform should then be used for tailoring end products to the needs of different market segments or customers. The platform approach reduces the incremental cost of addressing the specific needs of a market segment or of an individual customer. See also Figure 11.6 for an example of the modular approach in new product development. For simplicity, only the interaction between two product modules is illustrated.

The firm's advantages in using product modularity are:

- *reduction of development cost and time*. Parts and assembly processes developed for one end product can be used for other products.
- *reduction of variable costs*. When producing larger volumes of common components, companies achieve economies of scale, which cuts costs in materials management, logistics, distribution, inventory management, sales and service, and purchasing.
- *reduction of production investments*. Machinery, equipment, and tooling, and the engineering time needed to create them, can be shared across higher production volumes.

Figure 11.6 Principle of using modularity in creating product platforms

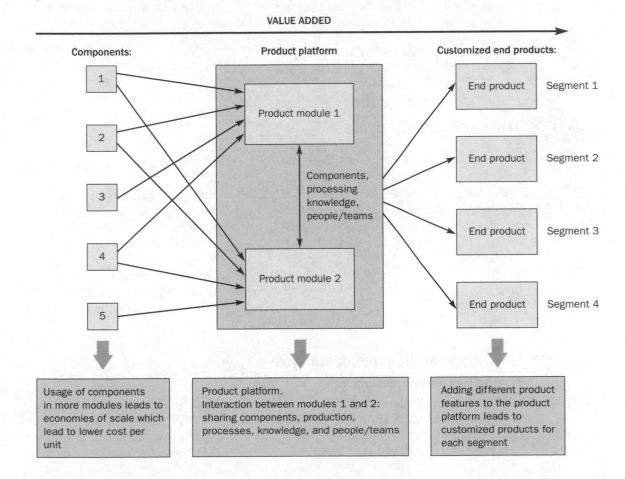

- *reduction of risks*. The lower investment required for each product developed from a platform results in decreased risk for each new product. Sharing components across products allows companies to stock fewer parts in their production and service parts inventories, which translates into better service levels and/or lower service costs.

Exhibit 11.2   **Kodak's modularity strategy**

In 1987, Fuji introduced the QuickSnap 35 mm single use camera into the US market. Kodak, which did not have a comparable product of its own, was caught unprepared in a market that was destined to grow by more than 50 per cent per year for the next eight years, from 3 million units in 1988 to 43 million in 1994. By the time Kodak introduced its first model almost a year later, Fuji had already developed a second model, the QuickSnap Flash. Yet Kodak won market share back from Fuji; by 1994, Kodak had captured more than 70 per cent of the US market.

The success of Kodak's response resulted from its strategy of developing many distinctively different models from a common platform. Between April 1989 and July 1990, Kodak redesigned its base model and introduced three additional models, all having common components and common production process steps. Because Kodak designed its four products to share component and process steps, it was able to develop its products faster and more cheaply. The different models appealed to different customer segments and gave Kodak twice as many products as Fuji, allowing it to capture precious retail space and substantial market share.

Source: adapted from Robertson and Ulrich (1998).

11.5   The product life cycle

The concept of the product life cycle (PLC) provides useful inputs into making product decisions and formulating product strategies.

Products, like individuals, pass through a series of stages. Each stage is identified by its sales performance and characterized by different levels of profitability, various degrees of competition and distinctive marketing programmes. The four stages of the product life cycle are introduction, growth, maturity and decline. The basic model of the PLC is shown in Figure 7.5.

The PLC emphasizes the need to review marketing objectives and strategies as products pass through various stages. It is helpful to think of marketing decisions during the lifetime of a product, but managers need to be aware of the limitations of the PLC so they are not misled by its prescriptions.

Limitations of the product life cycle

Misleading strategy prescriptions

The PLC is a dependent variable that is determined by the marketing mix; it is not an independent variable to which firms should adapt their marketing programmes (Dhalla and Yuspeh, 1976). If a product's sale is declining, management should not conclude that the brand is in the decline stage. If management withdraws market-

Exhibit 11.3	Using NVA time for creating value

Reducing customer 'NVA time' – that is non-value-added time – is a new source of competitive advantage, ripe for innovation. NVA time has long been a focus of companies' productivity enhancements. For a manufacturer, NVA time occurs when work in progress sits idle for one reason or another. The more NVA time, the higher the work-in-process inventory – and the lower the profits.

Although customers are not in a position to levy direct charges for their time spent waiting, the performance of companies like Amazon, which immediately confirms orders and informs customers of shipping and delays, has raised customers' expectations that their time will be valued.

As important as it is to reduce customers' NVA time, it may be even more useful to think about how to add value to the time customers spend with you. Disney has long understood this principle. It employs people and invests capital to entertain theme park visitors while they queue for their turn on a ride.

Some ATM machines are now installed with the Internet, which provides headlines, weather, and sports scores. This is especially useful at sites that use slow dial-up modems, such as convenience stores, where simple transactions can take a while.

Source: Meyer (2001).

ing resources from the brand, it will create a self-fulfilling prophecy and the brand's sales will continue to decline. Instead, management might increase marketing support in order to create a new cycle (see Figure 7.5). This could be realized by use of one or more of the following measures:

- product improvements (e.g. new product packaging)
- reposition perception of the product
- reach new users of the product (via new distribution outlets)
- promote more frequent use of the product (fulfilling same need)
- promote new uses of the product (fulfilling new needs).

Fads

Not all products follow the classic PLC curve. **Fads** are fashions that are adopted very quickly by the public, peak early and decline very fast. It is difficult to predict whether something will be only a fad, or how long it will last. The amount of mass-media attention together with other factors will influence the fad's duration.

Unpredictability

The duration of the PLC stages is unpredictable. Critics charge that markets can seldom tell what stage the product is in. A product may appear to be mature when actually it has only reached a temporary plateau prior to another upsurge.

Levels of the product life cycle

The PLC concept can be examined at various levels, from the life cycle of a whole industry or product form (the technological life cycle or TLC) (Popper and Buskirk, 1992) to the life cycle of a single model of a specific product. It is probably most useful to think in terms of the life cycle of a product form such as photocopiers or video cassette recorders. Life cycles for product forms include definable groups of direct and close competitors and a core technology. These characteristics make life cycles for product forms easier to identify and analyse, and would seem to have more stable and general implications. In Figure 11.7 an example of different PLC levels is shown.

Another example of a TLC shift happened when the compact disc (CD) format was introduced as a result of a joint development between Philips and Sony. A key success factor of the CD format in displacing the old LP record format was the ownership by Sony of CBS in the USA, and by Philips of Polygram in Europe, which are two of the biggest music companies in the world. This contributed to the new CD format establishing itself as the industry standard. However, there were also a number of barriers to the adoption of the new format. The potential users had already invested in LP record collections and the prices of discs and players were relatively high at the beginning of the TLC.

11.6 New products for the international market

Customer needs are the starting point for product development, whether for domestic or global markets. In addition to customer needs, conditions of use and ability to buy the product form a framework for decisions on new product development for the international market.

Developing new products/cutting the time to market

As a consequence of increasing international competition, speed is becoming a key success factor for an increasing number of companies that manufacture technologically sophisticated products.

Figure 11.7 Comparisons of TLC for different VCR systems and PLC of a single VCR model

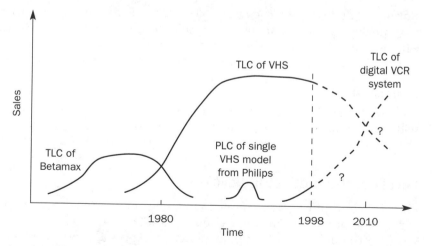

Source: Hollensen (2001), p. 403.

This speed of change in the environment is accelerating, leading to greater complexity and added 'turbulence', or discontinuity. Technological developments are combining to shorten product life cycles and speed up commercialization times. The increasing turbulence in the market makes it particularly difficult to predict. As a result planning time scales have been shortened. Where long-term plans in relatively predictable markets could span 10–15 years, very few companies today are able to plan beyond the next few years in any but the most general terms.

In parallel to shorter PLCs, the product development times for new products are being greatly reduced. This applies not only to technical products in the field of office communication equipment, but also to cars and consumer electronics. In some cases there have been reductions in development times of more than half.

Similarly, the time for marketing and selling, and hence also to pay off R&D costs, has gone down from about four years to only two years and less for a number of products like printers and computers, over a period of ten years (Töpfer, 1995, p. 68).

For all types of technological products it holds true that the manufactured product must be as good as required by the customer (i.e. as good as necessary), but not as good as is technically feasible. Too frequently, technological products are over-optimized and therefore too expensive from the customer's point of view.

Traditionally, Japanese and European suppliers to the car industry have had different approaches to the product development process. Normally the Japanese have been able to develop a product in a shorter time using the newest technology.

The reason for the better time competition of the Japanese manufacturers is the intensive use of:

- early integration of customers and suppliers
- multi-skilled project teams
- interlinking of R&D, production and marketing activities
- total quality management
- parallel planning of new products and the required production facilities (simultaneous engineering)
- high degree of outsourcing (reduction of internal manufacturing content).

Today product quality is not enough to reach and to satisfy the customer. Quality of design and appearance play an increasingly important role. Highly qualified product support staff and high quality customer service are also required.

Degrees of product newness

A new product can have several degrees of newness. A product may be an entirely new invention (new to the world) or it may be a slight modification of an existing product (cost reductions). In Figure 11.8 newness has two factors: newness to the market (consumers, channels and public policy) and newness to the company.

Let us briefly discuss the main categories in Figure 11.8.

New to international markets

These represent a small proportion of all new products introduced. Most new products modify and improve company's existing products. They are inventions that usually contain a significant development in technology such as a new discovery or manipulation of existing technology in a very different way leading to revolutionary new designs such as the Sony Discman. Other examples include Polaroid's instant camera and 3M's Post-its.

Figure 11.8 Different degrees of product newness

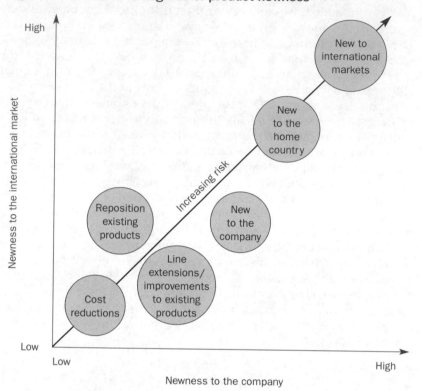

Source: Hollensen (2001), p. 409.

New to the company

Although not new to the marketplace, these products are new to the particular company. They provide an opportunity for the company to enter an established market for the first time. For example, Microsoft will be able to enter the games console market when it launches X-Box, ready to compete with Sony and Nintendo.

Line extensions

In this situation the company already has a line of products in the market. For example Virgin Soft Drink's Energy is an addition to its established line of cola brands.

Reposition existing products

This has more to do with new customer perception and branding than technical development. Therefore, this alternative may be new to the market (new perception) but not new to the company itself.

Exhibit 11.4	**Kodak's successful introduction of new products into the electronic imaging area**

Eastman Kodak's challenges are in competing in the traditional photography industry while also deciding how to compete with electronic imaging products. Kodak's cash cow is its traditional film business, and it must compete aggressively against Fuji in global markets. Yet management recognizes the escalating threat of electronic imaging.

The company's core competence centres on the development, production, and marketing of instant film, backed by a strong global brand name. During the 1990s Polaroid struggled to maintain a competitive edge. By 1999, it faced serious financial problems and a possible takeover by the Japanese film producer Fuji. At the centre of Polaroid's challenge is leveraging its capabilities to generate successful new products. Its instant film monopoly in the USA is affected negatively by electronic imaging and one-hour film developing services. In response to this threat, management has shifted research and development priorities toward digital products, though Polaroid will continue to protect its position with instant film products. The company has several products in the pipeline including plans for a digital camera that will offer instant prints. Of course, the more basic issue is whether instant film will become obsolete, and how fast.

Source: adapted from Cravens *et al*. (2000).

11.7 Product cannibalization

Introducing new brands that have a negative impact on the sales of existing products has often been regarded as a wrong product strategy. However, it is important that managers realize that pro-active **cannibalization** may be a sound strategy under certain conditions (Cravens *et al.*, 2000). This strategy ensures a continuing flow of new products, and recognizes that products need to be replaced as they move through their life cycles. Managers of innovative firms often resist the instinct to preserve the value of part of the investment in products. Instead, these companies pursue a continuing strategy of investing in new products that will cannibalize existing products (Chandy and Tellis, 1998).

Conditions for successful cannibalization

Successful cannibalization strategies are more likely to occur in companies where:

- effective market sensing capabilities have been developed, enabling the firms to form accurate visions about their markets and how they are most likely to change.
- some internal competition across business units is prevalent. Innovation is encouraged, and managers must compete for resources. Executives in these organizations accept cannibalization threats, but by encouraging competition across business units, they focus their attention on the most promising product concepts. Senior management must coordinate these processes towards optimal performance for the product portfolio.
- new product champions are able to influence corporate decisions. For example, the chief executive may play a central leadership role in new product development.

Some good examples of successful pro-active cannibalization are as follows (Cravens *et al.*, 2000).

Gillette, the global market leader in razors, introduced the Gillette sensor razor in 1989 with the objective of countering the sales growth of disposable razors. However, management knew the mature Atra Plus brand would also lose sales to Sensor. Sensor was a huge success, providing Gillette with impressive sales and profit growth. In 1998 Gillette introduced yet another new razor, Mach3. It was positioned as a significant improvement in shaving technology with development costs of over US$750 million and market entry costs of US$300 million in the first year of introduction. Management knew that while the Mach3 was priced above the SensorExcell, it was likely to cannibalize the existing brand's sales.

The German automobile group, Volkswagen (VW), now holds more than 18 per cent of the European market, six points clear of its nearest rival, Fiat. This gain has been achieved by VW's multi-brand strategy. The VW group includes automobiles from the VW brand portfolio, but also the Audi, Seat and Skoda operations. There are several platforms across the group and shared R&D. The brands compete directly with each other in several car segments across Europe, but have different strengths in different national markets. Although the VW brand's sales have been cannibalized, the result has been overall market leadership.

Exhibit 11.5 | **Mars is moving into the UK biscuit market**

UK market research data shows that 99% of households buy biscuits every year. In fact the UK consumes more biscuits per person than any other country. However, the UK market has also changed significantly in the past few years. Whereas people used to eat biscuits mostly with a cup of tea, 62% of consumers now describe biscuits as snacks in their own right. This means they are competing with crisps, confectionery and yogurt.

But closer investigation reveals that the UK market is worth £1.7 billion and certain parts of it are expanding fast. For instance, the children's biscuit segment is growing at almost 7% a year and healthier options by more than 17%.

The market leader in the UK is McVitie, which has over 22% of the UK biscuit market, more than three times that of its nearest competitor. But another challenger is about to enter the race – Mars, which will evolve some of its confectionery brands into biscuits starting with Bounty, M&Ms, Twix and Mars Bar.

The biscuit strategy allows Mars to capitalize on the popularity of existing brands and extend their shelf presence. The launch of biscuits is not Mars' first foray into biscuits. In 1999 it tested Twix Top, a flatter, single-finger variant of its Twix chocolate bar. Nor is it the first confectionery giant to turn its chocolates into biscuits. Nestlé recently launched Yorkie and Rolo biscuits. Cadbury's Time Out has a presence in the biscuit category by producing multipacks.

Source: adapted from Mason (2001).

11.8 Brand equity

A study by Citibank and Interbrand in 1997 found that companies that based their business on brands had outperformed the stock market for 15 years. The same study does, however, note the risky tendency of some brand owners to have reduced investments in brands in the mid-1990s with negative impacts on their performance (Hooley *et al.*, 1998, p. 120).

The following two examples show that brands add value for the customers.

The classic example is that in a blind test, 51 per cent of consumers prefer Pepsi to Coca-Cola, but in open tests 65 per cent prefer Coca-Cola to Pepsi: soft drink preferences are based on brand image, not taste (Hooley *et al.*, 1998, p. 119).

Skoda Cars (the Czech car manufacturer which before World War II had the status now enjoyed by BMW) used to display a negative **brand equity**. In the UK, Skoda cars have been best known as the butt of bad jokes, reflecting a widespread belief that the cars are of very low quality. In 1995, Skoda was preparing to launch a new model in the UK, and did blind and seen tests of the consumers' judgement of the vehicle. The vehicle was rated as better designed and worth more by those who did not know the make. With the Skoda name revealed, perceptions of the design were less favourable and estimated value was substantially lower. This leads us from the reputation of the company to branding (Hooley *et al.*, 1998, p. 117). The consumer perception of the value of Skoda cars and the likelihood of purchase was higher in some overseas markets when the Skoda badges and branding were removed from the vehicles. This signalled the need for major brand building efforts. The company has succeeded in turning the brand around and it now scores well in Europe. The management of Skoda has learned that one of the key factors in determining whether someone is likely to buy and drive a Skoda is not their age or where they live, but their attitude. Their strategy is to talk to people who are more rational in making decisions. These people are more likely to make purchases based on facts, such as high safety ratings, rather than on image (James, 2002).

Determining the value of a brand is believed to be important to firms for a number of reasons. Brands highly valued by customers produce competitive advantage in as much as brand equity comes about due to customers having greater confidence in the brand compared to competitors' brands (Lassar *et al.*, 1995). Brand equity may play a role in consumers' decisions to purchase certain brands over others (Swait *et al.*, 1993), and understanding brand equity can help develop marketing strategies (Keller, 1993). Brand equity also plays an important role in explaining the nature of brand and line extensions and in determining the effects of the name transfer from the parent brand to the extension (Swait *et al.*, 1993). Furthermore, brand equity may play an important role in co-branding. In certain co-branding situations, a well-known brand name is paired with another brand name (either well known in its own right or less well known) in order to enhance the lesser-known composite product. The general theory on line extensions is that the brand equity of the original brand will help the line extension gain favour in the eyes of consumers and channel members (Swait *et al.*, 1993). Co-branding is believed to limit the risk of entering into a new product category in which consumers may question the firm's expertise (Aaker, 1996).

Definitions of brand equity

Although the definition of brand equity is often debated, the term deals with the brand value, beyond the physical assets associated with its manufacture.

Brand equity has been measured in a number of ways:

- equalization price (Swait *et al.*, 1993)
- brand attributes (Lassar *et al.*, 1995)
- price premiums (Aaker, 1991)

- stock price analysis (Simon and Sullivan, 1990)
- replacement cost (Aaker, 1991)
- brand loyalty analysis (Feldwick, 1996).

Dr David Aaker of the University of California at Berkeley, one of the leading authorities on brand equity, has defined the term as 'a set of brand assets and liabilities linked to the brand, its name and symbol that add to or subtract from the value provided by a product or service to a firm or to the firm's customers' (Aaker, 1991, p.15).

Aaker has clustered those assets and liabilities into five categories.

1. *Brand loyalty*: encourages customers to buy a particular brand time after time and remain insensitive into competitors' offerings.
2. *Brand awareness*: brand names attract attention and convey images of familiarity. This can be translated into how large a percentage of the customers know the brand name.
3. *Perceived quality*: 'perceived' means that the customers decide upon the level of quality, not the company.
4. *Brand associations*: the values and the personality linked to the brand.
5. *Other proprietary brand assets*: including trademarks, patents, and market channel relationships.

Brand equity can be thought of as the additional cash flow achieved by associating a brand with the underlying values of the product or service. In this connection it is useful (although incomplete) to think of a brand's equity as the premium a customer or consumer would pay for the branded product or service compared to an identical unbranded version of the same product or service.

Hence, brand equity refers to the strength, depth, and character of the consumer-brand relationship. A strong equity implies a positive force that keeps the consumer and the brand together, in the face of resistance and tension. The strength, depth, and character of the customer-brand relationship is referred to as the brand relationship quality (BRQ) (Marketing Science Institute, 1995).

11.9 Branding

Branding is storytelling

A brand name is more than a label employed to differentiate among the manufacturers of a product. It is a complex symbol that represents a variety of ideas and attributes. It tells the consumer many things – not only by the way it sounds (and its literal meaning if it has one), but more importantly by the body of associations it has built up and acquired as a public object over a period of time. The net result is the public image, character or personality that may be more important for the customers. Figure 11.9 shows the communication of some **world-class brands** and what they stand for.

The concept of the brand represents an acceptance of the fact that all purchasing decisions for both products and services involve a combination of rational and emotional criteria. The rational criteria are the physical components or factual

Figure 11.9 Some world class brands

Company name	What they stand for	Brand attributes	Brand theme
Coca-Cola Company (www.coca-cola.com)	The spirit of refreshment. Only the original will do. Bringing people together.	Refreshing, exciting sociable, red	Always Coca-Cola
McDonald's Corporation (www.mcdonalds.com)	Affordable good food for the family.	Trust, convenience, value	To be the nation's favourite family restaurant
British Airways (www.british-airways.com)	The world's leading provider of travel services.	Global, caring	The world's favourite airline
Intel Corporation (www.intel.com)	To do a great job for our customers, stockholders and employees by being the pre-eminent building block supplier to the computer industry worldwide.	Safety, technology, leader, intelligence, unexpected	Intel inside ITANIUM
Nike Inc. (www.nike.com)	Experiencing the emotion of competition, winning and crushing competitors.	Performance, achievement, individualism, attitude	Just do it
American Express Company (www.americanexpress.com)	Personal enablement. Heroic customer service. Worldwide reliability of services.	Respect, worldliness, trust, security, success	Do more
BMW Group (www.bmw.com)	The best car company in the world.	Quality, performance, technology	The ultimate driving machine

Source: first published in *The Journal of Brand Management*, vol. 7, no. 4, in a paper by Dave Allen entitled 'The ACID Test™: a communications tool for leadership teams who want to interact with the whole organisation', Henry Stewart Publications (**www.henrystewart.co.uk**)

elements of the product or service in question. The emotional criteria are the sum of the impressions, ideas, opinions and random associations that the potential purchaser has stored in his or her mind about the product or service. Rational and emotional elements combine to form a brand image. The word 'brand' is used to represent everything that people know, think or feel about anything. There are a number of implications of this definition.

Successful brand management necessitates the firm innovating to stay abreast of constantly changing market conditions, ideally anticipating evolving tastes, and telling their brand stories to each new generation of consumers. The notion of story-telling is key. Well-managed brands are continually telling stories about themselves, and updating these stories to take account of underlying changes in society, though their core values usually remain constant. Clever brand management also involves decisions about the service element that supports a brand and the extent to which a brand should embrace some higher-order universal value.

Nike is the most quoted example of this phenomenon. This hugely successful worldwide brand rarely talks about the product itself, which is understandable as all manufacturing is outsourced, but about core values such as achievement, competitiveness and winning. Nike stories are parables, a tried and trusted technique for communicating desired messages. John Scully, the well-known chief executive of Apple, is another proponent of this approach. He is on record as saying that he doesn't want Apple advertising to mention anything to do with megabytes or memory or any other technical terms that could be employed to create a superior brand store for Apple computers. Scully believes that Apple's core value is that it believes that people with passion can change the world for the better (Fanning, 1999).

Branding decisions

The basic purposes of branding are the same everywhere in the world. In general, the functions of branding are as follows.

- To distinguish a company's offering and differentiate one particular product from its competitors.
- To create identification and brand awareness.
- To guarantee a certain level of quality and satisfaction.
- To help with promotion of the product.

All these purposes have the same ultimate goals: to create new sales (market share taken from competitors) or induce repeat sales (keep customers loyal).

As Figure 11.10 shows, there are four levels of branding decisions. Each alternative at the four levels has a number of advantages and disadvantages, which are presented in Table 11.2. We will discuss these options in more detail.

Brand versus no brand

Branding is associated with added costs in the form of marking, labelling, packaging and promotion. Commodities are unbranded or undifferentiated products. Examples of products with no brand are milk, metals, salt, beef and other agricultural products.

Figure 11.10 Branding decisions

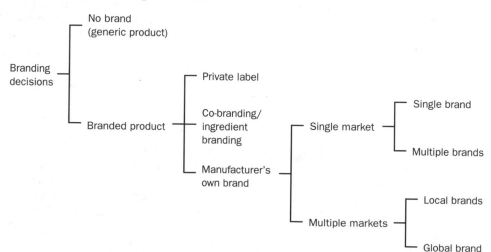

Source: Onkvisit and Shaw, 1993, p. 534, with permission from Pearson Education, Inc., Upper Saddle River, NJ.

Table 11.2 Advantages and disadvantages of branding alternatives

	Advantages	Disadvantages
No brand	Lower production cost. Lower marketing cost. Lower legal cost. Flexible quality control.	Severe price competition. Lack of market identity.
Branding	Better identification and awareness. Better chance for production differentiation. Possible brand loyalty. Possible premium pricing.	Higher production cost. Higher marketing cost. Higher legal cost.
Private label	Possibility of larger market share. No promotional problems.	Severe price competition. Lack of market identity.
Co-branding/ingredient branding	Adds more value to the brand. Sharing of production and promotion costs. Increases manufacturer's power in gaining access to retailer's shelves. Can develop into long-lasting relationships based on mutual commitment.	Consumers may become confused. Ingredient supplier is very dependent on the success of the final product. Promotion cost for ingredient supplier.
Manufacturer's own brand	Better price due to higher price inelasticity. Retention of brand loyalty. Better bargaining power. Better control of distribution.	Difficult for small manufacturer with unknown brand. Requires brand promotion.
Single market, single brand	Marketing efficiency. Permits more focused marketing. Eliminates brand confusion. Good for product with good reputation (halo effect).	Assumes market homogeneity. Existing brand's image harmed when trading up/down. Limited shelf space.
Single market/multiple brands	Market segmented for varying needs. Creates competitive spirit. Avoids negative connotation of existing brand. Gains more retail shelf space. Does not harm existing brand's image.	Higher marketing cost. Higher inventory cost. Loss of economies of scale.
Multiple markets, local brand	Meaningful names. Local identification. Avoidance of taxation on international brand. Allows variations of quantity and quality across markets.	Higher marketing cost. Higher inventory cost. Loss of economies of scale. Diffused image.
Multiple markets, global brands	Maximum marketing efficiency. Reduction of advertising costs. Elimination of brand confusion. Good for culture-free product. Good for prestigious product. Easy identification/recognition for international travellers. Uniform worldwide image.	Assumes market homogeneity. Problems with black and grey markets. Possibility of negative connotation. Requires quality and quantity consistency. LDCs' opposition and resentment. Legal complications.

Source: adapted from Onkvisit and Shaw (1989).

Private label versus co-branding versus manufacturer's own brand

These three options can be graded as shown in Figure 11.11.

The question of consumers having brand loyalty or shop loyalty is a crucial one. The competitive struggle between the manufacturer and the retailer emphasized the need for a better understanding of shopping behaviour. Both players need to be aware of the determinants of shop choice, shopping frequency and in-store behaviour. Where manufacturers pay little attention to the shopping behaviour of consumers, this information helps to anticipate the increasing power of certain retail chains.

Private label

Private labelling is most developed in the UK, where Marks & Spencer, for instance, only sells **own-label products**. At Sainsbury own labels account for 60 per cent of the sales. Contrary to the high share of private labelling in northern Europe, the share in southern Europe (e.g. Spain and Portugal) is no higher than 10 per cent.

The retailer's perspective

For the retailer there are two main advantages connected with own-label business.

- Own labels provide better profit margins. The cost of goods typically makes up 70–85 per cent of a retailer's total cost (The Economist, 1995). So if the retailer can buy a quality product from the manufacturer at a lower price, this will provide a better profit margin for the retailer. In fact, private labels have helped UK food retailers to achieve profit margins averaging 8 per cent of sales, which is high by international standards. The typical figure in France and the USA is 1–2 per cent.

- Own labels strengthen the retailer's image with its customers. Many retail chains try to establish loyalty to their particular chain of shops by offering their own quality products. In fact, premium private-label products (e.g. Marks & Spencer's St Michael) that compete in quality with manufacturers' top brands have seen a growth in market share, whereas the share of cheap generics is tiny and declining.

Figure 11.11 The three brand options

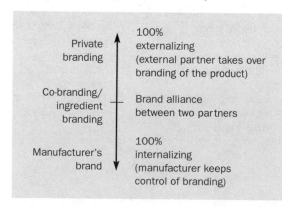

Source: Hollensen (2001), p. 417.

The manufacturer's perspective

Although private brands are normally regarded as threats for manufacturers, there may be situations where private branding is a preferable option.

- Since there are no promotional expenses associated with private branding for the producer, the strategy is especially suitable for SMEs with limited financial resources and limited competences in the downstream functions.
- The private brand manufacturer gains access to the shelves of the retail chains. With the increasing internationalization of the big retail chains, this may also result in export business for the SME, which has never been in international markets.

There are also a number of reasons why private branding is bad for the manufacturer.

- By not having its own identity, the manufacturer must compete mainly on price, because the retail chain can always switch supplier.
- The manufacturer loses control over how its products should be promoted. This may become critical if the retailer does not do a good job in pushing the product to the consumer.
- If the manufacturer is producing both its own brands and private brands, there is a danger that the private brands will cannibalize the manufacturer's brand name products.

Exhibit 11.6 shows an example with Kellogg, which has moved the other way, from a brand strategy to a private brand strategy.

Quelch and Harding (1996) argue that many manufacturers have over-reacted to the threat of private brands. Increasing numbers of manufacturers are beginning to make private-label products to take up excess production capacity. According to Quelch and Harding (1996), more than 50 per cent of the US manufacturers of branded consumer goods already make private-label goods as well.

Managers typically examine private-label production opportunities on an incremental marginal cost basis. The fixed overhead costs associated with the excess capacity used to make the private-label products would be incurred anyway. But if private-label manufacturing were evaluated on a full-cost basis rather than on an incremental basis, it would, in many cases, appear much less profitable. The more private-label production grows as a percentage of total production, the more an analysis based on full costs becomes relevant (Quelch and Harding, 1996).

Exhibit 11.6	**Kellogg is under pressure to produce Aldi's own-label goods**

In February 2000 Kellogg (the cereal giant) made an own-label deal with German supermarket chain Aldi. It is the first time that Kellogg has supplied own-label goods.

A slogan on Kellogg's cereal packets claims: 'If you don't see Kellogg's on the box ... it isn't Kellogg's in the box'. But now Kellogg has negotiated a deal with Aldi to supply products in Germany bearing a different brand name. Reports in Germany say that the deal was made after Aldi announced it would no longer pay brand suppliers' prices and threatened to cut top brands from its shelves.

Source: adapted from various public media.

Manufacturer's own brand

From World War II until the 1960s the brand manufacturers managed to build a bridge over the heads of the retailers to the consumers. They created consumer loyalty for their particular brand by using sophisticated advertising (culminating in TV advertising) and other promotional techniques.

Since the 1960s various sociological changes (notably the car) have encouraged the rise of large, efficient retailers. Nowadays the distribution system is being turned upside down. The traditional supply chain, powered by manufacturer push, is becoming a demand chain, driven by consumer pull. Retailers have won control over distribution not just because they decide the price at which goods are sold but also because individual shops and retail companies have become much bigger and more efficient. They are able to buy in bulk and to gain economies of scale, mainly due to advances in transport and, more recently, in information technology. Most retail chains have not only set up computer links between each store and the distribution warehouses, they are also linked to the computers of the firm's main suppliers, through an EDI (electronic data interchange) system.

After some decades of absence, private labels reappeared in the 1970s as **generic products** pioneered by Carrefour in France but were soon adopted by UK and US retailers. Ten years ago, there was a distinct gap in the level of quality between private-label and brand name products. Today the gap has narrowed: private-label quality levels are much higher than ever before, and they are more consistent, especially in categories historically characterized by little product innovation.

Co-branding/ingredient branding

This has already been discussed in Chapter 6.

Single brand versus multiple brands (single market)

A single brand or family brand (for a number of products) may be helpful in convincing consumers that each product is of the same quality or meets certain standards. In other words, when a single brand in a single market is marketed by the manufacturer, the brand is assured of receiving full attention for maximum impact.

The company may also choose to market several (multiple) brands on a single market. This is based on the assumption that the market is heterogeneous and consists of several segments.

Local brands versus a global brand (multiple markets)

A company has the option of using the same brand in most or all of its foreign markets, or using individual, local brands. A single, global brand is also known as an international or universal brand. A Eurobrand is a slight modification of this approach, as it is a single product for a single market of 12 or more European countries, with an emphasis on the search for inter-market similarities rather than differences.

A global brand is an appropriate approach when a product has a good reputation or is known for quality. In such a case, a company would be wise to extend the brand name to other products in the product line. Examples of global brands are

Coca-Cola, Shell and the Visa credit card. Although it is possible to find examples of global brands, local brands are probably more common among big multi-national companies than people realize (Hollensen, 2001, pp. 424–5).

11.10 Implications of Internet/e-commerce for product decisions

Types of products

The products sold in electronic markets were roughly grouped (in Chapter 10) into two categories: physical products and purely digital goods and services.

A virtual value chain can provide a number of options to customers to customize products and services. For example, customers can order through a credit card and download the required pieces of information. Or the firm may itself obtain the information from its suppliers electronically, which then can be automatically loaded on to the customers' computers. Also, a virtual value chain can be used to enhance the product and service offerings by providing additional information about the products and services. Moreover, with digital products and services, the virtual chain provides the possibility of their quick customization. For example, a student can pick a site from where he/she can choose research articles, magazine stories, and music video clips, published and created by different publishers and companies, and make one payment, instead of subscribing to many journals and videos.

Figure 11.12 shows some of the implications of the Internet on future product innovation.

Figure 11.12 Product innovation through the Internet

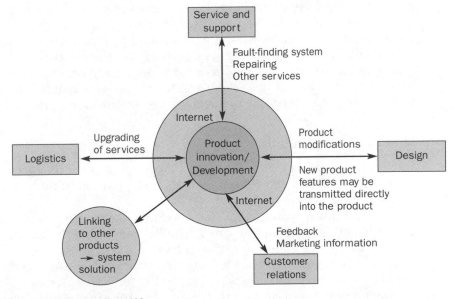

Source: Hollensen (2001), p. 428.

Design

Data is gathered directly from the product and is part of designing and developing the product. New qualities may be added to the product directly from the Internet.

Service and support

The service department can perform troubleshooting and correction directly through the Internet set-up.

Customer relations

Data gathered from the product may form part of statistics, comparisons between customers etc.

Logistics

Concurrently with the increasing demands of just-in-time deliveries, the Internet will automatically find the distribution and transport that will take the goods from the sub-supplier to the producer and then to the customers in the cheapest and most efficient way.

A fundamental shift in thinking is to replace the term supply chain with demand chain. The critical difference is that demand chain thinking starts with the customers and works backwards. This breaks out of parochial approaches that focus solely on reducing transport costs. It supports a mass customization viewpoint, in which bundles of goods and services are offered in ways that support customers' individual objectives.

This does not necessarily imply product differentiation. In fact, the service aspects often require differentiation. For example, a company such as Unilever will provide the same margarine to both Tesco and Sainsbury. However, the ways in which the product is delivered, transactions are processed and other parts of the relationship are managed, can and should be different, since these two competing supermarket chains each have their own ways of evaluating performance. The information systems required to coordinate companies along the demand chain require a new and different approach to that required within individual companies. Some managers believe that if they and their suppliers choose the same standard software package, such as SAP, they will be able to integrate their information systems.

Link to other products

Sometimes a product is used as a sub-component in other products. Through links in the Internet such sub-components may be essential inputs for more complex product solutions.

The car industry is an example of an industry that already makes a targeted effort in this direction. New 'stylish' cars are linked together by the Internet. In the wake of this development a new industry is created, the purpose of which is to provide integrated transport. In this new, integrated transport industry, developing and producing cars is only one of several important services. Instead, systems are to be developed that can diagnose cars (and correct the error) while the car is running; there will be systems for regulating traffic; and interactive systems that enable drivers to have the desired transport at their disposal when and where they want it without tiresome rental agreements etc.

The music industry is also undergoing a change. Today, you can buy portable players that can download music from the Internet using the MP3 format, and play the music that is stored in the player.

The CD is skipped – and so is the whole distribution facility. The music industry will have completely different economic conditions. Therefore the struggle will be about creating the best portal to the Internet, where the consumer can find the best information on music and the largest selection of music. The problems regarding rights are, however, still being discussed, and they have to find a final solution, before the market can increase significantly.

Thus, the innovative product development of the future demands that the company possesses the following characteristics.

- *Innovative product development and strategic thinking*: the product development will contain much technology and demand an inter-disciplinary, strategic overview and knowledge in order to find out what new services are worth aiming at.

- *Management of alliances*: few companies have all the necessary qualifications themselves – innovative product development and the resulting services demand that companies enter into alliances in a dynamic and structured way.

- *New customer relations*: the car industry example clearly shows that the customers are not car buyers any longer, but buyers of transport services, and that is quite another matter. This means that companies have to focus on understanding the customers' needs in a quite different way.

Developing brands on the Internet

Clearly, consumer product companies like Procter & Gamble, Colgate, Kraft Foods, and consumer durables and business-to-business companies like General Motors, General Electric, Allied Signal, and Caterpillar have crafted their business strategies by leveraging physical assets and developing powerful global brands supported by mass advertising and mass distribution. But remote links with customers apply equally well to these companies. Remote and continuous links with customers become critical as the concepts of brand identity and brand equity are redefined by the Internet.

Kraft Interactive Kitchen (**www.kraftfoods.com**) is an example of a consumer products company keeping in touch with its consumers by providing information-based services like meal planners, recipes, tips, and cooking techniques. Kraft's intention is to have remote connections and interactions with consumers in new ways.

However, some companies find it difficult to translate a strong offline brand (like Nike) to the Internet. In fact, many sites that are run by top brands register minimal online traffic, according to a report by Forrester Research. Forrester studied brand awareness and web surfing behaviour among 16 to 22-year-olds, who advertisers consider strongly brand-conscious.

The companies are taking a broad approach to branding, integrating it with an overall advertising and marketing strategy. On the Internet, branding is more than logos and colour schemes; it is about creating experiences and understanding customers. Consequently, web brand building is not cheap. Building a brand requires a persistent online presence. For some brands, that entails a mass-appeal site; for others, brand building requires a combination of initiatives, from banner advertising to sponsorship.

11.11 Summary

All goods and services consist of a core element that is surrounded by a variety of optional elements. If we look first at the core service products, we can assign them to one of three broad categories depending on their tangibility and the extent to which customers need to be physically present during service production.

The perceived service quality has two factors: a technical or outcome factor and a functional or process-related factor. The technical quality of a service process is normally a prerequisite for good quality. It has to be at an acceptable level.

After-sales service adds to the product's value and is often treated as an integral part of the product.

The traditional new product development models involve the following stages in product development: idea generation, screening, concept development and testing, business analysis, product development and testing, test marketing, commercialization or launch.

Products pass through a series of stages. Each stage is identified by its sales performance and characterized by different levels of profitability, various degrees of competition and distinctive marketing programmes. The four stages of the product life cycle are introduction, growth, maturity and decline.

A new product can have several degrees of newness. A product may be an entirely new invention (new to the world) or it may be a slight modification of an existing product.

Brand equity can be defined as 'a set of brand assets and liabilities linked to the brand, its name and symbol, that add to or subtract from the value provided by a product or service to a firm or to the firm's customers'.

Branding is a very important issue and alternatives have been discussed. For example, because large (often transnational) retail chains have won control over distribution, they try to develop their own labels. For the retailer, private labels provide better profit margins and strengthen the retailer's image with its customers. Because of the power shift to retailers, the percentage of retail grocery sales derived from private brands has increased in recent years.

The basic purposes of branding are the same everywhere in the world. In general, the functions of branding are:

- to distinguish a company's offering and differentiate one particular product from its competitors
- to create identification and brand awareness
- to guarantee a certain level of quality and satisfaction
- to help with promotion of the product.

The products sold over electronic markets and the Internet can be grouped into two categories: physical products and purely digital goods and services.

Case study 11.2 Joyco India

A bubblegum manufacturer outmanoeuvres Perfetti with Boomer in head-on competition

See Case study 6.2 for the history of Joyco and a description of its brands.

Joyco India started as a joint venture with Dabur India in 1995 with Joyco owning 51%. In 1999, the Indian company bought out Dabur's share in the joint venture. All Joyco's existing brands are being manufactured at its factory in India.

The confectionery market in India

Confectionery (of which bubblegum is a part), is driven by novelty, both at the consumer and distribution end. The size of the confectionery market in India is roughly Rs 1100 crore[1], of which toffees and candies account for Rs 600 crore. Joyco claims a 10% market share of the confectionery industry.

However, Joyco India has a clear goal. It wants to be the largest confectionery player in India in 2005 from being the third largest today, after Nutrine and Perfetti.

Boomer bubblegum

Boomer was launched in India in 1995 and in 2001 commanded a 50% share of the bubblegum segment. It is the flagship brand for the group, not just in India, but across markets, and has helped establish Joyco's presence in the confectionery industry worldwide.

In India, the gum market is highly competitive, with the presence of several global players. Joyco takes pride in claiming the position of market leader and fuelling growth in the category from a total market of Rs 35 crore in 1995 to Rs 300 crore in 2000 (about 15,000 tonnes of bubblegum). This market expansion has been possible with focused advertising and innovative consumer promotions.

Boomer is available in three formats – single unit, multi-pack and roll. The brand is synonymous with its super hero Boomerman, who with his dynamic looks and magical power is a proven winner with children around the country.

Around 1995, the Indian market for chewing gum and bubblegum was in a rut. Poor quality – the product was unpalatably rubbery – kept the market at Rs 35 crore annually. Perfetti entered the market in 1994 with Big Babol, followed by Generale De Confiteria (which later became Joyco).

Perfetti was first with Big Babol, about nine months ahead of Joyco's launch of Boomer in May 1995. Within a month of Boomer's launch, Perfetti dropped Big Babol's price to Rs 1, from Rs 1.50. Joyco, busy building its distribution, could not afford to react. For a full year, it sold at a Rs 0.50 premium to Big Babol. In mid-1996, it took Perfetti head-on by lowering Boomer's price.

Both the companies started off well by hiring executives from leading fast moving consumer goods and food companies. The focus was on building a strong distribution network. Over the next five years, the confectionery market changed dramatically. The gum market exploded at a compound annual growth rate of 60%. The gum market has grown nearly tenfold and is now worth over Rs 300 crore. Joyco India (a wholly owned subsidiary of Agrolimen), has emerged as the leader with a single brand: Boomer. Joyco India's total gum production of Rs 125 crore (5700 tonnes per year) is estimated to be 15–20% larger than that of Perfetti. In 1996, Perfetti's gum business was almost 2.5 times larger than that of Joyco.

All this time, Joyco stayed with a single product, except for minor deviations. Perfetti, on the other hand, introduced six brands in four categories and spent a great deal of money on advertising. Joyco spent far less on advertising, but Boomer is the country's largest selling gum brand.

The reason why Joyco is the leader in the bubble gum market is its single-minded focus on building that segment while others had their attention divided into too many segments. Perfetti wanted to reduce its risks by not depending on one product, says a former executive from a confectionery company. During the same period, Joyco had just two brands: Boomer bubblegum and Bonkers soft chew which apparently

---
[1] 1 US$ = 48 Rs (Indian Rupees), 1 crore = 10 million.

Case study 11.2 continued

did not do too well due to harsh climatic conditions. Yet its focus remained on bubblegum. It stepped into candies in early 1999 (Mickey and Donald). But candies are not strategic and were meant to test the company's distribution capabilities in products other than gum.

Joyco also took care to keep its major customers – children – constantly involved, with a barrage of innovative promotions and flavours. Children tend to have short attention spans that demand constant innovation. Joyco was the first company to act seriously on this factor. In 1997, it unleashed a big consumer promotion offering transfers with two single packs of Boomer. It was a runaway hit. The response actually took Joyco India by surprise. It had not anticipated the sudden upsurge in sales. The supply of Boomer could not meet the rising demand. Perfetti reacted with its own transfer scheme two months later. But by then children were associating Boomer with transfers. Perfetti's scheme was seen as a me-too product. Four months later, Boomer came back with the transfer promotion, stronger and better this time.

In 1997, when Perfetti began experimenting with plastic jars for retailers to display Big Babol, Joyco went further. In one go, it changed its entire supplies to jars. Transparent jars have become a big merchandising tool. And Joyco's swiftness has paid off. Today, most jars at retail outlets bear Boomer stickers.

The situation today

Boomer bubblegum constitutes about 60% of Joyco's overall sales in India, candies account for 25% of sales, followed by chocolates at 15%.

Today, Joyco India has 1650 distributors who reach about 400,000 outlets. The south and west of India have proved to be the biggest regions for the company as it entered markets that were already developed, thanks to the efforts of established players such as Perfetti and Nutrine India and Ravalgaon Sugar Farms.

In 2000, Joyco India launched the mouth freshener, Aqtimint. While all other Joyco brands are targeted at children, Aqtimint is the sole brand in its portfolio addressing the needs of Indian teenagers and young adults, for whom fresh breath is becoming more and more important. Approximately 80% of the Indian gum market consists of bubblegum. This percentage is much higher than in most western countries where sugar-free and dental chewing gum is much more popular than in India. Joyco India does not have a sugar-free chewing gum brand in its portfolio yet.

The management of Joyco India is now considering if it would be wise to launch a dental chewing gum brand for the Indian market. The Joyco managers are observing how Wrigley and Adams are slowly gaining market share with their sugar-free brands like Orbit, Trident, and Dentyne. These higher-priced brands are not important today, but what about the future?

Questions

1. What are the criteria for successful general marketing in the Indian bubblegum market?

2. What are the main reasons for Joyco's victory over Perfetti in the bubblegum market?

3. Should Joyco launch a sugar-free chewing gum brand for the Indian market?

Sources: adapted from The Business Standard, The Strategist (2000) Business Line (2001), India Infoline (2001), Joyco's English homepage: http://www.joycogroup.com/eng/ index_1.html

QUESTIONS FOR DISCUSSION

1. How would you distinguish between services and products? What are the main implications of this difference for the marketing of services?

2. What implications does the product life cycle theory have for product development strategy?

3. Why is the international product policy likely to be given a higher priority in most firms than other elements of the global marketing mix?

4. What are the requirements that must be met so that a commodity can effectively be transformed into a branded product?

5. Discuss the factors that need to be taken into account when making packaging decisions for a firm's products.

6. When is it appropriate to use multiple brands in (a) a single market and (b) several markets/countries?

7. What is the importance of 'country of origin' in international product marketing?

8. What are the distinguishing characteristics of services? Explain why these characteristics make it difficult to sell services in foreign markets.

9. Identify the major barriers to developing brands.

10. Discuss the decision to add or drop products to or from the product line in existing markets.

11. Why should customer-service levels differ internationally? Is it, for example, ethical to offer a lower customer-service level in developing countries than in industrialized countries?

12. What are the characteristics of a good international brand name?

REFERENCES

Aaker, D.A. (1991), *Managing Brand Equity*, The Free Press, New York, NY.

Aaker, D.A. (1996), Measuring brand equity across products and markets, *California Management Review*, vol. 38, no. 3, pp. 102–20.

Allen, A. (2000), The ACID test: a communication tool for leadership teams who want to interact with the whole organisation, *Journal of Brand Marketing*, no. 3, pp. 255–62.

Asugman, G., Johnson, J. L. and McCullough, J. L. (1997), The role of after sales service in international marketing, *Journal of International Marketing*, vol. 5, no. 4, pp. 11–28.

Baker, M. and Hart, S. (1999), *Product Strategy and Management*, Prentice Hall, Harlow.

Business Line (2001), Joyco to test-market 2 brands this year (**http://in.biz.yahoo.com/ 010905/17/1472h.html**), September 6.

Chandy, R. K. and Tellis, G. J. (1998), *Organizing for Radical Product Innovation*, Marketing Science Institute, report, no. 98–102.

Cravens, D. W., Piercy, N. G. and Prentice, A. (2000), Developing market-driven product strategies, *Journal of Product & Brand Management*, vol. 9, no. 6, pp. 369–88.

Czinkota, M. R. and Ronkainen, L. A. (1995), *International Marketing*, Dryden Press, Fort Worth, TX, 5th edn.

Dhalla, N. K. and Yuspeh, S. (1976), Forget the product life cycle concept, *Harvard Business Review*, January–February, pp. 102–12.

Driver, J. C. (2001), Airline marketing in regulatory context, *Marketing Intelligence Planning*, vol. 19, no. 2, pp. 125–35.

Fanning, J. (1999), Tell me a story: the future of branding, *Irish Marketing Review*, vol. 12, no. 2, pp. 3–15.

Feldwick, P. (1996), What is brand equity anyway, and how do you measure it?, *Journal of the Market Research Society*, vol. 38, no. 2, pp. 85–104.

Goffin, K. and New, C. (2001), Customer support and new product development, *International Journal of Operations & Production Management*, vol. 21, no. 3, pp. 275–301.

Grönroos, C. (2000), *Service Management and Marketing*, John Wiley & Sons, Chichester.

Herbig, P. A. and Palumbo, F. (1993), Serving the aftermarket in Japan and the United States, *Industrial Marketing Management*, vol. 22, pp. 339–46.

Hollensen, S. (2001), *Global Marketing: A market responsive approach*, Financial Times/Prentice Hall, Harlow, 2nd edn.

Hooley, G. J., Saunders, J. A. and Piercy, N. (1998), *Marketing Strategy and Competitive Positioning*, Prentice-Hall Europe, 2nd edn.

India infoline (2001), Joyco launches new milk candy – Solano (**http://www.indiainfoline.com/news/fmcg2001JUL18121114.html**), July 18 .

James, D. (2002), Skoda is taken from trash to treasure, *Marketing News*, February 8, pp. 4–5.

Keller, K. L. (1993), Conceptualizing, measuring, and managing customer-based brand equity, *Journal of Marketing*, vol. 57, no. 1, pp. 1–22.

Kotler, P. (2000), *Marketing Management*, Prentice-Hall, Englewood Cliffs, NJ.

Lassar, W., Mittal, B. and Sharma, A. (1995), Measuring customer-based brand equity, *Journal of Consumer Marketing*, vol. 12, pp. 11–19.

Lauterborn, R (1990), New marketing litany: 4Ps Passe: C-words take over, *Advertising Age*, October 1, pp. 25–7.

Levitt, T. (1983), After the sale is over…, *Harvard Business Review*, vol. 16, pp. 87–93.

Marketing Science Institute (1995), *Brand Equity and Marketing Mix: Creating customer value, conference summary*, Marketing Science Institute, report 95–111, September, p. 14.

Mason, T. (2001), Mars evolves brands into biscuit variants, *Marketing*, London, July 26, p. 19.

Meyer, C. (2001), While customers wait, add value, *Harvard Business Review*, vol. 79, no. 7, pp. 24–5.

Miskie, R. (1989), Documentation: not a 'necessary evil' but a valuable resource, *Network World*, vol. 6, no. 8, p. 35.

Onkvisit, S. and Shaw, J. J. (1993), *International Marketing: Analysis and Strategy*, Macmillan, London, 2nd edn.

Popper, E. T. and Buskirk, B. D. (1992), Technology life cycles in industrial markets, *Industrial Marketing Management*, vol. 21, no. 1, pp. 23–34.

Quelch, J. A. and Harding, D. (1996), Brands versus private labels: fighting to win, *Harvard Business Review*, January–February, pp. 99–109.

Robertson, D. and Ulrich, K. (1998), Planning for product platforms, *Sloan Management Review*, no. 4, Summer, pp. 19–31.

Ruyter, K. and Wetzels, M. (2000), Customer considerations in service recovery: a cross-industry perspective, *International Journal of Service Industry Management*, vol. 11, no. 1, pp. 91–108.

Samiee, S. (1999), The internationalisation of services: trends, obstacles and issues, *Journal of Services Marketing*, vol. 13, no. 4/5, pp. 319–28.

Simon, C. J. and Sullivan, M. W. (1990), *The Measurement and Determinants of Brand Equity: A financial approach*, Graduate School of Business, University of Chicago, Chicago, II, working paper.

Stremersch, S., Wuyts, S. and Frambach, R. T. (2001), The purchasing of full-service contracts, *Industrial Marketing Management*, vol. 30, pp. 1–12.

Swait, J., Erdem, T., Louvriere, J. and Dubelaar, C. (1993), The equalization price: a measure of consumer-perceived brand equity, *International Journal of Research in Marketing*, vol. 10, March 10, pp. 23–45.

The Business Standard, The Strategist (2000), Double Bubble (**http://www.bsstrategist.com/ 00apr18/1story.htm**), April 18.

The Economist (1995), Retailer's own labels – a threat for manufacturers, *The Economist*, March 4, p.10.

Töpfer, A. (1995), New products – cutting time to market, *Long Range Planning*, vol. 28, no. 2, pp. 61–78.

Wilson, T. L. (1999), International after-sales services, *Journal of Global Marketing*, vol. 13, no. 1, pp. 5–27.

Chapter 12

Pricing decisions

LEARNING OBJECTIVES

After studying this chapter you should be able to:

- understand why an appropriate customer value proposition is a useful guide to pricing strategy.
- explain how cost-based pricing methods work and what their primary drawbacks are.
- formulate pricing decisions for services.
- explain how internal and external variables influence pricing decisions.
- explain why and how prices escalate in different distribution channels.
- discuss the strategic options in determining the price level for a new product.
- undertake a break-even analysis.
- explain what is meant by experience curve pricing.
- evaluate reasons why base prices change over time in both business and consumer markets.
- understand the implications of the Internet for pricing behaviour in the market, particularly price 'customization'.

Case study 12.1 Electrolux

An alliance with Toshiba to break into the Japanese market for household appliances

Toshiba is a global leader in information and communication systems, electronic components and energy systems, as well as in consumer products such as PCs, TVs, videos, room air-conditioners, vacuum cleaners and white goods. Toshiba is one of the leading white goods companies in Japan. For the fiscal year ending March 1999, the company reported sales of ¥5300 billion (approximately £28 billion).

Electrolux and Toshiba of Japan signed an agreement to cooperate in household appliances which will cover transfer of technology and products, as well as components, environmental issues and purchasing, in addition to distribution, service and logistics in the Japanese market.

The global market for household appliances

Worldwide, production of major household appliances was expected to increase 2.9 per cent to 253 million units in 2001, well ahead of the increase in the number of households. The best product opportunities are in the market for automatic washing machines, which was expected to expand by almost 5 per cent to 55.6 million units in 2001. Much of the growth will take place in Asia, which will account for 70 per cent of the growth in worldwide demand.

This, according to the World Major Household Appliances report by Freedonia Group (2000), which projected that the Asia/Pacific market in

Case study 12.1 continued

2001 would be 80.8 million units, up more than 20 million from 1996 figures, showing a five-year annual growth rate of about 6 per cent. Excluding Japan, where the economy is still reeling, the five-year annual growth rate for Asia/Pacific would be nearly 9 per cent, led by China. By 2006, the Asia/Pasific market is expected to have climbed another 20 million units, the result of a five-year, 5 per cent annual growth rate.

Electrolux in the world market

Electrolux is the world's largest producer of power appliances for kitchen, cleaning and outdoor use, such as refrigerators, washing machines, cookers, vacuum cleaners, chain saws, lawn mowers, and garden tractors. In 2000, group sales were SEK 124.5 billion (£8.5 billion) and the group had 86,000 employees. Every year, customers in more than 150 countries buy more than 55 million Electrolux products for both consumer and professional use. The Electrolux includes famous appliance brands such as AEG, Electrolux, Zanussi, Frigidaire, Flymo, McCulloch, and Husqvarna.

Electrolux has the following market positions in the household appliances segment:

- white goods: market leader in Europe, third largest in the USA
- floor-care products: world leader, global market share approximately 20 per cent
- garden equipment: world's largest producer of such items as lawn mowers, garden tractors and lawn trimmers.

In 1999, white goods (i.e. refrigerators, freezers, cookers, washing machines, dishwashers and room air-conditioners) accounted for more than half of total Electrolux sales.

Electrolux and Toshiba announced on May 10, 2001 that they would launch a new series of home appliances that would bring European design values to the Japanese market under the brand name 'Electrolux by Toshiba'. The series was launched throughout Japan in June 2001, starting a phased introduction that will eventually cover ten categories of appliances. All Electrolux by Toshiba products express a modern design concept and bring the latest in European design into the Japanese home. Products in the series would be selected by Toshiba from the Electrolux catalogue or expressly designed by Electrolux and manufactured by Toshiba. Toshiba would support them with its present sales and services channels. Toshiba forecast that the series would achieve sales of ¥15 billion (€130 million) in 2003.

General barriers to the Japanese market

For many years foreign business executives have complained that Japan's distribution system is essentially closed and not easily accessible. In recent years, globalization has broken up the complex traditional Japanese distribution system. Japan's economic crisis and the subsequent Asian crisis have brought major changes to the business environment. Major problems in the financial sector have brought fear and uncertainty to domestic Japanese markets and curbed consumers' willingness to spend. Japan's unemployment is at its highest level since 1945 (4.4 per cent), and there is concern about the increasing 'Americanization' of Japanese corporations, which often includes major downsizing plans.

Czinkota and Kotabe (1999) identified the main barriers to entering the Japanese market. Their analysis showed that there are four main barriers. In order of importance, they are as follows.

Unique Japanese business practices

Keiretsu are considered the most important market impediment to foreign firms. Americans and Europeans have been suspicious of the keiretsu groups simply because they are linked together by means that are illegal in the USA, e.g. a combination of bank holdings, intercorporate shareholdings, and interlocking directorates. Also, the keiretsu are often accused of dealing predominantly with group members, thereby denying market access to foreigners.

Rigid quality and national standards

Japanese consumers' high quality and standards expectations and the government's bureaucratic practices are considered to be important.

Case study 12.1 continued

Consumers' expectations stem from the Japanese government's high quality standards that are stipulated in Japan Industrial Standards (JIS).

High price level and high operational cost
The high cost of doing business in Japan, and consequently higher prices, is still considered important. However expert observers believe that the situation will improve in the next five years, primarily as a result of the continued weakness of the Japanese economy.

Preference for products made in Japan
Foreign companies complain that due to the keiretsu or other business and government relationships, a strong 'buy Japanese' bias keeps out foreign products even when the quality and price are competitive or superior. However, the research results indicate that this factor is not so strong anymore.

Questions

1. Do you agree that the Electrolux management should focus on the Japanese market?

2. What have been the traditional reasons for relatively high prices in Japan?

3. Which of the major barriers to the Japanese market (identified by Czinkota and Kotabe, 1999) would be lower as a consequence of the relationship with Toshiba?

Source: adapted from www.electrolux.com.

12.1 Introduction

Pricing is the only element of the marketing mix to generate revenue. However, price affects not only the profit through its impact on revenue, it also affects the quantity sold through its influence on demand. Price has an interactive effect on the other elements of the marketing mix, so pricing decisions must be integrated with the other three Ps of the marketing mix. Price is the only area of the global marketing mix where policy can be changed rapidly without large direct cost implications. In addition, overseas consumers are often sensitive to price changes made in other areas of the firm's marketing programme. It is thus important that management realizes that constant fine tuning of prices in overseas markets should be avoided and that many problems are not best addressed by changing prices.

Generally, pricing policy is one of the most important yet often least recognized of all the elements in the marketing mix. The other elements in the marketing mix all lead to costs. The only source of profit to the firm comes from revenue, which in turn is dictated by pricing policy. In this chapter, we focus on a number of pricing issues of special interest to international marketers.

The objective of marketing is not simply to sell a product but to create value for the customer and the seller. Consequently, marketers should price products fairly, to reflect the value produced as well as received. Innovative marketers create value by offering, for example, a better product, faster delivery, better service, easier ordering, and more convenient locations. The greater the value perceived by customers, the more often they demand a company's products, and the higher the price they are willing to pay.

12.2 Pricing from an economist's perspective

Market demand and market growth are often dependent on price level. Wih high prices, at the beginning of the product life cycle, consumers simply cannot enter the market. As the price of mobile phones, CD players, and computers decreased more consumers entered these markets.

Ideally, the price maker would like information about the following two interrelated questions:

- what will be the quantity demanded at any given price?
- what will the effect of changes in price be on sales volume?

Figure 12.1 illustrates the principal issues with the help of a simple demand curve. It shows how market demand for a product varies as a function of price change. We normally refer to this as *price elasticity* of demand. It is important to distinguish between the demand curve for the industry as a whole and that faced by the individual company. In this chapter, the individual firm is analysed. Formally, price elasticity of demand can be calculated as follows:

$$\text{price elasticity of demand; } e = \frac{\text{percentage change in quantity demand}}{\text{percentage change in price}}$$

$$= \frac{\Delta Q / Q}{\Delta P / P}$$

Figure 12.1 shows that at each price along the diagonal demand curve, there is a different level of price elasticity.

Figure 12.1 Price elasticity on the demand curve

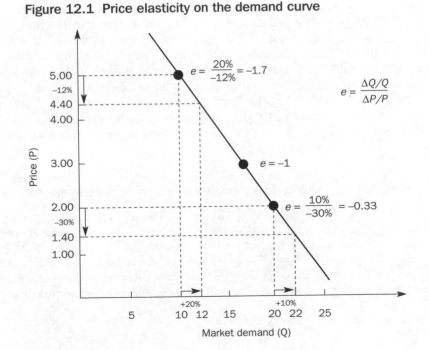

Measures of price elasticity commonly range through:

$e < 1$ Relatively price-inelastic – quantity demanded rises (falls) by a smaller percentage than price falls (rises).

$e = 1$ Neutral price elasticity – quantity demanded rises (falls) by the same percentage that price falls (rises).

$e > 1$ Relatively price-elastic – quantity demanded rises (falls) at a greater rate than price falls (rises).

While, by definition, the ratio usually has a negative sign (this is because as prices rise, demand usually falls), it is customary, in illustrating elasticities, to drop the sign (only mentioning the numerical value).

A business might continue to lower prices to grow demand, but when the price elasticity reaches –1.0, the sales revenue will have reached its maximum. At this point, raising or lowering prices will result in lower overall sales revenue. This is the price point at which a not-for-profit organization doing fund-raising events would be able to maximize the revenues received, if that is their objective. However, a business wanting to maximize profits may price above or below this price point, as we shall see in Section 12.2. Here, the optimum price change is dependent on the contribution margin.

The relationship between the price of one product and the quantity demanded of another is an important measure. It is known as the cross-price elasticity of demand (CPE). In this case:

● products are substitutes for one another if CPE > 0
● products are compliments to one another if CPE < 0.

Competitor price response

Many managers might ask, 'What will my competitors do in response to my price change?' If a business lowers prices to gain market share, and competitors follow, there is likely to be very little real gain. And at reduced margins, with a limited increase in volume, total contribution is likely to go down. On the other hand, if a business raises prices to improve margins and competitors do not follow, the business could lose market share and total contribution would be lower, even though margins are higher.

In any given market, competitor response to price change is going to depend on a variety of supply and demand forces, as outlined in Figure 12.2. As the forces shift from the left to the right, they will contribute to the likelihood of a full and fast competitor response to a price cut. Overall, there is generally a high degree of price

---

Exhibit 12.1

Johnny Walker whisky faced positive price elasticity in Japan

In Japanese markets, perceived value is a principal influence on product success. The images of quality significantly outweigh the actual value of the product, as quality is predominantly associated with high prices. This is demonstrated by the domination of Mercedes and BMW in the foreign import market. Johnny Walker whisky also represented images of high status. In an attempt to gain market share from its main rival Chivas, it reduced its price. Japanese consumers perceived the reduction in price to be a reduction in quality and status, resulting in a drastic decline in sales.

Source: adapted from Marsh (2000), p. 200.

Figure 12.2 Forces favouring competitive price response

	Probability of full and fast competitive response to price cut	
Competitor characteristics/internal forces:	Low	High
Variable cost structure	High ⟷	Low
Capacity utilization	Full ⟷	Low
Product perishability	None ⟷	High
Product differentiation	High ⟷	None
Competitor financial position	Poor ⟷	Strong
Strategic importance	Low ⟷	High
Demand forces:		
Price elasticity	Inelastic ⟷	Elastic
Efficiency in price shopping	Low ⟷	High
Customer loyalty	High ⟷	Low
Market growth rate	High ⟷	Low
Complementary products	None ⟷	Important
Substitute products	None ⟷	Many

Source: adapted from Best (2000), p. 186.

interdependence among competing firms. Lambin (1976) showed that the average competitor price response elasticity was 0.71. This means that if a business lowered its prices by 10 per cent, it could expect competitors to lower prices by 7.1 per cent.

12.3 Pricing from an accountant's perspective

In contrast to the economist's focus on demand, the accountant's approach to pricing is often based essentially on costs. **Break-even analysis** and **break-even pricing** are generally viewed as accounting concepts, but are extremely useful in evaluating the profit potential and risk associated with a pricing strategy, or any marketing strategy. The purpose of this section is to examine, from a marketing viewpoint, the usefulness of break-even volume.

For a given price strategy and marketing effort, it is useful to determine the number of units that need to be sold in order to break even, i.e. produce a net profit equal to zero. The break-even point is normally represented as that level of output where the total revenue from sales of a product or service matches exactly the total costs of its production and marketing (break-even quantity). Such an analysis of cost-revenue relationships can be very useful to the pricing decision maker.

One use of break-even analysis is to compare the break-even volumes associated with different prices for a product. A simplified example of this is shown in Figure 12.3.

The effect of charging a higher price is to steepen the total revenue curve and as a consequence lower the break-even volume. The pricing decision maker can then assess the effect of charging different prices in terms of what these different prices and break-even volumes mean to the company. Specifically, the information given by a break-even chart is:

● profit or losses at varying levels of output
● break-even points at varying levels of price
● effect on break-even point and profits or losses if costs change.

Figure 12.3 Break-even analysis for different prices

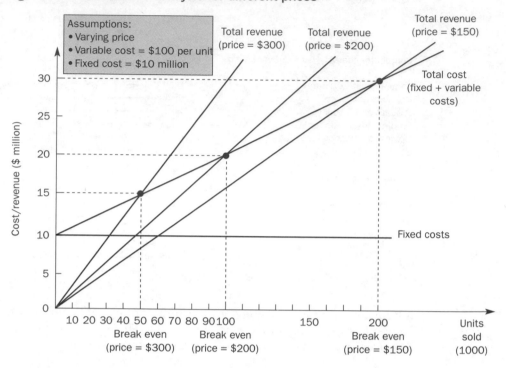

The break-even volume is the volume needed to cover the fixed costs on the basis of a particular contribution per unit. Although break-even volume can be estimated graphically, as illustrated in Figure 12.3, it can be computed more directly as follows:

$$\text{selling price} - \text{variable cost per unit} = \text{contribution per unit}$$

$$\text{break-even volume} = \frac{\text{fixed costs}}{\text{contribution per unit}}$$

The notion of contribution per unit is also a valuable addition to the price maker's armoury. It illustrates that, in the short term at least, it may pay a company to sell a product at a price that is less than the full cost of producing it. Remember that fixed costs are those that do not vary with the level of output. If a company produces and sells nothing, it will still incur these costs. At any price above the variable cost of producing each product, the company is receiving a contribution towards those fixed costs. In the long run, of course, a company must cover all its costs through the prices it sets on its products.

Break-even market share

Because break-even volume is an unconstrained number, the reasonableness of the break-even volume should be considered further. Because market share is constrained between 0 and 100 per cent, break-even market share provides a better framework from which to judge profit potential and risk. To compute break-even market share requires only that we divide the break-even volume by the size of the total market:

$$\text{break-even market share} = \frac{\text{break-even volume}}{\text{total market}} \times 100$$

If the total market for a product were 1 million units per year, then the break-even market share would be as follows using the three prices from Figure 12.3:

$$\text{Break-even market share (price} = \$300) = \frac{50,000}{1,000,000} \times 100 = 5\%$$

$$\text{Break-even market share (price} = \$200) = \frac{100,00}{1,000,000} \times 100 = 10\%$$

$$\text{Break-even market share (price} = \$150) = \frac{200,000}{1,000,000} \times 100 = 20\%$$

Of course management would feel much better if the break-even share was only 5 per cent instead of 20 per cent. In this example reducing the price by 50 per cent (from $300 to $150) would mean that the market share should be increased by 400 per cent.

It is clear that neither the economist's model of price setting (with help from the demand curve and price elasticity) nor the accountant's contribution of break-even analysis is in itself a sufficient basis on which to determine prices. Nevertheless, taken together, they do point to a clear-cut and universal assumption for delineating pricing decisions which can be incorporated into a more realistic and marketing-oriented approach to pricing. This more market-oriented approach to pricing will be discussed in the following sections.

12.4 A pricing framework

An SME which markets its products for the first time, with little knowledge of the market that it is entering, is likely to set a price that will ensure that the sales revenue generated at least covers the cost incurred. It is important that firms recognize that the cost structures of a product are very significant, but they should not be regarded as the sole determinants when setting prices.

Pricing policy is an important strategic and tactical competitive weapon that, in contrast to the other elements of the global marketing mix, is highly controllable and inexpensive to change and implement. Therefore, pricing strategies and actions should be integrated with the other elements of the global marketing mix.

Figure 12.4 presents a general framework for international pricing decisions. According to this model, factors affecting international pricing can be broken down into two main groups (internal and external factors) and four sub-groups, which we will now consider in more detail.

Firm-level factors

International pricing is influenced by past and current corporate philosophy, organization and managerial policies. The short-term tactical use of pricing in the form of discounts, product offers and reductions is often emphasized by managers at the expense of its strategic role. Yet pricing has played a very significant part in the restructuring of many industries, resulting in the growth of some businesses and the decline of others. In particular, Japanese firms have approached new markets with the intention of building market share over a period of years by reducing price levels,

Figure 12.4 Pricing framework

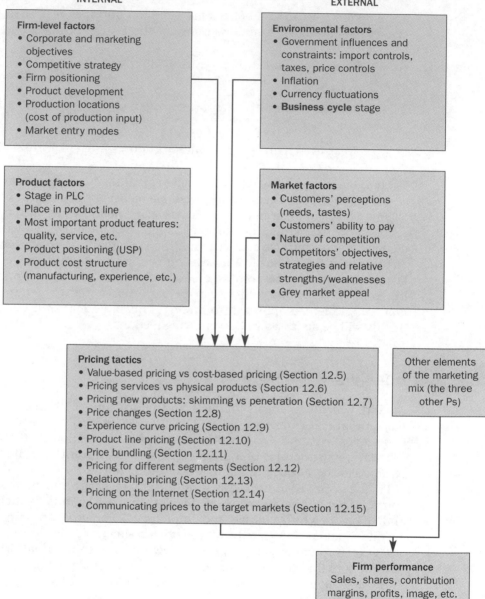

INTERNAL

Firm-level factors
- Corporate and marketing objectives
- Competitive strategy
- Firm positioning
- Product development
- Production locations (cost of production input)
- Market entry modes

Product factors
- Stage in PLC
- Place in product line
- Most important product features: quality, service, etc.
- Product positioning (USP)
- Product cost structure (manufacturing, experience, etc.)

EXTERNAL

Environmental factors
- Government influences and constraints: import controls, taxes, price controls
- Inflation
- Currency fluctuations
- **Business cycle** stage

Market factors
- Customers' perceptions (needs, tastes)
- Customers' ability to pay
- Nature of competition
- Competitors' objectives, strategies and relative strengths/weaknesses
- Grey market appeal

Pricing tactics
- Value-based pricing vs cost-based pricing (Section 12.5)
- Pricing services vs physical products (Section 12.6)
- Pricing new products: skimming vs penetration (Section 12.7)
- Price changes (Section 12.8)
- Experience curve pricing (Section 12.9)
- Product line pricing (Section 12.10)
- Price bundling (Section 12.11)
- Pricing for different segments (Section 12.12)
- Relationship pricing (Section 12.13)
- Pricing on the Internet (Section 12.14)
- Communicating prices to the target markets (Section 12.15)

Other elements of the marketing mix (the three other Ps)

Firm performance
Sales, shares, contribution margins, profits, image, etc.

establishing the brand name, and setting up effective distribution and servicing networks. The market share objective of the Japanese firms has usually been accomplished at the expense of short-term profits, as international Japanese firms have consistently taken a long-term perspective on profit. They are usually prepared to wait much longer for returns on investment than some of their western counterparts.

The choice of foreign market entry mode also affects the pricing policy. A manufacturer with a subsidiary in a foreign country has a high level of control over the pricing policy in that country.

Product factors

Key product factors include the unique and innovative features of the product and the availability of substitutes. These factors will have a major impact on the stage of the product life cycle, which will also depend on the market environment in target markets. Whether the product is a service, a manufactured product or a commodity sold into consumer or industrial markets is also significant.

The extent to which the organization has had to adapt or modify the product or service, and the level to which the market requires service around the core product, will also affect cost and thereby have some influence on pricing.

Costs are also helpful in estimating how rivals will react to the setting of a specific price, assuming that knowledge of one's own costs helps in the assessment of competitors' reactions. Added to the above is the intermediary cost, which depends on channel length, intermediary factors and logistical costs. All these factors add up and lead to price escalation through the distribution channel.

The example in Figure 12.5 shows that, due to additional shipping, insurance and distribution charges, the exported product costs 21 per cent more in the export market than at home. If there is an additional distribution link (an importer), the product will cost 39 per cent more abroad than at home.

Figure 12.5 Example of price escalation

	Domestic channel (a)	Foreign marketing channel (b)	Foreign marketing channel (c)
	£	£	£
Firm's net price	100	100	100
Insurance and shipping costs	—	10	10
Landed cost	—	110	110
Tariff (10% of landed cost)	—	11	11
Importer pays (cost)	—	—	121
Importer's margin/mark-up (15% of cost)	—	—	18
Wholesaler pays (cost)	100	121	139
Wholesaler's mark-up (20% of cost)	20	24	28
Retailer pays (cost)	120	145	167
Retail margin/mark-up (40% of cost)	48	58	67
Consumer pays (price) (exclusive VAT)	168	203	234
% price escalation over domestic channel	—	21	39

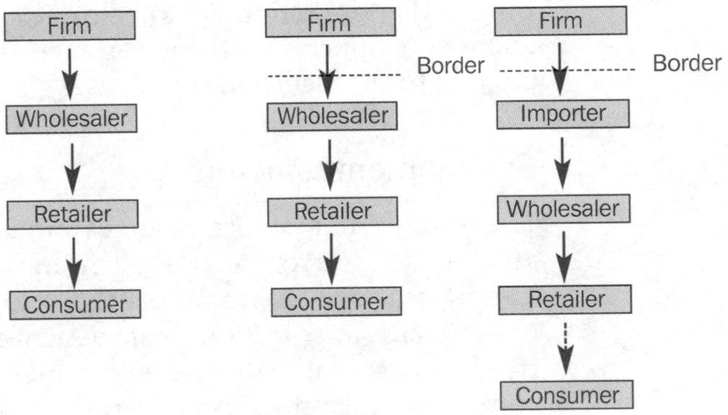

Source: Hollensen (2001), p. 450.

Many marketers are not aware of rapid price escalation; they are preoccupied with the price they charge to the importer. However, the final consumer price should be of vital concern because it is on this level that the consumer can compare prices of different competitive products and it is this price that plays a major role in determining the foreign demand.

Price escalation is not the only problem for marketers. It affects all firms involved in cross-border transactions. Companies that ship substantial amounts of goods and materials to subsidiaries in other countries are exposed to many of the additional charges that cause price escalation.

The following management options are available to counter price escalation:

- rationalizing the distribution process: one option is to reduce the number of links in the distribution process, either by doing more in-house or by circumventing some channel members.

- lowering the export price from the factory (firm's net price), thus reducing the multiplier effect of all the **mark-ups**.

- establishing local production of the product within the export market to eliminate some of the cost.

- pressuring channel members to accept lower profit margins. This may be appropriate if these intermediaries are dependent on the manufacturer for much of their turnover.

It may be dangerous to overlook traditional channel members. In Japan, for example, the complex nature of the distribution system, which often involves many different channel members, makes it tempting to consider radical change. However, existing intermediaries do not like to be overlooked, and their possible network with other channel members and the government may make it dangerous for a foreign firm to attempt to cut them out.

Environmental factors

The environmental factors are external to the firm and thus uncontrollable variables in the foreign market. The national government control of exports and imports is usually based on political and strategic considerations.

Generally, import controls are designed to limit imports in order to protect domestic producers or reduce the outflow of foreign exchange. Direct restrictions commonly take the form of tariffs, quotas and various **non-tariff trade barriers**. Tariffs directly increase the price of imports unless the exporter or importer is willing to absorb the tax and accept lower profit margins. Quotas have an indirect impact on prices. They restrict supply, thus causing the price of the import to increase.

Since tariff levels vary from country to country, there is an incentive for exporters to vary the price somewhat from country to country. In some countries with high customs duties and high price elasticity, the base price may have to be lower than in other countries if the product is to achieve a satisfactory volume in these markets. If demand is quite inelastic, the price may be set at a high level, with little loss of volume, unless competitors are selling at lower prices.

Government regulations on pricing can also affect the firm's pricing strategy. Many governments tend to have price controls on specific products related to health, education, food and other essential items. Another major environmental factor is fluctuations in the exchange rate. An increase (revaluation) or decrease

| Exhibit 12.2 | The use of prices to boost sales of bottled water in Italy |

In Italy this market has consistently increased in comparison to other soft drinks markets, over the last decade. Italian consumption of bottled water now ranks among the highest in Europe with average prices in Italy around 25 per cent lower than in neighbouring countries.

The demand decreased over the last two years for two reasons – first, the cool summer weather, and second, the industry has tended to use price to stimulate demand instead of other marketing techniques. It is now thought that as the market is reaching maturity and as prices are extremely low, demand cannot be further stimulated by lower prices with a high level of market concentration supporting this.

Source: adapted from Marsh (2000), p. 202.

(devaluation) in the relative value of a currency can affect the firm's pricing structure and profitability.

Market factors

One of the critical factors in the market is the purchasing power of the customers (the customer's ability to pay). The pressure of competitors may also affect international pricing. The firm has to offer a more competitive price if there are other sellers in the market. Thus, the nature of competition (e.g. **oligopoly** or monopoly) can influence the firm's pricing strategy.

Under conditions approximating pure competition, the price is set in the marketplace and tends to be just enough above costs to keep marginal producers in business. Thus, from the point of view of the price setter, the most important factor is costs. The more easily a product can be substituted, the closer prices must be, and the greater the influence of costs in determining prices (assuming that there is a large enough number of buyers and sellers).

Under a monopoly or imperfect competition, the seller has some discretion to vary the product quality, promotional efforts and channel politics in order to adapt the price of the total product to serve preselected market segments. Nevertheless, the freedom to set prices is still limited by what competitors charge, and any price differentials from competitors must be justified in the minds of customers on the basis of differential utility: that is, perceived value.

When considering how customers will respond to a given price strategy, Nagle (1987) has suggested nine factors which influence the sensitivity of customers to prices. Price sensitivity is reduced when:

- the product is more distinctive
- there is greater perceived quality of products
- consumers are less aware of substitutes in the market
- there is difficulty in making comparisons (e.g. in the quality of services such as consultancy or accountancy)
- the price of a product represents a small proportion of total expenditure of the customer
- the perceived benefit for the customer increases
- the product is used in association with a product bought previously, so that, for example, components and replacements are usually extremely highly priced

- costs are shared with other parties
- the product or service cannot be stored.

In the following sections we discuss the different pricing strategies that are available.

12.5 Market value-based pricing versus cost-based pricing

To arrive at the proper balance between the needs of the market and the needs of the firm, it is important to understand value-based pricing. Value-based pricing recognizes that price reflects value, not simply costs. Traditionally, firms assessed the costs of doing business, added a profit, and arrived at the price. Once it was set, the marketer's job was to convince customers that the product was worth it. If the marketer was not successful, then the price was lowered. If demand turned out to be higher than anticipated, then the price was raised. An important point is that the customer was the last person to be considered in this chain of events.

Value-based pricing begins by understanding customers and the competitive marketplace. The first step is to look at the value customers perceive in owning the product and to examine their options for acquiring similar products and brands.

Although cost-based pricing is easier, it ignores the customer and the competition. Marketers know that it is impossible to predict demand or competitors' actions simply by looking at their own costs. Consequently, cost-based pricing is becoming less popular.

Because prices send powerful messages, it is extremely important that they reflect the customer value the company delivers. Customer value is derived from the product itself, the services surrounding it, the company-customer interaction, and the image the customer associates with the product. Volvo, for example, has captured buyers at relatively high prices for years because of a reputation for durability and safety.

The firm is likely to incur higher costs when producing increased value. For example, it often costs more to make better products, create better distribution systems, or develop service facilities. The trick is to find a balance between what customers are willing to pay and the costs associated with the strategy.

It is not easy to establish precisely what price both buyers and seller agree is fair. We need to look at how customer value is derived, recognizing that people place different values on the products they buy as well as the relationship they have with companies. Several pricing strategies may work. It all depends on how price is perceived, how competitors act, and how a strategy is designed and implemented.

12.6 Pricing services versus physical product

The intangibility of service performance and the invisibility of the necessary facilities and labour makes it harder for customers to see what they are getting for their money than when they purchase a physical product.

Intangibles like services are inherently more difficult to price than goods, because it is harder to calculate the financial costs involved in serving a customer than it is to identify the labour, materials, machine time, storage and shipping costs associated with producing a physical product. The **variability** of both inputs and outputs means that units of service may not cost the same to produce, nor may they be of equal value to customers – especially if the variability extends to greater or lesser quality. Making matters even more complicated, it is not always easy to define a unit of service, raising questions as to what should be the basis of service pricing.

A very important distinction between goods and services is that many services have a much higher ratio of fixed costs to variable costs than is found in manufacturing firms. Service businesses with high fixed costs include those with an expensive physical facility (such as a hotel, a hospital, a college, or a theatre), or a network (such as a telecommunications company, an Internet provider, a railway). On the other hand, the variable costs of serving one extra customer may be minimal. Under these conditions, managers may feel that they have tremendous pricing flexibility and it is tempting to price very low in order to make an extra sale. However, there can be no profit at the end of the year unless all fixed costs have been recovered.

Another factor that influences service pricing concerns the importance of the time factor, since it may affect customer perceptions of value. In many instances, customers may be willing to pay more for a service delivered quickly than for one delivered more slowly. Sometimes greater speed increases operating costs, too – reflecting the need to pay overtime or use more expensive equipment.

Exhibit 12.3	Pricing in the airline business

As the marginal cost of carrying a passenger, rather than having the seat unfilled, is very low – meals, some extra fuel, and airport and over-flying charges – the price can be brought down to a sufficiently low level to sell those remaining seats as departure time approaches. However, experience also shows that associated with ticket flexibility there will be some passengers who do not turn up. The precise number is uncertain, but airlines typically overbook to allow for the passengers who do not turn up, though they run a risk of bumping passengers on to other flights at often relatively high prices if there are more passengers than available seats.

The pricing of scheduled airline tickets is complex, with features that are little appreciated by the traveller. For instance, irrespective of the product factors or service provision the price typically charged per kilometre is uniform neither for different passengers on a single flight nor in comparison with distance flown on other routes. The reason for this is that there are many categories of fare, which enables airlines to practise differential pricing by having special requirements or conditions. The principal methods are the amount of flexibility associated with the ticket, the period prior to flight when it was purchased and certain characteristics of the passenger, perhaps age or occupation.

Ticket flexibility on a scheduled flight enables the passenger to substitute another flight without notice or penalty and to book a flight virtually on demand. The desirability of doing this depends on the urgency of changing plans and the availability of alternative flights and it is possible to have reservations on many flights, where only one will be used. Arising from the airlines' responsibility to provide such flexibility enough capacity must be provided, thereby increasing costs. Typically this degree of flexibility is intended for the business traveller whose fare is paid by an employer.

Source: adapted from Driver (2001).

12.7   Pricing new products

Skimming vs penetration pricing

The strategic decision of pricing new products can be best understood by examining the policies at the boundaries of the continuum – from *skimming* (high initial price) to *penetration* (low initial price).

Skimming

A **skimming** approach, which is appropriate for a distinctly new product, provides the firm with an opportunity to profitably reach market segments that are not sensitive to the high initial price. As a product ages, as competitors enter the market, and as organizational buyers become accustomed to evaluating and purchasing the product, demand becomes more price elastic. The policy of using skimming at the outset, followed by penetration pricing as the product matures, is termed *time segmentation*. A skimming policy enables the marketer to capture early profits, then reduce the price to reach segments that are more price sensitive. It also enables the innovator to recover high developmental costs more quickly.

Problems with skimming are as follows:

- having a small market share makes the firm vulnerable to aggressive local competition.

- maintenance of a high-quality product requires a lot of resource (promotion, after-sales service) and a visible local presence, which may be difficult in distant markets.

- if the product is sold more cheaply at home or in another country, a **grey market** (**parallel import**) is likely.

Penetration

A **penetration** policy is appropriate when there is high price elasticity of demand, strong threat of imminent competition, and opportunity for a substantial reduction in production costs as volume expands. Drawing upon the experience effect, a firm that can quickly gain substantial market share and experience can gain a strategic advantage over competitors. The viability of this strategy increases with the potential size of the future market. By taking a large share of new sales, experience can be gained when there is a large market growth rate. Of course, the value of additional market share differs markedly between industries and often among products, markets, and competitors within a particular industry. Factors to be assessed in determining the value of additional market share include the investment requirements, potential benefits of experience, expected market trends, likely competitive reaction, and short- and long-term profit implications.

Penetration pricing can be effective for fixed periods of time and in the right competitive situation, but many firms overuse this approach and end up creating a market situation where everyone is forced to lower prices continually, driving some competitors from the market and guaranteeing that no one realizes a good return on investment. Managers can prevent the fruitless slide into kamikaze pricing by implementing a value-driven pricing strategy for the most profitable customers (Holden and Nayle, 1998).

Japanese companies have used penetration pricing intensively to gain market leadership in a number of markets, such as cars, home entertainment products and electronic components.

Figure 12.6 summarizes the main features of skimming and penetration pricing. Because neither is likely to achieve strong buyer loyalty in competitive markets, most companies use pricing approaches that fall somewhere between these extremes.

Market pricing

If similar products already exist in the target market, market pricing may be used. The final customer price is based on competitive prices. This approach requires the exporter to have a thorough knowledge of product costs, as well as confidence that the product life cycle is long enough to warrant entry into the market. It is a reactive approach and may lead to problems if sales volumes never rise to sufficient levels to produce a satisfactory return. Although firms typically use pricing as a differentiation tool, the global marketing manager may have no choice but to accept the prevailing world market price.

From the price that customers are willing to pay, it is possible to make a so-called retrograde calculation where the firm uses a 'reversed' price escalation to calculate backwards (from market price) to the necessary (ex-factory) net price. If this net price can create a satisfactory contribution margin, then the firm can go ahead.

12.8 Price changes

Price changes on existing products are called for when a new product has been launched or when changes occur in overall market conditions (such as fluctuating foreign exchange rates).

Table 12.1 shows the percentage sales volume increase or decrease required to maintain the level of profit. An example shows how the table functions. A firm has a product with a contribution margin of 20 per cent. The firm would like to know how much the sales volume should be increased as a consequence of a price reduction of 5 per cent, if it wishes to keep the same total profit contribution. The calculation is as follows:

Before price reduction

Per product	sales price	£100
	variable cost per unit	£80
	contribution margin	£20

Total contribution margin: 100 units @ £20 = £2000

After price reduction (5%)

Per product	sales price	£95
	variable cost per unit	£80
	contribution margin	£15

Total contribution margin: 133 units @ £15 = £2000

Figure 12.6 Two new product pricing strategies

	Skimming	Penetration pricing
Definition	Setting a relatively high price during the initial stage of a product's life. A strategy designed to obtain a relatively high price from relatively few consumers, who have the resources and desire to buy irrespective of price.	Setting a relatively low price during the initial stage of a product's life. A strategy that seeks the maximum number of buyers by charging low prices.
Objectives	To serve customers who are not price conscious while the market is at the upper end of the demand curve and competition has not yet entered the market. To recover a significant portion of promotional and research and development costs through a high margin.	To discourage competition from entering the market by quickly taking a large market share and by gaining a cost advantage through realizing economies of scale.
Requirements	Heavy promotional expenditure to introduce product, educate consumers, and induce early buying. Relatively inelastic demand at the upper end of the demand curve. Lack of direct competition and substitutes. If companies perceive they can obtain a monopoly position for a short time, then they may skim to generate profits that provide investment capital for further innovations. To sustain skimming, companies must offer unusual products of the highest quality or artistic value.	Product must appeal to a market large enough to support the cost advantage. Demand must be highly elastic in order for the firm to guard its cost advantage.
Expected results	Market segmented by price-conscious and not so price-conscious customers. High margin on sales that will cover promotion and research and development costs. During the first stages in the PLC, the firm is able to create a price umbrella because the competition cannot match the firm's relative advantage as shown here. As the demand for a high-priced segment is saturated, price can be lowered to systematically attract more customers until prices reach a level affordable to most potential customers.	High sales volume and large market share. Low margin on sales. Lower unit costs relative to competition due to economies of scale. A cost leadership position can enable a business to use penetration pricing to build market share and discourage competition from either entering the market or staying in the market. In this situation, the market leader is simply further down the cost curve and is able to price at a lower level and still maintain a satisfying contribution. If costs are sensitive to volume, then these will drop dramatically as share increases relative to competitors. This is a way to keep rivals from entering the market.
Illustrative examples/ problems	In the pharmaceutical industry many prescription drugs (like Pfizer's Viagra) are patented. Under this protection, the holder may create higher-than-normal prices. However, many times this strategy does not produce loyal customers, since subsequent entrants eventually offer better value at a lower price. In the past, IBM dominated personal computer sales, but as smaller companies entered the market it had to price more competitively.	Compaq Computer was an early entry in the personal computer market. Compaq priced aggresively to build market share in a market where all computer manufacturers could offer the same product. In these instances, product differentiation is minimal, customers are price-sensitive, there are many competitors or substitutes, and competitor entry is easy. The price leader can often both gain an early cost advantage with a large volume and charge lower prices, discouraging competitors from entering the market. The problem with penetration pricing is that losses are likely, especially in the short term. Because profit margins tend to be very small, demand must meet expectations in order to generate enough earnings. Furthermore, when customers buy only because of price, loyalty tends to be low. They are likely to switch to competition offering an even lower price or innovations of higher value at a higher price.

Table 12.1 Sales volume increase or decrease (%) required to maintain total profit contribution

Price reduction (%)	Profit contribution margin (price – variable cost per unit as % of the price)								
	5	10	15	20	25	30	35	40	50
	Sales volume increase (%) required to maintain total profit contribution								
2.0	67	25	15	11	9	7	7	5	4
3.0	150	43	25	18	14	11	9	8	6
4.0	400	67	36	25	19	15	13	11	9
5.0		100	50	33	25	20	17	14	11
7.5		300	100	60	43	33	27	23	18
10.0			200	100	67	50	40	33	25
15.0				300	150	100	75	60	43

Price increase (%)	Profit contribution margin (price – variable cost per unit as % of the price)								
	5	10	15	20	25	30	35	40	50
	Sales volume reduction (%) accepted to maintain total profit contribution								
2.0	29	17	12	9	7	6	5	5	4
3.0	27	23	17	13	11	9	8	7	6
4.0	44	29	21	17	14	12	10	9	7
5.0	50	33	25	20	17	14	12	11	9
7.5	60	43	33	27	23	20	18	16	13
10.0	67	50	40	33	29	25	22	20	17
15.0	75	60	50	43	37	33	30	27	23

Source: Hollensen (2001), p454.

As a consequence of a price reduction of 5 per cent, a 33 per cent increase in sales is required. If a decision is made to change prices, related changes must also be considered. For example, if an increase in price is required, it may be accompanied, at least initially, by increased promotional effort.

When changing prices, the degree of flexibility enjoyed by decision makers will tend to be less for existing products than for new products. This follows from the high probability that the existing product is now less unique, faces stronger competition and is aimed at a broader segment of the market. In this situation, the decision maker will be forced to pay more attention to competitive and cost factors in the pricing process.

The timing of price changes can be nearly as important as the changes themselves. For example, a simple tactic of announcing price increases after competitors can produce the perception among customers that you are the most customer-responsive supplier. The extent of the time lag can also be important.

In one company, an independent survey of customers (Garda, 1995) showed that the perception of being the most customer-responsive supplier was generated just as effectively by a six-week lag in following a competitor's price increase as by a six-month lag. A considerable amount of money would have been lost during the unnecessary four-and-a-half-month delay in announcing a price increase.

| Exhibit 12.4 | Heinz beats low-priced baked beans |

The following happened in the UK baked beans market in 1996.

End of 1995

As a consequence of increasing price competition in the UK, Heinz started manufacturing a low-priced brand for Sainsbury (Economy Baked Beans).

Beginning of 1996

Price situation

Brand	Cost per can (£)
Heinz	0.32
Sainsbury's own brand	0.26
Economy Baked Beans	0.10
Lowest priced brands	0.06

Source: adapted from BBC (1996).

April 1996

The market share of the Heinz brand decreased from 42% to 32%.

July 1996

The Heinz brand made a comeback with a price war and the result was a market share of 52%.

The chairman and CEO of Heinz, Tony O'Reilly, said: 'The housewives were increasingly suspicious of beans being given away for 6p when Heinz was charging 32p for them and had 52% of the market.'

This example shows that even large price premiums (compared to low price brands) can be justified, if the perceived brand quality is high.

Source: adapted from BBC (1996).

12.9   Experience curve pricing

Price changes usually follow changes in the product's stage in the life cycle. As the product matures, more pressure will be put on the price to keep the product competitive despite increased competition and less possibility of differentiation.

Let us also bring the cost aspect into the discussion. The experience curve has its roots in a commonly observed phenomenon called the learning curve, which states that as people repeat a task they learn to do it better and faster. The learning curve applies to the labour portion of manufacturing cost. The Boston Consulting Group extended the learning effect to cover all the value-added costs related to a product – manufacturing plus marketing, sales, administration etc.

The resulting experience curves, covering all value chain activities (see Figure 3.1 in Chapter 3), indicate that the total unit cost of a product in real terms can be reduced by a certain percentage with each doubling of cumulative production. The typical decline in cost is 30 per cent (termed a 70 per cent curve), although greater and lesser declines are observed.

If we combine the experience curve (average unit cost) with the typical market price development within an industry, we will have a relationship similar to that shown in Figure 12.7.

Figure 12.7 Product life cycle stages and the industry price experience curve

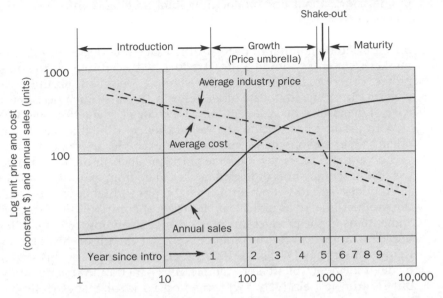

Source: Czepiel, 1992, p. 167.

Figure 12.7 shows that after the introduction stage (during part of which the price is below the total unit cost), profits begin to flow. Because supply is less than demand, prices do not fall as quickly as costs. Consequently, the gap between costs and prices widens, in effect creating a price umbrella, attracting new competitors. However, the competitive situation is not a stable one. At some point the umbrella will disappear as one or more competitors reduce prices in an attempt to gain market share. The result is that a shake-out phase will begin: inefficient producers will be shaken out by rapidly falling market prices, and only those with a competitive price/cost relationship will survive.

12.10 Product line pricing

As a business adds more product to its product line, it enhances sales growth but also increases the chances of cannibalization of existing product sales. It is necessary to know both a product's price elasticity and the degree to which there is a cross-elasticity with other products. Products that have a *positive* cross-elasticity are *substitutes*; lowering the price of one product will decrease the demand for the other product. Products that have a *negative* cross-elasticity are *complementary* products; lowering the price for one product will increase the demand for both products. Because the margins may be different for alternative products in a product line, one has to give careful consideration to any price change to ensure that the total profits are increased for the entire product line.

A firm may add to its product line – or even develop a new product line – to fit more precisely the needs of a particular market segment. If both the demand and the costs of individual product line items are interrelated, production and marketing decisions about one product line item inevitably influence both the revenues and costs of the others.

Are specific product line items substitutes or complements? Will a change in the price of one item enhance or retard the usage rate of this or other products in key market segments? Should a new product be priced high at the outset in order to protect other product line items (for example, potential substitutes) and in order to give the firm time to update other items in the line? Such decisions require knowledge of demand, costs, competition, and strategic marketing objective.

With product line pricing, the various items in the line may be differentiated by pricing them appropriately to indicate, for example, an economy version, a standard version and a superior version. One of the products in the line may be priced to protect against competitors or to gain market share from existing competitors.

Products with less competition may be priced higher to subsidize other parts of the product line, so as to make up for the lost contribution of such fighting brands. Some items in the product line may be priced very low to serve as **loss leaders** and induce customers to try the product. A special variant of this is the so-called buy in, follow on strategy (Weigand, 1991). A classic example of this strategy is the razor blade link where Gillette, for example, uses penetration pricing on its razor (buy in) but skimming (relatively high price) on its razor blades (follow on). Thus, the linked product or service – the follow on – is sold at a significant contribution margin. This inevitably attracts others who try to sell follow on products without incurring the cost of the buy in.

Other examples of the strategy are as follows:

● telephone companies sell mobile phones at a near giveaway price, hoping that the customer will be a heavy user of the profitable mobile telephone network.

● Nintendo often sells its game consoles at below cost but makes a handsome profit on the game software.

This kind of pricing is a particularly attractive strategy if it not only generates future sales but also creates an industry platform or standard to which all other rivals must use or conform (that is, a technological path dependency).

12.11 Price bundling

Products can be bundled or unbundled for pricing purposes. The bundled approach gives a single price for the entire offering. Bundling can be defined as the sale of two or more separate products in one package at a discount. For example, the direct online seller of PCs, Dell, markets to consumers who may want to buy a portable computer system consisting of a basic laptop, a modem, and a CD writer. It could sell these products as separate items, but they choose also to sell them as a price bundle by giving a discount to consumers if they buy all three products together (Stremersch and Tellis, 2002).

Many physical goods and services unite a core product with a variety of supplementary products at a set price. This has become a popular marketing strategy (Johnson *et al.*, 1999).

Manufacturers of industrial goods, such as machine tools, electronic components and chemical substances, frequently offer their products at a system price in conjunction with an assortment of services. In the service sector, travel companies bundle flights, rental cars, accommodation, and events into one package. Strategically this bundling activity is designed to benefit the consumer by reducing administration costs and consequently transaction costs.

Should such service packages be priced as a whole (referred to as the bundle), or should each element be priced separately? To the extent that people dislike having to make many small payments, bundled pricing may be preferable. But if customers do not like being charged for product elements they may not use, itemized pricing may be preferable.

Many firms offer an array of choices. Telephone subscribers, for instance, can select from several service options, ranging from paying a small monthly fee for basic service and then extra for each phone call made, or paying a higher flat rate and getting a certain number of local, regional or long-distance calls free. At the top of the scale is the option that provides business users with unlimited access to long-distance calls over a prescribed area – even internationally. Bundled prices offer a service firm a certain guaranteed revenue from each customer, while giving the latter a clear idea in advance of how much the bill will be. Unbundled pricing provides customers with flexibility in what they choose to acquire and pay for, but may also cause problems. For instance, customers may be put off by discovering that the ultimate price of what they want is substantially higher than the advertised base price that attracted them in the first place.

12.12 Pricing for different segments

Marketers very often have different marketing programmes for different consumer segments.

Geographic segments

It is possible that price sensitivity varies across geographic regions. For example, some grocery retailers have different price zones and prices are likely to vary across those zones. Competition and consumer profiles may differ between geographic segments. Products can be positioned with a high price in one country and a low price in another. This can be attributed to the pricing structure of international markets, viewed here as a major determinant of the product pricing policy. Consider the bottled water market in Italy (Exhibit 12.2).

Europe was a price differentiation paradise as long as markets were separated. But it is becoming increasingly difficult to retain the old price differentials. There are two developments which may force companies to standardize prices across European countries:

- international buying power of cross-European retail groups.
- parallel imports/grey markets. Because of differentiated prices across countries, buyers in one country are able to purchase at a lower price than in another country. As a result there will be an incentive for customers in lower-price markets to sell goods to higher-price markets in order to make a profit.

Simon and Kucher (1993) suggest a price 'corridor' (Figure 12.8). The prices in the individual countries may only vary within that range. Figure 12.8 is also interesting in the light of the euro, which was fully implemented in January 2002, when new euro notes and coins were circulated. But this does not mean that a uniform price across Europe is required. Price differences which can be justified by transport costs, short-term exchange rate fluctuations, etc. may still be maintained.

They recommend that business in smaller countries should be sacrificed, if necessary, in order to retain acceptable pricing levels in the big markets like France, Germany, the UK and Italy. For example, for a pharmaceutical manufacturer it is more profitable not to sell in the Portuguese pharmaceutical market than to accept a price reduction of 10 per cent in the German market due to parallel imports from Portugal.

Usage segments

It is common for marketers to recognize high volume users and reward them with different prices. For example, regular customers at a particular store who carry the stores' frequent shopper card will receive discounts at the checkout that other shoppers will not receive.

Time segments (off-peak pricing)

The most common form of usage segmentation pricing is based on the time of usage. Long-distance phone companies, electricity utilities, hotels, bars, restaurants, amusement parks, and cinemas all use off-peak demand pricing. For firms like these, demand for their products and services fluctuates over time, and they cannot store their production. Consequently, they have periods of under-utilization and often low incremental variable costs. At off-peak times, such companies welcome any additional revenue, as long as it makes some contribution toward their high fixed costs.

Figure 12.8 Development of prices in Europe

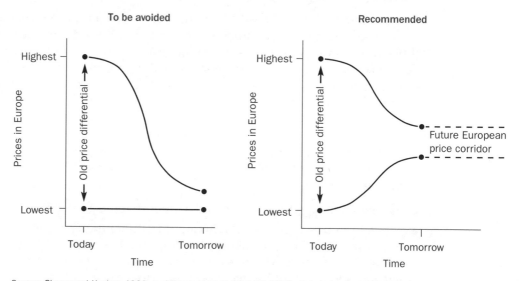

Source: Simon and Kucher, 1993, p. 26, copyright © ESOMAR 2001. Permission for using this material has been granted by ESOMAR®, Amsterdam, The Netherlands. For further information please refer to the ESOMAR® website: **www.esomar.nl**.

Off-peak pricing explains post-Christmas sales and end-of-season fashion sales. Unfortunately, some price sensitive shoppers learn when these sales occur and wait for them. This has the effect of reducing the overall average selling price and contribution margin.

Demographic segments

A concert hall might provide special prices for students or children to encourage attendance, or may give discounts to senior citizens. This is a common strategy used by museums, athletic events, and amusement parks.

Family recreational air travel is much more price sensitive than business travel. Because of this, airlines charge less for children and offer early booking discounts that effectively exclude businesspeople from purchasing such tickets. As with all forms of price discrimination, segment pricing works best when buyers in the high-priced target segment cannot buy the product or service directly or indirectly (through resale) at the lower price.

Exhibit 12.5 **The Body Shop concept is under pressure from the bottom end of the market**

Disruptive competition from the bottom end of the market may take several forms. The Body Shop achieved remarkable global expansion through the creation and production of innovative 'natural' cosmetics and personal care products, and its positioning as a uniquely ethical company. Nonetheless, the 1990s saw the collapse of the Body Shop's market position, in the face of lower cost competition – peppermint foot lotion can be produced more cheaply by competitors that are not carrying the overheads of the Body Shop's ethical and political programmes.

At the end of July 2001, it was announced that the Body Shop was planning to soften its campaigning image after admitting that its strategy of fighting for social and environmental causes has had mixed results.

Body Shop head of communications Steve McIvor said the mixture of politics and marketing 'has not always worked for us' and the brand will become 'less soap-boxy, patronizing and lecturing'.

Source: adapted from Curtis (2001).

12.13 Relationship pricing

When developing and maintaining long-term customer relationships, pricing strategy has an important role to play. Pricing low to win new business is not the best approach if a firm is seeking to attract customers who will remain loyal – those who are attracted by cut-price offers can easily be enticed away by another offer from a competitor. More creative pricing strategies focus on giving customers both price and non-price incentives to consolidate their business with a single supplier.

However, a strategy of discounting prices for large purchases can often be profitable for both parties, since the customer benefits from lower prices while the supplier may enjoy lower variable costs resulting from economies of scale. An alternative to volume discounting on a single service is for a firm to offer its customers discounts when two or more services are purchased together. The greater the number of different services a customer purchases from a single supplier, the closer the relationship is likely to be and the greater the exit barriers for the partners in the relationship. Both parties get to know each other better, and it is more inconvenient for the customer to shift its business.

Pricing is becoming more fluid. Even before the advent of the online medium, industrial markets and third-world bazaars have long followed a customized pricing mechanism based on bargaining and discount schedules. The online medium has made it feasible to apply flexible pricing more broadly. Online prices can be tailored to specific users and raised or lowered instantly for assessing price elasticity at different prices. The ability to create truly fluid pricing is only limited by customer acceptance. Technology is now available to vary pricing in ways that were not possible in the past. New in-store technology allows supermarkets to customize pricing based on specific times of the day through digital price labels or even to tailor discounts and coupons to individuals based on their past purchasing patterns.

Due to the influence of the online medium, we expect that all firms will be called upon to revamp their pricing strategies completely. The fixed one-price strategy of the past has been completely eroded over the past few years. In the years ahead, 'dynamic pricing' that takes advantage of instantaneous market conditions will become the norm. Interestingly, these developments do not necessarily mean that prices will decline. The convenience, time-saving aspects, and product matching features of online markets can increase the price a customer is willing to pay.

When customers become familiar and comfortable with a retail website it reduces their incentive to shift to other sites for lower prices. Further, if a company understands the customer (e.g. by tracking and understanding what customers do while visiting its website) and facilitates the creation of a co-production process to produce a product and service tailored to the customer's need, there is relatively little opportunity or incentive for customers to compare other shops based on price. Customization of the product or service adds so much value and strengthens the relationship that the price becomes a less important factor.

Establishing global pricing contracts (GPCs)

As globalization increases, the following is heard frequently among global suppliers and global customers: 'Give me a global pricing contract (GPC) and I'll consolidate my worldwide purchase with you.' Increasingly, global customers are demanding such contracts from suppliers. For example, in 1998, General Motor's Powertrain Group told suppliers of components used in GM's engines, transmissions and sub-assemblies to charge GM the same for parts from one region as they did for parts from another region.

Suppliers do not need to lose out when customers globalize. The most attractive global pricing opportunities are those that involve suppliers and customers working together to identify and eliminate inefficiencies that harm both. Sometimes suppliers do not have a choice. They do not want to shut themselves out of business with their largest and fastest-growing customers.

Suppliers and customers have different advantages and disadvantages with global pricing contracts. Table 12.2 illustrates some of them.

One chemicals manufacturer concentrated on relationships with a few select customers. It found out that its strength lay in value-added services but that potential

Table 12.2 Global pricing contracts (GPCs): advantages and disadvantages

Customers	Suppliers
Advantages	
● Lower prices worldwide coupled with higher levels of service.	● Easily gain access to new markets and grow the business.
● Standardization of products and services offered across markets.	● Consolidate operations and achieve economies of scale.
● Efficiencies in all processes, including new product development, manufacturing, inventory, logistics and customer service.	● Work with industry leaders and influence market development by using them as showcase accounts.
● Faster diffusion of innovations globally.	● Collaborate with customers and develop strong relationships that are difficult for potential competitors to break into.
	● Rectify price and service anomalies in a customer relationship across country markets.
Disadvantages	
● Customer might be less adaptable to local market variance and changes over time.	● Local managers sometimes resist change, and supplier may get caught in the crossfire between customer's HQ and country managers.
● Supplier might not have capabilities to provide consistent quality and performance across markets.	● Supplier might lose the ability to serve other attractive customers.
● Supplier might use customer's over-dependence to extract higher prices.	● Customer might not be able to deliver on promises.
● Local managers might resist global contracts and prefer dealing with local suppliers.	● Customer might take advantage of cost information shared in the relationship.
● Costs of monitoring global contracts might outstrip the benefits.	● Supplier might become over-dependent on one customer, even when there are other more attractive customers to serve.
	● Supplier might have a conflict with existing channels of distribution in the new markets.

Source: adapted from Narayandas *et al.* (2000), p. 63.

customers in emerging markets were more concerned with price. The select customers, however, were interested in money-saving supply and inventory management initiatives developed jointly with the supplier.

Global customers' demands for detailed cost information can also put suppliers at risk. Toyota, Honda, Xerox and others force suppliers to open their books for inspection. Their stated objectives are to help suppliers identify ways to improve processes and quality while reducing costs – and to build trust. But in an economic downturn, the global customer might also seek price reductions and supplementary services.

12.14 Pricing on the Internet

The virtual value chain offers different options on products and services to customers. The extra value obtained by the customer can be billed at a different price option also. In the simplest, mass produced products, a flat price may be appropriate. However, when customers can order from different sources to customize their choice, the Internet company, which is responsible for assembling this choice, may charge different prices. In the case of digital products, these options can also be extended with regard to time and place. For example, at peak times, when most of the customers are likely to log on to the site, the company may charge a premium price to minimize the Internet traffic. During off-peak hours the company may reduce the price of the products or services to keep the optimum level of Internet traffic on the site. Similarly, customers may have the option to obtain the product through the regular mail at a different price from when they directly download the product/service. Price variations can also be employed based on the need for the product or the service. For example, a customer who wants to search for and read a particular piece of information is likely to pay less than a person who will download and print the information. Similarly, a customer who wants to review only the summary of the information is likely to pay less than a person who needs the complete information. A customer who needs immediate access to new pieces of information is likely to be charged a higher price than a customer who can accept some delay in accessing the information.

A virtual value chain makes it easier for customers to compare the prices of similar offerings by different companies. Not only can customers obtain the price of the offerings, but they can also understand the prices charged for add-on features. With this information, customers can quickly customize their selections in products and services. Consequently, the Internet will lead to increased price competition and the standardization of prices across borders.

The ability to compare prices across all suppliers using the Internet and online shopping services will lead to increased price competition. Finally, the price of providing Internet-based services (especially information-based services) often contains little marginal costs. Thus, the ability of technology to offer services at a cheaper cost would make it difficult to determine the appropriate price for a consumer (Allen and Fjernestad, 2001).

Among the most popular applications of the Internet is the online auction in the consumer market. Online auctions attract thousands, sometimes millions, of bidders who compete with each other for items ranging from computer-related products to antiques. Companies such as eBay and Amazon.com have entered into the online auction business in a big way (Massad and Tucker, 2000).

In the B-t-B market many companies are likely to adopt online auctions as part of their ongoing purchasing process or perhaps even outsource the bulk of purchasing aided by new technology. It is an attractive technological solution for reducing costs, but it does not help uncover the root causes of poor cost management worked out by the buying firm (Emiliani, 2000).

12.15 Communicating prices to the target markets

Customers in the B-t-B market must be very price conscious. Each item they buy contributes to their costs and thus to their profits and competitiveness. Many of them keep extensive records using formalized purchasing systems designed to obtain the best value for the price. Consumers in the B-t-B market tend to be less aware of actual prices.

Consequently, the final task, once each of the other issues has been addressed, is to decide how the organization's pricing policies can best be communicated to the target market(s). People need to know the price for some product offerings well in advance of purchase; they may also need to know how, where and when that price is payable. This information must be presented in ways that are intelligible and unambiguous, so that customers will not be misled and question the ethical standards of the firm.

Managers must decide whether or not to include information on pricing in advertising for the service. It may be appropriate to relate the price to the costs of competing products or to show alternative ways of spending one's money. Certainly, salespeople and customer service representatives should be able to give prompt, accurate responses to show customer queries about pricing, payment and credit. Good signage at retail points of sale will save staff members from having to answer basic questions on prices.

12.16 Summary

In this chapter we have considered the role of pricing decisions in overall company and marketing strategies. Price setting is a complex decision which involves many factors. To establish a price, the manager must identify the firm's objectives and analyse the behaviour of demand, costs and competition.

A good deal of basic microeconomic theory is devoted to the relationship between price and demand. While many of the principles that have been developed have relevance to what happens in the real world, there are nevertheless many factors (other than demand and cost) that have to be taken into account.

Pricing strategies must balance the needs of both the customer and the firm. Value-based pricing, which includes the concepts of value in use and value in exchange, is increasingly popular. Since customers seeking differing types of value and competition have a broad range of choices in how to price, other strategies are viable as well. In devising a pricing strategy, it is important to identify a customer value proposition that matches the capabilities of the organization.

Pricing new products offers a different set of challenges. In general, two main opposing strategies are seen:

- *skimming*: high price, to skim off the short-term profit
- *penetration*: low price, to maximize long-term market share.

Practical pricing tactics may include experience curve pricing, product line pricing, price bundling, pricing on the Internet etc.

Case study 12.2 Harley-Davidson

Is the image justifying the price level?

Harley-Davidson's mission statement is 'We fulfil dreams through the experience of motorcycling'.

History

The Harley-Davidson Motorcycle Company was founded in 1903. Harley-Davidson soon became the world's leading manufacturer of motorcycles, based on a reputation of quality and reliability. After World War II, and the demise of the American Indian motorcycle, Harley-Davidson became the sole US manufacturer of motorcycles. In 1969, Harley-Davidson was sold to American Machine and Foundry (AMF).

AMF almost tripled production to 75,000 units annually over a four-year period to meet the increase in demand. Unfortunately, product quality deteriorated significantly as over half the motorcycles that came off the assembly line had parts missing and dealers had to repair in order to make sales. Little money was invested in improving design or engineering. The motorcycles leaked oil, vibrated, and could not match the excellent performance of the Japanese products.

During this time, Honda was beginning to penetrate the American motorcycle market and gain a significant market share. Honda manufacturing plants incorporated the principles of total quality management (TQM). Honda began producing motorcycles with constantly improving quality at a time when the quality of Harley-Davidson was drastically decreasing. By the early 1980s Honda almost totally dominated the world motorcycle market.

Japanese manufacturers also moved into the heavyweight motorcycle market and began selling Harley look-alike motorcycles. Yamaha was the first company to do so and was soon followed by the three other major Japanese manufacturers, Honda, Suzuki, and Kawasaki. Their products looked so similar to Harley-Davidson's that it was difficult to tell the difference without reading the name on the petrol tank. The Japanese companies also copied the style of the Harley-Davidson advertisements.

In order to stay in business while the necessary changes in design and production were being accomplished, the executives turned to William G. Davidson, Harley's styling vice president. Known as 'Willie G.' and a grandson of one of the company's founders, he designed a number of new models by combining components from existing models. These included the Super Glide, the Electra Glide, the Wide Glide, and the Low Rider. Each model was successful and other executives credit Davidson's skill with saving the company.

In 1982, Harley-Davidson faced new problems. Overall demand for motorcycles dropped dramatically and Harley-Davidson's share of this smaller market also continued to drop. The company had a large inventory of unsold products and could not continue in business with its level of production and expenses. Production was cut drastically, and more than 1800 of the 4000 employees were made redundant.

In 1983, President Reagan increased the tariffs on large Japanese motorcycles from 4.4 per cent to 49.4 per cent, but these would decline each year and be effective for only five years. While this did reduce the number of imports and gave Harley-Davidson some protection, Japanese manufacturers found ways to evade most of the tariffs, for example by assembling more of their heavyweight bikes in their US plants. In 1983, Harley-Davidson's share of the heavyweight motorcycle market slipped to 23 per cent, the lowest ever, although it did earn a slight profit.

Harley-Davidson today

The company now has a new direction. 'We are out of survival mode', said Jeff Bleustein, chairman and CEO of the Wisconsin-based Harley-Davidson Motor Co. 'We spent a lot of time putting together our business process, our values, issues, mission statement, all those things we believe in. We wanted to get everyone pointed in the same direction' (Milligan and Carbone, 2000).

Much of the value of a Harley resides in its tradition – the look, sound, and heritage that have made it an All-American symbol. The bikes 'represent something very basic – a desire for freedom, adventure, and individualism'.

Case study 12.2 continued

Harley-Davidson Inc. is the parent company for the following three companies.

Harley-Davidson Motor Company, the only major US-based motorcycle manufacturer, produces heavyweight motorcycles and offers a complete line of motorcycle parts, accessories, clothing, and general merchandise. Strategic licensing of the Harley-Davidson brand helps create future generations of Harley-Davidson enthusiasts. The US market launch of the Fisher-Price Power Wheels® Ride-On-Toy, a four-wheeled, battery-operated children's toy, became the most successful Power Wheels introduction in the last ten years.

Buell Motorcycle Company produces sport and sport-touring motorcycles.

Harley-Davidson Financial Services Inc. (HDFS) provides wholesale and retail financing, insurance and credit card programmes to Harley-Davidson dealers and customers. In 1999, there were over 200,000 Harley-Davidson Chrome Visa cardholders; nearly 55,000 riders funded their new and used vehicle purchase with the help of HDFS; over 110,000 enthusiasts were protected by an extended service plan; and 70,000 riders carried HDFS casualty insurance. The wholesale division of HDFS provides dealers with financing for motorcycles and related products, and store expansion or renovation.

Harley-Davidson faces the task of attracting younger customers, as its average customer's age increases and sales decrease. Part of reshaping their image includes releasing a new motorcycle, the Buell, designed for young professional men and women.

No one doubts that the women's market is real, although it accounts for only 8 per cent of the total motorcycling population, according to the Motorcycle Industry Council, an industry trade group based in Irvine, CA. In 1999, according to the council, nearly 10 per cent of new motorcycle purchasers were women.

The Buell does not appear to be cannibalizing Harley-Davidson sales because it is a very different kind of bike. The rider's position is thrust forward to create a racing feeling, while the Harley-Davidson is designed more for riders who want to cruise. Nor is a Buell as big or as heavy as a Harley-Davidson, and it is easier to manoeuvre.

To complicate things, Bleustein is trying this balancing act when the overall market for motorcycles is about 600,000 units per year, half what it was at its peak in 1972. The challenge of polishing a proud but ageing brand has confounded General Motors' Cadillac and Ford Motor's Lincoln divisions. Harley-Davidson is softening its bad-guy image to make biking more mainstream. It is encouraging the spread of Harley-Davidson owner groups, supporting charities, and taking toys to hospitals. But the company does not want to change its image too much. 'There are some upscale neurosurgeons and bankers who are riding Harleys because they want people to think there's a little bad in them', says CEO Bleustein. 'We don't want to completely squash that image' (Holstein, 2000).

The motorcycle market in the three main regions of the world is shown in Table 12.3.

For the fiscal year ended 2000, total Harley-Davidson motorcycle shipments were 204,592 units compared with 177,187 units in 1999, a 15.5 per cent increase. Harley-Davidson motorcycle revenue was US$2.25 billion, an increase of US$355.5 million (18.8 per cent).

Table 12.3 Registrations of heavyweight motorcycles (over 650cc), 1999

	North America	Europe	Asia/ Pacific
Total industry (1000s)	297.8	306.7	63.1
Market share	%	%	%
Harley-Davidson/Buell	49.0	6.5	19.6
Honda	17.0	22.2	22.4
Yamaha	7.6	18.0	19.0
Kawasaki	10.4	11.6	19.0
Suzuki	9.4	15.4	9.3
BMW	3.5	13.0	4.4
Ducati	–	5.4	3.2
Triumph	–	4.2	–
Others	3.1	3.7	3.1
Total	100	100	100

Source: Harley-Davidson Financial Report 1999, p. 54

Case study 12.2 continued

Total Buell motorcycle shipments were 10,189 units compared with 7767 units in 1999, a 31.2 per cent gain. Buell motorcycle revenue was US$58.1 million, a decrease of US$5.4 (8.5 per cent). The decline in revenue was driven primarily by a shift to production of lower-priced Buell Blast motorcycles, which target new riders.

Pricing

The price competition is getting tougher. Compared to similar models from Honda, Harley-Davidson still has about a 30 per cent price premium. Harley-Davidson owners still wear T-shirts saying 'I'd rather push a Harley than drive a Honda'.

Today, Harley-Davidson's overseas business outside the USA is around 25 per cent of its annual total. Europeans like cruiser bikes, but not Harley-Davidson prices. In fact some Harley-Davidson bikes have recently been shipped back from Europe due to lack of demand.

Questions

1. What are the main reasons for Harley-Davidson's enormous success over the last 15 years?
2. Describe Harley-Davidson's general pricing strategy. What does the company's positioning have to do with its pricing strategy?
3. Should Harley-Davidson alter its price, given that there are strong price pressures from rivals?
4. What should Harley-Davidson do to improve its market share in Europe?

Sources: Holstein (2000), Milligan and Carbone (2000).

QUESTIONS FOR DISCUSSION

1. What is value-based pricing? How does it differ from cost-based pricing?
2. (a) What does the economist contribute to the pricing decision?
   (b) What does the accountant contribute to the pricing decision?
3. What are skimming and penetration pricing?
4. What is umbrella pricing?
5. List three aspects of product line pricing.
6. Why is cost-based pricing particularly problematic in service industries?
7. How does competition affect a company's prices? Briefly describe a major competitor-based pricing approach.
8. Many firms enter a market as price leaders, but they end up dominating the bottom end of the market. What could be the reasons for this change?

REFERENCES

Allen, E. and Fjernestad, J. (2001), E-commerce marketing strategies: an integrated framework and case analysis, *Logistics Information Management*, vol. 14, no. 1, pp. 14–33.
BBC (1996), *Branded: Heinz case*, BBC TV.
Best, R. J. (2000), *Market-based Management*, Prentice Hall, Harlow, 2nd edn.
Curtis, J. (2001), Body Shop plans to scale down its political activity, *Marketing*, London, July 26, p. 3.
Czepiel, J. A. (1992), *Competative Marketing Strategy*, Prentice-Hall, Englewood Cliffs, NJ.
Czinkota, M. R. and Kotabe, M. (1999), Bypassing Japan's marketing barriers, *Marketing Management*, vol. 8, Winter, pp. 33–43.

Driver, J. C. (2001), Airline marketing in regulatory context, *Marketing Intelligence Planning*, vol. 19, no. 2, pp. 125–35.

Emiliani, M. L. (2000), Business-to-business online auctions. Key issues for purchasing process improvement, *Supply Chain Management: An International Journal*, vol. 5, no. 4, pp. 176–86.

Freedonia Group (2000), *World Major Household Appliances Report*, Freedonia Press, Cleveland.

Garda, R. A. (1995), Tactical pricing, *in* Paliwoda, S. J. and Ryans, J. K. (Eds), *International Marketing Reader*, Routledge, London.

Holden, R. K. and Nayle, T. T. (1998), Kamikaze pricing, *Marketing Management*, vol. 7, no. 2, Summer, pp. 30–9.

Hollensen, S. (2001), *Global Marketing: A market responsive approach*, Financial Times/Prentice Hall, Harlow, 2nd edn.

Holstein, W. (2000), 'Rebels with a cause: Harley revamps itself in a drive for new, young hog riders, *US News & World report*, no. 19, pp. 46–7.

Johnson, M. D., Hermann, A. and Baner, H. H. (1999), The effects of price bundling on consumer evaluations of product offerings, *International Journal of Research in Marketing*, vol. 16, pp. 129–42.

Lambin, J. (1976), *Advertising, Competition and Market Conduct in Oligopoly Over Time*, North Holland-Elsevier, Amsterdam.

Marsh, G. (2000), International pricing: a market perspective, *Marketing Intelligence & Planning*, vol. 18, no. 4, pp. 200–5.

Massad, V. J. and Tucker, J. M. (2000), Comparing bidding and pricing between in-person and online auction, *Journal of Product & Brand Management*, vol. 9, no. 5, pp. 325–32.

Milligan, B. and Carbone, J. (2000), Harley-Davidson win by getting suppliers on board, *Purchasing*, no. 5, Sept 21, pp. 52–65.

Nagle, T. T. (1987), *The Strategies and Tactics of Pricing*, Prentice-Hall, Englewood Cliffs, NJ.

Narayandas, D., Quelch, J. and Swartz, G. (2000), Prepare your company for global pricing, *Sloan Management Review*, Fall, pp. 61–70.

Simon, H. and Kucher, E. (1993), The European pricing bomb – and how to cope with it, *Marketing and Research Today*, February, pp. 25–36.

Stremersch, S. and Tellis, G. J. (2002). Strategic bundling of products and prices: a new synthesis for marketing, *Journal of Marketing*, vol. 66, January, pp. 55–72.

Weigand, R. E. (1991), Buy in – follow on strategies for profit, *Sloan Management Review*, Spring, pp. 29–38.

Chapter 13

Distribution decisions

LEARNING OBJECTIVES

After studying this chapter you should be able to:

- understand why relationships occur between manufacturer and distributor.
- explore the determinants of channel decisions.
- discuss the key points in putting together and managing marketing channels.
- discuss the factors influencing channel width (intensive, selective or exclusive coverage).
- explain what is meant by integration of the marketing channel.
- define and explain what is meant by logistics.
- discuss the role of retailing in modern marketing.

Case study 13.1 Denka Holding

A Danish furniture group in an international franchise expansion

Experts in the Danish furniture industry have repeatedly emphasized that most Danish furniture manufacturers produce furniture with too little value added. It is often standard furniture, which can be produced at a much lower price in eastern Europe or elsewhere. Danish producers have been requested to stake much more on design, branded goods, and profiling. Some of the furniture companies, e.g. Montana Møbler and Fritz Hansen, have embraced the message and marketed their products as brands. During recent years another Danish furniture group, Denka Holding, has begun profiling more strongly. As well as purchasing furniture through the retail trade (by way of the Club 8 brand), it has established it own franchise chain under the name BoConcept. In 2001 this international franchise chain opened a shop approximately every other week somewhere on the planet. There were about 100 franchise shops in February 2002.

Denka Holding consists of a several furniture companies, which today constitute one of Denmark's biggest furniture groups. The company was founded by two men in 1962. They began with small premises of 10 m². About 15 years ago the company went public in order to solve a generational change problem, and subsequently it acquired a small company, Zenia House, which was incorporated in Denka Møbler. In December 1988 the company bought Club 8, which at that time had an annual turnover of DKK 30–35 million. Over ten years the company has increased its turnover to more than DKK 300 million.

Economic development

In 1999–2000 the group's total turnover was DKK 540 million. Eighty per cent of this amount was realized outside the country. The largest markets for Denka Holding are Germany, the USA, and Japan.

Case study 13.1 continued

Group turnover has increased by 56 per cent. In 1995–6 the group lost DKK 15 million after tax, while in 1999–2000 it made a DKK 18 million profit. The net capital of the company is DKK 177 million.

New group structure

Until September 1999, the following companies were placed under Denka Holding (the 'age groups' for the furniture types are approximate):

● Club 8 Møbler A/S: sells children's furniture, 0–12 years (brand: Color 4 kids etc.), and adult furniture, 20–45 years (brand: Xilo, Transit etc.). The international retail furniture chain BoConcept was also part of this company.

● Denka Møbler A/S: sells adult furniture: 25–55 years.

● Zenia House A/S: the eco-conscious furniture consumer, 25–45 years. The furniture has been developed in cooperation with the firm of architects and designers Raunkjær & Kjærgaard. The cooperation has resulted in, among other things, the May-Flower line which is inspired by the lifestyle of Shakers – a puritan religious sect which was particularly popular in 19th century North America.

● Tensi A/S: sells youth furniture, 15–25 years.

● Vizone A/S: Denka Holding has a 50 per cent interest in this trading company, which primarily sells upholstered furniture (not Denka Holding's speciality).

● Dencon A/S: manufacturer of office furniture.

In September 1999, the group was restructured as shown in Figure 13.1.

The furniture has so far only been manufactured in Denmark. The manufacturing process is highly automated with wages accounting for a relatively small proportion of costs.

The only foreign factory in the Denka group is in Lithuania and it supplies furniture parts to Zenia House A/S.

The disadvantage of the old group structure was that customers might receive invoices from five different companies even though they had only been dealing with one company – Denka Holding. In the various markets, on the other hand, the group has in several cases, e.g. in Germany, had a joint subsidiary, which sold all product lines.

Figure 13.1 Denka Holding – new structure

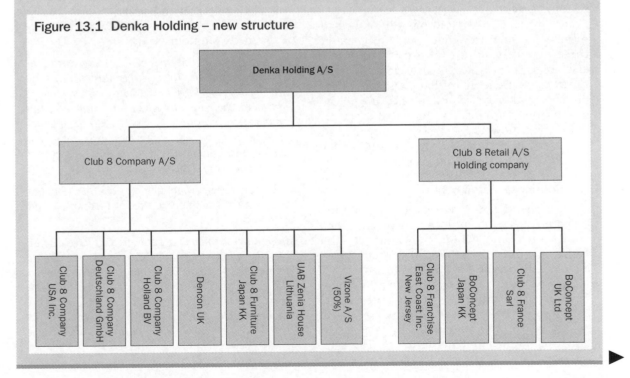

Case study 13.1 continued

However, the subsidiary in the UK has so far only been handling Dencon's office furniture.

A wish for simplification made Denka Holding A/S restructure the group (Figure 13.1) in September 1999. The new company structure gathers the Danish production and sales activities in one company called Club 8 Company A/S. The foreign subsidiaries are also in Club 8 Company A/S. All direct retail activities (BoConcept is now the only one) have been gathered in one independent company, Club 8 Company A/S, which now has its headquarters in Ølgod. The group's selling, financial and logistics departments are also managed from here. The group is also establishing a joint distribution centre for the group's manufacturing units here.

Denka Holding A/S has its headquarters in Herning, along with the retail department and the group's IT and marketing departments.

As a result of the new group structure, all administrative functions in the present companies have been merged. This means that the group has cut staff by 20, thereby reducing the group's costs by about DKK 7 million. The structural changes are also expected to produce some synergies, thereby improving the group's future earnings potential.

In future, Denka Holding will reduce the number of branded goods and only market three brands: Club 8 ('flat-pack' furniture to assemble), Zenia House (expensive lifestyle furniture) and Dencon (office furniture). These brands are already well established in the various customer groups, i.e. the distributors. The brands are, however, almost unknown to the end users. In this respect Denka Holding does not differ from other furniture producers.

The BoConcept retail chain

During the last 5–6 years Denka Holding's focus has been on building an international retail furniture chain, BoConcept, that addresses price-conscious and trendsetting people with a taste for designer furniture. The reason why price consciousness and designer furniture can harmonize with each other must be found in the fact that in its marketing the company tries to show its products as resembling well-known designer furniture. This often makes the consumers think that the furniture must be very expensive. They are then pleasantly surprised when told what the price is.

The whole concept is now contained in a separate company – Club 8 Retail A/S (see Figure 13.1). There are today 100 shops in over 20 countries. Denka Holding's goal is to gain half of the group's turnover through BoConcept in five years, the rest through the traditional furniture chains. At present the BoConcept shops represent about 30 per cent of the group's turnover.

The basic concept builds upon the idea of franchising. The franchisee invests a basic amount and subsequently he/she receives a franchise package from the franchisor. This package consists of shopfitting, display furniture for the shop, advertising material, suggestions for events on opening day, etc.

Club 8 Retail itself runs three shops in Tokyo and Paris. In these shops various furniture concepts are tested.

BoConcept furniture is produced primarily by Club 8, but the shops also sell accessories such as tablecloths, candlesticks and cutlery. In this connection BoConcept has initiated an international cooperation with Inspiration, the Danish chain of shops for art and design.

The product manager of Club 8 Company A/S, Betina B. Mølholm, said:

We have recorded good sales of accessories when consumers buy furniture. To strengthen this area we have therefore been looking for a business partner who has a finger on the pulse and who at the same time can combine the Danish eye for design with the international environment where our shops are found. In our opinion, Inspiration has an incredibly good eye for what are trendy and exciting goods right now.

Frank Skorstensgaard, managing director of Bocom Amba, which is a chain centre for Inspiration and Superkram, said:

Inspiration is making a great effort to have a sense of fashion and design all the time. We participate in fairs and seminars on fashion and trends around the world and we are holding our own in-house trend seminars in order to be at the forefront. This we use to find and to some extent design ourselves trendy goods from suppliers, partly in the East and partly elsewhere in the world.

Case study 13.1 continued

So far, the reports from the shops around the world indicate that the end users have been very positive towards this broad product concept, including accessories in the BoConcept shops.

Questions

1. As an input to Denka Holding's future international expansion strategy assess the franchise idea (the BoConcept shops) in relation to other relevant methods of distribution.

2. What problems and opportunities do you see in BoConcept's cooperation with the Inspiration chain?

3. What problems and opportunities do you see in the fact that in some markets (e.g. Germany) Denka Holding sells through both BoConcept franchise shops and large furniture chains?

Sources: Denka Holding press releases.

13.1 Introduction

A trading or distribution relationship is a relationship between a buyer and a seller who resells the goods and services. Trading relationships have been important since humans began to trade.

Access to international markets is a key decision area facing firms in the 21st century. In Chapter 9, we considered how a firm chooses an appropriate mode for entering a foreign market. After the firm has chosen a strategy to get its products into foreign markets, the next challenge is the distribution of products within national markets. The first part of this chapter concerns the structure and management of foreign distribution. The second part of the chapter is concerned with the management of logistics (Section 13.8).

A *distribution channel* is a set of organizations that make a product or service available for purchase by consumers or businesses. The distribution channel serves to connect a manufacturer, or a service provider, with consumers or users. In simple terms, a distribution channel is a pipeline or pathway to the market.

Distribution channels are needed because producers are separated from prospective customers.

A distribution channel consists of at least a producer and a customer. Most channels, however, use one or more intermediaries to help move products to the customer.

Intermediaries are independently owned organizations that act as links to move products between producers and the end user. The primary categories are brokers, wholesalers and distributors, and retailers. Agents do not purchase the goods they handle but instead negotiate the sale for the client. A familiar example is estate agents, who negotiate the sale of property for their customers. Companies have more control over the activities of brokers, including the final price to the customer, because brokers do not own the goods they sell. *Wholesalers* (also referred to as distributors) take title to products and resell them to retail, industrial, commercial, institutional, professional, or agricultural firms, as well as to other wholesalers.

Most distribution channels flow from the manufacturer to the end user, but goods sometimes move in the opposite direction. A *reverse channel* flows from the end user to the wholesaler and/or the manufacturer. An example is recycling of bottles and cans.

Recycling services have become increasingly important, given the growth of waste materials and the high costs associated with their disposal. Volunteer groups have been important in the recycling process, particularly in the collection and transport of waste to recycling plants. But the problem of disposing waste materials is growing so fast that more commercial solutions must be found despite the fact that many cities are mandating that consumers sort their waste to facilitate pickup and disposal. Some specialists have become more involved, including manufacturer-owned redemption centres and independent recycling centres, but on the whole current channels are not entirely satisfactory, and more cost-efficient ones are needed.

According to Bucklin *et al.* (1996), distribution channels typically account for 15–40 per cent of the retail price of goods and services in an industry.

Over the next few years, the challenges and opportunities for channel management will multiply, as technological developments accelerate channel evolution. Data networks are increasingly enabling end users to bypass traditional channels and deal directly with manufacturers and service providers.

Electronic data interchange (EDI) is now used for the exchange of orders and invoices between suppliers and their customers. By monitoring stock online, customers are also able to order directly from suppliers on a just-in-time (JIT) basis, and thereby to avoid holding stock altogether or to minimize the time it is held.

At the same time, new channels are continuing to emerge in one industry after another, opening up opportunities for companies to cut costs or improve their effectiveness in reaching specific market segments. Catalogue retailing, telephone ordering, cable TV shopping and Internet ordering are all becoming increasingly important to consumer goods manufacturers. Despite the scale and importance of these opportunities, however, few companies manage to take full advantage of them.

13.2 The basic functions of channel participants

The most common function of a marketing **channel member** is to resell the product into a market that could not be reached as efficiently or effectively by the original seller. Intermediaries have already established goodwill with their customers, and those customers trust the intermediary's buying judgements. Retailers often have multiple selling outlets that are both in prime geographical locations and have the right image. This gives the manufacturer both physical and psychological market positioning.

Figure 13.2 shows how the number of transactions (contact lines) between three manufacturers and three customers (using one intermediary) is reduced.

Intermediaries play a major role in bringing the product or service to the end user at the right time by transporting and storing it.

Many intermediaries also cooperate with the manufacturer to provide customer training, education, and after-sales maintenance and repair services.

Sometimes merchants do take risks with, for example, seasonal products and are caught with stock at the end of a season that has to be sold at a loss or carried over to the next year. However, the risk-taking and financing activities of channel intermediaries have been greatly reduced over the last hundred years. Nowadays, many new products are sold to retailers on consignment (retailers pay for what they sell and return the rest) or are purchased with buyback deals in the contract. Some retailers are even demanding up-front cash payments to compensate for the cost

Figure 13.2 How an intermediary increases distribution efficiency

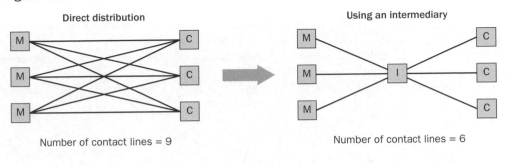

Direct distribution

Using an intermediary

Number of contact lines = 9

Number of contact lines = 6

M = Manufacturer

C = Customer

I = Intermediary

and the risk of placing a new product on their shelves. With established products, the credit allowances given to the wholesaler or retailer are such that a high-turnover product is often sold by the retailer before the wholesaler or retailer pays the manufacturer for the product.

Channel members are able to provide valuable customer feedback, but often the manufacturer also provides information down the channel to retailers that creates interest and support for its product. Hence, market research and information flows both ways with findings and data often being interpreted in different ways by the various parties.

13.3 Distributor portfolio analysis

A distributor analysis can be undertaken by reviewing the information on a distributor's growth rate and the firm's percentage of the distributor's total sales. Using Table 13.1 as an input, Figure 13.3 is an example of a manufacturing firm X, which within a SBU has four distributors each serving a different segment. The strategic recommendations in Figure 13.3 are only based on the variables included in the distributor portfolio (Table 13.1). Before making final recommendations, Firm X should also include its dependence on each distributor, e.g. by calculating how its total sales are distributed among its four distributors.

Table 13.1 A manufacturer's distributor portfolio analysis

Segment	Mainly served by	Percentage of firm X in distributor's total purchases	Distributor annual growth rate within the segment
Segment A	Distributor A	60%	50%
Segment B	Distributor B	30%	30%
Segment C	Distributor C	75%	−25%
Segment D	Distributor D	20%	−40%

Figure 13.3 A manufacturer's distributor portfolio analysis

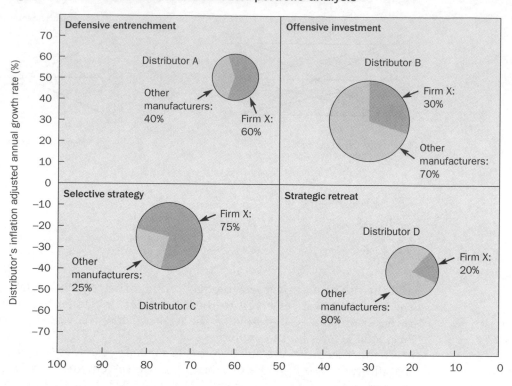

Penetration %: Firm X's share of distributor's product-line sales – the area of each circle is proportional to the value of the distributor's total purchase, from Firm X and others

Source: adapted from Dickson (1982).

13.4 Developing and managing relationships between manufacturer and distributor

A relationship occurs when there is a fit between the marketing strategies and implementation skills of the manufacturer and distributor in the process of adding customer value. Customer value is created by what each party brings to the relationship and how they work together to add additional customer services and marketing campaigns.

In addition to trading relationships and processes that raise the perceived quality of the product and supporting services, a unique trading relationship advantage can come from both the manufacturer and distributor working together to reduce the costs of doing business. If the cost-reduction drives and efforts of both parties are synchronized and if this synchronization between the manufacturer and distributor is better than any other trading relationship that manufacturers or distributors are in, then the trading relationship will have a unique competitive cost advantage towards customers.

It is always important to remember that the competitive advantage of a manufacturer-distributor relationship is managed by people at the manufacturer and distributor.

Historically, the way firms viewed personal relationships depended on their size. Among small firms, relationships mainly existed among owners. Larger firms operated under the sales representative/purchasing agent model. This model assumes that a firm's trading relationship is funnelled primarily through single agents: the personal relationship between the selling firm's salesperson (agent) and the buying firm's purchasing manager (agent). Other agency relationships were expected to develop among engineers working on supply-chain engineering specifications. But the salesperson acted as a gatekeeper to the buying organization.

The modern RM approach to the supply chain argues that this funnelling is unnecessarily restrictive. It proposes that trading relationships in the supply chain should be among cross-functional teams.

The new RM approach emphasizes that at the heart of the trading relationship is the set of relationship processes, such as decision making and learning, that integrate the operational and implementation processes between the two firms.

The reality of an important trading relationship is that it is held together by relationship processes and personal relationships among agents at several levels. At the strategic level, quality relationship processes have to enable senior management to initiate, agree on, and invest in creating a unique competitive position for the relationship. In addition, if senior managers get on well together, it makes a big difference in obtaining subordinates' cooperation in managing operations. The development of such inter-firm personal relationships is particularly valuable in very competitive markets when trading relationships are stressed and have to adapt creatively to new competitive realities. Such personal relationships nurture the personal trust and commitment that enables the relationship to survive market crises through creative, cooperative improvisation.

What is personal trust and commitment? Personal trust is when what the individual representatives say is their bond, and they are prepared to help each other to solve problems. Commitment is commitment to the goal of developing and nurturing the competitiveness of the relationship, compared to other competitive trading relationships. Mutual trust and commitment are determined by a history of shared values, open communication, both parties giving more to the relationship than to alternative relationships, and, particularly, not taking advantage of (or exploiting) the trust. The long-term return from the relationship is perceived to be higher than the return from nurturing other relationships. The driver of this long-term return is relationship process innovation: innovations in reducing process costs, increasing process speed, and increasing process output. Personal relationship goodwill and trust are needed when conflict arises and when attempts are initiated to improve systems and processes.

New information technology helps strengthen long-term relationships between manufacturers and distributors.

Integrated channel information systems (channel intranets) enable a manufacturer to assess the performance of distributors, the profitability of doing business with them, and the success of promotional programmes and new, more efficient operating processes. Not being a part of such an information system may become a real barrier to entering some markets. On the other hand, being part of the system may also limit the managerial options of the participant by limiting the company's ability to switch to alternative distribution options.

We will now look at a systematic approach to the major decisions in distribution by discussing the main variables influencing the distribution channel decision.

13.5 External and internal determinants of channel decisions

Customer characteristics

The customer, or final consumer, is the keystone in any channel design. Thus, the size, geographic distribution, shopping habits, outlet preferences and usage patterns of customer groups must be taken into account when making distribution decisions.

Consumer product channels tend to be longer than industrial product channels because the number of customers is greater, the customers are more geographically dispersed, and they buy in smaller quantities. Shopping habits, outlet preferences and usage patterns vary considerably from country to country and are strongly influenced by socio-cultural factors.

Nature of the product

Product characteristics play a key role in determining distribution strategy. For low-price, high-turnover **convenience products**, the requirement is an intensive distribution network. On the other hand, it is not necessary or even desirable for a prestigious product to have wide distribution. In this situation a manufacturer can shorten and narrow its distribution channel. Consumers are likely to do some comparison shopping and will actively seek information about all brands under consideration. In such cases, limited product exposure is not an impediment to market success.

Transportation and warehousing costs of the product are also critical issues in the distribution and sale of industrial goods such as bulk chemicals, metals and cement. Direct selling, servicing and repair, and warehousing spare parts dominate the distribution of such industrial products as computers, machinery and aircraft. The product's durability, ease of adulteration, amount and type of customer service required, unit costs and special handling requirements (such as cold storage) are also significant factors.

Nature of demand/location

The perceptions that the target customers hold about particular products can force distribution channels to be modified. Product perceptions are influenced by the customer's income and product experience, the product's end use, its life cycle position and the country's stage of economic development.

The geography of a country and the development of its transportation infrastructure can also affect the channel decision.

Competition

The channels used by competing products and close substitutes are important because channel arrangements that seek to serve the same market often compete with one another. Consumers generally expect to find particular products in particular outlets (e.g. speciality stores), or they have become accustomed to buying particular products from particular sources. In addition, local and global competitors may have agreements with the major wholesalers in a foreign country that effectively create barriers and exclude the company from key channels.

Sometimes the alternative is to use a distribution approach totally different from that of the competition and hope to develop a competitive advantage.

Legal regulations/local business practices

A country may have specific laws that rule out the use of particular channels or intermediaries. For example, until recently all alcoholic beverages in Sweden and Finland had to be distributed through state monopoly-owned outlets. Other countries prohibit the use of door-to-door selling. Channel coverage can also be affected by law. In general, exclusive representation may be viewed as a restraint of trade, especially if the product has a dominant market position. EU anti-trust authorities have increased their scrutiny of exclusive sales agreements. The Treaty of Rome prohibits distribution agreements (e.g. grants of exclusivity) that affect trade or restrict competition.

Furthermore, local business practices can interfere with efficiency and productivity and may force a manufacturer to employ a channel of distribution that is longer and wider than desired. Because of Japan's multi-tiered distribution system, which relies on numerous layers of intermediaries, foreign companies have long considered the complex Japanese distribution system as the most effective non-tariff barrier to the Japanese market.

Exhibit 13.1 shows how the Japanese distribution system differs from its counterparts in the USA and Europe. Let us now return to the major decisions concerning the structure of the distribution channel.

Exhibit 13.1	The distribution system in Japan

The distribution network in Japan has more wholesalers and retailers per capita than any other industrial country. The Japanese distribution channels are much longer and more complex than the western channels.

A consequence of the more complex Japanese distribution system is the considerable price escalation from producer to consumer. (The principle behind price escalation is shown in Figure 12.5.)

The first transaction shown in Figure 13.4 from producer to wholesaler is a vertical exchange, whereas the next transaction (from one wholesaler to another) is a horizontal exchange. Small Japanese distributors often lack adequate inventory to serve another distributor at the same vertical level (i.e. horizontal exchange). According to economic criteria, the Japanese distribution system would seem to be inefficient, resulting in higher consumer prices.

However, the complex Japanese distribution system exists to serve social as well as economic purposes. Channel members are like family members and their relations to each other are tightly interlocked by tradition and emotion. Because of these social considerations, inefficient channel members are sometimes retained and tolerated in order to maintain employment and income flows. For example, one of the primary concerns of Japanese channel managers is to help other channel members preserve their dignity.

►

Exhibit 13.1 continued

Figure 13.4   A hypothetical channel sequence in the Japanese consumer market

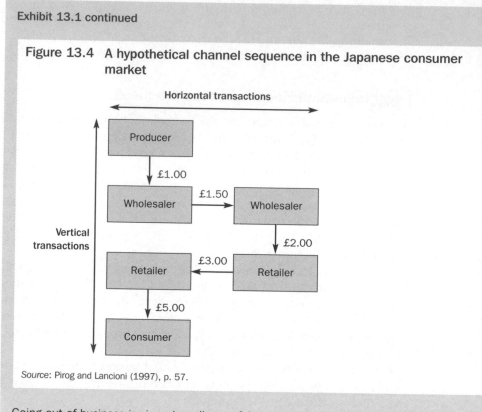

Source: Pirog and Lancioni (1997), p. 57.

Going out of business is viewed as disgraceful, so stronger channel members (typically producers) must often support weak distributors. The Japanese system is often seen as a trade barrier by western firms, but it is likely that these foreign firms have merely failed to understand the system.

Source: adapted from Hollensen (2001), p. 485.

13.6 The structure of the channel

Market coverage

The amount of market coverage that a channel member provides is important. Coverage is a flexible term. It can refer to geographical areas of a country (such as cities and major towns) or the number of retail outlets (as a percentage of all retail outlets). Regardless of the market coverage measure(s) used, the company has to create a distribution network (dealers, distributors and retailers) to meet its coverage goals.

As shown in Figure 13.5, three different approaches are available:

- *intensive coverage*: this calls for distributing the product through the largest number of different types of intermediary and the largest number of individual intermediaries of each type

Figure 13.5 Three strategies for market coverage

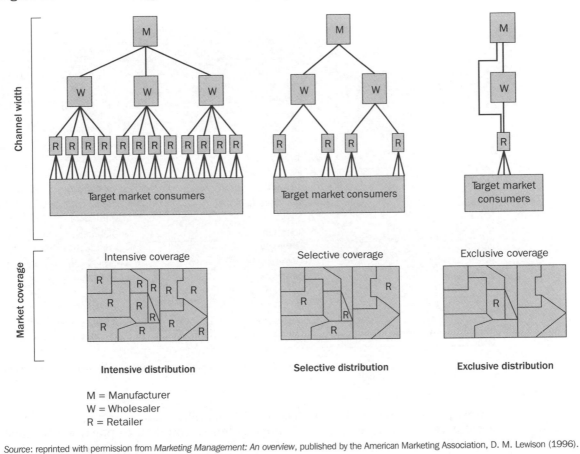

M = Manufacturer
W = Wholesaler
R = Retailer

Source: reprinted with permission from *Marketing Management: An overview*, published by the American Marketing Association, D. M. Lewison (1996).

- *selective coverage*: this entails choosing a number of intermediaries for each area to be penetrated
- *exclusive coverage*: this involves choosing only one intermediary in a market.

Channel coverage (or width) can be identified along a continuum ranging from wide channels (**intensive distribution**) to narrow channels (**exclusive distribution**). Figure 13.6 illustrates some factors favouring intensive, selective and exclusive distribution.

When analysing a channel's market coverage it is relevant to distinguish between market coverage of current and of new channels. To ensure the best possible market coverage, it is essential to have a view of what customer segment the current channel structure covers. This is necessary in order to identify any overlap between the channels' coverage of the identified segments (Figure 13.7).

In situation A, there is no overlap at all. Channels X and Y each work with their unique market segments, and there is no subject of conflict. On the other hand, the problem is that the entire market is not covered, which means lost earnings and a possibility of competitors moving into the open areas and then maybe even encroaching on the areas covered as well.

Figure 13.6 Factors influencing channel width

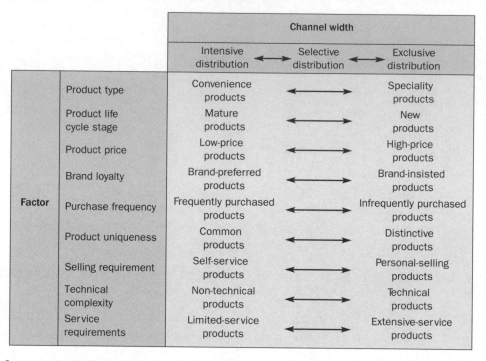

Factor	Channel width		
	Intensive distribution ↔	**Selective distribution** ↔	**Exclusive distribution**
Product type	Convenience products	← →	Speciality products
Product life cycle stage	Mature products	← →	New products
Product price	Low-price products	← →	High-price products
Brand loyalty	Brand-preferred products	← →	Brand-insisted products
Purchase frequency	Frequently purchased products	← →	Infrequently purchased products
Product uniqueness	Common products	← →	Distinctive products
Selling requirement	Self-service products	← →	Personal-selling products
Technical complexity	Non-technical products	← →	Technical products
Service requirements	Limited-service products	← →	Extensive-service products

Source: reprinted with permission from *Marketing Management: An overview*, published by the American Marketing Association, D. M. Lewison (1996).

In situation B, the scenario is close to optimal. The market coverage is complete and the overlap small with only minimal potential conflicts. In practice, the situation is seldom this simple. Often some of the channels will be more appropriate than others depending on the characteristics of the product and the strength of the intermediaries.

Finally, competitors can influence the market coverage. For example, in the consumer goods industry, leading brand name suppliers usually want to be represented by the same sales channel as other leading brand names. This ultimately results in excess coverage between the sales channels.

In situation C, both markets are covered, but there is significant overlap. This may result in conflict between the sales channels, and it is likely that the situation will not be the best possible based on the fundamental goal of creating profit. However, the situation may be tolerable, if this surplus supply acts as a shield against new competitors.

Channel length

This is determined by the number of levels or different types of intermediaries. Longer channels, those with several intermediaries, tend to be associated with convenience goods and mass distribution. As seen in Exhibit 13.1, Japan has longer channels for convenience goods because of the historical development of its system. One implication is that prices increase considerably for the final consumer (see Chapter 12 on price escalation).

Figure 13.7 Channel overlap

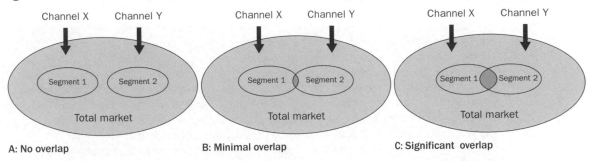

A: No overlap   B: Minimal overlap   C: Significant overlap

Control/cost

The control of one member in the vertical distribution channel is its ability to influence the decisions and actions of other channel members. Channel control is of critical concern to international marketers wanting to establish international brands and a consistent image of quality and service worldwide.

The company must decide how much control it wants to have over how each of its products is marketed. The answer is partly determined by the strategic role assigned to each market. It is also a function of the types of channel member available, the regulations and rules governing distribution activity in each foreign market, and to some extent the roles traditionally assigned to channel members.

Normally, a high degree of control is provided by the use of the firm's own sales force in international markets. The use of intermediaries will automatically lead to loss of some control over the marketing of the firm's products.

In getting its products to end users, a manufacturer must either perform all of the functions or shift some or all of them to intermediaries. As the old saying goes, 'You can eliminate the intermediary, but not the functions of the intermediary.'

In most marketing situations, there is a trade-off between a producer's ability to control important channel functions and the financial resources required to exercise that control. The more intermediaries involved in getting a supplier's product to user customers, the less control the supplier can generally exercise over the flow of its product through the channel and the way it is presented to customers. On the other hand, reducing the length and breadth of the distribution channel usually requires that the supplier perform more functions itself. In turn, this requires the supplier to allocate more financial resources to activities such as warehousing, shipping, credit, field selling or field service.

In summary, the decision to use an intermediary or to distribute via a company-owned sales force requires a major trade-off between the desire to control marketing efforts and the desire to minimize resource commitment costs.

Degree of integration

Control can also be exercised through integration. Channel integration is the process of incorporating all channel members into one channel system and uniting them under one leadership and one set of goals. Channel integration is relevant for the manufacturer to consider when high transaction costs occur between manufacturer and distributor, as a result of **channel conflicts** and/or bad cooperation. There are two different types of integration:

| Exhibit 13.2 | **Condomi's distribution alliance with Klosterfrau in Germany** |

At the end of July 2000 the German condom manufacturer, Condomi, and the successful MCM Klosterfrau GmbH announced a long-term distribution alliance. As of January 1, 2001 Klosterfrau, as German market leader for over-the-counter medical products (e.g. natural medicines like Klosterfrau Melissengeist, highly concentrated vitamin E, garlic, Franzbranntwein, Taxofit vitamins and minerals, neo angin sore throat medication and tiger balm), distributed Condomi's condom products. It is intended to achieve nearly complete distribution coverage in the German pharmacy, drug-store and retail store segments. By this cooperation Klosterfrau has ended its partnership with the condom manufacturer Durex (London).

The aim of the alliance is also to extend international presence into the segments covering European chemists, pharmaceutical markets and food retailers.

Both companies are based in Cologne, Germany. Condomi is the biggest manufacturer of condoms in Europe. Klosterfrau is the best-known brand in the product range of 'natural' medicine (especially the Klosterfrau Melissengeist – medicinal spirit). The emblem of three nuns framed with a pointed Gothic arc has an awareness of 94 per cent in Germany and has symbolized health and consumer confidence for generations. Its effects on the nerves, head, heart and stomach have been known for many years. The profile of traditional yet modern natural medicines has grown significantly in recent times.

Sources: adapted from www.klosterfrau.de; www.condomi-ag.de; Wall Street Journal (2000).

- *vertical integration*: seeking control of channel members at different levels of the channel

- *horizontal integration*: seeking control of channel members at the same level of the channel (i.e. competitors).

Integration is achieved either through acquisitions (ownership) or through tight cooperative relationships. Getting channel members to work together for their own mutual benefit can be a difficult task. However, today cooperative relationships are essential for efficient and effective channel operation.

Vertical integration (owning your supplier or reseller) offers the promise of potential efficiencies gained from a reduction in management overheads, integration of information systems, reduction or elimination of selling costs within the integrated channel, and better management and control of marketing campaigns and physical distribution logistics. It is sometimes the only way to introduce new technological advances into a channel. Integration enables unilateral decisions on who is going to do what and the more direct rewarding of key personnel down the channel for responding to the changes. It also gives the integrating firm more control over training and management succession. However, competitive market forces often make the use of independent channel agents more efficient, and vertical integration should be employed only when the market fails – when gross inefficiencies result from working with independent channel participants.

Figure 13.8 shows an example of vertical integration. The starting point in Figure 13.8 is the conventional marketing channels, where the channel consists of isolated and autonomous participating channel members. Channel coordination is here achieved through arm's-length bargaining. At this point, vertical integration can take two forms: forward and backward.

Figure 13.8 Vertical integration

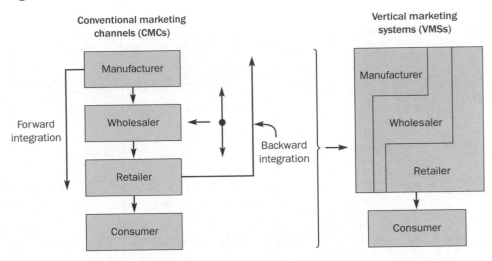

Source: Hollensen (2001), p. 489.

- The manufacturer can make forward integration, when it seeks control of businesses of the wholesale and retail levels of the channel.
- The retailer can make backward integration, seeking control of businesses at wholesale and manufacturer levels of the channel.
- The wholesaler has two possibilities: both forward and backward integration.

The result of these manoeuvres is the **vertical marketing system** (Figure 13.8). Here the channel consists of integrated participating members, where channel stability is high due to assured member loyalty and long-term commitments.

13.7 Managing and controlling distribution channels

Once the basic design of the channel has been determined, the international marketer must begin to fill it with the best available candidates, and must secure their cooperation.

Screening and selecting intermediaries

At this stage, the marketer knows the type of distributor that is needed. The potential candidates must now be compared and contrasted against determining criteria.

The example in Table 13.2 uses 13 criteria for screening potential channel members. The criteria to be used depend on the nature of a firm's business and its distribution objectives in given markets. The list of criteria should correspond closely to the marketer's own determinants of success – all the things that are important to beating the competition.

The hypothetical consumer packaged goods company used in Table 13.2 considered the distributor's marketing management expertise and financial soundness to

Table 13.2 Examples of distributor (dealer) selection criteria

Criteria (no ranking implied)	Weight	Distributor 1		Distributor 2		Distributor 3	
		Rating	Score	Rating	Score	Rating	Score
Financial soundness and depth of channel member	4	5	20	4	16	3	12
Marketing management expertise and sophistication	5	4	20	3	15	2	10
Satisfactory trade, customer relations and contacts	3	4	12	3	9	3	9
Capability of providing adequate sales coverage	4	3	12	3	12	3	12
Overall positive reputation and image as a company	3	5	15	4	12	4	12
Product compatibility (synergy or conflict?)	3	3	9	4	12	4	12
Pertinent technical know-how at staff level	–	–	–	–	–	–	–
Adequate technical facilities and service support	–	–	–	–	–	–	–
Adequate infrastructure in staff and facilities	1	5	5	3	3	3	3
Proven performance record with client companies	2	4	8	3	6	3	6
Positive attitude towards the company's products	1	3	3	3	3	3	3
Mature outlook regarding the company's inevitable progression in market management	1	3	3	3	3	3	3
Excellent government relations	1	4	4	3	3	3	3
Score			111		94		85

Scales:

Rating: 5 – Outstanding, 4 – Above average, 3 – Average, 2 – Below average, 1 – Unsatisfactory.

Weighting: 5 – Critical success factor, 4 – Prerequisite success factor, 3 – Important success factor, 2 – Of some importance, 1 – Standard.

Source: adapted from Toyne and Walters (1993), p. 520.

be of the greatest importance. These indicators will show whether the distributor is making money and is able to perform some of the necessary marketing functions such as extension of credit to customers and risk absorption. Financial reports are not always complete or reliable, or may lend themselves to differences of interpretation, pointing to the need for a third-party opinion. In the example, distributor 1 would be selected by the company.

Alternatively, an industrial goods company may consider the distributor's product compatibility, technical know-how, and technical facilities and service support to be of high importance, and the distributor's infrastructure, client performance and attitude toward its products to be of low importance. Quite often, global marketers find that the most desirable distributors in a given market are already handling competitive products and are therefore unavailable.

A high-technology consumer goods company, on the other hand, may favour financial soundness, marketing management expertise, reputation, technical know-how, technical facilities, service support and government relations. In some countries, religious or ethnic differences might make an agent suitable for one part of the market coverage but unsuitable for another. This can result in more channel members being required to give adequate market coverage.

Exhibit 13.3   ## Distribution of pharmaceutical products in China

The pharmaceutical industry undoubtedly plays an important role in China's economic development. In China, there are 60,000 hospitals, 125,000 clinics, 130 medical schools, and 2 million doctors.

In the past, healthcare in China was provided by the state. Since the promulgation of the socialist market economy, individuals in private sector companies have started to buy personal health insurance.

The government has promulgated a series of reforms in the public health insurance system, distribution system, legislation, and advertising policies. Although these new policies have invited more foreign pharmaceutical manufacturers to the Chinese market, these companies are operating in a very volatile environment.

At present, at least 70 per cent of the population (approximately 800 million people) do not have any health insurance, nor do they feel responsible for their medical care expenses.

Distribution system: before and now

Before the economic reform, China, as a planned economy, used to adopt a centralized purchasing and supply system. Both locally produced and imported pharmaceuticals were distributed through state-owned channels in three tiers, namely the primary, secondary and tertiary drug stations. No direct contact between foreign manufacturers and users/hospitals was allowed, except for those holding an import and export licence issued by the Ministry of Foreign Trade and Economic Cooperation. Therefore, the sales and distribution channels were lengthy and hence direct communication between marketers and users was hindered.

Nevertheless, the pharmaceutical industry has recently evolved from a planned economy to a market economy. The state is no longer responsible for all purchasing and supply, and the three-tier system has been completely replaced by a more market-oriented distribution system. Medicines produced domestically can now be sold directly to primary, secondary, and tertiary supply stores and designated hospitals. Marketers can also promote their pharmaceutical products directly to distributors and physicians. As a result, many pharmaceutical manufacturers have established their own sales and marketing teams to increase sales.

Source: adapted from Liu and Cheng (2000).

Contracting (distributor agreements)

When the international marketer has found a suitable intermediary, a foreign sales agreement is drawn up. Before final contractual arrangements are made, it is wise to make personal visits to the prospective channel member. The agreement itself can be relatively simple, but given the numerous differences in the market environments, certain elements are essential. These are listed in Table 13.3.

Table 13.3 Items to include in an agreement with a foreign intermediary (distributor)

- Names and addresses of both parties.
- Date when the agreement goes into effect.
- Duration of the agreement.
- Provisions for extending or terminating the agreement.
- Description of sales territory.
- Establishment of discount and/or commission schedules and determination of when and how paid.
- Provisions for revising the commission or discount schedules.
- Establishment of a policy governing resale prices.
- Maintenance of appropriate service facilities.
- Restrictions to prohibit the manufacture and sale of similar and competitive products.
- Designation of responsibility for patent and trade mark negotiations and/or pricing.
- The assignability or non-assignability of the agreement and any limiting factors.
- Designation of the country and state (if applicable) of contract jurisdiction in the case of dispute.

Source: adapted from Jain (1996), p. 523.

The long-term commitments involved in distribution channels can become particularly difficult if the contract between the company and the channel member is not carefully drafted. It is normal to prescribe a time limit and a minimum sales level to be achieved, in addition to the particular responsibilities of each party. If this is not carried out satisfactorily, the company may be stuck with a weak performer that either cannot be removed or is very costly to buy out from the contract.

Contract duration is important, especially when an agreement is signed with a new distributor. In general, distribution agreements should be for a specified, relatively short period (one or two years). The initial contract with a new distributor should stipulate a trial period of either three or six months, possibly with minimum purchase requirements. Duration is also dependent on the local laws and their stipulations on distributor agreements.

Geographic boundaries for the distributor should be determined with care, especially by smaller firms. Future expansion of the product market might be complicated if a distributor claims rights to certain territories. The marketer should retain the right to distribute products independently, reserving the right to certain customers.

The payment section of the contract should stipulate the methods of payment as well as how the distributor or agent is to draw compensation. Distributors derive compensation from various discounts, such as the functional discount, whereas agents earn a commission on a specific percentage of net sales (typically 10–20 per cent). Given the volatility of currency markets, the agreement should also state the currency to be used.

Product and conditions of sale need to be agreed on. The products or product lines included should be stipulated, as well as the functions and responsibilities of the intermediary in terms of carrying the goods in inventory, providing service in conjunction with them, and promoting them. Conditions of sale determine which party is to be responsible for some of the expenses (e.g. marketing expenses) involved, which will in turn have an effect on the price to the distributor. These conditions include credit and shipment terms.

Means of communication between the parties must be stipulated in the agreement if a marketer–distributor relationship is to succeed. The marketer should have access to all information concerning the marketing of its products in the distributor's territory, including past records, present situation assessments and market research.

Motivating

Geographic and cultural distance make the process of motivating channel members difficult. Motivating is also difficult because intermediaries are not owned by the company. Since intermediaries are independent firms, they will seek to achieve their own objectives, which will not always match the objective of the manufacturer. The marketer may offer both monetary and psychological rewards. Intermediaries will be strongly influenced by the earnings potential of the product. If the trade margin is poor and sales are difficult to achieve, intermediaries will lose interest in the product. They will concentrate upon products with a more rewarding response to selling efforts, since they make their sales and profits from their own assortment of products and services from different companies.

It is important to keep in regular contact with agents and distributors. A consistent flow of all relevant types of communication will stimulate interest and sales performance. The marketer may place one person in charge of distributor-related communications and put into effect an exchange of personnel so that both organizations gain further insight into the workings of the other.

Controlling

Control problems are reduced substantially if intermediaries are selected carefully. However, control should be sought through the common development of written performance objectives. These performance objectives might include some of the following: sales turnover per year, market share growth rate, introduction of new products, price charged and marketing communications support. Control should be exercised through periodic personal meetings.

Evaluation of performance has to be done against the changing environment. In some situations, economic recession or fierce competition prevents the possibility of objectives being met. However, if poor performance is established, the contract between the company and the channel member will have to be reconsidered and perhaps terminated.

Termination

Typical reasons for the termination of a channel relationship are as follows:

- the marketer has established a sales subsidiary in the country
- the marketer is unsatisfied with the performance of the intermediary.

Open communication is always needed to make the transition smooth. For example, the intermediary can be compensated for investments made, and major customers can be visited jointly to assure them that service will be uninterrupted.

Termination conditions are among the most important considerations in the distribution agreement. The causes of termination vary and the penalties for the international marketer may be substantial. It is especially important to find out what local laws say about termination and to check what type of experience other firms have had in the particular country.

In some countries terminating an ineffective intermediary can be time consuming and expensive. In the EU, one year's average commission is typical for termination without justification. A notice of termination has to be given three to six months in advance. If the cause for termination is the manufacturer's establishment of a local sales subsidiary, then the international marketer may consider engaging good employees from the intermediary as, for example, managers in the new sales subsidiary. This can prevent a loss of product know-how that has been created at the intermediary's firm. The marketer could also consider an acquisition of this firm if the intermediary is willing to sell.

13.8 Managing logistics

Logistics is used as a term to describe the movement of goods and services between suppliers and end users. It is about moving products to the right place in the right quantities at the right time, and in a cost-efficient manner.

Two major phases in the movement of materials are of logistical importance. The first phase is *materials management*, or the timely movement of raw materials, parts and supplies into and through the firm. The second phase is *physical distribution*, or the movement of the firm's finished product to its customers. The basic goal of logistics management is the effective coordination of both phases and their various components to result in maximum cost-effectiveness while maintaining service goals and requirements.

The primary area of concern in this section is the second phase: that is, order handling, transportation, inventory and storage/warehousing.

Order handling

Order handling refers to how the company receives, fills, and delivers orders to customers. New technologies, such as electronic data interchange and bar coding, have had a remarkable effect on system design, which in turn has improved the effectiveness and efficiency of order management. Electronic data interchange is an exchange by computer of orders and other business documents in standard formats.

Customer service standards will have a major bearing on the design of the physical distribution system. Companies that want good order fulfilment rate, order cycle time, delivery reliability, and invoice accuracy must be prepared to invest heavily in network design. Often, managers find they must lower the desired standard somewhat because the costs of achieving an ideal level are prohibitive. One approach is to recognize that all customers are not equal. As a general rule, a small percentage of a company's customers, often 20 per cent or less, provide over 80 per cent of its revenue. Customer service standards can be set higher for the firm's most important customers. Scarce resources can be saved by lowering customer service standards, at least to some extent, with less important customers.

Order cycles are shortened by rapid processing of orders, and the role of communications technology is critical in reducing the time factor. Not all countries have efficient and reliable communication systems; however, possessing an efficient international order-processing system would give a firm a competitive advantage.

Transportation

This deals primarily with the mode of transportation, which usually constitutes 10–15 per cent of the costs of imported goods. There are four main modes of transport: road, water, air and rail. You will find a more comprehensive explanation of the four transport modes in, for example, Hollensen (2001).

Freight forwarders

Freight forwarders provide an important service to exporters. The full-service foreign freight forwarder can relieve the producer of most of the burdens of distribution across national borders. This is particularly so for small and medium-sized companies and those that are inexperienced in exporting. Freight forwarders provide a wide range of services, but the general activities and services provided are:

- coordination of transport services
- preparation and processing of international transport documents
- provision of warehousing
- expert advice.

The traditional view of the freight forwarder is that of a provider of services, a company that does not own transport facilities but which buys from the most appropriate transport provider, and a company that acts as the agent of the exporter. Various changes have taken place which have had an impact on freight forwarders. There has been a tendency for transport companies to extend their activities to include an in-house forwarding function. In addition, larger and more experienced exporters have developed their own in-house transport and documentation expertise. Both these trends have threatened the freight forwarder.

Inventory (at the factory base)

The purpose of establishing inventory – to maintain product movement in the delivery pipeline, in order to satisfy demand – is the same for domestic and international inventory systems.

There are many different cost elements involved in managing an inventory: storage, interest on capital tied up, taxes, lost sales, etc. Since these costs may sometimes be sizeable, management must be concerned about inventory control. This involves determining the proper level of inventory to hold, so that a balance is maintained between customer service and inventory cost.

In deciding the level of inventory to be maintained, the marketer must consider two factors.

Order cycle time

This is the total time that passes between the placement of an order by a customer and the receipt of the goods. Depending on the choice of transportation mode, delivery times may vary considerably. As a result, the marketer has to keep a larger safety stock in order to be able to satisfy demand in any circumstance. However, the marketer could attempt to reduce order cycle time, thereby reducing costs, by altering the transportation method, changing inventory locations, or shifting order placement to direct entry on a computer.

Customer service levels

This is the ability to fulfil customer orders within a certain time. For example, if within three days 80 per cent of the orders can be fulfilled, the customer service level is 80 per cent within three days. The choice of customer service level for the firm has a major impact on the inventories needed. Because high customer service levels are costly (inventory constitutes tied-up capital), the goal should not be the highest level possible but rather an acceptable level, based on customer expectations. For some products, customers may not demand or expect quick delivery. In addition, if higher customer service levels result in higher prices, this may reduce the competitiveness of a firm's product.

Besides these two factors, international inventories can also be used as a strategic tool in dealing with exchange rate changes or hedging against inflation.

Storage/warehousing

Sometimes goods and materials need to be stored. However, this activity involves more than just storage. In addition to storing products in anticipation of consumer demand, warehousing encompasses a broad range of other activities, such as assembling, breaking bulk shipments into smaller sizes to meet customer needs, and preparing products for reshipment.

Warehousing decisions focus on three main issues:

- where the firm's customers are located
- the pattern of existing and future demands
- the customer service level required (i.e. how quickly a customer's order should be fulfilled).

The following general observations can be made about warehousing facilities:

- if products need to be delivered quickly, storage facilities will be required near the customer
- for high-value products (e.g. computer software), the location of the warehouse will be of minimal importance as these lightweight products can be moved by air.

Third-party logistics (contract logistics)

A growing preference among firms is to use outside logistical expertise. The main thrust behind the idea is that individual firms are experts in their industry and should therefore concentrate only on their operations. **Third-party logistics**

providers, on the other hand, are experts solely at logistics, with the knowledge and means to perform efficient and innovative services for those companies that require it. The goal is improved service at equal or lower cost.

One of the greatest benefits of contracting out the logistics function in a market is the ability to take advantage of an existing network complete with resources and experience. The local expertise and image are crucial when a business is just starting up.

One of the main arguments levelled against contract logistics is the loss of the firm's control in the supply chain. Yet contract logistics does not and should not require the handing over of control. Rather, it offers concentration on one's core competence, a division of labour. The control and responsibility towards the customer remain with the firm, even though operations may move to a highly trained outside organization.

13.9 Normative implications for selecting and managing distributors

Research shows that multi-nationals need to do a better job of selecting and working with local distributors. In particular, they must understand that distributors are implementers of marketing strategy, rather than marketing departments in the country markets (Arnold, 2000).

Manufacturers often face the classic trade-off: wanting to control their business expansion abroad, but at the same time benefit from local market knowledge and minimizing costs and risk.

Finding the right balance in this trade-off is very difficult for many manufacturers. Based on a field study of manufacturers' international distribution strategies in 250 new country markets, Arnold (2000) suggests the following seven guidlines for manufacturers planning to enter new international markets.

1. *Select distributors. Don't let them select you.* Entering a new international market should be the result of a pro-active market assessment.

2. *Look for distributors capable of developing markets, rather than those with a few obvious customer contacts.* The most obvious distributor is not necessarily the best partner in the long run. This means bypassing the obvious choice – a distributor who has the right customers and can therefore generate quick sales – in favour of a partner with a greater willingness to invest and an acceptance of an open relationship that draws on the manufacturers' experience in marketing its products.

3. *Treat the local distributors as long-term partners, not temporary market-entry vehicles.* This means structuring the relationships so that distributors become marketing partners willing to invest in long-term market development. One traditional way of doing this is to grant national exclusivity to a distributor, although such an agreement can become unproductive if conflicts of interest arise once entry is established. A more effective solution is to create an agreement with strong incentives for appropriate goals.

4. *Support market entry by committing money, managers, and proven marketing ideas.* Traditionally, manufacturers have demonstrated commitment by sending in technical and sales personnel or offering training to distributor employees. Such

support is good, but more experienced manufacturers now go further and do things earlier. In markets regarded as strategically important, they have started to take minority equity stakes in autonomous distribution companies. Although this increases investment and risk without achieving control, it opens the door to cooperative marketing based on shared information.

5. *From the start, maintain control over marketing strategy.* Manufacturers committed to maintaining early control over marketing strategy find that it is important to have employees on-site. Some send a few employees to work full time at the local distributor's offices. Others send their regional sales manager on frequent visits to the distributor's office to keep a close watch on distributor performance and local customer need.

6. *Make sure distributors provide you with detailed market and financial performance data.* In many countries, the distributors are the only sources of such information. A contract with a distributor must therefore require detailed market and financial performance data as the ability to exploit competitive advantages in a new market depends heavily on the quality of information obtained from the market.

7. *Build links among national distributors at the earliest opportunity.* After entering a new market, the manufacturer should try to create links among its regional distributors (in the country) as soon as possible. The transfer of marketing ideas among local distributors might improve performance in local markets and might be used as leverage in other similar markets, i.e. using marketing synergies across borders. The result of implementing these guidelines might be better working relationships between the manufacturer and the local distributor. Once the manufacturer understands that it can control its international operations through better relationship structures rather than simply through ownership, it might also find longer-term roles for local distributors.

13.10 Implications of the Internet for distribution decisions

The Internet has the power to change drastically the balance of power among consumers, retailers, distributors, manufacturers and service providers. Some participants in the distribution chain may experience an increase in their power and profitability. Others will experience the reverse; some may even find that they have been bypassed and have lost their market share.

Physical distributors and dealers of goods and services that are more conveniently ordered and/or delivered online are indeed subject to increasing pressure from e-commerce. This disintermediation process, with increasing direct sales through the Internet, leads manufacturers to compete with their resellers, which results in channel conflict.

The extent to which these effects are salient depends upon which of the following four Internet distribution strategies are adopted by the manufacturer.

Present only product information on the Internet

As less than 5 per cent of retail sales (in both Europe and the USA) currently occur over the Internet, only a few manufacturers would be willing to endanger their relationships with their distributors for that volume. The risk of distribution

| Exhibit 13.4 | Compaq creates distributor alliances |

In 1999, Compaq Computer Corp. decided to cut its distribution relationships from 39 to 4 in the United States, not only to keep better control of inventory, but also to improve its response time to changes in market conditions. The vendor uses inventory analysts to work with the four distributors to gain a better understanding of which products and models move better than others and why. Compaq's goal is to use the demand forecasts that are coming in from its field organizations and distributor partners and to make sure it has the right mix of product at the right time so it can meet customer expectations. As part of its distributor alliance programme, Compaq's inventory analysts work at the locations of the four distributors – Ingram Micro Inc., Merisel Inc., Tech Data Corp., and Inacom Corp.

Source: adapted from Rosa (1999).

conflicts with the existing distributors would be too great. So, manufacturers may decide not to sell their products through the Internet and prohibit their resellers also from using the Internet for sales. Only product information is provided on the Internet, with any customer queries being passed on to the appropriate channel member. In industries such as aircraft manufacturing, where sales are large, complex and customized, this may be an appropriate strategy.

Leave Internet business for distributors

Some companies prefer distributors to leave the Internet business for resellers and not to sell directly through the Internet. How effective this strategy is depends on the existing distribution structure. It can be effective when manufacturers assign exclusive territories to resellers, since resellers can be restricted to either delivering only to customers within their assigned territory or they can be compensated through profit pass-over agreements if they are adversely affected. Any leads generated by the manufacturer's website are passed on to the appropriate regional reseller.

In contrast, for intensively distributed products where resellers have no assigned territories, resellers simply compete with each other as they would do in the normal, physical marketplace. The global nature of the Internet creates price transparency, which may conflict with differential prices charged by the manufacturer in various markets. Another limitation of this approach is that most consumers search for manufacturers' websites rather than resellers' websites. Inability to purchase from the manufacturer's website can be frustrating for the consumer and can result in lost sales for the manufacturer.

Leave Internet business to the manufacturer

A third strategy for the manufacturer is to restrict Internet sales exclusively to itself. This strategy is only profitable if the manufacturer has a business model that is aligned with sales through the Internet. The business system of most manufacturers (such as consumer packaged goods companies) is not set up for sales to end users who place numerous small orders. Alternatively, by selling through the Internet a manufacturer may aim not to generate profits, but rather to learn about this new channel of distribution, collect information on consumers, or build its brand. But regardless of a manufacturer's objectives, resellers dislike having to yield the market space to manufacturers.

If a manufacturer uses this strategy it also risks channel conflicts, i.e. creating competition with its own customers (distributors). The PC manufacturer Compaq also realized this when it struggled to exploit the Internet, because to do so properly would mean bypassing its distributors. For Compaq it was difficult to remit sales through the Internet without upsetting distributors and jeopardizing its historically strong relationships with them. In order to limit the direct competition with its customers, Compaq introduced a differentiated product-line of PCs, Prosignia, for sales through the Internet (Kumar, 1999).

Open Internet business to everybody

The fourth strategy is to let the market decide the winners and open the Internet to everybody – for direct sales and resellers. Manufacturers who have ventured online, either through this strategy, or by restricting Internet sales to themselves, usually sell at retail prices and/or provide only a limited range because of their desire not to compete with their resellers. However, this limits the attractiveness of the Internet's value proposition.

Conclusion

The fear of cannibalizing existing distribution channels and potential channel conflict requires manufacturers to trade off existing sales through the traditional

---

Exhibit 13.5

Vin & Sprit achieves more control with worldwide distribution of Absolut Vodka in an alliance with Jim Beam brands

Absolut Vodka was distributed by Seagram for the six years up to June 2000. However, the decision by the Canadian conglomerate to pull out of spirits and concentrate on its media business left Vin & Sprit struggling to find a distributor for its premium brand.

Absolut Vodka was the world's seventh-largest spirits brand by value in 1999, selling around 6 million cases for a total value of US$1.23 billion. The company sold 7 million cases in 2000.

These sales figures are similar to famous brand names such as Johnnie Walker, Bacardi and Hennessy as well as value leader Stolichnaya vodka, but the Russian distiller's US$1.98 billion 1999 sales were generated on a far higher volume of 55 million cases.

In March 2001 Sweden's government-controlled Vin & Sprit and US-based Fortune Brands Inc. teamed up to distribute Absolut Vodka in a joint venture creating the number two spirits vendor in the USA.

Vin & Sprit paid US$270 million for a 49% stake in Future Brands LLC, a new jointly owned distribution company whose portfolio would include products such as Absolut, Jim Beam bourbon and DeKuyper fruit spirits.

The company would purchase a 10% equity stake in Jim Beam Brands worldwide unit for US$375 million, with an option to increase the stake by another 9.9% over the next few years.

Jim Beam Brands generated worldwide sales of more than US$1.2 billion in 2000, with more than half of its 28 million case volume sold in the USA.

The Absolut Vodka–Jim Beam relationship would help the two companies to achieve cost savings and scale in a consolidating retail environment.

Source: adapted from CNN (2001), Adweek (2001).

distribution network and potential future sales through the Internet. Unfortunately, history suggests that most companies tend to stay with declining distribution networks for too long.

13.11 Retailing

In the continuing integration of the world economy, internationalization not only concerns advertising, banking and manufacturing industries, it also affects the retailing business. The trend in all industrialized countries is towards larger units and more self-service. The number of retail outlets is dwindling, but the average size is increasing.

However, retailing still shows great differences between countries, reflecting different histories, geography, culture and economic development.

Trade marketing

For too long manufacturers have viewed vertical marketing channels as closed systems, operating as separate, static entities. The most important factors creating long-term, integrated strategic plans and fostering productive channel relationships were largely ignored. Fortunately, a new philosophy about channel management has emerged, but to understand its potential we must first understand how power has developed at the retailer level.

Power in channel relationships can be defined as the ability of a channel member to control the marketing decision variables of any other member in a channel at a different level of distribution. A classic example of this is the amount of power wielded by retailers against the food and grocery manufacturers. As the balance of power has shifted, more merchandise is controlled by fewer and fewer retailers.

There is a worldwide tendency towards concentration in retailing. A consequence of this development is that there has been a worldwide shift from manufacturer to retailer dominance. Power has become concentrated in the hands of fewer and fewer retailers, and the manufacturers have been left with little choice but to accede to their demands. This often results in manufacturing the retailers' own brands (private labels).

Therefore, we can see that traditional channel management, with its characteristics of power struggles, conflict and loose relationships, is no longer beneficial. New ideas are emerging to help channel relationships become more cooperative. This is what is known as **trade marketing**. Trade marketing is when the manufacturer (supplier) markets directly to the trade (retailers) to create a better fit between product and outlet. The objective is to create joint marketing and strategic plans for mutual profitability.

For the manufacturer (supplier), it means creating twin marketing strategies: one to the consumer and another to the trade (retailers). However, as Figure 13.9 shows, potential channel conflicts exist because of differences in the objectives of the channel members.

Despite potential channel conflicts, what both parties share, but often forget, is their common goal of consumer satisfaction. If the desired result is to create joint marketing plans, a prerequisite must be an improved understanding of the other's perspective and objectives.

Figure 13.9 Channel relationships and the concept of trade marketing

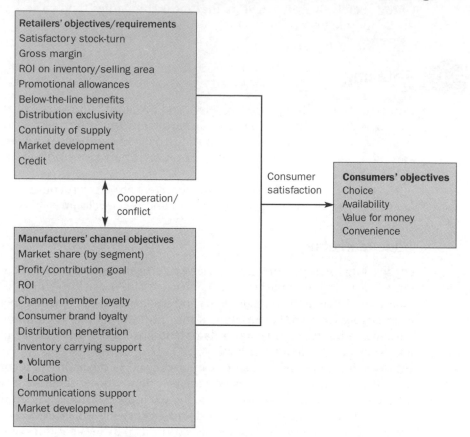

Source: Hollensen (2001), p. 507.

Retailers are looking for potential sales, profitability, exclusivity in promotions and volume. They are currently in the enviable position of being able to choose brands which fulfil those aims.

A private label manufacturer has to create different packages for different retailers. By carefully designing individual packages, the manufacturer gains a better chance of striking up a relationship with the best-matched retailer.

Manufacturers can offer retailers a total support package by stressing their own strengths. These include marketing knowledge and experience, market position, proven new product success, media support and exposure, and a high return on investment in shelf space.

If a joint strategy is going to be successful, manufacturers and retailers must work together at every level, perhaps by matching counterparts in each organization. As a consequence of the increasing importance of the individual customer, the concept of the key account (key customer) was introduced. Key accounts are often large retail chains with a large turnover (in total as well as of the supplier's products), which are able to decide quantity and price on behalf of different outlets.

Segmentation of customers is therefore no longer based only on size and geographic position, but also on customers' (retailers') structure of decision making. This results in a gradual restructuring of sales from a geographic division to a customer division. This reorganization is made visible by employing key account managers (managers responsible for customers).

ECR (efficient consumer response) in retailing

Twenty years ago, consumer goods manufacturers managed the distribution channel with advertising campaigns that pulled new products through the channel and with trade promotions used by a sales force that pushed the product down the channel. Such a push/pull strategy often does not work today, and the reason has to do with not only faster and more accurate ordering processes and cycles, but also faster and more reliable quick-response delivery processes that now use tracking information to move bar-coded products down the distribution channel. The combination of these new computer-driven order and delivery processes is called efficient consumer response.

Efficient consumer response (ECR) programmes are designed to improve the efficiency of replenishing, delivering, and stocking inventory while promoting customer value. Enhanced cooperation among channel members in order to eliminate activities that do not add value is a primary goal.

In the past, the presence of many slow-moving finished goods held in inventory by wholesalers and retailers helped manufacturers 'own' distribution channels because channel members had to move these mountains of manufacturers' goods to make a living. Now distribution channels carry small inventories of particular manufacturers' products, making the wholesalers and retailers less dependent on manufacturers. Conversely, with so little stock in distribution channels, what income manufacturers make next week almost literally depends on what they sell today. As a result, a problem with a major distribution channel has immediate effects on manufacturing and cash flow. A manufacturer has a short time to negotiate, to react, and at worst to switch some of its business to another distribution channel.

Exhibit 13.6 | **Xerox is 'promoting' channel conflicts**

Xerox General Market Operations (GMO) is a business of US$6 billion in sales and 6000 employees. Xerox uses a multiple channel approach, and it does not avoid channel conflicts.

According to Xerox Corporation's highest ranked female executive, Anne Mulcahy,

Those that don't aggressively embrace multiple channels for multiple products will get left behind. The inherent conflict in this business model is not only a reality of business; it's a sign of a healthy company.

Xerox's GMO, which offers products and software for networked groups and small/home office environments, recently launched a marketing campaign that uses the web and direct mail to generate leads for each of its product lines. Another significant source of leads is Xerox's website, where customers access product information and learn how to buy direct or through a partner. 'More and more customers are coming to the web to learn about products before they go to a retail store,' Mulcahy said.

A major focus for GMO is convincing account salespeople to represent Xerox's total solution, even though some of those products, such as printers, are typically fulfilled through an indirect channel. The goal is for account representatives to use their customer relationships to generate leads across all product lines.

Source: adapted from Cohen (2000).

13.12 Mystery shopping in retailing

Mystery shopping is a process for measuring service quality, with feedback, that is understandable to the front-line people in retailing. It is a form of participant observation, using researchers to act as customers or potential customers to monitor the quality of processes and procedures used in the delivery of a service. The need for specific performance information stems from the increasing emphasis being placed on service performance by service managers. While service standards are invariably set by head office staff and senior management, the task of delivering these standards falls to individual customer-facing personnel. Variations in service performance can have a major impact on customer satisfaction.

The stages in the mystery shopping process are now highlighted (Erstad, 1998; Wilson, 1998).

Step 1: The objectives

Know what you want to get out of the shopping programme. The objectives should be related to having satisfied customers as well as satisfied employees. Mystery shopping is meant to reinforce positive behaviour and modify improper behaviour, but not to punish.

The various objectives for mystery shopping programmes are:

- to act as a diagnostic tool identifying failings and weak points in an organization's service delivery, especially the customer contacts of the front-line personnel

- to encourage, develop and motivate service personnel by linking with appraisal, training and reward mechanisms; and to enable marketers to scrutinize and fine tune the human element

- to assess the competitiveness of an organization's service provision by benchmarking it against the offerings of others in an industry in order to identify areas that need training or further training. It can also be used to reveal how employee contact with customers is positive.

Step 2: The evaluation form

Use employees to define and set the measurable standards to be met. Find out what customers value and incorporate these into the evaluation form.

Often a significant amount of effort is put into positioning the mystery shopping research within an organization prior to the research being undertaken. Seminars, presentations and newsletters are used to explain the purpose of the research, the standards against which the service is being measured and the manner in which the mystery shopping result will feed into appraisal and reward systems. Pre-notification of this type was generally seen as being successful with most organizations, finding a high degree of staff acceptance.

In principle, there are two different ways of evaluating the service quality:

- most often mystery shoppers visit the shop posing as an average anonymous customer. Mystery shoppers do not want to call any attention to themselves, so they blend with the other customers in the shop, while observing the customer service and sales skills of the personnel. After leaving the shop, they file a report which is forwarded to the client.

- another way for mystery shoppers to obtain the information from front-line employees is to meet them in focus groups or individually to discuss the employee's impressions and experience with the customer and the service delivery system. Results from these interviews are then used to prepare a list of characteristics the employees view as important to customers.

Which main method to use is up to the company, but staff acceptance of mystery shopping is seen as being critical if the results are to be taken seriously by the service personnel and if industrial relations within the organization are not to suffer.

Shopper evaluations can be in the form of a checklist or an open, customized format which is more time consuming to complete. In formulating the specific shopper questions, a question asking 'Was the employee helpful?' does not provide concrete information on the service system. A question probing for more information is suggested: 'How did the employee describe the product or service?'

The service rating gives points on a scale of one to ten on the overall standard of service. Points are given for a specific action or attributes. For example, a welcoming smile is worth four points, being well-dressed is worth two points. Service standards that are to be evaluated must be made clear to the employee and should be easily measurable by the internal or external mystery shopper.

Step 3: The mystery shopper

Select, inform, and train the mystery shopper in line with the company's objectives. The shopper must match a customer profile that is appropriate for the scenario that is being enacted.

In selecting the mystery shopper, the company must also decide whether it will use in-house personnel or external shoppers. The in-house shoppers are usually quality control experts from corporate headquarters. The advantages with this type of shopper may be lower cost and better knowledge of the company's objectives and products. However, the cost of using corporate personnel may be hidden in the overall budget. Negative aspects of the in-house approach refer to employee reactions to being reported by someone within the company, and a stronger chance of the shopper being recognized.

External shoppers are employed temporarily, and do not require an ongoing salary, thus lowering overhead costs. The use of external mystery shoppers may have certain drawbacks. Obtaining consistent evaluations from external shoppers requires the shopper to be well briefed. A high turnover of mystery shoppers may also influence the quality of the evaluation.

Training and briefing the mystery shoppers is important, including data collection skills. Shoppers receive a detailed briefing on the scenario that they are to enact focusing on their personal characteristics, the questions they should ask and the behaviours they should adopt. They are then tested on these elements to ensure that the service encounter is realistic and reduce the opportunity for the true identity of the mystery shopper to be detected by the service personnel.

The training in data collection skills focuses on identifying the elements of the service to be observed as well as the retention and recording of the information. Retention and recording of information is particularly important, as the shoppers cannot complete an assessment form during the service encounter. Therefore shoppers should receive memory training and testing.

Step 4: Conducting the shop visit

Produce an unbiased, mainly objective evaluation (but include a limited amount of subjective information) of the shop.

With the objectives of the shopping visit in mind, an evaluation checklist or more subjective information collection form in hand, and any training that might be necessary, the mystery shopper is ready to conduct the visit.

Branches and employees involved in the mystery shopping programme could be forewarned of the visit. Some companies remind their employees continuously of the mystery shopper by using posters behind the counter where customers cannot see them. Other companies use stickers attached to workstations to remind employees of service standards.

Step 5: The analysis

Identify gaps in the service delivery and determine their origin.

The information obtained from the shopping visit is matched to the pre-established objectives and standards to determine outstanding performance as well as any gaps that might exist. Identifying the reasons for the gaps is the challenge of management and employees participating in the programme.

Results from mystery shopper visits should be analysed with the history of previous shopper visits in mind, not as a one-off event.

In order to increase the reliability, the mystery shopper evaluation can be cross-checked with results from other sources such as customer contact cards, management reports, and customer satisfaction surveys.

Step 6: The action needed

Develop a reward and incentive scheme related to employee performance in mystery shopping programmes. Provide coaching to further develop employees' technical and behavioural skills. Work on the service delivery system if gaps exist because of poor design. Repeat the mystery shopper visit.

The results of individual shopping visits should not go to senior management, but to the people directly involved, including the front-line employees. Data have to be communicated positively and in a way that is relevant to those involved. Once the programme has been completed with a series of visits and results have been tracked, recorded, and improvements made, a report of the mystery shopper study should be sent to senior management. Management must be informed of the value that has been obtained from the shopping programmes (Morrall, 1994) and any changes needed to improve customer service.

Coaching is the key to dealing with service delivery problems arising from lack of training. Mystery shopping evaluations provide information on what skills need to be developed. Employees can attend off-site training programmes in small groups where they perform role plays and work on service delivery.

In terms of motivation, the mystery shopping results can be used to reward those service teams who are performing well against the set service standards. Rewards mentioned by respondents ranged from simply taking the form of recognition through team league tables and team awards to being incorporated with sales per-

Exhibit 13.7	Mystery shopping at Bose Corporation

Bose Corporation (USA) has a reputation for excellence as a manufacturer of top quality loudspeakers and other audio equipment.

To make sure employees extend the pursuit of excellence to the retail setting, Bose has been using mystery shopping since 1995 to monitor performance of salespeople at its factory stores – which sell new and factory renewed products – and at its Bose showcase stores – which sell new merchandise. Mystery shopping is also conducted at department stores and electronic superstores where Bose products are sold.

For Bose, it is important for employees to greet customers within 10 seconds of arrival in the store. They should introduce themselves, or, if they are busy with another customer, acknowledge their presence with a nod or other gesture. Once with the customer they must be friendly, helpful and demonstrate product knowledge.

One of the key things the customers have told Bose that its salespeople can do to increase satisfaction is make the customers feel welcome.

The Bose mystery shopping has two parts. It begins with a phone call, in which the shopper calls to ask questions on specific products. Shoppers indicate if the employee performed tasks such as answering questions clearly. Employees are also rated on their friendliness, helpfulness, etc., using an excellent-satisfactory-unsatisfactory scale. Finally, shoppers have space to write about their interaction and support the ratings they gave the employee.

For the visit, shoppers describe how/if they were greeted, their evaluation of the employee in charge of the greater presentation (Bose stores contain a theatre for presenting a short audio-visual show which highlights Bose equipment), the employee's selling and closing skills and exploration of customer needs (did the employee use language which helped you picture having the product in your home?), product demonstration and knowledge (did the employee describe and demonstrate the benefits?), and overall impressions (did the Bose representative make you feel important, provide a comfortable environment?). At the factory stores, shoppers must note if the employee volunteered an explanation of factory-renewed products during their visit.

Mystery shoppers are instructed to complete the forms immediately after the experience, while everything is still fresh in their mind.

Mystery shoppers are also sent to other retailers that sell Bose equipment. The shopper notes how long it took to be noticed by a salesperson, when/if the salesperson steered them toward Bose products, if a demonstration was conducted and if the Bose equipment was in good order (no broken/missing parts) and positioned for optimal sound quality.

Each Bose store receives a quarterly summary showing the staff's overall performance. The district and store managers also get copies of the shopper's report. The stores use the mystery shopping data as a tool to show where they are doing well and where there are opportunities to do better. They can use it as a basis for a staff meeting, to look at things they can do to improve.

Depending on each store's overall performance, the employee team, including managers, are awarded a customer satisfaction bonus.

Individual employees are also noted only for outstanding service; however, they are not singled out if they perform poorly.

Source: adapted from Rydholm (1998).

formance in determining levels of financial reward. Financial rewards and incentives are becoming more common in almost all sectors, but particularly in financial services, travel agents and retail outlets.

In general, mystery shopping tends to lead to improvements in quality of service. However, in the longer term, the novelty of being 'shopped' can wear off leaving personnel complacent about their service and lacking motivation to take steps to improve it further. To overcome this, standards need to be constantly updated and staff need to see the ultimate consequences and rewards of mystery shopping.

13.13 Summary

In this chapter we have examined the management of international distribution channels and logistics. From the discussion it is evident that the marketer has a broad range of alternatives for selecting and developing an economical, efficient and high-volume international distribution channel.

In many instances, the channel structure is affected by external factors and it may vary from country to country. Physical distribution (external logistics) concerns the flow of goods from the manufacturer to the customer. This is one area where cost savings through efficiency are feasible, provided the decision is made systematically. The changing nature of retailing influences distribution planning. During the last decade, the balance of power (between manufacturers and retailers) has shifted in favour of the retailers. The manufacturer often has no other choice than to cooperate with large and increasingly concentrated retailers in terms of the 'trade marketing' concept.

Mystery shopping is getting a customer's view of the retail business and is widely recognized as a valuable marketing and customer service tool. Mystery shoppers visit the business, posing as an average customer. They evaluate what they find based on criteria established by the company.

Case study 13.2 Red Bull

The energy drink that gives you 'wings' attempts to penetrate US distribution channels

Having sprung from humble beginnings in Bangkok, Red Bull now sells 1 billion cans annually in 50 countries. In 1999, Red Bull sales were US$700 million; this increased to over US$1 billion in 2000. Single cans of the energy drink outsold single cans of Coke in the UK, according to Zenith International, a beverage consultancy. Its maker, Ted Bull GmbH, is estimated to be worth US$10 billion, making it Austria's most valuable enterprise.

This is not bad for a drink that was once dubbed 'the poor man's coffee' in Asia. Krating Daeng, as Red Bull is known in Thailand, is one of many health tonics sold in little brown bottles throughout Asia. A mixture of vitamin Bs, taurine (an animo acid that increases the metabolism), caffeine and sugar, most tonics taste like supersweet cough syrup. Found in pharmacies and **convenience stores** from Tokyo to Jakarta, they are caffeine-full favourites of worn-out people.

Thailand, in particular, is the land of 'energy in a bottle', as the Thais dub them. The health-tonic industry there generates 12 billion baht (US$285 million) a year. Krating Daeng is the best-selling label, accounting for half of the health tonic sold in the country.

Today, Dietrich Mateschitz is one of the richest men in Austria, but a lot has happened since

Case study 13.2 continued

he was a salesman for toothpaste and shampoo in Thailand. Mateschitz discovered Red Bull while selling toothpaste in Bangkok in 1984.

Believing the drink could be just as popular in Europe, he approached the Yoovidhya family, which owns TC Pharmaceuticals, the company that manufactures the drink. They sold Mateschitz foreign licensing rights in exchange for a 51 per cent stake in his Austrian Red Bull company. The family has remained a silent partner, leaving the entrepreneur to build and run his own business.

Armed with the secret formula, Mateschitz returned home and spent the next year tinkering with the taste and texture of the tonic. His version of Red Bull emerged as a carbonated, watered-down version of Krating Daeng's syrup. It was packaged in sleek silver and blue cans (Figure 13.10).

Next came the marketing plan. As a former Procter & Gamble salesman, Mateschitz realized the importance of branding. With Johannes Kastner, a friend who ran his own advertising agency, he set out to draft a strategy. It only took a year to formulate the drink, but it took two years to put a marketing strategy together.

And that has been the key to Mateschitz's success: investing time and money to make an entirely new brand image for a different market. It is something most Asian companies fail to do, assuming that what works at home will work just as well abroad. Even today, long after his brand has been established in most countries, Mateschitz pours 25 per cent of his earnings back into marketing.

He realized it would be impossible to convince middle-aged blue-collar workers in Austria to give up their morning coffee. Instead, he targeted 'active, modern people' who were 'endurance junkies'. The team created a Red Bull cartoon that was more New Yorker than Disney. Its tagline is: 'Red Bull gives you wiiings'.

Extreme sports, like snowboarding and Formula One racing, have been crucial to Red Bull's marketing. The company sponsors extreme-sports events in Europe like the mountain-biking competition Mountain Mayhem, and Flugtag, in which amateur pilots take to the air in home-made flying machines.

Figure 13.10 Red Bull

The extreme image has proved a winner. Red Bull has become the drink of choice for ravers, extreme-sports fanatics and Internet entrepreneurs.

Sales have grown from 1 million cans in 1987 to 920 million cans in 2000. The sales history is shown in Table 13.4.

Day and Robinson (2000) suggest that 59 per cent of consumers aged 18 to 24 are prepared to try new drink brands compared with only 47 per cent a decade before. But this increasing willingness to experiment is a double-edged sword for marketers. Although it has led to a growth in repertoire drinking (that is, changing brand choices according to time of day, location

▶

Case study 13.2 continued

Table 13.4 The expansion of the Red Bull brand

Year	Sales volume (million cans)	Sales revenue (€million)
1987	1	0.8
1988	2	1.6
1989	3	2.8
1990	7	5.2
1991	15	11.6
1992	25	19.6
1993	36	27.6
1994	114	90.8
1995	125	100.9
1996	142	107.5
1997	206	157.7
1998	320	252.8
1999	622	518.4
2000	920	740
2001	1320 (projected)	1100 (projected)
2002	1675 (projected)	1300 (projected)

Source: adapted from Clef (2001).

and who they are with) and expansion of consumers' drinks portfolios, it has also reduced brand loyalty. This has forced manufacturers to defend existing brands with increasing vigour – and expense.

With competition already intense in the low-growth beverages market, the trend towards greater brand promiscuity makes it even more important for manufacturers to get product offerings – new or old – right.

Consumers increasingly want products that comply exactly with their requirements at a particular time, so it is essential manufacturers identify and respond to these needs.

For most beverage manufacturers, the young adult market is perhaps the most important of all. Young adults are open to marketing messages, often have high levels of disposable income and devote much time to socializing.

It is also one of the most volatile markets for brand loyalty, as their tastes and values change quickly. But affinities made with brands in young adulthood can often be retained throughout later life.

Young adults are open to innovations in the majority of soft drink sectors, in particular bottled water, new-age beverages, such as herbal and health-enhancing drinks, juices, and energy drinks. The latter category is the most youth-oriented. Red Bull, for example, is now an almost iconic brand in youth marketing. It fits the perceived young adult lifestyle of working hard and playing hard, with connotations of club culture in its promotion and advertising.

While many drink Red Bull straight from the can, others quaff the energy tonic with alcoholic mixers. The drink has become a favourite cocktail ingredient – Red Bull claims almost 50 per cent of all sales are made in bars and clubs.

The European market for energy drinks

The UK market

The largest market for Red Bull in Europe is the UK market. Red Bull has become Britain's third biggest soft drink by value behind Coke and Pepsi, according to the Zenith International 2001 UK Energy and Sports Drinks report (Brabbs, 2001).

The report is the first of its kind to combine on and off trade (premise) figures and, as a result, Red Bull's sales, especially within bars and nightclubs, have risen above other soft drink brands such as Tango, Robinsons and Sunny Delight.

Within the retail sector alone, Coke had sales of £664.2 million in 2000, Pepsi £177.7 million and Red Bull £59.9 million. In 1999, Red Bull held a 75 per cent share of the functional energy drink market, growing in 2000 to an 86 per cent share.

The energy and sports drinks category is now worth over £700 million a year, with Red Bull's total sales in 2000 nearing £430 million. Lucozade's combined sales for its Energy and Sport brands was £210 million.

The report also shows, using A. C. Nielsen figures for retail and on-premise outlets, that functional energy drinks have almost doubled in sales value in 2000, after trebling in 1999. Sports drinks are also up by 50 per cent since 1998 (Brabbs, 2001).

Though Red Bull is the most popular drink in the energy drink sector, it faces increasing competition from the following.

Case study 13.2 continued

Anheuser-Busch (maker of Budweiser)
The new orange-flavoured drink, 180, contains vitamins B_6, B_{12} and C, as well as guarana, a plant-based energizer. The drink will be targeted at young professionals who want to increase their energy after a workout or while clubbing, or those needing a morning or afternoon pick-me-up.

Coca-Cola
Coke's energy drink Burn was launched in the UK before Christmas 2000 and the company says it is 'proving to be very popular' (Marketing Week, 2001a).

GlaxoSmithKline
GlaxoSmithKline (GSK) looks set to rethink its Lucozade Solstis brand, effectively admitting defeat to Red Bull in its challenge to take a slice of the high-energy drinks market. The company is understood to be 'reformulating' and developing an energy drink that will be repositioned as an 'afternoon pick-me-up' (Marketing Week, 2001b).

Scottish Courage
Scottish Courage is entering the energy drinks market with the launch of its non-alcoholic high-energy mixer Red Snapper. In a direct swipe at its best-selling rival, the product will be marketed under the strapline 'More bite than bull'. Red Snapper has been developed as a 'superstrength' energy mixer for clear spirits such as Vodka. But Harry Drnec, managing director of Red Bull, welcomes the competition, adding: 'We are extremely flattered that one of our customers wants to copy us so closely'.

In Central Europe (including Germany, Austria and Switzerland) new competitive brands are also coming up, like Flying Horse and Cult – both from Austria like Red Bull.

The German market
The German Red Bull market is the second largest in Europe. In 2000, the market share of Red Bull in the energy drink sector was 75 per cent. Flying Horse and private labels had 9 per cent and others 7 per cent. The unaided awareness (in the age group 14–29 years) of Red Bull was 69 per cent and the aided awareness in the same age group was 93 per cent (Clef, 2001).

These figures are also an indicator of the European strength of the brand.

Red Bull attacking the US market
Red Bull arrived in the USA in 1997 but is still available in only 25 states. Red Bull North America's unusual approach to marketing relies on a network of its own extreme sports to promote the brand. Unlike most marketers that sponsor an existing event, Red Bull goes out of its way to create its own, and that gives it a great deal more control in managing the events and influencing the athletes who participate. On the event schedule is the Red Bull Cliff Diving World Tour Finals in Hawaii. There is also Red Bull Wings Over Aspen, a hang-gliding event where competitors zoom through the gates of a downhill slalom ski course in Colorado at 110 km/h. Other annual events include death defying street luge competitions in San Francisco and the Snowthrill of Alaska winter sports event.

In addition to its events, Red Bull sponsors top athletes in a variety of extreme sports including bungee jumping, mountain biking and motocross. Red Bull also has animated commercials airing on network and cable TV, but it uses no print or Internet advertising.

Questions
1. What are the explanations for the international success of Red Bull?
2. Which threats and opportunities is Red Bull facing when planning a further increase in market share in the USA?
3. Outline the future Red Bull distribution plan for the US market. Please use Tables 13.5 and 13.6 as a starting point.

Sources: Beverage Industry (2000), Day and Robinson (2000), Fitzgerals (2000), Brabbs (2001), Clef (2001), Marketing Week (2001a, b, c).

Case study 13.2 continued

Table 13.5   Soft drinks sales in the USA (US$ million)

Segment	Supermarkets	Drug stores	Mass merchandise
Carbonated soft drinks	12,525.2	622.7	2,079.2
Bottled water	1,432.0	120.0	244.0
Coffee	2,868.0	49.9	547.7
Mixer drinks	629.6	5.2	103.0
Aseptic juice	645.9	5.5	127.1
Bottled juice (shelf-stable)	3,241.8	142.0	449.5
Canned juice (shelf-stable)	714.2	5.2	53.1
Instant tea	263.0	1.6	20.3
Loose tea and tea bags	638.9	14.8	77.0
Ready-to-drink tea	450.9	36.6	42.2
Isotonics	700.6	49.2	121.9
Milk	10,179.7	N/A	N/A

Source: adapted from Beverage Industry (2000), p. 29.

Table 13.6   Soft drink sales by US region 1999

Location	Value (US$ million)
Atlanta	146.7
Baltimore/Washington DC	286.1
Boise, Idaho	19.6
Boston	198.6
Charlotte, NC	108.1
Chicago	460.1
Cleveland	75.8
Dallas/Ft Worth	245.2
Denver	185.0
Detroit	227.9
Indianapolis	105.2
Little Rock, AK	37.2
Los Angeles	630.9
Memphis, TN	61.0
Miami/Ft Lauderdale	171.0
Minneapolis/St Paul	138.9
New Orleans/Mobile	164.4
New York City	593.8
Oklahoma City	50.4
Omaha, NE	48.2
Philadelphia	238.6
Phoenix/Tucson	175.7
Salt Lake City	77.1
San Francisco/Oakland	200.4
Seattle/Tacoma	131.4
St Louis	107.9
US category total	12,525.2

Source: adapted from Beverage Industry (2000), p. 30.

QUESTIONS FOR DISCUSSION

1. Discuss current distribution trends in world markets.
2. What are the factors that affect the length, width and number of marketing channels?
3. In attempting to optimize marketing channel performance, which of the following should a marketer emphasize: training, motivation or compensation? Why?
4. When would it be feasible and advisable for a company to centralize the coordination of its foreign market distribution systems? When would decentralization be more appropriate?
5. What is the idea behind 'mystery shopping' in retailing?
6. Why is physical distribution important to the success of global marketing?
7. Discuss the reasons why many exporters make extensive use of the services of freight forwarders.
8. Discuss the implications for the international marketer of the trend towards cross-border retailing.

9. Many markets have relatively large numbers of small retailers. How does this constrain the international marketer?

10. What services would the manufacturer like to receive from the retailer?

REFERENCES

Adweek (2001), Absolut find alternate US entry: Fortune Brands unveils a $740m distribution deal with Swedish firm, **www.adweek.com**. March 20.

Albaum, G., Strandskov, J., Duerr, E. and Dowd, L. (1994), *International Marketing and Export Management*, Addison Wesley, Reading, MA.

Arnold, D. (2000), Seven rules of international distribution, *Harvard Business Review*, November–December, pp. 131–7.

Barth, K., Karch, N. J., Mclaughlin, K. and Shi, C. S. (1996), Global retailing – tempting trouble, *The McKinsey Quarterly*, no. 1, pp. 117–25.

Beverage Industry (2000), Big news is behind the scenes, *Beverage Industry*, New York, March, no. 3, pp 24–32.

Brabbs , C. (2001), Red Bull soars into top three soft drinks, *Marketing*, London, February 8, p. 2.

Bucklin, C. B., Defalco, S. P., DeVincentis, J. R. and Levis III, J. P. (1996), Are you tough enough to manage your channels?, *The McKinsey Quarterly*, no. 1, pp. 105–14.

Cateora, P. R. (1993), *International Marketing*, Irwin, Homewood, IL, 8th edn.

Chee, H. and Harris, R. (1994), *Marketing: A global perspective*, Pitman, London.

Clef, U. (2001), Marketing verleiht Flüüügel, *Absatzwirtschaft, Sonderausgabe*, October, pp. 22–30.

CNN (2001) Vin & Sprit inks Absolut deal, **http://cnnfn.cnn.com**, Financial news.

Cohen, A. (2000), When channel conflict is good, *Sales and Marketing Management*, vol. 15, no. 4, pp. 13–14.

Day, J. and Robinson, R. (2000), Drink responds to fluid needs, *Marketing Week*, August 24 (**www.mad.co.uk**), pp. 25–6.

Dickson, P. R. (1982), Distributor portfolio analysis and channel dependence matrix, *Journal of Marketing*, vol. 47, Summer, pp. 35–44.

EIU (1995), *The EU50 – Corporate case studies in single market success*, Economist Intelligence Unit, Research Report, pp. 77–8.

Erstad, M. (1998), Mystery shopping programmes and human resource management, *International Journal of Contemporary Hospitality Management*, vol. 10, no. 1, pp. 34–8.

Fitzgerals, K. (2000), Red Bull charged up, *Advertising Age*, Chicago, August 22, pp. 26–8.

Hollensen, S. (2001), *Global Marketing: A market responsive approach*, Financial Times/Prentice-Hall, Harlow, 2nd edn.

Jain, S. (1996), *International Marketing Management*, South-Western College Publishing, Cincinnati, OH, 5th edn.

Kumar, N. (1999), Internet distribution strategies: dilemmas for the incumbent, *in Mastering Information Management, Part 7, Electronic Commerce, Financial Times*, March 15.

Lewison, D. M. (1996), *Marketing Management: An overview*, The Dryden Press/Harcourt Brace College Publishers, Fort Worth, TX.

Liu, S. S. and Cheng, M. (2000), Toward a framework for entering China's pharmaceutical market, *Marketing Intelligence & Planning*, May 18, pp. 227–35.

Marketing Week (2001a), Bud branches into energy drinks, *Marketing Week*, January 11, News.

Marketing Week (2001b), Drnec lashes out at rival energy drinks, *Marketing Week*, February 15, News.

Marketing Week (2001c), Scottish Courage to enter energy drinks market with Red Snapper, *Marketing Week*, March 22, News.

McGoldrick, P. J. and Davies, G. (1995), *International Retailing: Trends and strategies*, Pitman, London.

Morrall, K. (1994), Mystery shopping tests service and compliance, *Bank Marketing*, vol. 26, no. 2, pp. 13–15.

Onkvisit, S. and Shaw, J. J. (1993), *International Marketing: Analysis and strategy*, Macmillan, London, 2nd edn.

Paliwoda, S. (1993), *International Marketing*, Heinemann, Oxford.

Pirog III, S. F. and Lancioni, R. (1997), US–Japan distribution channel cost structures: is there a significant difference?, *International Journal of Physical Distribution and Logistics Management*, vol. 27, no. 1, pp. 53–66.

Rosa, J. (1999), Forming an alliance, *Computer Reseller News*, Manhasset, June 21, pp. 49–50.

Rydholm, J. (1998), *Quirk's Marketing Research Review*, January, Article no. 297.

Sletmo, G. K. and Picard, J. (1984), International distribution policies and the role of air freight, *Journal of Business Logistics*, vol. 6, pp. 35–52.

Spegel, R. (2000), Sony shocks Japanese dealers with direct sales web site, *E-Commerce Times*, February 1.

Toyne, B. and Walters, P. G. P. (1993), *Global Marketing Management: A strategic perspective*, Allyn & Bacon, Needham Heights, MA, 2nd edn.

Wall Street Journal (2000), Condomi in alliance with MCM Klosterfrau, *Wall Street Journal*, interactive section, press release, July 27.

Wilson, A. M. (1998), The role of mystery shopping in the measurement of service performance, *Managing Service Quality*, vol. 8, no. 6, pp. 414–20.

Communication decisions

Case study **14.1** Autoliv

The Autoliv–Volvo communication strategy for the launch of a post-crash safety system

Autoliv Inc. develops and manufactures car safety systems for all major car manufacturers in the world. Together with its joint ventures, Autoliv has close to 80 facilities with almost 30,000 employees in more than 30 countries. In addition, the company has eight technical centres, including 19 test tracks, more than any other car safety supplier. Sales in 2000 amounted to US$4.1 billion and net income US$170 million.

With its successful growth strategy, Autoliv has become the global leader in the expanding US$12 billion car safety market (also called the car occupant restraint market). Airbags account for just over 50% of that market, seat belts for almost 30% and electronics for nearly 20%.

Airbag market

The world market for airbags was an area of spectacular growth during the 1990s. In 2000, the number of frontal airbag units installed was approximately 90 million (up from about 35 million in 1995) and the number of side-impact airbags nearly 35 million. Much of the growth is currently offset, however, by strong pressure on prices.

In the USA, frontal airbags – both on the driver and the passenger side – are required by federal law in all new light vehicles sold after September 1, 1998. The US market for frontal airbags therefore fluctuates with the car production cycle, but sales of side airbags are now about to take off. They were installed in less

▶

Case study 14.1 continued

than 15% of new US light vehicles in 2000. Both Ford and General Motors have announced aggressive plans for curtain airbags such as Autoliv's inflatable curtain[1]. In addition, new regulations in the US will require vehicle manufacturers to phase in more valuable advanced airbags during a three year period starting on September 1, 2003.

In Europe, Autoliv estimates that currently over 90% of the new light vehicles have a driver airbag, and 75% also have an airbag for the other front seat occupant. Installations of side impact airbags began in 1994, but by 2000 over 50% of new cars in Europe had such systems for chest protection. In addition, 15% had separate side impact protection for the head (such as the inflatable curtain).

In Japan, where development started later than in Europe, installation rates for frontal airbags are already as high as in Europe, while the installation rate for side airbags is just over 10%.

In the rest of the world, installation rates vary greatly from country to country, but the average is still less than 40% for both driver and passenger airbags. Installation of side airbags has just started.

Seat belt market

The world market for seat belts keeps growing, despite the fact that seat belts were introduced (by Autoliv, among others) more than 40 years ago. This is mainly because seat belts are becoming increasingly sophisticated with such new features as automatic height adjusters and load limiters.

Autoliv's markets

Autoliv estimates that it currently has approximately one third of the global market for car occupant restraint products and that it has a somewhat higher global market share for airbags than for seat belts. For side airbags, which were

invented by Autoliv and introduced as recently as 1994, Autoliv's global market share is still approximately 50%. Autoliv's global market position is also strong in recent safety improvements.

Autoliv's percentage of sales in different geographical areas is shown in Table 14.1. The most important countries are the USA, Germany, France, Japan, Spain, the UK and Canada. Sweden accounts for almost 5% of sales.

Table 14.1 Autoliv's sales in different regions, 2000

Region	%
Europe	53
North America	33
Japan	9
Other countries	5
	100

Source: adapted from Autoliv's Annual Report (2000).

In North America, Autoliv estimates that, in 2000, it accounted for approximately one third of the airbag market and for one fifth of the seat belt market compared to just over 10% in 1999. Autoliv did not sell seat belts in the USA until 1993. In spring 2000, Autoliv acquired the North American seat belt business of NSK. Autoliv's market share for seat belts also increased as a result of new contracts, and the increasing number of new US vehicles with seat belt pretensioners. Steering wheel sales in the US started in 1998. Based on orders received so far, Autoliv expects its steering wheel market share to approach 10% in just a couple of years.

In Europe, Autoliv estimates its market share to be about 50% with a somewhat higher market share for seat belts than for airbags. The market share for steering wheels is approximately 15%.

In Japan, Autoliv has a strong position in the airbag inflator market and rapidly growing sales of airbag modules. Local assembly of airbag modules began there in 1998. In spring 2000, Autoliv acquired the second largest Japanese steering wheel company with a market share

---

[1] Introduced in 1998 on Volo, Mercedes, Toyota and Audi cars with one inflatable curtain on each side of the vehicle, the heads of the driver and all passengers seated next to the sides are protected in side collisions and roll-over accidents.

Case study 14.1 continued

exceeding 20%, and 40% of NSK's Asian seat belt operations with the option to increase its interest to 100% in two steps in 2002 and 2003. Including NSK's sales, Autoliv accounts for approximately a quarter of the Japanese seat belt market.

In other countries, such as Argentina, Australia, China, India, Malaysia, New Zealand, South Africa and Turkey, where Autoliv established production early, the company has often achieved strong market positions. An important reason for the strong market positions is the early establishment of joint ventures.

Customers

Autoliv's customer base has undergone considerable consolidation during the past five years. In 1995, the six largest vehicle producers accounted for less than 60% of global light vehicle production (about 50 million units per year). By 2000, these companies had increased their combined share to 80%. The largest company alone – GM with affiliates – now accounts for a quarter of global vehicle production.

The largest customers are BMW, Daimler-Chrysler, Ford/Volvo/Mazda, General Motors/Isuzu/Opel/Saab, Peugeot/Citroën, Renault/ Nissan, Toyota and Volkswagen/Audi/ Seat/Skoda. The Appendix to this case study contains a profile of the most important players in the car industry

No customer accounts for more than 10% of Autoliv's sales (not even after the merger of Daimler-Benz and Chrysler).

The contracts of the major manufacturers are typically divided among a car maker's different car models with each contract usually running as long as that car model is being produced. In the development of a new car model, which takes several years, Autoliv in many cases functions as a development partner. This means that Autoliv gives advice on new safety-enhancing products.

Competitors

In the late 1990s, the number of major suppliers of occupant restraint systems was reduced from nine to six. As a result of the consolidation among producers of light vehicles, the new groups that have been formed require suppliers to be cost efficient, and have the capability to deliver the same products to all the new group's plants worldwide.

The four leading car occupant restraint suppliers now account for 80% of the market instead of 50% five years ago. During this period, Autoliv has increased its share to slightly more than 30% and has replaced TRW (a US publicly-traded company) as the market leader. Other important car safety suppliers are Takata (a privately owned, Japanese company), Delphi (the world's largest automotive components supplier) and Breed (an American company which recently emerged from bankruptcy).

Autoliv and Volvo launch new safety system

In September 2000, Autoliv and the leading Swedish car manufacturer Volvo introduced one of the world's first post-crash safety systems, 'Volvo On Call'.

Volvo today has 76,400 employees, production in 25 countries and operates in more than 185 markets. The Volvo Group's total sales amounted to SEK 130 billion (£9 billion) in 2000. Volvo is one of the world's largest producers of trucks, buses and construction equipment and holds a leading position in the fields of marine and industrial power systems and aircraft engine components. From 1999 onwards, the Volvo Group focused exclusively on transport equipment for commercial use, which creates the conditions for increased synergies and improved competitiveness. The new safety system is a crash-robust system that automatically calls the EMS (emergency medical service) centre after a crash and gives the rescue team the exact location of the accident.

So far, passive car safety systems, such as airbags and seat belts, have mainly focused on 'in-crash' systems. These are systems that reduce the risk of injury when a crash happens.

The new concept represents a major step in Autoliv's total safety system strategy, which is to offer products ranging from pre-crash (installing infrared cameras in the car to improve a driver's night vision) and in-crash systems to post-crash systems.

►

Case study 14.1 continued

The system's main components are a cellular telephone, a built-in GPS unit and a multiplex communication unit.

In the Volvo On Call system notification is made almost instantly when any of the car's airbags are deployed. The car's electronic multiplex system registers this deployment and forwards the information to the car's integrated telephone, which sends a text message to a Volvo On Call alarm centre. In tandem, a voice line is opened so an operator at the alarm centre can try to talk to the car occupants and find out more about the accident. If, however, no one in the car is able to answer, the operator can send an ambulance directly to the vehicle. The vehicle's location is provided by the car's GPS unit and relayed as a part of the alarm text message.

The phone has, of course, been tested in collisions so that it can cope with extremely high stresses. In addition, it has its own back-up system with an integrated antenna and an emergency battery. This allows it to contact the alarm centre in the unlikely event that the phone is disconnected from its cradle by a very violent crash.

To resolve the concern of limited coverage in certain areas in North America, an additional satellite data link is provided in these markets to ensure uninterrupted access to the alarm centres. The sub-systems are integrated into one robust, easy-to-install unit that is designed to withstand very severe crashes. The new system is the result of a joint development project between Volvo and Autoliv, but the telecommunications company Ericsson has also been involved.

The driver can also press an SOS button to alert the alarm centre in the case of, for instance, an assault. There is also a button for road assistance if the car breaks down or there is traffic congestion and the driver wants to know the best way around it. Additionally, the system can be used to find the car if it has been stolen. The alarm centre can then obtain the location of the car, even if the phone is switched off. The owner can also get help if he or she has lost the car keys. By stating a security code, the alarm centre can contact the car's electrical system and unlock the doors.

The new Volvo On Call was introduced on the Volvo SGO, which was launched in August 2000.

Appendix: The global car (light vehicle) industry 2001–2

The world car industry is under pressure to consolidate, but it is already one of the most multi-national industries, with the biggest firms owning subsidiaries around the world. There are five major groups: General Motors, Ford, DaimlerChrysler, Toyota and Volkswagen.

Of these only Toyota relies on one global brand name. All the others have subsidiaries around the world. Both BMW and DaimlerChrysler have invested in major new facilities in North America. Others, including Audi and General Motors, are investing in countries on the periphery of the European Union – notably Hungary and Poland.

As the industry becomes truly a global concern, so the scope for shifting investment and production grows. However, a key problem in both Europe and North America is over-capacity.

Despite strong market growth, production in western Europe has stagnated at about 14.4 million cars a year. Yet the estimated capacity has grown to over 21 million cars per annum. That means Europe can produce over 6 million more cars than can be sold.

The following describes the world's biggest car producers.

General Motors (GM)

General Motors is the world's largest car company, based in Detroit, MI. It produces more than 8 million cars and trucks (light vehicles) a year (see Table 14.2). GM pioneered the development of different brands. In the USA it sells cars under the Cadillac, Chevrolet, Pontiac, Buick, and Oldsmobile marques, and more recently it developed the Saturn as a separate, Japanese-style quality car brand.

GM is one of the largest car producers in Europe, using the Vauxhall marque in the UK and Opel in the rest of Europe. More recently, it acquired a controlling stake in Sweden's Saab Motors which it continues to operate as a separate marque.

Appendix continued

In Australia, GM operates one of the country's most well-known marques, Holden. It also has a tie-up with the Japanese car and truck maker Isuzu. In Latin America the company has a major subsidiary in Brazil, which makes engines and Opel cars.

GM recently purchased a 20% stake in the world's seventh largest car maker, Fiat, and holds the right of first refusal to buy the rest. The two companies plan joint marketing and engine production in Europe and Latin America.

GM's profits in the USA have been dropping, and it recently announced plant closures in both Europe and America.

Ford

Ford, the main US rival to GM, is the world's second largest car company, and the most profitable, earning more than US$20 billion in 1999. However, Teather (2002) reported that Ford was 'bloated' and likely to report a loss of US$2 billion for 2001! Unlike GM, it has tended to market cars under its own label – until recently. It was one of the first US companies to set up production abroad, moving to Dagenham in the UK in the 1920s. In the USA it also markets cars under the Lincoln and Mercury marques.

In recent years, it has acquired the luxury car makers Jaguar and Aston Martin in the UK and a big stake in Japan's number three car company, Mazda.

Ford has been highly profitable in recent years and even after its purchase of Volvo it still has funds for further acquisitions. Ford acquired Land-Rover from BMW in 2000.

Volkswagen

Volkswagen, Germany's largest car maker, has been aggressive in acquiring other car companies throughout Europe. To complement its own cars and Germany's upmarket Audi marque which it bought in the 1970s, it has spent a great deal of money to try to acquire the Rolls-Royce car factory, only to be beaten by BMW, which will own the marque after 2003, leaving VW with the Bentley marque and the manufacturing plant.

It is still thought to be interested in acquiring BMW, its longstanding German rival.

It has moved into eastern Europe, buying the main car company in the Czech Republic, Skoda, which it has re-invigorated with its own reputation for quality. It operates the Seat subsidiary in Spain. Volkswagen has sought out more luxury marques to add to its range, buying up Italy's Lamborghini and Bugatti.

The company also produces cars in the USA and Latin America.

DaimlerChrysler

The merger of Germany's Daimler-Benz and the US-based Chrysler Corporation created the world's third largest car group. Chrysler markets cars under the Plymouth and Dodge marques, as well as sports utility vehicles under the Jeep marque. It has a very profitable range of minivans or people carriers.

The addition of Mercedes Benz cars gives the group a complete spread of models, from basic to luxury.

DaimlerChrysler has the world's largest truck business, marketing its Mercedes trucks and owning Freightliner in the USA. However, the merger has run into difficulties, with many Chrysler executives leaving the firm and profits in North America tumbling.

Toyota

Toyota is Japan's biggest car company and the most successful exporter of cars in the world. It has suffered like other Japanese car makers from the Japanese recession which hit sales in its home market, but its more efficient production methods and economies of scale have allowed it to remain independent, unlike other Japanese car makers. However, it had to cut back further on costs, squeezing its Japanese suppliers and moving some production overseas.

Toyota has been successful in Europe and the USA, with a reputation for reliability. The company has also created a successful luxury marque, the Lexus, which has overtaken many European luxury makes in the US market.

Renault/Nissan and the others

In the second tier are the European car makers Renault, Peugeot-Citroën, and Fiat, most of which lack a global presence.

Renault, formerly state owned, is the only one that has tried to become a global player in its own right, buying a controlling stake in Japan's Nissan, which was in financial difficulty. It has begun a sharp cost-cutting programme in Japan, as well as in its European plants. Nissan has major production plants in the UK and the USA.

Renault's main rival, Peugeot-Citroën, is looking increasingly vulnerable in the overcrowded European market, despite making a series of popular models.

▶

Appendix continued

Table 14.2 Total light vehicle production, 2002 (estimate – 000s)

Manufacturer	HQ	Europe	North America	Japan/ Korea	South America	Rest of the world[1]	Total worldwide
General Motors	USA	1989	4895	53	606	498	8041
Ford Motor Company	USA	2203	4047	844	303	377	7774
DaimlerChrysler	Germany/ USA	1664	2775	1100	56	808	6403
Toyota	Japan	342	1287	4035	69	1066	6799
Volkswagen	Germany	3571	382	–	619	528	5100
Renault/Nissan	France/ Japan	2524	625	1359	186	172	4866
Honda	Japan	188	1223	1307	56	184	2958
PSA (Citroën and Peugeot)	France	2627	–	–	117	99	2843
Fiat	Italy	1845	–	–	522	77	2444
Hyundai	S Korea	10	–	2105	14	49	2178
Suzuki	Japan	211	48	916	11	950	2136
Daewoo	S Korea	87	–	530	–	48	665
Fuji Heavy	Japan	–	116	445	–	–	561
BMW	Germany	768	115	–	–	48	931
Other manufacturers		1527	–	–	–	818	2345
Total light vehicle production		19,556	15,513	12,694	2559	5722	56,044

[1] Rest of world includes Australia, China, India, Indonesia, Malaysia, Philippines, South Africa, Taiwan, Thailand.

Fiat now owns the old Italian marques Alfa Romeo, Ferrari, Maserati and Lancia. But after many merger rumours, it has now sold a major stake to GM, and ruled out other merger partners.

BMW, the other main European car maker, and MG Rover, which it sold in 2000, both look too small to survive in the long term, although BMW is still profitable in the luxury niche.

Questions

1. Describe Autoliv's role as sub-supplier for large car manufacturers in a market that is characterized by consolidation.

2. Which car manufacturer should Autoliv target to strengthen its global competitive position (please refer to the Appendix)?

3. What strategic alternatives does Autoliv have to strengthen its competitive position outside Europe? Give a conclusion.

4. Suggest a communications strategy for the launch of the post-crash safety system (Volvo On Call) for customers other than Volvo.

Sources: adapted from: National Post (1999), Autoliv (2000), Autoliv annual report 2000, BBC (2000a, b), CSM (2002),

14.1 Introduction

Communication is the fourth part of the global marketing programme. The role of communication in global marketing is similar to that in domestic operations: to communicate with customers so as to provide the information that buyers need to make purchasing decisions. Although the communication mix carries information of interest to the customer, in the end it is designed to persuade the customer to buy a product, at the present time or in the future.

Marketers need to ensure that all elements of the marketing mix – product, price, promotion (communication), and place – are working together. This chapter deals with communication, which is broader than promotion but includes it within its scope.

Communication is the exchange of information between or among parties. It involves sharing points of view and is at the heart of forming relationships. You simply cannot connect with customers unless you communicate with them. Promotion is the process whereby marketers inform, educate, persuade, remind, and reinforce consumers through communication. It is designed to influence buyers and other groups. Although most marketing communications are aimed at consumers, a significant number also address shareholders, employees, channel members, suppliers, and society. In addition, we will see that effective communication works in two directions: receiving messages is often as important as sending them. **Integrated marketing communication (IMC)** is the coordination of advertising, sales promotion, personal selling, public relations and sponsorship to reach consumers with a powerful unified effect. These five elements should not be considered as separate entities. In fact, each element of the communication plan often has an effect on the other.

Clearly the Internet offers exciting new targeting opportunities that will increasingly affect the way marketers combine and orchestrate various communication activities to create the most effective IMC mix.

To communicate with and influence customers, several tools are available. Advertising is usually the most visible component of the promotion mix, but personal selling, exhibitions, sales promotions, publicity (PR) and direct marketing (including the Internet) are also part of a viable international promotion mix.

One important strategic consideration is whether to standardize the promotion mix worldwide or to adapt it to the environment of each country. Another consideration is the availability of media, which varies around the world.

For many years there has been considerable debate about how advertising works. Researchers agree that there can be no single all-embracing theory that explains how all advertising works.

One of the models is the frequently advocated **AIDA** model, where a person passes through the stages of awareness, interest, desire and action. According to this model, advertising is strong enough to increase people's knowledge and change people's attitudes and as a consequence is capable of persuading people who have not previously bought a brand. It is therefore a conversion theory of advertising: non-buyers are converted to buyers. Advertising is assumed to have a powerful influence on consumers.

Other hierarchy of effects models tend to describe the same processes from different viewpoints. After AIDA, the most quoted model within the advertising industry is DAGMAR (defining advertising goals for measuring advertising results) which splits the process into four steps of awareness, comprehension, conviction, and action.

These models are all limited by certain forces. Although they may work in a cold sales call, in other complex marketing situations they do not take into account time and experience. One major weakness is that they fail to take into account the history of the brand. Buying decisions are rarely made in isolation. They are an accumulation of months, even years, of experience on the part of the buyer.

14.2 The communication process

Opinion leadership

Marketing communications reach customers directly and indirectly. Figure 14.1 illustrates both paths. In *one-step communication*, all members of the target audience are simultaneously exposed to the same message. *Multiple-step communication* uses influential members of the target audience, known as **opinion leaders**, to filter a message before it reaches other group members, modifying its effect positively or negatively for the rest of the group.

Because of their important role, opinion leaders have often been called gatekeepers to indicate the control they have over ideas flowing into the group. Marketers interested in maximizing communication effectiveness nearly always attempt to identify opinion leaders. Opinion leaders are open to communication from all sources. They are more inclined to be aware of information regarding a broad range of subjects. They read a lot, talk with salespeople and other people who have information on products. Opinion leaders can intensify the strength of the message if they respond positively and pass it on to others, especially if it is going on through the mass media. Consequently, the resources used to gain support from opinion leaders are probably well spent.

Public figures are often opinion leaders. Consider the sales boost after Oprah Winfrey introduced her book of the month club feature. She has influenced so many consumers with her highly regarded opinion that her selections have become bestsellers.

Buyer initiative in the communication process

In considering the communication process we normally think about a manufacturer (sender) transmitting a message through any form of media to an identifiable

Figure 14.1 Opinion leadership in the communication process

One-step communication (direct)

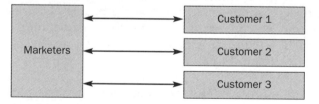

Multi-step communication

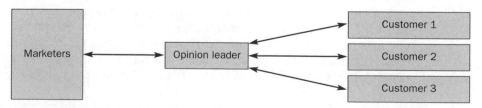

target segment audience. Here the seller is the initiator of the communication process. However, if the seller and the buyer have already established a relationship, it is likely that the initiative for the communication process will come from the buyer. If the buyer has a positive post-purchase experience with a given offering in one period of time, this may dispose the buyer to buy again on later occasions: that is, take initiatives in the form of making enquiries or placing orders (so-called reverse marketing).

The likely development of the split between total sales volume attributable to buyer and seller initiatives is shown in Figure 14.2. The relative share of sales volume attributable to buyer initiative will tend to increase over time. Present and future buyer initiatives are a function of all aspects of a firm's past market performance: that is, the extent, nature and timing of seller initiative, the competitiveness of offerings, post-purchase experience, the relationships developed with buyers as well as the way in which buyer initiative has been dealt with (Ottesen, 1995).

Key attributes of effective communication

All effective marketing communication has four elements: a sender, a message, a communication channel and a receiver (audience).

To communicate in an effective way, the sender needs to have a clear understanding of the purpose of the message, the audience to be reached and how this audience will interpret and respond to the message. However, sometimes the audience cannot hear clearly what the sender is trying to say about its product because of the 'noise' of rival manufacturers making similar and often contradictory claims about their products.

Figure 14.2 The shift from seller initiative to buyer initiative in buyer-seller relationships

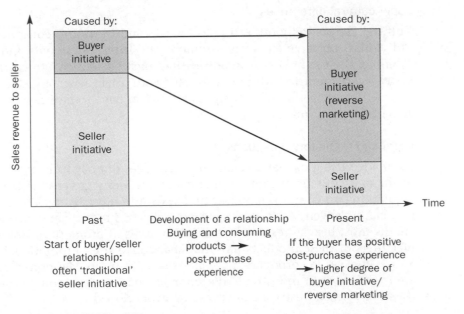

Source: Hollensen (2001), p. 516.

Another important point to consider is the degree of fit between medium and message. For example, a complex and wordy message would be better for the press than for a visual medium such as television or cinema.

Other factors affecting communication

Language differences

A slogan or advertising copy that is effective in one language may mean something different in another language. Thus, the trade names, sales presentation materials and advertisements used by firms in their domestic markets may have to be adapted and translated when used in other markets.

There are many examples of unfortunate translations of brand names and slogans. One of General Motors' models in the UK was called the Vauxhall Nova – in Spanish it means 'it does not go'. In Latin America, 'Avoid embarrassment – use Parker pens' was translated as 'Avoid pregnancy – use Parker pens'.

A Danish company made the following translation for its cat litter in the UK: 'Sand for cat piss'. Unsurprisingly, sales of the firm's cat litter did not increase! Another Danish company translated 'teats for baby bottles' as 'loose tits'. In Copenhagen Airport the following poster could be seen until recently: 'We take your baggage and send it in all directions'. A slogan thus used to express a wish of giving good service might give rise to some concern as to where the baggage might end up (Joensen, 1997).

Economic differences

In contrast to industrialized countries, developing countries may have radios but not television sets. In countries with low levels of literacy, written communication may not be as effective as visual or oral communication.

Socio-cultural differences

Cultural factors (religion, attitudes, social conditions and education) affect how individuals perceive their environment and interpret signals and symbols. For example, the use of colour in advertising must be sensitive to cultural norms. In many Asian countries, white is associated with grief; hence an advertisement for a detergent where whiteness is emphasized would have to be altered for promotional activities in, say, India.

Legal and regulatory conditions

Local advertising regulations and industry codes directly influence the selection of media and content of promotional materials. Many governments maintain tight regulations on content, language and sexism in advertising. The type of product that can be advertised is also regulated. Tobacco products and alcoholic beverages are the most heavily regulated products in terms of promotion. However, the manufacturers of these products have not abandoned their promotional efforts. Philip Morris engages in corporate-image advertising using its Marlboro man. Regulations are found more in industrialized economies than in developing economies, where the advertising industry is not yet as highly developed.

Competitive differences

As competitors vary from country to country in terms of number, size, type and promotional strategies used, a firm may have to adapt its promotional strategy and the timing of its efforts to the local environment.

Exhibit 14.1 **International advertising campaign to reduce birth rate among cats**

People for the Ethical Treatment of Animals (PETA), based in Norfolk, Virginia, has launched a cutting edge TV advert drawing attention to the international overpopulation of cats. Even with all the attention over the last decade on spaying and neutering, millions of cats and dogs are still being killed every year.

The spot entitled Bad Cats amusingly but realistically depicts cats having sex and encourages viewers to visit www.fixedcats.com for more information on spaying and neutering their pets. The spot was launched in early 2001 on The Tonight Show, which is shown across North America and in other parts of the world. Other markets and TV shows are under consideration for the spot.

Source: adapted from Adage Global (2001).

Push versus pull strategies

Where a marketer uses any form of distribution channel, he or she is faced with two extremes in terms of promotion. Marketers attempt to influence the market through either a **push** or **pull strategy**, as illustrated in Figure 14.3. In many cases they use both strategies.

Pull strategy

A pull strategy attempts to influence consumers directly. Communication is designed to build demand so consumers will pull the product through the channel of distribution. In other words, consumers ask retailers for the product, who in turn ask wholesalers, who in turn contact the manufacturer. When pursuing this strategy, a manufacturer focuses primarily on building selective demand and brand loyalty among potential customers through media advertising, consumer promotion, extended warranties and customer service, product improvements, line extensions, and other actions aimed at winning customer preference. Thus, by building strong consumer demand, the manufacturer increases its ability to promote economic rewards in the form of large sales volumes to its channel members in return for their cooperation.

Push strategy

The push strategy involves communicating to distribution channel members, who in turn promote to the end user. This is particularly common in industrial or business-to-business marketing. Marketers often train distribution channel members on the sales techniques they believe are most suited to their products. The push technique is also used in retail marketing.

Smaller firms with limited resources, those without established reputations as good marketers, and those attempting to gain better channel support for existing

Figure 14.3 Push versus pull strategies

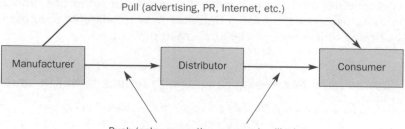

products with relatively small shares and volumes often have difficulty achieving relationships with end customers.

In such situations firms usually adopt a push strategy in which much of the product's marketing budget is devoted to direct inducements to gain the cooperation of wholesalers and/or retailers. Typically, a manufacturer offers channel members a number of rewards, each aimed at motivating them to perform a specific function or activity on the product's behalf. The rationale is that by motivating more wholesalers or retailers to carry and aggressively sell the product, more customers are exposed and persuaded to buy it.

It thus tends to revolve around sales promotion and is sometimes referred to as **'below the line'**. This term is derived from the days when advertising agencies managed all promotional activity, and the items on the accounts that did not relate to advertising were put below the line that divided the agency's main activity on the expenditure reports. This technique is particularly favoured by organizations without strong brands that are involved in price competition.

Often, a combined push-pull strategy is appropriate. The combination approach sells to the channel and to the end user. This can speed product adoption and strengthen market share. As we learned in Chapter 13, conflicts often occur between the marketing organization and its distributors. For example, in the food industry, retailers want to carry products that yield the greatest profitability. Since these may not be brands with the strongest pull, retailers may charge marketers for shelf space. Essentially, they are being paid to push the product to the end user. Using a pull strategy to create strong demand at the consumer level makes channel members more willing to handle the product.

With a pull strategy the marketer aims promotional effort (typically advertising) at the end customer in the belief that he or she will be motivated to 'pull' the product through the channel (by demanding it from retailers, for example). Due to its association with advertising, it is sometimes referred to as **'above the line'**. This technique is usually favoured by the owners of strong, differentiated brands, such as Procter & Gamble or Nestlé.

Mass customization, one-to-one marketing and the push-pull strategy

As shown in the following, new trends in product manufacturing have a great impact on the way that firms communicate more and more directly to the customer.

The phrase mass customization is striking, for it seems a contradiction in terms. Mass production implies uniform products, whereas customization connotes small-scale crafts. Combining the best of both promises exciting choices for consumers and new opportunities for business.

The concept of mass customization is about allowing companies to produce products tailored to customers' requirements. It is really an extension of product differentiation. The traditional form of product differentiation involves changing the product characteristics to differentiate one firm's product from another firm's. Differentiation can also assume the role of distinguishing several of a single firm's products from each other. The goal is to fit the product to the customer's needs better. The ultimate goal of mass customization is to fit the product and communication to the customer's needs perfectly. This one-to-one marketing relationship is difficult to achieve because of its nature and complexity.

Pitta (1998) proposed four basic steps companies must go through to practise one-to-one principles.

Identify customers

Companies must know their customers. It is vital to learn which are the heavy, medium, light and non-users of your products. When companies identify consumers who will never purchase their products at all, they can stop spending money and effort trying to win them over. They simply will not purchase. More important, it is vital to learn who are the loyal customers. They represent the best prospects for company success and are the company's most valued asset. It is important for companies to take the right actions to ensure they keep their business, forever.

Differentiate each customer

Identifying the most valuable customers, recognizing their unique preferences and needs, and treating them differently is the essence of one-to-one marketing. Customers have different needs from the firm, and from each other. Moreover, they have different values to the organization. The value of a customer determines how much time and investment should be allocated to that customer, and a customer's needs represent the key to keeping and to growing that customer's business. This applies both to individual consumers and to industrial customers.

Interact with each customer

Interacting with your customers is another one-to-one marketing fundamental. Every contact with a customer represents the opportunity to learn more about his needs and his value to the organization. In some cases, direct contact will be possible and considerable thought should go into how maximum learning can take place. In some cases, direct questions will be possible. In others, consumers will make choices and the firm can infer customer preferences.

Customize products for each customer

This seems logical and apparent, but producing and delivering a product customized to an individual customer is the most difficult principle to put into practice. It is difficult. If it were not, everyone would already be doing it. The difficulty depends in part on successful completion of the previous three steps.

Customization may create competitive advantages, but it is also a big challenge to implement it. It is only made possible by integrating the production process with a firm's customer feedback. A company that has been able to implement successful mass customization is Dell Computer. Dell's story is by now a familiar one. Over the web, customers select what they want from hundreds of different components to configure the computer of their choice, which Dell builds only when it has the money for it. The company has become the envy of manufacturers of all kinds.

But mass customization is not necessarily feasible for all goods. Assembling cars, for example, is more complex and difficult than building computers. Still, car companies such as BMW, Ford, and General Motors have high hopes for the build-to-order (BTO) approach (equivalent to one-to-one marketing), a variant of mass customization.

Agrawal *et al.* (2001) are very doubtful about the benefits of BTO in the car industry. Moving from a mass manufacturing (or push) system of production, which car makers have continually refined over the years, to a BTO (or pull) system, would require numerous operational and organizational changes throughout the car industry value chain (see Figure 14.4).

However, the payoff of a BTO strategy is unclear. Luxury-car buyers seem eager to specify their preferences in great detail. But it is still too early to tell whether mainstream customers want their vehicles built to order.

Figure 14.4 Push and pull strategies in the car industry value chain

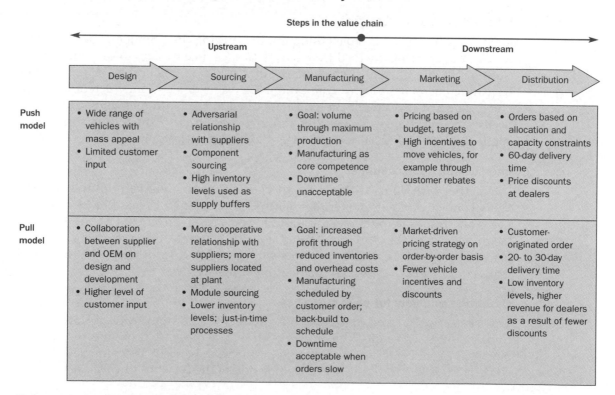

Source: adapted from Agrawal *et al.* (2000), p. 64.

Yet, a true pull system would mean a massive reduction in finished goods (for both the manufacturers and the dealers) and in component inventories (for both the manufacturers and the suppliers). Industry analysts estimate that if a majority of customers bought cars built to order, the industry could capture as much as 70 per cent of the capital lost or locked up in the present push system – lost when inventory becomes obsolete following a change in models, production processes, and assembly structures, or locked up in components stored to meet unanticipated demand.

Already today some degree of BTO is a reality. At the lowest level, customers (or sometimes dealers) can (via the Internet) check the inventories of various dealers within a given area to see whether a car being sought already exists. Customers can also ask their dealers to order cars from the manufacturer.

Also car makers are trying to achieve BTO by modularizing – that is, by fabricating individual cars not from thousands of distinct parts, but from mere dozens of larger mix-and-match modules. But car makers might have to carry a range of modules, some of which may vary slightly in colour, choice of fabric or even an individual part.

Thus it seems that a balanced selection would not be BTO, but rather locate-to-order. Customers should not care whether the car they purchased was built expressly for them or found for them somewhere in the supply chain, as long as it had the features they wanted and they got it in a reasonable amount of time. Certainly, Dell's customers do not know whether their PCs were actually made for them or pulled from an order queue. For car makers, this is a low-cost solution that is easier to implement than BTO yet likely to provide high customer satisfaction (Agrawal *et al.*, 2001).

Exhibit 14.2	Playtex's Wonderbra

In research, Playtex found that women want a bra that enhances the bust in a gentle, natural way. Wonderbra was developed to provide shape and comfort, but without thick padding.

When Playtex introduced the Wonderbra in 1994, push-up lingerie accounted for less than 3 per cent of the US bra market. By 2000 the figure was 10 per cent of all bra sales at department stores.

The main reason for the success of Wonderbra was the eye-catching 'Hello Boys' campaign, making the brand synonymous with the 'push-up' bra category.

Source: adapted from Kaufman (2000).

14.3 Communication tools

Earlier in this chapter we mentioned the major forms of promotion. In this section the different communication tools, listed in Table 14.3, will be further examined.

Advertising

Advertising is one of the most visible forms of communication. Because of its wide use and its limitations as a one-way method of communication, advertising in international markets is subject to a number of difficulties. Advertising is often the

Table 14.3 Typical communication tools (media)

One-way communication				Two-way communication
Advertising	Public relations	Sales promotion	Direct marketing	Personal selling
• Newspapers • Magazines • Journals • Directories • Radio • Television • Cinema • Outdoor	• Annual reports • Corporate image • House magazines • Press relations • Public relations • Events • Lobbying • Sponsorship	• Rebates and price discounts • Catalogues and brochures • Samples, coupons and gifts • Competitions	• Direct mail/database marketing • Internet marketing • Telemarketing	• Sales presentations • Sales force management • Trade fairs and exhibitions

Source: Hollensen (2001), p. 519.

most important part of the communications mix for consumer goods, where there are a large number of small-volume customers who can be reached through mass media. For most business-to-business markets, advertising is less important than the personal selling function.

The major decisions in advertising are shown in Figure 14.5. We will now discuss these different phases.

Objective setting

Although advertising methods may vary from country to country, the major **advertising objectives** remain the same. Major advertising objectives (and means) might include:

● increasing sales from existing customers by encouraging them to increase the frequency of their purchases; maintaining brand loyalty via a strategy that reminds customers of the key advantages of the product; and stimulating impulse purchases

● obtaining new customers by increasing consumer awareness of the firm's products and improving the firm's corporate image among a new target customer group.

Budget decisions

Controversial aspects of advertising include determining a proper method for deciding the size of the promotional budget, and its allocation across markets and over time.

In theory, the firm (in each of its markets) should continue to put more money into advertising, as money spent on advertising returns more money than money spent on anything else. In practice, it is not possible to set an optimum advertising budget. Therefore firms have developed more practical guidelines. The manager must also remember that the advertising budget cannot be regarded in isolation, but has to be seen as one element of the overall marketing mix.

Affordable approach/percentage of sales

These budgeting techniques link advertising expenditure directly to some measure of profits or, more commonly, to sales. The most popular of these methods is the

Figure 14.5 The major advertising decisions

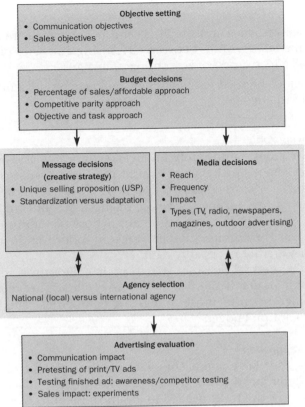

Source: Hollensen (2001), p. 520.

percentage of sales method, whereby the firm automatically allocates a fixed percentage of sales to the advertising budget.

Advantages of this method are:

- for firms selling in many countries, this simple method appears to guarantee equality among the markets. Each market seems to get the advertising it deserves.

- it is easy to justify in budget meetings.

- it guarantees that the firm only spends on advertising as much as it can afford. The method prevents wastage.

Disadvantages of this method are:

- it uses historical performance rather than future performance.

- it ignores the possibility that extra spending on advertising may be necessary when sales are declining, in order to reverse the sales trend by establishing a 'recycle' on the product life cycle curve (see Chapter 11).

- it does not take into account variations in the firm's marketing goals across countries.

- the percentage of sales method encourages local management to maximize sales by using the easiest and most flexible marketing tool: price (that is, lowering the price).

- the method's convenience and simplicity encourage management not to bother investigating the relationships between advertising and sales or analysing critically the overall effectiveness of advertising campaigns.

- the method cannot be used to launch new products or enter new markets (zero sales = zero advertising).

Competitive parity approach

The **competitive parity approach** involves estimating and duplicating the amounts spent on advertising by major rivals. Unfortunately, determining the marketing expenditures of foreign-based competitors is far more difficult than monitoring home country businesses, whose financial accounts (if they are limited companies) are open to public inspection and whose promotional activities are obvious the moment they occur. Another danger in following the practice of competitors is that they are not necessarily right.

Furthermore, the method does not recognize that the firm is in different situations in different markets. If the firm is new to a market, its relationships with customers are different from those of existing companies. This should also be reflected in its promotion budget.

Objective and task approach

The weaknesses of the above approaches have led some firms to follow the **objective and task approach**, which begins by determining the advertising objectives and then ascertaining the tasks needed to attain these objectives. This approach also includes a cost/benefit analysis, relating objectives to the cost of achieving them. To use this method, the firm must have good knowledge of the local market.

Hung and West (1991) showed that only 20 per cent of companies in the USA, Canada and the UK used the objective and task approach. Although it is the theoretically correct way of determining the promotion budget, it is sometimes more important to be operational and to use a percentage of sales approach. This is not necessarily a bad method if company experience shows it to be reasonably successful. If the percentage is flexible, it allows different percentages to be used in different markets.

Message decisions (creative strategy)

This concerns decisions about what **unique selling proposition (USP)** needs to be communicated, and what the communication is intended to achieve in terms of consumer behaviour in the country concerned. These decisions have important implications for the choice of advertising medium, since certain media can better accommodate specific creative requirements (use of colour, written description, high definition, demonstration of the product, etc.) than others.

An important decision for international marketers is whether an advertising campaign developed in the domestic market can be transferred to foreign markets with only minor modifications, such as translation into appropriate languages. Complete standardization of all aspects of a campaign over several foreign markets is rarely attainable. Standardization implies a common message, creative idea,

| Exhibit 14.3 | **Product placement – a marketing communication tool, but also difficult to control** |

Product placement (placing brands in, for example, films) is becoming increasingly important in many companies' communication strategies, as big brand manufacturers begin to recognize its effectiveness.

Reports by lawyers who broker agreements between companies and the film industry show that background brand placement does not generally gain large fees, but if the product constitutes an important element in the story line or is featured prominently during one or more scenes, a substantial fee (possibly several hundred thousand US dollars) may be paid by the manufacturer for the placement.

Here are some examples of product placement.

Mr Destiny

In the film Mr Destiny, Walt Disney Studios charged advertisers US$20,000 for showing a certain product, US$40,000 to show a product and have an actor mention the product name, and US$60,000 for an actor to be shown using a product.

Toy Story

Barbie history was made in Toy Story 2, in which the doll appears on the cinema screen for the first time, in a 'guest appearance'. Clad in her intergalactic mini-skirt and cap, Tour Guide Barbie inadvertently rescues Buzz Lightyear when she just happens to drive by in her zippy 4x4. It's not a major speaking part, and Barbie is certainly not a pivotal character; she has only three, short scenes.

The owner of Barbie, Mattel, refused to allow Barbie to appear in the original Toy Story because they thought the character written for her – a super-feminine action hero – was too strong. But they reconsidered when Toy Story became the third-highest-grossing animated film of all time, behind The Lion King and Aladdin. Mattel sold US$1.6 billion of Barbies in 1999, but it is also aware that girls are abandoning Barbies at younger and younger ages in favour of PCs, video games and other diversions. In response, the company has introduced a Barbie PC and licensed her image on a range of lifestyle, clothing and publishing products.

James Bond and Goldeneye

The 1995 film Goldeneye cost about £35 million to make and the same again to market globally. Striking a deal with BMW, Omega, Smirnoff, Bollinger, and Perrier generated an income of £35 million, enough to pay for marketing the film in 50 countries. BMW alone paid £17 million to ensure its sports car, the Z3, was the Bond car for that film.

PC and videogames

Designers of sports and car racing PC and videogames (e.g. EA (Electronic Arts)) have long sought to include brands associated with their sports, like Quaker Oats' Gatorade or Nike, to make the games look and feel more real. In the past, the games companies often paid licensing fees to display these brands. But as both sectors have become aware of the value of this type of brand exposure, gaming companies have been pushing more often for cross-marketing deals.

These examples show that product placement might be an effective and relatively cheap brand-marketing tool for the marketer. But, as the following Reebok example shows, it is a type of marketing where control is difficult, and the risk of wasting money is also real.

Reebok paid for a one-off uplifting advert, produced by its advertising agency Leo Burnett, to be included in a film. However, weeks before the film's final edit, Tristar executives told the company that the direction of the film had changed and the advert was cut.

▶

Sources: Adapted from Baird (1997), Irish Times (2000), Gunn (2001), Sargent et al. (2001),Schlosser (2001).

Exhibit 14.3 continued

But Reebok had spent £1 million providing products and technical assistance for the film Jerry Maguire. The script included a line saying 'Fuck Reebok' before finally including an uplifting commercial about the sports company towards the end of the film.

This illustrates the difficulty of this form of advertising. When it works, it can be a fairly cheap way of getting the brand worldwide awareness. But when it does not, there is the danger that the brand will not be noticed at all or, worse still, the brand will come out looking bad.

When shooting starts, major companies like Coca-Cola or Anheuser-Busch make sure they have a representative on the set during the shooting of scenes where the product appears. In post-production, that same representative will want to see as many of the rough cuts as possible, to see how the brand is being treated as the film progresses. The aim is to avoid the sort of surprise Reebok executives had when they sat down at a private screening to see that their brand did not come out well.

In Europe, much of product placement takes place on TV rather than film, and most deals are done free. The company provides the product, or gives its service simply to see it on the programme, like in the many European versions of Wheel of Fortune.

media and strategy, but it also requires that the firm's product has a USP that is clearly understood by customers in a cross-cultural environment.

Standardizing international advertising can lead to a number of advantages for the firm. For example, advertising costs will be reduced by centralizing the advertising campaign in the head office and transferring the same campaign from market to market, as opposed to running campaigns from different local offices.

However, running an advertising campaign in multiple markets requires a balance between conveying the message and allowing for local nuances. The adaptation of global ideas can be achieved by various tactics, such as adopting a modular approach, adapting international symbols and using international advertising agencies.

Media decisions

The selection of the media to be used for advertising campaigns needs to be done simultaneously with the development of the message. A key question in media selection is whether to use mass media or a targeted approach. The mass media (television, radio and newsprint) are effective when a significant percentage of the general public are potential customers. This percentage varies considerably by country for most products, depending on, for example, the distribution of incomes in different countries.

The selection of the media to be used in a particular campaign typically starts with some idea of the target market's demographic and psychological characteristics, regional strengths of the product, seasonality of sales, and so on. The media selected should be the result of a careful fit of local advertising objectives, media attributes and target market characteristics. Furthermore, media selection can be based on the following criteria:

- *Reach*: This is the total number of people in a target market exposed to at least one advertisement in a given time period (opportunity to see, or OTS).

- *Frequency*: This is the average number of times within a given time period that each potential customer is exposed to the same advertisement.

- *Impact*: This depends on compatibility between the medium used and the message. *Penthouse* magazine continues to attract advertisers for high-value-added consumer durables, such as cars, hi-fi equipment and clothes, which are geared primarily to a high-income male segment.

High reach is necessary when the firm enters a new market or introduces a new product so that information about, for example, a new product's availability is spread to the widest possible audience. A high level of frequency is appropriate when brand awareness already exists and the message is about informing the consumer that a campaign is under way. Sometimes a campaign should have both a high frequency and extensive reach, but limits on the advertising budget often create the need to trade off frequency against reach.

A media's **gross rating points (GRPs)** are the result of multiplying its reach by the frequency with which an advertisement appears within the media over a certain period. Hence it contains duplicated exposure, but indicates the critical mass of a media effort. GRPs may be estimated for individual vehicles, for entire classes of media or for a total campaign.

The cost of running a media campaign also has to be taken into consideration. Traditionally, media planning is based on a single measure, such as **cost per thousand** GRPs. When dealing with two or more national markets, the selection of media also has to take into account differences in:

- the firm's market objectives across countries
- media effectiveness across countries.

Since media availability and relative importance will not be the same in all countries, plans may require adjustment in cross-border campaigns.

As a way of distributing advertising messages through new communication channels, co-promotion now has a strong foothold.

Let us now take a closer look at the main media types.

Television

Television is an expensive but commonly used medium in attempting to reach broad national markets. In most developed countries, coverage is no problem. However, television is one of the most regulated communications media. Many countries have prohibited the advertising of cigarettes and alcohol other than beer. In other countries (e.g. Scandinavia, the UK) there are limits on the number of minutes that TV advertising is permitted to be shown. Some countries also prohibit commercial breaks in TV programmes.

Radio

Radio is a lower-cost broadcasting activity than television. Commercial radio started several decades before commercial television in many countries. Radio is often transmitted locally and therefore national campaigns have to be built up area by area.

Newspapers

In virtually all urban areas of the world, the population has access to daily newspapers. In fact, the problem for the advertiser is not having too few newspapers, but rather having too many of them. Most countries have one or more newspapers that can be said to have a truly national circulation. However, in many countries newspapers tend to be predominantly local or regional and, as such, serve as the primary medium for local advertisers. Attempting to use a series of local papers to reach a national market is considerably more complex and costly.

Many countries have English-language newspapers in addition to local-language newspapers. For example, the aim of the *Asian Wall Street Journal* is to supply economic information in English to influential Asian business people, politicians, senior government officials and intellectuals.

Magazines

In general, magazines have a narrower readership than newspapers. In most countries, magazines serve to reach specific segments of the population. For technical and industrial products, magazines can be quite effective. Technical business publications tend to be international in their coverage. These publications range from individual businesses (e.g. beverages, construction, textiles) to worldwide industrial magazines covering many industries.

Marketers of international products have the option of using international magazines that have regional editions (e.g. *Newsweek*, *Time* and *Business Week*). In the case of *Reader's Digest*, local-language editions are distributed.

Cinema

In countries where it is common to subsidize the cost of showing films by running commercials prior to the feature film, cinema advertising has become an important medium. India, for example, has a relatively high level of cinema attendance per capita (few have television at home). Therefore cinema advertisements play a much greater role in India than in, for example, the USA.

Cinema advertising has other advantages, one of the most important being that it has a truly captive audience (no channel hopping!).

Outdoor advertising

Outdoor advertising includes posters/billboards, shop signs and transit advertising. This medium shows the creative way in which space can be sold to customers. In the case of transit advertising, for example, a bus can be sold as an advertising medium. In Romania transit advertising is very effective. According to a survey by Mueller (1996), in Bucharest 91 per cent of all consumers surveyed said they remembered the content of transit advertisements, compared with 82 per cent who remembered the content of print adverts. The use of transit media is expanding rapidly in China as well. Outdoor posters/billboards can be used to develop the visual impact of advertising. France is a country associated with the effective use of poster and billboard advertising. In some countries, legal restrictions limit the amount of poster space available.

Agency selection

Confronted with the many complex problems that international advertising involves, many businesses instinctively turn to an advertising agency for advice and practical assistance. Agencies employ or have instant access to expert copywriters, translators, photographers, film makers, package designers and media planners who are skilled and experienced in the international field. Only the largest of big businesses can afford to employ such people in-house.

If the international marketer decides to outsource the international advertising functions, he or she has a variety of options including:

- using different national (local) agencies in the international markets where the firm is present
- using the services of a big international agency with domestic overseas offices.

In Table 14.4 the different factors favouring a national or an international agency are listed. The single European (pan-European) market is used as an example of an international agency. The criteria relevant to the choice of a national or an international agency include the following.

- *Policy of the company*: does the company have any realistic plans for a more standardized advertising approach?
- *Nature of the advertising to be undertaken*: corporate image advertising might be best undertaken by a single large multi-national agency which operates throughout the world via its own subsidiaries. For niche marketing in specialist country sectors, a local agency might be preferred.
- *Type of product*: the campaign for an item that is to be presented in a standardized format, using the same advertising layouts and messages in all countries, might be handled more conveniently by a single multi-national agency.

Table 14.4 European agency selection: national (local) or pan-European (international)

National (local)	Pan-European (international)
• Supports national subsidiary. • Investment in existing brand best handled nationally. • Closer to marketplace. • Smaller size more conducive to personalized service and greater creativity. • Diversity of ideas.	• Reflects new European reality and trends. • Economies of scale in new product development and branding. • Uniformity of treatment across Europe. • Resources and skills of major European or global agency. • Easier to manage one agency.

Source: adapted from Lynch (1994), Table 11.4.

Advertising evaluation

Advertising evaluation and testing is the final stage in the advertising decision process shown in Figure 14.5. Testing advertising effectiveness is normally more difficult in international markets than in domestic markets. An important reason for this is the distance and communication gap between domestic markets and foreign markets. Thus, it can be very difficult to transfer testing methods used in domestic markets to foreign markets. For example, the conditions for interviewing people can vary from country to country. Consequently, many firms try to use sales results as a measure of advertising effectiveness. First we will discuss some testing procedures (the following is primarily based on Griffin (1993)).

Pre-testing print advertisements and direct mail

When an advertising manager doubts which of two print advertisements should be used for a campaign, a split-run **pre-test** can be used to determine the reader response from the two versions. This technique can be used to test alternative headlines, illustrations and slogans. This is possible only where a newspaper or magazine to be used in the advertiser's media schedule can provide a split. Advertisements using, for example, two different headlines are produced. In all other respects, the advertisements are identical. The printing presses are then set to produce version A in every other paper or magazine coming off the press; the alternative paper or magazine carries version B. All advertisements carry the same offer to induce reader response, but they are coded differently so that it can be determined how many responses each version produced. In this way, the relative strengths of the two headlines, illustrations or slogans can be measured. This technique can be used equally well in testing alternative elements in a direct-mail campaign.

Pre-testing TV advertisements

The purpose of pre-testing TV adverts is similar. It is not the final version that will be tested, but a story board that is presented to potential customers. Simulation of the commercial in this manner will cost only a fraction of the finished product. This preliminary advertisement can be shown to individuals or a group in a central location. Afterwards, the viewers can be asked a number of questions:

- what went on?
- what was said?
- what was the main point of the commercial?
- what, if anything, was hard to understand?
- what was liked and disliked?
- what was the name of the product being advertised?

Results of this type of testing will either strengthen the advertiser's conviction that the commercial has the communication values sought, or lead to changes and improvements. Some drawbacks have been cited for preliminary message testing. Advertisements that have not been produced in final form may not include important details and may thereby reduce communication effectiveness. Subjects being interviewed may not represent the real target market. Because of the artificial environment, the results may be inaccurate.

Testing finished advertisements

More techniques exist for **post-testing** advertisements once they have been produced. Awareness testing is designed to measure the effectiveness of an advertising campaign after it has begun and is in progress. Brand awareness is of crucial importance during the early stages of a new product launch.

Telephone surveys (if telephones are available) are common during test market programmes and new product launches because of the need to obtain feedback as quickly as possible in order to find out if the advertising is producing the intended levels of awareness. Personal interviews are used when not only awareness but other types of information are sought. In conducting these surveys, it is necessary to qualify the respondent at the outset to make sure that he or she is in the target market. For awareness, the early questions may be of an unaided nature, as in the following example which lists questions concerning awareness of detergent brands.

Unaided awareness

1. What is the first brand that comes to mind when you think of detergent?
2. Please tell me all the other brands of detergent you have heard of.
3. Within the past six months, have you seen or heard any advertising for detergent?

Aided awareness:

4. Here is a list of different brands of detergent. Please read this list and tell me which brands you have heard of, including those you may already have mentioned.
5. Do you recall seeing or hearing any advertising for each brand not mentioned in question 3?
6. Where did you see or hear the advertising for each brand mentioned?
7. For each brand you saw or heard advertising for (ask separately), please tell me everything that you remember. What else do you remember seeing or hearing?

It is not only important to evaluate the advertisements of the particular firm. Sometimes it is relevant to compare the firm's advertisements against those of competitors.

Testing the impact of advertising on sales is very difficult because it is difficult to isolate the advertising effect. One way to solve this problem is to use a kind of experiment, where the markets of the firm are grouped according to similar characteristics. In each group of countries, one or two countries are used as test markets. Independent variables to be tested against the sales (dependent variable) might include the amount of advertising, the media mix, the unique selling proposition (USP) and the frequency of placement.

Exhibit 14.4	Big 'head-to-toe' contracts in the golf market

Tiger Woods' latest five-year contract with Nike is worth US$100 million, while David Duval in March 2001 signed a four-year deal worth about US$28 million.

Nike scored another coup by luring former number 1 player David Duval away from Acushnet, which makes Titleist balls and clubs and Foot-Joy shoes and gloves. Titleist, which has built its reputation as the leading maker of golf balls used by professionals, has sued Duval for breach of contract, but Woods and Duval have 'head-to-toe' contracts with Nike, meaning the golf ball and everything they wear is made by the company. Duval is even testing a prototype set of Nike irons, designed by Dallas-based Impact Technologies, which Nike acquired in 2001 to break into the golf club business.

By signing well-known professionals to use their products, golf companies are betting that recreational players will follow suit and boost sales. The 'Tiger effect' seems to be working for Nike, which has seen its share of the retail golf ball market grow from nothing to between 6 and 10 per cent in a year. Market leader is Titleist, with about 50 per cent market share.

While Nike is targeting the biggest names in professional golf, Titleist sees strength in numbers. Titleist thinks, 'it's not about a single player, it's about having the significant majority of players using our products. It's imperative to have plurality usage to establish credibility with the end user'.

Sources: adapted from Ferguson (2000), Steinbreder (2000), Writer and McLaughlin (2001).

Public relations

Word-of-mouth advertising is not only cheap, it is very effective. Public relations (PR) seeks to enhance corporate image building and influence favourable media treatment. PR (or publicity) is the marketing communications function that carries out programmes which are designed to earn public understanding and acceptance. It should be viewed as an integral part of the global marketing effort.

PR activities involve both internal and external communication. Internal communication is important to create an appropriate corporate culture. The target groups for public relations are shown in Table 14.5.

Table 14.5 Target groups for public relations

Public or target groups: domestic markets	Extra factors: international markets
Directly connected with the organization	
● Employees	● Wider range of cultural issues
● Shareholders	● The degree of remoteness of the corporate headquarters
Suppliers of raw materials and components	
● Providers of financial services	● Is this to be handled on a country-by-country basis, or is some overall standardization desirable?
● Providers of marketing services (e.g. marketing research, advertising, media)	
Customers of the organization	
● Existing customers	● May have less knowledge of the company
● Past customers	● The country-of-origin effect will influence communications
● Those capable of becoming customers	
Environment	
● The general public	● Wide range of general publics
● Government: local, regional, national	● Host governments
● Financial markets generally	● Regional grouping (e.g. EU), world groupings

Source: adapted from Phillips et al. (1994), p. 362.

The range of target groups is far wider in public relations than it is for the other communications tools. Target groups are likely to include the main stakeholder groups of employees, customers, distribution channel members and shareholders. For companies operating in international markets, this gives a very wide range of communication tasks. Internal communications in different country subsidiaries, employing people from a number of different countries, with different cultural values, will be particularly challenging.

In a more market-oriented sense, the PR activity is directed towards an influential, though relatively small, target audience of editors and journalists who work for newspapers/magazines, or towards broadcasting aimed at the firm's customers and stakeholders.

Since the target audience is small, it is relatively inexpensive to reach. Several methods can be used to gain PR. Such methods include the following.

● Contribution of prizes at different events.
● Sponsorship: according to Meenaghan (1996), one of the fastest growing aspects of marketing and marketing communications is the practice of corporate

Communication decisions 585

sponsorship. Sponsorship takes two forms: event sponsorship (such as athletic and entertainment events) and cause-oriented sponsorship. Event marketing is growing rapidly because it provides companies alternatives to the cluttered mass media, an ability to segment on a local or regional basis, and opportunities for reaching narrow lifestyle groups whose consumption behaviour can be linked with the local event. Cause-related marketing, a form of corporate philanthropy with benefits accruing to the sponsoring company, is based on the idea that a company will contribute to a cause every time the customer undertakes some action. In addition to helping worthy causes, corporations satisfy their own tactical and strategic objectives when undertaking cause-related efforts. By supporting a deserving cause, a company can enhance its corporate or brand image, generate incremental sales, increase brand awareness, broaden its customer base and reach new market segments. See also two examples of sponsorship in Exhibits 14.4 and 14.5.

- Press releases of news about the firm's products, plant and personnel.
- Announcements of the firm's promotional campaign.
- Lobbying (government).

The degree of control of the PR message is quite different. Journalists can use PR material to craft an article of so many words, or an interview of so many seconds. How material is used will depend on the journalist and the desired story line. On occasions a thoroughly negative story can result from a press release that was designed to enhance the company image.

Hence, PR activity includes anticipating criticism. Criticisms may range from general ones against all multinational corporations to more specific ones. They may also be based on a market; for example, doing business with prison factories in China.

Sales promotion

Sales promotion is defined as those selling activities that do not fall directly into the advertising or personal selling category. Sales promotion also relates to so-called below-the-line activities such as point-of-sale displays and demonstrations, leaflets, free trials, competitions and premiums such as 'two for the price of one'.

Exhibit 14.5 **Vodafone is sponsoring Formula One team Ferrari**

The Vodafone colour is red – the same as Ferrari. The Formula One team Ferrari received a massive cash boost after securing a £110 million sponsorship deal with telecommunications giant Vodafone. The three-year agreement dwarfs the £30 million Manchester United will receive during its four-year association with Vodafone.

Vodafone's biggest ever sponsorship deal will see its brand image on the sidepod, nose and front wing of the Ferraris from 2002. Michael Schumacher and team-mate Rubens Barrichello will also display the Vodafone brand on their overalls and helmets.

Ferrari is happy to cooperate with one of the biggest technology companies in the world. Vodafone has a presence in countries where Ferrari is very strong.

Vodafone wants to be associated with winners and Ferrari is a valuable supplement to its existing global sponsorship like Manchester United.

Source: adapted from BBC (2001).

Unlike media advertising which is above the line and earns a commission, below-the-line sales promotion does not. To an advertising agency, above the line means traditional media for which they are recognized by the media owners, entitling them to commission.

Sales promotion is a short-term effort directed primarily to the consumer and/or retailer, in order to achieve specific objectives such as:

- consumer product trial and/or immediate purchase
- consumer introduction to the shop
- encouraging retailers to use **point-of-sale displays** for the product
- encouraging shops to stock the product.

When a manufacturer owns two or more brands, current loyal customers are excellent candidates for *cross-selling*, promoting another of the brands or using one product to boost sales of another, often an unrelated product. Different companies also may work together to cross-sell.

In the USA, the sales promotion budgets for fast-moving consumer goods (FMCG) manufacturers are larger than the advertising budgets. In Europe, the European Commission estimates that the rate of spending growth on sales promotions was double that for conventional advertising throughout the period 1991–4 (Bennett, 1995, p. 321). Factors contributing to the expansion of sales promotion activities include:

- greater competition among retailers, combined with increasingly sophisticated retailing methods
- higher levels of brand awareness among consumers, leading to the need for manufacturers to defend brand market shares
- improved retail technology (e.g. electronic scanning devices that enable coupon redemptions etc. to be monitored instantly)
- greater integration of sales promotion, public relations and conventional media campaigns.

In markets where the consumer is hard to reach because of media limitations, the percentage of the total communication budget allocated to sales promotions is also relatively high. Some of the different types of sales promotion are as follows.

- *Price discounts* are very widely used. A variety of different price reduction techniques is available, such as cash-back deals.
- *Catalogues/brochures*: the buyer in a foreign market may be located at quite a distance from the closest sales office. In this situation, a foreign catalogue can be very effective. It must be able to close the gap between buyer and seller such that the potential buyer is supplied with all the necessary information, from prices, sizes, colours and quantities to packing, shipping time and acceptable form of payment. In addition to catalogues, brochures of various types are useful for salespeople, distributors and agents. Translations should be done in cooperation with overseas agents and/or distributors.
- *Coupons* are a classic tool for FMCG brands, especially in the USA. A variety of coupon distribution methods exists: door-to-door, on packs, in newspapers. Coupons are not allowed in all European countries.

- A *sample* gives the potential foreign buyer an idea of the quality that cannot be attained by even the best picture. Samples may prevent misunderstandings over style, sizes, models and so on.

- *Gifts*: most European countries have a limit on the value of the premium or gift given. Furthermore, in some countries it is illegal to offer premiums that are conditional on the purchase of another product. The USA does not allow beer to be offered as a free sample.

- *Competitions*: this type of sales promotion needs to be communicated to the potential customers. This can be done on the pack, in stores via leaflets or through media advertising.

The success of sales promotion depends on local adaptation. Major constraints are imposed by local laws which may not permit premiums or free gifts to be given. Some countries' laws control the amount of discount given at the retail level; others require permits for all sales promotions. Since it is impossible to know the specific laws of each and every country, international marketers should consult local lawyers and authorities before launching a promotional campaign.

Direct marketing

According to Onkvisit and Shaw (1993, p. 717), direct marketing is all the activities by which products and services are offered to market segments in one or more media for informational purposes or to solicit a direct response from a present or prospective customer or contributor by mail, telephone or personal visit.

Direct marketing covers direct mail (marketing database), telephone selling and marketing via the Internet. A number of factors have encouraged the rapid expansion of the international direct marketing industry (Bennett, 1995, p. 318):

- developments in mailing technology which have reduced the costs of distributing direct-mail literature

- escalating costs of other forms of advertising and sales promotion

- the increasing availability of good-quality lists of prospective customers

- developments in information technology (especially database technology and desktop publishing) which enable smaller companies to produce high-quality direct marketing materials in-house

- the increasing availability throughout the developed world of interactive television facilities, whereby consumers may order goods through a teletext system.

Direct mail

Direct mail is a viable medium in many countries. It is especially important when other media are not available. Direct mail offers a flexible, selective and potentially highly cost-effective means of reaching foreign consumers. Messages can be addressed exclusively to the target market, advertising budgets may be concentrated on the most promising market segments, and it will be some time before competitors realize that the firm has launched a campaign. In addition, the size, content, timing and geographical coverage of mailshots can be varied at will: the firm can spend as much or as little as necessary to achieve its objectives. There are no media space or airtime restrictions, and no copy or insertion deadlines to be met. All aspects of the direct-mail process are subject to the firm's immediate control, and it can experiment by varying the approach used in different countries. Direct mail can take many forms – letters, catalogues, technical literature – and it can serve as a vehicle for the distribution of samples. A major problem in the effective use of direct mail is the preparation of a suitable mailing list (marketing database).

European marketers are still far behind the United States in exploiting the medium and also with regard to the response to direct mail in the form of mail order. Per capita mail-order sales in the USA are more than double those of any European country (Desmet and Xardel, 1996, p. 58).

The use of direct mail in Japan is also below that in the USA. One reason for this discrepancy is that the Japanese feel printed material is too impersonal and insufficiently sincere.

Direct mail is not only relevant for the consumer market. However, effective use of direct mail for business-to-business purposes requires the preparation of an accurate customer profile (marketing database), including industry classification, size of target company (measured, for example, by turnover, number of employees or market share), the people to approach in each business (purchasing officer, project development engineer, product manager, etc.), industry purchasing procedures and (where known) supplier selection criteria and the buying motives of prospective customers.

Telemarketing is today used for both consumer and business-to-business campaigns throughout the industrialized world. The telephone can be used both to obtain orders and to conduct fast, low-cost market research. Telemarketing covers cold calling (unsolicited calls) by salespeople, market surveys conducted by telephone, calls designed to compile databases of possible sales prospects, and follow-ups to customer requests for further information, resulting from print and broadcast advertisements. Currently, the majority of cross-border telemarketing campaigns focus on business-to-business contacts, essentially because of the combined telephone/fax/database facilities that an increasing number of companies possess and, in consequence, the greater reliability of business-to-business communications.

The administration of international telemarketing normally requires the use of a commercial telemarketing agency. Language skills are required, plus considerable skills and experience in identifying decision makers in target firms.

In some European countries, cold calling consumers is receiving close scrutiny in the name of consumer protection and respect for privacy. For example, Germany has prohibited calls on the grounds of privacy invasion, and this ban even applies to an insurance salesperson's announcement of a visit.

In the light of the development within Internet technologies it is very relevant to consider the web as a direct marketing tool. This issue was discussed further in Chapter 13.

14.4   Personal selling

Because personal selling is relatively costly, a firm should devote a major portion of its promotional budget to the sales force only when its communications objectives can be accomplished more effectively by face-to-face communication than by any other method. As Table 14.6. summarizes, there are a number of strategic circumstances where personal selling is likely to play a major role in a business's promotional mix, circumstances which favour the unique advantages of one-to-one communication.

Table 14.6 Personal selling functions

Functions	Activities involved	Conditions where appropriate
Winning acceptance for new products.	Sales representatives build awareness and stimulate demand for new products or services among existing or potential customers.	Business pursuing prospector strategy; potential customers large or few; company's promotional resources limited; firm pursuing push distribution strategy.
Developing new customers.	Sales representatives find and cultivate new customers and/or expanded distribution for business's products or services.	Target market in growth stage or firm wishes to increase share of mature market; potential customers large or few; company's promotional resources limited; firm pursuing push distribution strategy.
Maintaining customer loyalty.	Sales representatives work to increase value delivered to customers by providing advice or training on product use, expediting orders, and facilitating product service.	Business pursuing differentiated defender strategy, firm has large share of mature market and wants to maintain loyalty of existing customers; product technically complex and/or competition for distribution support is strong.
Technical service to facilitate sales.	Sales representatives work to increase value to customers by helping integrate product or service with customer's other equipment or operations and by providing design, installation, and/or training.	Product technically complex; customers (or dealers) relatively few and large; product or service can be customized to fit needs of individual customers; products sold as parts of larger systems.
Communicating product information.	Sales representatives work to increase understanding of product's features and applications as basis for possible future sales and to educate people who may influence final purchase.	Product technically complex and/or in introductory or at growth stage of life cycle; lengthy purchase decision process; multiple influences on purchase decision.
Gathering information.	Sales representatives provide reports on competitors' actions, customers' requests or problems, and other market conditions, and conduct market research or intelligence activities.	Appropriate under all circumstances, but especially useful in industry introductory or growth stage, or when product technology or other factors are unstable; business implementing a prospector strategy.

Source: adapted from Boyd *et al.* (1998).

The steps in personal selling

Personal selling can be divided into four main stages, as follows.

Pre-approach and planning

Pre-approach refers to preparing and planning for the initial meeting by learning about the potential customer. In this stage, territory management is extremely important. Salespeople must determine how the company's target marketing and positioning can best be applied in their territory. Because each area is different, it is important to make adjustments based on local conditions. Exceptional sales skills are of little use if calls are not made to the appropriate accounts with the right frequency and intensity. *Territory planning* determines the pool of customers, their sales potential, and the frequency with which they will be contacted about various products. The fundamental objective is to allocate sales time and use company resources to obtain the best results. *Account planning* establishes sales goals and objectives for each major customer, such as the sales volume and profitability to be obtained. Increasingly, account objectives include customer satisfaction, often measured by loyalty (repeat business). Account plans are based on an understanding of the customer's business and how the seller's products contribute to it.

Approach

The approach is the first formal contact with the customer. The objective is to secure an initial meeting and gain customer interest. It is usually a good idea to schedule an appointment; that will save time and puts the prospect in the frame of mind for a sales call. Many times, a letter of introduction before calling will help in obtaining the first appointment.

Many techniques have been developed for the initial approach. The most successful ones focus on the potential customer's business, such as a brief explanation of how or why the seller's product can help. It is also important to determine not just when the meeting will take place but how long it will last and its objective. Organizations with a strong reputation generally have an advantage in the approach stage.

In the initial approach to a prospective customer, a sales representative should accomplish three things: develop a thorough understanding of the client's situation and the needs that the representative's products or services might help satisfy, determine who within the organization is likely to have the greatest influence and/or authority to make a purchase, and obtain the information needed to qualify the prospect as a worthwhile potential customer.

Building the relationship

The importance of a problem-solving sales approach as a basis for establishing an enduring relationship with a potential customer should be obvious. But as we have seen, organizational buying centres often consist of multiple individuals who have somewhat different concerns and play different roles in shaping the company's purchase decisions. Thus, it is important for salespeople to identify the key decision makers, their desires, and their relative influence.

The sales presentation is a two-way process: the salesperson listens in order to identify customer needs and then describes how the product will fulfil them. The most important part of any good presentation is listening. In fact, it is often said that successful selling is 90 per cent listening and 10 per cent talking. Unfortunately, many salespeople believe their role is to tell prospects about products. Instead, by asking questions, they should put the customer first and demonstrate that they have the customer's best interests in mind. The first contact is the first opportunity to connect with a customer.

Organizations generally have to train their sales force to be good listeners. This is a trait few people possess naturally. The training identifies ways to learn about the prospect's situation. It also teaches how to communicate that the salesperson is listening and is concerned about the customer's needs and wants. Empathy occurs when salespeople know precisely how prospects feel. Only when prospects know that the seller understands their wants and needs are they receptive to solutions the salesperson offers.

Closing the deal and building loyalty

One of the most important sales skills is the ability to overcome a buyer's objections. Assertive salespeople do not let the first objection stop the dialogue; they use it to advance the discussion. Most organizations have training programmes to teach salespeople how to manage objections. **Closing** means getting the first order. In many cases this is simple, such as asking directly if someone wants to buy the product or whether they will use cash or credit. In other cases, it involves elaborate contracts. Good salespeople know how important it is to help the buyer toward the final decision. In business-to-business situations, the salespeople may ask if the purchaser is ready to make a decision or would like to discuss the issue more thoroughly. A caution is in order regarding closing. If a buyer is not ready to make the commitment, then asking for an order prematurely can make the salesperson appear pushy and unconcerned with the buyer's needs. A great deal of sensitivity is required for an accurate reading of the buyer's state of mind.

There is a big difference between making a sale and gaining customer loyalty. In order to maintain relationships and gain customer loyalty, salespeople have to spend significant time servicing customers. They make sure products are delivered on schedule and operate to the buyer's liking. When there is a problem, the salesperson makes sure that it is resolved quickly and satisfactorily.

Follow-up occurs when a salesperson ensures that there is after-sale satisfaction in order to obtain repeat business. Follow-up also offers a way to identify additional sales opportunities. After the first sale is made, the second is easier. The salesperson who continues to work closely with the buying organization can uncover other needs to supply. Good service builds strong customer loyalty, which is the goal of relationship selling.

When the purchase decision is likely to be very complex, involving many people within the customer's organization, the seller might adopt a policy of multi-level selling or **team selling**. Team selling involves people from most parts of the organization, including senior executives, who work together to create relationships with the buying organization. In a high-technology business like aircraft manufacturing nearly every function is involved in the sales process. At Boeing it is the salesperson's job to coordinate contact between the company and the technical, financial, and planning personnel from the airline. Even if the CEO is brought in, it is not unusual for the salesperson to remain in charge of the sale using the CEO where appropriate. The salespeople perform the leadership function because they know all aspects of their customers' business. They must also be thoroughly familiar with Boeing's services.

There are some differences between advertising and personal selling. Advertising is a one-way communication process, whereas personal selling is a two-way communication process with immediate feedback and less 'noise'. Personal selling is an effective way to sell products, but it is expensive. It is used mainly to sell to distribution channel members and in business-to-business markets. However, personal selling is also used in some consumer markets – for example for cars and for consumer durable products. In some countries, labour costs are very low. In these instances, personal selling will be used to a greater extent than in high-cost countries.

If personal selling costs in business-to-business markets are relatively high, it is relevant to economize with personal selling resources, and use personal selling only at the end of the potential customer's buying process. Computerized database marketing (direct mail, etc.) is used in a customer screening process, to point out possible customers for the salesforce. Their job is to turn good customer candidates into real customers.

New technologies – particularly telemarketing systems – can help salespeople identify and qualify potential new customer leads.

The Internet is also proving to be a useful technology for providing leads for potential new customers. While increasing numbers of firms are soliciting orders directly via a home page on the Internet, many – particularly those selling relatively complex goods or services – use their Internet sites primarily to provide technical product information to customers or potential customers. These firms can then have their salespeople follow up technical enquiries from potential new accounts with a more traditional sales call.

Assessing sales force effectiveness

There are five essential questions to ask in assessing sales force effectiveness:

- *Is the selling effort structured for effective market coverage*? You should think about organization, size of sales force and territory deployment.
- *Is the sales force staffed with the right people*? You should think about the type of international sales force: (expatriates/host country/third country), age/tenure/education profile, interpersonal skills, technical capabilities and selling technique.
- *Is strong guidance provided*? You should think about written guidelines, key tasks/mission definition, call frequency, time allocation, people to be seen, market/account focus, territory planning and control tools, and on-the-job coaching.
- *Is adequate sales support in place*? You should think about training, technical back-up, in-house sales staff, and product and applications literature.
- *Does the sales compensation plan provide the proper motivation*? You should think about total compensation, split of **straight salary/straight commission**, incentive design/fit with management objectives and non-cash incentives.

In the following we will go into further detail with the first two questions.

Organization of the international sales force

In international markets, firms often organize their sales forces in a similar way to their domestic sales force, regardless of differences from one country to another. This means that the sales force is organized by geography, product, customer or some combination of these (Table 14.7).

A number of firms organize their international sales force along simple geographical territories within a given country or region. Firms that have broad product lines and a large sales volume, and/or operate in large, developed markets may prefer more specialized organizations, such as product or customer assignment. The firm may also organize the sales force based upon other factors such as culture or languages spoken in the targeted foreign markets. For example, firms often divide Switzerland into different regions reflecting French, Italian and German language usage.

Table 14.7 Sales force organizational structure

Structure	Factors favouring choice of organizational structure	Advantages	Disadvantages
Geographic	● Distinct languages/cultures ● Single product line ● Underdeveloped markets	● Clear, simple ● Incentive to cultivate local business and personal ties ● Travel expenses	● Breadth of customers ● Breadth of products
Product	● Established market ● Broad product lines	● Product knowledge	● Travel expenses ● Overlapping territories/customers ● Local business and personal ties
Customer[*]	● Broad product lines	● Market/customer knowledge	● Overlapping territories/products ● Local business and personal ties ● Travel expenses
Combination	● Large sales volume ● Large/developed markets ● Distinct language/cultures	● Maximum flexibility ● Travel expenses	● Complexity ● Sales management ● Product/market/geography overlap

[*] By type of industry, size of account, channel of distribution, individual company.

Source: Hollensen (2001), p. 538.

14.5 Trade fairs and exhibitions

Trade fairs, exhibitions or trade shows are major communication tools for marketers today. They account for about 20 per cent of the total communication budget for US industrial firms and about 25 per cent of the budget for European firms (Shoham, 1999).

A trade fair or exhibition is an event at which manufacturers, distributors and other vendors display their products and/or describe their services to current and prospective customers, suppliers, other business associates and the press. Figure 14.6 shows that trade fairs (TFs) are multi-purpose events involving many interactions between the TF exhibitor and numerous parties.

As TFs are very often annual affairs and have a mix of business and quasi-social events, buyers can maintain their contacts with sellers and other users. This is a long-term motive for a current buyer to attend and exhibit. Although they will not be repeating their purchase in the near term, it is important for them to maintain a relationship with sellers and others whom they may call upon for solutions to future problems.

TFs can enable a company to reach a group of interested prospects in a few days which might otherwise take several months to contact. Potential buyers can examine and compare the products of competing firms in a short period at the same place. They can see the latest developments and establish immediate contact with suppliers.

Figure 14.6 Three concepts of trade fairs: major interactions for a local exhibitor

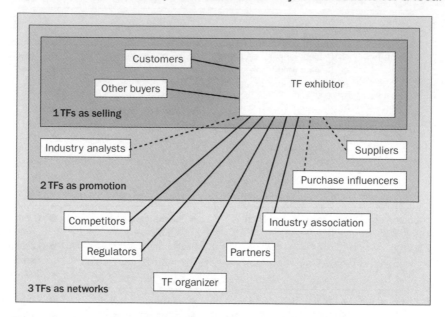

Source: adapted from Rosson and Seringhaus, 1995.

Traditionally, TFs have been regarded as a personal selling tool, but Sharland and Balogh (1996) conclude that TFs are an excellent environment for non-selling activities such as information exchange, relationship building and channel partner assessment. TFs offer international firms the opportunity to gather vital information quickly, easily and cheaply. For example, within a short period a firm can learn a considerable amount about its competitive environment, which would take much longer and cost much more to get through other sources (e.g. secondary information).

Attendance at TFs is often viewed by a company as a reward to its employees. This motivation is consistent with the motive ascribed to selling companies in prior research: the use of exhibitions as a tool to build the morale of the sales force (Godar and O'Connor, 2001).

We conclude this section by listing the arguments for and against participation in TFs.

Arguments for participation in TFs

- Marketers are able to reach a sizeable number of potential customers in a brief time period at a reasonable cost per contact. Orders may be obtained on the spot.

- Some products, by their very nature, are difficult to market without providing the potential customer with a chance to examine them or see them in action. TFs provide an excellent opportunity to introduce, promote and demonstrate new products.

- SMEs without extensive sales forces have the opportunity to present their products to large buying companies on the same face-to-face basis as large local rivals.

- Finding an intermediary may be one of the best reasons to attend a TF. A show is a cost-effective way to solicit and screen candidates to represent the firm, especially in a new market.

- Although many technical specialists and company executives refuse to see or take telephone calls from outsiders who try to sell them things at their places of work, these same managers often attend trade exhibitions. The customer goes to the exhibition in order to see the seller. This is also an important aspect in the concept of reverse marketing or buyer initiative (see, for example, Figure 14.2).

- An appearance also produces goodwill and improves the corporate image. Beyond the impact of displaying specific products, many firms place strong emphasis on 'waving the company flag' against competition. This facet also includes supporting the morale of the firm's sales personnel and intermediaries.

- TFs provide an excellent chance for market research and collecting competitive intelligence. The marketer is able to view most rivals at the same time and to test comparative buyer reactions.

- Visitors' names and addresses may be used for subsequent mailshots.

Arguments against participation in TFs

- There is a high cost in terms of the time and administrative effort needed to prepare an exhibition stand in a foreign country. However, a marketer can lower costs by sharing expenses with distributors or representatives. Furthermore, the costs of closing a sale through TFs are estimated to be much lower than those for a sale closed through personal representation.

- It is difficult to choose the appropriate TFs to attend. This is a critical decision. Because of scarce resources, many firms rely on suggestions from their foreign distributors on which TFs to attend and what specifically to exhibit.

- Coordination problems may arise. In LSEs with multiple divisions, more divisions may be required to participate in the same TF under the company banner. In SMEs coordination is required with distributors and agents if joint participation is desired, and this necessitates joint planning.

- Furthermore, the firm faces a lot of practical problems. For example, most people visit exhibitions to browse rather than to buy. How does the exhibiting firm obtain the names and addresses of the visitors who influence major buying decisions within their companies? Second, gimmicks may be highly effective in attracting visitors to a stand, but they can attract the wrong people. An audience may be greatly impressed by the music, dancing, demonstration or whatever is provided, yet not be remotely interested in the product. Third, how can the employees who staff a stand be prevented from treating the exercise as a holiday, paying more attention to the social aspects of their involvement with the exhibition than to finding customers? What specific targets can the staff be given and how can the attainment of targets be measured?

Whether a marketer should participate in a trade fair depends largely on the type of business relationship it wants to develop with a particular country. A company looking only for one-off or short-term sales might find the expense prohibitive, but a firm looking to build long-term relationships may find the investment worthwhile.

Trade fairs enable exhibitors to deliver their selling message to a large number of people at one time, thus providing an opportunity for face-to-face contact that is lacking in most other promotions and advertising media. This advantage is more important for internationally active firms, given the prohibitive costs of sales visits to foreign markets.

14.6 Implications of the Internet for communication decisions

In the marketplace different communication tools are used in the buying process of customers (see Figure 14.7). Traditional mass communication tools (print advertising, TV and radio) can create awareness and this can result in consumers' identification of new needs. From then on other elements of the communication mix take over, such as direct marketing (direct mail, personal selling) and in-store promotion. Unlike marketing in the marketplace the Internet encompasses the entire 'buying' process. However, many Internet-based companies also use a lot of mass communication media to attract customers to their sites.

Market communication strategies change dramatically in the online world. On the Internet, it is easier than ever to actually communicate a message to large numbers of people. However, in many cases, it is much harder for your message to be heard by your target audience above the noise. Various strategies for conducting online marketing have been developed in the past several years – from the most common (website linking) to the most expensive (banner advertising) to the most offensive (e-mail spamming), and everything in between. It is almost certain that a continual stream of new market communication strategies will emerge as the Internet evolves.

Although some companies do business exclusively on the web, for most the Internet offers exciting opportunities to develop an additional sales channel. This new channel can extend a company's reach significantly, enabling it to do business with a new customer base that was previously unreachable. Customer preferences are driving e-commerce as many consumers simply prefer online shopping because of the convenience, reach and availability of products and services. Companies that do not develop an Internet presence risk losing these customers to more aggressive competitors.

Developing a successful online marketing programme has the same objectives as in the physical world: how to create an audience. Audience development is the preferred phrase for online marketing, because it more precisely communicates the point of the activity.

Figure 14.7 **The role of Internet communication in the buying process of customers**

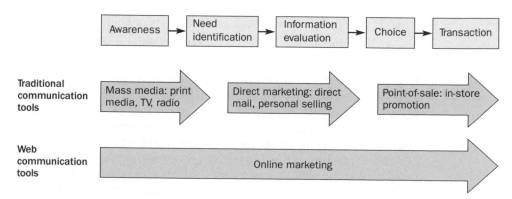

Source: Hollensen (2001), p. 545.

How, then, can a web audience be created? The web audience development process consists of the following six phases:

1. integration
2. design requirements that are unique
3. techniques for audience creation
4. methods of advertising the site
5. effective promotions that attract attention
6. measurement and analysis to ensure ongoing success.

Integration of Internet strategy into an overall business strategy

Before a company builds a website, it should determine how the site will fit into the company's overall business strategy. A holistic approach does not look at the website in isolation, but in the context of the overall marketing mix. How does a web marketing strategy fit together with the product sold, the price and the other parts of the distribution strategy plus the personal sales efforts? Marketers must understand the role of each medium within the company's marketing mix and utilize the strengths of each. Creating the right online corporate identity is the first step for audience development, the step from which all other components of a successful web marketing programme flow. Synergy and consistency are essential. Although individual messages may vary to apply the unique strengths of each medium, the overall message should be consistent across media.

All marketing and sales activities should work together, and each marketing objective should be supported across multiple media where possible. A company should cross-promote among media, for example promoting its website in brochures and print advertising.

Design requirements that are unique

Given the free flow of information in the market space and the potential for information overload, the marketer with the best-designed information package will generate competitive advantage.

While audience creation, advertising and promotions drive traffic to a website, it is the design that either encourages visitors to explore or drives them away in frustration. A good design is, of course, aesthetically pleasing. More importantly, though, it engages visitors, makes it easy for them to navigate the website and compels them to explore it further, purchase products and return. Attractive graphics that support the company's message are important, but large graphics that take a long time to load frustrate users. Many visitors will not wait long enough for the graphic to finish loading. Additionally, visitors are less likely to return to a website that has confusing navigational cues.

The design should use clear, consistent navigational cues that make it easy for visitors to determine where they are within the website. With more than a million websites competing for users' attention, first impressions are critical. A confusing, poorly organized structure can negate even the highest quality content.

Web design differs significantly from design for other media. The most important difference is that the web is interactive, incorporating hyperlinks and devices for immediate visitor feedback. Some sophisticated designs include dynamically generated pages that are customized to each visitor's interests, preferences and buying habits.

Techniques for audience creation

Developing traffic on a website requires expert knowledge of the numerous online search devices. The audience creation methods described in this section are highly cost-effective for generating a large number of repeat visitors.

Search engine optimization

Search engines and directories play a critical role in Internet marketing, because the majority of web surfers rely on these navigation guides to conduct their research. Because users typically explore only the first 10 or 20 sites on the list, an understanding of how search ranking works can make a huge difference in traffic volume. Effective optimization of search engine results requires carefully designed meta tags and other HTML code and pointer pages specialized for individual search engines.

Editorial placement in new media

In addition to using the Internet as a communications tool to contact traditional journalists, companies can reach out to the new and rapidly increasing breed of online-only news media. Most online stories contain hyperlinks to the websites of featured marketers. Because online stories are typically archived in news databases and indexed by search engines, they provide a source of new visitors for an indefinite period.

Strategic linking

A major differentiator between the web and other media is the use of hyperlinks, in which a user clicks on a link and is instantly transported to another site. The more inbound links a company establishes on other sites, the more qualified visitors the site will attract. Unlike banner adverts, links frequently stay in place for months and bear the credibility of editorial selection. Best of all, they are usually free. Some of the best investment of time marketers can make is to contact webmasters of affinity sites in an attempt to place inbound links on their sites. Webmasters of many popular sites actively seek out quality sites to which they can link.

Interactive public relations

Important sources for attracting web visitors are interactive public relations facilitates as well as direct interactivity with individuals. Newsgroups, mailing lists, forums, chat rooms, bulletin boards and other virtual communities are also of great importance.

One method for tapping into virtual communities is to employ interactive public relations with materials such as electronic press releases or other stories that may be of interest to specific groups.

Methods of advertising the site

To take full advantage of the power of Internet marketing, companies must understand the differences between online advertising and other more traditional media.

Banner advertising

Online banner adverts use eye-catching multimedia effects such as animation, interactivity, sound, video and 3D to attract attention and draw visitors to a site. Even commerce transactions in the banner are becoming common.

With online advertising, companies can target adverts with far greater precision than with any other medium. Today's advert server technology offers highly sophisticated, automatic targeting that uses factors such as demographic data and visitor behaviour while at the site. In addition, technology is emerging that allows online adverts to be tailored automatically to each visitor.

Marketers can take advantage of this targeting capability to place banner adverts on sites that attract visitors who match the demographic profile for companies' products. As a result, they can increase brand awareness among a carefully targeted audience and drive highly qualified traffic to their site.

Sponsorship

Exclusive sponsorship of site content is a growing trend. Sponsoring strategic editorial content is an effective way to establish long-term brand identification among target audiences.

Sponsorship of content or pages on certain sites – for example, a site maintained by an influential industry group or a leader in a particular industry – associates a company with that group or industry leader. This association lends credibility and helps increase customer interest and brand awareness.

Barter advertising

In addition to paid advertising, many sites are performing banner exchanges and advert barter arrangements. Even among top content sites, bartering is a common, cost-effective way to boost traffic. Companies can take advantage of this low-cost advertising method by establishing personal relationships and negotiating barter deals with other sites.

Effective promotions that attract attention

Promotions offer an excellent opportunity for public relations exposure and online community awareness. These promotions can take a variety of forms.

Competitions

Quizzes, sweepstakes and other competitions are sometimes effective components of online marketing. Companies can use competitions for a variety of purposes, including sales generation, brand recognition establishment, customer loyalty building and market research.

Loyalty programmes

It is well known that the cost of retaining a current customer is about one-tenth that of acquiring a new one. As a result, customer loyalty programmes can have a dramatic impact on the bottom line. Loyalty programmes and similar online campaigns can help retain customers and motivate them to recruit new customers by recommending a company's site or products to friends and associates.

Online events

Live events (for example live sporting events) in which users from around the world participate have proven tremendously popular with the online public. Promoters have seized on this trend to capture audiences for a variety of online events, including celebrity chats, live concert broadcasts, virtual conferences and auctions. Such events can be effective for gaining recognition among new users and positioning a company or site at the cutting edge of its market.

Measurement and analysis to ensure ongoing success

The Internet is one of the most measurable of all communications media. The ability to monitor the effectiveness and continually fine-tune websites and campaigns is one of the medium's greatest benefits.

Paul (1996) argues that the web has the ability to compile statistics about the reach (how many people have viewed each advertisement) and exposure time (how long the viewers have looked at the advertisement). This helps companies to measure the effectiveness of their advertisements.

Server logs and other performance data are valuable indicators that can be used to develop insights that are far beyond what any print circulation figures or TV ratings data can provide. It is important, however, to combine these quantitative measures with qualitative measures to achieve a meaningful evaluation of effectiveness. Tracking which external sources refer the most visitors to the home page is useful when evaluating the success of advert banners, affinity links and other promotional campaigns.

Audience qualification

Counting web page hits alone is not sufficient to determine effectiveness of audience development strategies. It is more important to determine who the visitors are. Are they prospective customers or simply confused and curious surfers who will never return? How many pages past the first home page does the average visitor explore from a particular banner advert? What percentage of visitors return again, and which ones become customers?

Customer feedback

Perhaps the most valuable form of analysis comes not from technology, but directly from site visitors. Sites that post their e-mail addresses or telephone numbers to encourage contact from visitors are sending a strong message that invites relationship building with prospects and customers. An interactive process that incorporates visitor feedback enables the company to raise the site to its full potential and keep it there.

Marketers can get information on visitors' perception of the site through online visitor surveys. Because they are convenient and even fun to respond to, response rates are typically high. For additional opinions, marketers can monitor discussions about the brand and general product category on discussion boards in newsgroups as well as other independent forums. Such feedback is a natural by-product of many online marketing activities and can be effectively incorporated into the other components of audience development.

14.7 Summary

Mass customization is the capability, realized by a few companies, to offer individually tailored products or services on a large scale. One-to-one marketing aims to customize a product offering so carefully that it fits the customer perfectly. Both trends mean that the firm has to communicate more and more directly to customers.

Five aspects of communication have been presented in this chapter:

1. advertising
2. public relations
3. sales promotion
4. direct marketing
5. personal selling.

As marketers manage the various elements of the promotional mix in differing environmental conditions, decisions must be made about what channels are to be used in the communication, the message, who is to execute or help execute the programme, and how the results of the communication plan are to be measured.

Personal selling is the marketing task involving face-to-face contact with the customer. Unlike advertising, promotion, sponsorship and other forms of non-personal communication, personal selling permits direct interaction between buyer and seller. This two-way communication means that the seller can identify the specific needs and problems of the buyer and tailor the sales presentation to provide this background information.

Some communication tools, especially personal selling, have to be localized to fit the conditions of individual markets. Another reason for localization of the personal selling tool is that distribution channel members are normally located firmly within a country. Consequently, decisions concerning recruitment, training, motivation and evaluation of salespeople have to be made at the local level.

A very important communication tool for the future is the Internet. Any company eager to take advantage of the Internet on a global scale must select a business model for its Internet ventures and estimate how information and transactions delivered through this new direct marketing medium will influence its existing distribution and communication system.

Case study 14.2 Heineken

Can the Heineken-Paulaner relationship provide new value for customers in the world beer market?

Heineken NV is the world's most international brewing group with production in more than 110 breweries in over 50 countries. The Heineken brand is sold in more than 170 countries. The company's product portfolio consists of over 80 brands. With 45 million hectolitres of beer sold in Europe (1999), Heineken is the largest European brewer. Heineken and Amstel are, respectively, the best and second best selling beer brands in Europe. The total group volume amounted in 1999 to 90.9 million hectolitres, giving it second place in the world after Anheuser-Busch (Budweiser). In 1999 the net turnover amounted to €7.1 billion with a net profit of €516 million. The Heineken group employed 36,733 people in 1999.

Europe

In Europe, Heineken is the leading brewer with leading positions in the Netherlands, Eire, Spain, Poland, France, Italy, Greece, Slovakia, Bulgaria and Macedonia Skopje. Heineken is also present in all other European countries.

America

Heineken was the first brewer to export to the USA after the lifting of Prohibition in April 1933 and has built up a strong position in the US beer market. Heineken beer remains America's favourite imported European premium beer. In Latin America, Heineken is present through exports, licensing partners and participation in several joint ventures.

Asia Pacific

Heineken has held a strong position in Indonesia since the 1920s. In the 1930s, Heineken and its partners founded Asia Pacific Breweries (APB). APB grew steadily and rapidly expanded its presence in Asia Pacific, e.g. Singapore, Malaysia, and New Zealand. In the 1990s new breweries were constructed in China, Cambodia, Vietnam and Thailand.

Africa

For many decades Heineken has been present in Africa. The most important African brands of the Heineken Group are Primus, Gulder, and Star. Heineken is the number two brewery group on this continent.

Starting with the export of Heineken beer to different countries has proved to be an excellent way of exploring a new market and building up the brand name and image. Exporting also offers the company an opportunity to assess the market potential for the Heineken brand and, where appropriate, to look for opportunities to acquire local brewing operations. This enables Heineken to support strong local brands by positioning Heineken beer in the premium segment.

In the 19th century, the Bavarian brewers played an important role in the birth of the Heineken brand. They also exported their knowledge and technique to most parts of the world.

However, Heineken has never been able to penetrate the German market successfully, which is the largest beer market in Europe. Today, Heineken can be obtained in several thousand German theme bars and restaurants, as well as in numerous convenience shops. However, the volume is still relatively small.

In February 2001, Heineken signed an agreement with Bayerische Brau Holding (BBH), owner of the Paulaner Brauerei. The two beer companies set up a joint venture company with the name Brauholding International AG.

Paulaner Brauerei

The Paulaner Brauerei is based in Bavaria. With its brands Paulaner, Hacker-Pschorr, Thur & Taxis, and AuerBrau and a sales volume of 2.8 million hectolitres in 2000, Paulaner Brauerei is one of the leading brewing groups in Germany. In 2000, sales of its Paulaner weissbeer exceeded 1 million hectolitre for the first time, strengthening its number two position in the German and international weissbeer segment. The company increased its exports by 9 per cent to 414,000 hectolitres.

Case study 14.2 continued

Paulaner produces 16 different kinds of beer. These include the famous 'white beers' (weissbier), the seasonal Oktoberfest beer and Salvator, Munich light and dark beer and the newly introduced Paulaner rye. Steady growth in exports has meant that Paulaner is found in over 30 countries.

The so-called microbreweries, Paulaner restaurants with their own breweries for people to visit, can be found in Singapore, Peking, Manila and Shanghai. The parent company of the microbreweries is based in Munich. Paulaner North America (PNA), a subsidiary in Denver, Colorado, is responsible for the North American market.

Paulaner is under the umbrella of the Schörghuber group, and is in partnership with the Kulmbacher brewery group, Coca-Cola Erfrischungsgetränke AG and the Chilean brewery, Compañia Cervecerias Unidas SA.

The Schörghuber group also operates internationally in the beverage, construction and real estate industries, as well as in the services sector (hotel, aircraft leasing etc.). It is a highly developed, financially strong group.

Questions

1. How could the relationship between Heineken and Paulaner Brauerei provide value to:
   (a) the customers around the world
   (b) each of the two partners?

2. Propose a plan for communicating the benefits of the relationship:
   (a) internally in the two companies
   (b) externally to customers.

Sources: Beverage industry (1999, 2000); Willram (2000), Heineken annual reports and press releases; Paulaner Brewery website.

QUESTIONS FOR DISCUSSION

1. What is the difference between 'mass customization' and one-to-one marketing?

2. What are the implications of one-to-one marketing for the communications strategy of a firm?

3. Identify and discuss problems associated with assessing advertising effectiveness in foreign markets.

4. Compare domestic communication with international communication. Explain why 'noise' is more likely to occur in the case of international communication processes.

5. Why do more companies not standardize advertising messages worldwide? Identify the environmental constraints that act as barriers to the development and implementation of standardized global advertising campaigns.

6. Explain how personal selling may differ overseas from how it is used in the home market.

7. What is meant by saying that advertising regulations vary around the world?

8. Evaluate the percentage of sales approach to setting advertising budgets in foreign markets.

9. Explain how the multi-national firm may have an advantage over local firms in training the sales force and evaluating its performance.

10. Identify and discuss problems associated with allocating the company's promotion budget across several foreign markets.

REFERENCES

Adage Global (2001), International campaign to reduce birth rate among cats, *Adage Global*, April 5, **http://www.adageglobal.com**.

Agrawal, M., Kumaresh, T.V. and Mercer, G.A. (2001), The false promise of mass customization, *McKinsey Quarterly*, no. 3, pp. 62–71.

Autoliv (2000), *Autoliv and Volvo launch new safety system*, Autoliv, press release, September 4.

Baird, R. (1997), Patent place, *Marketing Week*, March 14.

Balfour, F. (1993), Alcohol industry: companies in high spirits, *China Trade Report*, June, pp. 4–5.

BBC (2000a), *Analysis: Europe's car industry*, **http://news.bbc.co.uk** May 12.

BBC (2000b), *Automotives empire*, **http://news.bbc.co.uk** June 3.

BBC (2001), Ferrari fuelled by new deal, *BBC Business News*, **http://news.bbc.co.uk** May 25.

Bennett, R. (1995), *International Marketing: Strategy, planning, market entry and implementation*, Kogan Page, London.

Beverage Industry (1999), Beer is Dutch, *Beverage Industry*, New York, vol. 90, no. 9. p. 9.

Beverage Industry (2000), Europeans attack American brewers, *Beverage Industry*, New York, vol. 91, no. 1, p. 10.

Billing, C. (1994), No to Joe Camel, *China Trade Report*, December, p. 9.

Boddewyn, J. J., Soehl, R. and Picard, J. (1986), Standardization in international marketing: is Ted Levitt in fact right?, *Business Horizons*, pp. 69–75.

Boyd, H. W., Walker, O. C. and Larréché (1998) *Marketing Management – A strategic approach with a global orientation*, Irwin McGraw-Hill.

Business Week (1984), Advertising Europe's new Common Market, *Business Week*, July, pp. 62–5.

CSM Worldwide (2002), Automotive market forecast 2002, CSM Worldwide, Northville, MI (**www.csmauto.com/forecastsummary.html**).

Desmet, P. and Xardel, D. (1996), Challenges and pitfalls for direct mail across borders: the European example, *Journal of Direct Marketing*, vol. 10, no. 3, pp. 48–60.

Ferguson, D. (2000), Nike braces for earthquake if Woods switches golf balls, *Golfweek*, May 18, **http://www.golfweek.com**.

Godar, S.H. and O'Connor (2001), Same time next year – buyer trade show motives, *Industrial Marketing Management*, vol. 30, pp. 77–86.

Griffin, T. (1993), *International Marketing Communications*, Butterworth Heinemann, Oxford.

Gunn, E. (2001), Product placement prize, *Advertising Age*, Chicago, February 12, p. 72.

Harper, T. (1986), Polaroid clicks instantly in Moslem markets, *Advertising Age*, January 30, p. 12 (special report on Marketing to the Arab world).

Hite, R.E. and Frazer, C. (1988), International advertising strategies of multinational corporations, *Journal of Advertising Research*, vol. 28, August–September, pp. 9–17.

Hollensen, S. (2001), *Global Marketing: A market responsive approach*, Financial Times/Prentice Hall, Harlow, 2nd edn.

Honeycutt, E. D. and Ford, J. B. (1995), Guidelines for managing an international sales force, *Industrial Marketing Management*, vol. 24, pp. 135–44.

Hung, C. L. and West, D. C. (1991), Advertising budgeting methods in Canada, the UK and the USA, *International Journal of Advertising*, vol. 10, pp. 239–50.

Irish Times (2000), Barbie goes to Hollywood, *Irish Times*, January 26, pp. 11–12.

Joensen, S. (1997), What hedder it now on engelsk?, *Politikken* (Danish newspaper), April 24.

Kaufman, L. (2000), And now a few more words about breasts, *New York Times*, September 17, p. 43.

Lynch, R. (1994), *European Marketing*, Irwin, Homewood, IL.

MacNamee, B. and McDonnell, R. (1995), *The Marketing Casebook*, Routledge, London.

Meenaghan, T. (1996), Ambush marketing – a threat to corporate sponsorship, *Sloan Management Review*, Fall, pp. 103–13.

Mueller, B. (1996), *International Advertising: Communicating across cultures*, Wadsworth, Belmont, CA.

National Post (1999), Tilbury airbag plant to add 'curtains' *National Post*, October 15.

Nørmark, P. (1994), Co-promotion in growth, *Markedsføring* (Danish marketing magazine), no. 14, p. 14.

Onkvisit, S. and Shaw, J.J. (1993), *International Marketing: Analysis and strategy* Macmillan, London, 2nd edn.

Ottesen, O. (1995), Buyer initiative: ignored, but imperative for marketing management – towards a new view of market communication, *Tidsvise Skrifter*, no. 15, avdeling for Ákonomi, Kultur og Samfunnsfag ved Høgskolen i Stavanger.

Paul, P. (1996), Marketing on the Internet, *Journal of Consumer Marketing*, vol. 13, no. 4, pp. 27–39.

Phillips, C., Poole, I. and Lowe, R. (1994), *International Marketing Strategy: Analysis, development and implementation*, Routledge, London/New York.

Pitta, D. A. (1998), Marketing one-to-one and its dependence on knowledge discovery in databases, *Journal of Consumer Marketing*, vol. 15, no. 5, pp. 468–80.

Rosson, P. J. and Seringhaus, F. H. R. (1995), Visitor and exhibitor interaction at industrial trade fairs, *Journal of Business Research*, vol. 32, no. 1, pp. 81–90.

Sargent, J. D. *et al.* (2001), Brand appearances in contemporary cinema films and contributions to global marketing of cigarettes, *The Lancet*, London, January 6, pp. 29–32.

Schlosser, J. (2001), Plugging in the TV, *Broadcasting & Cable*, New York, January 29, p. 34.

Schmidt, K. V. (2000), Why SFA is a tough sell in Latin America, *Marketing News*, vol. 34, no. 1, pp. 4–5.

Sharland, A. and Balogh, D. (1996), The value of non selling activities at international trade shows, *Industrial Marketing Management*, vol. 25, pp. 59–66.

Shelly, B. (1995), Cool customer, *Unilever Magazine*, no. 2, pp. 13–17.

Shoham, A. (1999), Performance in trade shows and exhibitions – a synthesis and directions for future research, *Journal of Global Marketing*, vol. 12, no. 3, pp. 41–57.

Sorenson, R. Z. and Weichman, V. E. (1975), How multinationals view marketing standardization, *Harvard Business Review*, May–June, pp. 38–56.

Steinbreder, J. (2000), Nike deal is Woods' latest ace, *Golfweek*, September 23, **http://www.golfweek.com.**

Teather, D. (2002), 'Bloated' Ford sacks 35,000, *The Guardian*, London, January 12, p. 23.

USWeb/CKS (1999), *Audience Development: A comprehensive process for building a profitable customer base on the Internet*, White Paper, Washington, DC.

Willram, J. (2000), Miller takes a back seat in battle for global domination, *Financial Times, Companies and Finance: International*, April 8/9, p. 9.

Writer, S. and McLaughlin, M. (2001), Nike, Titleist wage ball battle, *CNN Financial News*, April 4, **http://cnnfn.cnn.com.**

Chapter 15

Establishing, developing and managing buyer-seller relationships

LEARNING OBJECTIVES

After studying this chapter you should be able to:

- understand the stages in the development of a dyadic buyer-seller relationship (acts, episodes, sequences and relationships).
- explain the importance of loyalty.
- identify the different categories (segments) of loyalty.
- describe the steps in building a loyalty-based, relationship-based strategy.
- explain how to create e-loyalty.
- understand the importance of customer lifetime value and how it is calculated.
- develop ideas for creating customer loyalty programmes.
- describe the stages in the KAM relationship development model.
- explain the purpose of a customer complaint management system.

Case study 15.1 Celador Productions

How to maintain relationships with the international entertainment market beyond the *Who Wants To Be A Millionaire?* show

The concept of *Who Wants To Be A Millionaire?* was brought to Celador Productions by David Briggs, now a producer of the show. He had a 'vague idea' which he scribbled down on a scrap of paper. The format was then further developed, but it took three years of discussion with ITV and changes of format before it finally made its debut in the UK on ITV (September 4, 1998). It was produced by London-based Celador Productions.

About the show

Following the preliminary fastest finger round in the studio, one or more contestants get the opportunity to show their skill and knowledge with Chris Tarrant in front of millions of TV viewers, knowing that a further 15 correct answers in a row will win them £1 million.

Once in the hot seat, contestants are shown each question and four possible answers before deciding whether to take the cash they have accumulated, or trust their knowledge in pursuit of a greater prize.

After every five correct questions, contestants bank whatever amount they have won so far (£1,000 for five, £32,000 for ten) knowing that one wrong answer at any stage in between will have increasingly devastating consequences as

Case study 15.1 continued

they are forced to make some of the hardest decisions of their lives.

By question 13, the contestant will be playing with a massive £125,000. A correct answer will double that sum to £250,000, but a wrong answer will knock them out of the game, but still taking home £32,000. Or they can opt not to answer the question, having seen it, and still walk away £125,000 better off.

Players are entitled to play three 'lifelines'. They can ask the audience, have the odds cut with 50:50 (where two incorrect answers are taken away) or they can phone a friend for advice.

In November 2000, garden designer Judith Keppel became the first person to win the top £1 million prize when she correctly answered 'Henry II' to the question 'Which king was married to Eleanor of Aquitane?'

The night Judith Keppel won, audience figures showed 13.9 million viewers watched *Who Wants To Be A Millionaire?* on ITV as opposed to 10.7 million for a BBC One comedy, starting 15 minutes later at 21:15 GMT.

The millionaire win – filmed the Sunday before it was broadcast – had been leaked to the press, and the resulting publicity helped ITV to a ratings victory over BBC One. ITV said a member of the audience, which had been sworn to secrecy, broke the story against its wishes.

Internationalization of the show

The show has been an enormous success in virtually every market in which it has been launched and was regularly the top-rated show in the USA.

It has been screened under licence in 90 countries including Spain, Australia, Israel, South Africa, India, and Russia. A CD-ROM, produced and marketed in the USA under licence to Disney Interactive, sold 1 million copies in December 1999 alone and it became the first product to top the PC, PlayStation, Dreamcast and all format charts at the same time. There is enormous potential for spin-off merchandising products in the UK and elsewhere.

The US market

The game is gaining international success, especially in the USA, which has enabled ABC – the network that carries it – to transform itself from being at the bottom of the ratings to being number one.

ABC Television has achieved extremely high viewing figures, topping the ratings for each night that the show has been broadcast with an average of 23.8 million viewers a night. The high ratings being achieved opened significant merchandising opportunities in the US market.

The Japanese market

In February 2000, Celador Productions licensed the show to Japanese broadcaster Fuji Television. This was the first time a western quiz show had been sold to a Japanese broadcaster by the UK. Fuji Television had commissioned an initial 26 60-minute episodes. The show would be broadcast in prime time every Thursday night from April 2000.

Paul Smith, Managing Director of Celador Productions and Executive Producer of *Who Wants To Be A Millionaire?* in Britain said,

'For years, Japan has been a notoriously hard market to break into for producers of television shows in the west. This is a groundbreaking deal for Celador. Who Wants To Be A Millionaire? has great international appeal and we are hopeful it will prove a hit with Japanese television audiences. Fuji Television is the perfect partner for Celador to make the show a success in Japan.

Mr Chihiro Kameyama, Senior director, Programming division of Fuji Television, commented,

Everyone at Fuji Television is very excited about the Who Wants To Be A Millionaire? *deal. It is both a big chance and a great challenge for us to create a reformatted version of a foreign hit programme and we will give it our all to make it successful. We have every confidence that* Who Wants To Be A Millionaire? *will be a great success in Japan, for history has proved that high-quality entertainment has no boundaries.*

▶

Case study 15.1 continued

Problems on the horizon

Good as the programme is, one day it will stop being the best-rated TV programme. Quiz shows generally have a limited life, but may last for a number of years.

In the USA, the audience for *Who Wants To Be A Millionaire?* is getting older and somewhat smaller, but ABC executives say the game show, whose multiple episodes continue to stay in the top ten in household viewing, still attracts viewers better than other programmes.

To bring back some younger viewers, two special *Millionaire* episodes on February 11 and 14, 2001 featured rock and pop stars, including Backstreet Boys' Nick Carter and Howie Dorough, Metallica drummer Lars Ulrich, Dixie Chick Emily Robison, Sugar Ray rocker Mark McGrath, Gene Simmons of Kiss and hitmaker Sisqo.

In contrast to the general trend, the number of viewers in Japan was surprisingly low. The failure surprised even media insiders because the Japanese have long had an insatiable appetite for British and US pop culture.

It seems that watching ordinary people winning money is not very enticing in Japan, a culture that has traditionally discouraged individuals from flaunting their wealth or achievements, says one media observer.

'Japan is like one big village,' said Mamoru Sakamoto, editor of the TV monthly *Galac*. 'Americans may really identify with somebody winning big bucks on TV, but Japanese are more apt to think, "What did he do to deserve that?"'

'Japanese people tend to be conservative when it comes to money,' said producer Toshihiko Matsuo. 'If they win 5 million yen on the show, they probably figure, "I might as well quit while I'm ahead and work for the rest".'

Money has never been the name of the game in Japan. That honour is reserved for weirdness.

'Game shows are supposed to be a form of entertainment, and the average person just isn't very entertaining,' said Tomohiro Maruyama, an accountant in his 30s.

Japan's hottest game show is *Tokyo Friend Park II*, which features a pair of celebrities competing in a series of oddball events – like flinging themselves against a wall-sized Velcro target to see who sticks (Wall Crash) or trying not to drop precariously balanced boxes of takeaway food while riding a motorbike simulator (Delivery Deluxe).

The prizes for completing these odd tasks are often just tokens. For example, after sitting through a recent episode of *Tokyo Friend Park II*, popular sumo wrestler Takatoriki was rewarded with a triple-decker bunk bed for his kids. And for those game shows that do feature average people as contestants, it is more often comic relief than gratuitous wealth on offer.

At the end of April 2001, Celador Productions was awarded the UK Queen's Award for Enterprise after the show's format became a huge success in countries such as the USA, India, Japan and Australia. However, during the summer and autumn of 2001 and spring 2002, the number of viewers in the original markets like the USA and the UK began to decrease.

Questions

1. How would you characterize the product life cycle of the *Who Wants To Be A Millionaire?* show?

2. How could Celador Productions extend the product life cycle of the show?

3. Why is the relationship approach important in this case?

4. How could Celador Productions' relations with the television companies be maintained?

Sources: BBC (2000, 2001a, b, c, 2002), Celador (2000), CNN (2000), Keveney (2001)

15.1 Introduction

Relationships in marketing encompass a range of exchange phenomena, from relationships between firms (B-t-B relationships) to relationships between firms and individual consumers.

Managing relationships with customers, suppliers, and competitors is now an integral part of a firm's strategic marketing agenda. This criticality is reflected in the growth in the importance of relationships in the academic literature. Subject areas such as RM, networks, alliances, partnering, and key account management encompass a growing set of theories and normative approaches to managing relationships. This chapter will concentrate on the relationship between the buyer (customer) and the seller (supplier).

Managing buyer-supplier relationships involves a consideration of a multiplicity of different relationship types. Webster (1992) conceived these types as representing a continuum from a price-based transaction to close interactive relationships. Whether relationship types can be thought of as a continuum, or as radically different approaches, is a matter for debate. However, the close and distant opposites are two types that can readily be understood and managed. Jackson (1985) examined the difference between close (lost-for-good) and transaction (always-a-share) accounts and developed a framework for managing this difference (Figure 6.4).

15.2 Building buyer-seller relationships in B-t-B markets

Why build a relationship in the first place? Relationships enhance value in several ways. The pooling of partners' knowledge may improve market vision. Combining the partners' unique competences and matching them to the most promising value opportunities may enhance customer value. The partnering of German car manufacturer Mercedes-Benz with the Swiss manufacturer of Swatch watches to collaborate in developing the SmartCar is a good example. Value migration opportunities that are not feasible for a single organization may be pursued via collaboration strategies.

In most business-to-business situations, especially where the benefits exceed the risks, it is desirable for both the seller and the customer to maintain a long-term relationship. A relationship is warranted in a situation where there is congruence between goals of the the seller and the customer, meaning where the organization and the customer realize that the potential gains from acting cooperatively will exceed the gains from acting opportunistically. From a strategic perspective, the seller wants to maintain a long-term relationship with a customer because it is generally much cheaper to keep an existing customer than to attract a new customer; a long-term customer can provide feedback on existing products and insights into new or re-engineered products; and a long-term customer almost becomes part of the selling team because it can provide recommendations and encourage new business. Also, as time passes and experience steps in, a long-term customer becomes easy to work with because communication channels will usually open and expand, the customer's needs and problems are known, and a comfortable working, and sometimes personal relationship exists between personnel in both firms.

Internal focus

Before any vendor can develop a relationship with another company, the selling organization must focus internally. The selling organization must determine its marketing goals and strategy, analyse its current culture, ensure that the strategy and culture match, and, if necessary, activate a customer service-oriented culture.

There seem to be three phases in the development of a dyadic relationship as illustrated in Figure 15.1.

The courtship phase

During courtship, purchasers express their desires to sellers, who develop proposals designed to satisfy the buyers' needs. This phase often begins when a company is placed on the buyer's approved supplier list, which means it meets at least minimum standards. The criteria usually include financial health, size, licensing qualification, and delivery capabilities.

Because quality has become so important, suppliers are often required to demonstrate quality control methods and records as a prerequisite to being approved.

Unlike many people, businesses tend to look before they leap. Often courtship takes a good deal of time. Each company is trying to understand the other's requirements, so there are many discussions about product specifications, product design, and order routines. Eventually, the organizations become closer. Often the buyer will grant the supplier a small order to test the water, including the response to any problems that occur. At this level of the relationship, the bonds that hold the two parties together are rather weak and can be broken without a great deal of disruption or cost to either party.

The relationship-building phase

The buyers and sellers work together for the first time in the relationship-building phase, which strengthens the bond between them. Unlike consumer marketing, business-to-business marketing tends to involve customizing the product, its deliv-

Figure 15.1 Developing buyer-seller relationships

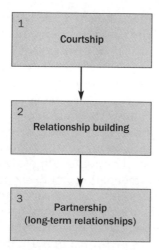

Source: adapted from Hutt and Speh (2001), p. 88–94.

ery, and its terms and conditions to each individual buyer. Buyers often grow to rely on suppliers for additional expertise, especially regarding new technologies. That is why trust, loyalty, and compromise become so important in organizational buying activities.

Due to the complexity and technical nature of most organizational purchasing, buyers and sellers must learn to work together. Each party may even adjust its internal practices to better satisfy the other's needs. Understanding the customer – and its customers – is critical.

During the relationship-building phase, the purchasing organization does not always have the upper hand. In fact, the relationship is sometimes said to be symmetrical, that is, the buyer and the seller may have equal power.

Both frequently feel a very strong need to interact in order to explore all options before signing a contract. This is particularly the case if a formal partnership is being considered. Sellers generally offer information to help buyers formulate ideas about the purchase decision. Buyers provide information that helps the sellers do a better job of matching products to needs.

The partnership phase

After numerous purchases have been completed satisfactorily and long-term agreements are reached, the partnership phase begins. Because the buyer and seller have extensive experience with each other, they spend less time on the relationship itself and more time on ways of improving the productive aspects of the exchange. The buying process becomes routine. The seller may become an exclusive supplier or a contract may guarantee that the buyer will purchase a certain amount within a certain period.

The seller can commit resources to the buyer because the business relationship will continue.

Partnerships can be informal or contractual. Informally, each party may work without any guarantee of long-term business. Usually, the benefits are such that the relationship is likely to last. A good example is an advertising agency and its client. Both invest a lot of time and energy, and share important information, so it is costly for either party to end the relationship.

A contractual partnership is formed when the buyer signs an agreement with a supplier for a specified period, usually three to five years. The trend in purchasing today is toward fewer suppliers, the use of programmes that certify the qualifications of suppliers and long-term contracts. Close relationships with suppliers help ensure quality. Many buying organizations find that contractual partnerships have considerable advantages. The long-term relationship with suppliers allows the buying organization to concentrate on its customers. The buyer and supplier work as a team, each contributing its own expertise, to provide products that better meet consumer needs. The longer the relationship, the better are the results in terms of cooperation, efficiency, quality control, and profits. Strong relationships mean greater dependence. If one partner experiences downsizing, strikes, or financial failure, then the other party feels the consequences.

In the development of a partnership (dyadic relationship) between buyer and seller, bonding can be described as a dynamic process that is progressive over time. The bonding process begins with the very basic force of the need for a seller to find a buyer for its product, and the desire for a buyer to purchase a product that will satisfy its needs. As time goes on, this relationship then advances toward interdependency between the buyer and the seller, which will finally lead to a situation between the two where there is total commitment on the part of both parties. Termination costs now restrict or almost prohibit an easy dissolution of the bond. At this advanced stage in the relationship, the bonds are so strong that they are almost impossible to break.

Bonding often begins as a result of the fulfilment of a basic business need on the part of both parties involved, and then grows as a social relationship develops between the vendor and the customer. One has a product or service to sell and the other has the need to purchase a product or service. Whether or not a bond will develop between the two parties depends on such factors as the fit between the vendor's product or service and the seller's needs, the price of the vendor's product or service, the expertise of the vendor at providing a high-quality product or service and high-quality follow-up service, and the ability of the seller to make and keep realistic promises to the customer.

After the basic business relationship has been established, and if the two parties like each other, a social bond begins to develop as time progresses and the two parties experience a more and more satisfying interaction.

The social bond is a product of personal relationships that develop between the parties involved from both the buyer and the seller. The better the fit (on the personal or social level) between the parties, the stronger the social bonds.

The ultimate service support is provided when the seller aids the customer with implementation of a new product. This process of implementation consists of all the necessary changes the organization needs to prepare for the acceptance of a new product. The implementation process also involves learning to use the product to its full potential. In the case of a high technology product such as a mainframe computer, seller involvement with implementation can provide much needed help to the customer.

Many suppliers also find contractual partnerships advantageous, but there are risks. The organizations often share highly secret market and technological information as well as sensitive strategic marketing plans. Contracts safeguard a supplier against an unethical buyer who might reveal those secrets to the supplier's competitors in an attempt to receive price reductions. When this occurs, most strong suppliers will refuse to market their newest technology to unethical buyers or in some cases refuse to sell to them altogether.

15.3 Building buyer-seller relationships in B-t-C markets

Firms that practise customer focus shift the power from the seller to the customer. Once the basic principle of shifting the power to customers is accepted, Internet technology makes it more achievable.

Customer focus promises to provide something that traditional strategies never could – increasing return. The value an organization derives from products diminishes over time, but the value of locking customers in can increase (Vandermerwe, 2000).

When a customer is locked in, it has no choice. There may be only one supplier with a monopoly for as long as its particular technology wave lasts. Or customers may have invested in one product and then find that the switching costs are too high. The customers are locked in a continuous relationship life cycle until an alternative comes along.

In Figure 15.2 a customer relationship life cycle of an airline transportation service is shown.

Vandermerwe (2000) has expanded the product or service space into a market space, which is an aggregation of all the customer-activity cycles in a particular segment. For example, in the air travel industry, the pre, during, and post phases of a customer-activity cycle might include: first deciding where to go and how, booking flights and getting to the airport; second, taking the trip, getting to and experiencing the destination; and finally, leaving the destination, finding transport, coming home and paying the bills. Customer-activity cycle methodology can help managers assess opportunities for providing new kinds of value to customers at each critical experience.

Any interruption in the flow of the customer-activity cycle creates value gaps, or discontinuities, that open access to competitors, unless the company fills the gaps first with added value services.

Figure 15.2 The customer relationship life cycle in the airline business

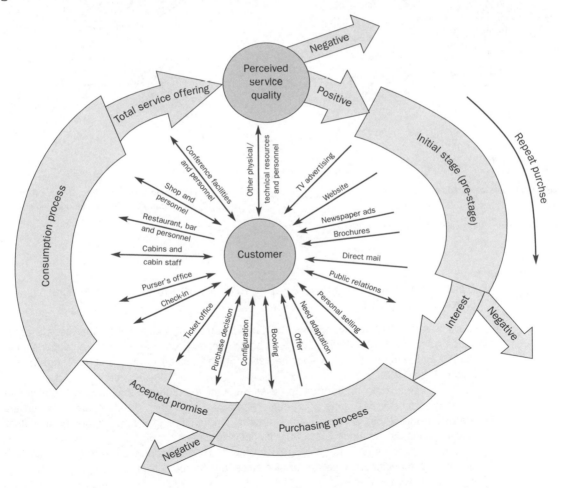

Source: after Grönroos (2000), p. 239.

In air travel, the British airline Virgin Atlantic challenged the diminishing returns, capacity managing thinking of conventional airlines by merging travel and leisure into one integrated customer experience (see Figure 15.3).

Virgin Atlantic has succeeded in turning a value added service into a strong competitive element. Virgin is always exploring new ways of increasing passenger comfort and offers superior service and quality. The price of an upper class ticket (comparable to business class on other airlines) includes a luxury limousine service

Figure 15.3 Virgin Atlantic's add-on service

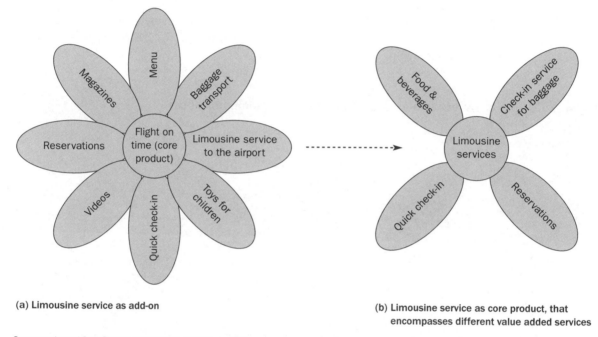

(a) Limousine service as add-on

(b) Limousine service as core product, that encompasses different value added services

Source: adapted from Thurau and Hansen (2000), p. 121.

| Exhibit 15.1 | **Boeing and Russian space agency RKA are launching commercial satellites together** |

2001 was the 40th anniversary of Yuri Gagarin's historic space flight. This year US aerospace giant Boeing and the Russian aviation and space agency RKA formed a relationship to launch commercial satellites and market a future Russian module for the International Space Station (ISS).

There was also an agreement to develop two new jetliners within the next four or five years, a business-class plane and a regional passenger aircraft. The agreement also covers the expansion of joint space research, Boeing's purchases of Russian titanium and other products, and the development of Russian polar air routes.

Boeing opened a research centre in Moscow in 1993, and now employs more than 500 scientists and engineers in seven Russian cities, the company said.

Source: adapted from BBC (2001).

that picks up passengers from their home, and brought on board an entertainment centre with a selection of videos, comfortable reclining seats, and masseurs who help passengers to relax on even the longest flights.

Other services are also incorporated, such as help with baggage at the check-in counter.

Virgin Atlantic creates value gaps in the customer-activity cycle and then fills them with added value services. Virgin's goal is to redistribute value for business class and first class customers over the whole activity cycle.

15.4 Relationship quality

In any commercial relationship between two parties, interaction is the key concept. Interactions are the basic phenomena in quality and value creation. The perception of relationship quality occurs in ongoing interactions, which may be either continuous, such as in security and cleaning services, or discrete, such as in bank services or goods transportation. Holmlund (2000) has developed a framework for understanding and analysing ongoing interactions. These interactions may be very different depending on the type of marketing situation involved. Some contacts are between people, some between customers and machines and systems, and some between systems of the supplier and customer, respectively. In every case interactions are involved. The framework is equally valid for describing and analysing relationships in consumer markets and relationships between organizations. Originally, the framework was developed for services, but it may also be used for suppliers of physical goods, but with some services involved.

The framework consists of a continuous flow of acts, episodes and sequences, which form the relationships. Figure 15.4 illustrates this relationship framework.

An act (A) is the smallest unit of analysis in the interaction process. Examples of acts include phone calls, plant visits, service calls and hotel registration. In service management literature they are often called *moments of truth*. Acts may be related to any kind of interaction elements, physical goods, services, information, financial aspects or social contacts.

Figure 15.4 Interaction levels in a relationship: acts, episodes and sequences

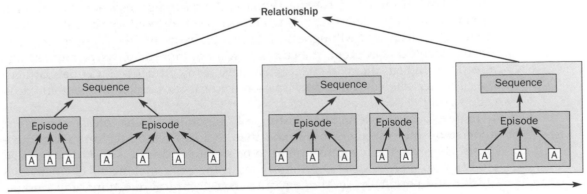

Source: adapted from Holmlund (2000), p. 96.

Interrelated acts form a minor part of a relationship. These are called episodes (or service encounters, to use a concept frequently found in the service management literature) and examples of these include paying bills from a home computer, visiting a bank to withdraw money, a negotiation, a shipment of goods, or dinner at a hotel restaurant during a stay at that hotel. Every episode includes a series of acts. For example, a shipment may include such acts as placing an order, assembling and packing the products, transporting the products, making a complaint, and payment.

Interrelated episodes form the next level of analysis in the interaction process, a sequence. Sequences can be defined in terms of a time period, a product introduction, a campaign or a project, or a combination of these. The analysis of a sequence may contain all kind of interactions related to a particular project, which may take up to a year or even longer. As an example, in a hotel context a sequence comprises everything that takes place during one stay at a particular hotel, including episodes such as accommodation, eating in the hotel restaurant, etc. Sequences may naturally overlap, so that episodes belonging to one sequence may also be part of another sequence.

The final and most aggregated level of analysis is the relationship. Several sequences form a relationship. Sequences may follow each other directly, may overlap or may follow after longer or shorter intervals depending, for example, on the type of business or on whether the service is of a continuous or discrete nature. This way of dividing the interaction process into several layers on different levels of aggregation gives the marketer a detailed enough instrument to be used in the analysis of interactions between a supplier or service provider and the customers.

All different types of elements in the interaction process – goods and service outcomes, service processes, information, social contacts, financial activities, etc. – can be identified and put into their correct perspective in the formation of a relationship over time.

The relationship between a customer and a salesperson is like a marriage. It starts with a courtship period, when both parties begin to know each other. Next a ceremony, or contract to do business, binds both parties to certain terms. The relationship is then maintained by developing high levels of trust and service norms that guide future interactions. If the relationship becomes unsatisfactory for either party, they divorce.

Developing strong relationships with customers gives a salesperson a sustainable competitive advantage in the marketplace. If a customer feels a certain level of commitment to the relationship, which has been fostered by the salesperson's attention to detail and willingness to do that bit extra in after-sales service, then, when a problem does occur, the customer will not immediately seek another supplier. Even though the marketplace may have many attractive potential partners, the customer will be loyal to a salesperson who has shown commitment and dedication over the long term.

To develop a long-term relationship, it is important for the salesperson to first understand the customer's needs and then to adapt selling techniques to those needs. However, the relationship has to be sustained, and it is sustained through attention to service, such as promptly returning calls, making special deliveries quickly and personally, seeking out answers to technical questions, and working with the customer to design the next generation of products and services.

Exhibit 15.2	Customer relationship management (CRM) in team sports

A growing number of major and minor league teams are beginning to use customer relationship management (CRM) strategies to stop fan defection. Part of the reason for adopting a CRM approach is that franchises today face a double threat. Consumers have more entertainment choices; even the most die-hard fans wince at the ever-increasing costs of attending a sporting event. If a team has a bad season, it is difficult to sell tickets. Until recently, sports teams have not had access to CRM strategies designed specifically for their use.

New technology is allowing developers of customer relationship programmes to manage the data they gather better. It is also helping marketers enhance their recruitment of new customers and keep current clients. Aided by technology, sports-specific strategies are helping marketers reconnect with their fans. Even when a team is winning and stadia are packed, CRM helps identify those fans most likely to buy season tickets or ticket packages in advance, by creating databases on fan attendance. A team can then target these prospects for season tickets the following year. Advance ticket sales are extremely valuable to sports teams, since they guarantee a certain revenue level for the season.

'Club cards' similar to credit cards are at the heart of fan loyalty programmes these days. Although programmes vary slightly from team to team, the idea is pretty much the same. Each time fans use their card, they gain attendance points which may be exchanged for promotional coupons or items such as food, drinks, and souvenirs. The more points they compile, the more 'rewards' they receive. In return, the teams get a database of information on their fans, which could lead to additional revenue streams. For example, when fans sign up for a typical club card, they must complete a form asking for their addresses, incomes, family configurations, and other basic personal information. And if teams want, the surveys could also include tailored questions like 'What's your favourite soft drink?' or 'What kind of car do you drive?'

Once a fan attends a game, there can be increased revenue generated from ancillary offerings such as food and merchandise. Loyalty programmes can help generate millions in additional revenue. An average fan at a US Major League Baseball game pays US$15 per ticket, and spends another US$15.40 on other items such as T-shirts, food, etc.

Hence, the CRM approach with a membership database may create a more personalized interaction with the fan base – from individualized e-mails to, perhaps, video highlights of sporting or entertainment events.

Source: adapted from Raymond (2001).

15.5 Categories of loyalty

If the above view of building relationships is accepted, then managing loyalty becomes crucial.

Defining loyalty: conceptual issues

Some marketers have mistakenly assumed that satisfied customers will automatically be loyal, and therefore measures of customer satisfaction have been widely used as proxy measures for loyalty. However, the use of satisfaction (or attitude) in measuring loyalty poses certain problems for marketers. While it certainly makes sense to suggest that dissatisfied customers are unlikely to be loyal, it seems that the corollary – that satisfied customers will be loyal – is not always true. Indeed, the link between a customer's words and actions in this case may only be tenuous.

Dick and Basu (1994) proposed a framework, which conceptualizes loyalty as 'the relationship between the relative attitude toward an entity (brand/service/store/vendor) and patronage behavior'. This definition combines both approaches, and results in four categories of loyalty, each of which has managerial implications. These four categories of loyalty provide a far richer conceptualization of loyalty than previously existed (see Table 15.1). In order to understand the categories used, it is important to understand the factors on which these categories are based.

Relative attitude focuses not only on attitude to the entity, but also incorporates comparison to other organizations or brands. For example, a customer may have a favourable attitude toward a national bank, but may prefer to deal with a local bank.

Patronage behaviour includes traditional retention measures, share of disposable income, purchase sequence, etc.

The four categories of loyalty are briefly explained below.

Table 15.1 Four categories of loyalty

Category	No loyalty	Spurious loyalty	Latent loyalty	Loyalty
Relative attitude	Low relative attitude.	Low relative attitude.	High relative attitude.	High relative attitude.
Patronage behaviour	Low repeat behaviour.	High repeat behaviour.	Low repeat behaviour.	High repeat behaviour.
Manifestation	Does not use the company, and does not wish to.	Uses the company, but does not have a high relative attitude. This may be as a result of other factors, including location, convenience, lack of alternatives.	In this case, the customer wishes to use the organization, but perhaps is not able to do so – store location may be inconvenient, favourite brands not stocked etc.	The individual enjoys a high relative attitude, together with high repeat patronage behaviour
Implications	Management may attempt to generate 'spurious loyalty'.	'Spurious loyalty' cannot be relied upon. The customer is clearly open to better offers.	Managerial efforts are best focused on removing the obstacles to patronage for the customer.	Loyalty must be continually reinforced, and the value offered must remain acceptable.

Source: adapted from Dick and Basu (1994).

No loyalty

There is an absence of loyalty where the consumer's relative attitude is low, and there is no evidence of purchase behaviour. For example, most petrol buyers are not loyal to any brand or location. Motorists tend to stop for petrol whenever it is most convenient for them to do so. In this and similar cases, the best that management can do is attempt to generate spurious loyalty through such means as in-store promotions, loyalty clubs and special offers.

Spurious loyalty

Spurious loyalty is very similar to the concept of inertia. That is, although behavioural data indicates that there is high repeat patronage, in reality the customer does not believe that the alternatives are highly differentiated. In such cases, repeat purchase may be based upon the availability of deals, special offers, convenience or the influence of other people. As a result, the consumer may only temporarily display such loyalty, and is likely to be very open to competing offers. The management objective in this case is to convert spurious loyalty into loyalty. This can be done by enhancing the customer's relative attitude by communicating specific advantages. Alternatively, where competing offers are generally undifferentiated, the manager can attempt to increase switching costs (effectively erecting a barrier to exit), that is, making it costly for a customer to switch between competing offers. One effective method of achieving this is through accruing points as used within many existing loyalty programmes. For example, airlines have for a long time run point accrual programmes.

These programmes aim to tie the customer into a particular supplier though the promise of future rewards. In this case, the points already accrued represent switching costs, because the customers lose the benefit of previous purchases if they switch suppliers.

Latent loyalty

This suggests that a customer has a high relative attitude toward the company or brand, but this is not evident in terms of purchase behaviour. This is probably as a result of situational influences – including inconvenient store locations, out-of-stock situations, or the influence of other people as in the case of restaurant patronage. Using the previous example, a motorist might have a preference for Q8, but it may be more convenient to purchase from BP, or his or her company may have a credit account at a Statoil station. In this case, despite a higher relative attitude for Q8, the motorist would not use Q8 much. In the case of latent loyalty, managerial efforts are best focused upon removing the obstacles to patronage, for example by extending the branch network or credit account.

Loyalty

When true loyalty exists, the customer regularly buys and does so because of strong preferences (high relative attitude). As such, this is clearly the most preferred of

---

Exhibit 15.3 | **Danone and Johnson & Johnson go into a relationship based on J&J's skin care.**

French food giant Danone and US-based Johnson & Johnson are teaming up on a new series of cosmetics and beauty/hygiene products to be marketed in retail chains and grocery stores under the Evian-Affinity brand name.

The products – including bath gels and moisturizing creams – aim to steal market share from leading brands including Beiersdorf-owned Nivea, Henkel-controlled Diadermine and L'Oréal-owned Plenitude.

Danone, which is contributing its Evian water as the base ingredient for the products as well as its well-known brand name, is relying on Johnson & Johnson for research and development, production and marketing of the new products.

Source: adapted from Adage Global (2001).

the four categories. Where loyalty exists, managerial efforts are best aimed at continually strengthening relative attitudes, particularly as the customer may be the focus of aggressive marketing by competing organizations. This may involve maintaining a price advantage, and/or offering additional services that are of value to the customers. In the case of petrol retailing, these might include car wash and oil-change facilities.

15.6 Managing loyalty

Managing loyalty means not only managing behaviour but also managing a state of mind. It means affecting the customer's attitude to doing business with the supplier over the long term – not merely until the next visit or the next purchase. This means that a properly managed approach to loyalty must make the customer want to do more business with the supplier over the long term or, at least, sustain its existing level of business.

Steps in a loyalty-based relationship strategy

Customer retention for all customers is key. There are six steps in a retention strategy as illustrated in Figure 15.5.

Define objectives

The need to develop a loyalty approach over and above existing marketing, sales and service approaches should be identified as part of an overall audit of customer management. Such an audit might reveal for example:

● competitive attempts to target precisely your best customers
● falling repurchase rate among your best customers

Figure 15.5 Steps in a relationship strategy

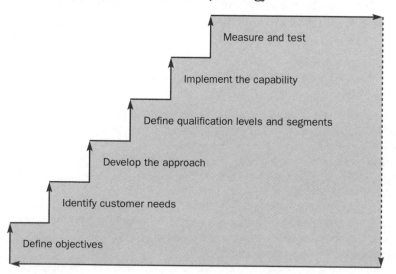

- falling levels of state-of-mind loyalty
- increasing numbers of customers switching away from your products and services.

Your objectives for the loyalty approach should be set in quantifiable terms, or else the approach will be impossible to evaluate, whether by research or through business performance. These objectives should always contain some financial component, or else the loyalty approach may be vulnerable to the criticism that it makes your customers feel good but has no effect on profits.

Identify your customers' needs (and their propensities to be loyal)

If you are considering introducing a loyalty approach, you must establish, usually through research and/or testing, the following:

- which groups of customers are strategically important to you?
- what is the propensity of these groups to respond to different marketing, sales and service approaches?
- how, and by how much, do they respond, and in particular, how does their loyalty increase mentally (as measured by research, perhaps) and behaviourally?

Remember that the customer base of the firm is the greatest potential market-research tool. It can provide market researchers with an excellent sampling frame, which is why the formal research process should be built into marketing contacts, involving where possible the use of questionnaires and structured telephone interviews. If executed properly, research will reinforce the brand and values you wish to transmit to customers.

Develop the approach

This involves the following. Find the best loyalty reinforcers. Identify those aspects of the marketing and service mix, which can be deployed most effectively (taking into account the nature of your target customers for the loyalty approach) to reinforce and build loyalty.

There is a tendency to focus first on promotional incentives (discounts, free or low-cost promotional products and services, etc.), but these have the disadvantage of focusing on specific behaviours, as the qualification to receive the incentive is usually fixed in terms of those behaviours. A key area of focus should be the interface with the customer. Put simply, how you deal with your customers, in terms of managing their requirements and exchanging information with them, should hold the key to sustaining and building their loyalty.

You should find the most valued reinforcers. Find those elements of the product or service mix which have the highest perceived value to your customers, but relatively low costs of provision. This may seem a strange point, but it is the key to most schemes that work in the long term. The justification of loyalty schemes is that they reduce marketing costs because:

- less has to be spent on acquiring new customers
- it costs less to sell more to existing customers, because we already know them and have access to them.

Loyalty schemes can also reduce service costs, partly because existing customers have learnt how to work with you. But these financial benefits may take some time to emerge.

Define qualification levels and segments

This is a detailed analysis of the profile of your best customers. We advise starting with a broad definition of best, rather than just the ones who buy the most.

A thorough profiling and tracking of purchase histories, transactional values, promotional responses, and sources is vital here. It also helps identify the potential market size of similar customers for the acquisition programme. This is sometimes referred to as a relationship marketing audit. Many financial institutions, when they have undertaken this activity, have been surprised to learn how many customers are multiple purchasers of the products.

You must work out to which groups of customers you wish to provide the benefits of your loyalty approach, and the divisions between these groups of customers. Conventionally, this is done in terms of how much they buy from you, but there are many other approaches:

- how much they buy of a key product or service
- how often they buy
- the spread of their purchases
- their potential future purchases
- their actual or potential importance as a recommender of your services
- how much you buy from them (for reciprocal approaches)
- how much information they give you

It is common to set tiered qualification levels, with increasing loyalty commitment from customers matched by increasing service levels and bonuses from you.

This makes sense provided that the customer's movement between tiers is normally upwards. Being downgraded is not a pleasant experience for customers in any context, but particularly disappointing for those who have been 'nurtured upwards' for a long period. One demotion can destroy a relationship built up over years.

Also it is important not to let temporary reductions in purchasing (which may be totally uncorrelated with loyalty) lead to downgrading. For example, a member of a frequent flyer scheme may temporarily fly less overall, rather than fly more with another airline. Demotivating them by downgrading them immediately makes little sense.

Implement the capability

Capability is defined as the support infrastructure necessary to deliver relationship marketing. It includes:

- briefing marketing service suppliers such as: advertising and direct marketing agencies, in-house magazine publishers, etc.
- customer service definition
- staff training and motivation approaches
- acquisitions, adaptations and development of customer-facing information systems
- setting pricing and terms of payment
- policy and process development.

The workload involved in all these is, of course, significant, but the point is that if your approach is developed logically, starting with proper strategic evaluation and with the right analysis of customer needs, behaviour, and experience, then the follow-through should be relatively straightforward, based on a phased approach.

Measure effectiveness

Loyalty approaches must in the end pay by producing better sales and profits than would have been yielded without the approach.

On a more detailed level, whatever stage of the life cycle a customer is at, it is always worth having a continued series of tests to establish optimum timing, frequency, offer, and creative treatments.

Wansink and Seed (2001) researched the effectiveness of different loyalty programmes in the B-t-C market and found that marketers need to understand that for a loyalty programme to be successful, it must offer obvious benefits to the consumer (see Table 15.2).

The products used in the study, Kellogg, Betty Crocker and Land O' Lakes, could be put into three categories: convenience foods, meal preparation items and perishable foods. Kellogg's cereals, for example, are an alternative to the traditional hot breakfast. The Betty Crocker products are not meals in themselves, but aid in the

Table 15.2 Loyalty implications for marketing managers

	Targeting non-users	*Targeting light users*	*Targeting heavy users*
Type of programme In general, the more obvious the benefits, the more effective the programme.	A programme with average benefits is the most effective in stimulating initial trial.	A programme with below average benefits and a programme with comparatively better benefits can generate a similar increase in purchases.	A programme with average benefits and a programme with comparatively better benefits can generate a similar increase in purchases.
Type of product, e.g. convenience foods A programme with attractive benefits is the most effective in increasing planned purchases.	A programme with average benefits is the most effective in stimulating initial trial.	A programme with very attractive benefits is the most effective in increasing planned purchases.	A programme with very attractive benefits is the most effective in increasing planned purchases.
Meal preparation items A programme with average benefits can increase purchases significantly more than programmes with better benefits.	A programme with average benefits is the most effective in stimulating initial trial.	A programme with average benefits can generate a greater increase in purchases than a programme with comparatively better benefits.	A programme with average benefits can generate a greater increase in purchases than a programme with comparatively better benefits.
Perishable foods A programme with average benefits and a programme with comparatively better benefits can generate a similar increase in purchases.	A programme with average benefits is the most effective in stimulating initial trial.	A programme with average benefits can generate a greater increase in purchases than a programme with comparatively better benefits.	A programme with very attractive benefits is the most effective in increasing planned purchases.

Source: first published in *The Journal of Brand Management*, vol. 8, no. 3 (2001), in a paper by Brian Wansink and Scott Seed entitled 'Making brand loyalty programs succeed', Henry Stewart Publications (**www.henrystewart.co.uk**)

preparation of main meal items and side dishes. The Land O' Lakes products fit into a category of perishable foods, since they have a limited shelf life and must be refrigerated.

These results indicate that marketers can motivate non-user and heavy-user segments to increase purchases with programmes offering only a moderate level of benefits.

Across all products, the moderate-reward programme was the only programme that motivated non-users to purchase. Perhaps the high-reward programme required too much involvement on the part of the non-user and the low-reward programme did not offer enough benefit to induce trial. The moderate-reward programme might have struck the right balance. As non-users become more familiar with the product, however, a programme with more benefits might be required to sustain interest.

Table 15.2 outlines the best reward programmes for three broad categories of products. For convenience foods, a programme with very attractive benefits (like the high-reward programme in the survey) is the most effective in increasing planned purchases. Specifically, light and heavy users of this category respond best to this level of loyalty programme. Since these products tend to have higher margins, the coupons in the survey's programme might be inducing additional purchases from consumers wanting more value.

For meal preparation items, a programme with average benefits can increase purchases significantly more than programmes with better benefits. Users of these products might already be content with the value they receive and are not attracted by the coupons. A quarterly newsletter, for example, might be of interest to those wanting new recipes for the products they are currently using. This interest could serve to increase involvement with the brand and positively affect planned purchases.

For perishable foods, a programme with average benefits can generate a similar increase in purchases as a programme with comparatively better benefits. Heavy users, however, should be targeted with an attractive programme. Since perishable items are difficult to stockpile without a good reason for use, perhaps heavy users are enticed with coupons that reduce the risk of purchasing items that might expire before consumption.

Exhibit 15.4 Developing service loyalty at Volkswagen

Volkswagen AG is the largest car manufacturer in Europe. Worldwide, there are more than 36 million Volkswagen vehicles on the road. In an increasingly competitive market, direct contact with customers takes on vital importance. In recent years, therefore, Volkswagen has been developing and extending its relationship management activities, as part of a strategic customer bonding concept. So what does relationship marketing mean for a company like Volkswagen?

The development of service loyalty is shown in Figure 15.6. It shows that the older a vehicle, the greater the demand for related services. However, loyalty to Volkswagen dealerships decreases over the same time period. A car has US$160–210 a year spent on it (for vehicle-related services) in the first few years after purchase, and VW has a market share of about 85%. Eleven years after purchase, annual spending rises to US$810, but VW's market share falls to only 25%. This means that VW is losing contact with the car owner after the first change of ownership (after an average 3.7 years). In reality, this means VW has no real information on many of its customers.

Exhibit 15.4 continued

Figure 15.6 The development of service loyalty

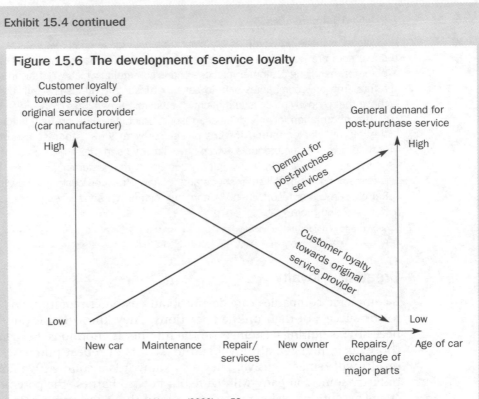

Source: adapted from Thurau and Hansen (2000), p. 52.

What is VW doing to give customers reasons to stay loyal towards VW services? For many years, VW has been a trendsetter in terms of service development in the car industry. It has developed services, which have not been offered by competitors, and these services have often been the reason why a customer has chosen to purchase their products. The services include a service guarantee, an emergency plan, a mobility guarantee, a customer club and a toll-free service telephone.

Volkswagen has bundled some service options into a premium concept called the Volkswagen Exclusive Service. This special service concept includes a mobility guarantee, service telephone hotline, a pick-up and delivery service and finally a courtesy car. These kinds of activities will be well known to experienced service marketers, but Volkswagen has now decided to go one important step further by extending these measures into a comprehensive club card concept.

The club card is a membership card which gives the customer out-of-hours access to the reception area of a Volkswagen dealership. The card also carries the mobility guarantee seal and is the first stage toward receiving a service card.

The bonus programme rewards customer loyalty by letting him or her collect bonus points every time he or she purchases something from Volkswagen (e.g. a car, accessory, or service) or from one of the partner organizations (e.g. Deutsche Bundesbahn). These bonus points can then only be exchanged for products and services from the Volkswagen organization. Research has shown that customers have a very positive impression of the programme; it strengthens the contact between customer and dealer and is an excellent instrument for binding customers to the dealer organization.

> **Exhibit 15.4 continued**
>
> None of these programmes are able to help increase customer satisfaction and loyalty if customers are not aware that they exist. Database management is therefore the starting point for managing customer relations and is something which will grow in importance in the future. The only companies able to construct lasting relationships with their customers are those that properly process and maintain a customer database.
>
> Key information for this database resource includes data on the customers themselves, the relevant dealer, the customer's present vehicle, the customer's use of the Volkswagen service card and the products, which have already been offered to him or her.
>
> VW also considers including information about the customer's hobbies. If VW knows that a customer's hobby is winter sports and it knows that the customer travels by car to his or her chosen winter resort, then VW can offer him or her snow tyres, snow chains, a roof rack (for skis) and more.
>
> *Source*: adapted from Thurau and Hansen (2000), Chapter 3.

Creating e-loyalty

E-commerce companies care deeply about customer retention and consider it vital to the success of their online operations. They know that loyalty is an economic necessity: acquiring customers on the Internet is enormously expensive, and unless those customers remain loyal and make lots of repeat purchases over the years, profits will remain elusive. They also know it is a competitive necessity: in every industry some company will figure out how to harness the potential of the web to create exceptional value for customers, and that company is going to lock in many profitable relationships at the expense of slow rivals. Without loyalty stickiness, even the best-designed e-business model will collapse.

Reichheld and Schefter (2000) studied e-loyalty and they found out that the web is actually a very sticky space in both the business-to-consumer and the business-to-business spheres. Most of today's online customers exhibit a clear proclivity toward loyalty, and web technologies, used correctly, reinforce that inherent loyalty. If executives do not quickly gain the loyalty of their most profitable existing customers and acquire the right new customers, they will face a dismal future left with only the most price-sensitive buyers.

It was shown that in e-industry after e-industry, the high cost of acquiring customers renders many customer relationships unprofitable during their early years. Only in later years, when the cost of serving loyal customers falls and the volume of their purchases rises, do relationships generate big returns.

At the beginning of a relationship, the outlays needed to acquire a customer are often considerably higher in e-commerce than in traditional retail channels. In clothing e-tailing, Reichheld and Schefter (2000) found that new customers cost 20–40 per cent more for pure Internet companies than for traditional retailers with both physical and online stores. That means that the losses in the early stages of relationships are larger.

However, web customers tend to consolidate their purchases with one primary supplier, to the extent that purchasing from the supplier's site becomes part of their daily routine. This phenomenon is particularly apparent in the business-to-business sector.

In the end, loyalty is not won with web technology. It is won through the delivery of a consistently superior customer experience. The Internet is a powerful tool for strengthening relationships, but the basic laws and rewards of building loyalty have not changed.

15.7 The CRM path to customer loyalty

The customer relationship management (CRM) loyalty development process is illustrated in Figure 15.7.

Stage 1: Customer acquisition (the courtship)

Before acquiring a customer, the firm must first get to know the potential customer. In this phase, loyalty is considered very weak because it is not based on relationships, but solely on look and feel – products and prices. In fact, the customer may switch to a competitor if its products and prices are better. The attitude is summed up as, 'what have you done for me lately?' A good example of this is the fierce competition in the mobile telephone market.

In stage 1, a company's main focus is customer acquisition. Attention is directed toward building a customer base through the use of technology and initiative-specific training to increase the effectiveness of salespeople. Stage 1 companies also spend a significant amount of time on best-practice benchmarking, analysing customer care processes and conducting initial customer research.

Stage 2: Customer retention (the relationship)

At this stage affection grows and a solid relationship is created. The firm engages with customer attitudes both before and after the purchase. It listens to the customer

Figure 15.7 Loyalty development in customer relationship management

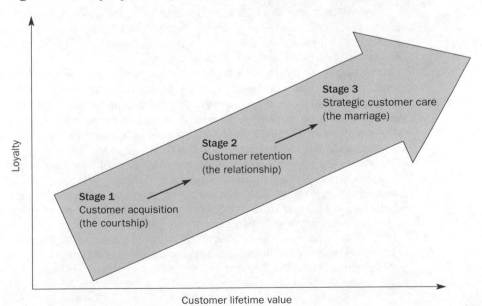

who is gradually getting to know the enterprise. Loyalty is no longer based on price and product alone. The relationship is also becoming a factor, even though there is no guarantee the customer will not go elsewhere. But the relationship is solid enough for loyalty to no longer be seen as fleeting. A mutual desire exists, and both parties begin to see a benefit in continuing to grow the relationship.

When a company enters stage 2, the focus has shifted to maximizing the customer relationships. A stage 2 company distinguishes itself from its stage 1 colleagues by beginning to segment its customers into groups with similar needs in order to serve each client group more effectively.

Stage 3: Strategic customer care (the marriage)

At this stage a long-lasting relationship is mutually agreeable, and both parties become inextricably linked. At this stage, loyalty is based on a high degree of satisfaction and the customer will get personally involved with the enterprise. As the marriage continues, the bonds between customer and enterprise are gradually strengthened. Here the feeling of customer satisfaction increases and with it loyalty to the enterprise. On the basis of such a relationship, one can speak of true loyalty and the beginning of customer dependency.

Exhibit 15.5 **Tenneco Automotive and Futaba Industrial Co. form a global strategic alliance**

Tenneco Automotive (USA) and Futaba Industrial Co. (Japan) announced in October 2000 that they had signed a strategic alliance to pursue opportunities to design, manufacture and market emission control products and systems for automotive original equipment manufacturers (OEMs). In connection with the alliance, the two companies had also established a joint venture at Burnley, UK.

The joint venture is known as Futaba-Tenneco UK Limited, and develops and produces emission control components and stamped products, mainly for automotive producers in the UK.

Tenneco Automotive is a US$3.3 billion manufacturing company headquartered in Lake Forest with 24,000 employees worldwide. Tenneco Automotive is one of the world's largest producers and marketers of ride control and exhaust systems and products, which are sold under the Monroe® and Walker® global brand names.

Futaba Industrial Co. Ltd. is a leading manufacturer and marketer of automotive equipment (including emission control components), office equipment parts and welding equipment. With 2500 employees, seven manufacturing facilities and two manufacturing subsidiaries in Japan, the company's customers include Toyota Motor Corp., Daihatsu Motor Co., Hino Motors Ltd., Mitsubishi Motors Corp., Honda Motor Co., Suzuki Motor Corp., Fuji Xerox Co., and Matshushita Electric Industrial Co.

As well as the joint venture in the UK, the strategic alliance will serve automotive OEMs, North American or European-based customers in Japan – whose global platforms require Japan-based engineering and/or manufacturing support. Drawing on Tenneco Automotive's worldwide presence and Futaba's engineering skills, the alliance will offer a combined solution to the ever-increasing demands of industry globalization.

The alliance partners will conduct product development, cost planning, and product preparation planning (upstream activities) in Japan, and then they will utilize Tenneco's global presence to sell the solutions to automotive producers worldwide.

Source: adapted from Tenneco Automotive (2000).

For the marriage or relationship to continue both the enterprise and customer must receive a positive benefit even though both parties will inevitably experience disappointments on the way to their final goal.

Stage 3 organizations have realized that they cannot be all things to all people. While most customers are potentially profitable, some hold more long-term promise than others. The ability to predict who these customers are is a necessary skill on the upward path to strategic customer care. By wisely applying the right technology and information tools (technology is not a solution on its own), companies at the stage of strategic customer care deliver a core level of service for all their customers and a distinctive, optimized level for their best customers. Equally important, stage 3 businesses have orchestrated a winning situation for both their clients and for themselves: the clients are dependent on the business for their success and vice versa.

15.8 Key account management (KAM)

KAM can be understood as a relationship-oriented marketing management approach focusing on dealing with major customers in the business-to-business market. Key accounts are customers in a business-to-business market identified by selling companies to be of strategic importance.

KAM is a management concept, including both organizational and selling strategies, to achieve long-lasting customer relationships. Key account manager is one of the most popular job titles today in the area of marketing management in companies operating in the business-to-business market. It has been used in several contexts, however the nature of this approach is very unclear and requires further conceptualization.

A key account manager is the person in the seller who represents the seller's capabilities to the buying company, the buyer's needs to the seller, and brings the two together. Successful KAM often requires an understanding of the logic of both product and service management. Moreover, excellent operational level capabilities are useless if strategic level management is inferior, and vice versa – the KAM approach combines strategic and operational level marketing management.

The starting point for the following is the firm that wishes to implement KAM. The development of KAM is examined from a dyadic perspective.

Implementation of KAM

The firm that wants to implement successful KAM with suitable key accounts may go through the following four steps (Ojasalo, 2001):

1. identifying the selling firm's key accounts
2. analysing the key accounts
3. selecting suitable strategies for the key accounts
4. developing operational level capabilities to build, grow, and maintain profitable and long-lasting relationships with key accounts.

Identifying the selling firm's key accounts

This means answering the following question: which existing or potential accounts are of strategic importance to us now and in the future?

The following criteria can be used to determine strategically important customers:

- sales volume
- age of the relationship
- the selling firm's share of customers' purchase: the new RM paradigm measures success in terms of long-term gains in its share of its customers' business, unlike mass marketing which counts wins or losses in terms of market share increases that may well be temporary (Peppers and Rogers, 1995)
- profitability of the customer to seller
- use of strategic resources: extent of executive/management commitment.

There is a positive correlation between the criteria and the likelihood of customers being identified as key accounts (strategic customers).

Analysing the key accounts

This includes activities such as analysing:

- *The basic characteristics of a key account*: includes assessing the relevant economic and activity aspects of their internal and external environment. This, for example, includes the account's internal value chain inputs, markets, suppliers, products, and economic situation.

- *The relationship history*: involves assessing the relevant economic and activity aspects of the relationship history. This includes volume of sales, profitability, key account's objectives, buying behaviour (the account's decision-making process), information exchange, special needs, buying frequency, and complaints. Among these aspects, knowing or estimating relationship value plays a particularly important role. The revenues from each key account (customer lifetime value) should exceed the costs of establishing and maintaining the relationship within a certain time span.

- *The level and development of commitment to the relationship*: the account's present and anticipated commitment to the relationship is important, since the extent of the business with the account depends on that.

- *Goal congruence*, or commonality of interests between buyer and seller, greatly affects their cooperation both at the strategic and operational levels. Common interests and relationship value together determine whether two companies can be partners, friends, or rivals that aims it sights lower than the sort of partnership relationship an account is looking for risks losing long-term share of that account's business.

- *Switching costs*: it is useful to estimate both the key account's and the selling company's switching costs in the event that the relationship dissolves. Switching costs are the costs of replacing an existing partner with another. These may be very different for the two parties and thus affect the power position in the relationship. Switching costs are also called transaction costs (Williamson, 1979), and they are affected by irretrievable investments in the relationship, the adaptations made, and the bonds that have developed. High switching costs may prevent a relationship from ending even though the key account's accumulated satisfaction with the selling company may be non-existent or negative.

Selecting suitable strategies for the key accounts

This depends greatly on the relative positions of the seller and the key account. The power structure within different accounts may vary significantly. Thus, the seller may typically not freely select the strategy – there is often only one strategic alternative to be chosen if there is a desire to retain the account.

Perhaps the seller might prefer to avoid very powerful accounts. Sometimes the seller realizes that accounts, which are less attractive today, may become attractive in future. Thus, with certain accounts, the objective of the strategy may be merely to keep the relationship alive for future opportunities.

Developing operational level capabilities

This refers to customization and development of capabilities related to the following.

Product/service development and performance

Joint R&D projects are typical between a selling company and a key account in industrial and high-technology markets. In addition, information technology (IT) applied in just-in-time production and distribution channels increases the possibilities of customizing the offering in consumer markets as well.

New products developed in a partnership are not automatically more successful than those developed in-house. However, R&D projects may bring other kinds of long-term benefits, such as access to account organization and learning. Improving capabilities for providing services to key accounts is extremely important, because even when the core product is a tangible good, it is often the related services that differentiate the seller from its competitors and provide competitive advantage.

Organizational structure

The seller's organizational ability to meet the key account's needs can be developed, for example, by adjusting the organizational structure to correspond to the key account's global and local needs and by increasing the number of interfaces between the seller and the account, and thus also the number of people interacting. Organizational capabilities can also be developed by organizing teams, consisting of people with the necessary competences and authorities, to take care of key accounts.

Individuals (human resources)

A company's capabilities related to individuals can be developed by selecting the right people for key account managers and key account teams, and by developing the skills of these people. The key account manager's responsibilities are often complex and varied, and therefore require a large number of skills and qualifications, which should be taken into account in the selection and development of key account managers.

It is quite common to find that the current set of key account managers may be good at maintaining their own relationships with their existing contacts but lack the skills required to lead an account team through a transition in the account relationship.

Therefore, an assessment of the total desired interfaces between the seller and the customer needs to be considered. It may be that a change is required by moving the relationship from a dependency on a one-to-one relationship (between the key account manager and the chief buyer) to a network of organizational relationships spanning many different projects, functions and countries.

Information exchange

Information exchange between the seller and a key account is particularly important in KAM. An important relationship-specific task is to search, filter, judge, and store information about the organization, strategies, goals, potentials, and problems of the partners. However, this mainly depends on the mutual trust and attitudes of the parties, and on the technical arrangements. A key account's trust is something that the seller has to earn over time by its performance, whereas the technical side can be developed, e.g. with IT.

Company and individual level benefits

Successful long-term KAM in a business-to-business context always requires the ability to offer both company and individual-level benefits to key accounts.

Company-level benefits are rational and may be either short or long term, direct or indirect, and typically contribute to the key account's turnover, profitability, cost savings, organizational efficiency and effectiveness, and image. Individual-level benefits in turn may be rational or emotional. From the relationship management point of view, the key individuals are the ones with the power to continue or terminate the relationship. Rational individual-level benefits contribute, for example, to the individual's own career, income, and ease of job. Emotional individual-level benefits include friendship, a sense of caring, and ego enhancement.

Customer complaint management (internal marketing)

Complaint management means satisfying the customer who has voiced the complaint and binding him or her to the company for the long term. Many firms have negative feelings about complaints. However, the firms stand to benefit if the personnel in contact with the dissatisfied customer handle the process skilfully, achieve the desired outcome, and also themselves derive satisfaction from the relevant tasks.

Customer complaints involve much more than just customers taking the initiative to articulate their dissatisfaction with products or services. They are complex psycho-sociological conflict management processes bounded by the relationship of the market partners. Within the framework of these processes, the qualifications required of contact personnel (in the form of appropriate interpersonal skills, for example) are of central importance.

Service personnel should be trained to handle complaints, so that they have consideration in the case of a service failure and allow customers to express frustration freely. Furthermore, service personnel should have the autonomy to help customers in real time. This means that service personnel must have the authority to offer a form of compensation without interference from management (Ruyter and Wetzels, 2000).

Therefore, internal marketing plays a key role here, creating the necessary psychological conditions for both the individual employee and the organization, and thereby ensuring the successful implementation and acceptance of an effective complaint management system.

It is not always advisable to handle the customer complaint on the spot because it is relatively resource demanding. The specific situation determines the most appropriate structural and operating organizations for complaint management. Relevant factors could include the nature of the product, the frequency and manner of customer contacts, and the business form of the firm. From a structural standpoint, one can differentiate between centralized, decentralized, and dual complaint management systems (Thurau and Hansen, 2000).

Centralized complaint management is advisable when a business has no personal contact with its customers, the complaint volume is relatively high, the types of complaints encountered are relatively simple and homogeneous, and changes in these conditions seldom occur. A key advantage is the routine nature of the work performed by the employees responsible for handling the complaints. Additionally, the employees are not subjected to those psychological pressure mechanisms associated with dealing with complaints, which they themselves have caused; the complaint handlers only deal with written or telephone complaints assigned to them by a centralized complaint management system.

Decentralized complaint management is advantageous when the relationships between the firm and customer are characterized by personal interactions distributed over a large number of customer contact points, and when the customer complaints are complex and less predictable. The biggest advantage of decentralization is the direct, prompt, appropriate and on-the-spot resolution of the problem. The main disadvantage is that it requires more human resources. Furthermore, employees are directly confronted with mistakes they themselves have made or which were caused at an earlier stage in the value chain (e.g. delivery delays).

Decentralized complaint management also makes it difficult to motivate employees to take a pro-active role in stimulating customers to lodge complaints.

In order to achieve a rapid resolution of complaints with a focus on pinpointing the underlying causes, employees have to be given wide-ranging authority in terms of decision-making responsibility, access to information and task assignment. This should ensure rapid and comprehensive solutions for the customers.

Dual complaint management combines the advantages of the centralized and decentralized approaches. It is appropriate for complex products and services, as well as for businesses featuring broad-based direct contact with customers (such as dealer networks).

Direct decentralized complaint management involves an interaction between employees and customers. It encompasses tasks related to the input, case handling and feedback functions. The quality and outcome of these processes is largely determined by the competences of the customer contact personnel. This is itself reflected in terms of how these staff perceive themselves and others, in their ability to engage in suitable interactions with customers, and in willingness to assume responsibility for complaints. We will now look at five ways to structure complaint management efficiently (Thurau and Hansen, 2000).

Personnel selection

The goal of personnel selection is to obtain customer-oriented, motivated and qualified employees who meet the general requirements of market and customer-oriented management. The personnel should be willing and able to perform general customer-related tasks (such as accepting and handling customer complaints) and to immerse themselves in the specific tasks asked of them (such as handling priority customer complaints on the telephone).

These employees must have a high degree of psycho-sociological competence. They are expected to react sensitively to the customer's situation and to turn critical situations in the relationship into positive contact experiences through the use of techniques designed to restore calm and defuse the conflict.

Personnel training

This task deals with the development and improvement of the psycho-sociological competence of those employees in direct contact with customers.

From a relationship-oriented perspective, training has two main objectives. First, employees should be informed about their tasks and functions in terms of how these relate to the relationship aspect of direct complaint management. Second, employees should receive the training necessary for complaint management to function effectively and in a customer-oriented manner. This training aims to teach employees the specific methods and skills they need to be able to identify customer and relationship types, engage in customer-centred communication concerning complaints, defuse conflict, and solve problems by focusing on the root causes. Key prospects for this training are those employees who are regularly confronted with customer complaints and, as a result, have high stress levels. As well as teaching specific skills when handling complaints, training also serves to familiarize employees at all levels of the organization with methods for conflict-free interaction.

Improving the quality of the relationship with the customer through internal interaction

The goal is to generate enthusiasm for customer-oriented behaviour and inform employees about their roles and responsibilities in achieving customer satisfaction and retention. This internal interaction is an underlying premise and a core component of successful personnel management. The character of those interactions taking place within the firm has a lasting influence on the quality of the interactions of employees who are in direct contact with customers.

Coaching supports complaint handling by strengthening the connection between the employee and the back office. Coaching makes use of qualified managers with expertise in social interaction. They observe the behaviour of employees in complaint situations and offer feedback, thereby helping these employees improve their performance both in horizontal relationships (such as the relationship between the complaints department and the quality control department) and in vertical relationships (such as the relationship between management and customer contact staff).

Support personal interaction by the use of internal and external mass communication

As personal interaction cannot communicate all of the information required for aligning the employee's behaviour with the wishes and demands of the customers, the goal of internal and external mass communication is to fill in any communication gaps and to further support personal interaction within the firm.

Classical instruments of external mass communication, such as advertisements or brochures, can help communicate positive models, which feature the tasks performed in the various steps of the direct complaint management process, such as a model for conflict-free and solution-oriented interactive processes.

These instruments can also be used to influence the opinions and images of the firm or individual departments positively, and to support entire groups of employees (such as hotline receptionists) in their need for internal and external recognition.

The use of internal market research (employee questionnaire and personal interview)

This instrument delivers the information required for planning and implementing internal marketing. In connection with complaint management, the employee questionnaire plays an important role. With this instrument, the attitudes, needs and expectations of customer complaint staff are identified, and appropriate support measures (e.g. specialized training or stress relief through job rotation) can then be set up. Another important tool for internal market research is the personal interview and the group discussion forum.

The personal interview can also be used to determine the relationship skills of the employees and their preferred relationship forms when stimulating, accepting and handling complaints. This provides an important information resource when planning relationship-oriented staff training initiatives.

It is important to find out the current status of the customer contact personnel in terms of how they perceive themselves. There also needs to be company-wide documentation of what effective complaint management means to staff, how they see their own roles as complaint managers and the kind of support they require. A comparison of the existing situation with the desired situation can identify gaps in quality and serve as a foundation for developing specific programmes to improve the relevant qualifications of customer contact personnel.

The effect of complaint management is at its greatest when management's existing external market orientation is expanded to include internal goals and, in particular, employee-related goals. In addition, internal marketing goes beyond the traditional goal-oriented interpretation of customer complaints to incorporate a relationship-oriented approach.

A lack of expertise and competence on the part of contact personnel can activate the latent potential for conflict and lead to an escalation of the complaint. This may not only lead to the termination of the relationship, but also to loss of sales and to damage to the company image through negative word of mouth spread by the dissatisfied customer.

The dyadic development of KAM

The model in Figure 15.8 describes and demonstrates the typical dyadic progression of a relationship between buyer and seller through five stages – pre-KAM, early KAM, mid-KAM, partnership KAM and synergistic KAM (Cheverton, 1999, McDonald *et al.*, 1997).

Pre-KAM stage

This describes preparation for KAM. A buyer is identified as having key account potential, and the seller starts to focus resources on winning some business with that prospect. Both seller and buyer are sending out signals (factual information) and exchanging messages (interactions) prior to the decision to engage in transactions.

Early KAM stage

At this stage, the seller is concerned with identifying the opportunities for account penetration once the account has been won. This is probably the most typical sales relationship, the classic bow-tie.

Adapted solutions are needed, and the key account manager will focus on understanding more about the customer and the market in which that customer is competing. The buyer will still be market testing other sellers. The seller must concentrate hard on product, service and intangibles – the buyer wants recognition that the product offering is the prime reason for the relationship – and expects it to work.

Figure 15.8 Key account relationship development model

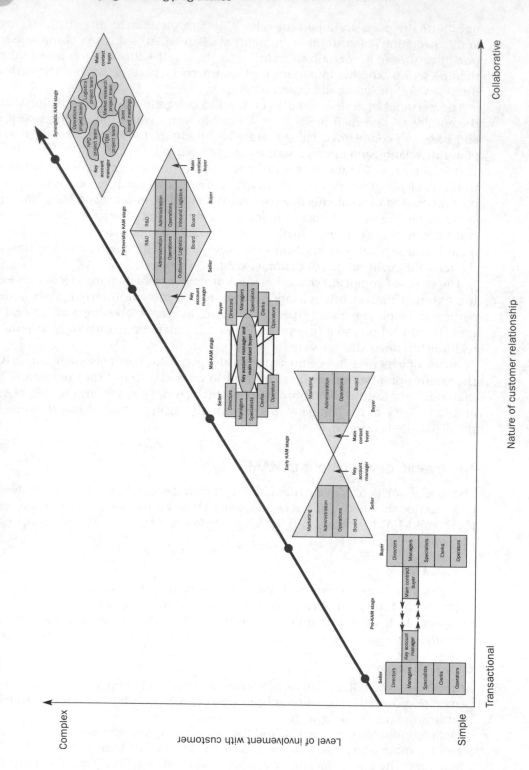

Sources: adapted from Cheverton (1999) and McDonald *et al.* (1997).

Mid-KAM stage

This is a transition stage between the classic bow-tie and the diamond of the partnership KAM stage.

At this stage the seller has established credibility with the buyer. Contacts between the two organizations increase at all levels and assume greater importance. Nevertheless, buyers still feel the need for alternative sources of supply. This may be driven by their own customers' desire for choice. The seller's offering is still periodically market tested, but is reliably perceived to be good value. The seller is now a preferred supplier.

Partnership KAM stage

This is the stage where benefits should start to flow. When partnership KAM is reached, the seller is seen by the buyer as a strategic external resource. The two companies will be sharing sensitive information and solving problems jointly. Pricing will be long term and stable, but it will have been established that each side will allow the other to make a profit.

If a major disadvantage of the bow-tie of early relationship KAM was the denial of access to customers' internal processes and to their market, the main advantage of the diamond relationship is in seeing those barriers of understanding opening up.

Key accounts will test all the seller's innovations so that they have first access to, and first benefit from, the latest technology. The buyer will expect to be guaranteed continuity of supply and access to the best material. Expertise will be shared. The buying company will also expect to gain from continuous improvement. There may be joint promotions, where appropriate.

Synergistic KAM stage

This stage is the ultimate stage in the relationship development model. The experience gained at the partnership stage – coordinating the team-sell, coaching the team on their interface roles – will be a good starting point for moving to synergistic KAM.

The seller understands that it still does not have an automatic right to the customer's business. Nevertheless, exit barriers have been built up. The buyer is confident that the relationship with the seller is delivering improved quality and reduced cost. Costing systems become transparent. Joint research and development will take place. There will be interfaces at every level and function between the organizations. Senior management commitment will be fulfilled through joint board meetings and reviews. There will be a joint business plan, joint strategies, joint market research. Information flow should be streamlined and information systems integration will be planned or in place as a consequence. Transaction costs will be reduced.

Though there are clear advantages for both partners in moving through the different KAM stages, there are also pitfalls. As the contacts proliferate through the stages, so does the speed of activity, and the risk of saying and doing the wrong things. Through the stages the key account manager changes from super salesperson to super-coach. In the last two stages the key account manager moves on to be a super-coordinator, who oversees everything.

If the key account manager does not move along, then the potential of losing control is great, resulting in well-meaning, but misdirected, individuals following their own quite separate courses.

Key account management requires process excellence and highly skilled professionals to manage relationships with strategic customers. For most companies, this represents a number of changes. A change is needed in the way activity is costed and costs are attributed, from product or geographical focus to customer focus. Currently, few financial or information systems in companies are sophisticated enough to support the higher levels of KAM. A transformation is needed in the way the person with responsibility for a customer relationship is developed, from an emphasis on selling skills to management skills, including cross-cultural management skills (McDonald *et al.*, 1997).

15.9 Summary

The future cash flow of a firm is generated by purchases from existing customers and purchases from new customers. Hence, if a firm makes sound investments in acquiring only the right customers and in developing existing customers it should, over time, continually enhance its value. This chapter has shown that both acquisition and retention are important for survival, and that marketers who focus only on the former are ignoring exciting opportunities and essential information.

In order to achieve customer loyalty you must start with a holistic picture of the customer. Remember, the customer is a strategic asset, one that is in short supply, one that must be treated with care. Therefore, regard customer information as a strategic asset. Once you have a customer, surround him or her with care. Establish team-based selling as the rule rather than the exception, and use each customer contact as an opportunity to create loyalty.

A loyalty programme is a long-term proposition, not a short-term promotion. Management has to be committed to a programme that will last for years, not months. Such commitment will help develop and maintain a strong lifetime relationship with customers. The result of such a close connection will bring many rewards to both sides.

KAM is the development towards customer focus and RM in business-to-business markets. It offers critical benefits and opportunities for profit enhancement to both sides of the seller-buyer relationship.

The scope of KAM is widening and becoming more complex. The skills of professionals involved in it at strategic and operational levels need to be constantly updated and developed.

Customer complaints are latent conflicts between customers and employees. The psycho-sociological dimension of the customer complaint is determined through the personality structures of the partners and the relationship itself.

Internal marketing provides a wide range of instruments for supporting the customer complaint management process.

The basic task of internal marketing is to convince staff of the economic benefits to be derived from effective complaint management and to overcome preconceived notions of how to handle dissatisfied customers. The associated business principles can be conveyed through specific internal communications instruments like the employee newsletter, intranet messages or staff meetings.

The goal of internal marketing is to positively influence internal relationships, thereby guaranteeing a positive external relationship experience for the employee and customer. One of the fundamental purposes of internal interactions between management and employees relates to the sensitivity of customer contact personnel to the important role they play in the interface between the firm and the customer.

Case study 15.2 Alcatel Space

Creating a network of relationships in the global satellite market

Alcatel Space, a leading French satellite indus-trialist, ranks among the world's leading space systems companies. With expertise in both civil and military applications, Alcatel Space develops innovative satellite technology for telecommunications, navigation, optical and radar observation, meteorology, environ-ment, science.

With partners around the world, subsidiaries throughout Europe, and a strong commitment to research and development, Alcatel Space plays an important role – as prime contractor, opera-tor, investor, or service provider – in a majority of ongoing space programmes. The company is also a European leader in the field of ground sys-tems operations and logistics support.

In 1999 Alcatel Space had a turnover of FFr9.3 billion (€1.4 billion), two-thirds of which comes from communication satellites. The com-pany employs 6000 people.

Alcatel Space Industries manages all the industrial and R&D resources in France, French Guyana, Belgium, Denmark, Germany, The Netherlands, Norway, Spain and Switzerland).

Alcatel Spacecom holds the Alcatel share-holdings in commercial satellite systems, including stakes in Skybridge, CyberStar, RESAM (Globalstar), Euteltracs, Europe*Star, Eurasiasat, and the future Bolivarsat and Rascom.

History

Alcatel Space's somewhat complicated history can be traced back as far as a major restructuring of the French electronics industry in 1983, when the space division of the state-owned Thomson-CSF was put into a privately held company and acquired by the Compagnie Générale d'Electricité (CGE). In 1991, this changed its name to Alcatel Alstholm, following a partnership with GEC-Alstholm that involved what has since become Britain's Marconi Group. The Alsthom connection remained in place until 1998.

As part of a plan to privatize, Thomson-CSF allied itself with privately held Alcatel, and ended up owning the 49% of Alcatel Space not held by Alcatel. Also the Alcatel group took a 15.84% stake in Thomson-CSF.

It is important to remember that Alcatel Space is only part of a very large electronics and telecommunicatons group with activities cover-ing almost every communications sector.

Alcatel Space has two major sub-units. Alcatel Space Industries manages its industrial resources in France (Nanterre (just outside Paris), Toulouse and Cannes), plus various ex-Thomson-CSF units and Sextant Avionique's Space Division in Valence. Satellite ground stations, previously the territory of Alcatel Telspace, which used to be a separate company, are also included. Space Industries also manages European subsidiaries in Belgium, plus those in Denmark, Germany, The Netherlands, Norway, Spain and Switzerland, and also Alcatel's investment in CNES operations such as Intespace, the satellite test centre at Toulouse.

The other main unit is Alcatel Spacecom, which controls Alcatel Space's numerous invest-ments in satellite operating companies. These are practically all joint ventures.

The world satellite market

Commercial spacecraft currently dominate the market, in 2000 representing about 61% of global satellite revenues, according to a Frost & Sullivan marketing study. The rest (39%) is the military market. That trend, forecast to continue well into the next century, is in sharp contrast

Figure 15.9 Structure of Alcatel

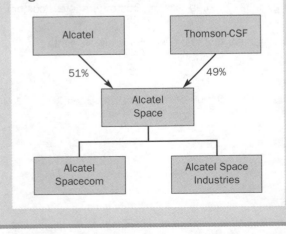

Case study 15.2 continued

with the mid-1980s when US payloads were roughly equally divided between NASA, the US Defense Department and commercial missions.

The world satellite market generated revenues of US$9.56 billion in 2000, according to the World Markets for Commercial, Military and Science Satellites study.

The forecast projected annual revenues would peak in 2003 at $16.12 billion, while the number of launches during the next five years could peak at 289 in 2002. More than 1300 satellites are expected to be launched from 1999 to 2005 with cumulative revenues of US$92.15 billion. The commercial satellite sector should continue to account for the highest revenues through 2005, the report noted.

The market is being driven by factors such as demand for Internet access, digital technology and implementation of broadband applications, the report said. But it has also been restrained by financial problems, national security considerations and competition from landline and terrestrial wireless technology.

The military market, which generated revenues of US$3.05 billion in 2000, is expected to remain relatively constant until 2005. The report projected annual military market revenues of between US$2.5 billion and US$3 billion until 2005 as a result of continuing requirements for space-based communications, early-warning, navigation, weather data and reconnaissance capabilities.

The customer

The customers for commercial satellites are typically telecommunications companies, television companies and providers of mobile satellite services.

The customers for the military satellites are mainly national governments, defence ministries and NATO.

Questions

1. Analyse the process related to the buying of a
   (a) commercial satellite
   (b) military satellite.

2. Why do you think that the networks and the relationships in the satellite business are so complicated?

Sources: Smith (1999), Brown (2000), Bullock (2000), Harbert (2000).

QUESTIONS FOR DISCUSSION

1. Identify the measures that can be used to encourage long-term relationships with customers.
2. What specific segmentation criteria could be used to categorize different loyalty segments?
3. Evaluate the strengths and weaknesses of frequent user programmes.
4. What are the arguments for spending money to keep existing customers loyal (customer retention)?
5. Put the arguments for and against the statement that 'the customer is always right'.
6. What are the motives for entering KAM?
7. Describe the different stages in KAM.
8. What is the purpose of implementing a customer complaint management system?

REFERENCES

Adage Global (2001), *Daily News*, **www.adageglobal.com**, February 19.

BBC (2000), Millionaire show earns owners a fortune, *BBC Business News*, December 14, (**http://news.bbc.co.uk/**).

BBC (2001), Boeing signs Russian space deal, *BBC Business News*, April 13, (**http://news.bbc.co.uk**).

BBC (2001a), Millionaire? Cleared of ratings 'fix', *BBC Business News*, January 15, (**http://news.bbc.co.uk/**).

BBC (2001b), Quiz show scoops business award, *BBC Business News*, April 20, (**http://news.bbc.co.uk/**)

BBC (2001c), Will ITC website capture the net? *BBC Business News*, April 25, (**http://news.bbc.co.uk**).

BBC (2002) TV's Millionaire misses the jackpot, *BBC Business News*, March 7 (**http://news.bbc.co.uk**).

Brown, P. J. (2000), Satellites: the next generation, *Broadcasting & Cable*, New York, July 31, pp. 48–50.

Bullock, C. (2000), Alcatel Space cashes in on global joint ventures, *Interavia*, Geneva, December, pp. 45–7.

Celador (2000), *Who Wants To Be A Millionaire?* format sold to Japan, Celador Productions press release, February 25.

Cheverton, P. (1999), *Key Account Management: The route to profitable supplier status*, Kogan Page, London.

CNN (2000), 'Millionaire' quiz show import doesn't find success in Japan, *CNN Business News*, August 9, (**http://www.cnn.com/2000/asianow**).

Dick, A. S. and Basu, K. (1994), Customer loyalty: toward an integrated conceptual framework, *Journal of the Academy of Marketing Science*, vol. 22, no. 2, pp. 99–113.

Grönroos, C. (2000), *Service Management and Marketing: A customer relationship management approach*, John Wiley, Chichester, 2nd edn.

Harbert, T. (2000), Beaming business abroad, *Electronic Business*, Highlands Ranch, June, pp. 76–84.

Holmlund, M. (2000), *Percieved Quality in Business Relationships*, Hanken, Swedish School of Economics, Helsinki/Helsingfros, Finland, CERS.

Hutt, M. D. and Speh, T. W. (2001), *Business Marketing Management*, Harcourt College Publishers, Orlando, FL, 7th edn.

Jackson, B. B. (1985), Build customer relationships that last, *Harward Business Review*, vol. 63, November/December, pp. 120–8.

Keveney, B. (2001), ABC still placing bets on 'Millionaire'. In 'good position' in event of strike, *USA Today*, Arlington, VA, January 15.

McDonald, M., Millman, T. and Rogers, B. (1997), Key account management: theory, practice and challenges, *Journal of Marketing Management*, vol. 13, pp. 737–57.

Ojasalo, J. (2001), Key account management at company and individual levels in business-to-business relationships, *Journal of Business and Industrial Marketing*, vol. 16, no. 3, pp. 199–218.

Peppers, D. and Rogers, M. (1995), A new marketing paradigm: share of customer, not market share, *Harvard Business Review*, July–August, pp. 105–13.

Raymond, J. (2001), Home field advantage, *American Demographics*, Ithaca, NY, April, pp. 34–6.

Reichheld, F. F. (1994), Loyalty and the renaissance of marketing management, *Marketing Management*, vol.12, no. 4, pp. 17–25.

Reichheld, F. F. and Schefter, P. (2000), E-loyalty: your secret weapon on the web, *Harvard Business Review*, vol. 7, no. 1, pp. 105–13.

Ruyter, K. and Wetzels, M. (2000), Customer considerations in service recovery: a cross-industry perspective, *International Journal of Service Industry Management*, vol. 11, no. 1, pp. 91–108.

Smith, B. A. (1999), New launchers seek commercial market share, *Aviation Week & Space Technology*, New York, December 13, pp. 50–2.

Tenneco Automotive (2000), Tenneco Automotive and Futaba Industrial Co. sign agreements to form a global strategic alliance and establish a joint venture in the UK, *Tenneco Automotive News*, October 30.

Thurau, T. H. and Hansen, U. (2000), *Relationship Marketing*, Springer-Verlag, Berlin-Heidelberg.

Vandermerwe, S. (2000), How increasing value to customers improves business results, *Sloan Management Review*, Fall, pp. 27–37.

Wansink, B. and Seed, S. (2001), Making brand loyalty programs succeed, *Brand Management*, vol. 8, no. 3, February, pp. 211–22.

Webster, Frederick E. (1992), The changing role of marketing in the corporation, *Journal of Marketing*, vol. 56, October, pp. 1–17.

Williamson, O. E. (1979), Transaction cost economics: the governance of contractual relations, *Journal of Law and Economics*, vol. 22, October, pp. 232–62.

Figure V.1 Structure of Part V

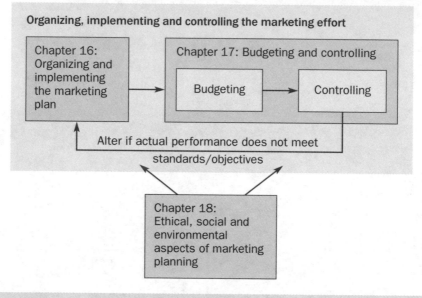

Organizing, implementing and controlling the marketing effort

Designing marketing strategies and programmes that meet current and future market requirements is a necessary but not a sufficient condition for corporate success. They need to be translated into action through effective implementation.

The purpose of Part V is to introduce the marketing plan, which is a mechanism for integrating and coordinating marketing programmes in the midst of uncertainty about the future.

A marketing plan (Chapter 16) is a detailed and systematic formulation of actions to take place, including the resources to be used. An action plan is a key step in ensuring that the marketing strategy has been executed effectively.

It is also a set of specific decision or marketing activities designed to carry out marketing strategies and accomplish a company's stated objectives and goals.

The structure of Part V is shown in Figure V.1

A good plan will address the product and customer relationships and employee/employer cooperation plan (internal marketing). The plan should also address the cooperative effort needed among engineering, manufacturing, research, sales, transportation, channel distribution, dealer and retailer relations, price, packaging, competition, sales, advertising, feedback, and promotion. This marketing plan reflects on past experience, assesses current trends and conditions, and forecasts future events.

The plan should incorporate all the assumptions, judgements, strategic options, and contingencies developed during the planning process.

Building a marketing plan (Chapter 16) is a creative effort to provide direction for marketing implementation. An action plan, as related to developing marketing activities, encompasses the information needed to complete marketing planning and includes answers to the following questions:

- what activities are to be completed in implementing the variables of the marketing mix?
- who will be responsible for each of these activities?
- when will the activities be initiated and completed?
- how will the activities be coordinated with each other?
- what resources are needed to carry out the activities?

The implementation of strategy decisions is further examined to address key issues as part of the marketing plan. Marketing managers have learned that strategy by itself is not enough; implementation is just as important.

A plan is not complete until it has been evaluated. In evaluating the marketing plan, the company's analysis of the past, present, and future, and adoption of marketing strategy will guide the marketing manager in formulating a specific plan. Also, a basic tool for evaluation could include a break-even analysis.

Marketing managers often use a control and budget system (Chapter 17) in monitoring the performance of marketing operations stated in terms of sales, market share, and/or profitability (see Figure V.1). Information requirements as part of the measurement system will also be discussed.

As marketing strategy is implemented, the marketing manager needs to track the results and monitor new developments in the environment, although it might be impossible to measure all relevant environmental changes. The company can count on one thing: the environment will change, and, when it does, the company will need to review and revise its strategies accordingly. The marketing manager must be aware of the nature of the changes taking place, and how the company and programme must be modified in order to adapt to these changes.

The last chapter (Chapter 18) in this part discusses the ethical, social and environmental aspects and how they will influence marketing planning (see Figure V.1). These issues are very complex and proposals on these problems have to take account of the cultural context. Codes vary across cultures, and the manager cannot assume that the firm and counterparts from another country share the same code.

Chapter 16

Organizing and implementing the marketing plan

LEARNING OBJECTIVES

After studying this chapter you should be able to:

- understand the need for an integrated approach to marketing and the role of marketing planning in that process.
- explain the background to preparing a marketing plan.
- explain the stages in the marketing planning process.
- outline and explain the structure and contents of a marketing plan.
- understand the important issues in implementing the marketing plan.
- understand the various ways of organizing the marketing department.

Case study 16.1 Adidas-Salomon

Split into three divisions to sharpen consumer focus

The Adidas name dates back to 1948, deriving from the first syllables of the founder Adi Dassler's name. One year later, Adi Dassler registered the three stripes as a trademark. Athletes wore running shoes produced by Dassler at the 1928 Olympic Games in Amsterdam. After a period spanning almost 70 years, the Dassler Family withdrew from the company in 1989, and the enterprise was transformed into a corporation (Aktiengesellschaft).

In 1997, Adidas acquired the Salomon Group, and the company's name changed to Adidas-Salomon AG. Adidas-Salomon AG is the second-largest company in the sporting goods industry (after Nike) with revenues of €5.8 billion in the financial year 2000. Adidas-Salomon AG is a global corporation with approximately 100 subsidiaries and with products present in all major markets around the world. The company's share of the world market for sporting goods is estimated at around 15%. Adidas-Salomon AG has approximately 13,000 employees worldwide.

The company markets its products under the brand names shown in Table 16.1. The company is based in Herzogenaurach, Germany.

Table 16.1 Brand names of Adidas-Salomon

Division	Products
Adidas	Footwear, clothing, and hardware such as bags and balls
Salomon	Skis, snowboards, snowblades, ski boots and bindings, summer sports products such as inline skates, hiking boots and trekking equipment
TaylorMade Adidas Golf	Golf clubs and golf balls, clothing and shoes, golf accessories
Mavic	Cycle components
Bonfire	Winter sports clothing
Erima	Team-sport clothing, swimwear and accessories

Case study 16.1 continued

In October 2000, Adidas-Salomon restructured into three new divisions: Forever Sport, Original, and Equipment. Each of the three divisions produces its own footwear and clothing lines. The positioning of the three divisions is shown in Figure 16.1. The characteristics of the three divisions are as follows.

Forever Sport division

The Forever Sport division features products that are developed for the sports performance market, but have design appeal, encouraging consumers to wear the products both on and off the court or playing field. With the footwear and clothing products in this division, Adidas targets athletes who want the highest level of functionality for their specific sport. Forever Sport products compete directly with Nike, Reebok, Puma and Fila.

Original division

The Original division targets consumers who want to buy products exclusively for leisure usage, but are still inspired by sports. This is the division that carries the majority of the leisure-oriented products that fit under Adidas' new brand positioning 'From competition to lifestyle'. The Original division has three different product segmentations: re-introduced, re-interpreted, and re-designed products. Re-introduced products will be limited volume re-makes of classic products. Re-interpreted products are based on the original authentic sport version, with updated colours, materials and details. Re-designed products are inspired by the old Adidas originals in style and craftsmanship, but put in today's fashion context. All products use the classic Adidas trefoil logo and compete against international brands such as

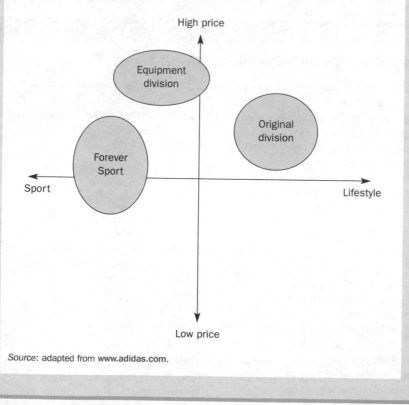

Figure 16.1 Positioning of the three Adidas divisions

Source: adapted from www.adidas.com.

Case study 16.1 continued

Gap, Tommy Hilfiger, and Ralph Lauren, as well as many local names.

Barbara Ambrus, an analyst at the Landesbank Baden Württemberg, is reported to estimate that 80% of sports clothing is now worn as leisurewear.

Equipment division

The Equipment division focuses on creating multi-functional sports products, with cutting-edge designs, for the prestigious consumer. It serves as the house of innovation for cross-performance clothing and footwear. Products in this category serve as the bridge between the Forever Sport and Original lines – between com-petition and lifestyle. The aim is to create a brand that is a status symbol on and off the court or playing field. All products use the new Adidas Equipment logo.

The first product launch is scheduled for autumn/winter 2002, with distribution in selected markets such as Germany, France and the USA.

Questions

1. What are the main motives for the new Adidas-Salomon organization?

2. Should a separate marketing plan be made for each of the three divisions?

16.1 Introduction

This chapter introduces the structure and outline of a marketing plan. The implementation of the marketing plan requires an organizational structure, form, and culture that is conducive to the firm's marketing effort. Within a marketing context, organizing consists of designing the internal and external relationships and establishing the policies and procedures, as well as creating the means and methods by which various participants in the marketing function can carry out their responsibilities in an effective and efficient manner.

Marketing implementation is that part of the marketing management process concerned with translating marketing plans into action.

16.2 Marketing audit

As the first formal step in marketing planning, the marketing audit should only involve bringing together the source material, which has already been collected throughout the year as part of the normal work of the marketing department.

A marketing audit is a comprehensive, systematic, independent and periodic examination of a company's – or business unit's – marketing environment, objectives, strategies, and activities with a view to determining problem areas and opportunities and recommending a plan of action to improve the company's marketing performance (Kotler, 2000).

Although some organizations have successfully employed external consultants to conduct marketing audits, they are generally best undertaken by management who 'own' the marketing process. This is partly because they are the best people to understand the company, and how the marketing plan has been made.

Even more important, though, the audit is the best possible learning process for these managers because it introduces them to the factors that are most important to their management of marketing. Finally, and most important of all, it ensures that those who will have to implement the results of the planning process understand, and are committed to, the assumptions that lie behind it.

It is apparent that a marketing audit can be a complex process, but the aim is simple; it is only to identify those existing (external and internal) factors that will have a significant impact on the future plans of the company.

It is clear that the basic input material for the marketing audit should be comprehensive. As suggested earlier, the best approach is to continuously accumulate this material as it becomes available. This method avoids the otherwise heavy workload involved in collecting it as part of the regular, typically annual, planning process itself – when time is usually at a premium.

There is much evidence to show that many highly successful companies also start their planning cycle each year with a formal review, through an audit-type process, of everything that has had an important influence on marketing activities. Certainly in many leading consumer goods companies, the annual self-audit is a tried and tested discipline integrated into the management process.

16.3   Building the marketing plan

Basically, the major functions of the marketing plan are to determine where the firm is, where it wants to go, and how it can get there.

Marketing planning is linked to planning in other functional areas and to overall corporate strategy. It takes place within the larger strategic marketing management process of the corporation. To survive and prosper, the business marketer must properly balance the firm's resources with the objectives and opportunities of the environment. Marketing planning is a continuous process that involves the active participation of other functional areas.

The marketing plan is responsive to both corporate and business unit strategy, and formally describes all the components of the marketing strategy – markets to be served, products or services to be marketed, price schedules, distribution methods, and so on. The key components of the marketing planning process are situational analysis, marketing objectives and goal, marketing strategies and programmes, budgets, and implementation and control. Note that the planning process format centres on clearly defined market segments, a thorough assessment of internal and external problems and opportunities, specific goals, and courses of action. Business market intelligence, market potential and sales forecasting (see Appendix) are fundamental in the planning process.

At a fundamental level, the marketing plan establishes specific objectives by market segment, defines marketing strategy and actions required to accomplish these objectives, and pinpoints responsibility for the implementation of these programmes. Ultimately, the marketing plan translates objectives and strategies into forecasts and budgets that provide a basis for planning by other functional areas of the firm.

A good marketing plan requires a great deal of information gathered from many sources. It is used to develop marketing strategy and tactics to reach a specific set of objectives and goals. The process is not necessarily difficult, but it does require organization, especially if the marketer is not developing this plan by himself and is depending on others to assist or to accomplish parts of the plan.

Every marketing plan should have a planned structure or outline before it is started. This ensures that no important information is omitted and that the material is presented in a logical manner. One outline to recommend is this:

- title page
- table of contents
- executive summary
- introduction
- situational analysis
- marketing objectives and goals
- marketing strategies and programmes
- budgets
- implementation and control
- conclusion.

However, there are other ways to organize a marketing plan that are equally good.

Let us examine each section of the marketing plan structure in further detail.

Title page

The title page provides the reader with the following essential information:

- the business unit for which the plan was prepared
- the individual or group of individuals for whom the plan was developed
- the names and addresses of the individuals or agencies who authored the plan
- the time period covered by the plan
- the date on which the plan was submitted.

Table of contents

The table of contents lists the subject matter of the plan, identifies where various topics are to be found within the report, and shows how the plan is organized and presented. The table of contents is usually a listing of titles and subtitles used within the text of the report together with the various types of illustration – tables, graphs, and photos.

A table of contents sounds rather superfluous, and the marketer may feel that it is unnecessary. The marketer might be especially inclined to discard the idea if the marketing plan is short. But a table of contents is absolutely necessary. It makes no difference whether the marketing plan is only a few pages or a hundred pages in length. It is required, never optional, because of a psychological factor that affects those who will evaluate the marketing plan for approval or rejection.

The need for a table of contents is especially critical when the plan is being submitted to venture capitalists, who put up large sums of money to businesses that already have a track record and a marketing plan for future growth.

You may have heard that venture capitalists look only at business plans. Marketing and business plan are very similar, especially in smaller companies and with start-ups and new products. When the marketer is trying to obtain resources from a venture capitalist, or any investor, the two plans are synonymous. Either the business plan must have a heavy marketing emphasis or the marketing plan must include complete financial, manufacturing, and technical data.

Executive summary

This is an overview of the entire plan, including a description of the product or service, the differential advantage, the required investment, and anticipated sales and profits.

The executive summary is a short (about one page) and concise summary of the key points of the marketing plan. It is designed to give busy executives a quick overview of the report and to inform them of key provisions of the organization's marketing effort with regard to a particular product or business unit. The executive summary centres on a brief description of the objectives to be achieved, the situations to be considered, and the programmes to be launched. Special issues that impact the marketing plan might also be reviewed.

Introduction

This includes the background of the project and a description of the product or service and how it fits into the market.

The introduction is the explanation of the details of your project. Unlike the executive summary, it is not an overview of the project. Its purpose is to give the background of the project and to describe the product or service so that any reader will understand exactly what is being proposed. The introduction can be a fairly large section.

Situational analysis

The **situational analysis** attempts to address the question 'where is the organization now?' The situational analysis contains a vast amount of information and, as the term indicates, is an analysis of the situation that you are facing with the proposed product or service.

The situational analysis is divided into four categories based on the SWOT analysis (see Chapter 7).

Internal assessment

This should describe strengths and weaknesses with regard to company resources (key personnel, skills and capabilities, and resources).

- Identify the organization's cultures and values – shared beliefs that will act as a catalyst for consistent actions by its members.
- Detail the marketing organization, i.e. structure and purpose; lines of authority; functions and responsibilities.
- Identify critical factors and skills for success in future activities of the organization.

Describe the current products, experience, and know-how, financial, human, capital resources, and suppliers. Do you enjoy favour with your customers or potential customers, and if so, why? Summarize the strengths and weaknesses as they apply to the project. In many respects this section includes the same items as the competitor section (see later).

External assessment

This should describe opportunities and threats with regard to the following factors.

- Demand and demand trends. What is the forecast demand for the product: is it growing or declining? Who is the decision maker? The purchase agent? How, when, where, what, and why do they buy?
- The target market: describe the target market segment in detail by using demographics, psychographics, geography, lifestyle, or whatever segmentation is appropriate. Why is this your target market? How large is it?
- Economic and business conditions for this product at this time and the geographical area selected including a description of trends in the **macroenvironment**.
- State of technology for this class of product. Is it high-technology and state of the art? Are newer products succeeding older ones frequently (short life cycle)? In short, how is technology affecting this product or service?
- Are politics (current or otherwise) in any way affecting the situation for marketing this product?
- What laws or regulations are applicable here?
- How does the availability or scarcity of funds affect the situation?
- Is current legislation in state, federal, or local government likely to affect marketing of this product or service?
- Media: what is happening in the media? Does current publicity favour this project?
- Special interests: aside from direct competitors, are any influential groups likely to affect the marketing plan?
- Describe your main competitors, their products, plans, experience, know-how, financial, human, and capital resources, suppliers, and strategy. Do they enjoy favour with their customers? If so, why? What marketing channels do the competitors use? What are their strengths and weaknesses?

Summarize your internal and external assessment in a SWOT matrix with the key points from the situational analysis.

Marketing objectives and goals

The marketing objectives and goals section of the marketing plan should answer the question 'where does the organization want to go?' State precisely the marketing objectives and goals in terms of sales volume, market share, return on investment (ROI), or other objectives or goals for the marketing plan and the time needed to achieve each of them.

What is the difference between a goal and an objective? An objective is an overall goal. It is more general and may not be quantified. 'To establish a product in the marketplace' is an objective. So is 'to become the market leader' or 'to dominate the market'. Goals are quantified. 'To sell 100,000 units a year' is a goal. Goals are also quantified in terms of sales, profits, market share, return on investment, or other measurements. There is one major cautionary note here: do not get trapped into setting objectives or goals that conflict. For example, your ability to capture a stated market share may require lower profits. Make sure that all the goals and objectives fit together. This is done by adjusting and reconfirming the goals and objectives after completing the financial portions of the plan.

Objectives may also include societal objectives. Societal objectives support the organization's philosophy that its marketing efforts should satisfy not only the market and financial objectives but also serve the best interests of society. Societal objectives can be classified as those related to **social responsibility** (e.g. specific standards regarding minimum age of employees, overtime pay, plant safety, and healthy working conditions) or ethical business practices (e.g. eliminate problems associated with job discrimination, unfair labour practices, operating violations, misleading warranties, false advertising claims, counterfeit products, price discrimination, price fixing, deceptive sales promotions or practices, and illegal distribution arrangements).

Marketing strategies and programmes

This section will describe what is to be done to reach the objectives and goals. Marketing strategy is a what-to-do section. Marketing programmes are sets of activities organized around the four general marketing functions of creating, distributing, pricing, and promoting products (the traditional marketing mix) plus how to establish and manage relationships with customers. All this was described in Part IV of this book. These marketing programmes are designed to satisfy the needs and tastes of a particular group of ultimate consumers or organizational buyers. It is at this point in the planning process that specific tactical actions are identified in sufficient detail to implement the annual marketing plan as well as plans that preceded it.

Marketing programmes are the means of achieving desired ends. They outline what needs to be done, how it will be done, when it will be done, and who will do it. The nature of the marketing programme suggests its decision-making character. That is, the development of the marketing programme is a series of decisions directed at the achievement of specific performance standards outlined by measurable objectives in the annual marketing plan.

Budgets

Having completed the major planning tasks, it is normal in this section to show the feasibility of the objectives and strategies in terms of the resulting market share, sales, costs, and other financial figures. In most cases there would be a marketing budget for the first two to three years of the strategic marketing plan, but there would also be a very detailed budget for the first year of the plan, which would be included in the one-year operational plan.

Remember to include all required resources and costs to reach the planned sales in the marketing budget. Budgeting is discussed further in Chapter 17.

Assessments of sales projections, cash flows, start-up costs and break-even points are required in this section.

Implementation and control

Include procedures for measuring and controlling the progress of planned actions as well as financial analyses. After implementing the marketing programme the marketer has to monitor the marketing plan. Thus, if the budget is exceeded you will know where to cut back or to reallocate resources. If sales are not what they should be, you will know where to focus your attention to improve them.

Conclusion

The conclusion is not a summary (you have the executive summary), but here you conclude what are the main contents of your marketing strategy, and why your plan will succeed.

It clearly states once again the differential advantage that the plan for this product or service has over the competition. The differential or competitive advantage is what you have that your competitors lack. The conclusion completes your marketing plan outline.

Exhibit 16.1

Successful reorganization of Kodak's dental business

Until late 1997 Kodak's US dental business sales and support team comprised regional sales representatives, product dealers, and an internal customer support group. Although it was a common business model, it was not working. Not only was maintaining the regional offices a big expense, but also morale was low in the absence of performance incentives. Plus, such rudimentary processes as taking orders and providing technical support were not standardized, making even simple transactions inefficient. As a result, both dealers and customers were unhappy with the level of service they were receiving. The business model could not provide enough satisfaction for dealers and dentists.

To turn things around, the dental business group was completely reorganized. Sales and customer support functions were combined into a single in-house organization accessed by a toll-free hotline. Employees were continually cross-trained on transaction-level processes to enable everything to be handled by one call. Plus, teams were put in place to offer support to specific dealers, ensuring a high level of service. And every employee continues to be given ample opportunities for advancement.

The result of the reorganization is that sales of X-ray film, chemicals, and dental anaesthetics are at an all-time high. Plus, blind surveys show employees are extremely satisfied with their jobs.

Source: adapted from Fisher (2000).

16.4 Organizing the marketing resources

Organization involves a coordinated effort, a resource allocation plan, and a system of checks and balances. Figure 16.2 outlines the three principal areas of concern when organizing the marketing effort.

Organizational structure

Lines of authority and areas of responsibility need to be carefully identified within the marketing organization. To accomplish this task, the marketing manager creates an organizational chart, which shows the formal relationships among various parts of the marketing organization and defines the roles and the decision-making authority of each team member. As identified in Figure 16.2, the organizational structure needs to answer three important questions:

1. should the organization be vertical or horizontal?
2. should the organization be centralized or decentralized?
3. should the organization be bureaucratic or adaptive?

Vertical or horizontal organization?

How many organizational levels are needed for the effective and efficient operation of the firm's marketing activities? The hierarchical structure of the marketing organization ranges from a vertical organization in which there are several levels separating the chief marketing officer from junior marketing employees to a horizontal organization, which restricts the number of line managers.

These lines of responsibility, areas of authority, and reporting relationships should be more clearly defined and established. On the other hand, horizontal organizations promote closer relationships and more adaptive personal interactions and lend themselves to team efforts and project management.

Centralized or decentralized organization?

What magnitude of managerial focus is needed to operate effectively and efficiently? In a centralized organization, decision-making authority is concentrated at the corporate or divisional level. Marketing managers who operate out of one centralized organization are responsible for most of the important operational and

Figure 16.2 Organizing the marketing effort

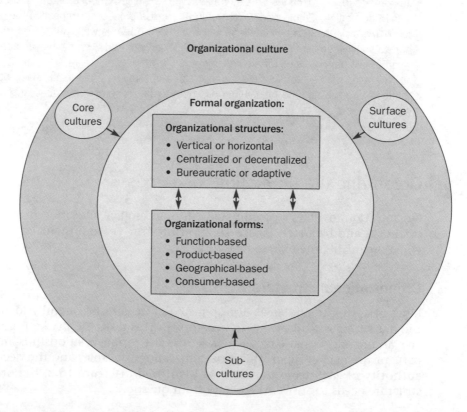

marketing decisions. Organizational structures in which the decision-making authority is delegated to marketing managers at the local operational level are classified as decentralized organizations. Greater control, better coordination, more consistency, and clearer direction are commonly cited strengths of the centralized marketing organization. A decentralized organization offers greater participation from all marketing personnel, which promotes higher morale, better understanding of customer needs (which results in closer relationships with the firm's customers), and quicker identification of operational and marketing problems (which allows faster response times to needed changes).

Bureaucratic or adaptive organization?

What degree of structural rigidity is needed to control the organization? From the perspective of structural design, marketing organizations can be classified along a continuum ranging from bureaucratic to adaptive organizations. Bureaucratic organizations are highly structured marketing organizations that tend to be characterized by high levels of centralized control, formal lines of authority, close supervision, and a less personal approach to work relationships. The bureaucratic marketing organization relies on rules and procedures for making decisions and solving problems. The adaptive organization is a loosely structured organizational design that features decentralized control, team problem solving, informal work relationships, and loose supervision. Employee participation and worker empowerment are two hallmarks of this form of organizational structure. In this type of learning organization, people working together with integrity, honesty and collective intelligence are profoundly more effective as a business than working relationships based on politics, game playing, and narrow self-interest. Whether management elects to go with a bureaucratic or adaptive organizational design or something in between depends on the particular circumstances facing the organization at a given point in time. When circumstances dictate a high level of control, organizations tend to become more bureaucratic. On the other hand, dynamic environmental changes require highly adaptive organizations.

Organizational forms

The organizational structure of marketing activities takes on many different forms. Marketing departments can be loosely classified as functional-, product-, geographical-, or customer-based organizations. The organizational form usually reflects the dominant nature of the marketing activity or problem. For example, a product-based organizational structure is needed when product considerations dominate decision making or are at the core of customers' problems.

Function-based organizations

The function-based organization is one founded on the basic marketing functions performed. Tasks are grouped and jobs are classified by such functional areas as marketing research, promotions, sales, and product and distribution management. Figure 16.3 illustrates one common function-based marketing organization. A high level of functional specialization, a more focused approach to task responsibilities, and relatively simple administration are the most relevant advantages of this form of organization. Safeguards must be initiated to overcome resistance to cross-functional activities. The function-based organization tends to be more effective in small companies and loses some of its effectiveness as the firm becomes larger.

Figure 16.3 The function-based marketing organization

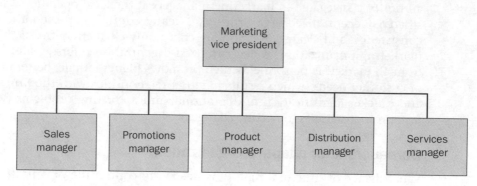

Product-based organizations

In a product-based organization, many of the marketing functions are organized along product and brand lines. In this form of organization, each product line, product category or brand often has its own marketing organization. This organizational format is shown in Figure 16.4. For marketing organizations that must manage an extensive and linked set of product lines, this form of organization is both efficient and effective. An organization that focuses on product specialization

Figure 16.4 The product-based marketing organization

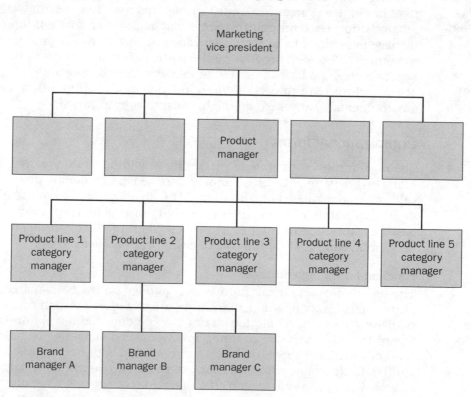

offers considerable benefits in attempting to tailor specific marketing programmes to targeted consumer groups. It is, however, an expensive approach to organizing the marketing effort.

Geographical-based organizations

When the firm must market its products in diverse market areas under different market conditions a geographical-based organization is appropriate. The vastly different demographic structures of market areas and the resulting differences in buying behaviour sometimes require that the organization adapt its marketing programmes from one region to another. These adaptive requirements are pronounced when moving from domestic to international markets. Geographic diversity is an operational reality that must be accommodated in some fashion. Many firms have elected to meet these realities by assigning a marketing manager and creating a marketing organization on the basis of geographical considerations. Figure 16.5 demonstrates this form or organizational structure.

Customer-based organizations

The customer-based organization recognizes that different customer segments have different needs; hence, the firm is organized around the type of customer being served. By structuring and tailoring the firm's marketing effort to take into account the specific needs of certain customer groups, the organization is better able to accommodate those differences and meet those needs. In reorganizing its international operations, IBM is organizing its marketing and sales staffs into 14 industry groups, rather than by country. Perhaps the most common form of a customer-based marketing organization involves dividing the firm into two customer divisions – business-to-business marketing and consumer-products marketing.

Figure 16.5 The geographical-based marketing organization

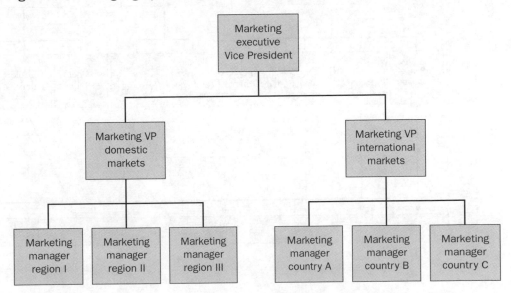

Exhibit 16.2	New customer oriented organization at Ciba Specialty Chemicals

Consolidation within the specialty chemicals industry as well as among customers and suppliers has posed a challenge to the specialty chemicals industry. There has been a fundamental change from simply selling products to providing a full package of solutions to customers. Customers are also demanding products more quickly and efficiently. This requires standardized and harmonized ways of delivering integrated solutions, a minimum of hierarchical levels and a full concentration on the core business.

In keeping with a trend toward decentralization and customer-focused emphasis, Ciba Specialty Chemicals recently restructured its businesses and divisions. The company hopes that the new structure will provide the framework for increased innovation and growth.

Innovation initiatives across the segments will be increased and gain importance under the leadership of the chief technology officer to ensure that the product portfolio and innovation efforts are successfully shared across segments.

The five industry focused segments are: plastic additives (polymer additives and process and lubricant additives), coating effects (imaging and coating additives, colours for inks, and paints and plastics), water and paper treatment, textile effects (colours for textiles and textile chemicals) and home and personal care.

The five segments are aligned on customer industries, have their own strategic initiatives and possess the critical size needed to maintain or gain market leadership.

Key customer markets for Ciba Specialty Chemicals include automotive, textiles, inks/paints, home and personal care, paper, pollution and extraction. Ciba estimates that roughly 40 per cent of its sales go into plastic materials in a number of the customer end markets mentioned.

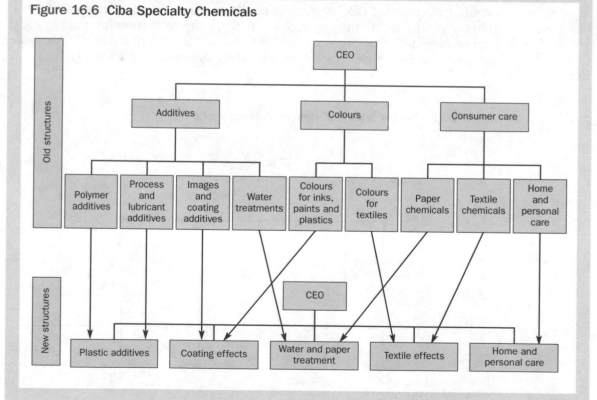

Figure 16.6 Ciba Specialty Chemicals

Exhibit 16.2 continued

In the car market there is a global overcapacity, and demand in the USA is expected to decrease, causing an overall global decrease in sales. While there is overcapacity in traditional inks, a healthy demand for environmentally friendly inks (8 per cent growth per year) and digital printing inks (13 per cent growth per year) is expected for the next few years. The global paints market is growing steadily at 2 per cent per year. In the home and personal care market, growth is expected to be 4–6 per cent per year, with fastest growth in the hair care and toothpaste segments. Both the oil and mineral extraction markets are seeing increasing demand.

Source: adapted from Challener (2001).

Transition from a product-focused to a customer-focused structure

The main aspects of this transition are illustrated in Figure 16.7. The shift towards a more customer-focused organization can be explained by the following factors.

● Production technologies allow 'mass customization', which results in a greater ability to target smaller customer segments with product features that are more appropriate for their needs.

Figure 16.7 Evolution from product-focused to customer-focused business units

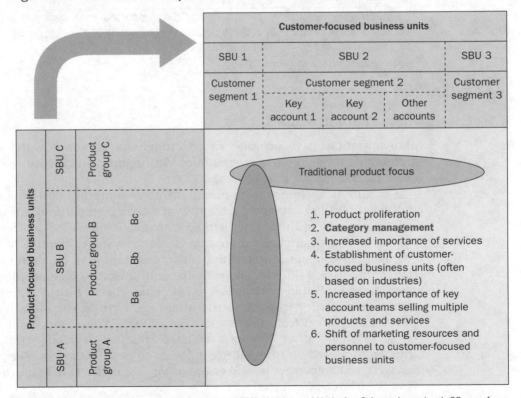

Source: C. Homburg, J. P. Workman Jr & O. Jensen (2000), *Academy of Marketing Science Journal*, vol. 28, no. 4, pp. 459–479, copyright © 2000 by Sage Publications, Inc., reprinted by permission of Sage Publications, Inc.

- Customer data warehouse and data mining techniques (see Appendix) make it possible to uncover previously unknown patterns of customer behaviour. These IT-based tools ultimately help marketers to make better decisions regarding relationships with customers.

- The increased number of products available often results in resellers wanting assistance at the overall category level, not the product level. Thus, firms have increasingly established managers responsible for entire product categories.

- There is an increased importance of services with many major firms receiving more profits from services than from products.

- Many firms reorganize their sales force around customer groups (often industry based) to develop coherent solutions out of the products and services from multiple divisions.

- Following on from such an industry segmentation, many firms then assign key account managers to be the single point of contact with major accounts, selling the entire range of products and services produced by their firm.

Exhibit 16.3 | **Wrigley (chewing gum) launches a new division**

The Wm Wrigley Jr Company has formed a new division, Wrigley Healthcare, to develop and market products that use chewing gum as a vehicle for functional health ingredients. Wrigley has outsourced some of the sales functions.

The Wrigley Healthcare sales team will be supported by Acosta Sales & Marketing Company, a national broker sales organization specializing in the sale, merchandising and distribution of over-the-counter drug products.

Source: adapted from Candy Industry (2000).

Organizational culture

All organizations have a culture, which strongly impacts on how that organization implements its marketing programmes. An organizational culture is created by accepting and sharing a set of values.

As companies attempt to re-orient themselves around customers, individual employees will have to come to terms with changing cultural norms, organizational structures and the way their performance is measured and rewarded. This requires an organizational culture that is adaptive and responsive to change, and the quality of communication within an organization is an important aspect of any change initiative. Failure to successfully communicate a change initiative and its implications for employees can lead to failure; an effective internal communication strategy needs to be in place so that there is buy-in to the initiative led by the senior management team (Ryals and Knox, 2001). When most or all of the members of an organization embrace a group of values, a prevailing set of traditions is created and passed on from older employees to new employees. The behaviour of managers and employees toward one another often reflects the type of culture that prevails within an organization.

An organization's culture exists at three levels. As shown in Figure 16.8 the core culture is the basic value system (the deep beliefs and understanding that shape and guide attitudes and actions) that serves as an invisible foundation for the

Figure 16.8 Organizational culture

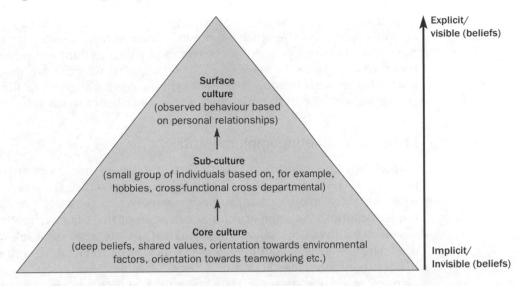

observable behaviour within the surface culture. The surface culture manifests itself in the form of behavioural and personal relationships that can be observed or heard by walking around the organization. It is how members of the marketing organization relate. Given the high level of interpersonal relationships that surround most marketing activities, core and surface cultures are vital to the successful completion of the marketing mission. Pleasant working relationships, supportive working environments, amiable motivational pressure, and strong marketing traditions are all benefits that organizational members hope to find within a well-established and tested cultural environment.

Under the surface culture of an organization, a number of subcultures exist in which small groups of individuals hold to the core value system, but have slightly different perspectives that usually reflect their particular set of circumstances. Subcultures are based on gender and racial differences, age and educational variations, and occupational and managerial positions. Creating the comfortable and productive organizational culture is one of the toughest challenges facing the marketing manager and crucial to the effective execution of the marketing effort.

16.5 Implementation of the marketing plan

Simply put, implementation refers to the 'how' part of the marketing plan. Because marketing implementation is a very broad term, it is often used but frequently misunderstood.

Some of this misunderstanding may stem from the fact that marketing strategies almost always turn out differently than anticipated because of the difference between intended marketing strategies and realized marketing strategy. Intended marketing strategy is what the organization wants to happen; it is the organization's planned strategic choice. The realized marketing strategy, on the other hand, is the strategy that actually takes place. More often than not, the difference between the intended and realized strategy is the result of the way the intended marketing strategy is implemented. This is not to say that an organization's realized marketing strategy is necessarily better or worse than the intended marketing strategy, just that it is different in some way. Such differences are often the result of internal and external environmental factors that change during implementation. As a result, when it comes to marketing implementation, Murphy's law usually applies: if anything can possibly go wrong, it will. This serves as a warning to all managers that the implementation of the marketing strategy should not be taken lightly.

Issues in marketing implementation

Marketing implementation is critical to the overall success of any organization because it is responsible for putting the marketing strategy into action. Unfortunately, many organizations repeatedly experience failures in marketing implementation. We often encounter examples of these failures in our daily lives – out-of-stock items at the local supermarket, overly aggressive salespeople at car dealerships, long checkout queues at the local department store, and unfriendly or inattentive employees at a hotel. Such examples illustrate that even the best planned marketing strategies are a waste of time without effective implementation to ensure their success. In short, a good marketing plan combined with bad marketing implementation is a guaranteed recipe for disaster.

One of the most interesting aspects of marketing implementation is its relationship to the strategic planning process. Many managers assume that planning and implementation are interdependent, but separate issues. In reality, planning and implementation are intertwined within the marketing planning process. Many of the problems of marketing implementation occur because of this relationship to strategic planning. We will now look at three of the most common issues.

Planning and implementation are interdependent processes

Many marketing managers assume that the planning and implementation process is sequential. That is, strategic planning comes first, followed by marketing implementation. Although it is true that the content of the marketing plan determines how it will be implemented, it is also true that how a marketing strategy is to be implemented determines the content of the marketing plan. This two-way relationship between marketing strategy and marketing implementation is depicted in Figure 16.9.

Certain marketing strategies will dictate some parts of their implementation. For example, a company such as Southwest Airlines with a strategy of improving customer service levels may turn to employee training programmes as an important part of that strategy's implementation. Through profit sharing, many Southwest Airlines employees are also shareholders with a vested interest in the firm's success. Employee training and profit-sharing programmes are commonly used in many companies to improve customer service. However, employee training, as a tool of implementation, can also dictate the content of the company's strategy. This leads us also to discuss the role of internal marketing.

Figure 16.9 Two-way relationship between marketing strategy and implementation

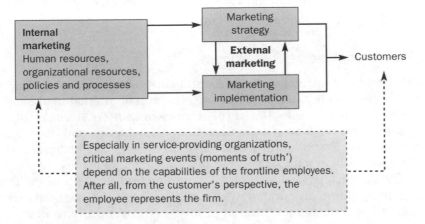

16.6

The role of internal marketing

As more companies come to appreciate the importance of people in the implementation process, they are becoming disappointed with traditional approaches to marketing implementation. These forces for change have been caused by several factors: high rates of employee turnover and its associated costs, and continuing problems in the implementation of marketing strategy. These problems have led many organizations to adopt alternative approaches to marketing implementation. One of these alternatives is internal marketing.

The internal marketing approach

The concept of internal marketing comes primarily from service organizations where it was first practised as a tactic for making all employees aware of the need for customer satisfaction. Generally speaking, internal marketing refers to the managerial actions necessary to make all members of the organization understand and accept their respective roles in implementing marketing strategy. This means that all employees, from the chief executive officer to front-line marketing personnel, must realize how each individual job assists in implementing the marketing strategy.

Under the internal marketing approach, every employee has two sets of customers: external and internal. For department store managers, for example, the people who shop in the store are called external customers, while the employees who work in the store are the manager's internal customers. In order for implementation to be successful, the store manager must serve the needs of both 'customer' groups. If the internal customers are not dealt with properly, then it is unlikely that the external customers will be completely satisfied.

This same pattern of internal and external customers is repeated throughout all levels of the organization. Even the CEO is responsible for serving the needs of his or her internal and external customers. Thus, unlike traditional approaches where the responsibility for implementation rests with lower levels of the organization, the internal marketing approach places this responsibility on all employees, regardless of organizational level. In the end, successful marketing implementation comes from an accumulation of individual actions where all employees are responsible for implementing the marketing strategy.

The internal marketing process

The process of internal marketing is straightforward and rests on many of the same principles used in external marketing. The overall internal marketing framework is presented in Figure 16.10. In this framework, internal marketing is seen as an output of and input to both marketing implementation and the external marketing programme. That is, neither the marketing strategy nor its implementation can be designed without some consideration for the internal marketing programme.

The product, price, distribution, and promotion elements of the internal marketing programme are similar, yet different from the elements of the external marketing programme. Internal products refer generally to marketing strategies that must be sold internally. More specifically, however, internal products refer to those employee tasks, behaviours, attitudes, and values necessary to ensure implementation of the marketing strategy. The implementation of any marketing strategy requires certain changes on the part of employees. They may have to work harder, change job assignments, or even change their attitudes and expand their abilities. The changes that employees must undergo in implementing the marketing strategy are called internal prices. Employees pay these prices through what they must do, change, or give up when implementing a new marketing strategy.

Internal distribution refers to how the marketing strategy is communicated internally. Planning sessions, workshops, formal reports, and personal conversations are all examples of internal distribution. Internal distribution also refers to employee training and education programmes designed to assist in the transition to a new marketing strategy. Finally, all communication aimed at informing and persuading employees about the merits of the marketing strategy comprise internal promotion. Internal promotion can take the form of speeches, video presentations, audiotapes, and/or internal company newsletters. With the vast age disparity of today's employees, it is unlikely that any one medium will communicate successfully with all employees. Managers must realize that telling employees important information once in a single format is not communicating. Until employees understand it, communication has not taken place.

Implementing an internal marketing approach

Successfully using an internal marketing approach requires the integration of many factors already discussed in this chapter. First, the recruitment, selection, and training of employees must be considered an important component of marketing implementation, with marketing having an input into the personnel function as necessary. This ensures that employees will be matched to the marketing tasks to be performed. Second, senior managers must be completely committed to the marketing strategy and overall marketing plan. It is naive to expect employees to be committed when senior managers are not. Simply put, the best planned strategy in the world cannot successfully proceed if the employees responsible for its implementation do not believe in it and are not committed to it.

Figure 16.10 Internal marketing framework

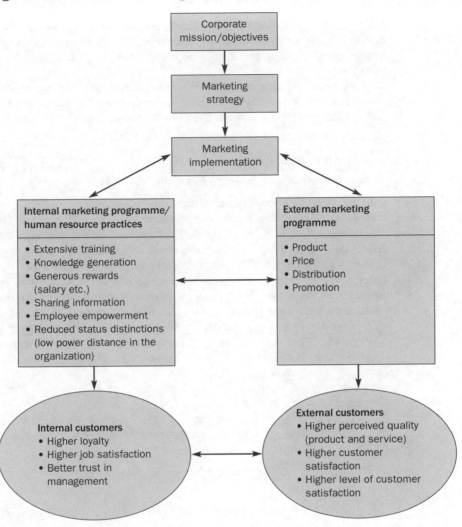

Source: adapted from Piercy (1992), p. 371.

Third, employee reward programmes must be linked to the implementation of the marketing strategy. This generally means that employees should be rewarded on the basis of their behaviours rather than on their work outcomes. In an organization guided by a strong culture and a shared marketing plan, outcome-based control systems may not adequately capture the effort put in by employees. Fourth, the organization should be characterized by open communication among all employees, regardless of organizational level. Through open, interactive communication, employees come to understand the support and commitment of senior managers, and how their jobs fit into the overall marketing implementation process.

Finally, organizational structures, policies, and processes should match the marketing strategy effectively. Although eliminating these constraints may mean that employees should be empowered to creatively fine-tune the marketing strategy or its

| Exhibit 16.4 | **Merger of Mars' European food, pet care and confectionery divisions** |

Mars Inc. is a diversified multi-functional company whose primary products include foods, pet care, confectionery, electronics, and drinks. Owned and controlled by the Mars family, this US giant is one of the world's biggest private companies, but also one of the most secretive.

Mars' decision in January 2000 to merge its food, pet care and confectionery divisions across Europe – and eventually with headquarters in the UK – has split the marketing industry.

The most well-known brands within the three divisions are:

- foods: Uncle Ben's Rice, Uncle Ben's sauces
- pet care: Whiskas, Pedigree
- confectionery: M&Ms, Snickers, Milky Way, Mars Bar.

Mars UK says the decision to pool the businesses was taken to strike at the company's international competitors in food and confectionery, such as Nestlé and Unilever. The move also coincides with plans to create a single European market and highlights the company's belief that its consumers' needs are the same across Europe.

But the combination of food and confectionery with pet care is not clear to all industry observers. One industry analyst made the comment: 'Generally speaking, Mars is doing the right thing by merging divisions to squeeze profits out of them. Before the advent of the euro it was acceptable to run separate companies in different European countries but not any more.'

Another analyst had this opinion: 'I can't imagine it marketing all three sides of the business together. They're too different. The only visible benefit appears to be an improvement in distribution. Tastes across European markets are very different, whether you're selling products for animals or people.'

'It's all very well Mars saying it will tackle competitors such as Nestlé and Unilever, but they are only rivals in food and confectionery.'

'If Mars starts laying down too many controls by merging all its businesses – and therefore also its marketing and management strategies – it may streamline communications, but could lose the creativity available in different regions.'

Source: adapted from McCawley (2000).

implementation, empowerment should be used only if the organization's culture can support it. However, if used correctly as a part of the internal marketing approach, the organization can gain more motivated, satisfied, and committed employees as well as enhanced customer satisfaction and improved business performance.

16.7 Summary

A marketing plan is like a map. It outlines where the business is, its desired destination (objectives), and the conditions it will face in its efforts to reach that destination. The plan helps to integrate activities, schedule resources, specify responsibilities and provide a means of measuring progress. Understanding the market situation reveals a set of key issues that need to be addressed in order to reach the desired destination. Situational analysis and identification of key performance issues are key inputs to the marketing plan.

In order to construct a realistic plan, managers need to estimate what total market demand might be. The marketing plan should have the following framework:

- title page
- table of contents
- executive summary
- introduction
- situational analysis
- marketing objectives and goals
- marketing strategies and programmes
- budgets
- implementation and control
- conclusion.

The marketing plan may be implemented around one of the following organizational forms: function-based, product-based, geographical-based or customer-based.

The development of a marketing plan involves process and structure, creativity and form.

If the marketing plan fails to produce the desired levels of performance, the marketing strategy needs to be re-examined.

Neither the marketing strategy nor its implementation can be designed without consideration for the internal marketing programme. Successful implementation of this can result in more motivated, satisfied and committed employees. In the end it can also improve business performance.

Case study 16.2 Teekanne GmbH

Marketing planning for international expansion of tea sales[1]

The Teekanne Group (total sales DM 550 million, 1700 employees) is a German producer of teabag machines and tea brands, like Teekanne (registered in 1888) and Teefix (registered in 1913). Whereas the tea bag machines have been sold all over the world (through the Teepack company), the two tea brands have mainly been sold in Germany where Teekanne is a market leader with 40–45 per cent share of the tea market. In the rest of Europe, market share is 2–5 per cent and outside Europe the market share is close to zero. Therefore, the Teekanne management is looking for some new expansion opportunities in the international market for its tea brands. Tea sales for various countries are given in Table 16.2.

[1] See also Case Study 3.1.

Background

According to Chinese legend, the story of tea began in 2737 BC. Emperor Shen Nung, who was known as the Divine Healer, always boiled his water before drinking it. He had observed that those who boiled their water had better health. One afternoon, as he knelt before his boiling water, some leaves from a nearby tree blew into the water. The emperor noted a delightful aroma and, upon sipping the beverage, proclaimed it heaven sent.

Shortly after Emperor Shen Nung's discovery, tea's popularity spread to Japan and the rest of the Far East. The Dutch first brought tea from China to Europe and the USA by 1650. In 1669, the East India Company began bringing tea

Case study 16.2 continued

Table 16.2 Total tea sales, (Estimated) 2002
            (US$ per capita)

Country	Value	Country	Value
Turkey	60.2	South Africa	4.4
Japan	28.2	Italy	4.4
Taiwan	25.6	South Korea	4.1
United Kingdom	22.4	Norway	4.2
Hong Kong	22.2	Slovakia	4.2
Ireland	18.1	Czech Republic	4.0
Australia	18.2	Morocco	3.4
Russia	16.7	China	2.7
Israel	12.2	Malaysia	2.7
New Zealand	12.2	Hungary	2.4
Germany	14.6	Denmark	2.3
Greece	8.9	India	1.8
Austria	9.5	Spain	1.9
Switzerland	9.2	Indonesia	1.5
Poland	9.5	Romania	1.2
Egypt	8.4	Vietnam	1.3
Singapore	7.7	Portugal	1.1
Chile	7.2	Belgium	1.0
Netherlands	6.9	Bulgaria	0.8
Finland	7.1	Venezuela	0.8
USA	6.2	Colombia	0.6
France	6.2	Mexico	0.5
Sweden	5.2	Brazil	0.5
Canada	4.9	Thailand	0.4
Argentina	4.6	Philippines	0.3

Source: adapted from Euromonitor figures.

leaves to England, and in 1721, the company was granted a monopoly on all tea imported into the British Empire. Initially, tea was very expensive and only royalty and the upper classes could afford it.

Broadly speaking, there are two types of tea, green and black tea. There are also herbal teas, which consist of leaves, flowers, and other ingredients from other plants.

Green and black tea originate from the same plant, *Camellia sinensis*. Green tea leaves are much less processed because they are not fermented (oxidized) like black tea. Green teas have a more delicate, fresh taste, where black teas are often more full-bodied and robust.

Black tea

Black tea gets its colour and character as a result of the fermentation process. The term 'ferment' has been used by the tea industry for years, but the process is more correctly defined as oxidation. The enzymes in the tea leaves are allowed to oxidize after rolling. Oxidation time is critical and greatly affects the flavour and quality of the tea. Tea estates employ skilled tea makers to oversee the process.

Black tea currently accounts for approximately 70 per cent of world tea consumption. The largest producer of black tea is India. Sri Lanka (Ceylon), China, Indonesia and Kenya are also major black tea sources. Other producers include Argentina, Brazil, Bangladesh, Malawi, Tanzania, and Uganda.

The quality of black tea is determined by the origin, growing conditions, and manufacturing skill of the tea estate manager. All tea comes from tropical or subtropical climates. Tea plants will flourish where it is warm and rainfall is heavy.

Green tea

Green tea, which is unfermented tea, remains the most popular tea in Asian countries such as China and Japan. In fact, up until the 18th century, it was also the most popular form of tea in Britain.

About 90 per cent of the world's green tea is produced in China. A cup of green tea is generally much lighter than other teas. While Asian cultures have believed for centuries that green tea has properties beneficial to human health, modern science is only now discovering that this may be true.

Teekanne is a marketer of black, green and herbal tea.

Tea calms nerves; however, in excess, it causes agitation, insomnia and indigestion. The tea leaf contains theine, similar to caffeine in that it stimulates the heart and the brain. It also contains a slightly poisonous substance called tannin. The amount of tannin in a drink is related to the length of time the leaves are left to steep. Generally, tea leaves should be left for a maximum of five minutes.

Case study 16.2 continued

Around the world, tea is served in different ways. The Chinese and Japanese tend to drink it plain, while the English and Irish add milk to a generally strong and dark brew. In Russia, sugar and lemon is added to the drink, which is presented in glasses rather than in cups. In Tibet and in central Asia, it is common to add salt and rancid butter to tea.

The European James Bond strategy

Adage Global (2000) announced on September 20, 2000 that Sean Connery ('James Bond') had been signed up by Teekanne to persuade European coffee-loving nations to drink more tea.

The image of tea has always been inferior to that of coffee in many European countries (except the UK). Tea has been advertised since the 1960s with images of traditional, happy families whereas coffee adverts are far more sexy. Sean Connery could bring qualities of masculinity, heroism and adventure to the idea of drinking tea – and he embodies the idea of Britishness.

The advert ran in Austria, Spain, the Czech Republic and Italy as well as in Germany. It headed a heavyweight campaign, which included a competition in which the top prize was a trip to Hollywood to meet Mr Connery himself – and share a pot of tea with him.

Teekanne heading for the American tea market

Against all odds the Teekanne management decided to try to penetrate the US tea market. The USA, of course, is still a coffee-drinking country, with Americans consuming 693 cups annually per capita, compared with 154 cups of tea.

But of the 50 billion cups of tea a year in the USA, the north east, including Connecticut, accounts for 33 per cent of the tea consumed. This does not include iced tea, which accounts for about 85 per cent of the tea consumed in the USA, the only country in the world that drinks more tea cold than hot.

The US hot drinks market, mainly tea and coffee, is highly consolidated. Multi-national producers dominate, and small manufacturers typically operate in speciality and niche markets.

Procter & Gamble and Philip Morris control nearly 70 per cent of the US hot drinks market.

Their dominance is due mostly to the popularity of Maxwell House (Philip Morris) and Folgers (Procter & Gamble). The buyout of Chock Full o'Nuts in 1999 by food conglomerate Sara Lee further consolidated the market.

Nestlé dominated the other hot drinks sector over the review period through its Nestlé Quick Instant Milk and Carnation Instant Milk brands.

Unilever is the market leader in the tea sector, accounting for 36.5 per cent of all sales in the sector. Despite Unilever's relatively low share in the hot drinks market as a whole it is still the market leader in the tea market (see Table 16.3).

Table 16.3 Manufacturers' market shares in the USA

Manufacturer	Market share (%)
Lipton (Unilever)	33
Celestial Seasonings	13
Bigelow	11
Private labels	7
Other (Luzianne, Tetley, Twinings, Red Rose, Saladu, etc.)	36
Total	100
Total market (tea bags/loose tea)	US$711 million

Source: adapted from Cosgrove (2000).

The total US tea market

In the US market the trend is that the big tea marketers become 'total tea' promoters. The same household may be drinking more than one type of tea (Table 16.4).

Table 16.4 US tea market: types and distribution channels, 1999 (US$ million)

Distribution channel	Tea bags/ loose tea	Instant tea mixes	Ready-to-drink (RTD) tea	Total tea
Food	626	271	441	1338
Drug stores	14	2	36	52
Mass	71	18	39	128
Total	711	291	516	1518

Source: adapted from Welham (1999).

Case study 16.2 continued

Older tea drinkers may be using tea bags, while the children are drinking instant or RTD iced tea. The traditional tea bag and instant tea mixes are mainly sold through supermarkets (food) whereas a larger percentage of RTD tea (iced tea) is sold through drugstores.

In Table 16.4 'speciality teas' are included in the tea bags/loose tea category. This is a small but vibrant segment growing 6–10 per cent per year. Indeed, speciality teas (including flavoured, herbal, and green teas) are expected to have 15–20 per cent of the US tea market by 2005, up from 10 per cent today.

The food service segment has always been tied tightly to the speciality tea segment. However, it takes more to prepare a good cup of tea than coffee, which has the advantage of equipment that helps to make the process foolproof.

The manufacturer's market shares in the tea bag/loose tea segment are shown in Table 16.3

Unilever

The company reported revenues of US$45.8 billion in 1999, a 2.9 per cent decrease from 1998. Over the same period, net income decreased by 9.9 per cent to US$3.1 billion.

Unilever's beverage business is centered on tea, and its Lipton brand is the leading bagged tea in the world. Lipton's range of teas includes Lipton Black and Yellow standard tea bags, Lipton Black standard loose tea, Lipton Black speciality tea bags, Lipton Black speciality loose tea and Lipton Green tea.

Unilever also participates in the 'ready-to-drink' tea market, through a joint venture with PepsiCo. Lipton's Iced Tea has been sold since 1992.

In recent years, it has focused its marketing and advertising efforts on Lipton Brisk, a ready-to-drink tea produced and sold like a soft drink, rather than on Lipton's Iced Tea, a more expensive bottled beverage made from real brewed tea.

In 2000, Lipton introduced Lipton Cold Brew Blend for consumers who like brewed iced tea, but who do not want to take the time to boil the water to make it. Cold Brew Blend (tea bags) steeps in cold water, unlike regular tea bags that require hot water to brew. The product is unsweetened and requires five minutes to steep.

Lipton Cold Brew is available in 24-bag pitcher size and 48 bag glass size packages.

Celestial Seasonings Inc.

Celestial Seasonings Inc. is the US leader in herbal tea, with about half the market in this segment. The company sells over 60 varieties of tea in supermarkets and natural foods stores in the USA and 50 other countries. Its products include Sleepytime, Red Zinger and Tension Tamer teas sold in brightly coloured boxes that often include recipes and homey sayings. The firm also makes herbal supplements and has licensing agreements with Warner-Lambert for throat drops, as well as Ferolito and Vultaggio for iced tea.

The largest brand in its portfolio, Celestial Seasonings, continues to be the best-selling speciality tea brand in the USA, ranking first in natural food stores, grocery, mass merchandisers, and drug stores. Celestial remains the leader in green tea, the fastest growing segment in the category. It intends to take green tea into the mainstream, as consumer recognition of its health benefits grows.

The Teekanne management has found some market data showing that about 80 per cent of regular black tea in bags is used for the preparation of iced tea. On average consumers spend about 40 minutes preparing iced tea. This is the reason why Lipton introduced Lipton Cold Brew Blend tea bags in the summer of 2000.

In Spring 2000, a market test was done on the product in the southern part of the USA. Results were encouraging enough to make the national launch of Cold Brew the centrepiece of Lipton's 2001 marketing plans.

The Teekanne management is impressed by the market feedback of this new Lipton Gold Brew product, and it wonders if such a new tea bag product could be good leverage to enter the US tea market.

Questions

1. Is it an advantage for the Teekanne Group that it is both a manufacturer of tea bag machines and a manufacturer of branded tea bags?

Case study 16.2 continued

2. Teekanne GmbH wants to expand its tea sales outside Germany. Which countries would you recommend Teekanne to concentrate on?

3. Teekanne thinks that Sean Connery should be able to replace the cosy image of tea with an adventurous, and even erotic one. Do you agree or disagree?

4. What kind of European promotion strategy could Teekanne have used as an alternative to the Sean Connery promotion to increase sales of the Teekanne brand in the European tea market?

5. Is the current product range of Teekanne (see www.teekanne.de) suitable for penetrating the US market? If not, what changes in the product concept would you recommend?

6. Through the sales of tea bag machines (through the Teepack company) Teekanne already has knowledge of and contacts with the main tea brand manufacturers in the US market. How could Teekanne use these contacts to plan the market penetration?

7. Produce a marketing plan for Teekanne to enter the US market. What are the critical moments in the implementation of your plan?

Sources: Beverage Industry (2000), Cosgrove (2000). Levere (2000), Thompson (1999), Welham (1999), Witteman (2001).)

QUESTIONS FOR DISCUSSION

1. Discuss the considerations involved in deciding marketing objectives.

2. What is a marketing audit and what is the purpose of it?

3. What are the principal decisions to be made when preparing the marketing plan?

4. What are the main criteria for the successful implementiation of a marketing plan?

5. Discuss the pros and cons of standardizing the marketing management process. Is a standardized process of more benefit to a company pursuing a national market strategy or a global market strategy?

REFERENCES

Adage Global (2000), German tea marketer enlists James Bond for mission, *Adage Global* New York, 20 September.

Beverage Industry (2000), Coffee and tea run hot and cold, *Beverage Industry*, New York, September, pp. NP24–5.

Candy Industry (2000), Wrigley launches new division, *Candy Industry*, no. 11, November, p. 13.

Challener, C. (2001), Customer-focused approach key for Ciba Speciality Chemicals, *Chemical Market Reporter*, New York, no. 13, pp. 10–14.

Cosgrove, J. (2000), Coffee and tea: two hot segments poised for increased growth, *Beverage Industry*, December, pp. 14–17.

Fisher. M. G. (2000), A picture-perfect reorganization, *Sales and Marketing Management*, November 21, pp. 5–6 (**http://www.salesandmarketing.com**).

Homburg, C., Workman Jr, J. P., Jensen, O. (2000), Fundamental changes in marketing organization: the movement toward a customer-focused organizational structure, *Academy of Marketing Science Journal*, Greenvale, vol. 28, no. 4, pp. 459–79.

Kotler, P. (2000), *Marketing Management*, Prentice Hall Inc., Englewood Cliffs, NJ.

Levere, J. L. (2000), A new campaign will try to differentiate Lipton's Iced Tea from its main competitors, *New York Times*, May 4, p. C7.

McCawley, I. (2000), Can Mars bridge gaps in merger? *Marketing Week*, January 13.

McDonald, M. (1999), *Marketing Plans: How to prepare them, how to use them*, Butterworth-Heinemann, Oxford, 4th edn.

Piercy, N. F. (1992), *Market-led Strategic Change*, Butterworth-Heinemann, Stoneham, MA.

Ryals, L. and Knox, S. (2001), Cross-functional issues in the implementation of relationship marketing through customer relationship mangement, *European Management Journal*, vol. 19, no. 5, pp. 534–42

Simkin, L. (2002), Barriers impeding effective implementation of marketing plans: a training agenda, *Journal of Business & Industrial Marketing*, vol. 17, no. 1, pp. 8–24.

Thompson, S. (1999), Lipton sets solid summer support for test of quick-iced-tea bag, *Brandweek*, New York, May 24, p. 14.

Welham, D. (1999), Back in black, *Supermarket Business*, New York, December 15, pp. 41–3.

Witteman, B. (2001), Infused in the industry, *New York Times*, February 11, p. CT1.

Chapter 17

Budgeting and controlling

After studying this chapter you should be able to:

- understand why customer profitability is important.
- define the concept customer lifetime value (CLTV).
- understand why CLTV is important.
- describe the key elements of the marketing control system.
- list the most important measures for marketing performance.
- understand the need for evaluation and control of marketing plans and their implementation.
- explain how a marketing budget is established.

Case study 17.1 Condomi

Marketing budget consequences of an aggressive pricing and promotion strategy in the British condom market

It is estimated that the global annual market for male condoms is 5.4 billion units. The world's three biggest markets are the USA, Japan, India, and China.

In March 2000, Condomi AG decided to undercut the established Durex condom brand by 70–80 per cent.

The German condom manufacturer, Condomi, is Europe's largest condom manufacturer with Germany as its main market. It produces 300 million condoms a year and it has about 15 per cent of the total European market (1.8 billion condoms a year). Until now its main condom market has been Germany.

The Durex brand is owned by the UK based SSL International that was formed in June 1999 by the merger of Seton Scholl Health Care with London International Group. Durex is the biggest condom brand around the world with a global market share of about 20 per cent.

Generally, the SSL managers run a brand-oriented strategy: 'We want Durex to be the Coca Cola of the condom world'.

Until 2000 Condomi's market share in the UK was below 5 per cent. Condomi was entering the UK consumer retail market through a deal with distributor Ceura Healthcare to obtain listings in supermarkets, wholesalers and Boots the Chemist.

Condomi claimed the UK's poor record on unwanted teenage pregnancies (it has the highest in Europe) and the increasing number of heterosexual HIV infections were linked to the high cost of condoms.

The market was dominated by Durex, which has a 70 per cent market share, and Mates, with about 20 per cent. The Condomi range of six condom variants costs £1.99 for a pack of three. This compares with £3.99 for Durex Gold, while Durex Fetherlite and Mates Ribbed cost

▶

Case study 17.1 continued

£2.25 for a pack of three. Durex Select, a mixed pack, costs £3.24 for three.

The total condom market in the UK is about 150 million per year. The distribution of condoms in the UK is shown in Table 17.1.

Table 17.1 Distribution of condoms in the UK

Distribution channel	
Supply to retailers and wholesalers for over the-counter sale in shops	60%
Supply to the National Health Service (NHS) for free distribution	23%
Supply via vending machines	17%
Total	100%

Source: adapted from various sources, including www.durex.com and www.condomi.com

Condomi director Ralph Patmore said: 'Condom prices here are far higher than in the rest of Europe – they don't need to be that expensive. For teenagers, condoms are expensive, and they could have a pint of beer instead.'

Questions

1. What is the underlying strategy behind Condomi's price cut in the UK?

2. Will Condomi succeed in capturing market share in the UK?

3. In order to reach its market share objectives Condomi considers launching a £2 million promotion campaign on radio and television. What would be the necessary sales and market shares before break-even would be reached? (Assume a contribution margin of 20 per cent).

17.1 Introduction

An organization needs to budget in order to ensure that its expenditure does not exceed its planned revenue. Therefore this chapter discusses how to use rational processes for developing budgets and allocating resources. Furthermore, the chapter will outline the need for a control system to oversee the marketing operations of the company.

17.2 Budgeting

The classic quantification of a marketing plan appears in the form of budgets. Because these are so rigorously quantified, they are particularly important. They should represent a projection of actions and expected results, and they should be capable of accurate monitoring. Indeed, performance against budget is the main (regular) management review process.

The purpose of a marketing budget is to pull all the revenues and costs involved in marketing together into one comprehensive document. It is a managerial tool that balances what needs to be spent against what can be afforded and helps make choices about priorities. It is then used to monitor the performance. The marketing budget is usually the most powerful tool with which you think through the relationship between desired results and available means. Its starting point should be the marketing strategies and plans that have already been formulated in the marketing plan itself. In practice, the two will run in parallel and will interact. At the very least, the rigorous, highly quantified budgets may cause some of the more optimistic elements of the plans to be reconsidered.

Budgeting is also an organizational process that involves making forecasts based on the proposed marketing strategy and programmes. The forecasts are then used to construct a budgeted **profit-and-loss statement**. An important aspect of budgeting is deciding how to allocate all of the available money across all of the proposed programmes within the marketing plan.

Profitability analysis

Regardless of the organizational level, control involves some form of profitability analysis. In brief, **profitability analysis** requires that analysts determine the costs associated with specific marketing activities to find out the profitability of such units in different market segments, products, customer accounts, and distribution channels (intermediaries).

Profitability is probably the single most important measure of performance, but it has limitations. These are that many objectives can best be measured in non-financial terms (maintaining market share); profit is a short-term measure and can be manipulated by taking actions that may prove counter-productive in the longer term (e.g. reducing R&D expenses); and profits can be affected by factors over which management has no control (the weather).

Analysts can use direct or full costing in determining the profitability of a product or market segment. In full costing, analysts assign both direct, or variable, and indirect costs to the unit of analysis. Indirect costs involve certain fixed joint costs that cannot be linked directly to a single unit of analysis. For example, office costs, general management, and the management of the sales force are all indirect costs for a multi-product company. Those who use full costing argue that only by allocating all costs to a product or a market can they obtain an accurate picture of its value.

Direct costing involves the use of contribution accounting. Those favouring the contribution margin approach argue there is really no accurate way to assign indirect costs. Further, because indirect costs are mostly fixed, a product or market may make a contribution to profits even if it shows a loss. Thus, even though the company must eventually absorb its overhead costs, the contribution method clearly indicates what is gained by adding or dropping a product or a customer.

Contribution analysis is helpful in determining the yield derived from the application of additional resources (for instance, to certain sales territories). Contribution analysis attempts to determine the amount of output (revenues) that can be expected from a given set of inputs (costs). You should be familiar with break-even analysis, which is a type of contribution analysis, used to determine the amount of revenue necessary to cover both variable and fixed costs (see Chapter 12).

There are three ways of building a marketing budget that is based on a specific strategic market plan and the tactical marketing strategy designed to achieve the target level of performance.

- *Top-down budget*: a new marketing budget based on projected sales objectives is determined, using past marketing expenses as a percentage of sales.
- *Customer mix budget*: the cost of customer acquisition and retention and the combination of new and retained customers are used to derive a new marketing budget.
- *Bottom-up budget*: each element of the marketing effort is budgeted for specific tasks identified in the marketing plan.

As this book has a customer-oriented approach the customer mix budget will be discussed in the following.

Customer mix budgets

Recognizing the customer as the primary unit of focus, a market-based business will expand its focus to customers and markets, not just products or units sold. This is an important strategic distinction because there is a finite number of potential customers, but a larger range of products and services can be sold to each customer. And, as shown in Figure 17.1, a business's volume is its customer share in a market with a finite number of customers at any point in time, not the number of units sold.

customer volume = market demand (from customers) × market share (percentage)

Figure 17.1 presents an overall flow chart of how market-based net profits are derived. Customer volume, at the top of this diagram, is derived from a certain level of customer market demand and a business's share of that customer demand. Without a sufficient volume of customers, net profit will be impossible to obtain. Marketing strategies that affect customer volume include marketing strategies that:

- attract new customers to grow market share
- grow the market demand by bringing more customers into a market
- enter new markets to create new sources of customer volume.

Each of these customer-focused marketing strategies affects net profits, invested assets, cash flow, and, as we will show later, shareholder value. Thus, a key component of profitability and financial performance is customer purchases and the collective customer volume produced. Without customer purchases, there is no positive cash flow or potential for net profits or shareholder value.

Figure 17.1 A customer-based model of marketing contribution and net profits (before tax)

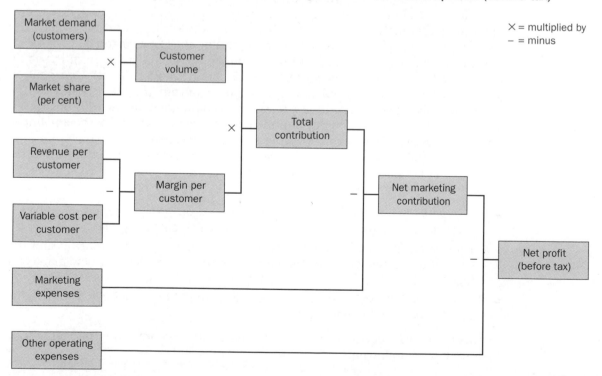

In the following, the different components of Figure 17.1 will be discussed (Best, 2000). Customer-based budgeting recognizes that companies are increasingly turning from traditional accounting methods, which identify costs according to various expense categories, to activity-based costing (ABC), which bases costs on the different tasks involved in performing a given activity.

Margin per customer (see Figure 17.1)

When customers decide to purchase an assortment of products and services from a business, the result is a certain revenue per customer. And, of course, a corresponding set of variable costs that go into each purchase and sales transaction must be taken into account to determine the margin per customer:

customer contribution margin= revenue per customer – variable cost per customer

This measure of customer profitability could be computed on a transaction basis (monthly or annually), or based on customer lifetime value (CLTV), which is discussed further in Section 17.3. The bottom line is that a business has to make a positive margin per customer or it will produce no profits and, therefore, no shareholder value. In many instances, new customers may produce a small or negative customer margin. Over time, we would expect a business to manage its marketing strategies so as to increase customer margin. If it does not, it has several alternatives to consider, one of which is to not continue to serve that customer as part of the business's marketing strategy. In general, marketing strategies designed to improve margin per customer can include marketing strategies that:

- grow revenue per customer by product line extensions
- grow revenue per customer by adding services that enhance customer value
- improve margin per customer with improved products and services for which the customer is willing to pay a premium price
- develop more cost-efficient marketing systems that lower variable sales and transaction costs
- eliminate customers that are not able to produce an acceptable level of customer margin.

As shown in Figure 17.1 revenue per customer and variable cost per customer come together to produce a certain level of margin per customer. Because the customer is the primary unit of focus of market-based management, it is the business's responsibility to develop marketing strategies that systematically build customer volume and customer margin.

Total contribution

Ultimately, whether tracking product revenues and variable product costs or tracking customer volume and margin per customer, the end result will be a total contribution produced by the marketing strategies that have been developed and implemented. Once again, both approaches are needed in managing different aspects of a business. However, those in marketing should be more concerned with a customer perspective and how to develop marketing strategies that affect both customers and the total contribution of the business.

total contribution = customer volume × customer margin

As shown in Figure 17.1, the total contribution produced by a marketing strategy is the product of the customer volume it produces and customer margin derived from customer purchases. The total contribution produced by a marketing strategy is an important component in the profitability equation because from this point forward only expenses are introduced. Hence, building market-based strategies that increase total contribution is an important priority in developing marketing strategies that deliver profitable growth.

Net marketing contribution

All marketing strategies require some level of marketing effort to achieve a certain level of market share. Expenses associated with sales effort, market communications, customer service, and market management are required to implement a marketing strategy designed to obtain a certain customer volume. The cost of this marketing effort is shown in Figure 17.1 as marketing expenses and must be deducted from the total contribution to produce a *net marketing contribution*. This is the net contribution produced after the marketing expenses are deducted from the total contribution produced.

net marketing contribution = total contribution – marketing expenses

In effect, this is how the marketing function contributes to the business's profits. If the marketing team develops a marketing strategy that fails and, therefore, produces a lower net marketing contribution, then that marketing strategy has, in effect, lowered the net profits of the business.

Marketing strategies are generally designed to affect total contribution, whether by increasing market demand, market share, or revenue per customer or by decreasing the variable cost per customer. The net marketing contribution equation should make it clear that such strategies are profitable only if the increase in total contribution exceeds the increase in marketing expenses required to produce that increase in total contribution. That is, for a marketing strategy to improve profits for the business, it has to improve net marketing contribution.

Net profit (before tax)

Although marketing strategies contribute to net profits through net marketing contribution, net profit (before tax) is generally beyond the control of the marketing function or the marketing management team. Marketing strategies produce a certain level of net marketing contribution from which all other business expenses must be deducted before a net profit is realized, as illustrated in Figure 17.1. These operating expenses include fixed expenses, such as human resources management, research and development, and administrative expenses, and other operating expenses, such as utilities, rent, and fees. In most instances, corporates overheads would also be allocated, which includes company expenses such as legal fees, corporate advertising, and executive salaries.

net profit (before tax) = net marketing expenses – other operating expenses

However, there are instances when a marketing strategy can affect other operating expenses. For example, a strategy to improve a product to attract more customers and build market share could involve research and development expenses to develop the new product.

Figure 17.1 is an illustration of the different budget element. Figure 17.2 illustrates the traditional marketing budget (per customer group) and its underlying determinants.

From Figure 17.2 the most important measures of marketing profitability may be defined as:

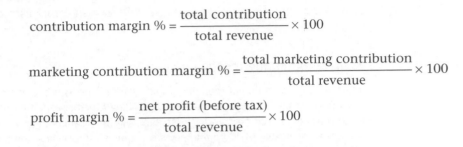

$$\text{contribution margin } \% = \frac{\text{total contribution}}{\text{total revenue}} \times 100$$

$$\text{marketing contribution margin } \% = \frac{\text{total marketing contribution}}{\text{total revenue}} \times 100$$

$$\text{profit margin } \% = \frac{\text{net profit (before tax)}}{\text{total revenue}} \times 100$$

Figure 17.2 A marketing budget and its underlying determinants

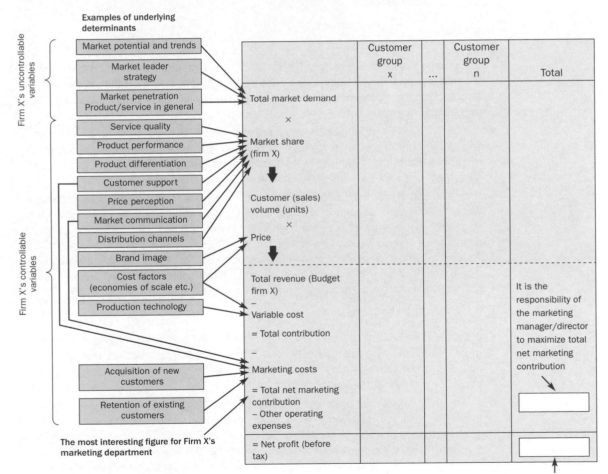

If we had information about the size of assets (accounts receivable + inventory + cash + plant + equipment) we could also define:

$$\text{return on assets (ROA)} = \frac{\text{net profit (before tax)}}{\text{assets}}$$

ROA is similar to the well-known measure, ROI (return on investment).

Exhibit 17.1

Alternative marketing metrics indicators

Marketing managers and chief marketing officers (CMO) need a supplementary set of indicators to monitor organizations' long-term marketing health. Marketing managers need to recognize that companies are moving from focusing on balance-sheet management to off-balance sheet management: from managing outcomes to processes and from managing the internal environment to the external environment.

Lusch (2000) identified ten indicators of marketing health in three areas: potential, people, and performance.

Potential

- Indicator 1: percentage of sales from products introduced in the last three years; and percentage of sales from markets (geographic or product) entered in the last three years. All products and markets have life cycles; they are born, and then they grow, mature, decline, and die. Companies that do not recognize this continue to live off past product and market successes.

- Indicator 2: percentage growth projected over the next three years in size of target market(s). Another indicator of potential is in the growth of the firm's target market(s). When companies fail to focus their marketing efforts toward the future, they may discover their markets do not have much of a future.

- Indicator 3: percentage of sales over the last three years from new marketing channels. Marketing channels respond to changes in how people would like to buy or source goods and services. Potential is necessary for long-term marketing health. However, potential alone is not sufficient. One also needs the 'right' people in the marketing organization. Today the 'people' element of marketing is seen most clearly in successful high-technology firms. It takes more than technology to have economically viable and highly sought-after products; it takes high-performance marketing personnel.

People

- Indicator 4: percentage of time the CEO and CMO spend on strategic marketing. The CEO must understand that new products, new markets, rapid growth target market(s), and new distribution channels are critical to success. The CEO and the CMO need to be thinking about these indicators and the future.

- Indicator 5: percentage of senior marketing executives whose work is central to their lives. We live in a world where work is becoming less central to life. As economies develop and mature and the quality of life increases, more time is spent on leisure and luxuries. Often, consumption becomes more central than work. However, for the CMO and his or her direct subordinates, the work of marketing must be central to their lives.

- Indicator 6: percentage of unsuccessful sales calls, unsuccessful new products, unsuccessful new advertising programmes, or unsuccessful marketing initiatives. If we

Exhibit 6.1 continued

succeed, we learn; if we fail, we learn. Learning is an important part of long-term health. And to learn the company must take risks. Undoubtedly, the problem with this measure is that one does not know the optimum level of failure. If a company always fails in its initiatives, it will eventually go bankrupt; however, if a firm never fails, it will not learn and will decline.

Performance

- Indicator 7: price-earnings ratio relative to the top competitor. Traditional performance measures include profitability measures such as return on sales, return on assets, or return on equity. Undoubtedly, these popular measures should not be ignored; however, they tend to characterize past performance as opposed to potential future performance. This indicator is share price divided by the earnings per share ratio and best represents the consensus of financial and market analysts, as well as individual and institutional investors, of the firm's future earnings. Within the same industry, if one firm has a substantially higher price-earnings ratio than its competitors, the consensus is that it has more potential.

- Indicator 8: share of total market valuation today vs five years ago. Rather than looking at how a firm's market share changes over time it is suggested that how a firm's share of the total market valuation in the industry has changed over time should be examined.

- Indicator 9: break-even sales as a percentage of current sales. Most firms have very high fixed costs, and reaching and exceeding break-even is a continuous challenge. For this reason, CEOs have been asking all functional areas to look at outsourcing arrangements in which fixed costs become variable costs and in which each area can contribute to reduction of costs in the firm's value chain. The net effect is to lower break-even points and make it economically feasible to operate profitably under more diverse economic conditions.

- Indicator 10: Percentage of customers over the last year who had an unsatisfactory service experience. Customers avoid organizations that provide poor service. In addition, they tell others of their bad service experiences. In short, poor or good service today is an excellent predictor of future failure or success.

Many CEOs and CMOs view marketing as an expense and not an asset. Marketing is much more than an operating expense. CMOs must take a leading role in promoting the long-term marketing health of their organization. To accomplish this, CMOs will need good communication and political skills. Marketers will need to learn more about finance and accounting so they can communicate with CEOs in a language they understand. Specifically, communicating the impact of marketing programmes on both the short and long-term profit and cash flow will be of paramount importance. Increasingly, marketing is managing business processes in the entire value chain and playing a pivotal role in managing the firm's external environment.

Source: adapted from Lusch (2000).

17.3 Customer profitability and customer lifetime value

Traditional accounting systems have viewed customers as sources of revenue. More and more firms, however, are beginning to use their accounting systems to view customers as assets, basing their decisions on customers as much as they would base their decisions on investments. Therefore we propose customer lifetime value (CLTV) to be the central unit of measurement for customer profitability. We define CLTV as the net present value (NPV) of the profit a firm stands to realize on the average new customer during a given number of years.

The transition from market share to customer share (share of disposable income) is a prevalent theme in the CRM debate about customer loyalty and lifetime value. One result of the debate is a growing understanding that a large market share is not equivalent to having loyal customers. What you have today can be gone tomorrow, if the customer is not locked in or dependent.

Loyal customers should be viewed as an asset by the firm, and it should work to create relationships that will maintain their loyalty.

Long-term contracts and repeat sales produce predictable sources of revenue. In fact, the worth of many businesses can be calculated by the size of the customer base, such as the number of subscribers of a mobile phone company. Customers are not viewed as prospects for a single sale or as targets for problem solving. Rather, they are partners in a relationship that produces long-term cash flows for the seller.

Ask yourself this question, what is the overall length of the relationship (retention) and how much will the customer buy in his or her lifetime?

Retention rate is used to measure customer turnover. It shows how large a percentage of its customer portfolio the enterprise retains yearly. The churn rate, on the other hand, shows how large a percentage of its customer portfolio the enterprise loses every year.

When an enterprise operates with a churn rate of 20 per cent – retention rate of 80 per cent – it means that it replaces one customer in five each year. In other words, it completely replaces all of its customers over a five-year period. In this case, the period over which the enterprise can generate income from the customer will be only five years – the so-called CLTV.

Retention rate has great significance for the creation of value. Research has shown that when the enterprise increases the retention rate from e.g. 80 to 90 per cent, it can double CLTV. Longevity creates value.

Realizing the full profit potential of a customer relationship

How much is a loyal customer worth in terms of profits? Reichheld (1994) analysed the profit per customer in different service businesses, categorized by the number of years that a customer had been with the firm. Reichheld found that the longer the customer remained with a firm in each of these industries, the more profitable they became to serve. Annual profits per customer, which have been indexed over a seven-year period for easier comparison, are summarized in Table 17.2. As shown in Table 17.2 it is more profitable to keep existing customers than acquire new ones. During the normal development of a customer relationship, the cost to market and sell to these customers gradually declines, and the potential for **gross margin** improvement increases.

Table 17.2 Calculation of CLTV for one mobile telephone customer

Period	Cash flow ($)	Present value of $1 (discount rate = 10%)	Net present value (NPV) of cash flow ($)
0	−50	1.000	−50
1	15	0.909	+ 13.6
2	40	0.826	+ 33.0
3	50	0.751	+ 37.6
4	60	0.683	+ 41.0
5	70	0.621	+ 43.5
6	80	0.564	+45.1
7	90	0.513	+46.2
CLTV			+210

The loyal customer rarely focuses on price alone but instead sees customer relationships in terms of value for money. In this way, the customer acts as an advocate for the enterprise and thus helps attract new customers.

Let us assume that Table 17.2 illustrates an example with average profit per mobile telephone customer generated over a seven-year period. Acquiring a new customer produces a loss of US$50 the first year. Consequently, the break-even of this customer is at the beginning of year 3. In this example, the average customer life is seven years, meaning that the churn rate is 14 per cent (1/7 × 100%). Working backward, we can estimate the customer retention rate to be 86 per cent as in Table 17.2.

Customer retention

To estimate the lifetime value of the customer at this rate of customer retention, we need to compute the net present value of the customer cash flow in Tale 17.2. In this example we assume that the yearly cash flow is equal to the yearly net profit. The calculation of present value is shown in Table 17.2 using a discount rate of 10 per cent.

The payback time of the investment ($50) in customer acquisition is a little more than two years. The CLTV per customer is $210. If the firm has 10,000 mobile telephone customers, the total CLTV would be $2.1 million.

If customer lifetime were only, say, four years, the customer value (net present value) would be considerably smaller. Thus, the higher rate of customer retention, the longer the average customer life expectancy and the greater the CLTV.

In Table 17.3 the CLTV calculation is a little more complex than in Table 17.2. Table 17.3 is based on an average of 1000 customers.

This spreadsheet might be typical of a firm marketing a magazine subscription. If we assume that the firm sells 1000 new subscriptions in year 1 at $150 each, then the calculation of net revenue and net costs at 50 per cent of revenue are both simple procedures. A further important issue is retention – in simple terms, how many customers at the beginning of a year are still subscribers at the year's end. Table 17.3 assumes a retention rate of 40 per cent at the end of year 1, then increases this gradually over the five-year period. Thus, 400 customers are still subscribers at the beginning of year 2, 180 at the beginning of year 3, and so forth. Naturally, the revenues and costs for a year are functions of the number of

Table 17.3 Calculating CLTV for an average of 1000 customers

	Year 1	Year 2	Year 3	Year 4	Year 5
Revenue					
Number of customers (left)	1000	400	180	90	50
Retention rate	40%	45%	50%	55%	60%
Average annual sales per customer	$150	$150	$150	$150	$150
Total revenue	$150,000	$60,000	$27,000	$13,500	$7,425
Costs					
Cost percentage	50%	50%	50%	50%	50%
Total costs	$75,000	$30,000	$13,500	$6,750	$3,713
Profits					
Gross profit	$75,000	$30,000	$13,500	$6,750	$3,713
Discount rate	1.00	1.20	1.44	1.73	2.07
NPV profit	$75,000	$25,000	$9,375	$3,906	$1,790
Cumulative NPV profit	$75,000	$100,000	$109,375	$113,281	$115,072
CLTV (per customer)	$75.00	$100.00	$109.38	$113.28	$115.07

Source: adapted from Pitt *et al*. (2000).

customers in the beginning of that year. Calculating gross profit is then a simple subtraction procedure.

As in all investments, the NPV for a customer five years from now is not worth what it is today. The discount rate we have chosen in Table 17.2 is 20 per cent – a discretionary figure, the choice of which will vary from firm to firm. Some may choose a premium bank rate, others an internal rate of return, still others some minimum rate of investment acceptability. The final calculation is a simple one: what is the CLTV of a customer who became a customer in year 1? The answer is the NPV of the cumulative gross profit for the year divided by the number of customers (1000) in year 1. Thus, the CLTV of one of these customers in year 4 would be $113.28; $115.07 in year 5, and so on.

An obvious application of this spreadsheet is its use in calculating what can be done to increase CLTV. The decision maker can change variables such as price, costs, the discount rate, the number of years an individual will be a customer, and the retention rate to determine the effects these will have on CLTV. In more general terms, however, it is worth considering what can be done from a marketing strategy perspective to maximize CLTV.

In summary we can increase CLTV by increasing the lifetime, increasing sales to customers and cutting the costs of serving a customer.

Increasing CLTV

Increasing customer life

There have been some excellent recent examples of firms extending the life of a customer by adapting the marketing strategy. Kimberly-Clark, manufacturer of Huggies disposable diapers, was subject to the limitations imposed by the fact that the 'life' of a Huggie customer (the baby) averaged only 18 months, until the child became toilet-trained. Market research also revealed a considerable degree of guilt among parents. Mothers and fathers felt guilty that little Johnny or Mary was still in 'nappies', while simultaneously feeling guilty at pushing a small child who might not be ready for parents. So Kimberly-Clark introduced 'trainer-pants', which fit like real pants but are disposable and have all the absorbency of the conventional nappy. No more guilt for parents. More important, Huggies have increased customer life by about six months. Though this might not seem much in real terms, it is effectively a 33 per cent average increase in customer life.

While the Huggies strategy has extended customer life, an alternative strategy would be to ask how a customer's life could start earlier. The Danish toy company Lego made building blocks that were played with by children between the ages of four and eight, on average. But this was a customer life of only about four years. So the company embarked on strategies that both began the customer life earlier and extended it for longer. In 1969 it launched Duplo – essentially, bigger Lego blocks that can be played with by children as young as two – thus adding two years to customer life. In 1977 it launched Lego Technic, an intricate set of construction blocks and fittings for older children (Pitt *et al.*, 2000).

Increasing retention rate

Current industry retention rates have a direct impact on long-term customer value. Where retention rates are 50 per cent or below, the average customer stays with the firm for two years or less. If a firm improves its retention rates from 50 per cent to 55 per cent, the average retention increases to 2.2 years from 2.0 years. In contrast, if average retention rates in an industry are relatively high, of the order of 75 per cent or greater, then an increase of 5 per cent in customer retention has a far greater impact. For example, improving retention rates from 75 per cent to 80 per cent improves customer retention from four years to five years. Here, long-term customer value is substantially greater and the leverage effect is more significant. The key to estimating and increasing average retention rates is to examine switching costs in the industry. To the extent that 'natural' or inherent switching costs exist, firms can retain their customer base with relatively less effort. These situations include monopolies, long-term contracts, warranties tied to service, and buying arrangements (e.g. a business has preferred rates with a hotel chain). Generally, higher switching costs will be related to higher retention rates. Industries that have higher switching costs will tend to have some or all of the following characteristics (Butcher *et al.*, 2001).

Membership based programmes
Membership services, such as banks, telephone firms, and credit card companies, have a formal tie or link with the customer. The customer must make an explicit decision to break the link and some effort is required to move to another firm. Further, from the provider's viewpoint, the formal link offers valuable customer information that may be used to enhance loyalty.

Loyalty based programmes
A vast range of industries focus on customer retention and loyalty nowadays, from airline frequent flyer schemes to supermarket **loyalty card** programmes. Even Coca-Cola now has an established loyalty programme. Many companies reward

customers simply by discounting or offering free products or services (airlines offering free flights, telephone companies discounting regular and frequent calls to friends and families). More and more firms are realizing that all customers are not the same, and that more individualized strategies will be more effective at retaining them.

Loyalty is a function of both the customer's unwillingness to exit and his or her ability to exert a voice, so managers should focus on loyalty by reducing the tendency to exit and providing opportunities to voice any concerns or complaints.

Some practical illustrations of these issues in recent times can be seen in the airline industry. Most frequent flyer schemes attempt to reduce exit by offering air miles to customers, who are then presumably unwilling to leave because they do not wish to lose those miles (we might refer to this as the economies of loyalty). But for customers this is a false loyalty, as they might endure poor quality of service (normally a reason for exiting) merely to avoid losing the miles. Besides, frequent flyers who put in hundreds of thousands of miles annually are not likely to be motivated by the reward of even more flying.

High degree of customer contact

The opportunity to establish a relationship with the customer through personal knowledge and customization to individual preferences will reduce risk and increase customer confidence in the firm. Professional service firms, hair stylists and financial services typically have either frequent contact and/or a long encounter when they meet their customers. The customer information gained during these encounters allows the firm to both meet and anticipate customer expectations.

Ability to differentiate

Services that are experience and/or credence based have a higher perceived risk (i.e. the cost of failure is high), and it is important to have a greater opportunity to be differentiated. Again, professional service firms, car repair services, delivery services and digital phone services can add customer value through offering various arrays of bundled services and/or better delivery of the core offering. Through effective differentiation these firms can improve retention rates.

Increasing sales to customers

This is done by raising either the firm's share of the customer's purchases or the customer's referral rate (the number of times the customer refers others to the firm's products and services). If the firm can segment and target high volume or usage customers, the revenue generated is substantial. In a number of industries, including financial services, the revenue generated from the high volume customers accounts for 70 per cent or more of the firm's business. Increasing the retention rates among these customers, or increasing their expenditure will be profitable. The key point is that the customer base must have varying spending rates and the high volume customers need to be identified. That is, the firm must be able to determine the average profitability per year by customer or segment.

Cutting the costs of serving a customer

The more the costs of serving customers can be reduced, the greater the profit margin on those customers that can be realized in the future. In many environments, it is also possible to cut costs by getting the customer to perform some of the work involved in service delivery – what Downes and Mui (1998) call 'outsourcing to the customer'. Surprisingly, customers often prefer this because it gives them greater control over the delivery process. When firms can develop systems to process customer transactions efficiently and effectively, servicing costs are also lower. This occurs with many financial services and business markets where large volumes of transactions are a characteristic of the industry.

The reasons why the profit per customer increases over time are schematically illustrated in Figure 17.3. The economic effect of customer loyalty can be attributed to the following factors: acquisition costs, revenue growth, reduced cost, **referrals** and price premiums.

The vertical axis in the figure is only an example (a mobile telephone customer), because the effects on profits of the various factors differ from industry to industry, firm to firm, and even customer to customer. However, the height of the sections gives some general indications of the relative importance of these factors. Every firm should, however, take the time and trouble to study its accounting and reporting system in order to make the necessary calculations of the influence on total profits per customer of these and possibly other profit drivers. It is a time-consuming task, because in most firms the figures needed are not readily available – revenues and costs are usually registered on a per product basis and not usually on a per customer basis. These factors are discussed overleaf.

Figure 17.3 Illustration of customer lifetime value

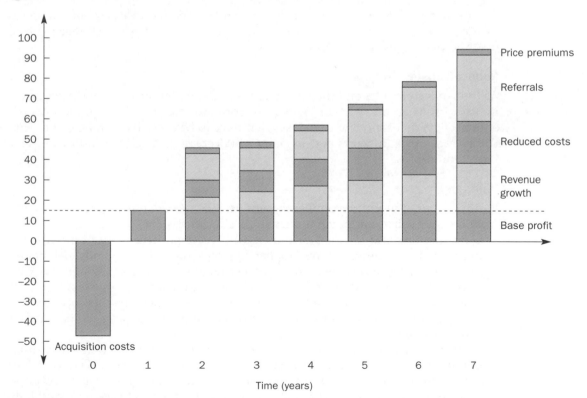

Source: adapted from Reichfeld (1994).

Acquisition costs

The active acquisition of new customers using sales and external marketing efforts is required in most businesses. As a rule of thumb, getting a new customer costs five to six times as much as the costs of normal service operations (sales calls, providing information about new goods or services, etc.) to keep an existing satisfied customer. In other words, it costs only 15–20 per cent of what has to be invested in getting a new customer to keep an existing customer. The economics of customer loyalty are very apparent. These figures of course vary from industry to industry, and situation to situation, but are nevertheless remarkable. In Figure 17.3 the acquisition cost per customer appears as a negative profit effect in the year before the customer relationship starts.

Base profit

In many service industries the price paid by customers during the first year or even the first few years does not cover the costs of producing the service. This is the base profit in the figure. After some years, depending on the industry and other factors, the accumulated base profits have covered the initial marketing costs of getting the customer.

Revenue growth

In most situations a long-standing customer will bring more business to the same service provider. Customers may decide to consolidate their purchases with a single supplier who provides high quality service.

This means that, on average, customers can be expected to contribute more to a firm's profit as the relationship grows. The annual revenue per customer increases over the years, thus contributing to growing profits.

Reduced costs

As the service provider and the customer learn about each other, and they get experience with what to expect and how to perform, service processes will be smoother and take less time, and fewer mistakes that have to be corrected will be made. Thus, the average operating costs per customer will decrease, which in turn has a positive impact on profits.

Referrals

Positive word-of-mouth recommendations are like free advertising, saving the firm from having to invest as much money in these activities.

Long-standing and satisfied customers will create positive word-of-mouth communication and recommend the supplier or service provider to friends, neighbours, business associates and others. The customer takes over the role of marketer without any additional costs to the firm. A large number of businesses, especially smaller ones, thrive on good referrals by satisfied customers. In this way new customers are brought in with lower than normal acquisition costs, which has an extra positive effect on profits.

With many services, particularly those that are primarily experience based (e.g. restaurants) or credence based (e.g. professional services, technical services like car tuning), word of mouth may be quite important in generating new business. Services that are high risk, which would include professional services, would also tend to have high impact from word of mouth.

Price premiums

New customers often benefit from introductory promotional discounts whereas long-term customers are more likely to pay regular (higher) prices. Moreover, when customers trust suppliers they may be more willing to pay higher prices at peak periods or for express work.

The argument is that the customer trusts the firm, values the relationship, and is therefore less sensitive to price increases.

Of course, it is not always the case that old customers pay a premium price. Sometimes, long-lasting relationships have given the customer a bargaining position based on power or social relationships, which keeps prices down. If this happens, a negative profit-eroding effect occurs.

Exhibit 17.2	Simulation of firm X's customer value (cumulative sales for firm X over periods 1 to 10) with different retention rates

The assumptions for Table 17.4 are:

- customer value is defined as accumulated sales for 100 customers of firm X from periods 1 to 10
- every customer makes one transaction per period
- every transaction is €100
- the costs of the transaction are not considered
- firm X's ability to attract new customers is not considered.

Table 17.4   Firm X's customer value under varying retention rates

Retention rate (repeat buying rate)	Number of customers left in each buying period										Number of transactions	Customer value: cumulative sales from periods 1 to 10	Growth of cumulative sales (%)
	1	2	3	4	5	6	7	8	9	10			
50%	100	50	25	13	7	4	2	1	0	0	202	20,200	
													24%
60%	100	60	36	22	13	8	5	3	2	1	250	25,000	
													30%
70%	100	70	49	34	24	17	12	8	6	4	324	32,400	
													38%
80%	100	80	64	51	41	33	26	21	17	14	447	44,700	
													46%
90%	100	90	81	73	66	59	53	48	43	39	652	65,200	

Table 17.4 shows that if firm X can increase its retention rate from 50% to 60% the customer value (here defined as cumulative sales from periods 1 to 10) will increase 24%, whereas an increase from 80% to 90% will increase cumulative sales by 46%. Hence, the higher the retention rate, the higher the increase in customer value.

17.4   Controlling the marketing programme

The final, but often neglected, stage of marketing planning is the control process. Not only is control important to evaluate how we have performed, but it completes the circle of planning by providing the feedback necessary for the start of the next planning cycle. Unfortunately, control is often viewed by the people of an organization as being negative. If individuals fear that the control process will be used not only to judge their performance, but as a basis for punishing them, then it will be feared and reviled.

The evaluation and control of marketing probably represents one of the weakest areas of marketing practice in many companies. Even the organizations that are otherwise strong in their strategic marketing planning have poor control and evaluation procedures for their global marketing. There are a number of possible reasons for this. First of all, there is no such thing as a standard system of control for marketing.

The function of the organizational structure is to provide a framework in which objectives can be met. However, a set of instruments and processes is needed to influence the behaviour and performance of organization members to meet the goals. The critical issue is the same as with organizational structures: what is the ideal amount of control? On the one hand, headquarters needs information to ensure that marketing activities contribute maximum benefit to the overall organization. On the other hand, controls should not be construed as a code of law.

The key question is to determine how to establish a control mechanism capable of early identification of emerging problems. Considered here are various criteria appropriate for the evaluation process, control styles, feedback and corrective action. These concepts are important for all businesses, but in the international arena they are vital.

Design of a control system

In designing a control system, management must consider the costs of establishing and maintaining it and trade them off against the benefits to be gained. Any control system will require investment in a management structure and in systems design.

The design of the control system can be divided into two groups which depend on the object of control:

- output control (typically based on financial measures)
- behavioural controls (typically based on non-financial measures).

Output control may consist of expenditure control, which involves regular monitoring of expenditure figures, comparison of these with budget targets, and taking decisions to cut or increase expenditure where any variance is believed to be harmful. Measures of output are accumulated at regular intervals and typically forwarded from the foreign subsidiary to headquarters, where they are evaluated and criticized based on comparison with the plan or budget.

Behavioural controls require the exercise of influence over behaviour. This influence can be achieved, for example, by providing sales manuals to subsidiary personnel or by fitting new employees into the corporate culture. Behavioural controls often require an extensive **socialization process**, and informal, personal interaction is central to the process. Substantial resources must be spent to train the individual to share the corporate culture: that is, the way things are done at the company.

To build a common vision and values, managers at the Japanese company Matsushita spend a substantial amount of their first months in what the company calls cultural and spiritual training. They study the company credo, the 'Seven Spirits of Matsushita', and the philosophy of the founder, Kanosuke Matsushita.

However, there remains a strong tradition of using output (financial) criteria. A fixation with output criteria leads companies to ignore the less tangible behavioural (non-financial) measures, although these are the real drivers of corporate success. However, there is a weakness in the behavioural performance measures. To date there has been little success in developing explicit links from behaviour to output criteria. Furthermore, companies and managers are still judged on financial criteria (profit contribution). Until a clear link is established, it is likely that behavioural criteria will continue to be treated with a degree of scepticism.

We will now develop a marketing control system based primarily on output controls. Marketing control is an essential element of the marketing planning process because it provides a review of how well marketing objectives have been achieved. A framework for controlling marketing activities is given in Figure 17.4.

The marketing control system begins with the company setting some marketing activities in motion (plans for implementation). This may be the result of certain objectives and strategies, each of which must be achieved within a given budget. Hence budgetary control is essential.

Figure 17.4 The marketing control system

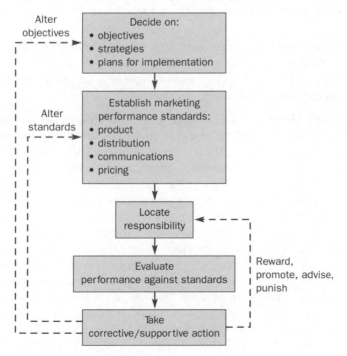

Source: Hollensen (2001), p. 600.

The next step in the control process is to establish specific performance standards which will need to be achieved for each area of activity if overall and sub-objectives are to be achieved. For example, in order to achieve a specified sales objective, a specific target of performance for each sales area may be required. In turn, this may require a specific standard of performance from each of the salespeople in the region with respect to, for example, number of calls, conversion rates and, of course, order value.

The next step is to locate responsibility. In some cases responsibility ultimately falls on one person (e.g. the brand manager); in others it is shared (e.g. the sales manager and sales force). It is important to consider this issue, since corrective or supportive action may need to focus on those responsible for the success of the marketing activity.

In order to be successful, the people involved and affected by the control process should be consulted in both the design and implementation stages of marketing control. Above all, they will need to be convinced that the purpose of control is to improve their own levels of success and that of the company. Subordinates need to be involved in setting and agreeing their own standards of performance, preferably through a system of management by objectives.

Performance is then evaluated against these standards, which relies on an efficient information system. A judgement has to be made about the degree of success and failure achieved and what corrective or supportive action is to be taken. This can take various forms.

- Failure which is attributed to the poor performance of individuals may result in the giving of advice regarding future attitudes and actions, training and/or punishment (e.g. criticism, lower pay, demotion, termination of employment). Success, on the other hand, should be rewarded with praise, promotion and/or higher pay.
- Failure which is attributed to unrealistic marketing objectives and performance may cause management to lower objectives or lower marketing standards (Figure 17.4). Success which is thought to reflect unambitious objectives and standards may cause them to be raised in the next period.

Many firms assume that corrective action needs to be taken only when results are less than those required or when budgets and costs are being exceeded. In fact, both negative (underachievement) and positive (overachievement) deviations may require corrective action. For example, failure to spend the amount budgeted for, say, sales force expenses may indicate that the initial sum allocated was excessive and needs to be reassessed, and/or that the sales force is not as active as it might be.

It is also necessary to determine such things as the frequency of measurement (e.g. daily, weekly, monthly or annually). More frequent and more detailed measurement usually means more cost. We need to be careful to ensure that the costs of measurement and the control process itself do not exceed the value of such measurements and do not overly interfere with the activities of those being measured.

The impact of the environment must also be taken into account when designing a control system. The control system should measure only factors over which the organization has control. Rewards make little sense if they are based on factors that may be relevant for overall corporate performance, but over which no influence can be exerted (e.g. price controls). Neglecting the factor of individual performance capability would send the wrong signals and severely impair the motivation of personnel.

Control systems should harmonize with local regulations and customs. In some cases, however, corporate behavioural controls have to be exercised against local customs even though overall operations may be affected negatively. This type of situation occurs, for example, when a subsidiary operates in markets where unauthorized facilitating payments are a common business practice.

Feedforward control

Much of the information provided by the firm's marketing control system is feedback on what has been accomplished in both financial (profits) and non-financial (customer satisfaction, market share) terms. As such, the control process is remedial in its outlook. It can be argued that control systems should be forward looking and preventive, and that the control process should start at the same time as the planning process. Such a form of control is feedforward control (Figure 17.5).

Feedforward control continuously evaluates plans, monitoring the environment to detect changes that would call for objectives and strategies to be revised. Feedforward control monitors variables other than performance; variables that may change before performance itself changes. The result is that deviations can be controlled before their full impact has been felt. Such a system is pro-active in that it anticipates environmental change, whereas other control systems are more reactive in that they deal with changes after they occur. Examples of early symptoms (early performance indicators) are presented in Table 17.5.

Feedforward control focuses on information that is prognostic: it tries to discover problems waiting to occur. Formal processes of feedforward control can be incorporated into the business marketer's total control programme to enhance its effectiveness considerably. Utilization of a feedforward approach would help ensure that planning and control are treated as concurrent activities.

Key areas for control in marketing

Kotler (2000) distinguishes four types of marketing control, each involving different approaches, different purposes and a different allocation of responsibilities. These are shown in Table 17.6. Here we will focus on annual plan control and profit control, since they are the most obvious areas of concern to firms with limited resources (e.g. SMEs).

Figure 17.5 Adjustment of the marketing strategy

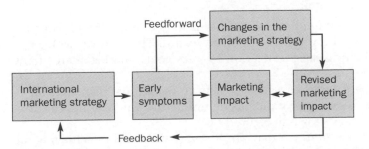

Source: Samli *et al.*, 1993, p. 425, with permission from Pearson Education, Inc., Upper Saddle River, NJ.

Table 17.5 Some key early performance indicators

Early performance indicators	Market implication
Sudden drop in quantities demanded.	Problem in marketing strategy or its implementation.
Sharp decrease or increase in sales volume.	Product gaining acceptance or being rejected quickly.
Customer complaints.	Product not debugged properly.
A notable decrease in competitors' business.	Product gaining acceptance quickly or market conditions deteriorating.
Large volumes of returned merchandise.	Problems in basic product design.
Excessive requests for parts or reported repairs.	Problems in basic product design, low standards.

Source: Samli *et al*. (1993), p. 421, with permission from Pearson Education, Inc., Upper Saddle River, NJ.

Table 17.6 Types of marketing control

Type of control	Prime responsibility	Purpose of control	Examples of techniques/approaches
Strategic control	• Senior management • Middle management	• To see if planned results are being achieved.	• Marketing effectiveness ratings • Marketing audit
Efficiency control	• Line and staff management • Marketing controller	• To examine ways of improving the efficiency of marketing.	• Sales force efficiency • Advertising efficiency • Distribution efficiency
Annual plan control	• Senior management • Middle management	• To see if planned results are being achieved.	• Sales analysis • Market share analysis • Marketing expenses to sales ratio • Customer tracking
Profit control (budget control)	• Marketing controller	• To examine where the company is making and losing money.	• Profitability by e.g. product, customer group or trade channel

Source: Kotler (2000), with permission from Pearson Education, Inc., Upper Saddle River, NJ.

Annual plan control

The purpose of annual plan control is to determine the extent to which marketing efforts over the year have been successful. This control will centre on measuring and evaluating sales in relation to sales goals, market share analysis and expense analysis.

Sales performance is a key element in the annual plan control. Sales control consists of a hierarchy of standards on different organizational control levels. These are interlinked, as shown in Figure 17.6.

We can see from the diagram that any variances in achieving sales targets at the corporate level are the result of variances in the performance of individual sales-

Figure 17.6 The hierarchy of sales and control

Source: Hollensen (2001), p. 605.

people at the operational level. At every level of sales control, variances must be studied with a view to determining their causes. In general, variances may be due to a combination of variances in volume and/or price.

Global profit control

In addition to the previously discussed control elements, all international marketers must be concerned to control their profit. The budgetary period is normally one year because budgets are tied to the accounting systems of the company.

Table 17.7 presents an example of a global marketing budget for a manufacturer of consumer goods. Included in the budget are those marketing variables which can be controlled and changed by the sales and marketing functions (departments) in the home country and in the export market. In Table 17.7 the only variable that cannot be controlled by the international sales and marketing departments is variable costs.

The global marketing budget system (as presented in Table 17.7) is used for the following (main) purposes:

● allocation of marketing resources among countries/markets to maximize profits. In Table 17.7 it is the responsibility of the global marketing director to maximize the total contribution 2 for the whole world.

● evaluation of country/market performance. In Table 17.7 it is the responsibility of export managers or country managers to maximize contribution 2 for each of their countries.

Please note that besides the marketing variables presented in Table 17.7, the global marketing budget normally contains inventory costs for finished goods. As the production runs of these goods are normally based on input from the sales and marketing department, the inventory of unsold goods will also be the responsibility of the international marketing manager or director.

Furthermore, the global marketing budget may also contain customer-specific or country-specific product development costs, if certain new products are preconditions for selling in certain markets.

Table 17.7 An example of an international marketing budget

| | Europe | | | America | Asia/Pacific | | | | |
International marketing	UK	Germany	France	USA	Japan	Korea	Other markets	Total World Σ
	B A	B A	B A	B A	B A	B A	B A	B A
budget year = _____								
Net sales (**gross sales less trade discounts, allowances, etc.**)								
÷ **Variable costs**								
= **Contribution 1**								
÷ **Marketing costs**								
Sales costs (salaries, commissions for agents, incentives, travelling, training, conferences)								
Consumer marketing costs (TV commercials, radio, print, sales promotion)								
Trade marketing costs (fairs, exhibitions, in-store promotions, contributions for retailer campaigns)								
= **Total contribution 2** (marketing contribution)								

B = budget figures; A = actual.

Note: On a short-term (one-year) basis, the export managers or country managers are responsible for maximizing the actual figures for each country and minimizing their deviation from budget figures. The international marketing manager/director is responsible for maximizing the actual figure for the total world and minimizing its deviation from the budget figure. Cooperation is required between the country managers and the international marketing manager/director to coordinate and allocate the total marketing resources in an optimum way. Sometimes certain inventory costs and product development costs may also be included in the total marketing budget (see main text).

Source: adapted from Hollensen (2001), p. 605.

In contrast to budgets, long-range plans extend over periods from two years up to ten years, and their content is more qualitative and judgemental in nature than that of budgets. For SMEs shorter periods (such as two years) are the norm because of the perceived uncertainty of diverse foreign environments.

Overall economic value with successful implementation of CRM

The CRM process creates value by working with the customer to improve performance and business processes (see Figure 17.7). For example, the firm may negotiate with the customer's team to implement a new inventory system. If the relationship

Figure 17.7 How customer relationship management affects economic value added (EVA)

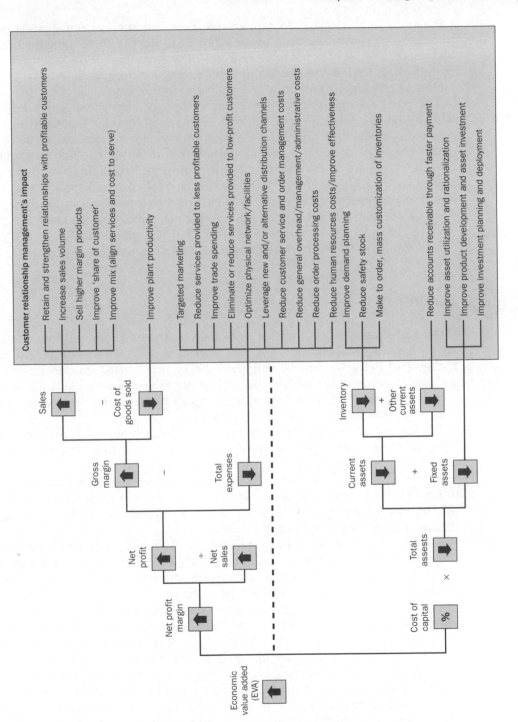

Source: adapted from Lambert and Pohlen (2001), p.10, with permission from International Logistics Research Institute Inc., www.ijlm.org

reduces costs and can yield a price reduction for the customer, revenues may increase as a result of increasing market share for the firm. Revenues may also increase as a result of better in-stock availability at the end of the supply chain. The cost of goods sold may decrease through better scheduling of material requirements and more efficient utilization of plant capacity and labour.

The cost-of-goods sold may be reduced through the leveraging of larger buys with a smaller group of suppliers. Other costs may increase due to reduced order processing and forecasting costs. Inventory carrying costs decrease as point-of-sale data are used to schedule shipments instead of forecasting requirements and maintaining safety stock. Better capacity utilization and collaborative planning and forecasting of requirements may reduce the need for customer specific assets. In the end, the process improvements obtained through successful implementation of CRM can be translated into increased shareholder value through the use of an economic value-added (EVA) model (Figure 17.7). By comparing net profit margin with cost of capital in Figure 17.7 the result would be a higher EVA.

17.5 Summary

Marketing strategies directly affect customers and sales revenue. However, they also affect margins, total contribution, and marketing costs. These effects, in turn, lead to the total net marketing contribution. Because operating (manufacturing) costs and overhead costs are beyond the control of marketing managers, net marketing contribution plays the most important role for the marketing department, to determine the profit impact of a marketing strategy.

Traditional accounting systems have viewed customers as sources of revenue. More and more firms are beginning to use their accounting systems to view customers as assets, basing their decisions on customers as much as they would base their decisions on investments. Therefore we propose *customer lifetime value* (CLTV) to be the central unit of measurement for customer equity. We define CLTV as the net present value (NPV) of the profit a firm stands to realize on the average new customer during a given number of years.

As marketing plans are being implemented, they have to be monitored and controlled. Control is the process of ensuring that global marketing activities are carried out as intended. It involves monitoring aspects of performance and taking corrective action where necessary. The global marketing control system consists of deciding marketing objectives, setting performance standards, locating responsibility, evaluating performance against standards, and taking corrective or supportive action.

In a conventional control system, managers wait until the end of the planning period to take corrective action. In a feedforward control system, corrective action is taken during the planning period by tracking early performance indicators and steering the organization back to its desired objectives if they are not being achieved.

The most obvious areas of control relate to the control of the annual marketing plan and the control of profitability. The purpose of the global marketing budget is mainly to allocate marketing resources across countries to maximize the worldwide total marketing contribution. The process improvements obtained through successful implementation of CRM can be translated into increased shareholder value through the use of an economic value-added (EVA) model.

Case study 17.2 SCA (Svenska Cellulosa Aktiebolaget)

Planning and budgeting for increased market share in the world tissue market

SCA was incorporated in 1929 as a holding company for ten forest industry companies producing sawn goods and paper pulp in northern Sweden. However, its roots are in companies that began exploiting the forests and hydroelectric power of northern Sweden on an industrial scale back in the 17th century.

Business concept

SCA sells hygiene products, packaging solutions and paper. Based on knowledge of end users' needs, and of the properties of papers, SCA offers its products and services. The products designed for private individuals shall add to the quality of life; SCA's products and service for institutions and companies shall offer increased product quality, safety, productivity and profitability.

SCA's net sales amounted to SEK67 billion (£5 billion) in 2000. Of this, hygiene products account for 46 per cent, packaging products for 37 per cent and paper for 17 per cent.

Western Europe is SCA's main market. The five biggest markets are the UK, Germany, France, Sweden and Italy. The group has acquired several companies in the region in recent years, thus strengthening the market positions for its hygiene products and packaging business areas. Concurrently, selective expansion is under way in America, central and eastern Europe as well as in Asia. SCA strives to increase the proportion of high-value-added products in order to generate stable and healthy profitability.

SCA's 12 largest markets in 2000 combined accounted for 85 per cent of net sales. Slightly more than 90 per cent of SCA's sales are outside Sweden.

SCA's hygiene products division

This division is one of Europe's leading manufacturers of tissue and soft paper products for personal hygiene and other applications.

Hygiene products have sales in more than 40 countries, with Europe as its main market. SCA holds a world-leading position in incontinence products and is Europe's largest supplier of tissue.

SCA's hygiene products consumer/retail market

The following products are sold to private consumers through retail outlets:

- toilet tissue and household towels
- incontinence products
- feminine hygiene products
- baby diapers
- paper handkerchiefs
- facial tissue
- napkins

SCA sells its products under its own name brands as well as retailers' brands. SCA brand names are Zewa and Edet for toilet and household paper, Libero for baby diapers, Nana, Nuvenia, Bodyform, Nosotras and Libresse for feminine hygiene products and Tena for incontinence products. Figure 17.8 shows one of SCA's main brands.

B-t-B market

The following products are sold to customers in companies and industries, hotels, restaurants and catering operations as well as institutions:

Figure 17.8 One of SCA's main brands

▶

Case study 17.2 continued

- complete systems for tissue products for wiping and cleaning
- incontinence products (primarily to the health and nursing care sectors)
- complete systems for personal hygiene.

Incontinence products are marketed under the Tena brand and Tork is the brand for a complete system of various products for good hygiene in, for example, public toilets and commercial kitchens.

The world market

The world market for absorbent hygiene products amounts to nearly SEK 460 billion (£32 billion), of which Europe accounts for slightly more than one quarter. Figure 17.9 shows the yearly capacity of the world's largest manufacturers of hygiene products.

Several large mergers and acquisitions during 2000 and 2001 have changed the landscape of the tissue business, with some old names disappearing and other giants being formed by the

transactions. During 2000 the biggest merger was between Georgia-Pacific and Fort James, which briefly made Georgia-Pacific the world's largest tissue producer. One driver for all the merger and acquisition activity may well have been the tough business conditions that most tissue companies were operating under in 2000. Rising pulp and raw material costs squeezed numerous companies during 2000. Profit margins were under pressure for much of 2000 and 2001. Share prices of all publicly traded tissue companies also performed rather poorly.

SCA is growing both organically and through acquisitions. Expansion is taking place primarily in the hygiene products and packaging business areas and the company's ambition is that an increasing percentage of its cash flow will be generated by these two units.

SCA is a world leader in incontinence products and is Europe's second-largest supplier of tissue products. The European market for tissue is about SEK150 billion (£10 billion) and is undergoing

Figure 17.9 The world's largest manufacturers of hygiene products

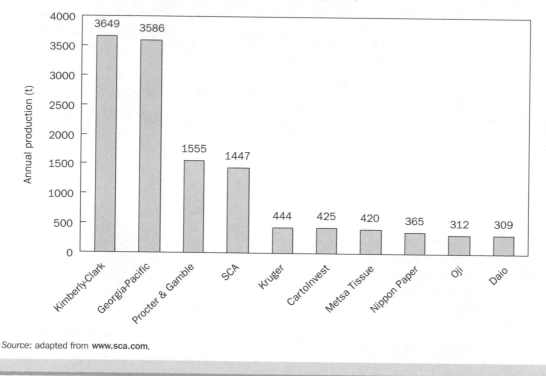

Source: adapted from **www.sca.com**.

Case study 17.2 continued

consolidation, which offers SCA favourable opportunities to grow through acquisitions. Since 1996 SCA's share of this market has increased from 17 to 20 per cent, mainly as a result of acquisitions (Table 17.8). The objective is to increase the market share to approximately 30 per cent.

Continued expansion in Europe will focus mainly on southern and eastern Europe. At the same time, priority will be given to the large and highly consolidated North American market.

Table 17.8 **Tissue market shares in Europe and North America**

Company	Europe	North America
SCA	22%	7%
Georgia-Pacific (incl. Fort James)	15%	35%
Kimberly-Clark	18%	24%
Procter & Gamble	4%	18%

Source: SCA (2001) *Financial Report*.

Table 17.8 shows that the four largest suppliers control about 60 per cent of the European market for tissue products. The sector is continuing its consolidation process and one of the clearest examples of this is Georgia-Pacific's acquisition of Fort James, which created the world's largest producer of tissue products.

American producers of hygiene products such as Procter & Gamble and Kimberly-Clark market their products mainly under their own brands. US-based Georgia-Pacific, and SCA, sell their products under their own and retailers' brands. SCA is strongest in northern and central Europe.

Tissue products are evenly split between manufacturers' brands and retailers' own brands. On average, 20 per cent of baby diapers and feminine hygiene products are sold under retailers' brands. However, there are large variations between products and countries.

The European retail sector has been characterized by consolidation and internationalization in recent years. This trend continued in 2000, and in the Nordic countries where the consolidation has progressed furthest, the three largest retailers represent up to 80 per cent of the market (Figure 17.10). As a consequence, the chains have a growing interest in selling high-quality hygiene products using their own brand names.

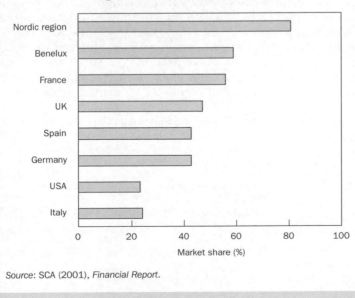

Figure 17.10 **Market share of top three retailers in various regions**

Source: SCA (2001), *Financial Report*.

Case study 17.2 continued

Retailing is more fragmented outside western European and US markets. Branded products are undergoing strong growth in these areas.

SCA's market share generally rose in 2000. Sales volume increased 10 per cent, of which acquired companies accounted for 7 per cent. Sales outside Europe rose by 25 per cent, due to rapidly rising sales in Latin America and the acqusition of Serenity (see below).

Acquisitions and alliances

SCA entered a cooperation agreement with the US hygiene company Johnson & Johnson. As a result of this agreement, SCA is buying Johnson & Johnson's Serenity incontinence brand in the North American market and the US company will provide the support of its sales organization to SCA. In addition, SCA will market Johnson & Johnson's consumer products to the retail trade in Nordic countries. In 2002, the licence for own brand tampons, which has been held by SCA, will be returned to Johnson & Johnson. The acquisition of Serenity provides access to the North American consumer products market and SCA will gradually introduce its own incontinence products to the US retail market.

In January 2001, SCA acquired US-based Georgia-Pacific's tissue paper operations for non-domestic uses for SEK8.1 billion (£550 million). The acquisition gave SCA national coverage in the US and a market share of 17 per cent in this segment. This means that SCA is third in this market after the merged Georgia-Pacific/Fort James and Kimberly-Clark.

Approximately 60 per cent of SCA's total sales of hygiene products are made through the retail trade. Libero diapers are strong in the Nordic region. An important factor underlying this success is the new marketing programme, with award-winning TV commercials and advertising.

Non-domestic tissue segment

In this market, mainly tissue products are sold to companies in the industrial, administration and service sectors, hotels, restaurants and catering (Horeca), healthcare institutions and other public establishments. Tissue products for hand-wiping and toilet tissue dominate, as do products for wiping and cleaning in industry. The products are distributed via wholesalers and service companies, or directly to individual customers. Consolidation and internationalization is also in progress among these customers.

The non-domestic market in Europe, which accounts for 30 per cent of global sales of tissue products, is valued at slightly more than SEK30 billion (£2 billion). Market growth amounts to about 3–4 per cent annually, and is controlled largely by economic conditions. Textiles represent one-third of the drying materials in this market, but are increasingly being replaced by tissue products. Awareness of good hygiene habits in manufacturing and construction and in offices and public buildings also affects growth potential, as does legislation governing good hygiene. Horeca is showing the strongest growth today, supported by the growing number of people who eat out.

Important competitive advantages include offering customers the complete products (paper and dispenser, etc.) along with good service and rapid deliveries.

SCA is Europe's second largest supplier of tissue products for the non-domestic market, with an 18 per cent market share. SCA's sales comprise a complete range for toilets and bathrooms, consisting of paper towels, toilet tissue, soap with matching dispensers, face towels and towels. The products are sold under the Tork brand. This range is sold to industry in combination with products for cleaning and wiping.

The concentration of suppliers to the European non-domestic tissue market is high, but even higher in the US market (Table 17.9).

Table 17.9 US non-domestic tissue segments market share

Company	Hand wiping	Toilet	Table napkins
Georgia-Pacific	44%	45%	45%
Kimberly-Clark	26%	31%	14%
SCA	14%	13%	37%
Top 3	84%	89%	96%

Source: adapted from Lindström, (2001), p. 18.

Case study 17.2 continued

Two main competitors

Kimberly-Clark

The company was founded in 1872 and incorporated as the Kimberly Clark Company in 1906. Historically, the company has been engaged in a wide variety of diversified businesses, including the manufacture and sale of consumer products, paper and forest products, airline services and various other businesses.

In 1995, the company acquired the Scott Paper Company which resulted in the company becoming a major force in the world disposable paper products market. However, as a result of the acquisition, Kimberly-Clark was forced to divest some operations by the US and European Union anti-trust authorities. The company operates three divisions: the tissue division produces facial and bathroom tissue, paper towels and wipes for household and non-domestic use; wet wipes; printing, premium business and correspondence papers; and related products. The personal care division produces disposable diapers; training and youth pants; feminine and incontinence care products; and related products. The health care and other products division produces health care products such as disposable medical devices for respiratory care, gastroenterology and cardiology surgical packs and gowns, sterilization wraps and disposable face masks; speciality and technical papers and related products; and other products. One of their most profitable brands is Kleenex.

Georgia-Pacific (GP) Corporation

The Georgia-Pacific Corporation is a manufacturing and distribution business. The company is one of the world's leading manufacturers of building and forest products, including container board, packaging, pulp and paper. The company also makes structural materials, such as wood panels, and lumber. It is the largest producer of gypsum board in North America. Georgia-Pacific comprises four main divisions: building products, distribution, container board and packaging, and pulp and paper. Within the pulp and paper segment, the company also has significant business as a private label supplier. Key consumer brands include Angel Soft and MD toilet tissue, Sparkle and Coronet kitchen towels, and Coronet napkins. Georgia-Pacific also derives substantial revenues from its wholesaling activities (the distribution division), which provide it with an outlet for its own products. Georgia-Pacific is an important manufacturer of branded disposable paper products, but not a leading one. Lacking the resources of Procter & Gamble or Kimberly-Clark, it neither advertises heavily nor leads with significant innovations. It is, in short, a market follower, albeit one that controls significant shares of the sub-sectors in which it operates.

When the Georgia-Pacific/Fort James deal was first announced in mid-2000, SCA quickly made it clear that it was potentially interested in purchasing some of the assets that Georgia-Pacific might be forced to sell in the USA to satisfy anti-trust concerns. It was no surprise when, in January 2001, the two parties announced that SCA was buying a major part of Georgia-Pacific's non-domestic tissue business in the USA.

Questions

1. What are the differences in buying behaviour between the consumer/retail and non-domestic B-t-B tissue markets?

2. SCA wants to increase market shares, both in Europe and the USA. How could SCA set up a budget system that would enable the company to control the budget if market objectives are met?

3. Explain the underlying determinants for the key figures/metrics in the marketing budget.

Sources: Lindström (2001), SCA (2000), Financial Report.

QUESTIONS FOR DISCUSSION

1. Why is customer profitability sometimes a better unit of measurement than market profitability?

2. Why is it important to consider customer lifetime value (CLTV)?

3. How can a firm increase CLTV?

4. Discuss why firms need marketing controls.

5. What is meant by performance indicators? What are they? Why does a firm need them?

6. Discuss the benefits gained by adopting a matrix organizational structure.

7. Discuss the problems involved in setting up and implementing a marketing control system.

8. To what general criteria should 'good' marketing objectives conform?

REFERENCES

Bartlett, C. and Ghoshal, S. (1989), *Managing Across Borders: The transnational solution*, Harvard University Press, Boston, MA.

Best, R. J. (2000), *Market-based management*, Prentice-Hall, NJ.

Butcher, K., Sparks, B. and O'Callaghan, F. (2001), Evaluative and relational influences on service loyalty, *International Journal of Service Industry Management*, vol. 12, no. 4, pp. 310–27.

Downes, L. and Mui, C. (1998), *Unleashing the Killer Approach: Digital strategies for market dominance*, Harvard Business School Press, Boston.

Hollensen, S. (2001), *Global Marketing: A market responsive approach*, Financial Times/Prentice Hall, Harlow, 2nd edn.

Jobber, D. (1995), *Principles and Practice of Marketing*, McGraw-Hill, New York.

Katayama, O. (1994), Not toying around, *Look Japan*, November, pp. 2–3.

Kotler, P. (2000), *Marketing Management: Analysis, planning, implementation and control*, Prentice-Hall, Englewood Cliffs, NJ, 10th edn.

Lambert, D. M. and Pohlen, T. L. (2001), Supply chain metrics, *The International Journal of Logistics Management*, vol. 12, no. 1, pp. 1–12.

Lindström, O. (2001), US acquisitions, *Pulp and Paper International*, San Francisco, vol. 43, January, pp. 15–20.

Lusch, R. F. (2000), Creating long-term marketing health, *Marketing Management*, vol. 9, no. 1, spring, pp. 18–22.

Ortman, R. F. and Bucklmann D. M. (1998), Estimating marketing costs using activity-based cost drivers, *Journal of Cost Management*, July–August, pp. 5–15.

Pitt, L. F., Ewing, M. T. and Berthon, P. (2000), Turning competitive advantages into customer equity, *Business Horizons*, September–October, pp. 11–18.

Quelch, J. A. (1992) The new country managers, *The McKinsey Quarterly*, no. 4, pp. 155–65.

Quelch, J. A. and Bloom, H. (1996), The return of the country manager, *The McKinsey Quarterly*, no. 2, pp. 30–43.

Reichheld, F. F. (1994), Loyalty and the renaissance of marketing management, *Marketing Management*, vol. 12, no. 4, pp. 17–25.

Samli, A.C., Still, R. and Hill, J. S. (1993), *International Marketing: Planning and practice*, Macmillan, London.

Shelly, B. (1995), Cool customer, *Unilever Magazine*, no. 2, pp. 12–17.

Unilever, (1996), *Introducing Unilever*, Unilever, Rotterdam.

Ethical, social and environmental aspects of marketing

After studying this chapter you should be able to:

- understand why ethical issues are important for the firm to consider in relationship building.
- explain how internal marketing is connected to ethical issues.
- define different degrees of ethical behaviour.
- understand the purpose of green alliances.
- discuss how social and environmental green issues can influence the firm's marketing strategy and marketing mix (the four Ps).

Case study 18.1 Pokémon

Ethical issues in marketing to children

Pokémon has enthralled the minds of children across the world since it was launched. Its success has spread to trading cards, comic books, a television series, film and toys, becoming a multi-billion-dollar enterprise that is enormously popular around the world.

Across Europe, schoolchildren have fought to get their hands on the cards of the 151 Pokémon characters, which are based on the Japanese cartoon, film and computer game. The game has been criticized in several countries, with a Christian church in Mexico calling it 'demonic', and organizations in Slovakia saying television shows based on the game were detrimental to children.

Now even Saudi Arabia's Mufti, the highest religious authority in the conservative Muslim state, has banned Pokémon, saying it promotes Zionism and involves gambling. The religious authority said that the Pokémon video game and cards have symbols that include the star of David, which is connected to international Zionism and is Israel's national emblem.

He protested that most of the cards feature symbols such as 'crosses, sacred for Christians and triangles, significant for Freemasons'. And he charged that the worldwide phenomenon of Pokémon launched in Japan in 1996 was a bad influence.

He also accused Pokémon of resembling gambling because of the competition that at times involves sums of money being exchanged between collectors of the cards.

In Tokyo, a Nintendo spokesman, speaking on condition of anonymity, denied that religious symbols are depicted on the Pokémon items. The card game involves a host of imaginary creatures, each with their own set of special powers. The goal is to win as many cards as possible. But he promised that the company would investigate the claims that have led to the ban.

Case study 18.1 continued

Questions

1. Try to explain the reason for the Pokémon marketing success.

2. Identify the main ethical issues in the case.

3. What effects would these allegations have on Pokémon's global sales?

4. What would you do about the allegations from Saudi Arabia if you were responsible for marketing in the Middle East?

Source: adapted from BBC (2001).

18.1 Introduction

Now that we have examined the basic framework for strategic marketing planning, we turn our attention to several important issues that should be considered during the planning process. The first of these is the role of ethics and social responsibility in the strategic marketing planning process. Being ethical and socially responsible is a necessity in the light of public demands and changes in national laws. We also believe that being ethical and socially responsible improves marketing performance and profits.

The relevance of ethical aspects in marketing has grown considerably over the last decades. In recent years, an increasing amount of attention has been devoted to ethics in business in general and the marketing function in particular.

Ethical considerations are important for the operation of an economy in many different ways. What happens in an economy depends on what people in that economy choose to do, and what they choose to do is influenced by the ethics of people. Since individual behaviour is central to the working of an economy and ethics are a critical influence on individual behaviour, ethical considerations are of profound importance for the nature and functioning of any economy. The importance of ethics is also clear if the role of government is considered. This is because operations in an economy are influenced also by public policies pursued by the government and other public institutions. These policies are influenced by the ethical priorities of the government and other public institutions.

Some recent events have indicated that the ethics of individuals and organizations involved in marketing can be questioned. Social pressures increasingly require marketers also to examine how they deal with consumers, competitors, suppliers, and the government from an ethical perspective. It seems that today many managers are looking for means which would help them solve the ethically troublesome issues facing their organization. They are willing to make the necessary adjustments so that their actions would be consistent with the social responsibilities perceived by them. In contemporary business life, it is increasingly necessary for marketers to examine their ethical responsibilities.

As more and more firms operate globally, an understanding of the effects of cultural differences on ethical decision making becomes increasingly important for avoiding potential business pitfalls and for designing effective international marketing management programmes.

Culture is a fundamental determinant of ethical decision making. It directly affects how an individual perceives ethical problems, alternatives, and consequences. In order to succeed in today's international markets, managers must recognize and understand how ideas, values, and moral standards differ across cultures, and how these in turn influence marketing decision making.

Some countries, such as India, are well known for 'requiring' small payments if customs officials are to allow goods to enter the country. While this may indeed be a bribe and illegal, the ethics of that country seem to allow it (at least to a certain extent). The company is then left with a problem: do they bribe the official, or do they wait for normal clearance and let their products sit in the customs warehouse for a considerably longer time?

Fees and commissions paid to a firm's foreign intermediary or to consultants for their services are a particular problem – when does the legal fee become a bribe? One reason for employing a foreign representative or consultant is to benefit from his or her contacts with decision makers, especially in a foreign administration. If the export intermediary uses part of the fee to bribe administrators, there is little that the firm can do.

Thus, every culture, nation, industry, organization or profession establishes a set of moral standards for business behaviour, that is, a code of business ethics. This set of standards influences all decisions and actions in a company, including, for example, what and how to manufacture (or not), what wages it is appropriate to pay, how many hours personnel should work and under what conditions, how to compete, and what communication guidelines to follow. Which actions are considered right or wrong, fair or unfair, in the conduct of business? Which are particularly susceptible to ethical norms and are heavily influenced by the culture in which they take place.

18.2 Ethical issues in a RM approach

Ethical problems occur only when an individual interacts with other people. Ethical conflicts then occur when people perceive that their duties towards one group are inconsistent with their duties and responsibilities towards some other group. Kavali *et al.* (1999) try to identify a number of potential ethical conflicts in the following marketing relationships:

- between different divisions in the company (e.g. between HQ and subsidiaries)
- between the company and its customers
- between the company and its competitors
- between the company and its suppliers.

Kavali *et al.* (1999) suggest that RM inputs can positively affect ethical behaviour by affecting categories of ethical factors and preventing a number of ethical problems from arising in the first place.

For example, relationships between marketers and their customers have traditionally been characterized as confrontational. Under this transactional regime, relationships are labelled as the manipulation of customers, exploiting their ignorance. Short-term strategies promoted a form of hit-and-run marketing, which sought a temporary increase in sales and resulted in ethical conflicts between the corporate interest and the interest of the customer. Ethical problems occurred as the customers were induced to use services that were not needed, exaggerated performance claims were made, higher prices were charged than by firms with similar product offerings, and overselling was a regular practice.

With RM there is a shift away from hard marketing to anonymous masses towards relationships with customers as 'co-producers' and 'members' of various marketing programmes, where value is created through long-term interactions between equal winning and respectful parties. As companies become more concerned with keeping satisfied customers, it becomes more evident that ethical behaviour is not only the moral thing to do but also good business. By adding more value to the core product (quality is improved, supporting services are included in the offering, etc.) companies try to improve customer satisfaction so that the bonds are strengthened and customer loyalty is achieved (Gummesen, 1999).

Moreover, the current emphasis on internal marketing is directly associated with more ethical behaviour and attempts to bridge inconsistencies between senior management and employees as the market inside the firm becomes equally important to the outside market. Relations with superiors can raise important ethical problems as employees frequently complain of superiors' pressure to support incorrect viewpoints, sign false documents, etc.

This means that assuming that higher level managers want the internal market to be motivated and committed to a total marketing function, senior management must provide moral guidance through its actions, set realistic goals, reduce ambiguities and reward ethical performance.

By providing for more ethical corporate practices, the RM philosophy has the potential to solve ethical problems previously associated with various outside constituencies through its core references to mutual cooperation and collaborative partnerships.

Despite the fact that RM is inherently a concept with strong ethical roots there is perhaps also a gap between the theory of RM and its actual practice.

The customer service and market research mentality under RM generates a demand for exchanging detailed customer profiles. Computerization allows the assembly and exchange of such databases. The ethical questions that arise are why various information is gathered, how it is used, who has access to it and whether consumers are informed as to what happens to the information in their personal profile. This manifests itself in what is generally termed invasions of privacy (Deighton *et al.*, 1994).

Inter-organizational relationships have also been particularly vulnerable to ethical criticism due to power differences. The way in which power is used in a relationship can lead to ethical problems, created when an action taken by one company causes harm to is relational partners.

On a global scale, partnership relationships have also been scrutinized as ethical problems occurred in relation to child labour, long hours and low pay. In response to dramatic price competition from countries with lower labour costs, Levi Strauss developed relationships with manufacturers in low wage countries in such areas as Latin America and South East Asia.

However, Levi Strauss was harmed when mass media in the USA found out that a few sub-supplier partners in the Far East did not behave according to the ethics code of Levi Strauss. In such a situation it is not always an advantage to be in a close relationship with your sub-suppliers.

However, as already suggested, the RM philosophy, by affecting factors that bear upon ethical decision making (organizational climate, senior management's actions, etc.), has the potential to affect ethical standards positively and reduce the limits for unethical behaviour not only among organizational members but also among other stakeholders and network partners.

Moreover, RM can bring about greater communication between partners, as its complex nature requires administrative mechanisms, which are not possible to bring into a contract because of RM's tacit nature.

Emphasis should therefore be placed on ethics as a foundation for RM where trust, equity, responsibility and commitment are required for honest relational exchanges to occur. It is through this dialogue that mutual understanding, confidence and respect can be cultivated and the capabilities and concerns of each party fully articulated and taken into account.

The following framework may be used as a guide for marketing managers to plan and implement morally justified RM operations (Takala and Uusitalo, 1996). The guide consists of four parts.

The ethics of keeping promises and telling the truth

Telling the truth is an issue often connected with the problems of keeping promises. As a general maxim it is often stated that you must always tell the truth, nothing but the truth, hide nothing, add nothing. This may be the ideal, but the practices of everyday life are more complicated and demand more fluid solutions.

The ethics of equal treatment of customers

In RM operations the equal treatment of the partner is an essential feature of action principles. The notion of fairness is widely recognized as essential for a mutually satisfying exchange. Fairness is also tied to the concept of distributive justice. Furthermore, ethics stresses equal treatment of all human beings.

The ethics of commitment

In RM, participants must be committed. Commitment can be defined as an affective attachment to an organization, the intensity of which can vary with the nature of the relationship. Thus commitment is conceived as the strength of an individual's identification with, and his/her involvement in, the organization. It is characterized by three factors. First, stability refers to a strong belief in and acceptance of the organization's goals and values. Second, sacrifice means a willingness to exert considerable effort for the benefit of the organization. Third, loyalty means a definite desire to maintain organizational membership.

The ethics of communication

Communication is a central element in RM. The basic ideal is that every individual has the right to domination-free action. An application to RM is that every buyer-seller relationship should be evaluated and reconstructed on a base of mutual communication.

18.3   Different levels of ethical behaviour

The ethical commitment of a company is illustrated in Figure 18.1 as a continuum from unacceptable ethical behaviour to most ethical decision making.

Figure 18.1 Ethical decision making

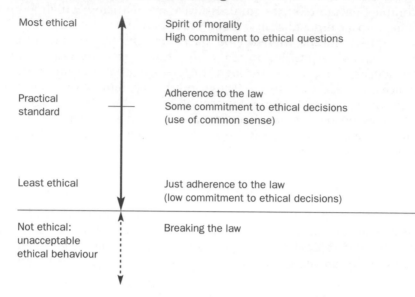

At the first level of the acceptable ethical behaviour, marketing ethics refer to principles and standards that define acceptable conduct as determined by the public, government regulators, private interest groups, competitors, and the organization itself. The most basic of these principles have been codified as laws and regulations to induce marketers to conform to society's expectations of conduct. However, it is important to understand that marketing ethics goes beyond legal issues: ethical marketing decisions foster trust, which helps build long-term marketing relationships.

Being ethical and responsible requires commitment. For this reason, many firms simply ignore these issues and focus instead on satisfying their economic and legal responsibilities, with the overall aim being profit maximization. While the firm may do nothing wrong, it misses out on the long-term benefits that can be derived from satisfying ethical and philanthropic responsibilities. Firms that choose to take these extra steps are concerned with increasing their overall positive impact on society, their local communities, and the environment, with the aim being increased goodwill toward the firm as well as increased profits.

A classification of a company as a highly ethical company requires that the firm's code of ethics should address the following six major issues:

- *organizational relations*, including competition, strategic alliances, and local sourcing
- *economic relations*, including financing, taxation, transfer prices, local reinvestment, equity participation
- *employee relations*, including compensation, safety, human rights, non-discrimination, collective bargaining, training, and the absence of sexual harassment
- *customer relations*, including pricing, quality, and advertising

- *industrial relations*, including technology transfer, research and development, infrastructure development, and organizational stability/longevity
- *political relations*, including legal compliance, bribery and other corrupt activities, subsidies, tax incentives, environmental protection, and political involvement.

It is easy to generalize about the ethics of political pay offs and other types of payments; it is much more difficult to make the decision to withhold payment of money when the consequences of not making the payment may affect the company's ability to do business profitably or at all. With the variety of ethical standards and levels of morality that exist in different cultures, the dilemma of ethics and pragmatism that faces international business cannot be resolved until more countries decide to deal effectively with the issue.

It is imperative that marketers become familiar with many of the ethical and social issues that may occur in marketing so that these issues can be identified and resolved when they occur. Some of these issues are shown in Figure 18.2. Essentially, any time an activity causes marketing managers, or customers in their

Figure 18.2 Possible ethical Issues in marketing

Product issues

- Reducing package size while holding prices constant.
- Product quality dishonesty (shortcuts in design/manufacture).
- Unsafe products (particularly for children).
- Poor service or no service after the sale.
- Adding useless features to command higher prices.

Promotion issues

- Bait-and-switch (comparitive) advertising
- Overstated claims for product
- Push money paid to salespeople
- Advertising to children
- Sex or fear as an advertising appeal
- Exaggerated product benefits
- High-pressure or misleading salespeople
- Bribery of salespeople or purchasing agents

Pricing issues

- Price fixing between competitors
- Predatory pricing
- Excessive pricing
- Misleading credit/financing practices
- Fraudulent warranty or refund policies

Distribution issues

- Opportunistic behaviour among channel members
- Slotting allowances paid to retailers to gain shelf space
- Extortion
- Tying contracts
- Distribution of counterfeit products

Sources: adapted from Peter and Donelly (1994), p. 274, and Pride and Ferrell (1997), p. 59.

target market, to feel manipulated or cheated, an ethical issue exists, regardless of the legality of the activity. Many ethical issues can develop into legal problems if they are not addressed in the planning process. Once an issue has been identified, marketers must decide how to deal with it.

Exhibit 18.1 **Ethical values at Levi Strauss & Co.**

In December 1991, NBC Nightly News aired a report accusing a Levi Strauss contractor in Saipan of forcing virtual slave-type conditions on its workers. For Levi Strauss, the world's largest brand-name clothing manufacturer, it was a painful moment.

Even before the NBC story broke, Levi Strauss had been drafting a programme designed to provide an ethics code and performance guidelines for its overseas suppliers, called the Business Partner Terms of Engagement.

Company teams investigated business practices as well as ethical, environmental, legal, health, and safety concerns in each of the 50 countries in which Levi Strauss did business. The result of this investigation was that out of 700 contractors, roughly 140 needed some kind of upgrading, ranging from better ventilation and improved lighting to increased attention to safety conditions and better wages.

Contractors unwilling or unable to comply had their contracts terminated. More significantly, Levi Strauss decided to give up its operations in Myanmar in late 1992 and most of its US$50 million-a-year operation in the blossoming market in China in March 1993.

But even the most carefully constructed questionnaire does not always achieve the right response. When another NBC report revealed unspeakable conditions in Bangladeshi factories producing for Wal-Mart, Levi Strauss auditors looked at the contractors there and found underage children working in the factories. On the surface it looked like an easy case, but here the company was also faced with a dilemma. These children provided the sole means of support for their families, who would starve without the income. The alternatives to factory work for the 12-year-olds were prostitution or begging on the street. To solve this dilemma Levi Strauss decided to pay the children's wages while they went to school until they reached legal working age.

Some countries, like China, dismiss the Terms of Engagement as rank interference.

In the long term, Levi Strauss' ethical code has become a benefit for the company and its contractors. Contractors value listing Levi Strauss as a customer. If the contractors can meet Levi Strauss' requirements it means that they can work for anybody in the industry.

Source: adapted from Rapaport (1993).

18.4 Incorporating ethics and social responsibility into strategic marketing planning

Ethics are our beliefs about what is right and what is wrong. The marketing planning process recognizes responsibilities to consumers, channel members, and the company. This responsibility is accomplished by designing a marketing strategy to satisfy the needs of each of these groups. The law and general public-policy issues also come into play. However, personal beliefs about what is right and what is wrong should also constrain our decision making. It is called exercising ethical standards.

Ultimately, marketing planners must live with their professional behaviour and decisions in the same way that they must live with their personal behaviour and decisions. Why are these ethics and values of marketing planners so important? Because supplier behaviour shapes consumer behaviour, the values of marketing planners are expressed in what they make and how they sell it. The resulting ethical dilemmas can be complex.

One of the more powerful arguments for including ethics and social responsibility in the strategic marketing planning process is increasing evidence of a link between social responsibility, ethics, and marketing performance. One study found that an ethical climate is associated with employee commitment to quality and intra-firm trust. Employee commitment, customer loyalty, market orientation, and profitability have also been associated with companies that are identified as socially responsible.

Research also suggests a relationship between a market orientation and ethics and social responsibility. Market-oriented businesses support the generation of thorough market intelligence and the use of this information at every level of the organization. This implies that in market-oriented organizations, employees are not only concerned about changes in market forces, but are also sensitive and responsive to the demands of customers and other stakeholders. Thus, by encouraging their employees to understand their markets, companies can help them respond to their stakeholders' demands.

In contrast, a competitive orientation in the workplace can be a negative force creating conflict and damaging the opportunity to improve ethics and social responsibility. A competitive orientation encourages personal success, which may come at the expense of openness and teamwork. Internal competition between employees may encourage the achievement of financial performance levels without regard for their potential effects on other parties both inside and outside the organization. Consequently, employees of such organizations are unlikely to incorporate the demands and concerns of society, business, and its customers in their decisions.

Many firms are integrating ethics and social responsibility into their strategic planning through ethics compliance programmes or integrity initiatives that make legal compliance, ethics, and social responsibility an issue throughout the organization. Such programmes establish, communicate, and monitor a firm's ethical values and legal requirements through codes of conduct, which are formalized rules and standards that describe what the company expects of its employees. One of the most widely adopted professional codes is that of the American Marketing Association, which has a code of conduct for advertising.

The marketing plan should include distinct elements of ethics and social responsibility as determined by senior marketing managers. Marketing strategy and implementation plans should be developed that reflect an understanding of the ethical and social consequences of strategic choices, and the values of organizational members and stakeholders. To help ensure success, senior managers must demonstrate their commitment to ethical and socially responsible behaviour through their actions – words are simply not enough. In the end, a marketing plan that ignores social responsibility – or is silent about ethical requirements – leaves the guidance of ethically and socially responsible behaviour to the work group, risking ethical breakdown and damage to the firm.

18.5 Green alliances between business and environmental groups/organizations

Strategic alliances with environmental groups (e.g. Greenpeace) can provide five benefits to marketers of consumer goods (Mendleson and Polonsky, 1995).

Increase consumer reliability on green products and their claims

It can be assumed that if an environmental group supports a firm, product or service, then consumers are more likely to believe the product's environmental claims. These types of strategic alliance also assist firms in minimizing consumer scepticism, as consumers are more likely to believe that the products are effective and environmentally responsible if they are supported by an environmental group.

Provide firms with access to environmental information

It is in their role as a source of information that environmental groups may be of immense benefit to organizations with whom they form strategic alliances. Manufacturers facing environmental problems may turn to their strategic partners for advice and information. In some cases environmental partners may actually have technical staff who can be used to assist in solving organizational problems or implementing existing solutions.

Give the marketer access to new markets

Most environmental groups have an extensive support base, which in many cases receives newsletters or other group mailings. Their members receive catalogues marketing a variety of licensed products, all of which are less environmentally harmful than other commercial alternatives. Environmental group members represent a potential market that can be utilized by producers, even if these groups do not produce specialized catalogues. An environmental group's newsletter may discuss how a firm has formed a strategic alliance with the group, as well as the firm's less environmentally harmful products. Inclusion of this information in a newsletter is also a useful form of publicity.

Provide positive publicity and reduce public criticism

Forming strategic alliances with environmental groups may also stimulate increased publicity. When the Sydney Olympic Bid Committee announced that Greenpeace was the successful designer for the year 2000 Olympic Village the story appeared in all major newspapers and on the national news. It is highly unlikely that this publicity would have been generated if a more conventional architect had been named as the designer of the Village. Once again the publicity associated with the alliance was positive and credible.

Educate consumers about key environmental issues to the firm and its product(s)

Environmental groups are valuable sources of environmental education information and materials. They educate consumers and the general public about environmental problems and also inform them about potential solutions. In many cases the public views these groups as credible sources of information, without a vested interest. Marketers can also play an important role as providers of environmental information through their marketing activities. In doing so they create environmental awareness for specific issues, their products, and their organizations.

For example, Kellogg in Norway educated consumers and promoted its environmental concern by placing environmental information on the packaging of its cereals relating to various regional environmental problems (World Wide Fund for Nature, 1993).

Choosing the correct alliance partner is not a simple task, as most environmental groups have different objectives and images. Some groups may be willing to form exclusive alliances, where they only partner one product in a given product category. Other groups may be willing to form alliances with all products that comply with their specific criteria.

The marketer must determine what capabilities and characteristics an alliance partner must bring to the alliance. As with any symbiotic relationship, each partner must contribute to the success of the activity. Poor definition of these characteristics will result in the firm possibly linking up with the wrong partner.

Exhibit 18.2 | **Environmental considerations at Fuji Photo Film**

Fuji Photo Film (Fujifilm) is a global company that began expanding sales worldwide from the second half of the 1960s. From the 1970s the firm began establishing a series of production bases overseas.

In 1970, Fujifilm established an environmental management department and in 1975 set up a materials safety testing office to independently assess the safety of new chemicals. The materials office assesses up to 5000 new types of chemical each year. In 1997, Fujifilm acquired ISO 14001 certification for all of its factories in Japan.

From development of new products through recycling of waste, the company has also adopted the concept of responsible care with respect to the environment and safety. For instance, Fujifilm has built a chemicals and environmental safety information database. The system enables the company to obtain safety information on chemicals and research related to Japanese and foreign regulations.

On the subject of the environment, Fujifilm is aggressively tackling the issue of recycling. In 1988 Fujifilm set up a system to recycle and reuse its Quick-Snap one-use cameras, which were a big hit. Then in 1992, the company developed an automated recycling system. In 1998, the company built a Quick-Snap recycling-oriented production factory based on the reverse manufacturing concept so that production, reuse, and recycling of the products could be carried out in an integrated fashion.

Fujifilm is developing and designing new products with a view to eventual reuse. Components (or parts) Fujifilm could reuse they would fix or restore automatically. Or they would turn a material into chips so that it could be used again later.

It should be noted that the company is able to reuse 90 per cent of parts with its latest 'Quick Snap Super-slim' camera.

Source: adapted from Katayama (2000).

18.6 Ethical issues in relation to the 4 Ps

Product

Environmental management in value chain perspective

Management cannot afford to be myopic in looking at the finished product without considering the manufacturing and R&D phases as they relate to consumers' perceptions of what constitutes a green product. Nor can a company use traditional marketing principles to gain product acceptance. Put differently, both the input and output activities associated with the design, manufacture, and delivery of products must be considered, and each step within the value-creating process must be weighed in the light of its overall environmental impact and consequences.

Figure 18.3 illustrates the resource conversion and pollutant generation relationships. As resources are used to create desired utilities, pollutants are implicitly produced as by-products during each step of the integrated supply chain process. For example, packaging is used to protect products from damage in transit and is a waste item once they are consumed. Proper management and awareness of the environmental implications of logistics activities can significantly reduce the negative impact.

Eco-labelling scheme

Over the years eco-labelling schemes have been implemented in a number of EU countries in an attempt to promote the use of products and production methods that are less harmful to the environment. The first scheme was introduced in West Germany in 1978. Today the organizers of the scheme claim that 80 per cent of German households are aware of the scheme and it receives widespread support from manufacturers.

The label should affect all businesses along the supply chain, because the suppliers will have to provide detailed information about their own components and their manufacturing process. The criteria for the award of an eco-label for a product are based on a life cycle assessment (Table 18.1)

National bodies, which award the eco-labels for products, assess the environmental performance of a product by reference to agreed specific environmental criteria for each product group.

Figure 18.3 Value adding logistics and the environment interface

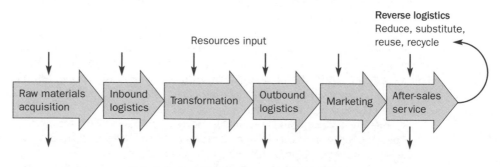

Pollutants (negative environmental impact)

Source: adapted from Wu and Dunn, 1995, p. 23.

Table 18.1 Eco-labelling scheme indicative assessment matrix

Environmental fields	Product life cycle				
	Pre-production	Production	Distribution	Utilization	Disposal
Waste relevance	xx	xx	xx	xx	xx
Soil pollution and degradation	xx	xx	xx	xx	xx
Water contamination	xx	xx	xx	xx	xx
Air contamination	xx	xx	xx	xx	xx
Noise	xx	xx	xx	xx	xx
Consumption of energy	xx	xx	xx	xx	xx
Consumption of natural resources	xx	xx	xx	xx	xx
Effects on eco-systems	xx	xx	xx	xx	xx

Source: adapted from Welford and Prescott (1996).

So firms need to incorporate environmental attributes into products and processes at the initial stages of new product development (NPD) along with other issues, such as quality. They can then use life-cycle analysis to evaluate a product's ecological impact for each production stage. This allows them to identify alternative methods of designing or producing goods, consequently opening up new, untapped industries and markets while cutting production costs.

Designing less harmful 'traditional' products is an integrated and complex process, requiring innovative designs. Hoover's New Wave washing machines had a redesigned water injection system to use less water and be easily disassembled for easier repair and recycling. Individual components were also designed to be less harmful. While some of these eco-changes were relatively minor, others required substantial engineering changes, thus demonstrating the importance of incorporating environmental issues into the early phases of NPD.

Green positioning is a question that needs to be asked early in an organization's development. In other words, what are the underlying environmental values and behaviours of the firm and its products? Truly green marketers demonstrate strategic greening by ensuring that all activities and behaviours thoroughly incorporate environmental values into decision-making processes. Environmental criteria should be considered as important as financial criteria.

Price

Price fixing occurs when one party attempts to control what another party will charge in the market. There are laws against vertical and horizontal price fixing. Vertical price fixing is an attempt by a manufacturer or distributor to control the final selling price at the retail level.

Price fixing among suppliers is the best-known illegal marketing tactic. It is an obvious conspiracy against the free market, unless of course the government does it in its regulation of a market. Price fixing has occurred in many and varied markets.

In the international market, one of the most common regulations relates to dumping, which is a form of price discrimination. Dumping occurs when a product is sold in a foreign country at a price lower than in the producing country and lower than its actual cost of production. Why do companies do this? It can be a very effective way to maximize profits, since global organizations cover may of their fixed costs through product pricing in the home market; they then price according to only their variable costs in other parts of the world. Dumping is illegal because it puts manufacturers in the local market at a disadvantage. In Latin America, for example, T-shirts have been imported from Asia and Panama for as little as 2 cents apiece.

Since 1990, China has been cited in more anti-dumping cases in the USA than in any other country.

Predatory dumping is pricing designed to drive local firms out of the market. A large market share is gained, competitors are put out of business, and then higher prices are charged. Some Japanese companies have engaged in this practice.

Container sizes for the same item can vary considerably. In some cases the package may have similar wording, such as 'giant' or 'large economy' size. This makes it difficult for consumers to compare the price of products based on the size and type of packaging.

Ethical issues in pricing abound. For price-sensitive products they revolve around the creation of demand and delivery of value based on price. For price inelastic products, particularly because of the captive audience, unscrupulous pricing is an issue.

Although laws protect customers against unscrupulous pricing, we still find questionable ways of using price to increase demand. For example, an advert for dramatically reduced airfares states (in tiny print) that some restrictions may apply. When you call, you learn that so many restrictions apply that your choices are limited to a few seats and times.

Horizontal price fixing is an agreement among manufacturers and other channel members to set prices at the retail level. According to national and EU trade laws horizontal price fixing is illegal. Signs of price fixing include: cooperation among competitors on discounting, credit terms, or conditions of sale; any discussions about pricing at association meetings; plans to issue price lists on the same date or on given dates; plans to withhold or rotate bids on contracts; agreements to limit production in order to increase prices; and any exchange of information among competitors on pricing. The intent is to prohibit communication among competitors about pricing or any aspects of the business that may influence pricing levels.

On the international level, there are anti-trust sanctions to ensure fair competition.

Green pricing

While green products are often priced higher than traditional goods, this does not always mean they cost more, especially when one considers all associated costs. Often, green goods have higher initial out-of-pocket expenses, but lower long-term costs. Long-life compact fluorescent light bulbs have a lower lifetime cost than cheaper tungsten light bulbs. Unfortunately, their longer payback period and higher initial cost discourage their use, making it difficult for many consumers to think of light bulbs as an investment warranting life cycle costing.

Place (channel management)

Resale price maintenance

Resale price maintenance is an attempt by companies to compel channel members to charge certain prices. The practice is illegal when title to the product changes hands. Since wholesalers and retailers normally purchase the products they sell, they can charge any price they choose. If manufacturers cross the line between persuasion and coercion, then legal problems can arise. For example, a manufacturer should never threaten to take a product away if prices are not raised.

Territorial and customer constraints

A territorial constraint exists when a company assigns an intermediary a specific geographic area in which to sell its products. That is, it can sell there but nowhere else. Such constraints are legal, as they are seen as protecting the investment of all neighbouring intermediaries who sell the company's products.

Another ethical issue arises when intermediaries have accepted territorial constraints and then choose to ignore them. They lack the courage to confront large intermediaries for selling outside their assigned territory. Such intermediaries often claim they will drop the product line and switch to competitors if they cannot broaden their market area.

A class-of-customer constraint is a company limit on the customer groups to which an intermediary can sell its product.

Exclusive dealing

Exclusive dealing occurs when a company restricts intermediaries from carrying competitive lines. Such constraints are legal, unless they are proved to be a substantial limit on competition in the marketplace.

Other practices may not be against the law but are ethically questionable. For example, franchisers often confront the issue of how close to place outlets. Market coverage improves with a greater number, but existing franchisees may be hurt. They have committed time and money to building their business, and they do not want to be crowded out by competition from their own company.

Retailers' listing fees

The power that a channel leader possesses can sometimes be misused. Manufacturers may take advantage of small retailers, and powerful retail chains might also take advantage of manufacturers. Given today's bargaining power of retailers, it has become practice for them to demand payments or free goods for listing a new item and stocking it. Retailers often argue that their valuable shelf space is for rent and slotting allowances represent nothing else but rent for shelf space.

From an ethical perspective these listing fees and slotting allowances have been heavily criticized, and some critics have referred to them as institutional bribery (Schlegelmilch, 1998).

Multi-level marketing (network marketing)

The major difference between direct marketing and multi-level marketing (MLM) is that in direct marketing the product is predominant, and sales of the product are emphasized, whereas in MLM the product is often secondary, and the emphasis is not placed on selling products but on recruiting other sales people to in turn recruit still others. MLM has two distinguishing features:

● the presence of sponsorship lines that create financial ties between distributors, ties that become the basis for intense social relationships.

● presence of recognition levels by a formal status hierarchy; a complete series of honorific titles is available.

MLMs appear at an ever increasing rate. Herbalife had 700,000 distributors by 1985 with sales of nearly $500 million (Herbig and Yelkar, 1997). MLMs tread the thin line between ethical and unethical behaviour. MLMs may become unethical when their primary purpose is to make money from recruiting instead of from selling products to users. It is perfectly legal to share commissions when the commissions are legitimately earned from selling products to consumers. It is not legal when a good deal of the commission money is derived from product sales to recruits themselves.

Grey markets

Grey markets or parallel importing can be defined as importing and selling products through market distribution channels which are not authorized by the manufacturer. It occurs when manufacturers have different prices across national boundaries, i.e. using significantly different market prices for the same product in different countries. This allows an unauthorized dealer (a wholesaler in Figure 18.4) to buy branded goods intended for one market at a low price and then sell them in another higher priced market at a higher profit than he could have obtained in the lower-price market.

Figure 18.4 Grey marketing (parallel importing)

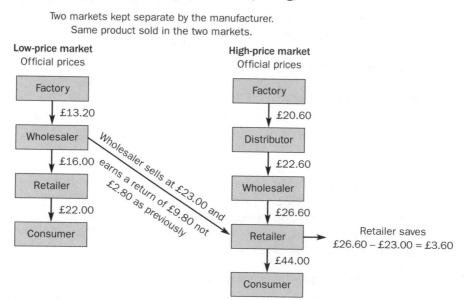

Two markets kept separate by the manufacturer.
Same product sold in the two markets.

Source: S. Paliwoda (1993) *International Marketing*, reprinted by permission of Elsevier Science.

To understand parallel exporting, one has to remember that countries have different tax regimes and that many have recommended resale price maintenance structures – making it virtually impossible for multi-national corporations to standardize price structure – and that, combined with rises and falls in foreign exchange rates, can create market opportunities for channel members.

Grey markets often occur because of the fluctuating value of currencies, which makes it attractive for the grey marketer to buy products in markets with weak currencies and sell in markets with strong currencies.

Grey markets can also be the result of a distributor in one country having an unexpected oversupply of a product. This distributor may be willing to sell his excess supply for less than the normal margin to recover his investment. Other reasons for lower prices in some countries (which can result in grey marketing) might be lower transport costs, fiercer competition or higher product taxes (high product taxes put downward pressure on the ex-works price to keep the end consumer price at an acceptable level).

The particular problem with grey markets for the manufacturer is that they result in authorized intermediaries losing motivation. The grey marketer usually only competes on price and pays little attention to providing marketing support and after-sales service.

Possible strategies to reduce grey markets

Sometimes companies hope that it is a short-term problem and that it will disappear. Indeed it might be if the price difference is a result of fluctuating currency values.

At other times a more pro-active approach to the problem is needed.

Seek legal redress

Although the legal option can be time consuming and expensive, some companies (e.g. Seiko) have chosen to prosecute grey marketers.

Change marketing mix

- *Product strategy*: the manufacturer can introduce a differentiated product concept with a different product for each main market.

- *Pricing strategy*: the manufacturer can change the ex-works prices to the channel members to minimize price differentials between markets. The manufacturer can also narrow the discount schedules it offers for large orders. This will reduce the incentive for intermediaries to over-order to get lower prices and later sell unsold stock on the grey market, still at a profit.

- *Warranty strategy*: the manufacturer may reduce or cancel the warranty period for grey-market products. This will require that the products can be identified through the channel system.

Green Logistics

Distribution is a typical concern, and one of the first functions targeted to minimize environmental costs. Firms have sought to reduce raw material use by modifying packaging, which can directly and indirectly lower distribution costs as well. Some concentrated laundry detergents now come in smaller packages, weigh less than regular ones (requiring less fuel to ship), and use less energy and raw material for equal cleaning performance.

Integrated transportation systems, the Internet, and other initiatives have further reduced the environmental impact of distribution activities by requiring fewer transport modes. However, the most complex advances in distribution are in the area of reverse logistics, whereby firms move packaging and used goods from the consumer back up the distribution channel to the firm.

Reverse logistics need not be simply a regulated activity that places costs on companies; it can also be a flow of inputs to production as well as a flow of goods, allowing firms to turn returned goods into major cash flows. Xerox markets reprocessed photocopiers as well as reprocessing parts from these machines to repair other machines. Reverse logistics, then, is not a cost by definition; it is an opportunity to generate more revenue. However, integrated reverse logistics do require extensive corporate commitment in terms of strategic focus, as well as additional financial and human resources.

Promotional and cross-cultural communication

Of all components of the marketing mix, promotion and advertising is, without debate, the most visible element.

The overstatement of claims in advertising has always been a reason for ethical discussions. In the EU and USA these overstatements are allowed if, and only if, they do not deceive the customer. The European directive on misleading advertising puts the burden of proof on the advertiser should claims be challenged.

Most countries agree that aggressive advertising towards children is unethical. There seems to be an agreement that children are especially vulnerable, as they are less able to make rational decisions and are more influenced by advertising. To act in a socially responsible manner, the marketer should make an effort to explain the product honestly and not exploit the vulnerability of children.

Types of ethical conflict in cross-cultural communication

Managers like clear guidelines to aid their decision making. A list of rules citing prohibitions and allowed practices is often helpful. Unfortunately, such lists are too simple to guide cross-cultural ethical interaction. For example, gift giving is not usually prohibited in most cultures. However, in a given culture, giving a gift may be ethical or unethical. In some societies, like China, presentation of a small, carefully chosen business gift conveys a great deal of respect and is a sign that the business relationship is valued by the giver. If there is a problem, it may rest with the receiver who may not trust the giver's motives. In this case, the issue can be understood as one of business etiquette.

Conversely, a gift whose purpose is to influence a decision-maker's judgement is actually or essentially a bribe. They are more universally recognized as such. This leads to a second issue involving basic values. What is the proper place of a bribe in the business context? In western cultures, bribes are usually not considered right or fair and are often against the law. In this case, the conflict deals with fundamental standards of fairness.

There is a continuum of ethical conflict ranging from the simple, rather innocuous practice like giving token gifts to serious issues like employing sweatshop or political prisoner labour. Judging the seriousness of the differences requires a look at the aspects of both the US and Chinese cultures (Pitta *et al.*, 1999).

Green promotion

One of the most difficult questions to address is: what environmental information should be communicated and how should it be communicated? A primary issue is that there must be something worthwhile to talk about. A good deal of environmental promotion has been labelled 'greenwash', having little if any real ecological meaning. This type of superficial tactical greening, i.e. doing the minimum possible, is no longer appropriate and both consumers and regulators are unwilling to accept it. Communicating substantive environmental information is a more appropriate approach to take, but requires real activity changes to be meaningful.

Before embarking on environmental promotion, the firm must consider what consumers perceive environmental information to be, and whether they actually understand what is being communicated.

As suggested earlier, many firms realize that green promotion alone is becoming less effective so they are shifting to promoting ecological attributes in addition to more traditional ones. It is questionable, for example, whether environmental sponsorship and cause-related marketing programmes will be effective, especially if they are seen as unrelated to a firm's core marketing activities or products. Thus, all green promotional activities need to be carefully evaluated to ensure that the firm is not criticized for greenwashing.

Green promotion needs to communicate substantive environmental information to consumers that have meaningful links to corporate activities. As such, it is unlikely to be an effective strategic tool unless it is supported by other corporate activities. A company might simply choose to sponsor a local environmental programme without modifying its other activities. This may seem to be an effective short-term strategy, but not necessarily from a long-term marketing perspective, especially if the firm is not seeking to achieve sustainable broader objectives. If consumers are sceptical of its motives, this opportunistic sponsorship could actually backfire. The publicity generated could even make consumers more critical of the firm's other, less eco-friendly activities.

18.7 Summary

Ethics are our beliefs about what is right and wrong. Personal beliefs about what is right and wrong should also constrain our decision making. It is called exercising ethical standards.

Every culture, nation, industry, organization and profession establishes a set of moral standards for business behaviour, that is, a code of business ethics. This set of standards influences all decisions and actions in a company, including, for example, what and how to manufacture (or not), what wages it is appropriate to pay, how many hours personnel should work and under what conditions, how to compete, and what communication guidelines to follow. Which actions are considered right or wrong, fair or unfair, in the conduct of business and which are particularly susceptible to ethical norms is heavily influenced by the culture in which they take place.

The need for a holistic approach in **green marketing** cannot be over-emphasized, considering the frequent problems associated with the non-integrated green market. Just like any integrated marketing approach, green marketing must involve extensive coordination across functional areas to be effective. The level of environmental promotion – strategic, quasi-strategic, or tactical – dictates exactly what activities should be undertaken. Strategic environmental promotion in one area may or may not be leveraged effectively in others. A firm could make substantial changes in production processes, but opt not to leverage them by positioning itself as an environmental leader. In short, green alliance partners can assist firms in implementing the activities. Although green alliances may be an effective way to achieve green marketing outcomes, they may take more time and effort to develop than traditional firm-to-firm alliances and require information to be shared in a way that is contrary to usual practices.

Case study 18.2 The Body Shop

A company with ethical values

It was in 1975, while Anita Roddick's husband was on an expedition on horseback from Buenos Aires to New York, that she had an idea to earn money while still spending time with her children. The first Body Shop opened in Brighton in March 1976, the walls painted the now familiar dark green, the only colour that would cover the damp patches.

The business concept was and is to produce products from a combination of traditional knowledge, ancient herbal recipes and modern scientific research. The Body Shop offers minimally packaged, natural-ingredient products that have not been tested on animals. It stands for environmental consciousness and Anita Roddick has become famous for her engagement in different environmental issues. She participated in a number of different projects, from increasing living standards for Indians in the Amazon to improving orphanages in Romania.

When Anita Roddick decided to use the franchising principle for The Body Shop, following the same concept as McDonald's and Burger King, the story became an adventure. The first Body Shop outside the UK opened in Belgium in 1978. The Body Shop became listed on the London Stock Exchange in 1984.

The Body Shop was arguably the most successful British enterprise of the 1980s and remains one of the best-known global brands to this day. But the company has had its share of downs, both financially and emotionally. However, Roddick created a fair-trade programme that buys goods directly from farmers, encouraging the growth of communities, not corporations.

In the middle of the 1990s, problems appeared. The Body Shop shares began to drop. One of the problems was the US market, where Roddick neglected to follow her own system for success. The Body Shop owned 113 of its 272 stores in the USA, and this was one of the key reasons for the company's stumble there, analysts say. Rather than perfecting sales in its existing shops, the company opened shops in the top malls, in the hope of gaining a foothold against the fast-expanding Bath & Body Works. But it did not work. The US operation lost money in 1996.

Bath & Body Works, by contrast, which had opened 412 stores from 1990 to 1995, was making a profit. Its chairman, Leslie H. Wexner, said his rival's background as a manufacturer (and foreigner) worked against her in the USA. 'They're not retailers', he said. 'We have an advantage – we know the territory'. 'It was just awesome to watch how fast they got into the market', Roddick admitted.

Roddick has ceded control of the company, but she is still the co-chairman of The Body Shop, but she says her first priority is writing. Her new book, *Business as Usual*, was published in the USA in January 2001, and she is working on another manuscript. 'I'm at a point in my life where I want to be heard', she explained. 'I have knowledge, and I want to pass it on'.

Today, The Body Shop operates 1840 stores around the world, 477 of them owned by the company (Table 18.2).

For 2000 and 2001, respectively, the total revenues were £330 million and £374 million with net profits of £29 million and £13 million. The sales are very seasonal. 70% of revenues are generated in the two months before Christmas.

Case study 18.2 continued

Table 18.2 The Body Shop stores by location

Region	Number
UK and Eire	310
Americas	415
Europe & Middle East	684
Asia Pacific	431
Total	1840

Source: based on various Body Shop sources

The business idea of The Body Shop is still:

- to dedicate the business to the pursuit of social and environmental change.
- to creatively balance the financial and human needs of stakeholders: employees, franchisees, customers, suppliers and shareholders.
- to courageously ensure that the business is ecologically sustainable: meeting the needs of the present without compromising the future.
- to meaningfully contribute to local and international communities in which the company trades, by adopting a code of conduct which ensures care, honesty, fairness and respect.
- to passionately campaign for the protection of the environment, human and civil rights, and against animal testing within the cosmetics and toiletries industry.
- to tirelessly work to narrow the gap between principle and practice, whilst making fun, passion and care part of our lives.

Product development

The Body Shop pioneered new approaches to the manufacturing, retailing and especially the marketing of cosmetics and toiletries. Now, however, there are many competitors using similar tactics to target the same consumer group.

In response to these new competitors, Patrick Gournay, CEO of The Body Shop, in 1998 announced the implementation of a major restructuring of the company. His initiative has revitalized the organization's sales, earnings and image. In working to become a world class brand retailer, The Body Shop has created centres of innovation in four regions: the UK, Asia, the USA and Europe. Innovation is expected to come from increased efforts in spa products and products geared toward well-being and health.

The product portfolio of The Body Shop

The overall Boston matrix of the portfolio is illustrated in Figure 18.5. As illustrated, the

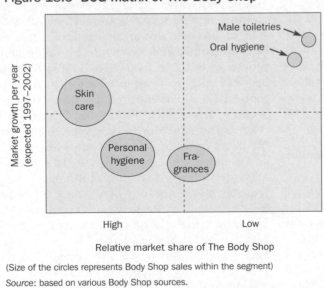

Figure 18.5 BCG-matrix of The Body Shop

(Size of the circles represents Body Shop sales within the segment)

Source: based on various Body Shop sources.

Case study 18.2 continued

Table 18.3 Skin care market real value medium forecast (US$ million, 1997 prices)

Segment	1997	1998	1999	2000	2001	2002	CAGR*
Facial care	2899	2890	2897	2921	2951	2995	0.9%
Hand and body care	1222	1224	1230	1239	1250	1266	0.7%
Sun care	749	766	786	808	831	857	2.7%
Medicated skin care	572	562	553	546	540	535	–1.3%
Lip care	225	232	239	245	251	257	2.7%
Depilatories	49	49	50	51	52	53	1.4%
Petroleum jelly	27	26	26	25	25	25	–1.6%
TOTAL	5743	5749	5781	5835	5900	5988	0.9%

*Compound annual growth rate.

Source: adapted from Datamonitor Cosmetics & Toiletries Database.

main market of the Body Shop is the skin care market. The development and structure of the skin care market (Western Europe and the USA) is shown in Table 18.3.

According to Datamonitor, the total market for skin care products is predicted to grow at a 0.9% compound annual growth rate (CAGR) in the period 1997–2002. This equates to a market value increase from US$5743 million in 1997 to US$5988 million in 2002.

Although medicated skin care is one of the slowest growth categories forecast, The Body Shop (as well as other manufacturers) is looking at new product development within this segment to encourage growth. In particular, The Body Shop developed the tea tree line in facial and body care that offers benefits for skin problems traditionally treated with medicated products.

A new facial and body (skin care) product is introduced

The Australian Aborigines have long recognized the virtues of the tea tree. When the rest of the world thought it was just a weed, they used the leaves to help skin blemishes and discolorations. The Body Shop's tea tree line uses the tea tree oil's valuable properties as a deep cleanser and antiseptic to make products geared toward consumers with oily or problem skin and irritated scalps.

The Body Shop's Tea Tree Oil contains a 15% tea tree oil solution for direct application to the skin, which helps discourage spots and blemishes. The product can be added to a warm bath for an aromatic and soothing soak and helps combat foot odour. The Tea Tree Oil Facial Scrub is a foaming scrub that contains ground tree leaves that act as exfoliating particles to remove excess oil, impurities and dead skin. It also contains anti-bacterial tea tree oil to help diminish spots while the astringent properties of tea tree oil help to tone the skin. Beeswax and pro-vitamin B5 are also added to moisturize and condition the skin. Another product, Tea Tree Oil Facial Wash, thoroughly cleanses the skin. Moisturizing vegetable glycerine helps condition the skin and leaves it soft and supple but not greasy. The Tea Tree Oil Face Mask, with deep cleansing kaolin, effectively removes grease and dirt by drawing them out from the skin while seaweed extract soothes and moisturizes the skin. Renowned for their skin conditioning properties, beeswax, shea butter and glycerine are also added. The Tea Tree Oil Freshener removes the last traces of makeup and daily grime after cleansing. It con-

Case study 18.2 continued

tains tea tree oil, witch hazel that acts as a gentle astringent, and vegetable glycerine to moisturize the skin. The Body Shop also recently launched its Tea Tree Oil Body Scrub, positioned as a body/bath scrub for people with acne-prone and oily skin.

The Tea Tree Oil Blemish Stick is a light, translucent gel and includes a sponge applicator that allows consumers to apply the gel directly to trouble spots. The stick also contains the soothing skin conditioners allantoin and bis-abolol. The Tea Tree Oil Cover Stick masks minor skin flaws from redness to blemishes without looking heavy or artificial. The natural tea tree oil helps soothe the skin and leaves it feeling fresh.

Industry experts predict that new product development will be one of the key factors in determining how much further the company can expand. The success of The Body Shop has spawned many imitators, especially in the USA. Bath & Body Works is financially stronger and more widespread in the USA than The Body Shop, but it has not enjoyed as much

success abroad. Competitors like Garden Botanika also present a potential international threat in the future.

New colours/new shop format

Lately, the colour of The Body Shop has been changed. The Body Shop has said goodbye to all the green and hello to orange, lime and blue. The new format, adapted from a design that originated in the UK (home of corporate parent Body Shop International) is intended to create 'greater clarity', Roddick says. The shelves are also less cluttered and the product categories more clearly segmented, creating the impression that the consumer is browsing through different boutiques within the same store.

Questions

1. What ethical values are transferred from The Body Shop to the customers?

2. Do you think that the new shop format can increase The Body Shop's market share?

Sources: Hartman and Beck-Dudley (1999), Tummell (1999), Buxton (2000), Pratt (2000), Cowell (2001), Hofman (2001).

QUESTIONS FOR DISCUSSION

1. What role do you think cultural differences play in ethical standards?
2. List the most important ethical issues to consider in preparing a marketing strategy.
3. What aspects of ethical behaviour are important to consider in building marketing relationships?

REFERENCES

BBC (2001), Saudi Arabia bans Pokémon, *BBC News*, http://news.bbc.co.uk, March 26.

Buxton, P. (2000), Companies with a social conscience, *Marketing*, London, April 27, pp. 34–5.

Cowell, A. (2001), A marriage of business and businesswoman, *New York Times*, February 11, pp. 3–6.

Deighton, J., Peppers, D. and Rogers, M. (1994), Consumer transaction databases: present status and prospects, *in The Marketing Information Revolution*, Harvard Business School Press, Boston, MA, pp. 58–79.

Gummesen, E. (2000), *Total Relationship Marketing: Rethinking marketing management: from 4 Ps to 30 Rs*, Butterworth-Heinemann, Oxford.

Hartman, C. L. and Beck-Dudley, C. L. (1999), Marketing strategies and the search for virtue: a case analysis of The Body Shop, International, *Journal of Business Ethics*, Dordrecht, July.

Herbig, P. and Yelkar, R. (1997), A review of multilevel marketing phenomenon, *Journal of Marketing Channels*, vol. 6, no. 1, pp. 17–33.

Hofman, M. (2001), Anita Roddick: The Body Shop International, established in 1976. *Inc*, Boston, April 30, vol. 23, no. 5, p. 61.

Katayama, O. (2000), *Color Positives*, **www.Lookjapan**, July 20.

Kavali, S. G., Tzokas, N. X. and Saren, N. J. (1999), Relationship marketing as an ethical approach: philosophical and managerial considerations, *Management Decision*, vol. 37, no. 7, pp. 573–81.

Mendleson, N. and Polonsky, M. J. (1995), Using strategic alliances to develop credible green marketing, *Journal of Consumer Marketing*, vol. 12, no. 2, pp. 4–18.

Paliwoda, S. (1993), *International Marketing*, Heinemann, Oxford.

Peter, J. P. and Donelly, Jr, J. H. (1994), *A Preface to Marketing Management*, Richard D. Irwin, Burr Ridge, IL, 6th edn.

Pitta, D. A., Fung, H.-G. and Isberg, S. (1999), Ethical issues across cultures: managing the differing perspectives of USA, *Journal of Consumer Marketing*, vol. 16, no. 3, pp. 240–56.

Pratt, L. (2000), Body Shop gets a makeover. Lightens up with new store design, *Pharmaceutical/Health & Beauty*, July 3.

Pride, W. M. and Ferrell, O. C. (1997), *Marketing: Concepts and strategies*, Houghton Mifflin Co., Boston, MA, 10th edn.

Rapaport, R. (1993), Import jeans, export values, *Fast Company*, November, pp. 24–6.

Schlegelmilch, B. (1998), *Marketing Ethics: An international perspective*, International Thomson Business Press, London.

Takala, T. and Uusitalo, O. (1996), An alternative view of relationship marketing: a framework for ethical analysis, *European Journal of Marketing*, vol. 20, no. 2, pp. 45–60.

Tummell, T. (1999), What's new at the Body Shop? *Global Cosmetic Industry*, New York, November, no. 5, pp. 16–18.

Welford, R. and Prescott, K. (1996), *European Business: An issue-based approach*, Pitman, London.

World Wide Fund for Nature (1993), *Corporate Relationships*, World Wide Fund for Nature, Sydney.

Wu, H. J. and Dunn, S. C. (1995), Environmentally responsible logistic systems, *International Journal of Physical Distribution and Logistics Management*, vol. 25, no. 2, pp. 20–38.

Market research and decision support system

After studying this appendix you should be able to:

- explain the concepts of data warehouses and data mining.
- explain the main contents of a B-t-B customer file.
- explain the importance of having a carefully designed international information system.
- link global market research to the decision-making process.
- discuss the key problems in gathering and using international market data.
- distinguish between different research approaches, data sources and data types.
- understand the relevance of the web as an important data source in global marketing research.

A.1 Introduction

The term market research refers to gathering, analysing and presenting information that is related to a well-defined problem. Hence the focus of market research is a specific problem or project with a beginning and an end.

Market research differs from a decision support system (DSS), which is information gathered and analysed on a continual basis. In practice, market research and DSS are often hard to differentiate, so they will be used interchangeably in this context.

Marketers have the idea that different customers should be treated differently to maximize the relationship with the best ones and minimize the involvement with the worst ones. Information technology helps to realize that desire. The reality comes at a cost, however, as relationship marketing presents a new set of challenges both to marketers and information systems managers. To succeed, an effective cross-functional team of information systems and marketing specialists must work harmoniously. In the past, the two groups barely understood or tolerated each other. On a positive note, a new breed of cross-disciplinary executives exists. They understand both marketing and technology. Overall, the most successful implementation will require true collaboration.

To be useful to organizations, knowledge tools must be accessible to mainstream users. They must be understandable and useful to marketing managers, not just statistical experts and information systems managers. To overcome potential problems in applicability, marketers must insist that several key goals be achieved. They include:

● putting the problem in the marketer's terms, including viewing the data from a marketing model perspective. Often the job of knowledge discovery is performed by analysts whose primary training is in statistics and data analysis. It is likely that these analysts do not have the same perspective as marketers. To be useful to marketing, the findings must be in a form that marketers can understand.

● presenting results in a manner that is useful for the business problem at hand. The foremost benefit of the analysis and the job of the analyst is to help solve business problems and increase or diminish the value of the analysis.

● providing support for specific key business analyses, marketers need to know about segmentation, market response, segment reachability. Knowledge discovery tools must support these analyses from the beginning.

● providing support for an extensive and iterative exploratory process. Realistic knowledge discovery is not simple and not linear. It is an interactive and iterative learning process. Initial results are fed back into the process to increase accuracy. The process takes time and can have a long lifespan.

The heart of RM (both for B-t-B and B-t-C marketing) is the database. The next section considers selected issues concerning data warehousing.

A.2 Data warehousing

A customer data warehouse can be defined as a large amounts of information about the customer, from sources both internal to the company and from the customer and third sources, such as the government, credit bureaus and market research firms. Data can include behaviours, preferences, lifestyle information, transactional data and data about communications with the firm before, during and after the sale. It may include information about customer profitability, satisfaction, retention, loyalty and referrals.

More generally, data warehouses can be described in terms of the processes and layers needed to automate and add value to communications with the customer and to facilitate mass customization.

Data warehousing enables companies to extract information from the underlying data to develop a better understanding of the most profitable relationships, for example. Data mining relies on statistical modelling and the other tools discussed below to spot rules and patterns in customer information from the data warehouse.

A.3 Data mining

Data mining is a process that employs information technology – both hardware and software – to uncover previously unknown patterns of behaviour, trends and issues from the assessment of warehoused data.

The focus is on finding, for example, buying patterns that help marketers make better decisions. These data mining techniques may depend on a series of interactive, structured databases (data warehouse).

With the explosion in supermarket scanner data, techniques were developed to analyse supermarket sales data. The results portrayed the most important changes in a particular product's volume and market share. The reports often broke the results down by location, product type, price level or other factor. The most important element was the clear understandable business language used to write the reports. They offer real value to marketing managers. Since the initial efforts, factors such as distribution channels, price changes, promotional levels and competitive initiatives have been related to changes in volume, profits and share.

Still other knowledge tools have concentrated on the movement of retail stock at a point of sale. Such information can support decisions about shelf-space allocation, store layout, promotional effectiveness, product location and product turnover.

Databases can be centralized for common usage, distributed locally or widely for access by multiple users, and can apply to a single user.

A.4 The customer information file

The benefits of a customer information file in RM are as follows (Gordon, 1998).

- Marketing effort becomes more efficient and more effective because the marketer is able to identify the most important customers and then present them with the right offer, product, or service at the right time.
- Computer technology is harnessed to manage the vast amounts of data the marketer requires to interact with the customers in a truly personalized manner.
- A true 'dialogue' can be maintained with consumers by tracking interactions over time, identifying changes in purchasing, and allowing the marketer to anticipate future changes.
- New product development is facilitated by knowing who has purchased a product, how satisfied he or she is and whether any changes would enhance the performance of the product.

An example of a customer information file (from the B-t-B market) is presented in Table A.1 (only the most important data are shown):

Table A.1 An example of a B-t-B customer file

Identification	• account or identification number • company name • main telephone number/fax/e-mail • website address
Background	• business demography – industry classification code (SIC) • history of company • geography • financial data, e.g. sales, growth rate and profitability, both overall and for relevant products; cash flow; return on investment; operating profit on net sales • market position: market size for customer's products; market segment participation; market share; major customers. • suppliers: major suppliers to this company and duration of relationships • overall business strategies

▶

Table A.1 continued

Pre-sale contact	• number of contacts prior to purchases • types of information sought • channels of communication initiated by customer (telephone, Internet, interactive voice response etc.), by type of information sought • call history – personal sales calls, by date, by audience
Purchases	• purchase behaviour • frequency with which purchases are made (per day, week, month, year) • amount spent on purchases • average margin on customer's purchase
Decision makers	• names, titles • staff who have relationships with these people
Decision making	• process (buying centre) • decision initiators • decision influencers • decision makers • executors of decision • gatekeepers
Purchase cycle	• time required to make decision, by type of decision: new buy, modified re-buy and re-buy
Customer's buying criteria	• supplier selection criteria • product selection criteria • key selection and patronage criteria, overall company • perceptions of company in respect of criteria • perceptions of competitors in respect of criteria
Post-purchase behaviour	• services required • items returned • condition in which returned • purchase amounts of returned product • tone and manner of return, customer • customer complaint frequency, recency • customer satisfaction: overall and specific product/service
Distribution channels used by customers	• intermediaries used for product/service, type and name • customer satisfaction with channel intermediaries
Pricing	• pricing history • pricing expectations • win/loss assessments: prices of winning vendors
Creditworthiness	• debt history • receivables on account • payment schedule • credit scoring and rating

A.5   Linking market research to the decision-making process

Market research should be linked to the decision-making process within the firm. The recognition that a situation requires action is the initiating factor in the decision-making process.

Even though most firms recognize the need for domestic market research, this need is not fully understood for global marketing activities. Most SMEs conduct no international market research before they enter a foreign market. Often, decisions concerning entry and expansion in overseas markets and the selection and appointment of distributors are made after a subjective assessment of the situation. The research done is usually less rigorous, less formal and less quantitative than in LSEs. Furthermore, once an SME has entered a foreign market, it is likely to discontinue any research of that market. Many business executives therefore appear to view foreign market research as relatively unimportant.

A major reason that firms are reluctant to engage in global market research is the lack of sensitivity to cross-cultural customer tastes and preferences. What information should the global market research/DSS provide?

Table A.2 summarizes the principal tasks of global market research, according to the major decision phases of the global marketing process. As can be seen, both internal (firm-specific) and external (market) data are needed. The role of a firm's internal information system in providing data for marketing decisions is often forgotten.

How the different types of information affect the major decisions have been thoroughly discussed in the different parts and chapters of this book. As well as the split between internal and external data, the two major sources of information are primary data and secondary data.

Primary data

These can be defined as information that is collected first-hand, generated by original research tailor-made to answer specific current research questions. The major advantage of primary data is that the information is specific ('fine grained'), relevant and up to date. The disadvantages of primary data are, however, the high costs and amount of time associated with its collection.

Secondary data

These can be defined as information that has already been collected for other purposes and is thus readily available. The major disadvantage is that the data are often more general and 'coarse grained' in nature. The advantages of secondary data are the low costs and amount of time associated with its collection. For those who are unclear on the terminology, secondary research is frequently referred to as desk research.

The two basic forms of research (primary and secondary research) will be discussed in further detail later in this appendix.

If we combine the split of internal/external data with primary/secondary data, it is possible to place data in four categories. In Figure A.1 this approach is used to

Table A.2 Information needed for major global marketing decisions

Global marketing decision	Information needed
Deciding whether to internationalize	• Assessment of global market opportunities (global demand) for the firm's products • Commitment of the management to internationalize • Competences and competitiveness of the firm compared to local and internationalcompetitors • Domestic versus international market opportunities
Deciding which markets to enter	• Ranking of world markets according to market potential of countries/regions • Local competition • Political risks • Trade barriers (tariff and non-tariff barriers) • Cultural/psychic 'distance' to potential market
Deciding how to enter foreign markets	• Desired control, flexibility and risks • Nature of the product (standard versus complex product) • Size of markets/segments • Behaviour of potential intermediaries • Behaviour of local competition • Transport costs • Government requirements
Designing the global marketing programme	• Buyer behaviour (consumers and intermediaries) • Competitive practice • Available distribution channels • Media and promotional channels
Implementing and controlling the global marketing programme	• Negotiation styles in different cultures • Sales by product line, sales force, customer type and country/region • Contribution margins, financial metrics • Marketing expenses per market

categorize indicator variables for answering the following marketing questions. Is there a market for the firm's product A in country B? If yes, how large is it and what is the possible market share for the firm to obtain? Note that in Figure A.1 only a limited number of indicator variables are shown.

As a rule, no primary research should be done without first searching for relevant secondary information, and secondary data should be used whenever available and appropriate. Besides, secondary data often help to define problems and research objectives. In most cases, however, secondary sources cannot provide all the information needed and the company must collect primary data.

In Figure A.1 the most difficult and costly kind of data to obtain is probably the strengths and weaknesses of the firm (internal and primary data). However, because it compares the profile of the firm with those of its main competitors, this quadrant is a very important indicator of the firm's international competitiveness. The following two sections discuss different forms of secondary research and primary research.

Figure A.1 Catgorization of data for assessment of market potential in a country

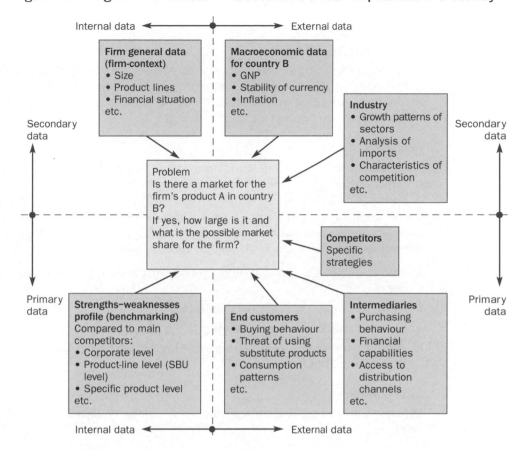

Source: Hollensen (2001), p. 629.

A.6 Secondary research

With many international markets to consider, it is essential that firms begin their market research by seeking and utilizing secondary data.

Advantages of secondary research

Secondary research conducted from the home base is less expensive and less time consuming than research conducted abroad. No contacts have to be made outside the home country, thus keeping commitment to possible future projects at a low level. Research undertaken in the home country about the foreign environment also has the benefit of objectivity. The researcher is not constrained by overseas customs. As a preliminary stage of a market-screening process, secondary research can quickly generate background information to eliminate many countries from the scope of enquiries.

Disadvantages of secondary research

Problems with secondary research are as follows.

Non-availability of data

In many developing countries, secondary data are very scarce. Weak economies have poor statistical services – many do not even carry out a population census. Information on retail and wholesale trade is especially difficult to obtain. In such cases, primary data collection becomes vital.

Reliability of data

Sometimes political considerations may affect the reliability of data. In some developing countries, governments may enhance the information to paint a rosy picture of the economic life in the country. In addition, due to the data collection procedures used, or the personnel who gathered the data, many data lack statistical accuracy. As a practical matter, the following questions should be asked to judge the reliability of data sources (Cateora, 1993, p. 346):

- who collected the data? Would there be any reason for purposely misrepresenting the facts?
- for what purpose was the data collected?
- how was the data collected (methodology)?
- are the data internally consistent and logical in the light of known data sources or market factors?

Data classification

In many countries, the data reported are too broadly classified for use at the micro level.

Comparability of data

International marketers often like to compare data from different countries. Unfortunately, the secondary data obtainable from different countries are not readily comparable because national definitions of statistical phenomena differ from one country to another.

Although the possibility of obtaining secondary data has increased dramatically, the international community has grown increasingly sensitive to the issue of data privacy. Readily accessible large-scale databases contain information valuable to marketers but considered sensitive by the individuals who have provided the data. The international marketer must therefore also pay careful attention to the privacy laws in different nations and to the possible consumer response to using such data. Neglecting these concerns may result in research backfiring and the corporate position being weakened.

In doing secondary research or building a decision support system, there are many information sources available. Generally, these secondary data sources can be divided into internal and external sources (Figure A.1). The latter can be classified as either international/global or regional/country-based sources.

Internal data sources

Internal company data can be a most fruitful source of information. However, it is often not utilized as fully as it should be.

The global marketing and sales departments are the main points of commercial interaction between an organization and its foreign customers. Consequently, a great deal of information should be available, including the following.

- Total sales. Every company keeps a record of its total sales over a defined time period: for example, weekly records, monthly records and so on.
- Sales by countries. Sales statistics should be split up by countries. This is partly to measure the progress and competence of the export manager or the salesperson (sometimes to influence earnings because commission may be paid on sales) and partly to measure the degree of market penetration in a particular country.
- Sales by products. Very few companies sell only one product. Most companies sell a range of products and keep records for each kind of product or, if the range is large, each product group.
- Sales volume by market segment. Such segmentation may be geographical or by type of industry. This will give an indication of segment trends in terms of whether they are static, declining or expanding.
- Sales volume by type of channel distribution. Where a company uses several different distribution channels, it is possible to calculate the effectiveness and profitability of each type of channel. Such information allows marketing management to identify and develop promising channel opportunities, and results in more effective channel marketing.
- Pricing information. Historical information relating to price adjustments by product allows the organization to establish the effect of price changes on demand.
- Communication mix information. This includes historical data on the effects of advertising campaigns, sponsorship and direct mail on sales. Such information can act as a guide to the likely effectiveness of future communication expenditure plans.
- Sales representatives' records and reports. Sales representatives should keep a record card or file on every 'live' customer. In addition, sales representatives often send reports to head office on such matters as orders lost to competitors and possible reasons why, as well as on firms that are planning future purchasing decisions. Such information could help to bring improvements in marketing strategy.

External data sources

A very basic method of finding international business information is to begin with a public library or a university library. The Internet can help in the search for data sources. The Internet has made available thousands of databases for intelligence research (i.e. research on competitors). In addition, electronic databases carry marketing information ranging from the latest news on product development to new thoughts in the academic and trade press and updates in international trade statistics. However, the Internet will not totally replace other sources of secondary data. Cost compared to data quality will still be a factor influencing a company's choice of secondary data sources.

Links to some relevant international data sources may be reached at **www.booksites.net/hollensen**.

A.7 Primary research

Qualitative and quantitative research

If a marketer's research questions are not adequately answered by secondary research, it may be necessary to search for additional information in primary data. These data can be collected by qualitative and quantitative research. Quantitative and qualitative techniques can be distinguished by the fact that quantitative techniques involve getting data from a large representative group of respondents.

The objective of qualitative research is to give a holistic view of the research problem, and therefore these techniques must have a large number of variables and few respondents (illustrated in Figure A.2). Choosing between quantitative and qualitative techniques is a question of trading off breadth and depth in the results of the analysis.

Other differences between the two research methodologies are summarized in Table A.3.

Data retrieval and analysis of quantitative data are based on a comparison of data between all respondents. This places heavy demands on the measuring instrument (the questionnaire), which must be well structured (with different answering categories) and tested before the survey takes place. All respondents are given identical stimuli: that is, the same questions. This approach will not usually give any problems, as long as the respondent group is homogeneous. However, if it is a heterogeneous group of respondents, it is possible that the same question will be understood in different ways. This problem becomes especially difficult in cross-cultural surveys.

Data retrieval and analysis of qualitative data, however, are characterized by a high degree of flexibility and adaptation to the individual respondent and his or her special background. Another considerable difference between qualitative and quantitative surveys is the source of data.

Quantitative techniques are characterized by a certain degree of distance as the construction of the questionnaire, data retrieval and data analysis take place in separate phases. Data retrieval is often done by people who have not had anything

Figure A.2 The trade-off in the choice between quantitative and qualitative research

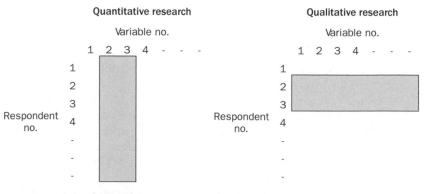

Source: Hollensen (2001), P. 632.

Table A.3 Quantitative versus qualitative research

Comparison dimension	Quantitative research (e.g. a postal questionnaire)	Qualitative research (e.g. a focus group interview or the case method
Objective	To quantify the data and generalize the results from the sample to the population of interest	To gain an initial and qualitative understanding of the underlying reasons and motives
Type of research	Descriptive and/or casual	Exploratory
Flexibility in research design	Low (as a result of a standardized and structured questionnaire: one-way communication)	High (as a result of the personal interview, where the interviewer can change questions during the interview: two-way communication)
Sample size	Large	Small
Choice of respondents	Representative sample of the population	Persons with considerable knowledge of the problem (key informants)
Information per respondent	Low	High
Data analysis	Statistical summarization	Subjective, interpretive
Ability to replicate with same result	High	Low
Interviewer requirements	No special skills required	Special skills required (an understanding of the interaction between interviewer and respondent)
Time consumption during the research	Design phase: high (formulation of questions must be correct) Analysis phase: low (the answers to the questions can be coded)	Design phase: low (no 'exact' questions are required before the interview) Analysis phase: high (as a result of much 'soft' data)

to do with the construction of the questionnaire. Here the measuring instrument (the questionnaire) is the critical element in the research process.

Qualitative techniques are characterized by proximity to the source of data, where data retrieval and analysis are done by the same person: namely, the interviewer. Data retrieval is characterized by interaction between the interviewer and the respondent, where each new question is to a certain degree dependent on the previous question. Here it is the interviewer and his or her competence which is the critical element in the research process.

Qualitative techniques imply a less sharp separation between data retrieval and analysis/interpretation, since data retrieval (for example, the next question in a personal interview) will be dependent on the interviewer's interpretation of the previous answer. The researcher's personal experience from field work (data retrieval) is generally a considerable input into the analysis phase.

It is often assumed that qualitative data requires no numbers. However, in for example focus groups the moderator often polls participants by hand votes or some form of rating or ranking exercise. Counting frequencies-of-mention, no matter how informal, is also a common qualitative technique, along with content analysis or mindmapping. The newer multivariate focus groups take this to a higher level and incorporate sophisticated analyses to help launch, guide and understand the discussion in a focus group (Wade, 2002).

The level of market information needed is dependent on the brand and the level of competition. In the lower left corner of Figure A.3, there is little competition and consequently only a little information is needed from market research. Information needs evolve according to the level of marketing sophistication, so in the upper right corner the information needs are extensive, and we will probably use a mixture of quantitative and qualitative research methods.

Qualitative research has now become a legitimate information source for decision makers in most areas of modern marketing. Its methodologies are now also commonly used in other areas of human activity, as well as commerce. The ubiquitous focus group has entered into the public domain and has become well established in market research.

Figure A.3 The evolution of market information needs

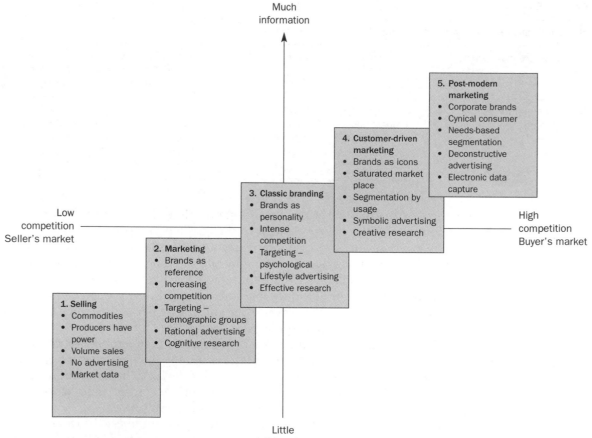

Source: Wright and Crimp (2000), p. 380.

Triangulation: mixing qualitative and quantitative research methods

The combined use of quantitative and qualitative research methods in the study of the same phenomenon is termed triangulation (Denzin, 1978; Jick, 1979). The triangulation metaphor is from navigation, where multiple reference points are used to locate an object's exact position. Similarly, market researchers can improve the accuracy and validity of their judgements by collecting both quantitative and qualitative data.

Sometimes it is relevant to use qualitative data collected by, for example, in-depth interview of a few key people as the exploratory input to the construction of the best possible questionnaire for the collection of data. In this way, triangulation can enrich our understanding of a research question before a structured and formalized questionnaire is designed.

The general stages in the market research process (integrating ethical issues) is shown in Figure A.4. Market research is conceptualized as a six step process (see Figure A.4) as outlined by Malhotra (1993).

From any one or all of these steps in the market research process, many different ethical dilemmas might arise – initiating the decision maker's entry into the first stage of the integrated model. The first step in the market research process is problem definition. This is a crucial step, as a well-defined problem is necessary for the research to be carried out efficiently and effectively. Ethical issues at this

Figure A.4 An integrated model for ethical decisions in market research

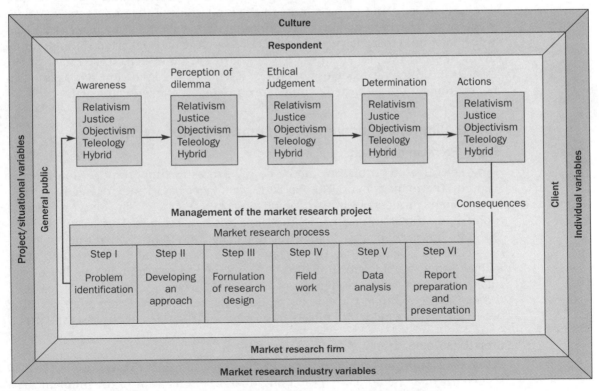

Source: adapted from Malhotra and Miller (1999), p. 218 with permission from Kluwer Academic Publishers.

stage might involve the researcher deciding whether to proceed with the research project if in defining the problem it comes to light that research or at least primary data collection is not necessary, or may be focused on whether the client chooses to disclose the true nature of the problem to the researcher and avoid withholding information.

Step two is concerned with developing an approach to the problem. At this point, attention is focused on things like case studies, simulations, developing hypotheses, models and research questions. Here the researcher should be sure to use information that is current and relevant.

Research design is the third step. This step encompasses everything from deciding on an exploratory, descriptive or causal design to secondary data sources, qualitative techniques, measurement and scaling, questionnaire design, and sampling techniques. Because this step includes several different activities, many ethical dilemmas can arise. Frequently occurring decisions might involve the researcher determining whether to inform respondents about the true purpose of the research at the start rather than debriefing them, or the misuse of focus groups due to the researcher treating the data as conclusive when they are not. There is also the issue of the client combining the research proposals submitted by different market research suppliers.

Data analysis is the fifth step. Ethical issues that commonly arise here are things like throwing out data that cause the analysis to give results other than what was hoped for, altering the results or the analysis to give the desired results, or using statistical techniques that are inappropriate for the data.

The final step is report preparation and presentation. Here ethical decisions may have to be made about the disclosure of the limitations of the project to the client, or avoiding misrepresentation of the findings. Thus, it should be recognized that ethical dilemmas that may exist in market research may be reflected throughout all the six steps of the process, just a few steps, or even one step. Since much of the research in ethics has made use of ethical dilemmas the following gives some further examples of the ethical dilemmas encountered in marketing research.

Ethical dilemmas encountered in marketing research

Step I: Problem definition

A market research problem could be defined so as to support a decision already made by the management. The marketing manager has already decided to introduce a new product without adequate market research. The market research problem is defined as how best to introduce this new product. This is done in spite of the preliminary analysis done by the researcher that indicates that the new product is likely to be a failure. The researcher thinks about advising the marketing manager that the problem should really be defined as determining whether or not the new product will succeed in the marketplace. However, given the enthusiasm of the marketing manager for the new product, the researcher refrains from pointing out that the new product is unlikely to succeed for fear of losing the assignment.

Step II: Developing an approach to the problem

While developing an approach to the problem the researcher makes use of secondary data, which are not current and only marginally relevant to the problem. In a project undertaken for a housebuilder the researcher has to estimate the population of high income households (annual household income more than $75,000) in 1994 in a given area. In doing so, the researcher makes use of the conveniently available 1990 population data knowing full well that there has been an influx of high income households into the area since 1990. Thus the 1990 population figures considerably underestimate the actual population in 1994. Furthermore, the 1990 data define a high income household as having an annual household income of more than $60,000 (rather than $75,000 required by the project), thus overestimating the number. The researcher concludes that these factors will compensate each other and does not report these sources of error to the client.

Step III: Formulation of research design

The client combines research proposals solicited from various market research suppliers to develop the best research design. Consider an instance where a toy manufacturer asked four research firms to develop competing approaches to the problem of researching attitudes of children toward toys. These four research firms develop competing research proposals including various theories, models, research questions, and data collection approaches. Obtaining information from children is an especially sensitive area. Research designs would tend to vary a great deal. These ideas are evaluated by the toy company, but instead of going with the best design the toy company uses the company that submits the lowest bid. This acceptance is contingent upon utilizing the best components of the other submitted research designs.

Step IV: Field work

The field work is conducted improperly. A field work agency contracted for data collection discovers that two of its interviewers have misunderstood some of the open ended questions and did not ask them properly. If the questionnaires administered by these interviewers are discarded, the agency will not be able to meet the deadline set in the contract. It would have to pay a penalty for the delay and perhaps lose favour with the client. So these questionnaires are not discarded but made part of the data set. Nothing is said to the client about this problem.

Step V: Data analysis

While the researcher realizes that non-metric regression rather than OLS (ordinary least square – a special statistical analysis which requires metric data) is the appropriate procedure, software to run non-metric regression is not available in-house and expertise is also lacking. So the data are analysed via OLS regression but the limitations of this analysis are not mentioned.

Step VI: Report preparation and presentation

Findings which seem intuitively implausible or which are difficult to explain are not reported. For example, in a study for a local bank, in one of the consumer banking segments, consumers are more willing to pay a higher monthly fee for a current account than a lower monthly fee.

Management of the market research project

There could be a conflict of interest in ownership of the research firm and management of the market research project. The market research firm contracted to assess the effectiveness of the current advertising campaign is a subsidiary of the advertising agency responsible for the advertising.

Research design

Figure A.5 shows that designing research for primary data collection calls for a number of decisions on research approaches, contact methods, sampling plan and research instruments. The following will look at the various elements of Figure A.5 in further detail.

Research problem/objectives

Companies are increasingly recognizing the need for primary international research. As the extent of a firm's international involvement increases, so does the importance and complexity of its international research. The primary research process should begin with a definition of the research problem and the establishment of specific objectives. The major difficulty here is translating the business problem into a research problem with a set of specific researchable objectives. In this initial stage, researchers often embark on the research process with only a vague grasp of the total problem. Symptoms are often mistaken for causes, and action determined by symptoms may be in the wrong direction.

Figure A.5 Primary data collection: research design

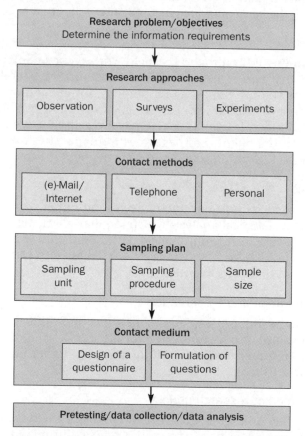

Source: Hollensen (2001), p. 635.

Research objectives may include obtaining detailed information for better penetrating the market, for designing and fine-tuning the marketing mix, or for monitoring the political climate of a country so that the firm can expand its operation successfully. The better defined the research objective is, the better the researcher will be able to determine the information requirement.

Research approaches

In Figure A.5 three possible research approaches are indicated: observation, surveys and experiments.

Observation

This approach to the generation of primary data is based on watching and sometimes recording market-related behaviour. Observational techniques are more suited to investigating what people do than why they do it. Here are some examples of this approach.

- Store checks: a food-products manufacturer sends researchers into supermarkets to find out the prices of competing brands or how much shelf space and display support retailers give its brands. To conduct in-store research in Europe, for example, store checks, photo audits of shelves and store interviews must be scheduled well in advance and need to be preceded by a full introduction of the researchers to store management and personnel.

- Mechanical observations are often used to measure TV viewership.

- Cash register scanners can be used to keep track of customer purchases and inventories.

Observational research can obtain information that people are unwilling or unable to provide. In some countries, individuals may be reluctant to discuss personal habits or consumption. In such cases, observation is the only way to obtain the necessary information. In contrast, some things are simply not observable, such as feelings, attitudes and motives, or private behaviour. Long-term or infrequent behaviour is also difficult to observe. Because of these limitations, researchers often use observation along with other data collection methods.

Experiments

Experiments gather casual information. They involve selecting matched groups of subjects, giving them different treatments, controlling unrelated factors and checking for differences in group responses. Thus experimental research tries to explain cause-and-effect relationships.

The most used market research application of experiments is in test marketing. This is a research technique in which a product under study is placed on sale in one or more selected localities or areas, and its reception by consumers and the trade is observed, recorded and analysed. In order to isolate, for example, the sales effects of advertising campaigns, it is necessary to use relatively self-contained marketing areas as test markets.

Performance in these test markets gives some indication of the performance to be expected when the product goes into general distribution. However, experiments are difficult to implement in global market research. The researcher faces the task of designing an experiment in which most variables are held constant or are comparable across cultures. To do so represents a major challenge. For example, an experiment that intends to determine a causal effect within the distribution system of one country may be difficult to transfer to another country, where the distribution system is different. As a result, experiments are used only rarely, even though their potential value to the international market researcher is recognized.

Surveys

The survey research method is based on the questioning of respondents and represents, both in volume and in value terms, perhaps the most important method of collecting data. Typically, the questioning is structured: a formal questionnaire is prepared and the questions are asked in a prearranged order. The questions may be asked verbally, in writing or via computer.

Survey research is used for a variety of marketing issues, including:

- customer attitudes
- customer buying habits
- potential market size
- market trends.

Unlike experimental research, survey research is usually aimed at generating descriptive rather than casual data. Unlike observational research, survey research usually involves the respondent.

Because of the importance and diversity of survey research in global marketing, it is on this particular aspect that we now concentrate.

Contact methods

The method of contact chosen is usually a balance between speed, degree of accuracy and costs. In principle, there are three possibilities when choosing a contact method: personal (face-to-face) interviews, telephone interviews and mail surveys. Each method has its own strengths and weaknesses. Table A.4 gives an overview of these.

Mail surveys

These can collect a large amount of data that can be quantified and coded into a computer. A low research budget combined with a widely dispersed population may mean that there is no alternative to the mail survey. However, the major problem is its potentially low response rate.

Telephone interviews

In some ways these are somewhere between personal and mail surveys. They generally have a response rate higher than mail questionnaires, but lower than face-to-face interviews; their cost is usually less than with personal interviews, and they allow a degree of flexibility when interviewing. However, the use of visual aids is not possible and there are limits to the number of questions that can be asked before respondents either terminate the interview or give quick (invalid) answers to speed up the process. The use of computer-aided telephone interviewing (CATI) is growing. Centrally located interviewers read questions from a computer monitor and input answers via the keyboard. Routing through the questionnaire is computer controlled, helping the process of interviewing. Some research firms set

Table A.4 Strengths and weaknesses of the three contact methods

Questions/questionnaire	Internet/mail	Telephone	Personal
Flexibility (ability to clarify problems)	Poor	Good	Excellent
Possibility of in-depth information (use of open-ended questions)	Fair	Fair	Excellent
Use of visual aids	Good	Poor	Good
Possibility of a widely dispersed sample	Excellent	Excellent	Fair
Response rates	Poor	Good	Good
Ask sensitive questions (anonymity of respondent is assumed)	Good	Poor	Fair
Control of interviewer effects (no interviewer bias)	Excellent	Fair	Poor
Speed of data collection	Poor	Excellent	Good
Costs	Good	Excellent	Poor

up terminals in shopping centres, where respondents sit down at a terminal, read questions from a screen and type their answers into the computer.

Personal interviews

Personal interviews take two forms – individual and group interviewing. Individual interviewing involves talking with people in their homes or offices, in the street, or in shopping arcades. The interviewer must gain the cooperation of the respondents. Group interviewing (focus groups) consists of inviting six to ten people to gather for a few hours with a trained moderator to talk about a product, service or organization. The moderator needs objectivity, knowledge of the subject and industry, and some understanding of group and consumer behaviour. The participants are normally paid a small sum for attending.

Personal interviewing is quite flexible and can collect large amounts of information. Trained interviewers can hold a respondent's attention for a long time and can explain difficult questions. They can guide interviews, explore issues and probe as the situation requires. Interviewers can show subjects actual products, advertisements or packages, and observe reactions and behaviour.

The main drawbacks of personal interviewing are the high costs and sampling problems. Group interview studies usually employ small sample sizes to keep time and costs down, but it may be hard to generalize from the results. Because interviewers have more freedom in personal interviews, the problem of interviewer bias is greater.

Thus, there is no 'best' contact method – it all depends on the situation. Sometimes it may even be appropriate to combine the three methods.

Sampling plan

Except in very restricted markets, it is both impractical and too expensive for a researcher to contact all the people who could have some relevance to the research problem. This total number is known statistically as the 'universe' or 'population'. In marketing terms, it comprises the total number of actual and potential users or customers of a particular product or service.

The population can also be defined in terms of elements and sampling units. Suppose that a lipstick manufacturer wants to assess the consumer response to a new line of lipsticks and wants to sample females over fifteen years of age. It may be possible to sample females of this age directly, in which case a sampling unit would be the same as an element. Alternatively, households might be sampled and all females over fifteen in each selected household then interviewed. Here, the sampling unit is the household, and the element is a female over fifteen years old.

What is usually done in practice is to contact a selected group of consumers/customers to be representative of the entire population. The total number of consumers who could be interviewed is known as the 'sample frame', while the number of people who are actually interviewed is known as the 'sample'.

Sampling procedure

There are several kinds of sampling procedure: probability and non-probability sampling.

In probability sampling, it is possible to specify in advance the chance that each element in the population will have of being included in a sample, although there is not necessarily an equal probability for each element. Examples are simple random sampling, systematic sampling, stratified sampling and cluster sampling (see Malhotra (1993) for more information).

With non-probability sampling, it is not possible to determine the probability or to estimate the sampling error. These procedures rely on the personal judgement of the researcher. Examples are convenience sampling, quota sampling and snowball sampling (see Malhotra (1993) for more information).

Given the disadvantages of non-probability samples (results cannot be projected to the total population, and sampling error cannot be computed), one may wonder why they are used so frequently by market researchers. The reasons relate to the inherent advantages of non-probability sampling:

- non-probability samples cost less than probability samples.
- if accuracy is not critical, non-probability sampling may have considerable appeal.
- non-probability sampling can be conducted more quickly than probability sampling.
- non-probability sampling, if executed properly, can produce samples of the population that are reasonably representative (e.g. by use of quota sampling) (Malhotra, 1993, p. 359).

Sample size

Once we have chosen the sampling procedure, the next step is to determine the appropriate sample size. Determining the sample size is a complex decision and involves financial, statistical and managerial considerations. Other things being equal, the larger the sample, the less the sampling error. However, larger samples cost more money, and the resources (money and time) available for a particular research project are always limited.

In addition, though, the cost of larger samples tends to increase on a linear basis, whereas the level of sampling error decreases at a rate only equal to the square root of the relative increase in sample size. For example, if sample size is quadrupled, data collection costs will be quadrupled too, but the level of sampling error will be reduced by only one-half. Among the methods for determining the sample size are:

- traditional statistical techniques (assuming the standard normal distribution).
- budget available. Although seemingly unscientific, this is a fact of life in a business environment based on the budgeting of financial resources. This approach forces the researcher to consider carefully the value of information in relation to its cost.
- rules of thumb. The justification for a specified sample size may boil down to a 'gut feeling' that this is an appropriate sample size, or it may be a result of common practice in the particular industry.
- number of subgroups to be analysed. Generally speaking, the more subgroups that need to be analysed, the larger the required total sample size.

In transnational market research, sampling procedures become a rather complicated matter. Ideally, a researcher wants to use the same sampling method for all countries in order to maintain consistency. Sampling desirability, however, often gives way to practicality and flexibility. Sampling procedures may have to vary across countries to ensure reasonable comparability of national groups. Thus, the relevance of a sampling method depends on whether it will yield a sample that is representative of a target group in a certain country, and on whether comparable samples can be obtained from similar groups in different countries.

Contact medium/measurement instrument

Designing the questionnaire

A good questionnaire cannot be designed until the precise information requirements are known. It is the vehicle whereby the research objectives are translated into specific questions. The type of information sought, and the type of respondents to be researched, will have a bearing upon the contact method to be used, and this in turn will influence whether the questionnaire is relatively unstructured (with **open-ended questions**) aimed at in-depth interviewing, or relatively structured (with closed questions) for on the street interviews.

In cross-cultural studies open-ended questions appear useful because they may help to identify the frame of reference of the respondents. Another issue is the choice between direct and indirect questions. Societies have different degrees of sensitivity to certain questions. Questions related to the income or age of the respondent may be accepted differently in different countries. Thus, the researcher must be sure that the questions are culturally acceptable. This may mean that questions that can be asked directly in some societies will have to be asked indirectly in others.

Formulation (wording) of questions

Once the researcher has decided on specific types of question, the next task is the actual writing of the questions. Four general guidelines are useful to bear in mind during the wording and sequencing of each question.

1. The wording must be clear. For example, try to avoid two questions in one.

2. Select words so as to avoid biasing the respondent. For example, try to avoid leading questions.

3. Consider the ability of the respondent to answer the question. For example, asking respondents about a brand or store that they have never encountered creates a problem. Since respondents may be forgetful, time periods should be relatively short. For example: 'Have you purchased one or more cola(s) in the last week?'

4. Consider the willingness of the respondent to answer the question. Embarrassing topics that deal with things like borrowing money, sexual activities and criminal records must be dealt with in a careful manner. One technique is to ask the question in the third person or to state that the behaviour or attitude is not unusual prior to asking the question. For example: 'Millions of people suffer from haemorrhoids. Do you or does any member of your family suffer from this problem?'

The impact of language and culture is of particular importance when wording questions. The goal for the global market researcher should be to ensure that the potential for misunderstandings and misinterpretations of spoken or written words is minimized. Both language and cultural differences make this issue an extremely sensitive one in the global market research process.

In many countries, different languages are spoken in different areas. In Switzerland, German is used in some areas and French and Italian in others. As we have seen, the meaning of words often differs from country to country. For example, in the USA the concept of 'family' generally refers only to the parents and children. In southern Europe, the Middle East and many Latin countries, it may also include grandparents, uncles, aunts, cousins and so forth.

When evaluating the questionnaire, the following items should be considered:

● is a certain question necessary? The phrase 'it would be nice to know' is often heard, but each question should either serve a purpose or be omitted.

● is the questionnaire too long?

● will the questions achieve the survey objectives?

Pre-testing

No matter how comfortable and experienced the researcher is in international research activities, an instrument should always be pre-tested. Ideally, such a pre-test should be carried out with a subset of the population under study, but a pre-test should at least be conducted with knowledgeable experts and/or individuals. The pre-test should also be conducted in the same mode as the final interview. If the study is to be on the street or in a shopping arcade, then the pre-test should be the same. Even though a pre-test may mean time delays and additional cost, the risks of poor research are simply too great for this process to be omitted.

Data collection

The global market researcher must check that the data are gathered correctly, efficiently and at a reasonable cost. The market researcher has to establish the parameters under which the research is conducted. Without clear instructions the interviews may be conducted in different ways by different interviewers. Therefore, the interviewers have to be instructed about the nature of the study, start and completion time, and sampling methodology. Sometimes a sample interview is included with detailed information on probing and quotas. Spot checks on these administration procedures are vital to ensure reasonable data quality.

Data analysis and interpretation

Once data have been collected, the final steps are the analysis and interpretation of findings in the light of the stated problem. Analysing data from cross-country studies calls for substantial creativity as well as scepticism. Not only are data often limited, but frequently results are significantly influenced by cultural differences. This suggests that there is a need for properly trained local personnel to function as supervisors and interviewers; alternatively the international market researchers require substantial advice from knowledgeable local research firms, which can also take care of the actual collection of data. Although data in cross-country analyses are often of a qualitative nature, the researcher should, of course, use the best and most appropriate tools available for analysis. On the other hand, international researchers should be cautioned against using overly sophisticated tools for unsophisticated data. Even the best of tools will not improve data quality. The quality of data must be matched with the quality of the research tools.

Problems with using primary research

Non-response

Non-response is the inability to reach selected elements in the sample frame. As a result, opinions of the sample elements who do not respond are not obtained or properly represented. A good sampling method can only identify elements who should be selected; there is no guarantee that such elements will ever be included.

The two main reasons for non-response errors are as follows. Not being at home. In countries where males are still dominant in the labour force, it may be difficult to contact a head of household at home during working hours. Frequently, only housewives or servants are home during the day.

Cultural habits in many countries virtually prohibit communication with a stranger, particularly for women. This is the case in the Middle East, much of the Mediterranean area and throughout most of south-east Asia – in fact, wherever strong traditional societies persist. Moreover, in many societies such matters as preferences for hygienic products and food products are too personal to be shared with an outsider. For example, in many Latin American countries, a woman may feel ashamed to talk with a researcher about her choice of a brand of sanitary towels, or even hair shampoo or perfume. Respondents may also suspect that the interviewers are agents of the government, seeking information for the imposition of additional taxes. Finally, privacy is becoming a big issue in many countries: for example, in Japan the middle class is showing increasing concern about the protection of personal information.

Measurement

The best research design is useless without proper measurements. A measurement method that works satisfactorily in one culture may fail to achieve the intended purpose in another country. Special care must therefore be taken to ensure the reliability and validity of the measurement method.

If we measure the same phenomenon over and over again with the same measurement device and we get similar results, then the method is reliable. There are two types of validity: internal and external.

Internal validity

If a measurement method lacks (internal) validity, it is not measuring what it is supposed to. The concepts of reliability and validity are illustrated in Figure A.6. In the diagram, the bull's eye is what the measurement device is supposed to hit.

Situation 1 shows holes all over the target. It could be due to the use of a bad measurement device. If a measurement instrument is not reliable, there are no circumstances under which it can be valid. However, just because an instrument is reliable, the instrument is not automatically valid. We see this in situation 2, where the instrument is reliable but is not measuring what it is supposed to measure. Situation 3 is the ideal situation for the researcher to be in. The measurement method is both reliable and valid.

An instrument proven to be reliable and valid in one country may not be so in another culture. The same measurement scales may have different reliabilities in different cultures because of various levels of consumers' product knowledge. Therefore, it may be dangerous simply to compare results in cross-country research. One way to minimize the problem is to adapt measurement scales to local cultures by pre-testing measures in each market of interest until they show similar and satisfactory levels of reliability.

External validity

External validity is concerned with the possible generalization of research results to other populations. For example, high external validity exists if research results obtained for a marketing problem in one country will be applicable to a similar marketing problem in another country. If such a relationship exists, it may be relevant to use the analogy method for estimating market demand in different countries. Estimating by analogy assumes, for example, that the demand for a product develops in much the same way in countries that are similar.

Figure A.6 Illustrations of possible reliability and validity situations in measurement

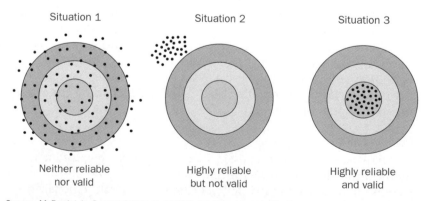

| Exhibit A.1 | Gathering and interpreting information in the Asia-Pacific region |

The Asia-Pacific market has been highlighted as a key market area for the coming decade, so obtaining reliable information in the region is of crucial importance to companies wishing to develop these markets. However, a recent survey by Lasserre (1993), with results from 167 European marketing and planning executives operating in the Asia-Pacific region, found that only in Japan, Singapore and Hong Kong were companies able easily to access data that were viewed as being of good quality.

Vietnamese data, in particular, are not trusted by researchers. The fact that Vietnam is characterized by an almost total lack of reliable data on virtually every aspect of doing business is confirmed by Dang and Speece (1996). The infrastructure to support market research is very bad in Vietnam. For example, telephones are rare and government development reached a telephone density of just 5 per cent by 2001. As mail is also a very difficult and slow contact method, face-to-face interviews seem to be the only way to learn something about what potential Vietnamese customers think and want.

The most important data sources in the Asia-Pacific region are the personal sources of companies (primary research, whether from customers, from other business relations, or from their own in-house surveys). The importance of primary research confirms the widely held opinion that business in the Asia-Pacific region depends more heavily on the network of personal relationships than on analysis of hard data (secondary research).

This pattern is valid from country to country, with the exception of Japan, where secondary data are both accessible and of good quality. The only problem for western firms here seems to be the cost of acquiring it. Government data sources are also important in Singapore. Generally, however, personal contacts and in-house surveys are very important data sources in the Asia-Pacific region.

Sources: Dang and Speece (1996); Lasserre (1993).

A.8 Other types of market research

A distinction is made between ad-hoc and continuous research.

Ad-hoc research

An ad-hoc study focuses on a specific marketing problem and collects data at one point in time from one sample of respondents. Examples of ad-hoc studies are usage and attitude surveys, and product and concept tests via custom-designed or multi-client studies. More general marketing problems (e.g. total market estimates for product groups) may be examined by use of Delphi studies (see below).

Custom-designed studies

These are based on the specific needs of the client. The research design is based on the research brief given to the marketing research agency or internal marketing researcher. Because they are tailor-made, such surveys can be expensive.

Multi-client studies

These are a relatively low-cost way for a company to answer specific questions without embarking on its own primary research. There are two types of multi-client study.

Independent research studies are carried out totally independently by research companies (e.g. Frost and Sullivan) and then offered for sale.

With **omnibus studies**, a research agency will target specified segments in a particular foreign market and companies will buy questions in the survey. Consequently, interviews (usually face-to-face or by telephone) may cover many topics. Clients will then receive an analysis of the questions purchased. For omnibus studies to be of use, the researcher must have clearly defined research needs and a corresponding target segment in order to obtain meaningful information.

Delphi studies

This type of research approach clearly aims at qualitative rather than quantitative measures by aggregating the information of a group of experts. It seeks to obtain answers from those who possess particular in-depth expertise instead of seeking the average responses of many with only limited knowledge.

The area of concern may be future developments in the international trading environment or long-term forecasts for market penetration of new products. Typically, 10–30 key informants are selected and asked to identify the major issues in the area of concern. They are also requested to rank their statements according to importance and explain the rationale behind the ranking. Next, the aggregated information is returned to all participants, who are encouraged to state clearly their agreements or disagreements with the various rank orders and comments. Statements can be challenged and then, in another round, participants can respond to the challenges. After several rounds of challenge and response, a reasonably coherent consensus is developed.

One drawback of the technique is that it requires several steps, and therefore months may elapse before the information is obtained. However, the emergence of e-mail may accelerate the process. If done properly, the Delphi method can provide insightful forecast data for the international information system of the firm.

Sales forecasting

A company can forecast its sales either by forecasting the market sales (called market forecasting) and then determining what share of this will accrue to the company or by forecasting the company's sales directly. Techniques for doing this are dealt with later in the appendix. The point is that planners are only interested in forecasts when the forecast comes down to individual products in the company.

We shall now examine the applicability and usefulness of the short-, medium- and long-term forecasts in so far as company planners are concerned and shall then look at each from individual company departmental viewpoints.

Short-term forecasts

These are usually for periods up to three months ahead, and as such are really of use for tactical matters such as production planning. The general trend of sales is less important here than short-term fluctuations.

Medium-term forecasts

These have direct implications for planners. They are of most importance in the area of business budgeting, the starting point for which is the sales forecast. Thus if the sales forecast is incorrect, then the entire budget is incorrect. If the forecast is over-optimistic, then the company will have unsold stock which must be financed out of working capital. If the forecast is pessimistic, then the firm may miss out on marketing opportunities because it is not geared up to produce the extra goods required by the market.

When forecasting is left to accountants, they will tend to err on the conservative side and will produce a forecast that is less than actual sales, the implications of which have just been described. This serves to re-emphasize the point that sales forecasting is the responsibility of the sales manager. Such medium-term forecasts are normally for one year ahead.

Long-term forecasts

These are usually for periods of three years and upwards depending upon the type of industry being considered. In industries such as computers three years is considered long term, whereas for steel manufacture ten years is long term. They are worked out from macro-environmental factors such as government policy, economic trends, etc.

Such forecasts are needed mainly by financial accountants for long-term resource implications, but such matters of course are board of directors' concerns. The board must decide what its policy is to be in establishing the levels of production needed to meet the forecast demand; such decisions might mean the construction of a new factory and the training of a workforce. Forecasts can be produced for different time scales starting at an international level, and then ranging down to national levels, by industry and then by company levels until we reach individual product-by-product forecasts. This is then broken down seasonally over the time span of the forecasting period, and geographically right down to individual salespeople. It is these latter levels that are of specific interest to sales management, or it is from this level of forecasting that the sales budgeting and remuneration system stems.

Figure A.7 shows an example of trend forecasting. The unit sales and trend are drawn in as in Figure A.7. The trend line is extended by sight (and it is here that

Figure A.7 An example of trend forecasting

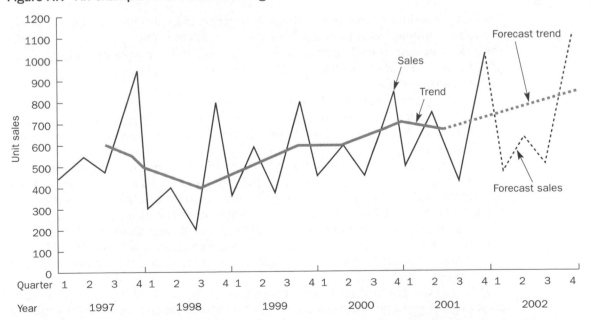

the forecaster's skill and intuition must come in). The deviations from trend are then applied to the trend line, and this provides the sales forecast.

In this particular example it can be seen that the trend line has been extended on a slow upwards trend similar to previous years. The technique, like many similar techniques, suffers from the fact that downturns and upturns cannot be predicted, and such data must be subjectively entered by the forecaster through manipulation of the extension to the trend line.

Continuous research (longitudinal designs)

A longitudinal design differs from ad-hoc research in that the sample or panel remains the same over time. In this way, a longitudinal study provides a series of pictures which give an in-depth view of developments taking place. The panel consists of a sample of respondents, who have agreed to provide information at specified intervals over an extended period.

There are two major types of panel. Consumer panels provide information on their purchases over time. For example, a grocery panel would record the brands, pack sizes, prices and stores used for a wide range of supermarket brands. By using the same households over a period of time, measures of brand loyalty and switching can be achieved together with a demographic profile of the type of person or household who buys particular brands.

Retailer panels can be set up by gaining the cooperation of retail outlets (e.g. supermarkets), and sales of brands can be measured by scanning the bar codes on goods as they pass through the checkout. Although brand loyalty and switching cannot be measured in this way, retail audits can provide accurate assessments of sales achieved by store. A major provider of retail data is A.C. Nielsen.

A.9 Summary

The basic objective of the market research function is to provide management with relevant information for more accurate decision making. The objective is the same for both domestic and global marketing. However, global marketing is more complex because of the difficulty of gathering information about multiple different foreign environments.

In this appendix, special attention has been given to the information collection process and the use of marketing information. This coverage is far from being exhaustive, and the reader should consult market research textbooks for specific details related to particular research topics.

Customer data warehouses can be defined as the relevant information about customers, e.g. their buying behaviour, lifestyle, transactional data, etc. Other marketing applications are more descriptive and focus on finding patterns that help marketers make better decisions. Such techniques are often called *data mining*.

An international marketer should initiate research by searching first for any relevant secondary data. Typically, a great deal of information is already available, and the researcher needs to know how to identify and locate the international sources of secondary data.

If it is necessary to gather primary data, the international marketer should be aware that it is simply not possible to replicate elsewhere the methodology used in one country. Some adaptation of the research method to different countries is usually necessary.

The firm should set up a decision support system to handle the information gathered efficiently. This system should integrate all information inputs, both internal and external. However, in the final analysis, every international marketer should keep in mind that an information system is no substitute for sound judgement.

QUESTIONS FOR DISCUSSION

1. Explore the reasons for using a marketing information system in the international market. What are the main types of information you would expect to use?
2. What are some of the problems that a global marketing manager can expect to encounter when creating a centralized marketing information system? How can these problems be solved?
3. What are the dangers of translating questionnaires that have been designed for one country for use in a multi-country study? How would you avoid these dangers?
4. Identify and classify the major groups of factors that must be taken into account when conducting a foreign market assessment.
5. What is the difference between 'data warehousing' and 'data mining'?
6. Identify and discuss the major considerations in deciding whether research should be centralized or decentralized.
7. Distinguish between internal and external validity. What are the implications of external validity for international marketers?
8. Would Tokyo be a good test market for a new brand planned to be marketed worldwide? Explain your reasoning.
9. If you had a contract to do market research in Saudi Arabia, what problems would you expect in obtaining primary data?
10. Do demographic variables have universal meanings? Is there a chance that they may be interpreted differently in different cultures?
11. In forecasting sales in international markets, to what extent can the past be used to predict the future?
12. How should the firm decide whether to gather its own intelligence or to buy it from outside?

REFERENCES

Cateora, P. R. (1993), *International Marketing*, Irwin, Homewood, IL, 8th edn.
Dang, T. and Speece, M. (1996), Marketing research in Vietnam, *Journal of International Marketing and Marketing Research*, vol. 21, no. 3, pp. 145–61.
Denzin, N. K. (1978), *The Research Act*, McGraw-Hill, New York, 2nd edn.
Gordon, I. (1998), *Relationship Marketing*, Wiley.
Hollensen, S. (2001), *Global Marketing: A market responsive approach*, Financial Times/Prentice Hall, Harlow, 2nd edn.
Jick, T. D. (1979), Mixing qualitative and quantitative methods: triangulation in action, *Administrative Science Quarterly*, vol. 24, December, pp. 602–11.
Lasserre, P. (1993), Gathering and interpreting strategic intelligence in Asia Pacific, *Long Range Planning*, vol. 26, no. 3, pp. 55–66.

Malhotra, N. K. (1993), *Marketing Research: An applied orientation*, Prentice-Hall, Englewood Cliffs, NJ.

Malhotra, N. K. and Miller, G. L. (1999), Social responsibility and the marketing educator: a focus on stakeholders, ethical theories, and related codes of ethics, *Journal of Business Ethics*, vol. 19, no. 2, pp. 211–24.

McDaniel Jr, S. and Gates, R. (1993), *Contemporary Market Research: An applied orientation*, Prentice-Hall, Englewood Cliffs, NJ.

Wade, K. (2002), Focus groups' research role is shifting, *Marketing News*, 4 March, p. 47.

Wright, L. T. and Crimp, M. (2000), *The Marketing Research Process*, Financial Times/Prentice Hall, Harlow, 5th edn.

Glossary

above-the-line advertising Advertising in the mass media, including press, radio, television, and posters.

account manager A manager who is responsible for taking care of the total relationship with a special group of customers, or sometimes only one customer.

adoption process The mental and behavioural stages through which a consumer passes before making a purchase or placing an order. The stages are awareness, interest, evaluation, trial, and adoption.

advertising Nonpersonal communication that is paid for by an identified sponsor, and involves either mass communication via newspapers, magazines, radio, television, and other media (e.g. billboards, bus stop signage) or direct-to-consumer communication via direct mail.

advertising agency A marketing services firm that assists companies in planning, preparing, implementing, and evaluating all or portions of their advertising programmes.

advertising objective A specific communication task to be accomplished with a specific target audience during a specific period of time.

affordable approach Setting the promotion budget at the level management thinks the company can afford.

agent A marketing intermediary who does not take title to the products but develops a marketing strategy and establishes contacts abroad.

AIDA Awareness, interest, desire, action – the stages through which a consumer is believed to pass before purchasing a product.

allowance Promotional money paid by manufacturers to retailers in return for an agreement to feature the manufacturer's products in some way.

always-a-share customers Customers who have low switching costs and do not value long-term relationships with suppliers, making them more suited to transaction marketing.

baby boom The major increase in the annual birth rate following World War II and lasting until the early 1960s. The 'baby boomers,' now moving into middle age, are a prime target for marketers.

below-the-line promotion Point-of-sale material, direct mail, exhibitions, i.e. any promotion which does not involve paid-for media channels.

benchmarking The process of comparing the company's products and processes to those of competitors or leading firms in other industries to find ways to improve quality and performance.

benefit segments Dividing the market into groups according to the different benefits that consumers seek from the product.

bottom-up method A sales forecasting method that starts with small-scale estimates (for example, product estimates) and works up to larger-scale ones. See also *break-down method*.

brand An identifying feature that distinguishes one product from another; more specifically, any name, term, symbol, sign, or design or a unifying combination of these.

brand equity The value of a brand, based on the extent to which it has high brand loyalty, name awareness, perceived quality, strong brand associations, and other assets such as patents, trademarks, and channel relationships.

brand extension Using a successful brand name to launch a new or modified product in a new category.

break-even analysis The calculation of the quantity needed to be sold to cover total costs.

break-even pricing Setting price to break even on the costs of making and marketing a product; or setting price to make a target profit.

bricks and mortar Physical retail stores.

broker A wholesaler who does not take title to goods and whose function is to bring buyers and sellers together and assist in negotiation.

browser Computer program such as Netscape Navigator or Microsoft Internet Explorer that enables users to view web pages.

business cycle Recurrent fluctuations in general economic activity. The four phases of the business cycle are prosperity, recession, depression, and recovery.

business model The fundamental strategy underlying the way a business unit operates.

business-to-business (B-t-B) Marketing which involves exchange relationships between two or more business customers and suppliers.

business-to-consumer (B-t-C) Marketing which involves exchange relationships between a firm and its end customers, perhaps via retailers.

buying centre A group who are involved in the buying decision. Also known as a decision-making unit (DMU).

bypass attack Circumventing the defender's position, usually through technological leap-frogging or diversification.

cannibalization A situation where a new brand gains sales at the expense of another of the company's brands.

cash cow A high market share product in a low-growth market.

category management The management of brands in a group, portfolio or category with specific emphasis on the retail trade's requirements.

chain store One of a group of two or more stores of a similar type, centrally owned and operated.

CI Competitor intelligence.

channel conflict Disagreement among marketing channel members on goals and roles – who should do what and for what rewards. A significant threat arising from the introduction of an Internet channel is that while disintermediation gives the opportunity for a company to sell direct and increase the profitability of products it also threatens distribution arrangements with existing partners.

channel member A layer of intermediaries that performs some work in bringing the product and its ownership closer to the final buyer.

clicks and mortar Online retailers who also have physical retail stores.

closing The step in the selling process in which the salesperson asks the customer for an order.

co-branding The practice of using the established brand of two different companies on the same product.

cognitive dissonance Buyer discomfort caused by post-purchase conflict.

competitive parity method Setting the promotion budget to match competitors' outlays.

competitor analysis The process of identifying key competitors; assessing their objectives, strategies, strengths and weaknesses, and reaction patterns; and selecting which competitors to attack or avoid.

contract manufacturing An agreement by which a domestic company allows a foreign producer to manufacture its product according to its specifications. Typically, the domestic company then handles foreign sales of the product.

control The process by which managers ensure that planned activities are completely and properly executed.

convenience product A relatively inexpensive, regularly purchased consumer product bought without much thought and with a minimum of shopping effort.

convenience store A small grocery store stressing convenient location and quick service and typically charging higher prices than other retailers selling similar products.

cookies Bits of information about website visitors created by websites and stored on client computers.

core competences The principal distinctive capabilities possessed by a company – what it is really good at.

cost leadership The achievement of the lowest cost position in an industry, serving many segments

cost per thousand (CPM) Calculated by dividing the cost of an ad placed in a particular advertising vehicle (e.g. certain magazine) by the number of people (expressed in thousands) who are exposed to that vehicle.

criteria for successful segmentation Includes target markets that are heterogeneous, substantial, actionable, and accessible.

cross-functional team A team made up of individuals from various organizational departments who share a common purpose.

cross-selling Marketing activities used to sell new services to customers of an existing service.

CRM Customer relationship management.

customer lifetime value The amount by which revenue from a given customer over time will exceed the company's costs of attracting, selling, and servicing that customer.

customer value The difference between the values the customer gains from owning and using a product and the costs of obtaining the product.

database marketing An interactive approach to marketing which uses individually addressable marketing media and channels to provide information to a target audience, stimulate demand and stay close to customers.

data warehousing (or mining) The storage and analysis of customer data gathered from their visits to websites for classification and modelling purposes so that products, promotions and price can be tailored to the specific needs of individual customers. The use of powerful computers to work through large volumes of data to discover purchasing patterns among an organization's customers.

decider The buying-centre role played by the organizational member who makes the actual purchasing decision.

decision support system A computer system that stores data and transforms them into accessible information. It includes databases and software.

demographics Measures such as age, gender, race, occupation, and income that are often used as a basis for selecting focus group members and market segments.

derived demand Demand for a product that depends on demand for another product.

diffusion The spread of a new product through society.

disintermediation The elimination of a layer of intermediaries from a marketing channel or the displacement of traditional resellers by radically new types of intermediaries.

diversification The market and product development strategy that involves expansion to a relatively large number of markets and products.

divest To improve short-term cash yield by dropping or selling off the product.

DMU (decision making unit): often identical with the buying centre in B-t-B. The initiator, the decider, the influencers, the purchaser, the gatekeeper, and the users.

early adopter A member of the group of consumers who purchase a product soon after it has been introduced, but after the innovators have purchased it.

early majority A group of consumers, usually solid, middle-class people, who purchase more deliberately and cautiously than early adopters.

e-commerce Electronic commerce or business dealings using electronic media, such as the Internet.

economies of scale and economies of scope Obtained by spreading the costs of distribution over a large quantity of products (scale) or over a wide variety of products (scope).

EDI Electronic data interchange, electronic links between suppliers and retailers allowing purchase orders, packing lists, delivery.

effectiveness Doing the right thing, making the correct strategic choice.

efficiency A way of managing business processes to a high standard, usually concerned with cost reduction.

electronic commerce (e-commerce) The general term for a buying and selling process that is supported by electronic means.

entrepreneur A risk-taking individual who sees an opportunity and is willing to undertake a venture to create a new product or service.

e-tailers Online retailers.

exclusive distribution An extreme form of selective distribution where only one wholesaler, retailer or industrial distributor is used in a geographical area to sell products of a supplier.

exhibition An event which brings buyers and sellers together in a commercial setting.

exit barrier The barriers to leaving an industry, e.g. cost of closing down plant.

experience curve (learning curve) The drop in the average per-unit production cost that comes with accumulated production experience.

extranet Connects computers outside the firm with the intranet at the firm. The portions of an organization's intranet that are shared by external collaborators, such as suppliers or customers.

fads Fashions that enter quickly are adopted with great zeal, peak early, and decline very fast.

family life cycle A series of stages through which most families pass.

four Ps of marketing The basic elements of the marketing mix: product, place (distribution), price, and promotion; also called the controllable variables of marketing, because they can be controlled and manipulated by the marketer.

franchise A contractual association between a manufacturer, wholesaler, or service organization (a franchiser) and independent businesspeople (franchisees) who buy the right to own and operate one or more units in the franchise system.

gap analysis A technique which compares future likely company performance against desired performance outcomes in order to identify any gaps.

gatekeeper Those who control the flow of information, e.g. secretaries who may allow or prevent access to a DMU member, or a buyer whose agreement must be sought before a supplier can contact other members of the DMU.

generic product, or generic brand A product that carries neither a manufacturer nor a distributor brand. The goods are plainly packaged with stark lettering that simply lists the contents.

global firm A firm that by operating in more than one country gains marketing, production, R&D, and financial advantages in its costs and reputation that are not available to purely domestic competitors.

green marketing Marketing ecologically sound products and promoting activities beneficial to the physical environment.

grey markets The marketing of authentic, legally trademarked goods through unauthorized channels.

gross margin The difference between net sales and cost of goods sold.

gross national product (GNP) The total value of all the goods and services produced by a nation's residents or corporations, regardless of their location.

gross rating points (GRPs) The accumulation of rating points including all vehicles in a media purchase over the span of a particular campaign.

gross sales The total amount that a company charges during a given period of time for merchandise (before any discounts).

idea generation stage The stage in new product development in which a marketer engages in a continuing search for product ideas consistent with target market needs and the organization's objectives.

idiosyncratic investment Specific investment in a single relationship.

influencer The buying-centre role played by organizational members (or outsiders) who affect the purchase decision by supplying advice or information.

inseparability A characteristic of services, namely that their production cannot be separated from their consumption.

intangibility A characteristic of services, namely that they cannot be touched, seen, tasted or smelled.

integrated marketing communications (IMC) A system of management and integration of marketing communication elements – advertising, publicity, sales promotion, sponsorship marketing, and point-of-sale communications – with the result that all elements adhere to the same message.

intensive distribution Stocking the product in as many outlets as possible.

internal marketing Marketing efforts aimed at a company's own employees.

Internet A worldwide network of interconnected computer networks that carry data and make information exchange possible.

intranets Connects the computers within a business together.

JIT The just-in-time (JIT) concept aims to minimize stocks by organizing a supply system which provides materials and components as they are required.

joint decisions Decisions made that are shared by all or some members of a group. Often, one decision maker dominates the process.

joint ventures The participation of two or more companies in an enterprise in which each party contributes assets, owns the new entity to some degree, and shares risk.

KAM (key account management) An approach to selling which focuses resources on major customers and uses a team selling approach.

key account manager A salesperson who concentrates on maintaining an ongoing relationship with existing customers.

key success factors (KSF) Those factors in a market which determine competitive success or failure in that market.

lead time The time gap between one event and another.

learning A change in the content of long-term memory. As humans, we learn because what we learn helps us respond better to our environment.

learning curves Track the decreasing cost of production and distribution of products or services over time as a result of learning by doing, innovation, and imitation.

licensing agreement An agreement in which one firm permits another to use its intellectual property in exchange for compensation, typically a royalty,

lifestyle An individual's activities, interests, opinions, and values as they affect his or her mode of living.

limited problem solving An intermediate level of decision making between routine response behaviour and extensive problem solving, in which the consumer has some purchasing experience, but is unfamiliar with stores, brands, or price options.

line extension Using a successful brand name to introduce additional items in a given product category under the same brand name, such as new flavours, forms, colours, added ingredients, or package sizes.

logistics The activities involved in moving raw materials and parts into a firm, moving in-process inventory through the firm, and moving finished goods out of the firm.

loss leader A product priced below cost to attract consumers, who may then make additional purchases.

lost-for-good customers Customers who have high switching costs and long-term horizons making them suitable for relationship marketing (RM).

loyalty card Usually a plastic card which is issued by a company to a customer and is used to record the frequency of the customer's purchases and calculate resulting discounts, rewards or allowances.

LSEs Large-scale enterprises (see also SMEs).

macro-environment Broad societal forces that shape the activities of every business and non-profit marketer. The physical environment, sociocultural forces, demographic factors, economic factors, technical knowledge, and political and legal factors are components of the macro-environment.

market development A strategy by which an organization attempts to draw new customers to an existing product, most commonly by introducing the product in a new geographical area.

marketing audit A systematic examination of a business' marketing environment, objectives, strategies, and activities with a view to identifying key strategic issues, problem areas and opportunities.

marketing information system A system in which marketing information is formally gathered, stored, analysed, and distributed to managers in accord with their informational needs on a regular, planned basis.

marketing management The process of planning, executing, and controlling marketing activities to attain marketing goals and objectives effectively and efficiently.

marketing myopia The failure of a company to define its organizational purpose from a broad consumer orientation.

marketing objective A statement of the level of performance that an organization, strategic business unit (SBU), or operating unit intends to achieve. Objectives define results in measurable terms.

market orientation view (MOV) Outside-in perspective. Adapting the firm's resources to market conditions and the competitive environment.

marketing plan A written statement of the marketing objectives and strategies to be followed and the specific courses of action to be taken when (or if) certain events occur.

marketing planning The process by which businesses analyse the environment and their capabilities, decide upon courses of marketing action and implement those decisions.

market penetration A strategy for company growth by increasing sales of current products to current market segments without changing the product.

market potential The upper limit of industry demand. That is, the expected sales volume for all brands of a particular product during a given period.

market space A virtual marketplace such as the Internet in which no direct contact occurs between buyers and sellers.

mark-up A mark-up expressed as a percentage of the cost of an item.

mass customization The ability to create tailored marketing messages or products for an individual customer or a group of similar customers yet retain the economies of scale and the capacity of mass marketing of production.

mass marketing One-to-many communications between a company and potential customers with limited tailoring of the message.

micro-environment A company, its customers, and the other economic actors that directly and regularly influence it marketing practices.

micro-segmentation Segmentation according to choice criteria, DMU structure, decision-making process, buying class, purchasing structure and organizational innovativeness.

modified re-buy A purchase where the buyers have experience in satisfying the need, but feel the situation warrants re-evaluation of a limited set of alternatives before making a decision.

moments of truth Staff-customer contact.

monopoly Exists if there is one seller in the market, such as a state-owned company, e.g. a local electricity supplier, postal service company or a gas company. The seller has the control over the market and can solely determine the price of its product.

nano-relationships Relations between internal customers, internal markets, divisions and business areas within organizations.

national account Large and important customers who may have centralized purchasing departments that buy or coordinate buying for decentralized, geographically dispersed business units.

new task buying An organizational buying situation in which a buyer is seeking to fill a need never before addressed. Uncertainty and lack of information about products and suppliers characterize this situation.

niche marketing The process of targeting a relatively small market segment with a specific, specialized marketing mix.

non-tariff trade barriers Non-monetary barriers to foreign products, such as biases against a foreign company's bids, or product standards that go against a foreign company's product features.

not-for-profit organization An organization which attempts to achieve an objective other than profit, for example relief of famine, animal rights, or public service.

objective and task approach Developing the promotion budget by defining specific objectives, determining the tasks that must be performed to achieve these objectives, and estimating the costs of performing these tasks. The sum of these costs is the proposed promotion budget.

OEM Original equipment manufacturer. In the OEM contract the customer is called the OEM or 'sourcer' whereas the parts suppliers are called manufacturers of OEM products.

oligopoly A market structure characterized by a small number of sellers who control the market.

omnibus study A regular survey usually operated by a market research specialist company which asks questions of respondents.

open-ended questions Allow respondents to determine the direction of the answer without being led by the question. They also prevent 'yes' or 'no' answers.

opinion leader Person within a reference group, who, because of special skills, knowledge, personality, or other characteristics, exerts influence on others.

order point The level of inventory at which re-ordering is advisable to avoid out-of-stocks caused by the lead-time to resupply.

organizational buying behaviour The decision-making activities of organizational buyers that lead to purchases of products.

outsourcing Using another firm for the manufacture of needed components or products or delivery of a service.

own-label products Brands created and owned by distributors or retailers (private labels).

packaging An auxiliary product component that includes labels, inserts, instructions, graphic design, shipping cartons, and sizes and types of containers.

paradigm A shared way of thinking, or meta-theory that provides a framework for theory.

parallel importing When importers buy products from distributors in one country and sell them in another to distributors who are not part of the manufacturer's normal distribution; caused by big price differences for the same product between different countries.

penetration Entering a new market.

penetration price A low introductory price meant to quickly establish a product in the market.

perceived risk Consumers' uncertainty about the consequences of their purchase decisions; the consumer's perception that a product may not do what it is expected to do.

percentage of sales Setting the promotion budget at a certain percentage of current or forecasted sales or as a percentage of the unit sales price.

perception The process by which people select, organize, and interpret sensory stimulation into a meaningful picture of the world.

personal selling Person-to-person interaction between a buyer and a seller wherein the seller's purpose is to persuade the buyer to accept a point of view, to convince the buyer to take a course of action, or to develop a customer relationship.

PIMS – profit impact of marketing strategy An empirical study, which seeks to identify the key factors underlying profitability and strategic success in an industry.

point-of-sale displays Includes all signage – posters, signs, shelf cards, and a variety of other visual materials – that are designed to influence buying decisions at the point of sale.

portal A website that acts as a gateway to the information on the Internet by providing search engines, directories and other services such as personalized news or free e-mail.

portfolio planning Managing groups of brands and product lines.

positioning The image that customers have about a product, especially in relation to the product's competitors.

post-testing In the context of advertising, testing that takes place after an advertisement has been run, to determine whether it has met the objectives set for it by management.

pre-testing Conducting limited trials of a questionnaire or some other aspect of a study to determine its suitability for the planned research project. In the context of advertising, research carried out beforehand on the effectiveness of an advertisement. It begins at the earliest stages of development and continues until the advertisement is ready for use.

price-bundling A strategy whereby the price of a group of products is lower than the total of the individual prices of the components. An example is selling a new car with an 'options package'.

primary data Data which is collected for the first time for the specific purpose of a particular market research study.

private brand (or label) A brand created and owned by a reseller (retailer) of a product or service.

product concept The end result of the marketing strategist's selection and blending of a product's primary and auxiliary components into a basic idea emphasizing a particular set of consumer benefits; also called the product positioning concept.

product life cycle (PLC) The course of a product's sales and profits over its lifetime. It involves five distinct stages: product development, introduction, growth, maturity, and decline.

product line pricing Setting the price steps between various products in a product line based on cost differences between the products, customer evaluations of different features, and competitors' prices.

product portfolio A collection of products balanced as a group. Product portfolio analysis focuses on the interrelationships of products within a product mix. The performance of the mix is emphasized rather than the performance of individual products.

profit-and-loss statement (operating statement, income statement) A financial statement that shows company sales, cost of goods sold, and expenses during a given period of time.

profitability analysis The calculation of sales revenues and costs for the purpose of calculating the profit performance of products, customers and/or distribution channels.

prospect An individual or organization that is a possible buyer of a product.

psychographics The characteristics of individuals that describe them in terms of their psychological and behavioural makeup.

pull strategy Involves a relatively heavy emphasis on consumer-oriented advertising to encourage consumer demand for a new brand and thereby obtain retail distribution. The brand is pulled through the channel system in the sense that there is a backward tug from the consumer to the retailer.

push strategy A promotional strategy whereby a supplier promotes a product to marketing intermediaries, with the aim of pushing the product through the channel of distribution.

qualitative research Research that aims to understand consumers' attitudes, values, behaviour, and beliefs.

reach The number of people exposed to an advertisement carried by a given medium.

reference group A group of people that influences an individual's attitude or behaviour.

referrals Usually obtained by the salesperson asking current customers if they know of someone else, or another company, who might have a need for the salesperson's product.

relationship marketing (RM) The process of creating, maintaining and enhancing strong long-term relationships with customers and other stakeholders through mutual exchange and trust. RM seeks to build a chain of relationships between the firm and its main stakeholders (see also transactional marketing (TM)).

reliability The consistency of data. It is often tested by re-examining customer opinions using the same survey on a different occasion or by another method of measurement.

repositioning A product strategy that involves changing the product design, formulation, brand image, or brand name so as to alter the product's competitive position.

resource based view (RBV) Inside-out perspective. Proactive quest for markets that allow exploitation of the firm's resources.

return on investment (ROI) A common measure of managerial effectiveness – the ratio of net profit to investment.

reverse auction A type of auction in which sellers bid prices for which they are willing to sell items or services.

reverse marketing The process whereby the buyer attempts to persuade the suppliers to provide exactly what the organization wants.

royalty The remuneration paid by one firm to another under licensing and franchising agreements.

screening The stage in new product or market development in which a marketer analyses ideas to determine their appropriateness and reasonableness in relation to the organization's goals and objectives.

secondary data Data which already exist but were collected in the first instance for another purpose.

selective distribution The use of a limited number of outlets in a geographical area to sell products of a supplier.

single sourcing Purchasing a product on a regular basis from a single vendor.

situational analysis The interpretation of environmental attributes and changes in light of an organization's ability to capitalize on potential opportunities.

skimming price A relatively high price, often charged at the beginning of a product's life. The price is systematically lowered as time goes by.

SMEs Small and medium sized enterprises (see also LSEs).

social responsibility The collection of marketing philosophies, policies, procedures, and actions intended primarily to enhance society's welfare.

socialization process The process by which a society transmits its values, norms, and roles to its members.

societal objectives Organizational philosophy that stresses the importance of considering the collective needs of society as well as individual consumers' desires and organizational profits.

sponsorship A business relationship between a provider of funds, resources or services and an individual, event, or organization, which offers in return some rights, and association that may be used for commercial advantage.

stakeholders Individuals or groups having a stake in the organization's well-being, e.g. shareholders, employees.

standardized concept The approach to international marketing in which the four Ps are marketed with little or no modification.

star A high-market-share product in a high-growth market.

straight commission Remuneration based strictly on sales performance.

straight re-buy A type of organizational buying characterized by automatic and regular purchases of familiar products from regular suppliers.

straight salary Compensation at a regular rate, not immediately tied to sales performance.

strategic alliances Informal or formal arrangements between two or more companies with a common business objective.

strategic business unit (SBU) A unit of the company that has a separate mission and objectives and that can be planned independently from other company businesses. A SBU can be a company division, a product line within a division, or sometimes a single product or brand.

subculture A group within a dominant culture that is distinct from the culture. Members of a subculture typically display some values or norms that differ from those of the overall culture.

subsidiary A company which is owned by another.

supply chain management How products are moved from the producer to the ultimate consumer with a view to achieving the most effective and efficient delivery system.

switching costs The costs to a buying organization of changing from one supplier to another.

tacit knowledge Consists of things customers know, but which are difficult or nearly impossible to articulate. This intuitive information, while frequently critical to product success in the marketplace, is the most difficult to provide to the NPD team during product development.

tariff A tax levied by a government against certain imported products. Tariffs are designed to raise revenue or to protect domestic firms.

team selling Using teams of people from sales, marketing, engineering, finance, technical support, and even upper management to service large, complex accounts.

telemarketing Using the telephone as the primary means of communicating with prospective customers. Telemarketers often use computers for order taking.

test marketing The stage of new product development where the product and marketing programme are tested in realistic market settings, such as a well-defined geographic area.

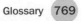

testimonial A type of advertising in which a person, usually a well-known or public figure, states that he or she owns, uses, or supports the product being advertised.

third-party logistics provider An independent logistics provider that performs any or all of the functions required to get its client's product to market.

time-based competition Competition based on providing time utility by delivering a product when the consumer wants it.

time to market The time it takes for a company to develop a new market and turn it into a product which people can buy.

top-down method A forecasting/planning approach based on objectives and works down to product/market estimates (see also build-up method).

total cost Fixed costs plus variable costs.

total quality management (TQM) Programmes designed to constantly improve the quality of products, services, and marketing processes.

trade-off Balancing of two different options. If you have chosen a certain option, you have also sorted out some possible advantages.

trade marketing Marketing to the retail trade.

trade show A meeting or convention of members of a particular industry where business-to-business contacts are routinely made.

transaction A trade of values between two parties.

transaction costs The total of all costs incurred by a buyer and seller as they gather information and negotiate a transaction.

transactional marketing (TM) The major focus of the marketing program (the four Ps) is to make customers buy. Independence among marketing actors ('arm's length') is considered vital for marketing efficiency (see also relationship marketing (RM)).

undifferentiated marketing A marketing effort not targeted at a specific market segment, but designed to appeal to a broad range of customers.

The approach is appropriate in a market that lacks diversity of interest.

unique selling proposition (USP) A unique characteristic of a product or brand identified by the marketer as the one on which to base a promotional campaign. It is often used in a product-differentiation approach to promotion.

user The buying-centre role played by the organizational member who will actually use the product.

value chain Chain of activities by which a company brings in materials, creates a good or service, markets it, and provides service after a sale is made. Each step creates more value for the consumer.

value chain based view (VBV) Building sustainable competitive advantages based on the firm's positioning in the value chain.

variability The characteristic of services referring to the fact that services are heterogeneous – that is, the quality of delivered services can vary widely.

variable cost A cost that varies directly with an organization's production or sales. Variable costs are a function of volume.

vertical marketing system A network of vertically aligned establishments that are managed professionally as a centrally administered distribution system.

wholesaler An organization or individual that serves as a marketing intermediary by facilitating transfer of products and title to them. Wholesalers do not produce the product, consume it, or sell it to ultimate consumers.

world-class brand A product that is widely distributed around the world with a single brand name that is common to all countries and is recognized in all its markets.

world wide web A portion of the Internet; a system of Internet server – computers that support specially formatted documents.

Index

Numbers in **bold** indicate glossary entries